RON SHANDLER's
Baseball
Forecaster

2004

Flying Infielder Edition

Shandler Enterprises, LLC
Roanoke, VA

Acknowledgments

Eighteen years ago, I started a statistical compilation for stat geeks and fantasy leaguers. I wrote it myself, on one of the first PC clones, using LOTUS 1-2-3 Version. 1A, on a 10 megabyte hard drive. This little project has grown so much since then that I should probably trade in that PC already, perhaps for one of those cool, super-fast 486's.

This book simply would not happen if not for the following people, places and things:

Paul Petera, Baseball HQ's Director of Data Analysis and the primary number-cruncher for this book.

Deric McKamey, Baseball HQ's Co-Director of Minor League Analysis and the source for all the expert prospect scouting information in these pages.

Rick Wilton, the alter-ego to Dr. HQ, and the voice on the phone that keeps saying, "you'll get through this."

John Burnson and Patrick Davitt, regular columnists at Baseball HQ, who constantly push the fanalytic envelope.

Doug Dennis, Al Melchior, Scott Monroe, Ray Murphy, Harold Nichols, Stephen Nickrand and Rod Truesdell, all regular HQ columnists as well, who picked up 35 pages of the player analyses and helped restore some of my sanity.

The *information sources that I relied on* to help fill in missing data and jog my memory... Rotowire.com, ESPN.com, BaseballAmerica.com, the *Baseball America Almanac*, and *The Sporting News Baseball Register*.

My *valued industry colleagues*, expert league competitors, conference speakers and friends... Greg Ambrosius, Jeff Barton, Matt Berry, Jim Callis, Jeff Erickson, John Hunt, Peter Kreutzer, Gene McCaffrey, Lenny Melnick, Lawr Michaels, Steve Moyer, Rob Neyer, Mat Olkin, Alex Patton, David Rawnsley, Peter Schoenke, John Sickels, Rick Wolf, John Zaleski and Irwin Zwilling.

The *incredible group of writers and analysts for the BaseballHQ.com web site*, those who I've not already mentioned... Neil Bonner, Matt Bruce, Matt Dodge, Jon Enriquez, Brent Hershey, Allen Hirsch, Gerald Holmes, Jeff Howard, Elliot Liffman, Terry Linhart, Rich Murawski, Frank Noto, Doug Ohlandt, Josh Paley, Joshua Randall, Michael Sanderson and Mike Shears. Their work is inspirational, and constantly reminds me why I'm in this business.

Kevin Goldstein and *Lynda Knezovich*, two key behind-the-scenes people without whom it would all come crashing down.

The *ladies of my life*, Sue, Darielle and Justina, for putting up with yet another year of late nights, missing weekends and random tirades. My girls are now pre-teens, which is very dangerous territory, but so far I haven't had too much trouble with the boys they've brought home. I keep my trusty New York Mets Official Insignia bat close by at all times. Except when Sue hides it from me.

Finally, thank *you, loyal readers*. All of this is for you. All the paper and the ink and the postage and the brain cells and the sweat. All of it. It's all your fault.

CONTENTS

I. FANALYTICS

Trot Nixon cost me a fantasy baseball title in 2003. This is particularly surprising for several reasons.

1. In his player commentary for last year's book, I wrote: "Recipe for a power breakout: Rising PX trend, declining G/F trend, stable contact rate, second half power surge, age 29. Thirty HRs could be a no-brainer."

2. He was clearly on pace to meet those expectations when he got hurt. Even with missing most of September, and losing about 50-60 AB, he posted a 28-87-.306 season, a career year in only 441 ABs.

3. I drafted him in the 12-team mixed Yoo Hoo League for $9.

He was mine. I owned him. But it wasn't enough.

Despite his excellent performance, 2003 didn't start off well. Two months into the season, he had punched out only three HRs, a dreadful 9-HR pace. To make matters worse, those homers were hit off of Cliff Politte, Kris Wilson and John Thomson, a trio with a combined HR/9 rate of 1.4. He wasn't exactly beating up on challenging skill sets.

The tide appeared to change as interleague play began in early June. Facing the Pirates on June 4 and 5, Nixon immediately doubled his full-season output by hitting three out, off of Brian Meadows, Jeff D'Amico and Scott Sauerbeck. One of the fantasy news services proclaimed, "Trot Nixon is finally turning it around. Grab him now before it's too late." And they were correct. He proceeded to hit 7 HRs in June, another 10 in July, and everyone lived happily ever after.

Well, not really.

You see, I take issue with these services making blanket recommendations based on a three-game sample size. While they were correct in this case, Nixon's mini-power display hardly guaranteed anything about his future performance.

Another player with high expectations was batting .206 on May 9. Over the next three games, he went 5 for 10 with 2 HRs and 3 RBIs. The news service proclaimed: "He's finally turning it around. His owners should rest easy." Unfortunately, after that brief outburst, Pat Burrell promptly went 1 for 14, en route to a .209 season.

These type of knee-jerk recommendations are feeding an obsession with micro-managing. Is that a bad thing? A recent Baseball HQ poll found that nearly one third of all leagues today allow some level of daily roster management. Shallow leagues – those that draft out of less than 75% of the player population – comprise over 50% of leagues, and are also high maintenance due to their deep free agent pool.

The Yoo Hoo League was one of these. Our rosters dipped into only 45% of the player population. The free agent pool represented the other 55%. That opens up lots of opportunities to tinker each week.

The problem with the short-term mindset required to play in these leagues is that they often force us to ignore the analytical end of the decision-making process.

There is a belief that making frequent roster decisions is empowering, but that perception is flawed. With a microscope on the minutia, there is a great inclination to treat random streaks and slumps as permanent reality. And that leads to over-managing every element of your roster.

A look at online reader forums back in early May revealed a startling demonstration of this phenomenon:

- Torii Hunter — too soon to panic?
- Should I give up on Aramis Ramirez and grab Stynes?
- Foppert = Floppert. Man, is this guy overrated.
- Mark Teixeira sucks. Should I pick up Randa?

The perceived empowerment of frequent transactions fosters an obsession with immediate gratification. If I draft a .300 hitter, *he absolutely has to hit .300 from Day One or I've got to find someone else who will*. Every slugger and speedster bears the burden of producing *a consistent stream of HRs and SBs, every day*. And this obsession can get ugly. On April 8, HQ columnist Neil Bonner wrote a sentence that was the most frightening thing I've read in a long time: "In ESPN leagues, Rey Ordonez is now owned in 82% of all AL leagues."

And as the short-term decision-maker wields his mighty sword, swinging wildly at anything that even marginally looks like an extra home run, save or steal, the game of fantasy baseball suffers. No longer is it a test of knowledge; it becomes a test of reflexes, a statistical video game controlled by the fleeting urges of the person holding the joystick. Power is just another mouse-click away.

It's easy to get caught up in that type of power. It's captivating, transforming an innocent game into a six-month adrenaline rush. And admittedly, it felt good to allow myself to be carried away by the current of the Yoo Hoo league.

However, my work over the past 18 years runs counter to this mode of play. And therein lies the conflict.

In last year's book, I kicked off a somewhat misguided campaign to change the name of fantasy baseball. There was a list of reasons why this made sense at the time, bolstered by about 200 e-mails from supporters. I felt that a name-change would help legitimize the hobby; the word "fantasy" was an affront to those of us who take a serious, scientific approach to the game. However, when I chose the new name in January, the world balked.

Fanalytics – a contraction of "fantasy" and "analytics" – drew more wrath than respect, but that's okay. It's better that we keep the name *fantasy* because there probably needs to be a distinction. We might consider that *fanalytic baseball* is a mode of play that requires a more strategic, long-term, quantitative approach to player analysis and game decisions. *Fantasy* can describe everything else.

This is not to diss other types of games. But there *is* a distinction between a competition that requires you to consider the possibility of churning a struggling front-liner versus one that requires a more macro view for success.

I suppose this is somewhat like the introduction of the term, *sabermetrics,* over two decades ago. In his book, *The Diamond Appraised,* co-author Craig Wright wrote:

1

"In the 1980 Baseball Abstract, Bill James was feeling the need for a distinct title for his work and christened it "sabermetrics." I cannot say the term hit me as a revelation. I had that Abstract for nearly a year before I considered endorsing the term. But the more I thought about it, the better it sounded…. It also turned out that people were going to have a hard time accepting the term "sabermetrician." The three major newspapers in Dallas and Fort Worth refused to use it… until the summer of 1984. Within the Rangers organization itself (where Wright was employed), some people balked at using the term…. Here in the late 1980s the term is beginning to settle in as a word with a specific meaning in a limited field."

The same book's other co-author, Tom House, provided another perspective:

"Tradition in baseball is an excuse for tunnel vision…. I always keep in mind Clarke's Laws, which demonstrate that the flow of revolutionary ideas in any field follow three steps:

First exposure: It's impossible – don't waste my time.

Second exposure: It's possible but not worth doing.

Third exposure: I said it was a good idea all along."

Fanalytics has spent its first year bouncing between first and second exposures, and there's no guarantee that it will get any further. However, just by virtue of it describing a type of analysis that is different from what many fantasy leaguers are using has value in itself. It helps us approach decision-making from the perspective that's most applicable to a given game format.

What is fanalytics, really? Fanalytics is a mode of analysis that takes player evaluation and prognostication to a new level. It shows us how to distinguish between skill and statistical output, how to break down statistics into their component parts and allow for — and even somewhat control — the effects of random chance. Fanalytics teaches us to look beyond the obvious and cast a cynical eye at media information, separating the news from the noise.

A fanalytic gamer uses traditional statistics as weapons against his competitors while running his team with underlying base skills indicators. He understands how the numbers work and will never hesitate to sell high or buy low, even when common wisdom dictates otherwise. He is willing to aggressively follow favorable percentage plays, while being willing to assume the risks that go along with that approach.

However, in pursuing this course, fanalytics teaches us to watch the season unfold from a perch far above the fray. Percentage plays bear their fruit over the long-term.

This is not to say that fanalytic gamers don't engage in any tactical decision-making. Our games do still require us to make well-thought-out tactical tweaks as situations present themselves. However, those moves have to be made with the bigger picture in mind. And that picture has certain time-tested tenets we need to remember…

1. The season is a marathon, not a sprint. Our players will be valued at season's end based upon the numbers they put up over six months of play. If they squeeze that full season of production into four, or three, or two months, it doesn't matter. All that matters is what their numbers are on October 1.

2. The path to .300 is paved with plenty of .250s and .350s. Nomar Garciaparra's .301 BA this year, on a month by month basis, looked like this: .273, .339, .398, .269, .325, .170. Few people looked at Joe Randa's .291 BA and knew that he batted well over .300 in four of the six months, and .344 after the All Star Break. And the panic button that was pushed for Mark Teixeira after hitting .188 in April would have negated the perfectly acceptable .269 level he hit from May 1 on.

3. Exhibit excruciating patience. It's my annual April mantra. Those who are patient are rewarded more often than those who act too early. It is frustrating to have to wait, but those players who have skill will eventually perform, especially those with a long-term track record.

4. Make decisions based exclusively on talent. When you are faced with a player decision, no matter what month of the season, ask yourself one simple question… Is the player you will be adding more *talented* than the one you will be giving up? If you're not gaining at least equal value, then sit tight.

5. Baseball reality is fluid. Fewer than 50% of today's Major League managerial decisions stick for more than a week or so; most are just tactical whims. Investing in anything more permanent is setting yourself up for failure.

And that's where I drowned in the Yoo Hoo League. I got caught up in the sprint, lost patience, and made a fateful decision based on a whim of the moment. I was in first place by 9 points, but saw a roster spot that was not pulling its weight. After two months, I had convinced myself that a 9-HR pace was a fixed reality and I could do better.

On June 4, Trot Nixon began his trek back to respectability. I cut him on June 2.

The HRs and RBIs that I tossed away would have netted me more than enough to close the 7.5 point gap between my team and the eventual league champion. I flat out blew it.

To be fair, following the rules of *fanalytics* is not an easy thing to do, for anyone. Fantasy baseball creates its own energy that draws us in, often forcing us to make decisions with our gut. And, the *fanalytic* learning curve can be steep; you have to do much of the work yourself.

That's what this book is about. There are no spoon-fed answers here. If you are a new reader, there *will* be a learning curve. However, *Forecaster* veterans will attest that it is well worth the effort, especially if your motivation is to win. **This book is all about winning.**

I'd like to think of the *Baseball Forecaster* as a teacher. In fact, I'd most liken it to Linda Harris' description of the *Mean Teacher:*

"A mean teacher has higher hopes for his students than they have for themselves. He gets them to create when they want to consume. He forces them to think when they want to be told. A mean teacher doesn't want his students to take his word, he wants them to find the words."

Find the words. *Your* words. Our analyses can provide the foundation, but there is a greater experience here, if you take the time. I'll try to lead you along as best I can, and make it all as intuitive as possible. But do take the time.

And hopefully, you won't be cutting any 30-HR hitters if they get off to a slow start next year.

How to Use This Book

For those new to the *Baseball Forecaster*, you are about to embark on a strange journey. This is a land where a career .250 hitter could be projected to challenge for a batting title. It's a place where today's frontline closers become tomorrow's mop-up men. Within these pages, you'll find performance breakouts and regressions that occur at odd times to unusual players. At face value, lots of what you read will look completely counter-intuitive. It's almost like we're making the whole thing up.

But we're not. In fact, this is probably the only book that provides complete analytical support to its projections. We don't go out and predict a player to experience a HR spike just because he shows up to spring training all bulked up. We don't believe that a chronically-injured player will suddenly become an icon of health just because he's quoted in the paper as saying he's ready to play 162 games. And we won't project this season's #1 ranked prospect to immediately become a franchise player just because media-puffed scouting reports make such good copy.

What we do is called "component skills analysis." We look at each player's raw skills behind their traditional stats, and draw conclusions from that evaluation. Then we apply a series of rules and percentage plays that have been developed from 18 years of research. For instance, in projecting HR output, we not only look at a player's HR history, but also at all extra base hits and fly balls. When we project a power spike, it's because we see an upward trend in those skills, coupled with a concurrent trend in a batter's tendency to hit fly balls. When projecting a pitcher's ERA, we never even look at past ERA; we evaluate the underlying skills of control, dominance and command. It's not just stats — there is a fair amount of logic as well.

As a result of these analyses, we do provide a baseline statistical projection for each player. But I caution you about putting too much credence into those inert numbers. Baseball statistics live in a highly volatile environment. A player can hit 45 HRs one year and only 29 the next and still be displaying the same level of skill (see Richie Sexson). Injury, untimely slumps and managerial whim can all affect the numbers. It's best to look at the data as a whole, glean a general sense of performance from the commentaries, and draw some of your own conclusions. This book can't really tell you how many HRs David Ortiz will hit next year — nobody can — but it can give you a general sense of what direction his power skills are heading.

Naturally, I think this approach is the most prudent in evaluating performance, but I'll let you decide for yourself. I do ask, however, that you keep an open mind as you begin this journey. There are ideas here that will likely challenge your own beliefs. These tools do work, but you may have to throw away some preconceptions in order to embrace the possibilities. In the end, concepts like strand rates, base performance values and the LIMA Plan have helped fantasy leaguers win their leagues. My staff and I have brought home championships in national experts competitions for six years in a row. Nobody can match that track record, so we must be doing something right.

The place to start your journey is in the next section, *The Tools of Victory*. It is here that you will read about some of the foundation principles of my approach. The most valuable reference section of the book is the **Forecaster's Toolbox**. This provides all of the rules and research results we use to draw conclusions about player performance. It contains the concepts for this book that have been developed over the past 18 years.

Take a quick scan through the **Sabermetric Glossary**, which is in the back of the book. You don't need to memorize the formulas, but a cursory knowledge can't hurt. At minimum, you should know where to go in case you run across an unfamiliar gauge. There are lots of them, but don't be intimidated. Not all of these formulas will have relevance for the particular game you play. As you read through the player commentaries, you'll get a sense of the ones that are best to have a working knowledge of.

It's good to have this foundation, because it will provide you with a far greater analytical arsenal when you jump into the meat of the book. That meat — the **Batter** and **Pitcher** sections — contains an incredible wealth of data.

There is a brief commentary for each player that provides an overall evaluation of performance and likely future direction. These are written by myself and seven of my respected writers, but we are just humans and likely no smarter than you. Your greatest value will be to use them as a springboard to your own analysis of the data. Odds are, if you take the time, you'll find hidden indicators that we might have missed.

Two sections, the **Pitcher Logs** and **Bullpen Indicators**, provide more support data in evaluating pitching. Unless your teams routinely finish first in ERA each year, you can never have enough pitching support data.

The *Minor League* section will help you evaluate those players with little or no major league experience. Deric McKamey's **Top Prospects** chart the trends for 54 newbies most likely to have an impact in 2004. There will be dozens more making appearances in the majors, and for those we provide complete **Major League Equivalencies**. One of the great in-season advantages of the *Forecaster* is that, when an unknown gets a call-up, you can check back on his past equivalent performances and see if it is someone worth pursuing. Of course, BaseballHQ.com subscribers get Deric's full analyses on these players all season long.

The *Draft Guide History* section has been in this book since 1988, and finds great value in providing player rankings and trends in a variety of categories. For those who play in simulation games, we have batters and pitchers ranked together in the **Runs Above Replacement** section.

Finally, there's the *2003 Greatest Hits* section, which includes some of the top columns I wrote for Baseball HQ in 2003. Over the past year, I began pulling away from shackles of obsessive analytical precision and tried to find some light in other places. Hopefully, you'll see some too.

What's New

For the *Forecaster* veterans, welcome back. Once again, we've got a bunch of new stuff this year...

1. Probably the biggest change in this year's book is something that, hopefully, you won't notice at all. For the first time, I've farmed out some of the writing of the player commentaries. This was not an easy decision to make. For years, readers have valued the singular voice of the analysis, something that is not found in any other book. But the overabundance of data that needs to be reviewed has made the task of analysis overwhelming. It was either push back the book's publication date or share the workload.

However, this is good news for you. The seven writers who share the billing are Baseball HQ veteran analysts whose skills I trust. Their individual perspectives provide more breadth to the commentary with absolutely no loss of insight. Their bylines appear on 35 of the 100 player pages, but that is the only thing that sets those pages apart.

2. John Burnson introduces the next iteration of **Expected Batting Average** and takes us to new places.

3. A few years ago, the sabermetric world was rocked by the findings of Voros McCracken, who concluded that pitchers have no control over the batted balls they allow. HQ's Patrick Davitt looks at the flipside – **Batting Hit Rates** – and makes some interesting discoveries.

4. The prognosticating process is not only the assessment of future skill but also the assessment of risk. In this year's player boxes, we break out the key factors for every player in a **Risk Table**. Now you can see the specific variables that contribute to each player's risk rating.

5. **ERA** and **Batting Average Percentage Plays** have been added to the player boxes. These provide insight into each player's potential to improve in those two categories.

6. When we introduced the Bullpen Indicator Charts last year, I also included a small table that tracked the changes in closer situations over time. That table is a regular feature now, and the **Closer Volatility Analysis** gives us a frightening look at where our saves dollars have been going.

7. **Japanese League Equivalencies**, inspired by research done by Jim Albright of BaseballGuru.com, have been applied to all JPN statistics in the player boxes. We've used similar conversions for other foreign and indy league stats, which help provide better input for the player projections.

8. Several readers have commented to me that the formulas we use for runs created and **Runs above Replacement** significantly overestimate value for batters. We've done an overhaul and updated those formulas.

9. We've overcome some space constraints, at least for this year. Strikeouts have been added to the pitching charts. We've also added SX to the batting MLE charts, and strand and hit rates to the pitching MLE charts. This year.

Other Stuff

The voluminous amount of information in each year's *Forecaster* is compiled and written over the course of seven weeks. In a project as large as this, there inevitably will be a few little things that slip through the cracks. We have set up an **Update page** online at www.baseballforecaster.com/bfupdates.shtml to catch these oversights.

As we get closer to Opening Day, we'll have a better handle on how playing time is going to be allocated, so our projections can become more and more accurate. As a buyer of this book, you get a **Free 2004 Projections Update** at the BaseballForecaster.com web site. These text and spreadsheet files will be posted on or about March 1, 2004.

This free update is only available online and only for those who own this Book. When you access the web site, have the book in front of you as it will ask for a password that appears somewhere in these pages. Also note that this is a single update. We revise the projections every week at Baseball HQ, so subsequent updates can be found there.

Beyond the Forecaster

This book is only the beginning of the process. Imagine having this information updated constantly during the year — daily player analyses, weekly projections, weekly pitching logs and bullpen charts. Imagine being able to access a player's complete record – current season stats, balance of year projections and more – at the click of your mouse. Imagine being able to create a profile of your fantasy team and use it to evaluate a trade proposal. Imagine getting scouting reports for hundreds of top prospects as well as daily analyses of every major league call-up. Imagine having all the player values customized to your own leagues. Imagine having access to a complete staff of experts who will answer your questions, at any time.

That's just *some* of what you get on **BaseballHQ.com**. There's more…

RotoHQ.com is the largest library of fantasy strategy essays and tools known to man. It includes over 300 essays, and is updated and restocked every January.

First Pitch Forums are a series of conferences we run all over the country, where you can meet some of the top baseball writers, and network with fellow fantasy leaguers. It begins each November in Phoenix with our big Arizona Fall League event. This past year's weekend of seminars, scouting and socializing drew over 100 fans and nearly two dozen national writers. Then, in March, we take the show on the road for half-day sessions in places like Chicago, New York, Boston and Baltimore. Keep an eye on the FirstPitchForums.com website for the upcoming schedule.

Details about all these products — and more — can be found in the back of this book.

If you have questions or comments, feel free to drop me a personal e-mail at ron@baseballhq.com. As my long-time readers can attest, I do read every e-mail and respond to as many as I can, as quickly as I can. However, don't ask me to analyze your roster or rank your keeper list because, if I agree to do that for you, then I'll have many thousands of other readers asking me to do it for them too, which will tie up so much of my time that I'll have to farm out the *entire* book, which would mean that most of the player commentaries would end up being written by a bunch of hack writers, and then this book would become an afterthought in the annals of baseball analysis, and the word *"fanalytic"* would disappear forever.

Don't say it.

— Ron Shandler

Command: Playing the Percentages

I spent a good part of the introduction to last year's *Baseball Forecaster* talking about how the quest for the perfect projections model is a perpetual process. As serious fanalytic gamers raise the bar of analysis each year, we have to constantly look at our past knowledge base and adjust our expectations.

Last year, new research showed that the correlation between a player's batting eye ratio (BB/K) and his batting average was not as predictive as we once thought. I took a different spin on the numbers and came to the conclusion that, while the statistical relationship was not as strong, there was still a moderately reasonable percentage play to hang our hats on.

In the end, I asked, "What are the odds that a player drafted with a 1.50 eye ratio will bat .300? What are the odds that he might bat under .250?" And these were the results...

BATTING EYE	BA	Pct who bat .300+	.250-
===========	=====	====	=====
1.51 +	.314	59%	4%
1.01 - 1.50	.300	51%	9%
0.76 - 1.00	.288	32%	14%
0.51 - 0.75	.278	18%	17%
0.26 - 0.50	.269	14%	26%
0.00 - 0.25	.259	7%	39%

The comfort level for a percentage play worth pursuing begins at 66%, so there are no clear winners here. However, we can say that a player with a 1.50 eye ratio has nearly a 6 in 10 chance of batting .300 and, at the same time, less than a 1 in 20 chance of batting under .250. There is still great value in that finding.

So it's now time to be a bit proactive with some of the gauges that we've been relying on. The next logical step in this analysis is to do a similar take with the pitching side of the equation.

Given two sets of numbers, our BPI analyses have become almost no-brainers...

PITCHER	bb/9	k/9	Cmd
=======	====	===	====
Pitcher A	2.2	9.4	4.2
Pitcher B	4.4	5.4	1.2

Based on these numbers alone, which player would you rather have on your team? The obvious answer would be Player A. Those BPIs belong to Javier Vazquez, who posted a 3.25 ERA last year. Player B? Wayne Franklin, who had a 5.52 ERA. But the numbers don't always tell you what you think they should...

PITCHER	bb/9	k/9	Cmd
=======	====	===	====
Pitcher C	2.2	6.9	3.1
Pitcher D	2.2	6.9	3.1

You would think that these two players would have put up fairly comparable ERAs. These BPIs certainly do not indicate anything like a 1.31 run differential in ERA, yet Player C posted a 3.21 mark and Player D just 4.52. The pitchers -- Livan Hernandez and Odalis Perez.

We have different tools that can explain this discrepancy, including strand and hit rates, and the like. But the BPIs above say that, from a purely skills standpoint, Hernandez and Perez are equivalent talents, and their ERAs should probably be closer than 1.31 runs apart.

We've been using the following chart as part of our analytical arsenal:

COMMAND	ERA	bb/9	k/9
========	=====	====	====
0.0 - 1.0	5.34	4.6	4.3
1.1 - 1.5	4.92	4.1	5.5
1.6 - 2.0	4.64	3.5	6.2
2.1 - 2.5	4.19	3.0	6.7
2.6 - 3.0	4.04	2.5	6.8
3.1 +	3.40	1.9	8.1

The data here represents the five year period of 1998-2002 and includes all pitchers who posted at least 100 IP in any year. And the numbers fall in line — the better the command, the better the ERA. The walk and strikeout rates also follow the trend, which we would expect.

But all is not what it seems. The mean values correlate up and down the scale, but like our batting eye analysis, the range of values within each group is wider than you would imagine...

COMMAND	ERA	Range
========	=====	============
0.0 - 1.0	5.34	3.93 - 6.90
1.1 - 1.5	4.92	2.92 - 8.59
1.6 - 2.0	4.64	2.89 - 6.83
2.1 - 2.5	4.19	2.47 - 6.87
2.6 - 3.0	4.04	2.59 - 7.32
3.1 +	3.40	1.74 - 4.86

We'd expect there to be outliers, and most of these spreads include their fair share. But the fact that there is such a wide range forces us to qualify our expectations. In the similar batting eye analysis, we were able to say, "The higher the batting eye ratio, the greater we can maximize our BA upside and minimize our BA downside," but that's not the case here. The downsides are consistently bad up and down the chart until you reach the 3.1 Command Elite.

This is where we can start trying to use percentage plays again. The goal — find a two-thirds (66%) play somewhere that we can use to anchor our analysis.

If we apply that 66% percentage play to the above chart, we get smaller ranges. We can now say, there is at least a 66% probability that a player with a certain command ratio will have an ERA within the stated range.

COMMAND	ERA	66% Range
0.0 - 1.0	5.34	5.12 - 6.05
1.1 - 1.5	4.92	4.06 - 5.75
1.6 - 2.0	4.64	4.04 - 5.38
2.1 - 2.5	4.19	3.48 - 5.09
2.6 - 3.0	4.04	3.30 - 4.83
3.1 +	3.40	2.65 - 4.06

The ranges, however, are still pretty wide. If I draft a pitcher with a superb 3.1 command ratio, there is still a chance that he'll have an ERA over 4.00. If I draft a pitcher with a horrible 1.1 command ratio, it is still within the 66% percentage play that he'll post an ERA better than the league average.

This brings us back to the performance range chart where we attempt to maximize our gains and minimize our risk relative to command ratios. We may have to come to terms with the reality that there is a high variability in the ERA to Command relationship, however, we can look to the far ends of the performance spectrum to get a better handle on upside and downside potential.

COMMAND	ERA	Pct who post 3.50-	4.50+
0.0 - 1.0	5.34	0%	87%
1.1 - 1.5	4.92	7%	67%
1.6 - 2.0	4.64	7%	57%
2.1 - 2.5	4.19	19%	35%
2.6 - 3.0	4.04	26%	25%
3.1 +	3.40	53%	5%

Unlike the batting chart, there are a few clear 66% winners here. With any Command ratio under 1.6, you run at least a 67% risk of your pitcher posting an ERA over 4.50. That risk declines as you go up the scale. At the 2.6 command level, pitchers have a 75% chance of posting an ERA under 4.50.

The quest for identifying the elite hurlers — those with ERAs of 3.50 and better — provides fewer clear percentage plays. In fact, the best we can do is say that just more than half of those arms with command ratios over 3.0 will return a 3.50 or better ERA, however... that group's risk of blowing up is only 5%. So, while you may not be able to guarantee a positive return with any confidence, you can guarantee a near-perfect level of damage control. In the world of pitching, there is something to be said for that.

In fact, let's take one more cut at this...

COMMAND	ERA	Pct who post 4.00-
0.0 - 1.0	5.34	7%
1.1 - 1.5	4.92	16%
1.6 - 2.0	4.64	16%
2.1 - 2.5	4.19	43%
2.6 - 3.0	4.04	45%
3.1 +	3.40	78%

I think we'd all be thrilled to find some way to ensure that we draft hurlers who'd post an ERA under 4.00. Unfortunately, we can't seem the get beyond that 3.0 command threshold. Anything under 3.0 still incurs a fair amount of risk.

So, what can we take away from this? From a percentage play perspective...

Never draft a pitcher with a command ratio of under 1.6. We used to use a 2.0 level as the delimiter here, but as the chart shows, it's still nearly a 50-50 percentage play to draft within the 1.6-2.0 range and avoid getting blown up.

What does this mean for the LIMA Plan? Well, higher command ratios are still better, but if your pool of LIMA-draftable hurlers begins to dwindle, you can cautiously tread among the 1.6-2.0 ratios and cherry-pick as best you can.

Never pass up an opportunity to grab a hurler with a ratio over 3.0. It is interesting to look at the group that comprised these elite arms in our study. There were 85 pitching seasons that qualified during the five years. The normal names you'd expect head up the list... Martinez, Maddux, Schilling, Johnson, Clemens, Brown...

But some of the lesser names are intriguing. Jon Lieber appears four times, the first three with ERAs over 4.00 before his 2001 breakout. Andy Pettitte is listed twice, with his 4.00 ERA in 2001 and then the improvement to 3.21 in 2002. In fact, there are virtually no pitchers on the list multiple times who have not posted at least one sub-4.00 ERA.

Except one.

If you are of the belief that a strong percentage play will eventually come through, then you have to expect that Eric Milton — twice on this list with ERAs over 4.80 — has to be on the cusp of major improvement. That improvement might have come in 2003 had he not been on the DL nearly the entire season. Perhaps we'll see it in 2004.

But the bottom line is that you absolutely have to roster any pitcher who has the potential to post a command ratio of over 3.0. And as the LIMA Plan states, this type of skill does not have to be expensive. There are typically over 50 pitchers each season who possess this skill, and nearly half of them will be valued at under $10. No matter if they ever see a save opportunity or win more than a handful of games, these arms will provide positive value to your roster.

Expected Batting Average: Take Two

by John Burnson

There is something about Yankees. Last year it was Alfonso Soriano. Now it's Derek Jeter.

In 2002, Soriano hit .300 despite having a ratio of walks to strikeouts of only 0.15. Such a low Batting Eye is more commonly associated with an anemic batting average. To explain Soriano's seemingly anomalous BA, we unveiled Expected Batting Average (xBA), which predicts batting average on the basis of three indicators: contact rate (CT%), a measure of power (Linear Weighted Power Index, or PX), and a measure of speed (Speed Score Index, or SX). The elements of xBA are arranged as follows:

$$xBA = CT\% * (a\ PX + b\ SX + c)$$

...where the terms in parentheses approximate the batter's hit rate on balls after contact (xH%). Given the exceptional power and speed shown by Soriano in 2002, xBA says that he deserved a batting average of about .285, even with his poor Batting Eye. Thus, a .300 BA was not unreasonable.

In the 2003 *Baseball Forecaster*, we established the predictive value of xBA both within seasons and across seasons. However, despite the general success of xBA, there is a troublesome cabal of outliers, membership in which is exemplified by Soriano's teammate, Derek Jeter:

	1998	1999	2000	2001	2002	2003
BA	.324	.349	.339	.311	.297	.324
xBA	.274	.291	.273	.282	.259	.256

Jeter's actual batting average is routinely fifty points higher than his Expected Batting Average. We could chalk up Jeter as an oddity, but we have observed this problem for other guys who can be called speedy ground-ball hitters.

The case of Jeter prodded us to dive back into xBA to try to refine it. In this column, we explore the most promising avenue: distinguishing between ground balls and fly balls.

We have two incentives for choosing this course. First, ground balls and fly balls might have inherently different hit rates. For example, research posted on Baseball HQ in 2003 suggested that, among balls in play (which exclude HR), ground balls fall for hits at a 20-25% higher rate than do fly balls. If ground balls and fly balls do have different underlying hit rates, then a hitter's batting average will be necessarily shaped by his ratio of ground balls to fly balls.

The second basis for divvying ground balls and fly balls is that our elements of hitter's hit rate – power and speed – could have different influences on each type of hit. A hit on a ground ball is plausibly a function of both power (so that you can swat the ball out of the infield) and speed (so that you can beat a throw to first base). However, power might matter more for a fly ball, and speed could matter less.

With this reasoning, we broke xH% into two sets of terms: one that represented a batter's expected hit rate on ground balls, and one on fly balls. As in our original formula, each new set of terms included linear functions of PX and SX; we were looking for an equation of this form:

$$xH\% = GB\% * (a\ PX + b\ SX + c)$$
$$+\ FB\% * (d\ PX + e\ SX + f)$$

So we went to work. And work. And work. Despite the additional terms and (we supposed) superior sensitivity, we made no progress. In fact, our regression *weakened*. For 2003, our original xH% had a correlation with actual H% of 65%; our new regression had a correlation of only 45%. Clearly, we had run outside the basepaths.

In retrospect, our oversight was obvious. We were basing our calculations on published ratios of ground balls to fly balls and classifying each ball-after-contact (BAC) as one or the other. However, ground balls and fly balls do not comprise all possibilities. There is a third case: line drives.

It is easy to overlook liners. In this matter, the prevalent ratio G/F is a willing accomplice, because it tells us nothing about line drives. A batter with a 1.0 G/F in 400 BAC could have 200 ground balls and 200 fly balls (and so 0 line drives), or 1 ground ball and 1 fly ball (and so 398 line drives). Those are not the same type of hitter. Even when we are led to notice line drives, we probably presume that they fall roughly between ground balls and fly balls in behavior. As we will see, the reality is quite different.

Taking a full view of things, then, our regression needs *nine* terms, not six:

$$xH\% = GB\% * (a\ PX + b\ SX + c)$$
$$+\ FB\% * (d\ PX + e\ SX + f)$$
$$+\ LD\% * (g\ PX + h\ SX + i)$$

That is, we sought an equation for H% in which power and speed contributed selectively to each of the three kinds of hits. For each line, the trailing constant would be the inherent hit rate for that type of hit, before power and speed are applied (assuming that they matter at all). We confined our analysis to players who had at least 300 BAC (our sample size for 2003 was a little over 200 hitters). Here are the results of our regression in a grid form, with the coefficients for each pair of variables at the intersections:

	PX	SX	constant
GB%	0.0022	0.0003	0.1005
FB%	NS	NS	0.1677
LD%	NS	NS	0.5902

Coefficients shown as "NS" were not significant to the regression; all other coefficients were significant at the 95% confidence level, and all but the SX term were significant beyond the level of 99.99%. Using this equation for xH%, our correlation with H% shot from 65% to 75%.

Here is the result in a more straightforward form, with the insignificant terms removed:

$$xH\% = GB\% * (0.0022\ PX + 0.0003\ SX + 0.1005)$$
$$+\ (0.1677 * FB\%) + (0.5902 * LD\%)$$

For an equation that is meant to predict hit rate, this formula is boggling. Of the five terms, only two – the products GB%*PX and GB%*SX – include any reference to actual hits (PX touches on 2B, 3B, and HR; SX mentions 1B, 3B, and HR). The other three terms – raw GB%, FB%, and LD% – say absolutely nothing about hits. They merely tabulate *the paths* taken by balls (land, sky, or in-between). And yet, this equation correlates with hit rate very well.

To establish that this result is not a fluke, let's check the same regression for 2001 and 2002. Here are the results:

	GB%PX	GB%SX	GB%	FB%	LD%
------	========	========	========	========	========
2001	0.0022	0.0002	0.0866	0.1702	0.6367
2002	0.0021	NS	0.1168	0.1593	0.6316
2003	0.0022	0.0003	0.1005	0.1677	0.5902

The similarity of the coefficients indicates that we have the right idea. However, there is one more base open to us: We can pool the data from all three seasons to boost our predictive power. If we do so, we find that the best regression has a slightly different form:

$$xH\% = GB\% * (0.0022\ PX + 0.0013\ SX)$$
$$+ FB\% * 0.1611$$
$$+ LD\% * (-0.0023\ SX + 0.8353)$$

We have lost the raw GB% term and boosted the product of GB% and SX, and we have added a term for the product of LD% and SX. This form is slightly superior to our prior one, even for 2003. Let's run through the terms one by one:

1. *SX doesn't matter for fly balls, and PX doesn't matter for liners.* These terms fell quickly from our regression. The fact that speed has no role in hits on fly balls is logical.

2. *PX almost matters for fly balls.* The product FB%*PX was significant at the 90% level but not at the 95% level. With more data, we perhaps would see a tiny role for PX.

The fact that PX does not figure into hits on line drives and fly balls is, at first blush, surprising. One possibility is that the act of hitting a line drive or a fly ball implies a certain amount of strength. However, there is another, more critical distinction to make: Our equation does not say that the hit rates for FB and LD are irrespective of power; rather, it says that the hit rates are irrespective of *PX*, and that is a very different thing. We regard PX as a window into physical power, but the fact of the matter is that, to a large extent, *PX is also a measure of fly-ball proclivity.*

To see why, consider the equation on which PX is based:

Power = ((2B * 0.8) + (3B * 0.8) + (HR * 1.4)) / AB

This formula, which rewards batters for extra-base hits per at-bat, looks reasonable, and it is. However, its efficacy relies on a veiled assumption: *The batter is a fly-ball hitter.*

Imagine that Barry Bonds had a brother Larry. Larry has the same physical prowess and bat speed as Barry, but whereas Barry has a ground-ball rate of 40%, Larry has a ground-ball rate of 90%. What would Larry's PX be if we sifted Barry's 2002 stats through Larry's ground-ball rate?

	GB%	AB	2B	3B	HR	PX
-------	======	=====	=====	=====	=====	=====
Barry	40%	403	31	2	46	225
Larry	90%	403	7	0	8	42

Larry emerges as a weenie, even though his only sin is putting the ball on the ground. The bulk of brother Barry's beefy PX owes not to his physical power but to his upward swing. Thus, FB% and LD% don't need extra terms for PX

not because PX is irrelevant but because PX is redundant.

PX is still a vital indicator. Most Roto batting categories rely on both power *and* flight – not only HR, but also RBI and Runs, both of which increase with extra-base hits. That said, because of its bias toward fly balls, PX might need to be reconsidered as our gauge for physical power in xBA.

3. *The intrinsic hit rate of line drives is much higher than that of other types of hits.* According to our equation, line drives have a raw hit rate of greater than 80%! By comparison, the rate for flies is only 16%. On reflection, line drives have several advantages over other types of hits. For one thing, line drives don't hit the earth in the infield as ground balls often do, so liners don't lose steam on their way past defenders. Also, line drives often go over the heads of infielders, so infielders can't stop them as easily. On the other hand, line drives have a lower trajectory than do fly balls, so outfielders have less time to react to liners.

If LD lead to more hits than do FB and GB, then LD% ought to have a higher correlation with BA. And so it does:

Correlation with Batting Average

	GB%	FB%	LD%
------	======	======	======
2001	0%	-11%	+23%
2002	2%	-14%	+28%
2003	0%	-6%	+14%

The message seems clear: Want hits? Hit line drives.

4. *SX has an influence on line drives, but it is a negative one.* This term is odd – how can speed hurt hit rate? Does this term reflect a true relationship between SX and liners? Does it indicate that we ought to have accepted a weaker regression that lacked this term? Or, as with PX and power, does it say that SX might not be exactly the representation of speed that we need for xBA? We will keep this term for now, but in time we expect to either justify it or discard it.

5. *There is no intrinsic hit rate for ground balls.* A hypothetical batter with a 0 PX and 0 SX would have a hit rate on ground balls of squat. Strength is not assumed here.

So… putting our new equation for H% into our equation for xBA, are we now able to predict Derek Jeter? Perhaps:

	2001	2002	2003
------	======	======	======
BA	.311	.297	.324
xBA2	.308	.275	.281

Our new equation is a much better fit; it might turn out that Jeter's real 2003 batting average is the aberration here. Consider, too, that xBA2 collars a seeming doppelganger of Jeter:

	GB/FB/LD	CT%	PX	SX	BA	xBA
----------	==========	=====	=====	=====	=====	=====
Jeter D	55/23/23	82%	83	102	.324	.281
Cedeno R	54/26/20	82%	73	112	.267	.266

Whether Jeter has a quirk – and whether we can name it – are puzzles for another year. For now, we believe that we have put another piece of Batting Average into its frame. Last year, we said that we wanted a batter who has power and speed and who makes good contact. This year, we add that we wouldn't mind if the guy also hits a lot of liners.

Misery Index

by John Burnson

When making in-season deals, we often try to capitalize on a player's early trends. However, it's not straightforward to chart the progress of a baseball player (or any human), and so it is problematic to determine whether a change in skills is genuine. Better flags would possess a large element of randomness, so that we could rely on a "natural" pull away from extreme values and toward average ones.

Two such stats for pitchers are hit rate (H%) and strand rate (S%). Hit and strand rates are not wholly random – hit rates tend to rise with ground-ball rates, and strand rates tend to fall with rising homer rates. Still, these rates can, and do, swing wildly over short spells. We can encapsulate deviations in hit rate and strand rate with a combined term:

Misery Index = (H% - 30%) + (70% - S%)

Misery Index (MI) rises as hit rate goes above 30% and as strand rate goes below 70%. Those percentages are not precisely league averages, but they are close enough. Note that a negative Misery indicates *favorable* circumstances.

We looked at all starters from 2003 who had at least 20 starts. We compared their MI after 10 starts (usually ending in late May or early June) with their stats in the remainder.

Pitchers who had an early Misery Index of 7 or higher (misfortunate) or -7 or lower (fortunate) reversed course sharply. Misfortunate starters had a median decline in Misery of 8 points, and their median MI for the rest of the season was a harmless 3. Fortunate pitchers had a median *rise* in Misery of 7 points, and their median MI for the duration was an unimpressive -3. These trends exactly capture the "pull" toward normalcy that we seek.

It is less risky to sell a fortunate player high than to buy a misfortunate player low, because misfortunate starters might not get enough innings to redeem themselves. So let's focus on the favored ones. Here are the pitchers from 2003 who had experienced the least Misery after 10 starts:

| | First 10 starts | | Balance of season | |
	MI	ERA	MI	ERA
Franklin R	-15	3.57	-10	3.56
Batista M	-15	2.29	+2	4.11
Nomo H	-15	3.04	-13	3.12
Webb B	-15	2.42	-6	3.12
Mulder M	-16	2.45	0	3.61
Vargas C	-16	3.02	+10	6.16
Loaiza E	-17	1.92	-3	3.31
Wells K	-17	3.32	-10	3.27
Cornejo N	-18	3.00	+6	5.35
Morris M	-18	2.53	+5	4.70
Zito B	-23	2.51	-4	3.63

Seven of these 11 starters had their ERA rise by at least a run in their remaining starts, and three of them had a rise of more than two runs. Even in those cases where Misery did not rise, *no pitcher improved measurably.* How could they? They were already getting the benefit of every bounce. Thus, Misery Index helps you to sell high with confidence.

Misery Index is not a replacement for skills analysis; the fact that a pitcher is unlucky does not mean that he is not also bad. But Misery can be an effective tool for sorting through your hot starters and deciding which to ditch.

The Next Esteban Loaiza

by John Burnson

The surprise player among starting pitchers in 2003 was undoubtedly Esteban Loaiza. We should not downplay the wonder of Loaiza's 21-Win season – his strikeout rate of 8.2 K/9 and homer rate of 0.7 HR/9 were both career bests, and his walk rate of 2.2 BB/9 was nearly so. Nevertheless, Loaiza's history bore hints that he could someday become, if not a great pitcher, then at least a good pitcher in fantasy terms. If we can name those hints, perhaps we can find the next starting pitcher who will earn $30 on a $3 investment.

After studying Loaiza's history, we identified five traits:

1. **The pitcher has a record of strikeout-to-walk ratios in the 2.0's.** The ability to neutralize one's walks with one's strikeouts is the key to pitching success. From 2000-2002, Loaiza had lofty Command ratios of 2.4, 2.8, and 2.5.

2. **The pitcher has been beset by above-average hit rates (i.e., above 30%).** From 1998-2002, Loaiza had hit rates of 31%, 31%, 32%, 33%, and 34%. In light of his strong Command, Loaiza needed only a little luck to turn a nice profit. In 2003, Loaiza got that luck, in a 29% hit rate.

3. **The pitcher has BPVs that are league average (i.e., around 50).** From 1999-2002, Loaiza's BPV's were 53, 46, 44, and 50. And because the formula for BPV considers Opponents' Batting Average, those decent BPV's were depressed – possibly unfairly – by Loaiza's high hit rates.

4. **The pitcher is at least 30 years old.** By 2003, Roto owners had grown bored with the 31-year-old Loaiza, who had logged 1,250 IP over eight repetitively lackluster years.

5. **The pitcher has at least one season of double-digit value.** This detail demonstrates that the pitcher possesses the ability to put it all together. In 2000, Loaiza earned $11.

We spotted five starters who fit these criteria well. Here is this year's cast of "Who Wants to Be a Roto Darling?":

Brian Anderson (age 32): Anderson's strikeout rate is low at about 4.0 K/9, but his walk rate is also low and the result tends to be a stellar Command. Anderson does have a high homer rate, but so did Loaiza, who entered 2003 having recorded a 1.3 HR/9 in three of the prior five years.

Pedro Astacio (age 34): Astacio's sidelining in 2003 does not augur a bright immediate future, but otherwise his indicators are Loaiza-perfect. Astacio's case affirms our approach, because we have seen him as a $30 pitcher – he earned $15 in the first half of 2002 before falling to fatigue.

John Halama (age 32): The 2003 season was an uncharacteristically poor one for Halama. However, in four of the previous five seasons, Halama had a respectable Command of at least 1.9 and BPV of at least 40. In three of those seasons, he was filleted by hit rates of at least 33%.

Sterling Hitchcock (age 33): In 1998 and 1999, Hitchcock earned $12 and $14 as a starter. However, in the four seasons since, he has averaged only 62 IP and -$2. Still, Hitchcock's Command ratios have stayed solid (2.3, 2.2, 1.9, 2.1), as have his BPV's (51, 48, 24, 47). Hitchcock might need only another manager who gives him 200 IP.

John Thomson (age 30): Thomson has never enjoyed major-league success, but a little something called Coors Field had something to do with that. His Command ratios in his last three seasons have been superb (2.8, 2.4, 2.8). Thomson earned $7 in 2003, and had he not endured a 65% strand rate despite a non-toxic 1.1 HR/9 and 30% hit rate, we might already be displaying him on velvet.

Batter Hit Rates

by Patrick Davitt

Over the last few years, the baseball-analysis community has been interested in pitchers' "Hit Rates" — the percent of balls they allow into the field of play that fall in for hits.

One theory suggests that once the ball is in play, it is largely a matter of luck whether it is hit right at someone or squeezed through for a hit. Indeed, pitchers' Hit Rates look well set at a 30% mean across MLB, and pitchers who vary from that mean can be expected to return to it.

So if Hit Rate can be used to forecast pitchers' success, why not also apply it to forecasting hitters' success? It seems intuitive that the same luck that plays a role for pitchers must also affect hitters.

But a study revealed that the MLB-wide mean Hit Rate does not apply to individual hitters; a player cannot be confidently forecast to regress to the MLB mean.

Instead, each hitter establishes an *individual* Hit Rate (H%) that stabilizes over time. In particular, we can forecast that a player who varies significantly from the H% he has established over the preceding three seasons is likely to regress to his individual H% mean.

Outliers

We looked at 232 hitters who had 900 ABs over the three seasons 2000-2002, and calculated the H% for every player, using the formula:

$$H\% = (H-HR) / (AB-HR-K)$$

The distribution of three-year H% fell as expected: a bell-shaped curve with a concentration at 30-31%. The median was 30%, the mean 31%. The chart also showed outliers, with three-year H%s from a low of 25% to a high of 38%.

We would expect outliers in any single-season study, and write them off to hitter's luck. But who were these hitters who had such high and low H% marks over three seasons?

Player	High H%
==============	======
Ramirez, Manny	38%
Edmonds, Jim	37%
Walker, Larry	36%
Jeter, Derek	36%
Helton, Todd	35%
Castillo, Luis	35%
Hernandez, Jose	35%
Abreu, Bobby	35%

Player	Low H%
==============	=======
Mondesi, Raul	26%
Hernandez, Ramon	26%
Palmeiro, Rafael	26%
Stairs, Matt	26%
Burnitz, Jeromy	26%
Batista, Tony	26%
Castilla, Vinny	26%
Ventura, Robin	25%

Ranges

Because a three-year result can be skewed by a single wild year, we looked at H% using rolling three-year averages, a tested method of leveling performance.

Looking again at our outliers, we see individual player H% ranges are very solidly established:

Player	H% 98-00	99-01	00-02	Range
==============	=====	=====	=====	=====
Ramirez, Manny	36%	38%	38%	2%
Edmonds, Jim	34%	35%	37%	3%
Walker, Larry	36%	36%	36%	0%
Jeter, Derek	39%	38%	36%	3%
Helton, Todd	33%	34%	35%	2%
Castillo, Luis	37%	36%	35%	2%
Hernandez, Jose	32%	33%	35%	3%
Abreu, Bobby	38%	36%	35%	3%
==============	=====	=====	=====	=====
Mondesi, Raul	29%	28%	26%	3%
Palmeiro, Rafael	29%	28%	26%	3%
Stairs, Matt	28%	27%	26%	2%
Burnitz, Jeromy	28%	27%	26%	2%
Batista, Tony	28%	27%	26%	2%
Castilla, Vinny	28%	27%	26%	2%
Ventura, Robin	29%	28%	25%	4%

Looking at all players active in 1998-2002, 76% performed within two-point H% ranges, and more than half of those were within one point. A few players show larger variations, but *most players establish narrow H% ranges over rolling three-year periods*.

Ranges and Rebounds

To make predictive use of this knowledge, we next need to examine whether players *stay* in their ranges in subsequent seasons.

We took players active in 98-02, comparing their "fourth years" following the 98-00 and 99-01 three-year averages. We found that while the odd player was 8 or 9 points outside his preceding three years, the overall distribution was again a bell curve, centered at −1 percentage point:

% Pt Diff	# in 2001 vs 98-00	# in 2002 vs 99-01	Total
====	=======	=======	========
+7-9	8	3	11 (3%)
+4-6	9	4	13 (4%)
+3	15	16	31 (8%)
+2	13	10	23 (6%)
+1	23	22	45 (12%)
0	23	21	44 (12%)
-1	30	32	62 (16%)
-2	20	20	40 (10%)
-3	17	16	33 (9%)
-4	18	17	35 (9%)
-5	5	11	16 (4%)
-6-8	11	20	31 (8%)

Overall, H% was within one percentage point of the preceding three-year average 40% of the time, within two points 56% of the time, and within three points 73% of the time.

So, combining what we learned earlier with what we have just found, we can say that *players establish reliable three-year H% levels, and the levels for a three-year period strongly predict the H% in the succeeding year*.

Regressing to the Mean

The next question is what happens to outliers who vary by unusual margins from their three-year H%. So we compared players' 2001 H% with their 1998-2000 three-year averages, sorted them by variance, and then looked at how they did the next year.

We would expect any "correction" to be stronger as the variance from the norm grew, with minimal effect among players whose 2001 H%s were within three percentage points of their three-year averages.

Indeed, that is the case:

		2002 Movement after 2001 variance				
2001 Diff	**Players**	**MIN**	**MAX**	**AVE**	**MEDIAN**	
+7 - +9 Pts	8	-8.0	-2.0	-5.9	-6.5	pts
+4 - +6 pts	9	-9.0	0.0	-3.7	-4.0	pts
+3	15	-10.0	+2.0	-2.1	-1.0	pts
+2	13	-9.0	+2.0	-2.9	-2.0	pts
+1	23	-7.0	+8.0	-2.0	-2.0	pts
0	23	-7.0	+2.0	-1.7	-2.0	pts
-1	30	-7.0	+6.0	-0.7	-0.5	pts
-2	20	-7.0	+4.0	-0.6	0.0	pts
-3	17	-5.0	+5.0	+0.5	+1.0	pts
-4	18	-1.0	+6.0	+2.8	+3.0	pts
-5 - -8	16	0.0	+7.0	+2.8	+2.5	pts

Players do move towards their three-year H% averages, and the effect is much sharper for players above their three-year averages. *Overperformers declined more than underperformers rose.*

Also, players right around their preceding three-year marks experience small declines. This seeming anomaly could lie in the study design: Including only players active in the preceding four years skews the sample towards the older part of the age range, where bat- and foot-speed declines start to set in.

Thus we might have a corollary to the overall theory: Declining H% for older players suggest the onset of an irreversible negative offensive trend more than a bounce-back opportunity.

Testing Predictive Value

Let's look in hindsight at outliers whose 2002 H% were more than five percentage points out of line with their 1999-01 three-year H%s. Their earlier rolling three-year averages are also shown as far back as they had 400-AB seasons. We would expect a regression to the mean in 2003, and generally that's what happened:

Player	98-00	99-01	02	+/-	03	Bounce
Hernandez, J	33%	33%	41%	+8%	31%	-10%
Wilson, Dan	30%	30%	37%	+7%	29%	- 8%
Bonds, Barry	26%	26%	33%	+7%	32%	- 1%
Clark, Tony	32%	33%	25%	-8%	26%	+ 1%
Lawton, Matt	30%	30%	23%	-7%	25%	+ 2%
Mayne, Brent	34%	34%	27%	-7%	28%	+ 1%
Tatis, F	33%	33%	26%	-7%	24%	- 2%
Stynes, Chris	31%	33%	26%	-7%	29%	+ 3%
Casey, Sean	34%	35%	28%	-7%	31%	+ 3%
Jenkins, Geoff	33%	35%	28%	-7%	34%	+ 6%
Alomar, R	33%	35%	29%	-6%	29%	0%
Cedeno, R	35%	36%	30%	-6%	31%	+ 1%
Graffanino, T	30%	35%	29%	-6%	28%	- 1%
Boone, Aaron	32%	32%	26%	-6%	28%	+ 2%

Bonds, Hernandez and Wilson should have had sharply lower H%s. And while Bonds is a special case (walks and HRs distort the formula), Hernandez and Wilson indeed regressed sharply back to their means.

Eight of the 11 H% underperformers in 2002 rebounded,

with Jenkins getting all the way back to his established norms. This is in line with expectations: Surges in H% followed by sharp declines, losses in H% followed by modest recoveries or continued losses. In fact, we can go as low as +/- 4% on both lists with similar results.

Looking to 2004

A number of players in 2003 had H% four or more percentage points above or below their 2000-2002 H% averages, implying a swing in H% next season:

	H%				
Batter	**98-00**	**99-01**	**00-02**	**03**	**Diff**
Mueller, Bill	31%	30%	29%	36%	+7%
Stairs, Matt	28%	27%	26%	31%	+5%
Grissom, M	29%	27%	27%	32%	+5%
Renteria, E	31%	30%	30%	35%	+5%
Grudzielanek,	32%	32%	31%	36%	+5%
Lieberthal, M	29%	30%	29%	33%	+4%
Guillen, Jose	30%	30%	29%	33%	+4%
Goodwin, Tom	33%	31%	31%	35%	+4%
Lopez, Javy	30%	31%	29%	33%	+4%
Cabrera, O	26%	26%	27%	31%	+4%
Dye, Jermaine	33%	33%	31%	19%	-12%
Giambi, Jason	33%	34%	34%	26%	-8%
Johnson, C	30%	32%	32%	25%	-7%
Konerko, Paul	30%	30%	30%	23%	-7%
Edmonds, Jim	34%	35%	37%	30%	-7%
Williams, B	35%	34%	34%	28%	-6%
Cordova, Marty	32%	33%	31%	25%	-6%
Bell, David	29%	28%	27%	21%	-6%
Young, Eric	30%	30%	30%	25%	-5%
Tatis, F	33%	33%	29%	24%	-5%
Clark, Tony	32%	33%	31%	26%	-5%
Higginson, B	30%	29%	30%	25%	-5%

In most cases, the 00-02 H% levels were in line with previous three-year averages, making the '03 shift seem even more out of place. All the players above look like good bets for either a sharp drop (first group) or recovery (2nd group), except Tatis, whose H% looks to be in steady decline, and Williams, whose other BPIs are dropping too fast to have any kind of confidence.

Conclusions

H% is not a magic formula. When using it, we have to look carefully at H% trends, other BPIs, and context. That said, we can assert with reasonable confidence that:

Each hitter establishes an individual H% that stabilizes over rolling three-year periods, and the levels for a three-year period strongly predict the H% in the succeeding year.

A player who varies significantly from his H% is likely to regress towards his individual H% mean, with overperformer declines both more likely and sharper than underperformer recoveries.

H% predictions should not be used within a season to anticipate short-term regressions. It should be used in pre-season draft calculations, and then only among veteran players with wide swings away from their norms and due attention to other factors.

There is still some work to do, particularly with regard to trend-spotting and the question of how soon young players establish reliable means. In the meantime, add H% to your toolbox and use it as part of your overall analytical set.

The Next Bret Boone

by Patrick Davitt

In trying to pick out potential draft bargains, we often focus on young players. But potential also exists in another place... among established journeymen who might be ready to raise their games to elite level.

Perhaps the best recent example was the sudden emergence in 2001 of Bret Boone. Boone was an established journeyman in 2000, when he went .251/19/74, with a .747 OPS. The next year, he erupted: .331/37/141 and an elite .957 OPS.

If we could identify some criteria in Boone's earlier years, we might be able to apply them pick out a hitter who could erupt.

Criteria

Age: Boone was 31 in his breakout year, so we want players who are no longer rising, but also not well into their decline years. Since players stay productive longer, we will set our age range as 30-34.

Journeyman Value: We'll be looking for players who have been consistent but unspectacular producers (Boone was an $11 player in 1999 and 2000), and haven't been above $15 in the last two seasons.

Regular PT: We also want steady performers who play regularly — an average of 450 AB in the preceding three years and at least 400 AB in each year.

Stats and BPIs: We want to match Boone's combined stats and key BPIs from 1998-2000, the three years before his big breakout:

- Contact Rate greater than 82%
- Walk Rate greater than 7%
- Linear Weighted Power (LWPr) greater than 37 (approximately 105 PX)
- OPS greater than .750
- AB/2B under 18.0
- Hit Rate (H%) under 30%. (Boone's preceding three-year mark was 28%, and his big year was 37%. We'll look for a player with room to cash in on luck.)

The Top Candidate

To test the concept, we applied our criteria to all hitters in the final stats for 2002 who also played in 1999-01. There were no perfect matches; Brian Giles and Shawn Green had six stat matches but are not journeymen by value.

Melvin Mora went four-for-six (short on the OPS and LWPr), and met the age and journeyman parameters. He had a breakout year in 2003.

One 2003 player met all the criteria. Scott Spiezio is 31, and has averaged 490 AB over the last three years earning $10, $12 and $14. He's a regular who will be somewhat under the radar at most drafts.

Spiezio also fits all six of our stat criteria for 2001-03:

Criterion	Standard	Spiezio
LWPr	37	40
OPS:	750	782
AB/2B	< 18.0	14.5

Contact Rate	82%	87%
Walk Rate	7%	8%
Hit %	< 30%	28%

Boone's breakthrough 2001 season also had a precursor — a "Hint Year" in 1998, when his production jumped significantly from 1997: He had 24 HR (up from 7), better AB/HR and AB/2B numbers, and his Contact Rate jumped to 82% from 77%.

Spiezio has not had quite such a dramatic "Hint Year." But in 1999, his AB/HR rate improved by 30% and his AB/2B rate doubled. His SLG rose 60 points. His value was muted by a 160-AB drop, and his H% fell to 26%, causing a BA decline. In 2000, Spiezio saw another spike in HR rate, to once every 17.5 AB, about 31 HR in a 550-AB season.

Finally, Boone's big year came after a team change, from weak San Diego to a loaded Seattle club. Spiezio is a free agent, so watch to see if he signs with an upper-tier team.

Other Players

No other players met all of the criteria though Robert Fick got five of six. Fick is not a great comp, however. He's slightly young (30 next Opening Day), and lacks the journeyman background. Worse, Fick's production against LHP has been consistently terrible. Any breakout will almost certainly have to be in a platoon, reducing its impact.

Two more 2003 players met the journeyman profile and had four stat matches: Todd Walker and Joe Randa. But while both players have a history of banging doubles and some high-value years, neither has nearly enough LWPr, and their peak value years were due to RBIs (Randa) a team stat, and SBs (Walker), which will be in short supply as he ages, especially if he stays in Boston.

Finally, the study uncovered the names of a few others who met five of the six criteria but were too young or are "name" players unlikely to sneak through draft. That said, these players could still step up to create value beyond established bid levels or draft placement: Mike Lowell, Orlando Cabrera, Aubrey Huff, Ivan Rodriguez, Ray Durham, Pat Burrell, Kevin Millar, Aramis Ramirez, Scott Rolen, Jose Vidro and Paul Konerko.

Tim Salmon was just high of the age range at 35, and has playing time issues, but otherwise met all but one of the criteria (two points shy of the 80% Ct%). Salmon could be a good rebound play.

Conclusion

As fanalytic players get wiser and deeper into the kind of BPI analysis *Forecaster* readers employ, it gets more difficult to stay ahead. The availability of detailed scouting data makes it tougher to find sleepers among rising stars.

For the next few years, one place to mine for gold will be among these undervalued journeymen. You likely won't snag "the next Bret Boone," because there likely won't *be* many stories like his. But being aware of the signs could provide added clues to uncovering important surplus value.

II.
The
TOOLS of
VICTORY

Foundation Philosophies

I cannot predict the future.

Nobody can. No matter what any other information source tells you. No matter how wonderfully complex and intricate their prognosticating model is. It is impossible to predict the future.

Nobody can tell you how many HRs Alex Rodriguez is going to hit next year. Nobody can tell you how many saves Eric Gagne is going to compile. And certainly, nobody can tell you whether Ken Griffey will ever see 500 ABs again.

Still, over the winter you will undoubtedly see advertisements for prognosticating services that proclaim amazing accuracy levels. "Accuracy" is a relative term, and frankly, it's overrated. Everyone has their own personal tolerance for how much "inaccuracy" they are willing to accept.

For instance, if I project that Alex Rodriguez is going to hit 45 HRs this year and he only hits 44, you will probably accept that level of inaccuracy. But what if he hits only 43? Or 42? Or 40? Or 39? At what point do we cross that imaginary line where the projection is "officially" deemed a failure? You might say "40." I might say, "Okay, so if A-Rod has 39 HRs on the final day of the season. and he hits a long fly ball that Darin Erstad makes an amazing over-the-wall leap to rob him of #40, has that one event been the difference between success and failure?"

You see, that imaginary line is a moving target.

So, how can we figure out how many home runs A-Rod is going to hit next year? Watch...

Forecasting is the systematic process of determining likely end results. In most disciplines, this process typically involves some large level of quantitative analysis. In baseball, most prognosticators attempt to do the same thing, with varying levels of success. But baseball forecasting is not the same animal, and that's where others tend to go wrong.

Baseball performance forecasting is inherently a high-risk exercise with a very modest accuracy rate. This is because the process involves not only statistics, but must also incorporate two very unscientific elements – random chance and human volatility. And even from within the statistical aspect there are multiple elements that need to be evaluated, from pure skills to playing time to a host of external variables.

Due to the abundance of all these variables, **baseball projections are prone to excessive noise**. For instance, projecting pitching wins requires the analysis and projection of not only the pitcher's skill, but the skills of his supporting offense, defense and bullpen, and the tendencies of his manager. A single win requires the input of *all* those elements, and so projecting wins requires that you be able to accurately project all those elements as well. It is an incredibly difficult task and is more apt to produce noise than any real expectation of future events.

Similarly, **projections of playing time can be an exercise in futility**. Beyond the small group of players who have guaranteed jobs each year, there are hundreds of others whose roles may or may not be nailed down at *any* subsequent time. Injuries, ill-timed slumps and managerial whim can all impact a player's chances to put up at bats and innings. Playing time is the most volatile element of the entire baseball forecasting process.

For the purposes of this book, we'd prefer not to tackle the playing time issue. Rather than making arbitrary decisions about who will play and who won't, this book focuses on performance. The playing time projections presented here are merely to help you better evaluate each player's talent. To what extent they will be able to use that talent won't be determined until much later. We do offer a pre-season projections update which provides more current projections based on how roles are being assigned.

An aspect of forecasting that others often ignore is that the process is not an isolated exercise to produce a set of inert numbers. **Baseball forecasting is dynamic, cyclical and ongoing.** Conditions are constantly changing and we must react to those changes by adjusting our expectations. A pre-season baseball projection is just a snapshot in time. Once the first batter steps to the plate on Opening Day, that projection has become obsolete. Its value to fantasy leaguers is merely to provide a starting point, a baseline for what is about to occur.

During the season, if a projection appears to have been invalidated by current performance, the process continues. It is then that we need to ask... What went wrong? What conditions have changed? In fact, has *anything* changed? We need to analyze the situation and revise our expectation, if necessary. This process must be ongoing, all year long.

Finally, the outcomes of forecasted events should not be confused with the process itself. Outcomes may be the components that are the most closely scrutinized, but as long as the process is sound, the forecast has done its job. It's tongue-in-cheek, but the shingle outside the professional forecaster's office always reads, **"There are no bad forecasts, only bad outcomes."**

Component Skills Analysis (CSA)

Familiar gauges like home runs and ERA have long been used to measure raw skill. In fact, these gauges only measure the outcome of an individual event, or series of events. They represent statistical output.

Raw skill is the talent beneath the stats, the individual elements of a player's makeup. For batters, skill includes the ability to see and follow pitches, the ability to make contact with the ball and the ability to hit with authority. For pitchers, skill includes the ability to get the ball over the plate, the ability to fool or dominate hitters and the ability to prevent batted balls from being hit with authority.

Players use these skills to create the individual events that we record using measures like HR and ERA. Why are these events not skills unto themselves? In tracking a batter's home run trend, for instance, what we are really trying to track is his *power* skills. And power skills are comprised of not only home runs, but *every* event that displays a batter's power — doubles, triples, fly outs, and even long foul balls.

Statistical output also includes an element that we're only first starting to get our arms around – *random chance*. From the perspective of a round bat meeting a round ball, it may be only a fraction of an inch at the point of contact that makes the difference between a homerun or a long foul ball. When a ball is hit safely, often it is only a few inches that separate a HR from a double. Yet we tend to neglect these facts in our analyses, although the outcomes — the doubles, the triples, the long fly balls — may be no less a measure of that batter's raw power skill. Similarly, we must look at the component events – both skill and chance – that contribute to other baseball talents, such as speed and pitching effectiveness.

In order for us to get a better read on raw skill, we use formulas that contain relevant raw statistical categories. Among these are linear weighted power (which includes weighted levels of HRs, doubles, and triples), batting eye, pitching command, and many others.

Why is all this important? Analysts complain about the lack of predictability of many traditional statistical gauges. The reason they find it difficult is that they are trying to project performance using gauges that are loaded with external noise. Raw skills gauges are more pure and follow better defined trends over the course of a player's career. And as we get a better handle on random chance, we can construct a complete picture of what a player's statistics really mean.

The next step in CSA is to assemble these peripheral evaluators in such a way that they can provide a more accurate view of performance. By creating a structure, sequence and organization to these gauges, we can paint a picture that can be used to validate our observations, analyze their relevance and project a likely future direction.

The beauty of CSA is it allows us to identify variances between statistical output and raw skill gauges, and from that, project changes in performance within a season or from one season to another. How it works...

In a perfect world, if a player's raw skills improve, then so should his statistical output. If his skills decline, then his stats should follow suit as well. Well, sometimes a player's skill may increase while the traditional stat category we use to measure that skill may decline. These variances may be due to a variety of factors, from the performances of other players on his team to random chance.

CSA is based on the philosophy that events tend to move towards universal order. This has been proven in other areas of baseball analysis... Players' performance tends to move towards their career averages, team Won/Loss records tend to move towards their statistical levels. CSA states that these variances will correct themselves over time. Statistical levels will eventually approach their associated raw skill levels. Aberrations in gauges we use to measure random chance almost always regress to the mean as well. And from this, we can identify players whose performance, as a whole, may change.

A batter whose HR output drops while his batting eye ratio and linear weighted power level increases has a high probability of improving his future HR output. A pitcher whose ERA improves while his command ratio and strikeout rate fall off is a good bet to see a spike in his ERA.

Leading Indicators

A player whose base performance indicators (BPIs) – those gauges that measure raw skill – follow a consistent, well-defined trend is rare. There are far more shades of greys than blacks and whites in baseball analysis. There are two basic types of indicators and trends that we encounter in our analyses.

Strong indicators are those that provide a solid foundation for drawing conclusions. A 10.0 strikeout rate and a 2.0 walk rate for a pitcher are two very strong indicators of success. For batters, a 95% contact rate is an important first step to a .300 batting average.

There can also be strong negative indicators. A rotation anchor with a 1.0 command ratio might fail in that role. A stolen base machine with an on base average under .300 might not get on base enough to use his speed skills.

Finally, there can be strong trends, which can be the most important support for our forecasting efforts. A batter who, over time, is showing a consistently rising power index in tandem with a rising fly ball rate could be a prime candidate for a home run spike. A reliever who has been demonstrating declining command in tandem with a falling saves conversion rate might be about to lose his role as a team's closer.

Conflicting indicators are those that do not provide a clear picture and often force us to make judgment calls. If a pitcher's strikeout rate is improving, but he is also giving up more home runs, what type of effect will that have on his future ERA? If a batter's contact rate is improving, but his batting average versus left-handed pitchers has been in a tailspin, what can we read into that?

It is often helpful to look at leading indicators in a hierarchy, of sorts. A pitcher's opponent batting average has less relevance than his command ratio, for instance. In fact, a hierarchy of the most important pitching BPIs might look like this: command (k/bb), control (bb/9), dominance (k/9), homerun rate and opposition batting average. For batters, contact rate might top the list, followed by on base average, batting eye (bb/k), power and speed.

Random Chance

When the analysis of leading indicators runs up against a wall, often we can look to random chance to shed light on a player's future. Recent research has shown that there are gauges that are not intrinsically skills-based, but do affect a player's statistical output. These gauges measure elements beyond the control of the player and can include defense, bullpen or managerial decision, as well as the random bounce of the ball.

And the beauty of these measures is that they tend to regress to the mean from year to year, or if not, are projectable by tracking their component elements.

For instance, pitching strand rates measure the percentage of runners who are prevented from scoring. This is a skill of the pitcher on the mound, but also a skill of the relievers that follow him. What's most important is that strand rates have a direct impact on a pitcher's ERA.

League average rates run about 72%, but research has shown that rates at the high and low end of the spectrum revert to the mean in 8 out of every 10 cases. This means that a low strand rate of 60% — which always indicates a high ERA — will improve 80% of the time, as will that pitcher's ERA. And if the law of averages doesn't kick in by itself, there are other external factors that can help in this case, for instance, the projected improvement in that team's bullpen.

None of this has anything to do with that pitcher's skill; his ERA would be projected to improve just because of the natural tendencies of a gauge like strand rate to move in a certain direction.

Performance Validation

I suppose, we could create projections out of nothing.

John Smith comes up to the plate. Nobody knows who he is or where he came from. Any expectation as to what he will do in this at bat is a shot in the dark. Any estimate of what statistics he might compile over the course of 162 games is an even greater unknown. However, with every time he comes to the plate, we start to build a profile of what his strengths and weaknesses are. Over time, that profile can help us form the basis of a future projection.

This would be the case if we were starting a new league. However, we have years and years of performance data already in the books, for virtually every player. Most prognosticating systems look at this history and calculate a projection from some series of formulas and rules. We do things a little bit differently here.

Our forecasting process starts the same way. We do have computer models that calculate a baseline projection, but from there, an entirely different process takes over.

We know that most people form an opinion on players based on the *previous year's performance*. Javy Lopez hit 43 HRs – can he repeat those numbers? Pat Burrell hit only .209 – can he rebound? Eric Gagne compiled 55 saves – can he keep up that level of dominance? Last season provides us with a point of reference, so it's a natural way to begin the process of looking at the future.

Given that, we start by attempting to *validate last year's performances*. Using our BPIs and looking at random chance, we get a general sense of whether the player's previous year's statistical output looks legitimate. A 10-HR spike but a drop in his power index? Perhaps that 40 HR performance was a bit inflated. A 2.50 ERA with a 80% strand rate? Let's see what that ERA looks like with a 72% rate. And, by using a series of statistical levers, we start adjusting last season's numbers to better represent the skill behind the stats.

Forecaster's Toolbox

Finally, we use a set of additional criteria and research results to help us add some final color to the picture of next season. These other criteria include the player's health, age, changes in role, home ballpark, and a variety of other risk factors. We'll incorporate our research results, looking at things like traditional periods of peak performance, the effects of crossing leagues, breakout profiles and factors impacting sophomore campaigns.

These are all described in detail in the next section.

Assimilating the Outside World

We will never know the entire truth.

The baseball gospel resides in the media. This is what we read, watch and listen to every day. This is the information upon which we create our fantasy baseball reality, manage our rosters and run our teams. This is where we seek the truth, but one that will be forever elusive to us.

Sometimes we overlook evidence ourselves. Sometimes we are unable to figure out the signs. And sometimes we are not made privy to complete information. Players, management and the media have absolute control over what we are allowed to know and what we cannot know.

And so... As long as we do not know all the variables, we cannot dismiss the possibility that any one variable does exist. No matter how outrageous it seems. No matter how often the media assures it, deplores it, or ignores it.

News is the lifeblood in which we assemble and run our teams, but this is just information comprised of other people's opinions... a manager who believes that a certain player has what it takes to be a regular, a scout whose observation is that a player has potential, a team physician whose diagnosis is that a player is healthy enough to play. These words from experts have some element of truth, especially in reference to current events, but cannot be wholly relied upon to provide an accurate expectation of future events.

The truth is that the news we rely on is really only part news and the rest noise. Our biggest challenge is to be able to distinguish between the two, so you need to develop an appropriate cynicism for what you read.

Four areas to be keenly aware of:

a. Full, prompt disclosure is something that is essentially non-existent.

From the players' perspective, there is often incentive to hide the truth, especially if it is information that might impact his future role with a team. For instance, if a player is struggling for no apparent reason, and there are complete denials about health issues, don't dismiss the possibility that an injury does, in fact, exist.

From the team's perspective, there are also incentives to conceal information. Internal confrontations between players and management might have an impact on future performance, but teams will naturally opt to keep this 'dirty laundry' in-house. Trade or contract negotiations may also be compromised if the media gets hold of inside information.

So we're left in the dark, sometimes legitimately, but sometimes not.

b. Medical reporting: Much of the prognosis reporting that goes on is pure speculation. Every player's ability to rehab from an injury is different. 15-day disabled list stays last 15 days only about half the time. Plus, ballclubs routinely refrain from reporting all information for fear that any perception of serious injury will significantly reduce a player's marketplace value. With the new HIPAA laws, there are now legal reasons to withhold medical information.

c. Fluidity of decision-making: Nothing lasts forever in major league baseball. In fact, everything lasts for a shorter time than you can possibly imagine.

The term, "firm decision," is an oxymoron. One decision begets a series of events that leads to another decision. And then another. Any reported action that could easily be reversed based on subsequent events is mostly noise (e.g. a rookie being handed a starting role prior to spring training, etc.). Decisions made in spring training are more benched in reality, but are still faulty. If a player looks good in 75 ABs or 15 IP against a mixture of major and minor league competition, is that really an accurate barometer of future major league success? For some managers, that's more than enough. Until, of course, the first 0 for 14 slump.

d. Direct quotes: Statements from players, scouts, coaches, managers and national columnists provide little more than isolated opinion and virtually no meaningful information. Always question whether there could be a hidden motive for someone making a particular statement. You'll be amazed at how noisy things can get.

We need the media to provide us with context for our analyses, and the *real* news they provide is valuable intelligence. But separating the news from the noise is difficult. In most cases, the only thing you can trust is how that player actually performs.

Embracing Imprecision

As a result of all the above, I've come to some startling conclusions.

Back in the 1994 edition of this book, I proclaimed that "numbers are everything." After all, that is what our games are all about. We play with numbers; we win or lose with numbers. Over the past few years, I've come to realize that, not only are numbers not everything, most of them hardly even matter at all, *especially* the numbers that we play our games with.

Precision and accuracy in baseball prognosticating is a fool's quest. There are far too many unexpected variables and noise, things that occur daily that render our expectations null and void. The truth is, the best we can ever hope for is to accurately forecast general tendencies. Using the following library of research results, built by myself and others, we've created a series of rules and have developed percentage plays for performance.

What is a percentage play? In its broadest sense, it is a series of statistical, logical or situational factors that provide a basis for some general level of performance. We can build percentage plays from individual factors. For instance, last March we could have said that, based on Jay Payton beginning a full season in Coors, and based on his .340 batting average in the second half of 2002, we were perhaps 80% confident that this .285 lifetime hitter would bat .300 in 2003.

Our goal is to find those percentage plays that give us at least a 67% chance of success. Ideally, we want to uncover those that provide us with 80% plays, though they are tougher to come by. And, of course, you also must remember the flipside: When you follow an 80% percentage play, you will still lose 20% of the time. Those 20% worth of outlying players are what skeptics like to use as proof that all prognosticators are frauds. HQ writer John Burnson once wrote: "The issue is not the success rate for one player, but the success rate for all players. No system is 100% reliable, and in trying to capture the outliers, you weaken the middle and thereby lose more predictive pull than you gain. At some level, everyone is an exception!"

So, long-term success dictates that you always chase the 80% and accept the fact that you will be wrong 20% of the time. Or, whatever that percentage play happens to be.

For our own fantasy league purposes, playing the percentages can take on an even less precise spin. The alternate reality of our game model suggests that the best projections are just the ones that are far enough away from the field of expectation to alter decision-making. In other words, it doesn't matter if I project Player X to bat .320 and he only bats .295. It matters that I projected .320, and everyone else projected .280.

Or, perhaps we should evaluate projections based upon their intrinsic value. For instance, coming into 2003, would it have been more important for me to tell you that Albert Pujols is going to hit 40 HRs or that Mike Lowell is going to hit a career high 26 HRs? By season's end, the Pujols projection would have been more accurate, but the Lowell projection would have been more *valuable*.

So, I can't really tell you what Sidney Ponson is going to do next year. However, I can tell you that, based on his solid command ratio, improved home run rate, increased ground ball rate and his first career xERA under 4.00, the odds were strong that his 3.75 ERA in 2003 was for real. I'll also say, with perhaps 75% confidence, that he has a good shot at maintaining that level in 2004. I'll even go one step further and say, based on his 3.53 ERA in the second half and being at a good age to take a step up, perhaps he might even improve upon that 3.75 ERA.

I say this even though 2003 represented his first sub-4.00 ERA ever. And I say this even though most other prognosticators will be projecting a natural regression to his career 4.00-plus levels.

And that should be enough. Actually, it *has* to be enough. Any tout who exactly projects Sidney Ponson's 2004 ERA was just lucky with his dart throws that day.

Forecaster's Toolbox

Over time, baseball analysts have amassed a large pool of research to help us understand how and why a player's performance changes from one year to another. The baseball prognosticating process, which relies on this research, has evolved into one where the best success can often be found by learning to play the percentages. This critical intelligence does not provide absolutes, but strong tendencies that we can use in evaluating talent.

The following tools, rules and findings represent the work of many authors. Much of our own research is here. There are findings of other baseball analysts. Bill James was the founding father of the seeds of this research, and many of his findings appear as well.

There are two types of information here. There are analytical tools, which are methods to put events and performances into some type of context. And there are actual research results. Generally, we only include the results of each particular piece of research, rather than take up space with all the methodologies and minutia. The back-up data has appeared in our other publications and on BaseballHQ.com in the past. Our purpose here is to give you the tools you need to make evaluations, and quickly. So pardon the lack of support data. Rest assured we're not making this stuff up.

Also remember that, since these research findings represent tendencies, not absolutes, they will occasionally be wrong. If we tell you that 96% of batters with eye ratios under 0.50 will not hit .300, don't send us hate mail if the spray hitter you passed on in the draft falls into the other 4%. It happens. It's not our fault. Consider this a universal disclaimer.

But beyond that, there is great value here. Consider this your own personal analytical arsenal. Use it to figure out why players perform how they do. Use it to help project what players might do in the future. Use it to help explain deviations from those expectations.

And use it to gain some perspective.

Validating Overall Performance

Performance Validation Criteria

The following list of criteria helps us validate that a player's performance is "for real." When a player puts up numbers that vary from expectation, we can assemble a set of support variables that can help us determine whether his statistical output is an accurate reflection of his skills, or if other variables have come into play that have skewed the stats. Essentially, we're asking, is this performance a "fact or fluke?"

1. The player's age... Is he at the stage of development when we might expect a change in performance?

2. Health status... Is he coming off an injury, reconditioned and healthy for the first time in years, or a habitual resident of the disabled list?

3. Minor league performance... Has he ever shown the potential for greater things at some level of the minors? Or does his minor league history show a poor skill set that might indicate a potential relapse?

4. Historical trends... Have his raw skill levels been on an upswing or downswing?

5. Hidden indicators within traditional stats... Looking beyond batting averages and ERAs, what do his support ratios look like?

6. Change in ballpark, team, league... Pitchers going to Colorado will see their ERA spike. Pitchers going to Shea Stadium will see their ERA improve. Stuff like that.

7. Change in team performance... Has a player's performance been affected by overall team chemistry or the environment fostered by a winning or losing club?

8. Change in batting stance, pitching style... Has a change in performance been due to an adjustment made during the off-season?

9. Change in usage, lineup position, etc.... Has a change in RBI opportunities been a result of moving further up or down in the batting order? Has pitching effectiveness been impacted by moving from the bullpen to the rotation?

10. Change in managerial strategy (opportunity)... Does his sudden change in performance have less to do with ability than with playing time, or perhaps not having a well-defined role?

11. Coaching effects... Has the coaching staff changed the way a player approaches his conditioning, or how he approaches the game itself?

12. Off-season activity... Has a player spent the winter frequenting workout rooms or banquet tables?

13. Personal factors... Has the player undergone a family crisis? Experienced spiritual rebirth? Given up red meat?

Skills Ownership

Once a player displays a skill, he owns it. That display could occur at any time... earlier in his career, back in the minors, or even in winter ball play. And while that skill may lie dormant after its initial display, the potential is always there for him to tap back into that skill at some point, barring injury or age. That dormant skill can reappear at any time given the right set of circumstances.

Caveats...

The initial display of skill must have occurred over an extended period of time. An isolated 1-hit shut-out in Single-A ball amidst a 5.00 ERA season is not enough. The shorter the display of skill in the past, the more likely it can be attributed to random chance. The longer the display, the more likely that any re-emergence of that skill is for real. Typically, you'd want to see a consistent level of performance over at least a several month period.

Once a player displays a vulnerability or skills deficiency, he owns that as well. That vulnerability could be an old injury problem, an inability to hit breaking pitches, or just a tendency to go into prolonged slumps.

The probability of a player addressing and correcting a skills deficiency declines with each year that deficiency continues to exist.

Categories of Surprises

Career year: These are players who have established a certain level of performance over several years, then suddenly put up exceptional numbers. Career years may be explained from the list of validation criteria, but are usually one-shot deals.

Maturation: These players have also established a certain level of performance over time, but the performance spike is truly indicative of their potential and will likely be maintained.

Off year: These are players who have established a certain level of performance over several years, then suddenly drop off. This could be a performance blip, an adjustment period or an injury-induced decline. These players have the potential to bounce back.

Comedown: These players have also established a certain level of performance over time, but their performance drop is indicative of a new level at which they will likely plateau. The typical thirtysomething syndrome.

Opportunity: Sometimes a surprise isn't a change in performance at all but the effect a change in playing time has on performance. Often, a solid role player gets thrust into a full-time job and suddenly puts up extraordinary numbers. This can work both ways — a player may rise to the occasion, or find that the regular day-to-day grind has an adverse effect on his numbers. Opportunity surprises are created by events like injuries or changes in managerial strategy and can last as long as the opportunity lasts.

No surprise: We sometimes form unrealistic expectations about players due to media hype or short-term performance levels. Rookies fall into this category, for instance, but the failure of unproven commodities should not be unexpected. In addition, frequently injured players who've lowered our expectations, then bounce back to previous productivity levels when healthy, should not be surprises either (except, perhaps, that they managed to stay healthy).

Aberration: These are the performances that simply cannot be adequately explained by the validation criteria. Chance occurrences do happen, and sometimes in bunches. There are stretches in a player's career when a spray hitter might see a few week's worth of fat, juicy homer balls, or a pitcher might face a string of wiffle bats. It just happens, then it stops. Most times, it will never happen again.

Assessing Forecast Risk

While forecasts are constructed with the best possible data available, there are many factors that can impact a player exceeding or falling short of expectation. One of the ways we deal with this is to assign each of our projections a risk level. The less certainty we can see in a data set, the higher the forecast risk.

The Risk Tables in the forecast boxes evaluate each player's risk for the following variables:

Experience (EXP): The greater the pool of major league history to draw from, the greater our ability to construct a viable forecast. Length of service is important, as is length of consistent service. So players who bounce up and down from the majors to the minors are higher risk players. And rookies are all high risk.

Consistency (CON): Consistent performers are easier to project and garner lower risk levels. Players that mix mediocrity, or worse, with occasional flashes of brilliance generate higher risk projections.

Playing time (PT): Fluctuating playing time is a sign of several possible problems. Players with an injury history — whether or not they are healthy right now — will generate higher risk projections. Also, any change in a player's role or usage will increase the risk of his projection being off. These changes could include a move from the bullpen into the rotation, a move to another position in the batting order, or the move from full-timer to a platoon role.

Stability (STB): Any player who has recently switched uniforms or has a history of frequent moves to different teams, or leagues, drops a notch in forecast confidence.

Age (AGE): Players will develop their skills to a certain level of performance, at which they will typically plateau for several years. However, during the rise of that skills curve, as well as during their late career descent, their performance will be more prone to fluctuation, and hence, higher risk.

Burnout potential (BRN): For a pitcher, workload levels need to be monitored, especially in the formative years of his career. Exceeding those levels elevates the risk of injury, burnout, or breakdown. More about this in the Pitcher's Toolbox, under Usage Warning Flags.

These main variables focus mostly on a player's own internal risk factors. There are also several external factors that can have equal impact on risk. For instance, are the manager's strategies and tendencies consistent or inconsistent? There are many unstable bullpen situations each year which make projecting saves a difficult task. Similarly, a speedster not knowing whether he will be at the top or middle of a lineup will impact his projected stolen base opportunities.

The player forecast boxes evaluate these criteria for each player and assign them an overall risk rating. You may be surprised at the paucity of lower risk players, but that is the reality of forecasting performance. It is inherently a high-risk game.

Half-Season Fallacies

A popular exercise at the midpoint of each season is to analyze those players who are *consistent* first half to second half surgers or faders. There are several fallacies with this analytical approach.

1. Half-season consistency is rare. There are very few players who show consistent changes in performance from one half of the season to the other.

Research results from a three-year study conducted in the late-1990s: The total of all batters who compiled a minimum of 300 full season ABs, and a minimum of 150 first half ABs in this study was 98. Of that group, 40% demonstrated a consistent first half to second half trend in at least one statistical category for all three years. Only 18% demonstrated any half-season tendency in more than one category. And only 3% demonstrated consistent tendencies in more than two categories over the three-year period.

The total of all pitchers who compiled a minimum of 100 full season IPs, and a minimum of 50 first half IPs in this study was only 42. Of that group, 57% demonstrated a consistent first half to second half trend in at least one stat category for all three years. Only 21% demonstrated any half-season tendency in more than one category. And only 5% had consistent tendencies in more than two categories.

When the analysis was stretched to a fourth year, only 1% of batters and pitchers showed consistency in even one category.

2. Analysts often use false indicators. Situational statistics provide us with tools that are often misused. Sources like ESPN.com's player pages and the now-defunct STATS, Inc. *Player Profiles* book offer up three and 5-year statistics intended to paint a picture of a long-term performance. Some analysts look at a player's half-season batting average swing over that muti-year period and conclude that he is demonstrating consistent performance.

The fallacy is that those scans may not show any consistency at all. They are not individual season performances but *aggregate* performances. A player whose 5-year ERA shows a 1-run rise in the 2nd half, for instance, may actually have experienced ERA *improvement* in several of those years, a fact that might have been offset by a huge ERA rise in one of the years.

3. It's arbitrary. Despite our use of half-season splits as one criteria for projecting forward, the season's midpoint is really an arbitrary delineator of performance swings. Some players are slow starters and might be more appropriately evaluated as pre-May 1 and post-May 1. Others bring their game up a notch with a pennant chase and might see a performance swing with August 15 as the cut-off point. Each player has his own individual tendency, if, in fact, one exists at all.. There's nothing magical about July 1 or the All Star Break as the analytical break point, and certainly not over a multi-year period.

Batting Toolbox
Batting Eye as a Leading Indicator

The raw ability to distinguish between balls and strikes — strike zone judgment — is a good descriptor of a batter's potential batting average, and in some cases, can be used as a predictor of future performance. Research findings:

1. There is a high correlation between a batter's eye ratio and his batting average.

Batting Eye	Batting Average				
	1999	2000	2001	2002	2003
0.00 - 0.25	.257	.253	.240	.251	.247
0.26 - 0.50	.269	.268	.257	.254	.261
0.51 - 0.75	.277	.273	.264	.266	.270
0.76 - 1.00	.283	.289	.277	.282	.281
1.01 and over	.299	.306	.304	.293	.294

2. Any batter with an eye ratio over 1.50 has about a 4% chance of hitting under .250 over 500 at bats.

3. Of all .300 hitters, those with ratios of at least 1.00 have a 65% chance of repeating as .300 hitters. Those with ratios under 1.00 have less than a 50% chance of repeating.

4. Sub-.250 batters with eye ratios under 1.00 are not likely to mature into .300 hitters the following year. Only 12% of those with ratios between 0.50 and 0.99, and only 4% of those with ratios under 0.50 will hit .300 in year #2.

5. Batters with eye ratios under 0.50 are a high risk group. They may hit over .300 at some point in their careers (some batters can hack their way to anything), but pitchers eventually figure out that they do not have to give these free-swingers anything good to hit. At that point, it takes a large scale adjustment on the part of the batter to return to the .300 plateau.

In a study covering 1995-2000, there were only 37 batters that had hit .300 or better with an eye ratio of 0.50 or less over at least 300 AB in a single season. Of this group, 30% exhibited the unique ability to accomplish this feat on a consistent basis. For the other 70%, a .300-plus BA and sub-0.50 eye ratio was a short-term aberration.

Contact Rate as a Leading Indicator

It follows intuitively that the more often a batter makes contact with the ball, the higher the likelihood that he will hit safely. Not rocket science here, but good to see that the numbers do typically bear this out.

Contact Rate	Batting Average			
	2000	2001	2002	2003
0% - 60%	.143	.170	.185	.161
61% - 65%	.212	.228	.233	.201
66% - 70%	.250	.233	.242	.240
71% - 75%	.262	.255	.247	.247
76% - 80%	.263	.259	.261	.264
81% - 85%	.275	.277	.268	.271
86% - 90%	.293	.278	.279	.280
Over 90%	.294	.291	.272	.284

Batting Eye and Power

We often ignore the batting eye ratio when evaluating power because so many batters achieve their lofty HR numbers by opening up their swing, thereby increasing their strikeout totals and depressing their eye ratio. However, this path to power success is a riskier one.

During the four-year study period, any batter who

slammed 30 HRs in a season had less than a 3 in 10 chance of improving his power skills in the following year. But by adding in the eye ratios of each batter, the power decline can be better defined...

Batting eye	YEAR 2	
	PX increased	PX declined
Less than 0.50	13%	87%
0.50 - 0.99	24%	76%
1.00 and over	31%	69%

Batters with lower eye ratios were more likely to experience a power drop-off in the year following a 30-HR campaign. We can use this information to our advantage when tracking a batter's power trends from year to year. Here are the various scenarios and explanations:

Power increases and batting eye increases: This is the most favorable scenario. The batter is seeing the ball better, exhibiting improved plate discipline, and the end result is an improvement in his power skills. These power surges are often long-term.

Power increases and batting eye decreases: The most likely scenario when a batter displays a spike in power. He opens up his swing and begins to drive the ball, the fallout often being an increase in strikeouts and a drop in batting average. The danger is that opposing pitchers often figure out that they do not have to give him anything good to hit. These batters are prone to prolonged streaks and slumps.

Power decreases and batting eye increases: This scenario occurs when a batter is trying to become more selective at the plate, often in response to a slump. In most cases, the power outage is short-term and the skills eventually return.

Power decreases and batting eye decreases: The least favorable scenario. The batter is slumping, but rather than working on being more selective at the plate, he begins to press, chase bad pitches, and the slump deepens. Large chunks of seasons can be lost when this scenario occurs.

Power Breakouts

It is not an easy task to predict which batters are going to put up an extraordinary power season. What we can do is categorize these power breakouts:

1. Increase in playing time. An unexpected increase in HR output might not be a product of any change in skills but the direct result of an increase in playing time, which may be expected or unexpected.

2. History of power skills. A player may have displayed power skills sometime in the past, be it in his early major league career or prior.

3. Distribution of extra base hits. There is not much difference in skill between a double and a HR. A HR breakout may merely be a random redistribution of already demonstrated extra base hit power.

4. Normal skills growth. The power spike may be a normal occurrence along a batter's growth curve. A batter's breakout year may have been easily predicted from a review of his power index (PX) trend.

5. Situational breakouts. No matter how impressive the HR-hitting feats of Vinny Castilla were in the past, the fact that he played half his games in Coors Field discounted any true spike in skills (even more noted since he's left Coors). Similar for any player moving into a more power-conducive venue, or moving *out* of a pitcher-friendly venue.

6. Fly ball tendency. Early research shows that a batter who increases his fly ball tendency may be trackable as a potential surger in power output.

7. The unexplained. Sometimes, a power spike makes no logical sense — Brady Anderson hitting 50 HRs, for instance. These power surges hold the lowest probability for a comparable follow-up performance.

Handedness Notes

1. While pure southpaws account for about 27% of total ABs (RHers about 55% and switch-hitters about 18%), they hit 31% of the triples and take 30% of the walks.

2. The average lefty posts a batting average about 10 points higher than the average RHer. The on base averages of pure LHers are nearly 20 points higher than RHers, but only 10 points higher than switch-hitters.

3. LHers tend to have a better batting eye ratio than RHers, but about the same as switch-hitters.

4. Pure righties and lefties have virtually identical power skills. Switch-hitters, however, tend to have less power, on average.

5. Switch-hitters tend to have the best speed, followed by LHers, and then RHers.

6. On an overall production basis, LHers have about an 8% advantage over RHers and about a 14% edge over switch-hitters.

Batting Average Perception

Early season batting average strugglers who surge later in the year get no respect because they have to live with the weight of their early numbers all season long. Conversely, quick starters who fade late get far more accolades than they deserve.

For instance, take Edgardo Alfonzo's 2003 month by month batting averages. Perception, which is typically based purely on a player's cumulative season level, was that he had a terrible year, from start to finish. Reality is different. How many people knew he batted over .280 in four of the six months, and .296 from July 1 on?

Month	BA	Cum BA
April	.174	.174
May	.283	.228
June	.230	.228
July	.306	.244
August	.284	.253
September	.296	.259

League Switching

Since the AL is a breaking ball league, right-handed NL hitters coming over to the AL tend to struggle at first until they adjust. Some never do.

AL free-swingers often have a difficult time when coming over to the NL and being fed a steady diet of fastballs.

Optimal Ages

Players develop at different paces, but in general terms, age can be helpful to determine where they should be along the developmental curve. From Bill James' research it has been accepted that batters tend to peak at about age 27. But further research has helped to refine these tendencies.

"26 With Experience" *(John Benson):* While batters may peak at about age 27, the players most likely to exhibit the most dramatic spike in performance are those aged 26 who have several years of major league experience.

Power: Batting power skills tend to grow consistently between ages 24 and 29. Many batters experience a power peak at about age 30-31. Catchers often experience a power spike in the mid-30's.

Speed: Baserunning and speed are skills of the young. When given the choice of two speedsters of fairly equivalent abilities and opportunity, always go after the younger one. A sharp drop-off in speed skills typically occurs at age 34.

Batting eye: For batters who continue to play into their 30's, this is a skill that can develop and grow throughout their career. A decline in this level, which can occur at any age, often indicates a decline in overall skills.

Thirtysomethings *(Ed Spaulding):* Batters tend to lose points on their batting average, steal fewer bases (and with a lower success rate) and draw more walks. While players on the outside of the defensive spectrum (1B, 3B, LF, RF, DH) often have their best seasons in their 30's, players in the middle (2B, SS, CF) tend to fade. Many former stars move to new positions (Ripken, Molitor, Banks, etc.).

Catchers *(Ed Spaulding):* Many catchers — particularly second line catchers — have their best seasons late in their careers. Some possible reasons why:

1. Catchers, like shortstops, often get to the big leagues for defensive reasons and not their offensive skills. These skills take longer to develop.

2. The heavy emphasis on learning the catching/defense/pitching side of the game detracts from their time to learn about, and practice, hitting.

3. Injuries often curtail their ability to show offensive skills, though these injuries (typically jammed fingers, bruises on the arms, rib injuries from collisions) often don't lead to time on the disabled list.

4. The time spent behind the plate has to impact the ability to recognize, and eventually hit, all kinds of pitches.

September Performance Declines *(Harold Brooks)*

Overall, batting average (-.002), on base average (-.002) and slugging average (-.006) decline after the end of August. Those who play every day of the season are more prone to decline. Throwing infielders (2B, 3B, SS) appear to suffer more than outfielders. As little as five days off during the season alleviates any of the problems in September, and with 10 days off, the chances of a September fade are very small.

Pitching Toolbox
The Global Fallacy

"There's no way to project pitchers accurately from year to year." — Bill James.

"Your most valuable commodity is a starting pitcher you can count on. The only problem is, you can't count on any of them." — Peter Golenbock

"Where else in the realm of fantasy sports can you have worse odds on success than from the wonderful world of the pitcher?" — Rod Beaton

"Starting pitchers are the most unreliable, unpredictable, unpleasant group of people in the world, statistically speaking that is." — John Benson

"No one, not the most astute major league scout nor the world's top number cruncher, can correctly project the statistical output of more than a couple of dozen of the game's 400 hurlers." — Steve Mann

While it's difficult to argue with the collective wisdom of these top baseball writers, their perception is tainted. Unreliable pitching performance is a fallacy driven by the practice of attempting to project performance using pitching gauges that are poor evaluators of talent.

In the *1991 Baseball Sabermetric*, Phil Birnbaum wrote about the perception of pitching inconsistency. He showed how small changes in batting statistics were equivalent to large changes in pitching statistics.

Birnbaum showed a player's batting line for two different years. In the first, this player hit .237 with 11 HRs and 52 RBIs. The second year he hit .264 with 15 HRs and 65 RBIs. Birnbaum notes, "you notice the improvement but you recognize that this is the same player; in fact, you might think these are pretty similar seasons." Yet, if these two lines represented the stats allowed by a pitcher, the first would have equated to an ERA of 3.29, the second, 4.55.

Birnbaum concludes that, although a pitcher's statistics tend to show great inconsistencies from year to year, his talent does not fluctuate any more than a batter's does.

The Fundamental Skills

How can we better evaluate pitching talent? There are three statistical categories generally unaffected by external factors, which solely capture the outcome of an individual pitcher versus batter match-up. A good or bad offense, defense or bullpen have no effect on these three stats...
Walks Allowed, Strikeouts and Homeruns Allowed

Even with only three stats to look at, there is a wealth of insight that these measures can provide. In fact, these three stats alone can measure several fundamental pitching skills.

Control (bb/9), the ability to get the ball over the plate.
Dominance (k/9), the ability to dominate hitters.
Command (k/bb), the overall ability to control the plate.
HR Rate (hr/9), the ability to keep the ball in the park.

These fundamental skills are the core components of the Base Performance Value (BPV) gauge (see the Glossary for a complete description). BPV also includes one more skill — the pitcher's ability to prevent hits. However, since this skill is impacted by the defense's ability to reach and successfully field the balls hit to them, and not entirely a measure of pure pitching skill, its role in the BPV formula is only as an adjustment measure.

Command Ratio as a Leading Indicator

The raw ability to get the ball over the plate — command of the strike zone — is one of the best leading indicators for future pitching performance. The command ratio (K/BB) can be used to project future potential in earned run average and other skills gauges as well.

In general, pitchers who maintain a command ratio of 2.5 have a high probability of long-term success. For fantasy drafting purposes, it is best to avoid pitchers with ratios of less than 2.0. Bullpen closers should be avoided if they have a command ratio under 2.5.

Research indicates that there is a high correlation between a pitcher's command ratio and his ERA (minimum 30 IP).

Command	Earned Run Average				
	1999	2000	2001	2002	2003
0.0 - 1.0	5.99	6.11	6.84	6.05	5.85
1.1 - 1.5	4.97	5.04	5.02	4.79	5.05
1.6 - 2.0	4.56	4.59	4.63	4.59	4.51
2.1 - 2.5	3.95	4.23	4.22	3.98	4.22
2.6 - 3.0	4.08	4.19	4.07	3.60	3.80
3.1 and over	3.46	3.54	3.45	3.15	3.30

Research also suggests that there is a strong correlation between a pitcher's command ratio and his propensity to win ballgames. Over three quarters of those with ratios over 3.0 posted winning records, and the collective W/L record of those command artists was nearly .600.

The command/winning correlation held up in both leagues, although the effect was much more pronounced in the NL. Over four times more NL hurlers than AL hurlers had command ratios over 3.0, and it appears that higher command ratios are required in the NL to maintain good winning percentages. While a ratio between 2.0 and 2.9 might be good enough for a winning record for over 70% of AL pitchers, that level of command in the NL will generate an above-.500 mark only slightly more than half the time.

In short, in order to have at least a 70% chance of drafting a pitcher with a winning record, you must target NL pitchers with at least a 3.0 command ratio. To achieve the same odds in the AL, a 2.0 command ratio will suffice.

Good Command versus Bad Command

While we can maximize our chances for assembling a good pitching staff by targeting pitchers with good command, we still have to be a little bit careful.

There are some pitchers that have excellent command, but still fare poorly. These pitchers are typically hard-throwers, but who have little movement on their pitches. Batters find that they don't need to wait on pitches and can usually make contact a high percentage of the time. The end result is a depressed control ratio (fewer walks allowed as batters make more contact) which, in turn, artificially pumps up a pitcher's command ratio. Poor opposition batting averages, and often poor strand rates also result.

These pitchers may still have good upside potential, especially those whose strikeout rates remain high. However, their development may be slower than other comparable pitchers, and their year-to-year consistency may be low. As such, their risk to you will be somewhat greater.

Strand Rates as a Leading Indicator

Strand Rate finds great utility in explaining variances between a pitcher's ERA and his performance indicators.

Pitchers with strand rates over 80% almost always have exemplary ERAs. Starters and middle relievers who post this level in a given season have an 80% likelihood of watching their ERA rise in the following year. The percentage drops to 50% for short relievers.

Pitchers with strand rates under 65% almost always have inflated ERAs, but have an 89% likelihood of watching their ERA improve in the following year. In addition, 83% will improve their ERA by more than one run.

Pitching and Defense *(Voros McCracken)*

In 2000, Voros McCracken published a study that concluded that "there is little if any difference among major league pitchers in their ability to prevent hits on balls hit in the field of play."

His assertion was that, while a Randy Johnson would have a better ability to prevent a batter from getting wood on a ball, or perhaps keeping the ball in the park, once that ball was hit in the field of play, the probability of it falling for a hit was virtually no different than for any other pitcher.

Among the findings in his study were:

- There is little correlation between what a pitcher does one year in the stat and what he will do the next. This is not true with other significant stats (BB, K, HR).
- You can better predict a pitcher's hits per balls in play from the rate of the rest of the pitcher's team than from the pitcher's own rate.

This last point brings a team's defense into the picture. It begs the question, when a batter gets a hit, is it because the pitcher made a bad pitch, the batter took a good swing, or the defense was not positioned correctly to field it? McCracken's findings take the onus away from the pitcher and put it on the shoulders of the batter and defense.

Pitchers will often post hit rates per balls in play (H%) that are far off from the league average, but then revert to the mean the following year. As such, we can use it in much the same way we use strand rate to project the direction of a pitcher's ERA.

This is not the final say on the matter. McCracken's research is controversial and has raised some flags in the sabermetric community. Essays by John Burnson and Patrick Davitt earlier in this book cast some new light on this work.

Ground Ball Pitchers *(John Burnson)*

Ground ball pitchers tend to give up fewer home runs than do flyball pitchers. We also have evidence that ground ball pitchers have higher hit rates... In other words, a ground ball has a higher chance of being a hit than does a fly ball that is not out of the park. Ground ball pitchers also have lower strikeout rates.

Overall, ground ball pitchers have a lower ERA than do fly ball pitchers but a higher WHIP. On balance, ground ball pitchers come out ahead, even when considering strikeouts, because a lower ERA also leads to more wins.

Projecting Wins

Using regression analyses, we can rank the importance of the variables that impact pitching win totals. In order:
1. Team offense (run support)
2. Pitching Effectiveness (base performance value)
3. Run Prevention (strand rate)
4. Bullpen support (inherited runners stranded %)
5. Managerial Tendencies (quick hooks/slow hooks)
6. Team Defense (fielding percentage)

As such, when a fantasy player needs to draft or beef up in the win category, the most prudent approach is always to target teams with good offensive support before looking at pitching performance data.

Optimal Ages

As with batters, pitchers develop at different rates, but in general terms, a look at their age can be helpful to determine where they should be along the developmental curve. Here are some tendencies...

While peaks vary, most all pitchers (who are still around) tend to experience a sharp drop-off in their skills at age 38.

Starting pitchers *(Rick Wilton)*: Their first productive season in the majors (10 wins, 150 IP, sub-4.00 ERA) is at age 25 or 26. Starters who experience a career year after age 31 are far less likely to repeat that performance than those who achieve their career year at a younger age.

Relief aces *(Rick Wilton)*: Their first 20-save season arrives at about age 26. About three of every four relievers who begin a run of 20-save seasons in their 20's will likely sustain that level for about four years, with their value beginning to decline at the beginning of the third year.

Many aces achieve a certain level of maturity in their 30's and can experience a run of 20-save seasons between ages 33 and 36. For some, this may be their first time in the role of bullpen closer. However, those who achieve their first 20-save season after age 34 are unlikely to repeat.

Thirtysomethings *(Ed Spaulding)*: Older pitchers, as they lose velocity and movement on the ball, must rely on more variety and better location. Thus, if strikeouts are a priority, you don't want many pitchers over 30. The over-30 set that tends to be surprising includes finesse types (Morgan, Moyer), career minor leaguers who break through for 2-3 seasons, often in relief (Telford, Vosberg, Shaw), and knuckleballers (a young knuckleballer is 31).

Career Year Drop-off *(Rick Wilton)*

Research shows that a pitcher's post-career year drop-off, on average, looks like this...
- ERA increases by 1.00
- WHIP increases by 0.14.
- Nearly 6 fewer wins

Usage Warning Flags

Research evidence suggests that there is a finite number of innings in a pitcher's arm. This number varies by pitcher, by development cycle, and by pitching style and repertoire. There are several gauges we can use to measure a pitcher's potential for future arm problems and/or reduced effectiveness. When this occurs in pitchers under the age of 28, we call it "early burnout."

- *Sharp increases in usage from one year to the next...* Any pitcher who increases his workload by 50 IP or more from year #1 to year #2 is a candidate to experience symptoms of burnout in year #3.
- *Starters' overuse...* Consistent "batters faced per game (BF/G) levels of 28.0 or higher, combined with consistent seasonal IP totals of 200 or more may indicate burnout potential. Within a season, a BF/G of over 30.0 with a projected IP total of 200 may indicate a late season fade.
- *Relievers' overuse...* Warning flags should be up for relievers who post in excess of 100 IP in a season, while averaging fewer than 2 IP per outing.

When focusing solely on minor league pitchers, research results are striking:

Stamina: Virtually every minor league pitcher who has had a BF/G of 28.5 or more in one season will experience a drop-off in BF/G the following year. Many will be unable to ever duplicate that previous level of durability.

Performance: Most pitchers experience an associated drop-off in their BPVs in the years following the 28.5 BF/G season. Some are able to salvage their effectiveness later on by moving to the bullpen.

Protecting Young Pitchers *(Craig Wright)*

There is a link between some degree of eventual arm trouble and a history of heavy workloads in a pitcher's formative years. Some recommendations from this research:

Teenagers (A-ball): No 200 IP seasons and no BF/G over 28.5 in any 150 IP span. No starts on three days rest.

Ages 20-22: Average no more than 105 pitches per start with a single game ceiling of 130 pitches.

Ages 23-24: Average no more than 110 pitches per start with a single game ceiling of 140 pitches.

When possible, a young rookie starter should be introduced to the major leagues in a long relief role before he goes into the rotation.

The Cubs' 2003 threesome: Mark Prior (age 23) averaged 113 pitches per start, Kerry Wood (26) averaged 110 per start and Carlos Zambrano (22) averaged 106 per start.

Catchers' Effect on Pitching *(Thomas Hanrahan)*

A typical catcher handles a pitching staff better after having been with a club for a few years. Research has shown that there is an improvement in team ERA of approximately 0.33 runs per game from a catcher's rookie season to his prime years with a club. Therefore, if a team has a veteran who has been catching for several seasons and are thinking of calling up a backstop from the minors, they can expect their short-term pitching results to drop off.

The Knuckleballers Rule

Knuckleballers don't follow any of the rules.

League Switching

American League left-handers often experience some early dominance upon coming over to the NL. This advantage over hitters normally lasts about one season. Pitchers then return to their previous performance levels.

Projecting Breakout Performances

Research has provided us with a set of criteria that can be used to identify candidates that have the potential to experience large-scale ERA improvement. For pitchers that have consistently posted ERAs at or above the league average, target those that...

- will be between 24 and 28 years of age (and eliminate anyone over 29)
- have a minimum of two full years of major league experience
- have a history of command ratios over 2.0 (although the most previous year may be below 2.0)
- have had consistent strikeout rates of 6.0 or above
- have had consistent opposition on base averages under .350
- have had strand rates of 70% or less and the promise of improved bullpen support in the next season.
- have had BPVs that showed potential for 50-plus levels, either via rising trends or minor league success.
- Very few pitchers will meet all eight criteria; target those who meet the most, with a minimum of five.

Origin of Closers

History has long maintained that ace closers are not easily recognizable early on in their careers, so that every season does see its share of the unexpected. Joe Borowski, Rocky Biddle, Danny Kolb, Tim Worrell, Aquilino Lopez... who would have thought it a year ago at this time?

Some accepted facts...

- You cannot find major league closers from pitchers who were closers in the minors.
- Closers begin their careers as starters.
- Closers are converted set-up men.
- Closers are pitchers who were unable to develop a third effective pitch.

All four statements are true. But the reality is a lot more simple... closers are a product of circumstance.

Are the minor leagues a place to look at all?

From a 1996 study... From 1990-1995, there were 104 incidences of 20-save performances in Double-A and Triple-A, which were accomplished by 89 different pitchers.

Of those 89, only 23 ever made it to the majors.

Of those 23, only 7 ever closed any game.

Of those 7, only 3 ever became full-time closers: John Wetteland, Mark Wohlers and Ricky Bottalico.

Three pitchers out of 89, a successful conversion rate of 3%. Not exactly a fertile ground.

The Rule of TOG

The task of finding future closing potential comes down to looking at three things, which we call the Rule of TOG:

Talent: The raw skills to mow down hitters for short periods of time. Pinpoint control, dominance and command are paramount. Optimal BPVs over 100, but not under 75.

Opportunity: The single most important element, and the one the pitcher has the least control over.

Guile: Gamesmanship, the innate mental makeup that allows a pitcher to make the most use of his talent in high-pressure situations. Guile is tough to project; we often can only assess it after the fact, when a pitcher is given an opportunity and either succeeds or fails. A good rule of thumb is to use a pitcher's saves success rate, or the percent of opportunities successfully converted. Proof of guile can be considered for those that convert at least 80% of their save opportunities.

The league's top closers possess all three qualities. The absence of any of the three significantly raises the risk of not accumulating saves.

There are pitchers that have *Talent and Guile, but not the Opportunity*. Often, these pitchers have proven that they can successfully close out games but are not given the full-time chance to do so, for a variety of reasons (e.g. being blocked by a solid frontliner in the pen, being left-handed, etc.) They are good to own because they will not likely hurt your pitching staff, but you cannot count on them for saves.

There are pitchers that have *Talent and Opportunity, but not the Guile*. Any pitcher with talent is good to own, and these pitchers have saves upside if they manage to overcome the obstacles to success. Failure, however, might incur some short-term impact to ERA and WHIP.

Finally, there are pitchers that have *Opportunity and Guile, but not the Talent*. MLB managers decide on who to give the ball to in the 9th inning based on their own perceptions about what skills are required to succeed. Sometimes the only criteria is "he has to be a hard-thrower who keeps the ball on the ground," even if those tendencies demonstrate little pure command or produce elevated opposition on base averages.

Those without any real command or dominance may have some initial short-term success, but their long-term prognosis is poor and they are high risks to your roster. Classic examples of the short life span of these types of pitchers include Matt Karchner and Heath Slocumb. You might be able to add Mike MacDougal to that list very soon.

Handedness Notes

1. Left-handed pitchers tend to peak about a year after right-handed pitchers.

2. While southpaws account for about 26% of total IPs, they post only 15% of the total saves. Typically, the few left-handers on a staff are reserved for specialized roles so few are given the job of frontline closer.

3. RHers have slightly better command and a slightly better HR rate.

4. But there is no statistically significant variance in LHer versus RHer ERAs.

5. On an overall productivity basis, RHers only have about a 6% advantage over LHers.

Minor League Toolbox

Minor League Information Management
(Terry Linhart)

The increased attention that the minor leagues are getting has created some dangerous analytical by-products.

Hype. With the minor leagues still largely uncovered by the media, one reporter's short-term observations can make their way into the mainstream as fact. This growing subjective information base is often not rooted in fact at all, yet drives perception about prospects.

There is a **rush** to scour the lower minors statistically for the next great phenom before anyone else does. But statistics alone do not tell the whole story. Often, there is an exaggerated emphasis on short-term performance in an environment (major league player development) that is supposed to focus on the long-term. Two poor outings don't mean a 21-year-old pitcher is washed up.

Other common factors that affect statistics:

League variances: Some leagues favor hitters or pitchers.

Ballpark variances: Dimensions and altitude create hitters parks and pitchers parks, but a factor rarely mentioned is that many ballparks in the lower minors are inconsistent in their field quality. Minor league clubs have limited resources to maintain their field conditions, and this can artificially depress defensive statistics while inflating gauges like batting average.

Widely variant skills: Some players' skills are so superior to the caliber of competition at their level that you can't truly get a picture of what they're going to do from their statistics alone.

Player development assignments: Many pitchers are told to work on secondary pitches while moving through the minors, throwing curveballs and change-ups on 3-2 or 2-2 counts to gain confidence in the pitch. The result is an increased number of walks affecting their command ratio. Again, the bigger picture is the long-term development for a major league club. They may be able to get hitters out with a sharp, moving fastball, but are trying to work on keeping hitters off-stride.

Pitching rotations: The #3, #4, and #5 pitchers in the lower minors are truly longshots to make the majors. They often possess only two pitches and can barely go five innings. The most obvious weakness is the inability to disguise the off-speed pitches with their delivery and arm speed. Hitters can see inflated statistics in these leagues.

Minor League Level versus Age

When evaluating minor league talent, you must look at the age of the prospect in relation to the median age of the league he is in:

Low level A	Between 19-20
Upper level A	Around 20
Double-A	21
Triple-A	22

These are the ideal ages for prospects at the particular level. If a prospect is younger than most and he holds his own against older and more experienced players, elevate his status. If a prospect is older than the median, reduce his status. These adjustments are taken into account in the Major League Equivalents section.

Law of Promotion *(Deric McKamey)*

Defense is what gets a minor league prospect to the majors; offense is what keeps him there.

Call-up Success Rates I

The overall probability that a promoted minor leaguer will immediately succeed at the major league level can vary depending upon the level of Triple-A experience that player has amassed at the time of call-up. Research conclusions:

The odds of a batter achieving immediate major league success, no matter what his minor league experience, remains slightly more than 50-50.

However, over 80% of all minor league pitchers promoted with less than a full year at Triple-A will struggle in their first year in the majors. Those pitchers who do have a full year of Triple-A experience increase their probability of success to a level equal to that of batters (about 50-50).

Another way to look at it... Pitchers with a full year at Triple-A are 3.5 times more likely to perform well in the majors in year #1 than those without a full year at Triple-A.

Call-up Success Rates II

Historical BPIs have some value in determining which minor league pitching call-ups fare well.

Based on a recent study, the percentage of hurlers that were good investments in the year that they were called up varied by the level of their historical BPIs *prior* to that year.

Pitchers who had:	Fared well	Fared poorly
Good indicators	79%	21%
Marginal or poor indicators	18%	82%

The minor league data used to classify these pitchers were MLE levels from the previous two years, not the season in which they were called up. What is the significance of this? Typically, it is solid current year performance in the minors that merits the call-up in the first place, but those minor league numbers had little bearing on who fared well. Early season performance in the minors is not a good indicator of short-term major league success, for two reasons:

1. The performance data set is too small, typically just a few month's worth of statistics. For pitchers, this is not nearly enough data to draw any reasonable conclusions.

2. For those pitchers putting up those stats at a new minor league level, there has not been enough time for the scouting reports to make their rounds, so we do not know if they have truly mastered that level yet.

Projecting Second Year Success

One of the most accurate indicators of a rookie's future potential is his performance during the second half of his debut season in the majors.

First year players often get off to particularly fast or slow starts. During their second tour of the league is when we get to see what they're truly made of. Have the slow starters adjusted to the level of play and brought their game up a notch? Has the rest of the league figured out the fast starters and taken them down a peg? That 2nd half "adjustment" performance level is the one you want to look at when projecting the sophomore campaign and beyond.

It also stands to reason that this phenomenon should occur at every level of professional baseball play.

When a player gets promoted to, say Triple-A, he is, in fact, a "rookie" during his first year at that level. An analysis of his second half Triple-A performance gives us a better indication of his true ability there.

And... premature major league call-ups often negate that ability to evaluate a player's true potential.

It happens all the time. A hotshot Double-A player opens the new season in Triple-A. After putting up solid numbers for a month or two, he gets a call to the big club... and then struggles. We wonder why. The fact is, at the point of call-up, we do not have enough evidence that the player has mastered the Triple-A level. We don't know whether the rest of the league would have caught up to him during his second tour of the league. But now he's an underperformer in the bigs. When someone says that a player needs a full season in Triple-A, there's a valid reason for it.

Older Prospects

There is some longshot potential talent in older prospects — age 26, 27 or higher — who, for whatever reason (untimely injury, circumstance, bad luck, etc.), don't reach the majors until they've lost their Official Prospect Status. Downgrading potential with age is an economic reality for Major League clubs, but not necessarily a skills reality.

Skills growth and decline is universal, whether it occurs at the major league level or in the minors. So a high skills journeyman in Triple-A is just as likely to peak at age 27, or thereabouts, as a major leaguer of the same age. The question becomes one of opportunity — will the parent club see fit to reap the benefits of that peak performance?

Most clubs approach the calling up of a minor leaguer in the same way as they approach all their future investments. They are more likely to take a chance on a 23-year-old who might return long-term dividends than a 29-year-old whose return is likely far lower, even if it is to fill a short-term roster opening. However, for those short-term openings, it is often a lower risk move to go with an older player at peak than a younger player still learning the craft. Look back on what the Athletics did in 2003 with long-gone names like Billy McMillon and Dave McCarty.

Since most clubs continue to ignore potential sources of talent from within their systems, prospecting these players for your fantasy team is, admittedly, a high risk endeavor.

In order to uncover next season's "Bull Durham" prospects, look for a player who is/has:

- Optimally, age 27-28 for overall peak skills, age 30-31 for power skills, or age 28-31 for pitchers.
- At least two seasons of experience at Triple-A. Career Double-A players are generally not good picks.
- Solid base skills levels.
- Shallow organizational depth at their position.
- Notable winter league or spring training performance.

Players who meet these conditions can often slip onto a 25-man roster by Opening Day, or become an early call-up. What should you do with these players? In general, these are typically not draftable players, but worthwhile reserve or Rotisserie-Ultra picks. Or grab them at FAAB time.

Team Toolbox

Not surprisingly, the following principles all come from the annals of Bill James and his *Baseball Abstracts* from the 1980's.

Johnson Effect *(Bryan Johnson)*: Teams whose actual won/loss record exceeds or falls short of their statistically projected record in one season will tend to revert to the level of their projection in the following season.

Law of Competitive Balance: The level at which a team (or player) will address its problems is inversely related to its current level of success. Losing teams/low performing players will tend to make changes to improve; winning teams/high performing players will not. This law is the explanation for the existence of the Plexiglass Principle and the Whirlpool Principle.

Plexiglass Principle: If a player or team improves markedly in one season, it will likely decline in the next. The opposite is also true but with a slightly lower frequency (because a poorer performing player will get fewer opportunities to rebound).

Whirlpool Principle: All team and player performances are forcefully drawn to the center. For teams, that center is a .500 record. For players, it represents their career average level of performance.

Japanese Baseball Toolbox

Japan's Pacific and Central Leagues are generally considered to be equivalent to very good Triple-A level ball, and the pitching may be even better.

As good as this league is, Japanese statistics are difficult to convert to a major league equivalent due to a variety of differences in the way the game is played there:

1. Japanese baseball's guiding philosophy centers on risk avoidance. Mistakes are not tolerated. Since fewer risks are taken, runners rarely take extra bases, batters focus on making contact rather than driving the ball, and managers play for one run at a time, rather than going for a big inning. As a result, offenses score fewer runs than they should given the number of hits produced. And pitching stats tend to look better than the talent behind them.

2. Stadiums in Japan have much shorter fences. Normally this would mean more HRs, but given #1 above, it is the American players who make up the majority of Japan's power elite. This skews offensive statistics.

3. There are more artificial turf fields, which increases the number of groundball singles.

4. The quality of umpiring is questionable. Far fewer errors are called (again, the cultural philosophy of low tolerance for mistakes).

5. Teams have smaller pitching staffs, often no more than about seven deep. Three-man pitching rotations are common, there is no relief specialization, and the best starters often work out of the pen between starts. Despite superior conditioning, Japanese pitchers tend to burn out early, often before age 30.

Other Diamonds

A-Rod 10-Step Path to Stardom: Not all well-hyped prospects hit the ground running. More often they follow an alternative path...

1. Prospect puts up phenomenal minor league numbers.
2. The media machine gets oiled up.
3. Prospect gets called up, but struggles, Year 1.
4. Prospect gets demoted.
5. Prospect tears it up in Triple-A, Year 2.
6. Prospect gets called up, but struggles, Year 2.
7. Prospect gets demoted.
8. The media turns their backs and fantasy leaguers reduce their expectations.
9. Prospect tears it up in Triple-A, Year 3. The public shrugs its collective shoulders.
10. Prospect is promoted in Year 3 and explodes. Some lucky fantasy leaguer lands a franchise player for under $5.

Some players that are currently stuck at one of the interim steps, and may or may not ever reach Step 10, include Brandon Phillips, Brandon Larson, Brandon Duckworth, um...

A-Rod's Rangers Rationalization: Money can't buy happiness, but it sure can make misery easier to live with.

The Bones-Olivares List: Pitcher with BPIs so incredibly horrible that you have to wonder how they can possibly draw a major league paycheck year after year.

Denver Doctrine: Coors does not turn bad hitters into good hitters; it only turns good hitters into better hitters.

The Dave Eiland Catch-22 *(John Sickels)*: There are minor league pitchers who would hold their own for a strong winning team because they are good enough to keep a game close, however, strong teams rarely promote this type of pitcher, so they end up losing for bad teams that can't provide the necessary offensive support.

Expos Law of Destiny: Glory may be fleeting, but obscurity lasts forever.

George Brett Path to Retirement: Get out while you're still putting up good numbers and the public perception of you is favorable. If Roger Clemens truly retires, he will be the first player in a long time to take this path. *(See Steve Carlton Path to Retirement.)*

Japan/Korea/Mexico Law of Perception: Foreign talent always seems better than home-grown talent.

Lance Painter Lesson: Six months of solid performance can be screwed up by one bad outing. (In 2000, Painter finished with an ERA of 4.76. However, prior to his final appearance of the year — in which he pitched 1 inning and gave up 8 earned runs — his ERA was 3.70.)

Law of Injury Estimation (Westheimer's Rule): To calculate an accurate projection of the amount of time a player will be out of action due to injury, first take the published time estimate, double it, and change the unit of measure to the next highest unit. Thus, a player estimated to be out two weeks will actually be out four months.

Law of Micro-management: The length of a team's transaction list is inversely proportional to its success.

Laws of Team Co-Dependency:

1. The one player that fails causes other players to fail.
2. No matter how many pieces have been assembled correctly, one mistake will cause the entire team to malfunction.
3. A $60 million team will be rendered useless by one $200,000 relief pitcher.

Official Colorado Procedures Manual for Recently Acquired Batters:

1. Arrive at Coors. Unpack.
2. Abandon plate patience. Swing at everything.
3. Post career best numbers.
4. Sign lucrative free agent contract somewhere else.
5. Ride out career.
6. Retire wealthy.

Steve Carlton Path to Retirement: Hang around the major leagues long enough for your numbers to become so wretched that people begin to forget your past successes.

Among the many players who have taken this path include Ken Caminiti, David Cone, Bobby Bonilla, Eric Davis, Doc Gooden, Orel Hershiser, Howard Johnson, Mark Langston, Don Mattingly, Hal Morris, Jack Morris, Dale Murphy, Tim Raines, Dave Stewart and of course, Steve Carlton. Current players who look to be on the same course include Jeff Fassero, Barry Larkin, Denny Neagle and Shane Reynolds. *(See George Brett Path to Retirement.)*

Rationalization for Not Trading an In-Season Underachiever *(Steve Moyer)*: If you hold on and he sucks, you've got an excuse. If you dump him and he comes around, you've got a nightmare.

Strawberry Postulate: It may be that your sole purpose in life is simply to serve as a warning to others.

Timlin Syndrome: A dreaded draft day malady in which you are unable to resist acquiring a player that has burned you multiple times in the past.

The Three Immutable Rules for Winners: If you cherish this hobby, you will live by them or die by them...

1. Revel in your success; fame is fleeting.
2. Exercise excruciating humility.
3. 100% of winnings must be spent on significant others.

The Final Pitch

"Forecasting is a business art, a marriage of quantitative technique and creative process, seeking not just truth but also beauty and elegance." — Unknown

"The best forecast combines sophisticated information management with good common sense." — Unknown

"Baseball is like this. Have one good year and you can fool them for five more, because for five more years they expect you to have another good one." — Frankie Frisch

III.
MAJOR
LEAGUES

The Batters

QUALIFICATION: All batters who accumulated at least 100 at bats in the majors in 2003 have been included. Nearly all who accumulated between 50 and 100 AB in 2003 are also included. A handful of players with fewer than 50 AB in 2003 are included if we believe that they will have an impact in 2004.

This book is designed to be an historical analysis, so players who will likely have a vital role in 2004, but spent the better part of 2003 on the sidelines or in the minors, are not included. We cover some of them briefly on page 146 and others in the Top Prospects section. All of these players will appear on BaseballHQ.com over the winter as their 2004 roles and projected impacts become clearer.

POSITIONS: Up to three positions are listed for each batter and represent those for which he appeared a minimum of 20 games in 2003.

AGE: Each batter's current age is shown, along with a description of the associated stage in his career.

BATS: Shows which side of the plate he bats from — right (R), left (L) or switch-hitter (S).

RISK TABLE: An analysis of each player's forecast risk, the variables that impact the viability of his projection. Atop the table is an overall risk level. In the grid below are five variables that contribute to the overall rating – experience (EXP), consistency (CON), playing time (PT), stability (STB) and age (AGE). (A full description of these variables appears in the Forecasters Toolbox.) If the variable appears in lower case, then it represents a small or moderate risk factor; UPPER CASE represents a significant risk factor.

LIMA GRADE: Rating that evaluates how well a batter would fit into a team using the LIMA Plan. Best grades go to batters who have excellent base skills (BPV), are expected to see a good amount of playing time, and are in the $10-$30 Rotisserie value range. Lowest grades will go to poor skills, few at bats and values under $5 or over $30.

BATTING AVERAGE PERCENTAGE PLAY (BA): The probability that a batter will improve his batting average in 2004 over 2003, based on an evaluation of contact rate, xBA variance and walk rate. These percentages are in 5% increments, ranging from 10% to 90%, though most will be centered closer to the mean. If a batter's BA says 60%, for instance, it means that he has a 60% chance of improving his batting average in 2004. It also means that he has a 40% of seeing no change, or a drop-off.

PLAYER STAT LINES: The past five year's statistics represent the total accumulated in the majors as well as in Triple-A, Double-A ball and various foreign leagues during each year. All non-major league stats used have been converted to their equivalent major league performance level. Minor league levels below AA are not included.

Nearly all baseball publications separate a player's statistical experiences in the major leagues from the minor leagues and outside leagues. While this may be an appropriate approach for the sake of official record-keeping, it is not an accurate measure of a player's complete performance for the year.

Bill James has proven that minor league statistics, at Double-A level or above, are accurate indicators of future potential. Other researchers have also devised conversion factors for foreign leagues that place them on a comparable playing field as MLB stats. If we can agree that these conversions are accurate barometers of potential performance, then we should be including them in the pool of historical data.

By limiting an analysis of a player's performance trends to major league numbers only, we ignore a wealth of valuable data. This data adds more depth to a player's historical trends, especially those with limited major league experience. So we include major league equivalencies as a part of each batter's and pitcher's yearly stats in this book.

TEAM DESIGNATIONS: An asterisk (*) appearing with a team name means that major league equivalent Triple-A and/or Double-A numbers are included in that year's stat line. A designation of "a/a" means the stats were accumulated at both Triple-A and Double-A levels that year. "JPN" means Japan, "MEX" means Mexico, "KOR" means Korea, "TWN" means Taiwan, "CUB" means Cuba and "ind" means independent league.

The designation "2TM" appears whenever a player was on more than one major league team, crossing leagues, in a season. "2AL" and "2NL" represent more than one team in the same league. Complete season stats are presented for players who crossed leagues during the season.

SABERMETRIC CATEGORIES: Descriptions of all the sabermetric categories appear in the glossary. The decimal point has been suppressed on several categories to conserve space.

2004 FORECASTS: It is far too early to be making definitive projections for 2004, especially on playing time. Focus on the skill levels and trends, then consult Baseball HQ for playing time revisions as players change teams and roles become finalized. A free projections update will also be available online at BaseballForecaster.com in March.

Forecasts are computed from a player's trends over the past five years. Adjustments were made for leading indicators and variances between skill and output. After reviewing the leading indicators, you might opt to make further adjustments.

Although each year's numbers include all playing time at the Double-A level or above, the 2004 forecast only represents potential playing time at the major league level, and again is highly preliminary.

CAPSULE COMMENTARIES: For each player, a brief analysis of their BPIs and the potential impact on performance in 2004 is provided. For those who played only a portion of 2003 at the major league level, and whose isolated MLB stats are significantly different from their full-season total, their MLB stats are listed here. Note that these commentaries generally look at performance related issues only. Playing time expectations may impact these analyses, so you will have to adjust accordingly, especially as we get closer to Opening Day. Upside and downside statistical potential appears for some players. These are less grounded in hard data and more speculative of longer-term potential.

Abreu,Bobby

Abreu,Bobby		Tm	AB	R	H	HR	RBI	SB	Avg	vL	vR	R$	OB	Slg	OPS	bb%	ct%	h%	Eye	xBA	PX	SX	G/F	RC/G	RAR
Pos RF	99	PHI	546	118	183	20	93	27	335	298	348	$34	446	549	995	17	79	39	0.96	305	130	165	1.53	9.32	63.1
Age 30 Past Peak	00	PHI	576	103	182	25	79	28	316	243	339	$32	417	554	971	15	80	36	0.86	303	142	154	1.20	8.60	54.5
Bats L	01	PHI	588	118	170	31	110	36	289	258	301	$37	398	543	940	15	77	33	0.77	296	155	128	1.14	7.55	33.8
R Very Low	02	PHI	572	102	176	20	85	31	308	302	310	$34	414	521	935	15	80	36	0.89	310	147	133	1.26	7.81	40.1
I	03	PHI	577	99	173	20	101	22	300	272	312	$30	411	468	879	16	78	35	0.87	287	110	86	1.84	6.93	21.4
S	1st Half		286	51	79	12	47	9	276			$13	391	458	849	16	78	32	0.84	287	116	74		6.23	5.2
K	2nd Half		291	48	94	8	54	13	323			$18	431	478	908	16	79	39	0.89	286	104	90		7.68	16.4
LIMA D+ BA: 45%	04	Proj	575	103	175	21	97	27	304			$33	413	486	899	16	78	36	0.86	295	117	99		7.27	29.0

Despite identical HR output in '03, his PX took a dive. Growing G/F ratio explains the trend and lends little hope for a return to the 30-HR level.

Alfonzo,Edgardo

Alfonzo,Edgardo		Tm	AB	R	H	HR	RBI	SB	Avg	vL	vR	R$	OB	Slg	OPS	bb%	ct%	h%	Eye	xBA	PX	SX	G/F	RC/G	RAR
Pos 3B	99	NYM	628	123	191	27	108	9	304	268	314	$27	387	502	889	12	86	32	1.00	279	124	80	0.72	7.14	47.9
Age 30 Past Peak	00	NYM	544	109	176	25	94	3	324	298	330	$26	424	542	966	15	87	34	1.36	307	134	63	0.70	8.61	62.2
Bats R	01	NYM	457	64	111	17	49	5	243	211	251	$8	319	403	722	10	86	25	0.82	250	97	70	0.58	4.39	-2.7
R Low	02	NYM	490	78	151	16	56	6	308	364	290	$20	386	459	845	11	89	32	1.13	290	102	71	0.71	6.63	27.1
I CON	03	SF	514	56	133	13	81	5	259	236	265	$13	334	391	725	10	92	26	1.41	284	87	65	0.90	4.48	3.4
S stb	1st Half		276	26	63	5	29	4	228			$2	302	330	631	10	93	23	1.53	276	64	81		3.31	-7.9
K	2nd Half		238	30	70	8	52	1	294			$10	371	462	833	11	91	30	1.32	292	113	34		6.12	12.4
LIMA B+ BA: 80%	04	Proj	500	69	144	16	74	5	288			$17	365	442	807	11	90	30	1.18	286	100	65		5.79	19.6

It was a poor season, in a tough ballpark, but there are still some positive signs. Excellent contact rate and batting eye, and 2H surge show there still something left in the tank. 80% odds of a BA rebound.

Almonte,Erick

Almonte,Erick		Tm	AB	R	H	HR	RBI	SB	Avg	vL	vR	R$	OB	Slg	OPS	bb%	ct%	h%	Eye	xBA	PX	SX	G/F	RC/G	RAR
Pos SS	99		0	0	0	0	0	0	0								0								
Age 26 Pre-Peak	00	aa	454	49	116	15	68	11	256			$12	303	405	708	6	75	31	0.28	247	86	101		4.26	4.3
Bats R	01	a/a	357	50	96	12	48	4	269			$10	343	431	774	10	76	32	0.48	251	99	71		4.88	9.6
R High	02	a/a	408	45	87	15	52	10	213			$7	282	365	647	9	75	25	0.38	241	93	84		3.35	-11.3
I EXP con	03	NYY	* 279	39	65	5	33	4	233	280	253	$3	289	351	640	7	77	28	0.35	241	80	86	2.39	3.29	-9.7
S pt stb	1st Half		97	16	26	1	11	1	268			$2	324	371	695	8	76	34	0.35	236	79	67		4.25	-0.5
K	2nd Half		182	23	39	4	22	3	214			$1	270	341	611	7	78	25	0.35	244	81	91		2.84	-9.1
LIMA F BA: 45%	04	Proj	150	20	36	4	19	3	240			$3	301	379	679	8	76	29	0.37	242	86	91		3.75	-3.1

1-11-.260 in 100 AB at NYY. Held his own as a stopgap, but BPIs say that .260 was over his head. Despite occasional pop in minors, he's not worth your time.

Alomar Jr.,Sandy

Alomar Jr.,Sandy		Tm	AB	R	H	HR	RBI	SB	Avg	vL	vR	R$	OB	Slg	OPS	bb%	ct%	h%	Eye	xBA	PX	SX	G/F	RC/G	RAR
Pos CA	99	CLE	* 199	34	59	8	39	1	296	353	291	$8	336	503	839	6	86	31	0.44	306	129	77	1.22	6.03	10.9
Age 37 Decline	00	CLE	356	44	103	7	42	2	289	351	273	$7	320	404	724	4	88	31	0.39	257	71	69	1.57	4.56	4.1
Bats R	01	CHW	220	17	54	4	21	1	245	273	239	$2	284	345	630	5	92	25	0.71	244	63	44	1.62	3.21	-4.3
R Very High	02	2TM	283	29	79	7	37	0	279	247	292	$7	301	410	711	3	88	30	0.27	271	86	37	1.46	4.37	4.0
I CON	03	CHW	194	22	52	5	26	0	268	233	284	$4	283	407	690	2	91	27	0.24	311	93	31	1.37	4.01	-0.4
S PT stb	1st Half		80	9	20	1	8	0	250			$1	277	338	615	4	98	25	1.50	308	63	35		3.18	-2.1
K AGE	2nd Half		114	13	32	4	18	0	281			$3	287	456	743	1	87	29	0.07	312	115	28		4.64	1.8
LIMA F BA: 60%	04	Proj	250	27	68	6	33	0	272			$5	294	411	705	3	90	28	0.32	307	90	49		4.20	1.9

Skills have eroded to the point where he no longer has any offensive value. High contact rate, but balls are going nowhere. Sub-.300 OB does nobody any good.

Alomar,Roberto

Alomar,Roberto		Tm	AB	R	H	HR	RBI	SB	Avg	vL	vR	R$	OB	Slg	OPS	bb%	ct%	h%	Eye	xBA	PX	SX	G/F	RC/G	RAR
Pos 2B	99	CLE	563	138	182	24	120	37	323	338	318	$39	424	533	957	15	83	36	1.03	307	129	135	1.18	8.77	72.8
Age 36 Decline	00	CLE	610	111	189	19	89	39	310	318	307	$33	375	475	851	9	87	33	0.78	310	103	126	1.54	6.90	50.6
Bats S	01	CLE	575	113	193	20	100	30	336	279	356	$37	417	541	958	12	88	36	1.13	324	122	167	1.27	8.77	69.5
R Moderate	02	NYM	590	73	157	11	53	16	266	205	290	$15	331	376	707	9	86	29	0.69	280	74	107	1.51	4.37	-0.7
I con	03	2TM	516	76	133	5	39	12	258	189	285	$7	334	349	683	10	85	29	0.77	275	66	102	1.78	4.08	-2.9
S stb	1st Half		263	34	69	2	22	6	262			$4	336	357	693	10	85	30	0.73	277	72	92		4.29	0.1
K AGE	2nd Half		253	42	64	3	17	6	253			$3	332	340	672	11	85	29	0.81	272	60	98		3.88	-3.0
LIMA B BA: 60%	04	Proj	500	79	133	9	52	11	266			$11	343	390	733	10	86	30	0.81	295	81	113		4.67	6.7

His 5-year BA vs LHers tells a story of declining skills. There's little here to indicate much of a rebound, but he can't continue on this current path and still remain gainfully employed. Expect a slight uptick.

Alou,Moises

Alou,Moises		Tm	AB	R	H	HR	RBI	SB	Avg	vL	vR	R$	OB	Slg	OPS	bb%	ct%	h%	Eye	xBA	PX	SX	G/F	RC/G	RAR
Pos LF	99	HOU	0	0	0	0	0	0	0								0			0					
Age 37 Decline	00	HOU	454	82	161	30	114	3	355	370	350	$33	421	623	1044	10	90	35	1.16	322	155	58	0.78	10.18	57.6
Bats R	01	HOU	513	79	170	27	108	5	331	424	309	$31	398	554	952	10	89	33	1.00	325	133	63	1.00	8.43	36.9
R Low	02	CHC	484	50	133	15	61	8	275	322	260	$15	339	419	758	9	87	29	0.77	295	96	73	1.08	5.11	-17.6
I con	03	CHC	565	83	158	22	91	3	280	346	260	$19	352	462	814	10	88	29	0.94	313	118	59	0.98	5.75	2.6
S stb	1st Half		299	42	88	10	50	2	294			$11	357	462	818	9	91	30	1.07	317	109	61		5.92	2.7
K AGE	2nd Half		266	41	70	12	41	1	263			$8	347	462	809	11	85	27	0.85	306	128	46		5.57	-0.1
LIMA C+ BA: 65%	04	Proj	500	71	149	21	84	2	298			$21	368	487	855	10	88	31	0.91	314	120	52		6.50	10.3

xBA says that he should be doing more flirting with .300 than he has been. Injury history does temper expectations, but don't be surprised to see another .300 season still in that bat.

Anderson,Garret

Anderson,Garret		Tm	AB	R	H	HR	RBI	SB	Avg	vL	vR	R$	OB	Slg	OPS	bb%	ct%	h%	Eye	xBA	PX	SX	G/F	RC/G	RAR
Pos LF	99	ANA	620	88	188	21	80	3	303	280	312	$19	339	469	809	5	87	32	0.42	299	103	59	1.53	5.71	10.9
Age 31 Past Peak	00	ANA	647	92	185	35	117	7	286	333	266	$25	311	519	831	4	87	29	0.28	312	135	79	1.11	5.60	9.4
Bats L	01	ANA	672	83	194	28	123	13	289	288	289	$29	316	478	794	4	85	31	0.27	304	116	77	1.09	5.32	13.1
R Very Low	02	ANA	638	93	195	29	123	6	306	284	316	$30	337	539	876	4	87	31	0.38	330	149	78	0.95	6.55	30.2
I con	03	ANA	638	80	201	29	116	6	315	310	318	$31	347	541	888	5	87	33	0.37	321	142	75	1.21	6.91	27.2
S	1st Half		324	44	102	19	68	4	315			$18	345	602	947	4	87	32	0.36	345	176	100		7.62	20.1
K	2nd Half		314	36	99	10	48	2	315			$13	348	478	826	5	87	34	0.39	295	107	41		6.16	7.0
LIMA C BA: 45%	04	Proj	625	82	192	27	112	7	307			$28	338	520	859	4	87	32	0.36	315	134	73		6.39	22.4

The past two seasons have generated higher PX levels than his 35 HR year, and he started '03 on pace to return to the 30-HR level. Will he get there? G/F says to not bet the rent; still, the skill is there.

Anderson,Marlon

Anderson,Marlon		Tm	AB	R	H	HR	RBI	SB	Avg	vL	vR	R$	OB	Slg	OPS	bb%	ct%	h%	Eye	xBA	PX	SX	G/F	RC/G	RAR
Pos 2B	99	PHI	452	48	114	5	54	13	252	297	245	$7	290	361	651	5	87	28	0.39	281	75	114	1.53	3.65	-7.6
Age 30 Past Peak	00	PHI	* 559	57	149	7	58	22	267	190	234	$14	322	383	705	8	89	29	0.77	287	73	120	2.20	4.07	-4.9
Bats L	01	PHI	522	69	153	11	61	8	293	327	285	$16	338	421	759	6	86	32	0.47	283	84	80	1.89	5.03	17.1
R Low	02	PHI	539	64	139	8	48	5	258	220	269	$8	312	380	692	7	87	28	0.59	292	86	107	1.64	4.09	-5.0
I con	03	TAM	482	59	130	6	67	19	270	315	262	$15	327	376	702	8	88	30	0.68	285	73	112	1.46	4.42	3.9
S pt stb	1st Half		244	27	66	4	42	11	270			$9	333	381	714	9	86	30	0.66	281	79	83		4.65	3.6
K	2nd Half		238	32	64	2	25	8	269			$5	320	370	690	7	89	29	0.72	288	68	128		4.18	0.3
LIMA C BA: 60%	04	Proj	450	55	124	6	53	12	276			$12	328	390	718	7	87	30	0.62	289	77	111		4.55	5.8

Fairly stable skill set, but xBA says he could be batting about 10 points higher than he has been. Late round pick.

Aurilia,Rich

Aurilia,Rich		Tm	AB	R	H	HR	RBI	SB	Avg	vL	vR	R$	OB	Slg	OPS	bb%	ct%	h%	Eye	xBA	PX	SX	G/F	RC/G	RAR
Pos SS	99	SF	558	68	157	22	80	2	281	296	276	$16	333	444	777	7	87	29	0.61	267	98	39	0.89	5.15	25.8
Age 32 Past Peak	00	SF	509	67	138	20	79	1	271	286	267	$14	341	444	785	10	82	30	0.60	258	102	46	0.89	5.23	25.9
Bats R	01	SF	636	114	206	37	97	1	324	322	325	$32	370	572	943	7	87	33	0.57	316	144	70	0.87	7.86	73.0
R Very Low	02	SF	538	76	138	15	61	1	257	241	261	$10	304	413	717	6	83	28	0.41	253	109	62	0.68	4.25	5.5
I con	03	SF	505	65	140	13	58	2	277	277	277	$12	325	410	735	7	84	31	0.44	280	88	54	0.95	4.65	7.8
S	1st Half		274	41	71	7	27	2	259			$5	316	398	714	8	87	28	0.64	296	95	62		4.31	1.6
K	2nd Half		231	24	69	6	31	0	299			$7	336	424	760	5	80	35	0.28	262	79	42		5.09	6.3
LIMA C BA: 50%	04	Proj	550	75	155	18	69	1	282			$15	329	439	769	7	84	31	0.44	289	101	55		5.07	18.0

Where has all the power gone? PX makes 2001 look like a major aberration. Pre and post-2001 levels are comparable, which means a 20-HR season is still possible.

Ausmus,Brad

Ausmus,Brad	Yr	Tm	AB	R	H	HR	RBI	SB	Avg	vL	vR	R$	OB	Slg	OPS	bb%	ct%	h%	Eye	xBA	PX	SX	G/F	RC/G	RAR
Pos CA	99	DET	458	62	126	9	54	12	275	264	277	$11	348	415	763	10	84	31	0.72	285	87	117	1.52	4.85	10.5
Age 35 Decline	00	DET	523	75	139	7	51	11	266	321	246	$8	351	365	717	12	85	30	0.87	276	64	93	1.45	4.43	4.3
Bats R	01	HOU	422	45	98	5	34	4	232	186	241	$1	283	341	624	7	85	26	0.47	253	73	100	1.01	3.22	-3.8
R Moderate	02	HOU	447	57	115	6	50	2	257	307	245	$6	315	353	669	8	84	29	0.54	250	67	74	1.66	3.75	-4.8
I CON	03	HOU	450	43	103	4	47	5	229	237	227	$2	300	291	592	9	85	26	0.70	237	42	70	1.58	2.87	-19.5
S stb	1st Half		225	19	46	2	24	2	204			($1)	275	271	546	9	88	23	0.79	244	46	63		2.39	-13.5
K age	2nd Half		225	24	57	2	23	3	253			$3	325	311	636	10	83	30	0.63	228	38	69		3.41	-5.9
LIMA D BA: 60%	04	Proj	**400**	**44**	**97**	**4**	**41**	**4**	**243**			**$4**	**309**	**329**	**637**	**9**	**85**	**28**	**0.62**	**241**	**58**	**84**		**3.37**	**-8.7**

The five-year xBA trend tells all you need to know. Even with the 60% likelihood of a BA rise, he'll still be below replacement level. Defense and leadership skills are unquestioned, but is that enough?

Baerga,Carlos

Baerga,Carlos	Yr	Tm	AB	R	H	HR	RBI	SB	Avg	vL	vR	R$	OB	Slg	OPS	bb%	ct%	h%	Eye	xBA	PX	SX	G/F	RC/G	RAR
Pos 1B	99	2TM	* 449	39	96	6	32	4	214			($2)	252	285	537	5	90	23	0.49	265	47	54	2.06	2.32	-44.9
Age 35 Decline	00		0	0	0	0	0	0	0								0								
Bats S	01	ind	203	36	60	5	42	3	294			$8	333	464	798	6	83	33	0.35	374	98	166		5.57	-3.6
R Very High	02	BOS	182	17	52	2	19	6	286	224	308	$6	312	379	691	4	89	31	0.35	285	69	75	2.74	4.43	-7.3
I exp CON	03	ARI	207	31	71	4	39	1	343	302	354	$10	396	464	859	8	90	37	0.90	307	86	44	2.35	7.03	8.1
S pt STB	1st Half		145	23	47	3	28	1	324			$7	355	476	831	5	92	34	0.64	333	113	59		6.43	3.5
K age	2nd Half		62	8	24	1	11	0	387			$4	479	435	915	15	85	44	1.22	251	25	23		8.22	4.1
LIMA F BA: 50%	04	Proj	**150**	**19**	**42**	**3**	**23**	**2**	**280**			**$4**	**337**	**385**	**722**	**8**	**88**	**31**	**0.71**	**300**	**68**	**80**		**4.56**	**-4.5**

Startling return to form, his best year since 1995. Huge second half h% jump masked big xBA drop, and makes a repeat seem unrealistic. Some value vs. RHP (.300+ BA two straight years).

Bagwell,Jeff

Bagwell,Jeff	Yr	Tm	AB	R	H	HR	RBI	SB	Avg	vL	vR	R$	OB	Slg	OPS	bb%	ct%	h%	Eye	xBA	PX	SX	G/F	RC/G	RAR
Pos 1B	99	HOU	562	143	171	42	126	30	304	354	289	$40	450	591	1041	21	77	33	1.17	278	169	86	0.78	9.61	67.9
Age 35 Decline	00	HOU	590	152	183	47	132	9	310	366	297	$37	416	615	1031	15	80	32	0.92	300	174	80	0.79	9.26	63.3
Bats R	01	HOU	600	126	173	39	130	11	288	296	287	$33	395	568	964	15	78	31	0.79	293	165	110	1.05	8.05	30.2
R Very Low	02	HOU	571	94	166	31	98	7	291	333	281	$28	397	518	916	15	77	33	0.78	266	144	72	0.89	7.36	28.2
I	03	HOU	605	109	168	39	100	11	278	327	267	$29	369	524	893	13	80	29	0.74	300	145	87	1.10	6.79	22.1
S	1st Half		316	49	87	14	38	3	275			$10	346	468	814	10	81	30	0.56	286	120	72		5.69	1.6
K age	2nd Half		289	60	81	25	62	8	280			$19	394	585	978	16	80	27	0.93	313	173	89		8.06	21.1
LIMA D+ BA: 60%	04	Proj	**600**	**115**	**171**	**40**	**112**	**12**	**285**			**$32**	**389**	**543**	**932**	**15**	**79**	**30**	**0.81**	**300**	**153**	**87**		**7.48**	**31.5**

Unusual h% and still-solid xBA mean a BA rebound is likely. Otherwise, a typical Bagwell season, punctuated by a nice second half. Age is beginning to creep into the BPIs, but expect another solid year.

Bako,Paul

Bako,Paul	Yr	Tm	AB	R	H	HR	RBI	SB	Avg	vL	vR	R$	OB	Slg	OPS	bb%	ct%	h%	Eye	xBA	PX	SX	G/F	RC/G	RAR
Pos CA	99	HOU	* 262	17	62	3	20	1	237	167	264	($0)	308	351	659	9	75	31	0.41	240	81	54	1.60	3.58	-3.0
Age 31 Past Peak	00	2NL	221	18	50	2	20	0	226	148	237	($1)	310	308	618	11	71	31	0.42	195	56	36	1.98	3.15	-5.7
Bats L	01	ATL	137	19	29	2	15	1	212	208	212	($0)	312	343	655	13	75	27	0.59	242	91	87	1.66	3.50	-0.1
R Very High	02	MIL	234	24	55	4	20	0	235	167	245	$1	295	329	624	8	80	28	0.43	249	63	47	1.74	3.12	-7.1
I CON	03	CHC	188	19	43	0	17	0	229	200	233	($1)	310	330	639	10	75	30	0.47	241	76	100	1.44	3.30	-5.7
S pt STB	1st Half		84	3	17	0	8	0	202			($1)	280	274	553	10	79	26	0.50	236	53	53		2.45	-4.8
K	2nd Half		104	16	26	0	9	0	250			$0	333	375	708	11	72	35	0.45	244	95	135		4.09	-0.6
LIMA F BA: 50%	04	Proj	**200**	**21**	**46**	**1**	**18**	**0**	**230**			**($0)**	**308**	**332**	**641**	**10**	**76**	**30**	**0.47**	**242**	**74**	**77**		**3.33**	**-4.7**

It's great to have a LH C, but not one with a consistent .650 OPS against RHP. On the other hand, he was darn close to replacement level in the second half. Just trying to look on the bright side....

Baldelli,Rocco

Baldelli,Rocco	Yr	Tm	AB	R	H	HR	RBI	SB	Avg	vL	vR	R$	OB	Slg	OPS	bb%	ct%	h%	Eye	xBA	PX	SX	G/F	RC/G	RAR
Pos CF	99		0	0	0	0	0	0	0								0								
Age 22 Growth	00		0	0	0	0	0	0	0								0								
Bats R	01		0	0	0	0	0	0	0								0								
R Very High	02	a/a	166	22	56	4	19	4	337			$8	353	494	847	2	84	39	0.15	277	103	109		5.41	2.8
I EXP con	03	TAM	637	89	185	11	78	27	290	298	285	$24	322	418	740	4	80	35	0.23	266	81	144	1.68	4.76	0.4
S pt stb	1st Half		309	40	97	5	39	14	314			$14	342	460	801	4	79	39	0.20	269	92	164		5.74	8.5
K AGE	2nd Half		328	49	88	6	39	13	268			$10	304	378	682	5	81	32	0.27	261	70	120		3.96	-7.5
LIMA C+ BA: 30%	04	Proj	**625**	**86**	**172**	**13**	**74**	**22**	**275**			**$19**	**307**	**411**	**718**	**4**	**82**	**32**	**0.25**	**270**	**86**	**126**		**4.03**	**-13.6**

The facts: BA fell to "correct" xBA levels, and he was below replacement level for most of the year. High ABs pad raw totals; he's better in Roto than Scoresheet. Certainly not bad for 21, but don't overbid now.

Banks,Brian

Banks,Brian	Yr	Tm	AB	R	H	HR	RBI	SB	Avg	vL	vR	R$	OB	Slg	OPS	bb%	ct%	h%	Eye	xBA	PX	SX	G/F	RC/G	RAR
Pos LF	99	MIL	219	34	53	5	22	6	242			$3	320	352	671	10	73	31	0.42	230	67	99		3.87	-7.7
Age 33 Decline	00	JPN	231	28	49	4	31	3	214			$1	297	303	600	11	78	26	0.54	236	56	62		2.99	-15.4
Bats S	01	aaa	396	56	87	17	52	4	220			$6	271	422	693	7	73	26	0.26	294	121	98		3.56	-19.6
R X HIGH	02	aaa	467	62	113	13	63	6	242			$9	315	400	716	10	85	26	0.69	280	107	77		4.13	-20.8
I exp CON	03	FLA	149	14	35	4	23	2	235	196	255	$3	345	383	727	14	74	29	0.66	238	90	98	0.83	4.37	-5.5
S pt STB	1st Half		96	10	21	4	17	1	219			$2	318	438	756	13	73	26	0.54	255	130	133		4.60	-2.9
K age	2nd Half		53	4	14	0	6	1	264			$1	391	283	674	17	77	34	0.92	205	17	33		3.72	-2.9
LIMA F BA: 50%	04	Proj	**150**	**17**	**36**	**4**	**20**	**2**	**240**			**$3**	**334**	**371**	**705**	**12**	**77**	**29**	**0.62**	**242**	**85**	**75**		**4.07**	**-7.6**

The walks are nice, but you've gotta have something to go along with them. Surely a spare corner OF with some upside could have better used these 150 AB. It's not as if he'd torn up Japan and Triple-A.

Barajas,Rod

Barajas,Rod	Yr	Tm	AB	R	H	HR	RBI	SB	Avg	vL	vR	R$	OB	Slg	OPS	bb%	ct%	h%	Eye	xBA	PX	SX	G/F	RC/G	RAR
Pos CA	99	aa	510	58	139	10	71	2	273			$10	296	408	704	3	89	29	0.30	290	92	66	0.33	4.25	3.5
Age 28 Peak	00	aaa	416	33	82	9	56	3	197			($1)	218	317	535	3	88	20	0.23	283	79	49	1.00	2.10	-26.1
Bats R	01	ARI	* 268	26	63	10	33	2	235	214	141	$4	265	403	668	4	83	25	0.24	278	104	47	0.48	3.53	0.1
R X HIGH	02	ARI	* 170	14	42	4	24	1	247	196	252	$3	293	382	675	6	85	27	0.42	271	98	35	0.56	3.82	-1.4
I EXP CON	03	ARI	220	19	48	3	28	0	218	244	212	$0	265	327	592	6	80	26	0.33	255	82	25	0.69	2.83	-9.9
S PT stb	1st Half		130	14	31	2	20	0	238			$1	261	377	638	3	82	28	0.17	266	107	36		3.30	-3.9
K	2nd Half		90	5	17	1	8	0	189			($1)	270	256	526	10	79	23	0.53	230	47	10		2.17	-6.1
LIMA F BA: 55%	04	Proj	**250**	**21**	**56**	**5**	**31**	**1**	**224**			**$1**	**271**	**344**	**615**	**6**	**82**	**25**	**0.37**	**259**	**85**	**34**		**3.06**	**-7.9**

Why he could surprise:
- consistently better past xBAs
- G/F ratio still low
- peak age, more experience

Why he probably won't:
- contact rate drop
- h% shows he's overmatched

Bard,Josh

Bard,Josh	Yr	Tm	AB	R	H	HR	RBI	SB	Avg	vL	vR	R$	OB	Slg	OPS	bb%	ct%	h%	Eye	xBA	PX	SX	G/F	RC/G	RAR
Pos CA	99		0	0	0	0	0	0	0								0								
Age 26 Pre-Peak	00		0	0	0	0	0	0	0								0								
Bats S	01	a/a	322	36	82	5	44	0	255			$4	320	373	693	9	86	28	0.70	271	85	28		4.03	3.2
R Moderate	02	CLE	* 434	42	118	9	61	0	272	229	218	$9	307	408	715	5	87	29	0.40	278	93	30	2.00	4.39	9.5
I EXP	03	CLE	* 418	38	110	13	55	1	263	289	227	$9	320	409	729	8	83	29	0.51	264	91	28	1.50	4.36	3.3
S pt stb	1st Half		217	12	53	3	19	1	244			$1	299	336	636	7	81	29	0.40	239	65	23		3.42	-4.3
K	2nd Half		201	26	57	10	36	0	284			$8	342	488	830	8	87	29	0.67	293	119	43		5.47	8.0
LIMA D BA: 50%	04	Proj	**350**	**35**	**94**	**10**	**49**	**0**	**269**			**$8**	**319**	**413**	**733**	**7**	**86**	**29**	**0.52**	**269**	**93**	**33**		**4.48**	**5.5**

8-36-.244 in 303 AB at CLE. There are the seeds of a hitter here. An impressive second half with improved bb%, a ct% rebound, and solid skills growth overall. Given the chance, he could help a lot of teams.

Barrett,Michael

Barrett,Michael	Yr	Tm	AB	R	H	HR	RBI	SB	Avg	vL	vR	R$	OB	Slg	OPS	bb%	ct%	h%	Eye	xBA	PX	SX	G/F	RC/G	RAR
Pos CA	99	MON	433	53	127	8	52	0	293	267	303	$9	342	436	778	7	91	31	0.82	309	99	49	1.32	5.28	16.0
Age 27 Peak	00	MON	* 391	47	98	3	39	1	251	160	237	$2	311	335	646	8	89	28	0.77	277	62	52	1.48	3.52	-5.5
Bats R	01	MON	472	42	118	6	38	2	250	254	249	$3	288	367	654	5	89	27	0.46	285	83	59	2.04	3.57	0.8
R Low	02	MON	376	41	99	12	49	6	263	261	264	$11	334	418	752	10	83	29	0.62	270	103	65	1.71	4.77	7.2
I CON	03	MON	226	33	47	10	30	0	208	205	209	$2	275	398	674	9	84	21	0.57	280	113	76	1.38	3.53	-5.4
S pt	1st Half		147	19	24	5	11	0	163			($2)	222	286	507	7	83	16	0.44	253	71	50		1.93	-11.4
K	2nd Half		79	14	23	5	19	0	291			$4	371	608	978	11	85	29	0.83	333	190	134		8.10	8.4
LIMA C+ BA: 65%	04	Proj	**400**	**53**	**105**	**15**	**57**	**1**	**263**			**$10**	**327**	**451**	**778**	**9**	**85**	**28**	**0.64**	**285**	**118**	**80**		**5.11**	**11.6**

A lost season, which held some promise going in. Injuries hit just as he was heating up. The reasons for optimism prior to '03 are still there, but he also may have lost the opportunity. Still, a decent sleeper.

ROD TRUESDELL

Batista,Tony

Pos 3B
Age 30 Past Peak
Bats R

R	Moderate	
I		CON
S		STB
K		

LIMA C **BA:** 60%

	Tm	AB	R	H	HR	RBI	SB	Avg	vL	vR	R$	OB	Slg	OPS	bb%	ct%	h%	Eye	xBA	PX	SX	G/F	RC/G	RAR
99	2TM	519	77	144	31	100	4	277	230	296	$21	327	518	845	7	82	29	0.40	267	142	68	0.64	6.03	24.1
00	TOR	620	96	163	41	114	5	263	235	273	$22	302	519	822	5	80	27	0.29	275	143	74	0.79	5.32	16.7
01	2AL	579	70	138	25	87	5	238	203	248	$13	278	435	713	5	80	26	0.28	245	115	98	0.76	4.03	-5.7
02	BAL	615	90	150	31	87	5	244	234	247	$16	301	457	758	8	83	25	0.47	249	129	66	0.54	4.55	1.5
03	BAL	631	76	148	26	99	4	235	193	249	$13	267	393	660	4	84	24	0.27	257	92	61	0.70	3.45	-20.3
1st Half		309	44	80	15	54	0	259			$9	293	443	737	5	83	27	0.29	263	105	50		4.34	-1.5
2nd Half		322	32	68	11	45	4	211			$4	242	345	587	4	84	22	0.26	251	79	62		2.70	-18.1
04	**Proj**	**625**	**80**	**149**	**28**	**96**	**4**	**238**			**$14**	**279**	**424**	**703**	**5**	**83**	**25**	**0.33**	**261**	**109**	**67**		**3.91**	**-10.5**

Overall BPIs have steadily declined, reaching a five-year low in 2003. Even his one bit of value, power, is now only league average. Not much to recommend here.

Bautista,Danny

Pos RF
Age 31 Past Peak
Bats R

R	High	
I		CON
S	PT	stb
K		

LIMA D+ **BA:** 45%

	Tm	AB	R	H	HR	RBI	SB	Avg	vL	vR	R$	OB	Slg	OPS	bb%	ct%	h%	Eye	xBA	PX	SX	G/F	RC/G	RAR
99	FLA	* 340	51	95	11	45	5	279	277	293	$10	304	438	742	3	87	29	0.27	290	98	93	1.59	4.61	-3.8
00	2NL	351	54	100	11	59	6	285	267	295	$12	332	476	808	7	86	31	0.50	300	112	147	1.50	5.62	4.7
01	ARI	222	26	67	5	26	3	302	239	343	$7	343	437	780	6	86	33	0.45	275	84	87	1.52	5.36	-1.2
02	ARI	154	22	50	6	23	4	325	362	308	$9	370	500	870	7	86	35	0.52	293	105	114	2.11	6.81	6.3
03	ARI	284	29	78	4	36	3	275	267	279	$6	325	394	719	7	82	32	0.42	264	82	91	2.05	4.43	-9.6
1st Half		173	14	45	1	18	2	260			$2	297	329	626	5	84	31	0.32	249	50	69		3.34	-11.5
2nd Half		111	15	33	3	18	1	297			$4	366	495	861	10	80	35	0.55	286	131	121		6.41	2.5
04	**Proj**	**300**	**38**	**89**	**8**	**42**	**5**	**297**			**$11**	**346**	**453**	**799**	**7**	**84**	**33**	**0.47**	**273**	**99**	**110**		**5.58**	**0.9**

Picked it up some in the 2nd half, but still disappointing. G/F ratios mean that power spike probably isn't going to happen. He still has the skills, but he's never seized the opportunities, and may not get many more.

Bellhorn,Mark

Pos 3B 2B
Age 29 Past Peak
Bats S

R	X HIGH	
I	EXP	CON
S	PT	STB
K		

LIMA D+ **BA:** 45%

	Tm	AB	R	H	HR	RBI	SB	Avg	vL	vR	R$	OB	Slg	OPS	bb%	ct%	h%	Eye	xBA	PX	SX	G/F	RC/G	RAR
99	aa	57	10	14	1	7	0	246			$0	348	333	682	14	74	32	0.60	221	57	40		3.93	-0.8
00	aaa	436	99	104	21	65	17	239			$14	360	454	814	16	74	28	0.72	261	116	183	1.33	5.50	15.1
01	OAK	* 230	34	44	10	31	2	191	118	140	$1	265	365	630	9	62	26	0.26	203	96	111	0.63	3.09	-9.3
02	CHC	445	86	115	27	56	7	258	303	241	$17	367	512	879	15	68	32	0.53	247	156	114	0.79	6.30	22.5
03	2NL	* 303	34	73	6	37	6	241	211	225	$5	361	363	724	16	72	32	0.66	225	81	78	1.50	4.22	-0.3
1st Half		161	17	33	2	22	4	205			$1	344	298	642	17	71	28	0.72	215	64	81		3.21	-5.4
2nd Half		142	17	40	4	15	2	282			$4	382	437	818	14	73	36	0.59	237	101	72		5.57	5.4
04	**Proj**	**300**	**45**	**73**	**11**	**38**	**5**	**243**			**$7**	**352**	**422**	**774**	**14**	**69**	**31**	**0.55**	**230**	**109**	**108**		**4.86**	**4.2**

He could rebound, because:
- full year in COL
- he still owns that '02 156 PX

But he probably won't, since:
- 2nd half lucky, not Coors (.237 xBA, .214 home BA)
- ultra-low ct% hurts at COL

Belliard,Ron

Pos 2B
Age 29 Past Peak
Bats R

R	Moderate	
I		CON
S	pt	stb
K		

LIMA C+ **BA:** 55%

	Tm	AB	R	H	HR	RBI	SB	Avg	vL	vR	R$	OB	Slg	OPS	bb%	ct%	h%	Eye	xBA	PX	SX	G/F	RC/G	RAR
99	MIL	* 565	70	158	9	64	13	280	273	304	$13	364	400	764	12	88	31	1.10	284	82	83	1.41	5.04	13.4
00	MIL	571	83	150	8	54	7	263	282	257	$8	355	389	744	13	85	30	0.98	277	79	115	1.61	4.70	5.6
01	MIL	364	69	96	11	36	5	264	284	259	$8	328	453	782	9	82	30	0.54	302	123	119	1.29	5.12	13.4
02	MIL	289	30	61	3	26	2	211	200	217	($1)	257	287	545	6	84	24	0.39	230	58	55	1.69	2.30	-19.1
03	COL	447	73	124	8	50	7	277	345	254	$11	349	409	758	10	84	32	0.69	295	94	97	1.87	5.05	8.3
1st Half		215	32	67	1	20	1	312			$5	393	405	798	12	82	38	0.74	272	78	45		5.83	8.3
2nd Half		232	41	57	7	30	6	246			$6	306	414	719	8	86	26	0.63	315	109	133		4.34	-0.5
04	**Proj**	**400**	**60**	**108**	**10**	**42**	**8**	**270**			**$10**	**334**	**421**	**755**	**9**	**84**	**30**	**0.61**	**298**	**101**	**97**		**4.90**	**6.8**

Appeared to come all the way back, but not when Coors is considered (home/road OPS .892/.656). 1st/2nd half splits mainly a function of h% (i.e. luck) rather than any skills issues. Expect a similar year.

Bell,David

Pos 3B
Age 31 Past Peak
Bats R

R	Moderate	
I		con
S	pt	stb
K		

LIMA C **BA:** 80%

	Tm	AB	R	H	HR	RBI	SB	Avg	vL	vR	R$	OB	Slg	OPS	bb%	ct%	h%	Eye	xBA	PX	SX	G/F	RC/G	RAR
99	SEA	597	92	160	21	78	7	268	220	280	$14	333	432	765	9	85	29	0.64	275	100	79	1.00	4.95	9.1
00	SEA	454	57	112	11	47	2	247	287	234	$4	310	381	692	8	85	27	0.64	260	83	60	0.86	3.92	-6.5
01	SEA	470	62	122	15	64	2	260	256	261	$10	301	415	716	6	87	27	0.47	269	100	50	0.65	4.29	-1.0
02	SF	552	82	144	20	73	1	261	263	260	$14	327	429	756	9	86	27	0.68	279	110	56	0.83	4.78	3.0
03	PHI	297	32	58	4	37	0	195	169	204	($2)	293	283	576	12	87	21	1.03	249	63	28	1.10	2.63	-15.3
1st Half		264	30	54	3	34	0	205			($1)	295	292	587	11	86	23	0.92	249	65	31		2.76	-12.3
2nd Half		33	2	4	1	3	0	121			($1)	275	212	487	17	91	10	2.33	250	47			1.69	-2.9
04	**Proj**	**450**	**59**	**117**	**17**	**62**	**1**	**260**			**$11**	**325**	**428**	**754**	**9**	**86**	**27**	**0.69**	**263**	**107**	**50**		**4.76**	**4.8**

Little doubt that his back woes were responsible for this debacle. Ironically, the best walk rate of his career (it must've hurt too much to swing). If he heals, it's another 15-20 HR and his usual replacement-level season.

Bell,Jay

Pos 2B
Age 38 Decline
Bats R

R	High	
I		CON
S	pt	stb
K	AGE	

LIMA F **BA:** 45%

	Tm	AB	R	H	HR	RBI	SB	Avg	vL	vR	R$	OB	Slg	OPS	bb%	ct%	h%	Eye	xBA	PX	SX	G/F	RC/G	RAR
99	ARI	589	132	170	38	112	7	289	339	268	$28	376	557	932	12	78	32	0.62	279	155	114	0.84	7.39	52.7
00	ARI	565	87	151	18	68	7	267	347	239	$13	348	437	785	11	84	29	0.80	265	102	103	0.83	5.27	14.8
01	ARI	428	59	106	13	46	0	248	224	256	$6	347	400	746	13	82	28	0.82	247	96	37	0.98	4.66	10.1
02	ARI	* 71	6	12	2	13	0	169	130	192	($0)	253	310	563	10	86	17	0.80	271	98		1.06	2.41	-4.6
03	NYM	116	11	21	0	3	0	181	139	200	($3)	312	190	501	16	67	27	0.58	186	8	23	0.69	1.84	-9.6
1st Half		57	6	12	0	3	0	211			($1)	392	211	602	23	67	32	0.89	181	0	17		2.66	-3.1
2nd Half		59	5	9	0	0	0	153			($2)	219	169	388	8	68	22	0.26	193	15	36		1.12	-6.5
04	**Proj**	**0**	**0**	**0**	**0**	**0**	**0**	**0**			**$0**					**0**				**0**	**0**			

A good player who parlayed a career 1999 into several more seasons of big league play and pay. Skills erosion, highlighted by RC/G slide, clearly shows hanging 'em up is a good decision.

Beltran,Carlos

Pos CF
Age 27 Peak
Bats S

R	Low	
I		con
S	pt	
K		

LIMA C **BA:** 55%

	Tm	AB	R	H	HR	RBI	SB	Avg	vL	vR	R$	OB	Slg	OPS	bb%	ct%	h%	Eye	xBA	PX	SX	G/F	RC/G	RAR
99	KC	663	112	194	22	108	27	293	273	298	$29	339	454	793	6	81	33	0.37	275	93	143	1.46	5.53	15.4
00	KC	372	49	92	7	44	13	247	310	233	$7	312	366	678	9	81	29	0.51	260	70	139	1.43	4.07	-6.4
01	KC	617	106	189	24	101	31	306	315	303	$34	360	514	874	8	81	35	0.43	298	121	181	1.36	7.12	38.2
02	KC	637	114	174	29	105	35	273	244	283	$33	346	501	847	10	79	31	0.53	304	139	156	1.39	6.17	25.7
03	KC	521	102	160	26	100	41	307	325	300	$38	391	522	913	12	84	32	0.89	311	116	185	1.42	7.91	45.4
1st Half		230	42	65	11	41	19	283			$15	384	465	850	14	84	30	1.03	276	99	137		6.87	13.8
2nd Half		291	60	95	15	59	22	326			$23	397	567	964	10	85	34	0.77	323	130	214		8.80	31.7
04	**Proj**	**600**	**110**	**189**	**30**	**115**	**45**	**315**			**$44**	**387**	**550**	**936**	**10**	**82**	**34**	**0.66**	**296**	**135**	**173**		**8.10**	**54.8**

xBA predicted the .300 BA, and suggests even better to come. BPI growth strong and across the board, especially in 2nd half. 26-with-experience, contract year also point to a breakout.

Beltre,Adrian

Pos 3B
Age 26 Pre-Peak
Bats R

R	Very Low	
I		con
S		
K		

LIMA C+ **BA:** 55%

	Tm	AB	R	H	HR	RBI	SB	Avg	vL	vR	R$	OB	Slg	OPS	bb%	ct%	h%	Eye	xBA	PX	SX	G/F	RC/G	RAR
99	LA	538	84	148	15	67	18	275	230	290	$17	349	428	776	10	80	32	0.58	257	95	116	1.16	5.20	13.0
00	LA	510	71	148	20	85	12	290	277	294	$21	360	475	835	10	84	31	0.70	286	112	81	1.07	6.07	25.3
01	LA	475	59	126	13	60	13	265	265	265	$14	306	411	717	6	83	30	0.34	266	88	117	1.09	4.35	-3.2
02	LA	587	70	151	21	75	7	257	302	245	$16	301	426	727	6	84	28	0.39	262	107	93	0.99	4.30	-4.9
03	LA	559	50	134	23	80	2	240	232	242	$12	287	424	711	6	82	26	0.36	278	116	44	1.14	4.03	-3.7
1st Half		264	22	58	6	28	1	220			$1	277	352	629	7	82	25	0.44	265	93	33		3.15	-8.9
2nd Half		295	28	76	17	52	1	258			$10	296	488	784	5	81	26	0.29	289	136	52		4.90	5.6
04	**Proj**	**550**	**60**	**139**	**25**	**87**	**6**	**253**			**$17**	**300**	**449**	**750**	**6**	**82**	**27**	**0.38**	**283**	**120**	**75**		**4.54**	**2.3**

Big September saved his season, but he didn't follow up on 2002 finish. High AB totals mask stagnant, mediocre skills. It's as if a switch was turned off after 2000. Think where he'd be now if that trend had continued.

Benard,Marvin

Pos CF
Age 33 Decline
Bats L

R	Moderate	
I		con
S	pt	
K	age	

LIMA F **BA:** 75%

	Tm	AB	R	H	HR	RBI	SB	Avg	vL	vR	R$	OB	Slg	OPS	bb%	ct%	h%	Eye	xBA	PX	SX	G/F	RC/G	RAR
99	SF	562	100	163	16	64	27	290	263	297	$22	353	457	811	9	83	33	0.57	289	107	126	1.29	5.55	20.0
00	SF	560	102	147	12	55	22	263	216	273	$14	337	396	734	10	83	30	0.65	272	82	140	1.62	4.63	5.1
01	SF	392	70	104	15	44	10	265	390	251	$12	316	439	755	7	83	29	0.44	281	103	115	1.16	4.70	9.7
02	SF	123	16	34	1	13	5	276	389	257	$4	315	407	722	5	79	34	0.27	264	96	156	1.06	4.60	-1.0
03	SF	* 121	10	22	1	9	3	182		215	($1)	214	273	487	4	90	19	0.42	277	65	110	1.83	1.91	-11.9
1st Half		63	6	11	0	4	1	175			($1)	235	254	489	7	90	19	0.83	275	57	122		1.91	-6.3
2nd Half		58	4	11	1	5	2	190			$0	190	293	483	0	90	20	0.00	277	73	80		1.86	-5.7
04	**Proj**	**150**	**18**	**40**	**4**	**14**	**5**	**267**			**$4**	**303**	**420**	**722**	**5**	**85**	**29**	**0.36**	**279**	**98**	**102**		**4.48**	**-1.0**

0-4-.197 in 71 AB at SF. His second straight season plagued by knee injuries. A paltry 19% hit rate means toss out the '03 stats, and he has been a serviceable player. But the knees make him too risky.

ROD TRUESDELL

Bennett,Gary

Pos CA
Age 32 Past Peak
Bats R
R: X HIGH
I: CON
S: PT | STB
K:
LIMA D | BA: 55%

Yr	Tm	AB	R	H	HR	RBI	SB	Avg	vL	vR	R$	OB	Slg	OPS	bb%	ct%	h%	Eye	xBA	PX	SX	G/F	RC/G	RAR
99	PHI	88	7	24	1	21	0	273	273	273	$2	304	352	657	4	88	30	0.36	286	57		2.11	3.76	-0.5
00	PHI	* 391	46	108	11	48	1	276	364	192	$8	354	440	794	11	86	30	0.87	296	109	33	1.10	5.50	16.7
01	2NL	* 198	21	49	4	22	0	247	185	260	$2	304	374	677	7	81	29	0.43	259	82	46	1.50	3.85	1.9
02	COL	291	26	77	4	26	1	265	365	237	$4	301	354	655	5	85	30	0.33	256	60	58	2.06	3.54	-4.9
03	SD	307	26	73	2	42	3	238	218	248	$3	293	306	599	7	84	28	0.50	256	54	54	1.64	3.05	-11.4
1st Half		142	12	29	1	12	0	204			($2)	252	268	519	6	82	24	0.36	245	49	28		2.16	-9.5
2nd Half		165	14	44	1	30	3	267			$4	328	339	667	8	86	30	0.65	264	58	54		3.98	-1.5
04	**Proj**	**300**	**28**	**76**	**4**	**37**	**2**	**253**			**$4**	**307**	**348**	**654**	**7**	**84**	**29**	**0.49**	**261**	**67**	**56**		**3.64**	**-4.1**

Got another 300 AB, and did nothing with them. BPIs have been all over the place. Hit rate shows some first-half bad luck, but a .306 SLG? Really awful. That solid 2000 season looks a long way off now.

Berg,Dave

Pos 2B
Age 33 Decline
Bats R
R: High
I: CON
S: PT | stb
K: age
LIMA F | BA: 40%

Yr	Tm	AB	R	H	HR	RBI	SB	Avg	vL	vR	R$	OB	Slg	OPS	bb%	ct%	h%	Eye	xBA	PX	SX	G/F	RC/G	RAR
99	FLA	304	42	87	3	25	2	286	241	303	$5	344	382	726	8	81	35	0.46	270	70	61	1.14	4.61	3.4
00	FLA	210	23	53	1	21	3	252	270	245	$2	332	343	675	11	78	32	0.54	253	68	75	0.98	3.97	-2.4
01	FLA	215	26	52	4	16	0	242	211	253	$1	288	363	651	6	82	28	0.36	248	80	59	0.67	3.44	-2.7
02	TOR	374	42	101	4	39	0	270	264	272	$5	318	382	700	7	85	31	0.46	278	81	50	0.97	4.14	1.1
03	TOR	161	26	41	4	18	0	255	304	207	$2	302	379	681	6	79	30	0.32	252	76	77	1.02	3.81	-1.6
1st Half		101	17	28	3	13	0	277			$2	311	416	727	5	79	32	0.24	260	88	48		4.57	1.2
2nd Half		60	9	13	1	5	0	217			($0)	288	317	605	9	78	26	0.46	239	54	123		2.75	-2.6
04	**Proj**	**200**	**27**	**50**	**4**	**19**	**0**	**250**			**$2**	**304**	**371**	**675**	**7**	**81**	**29**	**0.40**	**255**	**77**	**63**		**3.72**	**-2.3**

Appeared at every position but CF and C in 2003. That helps him remain employed in an exciting, high-paying career, but you have to wonder if his clubs are getting their money's worth with this level of output.

Berkman,Lance

Pos LF
Age 28 Peak
Bats S
R: Very Low
I: con
S: pt
K:
LIMA C | BA: 55%

Yr	Tm	AB	R	H	HR	RBI	SB	Avg	vL	vR	R$	OB	Slg	OPS	bb%	ct%	h%	Eye	xBA	PX	SX	G/F	RC/G	RAR
99	HOU	* 319	42	84	9	52	10	263	154	250	$10	345	411	756	11	82	30	0.68	271	98	73	1.16	4.99	-0.5
00	HOU	353	76	105	21	67	6	297	218	320	$18	394	561	955	14	79	32	0.77	298	159	85	1.14	7.98	27.1
01	HOU	577	110	191	34	126	7	331	308	337	$37	423	620	1043	14	79	37	0.76	310	178	88	1.02	9.57	60.0
02	HOU	578	106	169	42	128	8	292	240	307	$36	403	578	981	16	80	30	0.91	303	176	74	0.95	8.30	31.0
03	HOU	538	110	155	25	93	5	288	282	290	$23	406	515	921	17	80	32	0.99	294	141	108	1.09	7.42	27.7
1st Half		267	54	75	14	47	1	281			$11	396	494	891	16	80	31	0.94	283	129	61		6.79	9.2
2nd Half		271	56	80	11	46	4	295			$12	416	535	951	17	80	33	1.04	305	153	145		8.07	18.7
04	**Proj**	**550**	**107**	**163**	**37**	**106**	**7**	**296**			**$30**	**406**	**586**	**992**	**16**	**80**	**31**	**0.91**	**304**	**176**	**99**		**8.50**	**42.1**

Numbers tainted from the start by injury-induced April slump, otherwise would be about what we've come to expect. 2001 was a hit-rate aberration, but we'll take a 950+ OPS to the bank. Looks good for rebound.

Berroa,Angel

Pos SS
Age 24 Growth
Bats R
R: Very High
I: EXP | con
S: pt | stb
K: age
LIMA C | BA: 45%

Yr	Tm	AB	R	H	HR	RBI	SB	Avg	vL	vR	R$	OB	Slg	OPS	bb%	ct%	h%	Eye	xBA	PX	SX	G/F	RC/G	RAR
99		0	0	0	0	0	0	0								0								
00		0	0	0	0	0	0	0								0								
01	aa	357	57	99	6	37	14	277			$11	308	403	712	4	86	31	0.32	279	83	130	1.58	4.23	2.7
02	aaa	372	38	76	7	33	8	204			$1	243	328	571	5	80	24	0.25	252	80	122	0.77	2.46	-20.9
03	KC	567	92	164	17	73	21	289	313	276	$23	324	453	777	5	82	33	0.29	291	100	149	1.34	5.29	13.9
1st Half		269	38	76	8	29	3	283			$7	320	457	778	5	80	33	0.28	288	110	106		5.11	5.2
2nd Half		298	54	88	9	44	18	295			$15	327	450	777	4	85	33	0.30	293	90	167		5.47	8.7
04	**Proj**	**550**	**78**	**154**	**18**	**77**	**19**	**280**			**$21**	**314**	**451**	**765**	**5**	**82**	**31**	**0.28**	**292**	**102**	**132**		**4.94**	**7.9**

Exciting growth season. Low h% and injuries suggest '02 was the outlier. Numbers fully supported by skills growth. A little more plate patience would be nice, but that's nitpicking. The Dye trade isn't looking so bad, is it?

Bigbie,Larry

Pos LF
Age 26 Pre-Peak
Bats L
R: Very High
I: EXP | con
S: pt | STB
K:
LIMA C+ | BA: 30%

Yr	Tm	AB	R	H	HR	RBI	SB	Avg	vL	vR	R$	OB	Slg	OPS	bb%	ct%	h%	Eye	xBA	PX	SX	G/F	RC/G	RAR
99		0	0	0	0	0	0	0								0								
00	aa	112	10	23	0	5	3	205			($1)	270	250	520	8	77	27	0.38	223	38	67		2.30	-10.0
01	BAL	* 435	57	112	11	43	14	257	185	240	$11	345	389	733	12	77	31	0.59	243	82	82	2.08	4.39	-3.1
02	aaa	348	37	95	2	31	6	273			$6	331	353	684	8	80	34	0.42	238	63	73	8.50	4.06	-15.5
03	BAL	* 404	65	124	12	51	7	307	324	296	$15	372	478	850	9	78	37	0.47	261	110	104	2.69	6.61	14.1
1st Half		151	22	42	3	18	2	278			$4	351	424	775	10	75	35	0.46	244	94	114		5.35	0.1
2nd Half		253	43	82	9	33	5	324			$12	385	510	895	9	79	38	0.48	271	120	86		7.45	14.3
04	**Proj**	**500**	**68**	**140**	**15**	**52**	**10**	**280**			**$15**	**347**	**440**	**787**	**9**	**78**	**33**	**0.47**	**259**	**101**	**94**		**5.39**	**4.5**

37% hit rate means another .300 BA is unlikely. PX gains were real, though very high G/F might mean his upside is limited. Some positive signs, even if .280 is more likely in 2004.

Biggio,Craig

Pos CF
Age 38 Decline
Bats R
R: High
I: CON
S: pt
K: AGE
LIMA C+ | BA: 55%

Yr	Tm	AB	R	H	HR	RBI	SB	Avg	vL	vR	R$	OB	Slg	OPS	bb%	ct%	h%	Eye	xBA	PX	SX	G/F	RC/G	RAR
99	HOU	639	123	188	16	73	28	294	307	290	$24	380	457	837	12	83	33	0.82	291	115	90	1.40	6.08	32.2
00	HOU	377	67	101	8	35	12	268	235	275	$9	370	393	762	14	81	31	0.84	247	72	138	1.59	5.18	9.3
01	HOU	617	118	180	20	70	7	292	222	306	$20	360	455	816	10	84	32	0.66	273	102	95	1.25	5.84	34.3
02	HOU	577	96	146	15	58	16	253	183	271	$14	313	404	716	8	81	29	0.45	267	104	128	1.31	4.41	-7.9
03	HOU	628	102	166	15	62	8	264	267	264	$13	326	412	738	8	82	30	0.49	286	103	91	1.44	4.61	-6.8
1st Half		325	50	88	9	31	5	271			$8	319	431	750	7	80	31	0.36	285	112	75		4.71	-2.6
2nd Half		303	52	78	6	31	3	257			$5	332	393	725	10	83	29	0.65	286	93	99		4.48	-4.4
04	**Proj**	**600**	**103**	**160**	**14**	**61**	**6**	**267**			**$12**	**334**	**412**	**746**	**9**	**82**	**31**	**0.55**	**287**	**99**	**99**		**4.79**	**1.3**

Mixed BPI signals, but one thing is clear: age is taking its toll. Mind you, he's not awful... but he's fast becoming one of those players whose reputation so far outweighs his actual value, he's basically un-ownable.

Blake,Casey

Pos 3B 1B
Age 30 Past Peak
Bats R
R: High
I: EXP | con
S: | stb
K:
LIMA C | BA: 50%

Yr	Tm	AB	R	H	HR	RBI	SB	Avg	vL	vR	R$	OB	Slg	OPS	bb%	ct%	h%	Eye	xBA	PX	SX	G/F	RC/G	RAR
99	aaa	387	53	80	16	58	7	207			$5	294	375	669	11	82	21	0.68	271	98	73	2.11	3.40	-12.1
00	aaa	399	54	103	11	47	6	258			$8	320	419	738	8	83	29	0.52	280	102	80	0.29	4.40	0.5
01	aaa	412	50	108	8	39	13	262			$10	309	393	702	6	84	30	0.42	271	84	119	2.00	4.20	-3.3
02	aaa	502	60	123	12	39	16	245			$10	297	371	667	7	86	27	0.51	270	82	94	1.00	3.55	-14.9
03	CLE	557	80	143	17	67	7	257	245	261	$12	304	411	715	6	80	29	0.35	268	101	63	1.14	4.06	-7.5
1st Half		244	36	65	8	28	3	266			$6	330	430	760	9	78	31	0.43	259	107	56		4.68	1.2
2nd Half		313	44	78	9	39	4	249			$6	284	396	680	5	82	28	0.27	271	97	68		3.60	-8.6
04	**Proj**	**500**	**67**	**126**	**14**	**54**	**10**	**252**			**$10**	**303**	**395**	**697**	**7**	**82**	**28**	**0.41**	**265**	**92**	**79**		**3.90**	**-8.5**

Did pretty much what his MLEs said he would, with a bit more pop. At 30, there's not much upside in these numbers. But he's unheralded, and figures to return 10 bucks. So if you get him for five, he's a bargain.

Blalock,Hank

Pos 3B
Age 23 Growth
Bats L
R: Very High
I: EXP | con
S: pt | stb
K: AGE
LIMA C+ | BA: 50%

Yr	Tm	AB	R	H	HR	RBI	SB	Avg	vL	vR	R$	OB	Slg	OPS	bb%	ct%	h%	Eye	xBA	PX	SX	G/F	RC/G	RAR
99		0	0	0	0	0	0	0								0								
00		0	0	0	0	0	0	0								0								
01	aa	272	44	87	11	54	3	320			$14	399	529	929	12	89	33	1.24	313	128	87		7.70	23.8
02	TEX	* 534	69	148	10	69	2	277	67	248	$12	338	412	750	8	84	31	0.58	270	95	54	0.95	4.90	6.5
03	TEX	567	89	170	29	90	2	300	209	329	$24	350	522	872	7	83	32	0.45	301	133	63	0.74	6.54	31.8
1st Half		274	46	91	12	46	0	332			$13	388	536	924	8	83	37	0.53	296	127	46		7.73	23.3
2nd Half		293	43	79	17	44	2	270			$10	314	509	823	6	83	27	0.38	306	139	79		5.53	8.6
04	**Proj**	**550**	**81**	**161**	**28**	**84**	**3**	**293**			**$22**	**351**	**524**	**875**	**8**	**84**	**30**	**0.57**	**306**	**140**	**64**		**6.53**	**31.7**

Hit rate shows he was over his head in the first half, but also that the second half slide wasn't as bad as it looked. Still needs work vs. LHP, but overall, a terrific season. Unsteady growth should continue.

Blanco,Henry

Pos CA
Age 32 Past Peak
Bats R
R: High
I: CON
S: pt | stb
K:
LIMA F | BA: 70%

Yr	Tm	AB	R	H	HR	RBI	SB	Avg	vL	vR	R$	OB	Slg	OPS	bb%	ct%	h%	Eye	xBA	PX	SX	G/F	RC/G	RAR
99	COL	* 320	35	79	8	36	1	247	222	238	$3	321	391	712	10	86	27	0.78	281	90	64	0.64	4.16	1.9
00	MIL	284	29	67	7	31	0	236	306	216	$2	322	394	716	11	79	28	0.60	252	109	20	0.71	4.06	0.5
01	MIL	314	33	66	6	31	3	210	164	224	$0	287	344	631	10	77	25	0.47	223	86	96	0.57	3.19	-3.2
02	ATL	221	17	45	6	22	0	204	211	202	($0)	270	335	605	8	77	24	0.39	213	86	38	0.79	2.77	-9.4
03	ATL	151	11	30	1	13	0	199	281	176	($2)	248	272	520	6	86	22	0.48	253	58	23	0.62	2.15	-10.2
1st Half		84	5	15	0	6	0	179			($2)	225	238	463	6	87	21	0.45	253	53	22		1.66	-7.1
2nd Half		67	6	15	1	7	0	224			$0	278	313	591	7	85	25	0.50	253	63	24		2.86	-2.9
04	**Proj**	**150**	**13**	**31**	**2**	**14**	**0**	**207**			**($1)**	**269**	**310**	**579**	**8**	**82**	**24**	**0.47**	**252**	**74**	**31**		**2.64**	**-6.8**

You know, Eddie Perez, Charlie O'Brien, Paul Bako, and Henry Blanco should chip in after Greg Maddux retires and buy him some golf clubs or a nice pen set with their MLB pension money.

ROD TRUESDELL

Bloomquist,Willie

Pos 3B | Age 26 Pre-Peak | Bats R
R: X HIGH | I: EXP, CON | S: PT, STB | K:
LIMA F | BA: 45%

Yr	Tm	AB	R	H	HR	RBI	SB	Avg	vL	vR	R$	OB	Slg	OPS	bb%	ct%	h%	Eye	xBA	PX	SX	G/F	RC/G	RAR
99		0	0	0	0	0	0	0								0								
00	aaa	191	18	41	1	23	5	215			$0	242	267	509	4	85	25	0.25	247	34	102		2.22	-12.6
01	aa	491	52	108	0	24	30	220			$5	259	263	522	5	89	25	0.47	257	35	113		2.26	-34.1
02	aaa	337	42	82	5	42	18	243			$10	298	338	636	7	88	26	0.67	268	63	114		3.17	-14.1
03	SEA	196	30	49	1	14	4	250	242	257	$2	316	321	638	9	80	31	0.49	235	48	118	1.64	3.50	-5.9
1st Half		67	11	13	0	3	1	194			($1)	280	239	519	11	85	23	0.80	236	26	131		2.19	-4.9
2nd Half		129	19	36	1	11	3	279			$3	336	364	700	8	78	35	0.38	234	59	103		4.34	-0.6
04	**Proj**	**150**	**20**	**37**	**1**	**13**	**7**	**247**			**$3**	**315**	**313**	**628**	**9**	**84**	**29**	**0.64**	**241**	**45**	**112**		**3.42**	**-4.7**

Leg problems plagued him throughout 2003. If healthy, OB and SX trends give hope for brighter future. Does not hit well enough to warrant everyday duty but could develop into hidden speed source.

Blum,Geoff

Pos 3B 2B | Age 31 Past Peak | Bats S
R: Moderate | I: CON | S: pt, stb | K:
LIMA D | BA: 55%

Yr	Tm	AB	R	H	HR	RBI	SB	Avg	vL	vR	R$	OB	Slg	OPS	bb%	ct%	h%	Eye	xBA	PX	SX	G/F	RC/G	RAR
99	MON	* 401	58	98	16	50	6	244	190	250	$8	328	431	760	11	86	25	0.86	293	113	93	0.82	4.82	5.5
00	MON	343	40	97	11	45	1	283	292	280	$9	333	449	782	7	83	32	0.43	281	102	51	0.93	5.08	7.5
01	MON	453	57	107	9	50	9	236	263	229	$6	302	351	653	9	79	28	0.46	242	77	73	1.01	3.48	-15.2
02	HOU	368	45	104	10	52	2	283	185	304	$11	367	440	807	12	81	33	0.70	255	104	88	1.03	5.78	12.3
03	HOU	420	51	110	10	52	0	262	135	274	$7	295	379	674	5	88	28	0.40	281	78	34	1.22	3.86	-4.7
1st Half		218	25	57	6	24	0	261			$4	306	404	710	6	86	28	0.47	286	96	27		4.27	0.1
2nd Half		202	26	53	4	28	0	262			$4	284	351	635	3	90	28	0.30	276	58	41		3.45	-4.7
04	**Proj**	**400**	**50**	**108**	**10**	**51**	**2**	**270**			**$9**	**324**	**397**	**721**	**7**	**85**	**30**	**0.52**	**280**	**83**	**58**		**4.48**	**0.9**

Made best contact of career but his incompetence against LHers keeps on growing. Makes little sense to keep giving this guy 400 AB every year. xBA trend gives some hope that he can push his BA back towards .280.

Bonds,Barry

Pos LF | Age 39 Decline | Bats L
R: Moderate | I: con | S: pt | K: AGE
LIMA D+ | BA: 70%

Yr	Tm	AB	R	H	HR	RBI	SB	Avg	vL	vR	R$	OB	Slg	OPS	bb%	ct%	h%	Eye	xBA	PX	SX	G/F	RC/G	RAR
99	SF	355	91	93	34	83	15	262	266	260	$23	388	617	1005	17	83	23	1.18	296	200	122	0.62	8.41	34.8
00	SF	480	129	147	49	106	11	306	230	340	$34	442	688	1130	20	84	28	1.52	306	209	112	0.57	11.15	78.2
01	SF	476	129	156	73	137	13	328	312	334	$51	510	863	1373	27	80	27	1.90	334	292	84	0.56	16.68	139.2
02	SF	403	117	149	46	110	9	370	384	363	$44	577	799	1376	33	88	33	4.21	371	260	80	0.65	18.70	123.6
03	SF	390	111	133	45	90	7	341	363	331	$36	522	749	1271	28	85	31	2.55	355	233	79	0.66	15.33	98.2
1st Half		222	54	67	22	47	7	302			$17	476	649	1125	25	84	27	2.11	331	195	91		11.59	36.5
2nd Half		168	57	66	23	43	0	393			$19	579	881	1459	31	86	35	3.22	383	283	27		21.40	63.3
04	**Proj**	**350**	**101**	**117**	**40**	**89**	**4**	**334**			**$31**	**520**	**747**	**1267**	**28**	**84**	**30**	**2.38**	**354**	**239**	**66**		**14.86**	**83.5**

Skills remain other-worldly but AB trend in last four seasons will continue to eat away at his HR and RBI totals. No longer a speed threat. Time to start tempering expectations to a more worldly level.

Boone,Aaron

Pos 3B | Age 31 Past Peak | Bats R
R: Moderate | I: con | S: PT, stb | K:
LIMA C+ | BA: 55%

Yr	Tm	AB	R	H	HR	RBI	SB	Avg	vL	vR	R$	OB	Slg	OPS	bb%	ct%	h%	Eye	xBA	PX	SX	G/F	RC/G	RAR
99	CIN	* 513	61	144	14	77	19	281	219	297	$19	323	441	763	6	84	31	0.39	282	100	119	1.03	4.93	8.4
00	CIN	291	44	83	12	43	6	285	302	382	$11	340	471	810	8	82	31	0.46	271	114	73	0.79	5.76	11.8
01	CIN	381	54	112	14	62	6	294	306	290	$16	344	483	827	7	81	33	0.41	277	118	87	1.00	5.91	14.1
02	CIN	606	83	146	26	87	32	241	233	243	$25	305	439	744	8	82	26	0.50	284	130	117	1.01	4.53	-1.1
03	2TM	592	92	158	24	96	23	267	216	285	$25	320	453	772	7	82	29	0.44	283	115	124	0.95	5.16	13.3
1st Half		298	45	79	15	47	11	265			$13	322	480	802	8	81	28	0.44	286	128	120		5.51	9.7
2nd Half		294	47	79	9	49	12	269			$12	317	425	743	7	84	29	0.45	280	101	115		4.81	3.6
04	**Proj**	**600**	**88**	**165**	**23**	**104**	**28**	**275**			**$29**	**329**	**460**	**789**	**7**	**82**	**30**	**0.45**	**286**	**116**	**116**		**5.31**	**15.2**

Overall production suffered after trade to NYY but his skills remained similar. SX and OB improved but SB went down -- that should change. xBA says BA should continue its ascent.

Boone,Bret

Pos 2B | Age 35 Decline | Bats R
R: High | I: CON | S: pt, stb | K: age
LIMA C+ | BA: 45%

Yr	Tm	AB	R	H	HR	RBI	SB	Avg	vL	vR	R$	OB	Slg	OPS	bb%	ct%	h%	Eye	xBA	PX	SX	G/F	RC/G	RAR
99	ATL	608	102	153	20	63	14	252	280	241	$12	305	416	721	7	82	28	0.42	271	106	91	1.11	4.18	-0.7
00	SD	463	61	116	19	74	8	251	235	257	$12	324	421	745	10	79	28	0.52	247	98	78	0.98	4.57	2.9
01	SEA	623	118	206	37	141	5	331	444	296	$38	371	578	949	6	82	36	0.36	288	146	75	1.13	7.97	62.3
02	SEA	608	88	169	24	107	12	278	295	272	$24	336	462	798	8	83	30	0.52	287	113	93	1.68	5.42	24.1
03	SEA	622	111	183	35	117	16	294	257	308	$32	364	535	899	10	80	32	0.54	297	142	119	1.22	7.09	51.1
1st Half		319	61	100	22	66	6	313			$20	372	592	965	9	83	32	0.55	323	168	76		8.24	35.4
2nd Half		303	50	83	13	51	10	274			$13	355	475	830	11	77	32	0.54	270	114	152		5.99	16.1
04	**Proj**	**625**	**105**	**181**	**31**	**114**	**12**	**290**			**$28**	**352**	**507**	**860**	**9**	**81**	**32**	**0.51**	**294**	**129**	**107**		**6.37**	**39.8**

BA trend against LHers and second half BA swoon will make another near-.300 BA season unlikely. Speed came on strong down the stretch, but age will start to eat away at those skills.

Borchard,Joe

Pos CF | Age 25 Pre-Peak | Bats S
R: High | I: EXP, con | S: stb | K: age
LIMA F | BA: 45%

Yr	Tm	AB	R	H	HR	RBI	SB	Avg	vL	vR	R$	OB	Slg	OPS	bb%	ct%	h%	Eye	xBA	PX	SX	G/F	RC/G	RAR
99		0	0	0	0	0	0	0								0								
00		0	0	0	0	0	0	0								0								
01	aa	515	79	141	25	82	4	274			$18	346	472	818	10	75	32	0.44	253	117	55		5.57	18.1
02	aaa	474	60	120	22	57	2	253			$12	321	464	785	9	71	31	0.34	247	135	46	1.13	4.93	1.5
03	CHW	* 484	59	112	14	51	2	231	176	188	$5	276	362	638	6	78	27	0.28	242	80	53	2.50	3.17	-23.1
1st Half		246	27	50	6	28	1	203			($0)	246	321	567	7	77	24	0.25	235	73	65		2.39	-18.3
2nd Half		238	32	62	8	23	1	261			$4	307	403	710	6	79	30	0.32	249	88	45		4.14	-4.2
04	**Proj**	**250**	**32**	**62**	**10**	**29**	**1**	**248**			**$5**	**306**	**415**	**721**	**8**	**75**	**29**	**0.33**	**244**	**103**	**42**		**4.16**	**-4.5**

1-5-.184 in 49 AB at CHW. Still struggling to understand the benefit of drawing a walk. 2001 line will still draw bidders, but he needs more time to get back to that level. Check back in a year or two.

Bordick,Mike

Pos SS 3B | Age 38 Decline | Bats R
R: X HIGH | I: CON | S: pt, STB | K: AGE
LIMA F | BA: 45%

Yr	Tm	AB	R	H	HR	RBI	SB	Avg	vL	vR	R$	OB	Slg	OPS	bb%	ct%	h%	Eye	xBA	PX	SX	G/F	RC/G	RAR
99	BAL	631	93	175	10	77	14	277	402	252	$15	334	403	737	8	84	32	0.53	263	81	127	1.05	4.77	10.8
00	2TM	583	88	166	20	80	9	285	307	277	$18	340	443	783	8	83	31	0.49	271	96	72	1.06	5.24	21.6
01	BAL	229	32	57	7	30	9	249	333	217	$7	301	397	698	7	84	27	0.47	260	95	86	0.98	4.04	-2.3
02	BAL	367	37	85	8	36	7	232	236	230	$5	299	365	664	9	83	26	0.56	248	85	92	0.88	3.55	-11.6
03	TOR	343	39	94	5	54	3	274	347	246	$8	338	382	720	9	83	32	0.55	265	73	72	1.15	4.53	1.1
1st Half		144	15	35	2	27	2	243			$3	297	382	679	7	81	29	0.39	260	94	110		3.89	-2.3
2nd Half		199	24	59	3	27	1	296			$5	367	382	748	10	84	34	0.69	258	58	37		5.01	3.2
04	**Proj**	**0**	**0**	**0**	**0**	**0**	**0**	**0**			**$0**					**0**				**0**	**0**			

If this is the end of the road, he rebounded to replacement-level value in his final season. Still would make a contribution in a platoon role against LHers.

Bradley,Milton

Pos CF | Age 26 Pre-Peak | Bats S
R: X HIGH | I: EXP, CON | S: pt, STB | K:
LIMA B+ | BA: 45%

Yr	Tm	AB	R	H	HR	RBI	SB	Avg	vL	vR	R$	OB	Slg	OPS	bb%	ct%	h%	Eye	xBA	PX	SX	G/F	RC/G	RAR
99	aa	346	53	105	9	43	12	303			$14	356	465	821	7	85	34	0.54	287	102	115		5.40	8.9
00	MON	* 496	71	131	8	40	11	264	261	204	$8	334	375	709	9	83	30	0.63	268	74	76	1.57	3.85	-7.1
01	2TM	* 488	57	115	8	44	29	236	156	247	$12	317	361	678	11	75	30	0.48	243	81	135	1.90	3.88	-7.0
02	CLE	* 359	52	90	9	42	8	251	293	230	$8	319	396	715	9	82	28	0.57	264	91	107	1.70	4.17	-6.5
03	CLE	377	61	121	10	56	17	321	402	287	$20	420	501	921	15	81	38	0.88	311	124	97	1.28	7.76	31.2
1st Half		246	42	84	6	37	13	341			$15	439	516	956	15	80	41	0.86	308	126	80		8.77	26.2
2nd Half		131	19	37	4	19	4	282			$5	382	473	855	14	82	32	0.91	316	120	118		6.11	5.2
04	**Proj**	**500**	**73**	**140**	**17**	**63**	**11**	**280**			**$17**	**366**	**469**	**834**	**12**	**81**	**32**	**0.71**	**310**	**119**	**97**		**5.99**	**17.7**

One of the best skill sets in the 1st half before the DL beckoned again. Back problem could make him hesitant on basepaths. Is a legit 20 HR threat if we carry out his PX trend one more year and he stays healthy.

Bragg,Darren

Pos RF LF CF | Age 34 Decline | Bats L
R: X HIGH | I: CON | S: PT, STB | K: age
LIMA F | BA: 35%

Yr	Tm	AB	R	H	HR	RBI	SB	Avg	vL	vR	R$	OB	Slg	OPS	bb%	ct%	h%	Eye	xBA	PX	SX	G/F	RC/G	RAR
99	STL	273	38	71	6	26	3	260	230	269	$4	363	377	740	14	75	33	0.66	245	75	69	1.51	4.79	-1.6
00	COL	149	16	33	3	21	4	221	63	241	$2	301	342	643	10	72	29	0.41	214	76	92	1.82	3.42	-7.9
01	2TM	* 359	48	93	9	28	9	259	333	259	$7	342	401	743	11	71	34	0.44	232	91	90	2.13	4.56	-7.5
02	ATL	* 287	46	75	4	21	9	261	308	263	$6	350	387	736	12	77	33	0.59	251	93	114	1.20	4.62	-5.8
03	ATL	161	21	38	0	9	2	236	292	219	($0)	293	280	573	7	76	31	0.34	224	33	94	1.07	2.72	-14.0
1st Half		85	5	13	0	3	2	153			($2)	191	165	356	4	78	20	0.21	213	11	66		0.95	-13.3
2nd Half		76	16	25	0	6	0	329			$2	400	408	808	11	75	44	0.47	234	59	106		6.20	1.2
04	**Proj**	**200**	**29**	**47**	**2**	**15**	**4**	**235**			**$1**	**312**	**323**	**635**	**10**	**75**	**30**	**0.45**	**231**	**64**	**96**		**3.34**	**-12.9**

Actually played quite well down the stretch but does not make enough contact or hit for enough power to make a bigger impact. Consistently low xBA gives him very little chance of significantly raising his BA.

STEPHEN NICKRAND

Branyan,Russ

Pos 3B
Age 28 Peak
Bats L
R: Moderate
I: exp | con
S: pt | STB
K:
LIMA D | BA: 30%

	Tm	AB	R	H	HR	RBI	SB	Avg	vL	vR	R$	OB	Slg	OPS	bb%	ct%	h%	Eye	xBA	PX	SX	G/F	RC/G	RAR
99	aaa	395	43	76	25	57	7	192			$6	275	413	688	10	60	24	0.28	206	120	67	0.50	3.54	-10.7
00	CLE	* 422	72	99	35	90	1	235	200	242	$14	310	533	843	10	64	27	0.30	243	157	84	0.59	5.46	13.5
01	CLE	315	48	73	20	54	1	232	325	218	$8	314	486	800	11	58	33	0.29	194	146	76	0.56	5.02	6.3
02	2TM	378	50	86	24	56	4	228	233	226	$11	319	458	777	12	60	31	0.34	203	133	61	0.88	4.73	2.3
03	CIN	176	22	38	9	26	0	216	250	205	$3	320	438	758	13	61	30	0.39	215	141	20	0.63	4.56	1.6
1st Half		31	4	6	1	4	0	194			($0)	342	355	697	18	61	28	0.58	204	108	22		3.84	-0.4
2nd Half		145	18	32	8	22	0	221			$3	315	455	770	12	61	30	0.35	218	148	19		4.69	1.9
04	Proj	**300**	**41**	**67**	**19**	**49**	**2**	**223**			**$8**	**310**	**468**	**779**	**11**	**60**	**30**	**0.32**	**218**	**144**	**61**		**4.73**	**3.1**

No change in contact rate, but walk rate keeps getting better. xBA slowly improving but not quickly enough to give him another 400 AB season. His chances for a breakout get smaller every year.

Broussard,Ben

Pos 1B
Age 27 Peak
Bats L
R: Very High
I: EXP | CON
S: pt | stb
K:
LIMA C+ | BA: 45%

	Tm	AB	R	H	HR	RBI	SB	Avg	vL	vR	R$	OB	Slg	OPS	bb%	ct%	h%	Eye	xBA	PX	SX	G/F	RC/G	RAR
99	aa	127	20	23	7	16	1	181			$0	235	386	621	7	73	19	0.26	252	117	76		2.86	-10.9
00	aa	286	48	64	11	39	11	224			$6	351	388	739	16	78	25	0.88	257	89	128		4.60	-9.2
01	aa	353	59	95	17	50	7	269			$13	352	479	831	11	83	28	0.75	289	129	68		5.75	-4.6
02	CLE	* 452	64	109	20	55	4	241	167	255	$10	325	431	756	11	78	27	0.55	262	115	68	1.12	4.72	-15.4
03	CLE	* 506	67	123	19	68	8	243	175	276	$11	299	417	716	7	80	27	0.39	263	104	105	1.02	4.21	-17.7
1st Half		260	33	63	8	31	4	242			$5	301	385	686	8	77	29	0.37	242	84	96		3.92	-11.3
2nd Half		246	34	60	11	37	4	244			$7	295	451	747	7	83	26	0.42	286	125	101		4.50	-6.4
04	Proj	**500**	**72**	**126**	**21**	**67**	**8**	**252**			**$13**	**321**	**442**	**763**	**9**	**80**	**28**	**0.50**	**266**	**113**	**94**		**4.84**	**-12.2**

16-55-.249 in 386 AB at CLE. MLB production tailed off a bit down the stretch. Skills have remained relatively flat for a few years now. Needs to reverse OB and Slg trends before taking a step up.

Brown,Dee

Pos LF
Age 26 Pre-Peak
Bats L
R: X HIGH
I: EXP | CON
S: pt | stb
K:
LIMA D | BA: 40%

	Tm	AB	R	H	HR	RBI	SB	Avg	vL	vR	R$	OB	Slg	OPS	bb%	ct%	h%	Eye	xBA	PX	SX	G/F	RC/G	RAR
99	aa	235	48	77	10	46	8	328			$14	399	532	931	11	86	35	0.88	303	119	121		7.21	14.1
00	aaa	479	63	126	20	59	17	263			$16	305	455	760	6	83	28	0.36	289	111	121	2.00	4.83	-4.6
01	KC	* 417	43	103	9	45	5	247	258	241	$6	288	357	645	5	80	29	0.28	242	72	54	1.81	3.43	-14.8
02	KC	* 509	59	128	15	68	8	251	91	275	$12	303	395	698	7	79	29	0.36	251	89	78	0.47	3.99	-12.7
03	KC	* 179	21	42	4	21	2	235	259	219	$2	279	352	631	6	75	29	0.25	232	78	59	0.87	3.24	-11.3
1st Half		79	11	19	2	10	0	241			$1	277	367	644	5	75	30	0.20	233	83	55		3.21	-5.1
2nd Half		100	10	23	2	11	2	230			$1	280	340	620	7	76	28	0.29	232	74	58		3.26	-6.3
04	Proj	**350**	**42**	**86**	**9**	**43**	**5**	**246**			**$6**	**293**	**378**	**671**	**6**	**78**	**29**	**0.31**	**239**	**84**	**75**		**3.68**	**-14.6**

2-14-.227 in 132 AB at KC. Still young enough to emerge as a force but skill set remains stagnant. Will not break out unless he overhauls his approach at the plate.

Bruntlett,Eric

Pos SS
Age 26 Pre-Peak
Bats R
R: High
I: EXP | con
S: pt | stb
K:
LIMA F | BA: 50%

	Tm	AB	R	H	HR	RBI	SB	Avg	vL	vR	R$	OB	Slg	OPS	bb%	ct%	h%	Eye	xBA	PX	SX	G/F	RC/G	RAR
99		0	0	0	0	0	0	0								0								
00		0	0	0	0	0	0	0								0								
01	a/a	519	73	127	3	34	19	245			$7	302	314	617	8	87	28	0.65	261	50	107		3.19	-12.2
02	a/a	532	75	127	2	41	30	239			$11	309	301	610	9	89	27	0.90	259	48	115		3.04	-19.8
03	HOU	* 378	46	94	3	28	8	249	190	303	$4	306	307	613	8	85	29	0.55	246	43	74	0.80	3.15	-10.8
1st Half		309	41	75	2	24	8	243			$3	306	294	600	8	85	28	0.61	244	39	81		3.00	-10.3
2nd Half		69	5	19	1	4	0	275			$1	306	362	668	4	86	31	0.30	251	62	14		3.90	-0.4
04	Proj	**150**	**18**	**38**	**1**	**10**	**5**	**253**			**$2**	**308**	**317**	**625**	**7**	**87**	**29**	**0.60**	**251**	**48**	**74**		**3.29**	**-2.8**

His history indicates some speed potential, but his OB levels just will not cut it. These speedsters who can't find 1B with a telescope are littered throughout Triple-A, giving him little room for error.

Buchanan,Brian

Pos RF 1B
Age 30 Past Peak
Bats R
R: Moderate
I: exp | con
S: pt | STB
K:
LIMA D | BA: 45%

	Tm	AB	R	H	HR	RBI	SB	Avg	vL	vR	R$	OB	Slg	OPS	bb%	ct%	h%	Eye	xBA	PX	SX	G/F	RC/G	RAR
99	aaa	391	48	99	7	43	8	253			$6	291	368	660	5	83	29	0.31	264	78	88		3.69	-15.0
00	MIN	* 446	73	116	21	87	4	260	303	184	$13	320	455	775	8	82	28	0.49	283	112	73	1.75	4.92	0.1
01	MIN	197	28	54	10	32	1	274	284	268	$7	338	487	825	9	71	34	0.33	246	130	39	1.11	5.70	4.1
02	2TM	227	31	61	11	28	2	269	225	304	$7	314	467	781	6	74	32	0.25	253	119	71	1.46	4.97	-1.2
03	SD	198	29	52	8	29	6	263	302	217	$7	342	455	797	11	74	32	0.47	267	117	120	1.39	5.36	-1.4
1st Half		118	17	34	7	22	4	288			$7	349	534	883	9	75	33	0.38	285	153	69		6.67	3.5
2nd Half		80	12	18	1	7	2	225			$1	333	337	671	14	73	30	0.59	240	64	180		3.67	-4.8
04	Proj	**250**	**36**	**65**	**10**	**33**	**5**	**260**			**$7**	**331**	**440**	**770**	**10**	**74**	**31**	**0.41**	**265**	**110**	**102**		**4.94**	**-3.9**

Typically mashes LHers, but liability on defense and poor contact ability limits his AB. Still has the power skills to surprise with a 30 HR season if given the chance.

Burks,Ellis

Pos DH
Age 39 Decline
Bats R
R: High
I: CON
S: pt | stb
K: AGE
LIMA D | BA: 45%

	Tm	AB	R	H	HR	RBI	SB	Avg	vL	vR	R$	OB	Slg	OPS	bb%	ct%	h%	Eye	xBA	PX	SX	G/F	RC/G	RAR
99	SF	390	73	110	31	96	7	282	345	255	$22	390	569	959	15	78	29	0.80	274	164	54	0.89	7.66	27.6
00	SF	393	74	135	24	96	5	344	360	338	$27	425	606	1031	12	88	35	1.14	320	147	106	1.25	10.03	50.2
01	CLE	439	83	123	28	74	5	280	245	292	$19	369	542	911	12	81	29	0.73	294	156	73	1.11	7.11	23.4
02	CLE	518	92	156	32	91	2	301	316	296	$25	356	541	896	8	79	33	0.41	285	141	47	1.34	6.88	19.4
03	CLE	198	27	52	6	28	1	263	322	237	$4	351	419	770	12	77	32	0.59	268	99	61	2.05	5.02	2.4
1st Half		198	27	52	6	28	1	263			$4	351	419	770	12	77	32	0.59	268	99	61		5.02	2.4
2nd Half		0	0	0	0	0	0	0			($0)					0			0					
04	Proj	**300**	**51**	**82**	**10**	**54**	**3**	**273**			**$10**	**358**	**440**	**798**	**12**	**80**	**31**	**0.66**	**275**	**104**	**71**		**5.49**	**4.3**

Elbow surgery negated his season. Great skills, but his injury risk heading into 2004 is high. Declining power skills suggest the end is near. xBA indicates another .300 BA season is unlikely.

Burnitz,Jeromy

Pos LF RF CF
Age 35 Decline
Bats L
R: Moderate
I: CON
S: stb
K: age
LIMA C+ | BA: 55%

	Tm	AB	R	H	HR	RBI	SB	Avg	vL	vR	R$	OB	Slg	OPS	bb%	ct%	h%	Eye	xBA	PX	SX	G/F	RC/G	RAR
99	MIL	467	87	126	33	103	7	270	247	282	$22	389	561	950	16	73	30	0.73	271	173	77	0.79	7.56	33.9
00	MIL	564	91	131	31	98	6	232	238	230	$14	347	456	803	15	79	24	0.82	261	129	68	0.92	5.18	-0.7
01	MIL	562	104	141	34	100	0	251	224	262	$18	344	504	848	12	73	28	0.53	260	146	67	0.79	5.74	0.8
02	NYM	479	65	103	19	54	10	215	174	229	$8	300	365	665	11	72	26	0.43	211	93	70	0.83	3.45	-44.1
03	2NL	464	63	111	31	77	5	239	250	235	$16	293	487	780	7	76	25	0.31	270	147	55	0.73	4.65	-13.2
1st Half		190	29	53	14	35	1	279			$9	328	579	907	7	76	30	0.31	288	186	43		6.17	3.2
2nd Half		274	34	58	17	42	4	212			$6	268	423	691	7	76	22	0.31	256	120	66		3.74	-15.7
04	Proj	**500**	**73**	**118**	**29**	**79**	**6**	**236**			**$15**	**298**	**462**	**760**	**8**	**74**	**26**	**0.34**	**261**	**134**	**72**		**4.46**	**-19.7**

A bit of a rebound — especially in first half — but really nothing we have not seen before. Walk rate trend is very worrisome. Do not expect many more surges, especially while in LA.

Burrell,Pat

Pos LF
Age 27 Peak
Bats R
R: Moderate
I: exp | CON
S: stb
K:
LIMA C+ | BA: 60%

	Tm	AB	R	H	HR	RBI	SB	Avg	vL	vR	R$	OB	Slg	OPS	bb%	ct%	h%	Eye	xBA	PX	SX	G/F	RC/G	RAR
99	a/a	450	72	134	24	77	2	298			$18	392	538	930	13	79	33	0.74	284	142	68		7.39	29.4
00	PHI	* 551	82	146	21	99	1	265	282	254	$15	368	465	833	14	69	35	0.53	245	126	51	0.97	5.91	11.0
01	PHI	539	70	139	27	89	2	258	265	256	$16	343	469	813	11	70	32	0.43	243	125	56	0.84	5.52	-2.8
02	PHI	586	96	165	37	116	1	282	311	274	$28	376	544	921	13	74	32	0.58	279	167	54	0.76	7.28	14.8
03	PHI	522	57	109	21	64	0	209	198	212	$4	305	404	709	12	73	25	0.51	248	123	54	0.79	3.97	-26.2
1st Half		276	34	55	11	29	0	199			$0	305	399	704	13	69	25	0.49	237	130	42		3.87	-14.9
2nd Half		246	23	54	10	35	0	220			$3	304	411	715	11	77	24	0.54	260	115	66		4.08	-11.3
04	Proj	**550**	**71**	**139**	**26**	**86**	**1**	**253**			**$15**	**345**	**471**	**816**	**12**	**73**	**30**	**0.53**	**253**	**135**	**62**		**5.53**	**-3.6**

Production was disappointing but skills did not get that much worse. H% says to expect a BA rebound, but BA will still continue to be a liability. Do not expect a huge spike back towards 2002 levels just yet.

Burroughs,Sean

Pos 3B
Age 23 Growth
Bats L
R: Very High
I: EXP | con
S: pt | stb
K: AGE
LIMA C+ | BA: 50%

	Tm	AB	R	H	HR	RBI	SB	Avg	vL	vR	R$	OB	Slg	OPS	bb%	ct%	h%	Eye	xBA	PX	SX	G/F	RC/G	RAR
99		0	0	0	0	0	0	0								0								
00	aa	392	39	103	2	35	5	263			$4	339	360	698	10	91	29	1.25	285	70	66		3.83	-6.2
01	aaa	394	58	125	8	53	9	317			$16	370	454	824	8	89	34	0.73	289	94	84		6.32	19.7
02	SD	* 371	44	102	3	32	3	275	218	292	$6	331	364	695	8	88	31	0.70	269	68	80	2.09	4.29	-3.2
03	SD	517	62	148	7	58	7	286	260	296	$13	342	402	745	8	85	32	0.59	292	78	110	1.75	4.93	9.9
1st Half		249	25	75	4	29	3	301			$8	358	430	788	8	85	34	0.59	294	90	81		5.70	9.9
2nd Half		268	37	73	3	29	4	272			$5	328	377	704	8	86	31	0.58	288	68	125		4.28	0.2
04	Proj	**500**	**62**	**146**	**9**	**53**	**7**	**292**			**$14**	**349**	**418**	**767**	**8**	**87**	**32**	**0.68**	**296**	**85**	**91**		**5.23**	**11.6**

Not the production you would expect from a 3B but still plenty of time to grow into the role. G/F ratio still indicates that a power surge is not on the horizon. Patience is required with this one.

STEPHEN NICKRAND

Butler,Brent

	Yr	Tm	AB	R	H	HR	RBI	SB	Avg	vL	vR	R$	OB	Slg	OPS	bb%	ct%	h%	Eye	xBA	PX	SX	G/F	RC/G	RAR
Pos 2B	99	aa	528	61	133	12	48	0	252			$4	284	362	646	4	92	25	0.59	284	69	35		3.38	-11.1
Age 26 Pre-Peak	00	aaa	438	55	126	7	40	1	288			$7	339	420	759	7	93	30	1.13	307	93	42		4.92	10.0
Bats R	01	COL	* 391	52	113	7	40	4	289	205	263	$10	320	422	742	4	94	29	0.75	306	88	87	1.46	4.69	9.2
R High	02	COL	* 449	68	121	11	53	2	269	237	265	$10	292	423	715	3	90	28	0.30	297	103	101	1.09	4.07	-4.5
I EXP con	03	COL	* 295	41	83	7	24	1	281	154	234	$6	329	437	766	7	91	29	0.78	300	107	73	0.91	5.06	5.4
S pt stb	1st Half		90	13	19	1	4	1	211			($1)	268	300	568	7	86	24	0.54	259	57	116		2.65	-4.9
K	2nd Half		205	28	64	6	20	0	312			$7	356	498	854	6	93	31	1.00	318	129	51		6.44	11.3
LIMA D BA: 65%	04	Proj	**300**	**42**	**87**	**7**	**28**	**1**	**290**			**$7**	**328**	**432**	**760**	**5**	**91**	**30**	**0.62**	**298**	**96**	**75**		**4.97**	**5.5**

1-4-.211 in 90 AB at COL. Bat emerged in Triple-A but fizzled in COL. Great contact rate in Coors will eventually make him a .300 hitter but the rest of his skills shows little flair.

Byrd,Marlon

	Yr	Tm	AB	R	H	HR	RBI	SB	Avg	vL	vR	R$	OB	Slg	OPS	bb%	ct%	h%	Eye	xBA	PX	SX	G/F	RC/G	RAR
Pos CF	99		0	0	0	0	0	0	0								0								
Age 26 Pre-Peak	00		0	0	0	0	0	0	0								0								
Bats R	01	aa	510	85	141	20	69	25	276			$23	333	467	799	8	83	30	0.49	287	110	156		5.51	17.0
R Moderate	02	aaa	538	85	147	12	52	13	273			$15	325	429	754	7	83	31	0.46	280	107	136		5.00	2.8
I EXP	03	PHI	495	86	150	7	45	11	303	315	299	$16	360	418	778	8	81	36	0.47	280	80	128	1.98	5.62	8.7
S stb	1st Half		149	21	40	1	11	2	268			$2	339	362	702	10	74	36	0.41	248	77	65		4.37	-2.6
K	2nd Half		346	65	110	6	34	9	318			$14	369	442	811	7	84	36	0.51	294	81	142		6.23	11.6
LIMA B BA: 35%	04	Proj	**500**	**82**	**143**	**10**	**49**	**13**	**286**			**$15**	**342**	**423**	**765**	**8**	**82**	**33**	**0.46**	**286**	**92**	**129**		**5.27**	**7.8**

H% was nice but skills remained the same. Last season was not a point on a growth curve, but strong finish could mean some small growth in '04. Off-season shoulder surgery but expected to be ready by spring training.

Byrnes,Eric

	Yr	Tm	AB	R	H	HR	RBI	SB	Avg	vL	vR	R$	OB	Slg	OPS	bb%	ct%	h%	Eye	xBA	PX	SX	G/F	RC/G	RAR
Pos CF LF	99	aa	164	16	31	1	15	4	189			($2)	240	274	514	6	87	21	0.50	269	67	74		1.91	-14.0
Age 28 Peak	00	a/a	502	83	138	11	67	26	275			$18	351	430	781	11	89	29	1.07	304	105	103	0.40	4.83	5.1
Bats R	01	aaa	453	72	112	19	45	21	247			$15	294	424	718	6	87	25	0.50	293	105	117	1.08	4.30	-0.7
R X HIGH	02	OAK	* 213	36	48	6	23	7	225	279	216	$4	257	376	632	4	87	23	0.32	281	92	155	0.88	3.25	-9.9
I EXP CON	03	OAK	414	64	109	12	51	10	263	286	251	$11	331	459	790	9	83	29	0.59	280	120	168	0.86	5.31	6.8
S PT STB	1st Half		257	50	86	11	41	7	335			$15	400	576	976	10	86	36	0.76	304	143	170		8.93	28.2
K	2nd Half		157	14	23	1	10	3	146			($4)	216	268	484	8	78	18	0.41	242	82	150		1.74	-15.9
LIMA D+ BA: 55%	04	Proj	**400**	**58**	**100**	**10**	**42**	**12**	**250**			**$9**	**304**	**408**	**713**	**7**	**84**	**28**	**0.49**	**276**	**99**	**138**		**4.24**	**-6.2**

Dynamic first half coupled with futile effort in second half. Skills supported strong start but AL pitchers carved him apart and he could not adjust. Temper your expectations but do not take him off your radar.

Cabrera,Jolbert

	Yr	Tm	AB	R	H	HR	RBI	SB	Avg	vL	vR	R$	OB	Slg	OPS	bb%	ct%	h%	Eye	xBA	PX	SX	G/F	RC/G	RAR
Pos 2B CF LF	99	aaa	279	35	66	0	22	16	237			$4	290	297	587	7	86	28	0.54	260	43	140	2.14	2.98	-9.4
Age 31 Past Peak	00	CLE	* 249	43	68	5	25	8	273	210	274	$6	307	386	692	5	91	28	0.55	284	66	126	1.22	3.96	0.7
Bats R	01	CLE	287	50	75	1	38	10	261	257	264	$6	300	348	649	5	86	30	0.39	267	63	139	1.30	3.58	-5.3
R Very High	02	2TM	* 277	33	58	1	20	5	209	256	44	($1)	268	264	531	7	87	24	0.59	248	44	71	1.00	2.09	-18.9
I exp CON	03	LA	345	43	98	6	37	6	284	307	267	$9	318	441	758	5	82	33	0.28	305	115	93	1.24	4.84	4.2
S STB	1st Half		138	21	37	4	17	4	268			$4	318	478	796	7	80	31	0.36	317	143	147		5.30	3.6
K	2nd Half		207	22	61	2	20	2	295			$5	318	415	733	3	84	34	0.21	296	97	51		4.53	0.7
LIMA D BA: 45%	04	Proj	**350**	**47**	**91**	**4**	**35**	**8**	**260**			**$6**	**301**	**373**	**675**	**6**	**85**	**30**	**0.38**	**301**	**84**	**102**		**3.73**	**-6.1**

Rode a near .300 BA down the stretch thanks to newfound power skills. Given contact rate trend and lack of previous power displays, it is hard to project a better 2004.

Cabrera,Miguel

	Yr	Tm	AB	R	H	HR	RBI	SB	Avg	vL	vR	R$	OB	Slg	OPS	bb%	ct%	h%	Eye	xBA	PX	SX	G/F	RC/G	RAR
Pos LF 3B	99		0	0	0	0	0	0	0								0								
Age 21 Growth	00		0	0	0	0	0	0	0								0								
Bats R	01		0	0	0	0	0	0	0								0								
R Moderate	02		0	0	0	0	0	0	0								0								
I EXP	03	FLA	* 580	82	179	20	117	8	309	364	247	$28	368	519	886	9	78	37	0.43	278	140	101	1.50	6.80	19.4
S	1st Half		304	47	101	9	61	8	332			$18	394	549	943	9	83	38	0.60	301	149	122		7.97	19.4
K AGE	2nd Half		276	35	78	11	56	0	283			$10	338	486	823	8	73	35	0.31	245	130			5.66	0.5
LIMA B BA: 30%	04	Proj	**500**	**69**	**131**	**18**	**81**	**5**	**262**			**$15**	**330**	**471**	**801**	**9**	**77**	**31**	**0.44**	**275**	**138**	**98**		**5.19**	**-8.3**

12-62-.268 in 314 AB at FLA. Future star, but not quite yet. Made terrible contact in second half. The power is for real, but expect a BA plunge until he changes his approach.

Cabrera,Orlando

	Yr	Tm	AB	R	H	HR	RBI	SB	Avg	vL	vR	R$	OB	Slg	OPS	bb%	ct%	h%	Eye	xBA	PX	SX	G/F	RC/G	RAR
Pos SS	99	MON	382	48	97	8	39	2	254	333	228	$4	288	403	691	5	90	26	0.47	290	96	97	1.28	3.89	4.1
Age 29 Past Peak	00	MON	422	47	100	13	55	4	237	286	221	$6	280	393	673	6	93	23	0.89	282	98	60	1.23	3.56	1.3
Bats R	01	MON	626	64	173	14	96	19	276	268	279	$22	323	428	751	6	91	28	0.80	295	98	109	1.20	4.82	22.8
R Low	02	MON	563	64	148	7	56	25	263	264	263	$16	321	380	701	8	91	28	0.91	292	92	99	1.26	4.26	5.9
I con	03	MON	626	95	186	17	80	24	297	311	293	$27	351	460	811	8	90	31	0.81	307	113	115	1.03	6.05	33.6
S pt	1st Half		312	52	93	11	45	10	298			$15	362	481	842	9	88	31	0.82	304	121	104		6.46	20.3
K	2nd Half		314	43	93	6	35	14	296			$13	340	439	780	6	92	31	0.81	308	104	111		5.65	13.4
LIMA B+ BA: 60%	04	Proj	**625**	**81**	**190**	**19**	**76**	**28**	**304**			**$30**	**358**	**477**	**835**	**8**	**91**	**31**	**0.90**	**310**	**117**	**105**		**6.27**	**40.9**

One of the more stable skill sets around. OB is slowly trending upward, meaning a 30 SB season is around the corner. He has not reached his peak just yet.

Cairo,Miguel

	Yr	Tm	AB	R	H	HR	RBI	SB	Avg	vL	vR	R$	OB	Slg	OPS	bb%	ct%	h%	Eye	xBA	PX	SX	G/F	RC/G	RAR
Pos 2B LF	99	TAM	465	61	137	3	36	22	295	384	274	$14	329	368	697	5	90	32	0.52	269	46	132	1.35	4.39	5.5
Age 29 Past Peak	00	TAM	375	49	98	1	34	28	261	270	259	$11	314	328	642	7	91	29	0.85	272	49	128	1.19	3.69	-1.9
Bats R	01	2TM	* 279	43	77	5	27	5	276	409	250	$6	336	394	730	8	88	30	0.74	277	76	91	1.55	4.37	2.7
R High	02	STL	184	28	46	2	23	1	250	273	237	$2	299	353	653	7	80	30	0.36	242	73	109	1.30	3.54	-4.7
I CON	03	STL	261	41	64	5	32	4	245	244	246	$4	281	375	657	5	89	26	0.49	274	88	120	0.97	3.58	-6.4
S pt stb	1st Half		161	24	41	2	15	1	255			$2	277	385	662	3	88	28	0.26	287	92	119		3.57	-4.0
K	2nd Half		100	17	23	3	17	3	230			$2	287	360	647	7	89	23	0.73	270	83	97		3.58	-2.5
LIMA D BA: 60%	04	Proj	**200**	**31**	**50**	**3**	**25**	**4**	**250**			**$4**	**298**	**362**	**660**	**6**	**87**	**27**	**0.51**	**273**	**76**	**105**		**3.65**	**-3.9**

SX is going up but OB is going down. History says that his good contact skills will boost his BA, but not enough to make him draft worthy.

Calloway,Ron

	Yr	Tm	AB	R	H	HR	RBI	SB	Avg	vL	vR	R$	OB	Slg	OPS	bb%	ct%	h%	Eye	xBA	PX	SX	G/F	RC/G	RAR
Pos LF RF	99		0	0	0	0	0	0	0								0								
Age 27 Peak	00		0	0	0	0	0	0	0								0								
Bats L	01	a/a	518	66	144	18	72	32	278			$25	322	458	780	6	81	32	0.34	277	112	120		5.19	0.5
R High	02	aaa	447	61	108	12	50	14	242			$10	300	383	682	8	83	27	0.47	265	90	106		3.53	-28.7
I EXP con	03	MON	340	36	81	9	52	9	238	169	253	$8	281	374	654	6	76	29	0.25	267	89	92	2.63	3.55	-20.9
S pt stb	1st Half		157	20	38	7	31	4	242			$6	296	433	729	7	78	27	0.34	287	115	98		4.20	-6.6
K	2nd Half		183	16	43	2	21	5	235			$2	267	322	589	4	75	30	0.18	250	66	77		3.00	-14.2
LIMA F BA: 45%	04	Proj	**200**	**24**	**48**	**5**	**27**	**5**	**240**			**$4**	**288**	**380**	**668**	**6**	**79**	**28**	**0.32**	**273**	**91**	**93**		**3.62**	**-12.9**

340 AB for a 27 year-old with these skills? Does not draw BB, makes marginal contact, and offers little power or speed. Faltered mightily down the stretch.

Cameron,Mike

	Yr	Tm	AB	R	H	HR	RBI	SB	Avg	vL	vR	R$	OB	Slg	OPS	bb%	ct%	h%	Eye	xBA	PX	SX	G/F	RC/G	RAR
Pos CF	99	CIN	542	93	139	21	66	38	256	292	246	$22	352	469	821	13	73	31	0.55	269	128	171	1.17	5.62	21.3
Age 31 Past Peak	00	SEA	543	96	145	19	78	24	267	273	266	$19	359	438	797	13	76	32	0.59	249	100	128	0.86	5.50	13.4
Bats R	01	SEA	540	99	144	25	110	34	267	301	255	$29	350	480	829	11	71	33	0.45	223	126	147	0.64	6.03	18.6
R Very Low	02	SEA	545	84	130	25	80	31	239	239	238	$22	335	442	777	13	68	31	0.45	221	119	143	0.80	5.01	3.9
I	03	SEA	534	74	135	18	76	17	253	286	240	$16	339	431	770	12	74	31	0.51	259	110	116	0.79	4.93	3.0
S stb	1st Half		266	44	73	12	50	7	274			$11	363	500	863	12	74	33	0.54	274	138	119		6.20	11.3
K	2nd Half		268	30	62	6	26	10	231			$5	316	362	678	11	75	29	0.49	243	83	106		3.82	-7.5
LIMA B BA: 45%	04	Proj	**550**	**83**	**138**	**21**	**81**	**25**	**251**			**$20**	**340**	**437**	**777**	**12**	**72**	**31**	**0.49**	**257**	**113**	**130**		**5.08**	**5.2**

OB improved, contact improved, but speed went south. Why? His SB attempts were reduced 37%. Getting out of Safeco field could bring some life back into his output.

STEPHEN NICKRAND

Carroll,Jamey

	Yr	Tm	AB	R	H	HR	RBI	SB	Avg	vL	vR	R$	OB	Slg	OPS	bb%	ct%	h%	Eye	xBA	PX	SX	G/F	RC/G	RAR
Pos 3B	99	aa	561	63	143	4	51	17	255			$8	302	346	648	6	91	28	0.73	283	65	100		3.46	-15.6
Age 30 Past Peak	00	a/a	518	65	133	2	35	12	257			$5	308	324	632	7	92	27	0.97	276	46	103		3.38	-15.0
Bats R	01	aaa	267	23	57	0	14	5	213			($2)	255	258	514	5	85	25	0.38	242	32	89		2.02	-20.7
R X HIGH	02	MON	* 501	62	127	8	45	6	253	400	295	$7	302	363	666	7	91	27	0.76	283	76	85		3.49	-16.6
I EXP CON	03	MON	227	31	59	1	10	5	260	268	255	$2	317	326	643	8	83	31	0.49	246	50	95	1.52	3.56	-4.6
S PT STB	1st Half		91	12	25	0	4	3	275			$2	320	385	704	6	81	34	0.35	265	88	125		4.31	0.2
K	2nd Half		136	19	34	1	6	2	250			$1	315	287	602	9	84	29	0.59	232	25	66		3.06	-4.8
LIMA F BA: 45%	04	Proj	**150**	**19**	**38**	**1**	**9**	**3**	**253**			**$1**	**305**	**327**	**632**	**7**	**86**	**29**	**0.54**	**252**	**52**	**93**		**3.31**	**-4.8**

As he got more exposure to NL pitchers, power and speed dropped. Hasn't exceeded replacement value once in past five years. No fantasy value.

Casey,Sean

	Yr	Tm	AB	R	H	HR	RBI	SB	Avg	vL	vR	R$	OB	Slg	OPS	bb%	ct%	h%	Eye	xBA	PX	SX	G/F	RC/G	RAR
Pos 1B	99	CIN	594	103	197	25	99	0	332	271	356	$27	394	539	933	9	85	36	0.69	341	130	47	1.76	7.99	42.1
Age 29 Past Peak	00	CIN	480	69	151	20	85	1	315	250	332	$21	382	517	898	10	83	34	0.65	311	124	51	1.57	7.35	25.9
Bats L	01	CIN	533	69	165	13	89	3	310	276	324	$20	361	458	819	7	88	33	0.68	312	101	50	1.77	6.10	-2.2
R Very Low	02	CIN	433	58	115	7	44	2	266	231	275	$7	333	372	705	9	89	28	0.94	290	79	51	1.62	4.29	-16.3
I con	03	CIN	573	71	167	14	80	4	291	320	278	$18	349	408	758	8	90	31	0.88	307	73	77	1.65	5.18	-5.3
S pt	1st Half		308	44	92	8	39	4	299			$11	349	425	775	7	89	32	0.69	309	81	81		5.49	-0.2
K	2nd Half		265	27	75	6	41	0	283			$7	349	389	738	9	91	29	1.17	302	62	45		4.83	-5.1
LIMA C+ BA: 60%	04	Proj	**550**	**70**	**163**	**11**	**77**	**3**	**296**			**$17**	**357**	**412**	**769**	**9**	**89**	**32**	**0.86**	**307**	**77**	**62**		**5.34**	**-4.4**

Four year trend of declining PX makes 10 HR more likely than 20. Other BPI stable, but note that he has been below replacement value for three consecutive years. Looks like 1999 was his career season.

Castilla,Vinny

	Yr	Tm	AB	R	H	HR	RBI	SB	Avg	vL	vR	R$	OB	Slg	OPS	bb%	ct%	h%	Eye	xBA	PX	SX	G/F	RC/G	RAR
Pos 3B	99	COL	615	83	169	33	102	2	275	225	294	$21	332	478	810	8	88	27	0.71	299	117	39	1.25	5.49	20.0
Age 36 Decline	00	TAM	331	22	73	6	42	1	221	203	225	$0	252	308	560	4	88	24	0.34	217	52	38	1.76	2.48	-19.6
Bats R	01	2TM	538	69	140	25	91	1	260	253	261	$16	305	467	772	6	80	28	0.32	270	126	39	1.36	4.76	4.5
R X HIGH	02	ATL	543	56	126	12	61	4	232	224	233	$6	262	348	610	4	87	25	0.32	255	78	76	1.05	3.03	-25.5
I CON	03	ATL	542	65	150	22	76	1	277	290	273	$17	310	461	771	5	84	29	0.30	278	115	56	1.57	4.97	11.0
S pt STB	1st Half		275	36	69	12	35	0	251			$6	292	433	725	5	85	26	0.40	280	111	50		4.23	-0.2
K AGE	2nd Half		267	29	81	10	41	1	303			$11	329	491	819	4	83	34	0.22	277	119	65		5.83	11.5
LIMA C BA: 45%	04	Proj	**550**	**63**	**138**	**18**	**77**	**2**	**251**			**$11**	**286**	**406**	**692**	**5**	**85**	**27**	**0.32**	**276**	**99**	**58**		**3.90**	**-8.0**

Nice rebound season fueled by 34% hit rate in second half. Two reasons he won't repeat: His BA fluctuates with his hit rate, which his history says will drop. Increased G/F means fewer HR.

Castillo,Luis

	Yr	Tm	AB	R	H	HR	RBI	SB	Avg	vL	vR	R$	OB	Slg	OPS	bb%	ct%	h%	Eye	xBA	PX	SX	G/F	RC/G	RAR
Pos 2B	99	FLA	487	76	147	0	28	50	302	310	300	$22	386	366	752	12	83	37	0.79	267	48	130	4.88	5.22	14.1
Age 28 Peak	00	FLA	539	101	180	2	17	62	334	291	350	$32	418	388	806	13	84	39	0.91	251	37	126	4.74	6.22	27.8
Bats S	01	FLA	537	76	141	2	45	33	263	281	257	$15	344	341	685	11	83	31	0.74	261	47	166	2.59	3.96	1.6
R Low	02	FLA	606	86	185	2	39	48	305	329	297	$28	363	361	724	8	87	35	0.72	264	40	135	3.39	4.89	8.1
I CON	03	FLA	595	99	187	6	39	21	314	320	312	$21	380	397	777	10	90	34	1.05	292	53	114	3.07	5.19	13.1
S	1st Half		313	51	97	5	23	14	310			$13	370	403	773	9	92	32	1.25	302	56	119		5.21	7.1
K	2nd Half		282	48	90	1	16	7	319			$9	390	390	781	10	87	36	0.92	280	50	106		5.16	5.9
LIMA B BA: 50%	04	Proj	**600**	**95**	**183**	**3**	**39**	**24**	**305**			**$19**	**374**	**376**	**750**	**10**	**87**	**34**	**0.87**	**287**	**48**	**121**		**5.00**	**11.5**

Contact rate and batting eye indicate legit .300 hitter. Increased HR didn't boost PX much, so don't expect a repeat. Speed in three year decline, so don't expect increase in SB. Might plateau at current level.

Castro,Juan

	Yr	Tm	AB	R	H	HR	RBI	SB	Avg	vL	vR	R$	OB	Slg	OPS	bb%	ct%	h%	Eye	xBA	PX	SX	G/F	RC/G	RAR
Pos 2B 3B SS	99	aaa	423	36	88	5	35	2	208			($3)	249	298	547	5	86	23	0.40	263	61	57		2.29	-23.9
Age 31 Past Peak	00	CIN	* 284	27	71	6	31	0	250	244	240	$3	306	394	701	7	85	28	0.55	283	91	60	1.70	3.92	-3.8
Bats R	01	CIN	242	27	54	3	13	0	223	246	216	($1)	263	302	564	5	79	27	0.26	227	54	38	1.11	2.60	-9.3
R Very High	02	CIN	* 99	7	21	2	13	0	212	222	217	$0	271	303	574	7	80	25	0.40	233	61		1.46	2.66	-5.4
I exp CON	03	CIN	320	28	81	9	33	2	253	193	276	$5	293	388	680	5	82	28	0.31	256	86	47	1.07	3.74	-6.3
S PT stb	1st Half		172	13	41	4	13	1	238			$1	260	360	620	3	82	27	0.16	253	78	59		2.98	-7.4
K	2nd Half		148	15	40	5	20	1	270			$4	329	419	748	8	82	30	0.48	259	95	34		4.73	1.4
LIMA F BA: 45%	04	Proj	**250**	**24**	**59**	**6**	**23**	**1**	**236**			**$2**	**281**	**359**	**640**	**6**	**82**	**27**	**0.35**	**256**	**81**	**53**		**3.28**	**-7.8**

Mini-surge fueled by a career year vs RHP. That looks like an anomaly. Don't believe it until he does it again. Below replacement value for his entire 9-year career.

Castro,Ramon

	Yr	Tm	AB	R	H	HR	RBI	SB	Avg	vL	vR	R$	OB	Slg	OPS	bb%	ct%	h%	Eye	xBA	PX	SX	G/F	RC/G	RAR
Pos CA	99	FLA	* 416	36	86	12	49	0	207	167	182	($0)	257	346	603	6	85	22	0.45	275	90		0.64	2.86	-14.3
Age 28 Peak	00	FLA	* 356	43	96	12	48	0	270	200	248	$8	323	435	758	7	81	30	0.42	277	105	24	0.65	4.91	9.3
Bats R	01	aaa	401	56	110	18	63	1	274			$13	322	479	800	7	86	28	0.49	296	128	41	0.43	5.37	19.2
R Very High	02	FLA	101	11	24	6	18	0	238	160	263	$3	330	455	786	12	76	25	0.58	263	133		0.74	5.03	2.8
I exp CON	03	FLA	53	6	15	5	8	0	283	409	194	$3	333	604	937	7	79	27	0.36	334	181	-1	0.45	7.16	4.3
S pt stb	1st Half		31	1	8	1	2	0	258			$0	343	355	698	11	84	28	0.80	271	50	-10		4.18	-0.1
K	2nd Half		22	5	7	4	6	0	318			$2	318	955	1273	0	73	25	0.00	409	366	33		11.36	4.2
LIMA F BA: 50%	04	Proj	**200**	**23**	**50**	**10**	**30**	**0**	**250**			**$5**	**314**	**449**	**763**	**9**	**81**	**26**	**0.50**	**323**	**124**	**24**		**4.78**	**4.0**

Opened his swing in the second half and hit one HR every 5 AB. Pitchers will adjust, but note the five-year rising power trend. Could do some serious damage if he gets playing time. A good one buck bet.

Catalanotto,Frank

	Yr	Tm	AB	R	H	HR	RBI	SB	Avg	vL	vR	R$	OB	Slg	OPS	bb%	ct%	h%	Eye	xBA	PX	SX	G/F	RC/G	RAR
Pos LF RF DH	99	DET	286	41	79	11	35	3	276	269	277	$8	312	458	770	5	83	30	0.31	281	114	59	1.00	4.79	-2.3
Age 30 Past Peak	00	TEX	282	55	82	10	42	6	291	263	293	$10	365	457	823	10	87	31	0.92	283	96	108	1.21	5.99	7.1
Bats L	01	TEX	463	77	153	11	54	15	330	326	331	$22	382	490	873	8	88	36	0.71	321	103	118	1.47	7.09	30.5
R Moderate	02	TEX	228	43	59	3	25	9	259	231	274	$6	335	430	764	10	88	28	0.93	316	108	211	1.37	4.75	-0.5
I con	03	TOR	489	83	146	13	59	2	299	176	318	$14	345	472	818	7	87	32	0.56	313	112	101	1.26	5.86	7.2
S PT stb	1st Half		304	57	92	7	41	1	303			$9	340	480	820	5	88	33	0.45	299	118	109		5.82	4.1
K	2nd Half		185	26	54	6	18	1	292			$5	355	459	814	9	87	31	0.75	303	101	83		5.91	3.0
LIMA B+ BA: 55%	04	Proj	**400**	**67**	**116**	**12**	**46**	**7**	**290**			**$13**	**349**	**475**	**823**	**8**	**87**	**31**	**0.71**	**298**	**115**	**130**		**5.84**	**8.6**

Nice comeback as predicted. Could he do better? Pro: xBA consistently .300+, rising PX and falling G/F. Con: sore back and declining BA vs LHP. If he gets 500 AB could produce strong numbers, but it's a gamble.

Cedeno,Roger

	Yr	Tm	AB	R	H	HR	RBI	SB	Avg	vL	vR	R$	OB	Slg	OPS	bb%	ct%	h%	Eye	xBA	PX	SX	G/F	RC/G	RAR
Pos RF	99	NYM	453	90	142	4	36	66	313	194	334	$31	394	408	802	12	78	40	0.60	262	66	155	2.23	6.20	15.5
Age 29 Past Peak	00	HOU	259	54	73	6	26	25	282	313	275	$13	384	398	782	14	82	33	0.91	263	58	179	2.25	5.25	0.9
Bats S	01	DET	523	79	153	6	48	55	293	282	297	$28	338	396	734	6	84	34	0.43	283	59	188	2.52	4.89	-1.3
R High	02	NYM	511	65	133	7	41	25	260	231	273	$14	316	346	663	8	82	31	0.46	264	60	118	2.03	3.94	-20.4
I con	03	NYM	484	70	129	7	37	14	267	241	274	$10	320	378	698	7	82	31	0.44	276	76	117	2.15	4.04	-22.3
S pt STB	1st Half		223	28	59	3	18	7	265			$5	333	363	697	9	81	31	0.55	265	65	104		3.86	-11.7
K	2nd Half		261	42	70	4	19	7	268			$5	308	391	699	5	83	31	0.34	286	86	127		4.21	-10.6
LIMA C+ BA: 50%	04	Proj	**500**	**74**	**136**	**7**	**40**	**17**	**272**			**$13**	**328**	**376**	**704**	**8**	**82**	**32**	**0.47**	**275**	**68**	**127**		**4.19**	**-18.7**

OB below .320 for second straight season. SX has plummeted in past two years. Should probably be counted on for less than 20 SB per year, which limits his value.

Chavez,Endy

	Yr	Tm	AB	R	H	HR	RBI	SB	Avg	vL	vR	R$	OB	Slg	OPS	bb%	ct%	h%	Eye	xBA	PX	SX	G/F	RC/G	RAR
Pos CF	99		0	0	0	0	0	0	0								0						1.21		
Age 26 Pre-Peak	00		0	0	0	0	0	0	0								0						0.92		
Bats L	01	KC	* 349	40	95	1	18	12	272	286	200	$6	302	324	626	4	92	29	0.56	263	39	80	2.25	3.04	-18.9
R High	02	MON	* 530	79	169	5	45	21	319	316	292	$22	359	447	806	6	91	34	0.69	299	94	137	2.20	5.42	8.2
I EXP con	03	MON	483	66	121	5	47	18	251	304	238	$10	296	354	650	6	88	28	0.53	302	72	138	2.37	3.53	-21.0
S pt stb	1st Half		302	41	78	4	27	14	258			$8	291	361	652	4	89	28	0.41	303	68	139		3.52	-13.1
K	2nd Half		181	25	43	1	20	4	238			$2	303	343	646	9	86	27	0.68	298	78	123		3.51	-8.0
LIMA B BA: 60%	04	Proj	**500**	**69**	**138**	**4**	**44**	**17**	**276**			**$13**	**321**	**382**	**703**	**6**	**89**	**30**	**0.61**	**305**	**75**	**130**		**4.08**	**-9.3**

BA by month: .296, .216, .268, .230, .278, .188. Lack of consistency cost him PT. xBA and ct% indicate potential .300 BA. If that happens, he will produce SB. 2nd half fade says he might be a year away.

HAROLD NICHOLS

38

Chavez,Eric

Pos 3B | Age 26 Pre-Peak | Bats L
R: Very Low | I: con | S: pt | K:
LIMA B | BA: 65%

Yr	Tm	AB	R	H	HR	RBI	SB	Avg	vL	vR	R$	OB	Slg	OPS	bb%	ct%	h%	Eye	xBA	PX	SX	G/F	RC/G	RAR
99	OAK	356	47	88	13	50	1	247	184	257	$6	333	427	760	11	84	26	0.82	269	110	59	1.21	4.78	3.8
00	OAK	501	89	139	26	86	2	277	197	303	$16	357	495	852	11	81	30	0.66	260	121	82	0.92	6.17	25.2
01	OAK	552	91	159	32	114	8	288	257	304	$27	337	540	877	7	82	30	0.41	303	155	72	1.18	6.52	33.4
02	OAK	585	87	161	34	109	8	275	209	301	$26	348	513	861	10	80	29	0.55	265	139	83	0.74	6.24	29.6
03	OAK	588	94	166	29	101	8	282	220	312	$24	351	514	864	10	85	29	0.70	324	140	99	1.12	6.36	30.9
1st Half		294	42	76	16	46	6	259			$11	325	480	805	9	83	26	0.59	310	130	79		5.33	7.1
2nd Half		294	52	90	13	55	2	306			$13	376	548	924	10	86	32	0.83	337	150	105		7.52	24.2
04	Proj	**575**	**91**	**167**	**35**	**104**	**7**	**290**			**$27**	**358**	**550**	**908**	**9**	**83**	**30**	**0.62**	**325**	**154**	**88**		**7.03**	**41.3**

Only thing holding him back is BA vs LH. When he solves that, watch out. Second half surge in BA, contact rate, batting eye, xBA, and power indicates he could explode in 2004. Upside: 40 HR, .300 BA.

Choi,Hee Seop

Pos 1B | Age 25 Pre-Peak | Bats L
R: X HIGH | I: EXP CON | S: PT stb | K: age
LIMA D+ | BA: 45%

Yr	Tm	AB	R	H	HR	RBI	SB	Avg	vL	vR	R$	OB	Slg	OPS	bb%	ct%	h%	Eye	xBA	PX	SX	G/F	RC/G	RAR
99		0	0	0	0	0	0	0								0								
00	aa	122	24	34	9	24	3	279			$6	397	566	963	16	70	33	0.65	267	164	61		7.90	7.9
01	aaa	266	34	56	11	40	4	211			$4	291	368	659	10	79	23	0.55	256	92	62		3.48	-22.5
02	aaa	528	72	124	20	72	2	235			$10	330	396	726	12	81	25	0.75	262	98	54	0.87	4.28	-23.2
03	CHC	* 268	41	59	13	42	1	220	59	232	$5	332	448	780	14	67	28	0.51	238	146	60	1.06	4.75	-6.3
1st Half		160	30	37	8	25	1	231			$4	359	475	834	17	68	29	0.62	246	162	54		5.70	0.9
2nd Half		108	11	22	5	17	0	204			$1	289	407	697	11	67	25	0.36	227	122	74		3.48	-7.0
04	Proj	**400**	**56**	**90**	**19**	**62**	**3**	**225**			**$8**	**325**	**426**	**751**	**13**	**73**	**26**	**0.54**	**243**	**125**	**57**		**4.44**	**-14.5**

8-28-.218 in 202 AB at CHC. Prodigious power but struggled vs LH and made limited contact vs everyone. Right now just another high power, low avg hitter. Excellent walk rate gives hope. Still a couple years away.

Christenson,Ryan

Pos CF | Age 30 Past Peak | Bats R
R: High | I: EXP con | S: pt STB | K:
LIMA F | BA: 50%

Yr	Tm	AB	R	H	HR	RBI	SB	Avg	vL	vR	R$	OB	Slg	OPS	bb%	ct%	h%	Eye	xBA	PX	SX	G/F	RC/G	RAR
99	OAK	* 396	67	97	5	38	13	245	301	160	$5	338	343	682	12	81	29	0.75	253	66	107	1.23	3.85	-10.2
00	OAK	129	31	32	4	18	1	248	167	307	$2	345	388	732	13	74	30	0.58	228	71	146	1.45	4.31	-1.3
01	aaa	285	29	64	5	23	5	225			$1	275	344	619	7	84	25	0.44	267	84	65	4.00	3.10	-11.0
02	MIL	* 318	37	67	6	28	9	211	118	171	$2	257	333	591	6	87	22	0.50	281	89	100	1.60	2.68	-22.0
03	TEX	* 360	46	82	7	35	11	228	109	209	$5	302	350	652	10	76	28	0.44	239	83	95	1.18	3.52	-13.4
1st Half		187	25	45	3	20	6	241			$3	314	353	667	10	78	29	0.49	243	80	77		3.65	-6.2
2nd Half		173	21	37	4	15	5	214			$1	288	347	635	9	74	27	0.40	234	86	104		3.39	-7.2
04	Proj	**100**	**13**	**22**	**2**	**9**	**3**	**220**			**$1**	**287**	**339**	**626**	**9**	**80**	**26**	**0.47**	**245**	**82**	**73**		**3.17**	**-4.9**

2-16-.176 in 165 AB at TEX. Excellent defense, but that doesn't help in fantasy. And when you hit below the Mendoza Line, it doesn't help in MLB either. Can't hit LH at all and can't hit righties much.

Cintron,Alex

Pos SS | Age 25 Pre-Peak | Bats S
R: Very High | I: EXP con | S: pt stb | K: age
LIMA B | BA: 55%

Yr	Tm	AB	R	H	HR	RBI	SB	Avg	vL	vR	R$	OB	Slg	OPS	bb%	ct%	h%	Eye	xBA	PX	SX	G/F	RC/G	RAR
99		0	0	0	0	0	0	0								0								
00	aa	522	65	142	3	46	7	272			$7	303	358	661	4	92	29	0.53	282	60	86		3.52	-6.5
01	aaa	432	44	120	2	29	7	278			$7	299	359	658	3	92	30	0.37	278	59	83	0.50	3.60	-4.6
02	ARI	* 426	51	119	3	24	7	279	182	226	$7	312	371	683	4	91	30	0.54	282	72	84	2.24	3.93	0.4
03	ARI	* 555	86	181	15	67	3	326	365	296	$22	366	501	867	6	93	33	0.92	315	113	103	1.55	6.83	40.2
1st Half		264	48	87	9	40	2	330			$13	368	534	902	6	95	32	1.14	334	135	108		7.53	23.7
2nd Half		291	38	94	6	27	1	323			$10	365	471	835	6	92	34	0.79	298	94	98		6.22	16.6
04	Proj	**500**	**67**	**146**	**10**	**46**	**5**	**292**			**$13**	**327**	**432**	**759**	**5**	**92**	**30**	**0.68**	**308**	**94**	**94**		**4.92**	**14.1**

13-51-.317 in 448 AB at ARI. Contact rate and eye say he's a legit .300 hitter. Rising PX and falling G/F legitimize his power outburst. 2nd half fade suggests possible sophomore slump, but he looks like a good one.

Cirillo,Jeff

Pos 3B | Age 34 Decline | Bats R
R: Moderate | I: con | S: pt stb | K: age
LIMA D | BA: 75%

Yr	Tm	AB	R	H	HR	RBI	SB	Avg	vL	vR	R$	OB	Slg	OPS	bb%	ct%	h%	Eye	xBA	PX	SX	G/F	RC/G	RAR
99	MIL	607	98	198	15	88	7	326	323	327	$24	400	461	862	11	86	36	0.90	302	90	62	1.03	6.91	41.3
00	COL	598	111	195	11	115	3	326	379	311	$24	394	477	871	10	88	36	0.93	323	106	64	1.55	6.97	42.3
01	COL	528	72	165	17	83	12	313	264	327	$25	364	473	838	8	88	33	0.68	304	97	105	1.20	6.47	26.9
02	SEA	485	51	121	6	54	8	249	304	226	$7	295	328	622	6	86	28	0.46	232	55	66	0.99	3.25	-17.6
03	SEA	258	24	53	2	23	1	205	227	194	($2)	273	271	544	9	88	23	0.75	258	49	40	1.07	2.35	-17.4
1st Half		213	21	49	2	21	1	230			$0	299	300	600	9	88	25	0.84	261	51	39		2.94	-10.2
2nd Half		45	3	4	0	2	0	89			($2)	146	133	279	6	84	11	0.43	240	39			0.54	-6.4
04	Proj	**400**	**51**	**103**	**7**	**54**	**5**	**258**			**$8**	**320**	**371**	**691**	**8**	**88**	**28**	**0.74**	**268**	**76**	**71**		**4.05**	**-4.9**

A low hit rate (11% in second half) was responsible for this debacle. Ct% and batting eye were stable, so BA should rebound, but PX trend indicates that his power is gone.

Clark,Brady

Pos RF LF | Age 31 Past Peak | Bats R
R: X HIGH | I: EXP CON | S: PT STB | K:
LIMA D | BA: 55%

Yr	Tm	AB	R	H	HR	RBI	SB	Avg	vL	vR	R$	OB	Slg	OPS	bb%	ct%	h%	Eye	xBA	PX	SX	G/F	RC/G	RAR
99	aa	506	73	130	12	53	17	257			$11	344	399	743	12	89	27	1.24	294	92	90		4.31	-10.4
00	aaa	487	66	127	12	57	9	261			$10	335	427	762	10	92	26	1.35	315	107	88	6.00	4.64	-5.7
01	CIN	* 296	40	72	8	32	9	243	279	256	$6	325	358	683	11	90	25	1.20	279	67	90	0.86	3.94	-14.4
02	2NL	* 187	21	42	1	22	1	225	143	220	$0	260	294	554	5	90	25	0.47	266	58	57	1.63	2.28	-17.6
03	MIL	* 349	37	93	6	43	14	266	263	279	$11	312	393	704	6	87	29	0.50	281	91	100	1.17	4.38	-12.4
1st Half		149	12	35	1	22	5	235			$3	278	309	587	6	87	27	0.45	259	59	72		2.94	-12.0
2nd Half		200	25	58	5	21	9	290			$8	336	455	791	7	87	31	0.54	296	115	108		5.68	0.4
04	Proj	**350**	**41**	**93**	**6**	**41**	**10**	**266**			**$9**	**317**	**381**	**699**	**7**	**88**	**29**	**0.65**	**281**	**82**	**86**		**4.15**	**-13.6**

6-40-.273 in 315 AB at MIL. Given an opportunity, he produced $10 in roto-value. A history of high contact rate and batting eye, plus a solid second half indicate he could repeat if given the chance.

Clark,Howie

Pos 2B | Age 30 Past Peak | Bats L
R: X HIGH | I: EXP CON | S: PT STB | K:
LIMA F | BA: 70%

Yr	Tm	AB	R	H	HR	RBI	SB	Avg	vL	vR	R$	OB	Slg	OPS	bb%	ct%	h%	Eye	xBA	PX	SX	G/F	RC/G	RAR
99	a/a	405	42	103	7	33	3	254			$3	314	373	686	8	92	26	1.03	291	77	70		3.96	-1.6
00	a/a	242	32	63	4	26	3	260			$3	332	364	696	10	92	27	1.37	289	70	59		4.17	0.4
01	MEX	493	65	153	3	61	5	310			$14	350	457	807	6	92	33	0.83	311	100	132		5.79	23.7
02	BAL	* 471	50	126	6	39	3	268		320	$7	320	367	687	7	93	28	1.09	279	67	62	1.25	3.94	-1.3
03	TOR	* 322	32	81	4	31	1	252		362	$3	295	351	646	6	92	26	0.80	277	68	59	2.20	3.50	-6.1
1st Half		176	18	45	4	15	1	256			$2	307	386	693	7	92	26	0.93	288	84	59		4.09	-0.2
2nd Half		146	14	36	0	16	0	247			$0	281	308	589	5	92	27	0.64	263	48	59		2.84	-5.7
04	Proj	**150**	**16**	**40**	**2**	**15**	**1**	**267**			**$2**	**313**	**364**	**677**	**6**	**92**	**28**	**0.89**	**279**	**68**	**65**		**3.89**	**-0.9**

0-7-.357 in 70 AB at TOR. Contact rate and batting eye indicate a legitimate .300 hitter, but this is an otherwise empty skills set with no power and no speed. And at age 30, probably no opportunity.

Clark,Tony

Pos 1B | Age 31 Past Peak | Bats S
R: High | I: con | S: PT stb | K:
LIMA F | BA: 45%

Yr	Tm	AB	R	H	HR	RBI	SB	Avg	vL	vR	R$	OB	Slg	OPS	bb%	ct%	h%	Eye	xBA	PX	SX	G/F	RC/G	RAR
99	DET	536	74	150	31	99	2	280	262	284	$20	357	507	864	11	75	32	0.48	269	133	37	1.17	6.39	9.2
00	DET	208	32	57	13	37	0	274	308	266	$7	349	529	878	10	75	31	0.47	273	148	25	1.36	6.49	3.2
01	DET	428	67	123	16	75	0	287	321	271	$14	378	481	859	13	75	35	0.57	284	121	56	2.04	6.45	3.6
02	BOS	275	25	57	3	29	0	207	159	228	($1)	264	291	554	7	79	25	0.37	205	58	41	1.40	2.47	-29.0
03	NYM	254	29	59	16	43	0	232	279	215	$7	299	472	771	9	71	26	0.33	261	144	15	1.49	4.69	-6.3
1st Half		127	15	27	9	25	0	213			$3	275	472	748	8	72	22	0.31	267	153	17		4.21	-5.1
2nd Half		127	14	32	7	18	0	252			$3	321	472	794	9	71	30	0.35	256	136	14		5.18	-1.3
04	Proj	**200**	**23**	**48**	**9**	**31**	**0**	**240**			**$4**	**309**	**430**	**740**	**9**	**74**	**28**	**0.39**	**262**	**119**	**25**		**4.46**	**-7.0**

Power rebounded nicely, but falling batting eye and ct%, plus increasing struggles vs RHP, indicate that his BA is unlikely to do the same.

Clayton,Royce

Pos SS | Age 34 Decline | Bats R
R: High | I: CON | S: pt stb | K: age
LIMA D | BA: 55%

Yr	Tm	AB	R	H	HR	RBI	SB	Avg	vL	vR	R$	OB	Slg	OPS	bb%	ct%	h%	Eye	xBA	PX	SX	G/F	RC/G	RAR
99	TEX	465	69	134	14	52	8	288	306	283	$13	343	445	788	8	78	34	0.39	283	93	110	2.03	5.30	15.0
00	TEX	513	70	124	14	54	11	242	196	254	$7	299	384	683	8	82	27	0.46	258	82	115	1.53	3.75	-10.4
01	CHW	433	62	114	9	60	10	263	333	242	$11	315	393	708	7	83	30	0.46	269	81	106	2.04	4.12	-3.2
02	CHW	342	51	86	7	35	5	251	238	257	$6	293	365	658	6	80	29	0.30	260	72	107	1.96	3.68	-9.1
03	MIL	483	49	110	11	39	5	228	240	225	$3	299	333	632	9	81	26	0.53	230	67	63	1.84	3.29	-12.1
1st Half		260	28	58	8	24	2	223			$2	303	362	665	10	82	25	0.63	241	86	58		3.53	-4.7
2nd Half		223	21	52	3	15	3	233			$1	293	300	594	8	80	28	0.43	217	45	57		3.00	-7.4
04	Proj	**450**	**55**	**110**	**10**	**43**	**7**	**244**			**$6**	**302**	**355**	**657**	**8**	**81**	**28**	**0.44**	**233**	**71**	**86**		**3.61**	**-4.1**

Power and speed have been in decline for past four years. xBA says that his batting average was where it belonged. Has been below replacement value for four seasons and will stay there.

HAROLD NICHOLS

Colbrunn,Greg

Pos 1B
Age 34 Decline
Bats R

R	High	
I		con
S	PT	stb
K	age	

LIMA D BA: 25%

	Tm	AB	R	H	HR	RBI	SB	Avg	vL	vR	R$	OB	Slg	OPS	bb%	ct%	h%	Eye	xBA	PX	SX	G/F	RC/G	RAR
99	ARI	135	20	44	5	24	1	326	361	237	$6	381	519	899	8	83	36	0.52	259	108	125	0.75	7.32	7.3
00	ARI	329	48	103	15	57	0	313	285	333	$14	392	523	915	12	86	33	0.96	293	127	34	1.07	7.53	19.5
01	ARI	97	12	28	4	18	0	289	235	317	$4	349	495	844	8	86	30	0.64	327	133	21	1.14	6.19	-0.2
02	ARI	* 196	35	64	12	32	0	327	368	259	$11	374	628	1002	7	89	32	0.71	348	198	73	1.12	8.90	17.1
03	SEA	58	7	16	3	7	0	276	250	400	$2	323	483	805	6	72	33	0.25	232	109	110	0.94	5.09	-0.5
1st Half		48	7	14	3	6	0	292			$2	346	521	867	8	79	31	0.40	257	113	124		5.95	0.8
2nd Half		10	0	2	0	1	0	200			($0)	200	300	500	0	40	50	0.00	120	87	-9		1.91	-1.1
04	**Proj**	**150**	**24**	**45**	**7**	**26**	**0**	**300**			**$6**	**361**	**536**	**897**	**9**	**86**	**31**	**0.68**	**265**	**142**	**91**		**6.96**	**5.4**

Injuries ruined his season, which ended with wrist surgery. His excellent ct%, batting eye, and rising power still lurk waiting for health and opportunity. If he ever got a full season of AB, it could be a big one.

Conine,Jeff

Pos 1B LF
Age 37 Decline
Bats R

R	Moderate	
I		
S	pt	stb
K	AGE	

LIMA B BA: 60%

	Tm	AB	R	H	HR	RBI	SB	Avg	vL	vR	R$	OB	Slg	OPS	bb%	ct%	h%	Eye	xBA	PX	SX	G/F	RC/G	RAR
99	2AL	444	54	129	13	75	0	291	280	293	$12	335	453	788	6	91	30	0.75	311	105	32	0.98	5.30	-6.0
00	BAL	409	53	116	13	46	4	284	333	263	$10	342	438	779	8	87	30	0.68	262	91	69	1.01	5.23	-8.3
01	BAL	524	75	163	14	97	12	311	376	291	$24	386	443	829	11	86	34	0.85	278	82	72	1.05	6.14	-0.0
02	BAL	451	44	123	15	63	8	273	292	266	$14	311	448	759	5	85	29	0.38	267	108	101	0.95	4.99	-11.2
03	2TM	577	88	163	20	95	5	282	288	281	$20	340	459	799	8	88	29	0.71	305	113	90	0.97	5.60	2.5
1st Half		311	46	85	9	53	4	273			$10	331	441	772	8	86	29	0.63	297	110	96		5.20	-2.1
2nd Half		266	42	78	11	42	1	293			$10	349	481	831	8	90	29	0.85	312	117	62		6.09	4.8
04	**Proj**	**500**	**68**	**143**	**17**	**79**	**6**	**286**			**$18**	**341**	**457**	**798**	**8**	**87**	**30**	**0.65**	**305**	**108**	**86**		**5.57**	**-1.0**

At age 36, BPIs rose across the board, and he surged in the second half. One of these days he will begin to show his age, but there are no signs of it yet.

Conti,Jason

Pos RF
Age 29 Past Peak
Bats L

R	X HIGH	
I	EXP	CON
S	pt	STB
K		

LIMA F BA: 40%

	Tm	AB	R	H	HR	RBI	SB	Avg	vL	vR	R$	OB	Slg	OPS	bb%	ct%	h%	Eye	xBA	PX	SX	G/F	RC/G	RAR
99	aaa	520	77	136	7	44	17	262			$9	314	369	684	7	88	29	0.63	278	67	134		3.86	-17.3
00	ARI	* 474	69	126	9	59	11	266	250	229	$11	303	395	697	5	85	30	0.34	275	79	133	1.15	4.12	-14.1
01	aaa	523	72	148	10	53	4	283			$12	326	417	742	6	87	31	0.47	279	88	78		4.60	-10.0
02	TAM	222	26	57	3	21	4	257	367	240	$4	313	383	695	8	75	33	0.33	257	87	103	0.94	4.05	-6.3
03	MIL	* 504	51	110	10	40	11	218		250	$3	251	319	570	4	73	28	0.16	223	65	92	0.67	2.47	-49.6
1st Half		278	30	49	5	21	7	176			($2)	224	266	490	6	75	22	0.25	227	57	103		1.75	-35.4
2nd Half		226	21	61	5	19	4	270			$5	286	385	671	2	71	36	0.08	219	74	77		3.61	-13.2
04	**Proj**	**150**	**17**	**35**	**3**	**13**	**3**	**233**			**$1**	**273**	**348**	**621**	**5**	**77**	**29**	**0.24**	**232**	**76**	**97**		**3.03**	**-11.2**

2-7-.229 in 48 AB at MIL. An amazing 50 runs below replacement level. Is this the RAR futility equivalent of the Mendoza line?

"The Conti Line"

It does have a certain ring to it.

Coomer,Ron

Pos 1B
Age 37 Decline
Bats R

R	High	
I		con
S	pt	STB
K	AGE	

LIMA F BA: 60%

	Tm	AB	R	H	HR	RBI	SB	Avg	vL	vR	R$	OB	Slg	OPS	bb%	ct%	h%	Eye	xBA	PX	SX	G/F	RC/G	RAR
99	MIN	467	53	123	16	65	2	263	278	259	$10	308	424	732	6	85	28	0.43	263	99	51	1.22	4.50	-17.3
00	MIN	544	64	147	16	82	2	270	256	274	$11	316	415	731	6	91	27	0.72	268	89	54	1.37	4.60	-20.9
01	2TM	349	25	91	8	53	0	261	292	249	$7	317	390	707	8	80	31	0.41	241	84	20	1.15	4.27	-19.5
02	NYY	148	14	39	3	17	0	264	288	235	$2	292	372	664	4	84	30	0.26	256	72	23	1.54	3.76	-9.0
03	LA	125	11	30	4	15	0	240	355	127	$2	296	368	664	7	85	25	0.53	262	79	15	1.40	3.66	-6.9
1st Half		77	7	17	1	7	0	221			($0)	286	299	584	8	84	25	0.58	248	55	23		2.79	-6.4
2nd Half		48	4	13	3	8	0	271			$2	314	479	793	6	85	26	0.43	283	116	-0		5.26	-0.4
04	**Proj**	**150**	**14**	**38**	**3**	**19**	**0**	**253**			**$2**	**304**	**365**	**668**	**7**	**84**	**28**	**0.46**	**262**	**75**	**26**		**3.78**	**-8.1**

Achieved a new level of futility vs RHP. No power. No speed. Same age as Conine but began declining 3 years ago. Now worthless.

Cora,Alex

Pos 2B
Age 28 Peak
Bats L

R	Very High	
I	exp	CON
S	PT	stb
K		

LIMA D BA: 50%

	Tm	AB	R	H	HR	RBI	SB	Avg	vL	vR	R$	OB	Slg	OPS	bb%	ct%	h%	Eye	xBA	PX	SX	G/F	RC/G	RAR
99	aaa	302	40	79	3	29	7	262			$4	283	348	631	3	91	28	0.32	278	52	124	1.11	3.20	-8.0
00	LA	* 463	53	119	4	48	8	257	226	241	$6	304	371	675	6	87	29	0.51	280	74	127	1.52	3.78	-7.9
01	LA	405	38	88	4	29	0	217	293	209	($3)	273	306	579	7	86	24	0.53	262	59	56	1.47	2.66	-15.0
02	LA	258	37	75	5	28	7	291	318	288	$9	356	434	790	9	85	33	0.68	291	96	137	1.61	5.57	8.4
03	LA	477	39	119	4	34	4	249	308	240	$3	274	338	611	3	88	28	0.27	264	64	76	1.38	3.12	-18.2
1st Half		242	19	55	0	17	2	227			($1)	258	302	560	4	84	27	0.26	252	59	82		2.50	-14.1
2nd Half		235	20	64	4	17	2	272			$4	290	374	665	2	91	29	0.29	275	69	63		3.86	-3.7
04	**Proj**	**450**	**47**	**116**	**6**	**38**	**6**	**258**			**$6**	**298**	**362**	**660**	**5**	**87**	**29**	**0.45**	**267**	**71**	**95**		**3.68**	**-8.4**

Became more aggressive at the plate and lost 80 pts in on-base percentage. Since OB was his only real skill, he has little value unless he can turn things around.

Cordero,Wil

Pos 1B
Age 32 Past Peak
Bats R

R	Very High	
I		con
S	PT	STB
K		

LIMA D+ BA: 45%

	Tm	AB	R	H	HR	RBI	SB	Avg	vL	vR	R$	OB	Slg	OPS	bb%	ct%	h%	Eye	xBA	PX	SX	G/F	RC/G	RAR
99	CLE	194	35	58	8	32	2	299	255	317	$7	349	500	849	7	81	34	0.41	306	128	69	1.31	6.42	3.4
00	2TM	496	64	137	16	68	1	276	323	260	$11	320	464	784	6	85	30	0.42	295	116	75	1.02	5.15	-7.0
01	CLE	268	30	67	4	21	0	250	298	228	$2	307	343	650	8	81	29	0.44	229	61	41	1.11	3.58	-20.2
02	2TM	161	22	43	6	30	2	267	258	279	$6	337	435	772	10	82	29	0.59	277	109	56	0.94	5.18	-2.5
03	MON	436	57	121	16	71	1	278	324	262	$14	351	450	800	10	79	32	0.54	275	113	35	1.00	5.53	0.2
1st Half		217	23	59	7	31	1	272			$6	344	433	778	10	83	30	0.65	284	108	33		5.26	-1.6
2nd Half		219	34	62	9	40	0	283			$8	357	466	822	10	76	34	0.47	265	117	35		5.80	1.8
04	**Proj**	**450**	**60**	**123**	**15**	**71**	**2**	**273**			**$13**	**341**	**433**	**774**	**9**	**80**	**31**	**0.52**	**276**	**105**	**47**		**5.18**	**-5.8**

His most recent previous season with 400 AB was 2000, and he produced almost identical results. This is his established performance level if the gets the playing time.

Cordova,Marty

Pos DH
Age 34 Decline
Bats R

R	Very High	
I		CON
S	PT	STB
K	age	

LIMA D BA: 75%

	Tm	AB	R	H	HR	RBI	SB	Avg	vL	vR	R$	OB	Slg	OPS	bb%	ct%	h%	Eye	xBA	PX	SX	G/F	RC/G	RAR
99	MIN	425	62	121	14	70	13	285	206	310	$16	357	464	821	10	77	34	0.50	264	111	108	1.56	5.90	8.5
00	2AL	200	23	49	4	18	3	245	212	261	$2	307	340	647	8	83	28	0.51	210	59	56	1.38	3.46	-9.7
01	CLE	409	61	123	20	69	0	301	333	289	$17	338	506	844	5	80	33	0.28	284	121	48	1.39	6.05	9.2
02	BAL	458	55	116	18	64	1	253	274	245	$11	323	434	757	9	76	30	0.42	235	111	44	1.15	4.55	-13.4
03	BAL	30	5	7	1	4	1	233	375	182	$1	395	367	761	21	83	25	1.60	254	80	52	1.00	5.05	0.4
1st Half		30	5	7	1	4	1	233			$1	395	367	761	21	83	25	1.60	258	80	52		5.05	0.4
2nd Half		0	0	0	0	0	0	0			($0)					0			0					
04	**Proj**	**450**	**58**	**113**	**15**	**59**	**5**	**251**			**$10**	**313**	**409**	**723**	**8**	**79**	**29**	**0.44**	**257**	**97**	**70**		**4.24**	**-10.1**

Season ended by elbow problems which required Tommy John surgery. Will he take the Jeff Conine or the Ron Coomer path to retirement? Contact rate decline in '02 looks like Coomer. Approach warily in 2004.

Counsell,Craig

Pos 3B SS
Age 33 Decline
Bats L

R	High	
I		CON
S	pt	stb
K	age	

LIMA D+ BA: 75%

	Tm	AB	R	H	HR	RBI	SB	Avg	vL	vR	R$	OB	Slg	OPS	bb%	ct%	h%	Eye	xBA	PX	SX	G/F	RC/G	RAR
99	2NL	174	24	38	0	11	1	218	250	312	($2)	277	259	535	7	86	25	0.58	220	35	62	1.41	2.36	-10.7
00	ARI	152	23	48	2	11	3	316	267	321	$5	395	421	816	12	88	35	1.11	261	70	78	1.50	5.91	6.7
01	ARI	458	76	126	4	38	6	275	337	258	$8	360	362	723	12	83	32	0.80	254	60	87	1.65	4.38	-2.8
02	ARI	436	63	123	2	51	7	282	269	289	$10	349	351	700	9	88	32	0.87	255	56	76	1.82	4.26	-4.1
03	ARI	303	40	71	3	21	11	234	219	239	$4	326	304	629	12	89	25	1.28	261	42	118	1.86	3.33	-8.6
1st Half		116	18	32	1	10	5	276			$3	382	353	736	15	86	31	1.25	256	52	108		4.77	1.7
2nd Half		187	22	39	2	11	6	209			$0	288	273	561	10	91	22	1.31	263	36	117		2.57	-9.9
04	**Proj**	**300**	**43**	**77**	**2**	**25**	**8**	**257**			**$5**	**339**	**327**	**666**	**11**	**88**	**29**	**1.03**	**260**	**48**	**99**		**3.77**	**-5.6**

21% hit rate in second half killed his BA. Already strong contact rate and batting eye improved in second half, so BA should rebound. Beyond that, he doesn't offer much.

Crawford,Carl

Pos LF
Age 22 Growth
Bats L

R	High	
I	EXP	con
S		stb
K	AGE	

LIMA D BA: 40%

	Tm	AB	R	H	HR	RBI	SB	Avg	vL	vR	R$	OB	Slg	OPS	bb%	ct%	h%	Eye	xBA	PX	SX	G/F	RC/G	RAR
99		0	0	0	0	0	0	0								0								
00		0	0	0	0	0	0	0								0								
01	aa	537	64	149	4	51	36	277			$19	324	358	682	6	85	32	0.46	258	56	111		3.76	-22.4
02	TAM	* 612	79	176	9	80	34	288	200	276	$26	319	430	748	4	84	33	0.29	271	86	191	2.00	4.70	-2.3
03	TAM	630	80	177	5	54	55	281	263	288	$27	309	362	671	4	84	33	0.25	265	49	169	2.28	4.18	-20.8
1st Half		289	34	73	1	22	19	253			$7	292	322	614	5	79	32	0.26	245	44	160		3.40	-16.6
2nd Half		341	46	104	4	32	36	305			$20	325	396	721	3	88	34	0.25	282	54	170		4.93	-3.8
04	**Proj**	**625**	**79**	**178**	**7**	**65**	**61**	**285**			**$32**	**316**	**387**	**703**	**4**	**84**	**33**	**0.30**	**273**	**63**	**173**		**4.38**	**-12.6**

As he learned the pitchers and catchers, he increased his BA, ct%, xBA, SX, and stolen base success rate in second half. At his young age, that's scary. If he can keep his OB up, could top 70 SB in 2004.

HAROLD NICHOLS

Crede,Joe

Pos 3B | Age 26 Pre-Peak | Bats R | R: Very High | I: EXP, CON | S: pt, stb | K: | LIMA C | BA: 60%

Yr	Tm	AB	R	H	HR	RBI	SB	Avg	vL	vR	R$	OB	Slg	OPS	bb%	ct%	h%	Eye	xBA	PX	SX	G/F	RC/G	RAR
99	aa	291	34	68	4	38	2	234			$1	283	330	613	6	86	26	0.48	264	65	60		2.85	-13.8
00	aa	533	78	158	22	87	3	296			$19	360	482	842	9	81	33	0.52	279	113	42	0.29	6.15	26.6
01	aaa	513	62	134	18	66	3	261			$12	322	439	761	8	82	29	0.51	277	112	63	0.94	4.87	5.9
02	CHW	* 559	78	164	36	92	0	293	259	295	$25	333	538	871	6	85	29	0.40	303	143	21	0.74	6.32	28.9
03	CHW	536	68	140	19	75	1	261	300	246	$12	303	433	736	6	86	27	0.43	283	108	54	0.81	4.50	-0.2
1st Half		270	24	62	7	32	0	230			$2	265	348	613	5	85	25	0.32	256	75	25		3.00	-12.4
2nd Half		266	44	78	12	43	1	293			$10	340	519	859	7	87	30	0.56	310	141	80		6.40	13.9
04	**Proj**	**550**	**73**	**150**	**24**	**81**	**1**	**273**			**$16**	**319**	**467**	**786**	**6**	**85**	**28**	**0.45**	**285**	**119**	**52**		**5.15**	**10.7**

Made adjustments after a lousy 1st half and doubled his PX, Eye, ct%, SX and OB. Likely to continue this growth in 2004. Upside: 25-80-.300.

Crisp,Coco

Pos CF LF | Age 24 Growth | Bats S | R: Moderate | I: EXP | S: pt | K: age | LIMA C+ | BA: 50%

Yr	Tm	AB	R	H	HR	RBI	SB	Avg	vL	vR	R$	OB	Slg	OPS	bb%	ct%	h%	Eye	xBA	PX	SX	G/F	RC/G	RAR
99		0	0	0	0	0	0	0								0								
00		0	0	0	0	0	0	0								0								
01		0	0	0	0	0	0	0								0								
02	CLE	* 461	79	135	9	52	33	293	270	256	$23	347	406	752	8	85	33	0.56	263	75	118	1.05	4.95	2.3
03	CLE	* 639	94	187	4	49	33	293	321	245	$21	341	396	737	7	89	33	0.64	271	70	148	1.52	4.63	-2.0
1st Half		301	53	93	1	26	22	309			$14	377	432	809	10	91	34	1.27	292	86	169		5.77	8.8
2nd Half		338	41	94	3	23	11	278			$7	307	364	671	4	86	32	0.30	252	55	120		3.71	-10.2
04	**Proj**	**400**	**62**	**112**	**5**	**36**	**23**	**280**			**$14**	**330**	**385**	**715**	**7**	**87**	**31**	**0.58**	**270**	**70**	**136**		**4.33**	**-5.1**

3-27-.266 in 414 ABs for CLE. Nice OB, low PX, solid SX make him a decent source of steals.

Upside: 30 steals.

Cruz,Deivi

Pos SS | Age 31 Past Peak | Bats R | R: Moderate | I: con | S: pt, stb | K: | LIMA D | BA: 65%

Yr	Tm	AB	R	H	HR	RBI	SB	Avg	vL	vR	R$	OB	Slg	OPS	bb%	ct%	h%	Eye	xBA	PX	SX	G/F	RC/G	RAR
99	DET	518	64	147	13	58	1	284	290	282	$10	300	427	727	2	89	30	0.21	293	95	39	1.58	4.41	3.5
00	DET	583	68	176	10	82	1	302	345	288	$14	317	449	767	2	93	31	0.30	324	98	65	1.27	5.06	10.3
01	DET	414	39	106	7	52	4	256	223	268	$7	285	379	665	4	89	27	0.37	284	86	62	1.33	3.72	-7.9
02	SD	514	49	135	7	47	2	263	242	272	$7	293	366	659	4	89	29	0.38	272	76	54	1.49	3.63	-4.1
03	BAL	548	61	137	14	65	1	250	286	238	$8	267	378	645	2	91	25	0.27	285	80	54	1.41	3.38	-16.9
1st Half		261	32	68	10	37	1	261			$6	272	421	693	2	93	25	0.21	301	95	64		3.97	-3.5
2nd Half		287	29	69	4	28	0	240			$1	264	338	601	3	90	26	0.30	270	67	47		2.89	-13.3
04	**Proj**	**400**	**42**	**96**	**8**	**45**	**1**	**240**			**$4**	**263**	**357**	**620**	**3**	**90**	**25**	**0.32**	**282**	**78**	**54**		**3.10**	**-16.1**

Declining skill set with OB down nearer to .260 than even .300. Free swinging/low PX is a bad combination. Should have a lower BA, SB and RBI output in 2004.

Cruz,Enrique

Pos SS | Age 22 Growth | Bats R | R: Moderate | I: EXP | S: | K: AGE | LIMA F | BA: 50%

Yr	Tm	AB	R	H	HR	RBI	SB	Avg	vL	vR	R$	OB	Slg	OPS	bb%	ct%	h%	Eye	xBA	PX	SX	G/F	RC/G	RAR
99		0	0	0	0	0	0	0								0								
00		0	0	0	0	0	0	0								0								
01		0	0	0	0	0	0	0								0								
02		0	0	0	0	0	0	0								0								
03	MIL	71	6	6	0	2	0	85		100	($4)	133	99	232	5	58	15	0.13	143	13	66	3.57	0.37	-9.5
1st Half		47	3	5	0	2	0	106			($2)	176	128	304	8	62	17	0.22	152	19	33		0.64	-5.7
2nd Half		24	3	1	0	0	0	42			($2)	42	42	83	0	50	8	0.00	137	0	372		0.05	-3.7
04	**Proj**	**50**	**5**	**8**	**0**	**1**	**0**	**160**			**($2)**	**188**	**160**	**348**	**3**	**55**	**29**	**0.08**	**137**	**0**	**56**		**0.91**	**-4.9**

Rule 5 pick was robbed of development time wasting on the Brewers bench. Had a so-so Single A season at St.Lucie in 2002 and has some speed, but he is overmatched at this level.

Cruz,Jose

Pos RF | Age 30 Past Peak | Bats S | R: Low | I: CON | S: stb | K: | LIMA B | BA: 55%

Yr	Tm	AB	R	H	HR	RBI	SB	Avg	vL	vR	R$	OB	Slg	OPS	bb%	ct%	h%	Eye	xBA	PX	SX	G/F	RC/G	RAR
99	TOR	* 452	80	103	17	59	19	228	275	230	$11	358	407	766	17	75	27	0.82	259	105	131	1.14	4.93	-0.5
00	TOR	603	91	146	31	76	15	242	290	224	$15	322	466	788	11	79	26	0.55	274	127	116	1.09	5.02	1.9
01	TOR	577	92	158	34	88	32	274	290	269	$31	326	530	857	7	76	31	0.33	288	152	131	1.01	6.20	20.2
02	TOR	466	64	114	18	70	7	245	225	253	$12	319	438	757	10	77	28	0.48	258	116	117	0.96	4.76	-3.5
03	SF	539	90	135	20	68	5	250	304	233	$12	370	414	783	16	78	29	0.84	257	103	55	1.07	4.99	-10.0
1st Half		281	49	72	12	33	5	256			$8	372	441	814	16	77	29	0.80	262	115	77		5.47	-1.2
2nd Half		258	41	63	8	35	0	244			$4	367	384	751	16	78	28	0.89	247	90			4.49	-8.7
04	**Proj**	**500**	**79**	**125**	**20**	**69**	**4**	**250**			**$12**	**348**	**436**	**784**	**13**	**77**	**29**	**0.66**	**262**	**115**	**82**		**5.10**	**-5.5**

Despite the low BA, this was a growth season. 16% BB rate raised his OB 50 points while his contact rate and hit rate did not change. His team did not run, ruining any SB value.

Cuddyer,Michael

Pos RF | Age 25 Pre-Peak | Bats R | R: High | I: EXP, con | S: pt, stb | K: age | LIMA F | BA: 40%

Yr	Tm	AB	R	H	HR	RBI	SB	Avg	vL	vR	R$	OB	Slg	OPS	bb%	ct%	h%	Eye	xBA	PX	SX	G/F	RC/G	RAR
99		0	0	0	0	0	0	0								0								
00	aa	490	63	123	5	53	4	251			$4	317	367	684	9	83	29	0.58	268	77	100		3.87	-16.9
01	aa	527	96	157	29	88	6	298			$24	386	550	937	13	79	33	0.68	289	153	74	0.67	7.33	30.7
02	MIN	442	63	119	18	52	11	269			$15	321	468	790	7	80	30	0.38	399	117	127	1.52	4.95	-0.9
03	MIN	* 288	36	80	6	39	5	278	245	262	$8	354	424	778	11	78	34	0.53	251	95	94	1.71	5.06	-0.8
1st Half		139	22	40	3	13	3	288			$4	385	432	817	14	79	35	0.76	250	83	140		5.35	0.8
2nd Half		149	14	40	3	26	2	268			$4	323	416	739	7	77	33	0.34	252	107	47		4.77	-1.6
04	**Proj**	**150**	**20**	**41**	**4**	**20**	**3**	**273**			**$4**	**343**	**436**	**779**	**10**	**79**	**32**	**0.50**	**256**	**103**	**82**		**5.03**	**-0.2**

4-8-.245 in 102 ABs at MIN. PX and SX combination is too low for an OF. Hit rate should drop and with it, his BA, eliminating any value. Still a chance he could bump up PX but time is running out.

Cust,Jack

Pos DH | Age 25 Pre-Peak | Bats L | R: High | I: EXP | S: stb | K: age | LIMA D | BA: 40%

Yr	Tm	AB	R	H	HR	RBI	SB	Avg	vL	vR	R$	OB	Slg	OPS	bb%	ct%	h%	Eye	xBA	PX	SX	G/F	RC/G	RAR
99		0	0	0	0	0	0	0								0								
00	aa	447	78	118	15	59	9	264			$12	388	450	838	17	74	32	0.79	258	114	95		5.68	8.0
01	aaa	442	67	116	21	65	5	262			$14	380	462	842	16	73	31	0.71	249	118	56		5.95	9.3
02	aaa	424	55	98	20	43	4	231			$8	333	427	760	13	76	26	0.63	257	123	42	1.45	4.56	-12.6
03	BAL	* 406	58	107	13	65	5	264	364	242	$11	391	419	810	17	73	33	0.77	236	98	61	1.06	5.66	12.4
1st Half		249	39	63	8	41	4	253			$7	394	398	792	19	73	31	0.88	233	91	52		5.32	5.2
2nd Half		157	19	44	5	24	1	280			$5	386	452	838	15	72	36	0.61	239	110	61		6.23	7.2
04	**Proj**	**300**	**42**	**77**	**11**	**42**	**3**	**257**			**$8**	**373**	**435**	**808**	**16**	**74**	**31**	**0.70**	**245**	**110**	**59**		**5.47**	**4.3**

4-11-.260 in 73 ABs at BAL. Extreme patience jacked up his OB to nearly .400. PX plunged down, but there is little doubt that he can hit if given regular playing time.
Upside: 20-60-.260.

Damon,Johnny

Pos CF | Age 30 Past Peak | Bats L | R: Low | I: con | S: stb | K: | LIMA B+ | BA: 65%

Yr	Tm	AB	R	H	HR	RBI	SB	Avg	vL	vR	R$	OB	Slg	OPS	bb%	ct%	h%	Eye	xBA	PX	SX	G/F	RC/G	RAR
99	KC	583	101	179	14	77	36	307	329	300	$29	378	477	855	10	91	32	1.34	325	106	161	1.39	6.84	34.3
00	KC	655	136	214	16	88	46	327	357	316	$37	388	495	882	9	91	34	1.08	328	102	173	1.49	7.42	48.8
01	OAK	644	108	165	9	49	27	256	265	252	$14	321	363	684	9	89	28	0.87	282	72	118	1.15	3.92	-17.9
02	BOS	623	118	178	14	63	31	286	306	279	$25	353	443	796	9	89	30	0.93	306	97	177	1.29	5.71	16.5
03	BOS	609	103	166	12	67	30	273	275	272	$21	346	404	750	10	88	29	0.92	297	84	140	1.47	5.02	4.9
1st Half		322	57	84	6	36	14	261			$9	330	410	740	9	88	28	0.87	309	99	151		4.81	0.6
2nd Half		287	46	82	6	31	16	286			$12	363	397	761	11	87	31	0.97	283	68	118		5.26	4.2
04	**Proj**	**650**	**114**	**182**	**13**	**68**	**33**	**280**			**$23**	**350**	**414**	**764**	**10**	**89**	**30**	**0.94**	**299**	**85**	**144**		**5.23**	**8.8**

Still good patience and OB, consistent BPIs make him a solid low power/high SB player. xBA indicates that he can still hit .300, although he has not since 2000 with KC.

Daubach,Brian

Pos 1B | Age 32 Past Peak | Bats L | R: Moderate | I: CON | S: pt, stb | K: | LIMA F | BA: 50%

Yr	Tm	AB	R	H	HR	RBI	SB	Avg	vL	vR	R$	OB	Slg	OPS	bb%	ct%	h%	Eye	xBA	PX	SX	G/F	RC/G	RAR
99	BOS	* 412	64	121	22	78	0	294	273	297	$16	358	553	911	9	76	34	0.41	283	159	61	0.96	7.08	14.8
00	BOS	495	55	123	21	76	1	248	216	257	$9	310	448	758	8	74	30	0.34	261	120	49	1.06	4.69	-18.4
01	BOS	407	54	107	22	71	1	263	169	279	$13	348	509	856	12	73	31	0.49	271	148	63	0.89	6.14	-0.1
02	BOS	444	62	118	20	78	2	266	242	270	$15	341	464	805	10	72	33	0.40	252	119	65	1.02	5.48	-4.9
03	CHW	183	26	42	6	21	1	230	188	234	$2	350	388	738	16	70	29	0.63	239	102	42	1.08	4.53	-4.7
1st Half		105	13	25	2	11	1	238			$1	344	371	716	14	74	30	0.63	248	95	43		4.34	-3.3
2nd Half		78	13	17	4	10	0	218			$1	358	410	768	18	65	28	0.63	226	112	27		4.79	-1.4
04	**Proj**	**150**	**21**	**37**	**7**	**22**	**1**	**247**			**$3**	**348**	**437**	**785**	**13**	**69**	**31**	**0.50**	**240**	**118**	**36**		**5.15**	**-2.3**

Declining BPIs evident, but reduced playing time makes him a risky selection. At 32, he can be expected to decline further, even as BB rate goes up, due to falling PX and contact rate.

DOUG DENNIS

DaVanon,Jeff

	Yr	Tm	AB	R	H	HR	RBI	SB	Avg	vL	vR	R$	OB	Slg	OPS	bb%	ct%	h%	Eye	xBA	PX	SX	G/F	RC/G	RAR
Pos RF CF	99	a/a	506	102	151	14	66	24	298			$22	375	488	863	11	83	34	0.70	292	115	176	1.20	6.25	18.4
Age 30 Past Peak	00		0	0	0	0	0	0	0								0								
Bats S	01	ANA	* 344	40	84	13	44	7	244	280	159	$8	312	445	757	9	79	28	0.47	272	118	122	0.88	4.40	-6.1
R X HIGH	02	aaa	130	18	32	5	17	5	246			$4	319	462	781	10	81	27	0.56	290	143	109	0.50	4.58	-2.3
I EXP con	03	ANA	* 390	64	108	14	53	20	277	342	274	$17	356	446	802	11	83	30	0.72	274	104	112	1.17	5.61	5.2
S PT STB	1st Half		197	37	62	12	35	11	315			$14	363	548	911	7	84	33	0.47	296	133	118		7.51	12.7
K	2nd Half		193	27	46	2	18	9	238			$3	350	342	692	15	82	28	0.94	252	75	98		3.98	-7.0
LIMA D BA: 50%	04	Proj	**200**	**30**	**48**	**6**	**30**	**6**	**240**			**$5**	**306**	**405**	**711**	**9**	**80**	**27**	**0.48**	**270**	**104**	**118**		**3.92**	**-7.0**

12-43-.282 in 330 ABs for ANA. Surprising SBs, but unlikely to see it again. OB solid, but low BA, PX and hit rate in the 2nd half indicate that a drop off is likely the norm.

Davis,Ben

	Yr	Tm	AB	R	H	HR	RBI	SB	Avg	vL	vR	R$	OB	Slg	OPS	bb%	ct%	h%	Eye	xBA	PX	SX	G/F	RC/G	RAR
Pos CA	99	SD	* 467	49	117	11	62	5	251	239	246	$7	312	392	704	8	78	30	0.42	258	94	68	1.70	4.15	2.6
Age 27 Peak	00	SD	* 351	45	81	9	49	5	231	194	234	$4	318	370	689	11	79	27	0.60	260	89	69	0.97	3.85	-1.5
Bats S	01	SD	448	56	107	11	57	4	239	241	238	$6	337	357	694	13	75	30	0.59	227	75	46	1.20	3.94	5.7
R Moderate	02	SEA	228	24	59	7	43	1	259	235	266	$6	313	404	717	7	75	32	0.31	238	89	54	1.03	4.29	4.5
I con	03	SEA	246	25	58	6	42	0	236	281	222	$3	288	382	670	7	75	29	0.30	266	101	24	1.55	3.67	-3.1
S pt stb	1st Half		133	17	37	5	28	0	278			$5	319	489	808	6	74	34	0.24	290	143	27		5.51	5.3
K	2nd Half		113	8	21	1	14	0	186			($1)	252	257	509	8	76	24	0.37	238	52	19		2.03	-7.5
LIMA F BA: 50%	04	Proj	**250**	**26**	**59**	**6**	**40**	**1**	**236**			**$3**	**300**	**364**	**664**	**8**	**75**	**29**	**0.37**	**262**	**85**	**36**		**3.61**	**-2.4**

Played over his head in the 1st half, but underwater the 2nd half, left him with his usual results. PX, SX, hit rate all dropped so precipitously that his future may be in doubt.

Delgado,Carlos

	Yr	Tm	AB	R	H	HR	RBI	SB	Avg	vL	vR	R$	OB	Slg	OPS	bb%	ct%	h%	Eye	xBA	PX	SX	G/F	RC/G	RAR
Pos 1B	99	TOR	573	113	156	44	134	1	272	309	259	$26	367	571	938	13	75	29	0.61	281	173	43	0.79	7.31	25.0
Age 31 Past Peak	00	TOR	569	115	196	41	137	0	344	319	357	$36	461	664	1125	18	82	37	1.18	350	191	30	1.33	11.84	86.5
Bats L	01	TOR	574	102	160	39	102	3	279	246	293	$25	396	540	936	16	76	30	0.82	287	151	55	1.12	7.59	23.5
R Very Low	02	TOR	505	103	140	33	108	1	277	238	297	$23	399	549	947	17	75	31	0.81	263	161	63	0.77	7.73	26.8
I con	03	TOR	570	117	172	42	145	0	302	284	310	$33	414	593	1007	16	76	33	0.80	310	172	37	0.92	8.96	55.9
S	1st Half		298	68	91	26	89	0	305			$20	415	644	1060	16	77	32	0.82	333	200	33		9.82	36.1
K	2nd Half		272	49	81	16	56	0	298			$13	412	537	949	16	75	35	0.77	285	141	41		8.04	19.9
LIMA B BA: 50%	04	Proj	**550**	**109**	**161**	**38**	**124**	**1**	**293**			**$28**	**408**	**569**	**977**	**16**	**76**	**32**	**0.80**	**307**	**163**	**46**		**8.37**	**41.3**

Awesome PX spike, especially in the 1st half. Will decline some, but this is still an elite skill set, and the lower 2nd half numbers are more than acceptable.

Delgado,Wilson

	Yr	Tm	AB	R	H	HR	RBI	SB	Avg	vL	vR	R$	OB	Slg	OPS	bb%	ct%	h%	Eye	xBA	PX	SX	G/F	RC/G	RAR
Pos 3B SS	99	SF	* 284	28	72	1	28	4	254	333	213	$2	300	324	624	6	87	29	0.51	264	48	92	1.52	3.30	-8.9
Age 31 Past Peak	00	2AL	128	21	33	1	11	2	258	241	263	$1	317	297	613	8	80	32	0.42	190	24	75	4.00	3.21	-4.5
Bats S	01	aaa	255	18	56	3	23	6	220			$1	255	302	557	4	87	24	0.36	260	55	74		2.47	-15.9
R X HIGH	02	aaa	365	23	77	5	27	2	211			($1)	248	299	547	5	86	23	0.36	255	61	41	0.83	2.25	-26.2
I EXP CON	03	2TM	* 213	21	46	2	17	2	216	195	244	($1)	283	268	551	9	84	25	0.59	233	35	51	1.84	2.46	-12.7
S PT STB	1st Half		68	8	12	0	2	0	176			($2)	211	221	432	4	87	20	0.33	244	39	57		1.44	-6.5
K	2nd Half		145	13	34	2	15	2	234			$1	315	290	604	10	83	27	0.68	228	34	44		3.03	-5.9
LIMA F BA: 60%	04	Proj	**150**	**13**	**33**	**1**	**12**	**2**	**220**			**($0)**	**272**	**283**	**555**	**7**	**85**	**25**	**0.48**	**241**	**45**	**49**		**2.47**	**-9.1**

0-7-.228 in 127 ABs for ANA and STL. Not a rosterable skill set. It is hard to fathom how a 35 PX hitter gets 127 ABs.

Dellucci,David

	Yr	Tm	AB	R	H	HR	RBI	SB	Avg	vL	vR	R$	OB	Slg	OPS	bb%	ct%	h%	Eye	xBA	PX	SX	G/F	RC/G	RAR
Pos RF	99	ARI	109	27	43	1	15	2	394	250	419	$6	450	505	955	9	78	50	0.46	281	78	110	3.13	9.75	12.3
Age 30 Past Peak	00	ARI	* 172	13	39	2	14	3	227		300	$0	285	331	616	8	88	25	0.67	278	67	92	6.20	3.20	-10.1
Bats L	01	ARI	217	28	60	10	40	2	276	231	283	$8	343	479	822	9	76	32	0.42	280	117	86	1.83	5.75	1.2
R High	02	ARI	* 244	35	58	7	30	2	238	111	262	$4	319	389	708	11	76	28	0.50	249	99	88	2.16	3.92	-10.3
I CON	03	2TM	216	26	49	3	23	12	227	132	247	$4	301	352	653	10	73	30	0.40	243	83	162	1.45	3.80	-10.3
S pt stb	1st Half		127	16	35	2	19	6	276			$5	352	457	809	11	74	36	0.45	269	122	185		5.98	2.2
K	2nd Half		89	10	14	1	4	6	157			($0)	227	202	429	8	72	21	0.32	206	27	109		1.64	-11.0
LIMA F BA: 40%	04	Proj	**150**	**20**	**35**	**3**	**17**	**5**	**233**			**$3**	**306**	**358**	**664**	**9**	**75**	**29**	**0.42**	**247**	**80**	**110**		**3.76**	**-6.8**

1st half was quite good, but the 2nd half was an unmitigated disaster. Why?

1st half PX: 122
2d half PX: 27

Yes, a 27 PX causes a 21 H%.

DeRosa,Mark

	Yr	Tm	AB	R	H	HR	RBI	SB	Avg	vL	vR	R$	OB	Slg	OPS	bb%	ct%	h%	Eye	xBA	PX	SX	G/F	RC/G	RAR
Pos 2B 3B SS	99	aaa	364	35	90	1	34	6	247			$2	283	308	590	5	88	28	0.43	262	45	76		2.77	-14.6
Age 29 Past Peak	00	aaa	370	52	98	2	30	11	265			$6	325	346	671	8	92	28	1.10	282	58	101	1.25	3.86	-2.8
Bats R	01	ATL	* 350	54	97	5	35	8	277	417	250	$9	331	389	719	7	89	30	0.72	284	80	83	2.08	4.46	6.0
R Moderate	02	ATL	* 267	32	75	5	28	4	281	293	299	$7	322	397	719	6	90	30	0.62	283	79	87	1.70	4.40	-0.1
I EXP con	03	ATL	266	40	70	6	22	1	263	277	257	$4	305	383	688	6	82	30	0.33	256	82	60	1.31	4.07	-2.6
S pt stb	1st Half		107	18	24	4	12	0	224			$1	272	374	646	6	76	26	0.27	242	92	56		3.34	-3.5
K	2nd Half		159	22	46	2	10	1	289			$3	327	390	717	5	86	33	0.39	265	76	57		4.62	1.0
LIMA D BA: 40%	04	Proj	**300**	**42**	**81**	**6**	**27**	**3**	**270**			**$6**	**314**	**385**	**699**	**6**	**86**	**30**	**0.45**	**264**	**79**	**80**		**4.18**	**-1.2**

Acceptable contact rate, but he really should generate a higher PX if he wants to play every day. Versatility will keep him getting utility ABs.

Diaz,Einar

	Yr	Tm	AB	R	H	HR	RBI	SB	Avg	vL	vR	R$	OB	Slg	OPS	bb%	ct%	h%	Eye	xBA	PX	SX	G/F	RC/G	RAR
Pos CA	99	CLE	392	43	110	3	32	11	281	213	302	$8	320	362	683	6	90	31	0.56	274	59	85	1.25	4.10	0.4
Age 31 Past Peak	00	CLE	250	29	68	4	25	4	272	263	275	$4	303	392	695	4	88	29	0.38	260	77	94	1.74	4.10	-0.4
Bats R	01	CLE	437	54	121	4	56	1	277	196	305	$8	304	387	691	4	90	30	0.39	283	83	51	1.17	4.07	2.6
R Moderate	02	CLE	320	34	66	2	16	0	206	225	201	($4)	246	284	531	5	92	22	0.63	259	61	43	1.48	2.21	-14.0
I con	03	TEX	334	30	86	4	35	3	257	253	259	$4	277	341	618	3	90	28	0.28	285	57	63	1.18	3.25	-8.3
S PT stb	1st Half		191	16	50	2	20	2	262			$3	288	356	644	4	88	29	0.30	263	66	65		3.51	-3.2
K	2nd Half		143	14	36	2	15	1	252			$2	262	322	584	1	94	26	0.22	286	46	51		2.91	-5.0
LIMA D BA: 55%	04	Proj	**350**	**36**	**87**	**4**	**33**	**2**	**249**			**$3**	**275**	**337**	**611**	**3**	**91**	**26**	**0.40**	**271**	**63**	**64**		**3.12**	**-8.5**

Excellent contact rate, but crummy PX will always depress his BA versus his xBA. It would not hurt him to take a walk once in a while, either. Best OB since '00 is .304. Better to have a part-timer.

DiFelice,Mike

	Yr	Tm	AB	R	H	HR	RBI	SB	Avg	vL	vR	R$	OB	Slg	OPS	bb%	ct%	h%	Eye	xBA	PX	SX	G/F	RC/G	RAR
Pos CA	99	TAM	179	21	55	6	27	0	307	286	315	$6	337	469	806	4	87	33	0.35	310	103	23	1.25	5.82	8.5
Age 34 Decline	00	TAM	204	23	49	6	19	0	240	225	244	$1	282	402	684	6	80	27	0.30	252	100	49	1.11	3.81	-2.1
Bats R	01	2TM	* 196	19	39	3	12	1	199	151	205	($2)	238	281	518	5	72	26	0.18	212	49	72	0.91	2.09	-9.9
R High	02	STL	174	17	40	4	19	0	230	216	236	$1	298	362	660	9	76	28	0.40	238	95	21	0.93	3.58	-2.8
I CON	03	KC	189	29	48	3	25	1	254	313	224	$3	288	397	685	5	84	29	0.30	286	103	87	1.08	3.93	-0.9
S STB	1st Half		109	17	30	2	15	0	275			$2	301	431	732	4	84	31	0.24	290	108	82		4.56	1.5
K age	2nd Half		80	12	18	1	10	1	225			$0	271	350	621	6	84	26	0.38	279	95	77		3.18	-2.2
LIMA F BA: 50%	04	Proj	**100**	**13**	**23**	**1**	**10**	**1**	**230**			**$0**	**276**	**326**	**602**	**6**	**80**	**28**	**0.32**	**270**	**74**	**69**		**3.04**	**-2.7**

Was a good 2nd catcher... a long time ago. Nice revival in '03 in BPIs, but low OB in the 2nd half and age (34) will combine to prevent any kind of repeat. Not rosterable.

Drew,J.D.

	Yr	Tm	AB	R	H	HR	RBI	SB	Avg	vL	vR	R$	OB	Slg	OPS	bb%	ct%	h%	Eye	xBA	PX	SX	G/F	RC/G	RAR
Pos RF CF	99	STL	* 455	82	113	15	52	24	248	264	233	$14	332	424	756	11	79	28	0.60	270	104	166	0.88	4.93	-1.0
Age 28 Peak	00	STL	407	73	120	18	57	17	295	257	303	$19	395	479	874	14	76	35	0.68	267	106	97	1.19	6.61	17.1
Bats L	01	STL	375	80	121	27	73	13	323	289	332	$27	412	613	1025	13	80	34	0.76	316	161	145	1.18	9.53	40.1
R Moderate	02	STL	424	61	107	18	56	8	252	262	250	$13	341	429	770	12	75	29	0.55	250	112	81	1.07	5.02	-3.5
I CON	03	STL	287	60	83	15	42	2	289	218	306	$12	368	512	881	11	83	30	0.75	315	132	106	1.36	6.64	8.3
S pt	1st Half		149	33	46	9	25	2	309			$8	368	564	932	9	85	32	0.61	332	143	158		7.55	7.9
K	2nd Half		138	27	37	6	17	0	268			$4	369	457	825	14	82	29	0.88	297	120	46		5.71	0.4
LIMA C+ BA: 55%	04	Proj	**350**	**66**	**102**	**18**	**51**	**6**	**291**			**$16**	**377**	**505**	**883**	**12**	**80**	**32**	**0.69**	**309**	**127**	**108**		**6.80**	**13.0**

A repeat of 2001 is possible at any time, but it is getting to the point where you have to wonder if he will ever be healthy again. Struggles against LHers is a concern.

Upside: 30-90-.300.

DOUG DENNIS

Duncan,Jeff

Pos CF
Age 25 Pre-Peak
Bats L
R Moderate / I EXP / S / K age
LIMA F BA: 50%

Yr	Tm	AB	R	H	HR	RBI	SB	Avg	vL	vR	R$	OB	Slg	OPS	bb%	ct%	h%	Eye	xBA	PX	SX	G/F	RC/G	RAR
99		0	0	0	0	0	0	0								0								
00		0	0	0	0	0	0	0								0								
01		0	0	0	0	0	0	0								0								
02		0	0	0	0	0	0	0								0								
03	NYM	* 432	56	100	6	32	25	231	67	210	$9	307	322	629	10	76	29	0.46	233	55	144	1.52	3.16	-24.6
1st Half		256	33	59	3	18	16	230			$5	289	316	605	8	80	28	0.41	244	57	133		2.85	-17.2
2nd Half		176	23	41	3	14	9	233			$3	332	330	661	13	71	31	0.51	217	52	160		3.60	-7.5
04	**Proj**	**100**	**13**	**23**	**1**	**8**	**6**	**230**			**$2**	**313**	**315**	**628**	**11**	**75**	**29**	**0.48**	**229**	**50**	**127**		**3.19**	**-4.8**

Given a chance to win a job with his legs, but poor OB and base skills make him a good pick only if desperate for steals and he is getting unexpected playing time.

Dunn,Adam

Pos LF
Age 24 Growth
Bats L
R Moderate / I EXP con / S pt / K age
LIMA B+ BA: 50%

Yr	Tm	AB	R	H	HR	RBI	SB	Avg	vL	vR	R$	OB	Slg	OPS	bb%	ct%	h%	Eye	xBA	PX	SX	G/F	RC/G	RAR
99		0	0	0	0	0	0	0								0								
00		0	0	0	0	0	0	0								0								
01	CIN	* 594	120	184	49	118	14	310	282	254	$40	405	630	1035	14	78	33	0.71	305	185	78	0.80	9.16	56.8
02	CIN	535	84	133	26	71	19	249	254	246	$20	394	454	848	19	68	32	0.75	239	130	88	1.01	5.98	-6.6
03	CIN	381	70	82	27	57	8	215	202	221	$11	343	465	807	16	67	24	0.59	219	141	90	0.62	5.20	-4.6
1st Half		241	51	50	23	46	7	207			$10	339	519	858	17	61	22	0.52	212	172	84		5.66	0.5
2nd Half		140	19	32	4	11	1	229			$1	349	371	721	16	76	27	0.79	225	89	74		4.34	-5.3
04	**Proj**	**500**	**84**	**114**	**29**	**69**	**12**	**228**			**$15**	**358**	**453**	**812**	**17**	**71**	**26**	**0.69**	**224**	**134**	**91**		**5.33**	**-6.5**

Horrendous trend in contact rate and PX, leading to miserable xBA. Has power potential, but needs to change his approach at the plate in order to maintain enough contact and PX to be an impact hitter. Use caution.

Durazo,Erubiel

Pos 1B DH
Age 30 Past Peak
Bats L
R High / I CON / S PT stb / K
LIMA B BA: 60%

Yr	Tm	AB	R	H	HR	RBI	SB	Avg	vL	vR	R$	OB	Slg	OPS	bb%	ct%	h%	Eye	xBA	PX	SX	G/F	RC/G	RAR
99	ARI	* 499	92	176	28	93	3	353	222	343	$30	428	589	1017	12	84	38	0.80	298	138	75	0.85	9.85	58.0
00	ARI	196	35	52	8	33	1	265	318	259	$5	374	444	818	15	78	30	0.79	244	109	48	1.28	5.80	2.5
01	ARI	175	34	47	12	38	0	269	188	287	$8	369	537	907	14	72	31	0.57	254	157	34	1.10	6.92	3.3
02	ARI	* 258	53	69	18	55	0	267	167	292	$12	390	562	952	17	76	29	0.84	289	181	90	0.97	7.53	14.4
03	OAK	537	92	139	21	77	1	259	283	247	$13	375	430	805	16	80	29	0.95	266	107	39	1.01	5.53	2.3
1st Half		263	44	74	9	43	0	281			$8	404	460	864	17	80	32	1.02	271	118	26		6.59	9.0
2nd Half		274	48	65	12	34	1	237			$5	347	401	748	14	81	25	0.88	261	95	47		4.61	-6.3
04	**Proj**	**550**	**102**	**146**	**29**	**95**	**1**	**265**			**$18**	**378**	**485**	**863**	**15**	**78**	**29**	**0.83**	**270**	**130**	**54**		**6.33**	**10.5**

Full-time ABs exposed him to LHers, but he did well against them. PX, however, plunged in 2003. Eye maintained, so there is some hope that he can pump up his PX and produce better numbers in '04.

Durham,Ray

Pos 2B
Age 32 Past Peak
Bats S
R Low / I / S pt stb / K
LIMA B+ BA: 45%

Yr	Tm	AB	R	H	HR	RBI	SB	Avg	vL	vR	R$	OB	Slg	OPS	bb%	ct%	h%	Eye	xBA	PX	SX	G/F	RC/G	RAR
99	CHW	612	109	181	13	60	34	296	301	294	$24	371	435	805	11	83	34	0.70	290	85	152	1.76	5.83	32.2
00	CHW	614	121	172	17	75	25	280	248	289	$21	358	450	808	11	83	32	0.71	294	100	155	1.57	5.52	29.4
01	CHW	611	104	163	20	65	23	267	259	269	$20	336	466	803	9	82	30	0.58	290	123	152	1.09	5.33	20.2
02	2AL	564	114	163	15	70	26	289	255	301	$24	370	450	821	11	84	32	0.78	283	102	147	1.22	6.03	31.8
03	SF	410	61	117	8	33	7	285	370	258	$10	363	441	805	11	80	34	0.61	281	107	112	1.18	5.47	12.5
1st Half		229	33	72	3	15	6	314			$8	405	441	846	13	78	39	0.69	264	91	103		6.65	14.0
2nd Half		181	28	45	5	18	1	249			$3	306	442	748	8	83	28	0.48	305	127	126		4.09	-1.8
04	**Proj**	**550**	**94**	**153**	**14**	**56**	**11**	**278**			**$15**	**353**	**446**	**799**	**10**	**82**	**32**	**0.64**	**287**	**110**	**128**		**5.43**	**17.6**

Steady BPIs, but injuries knocked 200 ABs off his usual totals, as well permitting him to run far less often. BPIs can be expected to decline, but regular PT should provide a rebound to a level between '02 and '03.

Dye,Jermaine

Pos RF
Age 30 Past Peak
Bats R
R Moderate / I con / S pt stb / K
LIMA C BA: 70%

Yr	Tm	AB	R	H	HR	RBI	SB	Avg	vL	vR	R$	OB	Slg	OPS	bb%	ct%	h%	Eye	xBA	PX	SX	G/F	RC/G	RAR
99	KC	608	96	179	27	119	2	294	267	300	$23	356	526	882	9	80	33	0.49	294	139	96	1.23	6.66	28.6
00	KC	601	107	193	33	118	0	321	323	321	$28	391	561	952	10	84	34	0.70	319	140	44	1.15	8.18	52.4
01	2AL	599	91	169	26	106	9	282	293	278	$24	345	467	812	9	81	31	0.51	281	112	78	1.23	5.78	13.6
02	OAK	504	76	125	24	87	2	248	212	262	$14	320	452	772	10	78	27	0.49	261	124	63	0.91	4.93	-1.4
03	OAK	* 270	34	49	6	26	1	181	260	146	($3)	271	278	548	11	81	20	0.63	237	60	51	0.88	2.36	-24.2
1st Half		150	20	25	3	13	0	167			($3)	260	253	514	11	81	18	0.68	235	54	41		2.02	-15.4
2nd Half		120	14	24	3	13	1	200			($0)	284	308	592	10	80	23	0.58	239	67	48		2.83	-8.7
04	**Proj**	**500**	**69**	**130**	**22**	**70**	**3**	**260**			**$13**	**334**	**443**	**777**	**10**	**80**	**28**	**0.56**	**252**	**108**	**59**		**5.12**	**0.8**

4-20-.172 in 221 ABs at OAK. Season was a complete loss due to injuries and a 20% hit rate caused largely by a poor PX. Should return to power norms, but may never hit for average as in years past.

Easley,Damion

Pos 3B
Age 34 Decline
Bats R
R High / I CON / S pt stb / K age
LIMA F BA: 60%

Yr	Tm	AB	R	H	HR	RBI	SB	Avg	vL	vR	R$	OB	Slg	OPS	bb%	ct%	h%	Eye	xBA	PX	SX	G/F	RC/G	RAR
99	DET	549	83	146	20	65	11	266	291	261	$14	328	434	762	9	77	31	0.41	261	103	88	1.28	4.96	8.5
00	DET	464	76	120	14	58	13	259	280	251	$11	337	416	753	11	83	29	0.70	278	96	104	1.18	4.83	5.9
01	DET	585	77	146	11	65	10	250	236	254	$9	311	376	687	8	85	28	0.58	264	79	111	1.45	3.92	-7.6
02	DET	* 330	33	71	8	30	1	215	313	198	$1	285	339	624	9	87	23	0.74	268	79	42	0.97	2.94	-15.8
03	TAM	107	8	20	1	7	0	187	184	188	($2)	202	262	464	2	83	22	0.11	232	47	66	1.29	1.66	-9.7
1st Half		107	8	20	1	7	0	187			($2)	202	262	464	2	83	22	0.11	232	47	66		1.66	-9.7
2nd Half		0	0	0	0	0	0	0			($0)					0			0					
04	**Proj**	**100**	**12**	**23**	**1**	**10**	**1**	**230**			**$0**	**283**	**302**	**585**	**7**	**84**	**27**	**0.46**	**233**	**42**	**93**		**2.79**	**-5.1**

Career is likely over. Still makes good contact, but tiny PX and low BB rate render him useless at the plate.

Eckstein,David

Pos SS
Age 29 Past Peak
Bats R
R High / I exp CON / S pt stb / K
LIMA C+ BA: 65%

Yr	Tm	AB	R	H	HR	RBI	SB	Avg	vL	vR	R$	OB	Slg	OPS	bb%	ct%	h%	Eye	xBA	PX	SX	G/F	RC/G	RAR
99	aa	483	88	135	5	43	26	280			$14	372	371	742	13	91	30	1.61	283	60	120		4.72	12.4
00	aaa	474	81	116	3	34	14	245			$4	326	321	646	11	92	26	1.43	280	57	85		3.34	-8.7
01	ANA	582	82	166	4	41	29	285	303	278	$17	334	357	692	7	90	31	0.72	283	52	111	1.58	4.46	1.5
02	ANA	608	107	178	8	63	21	293	302	289	$20	342	388	730	7	93	31	1.02	291	60	127	1.26	4.58	0.0
03	ANA	452	59	114	3	31	16	252	256	251	$7	307	325	633	7	90	27	0.80	264	54	98	1.68	3.44	-13.2
1st Half		284	41	67	3	19	9	236			$3	295	313	609	8	90	25	0.89	263	53	103		3.11	-11.3
2nd Half		168	18	47	0	12	7	280			$4	328	345	673	7	89	31	0.67	262	57	77		4.06	-1.8
04	**Proj**	**500**	**72**	**137**	**4**	**40**	**20**	**274**			**$12**	**329**	**352**	**680**	**8**	**91**	**30**	**0.87**	**268**	**56**	**105**		**4.05**	**-5.7**

Maintained high contact rate, but declining hit rate and SX hurt his OB and dropped his results across the board. Should rebound some if healthy, but unlikely to see 600 ABs again.

Edmonds,Jim

Pos CF
Age 33 Decline
Bats L
R Low / I con / S pt stb / K age
LIMA B BA: 50%

Yr	Tm	AB	R	H	HR	RBI	SB	Avg	vL	vR	R$	OB	Slg	OPS	bb%	ct%	h%	Eye	xBA	PX	SX	G/F	RC/G	RAR
99	ANA	204	34	51	5	23	5	250	190	277	$4	341	426	767	12	78	30	0.62	274	116	115	1.21	4.71	0.1
00	STL	525	129	155	42	108	10	295	270	306	$31	411	583	994	16	68	36	0.70	254	160	79	0.73	8.65	63.2
01	STL	500	95	152	30	110	5	304	246	323	$28	413	564	977	16	73	37	0.68	281	157	60	1.07	8.33	61.9
02	STL	476	96	148	28	83	4	311	262	329	$26	416	561	977	15	72	38	0.64	281	159	74	0.98	8.52	47.4
03	STL	447	89	123	39	89	1	275	225	292	$24	382	617	999	15	72	30	0.61	280	205	59	0.72	8.11	40.1
1st Half		262	53	82	25	59	1	313			$19	398	695	1093	12	76	33	0.59	310	231	58		10.01	35.9
2nd Half		185	36	41	14	30	0	222			$5	360	508	868	18	65	25	0.63	240	167	66		5.88	5.1
04	**Proj**	**500**	**99**	**140**	**35**	**93**	**3**	**280**			**$24**	**391**	**566**	**957**	**15**	**71**	**33**	**0.63**	**272**	**173**	**68**		**7.69**	**42.4**

Nice power spike at age 33, but hit rate dropped in the 2nd half. PX should drop a little, hit rate will rebound a little, and, a slight decline should be expected overall.

Ellis,Mark

Pos 2B
Age 26 Pre-Peak
Bats R
R Very High / I EXP CON / S pt stb / K
LIMA D+ BA: 55%

Yr	Tm	AB	R	H	HR	RBI	SB	Avg	vL	vR	R$	OB	Slg	OPS	bb%	ct%	h%	Eye	xBA	PX	SX	G/F	RC/G	RAR
99		0	0	0	0	0	0	0								0								
00	aa	22	3	6	0	3	1	273			$1	385	318	703	15	73	38	0.67	211	38	58		4.63	0.3
01	aaa	472	56	111	8	42	17	235			$7	299	354	653	8	87	26	0.69	277	84	81		3.42	-8.9
02	OAK	* 429	68	115	6	39	7	268	296	268	$8	342	389	731	10	85	30	0.75	266	80	121	0.73	4.65	7.6
03	OAK	553	78	137	9	52	6	248	217	259	$6	308	371	679	8	83	28	0.51	264	82	106	1.04	3.87	-4.4
1st Half		275	37	69	5	23	1	251			$2	327	382	709	10	82	29	0.63	265	88	70		4.14	0.0
2nd Half		278	41	68	4	29	5	245			$3	288	360	648	6	84	28	0.38	264	75	129		3.59	-4.5
04	**Proj**	**550**	**79**	**139**	**8**	**51**	**9**	**253**			**$8**	**317**	**373**	**690**	**9**	**84**	**29**	**0.60**	**267**	**80**	**112**		**4.04**	**-1.1**

Lousy OB, low PX and average SX make him replacement level. Any value he adds to your team is held in ABs alone.

DOUG DENNIS

Encarnacion,Juan

Pos RF | Age 28 Peak | Bats R
R Moderate | I con | S pt stb | K
LIMA C+ | BA: 60%

Yr	Tm	AB	R	H	HR	RBI	SB	Avg	vL	vR	R$	OB	Slg	OPS	bb%	ct%	h%	Eye	xBA	PX	SX	G/F	RC/G	RAR
99	DET	509	62	130	19	74	33	255	263	254	$21	275	450	725	3	78	29	0.12	283	116	159	1.32	4.07	-13.8
00	DET	547	75	158	14	72	16	289	314	280	$18	325	433	758	5	84	33	0.32	281	85	131	1.67	5.07	2.3
01	DET	417	52	101	12	52	9	242	259	236	$8	285	408	693	6	78	29	0.27	260	98	138	1.11	3.80	-14.8
02	2NL	584	77	158	24	85	21	271	233	282	$25	324	449	772	7	81	30	0.41	280	109	118	1.19	4.96	-5.7
03	FLA	601	80	162	19	94	19	270	267	270	$23	312	446	758	6	86	29	0.45	301	113	126	1.15	4.76	-14.9
1st Half		319	44	91	11	52	13	285			$15	329	476	806	6	89	29	0.60	316	118	146		5.48	-1.2
2nd Half		282	36	71	8	42	6	252			$7	292	411	703	5	83	28	0.34	284	108	91		4.01	-13.4
04	Proj	600	78	158	20	88	19	263			$21	307	436	743	6	83	29	0.36	294	108	126		4.53	-16.5

A player to trade around mid-season. He's nowhere close to replacement level in the 2nd half.

OPS	1st half	2nd half
2001	.768	.571
2002	.804	.735
2003	.795	.709

Ensberg,Morgan

Pos 3B | Age 28 Peak | Bats R
R High | I EXP con | S pt stb | K
LIMA B | BA: 60%

Yr	Tm	AB	R	H	HR	RBI	SB	Avg	vL	vR	R$	OB	Slg	OPS	bb%	ct%	h%	Eye	xBA	PX	SX	G/F	RC/G	RAR
99	0	0	0	0	0	0	0	0								0								
00	0	0	0	0	0	0	0	0								0								
01	aaa	316	53	90	20	50	5	285			$15	360	535	895	10	83	29	0.69	299	147	59		6.72	20.2
02	HOU	* 424	56	109	10	50	10	257	320	224	$11	349	394	743	12	82	29	0.77	264	88	115	1.00	4.66	0.9
03	HOU	385	69	112	25	60	7	291	316	282	$20	370	530	899	11	84	29	0.80	303	139	82	0.92	7.03	30.0
1st Half		152	36	47	14	37	4	309			$12	403	625	1028	14	81	30	0.83	312	174	107		9.30	21.0
2nd Half		233	33	65	11	23	3	279			$8	346	468	814	9	87	28	0.77	296	116	56		5.72	9.7
04	Proj	450	73	125	23	64	9	278			$18	361	480	841	11	83	29	0.77	297	120	87		6.06	21.4

Played over his head in the 1st half, but the overall result was encouraging. There are worse things to be than a 28-year-old right-handed version of Bill Mueller.

Erstad,Darin

Pos CF | Age 29 Past Peak | Bats L
R Low | I CON | S pt | K
LIMA C | BA: 50%

Yr	Tm	AB	R	H	HR	RBI	SB	Avg	vL	vR	R$	OB	Slg	OPS	bb%	ct%	h%	Eye	xBA	PX	SX	G/F	RC/G	RAR
99	ANA	585	84	148	13	53	13	253	274	245	$9	309	374	683	7	83	29	0.47	259	73	114	1.65	3.86	-14.6
00	ANA	676	121	240	25	100	28	355	338	363	$41	411	541	952	9	88	38	0.78	325	110	123	1.61	8.76	71.5
01	ANA	631	89	163	9	63	24	258	204	283	$14	325	360	684	9	82	30	0.55	244	71	91	1.67	3.98	-16.4
02	ANA	625	99	177	10	73	23	283	280	285	$21	313	389	702	4	89	30	0.40	282	69	135	1.51	4.46	-5.7
03	ANA	258	35	65	4	17	9	252	302	227	$4	301	333	634	7	84	29	0.45	258	51	106	1.83	3.55	-9.0
1st Half		141	22	40	3	12	5	284			$4	331	362	693	7	89	30	0.63	266	45	84		4.36	-1.5
2nd Half		117	13	25	1	5	4	214			$0	264	299	563	6	79	26	0.33	248	58	117		2.72	-7.3
04	Proj	600	85	156	10	52	21	260			$13	308	358	666	6	85	29	0.45	264	63	118		3.89	-15.2

Continues to be the bane of fantasy owners everywhere. In his defense, he's an outstanding defensive replacement in sim formats...as long as his hammy holds up.

Escobar,Alex

Pos RF | Age 25 Pre-Peak | Bats R
R Very High | I EXP con | S pt stb | K age
LIMA C | BA: 35%

Yr	Tm	AB	R	H	HR	RBI	SB	Avg	vL	vR	R$	OB	Slg	OPS	bb%	ct%	h%	Eye	xBA	PX	SX	G/F	RC/G	RAR
99		0	0	0	0	0	0	0								0								
00	aa	437	68	114	13	58	21	261			$15	334	426	760	10	76	31	0.47	259	98	144		4.92	-1.3
01	NYM	* 447	54	109	13	56	18	244			$13	299	391	690	7	64	35	0.22	211	90	129	0.75	4.04	-20.2
02	CLE	0	0	0	0	0	0	0								0								
03	CLE	* 538	72	131	28	84	8	243	350	220	$16	282	446	728	5	71	29	0.18	241	118	80	1.38	4.21	-15.1
1st Half		293	34	64	11	44	4	218			$5	252	389	641	4	71	27	0.15	236	105	89		3.26	-17.0
2nd Half		245	38	67	17	40	4	273			$11	318	514	832	6	70	32	0.22	247	134	61		5.54	2.7
04	Proj	400	54	100	17	57	12	250			$13	301	434	734	7	69	32	0.23	236	109	106		4.43	-7.6

5-14-.273 in 99 AB at CLE. Good news: drew 7 walks in 76 September PAs. Bad news: 20 Ks during the same period. Development of power is a positive sign, but he's generally going in the wrong direction.

Estalella,Bobby

Pos CA | Age 29 Past Peak | Bats R
R Very High | I exp CON | S pt STB | K
LIMA D | BA: 30%

Yr	Tm	AB	R	H	HR	RBI	SB	Avg	vL	vR	R$	OB	Slg	OPS	bb%	ct%	h%	Eye	xBA	PX	SX	G/F	RC/G	RAR
99	aaa	386	46	80	13	49	3	207			$2	290	368	658	10	77	23	0.52	257	100	63	1.00	3.43	-7.0
00	SF	299	45	70	14	53	3	234	250	229	$7	357	468	825	16	69	29	0.62	233	141	100	0.72	5.63	14.7
01	2TM	* 290	33	60	11	39	0	207	222	190	$2	274	386	661	9	76	24	0.38	251	108	58	0.64	3.25	-4.0
02	COL	* 191	26	43	13	37	0	225	136	222	$6	302	508	810	10	76	23	0.46	284	182	29	0.46	4.93	4.8
03	COL	140	17	28	7	21	2	200	294	187	$2	296	400	696	12	61	27	0.35	190	123	53	0.69	3.84	-2.0
1st Half		92	13	21	5	18	1	228			$3	324	435	759	12	61	31	0.36	190	124	47		4.72	1.2
2nd Half		48	4	7	2	3	1	146			($1)	241	333	574	11	60	19	0.32	188	121	46		2.48	-2.9
04	Proj	250	33	55	12	43	1	220			$5	308	437	746	11	70	26	0.43	209	135	63		4.37	2.1

Had surgery on right elbow in August. Always good for a handful of homers, even in limited playing time, but a 61% contact rate won't do wonders for his Avg.

Estrada,Johnny

Pos CA | Age 27 Peak | Bats S
R High | I EXP con | S STB | K
LIMA D | BA: 60%

Yr	Tm	AB	R	H	HR	RBI	SB	Avg	vL	vR	R$	OB	Slg	OPS	bb%	ct%	h%	Eye	xBA	PX	SX	G/F	RC/G	RAR
99		0	0	0	0	0	0	0								0								
00	aa	356	32	92	9	32	1	258			$4	277	388	664	2	95	25	0.47	304	82	36		3.70	-3.8
01	PHI	* 429	38	106	8	52	0	247	218	230	$5	282	373	655	5	91	26	0.55	292	88	22	1.35	3.56	0.6
02	aaa	451	40	110	9	56	1	244			$6	282	364	646	5	89	26	0.47	277	85	36	1.60	3.47	-5.3
03	ATL	* 390	38	117	10	62	0	300	167	333	$13	345	446	791	6	92	31	0.84	294	102	17	1.17	5.61	14.1
1st Half		238	25	76	6	41	0	319			$10	367	475	842	7	92	33	1.00	302	111	18		6.53	14.2
2nd Half		152	13	41	4	21	0	270			$3	311	401	712	6	91	28	0.64	283	88	15		4.35	0.3
04	Proj	350	32	94	8	47	0	269			$7	307	401	709	5	91	28	0.63	292	92	25		4.30	2.1

0-2-.306 in 36 AB at ATL. Steadily developing patience and power while maintaining contact skills. Still not worth a staff ace straight up, but could be a solid regular as soon as next year.

Everett,Adam

Pos SS | Age 27 Peak | Bats R
R High | I EXP con | S pt stb | K
LIMA D | BA: 55%

Yr	Tm	AB	R	H	HR	RBI	SB	Avg	vL	vR	R$	OB	Slg	OPS	bb%	ct%	h%	Eye	xBA	PX	SX	G/F	RC/G	RAR
99	aa	338	48	83	8	38	18	246			$9	316	349	665	9	83	27	0.63	259	64	93		3.75	-1.0
00	aaa	453	71	105	5	32	11	232			$2	327	329	656	12	81	28	0.73	252	67	100		3.58	-4.9
01	aaa	444	59	103	5	34	21	232			$7	285	338	623	7	85	26	0.51	270	67	152		3.24	-9.9
02	HOU	* 433	56	108	2	26	14	249	261	169	$6	303	339	642	7	83	30	0.45	259	63	159	0.70	3.56	-4.3
03	HOU	* 487	71	122	9	59	11	251	324	240	$10	299	372	671	7	84	28	0.43	267	80	127	0.99	3.84	-3.9
1st Half		251	45	62	5	27	9	247			$6	292	378	671	6	82	28	0.36	270	88	148		3.80	-2.3
2nd Half		236	26	60	4	32	2	254			$4	307	364	671	7	85	29	0.50	262	72	86		3.88	-1.6
04	Proj	250	34	62	3	24	7	248			$4	302	357	659	7	84	28	0.48	264	71	134		3.71	-1.5

8-51-.256 in 387 AB at HOU. Added some pop without eroding his batting eye. Still not enough to make him useful in any Roto category other than SB.

Everett,Carl

Pos CF LF RF | Age 33 Decline | Bats S
R High | I con | S pt STB | K age
LIMA C+ | BA: 55%

Yr	Tm	AB	R	H	HR	RBI	SB	Avg	vL	vR	R$	OB	Slg	OPS	bb%	ct%	h%	Eye	xBA	PX	SX	G/F	RC/G	RAR
99	HOU	464	86	151	25	108	27	325	325	326	$34	391	571	962	10	80	37	0.53	290	150	120	1.00	8.42	51.5
00	BOS	496	82	149	34	108	11	300	348	283	$27	367	587	953	9	77	33	0.46	286	161	107	0.88	7.76	42.7
01	BOS	409	61	105	14	58	9	257	197	285	$11	303	438	740	6	75	31	0.26	264	111	124	1.13	4.57	-3.4
02	TEX	374	47	100	16	62	2	267	220	283	$12	327	439	765	8	79	30	0.43	244	102	38	1.01	4.85	0.9
03	2AL	526	93	151	28	92	8	287	254	299	$23	352	510	862	9	84	30	0.63	297	131	92	0.80	6.33	23.6
1st Half		270	53	74	18	51	4	274			$13	349	544	893	10	82	27	0.65	306	153	118		6.67	14.9
2nd Half		256	40	77	10	41	4	301			$11	356	473	829	8	86	32	0.61	286	107	60		5.96	8.7
04	Proj	500	79	141	21	86	8	282			$19	342	465	807	8	81	31	0.48	285	111	85		5.57	11.5

Reasons to bid very cautiously:
- Still struggling vs. lefties
- Walk rate, PX and SX regressed dramatically in 2nd half.

Febles,Carlos

Pos 2B | Age 27 Peak | Bats R
R Moderate | I exp CON | S pt | K
LIMA F | BA: 50%

Yr	Tm	AB	R	H	HR	RBI	SB	Avg	vL	vR	R$	OB	Slg	OPS	bb%	ct%	h%	Eye	xBA	PX	SX	G/F	RC/G	RAR
99	KC	453	71	116	10	53	20	256	278	250	$12	326	411	737	9	80	30	0.52	298	91	182	2.54	4.68	9.6
00	KC	339	59	87	2	29	17	257	272	251	$7	328	316	644	10	86	29	0.75	270	41	116	2.85	3.59	-2.8
01	KC	* 390	63	100	10	32	10	256	226	241	$8	308	390	698	7	82	29	0.42	263	81	115	1.92	4.08	-1.5
02	KC	* 405	52	97	5	30	18	240	229	250	$7	314	346	660	10	83	28	0.66	254	68	138	2.44	3.66	-4.7
03	KC	* 228	37	55	0	16	8	241	333	188	$2	288	281	569	6	85	28	0.43	234	34	105	1.98	2.79	-9.3
1st Half		129	15	31	0	10	6	240			$2	269	271	540	4	85	28	0.26	231	27	97		2.68	-5.6
2nd Half		99	22	24	0	6	2	242			$0	312	293	605	9	84	29	0.63	238	44	98		2.93	-3.7
04	Proj	250	41	61	2	19	9	244			$3	304	321	625	8	84	28	0.53	240	54	112		3.31	-6.0

0-11-.235 in 196 AB at KC. Still hasn't developed into the on-base machine that many expected him to be. Power has been MIA since 2001, and he won't be able to elevate his Avg or OB unless it returns.

AL MELCHIOR

Feliz,Pedro

Pos 3B
Age 29 Past Peak
Bats R

RISK		
R	X HIGH	
I	exp	CON
S	PT	stb
K		

LIMA F BA: 55%

Yr	Tm	AB	R	H	HR	RBI	SB	Avg	vL	vR	R$	OB	Slg	OPS	bb%	ct%	h%	Eye	xBA	PX	SX	G/F	RC/G	RAR
99	aa	491	49	115	12	73	4	234			$6	261	373	634	4	81	27	0.20	264	84	95		3.22	-17.4
00	aaa	503	64	129	24	80	1	256			$12	288	463	751	4	86	26	0.31	303	123	48		4.54	2.6
01	SF	220	23	50	7	22	2	227	397	167	$2	261	373	634	4	77	26	0.20	240	87	74	1.12	3.18	-9.4
02	SF	146	14	37	2	13	0	253	184	289	$1	283	336	619	4	82	30	0.22	235	54	55	1.14	3.24	-5.8
03	SF	235	31	58	16	48	2	247	231	251	$9	278	515	792	4	77	25	0.19	296	152	110	1.26	4.69	3.0
1st Half		109	19	28	8	25	0	257			$5	296	541	837	5	78	26	0.25	303	164	96		5.26	3.3
2nd Half		126	12	30	8	23	2	238			$4	262	492	754	3	77	25	0.14	289	142	117		4.21	-0.2
04	**Proj**	**250**	**29**	**61**	**11**	**38**	**2**	**244**			**$6**	**274**	**433**	**707**	**4**	**79**	**27**	**0.20**	**287**	**110**	**82**		**3.93**	**-3.4**

Happy Pedro hacked his way to a career-high 16 HR in just 235 AB. 2nd half decline demonstrates how you can't sustain productivity with a sub-0.20 batting eye.

Fick,Robert

Pos 1B
Age 30 Past Peak
Bats L

RISK		
R	High	
I		con
S	PT	stb
K		

LIMA C+ BA: 65%

Yr	Tm	AB	R	H	HR	RBI	SB	Avg	vL	vR	R$	OB	Slg	OPS	bb%	ct%	h%	Eye	xBA	PX	SX	G/F	RC/G	RAR
99	DET	* 89	16	22	4	16	1	247			$2	350	382	732	14	85	25	1.08	261	67	56	0.58	4.40	-3.7
00	DET	* 231	22	50	4	28	3	216	194	265	$0	298	338	636	10	79	26	0.56	251	76	86	0.79	3.29	-19.0
01	DET	401	62	109	19	61	0	272	237	280	$12	336	476	813	9	85	28	0.63	289	121	48	0.97	5.44	-8.1
02	DET	556	66	150	17	63	0	270	281	265	$12	326	433	759	8	84	30	0.51	273	106	39	0.94	4.89	-15.5
03	ATL	409	52	110	11	80	1	269	135	289	$12	337	418	755	9	89	28	0.89	302	101	50	0.86	4.93	-6.8
1st Half		204	28	64	7	44	1	314			$10	372	500	872	9	91	32	1.00	325	128	42		6.95	7.9
2nd Half		205	24	46	4	36	0	224			$2	303	337	639	10	86	24	0.82	278	74	48		3.35	-13.5
04	**Proj**	**500**	**62**	**130**	**15**	**80**	**1**	**260**			**$12**	**327**	**416**	**742**	**9**	**86**	**28**	**0.69**	**299**	**103**	**54**		**4.66**	**-14.1**

Track record doesn't show much hope for much improvement over mediocre '03 stats. Since he lacks above-average power and speed, he's reliant on free passes to keep his OB respectable.

Figgins,Chone

Pos CF
Age 26 Pre-Peak
Bats S

RISK		
R	High	
I	EXP	con
S		stb
K		

LIMA D+ BA: 50%

Yr	Tm	AB	R	H	HR	RBI	SB	Avg	vL	vR	R$	OB	Slg	OPS	bb%	ct%	h%	Eye	xBA	PX	SX	G/F	RC/G	RAR
99		0	0	0	0	0	0	0								0								
00		0	0	0	0	0	0	0								0								
01	aa	470	47	95	2	28	26	202			$3	266	283	549	8	84	24	0.54	257	56	133		2.36	-30.3
02	aaa	511	77	136	6	47	30	266			$17	319	380	699	7	88	29	0.65	277	73	173		4.20	-9.4
03	ANA	* 525	78	149	3	51	26	284	284	303	$16	338	392	730	8	87	32	0.65	267	67	180	1.55	4.51	-3.5
1st Half		265	44	73	2	24	15	275			$8	326	396	723	7	91	30	0.80	281	71	207		4.38	-2.8
2nd Half		260	34	76	1	27	11	292			$8	350	388	738	8	84	34	0.56	253	63	147		4.65	-0.7
04	**Proj**	**250**	**35**	**67**	**2**	**23**	**13**	**268**			**$7**	**324**	**374**	**698**	**8**	**87**	**30**	**0.62**	**267**	**67**	**164**		**4.10**	**-4.9**

0-27-.296 in 240 AB at ANA. Take Juan Pierre, add a touch more power and some extra K's and you have something close to Figgins. While he doesn't yet have Pierre's résumé, he'll come much cheaper.

Finley,Steve

Pos CF
Age 38 Decline
Bats L

RISK		
R	Low	
I		con
S		
K	AGE	

LIMA B+ BA: 55%

Yr	Tm	AB	R	H	HR	RBI	SB	Avg	vL	vR	R$	OB	Slg	OPS	bb%	ct%	h%	Eye	xBA	PX	SX	G/F	RC/G	RAR
99	ARI	590	100	156	34	103	8	264	259	267	$21	335	525	861	10	84	26	0.67	307	150	131	1.04	6.03	29.5
00	ARI	539	100	151	35	96	12	280	274	283	$25	358	544	901	11	84	28	0.75	297	147	111	1.03	6.74	37.3
01	ARI	495	66	136	14	73	11	275	235	285	$16	338	430	768	9	86	29	0.70	264	96	99	1.06	4.96	15.9
02	ARI	505	82	145	25	89	16	287	297	282	$27	368	499	867	11	86	29	0.89	296	131	115	1.13	6.60	24.7
03	ARI	516	82	148	22	70	15	287	245	306	$22	358	500	858	10	82	32	0.61	297	126	157	1.18	6.21	18.1
1st Half		237	43	70	10	34	5	295			$10	379	506	886	12	78	34	0.62	283	126	143		6.78	12.0
2nd Half		279	39	78	12	36	10	280			$12	339	495	833	8	85	29	0.60	309	125	162		5.73	6.0
04	**Proj**	**500**	**78**	**142**	**22**	**76**	**14**	**284**			**$22**	**356**	**492**	**848**	**10**	**84**	**30**	**0.69**	**300**	**124**	**133**		**6.12**	**20.0**

BPIs don't show any sign of imminent decline, though the dip in his Avg vs. lefties is something to watch.

Flaherty,John

Pos CA
Age 36 Decline
Bats R

RISK		
R	High	
I		con
S	pt	stb
K	AGE	

LIMA F BA: 45%

Yr	Tm	AB	R	H	HR	RBI	SB	Avg	vL	vR	R$	OB	Slg	OPS	bb%	ct%	h%	Eye	xBA	PX	SX	G/F	RC/G	RAR
99	TAM	446	53	124	14	71	0	278	175	301	$11	308	415	722	4	86	30	0.30	263	83	28	1.11	4.42	4.4
00	TAM	394	36	103	10	39	0	261	270	259	$4	297	376	673	5	86	28	0.35	256	69		0.89	3.85	-3.4
01	TAM	248	20	59	4	29	1	238	286	230	$2	267	363	630	4	87	26	0.30	252	87	50	0.83	3.27	-4.4
02	TAM	281	27	73	4	33	2	260	250	262	$4	297	374	671	5	82	30	0.30	243	83	45	0.63	3.74	1.0
03	NYY	105	16	28	4	14	0	267	297	250	$2	294	457	751	4	82	29	0.21	266	124	43	0.82	4.67	1.7
1st Half		56	9	15	1	5	0	268			$1	293	393	686	3	86	30	0.25	256	89	52		4.01	-0.1
2nd Half		49	7	13	3	9	0	265			$2	294	531	825	4	78	29	0.18	272	165			5.42	1.9
04	**Proj**	**100**	**11**	**26**	**2**	**11**	**0**	**260**			**$1**	**291**	**378**	**668**	**4**	**85**	**29**	**0.29**	**258**	**81**	**41**		**3.76**	**-0.5**

Hit .313/.353/.604 on the road in 48 AB. Ah, the beauty of small sample sizes. At this point in his career, those sample sizes will just keep getting smaller.

Floyd,Cliff

Pos LF
Age 31 Past Peak
Bats L

RISK		
R	Moderate	
I		
S	PT	stb
K		

LIMA B BA: 50%

Yr	Tm	AB	R	H	HR	RBI	SB	Avg	vL	vR	R$	OB	Slg	OPS	bb%	ct%	h%	Eye	xBA	PX	SX	G/F	RC/G	RAR
99	FLA	251	37	76	11	49	5	303	305	302	$12	377	518	895	11	81	34	0.64	313	137	66	1.44	6.66	11.4
00	FLA	420	75	126	22	91	24	300	333	286	$27	374	529	903	11	80	33	0.61	277	139	100	0.90	7.43	25.8
01	FLA	555	123	176	31	103	18	317	311	319	$35	383	578	961	10	82	34	0.58	303	158	136	0.91	8.35	39.7
02	2TM	520	86	150	28	79	15	288	247	306	$26	379	533	912	13	80	32	0.72	313	159	77	1.18	7.19	23.3
03	NYM	365	57	106	18	68	3	290	262	305	$16	377	518	895	12	82	31	0.77	286	143	78	0.86	7.08	15.2
1st Half		257	38	70	14	43	0	272			$9	366	521	888	13	81	29	0.78	286	158	39		6.69	8.1
2nd Half		108	19	36	4	25	3	333			$7	405	509	914	11	84	37	0.76	277	108	107		8.12	7.2
04	**Proj**	**500**	**87**	**152**	**24**	**95**	**12**	**304**			**$27**	**384**	**528**	**912**	**12**	**82**	**33**	**0.71**	**287**	**142**	**97**		**7.48**	**23.7**

Missed significant time due to injury for the first time in three years. Has been a model of consistency when healthy. He should pick up where he left off when he returns in the spring.

Fordyce,Brook

Pos CA
Age 33 Decline
Bats R

RISK		
R	High	
I		CON
S	pt	stb
K	age	

LIMA F BA: 55%

Yr	Tm	AB	R	H	HR	RBI	SB	Avg	vL	vR	R$	OB	Slg	OPS	bb%	ct%	h%	Eye	xBA	PX	SX	G/F	RC/G	RAR
99	2TM	333	36	99	9	49	2	297	333	283	$10	339	459	798	6	86	33	0.44	309	108	54	1.45	5.69	15.4
00	2AL	302	41	91	14	49	0	301	347	287	$11	339	507	845	5	83	32	0.34	275	120	39	0.85	6.26	17.5
01	BAL	292	30	61	5	19	1	209	282	186	($2)	262	322	584	7	81	24	0.38	242	79	42	1.21	2.64	-11.1
02	BAL	130	7	30	1	8	1	231	103	267	($0)	281	315	596	6	85	26	0.47	250	65	30	2.07	2.97	-2.5
03	BAL	348	28	95	6	31	2	273	345	250	$6	311	371	681	5	87	30	0.43	285	61	51	1.42	3.92	-1.7
1st Half		131	10	35	1	6	1	267			$1	304	328	633	5	84	31	0.33	236	45	35		3.40	-2.6
2nd Half		217	18	60	5	25	1	276			$5	314	396	711	5	89	29	0.52	300	71	60		4.24	0.9
04	**Proj**	**250**	**20**	**64**	**4**	**21**	**1**	**256**			**$3**	**299**	**362**	**661**	**6**	**86**	**29**	**0.42**	**258**	**70**	**48**		**3.65**	**-2.1**

Best season since 2000 was supported by an improved contact rate. At 33, this is as good as it gets and there are plenty of replacement-level catchers out there. Pass.

Ford,Lew

Pos CF
Age 27 Peak
Bats R

RISK		
R	Very High	
I	EXP	con
S	pt	stb
K		

LIMA F BA: 50%

Yr	Tm	AB	R	H	HR	RBI	SB	Avg	vL	vR	R$	OB	Slg	OPS	bb%	ct%	h%	Eye	xBA	PX	SX	G/F	RC/G	RAR
99		0	0	0	0	0	0	0								0								
00		0	0	0	0	0	0	0								0								
01	aa	252	27	50	6	23	5	198			$0	252	325	577	7	85	21	0.46	267	74	111		2.44	-15.5
02	a/a	566	85	147	14	52	20	260			$16	312	403	715	7	89	27	0.70	291	96	119		4.33	-8.2
03	MIN	* 284	45	82	5	42	6	289	329	361	$9	329	447	776	6	87	32	0.47	293	110	115	1.27	5.01	2.2
1st Half		215	32	65	4	31	4	302			$8	339	460	800	5	89	33	0.50	297	109	101		5.39	3.9
2nd Half		69	13	17	1	11	2	246			$2	297	406	703	7	83	29	0.42	279	111	154		3.97	-1.6
04	**Proj**	**150**	**23**	**38**	**3**	**18**	**4**	**253**			**$3**	**302**	**394**	**697**	**7**	**86**	**28**	**0.52**	**287**	**94**	**109**		**3.96**	**-3.6**

3-15-.329 in 73 AB at MIN. With a better walk rate, he could be a good leadoff hitter. Unfortunately, his walk rate declined in '03, and that next step up may never happen.

Fox,Andy

Pos 2B
Age 33 Decline
Bats L

RISK		
R	Very High	
I		CON
S	PT	stb
K	age	

LIMA D BA: 50%

Yr	Tm	AB	R	H	HR	RBI	SB	Avg	vL	vR	R$	OB	Slg	OPS	bb%	ct%	h%	Eye	xBA	PX	SX	G/F	RC/G	RAR
99	ARI	274	34	70	6	33	4	255	152	276	$4	336	380	715	11	78	31	0.54	236	78	85	1.26	4.39	1.4
00	2NL	250	29	58	4	20	10	232	250	230	$3	294	328	622	8	79	28	0.42	226	58	112	1.62	3.18	-9.1
01	FLA	* 123	14	29	4	12	2	236		195	$2	329	382	711	12	85	25	0.89	270	77	111	1.57	4.15	1.1
02	FLA	435	55	109	4	41	31	251	148	277	$14	326	333	660	10	78	31	0.52	241	55	152	1.43	3.87	-7.1
03	FLA	108	12	21	0	8	1	194	364	175	($2)	243	259	503	6	73	27	0.24	226	50	109	2.00	1.85	-8.9
1st Half		67	8	14	0	5	1	209			($1)	264	299	562	7	67	31	0.23	218	67	145		2.25	-4.7
2nd Half		41	4	7	0	3	0	171			($1)	209	195	404	5	83	21	0.29	234	22	47		1.26	-4.2
04	**Proj**	**250**	**30**	**58**	**4**	**22**	**8**	**232**			**$3**	**305**	**336**	**640**	**9**	**77**	**29**	**0.45**	**236**	**66**	**125**		**3.31**	**-7.7**

Season's highlight: Spared from wearing "A. Fox" on his uniform upon FLA's acquisition of Chad Fox. A bad year, and now has little chance of regaining a regular role.

AL MELCHIOR

Franco,Julio

Pos 1B | Age 45 Decline | Bats R

R	X HIGH	
I		CON
S	PT	STB
K	AGE	

LIMA F | BA: 40%

Yr	Tm	AB	R	H	HR	RBI	SB	Avg	vL	vR	R$	OB	Slg	OPS	bb%	ct%	h%	Eye	xBA	PX	SX	G/F	RC/G	RAR
99	MEX	326	86	129	8	73	0	395			$21	494	597	1091	16	87	44	1.46	307	121	146		12.42	53.2
00	KOR	477	76	145	13	90	0	305			$16	374	440	813	10	77	37	0.48	248	85	32		6.02	4.9
01	MEX	497	103	205	21	101	15	412	400	262	$43	476	636	1112	11	85	46	0.79	305	138	113		12.90	78.3
02	ATL	* 338	51	96	6	30	5	284	382	256	$9	358	382	740	10	78	35	0.52	318	67	83	1.61	4.91	-6.5
03	ATL	197	28	58	5	31	0	294	351	243	$6	374	447	821	11	78	36	0.58	289	99	74	2.74	5.92	2.2
1st Half		107	14	31	1	15	0	290			$2	367	402	769	11	79	36	0.57	279	81	67		5.29	-0.7
2nd Half		90	14	27	4	16	0	300			$4	382	500	882	12	78	35	0.60	300	119	83		6.68	2.9
04	**Proj**	**100**	**14**	**32**	**3**	**15**	**0**	**320**			**$4**	**396**	**476**	**872**	**11**	**79**	**38**	**0.61**	**292**	**98**	**77**		**6.95**	**3.6**

Can still get on-base and even took his power game up a notch over last year. Of course, he's repeated this level several times and is playing against much younger prospects.

Franco,Matt

Pos 1B | Age 34 Decline | Bats L

R	X HIGH	
I	exp	CON
S	PT	stb
K	age	

LIMA F | BA: 45%

Yr	Tm	AB	R	H	HR	RBI	SB	Avg	vL	vR	R$	OB	Slg	OPS	bb%	ct%	h%	Eye	xBA	PX	SX	G/F	RC/G	RAR
99	NYM	132	18	31	4	21	0	235		248	$1	369	364	732	18	84	25	1.33	248	79	21	1.68	4.47	-3.3
00	NYM	* 185	11	38	2	15	0	205	200	242	($2)	293	265	558	11	83	24	0.74	246	39		1.12	2.49	-16.4
01	aaa	433	41	89	6	39	5	206			($1)	276	303	578	9	82	24	0.54	250	67	66		2.68	-47.8
02	ATL	* 378	44	106	11	53	2	280	333	317	$12	346	452	799	9	87	30	0.78	293	115	85	1.61	5.58	-0.1
03	ATL	134	11	33	3	15	0	246	333	240	$1	303	358	662	8	81	29	0.42	227	75	22	1.65	3.56	-7.8
1st Half		74	7	23	2	8	0	311			$2	346	446	792	5	86	34	0.40	252	91	26		5.39	-0.2
2nd Half		60	4	10	1	7	0	167			($1)	254	250	504	10	73	21	0.44	198	56	14		1.94	-7.0
04	**Proj**	**150**	**14**	**35**	**3**	**18**	**0**	**233**			**$1**	**304**	**345**	**650**	**9**	**82**	**27**	**0.56**	**230**	**76**	**30**		**3.46**	**-9.8**

Unlike the elder Franco, Matt has experienced a steady decline in his BPIs. Walk rate is still acceptable, but his Avg isn't high enough to make him draftable.

Freel,Ryan

Pos CF | Age 28 Peak | Bats R

R	Very High	
I	EXP	con
S	pt	stb
K		

LIMA D | BA: 60%

Yr	Tm	AB	R	H	HR	RBI	SB	Avg	vL	vR	R$	OB	Slg	OPS	bb%	ct%	h%	Eye	xBA	PX	SX	G/F	RC/G	RAR
99	a/a	123	19	32	1	16	11	260			$5	331	382	713	10	89	28	1.00	295	83	159		4.00	-1.9
00	a/a	327	59	86	8	30	26	263			$13	332	413	745	9	88	28	0.87	294	90	156		4.50	0.1
01	aaa	341	51	83	4	31	21	243			$9	316	355	670	10	89	27	0.92	283	78	121	1.33	3.60	-7.9
02	aaa	448	54	107	7	41	31	239			$13	288	359	647	6	90	25	0.67	286	83	140		3.42	-19.4
03	CIN	* 352	52	92	7	22	28	261	326	266	$13	310	378	688	7	89	28	0.64	283	77	135	1.64	3.93	-11.2
1st Half		159	25	43	2	9	11	270			$5	329	371	701	8	92	28	1.17	290	70	130		4.35	-2.9
2nd Half		193	27	49	5	13	17	254			$8	294	383	678	5	86	27	0.41	277	82	134		3.56	-8.4
04	**Proj**	**150**	**21**	**38**	**3**	**12**	**11**	**253**			**$5**	**308**	**373**	**680**	**7**	**89**	**27**	**0.70**	**284**	**81**	**131**		**3.78**	**-4.3**

4-12-.285 in 137 AB at CIN. Had a nice late-season run after coming off the DL, but he's a long shot to become more than a 4th OF. Still has some value in deeper leagues as a SB threat.

Fullmer,Brad

Pos DH | Age 29 Past Peak | Bats L

R	Moderate	
I		con
S	pt	stb
K		

LIMA C+ | BA: 55%

Yr	Tm	AB	R	H	HR	RBI	SB	Avg	vL	vR	R$	OB	Slg	OPS	bb%	ct%	h%	Eye	xBA	PX	SX	G/F	RC/G	RAR
99	MON	* 489	65	138	18	75	4	282	240	283	$15	328	489	816	6	90	28	0.67	319	137	62	1.18	5.49	4.2
00	TOR	482	76	142	32	104	3	295	226	311	$23	336	558	894	6	86	29	0.44	311	149	63	0.93	6.76	22.4
01	TOR	522	71	143	18	83	5	274	202	295	$16	323	444	768	7	83	30	0.43	267	107	72	0.87	5.02	-3.2
02	ANA	429	75	124	19	59	10	289	222	301	$18	338	531	870	7	90	29	0.73	315	150	141	0.70	6.42	10.7
03	ANA	206	32	63	9	35	5	306	267	313	$10	384	500	884	11	85	33	0.84	299	113	95	1.09	6.72	12.1
1st Half		206	32	63	9	35	5	306			$10	384	500	884	11	85	33	0.84	299	113	95		6.72	12.1
2nd Half		0	0	0	0	0	0	0			($0)					0			0					
04	**Proj**	**450**	**69**	**131**	**20**	**75**	**7**	**291**			**$19**	**348**	**499**	**847**	**8**	**86**	**30**	**0.63**	**306**	**127**	**89**		**6.12**	**14.3**

Was having a whale of a season before going down with a torn patella tendon in June. If he can couple power skills with his newfound batting eye, this projection could be conservative.

Furcal,Rafael

Pos SS | Age 26 Pre-Peak | Bats S

R	Moderate	
I		con
S	pt	
K		

LIMA B | BA: 60%

Yr	Tm	AB	R	H	HR	RBI	SB	Avg	vL	vR	R$	OB	Slg	OPS	bb%	ct%	h%	Eye	xBA	PX	SX	G/F	RC/G	RAR
99		0	0	0	0	0	0	0								0								
00	ATL	455	87	134	4	37	40	295	250	306	$21	392	382	774	14	82	35	0.91	270	58	137	2.24	5.45	26.2
01	ATL	324	39	89	4	30	22	275	349	249	$12	325	370	695	7	83	32	0.43	259	69	100	1.82	4.30	7.0
02	ATL	636	95	175	8	47	27	275	288	272	$18	321	387	708	6	82	32	0.38	279	77	147	1.76	4.18	5.2
03	ATL	664	130	194	15	61	25	292	247	306	$24	351	443	794	8	89	31	0.79	317	96	174	1.68	5.79	31.0
1st Half		327	63	96	10	28	14	294			$13	357	489	846	9	88	31	0.82	332	119	203		6.52	21.9
2nd Half		337	67	98	5	33	11	291			$11	345	398	743	8	89	32	0.76	300	74	133		5.10	9.3
04	**Proj**	**650**	**112**	**192**	**11**	**57**	**29**	**295**			**$24**	**353**	**417**	**770**	**8**	**85**	**33**	**0.61**	**305**	**81**	**145**		**5.34**	**26.2**

Nice comeback year. Power trailed off in the 2nd half, but the rebound in ct% and batting eye lasted all season. Looks like one of the best NL shortstops after all.

Galarraga,Andres

Pos 1B | Age 42 Decline | Bats R

R	Very High	
I		CON
S	pt	STB
K	AGE	

LIMA F | BA: 35%

Yr	Tm	AB	R	H	HR	RBI	SB	Avg	vL	vR	R$	OB	Slg	OPS	bb%	ct%	h%	Eye	xBA	PX	SX	G/F	RC/G	RAR
99	ATL	0	0	0	0	0	0	0								0			0					
00	ATL	494	67	149	28	100	3	302	347	287	$24	349	526	875	7	74	36	0.29	285	129	44	1.41	6.47	15.5
01	2TM	399	50	102	17	69	1	256	268	251	$11	309	459	768	7	71	32	0.26	229	127	45	1.00	4.72	-17.4
02	MON	292	30	76	9	40	2	260	294	246	$7	329	394	723	9	72	33	0.37	219	88	36	1.45	4.39	-10.4
03	SF	272	36	82	12	42	1	301	309	298	$11	347	489	836	7	78	35	0.31	310	118	35	1.41	5.94	3.3
1st Half		116	15	37	6	20	0	319			$6	363	534	897	6	78	37	0.31	320	135	28		6.77	4.0
2nd Half		156	21	45	6	22	1	288			$6	335	455	790	7	78	34	0.31	304	106	46		5.37	-0.6
04	**Proj**	**200**	**25**	**57**	**8**	**31**	**1**	**285**			**$7**	**338**	**465**	**803**	**7**	**75**	**34**	**0.32**	**305**	**114**	**36**		**5.42**	**-1.2**

Not out of juice just yet. Still an inspiration at 42, but less risky fantasy options abound.

Garciaparra,Nomar

Pos SS | Age 30 Past Peak | Bats R

R	Low	
I		con
S	pt	
K		

LIMA C | BA: 60%

Yr	Tm	AB	R	H	HR	RBI	SB	Avg	vL	vR	R$	OB	Slg	OPS	bb%	ct%	h%	Eye	xBA	PX	SX	G/F	RC/G	RAR
99	BOS	532	103	190	27	104	14	357	400	346	$35	413	603	1017	9	93	35	1.31	359	150	112	1.16	9.92	77.8
00	BOS	529	104	197	21	96	5	372	383	369	$31	437	599	1037	10	91	38	1.22	359	143	83	1.17	10.59	80.9
01	BOS	* 99	16	31	5	11	0	313	313	284	$4	364	515	880	7	89	31	0.73	297	120	36	0.87	6.69	6.3
02	BOS	635	101	197	24	120	5	310	305	311	$29	352	528	880	6	90	32	0.65	312	141	93	0.71	6.83	38.9
03	BOS	658	120	198	28	105	19	301	357	281	$31	340	524	864	6	91	30	0.64	303	131	169	0.71	6.49	37.6
1st Half		337	70	114	12	56	8	338			$19	374	585	958	5	92	34	0.73	339	145	214		8.30	34.3
2nd Half		321	50	84	16	49	11	262			$13	305	461	766	6	89	25	0.57	285	117	105		4.92	4.6
04	**Proj**	**650**	**115**	**205**	**30**	**112**	**14**	**315**			**$33**	**362**	**548**	**910**	**7**	**91**	**31**	**0.77**	**328**	**141**	**129**		**7.37**	**51.5**

Steady as ever. Even the apparent three-year dip in walk rate is mostly an artifact of 20 intentional walks in 2000.

Garcia,Danny

Pos 2B | Age 23 Growth | Bats R

R	Moderate	
I	EXP	
S		
K	AGE	

LIMA F | BA: 55%

Yr	Tm	AB	R	H	HR	RBI	SB	Avg	vL	vR	R$	OB	Slg	OPS	bb%	ct%	h%	Eye	xBA	PX	SX	G/F	RC/G	RAR
99		0	0	0	0	0	0	0								0								
00		0	0	0	0	0	0	0								0								
01		0	0	0	0	0	0	0								0								
02		0	0	0	0	0	0	0								0								
03	NYM	* 561	63	138	8	72	11	246	333	158	$10	283	358	641	5	85	28	0.35	270	80	103	2.08	3.45	-16.1
1st Half		280	36	77	3	39	7	275			$8	319	386	705	6	86	31	0.47	275	84	95		4.34	-0.5
2nd Half		281	27	61	5	33	4	217			$2	247	331	578	4	84	24	0.25	264	76	98		2.67	-15.0
04	**Proj**	**150**	**16**	**36**	**2**	**19**	**3**	**240**			**$2**	**276**	**352**	**627**	**5**	**85**	**27**	**0.33**	**269**	**77**	**95**		**3.27**	**-4.7**

2-6-.214 in 56 AB at NYM. Showed moderate pop at AAA and in the bigs, but needs to develop his batting eye. At 22, there is still time. Won't help much in '04, but he's a worthy keeper pick.

Garcia,Karim

Pos RF | Age 28 Peak | Bats L

R	Very High	
I	EXP	con
S	pt	STB
K		

LIMA D | BA: 40%

Yr	Tm	AB	R	H	HR	RBI	SB	Avg	vL	vR	R$	OB	Slg	OPS	bb%	ct%	h%	Eye	xBA	PX	SX	G/F	RC/G	RAR
99	DET	288	38	69	14	32	2	240			$5	289	441	730	6	77	27	0.30	252	111	98	1.02	4.24	-6.3
00	aaa	425	55	107	19	73	4	252			$11	310	447	757	8	82	27	0.47	284	114	67		4.54	-6.2
01	aaa	507	71	129	34	83	4	254			$18	311	503	814	8	79	26	0.40	282	137	70	1.15	5.22	-0.7
02	CLE	* 581	83	167	31	115	1	287	278	308	$25	325	511	836	5	83	30	0.32	288	130	57	1.14	5.56	9.0
03	2AL	* 304	30	78	11	41	2	257	164	291	$7	294	405	698	5	77	30	0.23	244	90	36	1.08	3.93	-11.0
1st Half		163	15	37	6	22	2	227			$3	263	380	644	5	75	26	0.20	241	94	46		3.16	-10.0
2nd Half		141	15	41	5	19	0	291			$4	329	433	761	5	79	34	0.28	248	85	24		4.96	-0.7
04	**Proj**	**300**	**36**	**80**	**14**	**47**	**1**	**267**			**$9**	**309**	**452**	**760**	**6**	**79**	**29**	**0.30**	**253**	**107**	**50**		**4.65**	**-3.6**

11-35-.262 in 244 AB at NYY. BPIs tumbled from career year. Track record suggests a rebound, though another season like '02 is unlikely.

AL MELCHIOR

Gerut,Jody

Pos RF LF | Age 26 Pre-Peak | Bats L
R: Very High | I: EXP con | S: pt stb | K:
LIMA B+ | BA: 60%

	AB	R	H	HR	RBI	SB	Avg	vL	vR	R$	OB	Slg	OPS	bb%	ct%	h%	Eye	xBA	PX	SX	G/F	RC/G	RAR
99	0	0	0	0	0	0	0								0								
00 aa	362	41	101	3	49	16	279			$11	390	401	791	15	87	31	1.43	287	89	82		5.20	1.9
01	0	0	0	0	0	0	0								0								
02 a/a	439	65	120	10	51	17	273			$15	346	401	747	10	89	29	1.02	281	83	104		4.55	-7.9
03 CLE	* 545	78	150	27	91	8	275	209	306	$21	331	501	831	8	85	28	0.56	304	140	76	1.13	5.69	8.5
1st Half	247	38	67	13	47	5	271			$11	336	522	858	9	85	27	0.67	317	158	84		6.06	6.5
2nd Half	298	40	83	14	44	3	279			$11	326	483	809	7	85	29	0.48	293	124	62		5.39	2.1
04 Proj	**500**	**70**	**138**	**17**	**72**	**14**	**276**			**$18**	**346**	**452**	**797**	**10**	**87**	**29**	**0.82**	**298**	**110**	**89**		**5.24**	**2.5**

22-75-4-.275 in 480 AB at CLE. Four reasons why he won't repeat HR numbers or R$:
1. Can't hit LHPs;
2. Drop in Eye, OBP, bb%, ct%;
3. Previous HR high was 10;
4. PX unsupported by G/F ratio.

Giambi,Jason

Pos 1B DH | Age 33 Decline | Bats L
R: Moderate | I: CON | S: stb | K: age
LIMA B+ | BA: 55%

	AB	R	H	HR	RBI	SB	Avg	vL	vR	R$	OB	Slg	OPS	bb%	ct%	h%	Eye	xBA	PX	SX	G/F	RC/G	RAR
99 OAK	575	115	181	33	123	1	315	282	330	$28	421	553	974	15	82	34	0.99	298	141	46	0.84	8.62	43.9
00 OAK	510	108	170	43	137	2	333	324	349	$35	474	647	1122	21	81	34	1.43	295	173	49	0.71	11.78	77.8
01 OAK	520	109	178	38	120	2	342	333	347	$36	473	660	1133	20	84	35	1.55	327	192	55	0.74	12.14	80.4
02 NYY	560	120	176	41	122	2	314	299	320	$34	426	598	1024	16	80	33	0.97	302	165	51	0.70	9.39	53.5
03 NYY	535	97	134	41	107	2	250	192	272	$22	396	527	923	19	74	26	0.92	253	158	37	0.52	7.09	26.9
1st Half	277	52	75	22	63	1	271			$14	414	545	960	20	76	28	1.01	257	153	34		7.93	20.2
2nd Half	258	45	59	19	44	1	229			$8	376	508	884	19	72	24	0.84	248	163	34		6.26	6.9
04 Proj	**550**	**108**	**157**	**41**	**115**	**2**	**285**			**$28**	**418**	**572**	**990**	**19**	**77**	**30**	**1.01**	**262**	**166**	**47**		**8.51**	**44.0**

Sore knee and staph infections in eyes affected performance. But can injuries be blamed completely for the drop in BA, inability to hit LHPs, drop in ct% and Eye, and a drop in PX despite extreme FB tendencies?

Giambi,Jeremy

Pos DH | Age 29 Past Peak | Bats L
R: Very High | I: exp con | S: PT STB | K:
LIMA D | BA: 45%

	AB	R	H	HR	RBI	SB	Avg	vL	vR	R$	OB	Slg	OPS	bb%	ct%	h%	Eye	xBA	PX	SX	G/F	RC/G	RAR
99 KC	* 415	60	122	13	57	1	294	292	283	$11	390	441	831	14	78	35	0.72	251	88	54	1.50	6.17	11.2
00 OAK	260	42	66	10	50	0	254	266	250	$6	336	423	759	11	77	30	0.52	242	95	69	1.06	4.85	-1.8
01 OAK	* 398	65	113	12	58	0	284	250	291	$11	383	442	825	14	78	34	0.73	251	104	29	1.08	5.98	8.4
02 2TM	313	58	81	20	45	0	259	286	251	$11	408	505	913	20	70	31	0.84	257	149	26	0.89	7.01	13.6
03 BOS	* 162	20	32	6	18	1	198	125	214	$0	326	364	691	16	65	26	0.55	214	105	38	0.83	3.81	-4.1
1st Half	110	13	19	5	13	0	173			($0)	321	355	675	18	67	20	0.67	222	109	16		3.51	-4.0
2nd Half	52	7	13	1	5	1	250			$1	339	385	724	12	62	39	0.35	198	96	54		4.55	-0.1
04 Proj	**350**	**53**	**85**	**14**	**44**	**2**	**243**			**$6**	**361**	**419**	**781**	**16**	**69**	**31**	**0.59**	**222**	**111**	**46**		**5.12**	**1.3**

5-15-1-.197 in 127 AB at BOS. Still searching for a 400 AB season. Shoulder problems surely contributed to lost year, but don't explain everything. Time is running out for him to prove he's an everyday player.

Gibbons,Jay

Pos RF | Age 27 Peak | Bats L
R: Moderate | I: exp | S: PT stb | K:
LIMA D+ | BA: 60%

	AB	R	H	HR	RBI	SB	Avg	vL	vR	R$	OB	Slg	OPS	bb%	ct%	h%	Eye	xBA	PX	SX	G/F	RC/G	RAR
99	0	0	0	0	0	0	0								0								
00 aa	474	64	134	15	57	2	283			$11	346	458	804	9	89	29	0.87	306	113	52		5.61	7.8
01 BAL	225	27	53	15	36	0	236	370	217	$6	289	480	769	7	83	22	0.44	279	139	22	0.99	4.54	-3.0
02 BAL	490	71	121	28	69	1	247	235	250	$13	310	482	792	8	87	23	0.68	282	140	44	0.92	4.94	-1.2
03 BAL	625	80	173	23	100	0	277	273	279	$18	329	456	785	7	86	29	0.55	305	113	38	1.11	5.26	2.0
1st Half	306	42	87	14	59	0	284			$11	348	490	838	9	87	29	0.75	318	127	38		6.00	7.4
2nd Half	319	38	86	9	41	0	270			$7	311	423	734	6	85	30	0.39	292	100	39		4.59	-5.1
04 Proj	**625**	**82**	**179**	**28**	**103**	**1**	**286**			**$22**	**340**	**486**	**826**	**8**	**86**	**30**	**0.57**	**307**	**122**	**33**		**5.83**	**13.4**

Now reaching peak years with three solid growth years behind him. xBA says he can hit .300, and 30+ HRs are not out of reach. Trends are very favorable for him to break out in a big way.

Giles,Brian

Pos LF | Age 33 Decline | Bats L
R: Very Low | I: | S: stb | K: age
LIMA A | BA: 70%

	AB	R	H	HR	RBI	SB	Avg	vL	vR	R$	OB	Slg	OPS	bb%	ct%	h%	Eye	xBA	PX	SX	G/F	RC/G	RAR
99 PIT	521	109	164	39	115	6	315	299	323	$32	420	614	1035	15	85	31	1.19	316	175	81	0.81	9.58	63.8
00 PIT	559	111	176	35	123	6	315	293	323	$32	431	594	1025	17	88	31	1.65	323	160	110	0.99	9.62	66.1
01 PIT	576	116	178	37	95	13	309	267	322	$33	402	590	993	14	88	30	1.34	324	162	123	0.88	8.62	46.4
02 PIT	497	95	148	38	103	15	298	231	325	$34	448	622	1070	21	85	29	1.82	312	202	106	0.58	9.99	50.2
03 2NL	492	93	147	20	88	4	299	286	305	$21	422	514	936	18	88	31	1.81	312	136	97	0.78	7.80	30.2
1st Half	200	38	60	7	35	0	300			$8	440	485	925	20	90	31	2.50	305	122	49		7.65	11.4
2nd Half	292	55	87	13	53	4	298			$14	409	534	943	16	87	31	1.45	317	146	126		7.86	18.5
04 Proj	**550**	**106**	**166**	**31**	**103**	**9**	**302**			**$29**	**426**	**561**	**987**	**18**	**87**	**30**	**1.70**	**318**	**159**	**104**		**8.64**	**43.9**

Corrected problem vs LHPs, but power dropoff is troubling. All other BPIs were unchanged and the power should return, as it's not like he suddenly became a GB or gap hitter. Could be discounted in many drafts.

Giles,Marcus

Pos 2B | Age 25 Pre-Peak | Bats R
R: High | I: EXP con | S: pt stb | K: age
LIMA B | BA: 50%

	AB	R	H	HR	RBI	SB	Avg	vL	vR	R$	OB	Slg	OPS	bb%	ct%	h%	Eye	xBA	PX	SX	G/F	RC/G	RAR
99	0	0	0	0	0	0	0								0								
00 aa	458	60	120	14	51	20	262			$14	347	413	760	12	87	27	1.03	290	93	89		4.98	11.7
01 ATL	* 496	79	143	14	70	14	288	286	256	$19	351	442	793	9	84	32	0.60	279	96	101	1.56	5.25	19.9
02 ATL	* 328	49	83	11	37	4	253	158	246	$8	327	409	735	10	84	27	0.67	274	102	80	1.08	4.58	1.6
03 ATL	551	101	174	21	69	14	316	283	325	$27	382	526	908	10	85	34	0.74	318	142	102	1.10	7.48	45.9
1st Half	276	47	80	8	36	7	290			$10	357	478	836	10	86	31	0.76	315	133	101		6.23	14.1
2nd Half	275	54	94	13	33	7	342			$16	407	575	981	10	85	37	0.71	319	152	92		8.90	32.4
04 Proj	**550**	**92**	**166**	**23**	**77**	**13**	**302**			**$25**	**370**	**503**	**874**	**10**	**85**	**32**	**0.72**	**313**	**131**	**94**		**6.74**	**37.0**

2003 Forecaster said "he needs to write off 2002 and start again", which he certainly did. BPIs were strong across the board, and he really turned it up in 2nd half. Should remain at this level for years to come.

Gil,Benji

Pos 2B SS | Age 31 Past Peak | Bats R
R: High | I: exp CON | S: pt stb | K:
LIMA F | BA: 55%

	AB	R	H	HR	RBI	SB	Avg	vL	vR	R$	OB	Slg	OPS	bb%	ct%	h%	Eye	xBA	PX	SX	G/F	RC/G	RAR
99 aaa	412	50	87	11	43	12	211			$3	246	352	598	4	80	24	0.23	262	91	103		2.75	-17.4
00 ANA	301	28	72	6	23	10	239	301	202	$4	308	352	660	9	80	28	0.51	254	71	77	1.51	3.51	-3.3
01 ANA	260	33	77	8	39	3	296	294	299	$9	332	477	809	5	78	35	0.25	278	110	109	1.45	5.44	9.1
02 ANA	* 154	14	45	5	25	2	292	310	233	$6	319	500	819	4	77	35	0.17	270	134	97	1.23	5.18	5.0
03 ANA	* 161	16	29	3	14	5	180	177	217	($0)	200	286	486	2	73	23	0.09	222	66	124	1.19	1.81	-12.1
1st Half	90	8	16	1	7	2	178			($1)	213	267	479	4	72	23	0.16	212	56	121		1.84	-6.7
2nd Half	71	8	13	2	7	3	183			$0	183	310	493	0	75	22	0.00	233	80	118		1.73	-5.6
04 Proj	**100**	**10**	**23**	**3**	**12**	**3**	**230**			**$2**	**255**	**377**	**633**	**3**	**76**	**28**	**0.14**	**244**	**91**	**113**		**3.07**	**-3.2**

1-9-5-.192 in 125 AB at ANA. Minimal plate patience became even more miniscule in 2003 as he established a new career low in batting eye. Think any team will be hard-pressed to give him 250 AB again?

Gil,Geronimo

Pos CA | Age 28 Peak | Bats R
R: High | I: EXP con | S: pt stb | K:
LIMA F | BA: 35%

	AB	R	H	HR	RBI	SB	Avg	vL	vR	R$	OB	Slg	OPS	bb%	ct%	h%	Eye	xBA	PX	SX	G/F	RC/G	RAR
99 aa	343	36	80	11	46	2	233			$4	306	397	703	9	86	24	0.75	287	104	53		4.07	0.6
00 a/a	402	41	100	10	63	2	249			$6	301	378	679	7	85	27	0.48	271	81	44		3.72	-4.2
01 BAL	* 421	37	101	8	46	0	240	571	255	$3	269	344	614	4	83	27	0.24	247	68	33	1.53	3.08	-9.9
02 BAL	422	33	98	12	45	2	232	239	230	$5	269	363	631	5	79	27	0.24	258	82	33	1.50	3.18	-5.5
03 BAL	* 303	35	81	4	31	0	267	293	219	$4	311	347	657	6	80	32	0.31	230	55	31	1.12	3.58	-4.5
1st Half	148	22	35	3	16	0	236			$1	289	324	614	7	82	27	0.41	236	54	45		3.13	-4.2
2nd Half	155	13	46	1	15	0	297			$3	331	368	699	5	77	38	0.23	223	55	24		4.06	-0.1
04 Proj	**200**	**20**	**51**	**4**	**22**	**0**	**255**			**$2**	**296**	**356**	**652**	**5**	**80**	**30**	**0.29**	**235**	**68**	**32**		**3.49**	**-2.7**

3-16-0-.237 in 169 AB at BAL. He shouldn't approach double figures in HR again with those BPIs. Could platoon against LHPs and see some small success. A prototypical $1 catcher, if you're so inclined.

Ginter,Keith

Pos 2B 3B | Age 27 Peak | Bats R
R: High | I: EXP con | S: pt STB | K:
LIMA D+ | BA: 45%

	AB	R	H	HR	RBI	SB	Avg	vL	vR	R$	OB	Slg	OPS	bb%	ct%	h%	Eye	xBA	PX	SX	G/F	RC/G	RAR
99	0	0	0	0	0	0	0								0								
00 aa	462	92	143	25	79	21	310			$27	400	548	948	13	73	38	0.57	269	138	113	0.25	7.76	47.2
01 aaa	458	63	115	15	58	7	251			$10	325	434	759	10	72	32	0.39	248	115	97		4.60	7.7
02 2NL	* 516	67	127	13	55	3	246	154	250	$8	330	395	726	11	80	29	0.62	261	107	53	0.88	4.32	-1.4
03 MIL	358	51	92	14	44	1	257	224	267	$8	327	427	754	9	76	30	0.43	253	104	68	0.94	4.75	3.6
1st Half	136	15	38	2	15	1	279			$3	333	360	694	7	74	36	0.31	222	49	75		4.17	-0.9
2nd Half	222	36	54	12	29	0	243			$5	323	468	791	10	77	27	0.50	272	137	55		5.09	4.5
04 Proj	**400**	**57**	**101**	**10**	**50**	**4**	**253**			**$8**	**329**	**405**	**734**	**10**	**76**	**31**	**0.47**	**254**	**103**	**80**		**4.46**	**1.7**

Continued three-year trend of flat or decreasing BPIs. Again exhibited reverse split tendency, which should inhibit overall ABs. However, he has displayed decent skills and is entering peak, so has a 20-HR upside.

SCOTT MONROE

Glanville,Doug

Pos CF | Age 33 Decline | Bats R
R Moderate | I con | S pt stb | K age
LIMA F | BA: 55%

	Tm	AB	R	H	HR	RBI	SB	Avg	vL	vR	R$	OB	Slg	OPS	bb%	ct%	h%	Eye	xBA	PX	SX	G/F	RC/G	RAR
99	PHI	628	101	204	11	73	34	325	250	346	$30	373	457	830	7	87	36	0.59	301	88	138	1.45	6.77	41.0
00	PHI	637	89	175	8	52	31	275	237	285	$18	308	374	682	5	88	30	0.41	273	63	136	1.52	4.10	-4.1
01	PHI	634	74	166	14	55	28	262	290	254	$18	283	375	659	3	86	29	0.21	269	70	121	1.17	3.74	-2.1
02	PHI	422	49	105	6	29	19	249	250	248	$9	291	344	634	6	86	28	0.44	263	65	130	1.10	3.56	-16.4
03	2TM	* 298	28	71	5	18	5	238	280	255	$2	263	305	568	3	88	26	0.27	248	41	67	1.04	2.72	-19.1
1st Half		176	13	31	2	6	4	176			($3)	208	216	424	4	85	20	0.26	229	23	73		1.47	-19.3
2nd Half		122	15	40	3	12	1	328			$5	344	434	778	2	92	34	0.30	275	67	46		5.53	2.2
04	**Proj**	**250**	**28**	**61**	**5**	**19**	**4**	**244**			**$2**	**274**	**338**	**612**	**4**	**88**	**26**	**0.33**	**258**	**59**	**81**		**3.10**	**-12.2**

5-16-4-.264 in 246 AB with TEX and CHC. Is a mere shadow of peak year in 1999. BA, xBA and OPS have declined each year since then, and what was his only remaining skill -- SB -- has now eroded almost completely.

Glaus,Troy

Pos 3B | Age 27 Peak | Bats R
R Low | I con | S pt | K
LIMA B | BA: 55%

	Tm	AB	R	H	HR	RBI	SB	Avg	vL	vR	R$	OB	Slg	OPS	bb%	ct%	h%	Eye	xBA	PX	SX	G/F	RC/G	RAR
99	ANA	551	85	132	29	79	5	240	316	246	$12	326	450	776	11	74	27	0.50	250	124	63	0.83	4.94	8.6
00	ANA	563	120	160	47	102	14	284	369	259	$30	403	604	1007	17	71	32	0.69	275	179	76	0.76	8.28	63.0
01	ANA	588	100	147	41	108	10	250	252	249	$24	365	531	896	15	73	27	0.68	255	165	78	0.76	6.59	38.7
02	ANA	569	99	142	30	111	10	250	298	230	$21	350	453	804	13	75	28	0.61	253	118	83	0.94	5.40	15.7
03	ANA	319	53	79	16	50	7	248	303	226	$10	342	464	806	13	77	27	0.63	268	128	100	0.80	5.39	8.4
1st Half		261	47	68	14	44	7	261			$10	357	490	847	13	75	30	0.60	265	135	113		6.12	12.3
2nd Half		58	6	11	2	6	0	190			($0)	277	345	622	11	86	19	0.88	276	98	35		2.78	-3.3
04	**Proj**	**500**	**77**	**126**	**29**	**99**	**7**	**252**			**$19**	**349**	**481**	**829**	**13**	**78**	**27**	**0.67**	**270**	**134**	**64**		**5.60**	**16.9**

Partially torn rotator cuff could continue to inhibit power. Still, there are some positives that foreshadow a modest rebound:
- slight improvment vs LHers
- rise in ct% and xBA
- reversal of PX/GB trends

Gomez,Chris

Pos 2B | Age 32 Past Peak | Bats R
R Very High | I CON | S PT STB | K
LIMA F | BA: 70%

	Tm	AB	R	H	HR	RBI	SB	Avg	vL	vR	R$	OB	Slg	OPS	bb%	ct%	h%	Eye	xBA	PX	SX	G/F	RC/G	RAR
99	SD	234	20	59	1	15	1	252	294	235	$0	330	308	637	10	79	32	0.55	224	40	44	1.70	3.36	-5.9
00	SD	54	4	12	0	3	0	222	227	219	($1)	311	222	534	11	91	24	1.40	246			1.40	2.27	-3.4
01	2TM	* 434	53	110	12	60	6	253	243	264	$10	297	399	696	6	89	26	0.57	290	93	78	1.05	4.08	0.6
02	TAM	461	51	122	10	46	1	265	172	286	$8	297	410	707	4	87	28	0.36	279	97	60	1.01	4.11	0.9
03	MIN	175	14	44	1	15	2	251	251	252	$1	280	354	635	4	93	27	0.54	294	68	106	1.57	3.35	-4.1
1st Half		77	9	23	0	5	1	299			$1	333	429	762	5	92	32	0.67	311	91	141		4.99	1.8
2nd Half		98	5	21	1	10	1	214			($0)	238	296	534	3	93	22	0.43	280	51	69		2.33	-5.5
04	**Proj**	**150**	**14**	**38**	**2**	**14**	**1**	**253**			**$2**	**290**	**373**	**663**	**5**	**89**	**27**	**0.49**	**292**	**78**	**92**		**3.65**	**-2.0**

Upside indicated by rising PX in 2001-02 is now gone, and all that's left is a slap hitter who no longer takes a walk, which makes him completely undraftworthy.

Gonzalez,Alex

Pos SS | Age 27 Peak | Bats R
R High | I CON | S PT | K
LIMA D+ | BA: 45%

	Tm	AB	R	H	HR	RBI	SB	Avg	vL	vR	R$	OB	Slg	OPS	bb%	ct%	h%	Eye	xBA	PX	SX	G/F	RC/G	RAR
99	FLA	560	81	155	14	59	3	277	254	283	$11	296	430	726	3	80	33	0.13	263	94	111	0.97	4.33	12.9
00	FLA	385	35	77	7	42	7	200	245	185	($0)	226	319	546	3	80	23	0.17	234	74	119	0.83	2.34	-13.5
01	FLA	515	57	129	9	48	2	250	235	255	$5	292	377	668	6	79	30	0.28	248	88	55	0.87	3.69	2.1
02	FLA	151	15	34	2	18	3	225	200	231	$2	282	325	607	7	79	27	0.38	239	70	91	0.63	3.02	-4.1
03	FLA	528	52	135	18	77	0	256	274	251	$12	299	443	743	6	80	29	0.31	263	119	64	0.77	4.39	4.4
1st Half		279	33	85	12	51	0	305			$12	338	548	886	5	84	33	0.30	297	154	96		6.39	17.7
2nd Half		249	19	50	6	26	0	201			($1)	257	325	583	7	76	24	0.32	229	81	34		2.67	-11.2
04	**Proj**	**500**	**50**	**124**	**12**	**61**	**3**	**248**			**$8**	**294**	**392**	**685**	**6**	**79**	**29**	**0.31**	**257**	**94**	**79**		**3.84**	**-1.1**

2003 Forecaster said that G/F ratio "suggests possible power potential." He continued that trend in '03, and career highs in HR, RBI, Slg, OPS and PX resulted. Other BPIs remained flat, so don't expect BA to climb.

Gonzalez,Alex S.

Pos SS | Age 31 Past Peak | Bats R
R Moderate | I CON | S pt stb | K
LIMA D+ | BA: 55%

	Tm	AB	R	H	HR	RBI	SB	Avg	vL	vR	R$	OB	Slg	OPS	bb%	ct%	h%	Eye	xBA	PX	SX	G/F	RC/G	RAR
99	TOR	154	22	45	2	12	4	292	268	301	$4	359	416	774	9	85	33	0.70	278	91	69	1.19	5.28	4.8
00	TOR	527	68	133	15	69	4	252	228	259	$8	309	404	713	8	79	30	0.38	256	94	69	1.37	4.16	-4.0
01	TOR	636	79	161	17	76	18	253	336	233	$15	300	388	689	6	77	31	0.29	253	81	105	1.52	3.83	-10.3
02	CHC	513	58	127	18	61	5	248	237	251	$11	309	425	734	8	73	30	0.34	260	114	97	1.18	4.40	7.7
03	CHC	536	71	122	20	59	3	228	228	228	$7	290	409	698	8	77	26	0.38	263	120	54	1.08	3.84	-4.4
1st Half		301	43	73	9	29	0	243			$3	292	405	697	7	82	27	0.39	275	112	44		3.81	-2.8
2nd Half		235	28	49	11	30	3	209			$3	287	413	700	10	71	25	0.38	246	130	59		3.89	-1.6
04	**Proj**	**550**	**69**	**131**	**19**	**64**	**7**	**238**			**$10**	**300**	**410**	**711**	**8**	**76**	**28**	**0.37**	**260**	**111**	**78**		**4.06**	**2.5**

xBA says he was unlucky in the hits department, and the rise in ct% and Eye support that. PX rise the past two years was accompanied by a decrease in G/F – could be a conscious effort from playing in Wrigley.

Gonzalez,Juan

Pos RF DH | Age 34 Decline | Bats R
R Very High | I CON | S pt STB | K age
LIMA D+ | BA: 40%

	Tm	AB	R	H	HR	RBI	SB	Avg	vL	vR	R$	OB	Slg	OPS	bb%	ct%	h%	Eye	xBA	PX	SX	G/F	RC/G	RAR
99	TEX	562	114	183	39	128	3	326	342	321	$33	382	601	983	8	81	34	0.49	296	160	63	0.70	8.54	53.6
00	DET	461	69	133	22	67	1	289	360	265	$14	335	505	840	6	82	31	0.38	298	128	58	0.94	5.97	13.6
01	CLE	532	97	173	35	140	1	325	368	313	$34	373	590	964	7	82	34	0.44	304	157	51	0.89	8.34	47.4
02	TEX	277	38	78	8	35	2	282	358	250	$8	323	451	774	6	80	33	0.30	285	113	73	0.95	5.22	1.6
03	TEX	327	49	96	24	70	1	294	273	303	$17	323	572	894	4	78	31	0.19	310	160	53	0.84	6.59	13.1
1st Half		274	39	79	18	52	1	288			$13	323	544	867	5	76	32	0.22	297	148	55		6.22	8.2
2nd Half		53	10	17	6	18	0	321			$5	321	717	1038	0	85	28	0.00	382	222	35		8.63	4.9
04	**Proj**	**400**	**66**	**122**	**28**	**92**	**1**	**305**			**$23**	**335**	**583**	**918**	**4**	**81**	**32**	**0.24**	**318**	**163**	**58**		**7.15**	**22.7**

Last year it was his thumb, this year his calf. Either way, he hasn't played a game past July since 2001. Skills are declining along with health and attitude – it looks like $30 (or even $25) won't be reached again.

Gonzalez,Luis

Pos LF | Age 36 Decline | Bats L
R Moderate | I CON | S | K AGE
LIMA A | BA: 70%

	Tm	AB	R	H	HR	RBI	SB	Avg	vL	vR	R$	OB	Slg	OPS	bb%	ct%	h%	Eye	xBA	PX	SX	G/F	RC/G	RAR
99	ARI	614	112	206	26	111	9	336	327	339	$32	400	549	949	10	90	34	1.05	318	134	86	1.11	8.29	52.5
00	ARI	618	106	192	31	114	2	311	254	333	$28	388	544	932	11	86	32	0.92	293	142	49	0.86	7.64	40.9
01	ARI	609	128	198	57	142	1	325	312	331	$43	420	688	1108	14	86	30	1.20	334	201	84	0.78	10.88	83.8
02	ARI	524	90	151	28	103	9	288	272	297	$27	399	496	896	16	85	29	1.28	288	125	90	0.97	7.14	11.1
03	ARI	579	92	176	26	104	5	304	223	354	$27	401	532	933	14	88	31	1.40	325	148	76	1.00	7.74	34.3
1st Half		307	54	98	17	60	4	319			$18	392	580	972	11	90	31	1.23	334	168	72		8.42	23.4
2nd Half		272	38	78	9	44	1	287			$9	410	478	888	17	86	31	1.54	304	124	73		6.95	10.4
04	**Proj**	**550**	**93**	**167**	**29**	**104**	**5**	**304**			**$28**	**405**	**541**	**945**	**14**	**87**	**31**	**1.31**	**313**	**146**	**80**		**7.96**	**33.4**

Could plateau at this level for another couple of seasons. Starting to hit more GB and improved his ct% and eye, which bodes well for .300 but not so good for a return to 30 HR territory.

Gonzalez,Raul

Pos LF RF CF | Age 30 Past Peak | Bats R
R X HIGH | I EXP CON | S PT STB | K
LIMA F | BA: 55%

	Tm	AB	R	H	HR	RBI	SB	Avg	vL	vR	R$	OB	Slg	OPS	bb%	ct%	h%	Eye	xBA	PX	SX	G/F	RC/G	RAR
99	aa	505	62	143	13	80	9	283			$15	335	432	766	7	86	31	0.57	286	95	87		5.13	1.0
00	aaa	241	29	54	3	27	4	224			$1	275	315	591	7	93	23	0.94	285	60	79		2.60	-19.3
01	aaa	539	69	143	9	51	5	265			$9	329	386	715	9	89	28	0.86	281	84	53	2.00	4.16	-15.9
02	2NL	* 536	79	149	13	62	11	278	273	254	$17	338	405	743	8	87	30	0.71	277	87	75	3.67	4.57	-28.3
03	NYM	* 337	43	86	5	36	8	255	240	223	$6	334	362	696	11	83	30	0.69	258	71	110	1.88	4.19	-13.9
1st Half		207	29	57	5	25	7	275			$7	359	406	765	12	81	32	0.69	259	85	95		5.16	-2.5
2nd Half		130	14	29	0	11	1	223			($1)	294	292	586	9	85	26	0.68	253	48	109		2.86	-10.8
04	**Proj**	**150**	**19**	**38**	**2**	**16**	**3**	**253**			**$2**	**322**	**359**	**681**	**9**	**86**	**28**	**0.71**	**262**	**71**	**87**		**3.86**	**-8.4**

2-21-3-.230 in 217 AB at NYM. What little power he had went south, although if bb% was a category, he'd be valuable. But there's not much demand for a .260 slap hitting OFer with average speed on most rosters.

Gonzalez,Wiki

Pos CA | Age 29 Past Peak | Bats R
R Moderate | I CON | S pt | K
LIMA F | BA: 75%

	Tm	AB	R	H	HR	RBI	SB	Avg	vL	vR	R$	OB	Slg	OPS	bb%	ct%	h%	Eye	xBA	PX	SX	G/F	RC/G	RAR
99	SD	* 400	46	108	16	58	0	270	150	349	$10	315	450	765	6	91	27	0.70	306	109	38	1.48	4.94	11.3
00	SD	284	25	66	5	30	1	232	277	214	$1	306	345	651	10	89	25	0.97	273	74	40	1.45	3.42	-5.0
01	SD	160	16	44	8	27	2	275	345	235	$6	322	463	784	6	83	29	0.39	274	107	41	1.43	5.31	8.2
02	SD	164	16	36	1	20	0	220	310	189	($0)	330	299	629	14	85	25	1.13	229	61	44	2.47	3.22	-4.5
03	SD	* 214	14	46	3	25	1	215	214	196	$0	282	318	600	9	89	23	0.83	270	72	47	1.21	2.93	-8.9
1st Half		168	9	34	2	19	1	202			($1)	276	286	561	9	87	22	0.77	256	61	27		2.55	-9.2
2nd Half		46	5	12	1	6	0	261			$1	306	435	741	6	96	26	1.50	322	112	100		4.59	0.4
04	**Proj**	**200**	**17**	**47**	**5**	**26**	**1**	**235**			**$2**	**306**	**352**	**658**	**9**	**86**	**25**	**0.75**	**268**	**78**	**33**		**3.61**	**-3.0**

0-10-0-.200 in 65 AB at SD. Two signs that you should be worried about your job security:
- Gary Bennett outhits and outhomers you
- There's still a few years before that catcher power spike.

SCOTT MONROE

Goodwin,Tom

Pos CF
Age 35 Decline
Bats L
R Very High
I CON
S pt STB
K age
LIMA F BA: 30%

Tm		AB	R	H	HR	RBI	SB	Avg	vL	vR	R$	OB	Slg	OPS	bb%	ct%	h%	Eye	xBA	PX	SX	G/F	RC/G	RAR
99	TEX	405	63	105	3	33	39	259	262	259	$15	326	341	667	9	85	30	0.66	264	49	173	1.89	3.94	-9.4
00	2NL	528	94	139	6	58	55	263	340	244	$24	347	352	700	11	78	33	0.58	242	49	188	1.81	4.57	3.8
01	LA	286	51	66	4	22	22	231	250	228	$8	288	336	624	7	80	28	0.40	255	60	203	1.71	3.17	-6.1
02	SF	* 216	32	52	1	22	19	241	53	289	$7	305	319	625	8	85	28	0.61	261	54	174	1.79	3.47	-9.2
03	CHC	171	26	49	1	12	19	287	238	302	$9	330	363	692	6	81	35	0.33	264	61	124	2.03	4.40	-2.9
1st Half		92	12	23	1	6	11	250			$4	281	315	596	4	84	29	0.27	265	46	125		3.10	-5.3
2nd Half		79	14	26	0	6	8	329			$5	384	418	801	8	77	43	0.39	261	79	111		6.25	2.7
04	Proj	**150**	**24**	**40**	**1**	**12**	**15**	**267**			**$7**	**322**	**346**	**668**	**8**	**81**	**32**	**0.44**	**265**	**58**	**147**		**4.01**	**-3.1**

He does only one thing, but if the playing time is there he can make a difference. He's slowed down significantly over the past two years, but could still make a good $1 flier.

Grace,Mark

Pos 1B
Age 39 Decline
Bats L
R High
I con
S pt stb
K AGE
LIMA F BA: 80%

Tm		AB	R	H	HR	RBI	SB	Avg	vL	vR	R$	OB	Slg	OPS	bb%	ct%	h%	Eye	xBA	PX	SX	G/F	RC/G	RAR
99	CHC	593	107	183	16	91	3	309	307	310	$20	393	481	874	12	93	31	1.89	329	113	74	1.07	6.84	25.0
00	CHC	510	75	143	11	82	1	280	305	272	$12	393	429	823	16	95	28	3.39	324	102	37	1.19	5.92	8.3
01	ARI	476	66	142	15	78	1	298	295	300	$17	385	466	851	12	92	30	1.86	302	107	51	1.15	6.54	3.8
02	ARI	298	43	75	7	48	2	252	321	226	$7	352	386	738	13	90	26	1.53	275	97	54	1.31	4.67	-8.1
03	ARI	135	13	27	3	16	0	200	217	196	($0)	285	304	588	11	89	21	1.07	269	68	22	1.04	2.76	-11.7
1st Half		106	12	22	3	15	0	208			$0	306	330	636	12	92	20	1.67	284	78	24		3.25	-7.5
2nd Half		29	1	5	0	1	0	172			($1)	200	207	407	3	79	22	0.17	220	31	11		1.27	-4.0
04	Proj	**0**	**0**	**0**	**0**	**0**	**0**	**0**			**$0**					**0**				**0**	**0**			

Announced his retirement in September. A class act all the way. Ends his career with a .303 BA, 173 HR and 1146 RBI. Most similar in career to Keith Hernandez, according to Baseball-Reference.com.

Graffanino,Tony

Pos SS 2B 3B
Age 31 Past Peak
Bats R
R Moderate
I con
S pt stb
K
LIMA D+ BA: 65%

Tm		AB	R	H	HR	RBI	SB	Avg	vL	vR	R$	OB	Slg	OPS	bb%	ct%	h%	Eye	xBA	PX	SX	G/F	RC/G	RAR
99	TAM	* 475	76	142	11	69	17	299	367	300	$18	352	472	824	8	87	32	0.65	305	108	147	0.88	5.72	21.0
00	2AL	168	33	46	2	17	7	274	224	300	$4	358	357	715	12	84	32	0.81	232	52	115	1.17	4.35	-0.3
01	CHW	145	23	44	2	15	4	303	319	296	$5	373	407	780	10	80	37	0.55	264	75	70	1.67	5.61	4.9
02	CHW	229	35	60	6	31	2	262	261	263	$5	327	428	755	9	83	29	0.58	276	100	128	1.20	4.80	1.4
03	CHW	250	51	65	7	23	8	260	303	176	$6	325	428	753	9	85	28	0.65	304	105	155	1.28	4.99	4.1
1st Half		120	24	29	4	10	3	242			$2	326	408	734	11	79	27	0.60	282	109	90		4.63	0.7
2nd Half		130	27	36	3	13	5	277			$4	324	446	770	6	91	29	0.75	324	102	191		5.34	3.4
04	Proj	**250**	**46**	**68**	**6**	**27**	**7**	**272**			**$7**	**336**	**424**	**760**	**9**	**84**	**30**	**0.62**	**300**	**95**	**137**		**5.07**	**4.5**

Showed modest improvement in BPIs over previous two seasons, even though BA didn't show it. Will continue to make an excellent reserve player, as stats should maintain.

Greene,Todd

Pos CA
Age 32 Past Peak
Bats R
R X HIGH
I exp CON
S PT STB
K
LIMA F BA: 50%

Tm		AB	R	H	HR	RBI	SB	Avg	vL	vR	R$	OB	Slg	OPS	bb%	ct%	h%	Eye	xBA	PX	SX	G/F	RC/G	RAR
99	ANA	* 395	47	95	19	57	1	241	253	239	$7	263	451	714	3	81	25	0.16	281	128	41	0.82	3.79	-3.3
00	TOR	* 176	23	45	11	22	1	256	260	200	$4	296	472	767	5	82	25	0.32	284	115	43	0.93	4.81	3.4
01	NYY	* 227	22	48	6	24	3	211	250	200	$1	232	335	567	3	83	23	0.15	256	78	61	0.79	2.44	-10.1
02	TEX	* 389	48	103	22	68	2	265	271	266	$14	283	491	774	3	84	27	0.16	295	135	51	0.67	4.85	13.8
03	TEX	205	25	47	10	20	0	229	211	240	$3	237	434	671	1	77	25	0.04	265	121	58	0.68	3.40	-4.3
1st Half		85	10	18	3	5	0	212			($0)	221	388	609	1	73	25	0.04	243	105	96		2.77	-3.5
2nd Half		120	15	29	7	15	0	242			$3	248	467	715	1	80	25	0.04	281	133	33		3.89	-0.7
04	Proj	**250**	**30**	**59**	**12**	**31**	**1**	**236**			**$5**	**251**	**437**	**687**	**2**	**80**	**25**	**0.10**	**270**	**118**	**65**		**3.63**	**-2.3**

Abandoned any pretense of plate patience, evidenced by a ratio of two BBs against 47 Ks. PX stayed high, but a .237 OBP is just ugly. You'll need plenty of high BA hitters to overcome his hacking if you dare.

Green,Shawn

Pos RF
Age 31 Past Peak
Bats L
R Low
I CON
S stb
K
LIMA B BA: 55%

Tm		AB	R	H	HR	RBI	SB	Avg	vL	vR	R$	OB	Slg	OPS	bb%	ct%	h%	Eye	xBA	PX	SX	G/F	RC/G	RAR
99	TOR	614	134	190	42	123	20	309	280	320	$37	376	588	964	10	81	33	0.56	333	165	97	1.55	8.06	52.2
00	LA	610	98	164	24	99	24	269	259	273	$24	363	472	835	13	80	30	0.74	299	126	114	1.34	6.06	16.2
01	LA	619	121	184	49	125	20	297	298	297	$41	370	598	968	10	83	29	0.67	331	167	120	1.27	8.07	43.3
02	LA	582	110	166	42	114	8	285	270	291	$33	384	558	942	14	81	29	0.83	332	167	69	1.78	7.51	36.5
03	LA	611	84	171	19	85	6	280	252	295	$19	352	460	812	10	82	32	0.61	296	123	74	1.50	5.72	2.0
1st Half		310	36	78	8	39	2	252			$5	312	419	731	8	80	29	0.43	285	118	63		4.43	-10.8
2nd Half		301	48	93	11	46	4	309			$13	392	502	893	12	84	34	0.84	307	129	74		7.27	13.6
04	Proj	**600**	**100**	**173**	**36**	**101**	**10**	**288**			**$29**	**369**	**543**	**912**	**11**	**82**	**30**	**0.70**	**307**	**157**	**84**		**7.15**	**28.3**

Announced in Sept that he had shoulder problems all season, which would explain power woes. Rest of BPIs stayed relatively consistent, so it's reasonable to expect a sizable rebound. Big bargain without huge risk.

Grieve,Ben

Pos DH
Age 27 Peak
Bats L
R Moderate
I CON
S pt stb
K
LIMA C+ BA: 50%

Tm		AB	R	H	HR	RBI	SB	Avg	vL	vR	R$	OB	Slg	OPS	bb%	ct%	h%	Eye	xBA	PX	SX	G/F	RC/G	RAR
99	OAK	486	80	129	28	86	4	265	156	297	$16	350	481	831	11	78	29	0.58	275	123	62	1.42	5.90	9.9
00	OAK	594	92	166	27	104	3	279	268	285	$19	358	487	845	11	78	32	0.56	298	124	62	1.51	6.20	18.8
01	TAM	542	72	143	11	72	7	264	293	253	$12	366	387	753	14	71	35	0.55	232	82	76	2.13	4.96	-4.2
02	TAM	482	62	121	19	64	8	251	221	262	$13	345	432	776	13	75	30	0.57	266	114	62	2.08	5.09	-6.2
03	TAM	165	28	38	4	17	0	230	208	241	$1	355	345	701	16	75	28	0.78	221	74	35	2.40	4.07	-2.7
1st Half		131	25	30	4	14	0	229			$1	369	351	720	18	78	27	1.00	228	73	37		4.28	-1.3
2nd Half		34	3	8	0	3	0	235			($0)	297	324	621	8	65	36	0.25	191	77	24		3.21	-1.4
04	Proj	**500**	**78**	**127**	**14**	**68**	**4**	**254**			**$10**	**361**	**394**	**755**	**14**	**75**	**31**	**0.68**	**226**	**89**	**67**		**4.89**	**-1.5**

Suffered from a blood clot which ended his season in July. This doesn't explain his huge drop in power, but increasing G/F ratio does. Will be lucky to get near 20 HRs - 10 to 15 is more like it.

Griffey Jr.,Ken

Pos CF
Age 34 Decline
Bats L
R Moderate
I con
S pt stb
K age
LIMA C+ BA: 60%

Tm		AB	R	H	HR	RBI	SB	Avg	vL	vR	R$	OB	Slg	OPS	bb%	ct%	h%	Eye	xBA	PX	SX	G/F	RC/G	RAR
99	SEA	606	123	173	48	134	24	285	229	307	$38	379	576	955	13	82	28	0.84	291	159	111	0.77	7.74	52.4
00	CIN	520	100	141	40	118	6	271	263	274	$26	383	556	939	15	78	28	0.80	264	156	79	0.69	7.32	45.0
01	CIN	364	57	104	22	65	2	286	254	303	$16	363	533	896	11	80	30	0.61	294	143	72	0.92	6.94	31.5
02	CIN	197	17	52	8	23	1	264	217	285	$5	356	426	782	12	80	29	0.72	269	103		0.92	5.08	1.2
03	CIN	166	34	41	13	26	1	247	250	245	$6	352	566	919	14	73	26	0.61	306	193	86	0.96	6.80	8.9
1st Half		131	26	32	8	20	1	244			$4	344	504	848	13	72	28	0.54	263	157	99		5.90	3.6
2nd Half		35	8	9	5	6	0	257			$2	381	800	1181	17	80	17	1.00	401	326	25		10.46	5.6
04	Proj	**350**	**58**	**93**	**21**	**59**	**4**	**266**			**$14**	**360**	**512**	**871**	**13**	**77**	**29**	**0.65**	**278**	**146**	**81**		**6.35**	**16.6**

It's become an annual event to predict when he will get hurt. Very unfortunate, especially since his power was coming back in a big way before his Achilles injury. But predicting even 400 AB is too risky.

Grissom,Marquis

Pos CF
Age 37 Decline
Bats R
R Very High
I CON
S pt stb
K AGE
LIMA C+ BA: 45%

Tm		AB	R	H	HR	RBI	SB	Avg	vL	vR	R$	OB	Slg	OPS	bb%	ct%	h%	Eye	xBA	PX	SX	G/F	RC/G	RAR
99	MIL	603	92	161	20	83	24	267	322	245	$20	322	415	737	8	82	30	0.45	268	91	100	1.29	4.69	6.6
00	MIL	595	67	145	14	62	20	244	304	228	$11	290	351	641	6	83	27	0.39	237	64	90	1.48	3.35	-17.6
01	LA	448	56	99	21	60	7	221	254	207	$9	248	404	652	3	76	24	0.15	243	105	86	1.31	3.16	-9.6
02	LA	343	57	95	17	60	5	277	293	267	$15	321	510	831	6	80	30	0.32	303	147	130	1.14	5.79	8.9
03	SF	587	82	176	20	79	11	300	364	280	$24	323	468	791	3	86	32	0.24	291	108	102	1.35	5.50	8.5
1st Half		303	39	93	11	38	7	307			$14	338	488	826	4	86	33	0.33	294	113	108		5.96	8.2
2nd Half		284	43	83	9	41	4	292			$11	307	447	754	2	86	31	0.15	285	103	84		5.03	0.4
04	Proj	**500**	**72**	**138**	**20**	**72**	**9**	**276**			**$18**	**307**	**459**	**766**	**4**	**83**	**30**	**0.26**	**288**	**114**	**107**		**4.94**	**3.2**

Only 2nd .300 season in 15-year career. Managed the feat by destroying LHPs and raising ct%, at 36 no less. Can he make it three straight years of 15+ R$? Don't bet against it.

Grudzielanek,Mark

Pos 2B
Age 33 Decline
Bats R
R Low
I con
S pt stb
K age
LIMA D+ BA: 45%

Tm		AB	R	H	HR	RBI	SB	Avg	vL	vR	R$	OB	Slg	OPS	bb%	ct%	h%	Eye	xBA	PX	SX	G/F	RC/G	RAR
99	LA	488	72	159	7	46	6	326	389	299	$15	366	436	803	6	87	37	0.48	281	72	92	1.66	5.84	21.3
00	LA	617	101	172	7	49	12	279	250	290	$11	328	389	717	7	87	31	0.56	287	73	124	1.81	4.54	3.1
01	LA	539	83	146	13	55	4	271	295	264	$11	307	393	700	5	85	30	0.34	270	74	88	1.49	4.13	4.1
02	LA	536	56	145	9	50	4	271	257	274	$10	299	364	663	4	83	31	0.25	259	67	58	1.39	3.82	-9.2
03	CHC	481	73	151	3	38	6	314	360	302	$13	354	416	770	6	87	36	0.47	304	82	83	1.86	5.47	13.8
1st Half		296	44	88	2	15	2	297			$5	338	385	723	6	85	34	0.42	290	71	60		4.63	1.8
2nd Half		185	29	63	1	23	4	341			$8	381	465	846	6	89	38	0.57	324	100	99		7.02	12.5
04	Proj	**450**	**64**	**130**	**5**	**43**	**6**	**289**			**$10**	**327**	**398**	**725**	**5**	**86**	**33**	**0.40**	**303**	**80**	**91**		**4.67**	**4.5**

Essentially jumped over three lesser years to get back to 1999's levels. If you base your expectations on $10 of value, you shouldn't be disappointed.

SCOTT MONROE

49

Guerrero,Vladimir

	Yr	Tm	AB	R	H	HR	RBI	SB	Avg	vL	vR	R$	OB	Slg	OPS	bb%	ct%	h%	Eye	xBA	PX	SX	G/F	RC/G	RAR
Pos RF	99	MON	610	102	193	42	131	14	316	287	324	$38	373	600	973	8	90	30	0.89	349	165	96	1.17	8.15	52.3
Age 28 Peak	00	MON	571	101	197	44	123	9	345	376	336	$41	405	664	1069	9	87	34	0.78	355	173	123	1.29	9.93	72.1
Bats R	01	MON	599	107	184	34	108	37	307	319	304	$42	370	566	936	9	85	31	0.68	338	155	127	1.39	7.36	30.4
R Very Low	02	MON	614	106	206	39	111	40	336	290	347	$52	415	593	1008	12	89	33	1.20	341	161	97	1.13	8.90	60.4
I	03	MON	394	71	130	25	79	9	330	393	313	$27	422	586	1009	14	87	33	1.19	336	152	92	1.31	9.20	37.9
S pt	1st Half		176	31	53	8	33	5	301			$10	414	494	909	16	86	31	1.42	314	122	63		7.27	8.2
K	2nd Half		218	40	77	17	46	4	353			$18	429	661	1090	12	87	35	1.00	353	175	110		10.98	30.1
LIMA C BA: 60%	04	Proj	**600**	**106**	**198**	**40**	**117**	**13**	**330**			**$41**	**411**	**598**	**1008**	**12**	**87**	**33**	**1.06**	**340**	**159**	**85**		**8.87**	**55.2**

Back injuries are always a concern, but post-injury BPIs were simply sterling. Managed to sustain 2002's gains in BB% and Eye, PX and SX actually jumped in 2nd half. All signs say that his back is fine.

Guiel,Aaron

	Yr	Tm	AB	R	H	HR	RBI	SB	Avg	vL	vR	R$	OB	Slg	OPS	bb%	ct%	h%	Eye	xBA	PX	SX	G/F	RC/G	RAR
Pos RF	99	aaa	257	36	50	9	31	4	195			$1	286	385	671	11	66	25	0.38	231	124	83		3.27	-14.2
Age 31 Past Peak	00	aaa	258	34	64	10	30	5	248			$5	314	422	737	9	83	26	0.57	282	103	86		4.62	-3.1
Bats L	01	aaa	442	56	99	15	53	5	224			$6	281	387	668	7	83	24	0.46	273	100	77		3.44	-24.9
R Very High	02	KC	* 455	62	120	11	75	7	264	169	254	$13	323	389	712	8	80	31	0.44	249	81	72	1.40	4.21	-10.9
I EXP CON	03	KC	* 544	90	143	21	74	5	263	275	278	$14	325	454	779	8	82	29	0.51	280	121	77	1.07	4.96	-3.0
S pt stb	1st Half		260	39	64	8	31	2	246			$4	317	408	725	9	79	28	0.50	259	101	87		4.28	-6.8
K	2nd Half		284	51	79	13	43	3	278			$10	332	496	829	7	84	29	0.51	300	140	67		5.64	4.0
LIMA D BA: 55%	04	Proj	**250**	**38**	**64**	**9**	**35**	**3**	**256**			**$6**	**318**	**428**	**746**	**8**	**81**	**29**	**0.47**	**275**	**108**	**77**		**4.52**	**-4.1**

15-52-.277 in 354 AB at KC. Nice power surge on his arrival in KC, driven by a free-swinging approach. Cooled after a hot July, as pitchers learned to exploit his aggression. Overall, skill set is stable and unexciting.

Guillen,Carlos

	Yr	Tm	AB	R	H	HR	RBI	SB	Avg	vL	vR	R$	OB	Slg	OPS	bb%	ct%	h%	Eye	xBA	PX	SX	G/F	RC/G	RAR
Pos SS 3B	99	SEA	0	0	0	0	0	0	0								0			0			1.17		
Age 28 Peak	00	SEA	* 375	64	98	9	53	5	261	320	244	$7	333	400	733	10	81	30	0.56	263	84	103	1.24	4.48	0.6
Bats S	01	SEA	456	72	118	5	53	4	259	295	243	$6	336	355	691	10	80	31	0.60	246	64	98	1.30	4.13	-3.3
R Very Low	02	SEA	475	73	124	9	56	4	261	221	275	$9	326	394	720	9	81	31	0.51	249	84	109	1.06	4.29	-4.0
I con	03	SEA	388	63	107	7	52	4	276	265	280	$9	361	394	756	12	84	32	0.81	272	77	85	1.31	4.89	5.2
S	1st Half		237	39	67	3	25	0	283			$4	354	397	750	10	84	33	0.68	272	74	89		4.90	3.2
K	2nd Half		151	24	40	4	27	4	265			$5	373	391	764	15	83	30	1.00	272	81	62		4.87	2.0
LIMA D BA: 55%	04	Proj	**350**	**56**	**95**	**7**	**48**	**4**	**271**			**$8**	**353**	**395**	**748**	**11**	**82**	**31**	**0.70**	**271**	**79**	**93**		**4.76**	**3.2**

Reasons why BA improvement might be sustainable:
- Increased BB%
- Improved Eye
- xBA supports it

Still, given the weak PX and SX, he won't offer much else.

Guillen,Jose

	Yr	Tm	AB	R	H	HR	RBI	SB	Avg	vL	vR	R$	OB	Slg	OPS	bb%	ct%	h%	Eye	xBA	PX	SX	G/F	RC/G	RAR
Pos RF LF	99	2TM	* 454	73	127	11	60	1	280	256	240	$10	327	412	739	7	82	32	0.40	265	88	49	1.55	4.70	-3.7
Age 27 Peak	00	TAM	* 394	55	110	17	64	3	279	195	275	$12	321	497	818	6	81	31	0.33	292	125	116	1.37	5.57	7.3
Bats R	01	TAM	* 254	30	70	9	37	2	276	375	252	$7	300	437	737	3	80	31	0.18	259	101	45	1.88	4.42	-4.1
R X HIGH	02	CIN	* 286	30	71	10	40	4	248	252	226	$7	286	399	684	5	83	27	0.31	267	98	51	1.95	3.56	-15.0
I exp CON	03	2TM	485	77	151	31	86	1	311	315	310	$25	344	569	913	5	80	33	0.25	321	153	54	1.39	7.07	22.4
S pt STB	1st Half		200	31	69	14	39	0	345			$13	385	630	1015	6	82	37	0.35	336	170	46		8.89	18.5
K	2nd Half		285	46	82	17	47	1	288			$12	314	526	841	4	80	31	0.19	312	142	69		5.94	4.5
LIMA C BA: 40%	04	Proj	**500**	**69**	**143**	**25**	**80**	**3**	**286**			**$20**	**320**	**492**	**812**	**5**	**81**	**31**	**0.26**	**317**	**125**	**53**		**5.40**	**1.8**

Dramatic power spike was driven by decline in G/F ratio, as other indicators remained stable. As for that .311 BA: note how well his BA tracks against H%. As that elevated H% from 2003 regresses, so will his BA.

Gutierrez,Ricky

	Yr	Tm	AB	R	H	HR	RBI	SB	Avg	vL	vR	R$	OB	Slg	OPS	bb%	ct%	h%	Eye	xBA	PX	SX	G/F	RC/G	RAR
Pos SS	99	HOU	268	33	70	1	25	2	261	379	223	$2	351	336	687	12	83	31	0.82	240	45	105	2.91	3.83	2.4
Age 33 Decline	00	CHC	449	73	124	11	56	8	276	356	256	$12	369	401	770	13	87	30	1.14	276	76	87	2.17	5.25	23.0
Bats R	01	CHC	528	76	153	10	66	4	290	258	300	$14	340	402	741	7	89	31	0.71	281	71	79	2.13	4.83	18.9
R High	02	CLE	353	38	97	4	38	0	275	371	242	$6	314	346	659	5	86	31	0.42	235	49	30	2.14	3.76	-8.2
I con	03	CLE	* 115	8	29	0	8	4	252	313	235	$1	295	313	608	6	90	28	0.64	257	45	91	4.43	3.21	-4.1
S PT stb	1st Half		86	8	21	0	8	4	244			$1	293	314	607	7	88	28	0.60	256	51	115		3.19	-3.2
K age	2nd Half		29	0	8	0	0	0	276			$0	300	310	610	3	97	29	1.00	259	30			3.28	-0.9
LIMA F BA: 60%	04	Proj	**200**	**24**	**54**	**2**	**22**	**4**	**270**			**$4**	**328**	**353**	**682**	**8**	**88**	**30**	**0.70**	**257**	**56**	**80**		**4.04**	**-2.4**

0-3-.260 in 50 AB at CLE. Briefly made it all the way back to the majors after off-season neck surgery, but was quickly shut down again. Will reportedly try again this spring, but don't expect much.

Guzman,Cristian

	Yr	Tm	AB	R	H	HR	RBI	SB	Avg	vL	vR	R$	OB	Slg	OPS	bb%	ct%	h%	Eye	xBA	PX	SX	G/F	RC/G	RAR
Pos SS	99	MIN	420	47	95	1	26	9	226	296	200	($1)	265	276	541	5	79	29	0.24	213	34	105	3.15	2.31	-24.1
Age 26 Pre-Peak	00	MIN	631	89	156	8	54	28	247	209	261	$11	298	388	687	7	84	28	0.46	298	78	224	1.99	3.88	-10.2
Bats S	01	MIN	493	80	149	10	51	25	302	312	299	$21	331	477	807	4	84	34	0.27	310	104	205	1.65	5.68	18.1
R Low	02	MIN	623	80	170	9	59	12	273	257	281	$14	292	385	677	3	87	30	0.22	277	73	109	2.04	3.67	-16.7
I CON	03	MIN	534	78	142	3	53	18	266	268	276	$11	305	363	668	5	85	31	0.38	269	56	188	1.71	3.75	-10.7
S pt	1st Half		309	44	80	0	19	7	259			$3	284	346	631	3	86	30	0.25	267	51	191		3.25	-10.8
K	2nd Half		225	34	62	3	34	11	276			$8	332	387	719	8	84	32	0.54	270	63	174		4.48	0.4
LIMA B BA: 45%	04	Proj	**500**	**71**	**136**	**6**	**52**	**22**	**272**			**$14**	**308**	**388**	**696**	**5**	**85**	**31**	**0.35**	**274**	**69**	**180**		**4.11**	**-4.9**

Made some gains in bb% and eye. When combined with the rebound in SX, there is potential for his SB totals to rebound to 2000-01 levels. Based on the continued PX decline, speed will remain his only fantasy asset.

Guzman,Edwards

	Yr	Tm	AB	R	H	HR	RBI	SB	Avg	vL	vR	R$	OB	Slg	OPS	bb%	ct%	h%	Eye	xBA	PX	SX	G/F	RC/G	RAR
Pos 3B	99	aaa	358	36	83	5	36	5	232			$2	259	304	563	4	89	25	0.33	263	48	59		2.46	-21.3
Age 27 Peak	00	aaa	421	39	101	4	39	1	240			$0	261	323	584	3	92	25	0.38	281	58	44		2.64	-22.0
Bats L	01	SF	* 187	18	51	3	15	0	273	111	255	$3	303	380	682	4	90	29	0.44	280	70	48	1.29	3.93	-3.5
R X HIGH	02	aaa	390	39	103	4	48	1	264			$6	290	349	638	3	94	27	0.58	279	64	38		3.39	-13.0
I EXP con	03	MON	* 359	34	99	3	34	4	276	200	248	$6	297	351	648	3	91	30	0.34	270	55	70	3.21	3.69	-5.8
S pt STB	1st Half		277	25	84	3	29	4	303			$8	320	386	707	2	92	32	0.33	276	59	69		4.55	2.2
K	2nd Half		82	9	15	0	5	0	183			($2)	221	232	453	5	87	21	0.36	248	44	50		1.60	-7.0
LIMA F BA: 50%	04	Proj	**150**	**15**	**37**	**1**	**14**	**1**	**247**			**$1**	**274**	**318**	**593**	**4**	**91**	**27**	**0.41**	**267**	**55**	**47**		**2.91**	**-6.6**

1-5-.240 in 146 AB at MON. Acquired from SF in the Livan Hernandez trade. Free swinger who makes a lot of contact, but cannot drive the ball. At age 27 with no signs of BPI growth, has no fantasy value.

Hafner,Travis

	Yr	Tm	AB	R	H	HR	RBI	SB	Avg	vL	vR	R$	OB	Slg	OPS	bb%	ct%	h%	Eye	xBA	PX	SX	G/F	RC/G	RAR
Pos 1B	99		0	0	0	0	0	0	0								0								
Age 26 Pre-Peak	00		0	0	0	0	0	0	0								0								
Bats L	01	aa	323	47	82	18	59	2	254			$11	350	492	843	13	79	27	0.72	283	145	42		5.87	-3.2
R High	02	TEX	* 463	66	137	18	64	2	296	333	232	$17	386	473	859	13	84	32	0.93	279	108	53	0.86	6.54	8.8
I EXP con	03	CLE	* 391	49	99	16	49	4	253	190	280	$9	327	450	777	10	73	31	0.41	249	120	84	1.22	4.99	-4.5
S pt stb	1st Half		162	17	37	4	16	3	228			$2	339	358	697	14	73	29	0.61	228	86	48		4.02	-6.7
K	2nd Half		229	32	62	12	33	1	271			$7	318	515	834	7	73	32	0.26	264	145	102		5.66	1.8
LIMA C+ BA: 40%	04	Proj	**500**	**67**	**134**	**21**	**69**	**4**	**268**			**$14**	**351**	**466**	**817**	**11**	**78**	**31**	**0.58**	**257**	**120**	**70**		**5.65**	**-0.2**

14-40-.254 in 291 AB at CLE. Opened up his swing in the 2nd half, as his PX jumped while bb% and eye plunged. That approach won't work long-term. BPIs hold some promise, but may struggle in the short-term.

Hairston Jr.,Jerry

	Yr	Tm	AB	R	H	HR	RBI	SB	Avg	vL	vR	R$	OB	Slg	OPS	bb%	ct%	h%	Eye	xBA	PX	SX	G/F	RC/G	RAR
Pos 2B	99	BAL	* 588	86	158	11	61	27	269	333	257	$17	313	396	709	6	88	29	0.53	287	83	122	1.42	4.14	3.0
Age 27 Peak	00	BAL	* 381	66	99	9	38	13	260	244	259	$8	343	383	726	11	87	28	0.94	275	76	94	1.44	4.32	5.2
Bats R	01	BAL	532	63	124	8	47	29	233	290	216	$11	292	344	636	8	86	26	0.60	262	72	125	1.06	3.30	-14.9
R Moderate	02	BAL	426	55	114	5	32	21	268	263	269	$12	322	376	697	7	87	30	0.62	281	75	122	0.96	4.25	2.6
I con	03	BAL	218	25	59	2	21	14	271	255	276	$7	340	372	712	10	89	30	0.92	277	70	117	0.95	4.41	1.7
S PT	1st Half		157	22	45	2	16	14	287			$8	371	382	753	12	88	32	1.11	271	64	114		5.06	4.2
K	2nd Half		61	3	14	0	5	0	230			($0)	254	344	598	3	90	25	0.33	291	86	69		2.89	-2.3
LIMA B+ BA: 60%	04	Proj	**500**	**54**	**137**	**5**	**44**	**31**	**274**			**$17**	**345**	**384**	**729**	**10**	**88**	**30**	**0.91**	**280**	**76**	**124**		**4.76**	**9.6**

Foot injury in May derailed a very promising start. Pre-injury, his bb% and eye were spiking, and he was on pace for a career high in SB as a result. Likely to be undervalued on draft day.

RAY MURPHY

Hall,Bill

Pos 2B
Age 24 Growth
Bats R
R: Very High
I: EXP | con
S: pt | stb
K: age
LIMA D | BA: 40%

Yr	Tm	AB	R	H	HR	RBI	SB	Avg	vL	vR	R$	OB	Slg	OPS	bb%	ct%	h%	Eye	xBA	PX	SX	G/F	RC/G	RAR
99		0	0	0	0	0	0	0								0								
00		0	0	0	0	0	0	0								0								
01	aa	160	13	39	3	13	5	244			$3	267	363	629	3	74	31	0.12	235	77	92		3.10	-4.5
02	aaa	465	34	105	4	29	16	226			$4	262	299	561	5	81	27	0.26	237	54	78		2.41	-26.5
03	MIL	* 496	75	131	10	49	10	264	185	278	$11	307	403	711	6	80	31	0.31	261	96	101	1.62	3.88	-7.8
1st Half		281	39	69	4	20	6	246			$3	293	352	646	6	79	30	0.33	248	76	89		3.06	-11.8
2nd Half		215	36	62	6	29	4	288			$8	326	470	796	5	80	34	0.29	278	123	118		5.17	4.7
04	**Proj**	**450**	**52**	**113**	**8**	**40**	**12**	**251**			**$8**	**288**	**369**	**657**	**5**	**79**	**30**	**0.25**	**257**	**82**	**93**		**3.35**	**-13.2**

5-20-.261 in 142 AB at MIL. Showed some growth while repeating Triple-A. Much of 2nd half improvement is rooted in H% gain, so that must be viewed skeptically. Risky choice as anything more than roster filler.

Hall,Toby

Pos CA
Age 28 Peak
Bats R
R: X HIGH
I: EXP | CON
S: PT | stb
K:
LIMA D+ | BA: 70%

Yr	Tm	AB	R	H	HR	RBI	SB	Avg	vL	vR	R$	OB	Slg	OPS	bb%	ct%	h%	Eye	xBA	PX	SX	G/F	RC/G	RAR
99	aa	173	15	38	8	27	1	220			$2	233	399	632	2	95	19	0.38	317	105	37		2.96	-5.6
00	a/a	455	46	133	13	66	2	292			$13	316	437	754	3	93	29	0.48	305	92	36	1.00	4.92	10.7
01	TAM	* 561	80	174	22	93	3	310	298	298	$23	345	510	855	5	94	30	0.86	320	129	48	0.96	6.30	37.5
02	TAM	* 422	48	114	8	58	0	270	200	272	$8	303	386	689	5	91	28	0.56	281	78	40	1.03	4.05	5.2
03	TAM	463	50	117	12	47	0	253	253	252	$6	288	380	668	5	91	26	0.58	292	83	28	0.73	3.70	-5.3
1st Half		222	22	60	5	23	0	270			$4	316	378	695	6	94	27	1.15	291	70	20		4.18	0.6
2nd Half		241	28	57	7	24	0	237			$2	261	382	643	3	89	24	0.30	293	95	40		3.26	-6.0
04	**Proj**	**450**	**51**	**122**	**15**	**56**	**1**	**271**			**$11**	**303**	**429**	**733**	**4**	**92**	**27**	**0.56**	**299**	**100**	**31**		**4.49**	**7.1**

Showed terrific ct% and eye in 1st half. Unsatisfied with the results, he got overly aggressive in 2nd half, with worse results. Depressed H% says BA should recover, and declining G/F plus PX history hints at more power.

Halter,Shane

Pos 3B SS 2B
Age 34 Decline
Bats R
R: Very High
I: | CON
S: pt | stb
K: age
LIMA F | BA: 55%

Yr	Tm	AB	R	H	HR	RBI	SB	Avg	vL	vR	R$	OB	Slg	OPS	bb%	ct%	h%	Eye	xBA	PX	SX	G/F	RC/G	RAR
99	aaa	474	52	94	4	24	13	198			($3)	262	266	528	8	80	24	0.43	238	46	87		1.96	-37.8
00	DET	238	26	62	3	27	5	261	286	245	$4	302	366	667	6	79	32	0.29	252	68	102	1.29	3.78	-4.4
01	DET	450	53	128	12	65	3	284	291	282	$13	339	467	805	8	78	34	0.37	276	115	102	1.07	5.52	14.8
02	DET	410	46	98	10	39	0	239	243	238	$3	305	395	700	9	78	29	0.42	252	96	85	1.22	3.87	-7.4
03	DET	360	33	78	12	30	2	217	243	197	$2	271	342	613	7	79	24	0.35	232	68	56	1.20	2.93	-17.7
1st Half		178	16	39	5	15	1	219			$1	265	348	613	6	77	26	0.27	231	72	83		2.87	-9.1
2nd Half		182	17	39	7	15	1	214			$1	278	335	613	8	80	23	0.44	234	63	32		2.97	-8.7
04	**Proj**	**200**	**21**	**47**	**6**	**19**	**1**	**235**			**$2**	**293**	**375**	**668**	**8**	**78**	**27**	**0.38**	**237**	**82**	**79**		**3.54**	**-5.6**

Only a 119-loss team could find 360 AB for this skill set. Note the 3-year PX decline, which effectively kills off any value he once had. At age 34, he is highly unlikely to reverse the downward spiral.

Hammock,Robby

Pos CA
Age 26 Pre-Peak
Bats R
R: X HIGH
I: EXP | CON
S: PT | stb
K:
LIMA D | BA: 45%

Yr	Tm	AB	R	H	HR	RBI	SB	Avg	vL	vR	R$	OB	Slg	OPS	bb%	ct%	h%	Eye	xBA	PX	SX	G/F	RC/G	RAR
99		0	0	0	0	0	0	0								0								
00	aa	140	16	30	1	12	1	214			($1)	262	286	547	6	86	24	0.45	255	47	83		2.29	-7.8
01	aa	74	4	10	0	3	1	135			($3)	190	189	379	6	81	17	0.36	235	47	57		0.93	-7.2
02	aa	441	48	105	8	51	4	238			$5	287	358	645	6	87	26	0.53	272	81	78		3.31	-7.5
03	ARI	* 311	41	83	10	41	4	267	308	265	$9	323	441	764	8	80	31	0.41	268	108	115	1.54	4.90	5.5
1st Half		162	23	47	6	28	2	290			$7	324	512	836	5	85	31	0.32	304	135	159		5.71	6.5
2nd Half		149	18	36	4	13	2	242			$2	323	362	686	11	74	30	0.47	230	78	54		4.02	-1.2
04	**Proj**	**200**	**24**	**49**	**8**	**23**	**4**	**245**			**$5**	**301**	**429**	**729**	**7**	**83**	**26**	**0.46**	**274**	**113**	**105**		**4.30**	**1.2**

8-28-.282 in 195 AB at ARI. PX and SX are positive, but:
- ct% (77%) and eye (0.38) both suffered in ARI.
- Spike in H% propped up BA.
The power looks legitimate, but expect BA to deteriorate.

Hammonds,Jeffrey

Pos LF
Age 33 Decline
Bats R
R: Very High
I: | con
S: PT | STB
K: age
LIMA D | BA: 55%

Yr	Tm	AB	R	H	HR	RBI	SB	Avg	vL	vR	R$	OB	Slg	OPS	bb%	ct%	h%	Eye	xBA	PX	SX	G/F	RC/G	RAR
99	CIN	262	43	73	17	41	3	279	300	254	$11	346	523	869	9	76	31	0.42	281	142	47	0.95	5.90	6.5
00	COL	454	94	152	20	106	14	335	378	323	$29	394	529	922	9	82	38	0.53	286	114	102	0.94	7.76	30.8
01	MIL	174	20	43	6	21	5	247	237	250	$5	303	425	728	7	76	29	0.33	263	111	94	0.98	4.20	-7.9
02	MIL	448	47	115	9	41	4	257	298	247	$7	334	397	731	10	81	30	0.60	252	96	86	0.99	4.40	-26.2
03	2NL	132	22	32	4	13	1	242	360	215	$2	324	424	749	11	79	28	0.57	288	129	62	0.90	4.68	-3.6
1st Half		38	2	6	1	3	0	158			($1)	220	289	509	7	82	17	0.43	270	88	6		1.92	-4.6
2nd Half		94	20	26	3	10	1	277			$3	364	479	843	12	78	33	0.62	294	145	72		6.23	1.7
04	**Proj**	**250**	**40**	**69**	**9**	**33**	**4**	**276**			**$8**	**348**	**462**	**809**	**10**	**78**	**32**	**0.50**	**288**	**123**	**86**		**5.52**	**-1.7**

2003 BPIs in part-time role actually compare reasonably well to 2000 career year, with a key difference in H%. 2nd half performance in SF, especially PX, says there is still some value here, in the right situation.

Hansen,Dave

Pos 1B
Age 35 Decline
Bats L
R: Moderate
I: | CON
S: | stb
K: age
LIMA F | BA: 60%

Yr	Tm	AB	R	H	HR	RBI	SB	Avg	vL	vR	R$	OB	Slg	OPS	bb%	ct%	h%	Eye	xBA	PX	SX	G/F	RC/G	RAR
99	LA	107	14	27	2	17	0	252	267	250	$1	398	402	800	20	81	29	1.30	297	102	53	1.17	5.46	0.5
00	LA	121	18	35	8	26	0	289		310	$6	415	570	985	18	74	33	0.81	292	155	93	1.57	8.25	9.9
01	LA	140	13	33	2	20	0	236	100	246	$1	378	350	728	19	79	28	1.10	232	83		1.28	4.30	-8.2
02	LA	120	15	35	2	17	1	292	125	304	$4	366	392	757	10	82	34	0.64	230	73	44	1.34	5.22	-1.3
03	SD	135	13	33	2	15	1	244	500	233	$1	354	333	688	15	81	29	0.92	264	56	63	2.38	4.04	-5.9
1st Half		76	6	20	0	9	0	263			$1	398	316	714	18	83	32	1.31	257	47	11		4.35	-2.6
2nd Half		59	7	13	2	6	1	220			$1	292	356	648	9	80	24	0.50	271	68	124		3.49	-3.6
04	**Proj**	**150**	**17**	**38**	**3**	**19**	**1**	**253**			**$3**	**357**	**369**	**726**	**14**	**81**	**30**	**0.83**	**268**	**74**	**64**		**4.52**	**-4.9**

Still controls the strike zone very well. But four-year PX decline, and spike in G/F ratio, says that his days as an end-game power source are gone. Sample sizes are small, though, so don't give up on him entirely.

Harris,Lenny

Pos 3B
Age 39 Decline
Bats L
R: X HIGH
I: | CON
S: PT | STB
K: AGE
LIMA F | BA: 75%

Yr	Tm	AB	R	H	HR	RBI	SB	Avg	vL	vR	R$	OB	Slg	OPS	bb%	ct%	h%	Eye	xBA	PX	SX	G/F	RC/G	RAR
99	2NL	187	17	58	1	20	2	310	412	300	$5	332	396	727	3	96	32	0.86	289	69	44	1.72	4.81	2.3
00	2NL	223	31	58	4	26	13	260	158	270	$7	321	381	702	8	90	27	0.91	287	69	161	2.04	4.49	1.1
01	NYM	135	12	30	0	9	3	222		226	($0)	266	274	540	6	93	24	0.89	248	38	91	2.15	2.32	-9.5
02	MIL	197	23	60	3	17	4	305	467	291	$6	351	411	762	7	91	32	0.82	277	71	99	1.83	5.32	3.9
03	FLA	145	14	28	1	8	1	193	50	216	($2)	273	234	508	10	86	22	0.76	250	29	47	2.64	2.06	-10.1
1st Half		104	7	18	1	7	0	173			($2)	246	221	467	9	85	20	0.63	233	32	18		1.68	-8.7
2nd Half		41	7	10	0	1	1	244			$0	340	268	609	13	88	28	1.20	255	22	72		3.23	-1.2
04	**Proj**	**100**	**10**	**22**	**1**	**8**	**2**	**220**			**$0**	**274**	**297**	**572**	**7**	**90**	**24**	**0.76**	**268**	**50**	**96**		**2.69**	**-5.3**

Signs he's finally finished at 39:
- Sharp PX and SX declines.
- Spike in G/F.
He surprised us back in 2001 with a late-career rebound. Odds are strongly against another one, though.

Harris,Willie

Pos CF
Age 25 Pre-Peak
Bats L
R: Very High
I: EXP | con
S: pt | stb
K: age
LIMA D+ | BA: 45%

Yr	Tm	AB	R	H	HR	RBI	SB	Avg	vL	vR	R$	OB	Slg	OPS	bb%	ct%	h%	Eye	xBA	PX	SX	G/F	RC/G	RAR
99		0	0	0	0	0	0	0								0								
00		0	0	0	0	0	0	0								0								
01	aa	549	76	145	8	43	48	264			$22	316	361	677	7	87	29	0.57	269	63	129		3.91	-7.3
02	CHW	* 523	62	133	7	41	36	254	237	232	$17	307	342	650	7	85	29	0.53	252	57	120	1.55	3.51	-20.1
03	CHW	* 237	38	64	6	16	20	270	105	220	$10	342	401	743	10	81	31	0.58	253	79	139	2.00	4.91	1.2
1st Half		192	26	54	6	14	12	281			$8	343	432	775	9	81	32	0.50	260	89	127		5.21	2.6
2nd Half		45	12	10	0	2	8	222			$2	340	267	606	15	80	28	0.89	226	39	150		3.73	-1.4
04	**Proj**	**350**	**46**	**94**	**7**	**27**	**26**	**269**			**$13**	**324**	**386**	**710**	**8**	**84**	**30**	**0.53**	**258**	**73**	**130**		**4.30**	**-4.8**

0-5-.204 in 137 AB at CHW. Started year with terrific 100 AB in AAA, but suffered shoulder injury soon after callup. Has improved plate discipline in minors, but not yet translated to majors. There's still time.

Hart,Bo

Pos 2B
Age 27 Peak
Bats R
R: High
I: EXP | con
S: pt | stb
K:
LIMA F | BA: 35%

Yr	Tm	AB	R	H	HR	RBI	SB	Avg	vL	vR	R$	OB	Slg	OPS	bb%	ct%	h%	Eye	xBA	PX	SX	G/F	RC/G	RAR
99		0	0	0	0	0	0	0								0								
00		0	0	0	0	0	0	0								0								
01		0	0	0	0	0	0	0								0								
02	aa	405	42	77	3	27	10	190			($2)	248	259	507	7	82	23	0.42	238	47	109		1.95	-29.9
03	STL	* 562	73	153	11	56	7	272	300	267	$12	304	397	701	4	79	33	0.22	251	80	117	1.48	4.20	-3.3
1st Half		319	39	94	8	34	4	295			$10	328	436	764	5	80	35	0.25	257	90	98		5.11	6.3
2nd Half		243	34	59	3	22	3	243			$2	273	346	618	4	77	30	0.18	241	67	133		3.17	-8.9
04	**Proj**	**200**	**24**	**47**	**3**	**17**	**3**	**235**			**$2**	**277**	**336**	**612**	**5**	**80**	**28**	**0.28**	**249**	**66**	**113**		**3.04**	**-7.8**

4-28-.277 in 296 AB at STL. Swung at everything upon arriving in STL, which worked for his first 50 AB before he cooled off. 2nd half numbers are a better sign of what to expect if he continues that approach.

RAY MURPHY

Harvey,Ken

	Yr	Tm	AB	R	H	HR	RBI	SB	Avg	vL	vR	R$	OB	Slg	OPS	bb%	ct%	h%	Eye	xBA	PX	SX	G/F	RC/G	RAR
Pos 1B DH	99		0	0	0	0	0	0	0								0								
Age 26 Pre-Peak	00		0	0	0	0	0	0	0								0								
Bats R	01	aa	326	42	98	7	50	2	301			$11	329	436	765	4	85	34	0.29	273	88	74	4.00	5.20	-8.9
R High	02	aaa	488	61	124	17	61	7	254			$12	301	418	719	6	86	27	0.49	284	106	75		4.27	-21.0
I EXP	03	KC	485	50	129	13	64	2	266	333	234	$10	307	408	716	6	81	31	0.31	263	95	35	2.46	4.26	-15.7
S pt stb	1st Half		233	28	60	8	36	1	258			$5	300	425	724	6	79	30	0.29	266	108	43		4.31	-7.3
K	2nd Half		252	22	69	5	28	1	274			$5	315	393	707	6	82	32	0.33	259	82	29		4.21	-8.5
LIMA D+ BA: 40%	04	Proj	**450**	**51**	**120**	**13**	**59**	**4**	**267**			**$10**	**308**	**414**	**722**	**6**	**83**	**30**	**0.36**	**268**	**95**	**57**		**4.36**	**-16.9**

2003 vLHP vRHP
OPS 941 616
PX 146 65
Should have a career as a lefty-killer, but at this point that's the extent of his value.

Hatteberg,Scott

	Yr	Tm	AB	R	H	HR	RBI	SB	Avg	vL	vR	R$	OB	Slg	OPS	bb%	ct%	h%	Eye	xBA	PX	SX	G/F	RC/G	RAR
Pos 1B	99	BOS	* 114	15	28	1	14	0	246	267	277	$0	363	333	696	16	83	29	1.11	250	66	27	1.38	4.09	-5.7
Age 34 Decline	00	BOS	230	21	61	8	36	0	265	189	280	$5	369	435	804	14	83	29	0.97	297	105		1.36	5.49	-3.1
Bats L	01	BOS	278	34	68	3	25	1	245	176	260	$1	325	345	670	11	91	26	1.27	298	76	40	1.55	3.75	-19.8
R High	02	OAK	492	58	138	15	61	0	280	233	291	$13	368	433	801	12	89	29	1.21	273	92	48	1.24	5.64	-3.0
I CON	03	OAK	541	63	137	12	61	0	253	255	253	$7	334	383	717	11	90	26	1.25	284	89	24	1.31	4.34	-16.5
S pt stb	1st Half		285	35	76	6	38	0	267			$5	345	389	734	11	90	28	1.21	281	84	25		4.67	-5.8
K age	2nd Half		256	28	61	6	23	0	238			$2	323	375	698	11	90	24	1.28	288	94	25		3.99	-10.7
LIMA C BA: 75%	04	Proj	**550**	**64**	**146**	**13**	**62**	**0**	**265**			**$9**	**351**	**403**	**753**	**12**	**89**	**28**	**1.21**	**283**	**91**	**30**		**4.87**	**-12.6**

Skill set is stable and remains very attractive for the Moneyball poster boy. He's even starting to figure out how to hit LHers. At 34, though, it's unrealistic to expect any significant growth.

Helms,Wes

	Yr	Tm	AB	R	H	HR	RBI	SB	Avg	vL	vR	R$	OB	Slg	OPS	bb%	ct%	h%	Eye	xBA	PX	SX	G/F	RC/G	RAR
Pos 3B	99	aa	113	12	29	6	20	1	257			$3	294	469	763	5	74	29	0.21	257	126	37		4.78	1.3
Age 27 Peak	00	aaa	539	63	142	16	75	0	263			$10	294	417	711	4	86	28	0.30	282	91	59	1.00	3.99	-5.8
Bats R	01	ATL	216	28	48	10	36	1	222	203	234	$4	291	435	726	9	74	25	0.38	238	121	109	0.65	4.09	-3.3
R Very High	02	ATL	210	20	51	6	22	1	243	167	269	$3	281	405	685	5	73	31	0.19	229	116	40	0.81	3.76	-5.2
I exp con	03	MIL	476	56	124	23	67	0	261	314	249	$13	322	450	771	8	72	31	0.33	249	115	20	1.00	4.94	9.6
S PT STB	1st Half		265	34	64	13	43	0	242			$6	307	434	741	9	72	29	0.33	248	117	29		4.41	1.2
K	2nd Half		211	22	60	10	24	0	284			$7	341	469	810	8	73	34	0.32	251	112	13		5.69	8.5
LIMA C BA: 35%	04	Proj	**500**	**56**	**127**	**21**	**67**	**1**	**254**			**$12**	**307**	**437**	**744**	**7**	**74**	**30**	**0.29**	**253**	**114**	**40**		**4.54**	**2.0**

2003 vLHP vRHP
OPS 1006 728
PX 150 98
AB 86 390
Didn't anyone throw LHers at MIL in 2003? Like Harvey, he's best utilized in a platoon.

Helton,Todd

	Yr	Tm	AB	R	H	HR	RBI	SB	Avg	vL	vR	R$	OB	Slg	OPS	bb%	ct%	h%	Eye	xBA	PX	SX	G/F	RC/G	RAR
Pos 1B	99	COL	578	114	185	35	113	7	320	245	349	$32	392	587	978	11	87	32	0.88	324	159	91	0.96	8.38	48.1
Age 30 Past Peak	00	COL	580	138	216	42	147	5	372	329	387	$46	467	698	1165	15	89	36	1.69	384	197	69	1.08	13.11	111.7
Bats L	01	COL	587	132	197	49	146	7	336	290	354	$45	431	685	1115	14	82	34	0.94	352	207	76	0.96	11.09	75.0
R Very Low	02	COL	553	107	182	30	109	5	329	327	331	$34	431	577	1008	15	84	35	1.09	331	159	90	1.02	9.47	56.5
I con	03	COL	583	135	209	33	117	0	358	387	344	$38	461	630	1091	16	88	37	1.54	357	171	62	0.83	11.27	85.4
S	1st Half		307	71	103	14	64	0	336			$18	436	577	1013	15	88	35	1.53	352	159	67		9.55	32.4
K	2nd Half		276	64	106	19	53	0	384			$22	488	688	1176	17	87	39	1.56	364	186	72		13.41	53.6
LIMA C BA: 60%	04	Proj	**550**	**121**	**192**	**39**	**115**	**3**	**349**			**$39**	**449**	**660**	**1109**	**15**	**86**	**35**	**1.27**	**361**	**191**	**74**		**11.41**	**82.0**

Nice rebound from a comparatively sub-par 2002. 2nd-half BPIs were very similar to those of his monster 2000 season. Could return to the 40 HR level in 2004.

Henderson,Rickey

	Yr	Tm	AB	R	H	HR	RBI	SB	Avg	vL	vR	R$	OB	Slg	OPS	bb%	ct%	h%	Eye	xBA	PX	SX	G/F	RC/G	RAR
Pos LF	99	NYM	438	89	138	12	42	37	315	343	306	$25	423	466	889	16	81	37	1.00	285	102	96	1.12	7.22	26.7
Age 45 Decline	00	2TM	420	75	98	4	32	36	233	200	242	$11	366	305	671	17	82	28	1.17	225	46	122	1.07	3.90	-16.4
Bats R	01	SD	* 419	74	95	8	44	26	227	210	235	$11	353	346	699	16	78	27	0.88	250	76	134	1.13	4.16	-19.9
R Very High	02	BOS	179	40	40	5	16	8	223	200	245	$4	359	352	711	18	74	28	0.81	226	76	124	1.41	4.27	-3.1
I con	03	LA	72	7	15	2	5	3	208	167	250	$1	313	306	619	13	78	24	0.69	257	56	60	1.35	3.31	-5.1
S pt STB	1st Half		0	0	0	0	0	0	0			($0)					0			0	0				
K AGE	2nd Half		72	7	15	2	5	3	208			$1	313	306	619	13	78	24	0.69	257	56	60		3.32	-5.1
LIMA D BA: 70%	04	Proj	**150**	**25**	**35**	**3**	**13**	**4**	**233**			**$2**	**354**	**349**	**703**	**16**	**78**	**28**	**0.85**	**264**	**71**	**97**		**4.06**	**-7.8**

Plate discipline is still there, but SX says the legs finally gave out. The sample size is small, though. If this is in fact the end of the line, we bid a fond farewell to one of the original roto-gods.

Hernandez,Jose

	Yr	Tm	AB	R	H	HR	RBI	SB	Avg	vL	vR	R$	OB	Slg	OPS	bb%	ct%	h%	Eye	xBA	PX	SX	G/F	RC/G	RAR
Pos 3B SS	99	2NL	508	79	135	19	62	11	266	292	253	$14	334	425	759	9	71	34	0.36	244	95	94	1.50	4.95	8.7
Age 34 Decline	00	MIL	446	51	109	11	59	3	244	212	255	$6	308	372	680	8	72	32	0.33	224	81	48	1.99	3.65	-9.0
Bats R	01	MIL	542	67	135	25	78	5	249	339	226	$14	299	443	742	7	66	33	0.21	232	114	72	1.43	4.41	-2.9
R High	02	MIL	525	72	151	24	73	3	288	253	296	$20	352	478	830	9	64	41	0.28	235	120	58	1.68	5.83	18.5
I CON	03	2NL	519	58	117	13	57	2	225	235	221	$4	288	347	635	8	66	32	0.26	205	75	76	1.44	3.29	-15.3
S stb	1st Half		273	34	62	9	28	1	227			$2	301	355	657	10	63	33	0.29	194	75	62		3.50	-6.3
K age	2nd Half		246	24	55	4	29	1	224			$1	274	337	611	6	69	31	0.22	216	76	83		3.05	-9.0
LIMA D BA: 30%	04	Proj	**450**	**54**	**108**	**15**	**56**	**3**	**240**			**$7**	**301**	**390**	**691**	**8**	**66**	**33**	**0.26**	**210**	**93**	**70**		**3.88**	**-7.0**

The introduction of H% as a metric goes a long way toward explaining 2002's BA surge. Even a half-season in COL couldn't stop the regression. Sharp drop in PX at his age is a potential warning sign as well.

Hernandez,Ramon

	Yr	Tm	AB	R	H	HR	RBI	SB	Avg	vL	vR	R$	OB	Slg	OPS	bb%	ct%	h%	Eye	xBA	PX	SX	G/F	RC/G	RAR
Pos CA	99	OAK	* 427	46	109	14	68	2	255	357	245	$8	315	405	720	8	90	26	0.88	289	89	53	1.24	4.31	3.0
Age 27 Peak	00	OAK	419	52	101	14	62	1	241	243	240	$5	304	387	691	8	85	26	0.59	251	87	42	1.26	3.96	-2.3
Bats R	01	OAK	453	55	115	15	60	1	254	241	261	$9	310	408	719	8	85	27	0.54	289	98	36	1.45	4.30	5.8
R Very Low	02	OAK	403	51	94	7	42	0	233	257	224	$2	307	335	642	10	84	26	0.67	239	69	33	1.45	3.42	-2.4
I con	03	OAK	483	70	132	21	78	0	273	208	302	$15	320	458	777	6	84	29	0.42	286	111	40	1.10	5.13	14.3
S	1st Half		244	36	66	10	35	0	270			$7	313	463	776	6	84	29	0.39	287	120	51		5.06	6.8
K	2nd Half		239	34	66	11	43	0	276			$8	327	452	779	7	83	29	0.44	278	103	29		5.20	7.5
LIMA D+ BA: 55%	04	Proj	**450**	**60**	**117**	**18**	**65**	**0**	**260**			**$11**	**317**	**426**	**743**	**8**	**84**	**27**	**0.53**	**274**	**102**	**34**		**4.64**	**9.1**

Got more aggressive at the plate, and it worked for him all year. Note that H% says the BA improvement may not be sustainable. But the PX rebound and declining G/F say that the power surge is more legitimate.

Hidalgo,Richard

	Yr	Tm	AB	R	H	HR	RBI	SB	Avg	vL	vR	R$	OB	Slg	OPS	bb%	ct%	h%	Eye	xBA	PX	SX	G/F	RC/G	RAR
Pos RF	99	HOU	383	49	87	15	56	8	227	224	228	$7	326	420	746	13	81	24	0.77	252	121	78	0.79	4.40	-7.0
Age 28 Peak	00	HOU	558	118	175	44	122	13	314	333	308	$37	376	636	1012	9	80	32	0.51	281	186	104	0.58	8.70	54.3
Bats R	01	HOU	512	70	141	19	80	3	275	286	273	$16	345	455	800	10	79	32	0.50	245	109	66	0.72	5.34	-3.2
R Moderate	02	HOU	388	54	91	15	48	6	235	263	228	$8	311	415	726	10	78	26	0.51	246	112	114	0.76	4.29	-11.8
I CON	03	HOU	514	91	159	28	88	9	309	307	310	$28	379	572	951	10	80	34	0.56	301	167	100	0.75	7.73	30.1
S pt	1st Half		227	41	72	11	36	4	317			$12	395	551	945	11	83	34	0.74	302	155	61		7.73	13.2
K	2nd Half		287	50	87	17	52	5	303			$16	367	589	956	9	77	34	0.45	300	177	130		7.71	16.8
LIMA B BA: 40%	04	Proj	**550**	**88**	**160**	**32**	**102**	**9**	**291**			**$28**	**362**	**546**	**908**	**10**	**79**	**32**	**0.54**	**298**	**157**	**93**		**6.93**	**22.6**

Fantastic comeback, 2003 skill set was in line with his monster 2000 campaign. In fact, most BPIs (except PX and SX) were stable all along. Health was the missing element. 2H PX and SX say that there's more to come.

Higginson,Bobby

	Yr	Tm	AB	R	H	HR	RBI	SB	Avg	vL	vR	R$	OB	Slg	OPS	bb%	ct%	h%	Eye	xBA	PX	SX	G/F	RC/G	RAR
Pos RF	99	DET	377	51	90	12	46	4	239	265	231	$5	349	382	731	15	82	26	0.97	270	88	43	0.74	4.27	-8.0
Age 33 Decline	00	DET	597	104	179	30	102	15	300	264	316	$27	377	538	915	11	83	32	0.75	290	141	110	0.69	7.43	41.5
Bats L	01	DET	541	84	150	17	71	20	277	293	271	$20	370	445	816	13	88	29	1.23	272	102	110	0.74	5.60	9.8
R Low	02	DET	444	50	125	10	63	12	282	241	299	$15	342	417	759	8	90	30	0.91	277	87	92	0.82	5.01	-0.2
I con	03	DET	469	61	110	14	52	8	235	227	238	$7	320	369	689	11	84	25	0.81	266	77	88	1.05	3.76	-20.0
S pt	1st Half		268	36	63	5	23	7	235			$3	328	332	660	12	84	26	0.86	253	61	80		3.51	-13.5
K age	2nd Half		201	25	47	9	29	1	234			$4	309	418	727	10	85	23	0.73	283	99	92		4.06	-6.7
LIMA B BA: 70%	04	Proj	**500**	**66**	**135**	**16**	**65**	**10**	**270**			**$15**	**348**	**421**	**769**	**11**	**86**	**29**	**0.88**	**274**	**90**	**88**		**4.95**	**-1.8**

Here is a case where H% predicts a BA rebound in 2004. PX trend is troubling, although year-long battle with hamstring injury may be a factor. If the bidding stops under $10, you'll make a nice profit.

RAY MURPHY

Hillenbrand,Shea

Pos 1B 3B
Age 28 Peak
Bats R
R: High
I: exp con
S: pt stb
K:
LIMA C BA: 55%

Yr	Tm	AB	R	H	HR	RBI	SB	Avg	vL	vR	R$	OB	Slg	OPS	bb%	ct%	h%	Eye	xBA	PX	SX	G/F	RC/G	RAR
99	aa	282	33	65	6	29	5	230			$2	259	344	603	4	91	23	0.46	289	75	69		2.73	-24.6
00	aa	529	60	147	7	62	3	278			$9	297	384	680	3	93	29	0.37	293	72	64		3.94	-25.7
01	BOS	468	52	123	12	49	3	263	227	277	$8	283	391	674	3	87	28	0.21	267	80	61	1.55	3.70	-33.4
02	BOS	634	94	186	18	83	4	293	269	299	$20	320	459	779	4	85	32	0.26	298	107	89	1.50	5.27	-10.4
03	2TM	515	60	144	20	97	1	280	298	271	$18	312	468	780	4	86	29	0.34	325	122	45	1.40	5.17	-3.9
1st Half		219	24	65	4	44	1	297			$8	325	452	777	4	87	33	0.31	321	113	60		5.35	-0.6
2nd Half		296	36	79	16	53	0	267			$10	302	480	782	5	86	26	0.37	326	128	22		5.04	-3.4
04	Proj	**550**	**68**	**153**	**18**	**84**	**1**	**278**			**$16**	**306**	**454**	**760**	**4**	**87**	**29**	**0.31**	**329**	**116**	**51**		**4.88**	**-11.9**

Positive trends, but we're probably seeing about the best that it's going to get. High G/F puts a cap on power potential. Low OB limits his overall value. And sub-zero RAR tells sim players all they need to know.

Hinch,A.J.

Pos CA
Age 29 Past Peak
Bats R
R: Very High
I: EXP CON
S: PT stb
K:
LIMA F BA: 55%

Yr	Tm	AB	R	H	HR	RBI	SB	Avg	vL	vR	R$	OB	Slg	OPS	bb%	ct%	h%	Eye	xBA	PX	SX	G/F	RC/G	RAR
99	OAK	* 266	33	64	8	29	6	241	224	212	$4	276	361	637	5	79	28	0.23	246	67	93	1.12	3.34	-5.8
00	aaa	417	58	99	6	42	5	237			$2	304	333	637	9	85	27	0.63	262	64	72	4.00	3.28	-10.0
01	KC	* 289	31	67	14	40	2	232	194	141	$6	272	429	701	5	82	24	0.31	273	118	42	1.02	3.85	-0.1
02	KC	197	25	49	7	27	3	249	276	231	$5	312	401	713	8	82	27	0.51	252	89	75	0.94	4.05	2.6
03	DET	* 259	24	55	6	31	0	212	190	208	$0	255	355	611	5	79	25	0.27	251	93	61	0.80	2.88	-9.7
1st Half		198	17	43	4	24	0	217			$0	258	364	622	5	78	26	0.26	253	97	69		2.98	-6.8
2nd Half		61	7	12	2	7	0	197			($0)	246	328	574	6	80	21	0.33	247	79	34		2.56	-2.9
04	Proj	**150**	**17**	**33**	**5**	**19**	**1**	**220**			**$1**	**270**	**370**	**641**	**6**	**81**	**24**	**0.36**	**257**	**89**	**74**		**3.21**	**-3.4**

3-11-.203 in 74 AB. Successive groin injuries derailed his 2nd half, but you'd hardly notice from the numbers. Consistently low hit rates show that the bar is very low here. Pass.

Hinske,Eric

Pos 3B
Age 26 Pre-Peak
Bats L
R: High
I: EXP con
S: pt stb
K:
LIMA B BA: 55%

Yr	Tm	AB	R	H	HR	RBI	SB	Avg	vL	vR	R$	OB	Slg	OPS	bb%	ct%	h%	Eye	xBA	PX	SX	G/F	RC/G	RAR
99	aaa	15	3	4	1	2	0	267			$0	313	600	913	6	73	30	0.25	294	158	353		6.52	0.9
00	aa	436	70	100	17	67	13	229			$10	339	415	754	14	69	29	0.54	239	104	143		4.63	3.6
01	aaa	436	56	106	20	62	16	243			$15	311	438	749	9	79	26	0.48	271	117	84		4.39	-1.1
02	TOR	566	99	158	24	84	13	279	202	301	$22	365	481	846	12	76	33	0.56	268	126	104	1.04	6.33	29.9
03	TOR	449	74	109	12	63	12	243	256	237	$10	331	437	767	12	77	29	0.57	282	134	120	0.93	4.94	5.7
1st Half		174	26	40	2	22	2	230			$1	313	379	692	11	75	29	0.49	264	118	67		3.90	-3.2
2nd Half		275	48	69	10	41	10	251			$9	342	473	815	12	78	29	0.62	293	144	140		5.65	9.3
04	Proj	**550**	**89**	**153**	**25**	**94**	**15**	**278**			**$24**	**362**	**504**	**866**	**12**	**76**	**32**	**0.55**	**284**	**142**	**104**		**6.46**	**31.3**

Chalk this disappointing season up to a broken hand. Still, there are a few exciting BPIs that point to good times ahead... Stable bb% and ct% despite injury, rising power, declining G/F all point to a solid rebound in '04.

Hocking,Denny

Pos 2B 3B
Age 34 Decline
Bats S
R: Low
I: con
S: pt
K: age
LIMA F BA: 55%

Yr	Tm	AB	R	H	HR	RBI	SB	Avg	vL	vR	R$	OB	Slg	OPS	bb%	ct%	h%	Eye	xBA	PX	SX	G/F	RC/G	RAR
99	MIN	386	47	103	7	41	11	267	242	279	$8	306	378	685	5	86	30	0.41	275	71	95	1.27	3.87	-1.2
00	MIN	373	52	111	4	47	7	298	279	305	$10	378	416	793	11	79	37	0.62	243	78	103	1.40	5.55	17.6
01	MIN	327	34	82	3	25	6	251	222	260	$3	312	339	651	8	80	31	0.43	238	62	87	1.34	3.66	-5.2
02	MIN	260	28	65	2	25	0	250	342	212	$2	313	323	636	8	83	29	0.55	227	55	30	1.35	3.33	-5.5
03	MIN	188	22	45	3	22	0	239	239	274	$1	296	362	657	7	80	28	0.41	255	80	78	1.69	3.50	-3.6
1st Half		76	9	19	1	7	0	250			$0	305	382	686	7	82	30	0.43	266	89	93		3.73	-0.9
2nd Half		112	13	26	2	15	0	232			$1	289	348	637	7	79	28	0.39	248	74	66		3.34	-2.7
04	Proj	**150**	**17**	**37**	**2**	**16**	**1**	**247**			**$1**	**306**	**352**	**658**	**8**	**81**	**29**	**0.45**	**253**	**71**	**70**		**3.57**	**-2.4**

This projection follows the logical 5-year trend of his playing time. This is confirmed by the concurrent trends in OB, bb%, and roto value. Pass.

Hollandsworth,Tod

Pos LF
Age 31 Past Peak
Bats L
R: High
I: con
S: PT stb
K:
LIMA C BA: 50%

Yr	Tm	AB	R	H	HR	RBI	SB	Avg	vL	vR	R$	OB	Slg	OPS	bb%	ct%	h%	Eye	xBA	PX	SX	G/F	RC/G	RAR
99	LA	261	39	74	9	32	5	284	310	280	$8	344	448	792	8	77	34	0.39	276	100	96	1.68	5.44	2.9
00	2NL	428	81	115	19	47	18	269	250	272	$16	333	449	781	9	77	31	0.41	265	106	99	1.35	5.11	-1.3
01	COL	117	21	43	6	19	5	368	158	408	$9	408	667	1075	6	83	41	0.40	378	194	121	1.68	11.35	16.4
02	2TM	430	55	122	16	67	8	284	228	292	$17	345	463	807	9	77	34	0.41	266	117	65	1.71	5.38	-2.9
03	FLA	228	32	58	3	20	2	254	250	255	$2	320	421	741	9	76	32	0.40	269	123	116	1.09	4.41	-8.0
1st Half		187	27	47	2	14	2	251			$2	307	422	729	7	74	33	0.31	268	132	115		4.17	-7.9
2nd Half		41	5	11	1	6	0	268			$1	375	415	790	15	83	30	1.00	272	82	116		5.42	-0.2
04	Proj	**350**	**55**	**97**	**12**	**43**	**9**	**277**			**$12**	**333**	**481**	**813**	**8**	**78**	**33**	**0.37**	**285**	**139**	**109**		**5.53**	**-2.3**

A pulled hamstring in May dogged him for most of the year, and FLA found other options. BPIs are stable, after 2001's short-term aberration, and the promise of a ROY season long ago are long gone.

Houston,Tyler

Pos 3B
Age 33 Decline
Bats L
R: Moderate
I: con
S: pt stb
K: age
LIMA F BA: 45%

Yr	Tm	AB	R	H	HR	RBI	SB	Avg	vL	vR	R$	OB	Slg	OPS	bb%	ct%	h%	Eye	xBA	PX	SX	G/F	RC/G	RAR
99	CLE	276	28	62	10	30	1	225	333	125	$2	303	377	680	10	72	28	0.40	248	88	47	1.26	3.72	-5.9
00	MIL	284	30	71	18	43	2	250	182	256	$8	292	493	785	6	75	27	0.24	279	139	34	1.04	4.86	4.5
01	MIL	235	36	68	12	38	0	289	280	290	$9	340	472	812	7	74	35	0.29	275	102	31	1.25	5.76	7.7
02	LA	320	34	90	7	40	1	281	259	283	$8	315	428	744	5	81	33	0.26	262	102	79	1.32	4.81	2.0
03	PHI	* 120	9	31	2	14	0	258	333	277	$2	299	383	683	6	83	30	0.35	261	86	47	2.21	3.94	-1.1
1st Half		36	4	12	1	7	0	333			$2	368	472	841	5	83	38	0.33	262	93	20		6.65	2.3
2nd Half		84	5	19	1	7	0	226			($0)	270	345	615	6	83	26	0.36	261	83	58		3.07	-3.0
04	Proj	**250**	**26**	**67**	**8**	**31**	**1**	**268**			**$6**	**314**	**426**	**740**	**6**	**78**	**31**	**0.30**	**253**	**99**	**47**		**4.65**	**1.8**

The Phil's insurance policy in case a vet got hurt, he never got much of a chance, and likely played pissed-off for most of the 2nd half. There is still some latent talent here, but the latent attitude might get in the way.

Hudson,Orlando

Pos 2B
Age 26 Pre-Peak
Bats S
R: High
I: EXP con
S: pt stb
K:
LIMA C+ BA: 50%

Yr	Tm	AB	R	H	HR	RBI	SB	Avg	vL	vR	R$	OB	Slg	OPS	bb%	ct%	h%	Eye	xBA	PX	SX	G/F	RC/G	RAR
99		0	0	0	0	0	0	0								0								
00	aa	134	13	29	2	12	2	216			($0)	276	321	597	8	90	23	0.79	276	60	105		2.75	-5.7
01	a/a	500	70	144	7	67	16	288			$17	353	438	791	9	87	32	0.79	294	99	144		5.44	20.0
02	TOR	* 609	70	168	12	53	6	276	184	308	$12	319	419	738	6	89	30	0.56	284	93	92	1.25	4.54	8.8
03	TOR	474	54	127	9	57	5	268	160	297	$10	324	395	718	8	82	31	0.45	279	79	99	1.68	4.35	2.9
1st Half		255	33	75	5	36	4	294			$8	341	431	772	7	83	34	0.41	288	85	120		5.24	7.9
2nd Half		219	21	52	4	21	1	237			$1	304	352	656	9	80	28	0.49	269	72	69		3.46	-4.5
04	Proj	**550**	**63**	**155**	**12**	**59**	**10**	**282**			**$15**	**336**	**423**	**759**	**8**	**85**	**31**	**0.54**	**299**	**88**	**107**		**4.94**	**13.3**

Reasons why this was not a sophomore slump:
- 1st half showed BPI growth
- Naggy groin hurt 2nd half
- I hate when the media slaps stereotypical labels on players.

Huff,Aubrey

Pos RF DH 1B
Age 27 Peak
Bats L
R: Low
I: EXP con
S:
K:
LIMA C BA: 60%

Yr	Tm	AB	R	H	HR	RBI	SB	Avg	vL	vR	R$	OB	Slg	OPS	bb%	ct%	h%	Eye	xBA	PX	SX	G/F	RC/G	RAR
99	aa	491	70	136	19	64	2	277			$13	345	479	824	9	87	29	0.81	305	129	55		5.71	10.2
00	TAM	* 530	66	148	19	70	1	279	250	291	$12	333	470	803	8	87	29	0.61	302	119	43	1.54	5.38	7.0
01	TAM	* 477	54	120	11	54	1	252	172	269	$6	292	390	682	5	84	28	0.35	264	93	43	2.04	3.78	-17.0
02	TAM	* 580	83	180	26	76	4	310	307	315	$24	362	503	865	7	89	32	0.71	301	119	53	1.31	6.74	27.1
03	TAM	636	91	198	34	107	2	311	318	308	$29	364	555	919	8	87	31	0.66	340	150	51	1.49	7.37	38.4
1st Half		311	45	94	15	45	1	302			$12	352	547	899	7	85	32	0.51	335	158	50		6.88	14.8
2nd Half		325	46	104	19	62	1	320			$17	376	563	939	8	90	31	0.88	344	143	54		7.86	23.6
04	Proj	**625**	**86**	**202**	**28**	**108**	**2**	**323**			**$30**	**373**	**534**	**907**	**7**	**87**	**34**	**0.63**	**325**	**130**	**48**		**7.41**	**39.1**

Two intriguing indicators...
- xBA says that there is some exciting BA upside, confirmed by his 2nd half contact rate.
- High G/F ratios might indicate that 2003's power output is a bit over his head.

Hundley,Todd

Pos CA
Age 34 Decline
Bats S
R: Moderate
I: CON
S: pt stb
K: age
LIMA F BA: 50%

Yr	Tm	AB	R	H	HR	RBI	SB	Avg	vL	vR	R$	OB	Slg	OPS	bb%	ct%	h%	Eye	xBA	PX	SX	G/F	RC/G	RAR
99	LA	376	49	78	24	55	3	207	105	226	$6	290	436	727	10	70	23	0.39	221	130	50	0.88	4.12	1.8
00	LA	299	49	85	24	70	0	284	237	300	$15	378	579	957	13	77	30	0.65	277	165	21	0.83	7.69	31.2
01	CHC	* 309	29	57	14	38	0	184	292	176	$0	254	362	617	9	63	24	0.25	207	104		0.93	2.88	-6.3
02	CHC	275	33	58	17	38	0	211	217	209	$5	295	425	721	11	71	23	0.41	231	127		0.78	4.06	-0.4
03	LA	33	2	6	2	11	0	182		222	$1	341	394	735	20	61	22	0.62	179	122	7	0.55	3.75	-0.6
1st Half		25	1	5	1	8	0	200			$1	394	360	754	24	68	25	1.00	191	98	7		3.97	-0.3
2nd Half		8	1	1	1	3	0	125			$0	125	500	625	0	38	0	0.00	0	196			1.82	-0.7
04	Proj	**150**	**20**	**35**	**9**	**25**	**0**	**233**			**$4**	**319**	**449**	**768**	**11**	**71**	**27**	**0.43**	**215**	**127**	**28**		**4.74**	**2.9**

In even 33 AB, we can still see small signs of life. His constant health woes have conditioned us to expect the worst, but with a little bit of health, he could provide an unexpected return on investment.

Hunter,Brian L.

	Yr	Tm	AB	R	H	HR	RBI	SB	Avg	vL	vR	R$	OB	Slg	OPS	bb%	ct%	h%	Eye	xBA	PX	SX	G/F	RC/G	RAR
Pos RF	99	SEA	539	79	125	4	34	44	232	186	243	$12	281	301	582	6	83	27	0.41	244	41	171	1.86	3.01	-32.4
Age 33 Decline	00	2NL	240	47	64	1	14	20	267	223	295	$8	341	308	649	10	83	32	0.68	240	27	136	2.64	3.99	-8.1
Bats R	01	PHI	145	22	40	2	16	14	276	232	303	$7	348	359	706	10	83	32	0.64	239	56	109	1.39	4.64	-3.9
R Very High	02	HOU	201	32	54	3	20	5	269	241	301	$5	323	423	745	7	81	32	0.41	292	111	153	1.55	4.91	-2.2
I CON	03	HOU	98	13	23	0	13	0	235	263	217	$0	279	316	595	6	79	30	0.29	203	64	88	1.69	2.94	-7.9
S PT stb	1st Half		78	13	20	0	11	0	256			$1	310	321	630	7	81	32	0.40	203	57	54		3.40	-5.0
K age	2nd Half		20	0	3	0	2	0	150			($1)	150	300	450	0	70	21	0.00	200	89	217		1.35	-2.8
LIMA F BA: 35%	04	Proj	**150**	**25**	**36**	**1**	**16**	**7**	**240**			**$3**	**303**	**330**	**633**	**8**	**82**	**29**	**0.50**	**216**	**66**	**135**		**3.50**	**-8.9**

Cut on 7/28 after failing to score from 2nd on a double because he misjudged a fly ball. When your value dips below a certain level, there is little margin for error. Odds are Barry Bonds would not have been cut.

Hunter,Torii

	Yr	Tm	AB	R	H	HR	RBI	SB	Avg	vL	vR	R$	OB	Slg	OPS	bb%	ct%	h%	Eye	xBA	PX	SX	G/F	RC/G	RAR
Pos CF	99	MIN	384	52	98	9	35	10	255	295	239	$7	302	380	683	6	81	29	0.36	243	77	100	1.64	3.81	-10.3
Age 28 Peak	00	MIN	* 545	89	164	19	91	13	301	241	292	$22	333	490	823	5	83	33	0.29	290	109	142	1.44	5.77	17.0
Bats R	01	MIN	564	82	147	27	92	9	261	256	262	$19	297	479	776	5	78	29	0.23	283	129	106	1.36	4.75	-1.6
R Low	02	MIN	561	89	162	29	94	23	289	296	286	$30	331	524	855	6	79	32	0.30	301	142	126	1.50	6.09	21.0
I CON	03	MIN	581	83	145	26	102	6	250	250	249	$17	309	451	760	8	82	27	0.47	287	121	83	1.40	4.55	-3.3
S pt	1st Half		295	39	75	11	50	3	254			$8	325	437	762	10	81	28	0.56	280	113	71		4.46	-2.5
K	2nd Half		286	44	70	15	52	3	245			$9	292	465	757	6	82	25	0.37	294	129	99		4.64	-0.9
LIMA C+ BA: 60%	04	Proj	**550**	**82**	**154**	**25**	**92**	**11**	**280**			**$22**	**327**	**490**	**817**	**7**	**81**	**31**	**0.36**	**287**	**125**	**101**		**5.53**	**12.1**

Dug himself a .227 hole by 5/1, which was tough to climb out of, but BPIs were not that bad. Oddly, most of the negative focus was on his BA, but it was his power that was truly off from 2003. G/F limits expectations.

Hyzdu,Adam

	Yr	Tm	AB	R	H	HR	RBI	SB	Avg	vL	vR	R$	OB	Slg	OPS	bb%	ct%	h%	Eye	xBA	PX	SX	G/F	RC/G	RAR
Pos CF	99	a/a	424	53	103	23	70	6	243			$12	299	469	768	7	80	25	0.41	285	133	74		4.61	1.3
Age 32 Past Peak	00	aa	514	66	110	22	73	2	214			$5	301	409	710	11	77	23	0.55	269	116	51	1.00	3.82	-10.8
Bats R	01	PIT	* 333	34	77	13	37	1	231	167	229	$4	269	402	671	5	77	26	0.22	255	102	46	0.92	3.34	-5.2
R High	02	PIT	* 398	48	85	18	71	1	214	204	245	$8	290	399	690	10	76	24	0.45	254	119	35	0.60	3.69	-14.6
I EXP con	03	PIT	* 198	33	45	6	22	2	227	188	226	$2	311	399	710	11	76	27	0.51	258	115	90	1.40	3.98	-6.1
S PT	1st Half		87	20	19	3	14	1	218			$1	333	425	759	15	78	25	0.79	279	146	84		4.29	-1.9
K	2nd Half		111	13	26	3	8	1	234			$1	292	378	670	7	75	29	0.32	241	91	91		3.72	-4.2
LIMA F BA: 55%	04	Proj	**100**	**14**	**22**	**4**	**13**	**1**	**220**			**$1**	**293**	**391**	**684**	**9**	**76**	**25**	**0.44**	**255**	**111**	**55**		**3.64**	**-3.3**

1-8-.206 in 63 AB at PIT, but for the 2nd season in a row, he included a .300-plus run in those stats. Unfortunately, we cannot call you a legitimate .300 hitter unless you can sustain it for more than 50 AB.

Ibanez,Raul

	Yr	Tm	AB	R	H	HR	RBI	SB	Avg	vL	vR	R$	OB	Slg	OPS	bb%	ct%	h%	Eye	xBA	PX	SX	G/F	RC/G	RAR
Pos LF 1B	99	SEA	* 240	28	64	12	31	6	267	238	261	$8	318	450	768	7	84	28	0.46	279	103	64	1.13	5.03	-0.2
Age 31 Past Peak	00	SEA	* 180	24	41	2	21	2	228	333	221	$0	287	328	615	8	84	26	0.54	263	72	69	0.86	3.17	-10.5
Bats L	01	KC	* 306	46	82	15	58	0	268	200	286	$10	339	487	826	10	81	29	0.56	278	122	92	1.03	5.60	8.7
R High	02	KC	497	70	146	24	103	5	294	274	300	$23	346	537	884	7	85	31	0.53	313	148	102	1.06	6.62	24.8
I exp CON	03	KC	608	95	179	18	90	8	294	245	319	$21	347	454	801	7	87	32	0.60	296	100	98	1.17	5.63	5.1
S pt	1st Half		310	51	89	10	45	2	287			$10	338	461	800	7	87	30	0.60	304	111	83		5.55	1.9
K	2nd Half		298	44	90	8	45	6	302			$12	356	446	802	8	86	33	0.61	286	88	103		5.71	3.1
LIMA C+ BA: 55%	04	Proj	**550**	**81**	**166**	**20**	**92**	**6**	**302**			**$22**	**356**	**487**	**844**	**8**	**85**	**33**	**0.57**	**300**	**113**	**93**		**6.26**	**18.1**

A near-identical season to 2002, except for the power drop-off. Given his G/F ratio, he's probably reached his power ceiling anyway. Could flirt with .300 in 2004.

Infante,Omar

	Yr	Tm	AB	R	H	HR	RBI	SB	Avg	vL	vR	R$	OB	Slg	OPS	bb%	ct%	h%	Eye	xBA	PX	SX	G/F	RC/G	RAR
Pos SS	99		0	0	0	0	0	0	0								0								
Age 22 Growth	00		0	0	0	0	0	0	0								0								
Bats R	01	aa	540	79	167	1	57	25	309			$20	359	369	728	7	89	35	0.69	261	44	105		4.66	10.6
R High	02	aaa	436	51	127	3	53	20	291			$16	338	394	733	7	92	31	0.84	281	64	156	0.95	4.28	0.5
I EXP con	03	DET	* 445	54	100	2	27	29	225	155	253	$7	290	279	569	8	86	26	0.65	242	40	113	1.29	2.80	-22.5
S stb	1st Half		208	20	43	0	7	6	207			($1)	273	236	509	8	83	25	0.53	220	21	89		2.06	-15.6
K AGE	2nd Half		237	34	57	2	20	23	241			$8	305	316	621	8	89	26	0.81	261	57	119		3.52	-6.6
LIMA D BA: 65%	04	Proj	**250**	**31**	**60**	**1**	**23**	**11**	**240**			**$4**	**298**	**312**	**610**	**8**	**88**	**27**	**0.72**	**258**	**50**	**115**		**2.99**	**-11.2**

0-8-6-.222 in 221 AB at DET, then was demoted and put up marginally better MLEs at AAA. Earlier history shows signs of good lead-off style skill, but he needs much more development time.

Inge,Brandon

	Yr	Tm	AB	R	H	HR	RBI	SB	Avg	vL	vR	R$	OB	Slg	OPS	bb%	ct%	h%	Eye	xBA	PX	SX	G/F	RC/G	RAR
Pos CA	99		0	0	0	0	0	0	0								0								
Age 26 Pre-Peak	00	a/a	488	51	108	7	59	10	221			$3	271	344	615	6	81	26	0.36	264	83	98		3.00	-16.2
Bats S	01	DET	* 279	22	58	1	27	2	208	218	164	($2)	248	305	553	5	79	26	0.25	242	77	58	1.18	2.29	-13.9
R High	02	DET	* 386	36	82	9	36	2	212	229	195	$1	276	368	644	8	70	28	0.30	227	92	129	1.01	3.08	-6.5
I EXP con	03	DET	* 472	46	102	12	44	7	216	245	182	$3	270	354	624	7	79	25	0.35	248	87	83	1.12	3.02	-15.7
S pt	1st Half		194	14	31	4	11	0	160			($4)	220	273	493	7	75	19	0.31	225	67	72		1.63	-16.1
K	2nd Half		278	32	71	8	33	7	255			$7	305	410	715	7	81	29	0.38	266	100	88		4.36	2.2
LIMA D BA: 55%	04	Proj	**350**	**33**	**80**	**7**	**34**	**4**	**229**			**$3**	**282**	**362**	**643**	**7**	**77**	**28**	**0.32**	**243**	**86**	**84**		**3.24**	**-7.6**

8-30-.203 in 330 AB at DET. He's shown power potential... but has yet to crack a league average 100 PX. His xBA shows .240 BA potential ... but in four seasons, his REAL BA has yet to crack .221.

Izturis,Cesar

	Yr	Tm	AB	R	H	HR	RBI	SB	Avg	vL	vR	R$	OB	Slg	OPS	bb%	ct%	h%	Eye	xBA	PX	SX	G/F	RC/G	RAR
Pos SS	99		0	0	0	0	0	0	0								0								
Age 24 Growth	00	aaa	435	51	100	0	25	20	230			$3	260	294	555	4	93	25	0.60	278	45	135		2.30	-22.4
Bats S	01	TOR	* 476	49	138	4	42	30	290	200	288	$18	306	382	688	2	93	30	0.35	288	64	117	1.58	4.07	-4.2
R Moderate	02	LA	439	43	102	1	31	7	232	306	195	$1	256	303	559	3	91	25	0.36	275	58	86	1.99	2.44	-19.7
I EXP con	03	LA	558	47	140	1	40	10	251	263	246	$4	283	315	598	4	87	29	0.36	270	46	106	1.96	3.00	-18.4
S pt stb	1st Half		269	22	67	0	17	5	249			$2	286	294	580	5	87	29	0.40	259	33	89		2.85	-10.1
K age	2nd Half		289	25	73	1	23	5	253			$3	280	336	616	4	88	28	0.31	280	58	113		3.14	-8.4
LIMA D+ BA: 50%	04	Proj	**550**	**52**	**148**	**2**	**40**	**15**	**269**			**$9**	**295**	**341**	**637**	**4**	**90**	**30**	**0.37**	**283**	**53**	**106**		**3.41**	**-8.1**

The good signs...
- 90% contact rate potential
- Plus speed potential

The bad signs...
- That contact rate is declining.
- Empty, sub-.300 OB
- Can't take advantage of speed

Jackson,Damian

	Yr	Tm	AB	R	H	HR	RBI	SB	Avg	vL	vR	R$	OB	Slg	OPS	bb%	ct%	h%	Eye	xBA	PX	SX	G/F	RC/G	RAR
Pos 2B	99	SD	388	56	87	9	39	34	224	188	240	$12	317	356	673	12	73	28	0.50	223	85	126	0.56	3.79	-5.2
Age 30 Past Peak	00	SD	470	68	120	6	37	28	255	223	266	$12	342	377	719	12	77	32	0.57	245	79	149	0.99	4.56	2.7
Bats R	01	SD	440	67	106	4	38	23	241	319	214	$9	310	343	653	9	71	33	0.34	217	66	172	0.94	3.65	-2.8
R High	02	DET	245	31	63	1	25	12	257	217	270	$6	316	359	675	8	85	30	0.58	261	81	111	1.09	3.97	-0.5
I CON	03	BOS	161	34	42	1	13	16	261	241	284	$6	296	323	619	5	83	31	0.29	259	47	144	0.73	3.03	-5.5
S pt stb	1st Half		64	12	16	0	4	11	250			$4	304	281	586	7	81	31	0.42	241	27	143		3.14	-2.0
K	2nd Half		97	22	26	1	9	5	268			$3	290	351	641	3	84	31	0.19	271	61	132		2.96	-3.5
LIMA D BA: 40%	04	Proj	**200**	**35**	**51**	**1**	**18**	**15**	**255**			**$6**	**307**	**342**	**649**	**7**	**81**	**31**	**0.39**	**266**	**63**	**139**		**3.50**	**-3.7**

Over the past few years, his plate patience has declined as his opportunities to come to the plate have declined... a natural cause and effect, I suppose. But it's done nothing for his BPIs and has left his output flat.

Jenkins,Geoff

	Yr	Tm	AB	R	H	HR	RBI	SB	Avg	vL	vR	R$	OB	Slg	OPS	bb%	ct%	h%	Eye	xBA	PX	SX	G/F	RC/G	RAR
Pos LF	99	MIL	447	70	140	21	82	5	313	259	326	$21	363	564	927	7	81	35	0.40	335	162	88	1.28	7.61	31.0
Age 29 Past Peak	00	MIL	512	100	155	34	94	11	303	283	309	$28	345	588	933	6	74	35	0.24	295	165	130	1.21	7.50	32.1
Bats L	01	MIL	397	60	105	20	63	4	264	316	244	$14	326	474	799	8	70	33	0.30	246	123	73	1.10	5.30	-4.6
R Low	02	MIL	243	35	59	10	29	1	243	200	258	$5	306	444	750	8	75	28	0.37	267	135	68	1.44	4.44	-14.2
I con	03	MIL	487	81	144	28	95	0	296	270	308	$23	371	538	909	11	75	34	0.48	299	149	48	1.26	7.22	21.9
S pt	1st Half		287	51	81	19	61	0	282			$14	354	547	901	10	71	34	0.38	287	160	51		6.88	10.5
K	2nd Half		200	30	63	9	34	0	315			$9	394	525	919	12	82	35	0.72	316	133	44		7.70	11.3
LIMA D+ BA: 40%	04	Proj	**450**	**71**	**132**	**26**	**84**	**0**	**293**			**$21**	**360**	**537**	**898**	**9**	**76**	**34**	**0.43**	**304**	**150**	**52**		**6.91**	**14.4**

Broken thumb ended a solid rebound season, but injury history begs the question - what are the odds that he'll see 500 AB for only the 2nd time in his career? If he does, BPIs say he'll return full value.

Jeter,Derek

Jeter,Derek		Tm	AB	R	H	HR	RBI	SB	Avg	vL	vR	R$	OB	Slg	OPS	bb%	ct%	h%	Eye	xBA	PX	SX	G/F	RC/G	RAR
Pos SS	99	NYY	627	134	219	24	102	19	349	282	366	$36	432	552	984	13	81	40	0.78	305	120	141	1.63	9.19	82.0
Age 29 Past Peak	00	NYY	593	119	201	15	73	22	339	395	321	$29	407	481	888	10	83	39	0.69	298	86	125	2.10	7.67	50.5
Bats R	01	NYY	614	110	191	21	74	27	311	333	305	$30	369	480	849	8	84	34	0.57	304	105	118	1.96	6.75	39.8
R Very Low	02	NYY	644	124	191	18	75	32	297	315	292	$29	368	421	789	10	82	34	0.64	275	77	113	2.23	5.87	23.2
I con	03	NYY	482	87	156	10	52	11	324	370	312	$19	379	450	829	8	82	38	0.49	290	82	104	2.54	6.35	25.0
S pt	1st Half		194	35	54	5	19	4	278			$5	336	423	759	8	80	33	0.44	289	89	123		5.05	3.5
K	2nd Half		288	52	102	5	33	7	354			$14	408	469	876	8	83	41	0.53	290	78	85		7.36	21.9
LIMA C BA: 30%	04	Proj	**600**	**112**	**179**	**13**	**69**	**15**	**298**			**$21**	**362**	**425**	**787**	**9**	**82**	**34**	**0.56**	**293**	**82**	**109**		**5.60**	**19.3**

I'm really not a Yankee-hater, but I can't fathom the fascination with a player whose production has dropped 50% in the past 5 years. xBA says his BA will come down too, and G/F says that his power is not coming back.

Jimenez,D'Angelo

Jimenez,D'Angelo		Tm	AB	R	H	HR	RBI	SB	Avg	vL	vR	R$	OB	Slg	OPS	bb%	ct%	h%	Eye	xBA	PX	SX	G/F	RC/G	RAR
Pos 2B	99	aaa	526	83	164	12	75	22	312			$23	372	452	824	9	90	33	0.93	296	92	95	1.50	5.62	22.9
Age 26 Pre-Peak	00	aaa	73	10	16	1	4	1	219			($0)	278	288	566	8	81	26	0.43	238	43	67		2.52	-3.6
Bats S	01	SD	* 522	73	137	8	49	6	262	241	290	$8	338	368	706	10	82	31	0.64	256	72	61	1.51	4.05	2.9
R Very High	02	2TM	* 586	82	149	10	60	11	254	261	247	$11	337	375	712	11	85	28	0.85	268	77	124	1.65	4.29	1.2
I EXP CON	03	2TM	561	69	153	14	57	11	273	273	273	$14	349	415	765	11	84	30	0.74	293	87	108	1.35	4.97	11.3
S pt stb	1st Half		271	35	69	7	26	4	255			$5	333	410	743	11	83	28	0.70	293	92	127		4.55	2.3
K	2nd Half		290	34	84	7	31	7	290			$9	364	421	785	10	85	32	0.79	291	83	83		5.38	9.1
LIMA B BA: 55%	04	Proj	**550**	**73**	**159**	**16**	**58**	**12**	**289**			**$18**	**363**	**444**	**807**	**10**	**85**	**32**	**0.77**	**306**	**95**	**103**		**5.60**	**21.9**

Good growth year, but we're probably looking at a 20-HR, .290 ceiling once he peaks. That probably won't happen for another 2-3 years, but the trek to those levels should continue in 2004.

Johnson,Charles

Johnson,Charles		Tm	AB	R	H	HR	RBI	SB	Avg	vL	vR	R$	OB	Slg	OPS	bb%	ct%	h%	Eye	xBA	PX	SX	G/F	RC/G	RAR
Pos CA	99	BAL	426	58	107	16	54	0	251	355	234	$7	337	413	750	11	75	30	0.51	248	96	36	1.19	4.74	8.4
Age 32 Past Peak	00	2AL	421	76	128	31	91	2	304	252	324	$22	381	582	962	11	75	34	0.49	292	155	50	1.21	8.15	46.0
Bats R	01	FLA	451	51	117	18	75	0	259	245	261	$12	317	450	767	8	71	33	0.29	247	121	21	0.94	4.91	18.3
R High	02	FLA	244	18	53	6	36	0	217	275	202	$2	305	369	674	11	75	27	0.51	238	112		1.25	3.67	-3.3
I CON	03	COL	356	49	82	20	61	1	230	250	223	$9	323	455	779	12	76	25	0.58	256	138	32	0.82	4.73	4.8
S pt stb	1st Half		195	23	46	9	37	0	236			$5	332	426	757	13	76	26	0.61	246	118	22		4.62	1.9
K	2nd Half		161	26	36	11	24	1	224			$4	313	491	804	12	76	22	0.55	270	162	50		4.83	2.7
LIMA D BA: 60%	04	Proj	**350**	**43**	**82**	**19**	**57**	**1**	**234**			**$8**	**319**	**462**	**782**	**11**	**75**	**26**	**0.50**	**256**	**144**	**28**		**4.83**	**7.8**

His 2nd half PX says that the 31-HR season in 2000 wasn't a complete anomaly, but seeing 420 AB again might be a stretch. Home/road splits were brutal -- .306/.153 -- which further limits his upside.

Johnson,Nick

Johnson,Nick		Tm	AB	R	H	HR	RBI	SB	Avg	vL	vR	R$	OB	Slg	OPS	bb%	ct%	h%	Eye	xBA	PX	SX	G/F	RC/G	RAR
Pos 1B DH	99	aa	420	100	132	12	77	7	314			$18	454	488	942	20	81	36	1.35	278	113	88		7.95	27.8
Age 25 Pre-Peak	00	NYY	0	0	0	0	0	0	0								0			0					
Bats L	01	NYY	* 426	64	99	19	50	8	232			$9	349	413	762	15	76	26	0.74	250	108	64	1.44	4.82	-17.1
R Moderate	02	NYY	389	57	93	15	58	1	239	175	257	$8	324	393	718	11	74	29	0.49	240	92	39	1.23	4.16	-20.0
I exp CON	03	NYY	324	60	92	14	47	5	284	282	285	$12	411	472	883	18	82	31	1.23	318	117	59	1.62	6.89	13.9
S pt	1st Half		120	29	37	5	18	2	308			$5	458	517	974	22	82	34	1.50	329	136	61		8.87	11.4
K age	2nd Half		204	31	55	9	29	3	270			$7	382	446	828	15	83	29	1.06	311	106	48		5.84	2.7
LIMA C+ BA: 65%	04	Proj	**550**	**97**	**163**	**22**	**90**	**7**	**296**			**$22**	**410**	**473**	**883**	**16**	**79**	**34**	**0.93**	**300**	**109**	**56**		**6.96**	**19.9**

Has battled chronic hand injuries, but if he can finally stay healthy, this is what his future looks like. BPI trends are exciting.

Johnson,Reed

Johnson,Reed		Tm	AB	R	H	HR	RBI	SB	Avg	vL	vR	R$	OB	Slg	OPS	bb%	ct%	h%	Eye	xBA	PX	SX	G/F	RC/G	RAR
Pos RF LF	99		0	0	0	0	0	0	0								0								
Age 27 Peak	00		0	0	0	0	0	0	0								0								
Bats R	01	aa	554	85	155	11	60	34	280			$22	324	401	724	6	88	30	0.52	280	78	124		4.49	-12.5
R Very High	02	aaa	159	21	33	2	8	1	208			($1)	254	321	575	6	89	22	0.56	277	76	114		2.26	-14.9
I EXP con	03	TOR	* 513	91	151	12	66	8	294	328	279	$16	325	425	750	4	85	33	0.29	267	83	107	1.47	4.91	-3.4
S pt stb	1st Half		242	47	76	8	34	3	314			$10	339	479	818	4	90	32	0.38	295	101	105		5.70	3.6
K	2nd Half		271	44	75	4	32	5	277			$6	312	376	689	5	80	33	0.26	242	68	104		4.26	-6.9
LIMA D+ BA: 40%	04	Proj	**500**	**78**	**131**	**9**	**49**	**10**	**262**			**$9**	**300**	**383**	**684**	**5**	**86**	**29**	**0.40**	**270**	**78**	**110**		**3.77**	**-19.3**

10-52-.294 in 412 AB at TOR, but there are concerns. 2nd half fade by this rookie puts a ceiling on his 2004 potential, and TOR expectations of him owning the lead-off spot seem ill-advised by his middling OB avg.

Jones,Andruw

Jones,Andruw		Tm	AB	R	H	HR	RBI	SB	Avg	vL	vR	R$	OB	Slg	OPS	bb%	ct%	h%	Eye	xBA	PX	SX	G/F	RC/G	RAR
Pos CF	99	ATL	592	97	163	26	84	24	275	271	277	$24	358	483	841	11	83	30	0.74	292	126	112	1.05	5.88	27.1
Age 26 Pre-Peak	00	ATL	656	122	199	36	104	21	303	313	301	$34	361	541	902	8	85	31	0.59	314	136	126	1.25	7.12	50.7
Bats R	01	ATL	625	104	157	34	104	11	251	252	251	$22	313	461	774	8	77	27	0.39	254	119	98	1.11	4.88	19.0
R Very Low	02	ATL	560	91	148	35	94	8	264	228	270	$25	359	513	872	13	76	29	0.61	277	157	64	1.06	6.35	24.1
I con	03	ATL	595	101	165	36	116	4	277	260	282	$27	336	513	849	8	79	30	0.42	282	140	73	0.98	6.00	17.4
S	1st Half		294	52	85	20	57	2	289			$15	359	541	900	10	78	31	0.50	282	146	68		6.92	16.0
K	2nd Half		301	49	80	16	59	2	266			$12	314	485	799	7	80	29	0.34	282	134	74		5.17	1.7
LIMA D BA: 50%	04	Proj	**600**	**100**	**172**	**40**	**108**	**8**	**287**			**$30**	**354**	**545**	**899**	**9**	**78**	**31**	**0.48**	**290**	**153**	**79**		**6.81**	**35.4**

We were projecting his first 40-HR season for '03, and he got off to that pace before fading, thanks to a lingering oblique muscle strain. His BPIs still support that potential so we'll ink that in again for 2004.

Jones,Chipper

Jones,Chipper		Tm	AB	R	H	HR	RBI	SB	Avg	vL	vR	R$	OB	Slg	OPS	bb%	ct%	h%	Eye	xBA	PX	SX	G/F	RC/G	RAR
Pos LF	99	ATL	567	116	181	45	110	25	319	352	308	$41	443	633	1076	18	83	32	1.34	352	186	89	1.24	10.72	86.5
Age 31 Past Peak	00	ATL	579	118	180	36	111	14	311	415	281	$33	408	566	975	14	89	30	1.48	330	150	78	1.09	8.38	50.4
Bats S	01	ATL	572	113	189	38	102	9	330	376	320	$36	428	605	1033	15	86	33	1.20	333	157	89	1.26	9.41	57.3
R Very Low	02	ATL	548	90	179	26	100	8	327	320	328	$32	437	536	973	16	84	35	1.20	310	137	67	1.15	8.89	36.5
I	03	ATL	555	103	169	27	106	2	305	306	304	$26	405	517	922	14	85	32	1.13	305	133	58	0.96	7.61	30.8
S	1st Half		269	45	80	13	43	1	297			$11	404	498	902	15	86	31	1.23	301	126	40		7.33	12.9
K	2nd Half		286	58	89	14	63	1	311			$15	407	535	942	14	85	33	1.05	309	139	74		7.88	17.9
LIMA C BA: 60%	04	Proj	**550**	**102**	**174**	**34**	**104**	**6**	**316**			**$32**	**420**	**572**	**992**	**15**	**85**	**32**	**1.18**	**321**	**156**	**69**		**8.85**	**46.1**

Disappointing power output for the 2nd consecutive year, but was bothered by a sore wrist, has a history of better, and a G/F trend that supports bigger numbers. Don't write off a return to the 30-HR level just yet.

Jones,Jacque

Jones,Jacque		Tm	AB	R	H	HR	RBI	SB	Avg	vL	vR	R$	OB	Slg	OPS	bb%	ct%	h%	Eye	xBA	PX	SX	G/F	RC/G	RAR
Pos LF DH	99	MIN	* 520	81	147	12	66	10	283	222	297	$14	314	433	747	4	82	33	0.26	275	99	106	1.54	4.70	-5.4
Age 28 Peak	00	MIN	523	66	149	19	76	7	285	230	294	$16	319	463	781	5	79	33	0.23	280	103	99	2.07	5.12	0.5
Bats L	01	MIN	475	57	131	14	49	12	276	182	288	$14	331	417	748	8	81	32	0.42	267	90	60	2.12	4.63	0.1
R Very Low	02	MIN	577	96	173	27	85	6	300	213	333	$25	342	511	853	6	78	35	0.29	283	130	76	1.86	6.12	20.7
I con	03	MIN	517	76	157	16	69	12	304	304	317	$21	331	462	793	4	80	36	0.20	290	103	97	2.78	5.71	5.3
S	1st Half		300	46	90	10	35	6	300			$11	316	473	789	2	79	35	0.11	294	112	98		5.49	1.3
K	2nd Half		217	30	67	6	34	6	309			$10	351	447	798	6	81	36	0.33	284	90	77		5.98	3.8
LIMA D+ BA: 30%	04	Proj	**550**	**80**	**162**	**19**	**75**	**11**	**295**			**$21**	**333**	**460**	**793**	**5**	**80**	**34**	**0.28**	**292**	**105**	**84**		**5.49**	**6.4**

Strained groin slowed him down in the 2nd half, but not enough to prevent him from posting a grossly inflated BA. His .300 potential is borderline, despite '02-'03 levels. G/F says to bet against a return to 25-HR level.

Jones,Jason

Jones,Jason		Tm	AB	R	H	HR	RBI	SB	Avg	vL	vR	R$	OB	Slg	OPS	bb%	ct%	h%	Eye	xBA	PX	SX	G/F	RC/G	RAR
Pos LF	99		0	0	0	0	0	0	0								0								
Age 20 Green	00		0	0	0	0	0	0	0								0								
Bats S	01	aa	107	7	20	2	7	0	187			($2)	209	299	508	3	87	20	0.21	267	77	20		1.96	-10.9
R High	02	aa	471	66	120	11	60	10	255			$11	351	393	744	13	80	30	0.75	258	94	82		4.59	-14.3
I EXP con	03	TEX	* 482	55	124	12	58	7	257	182	224	$10	331	402	733	10	81	30	0.58	263	99	57	1.00	4.55	-11.1
S pt stb	1st Half		309	33	83	4	37	6	269			$7	341	379	720	10	81	32	0.57	251	82	59		4.51	-7.3
K AGE	2nd Half		173	22	41	8	21	1	237			$3	312	445	758	10	82	25	0.61	286	131	41		4.57	-4.6
LIMA F BA: 50%	04	Proj	**150**	**18**	**36**	**4**	**17**	**2**	**240**			**$2**	**316**	**389**	**705**	**10**	**82**	**27**	**0.61**	**266**	**99**	**51**		**4.06**	**-4.6**

3-11-.224 in 107 AB at TEX. BPIs are nothing special -- yet -- but he's way too young to be thrown to the wolves. Another year in the minors, at least, please.

Jordan,Brian

	Yr	Tm	AB	R	H	HR	RBI	SB	Avg	vL	vR	R$	OB	Slg	OPS	bb%	ct%	h%	Eye	xBA	PX	SX	G/F	RC/G	RAR
Pos LF	99	ATL	576	100	163	23	115	13	283	331	270	$24	341	465	807	8	86	30	0.63	288	110	102	1.16	5.48	7.1
Age 37 Decline	00	ATL	489	71	129	17	77	10	264	402	223	$14	317	421	738	7	84	29	0.48	262	97	80	1.15	4.66	-7.8
Bats R	01	ATL	560	82	165	25	97	3	295	292	295	$23	332	496	828	5	84	31	0.35	291	121	75	1.05	5.90	3.2
R Moderate	02	LA	471	65	134	18	80	2	285	303	279	$18	333	469	802	7	82	32	0.40	284	121	72	1.17	5.49	-11.9
I con	03	LA	224	28	67	6	28	1	299	397	265	$7	364	420	784	9	87	32	0.77	255	78	37	1.67	5.50	-0.6
S pt stb	1st Half		224	28	67	6	28	1	299			$7	364	420	784	9	87	32	0.77	255	78	37		5.50	-0.6
K AGE	2nd Half		0	0	0	0	0	0	0			($0)					0			0					
LIMA D+ BA: 45%	04	Proj	**350**	**49**	**95**	**10**	**55**	**3**	**271**			**$10**	**325**	**411**	**736**	**7**	**85**	**30**	**0.51**	**258**	**91**	**71**		**4.63**	**-11.3**

Knee surgery ended his season early, but BPIs were already showing that this would be a down year. At 37, with his history, the pct play would be to let someone else assume the risk.

Kapler,Gabe

	Yr	Tm	AB	R	H	HR	RBI	SB	Avg	vL	vR	R$	OB	Slg	OPS	bb%	ct%	h%	Eye	xBA	PX	SX	G/F	RC/G	RAR
Pos RF LF	99	DET	* 470	70	118	21	62	11	251	280	238	$12	324	468	792	10	82	27	0.61	296	127	125	1.15	5.04	1.0
Age 28 Peak	00	TEX	444	59	134	14	66	8	302	286	306	$16	362	473	835	9	87	32	0.74	302	108	70	1.22	6.16	15.3
Bats R	01	TEX	483	77	129	17	72	23	267	269	266	$20	349	437	786	11	86	28	0.87	283	107	97	1.01	5.36	5.4
R Moderate	02	2TM	* 332	42	95	3	38	12	286	250	293	$11	323	392	714	5	83	34	0.33	260	74	134	1.23	4.50	-6.2
I exp con	03	2TM	* 263	43	67	4	29	9	255	326	233	$6	324	376	701	9	80	30	0.52	256	84	126	1.53	4.25	-8.8
S pt stb	1st Half		114	18	28	2	13	5	246			$3	323	395	718	10	74	32	0.43	244	97	170		4.57	-2.7
K	2nd Half		149	25	39	2	16	4	262			$3	325	362	688	9	85	30	0.64	263	74	85		4.00	-6.0
LIMA D+ BA: 50%	04	Proj	**300**	**45**	**80**	**6**	**36**	**11**	**267**			**$9**	**329**	**397**	**726**	**9**	**82**	**31**	**0.53**	**263**	**88**	**116**		**4.57**	**-6.1**

4-27-6-.271 in 225 AB at COL and BOS. Since leaving TEX, he's become another player, and not a very good one. Rising G/F and below average PX spells doom for a bulked up power hitter.

Karros,Eric

	Yr	Tm	AB	R	H	HR	RBI	SB	Avg	vL	vR	R$	OB	Slg	OPS	bb%	ct%	h%	Eye	xBA	PX	SX	G/F	RC/G	RAR
Pos 1B	99	LA	578	74	176	34	112	8	304	308	303	$29	363	550	913	8	79	33	0.45	288	150	46	0.88	7.17	29.8
Age 36 Decline	00	LA	584	84	146	31	106	4	250	286	239	$17	323	459	782	10	79	27	0.52	249	121	48	0.66	4.97	-6.4
Bats R	01	LA	438	42	103	15	63	3	235	255	230	$7	301	388	689	9	77	27	0.41	249	95	43	0.95	3.89	-31.1
R Very High	02	LA	524	52	142	13	73	4	271	317	260	$14	319	399	718	7	86	30	0.50	283	88	54	1.36	4.43	-17.7
I CON	03	CHC	336	37	96	12	40	1	286	366	246	$10	341	446	787	8	86	30	0.61	312	101	42	1.16	5.38	-1.2
S pt stb	1st Half		165	16	50	7	18	0	303			$6	372	485	856	10	90	30	1.06	330	110	36		6.44	4.2
K AGE	2nd Half		171	21	46	5	22	1	269			$4	309	409	719	6	83	30	0.34	296	93	49		4.45	-5.2
LIMA D+ BA: 60%	04	Proj	**350**	**38**	**102**	**12**	**47**	**1**	**291**			**$11**	**345**	**451**	**796**	**7**	**84**	**32**	**0.50**	**309**	**102**	**41**		**5.54**	**-0.8**

Pre-2003, faced LHers in about 20% of his plate appearances; in 2003, 35%, and you can see how it helped his BPIs. G/F says his power is not coming back, but he still makes a dandy platoon player. Feed him LHers.

Kata,Matt

	Yr	Tm	AB	R	H	HR	RBI	SB	Avg	vL	vR	R$	OB	Slg	OPS	bb%	ct%	h%	Eye	xBA	PX	SX	G/F	RC/G	RAR
Pos 2B 3B	99		0	0	0	0	0	0	0								0								
Age 26 Pre-Peak	00		0	0	0	0	0	0	0								0								
Bats S	01	aa	16	3	6	0	3	0	375			$1	444	500	944	11	88	43	1.00	291	108	60		7.21	1.4
R High	02	aa	578	70	150	9	43	9	260			$9	293	384	677	4	89	28	0.43	282	82	119		3.71	-8.8
I EXP con	03	ARI	* 489	66	127	9	48	5	260	299	236	$8	305	409	714	6	85	29	0.43	280	96	133	1.38	4.13	-4.0
S pt stb	1st Half		249	33	71	5	26	2	285			$6	323	446	769	5	87	31	0.44	292	107	112		4.75	2.5
K	2nd Half		240	33	56	4	22	3	233			$2	287	371	658	7	82	27	0.42	268	86	157		3.54	-6.3
LIMA D BA: 55%	04	Proj	**250**	**32**	**60**	**4**	**22**	**3**	**240**			**$2**	**282**	**375**	**658**	**6**	**86**	**26**	**0.43**	**280**	**87**	**129**		**3.42**	**-6.8**

7-29-.257 in 288 AB at ARI. 2nd half fade shows that he could not adjust to the competition the second time through the league. Reduce your expectations for 2004.

Kearns,Austin

	Yr	Tm	AB	R	H	HR	RBI	SB	Avg	vL	vR	R$	OB	Slg	OPS	bb%	ct%	h%	Eye	xBA	PX	SX	G/F	RC/G	RAR
Pos RF CF	99		0	0	0	0	0	0	0								0								
Age 23 Growth	00		0	0	0	0	0	0	0								0								
Bats R	01	aa	205	24	51	5	29	6	249			$5	319	385	704	9	84	28	0.64	270	87	80		3.83	-9.0
R Very High	02	CIN	* 417	76	130	17	68	7	312	330	310	$21	401	516	916	13	79	36	0.70	277	134	99	1.37	7.59	26.1
I EXP con	03	CIN	292	39	77	15	58	6	264	266	263	$13	354	455	810	12	77	30	0.60	270	114	59	1.77	5.58	-0.2
S pt stb	1st Half		276	39	75	15	57	5	272			$13	364	475	839	13	76	31	0.62	273	121	56		6.01	3.2
K AGE	2nd Half		16	0	2	0	1	1	125			($0)	176	125	301	6	81	15	0.33	221	0	39		0.82	-2.6
LIMA B BA: 50%	04	Proj	**500**	**71**	**136**	**19**	**85**	**11**	**272**			**$19**	**355**	**449**	**804**	**11**	**80**	**31**	**0.65**	**277**	**111**	**80**		**5.39**	**-1.2**

Shoulder surgery ended his season, but not before he put up some interesting numbers. HR output looks like growth, but cancelled out by 20 fewer 2B/3B. High G/F tempers expectations for power growth in 2004.

Kendall,Jason

	Yr	Tm	AB	R	H	HR	RBI	SB	Avg	vL	vR	R$	OB	Slg	OPS	bb%	ct%	h%	Eye	xBA	PX	SX	G/F	RC/G	RAR
Pos CA	99	PIT	280	61	93	8	41	22	332	271	348	$19	412	511	923	12	89	35	1.19	328	115	146	1.47	8.38	32.9
Age 29 Past Peak	00	PIT	579	112	185	14	58	22	320	331	316	$25	401	470	871	12	86	35	1.00	296	93	120	1.34	6.83	45.2
Bats R	01	PIT	606	84	161	10	53	13	266	279	263	$12	315	358	673	7	92	28	0.92	251	59	83	1.20	3.66	2.5
R Low	02	PIT	545	59	154	3	44	15	283	275	284	$13	342	356	698	8	95	29	1.69	276	56	89	1.72	4.24	2.0
I con	03	PIT	587	84	191	6	58	8	325	310	331	$20	377	416	793	8	93	34	1.23	302	65	77	1.72	5.76	23.2
S pt	1st Half		279	42	83	4	32	5	297			$9	364	391	754	9	90	32	1.07	292	61	90		5.00	5.5
K	2nd Half		308	42	108	2	26	3	351			$12	390	438	829	6	96	36	1.54	311	68	62		6.54	17.9
LIMA B+ BA: 55%	04	Proj	**550**	**77**	**169**	**6**	**52**	**12**	**307**			**$18**	**363**	**401**	**764**	**8**	**93**	**32**	**1.25**	**304**	**66**	**89**		**5.21**	**17.0**

A .325 BA was probably a bit over his head, but not by much. With any lingering power or speed skills probably gone, all he has left is BA, but as a CA, that's more than enough.

Kennedy,Adam

	Yr	Tm	AB	R	H	HR	RBI	SB	Avg	vL	vR	R$	OB	Slg	OPS	bb%	ct%	h%	Eye	xBA	PX	SX	G/F	RC/G	RAR
Pos 2B	99	STL	* 469	72	136	9	71	17	290	250	256	$17	331	429	760	6	91	30	0.73	304	94	110	0.83	5.01	10.6
Age 28 Peak	00	ANA	598	82	159	9	72	22	266	275	263	$14	299	403	702	4	88	29	0.38	277	84	166	0.91	4.13	4.6
Bats L	01	ANA	478	48	129	6	40	12	270	242	277	$9	309	372	681	5	85	31	0.38	257	70	86	0.84	3.90	-4.2
R Moderate	02	ANA	474	65	148	7	52	17	312	275	319	$19	339	449	788	4	83	36	0.24	273	92	142	0.83	5.68	21.3
I CON	03	ANA	449	71	121	13	49	22	269	235	281	$16	336	399	735	9	84	30	0.62	272	79	101	0.75	4.60	6.0
S pt stb	1st Half		198	28	53	3	21	11	268			$6	332	343	675	9	83	31	0.58	250	50	88		3.89	-1.5
K	2nd Half		251	43	68	10	28	11	271			$10	339	442	782	9	84	29	0.65	289	102	106		5.19	7.7
LIMA C+ BA: 55%	04	Proj	**500**	**72**	**139**	**16**	**54**	**20**	**278**			**$18**	**328**	**437**	**765**	**7**	**84**	**30**	**0.48**	**280**	**98**	**111**		**4.98**	**12.6**

Was that 2H power outburst for real? Most likely, and he's probably not done yet. In fact, if you're willing to make a 2-year investment, you could be looking at a 20-20 season by 2005.

Kent,Jeff

	Yr	Tm	AB	R	H	HR	RBI	SB	Avg	vL	vR	R$	OB	Slg	OPS	bb%	ct%	h%	Eye	xBA	PX	SX	G/F	RC/G	RAR
Pos 2B	99	SF	511	86	148	23	101	13	290	273	296	$23	365	511	876	11	78	33	0.54	259	141	89	0.78	6.58	34.2
Age 36 Decline	00	SF	587	114	196	33	125	12	334	324	335	$37	422	596	1019	13	82	36	0.84	285	153	109	0.73	9.30	77.5
Bats R	01	SF	607	84	181	22	106	7	298	295	299	$25	366	507	873	10	84	33	0.68	291	132	91	0.94	6.57	46.0
R Moderate	02	SF	623	102	195	37	108	5	313	366	297	$35	366	565	931	8	84	33	0.51	303	161	76	0.80	7.68	55.1
I con	03	HOU	505	77	150	22	93	6	297	361	282	$23	347	509	856	7	83	32	0.46	295	139	76	0.84	6.39	27.8
S stb	1st Half		265	42	83	11	50	4	313			$14	370	521	891	8	84	34	0.56	296	139	66		7.17	19.8
K AGE	2nd Half		240	35	67	11	43	2	279			$9	322	496	817	6	83	30	0.36	292	139	75		5.59	8.1
LIMA C+ BA: 45%	04	Proj	**600**	**93**	**179**	**28**	**109**	**7**	**298**			**$28**	**355**	**526**	**880**	**8**	**83**	**32**	**0.52**	**298**	**145**	**85**		**6.71**	**39.9**

Moving from Pac Bell to Minute Maid should have boosted his power, but it didn't. At 37, his window for a late power surge is probably past, but he's still one of the best middle infielders you can own.

Kielty,Bobby

	Yr	Tm	AB	R	H	HR	RBI	SB	Avg	vL	vR	R$	OB	Slg	OPS	bb%	ct%	h%	Eye	xBA	PX	SX	G/F	RC/G	RAR
Pos RF DH	99		0	0	0	0	0	0	0								0								
Age 27 Peak	00	a/a	484	71	117	11	55	5	242			$5	355	386	741	15	80	28	0.88	266	95	67		4.50	-7.7
Bats S	01	aaa	341	45	88	9	39	4	258			$7	338	413	751	11	82	29	0.68	273	103	73	0.94	4.87	-3.9
R Very High	02	MIN	296	49	87	12	46	4	294	264	303	$12	401	486	888	15	77	35	0.79	259	114	100	0.93	7.07	16.9
I EXP con	03	2AL	427	71	104	13	57	8	244	300	216	$9	351	400	752	14	78	28	0.77	266	102	82	0.97	4.74	-5.3
S pt STB	1st Half		193	33	49	9	31	4	254			$5	368	446	814	15	75	33	0.71	261	116	67		5.75	3.4
K	2nd Half		234	38	55	4	26	4	235			$3	337	363	700	13	82	27	0.84	269	89	84		3.98	-8.3
LIMA B BA: 55%	04	Proj	**500**	**79**	**129**	**15**	**66**	**8**	**258**			**$12**	**362**	**418**	**780**	**14**	**79**	**30**	**0.78**	**268**	**102**	**82**		**5.20**	**1.9**

A scan of his hit rates indicates that '02's .294 BA was probably an aberration, further supported by his xBA. So we're probably looking at a .260ish hitter at best, with a HR upside in the 15-20 range. Bid accordingly.

Kieschnick,Brooks

Kieschnick,Brooks	Yr	Tm	AB	R	H	HR	RBI	SB	Avg	vL	vR	R$	OB	Slg	OPS	bb%	ct%	h%	Eye	xBA	PX	SX	G/F	RC/G	RAR
Pos RF	99	aaa	371	44	87	18	58	0	235			$6	270	445	715	5	82	24	0.26	283	125	51		3.95	-11.6
Age 31 Past Peak	00	aaa	440	48	103	19	64	2	234			$7	280	434	714	6	80	25	0.33	283	123	43		4.03	-13.3
Bats L	01	COL	* 294	32	73	14	37	2	248			$7	292	442	734	6	78	27	0.28	263	107	83	0.91	4.21	-11.8
R X HIGH	02	aaa	189	25	44	12	32	0	233			$5	279	471	750	6	76	24	0.26	266	142	28		4.36	-4.5
I EXP con	03	MIL	* 80	12	21	7	12	0	263	125	323	$3	322	538	859	8	79	25	0.41	276	148	20	1.23	5.98	0.9
S PT STB	1st Half		50	8	13	4	6	0	260			$2	275	520	795	2	82	24	0.11	287	143	41		4.92	-1.0
K	2nd Half		30	4	8	3	6	0	267			$2	389	567	956	17	73	26	0.75	260	157	2		7.66	1.8
LIMA F BA: 55%	04	Proj	**100**	**13**	**25**	**6**	**14**	**0**	**250**			**$3**	**285**	**470**	**754**	**5**	**79**	**26**	**0.24**	**275**	**129**	**39**		**4.49**	**-2.9**

7-12-.300 in 70 AB at MIL. On the batting side... While his poor OB has limited his value, he has a history of hitting in bad luck, as shown by consistently low hit rates and xBAs 20 points higher than his BAs.

Kingsale,Gene

Kingsale,Gene	Yr	Tm	AB	R	H	HR	RBI	SB	Avg	vL	vR	R$	OB	Slg	OPS	bb%	ct%	h%	Eye	xBA	PX	SX	G/F	RC/G	RAR
Pos CF	99	BAL	* 544	77	134	5	47	23	246	250	247	$9	306	322	628	8	85	28	0.59	257	50	107	1.67	2.98	-29.2
Age 27 Peak	00	BAL	* 109	20	29	1	15	3	266	190	257	$2	298	358	656	4	87	30	0.36	267	59	132	1.95	3.40	-4.1
Bats S	01	aaa	478	56	102	2	35	27	213			$5	264	291	555	6	86	25	0.48	262	55	138	4.50	2.54	-27.3
R X HIGH	02	2TM	* 407	48	105	7	50	18	258	293	281	$12	314	393	707	8	82	30	0.45	266	91	140	1.51	4.27	-6.7
I EXP CON	03	DET	* 280	28	61	1	18	9	218	270	181	$0	270	307	577	7	86	25	0.51	252	52	163	1.74	2.49	-20.1
S PT STB	1st Half		136	14	29	1	9	3	213			($0)	272	294	566	7	85	24	0.55	247	50	117		2.43	-10.0
K	2nd Half		144	14	32	0	9	6	222			$1	268	319	587	6	87	26	0.47	258	54	202		2.53	-10.1
LIMA D BA: 65%	04	Proj	**150**	**17**	**35**	**1**	**13**	**6**	**233**			**$2**	**285**	**335**	**620**	**7**	**85**	**27**	**0.48**	**256**	**63**	**154**		**3.03**	**-8.1**

1-8-1-.208 in 120 AB at DET, not good for someone who needs to make his living on speed, and could have made a statement on a team in search of any type of talent. He will improve, but will anyone notice?

Kinkade,Mike

Kinkade,Mike	Yr	Tm	AB	R	H	HR	RBI	SB	Avg	vL	vR	R$	OB	Slg	OPS	bb%	ct%	h%	Eye	xBA	PX	SX	G/F	RC/G	RAR
Pos LF	99	NYM	* 358	46	91	8	46	7	254	211	185	$7	294	385	679	5	90	27	0.54	292	85	94	2.10	3.88	-12.3
Age 30 Past Peak	00	aa	399	61	109	11	62	13	273			$13	336	419	755	9	84	30	0.59	277	89	100	2.50	4.79	-4.2
Bats R	01	BAL	160	19	44	4	16	2	275	284	264	$4	333	381	715	8	81	32	0.45	257	65	47	1.16	4.43	-0.9
R X HIGH	02	LA	* 337	48	93	9	44	5	276	400	350	$10	322	436	758	6	85	30	0.46	286	109	104	1.31	4.85	-14.8
I exp CON	03	LA	162	25	35	5	14	1	216	370	139	$1	274	352	626	7	77	25	0.34	238	87	67	1.30	2.90	-13.7
S PT STB	1st Half		96	18	25	4	8	1	260			$2	324	438	761	9	83	28	0.56	273	112	72		4.53	-3.0
K	2nd Half		66	7	10	1	6	0	152			($2)	200	227	427	6	67	21	0.18	192	51	65		1.25	-9.7
LIMA F BA: 50%	04	Proj	**150**	**21**	**38**	**4**	**16**	**2**	**253**			**$3**	**305**	**377**	**683**	**7**	**79**	**30**	**0.35**	**241**	**82**	**59**		**3.77**	**-8.9**

What was it that turned his first half promise into a second half debacle? A sore shoulder? Distress over his grandmother's passing? We can chart the path, but we're not always privy to the reasons things happen.

Klassen,Danny

Klassen,Danny	Yr	Tm	AB	R	H	HR	RBI	SB	Avg	vL	vR	R$	OB	Slg	OPS	bb%	ct%	h%	Eye	xBA	PX	SX	G/F	RC/G	RAR
Pos 3B	99	aaa	245	29	59	4	25	4	241			$2	282	371	653	5	85	27	0.38	277	85	110		3.33	-7.9
Age 28 Peak	00	ARI	* 173	32	46	3	19	2	266	243	231	$3	352	382	734	12	76	33	0.56	246	75	87	1.75	4.43	0.6
Bats R	01	aaa	18	4	4	1	2	0	222			$0	300	389	689	10	89	20	1.00	282	84	64		3.83	-0.4
R X HIGH	02	a/a	426	35	81	3	32	4	190			($4)	223	270	493	4	74	25	0.17	221	57	97	2.00	1.91	-35.6
I EXP CON	03	DET	* 480	65	105	9	50	10	219	281	220	$4	263	340	603	6	73	28	0.22	225	74	140	1.25	2.84	-25.0
S pt STB	1st Half		285	42	60	5	30	8	211			$2	260	333	593	6	75	26	0.26	231	73	173		2.78	-15.5
K	2nd Half		195	23	45	4	20	2	231			$1	268	349	617	5	70	31	0.17	215	76	82		2.92	-9.5
LIMA F BA: 40%	04	Proj	**250**	**31**	**56**	**4**	**24**	**4**	**224**			**$1**	**271**	**331**	**602**	**6**	**74**	**29**	**0.25**	**226**	**69**	**103**		**2.86**	**-12.4**

1-7-.247 in 73 AB at DET, though hasn't seen even a .225 BA over a full season since the turn of the century. Remarkably, his BPIs fully support that feeble level of performance, and there are no signs of any growth.

Klesko,Ryan

Klesko,Ryan	Yr	Tm	AB	R	H	HR	RBI	SB	Avg	vL	vR	R$	OB	Slg	OPS	bb%	ct%	h%	Eye	xBA	PX	SX	G/F	RC/G	RAR
Pos 1B	99	ATL	404	55	120	21	80	5	297	102	324	$19	379	532	911	12	83	32	0.77	294	144	66	1.02	7.26	22.0
Age 32 Past Peak	00	SD	494	88	140	26	92	23	283	256	292	$26	395	516	911	16	84	29	1.12	314	139	98	1.20	7.24	26.8
Bats L	01	SD	538	105	154	30	113	23	286	256	299	$32	387	539	926	14	83	30	0.99	305	148	143	0.97	7.56	19.9
R Low	02	SD	540	90	162	29	95	6	300	287	305	$28	386	537	923	12	84	31	0.88	316	155	68	1.02	7.54	28.9
I con	03	SD	397	47	100	21	67	2	252	194	272	$12	357	456	813	14	79	27	0.78	253	123	23	0.91	5.33	-2.2
S pt stb	1st Half		238	32	60	15	43	1	252			$9	360	492	851	14	80	26	0.85	267	144	26		5.78	1.9
K	2nd Half		159	15	40	6	24	1	252			$4	353	403	756	14	77	29	0.69	233	93	24		4.66	-4.1
LIMA B BA: 55%	04	Proj	**550**	**78**	**160**	**31**	**102**	**8**	**291**			**$27**	**387**	**529**	**916**	**14**	**81**	**31**	**0.83**	**265**	**148**	**58**		**7.22**	**24.8**

Shoulder woes depressed his numbers all season. He's had surgery and is expected to return healthy in 2004.

Konerko,Paul

Konerko,Paul	Yr	Tm	AB	R	H	HR	RBI	SB	Avg	vL	vR	R$	OB	Slg	OPS	bb%	ct%	h%	Eye	xBA	PX	SX	G/F	RC/G	RAR
Pos 1B	99	CHW	513	71	151	24	81	1	294	319	287	$18	351	511	862	8	87	30	0.66	306	128	67	1.23	6.50	10.1
Age 28 Peak	00	CHW	524	84	156	21	97	1	298	302	297	$18	356	481	836	8	86	31	0.65	300	110	54	1.13	6.22	4.0
Bats R	01	CHW	582	92	164	32	99	1	282	297	278	$22	343	507	850	8	85	29	0.61	296	135	41	1.10	6.18	0.6
R Very Low	02	CHW	570	81	173	27	104	0	304	279	310	$25	353	498	852	7	87	31	0.61	288	118	26	1.17	6.45	9.1
I con	03	CHW	444	49	104	18	65	0	234	327	187	$7	302	399	700	9	89	23	0.86	296	99	20	1.07	4.01	-18.3
S	1st Half		211	16	39	3	17	0	185			($3)	255	265	521	9	89	19	0.87	265	55	19		2.12	-22.0
K	2nd Half		233	33	65	15	48	0	279			$10	344	519	863	9	88	26	0.85	323	139	21		6.31	6.2
LIMA C BA: 75%	04	Proj	**550**	**73**	**158**	**31**	**101**	**0**	**287**			**$22**	**347**	**503**	**850**	**8**	**88**	**28**	**0.73**	**303**	**127**	**24**		**6.24**	**8.9**

How unlucky was he in the 1st half? A 19% hit rate turned a .265 xBA into .185. The 2nd half was more on par with expected levels and bodes well for a full rebound in 2004.

Koskie,Corey

Koskie,Corey	Yr	Tm	AB	R	H	HR	RBI	SB	Avg	vL	vR	R$	OB	Slg	OPS	bb%	ct%	h%	Eye	xBA	PX	SX	G/F	RC/G	RAR
Pos 3B	99	MIN	342	42	106	11	58	4	310	267	316	$13	382	468	850	10	79	37	0.56	266	100	42	1.22	6.41	18.7
Age 30 Past Peak	00	MIN	474	79	142	9	65	5	300	333	292	$13	397	441	838	14	78	37	0.74	263	91	90	1.48	6.27	24.7
Bats L	01	MIN	562	100	155	26	103	27	276	242	290	$28	354	488	842	11	79	31	0.58	279	130	110	1.16	6.14	28.9
R Very Low	02	MIN	490	71	131	15	69	10	267	253	274	$15	361	447	808	13	74	33	0.57	252	117	85	1.06	5.29	11.9
I	03	MIN	469	76	137	14	69	11	292	292	331	$18	392	452	844	14	76	36	0.68	268	103	85	1.04	6.32	23.8
S pt	1st Half		282	46	87	12	50	6	309			$14	404	507	911	14	77	36	0.70	285	124	74		7.43	22.7
K	2nd Half		187	30	50	2	19	5	267			$4	374	369	743	15	74	35	0.65	242	72	92		4.81	1.6
LIMA B BA: 40%	04	Proj	**500**	**79**	**137**	**18**	**72**	**10**	**274**			**$17**	**370**	**459**	**828**	**13**	**76**	**33**	**0.63**	**272**	**117**	**79**		**5.80**	**19.3**

Only after the season had ended did he reveal that his homerless Sept was due to him playing with a broken bone in his hand. He never did reveal the reason for his homerless August, though.

Kotsay,Mark

Kotsay,Mark	Yr	Tm	AB	R	H	HR	RBI	SB	Avg	vL	vR	R$	OB	Slg	OPS	bb%	ct%	h%	Eye	xBA	PX	SX	G/F	RC/G	RAR
Pos CF	99	FLA	495	57	134	8	50	7	271	272	271	$8	311	402	713	6	90	29	0.58	275	81	118	1.09	4.22	-1.3
Age 28 Peak	00	FLA	530	87	158	12	57	19	298	308	296	$19	350	443	793	7	91	31	0.91	305	92	120	1.52	5.49	17.3
Bats L	01	SD	406	67	118	10	58	13	291	215	318	$16	366	441	807	11	86	32	0.83	303	100	95	1.33	5.75	21.8
R Low	02	SD	578	82	169	17	61	11	292	324	277	$20	358	452	809	9	85	32	0.66	292	102	110	1.11	5.60	12.0
I con	03	SD	482	64	128	7	38	6	266	236	278	$7	342	384	726	10	83	31	0.68	284	82	95	1.57	4.53	-6.4
S pt stb	1st Half		217	29	53	3	13	4	244			$2	336	341	677	12	86	27	1.00	284	67	79		3.77	-7.9
K	2nd Half		265	35	75	4	25	2	283			$6	347	419	766	9	80	34	0.50	283	94	101		5.22	1.8
LIMA B BA: 55%	04	Proj	**550**	**77**	**160**	**16**	**69**	**10**	**291**			**$19**	**360**	**454**	**813**	**10**	**84**	**32**	**0.69**	**294**	**104**	**100**		**5.76**	**16.2**

Back woes sidetracked the growth curve, so he should rebound if healthy. However, keep the expectations in check; despite consistent power growth coming into '03, BPIs point to no more than a 20 HR ceiling.

Laird,Gerald

Laird,Gerald	Yr	Tm	AB	R	H	HR	RBI	SB	Avg	vL	vR	R$	OB	Slg	OPS	bb%	ct%	h%	Eye	xBA	PX	SX	G/F	RC/G	RAR
Pos CA	99		0	0	0	0	0	0	0								0								
Age 24 Growth	00		0	0	0	0	0	0	0								0								
Bats R	01		0	0	0	0	0	0	0								0								
R Moderate	02	aa	442	62	116	10	60	7	262			$11	324	389	713	8	81	30	0.49	256	82	91		4.16	3.9
I EXP	03	TEX	* 382	53	96	10	41	8	251	294	259	$8	319	411	730	9	84	28	0.60	274	99	124	1.09	4.44	4.0
S stb	1st Half		177	21	45	4	19	2	254			$3	302	412	714	6	83	29	0.40	269	94	141		4.21	0.6
K age	2nd Half		205	32	51	6	22	6	249			$5	333	410	743	11	84	27	0.79	277	104	97		4.63	3.3
LIMA D+ BA: 60%	04	Proj	**350**	**49**	**89**	**9**	**42**	**7**	**254**			**$7**	**321**	**403**	**724**	**9**	**83**	**29**	**0.56**	**271**	**92**	**113**		**4.33**	**4.1**

1-4-.273 in 44 AB at TEX. There is some marginal value here as a rising CA. If nothing else, getting a half dozen steals from a CA slot is worth a buck alone on draft day.

Laker,Tim

Laker,Tim		Tm	AB	R	H	HR	RBI	SB	Avg	vL	vR	R$	OB	Slg	OPS	bb%	ct%	h%	Eye	xBA	PX	SX	G/F	RC/G	RAR
Pos CA	99	aaa	405	32	81	8	42	2	200			($2)	236	326	562	4	84	22	0.29	268	83	65	1.50	2.47	-19.6
Age 34 Decline	00	aaa	421	50	83	14	53	4	197			$1	264	366	629	8	84	20	0.56	284	101	95		3.11	-12.8
Bats R	01	CLE	* 353	41	74	18	50	2	210			$5	270	394	663	8	84	20	0.50	271	104	43	1.09	3.41	-5.0
R X HIGH	02	aaa	216	19	42	4	23	2	194			($1)	253	292	545	7	75	24	0.32	226	66	52		2.38	-10.1
I EXP CON	03	CLE	162	17	39	3	21	2	241	189	266	$2	281	364	645	5	77	30	0.24	264	87	55	1.51	3.30	-3.9
S pt STB	1st Half		84	10	22	2	13	1	262			$2	295	417	712	5	77	32	0.21	281	109	57		4.09	-0.0
K age	2nd Half		78	7	17	1	8	1	218			$0	265	308	573	6	76	28	0.26	246	64	51		2.55	-3.7
LIMA F BA: 45%	04	Proj	**150**	**15**	**33**	**4**	**18**	**2**	**220**			**$1**	**269**	**344**	**613**	**6**	**78**	**26**	**0.31**	**264**	**82**	**50**		**2.98**	**-4.4**

He's spent so little time in the majors over the past 5 years that '03 was almost like a rookie season, with pitchers getting their first look at him. That worked well for half the year, until that dreaded "2nd look."

Larkin,Barry

Larkin,Barry		Tm	AB	R	H	HR	RBI	SB	Avg	vL	vR	R$	OB	Slg	OPS	bb%	ct%	h%	Eye	xBA	PX	SX	G/F	RC/G	RAR
Pos SS	99	CIN	583	108	171	12	75	30	293	259	305	$24	391	420	811	14	90	31	1.63	295	82	116	1.47	6.01	40.9
Age 39 Decline	00	CIN	396	71	124	11	41	14	313	307	315	$17	387	487	875	11	92	32	1.55	324	108	125	1.22	6.88	37.3
Bats R	01	CIN	156	29	40	2	17	3	256	333	231	$3	366	372	738	15	84	29	1.08	256	85	72	1.42	4.58	4.7
R High	02	CIN	507	72	124	7	47	13	245	189	262	$8	305	367	672	8	89	26	0.77	274	93	107	1.18	3.79	-1.7
I con	03	CIN	241	39	68	2	18	2	282	200	309	$4	342	382	724	8	87	32	0.69	290	76	84	1.82	4.70	4.0
S PT	1st Half		114	21	31	1	9	1	272			$2	346	377	724	10	89	30	1.08	302	76	100		4.64	1.7
K AGE	2nd Half		127	18	37	1	9	1	291			$2	338	386	724	7	84	34	0.45	279	76	58		4.75	2.3
LIMA D BA: 55%	04	Proj	**200**	**32**	**54**	**2**	**18**	**2**	**270**			**$3**	**340**	**386**	**726**	**10**	**87**	**30**	**0.82**	**295**	**86**	**80**		**4.53**	**3.6**

Continues to squeeze every last bit of productivity out of his declining career, and though he can no longer hit LHers, or hit HRs, or steal bases, or bat lead-off (really), he's still worth an end-game flyer.

Larson,Brandon

Larson,Brandon		Tm	AB	R	H	HR	RBI	SB	Avg	vL	vR	R$	OB	Slg	OPS	bb%	ct%	h%	Eye	xBA	PX	SX	G/F	RC/G	RAR
Pos 3B	99	aa	172	22	43	10	33	3	250			$6	287	483	770	5	76	28	0.21	269	138	57		4.06	-1.7
Age 27 Peak	00	a/a	490	56	122	18	53	12	249			$11	290	427	716	5	79	28	0.27	270	109	81		4.09	-4.0
Bats R	01	aaa	457	51	103	12	46	4	225			$4	261	359	620	5	76	27	0.20	242	85	62		2.89	-22.4
R X HIGH	02	CIN	* 348	44	103	24	65	2	296	308	240	$19	340	566	906	6	82	30	0.36	299	167	49	0.94	6.92	22.5
I EXP CON	03	CIN	* 371	46	92	18	66	4	248	143	82	$12	313	453	766	9	76	28	0.39	260	127	65	1.17	4.76	5.5
S pt STB	1st Half		243	33	65	10	41	3	267			$8	326	449	774	8	77	31	0.38	257	112	77		5.08	5.8
K	2nd Half		128	13	27	8	25	1	211			$3	289	461	750	10	74	22	0.42	264	154	32		4.19	-0.2
LIMA D+ BA: 45%	04	Proj	**350**	**41**	**88**	**19**	**59**	**3**	**251**			**$11**	**306**	**473**	**779**	**7**	**77**	**28**	**0.35**	**265**	**136**	**58**		**4.81**	**4.3**

1-9-.101 in 89 AB at CIN, a resounding flop after 2002's promise. Season ended with surgery and one has to wonder whether the bum shoulder had anything to do with his struggles. Worth another shot.

LaRue,Jason

LaRue,Jason		Tm	AB	R	H	HR	RBI	SB	Avg	vL	vR	R$	OB	Slg	OPS	bb%	ct%	h%	Eye	xBA	PX	SX	G/F	RC/G	RAR
Pos CA	99	CIN	* 353	43	76	12	38	4	215	162	245	$2	263	374	637	6	80	24	0.33	267	99	71	1.47	3.08	-9.7
Age 30 Past Peak	00	CIN	* 405	53	93	16	48	2	230	300	218	$5	269	412	682	5	86	23	0.38	296	111	63	1.23	3.61	-4.7
Bats R	01	CIN	364	39	86	12	43	3	236	267	227	$5	289	404	693	7	71	30	0.25	234	104	73	0.96	3.80	3.1
R Very Low	02	CIN	353	42	88	12	52	1	249	207	264	$8	303	405	708	7	67	34	0.23	223	102	52	1.23	4.08	-0.4
I con	03	CIN	379	52	87	16	50	3	230	210	237	$7	291	422	713	8	71	28	0.30	237	123	70	1.02	3.97	-3.7
S	1st Half		204	25	50	10	28	3	245			$6	309	471	780	9	71	30	0.32	247	147	55		4.80	3.1
K	2nd Half		175	27	37	6	22	0	211			$1	270	366	636	7	71	26	0.27	226	95	83		3.11	-6.5
LIMA D BA: 40%	04	Proj	**350**	**45**	**81**	**14**	**46**	**2**	**231**			**$6**	**288**	**417**	**705**	**7**	**71**	**29**	**0.27**	**238**	**119**	**64**		**3.88**	**-2.3**

A catcher with pop will always have some end-game value, however you must consider:
1. Does your team have enough to offset the .230 BA?
2. His power skills are not likely to get any better than this.

Lawton,Matt

Lawton,Matt		Tm	AB	R	H	HR	RBI	SB	Avg	vL	vR	R$	OB	Slg	OPS	bb%	ct%	h%	Eye	xBA	PX	SX	G/F	RC/G	RAR
Pos LF DH	99	MIN	406	58	105	7	54	26	259	290	248	$14	350	355	705	12	90	27	1.36	261	64	100	1.77	4.52	-6.6
Age 32 Past Peak	00	MIN	561	84	171	13	88	23	305	294	309	$24	402	460	862	14	89	33	1.44	294	102	93	1.74	6.80	26.6
Bats L	01	2TM	559	95	155	13	64	29	277	244	287	$21	373	415	788	13	86	30	1.06	278	92	101	1.81	5.53	6.0
R Moderate	02	CLE	426	72	98	15	57	8	230	178	258	$9	326	390	716	13	92	22	1.74	299	96	86	1.42	3.97	-11.4
I con	03	CLE	374	57	93	15	53	10	249	183	270	$11	333	420	752	11	87	25	1.00	312	105	78	1.30	4.75	-6.5
S pt stb	1st Half		286	39	69	11	40	8	241			$8	328	413	741	11	87	24	0.97	311	107	70		4.52	-7.0
K	2nd Half		88	18	24	4	13	2	273			$3	347	443	790	10	90	27	1.11	316	99	79		5.54	0.5
LIMA B+ BA: 75%	04	Proj	**400**	**68**	**107**	**14**	**55**	**9**	**268**			**$13**	**354**	**427**	**781**	**12**	**89**	**27**	**1.21**	**313**	**97**	**84**		**5.19**	**1.4**

I think we can officially label him now as an injury-prone under-achiever. It's sad because he's got such terrific upside, but the list of risk factors is growing and even a cautious investment might not pay off.

LeCroy,Matt

LeCroy,Matt		Tm	AB	R	H	HR	RBI	SB	Avg	vL	vR	R$	OB	Slg	OPS	bb%	ct%	h%	Eye	xBA	PX	SX	G/F	RC/G	RAR
Pos CA	99	aaa	119	17	32	7	23	0	269			$4	293	496	788	3	86	26	0.24	300	125	73		4.86	2.9
Age 28 Peak	00	MIN	* 427	59	99	18	62	0	232	169	176	$5	305	426	731	10	82	24	0.59	284	117	40	0.67	4.32	2.2
Bats R	01	MIN	40	6	17	3	12	0	425			$4	425	775	1200	0	80	48	0.00	361	222		1.27	13.18	8.8
R High	02	MIN	* 355	45	99	15	63	1	279	289	231	$13	326	468	794	7	82	31	0.38	274	113	58	0.88	5.28	16.9
I exp con	03	MIN	345	39	99	17	64	0	287	287	280	$13	335	490	825	7	76	33	0.30	279	123	18	1.08	5.80	16.5
S PT stb	1st Half		146	13	43	6	28	0	295			$6	318	473	790	3	77	35	0.15	274	110	11		5.43	5.4
K	2nd Half		199	26	56	11	36	0	281			$8	347	503	850	9	75	32	0.41	281	132	23		6.06	11.1
LIMA D+ BA: 35%	04	Proj	**400**	**49**	**113**	**19**	**71**	**0**	**283**			**$15**	**332**	**483**	**815**	**7**	**79**	**31**	**0.36**	**283**	**120**	**35**		**5.61**	**18.9**

It's amazing what a little regular playing time can do. A gander at his 2nd half reveals the potential. His platoon splits have leveled out; now he only needs the opportunity.

Ledee,Ricky

Ledee,Ricky		Tm	AB	R	H	HR	RBI	SB	Avg	vL	vR	R$	OB	Slg	OPS	bb%	ct%	h%	Eye	xBA	PX	SX	G/F	RC/G	RAR
Pos CF LF	99	NYY	* 365	60	96	12	53	7	263	282	275	$9	339	447	786	10	73	33	0.43	256	108	145	1.00	5.07	4.0
Age 30 Past Peak	00	2AL	467	59	110	13	77	13	236	241	234	$9	321	381	702	11	79	27	0.60	243	84	116	1.10	4.03	-8.9
Bats L	01	TEX	242	33	56	2	36	3	231	267	226	$2	298	351	649	9	76	30	0.40	252	91	80	1.12	3.35	-11.1
R High	02	PHI	203	33	46	8	23	1	227	80	247	$3	340	419	759	15	75	26	0.70	260	127	69	0.86	4.55	-2.0
I CON	03	PHI	255	37	63	13	46	0	247	250	247	$7	336	475	810	12	77	27	0.58	283	139	61	1.11	5.39	3.1
S pt STB	1st Half		151	22	36	7	23	0	238			$3	339	450	789	13	78	26	0.70	283	132	56		5.11	0.6
K	2nd Half		104	15	27	6	23	0	260			$4	330	510	840	10	75	29	0.42	283	150	70		5.80	2.5
LIMA D BA: 55%	04	Proj	**250**	**37**	**60**	**10**	**41**	**1**	**240**			**$6**	**328**	**442**	**771**	**12**	**76**	**28**	**0.55**	**280**	**128**	**83**		**4.79**	**0.6**

Nice skills development that progressed into the 2nd half and would be poised to take a step up in 2004 if there was some guarantee of playing time. Without regular play, the trend may stagnate, or regress.

Lee,Carlos

Lee,Carlos		Tm	AB	R	H	HR	RBI	SB	Avg	vL	vR	R$	OB	Slg	OPS	bb%	ct%	h%	Eye	xBA	PX	SX	G/F	RC/G	RAR
Pos LF	99	CHW	* 586	79	173	19	101	6	295	301	291	$20	318	461	779	3	86	32	0.24	288	104	78	0.98	5.25	3.0
Age 27 Peak	00	CHW	572	107	172	24	92	13	301	327	295	$24	344	484	829	6	84	33	0.40	283	107	107	1.30	6.06	15.3
Bats R	01	CHW	558	75	150	24	84	17	269	243	275	$21	315	468	783	6	85	28	0.45	283	121	97	0.98	5.04	6.8
R Very Low	02	CHW	492	82	130	26	80	1	264	295	255	$16	362	484	845	13	85	26	1.03	288	130	49	0.67	5.89	15.2
I con	03	CHW	623	100	181	31	113	18	291	218	317	$31	330	499	830	6	85	30	0.41	299	126	97	0.97	5.95	10.8
S	1st Half		296	41	80	13	49	8	270			$12	319	459	778	7	82	29	0.40	282	117	77		5.13	-1.7
K	2nd Half		327	59	101	18	64	10	309			$19	341	535	876	5	88	31	0.41	315	135	104		6.77	12.8
LIMA D BA: 55%	04	Proj	**600**	**96**	**179**	**34**	**103**	**13**	**298**			**$30**	**352**	**531**	**883**	**8**	**85**	**30**	**0.56**	**303**	**137**	**87**		**6.72**	**27.5**

BPIs fully support this season, and 2nd half surge sets the stage for another step up for this peaking 27-year-old.

Lee,Derrek

Lee,Derrek		Tm	AB	R	H	HR	RBI	SB	Avg	vL	vR	R$	OB	Slg	OPS	bb%	ct%	h%	Eye	xBA	PX	SX	G/F	RC/G	RAR
Pos 1B	99	FLA	* 557	65	125	18	74	4	224	234	199	$5	276	375	652	7	75	27	0.29	248	93	63	1.31	3.30	-34.3
Age 28 Peak	00	FLA	477	70	134	28	70	0	281	228	295	$17	365	507	872	12	74	33	0.51	258	125	46	1.07	6.41	14.4
Bats R	01	FLA	561	83	158	21	75	4	282	310	274	$18	340	474	815	8	78	33	0.40	267	119	89	0.98	5.69	-8.9
R Very Low	02	FLA	581	95	157	27	86	19	270	264	272	$26	376	494	870	14	72	33	0.60	257	142	134	0.83	6.35	12.7
I con	03	FLA	539	91	146	31	92	21	271	333	256	$28	373	508	882	14	76	31	0.67	289	145	99	1.19	6.55	16.2
S	1st Half		293	46	77	16	44	14	263			$14	372	485	857	15	78	29	0.78	291	137	81		6.25	6.4
K	2nd Half		246	45	69	15	48	7	280			$13	375	537	911	13	73	33	0.56	285	154	111		6.90	9.8
LIMA B BA: 50%	04	Proj	**550**	**89**	**153**	**28**	**98**	**15**	**278**			**$26**	**370**	**504**	**874**	**13**	**75**	**33**	**0.57**	**286**	**138**	**107**		**6.47**	**13.3**

Despite rising PX trend, G/F levels temper expectations a bit. 35-40 HRs might ordinarily be the next logical step; more likely he'll continue to hover around 30 for another year.

Lee,Travis

		Tm	AB	R	H	HR	RBI	SB	Avg	vL	vR	R$	OB	Slg	OPS	bb%	ct%	h%	Eye	xBA	PX	SX	G/F	RC/G	RAR
Pos 1B	99	ARI	375	57	89	9	50	17	237	216	245	$9	339	363	702	13	87	25	1.16	261	79	108	1.42	4.27	-11.7
Age 28 Peak	00	2NL	404	53	95	9	54	8	235	205	242	$6	341	366	707	14	80	27	0.82	248	86	79	1.49	4.25	-13.3
Bats L	01	PHI	555	75	143	20	90	3	258	265	255	$14	342	434	776	11	80	29	0.65	269	110	56	1.22	4.99	-20.6
R High	02	PHI	536	55	142	13	70	5	265	282	259	$13	332	394	726	9	81	31	0.52	269	87	62	1.30	4.49	-17.2
I CON	03	TAM	542	75	149	19	70	6	275	285	269	$16	351	459	811	11	82	31	0.66	282	118	80	1.11	5.67	4.5
S pt STB	1st Half		248	34	63	6	25	1	254			$3	317	415	733	8	81	29	0.49	272	107	79		4.45	-6.8
K	2nd Half		294	41	86	13	45	5	293			$12	379	497	876	12	83	32	0.82	290	127	70		6.83	11.9
LIMA C+ BA: 55%	04	Proj	**550**	**71**	**155**	**23**	**85**	**7**	**282**			**$20**	**359**	**472**	**831**	**11**	**82**	**31**	**0.66**	**281**	**117**	**68**		**5.99**	**5.1**

Finally, some signs of growth, bolstered by an impressive 2nd half. A springboard to further improvement? Possibly, but BPIs are not optimistic enough to project any type of major breakout.

Leon,Jose

		Tm	AB	R	H	HR	RBI	SB	Avg	vL	vR	R$	OB	Slg	OPS	bb%	ct%	h%	Eye	xBA	PX	SX	G/F	RC/G	RAR
Pos 3B	99	aa	335	33	73	16	48	3	218			$5	268	409	677	6	71	26	0.23	239	113	41		3.47	-9.6
Age 27 Peak	00	aa	365	42	85	14	41	6	233			$5	269	397	666	5	80	26	0.24	265	94	89		3.49	-9.7
Bats R	01	a/a	511	66	137	15	67	7	268			$13	310	417	727	6	79	31	0.29	256	91	88		4.43	-0.7
R Very High	02	BAL	* 401	42	100	10	45	1	249	290	148	$6	283	369	652	5	83	28	0.28	253	75	51	2.12	3.57	-10.6
I EXP CON	03	BAL	* 363	36	86	4	35	1	237	286	158	$1	271	322	593	4	83	28	0.27	244	60	53	2.00	2.89	-17.6
S pt stb	1st Half		202	21	48	4	23	0	238			$1	277	356	633	5	84	27	0.34	258	78	47		3.30	-7.3
K	2nd Half		161	15	38	0	12	1	236			($0)	263	280	543	4	81	29	0.20	225	38	50		2.41	-10.2
LIMA F BA: 45%	04	Proj	**150**	**16**	**37**	**3**	**16**	**1**	**247**			**$2**	**282**	**350**	**632**	**5**	**81**	**29**	**0.26**	**244**	**69**	**46**		**3.31**	**-5.2**

0-0-.241 in 54 AB at BAL. Despite minor promise shown in 2001, this is a weak hitter who is completely tied into knots by RHers -- not a good thing when you have to face RHers 75% of the time.

Lieberthal,Mike

		Tm	AB	R	H	HR	RBI	SB	Avg	vL	vR	R$	OB	Slg	OPS	bb%	ct%	h%	Eye	xBA	PX	SX	G/F	RC/G	RAR
Pos CA	99	PHI	510	84	153	31	96	0	300	377	276	$23	356	551	907	8	83	31	0.51	302	151	36	0.94	7.14	44.5
Age 32 Past Peak	00	PHI	389	55	108	15	71	2	278	350	259	$12	345	470	815	9	86	29	0.75	299	123	49	0.90	5.76	19.5
Bats R	01	PHI	121	21	28	2	11	0	231	417	186	$0	301	347	648	9	83	27	0.57	252	82	54	0.68	3.46	-0.2
R Low	02	PHI	476	46	133	15	52	0	279	346	260	$12	333	443	776	7	88	29	0.66	300	111	32	0.88	5.17	14.3
I con	03	PHI	508	68	159	13	81	0	313	319	311	$19	361	453	814	7	88	33	0.64	311	95	35	0.99	6.06	24.2
S pt	1st Half		243	32	80	5	34	0	329			$10	387	453	840	9	90	35	0.92	309	84	40		6.66	15.2
K	2nd Half		265	36	79	8	47	0	298			$10	336	453	789	5	87	32	0.44	313	105	32		5.52	9.0
LIMA C BA: 50%	04	Proj	**500**	**66**	**151**	**14**	**70**	**0**	**302**			**$17**	**354**	**453**	**807**	**7**	**87**	**33**	**0.61**	**312**	**102**	**38**		**5.85**	**24.0**

xBAs have shown that he retained .300 BA skills after 1999, but this was the first year back at that level since then. This year's productivity is about where he'll likely plateau as long as he stays healthy.

Liefer,Jeff

		Tm	AB	R	H	HR	RBI	SB	Avg	vL	vR	R$	OB	Slg	OPS	bb%	ct%	h%	Eye	xBA	PX	SX	G/F	RC/G	RAR
Pos CF	99	CHW	* 284	35	77	7	40	4	271	124	257	$7	328	440	768	8	83	31	0.49	284	112	86	1.96	4.99	2.3
Age 29 Past Peak	00	aaa	445	56	110	27	69	2	247			$12	311	490	801	8	81	25	0.48	294	139	41	1.00	4.98	6.6
Bats L	01	CHW	* 373	56	96	24	57	3	257	105	268	$13	318	504	822	8	71	30	0.31	250	144	50	0.86	5.42	6.2
R Very High	02	CHW	204	28	47	7	26	0	230	300	227	$2	296	373	669	9	71	29	0.32	228	86	35	1.40	3.65	-6.9
I EXP con	03	2TM	* 270	26	55	9	40	0	204	125	186	$1	251	374	625	6	68	26	0.20	223	104	83	1.27	2.95	-16.2
S PT STB	1st Half		100	6	18	3	19	0	180			$0	212	300	512	4	67	23	0.12	202	73	23		1.86	-9.8
K	2nd Half		170	20	37	6	21	0	218			$1	273	418	691	7	68	28	0.24	235	122	115		3.72	-5.9
LIMA F BA: 40%	04	Proj	**200**	**23**	**45**	**8**	**29**	**0**	**225**			**$3**	**280**	**402**	**682**	**7**	**70**	**28**	**0.26**	**231**	**109**	**62**		**3.65**	**-6.6**

4-21-.177 in 113 AB at MON and TAM. After two straight down years, the window of opportunity is likely closing for this 29-year-old.

Lockhart,Keith

		Tm	AB	R	H	HR	RBI	SB	Avg	vL	vR	R$	OB	Slg	OPS	bb%	ct%	h%	Eye	xBA	PX	SX	G/F	RC/G	RAR
Pos 2B	99	ATL	161	20	42	1	21	3	261	83	275	$2	339	311	649	11	87	29	0.90	230	31	79	1.24	3.66	-2.6
Age 39 Decline	00	ATL	275	32	73	2	32	4	265	375	251	$4	336	353	688	10	89	29	0.94	251	57	96	1.20	4.14	-1.8
Bats L	01	ATL	178	17	39	3	12	1	219	111	225	($0)	284	303	587	8	88	24	0.73	227	54	40	0.93	2.70	-6.4
R X HIGH	02	ATL	296	34	64	5	32	0	216	67	224	$0	282	331	613	8	83	24	0.54	234	77	76	0.91	2.99	-13.0
I CON	03	SD	95	18	23	3	8	0	242	100	259	$1	333	411	744	12	80	27	0.68	257	106	100	0.64	4.41	0.0
S PT stb	1st Half		87	18	22	3	6	0	253			$1	343	437	780	12	83	28	0.80	272	116	107		4.89	1.3
K AGE	2nd Half		8	0	1	0	2	0	125			($0)	222	125	347	11	50	25	0.25	122	0			0.81	-1.0
LIMA F BA: 55%	04	Proj	**150**	**21**	**36**	**3**	**13**	**1**	**240**			**$1**	**315**	**352**	**667**	**10**	**85**	**26**	**0.75**	**256**	**72**	**76**		**3.63**	**-3.1**

Minor inklings of remnant skill remain, but at 39, he's not likely going to find a team willing to pick through the scraps of career residue to exhume those last buried nuggets of value. Not my team, anyway.

LoDuca,Paul

		Tm	AB	R	H	HR	RBI	SB	Avg	vL	vR	R$	OB	Slg	OPS	bb%	ct%	h%	Eye	xBA	PX	SX	G/F	RC/G	RAR
Pos CA 1B	99	LA	* 171	24	45	4	17	2	263	278	171	$3	333	380	713	10	94	26	1.80	299	77	51	1.14	4.15	1.0
Age 32 Past Peak	00	LA	* 344	43	99	5	51	6	288	240	250	$10	348	413	761	9	94	29	1.60	310	86	72	1.25	4.79	7.9
Bats R	01	LA	460	71	147	25	90	2	320	411	290	$25	373	543	916	8	93	30	1.30	339	134	37	1.08	7.37	47.8
R Moderate	02	LA	580	74	163	10	64	3	281	307	273	$13	321	402	723	6	95	28	1.10	311	90	64	1.37	4.57	7.5
I con	03	LA	568	64	155	7	52	0	273	281	270	$8	325	377	702	7	90	29	0.81	310	76	39	1.55	4.23	-1.0
S pt	1st Half		280	30	89	5	28	0	318			$9	368	454	821	7	91	34	0.85	324	95	48		6.14	13.9
K	2nd Half		288	34	66	2	24	0	229			($1)	284	302	586	7	90	25	0.79	297	57	41		2.79	-13.1
LIMA C BA: 70%	04	Proj	**450**	**56**	**131**	**9**	**51**	**2**	**291**			**$12**	**341**	**416**	**757**	**7**	**92**	**30**	**0.99**	**318**	**87**	**47**		**5.01**	**11.4**

The fallout of full-time play...

	1st half	2nd half
2001	.344	.304*
		*.221 in Sept.
2002	.318	.248
2003	.318	.229

Hello, LA? Anyone listening?

Lofton,Kenny

		Tm	AB	R	H	HR	RBI	SB	Avg	vL	vR	R$	OB	Slg	OPS	bb%	ct%	h%	Eye	xBA	PX	SX	G/F	RC/G	RAR
Pos CF	99	CLE	465	110	140	7	39	25	301	224	327	$17	403	432	835	15	82	36	0.94	279	85	161	1.24	6.48	23.0
Age 36 Decline	00	CLE	543	107	151	15	73	30	278	260	283	$21	370	422	792	13	87	30	1.10	278	84	142	1.17	5.63	15.2
Bats L	01	CLE	517	91	135	14	66	16	261	246	266	$15	323	398	721	8	87	28	0.68	284	83	117	1.12	4.33	-7.9
R Moderate	02	2TM	532	98	139	11	51	29	261	248	265	$18	349	414	763	12	86	29	0.99	290	98	170	1.14	4.93	1.7
I con	03	2NL	547	97	162	12	46	30	296	244	313	$23	351	450	800	8	91	31	0.90	309	100	164	1.22	5.70	11.2
S stb	1st Half		281	51	79	8	25	14	281			$11	340	441	781	8	91	29	1.00	310	102	146		5.33	2.8
K AGE	2nd Half		266	46	83	4	21	16	312			$13	362	459	821	7	90	33	0.81	307	98	174		6.12	8.4
LIMA A BA: 65%	04	Proj	**550**	**100**	**156**	**12**	**53**	**28**	**284**			**$21**	**352**	**432**	**784**	**9**	**88**	**30**	**0.89**	**304**	**95**	**161**		**5.38**	**10.4**

It is not unusual for a player to improve his bat control and plate patience as he gets older, but usually to offset the erosion of other skills, like power. Not here. He's on an overall skills surge, at 36. Pretty cool.

Long,Terrence

		Tm	AB	R	H	HR	RBI	SB	Avg	vL	vR	R$	OB	Slg	OPS	bb%	ct%	h%	Eye	xBA	PX	SX	G/F	RC/G	RAR
Pos LF RF	99	aaa	458	48	123	7	58	18	269			$12	311	384	695	6	87	30	0.47	278	76	104		3.87	-16.2
Age 28 Peak	00	OAK	* 644	114	190	21	94	5	295	263	298	$19	343	467	810	7	87	31	0.58	298	105	93	1.32	5.74	11.6
Bats L	01	OAK	629	90	178	12	85	9	283	278	286	$17	338	412	750	8	84	32	0.50	279	85	93	1.34	4.94	5.6
R Moderate	02	OAK	587	71	141	16	67	3	240	250	237	$8	298	390	688	8	84	26	0.50	269	95	69	1.17	3.75	-19.2
I exp CON	03	OAK	486	64	119	14	61	4	245	236	249	$8	290	385	675	6	86	26	0.46	274	87	80	1.32	3.78	-22.4
S pt stb	1st Half		258	36	64	8	31	1	248			$4	300	391	691	7	86	26	0.53	273	88	66		4.00	-10.1
K	2nd Half		228	28	55	6	30	3	241			$4	279	377	656	5	86	26	0.39	274	86	82		3.53	-12.3
LIMA D BA: 60%	04	Proj	**450**	**59**	**114**	**12**	**57**	**5**	**253**			**$8**	**302**	**392**	**694**	**7**	**85**	**27**	**0.48**	**273**	**88**	**78**		**3.99**	**-14.4**

The Anti-Beane... Over 1000 AB of sub-.300 OB Avg over the past two years. That's what OAK is getting for signing him to a 4-year deal that runs through 2005. xBA says it might get a little better, but not enough.

Lopez,Felipe

		Tm	AB	R	H	HR	RBI	SB	Avg	vL	vR	R$	OB	Slg	OPS	bb%	ct%	h%	Eye	xBA	PX	SX	G/F	RC/G	RAR
Pos SS	99		0	0	0	0	0	0	0								0								
Age 23 Growth	00	aa	463	42	112	7	34	9	242			$3	281	339	620	5	83	28	0.32	255	61	77		2.85	-15.5
Bats S	01	TOR	* 607	93	166	23	68	19	273	293	244	$21	327	470	796	7	79	31	0.38	274	113	148	1.24	5.06	12.2
R X HIGH	02	TOR	* 455	64	117	10	48	16	257	303	204	$12	327	400	727	9	74	33	0.40	239	93	128	1.52	4.53	-0.6
I EXP CON	03	CIN	* 340	46	80	4	28	10	235	196	219	$4	312	335	647	10	74	31	0.43	229	71	101	1.84	3.18	-9.9
S pt stb	1st Half		258	38	60	2	20	9	233			$3	320	326	645	11	72	31	0.46	225	68	119		3.32	-6.3
K AGE	2nd Half		82	8	20	2	8	1	244			$1	287	366	653	6	78	29	0.28	243	82	52		2.67	-3.8
LIMA D BA: 40%	04	Proj	**350**	**44**	**87**	**8**	**33**	**9**	**249**			**$7**	**309**	**376**	**685**	**8**	**77**	**31**	**0.37**	**237**	**85**	**92**		**3.55**	**-3.8**

2-13-8-.213 in 197 AB at CIN... and more errors than RBIs. His BPIs have been in a nosedive, but ended mercifully in July by a dislocated ankle. Poised to take over SS from Larkin. Um, yeah.

Lopez,Javy

	Yr	Tm	AB	R	H	HR	RBI	SB	Avg	vL	vR	R$	OB	Slg	OPS	bb%	ct%	h%	Eye	xBA	PX	SX	G/F	RC/G	RAR
Pos CA	99	ATL	246	34	78	11	45	0	317	340	311	$11	368	533	901	8	83	35	0.49	318	136	39	1.78	6.98	20.2
Age 33 Decline	00	ATL	481	60	138	24	89	0	287	277	289	$18	335	484	820	7	83	30	0.44	276	113	28	1.47	5.81	24.4
Bats R	01	ATL	438	45	117	17	66	1	267	212	280	$12	311	425	736	6	81	29	0.34	241	92	41	1.39	4.61	13.8
R Moderate	02	ATL	347	31	81	11	52	0	233	255	230	$6	287	372	659	7	82	26	0.41	244	91		1.67	3.50	-6.4
I CON	03	ATL	457	89	150	43	109	0	328	336	326	$34	373	687	1061	7	80	33	0.37	349	210	63	1.06	9.66	64.8
S pt	1st Half		217	40	68	23	48	0	313			$16	361	696	1056	7	82	29	0.40	358	215	67		9.32	29.4
K age	2nd Half		240	49	82	20	61	0	342			$19	385	679	1064	7	79	36	0.34	341	205	60		9.97	35.4
LIMA D+ BA: 45%	04	Proj	**400**	**60**	**118**	**26**	**80**	**0**	**295**			**$20**	**342**	**549**	**891**	**7**	**81**	**31**	**0.38**	**334**	**152**	**39**		**6.73**	**29.2**

Can you say, Contract Year? It was the motivation he needed to lose 32 lbs and post a monster season. The big question now is -- what happens AFTER he signs a new contract? Odds are to expect a significant drop-off.

Lopez,Mendy

	Yr	Tm	AB	R	H	HR	RBI	SB	Avg	vL	vR	R$	OB	Slg	OPS	bb%	ct%	h%	Eye	xBA	PX	SX	G/F	RC/G	RAR
Pos 1B	99	aaa	222	31	60	10	31	2	270			$6	314	437	750	6	86	28	0.44	280	95	51	7.00	4.65	-5.7
Age 29 Past Peak	00	aaa	225	25	61	5	21	1	271			$3	302	422	724	4	86	30	0.32	290	100	60		4.40	-8.1
Bats R	01	2NL	* 266	38	67	14	36	2	252	250	235	$7	307	477	784	7	76	28	0.33	271	131	86	1.06	4.87	-10.9
R Very High	02	aaa	385	47	85	8	56	3	221			$4	272	345	617	7	79	26	0.33	250	88	65		3.07	-31.4
I EXP con	03	KC	94	13	26	3	11	2	277	316	250	$3	306	447	753	4	70	37	0.14	259	104	118	1.53	4.95	-1.2
S pt STB	1st Half		43	5	12	0	3	2	279			$1	295	349	644	2	77	36	0.10	253	61	81		3.91	-1.8
K	2nd Half		51	8	14	3	8	0	275			$2	315	529	844	6	65	37	0.17	259	141	136		5.86	0.7
LIMA F BA: 25%	04	Proj	**100**	**14**	**25**	**4**	**14**	**1**	**250**			**$2**	**295**	**448**	**744**	**6**	**76**	**29**	**0.27**	**273**	**117**	**92**		**4.45**	**-3.6**

Let's play DL Games! Placed on the DL on 6/15 with a strained calf muscle, concurrently with Carlos Febles being activated. Was it a real injury? Activated on 8/12 -- Does a strained calf take two months to heal? Hmm.

Loretta,Mark

	Yr	Tm	AB	R	H	HR	RBI	SB	Avg	vL	vR	R$	OB	Slg	OPS	bb%	ct%	h%	Eye	xBA	PX	SX	G/F	RC/G	RAR
Pos 2B	99	MIL	587	93	170	5	67	4	290	300	286	$11	347	390	738	8	90	32	0.88	288	71	93	1.03	4.88	10.9
Age 32 Past Peak	00	MIL	352	49	99	7	40	0	281	333	266	$7	350	406	756	10	89	30	0.97	308	83	39	1.68	4.87	5.1
Bats R	01	MIL	384	40	111	2	29	1	289	313	281	$6	337	352	689	7	88	32	0.61	288	44	53	1.19	4.18	3.4
R Moderate	02	2NL	283	33	86	4	27	1	304	309	302	$8	375	410	784	10	87	34	0.86	285	82	35	1.03	5.58	9.0
I con	03	SD	589	74	186	13	72	5	316	307	318	$21	373	445	818	8	89	34	0.87	325	85	72	1.09	6.09	26.8
S pt stb	1st Half		283	34	85	6	29	3	300			$9	367	431	799	10	89	32	1.00	326	87	76		5.77	10.6
K	2nd Half		306	40	101	7	43	2	330			$13	379	458	836	7	90	35	0.75	323	83	64		6.40	16.2
LIMA C+ BA: 55%	04	Proj	**550**	**68**	**169**	**12**	**65**	**3**	**307**			**$18**	**367**	**436**	**803**	**9**	**89**	**33**	**0.82**	**324**	**85**	**61**		**5.79**	**22.2**

Excellent breakout season, fully supported by his BPIs. At 32, there's probably not much further to go, but you can't ask for more from a middle infielder.

Lowell,Mike

	Yr	Tm	AB	R	H	HR	RBI	SB	Avg	vL	vR	R$	OB	Slg	OPS	bb%	ct%	h%	Eye	xBA	PX	SX	G/F	RC/G	RAR
Pos 3B	99	FLA	* 391	40	100	13	54	0	256	250	254	$7	312	399	711	8	79	29	0.39	254	89		0.69	4.27	-1.1
Age 30 Past Peak	00	FLA	508	73	137	22	91	4	270	257	273	$16	340	474	814	10	85	28	0.72	286	128	59	0.67	5.68	19.8
Bats R	01	FLA	551	65	156	18	100	1	283	283	283	$18	335	448	783	7	86	30	0.54	283	107	31	0.65	5.27	10.7
R Very Low	02	FLA	597	88	165	24	92	4	276	255	283	$21	347	471	818	10	85	29	0.71	288	133	52	0.61	5.69	18.8
I con	03	FLA	492	76	136	32	105	3	276	295	271	$24	350	530	881	10	84	27	0.72	306	153	58	0.73	6.54	32.0
S pt	1st Half		317	55	91	25	68	2	287			$18	354	599	954	9	84	28	0.63	325	188	64		7.54	29.3
K	2nd Half		175	21	45	7	37	1	257			$6	343	406	749	12	85	27	0.88	272	88	36		4.82	2.9
LIMA D BA: 60%	04	Proj	**600**	**83**	**178**	**40**	**123**	**3**	**297**			**$32**	**366**	**553**	**919**	**10**	**84**	**30**	**0.70**	**308**	**154**	**39**		**7.30**	**48.2**

Was en route to a monster year when a groin injury and broken hand put on the brakes. If healthy, he could get right back on track and post some extraordinary numbers.

Ludwick,Ryan

	Yr	Tm	AB	R	H	HR	RBI	SB	Avg	vL	vR	R$	OB	Slg	OPS	bb%	ct%	h%	Eye	xBA	PX	SX	G/F	RC/G	RAR
Pos RF	99		0	0	0	0	0	0	0								0								
Age 25 Pre-Peak	00		0	0	0	0	0	0	0								0								
Bats R	01	a/a	500	73	114	21	81	9	228			$12	293	406	699	8	80	25	0.45	266	105	82		3.61	-25.8
R High	02	TEX	* 386	57	97	13	49	4	251			$9	315	446	761	9	79	29	0.45	275	125	95	0.92	4.69	-3.8
I EXP con	03	2AL	* 479	61	131	23	80	3	273	220	262	$17	331	495	826	8	77	31	0.38	272	135	73	0.49	5.73	8.0
S stb	1st Half		314	44	90	16	52	1	287			$12	345	522	867	8	81	31	0.47	291	144	62		6.38	10.8
K age	2nd Half		165	17	41	7	28	2	248			$5	303	442	746	7	70	31	0.27	238	118	73		4.62	-2.6
LIMA D BA: 40%	04	Proj	**350**	**46**	**89**	**14**	**53**	**4**	**254**			**$9**	**315**	**452**	**766**	**8**	**77**	**29**	**0.38**	**268**	**122**	**79**		**4.78**	**-3.1**

7-26-.247 in 162 AB at TEX and CLE. A future major power source, his PX and G/F trends are already making a statement. A warning sign, however, is a declining ct% as he moves up levels. Bid with caution.

Lugo,Julio

	Yr	Tm	AB	R	H	HR	RBI	SB	Avg	vL	vR	R$	OB	Slg	OPS	bb%	ct%	h%	Eye	xBA	PX	SX	G/F	RC/G	RAR
Pos SS	99	aa	445	67	124	8	37	22	279			$13	334	409	743	8	88	30	0.67	287	83	131		4.64	10.3
Age 28 Peak	00	HOU	* 521	97	150	13	50	32	288	239	300	$22	346	436	781	8	79	35	0.41	262	89	150	1.52	5.07	24.6
Bats R	01	HOU	513	93	135	10	37	12	263	299	254	$10	324	372	696	8	77	32	0.40	239	68	112	1.20	3.94	5.8
R Moderate	02	HOU	322	45	84	8	35	9	261	270	258	$9	320	388	708	8	77	32	0.38	251	86	96	1.46	4.28	3.6
I exp con	03	2TM	498	64	135	15	55	12	271	240	284	$15	330	410	740	8	80	31	0.44	268	82	106	1.59	4.72	6.6
S pt stb	1st Half		210	18	52	2	15	6	248			$3	307	333	640	8	79	31	0.40	249	61	83		3.48	-4.9
K	2nd Half		288	46	83	13	40	6	288			$12	347	465	812	8	81	32	0.47	281	97	114		5.76	12.1
LIMA C BA: 45%	04	Proj	**500**	**72**	**139**	**16**	**56**	**11**	**278**			**$16**	**336**	**426**	**763**	**8**	**79**	**32**	**0.42**	**271**	**89**	**96**		**4.95**	**11.1**

Excellent 2nd half, but it only served to offset his poor 1st half and net out at virtually no BPI gain over previous years. It's possible he might have a slight uptick in performance in 2004.

Mabry,John

	Yr	Tm	AB	R	H	HR	RBI	SB	Avg	vL	vR	R$	OB	Slg	OPS	bb%	ct%	h%	Eye	xBA	PX	SX	G/F	RC/G	RAR
Pos RF	99	SEA	262	34	64	9	33	2	244	250	244	$4	298	401	699	7	77	28	0.33	253	97	55	1.09	4.00	-7.5
Age 33 Decline	00	2TM	226	35	53	8	32	0	235		264	$3	282	398	680	6	69	30	0.22	244	101	51	1.19	3.67	-9.3
Bats L	01	2NL	154	14	32	6	20	1	208	214	207	$1	269	370	640	8	70	25	0.28	208	98	36	1.02	3.24	-11.1
R X HIGH	02	2TM	214	28	59	11	43	1	276	192	287	$9	323	500	823	7	80	30	0.36	267	139	60	1.00	5.60	2.7
I CON	03	SEA	104	12	22	3	16	0	212		224	$1	311	356	667	13	80	24	0.71	247	94	23	1.43	3.58	-5.1
S PT STB	1st Half		37	5	6	2	7	0	162			$0	225	378	603	8	70	17	0.27	237	130	43		2.59	-3.1
K age	2nd Half		67	7	16	1	9	0	239			$0	354	343	698	15	85	27	1.20	251	75	18		4.08	-2.1
LIMA F BA: 65%	04	Proj	**200**	**23**	**49**	**7**	**29**	**1**	**245**			**$4**	**318**	**400**	**717**	**10**	**77**	**29**	**0.47**	**245**	**98**	**35**		**4.27**	**-4.7**

Battled a strained shoulder all season long and should bounce back with more representative numbers in 2004. For whatever that's worth.

Machado,Robert

	Yr	Tm	AB	R	H	HR	RBI	SB	Avg	vL	vR	R$	OB	Slg	OPS	bb%	ct%	h%	Eye	xBA	PX	SX	G/F	RC/G	RAR
Pos CA	99	aaa	129	9	25	2	9	0	194			($2)	212	302	514	2	82	22	0.13	257	77	34	0.50	1.94	-8.5
Age 30 Past Peak	00	aaa	330	38	86	8	54	1	261			$6	318	385	703	8	86	28	0.60	273	79	32	0.33	3.98	-0.9
Bats R	01	CHC	* 315	29	72	8	37	0	229	278	185	$2	264	362	626	5	81	26	0.25	259	87	24	1.27	3.15	-3.5
R X HIGH	02	MIL	211	19	55	3	22	0	261	226	290	$3	316	379	695	7	81	31	0.41	240	89	39	1.10	4.13	0.1
I EXP CON	03	BAL	* 270	33	75	8	35	0	278	600	179	$6	328	422	750	7	82	31	0.41	261	94	26	1.15	4.88	6.1
S PT STB	1st Half		163	20	42	5	23	0	258			$3	301	405	705	6	83	28	0.36	265	95	30		4.18	0.4
K	2nd Half		107	13	33	3	12	0	308			$3	368	449	816	9	80	36	0.48	254	92	21		6.08	5.8
LIMA F BA: 45%	04	Proj	**150**	**16**	**40**	**4**	**18**	**0**	**267**			**$3**	**317**	**398**	**715**	**7**	**81**	**31**	**0.39**	**258**	**88**	**27**		**4.36**	**1.8**

1-3-.265 in 49 AB at BAL. Intriguing 2nd half showed outward signs of hidden BA skill, but xBA puts that to rest.

Macias,Jose

	Yr	Tm	AB	R	H	HR	RBI	SB	Avg	vL	vR	R$	OB	Slg	OPS	bb%	ct%	h%	Eye	xBA	PX	SX	G/F	RC/G	RAR
Pos LF 3B	99	aaa	438	34	89	2	28	8	203			($4)	253	279	531	6	88	23	0.57	267	48	107	1.00	2.18	-40.1
Age 32 Past Peak	00	DET	* 303	40	71	2	30	4	234	350	226	$0	305	314	619	9	88	26	0.86	260	46	124	1.23	3.13	-18.1
Bats S	01	DET	488	62	131	8	51	21	268	238	279	$14	313	391	705	6	89	29	0.59	293	78	131	1.62	4.30	-4.7
R Very High	02	2TM	338	43	84	7	39	8	249	250	248	$7	292	379	671	6	83	28	0.37	277	91	86	1.35	3.48	-21.8
I exp CON	03	MON	272	31	65	4	22	4	239	250	231	$2	269	353	621	4	83	27	0.24	272	79	100	1.50	3.08	-20.7
S PT STB	1st Half		135	20	36	3	10	3	267			$3	313	400	713	6	85	29	0.45	285	88	107		4.34	-4.9
K	2nd Half		137	11	29	1	12	1	212			($1)	223	307	530	1	81	25	0.08	259	70	86		2.06	-15.2
LIMA F BA: 50%	04	Proj	**250**	**29**	**60**	**4**	**23**	**5**	**240**			**$3**	**277**	**352**	**630**	**5**	**84**	**27**	**0.33**	**274**	**77**	**104**		**3.15**	**-19.8**

Consistently underperforms his xBA by nearly 30 points, but with his declining trends, the odds of him closing the gap decrease every year.

Mackowiak,Rob

Pos RF
Age 27 Peak
Bats L

RISK		
R	High	
I	EXP	con
S	pt	stb
K		

LIMA F BA: 45%

	Tm	AB	R	H	HR	RBI	SB	Avg	vL	vR	R$	OB	Slg	OPS	bb%	ct%	h%	Eye	xBA	PX	SX	G/F	RC/G	RAR
99	aa	195	17	47	3	22	0	241			$1	267	385	652	3	84	27	0.23	279	99	69		3.28	-10.0
00	aa	526	67	136	11	71	15	259			$12	283	390	673	3	82	30	0.19	269	84	112		3.74	-20.1
01	PIT	* 332	41	85	7	32	5	256	167	269	$6	300	392	692	6	75	32	0.25	245	89	92	1.26	3.90	-16.3
02	PIT	385	57	94	16	48	9	244	302	237	$11	319	426	744	10	69	31	0.35	228	120	80	1.11	4.56	-8.5
03	PIT	* 391	37	92	8	38	12	235	257	273	$7	288	358	646	7	75	29	0.30	239	75	133	1.76	3.48	-25.2
1st Half		144	10	25	2	6	2	174			($3)	232	236	468	7	72	23	0.28	205	34	82		1.75	-18.0
2nd Half		247	27	67	6	32	10	271			$9	321	429	750	7	77	33	0.32	259	100	149		4.81	-5.7
04	Proj	250	28	60	6	26	6	240			$5	295	380	675	7	74	30	0.30	240	90	107		3.75	-13.0

6-19-6-.270 in 174 AB at PIT. Could not follow up on his surprising 2002 line. Given his poor skill set, this is not all that surprising. What IS surprising is that PIT still projects him as a possible regular. But not I.

Marrero,Eli

Pos RF
Age 30 Past Peak
Bats R

RISK		
R	High	
I		CON
S	PT	
K		

LIMA D BA: 50%

	Tm	AB	R	H	HR	RBI	SB	Avg	vL	vR	R$	OB	Slg	OPS	bb%	ct%	h%	Eye	xBA	PX	SX	G/F	RC/G	RAR
99	STL	317	32	61	6	34	11	192	203	189	$0	236	297	532	5	82	22	0.32	238	67	102	1.22	2.27	-27.6
00	STL	102	21	23	5	17	5	225	200	232	$3	288	422	710	8	84	22	0.56	298	106	155	1.28	4.26	-2.7
01	STL	203	37	54	6	23	6	266	256	269	$6	317	438	755	7	82	30	0.42	294	104	156	1.61	4.69	-5.2
02	STL	397	63	104	18	66	14	262	227	273	$18	330	451	780	9	82	28	0.56	274	120	106	0.83	5.24	-0.6
03	STL	107	10	24	2	20	0	224	259	222	$1	272	355	627	6	83	25	0.39	226	79	108	0.67	3.04	-8.5
1st Half		75	8	17	2	15	0	227			$1	284	373	657	7	85	24	0.55	235	89	90		3.29	-5.4
2nd Half		32	2	7	0	5	0	219			($0)	242	312	555	3	78	28	0.14	206	56	149		2.47	-3.1
04	Proj	250	38	60	9	39	1	240			$5	297	413	710	8	83	25	0.49	233	105	89		4.05	-10.6

On May 11, he slipped on wet outfield grass and tore ankle ligaments. Medical experts said he'd be out for 2-6 weeks. He was out for 4 months. Refer to the Forecaster's Toolbox for Westheimer's Rule.

Martinez,Edgar

Pos DH
Age 41 Decline
Bats R

RISK		
R	Low	
I		
S	pt	
K	AGE	

LIMA C BA: 55%

	Tm	AB	R	H	HR	RBI	SB	Avg	vL	vR	R$	OB	Slg	OPS	bb%	ct%	h%	Eye	xBA	PX	SX	G/F	RC/G	RAR
99	SEA	502	86	169	24	86	7	337	358	331	$26	444	554	998	16	80	38	0.98	305	133	65	1.40	9.46	56.0
00	SEA	556	100	180	37	145	3	324	359	317	$33	423	579	1002	15	83	34	1.01	298	144	49	0.95	9.29	62.0
01	SEA	470	80	144	23	116	4	306	246	328	$25	421	543	964	17	81	34	1.03	289	150	57	0.95	8.41	40.7
02	SEA	328	42	91	15	59	1	277	306	267	$12	400	485	885	17	79	31	0.97	260	130	25	0.86	6.79	11.8
03	SEA	497	72	146	24	98	0	294	301	291	$21	404	489	893	16	81	32	0.97	284	117	18	1.16	7.08	34.1
1st Half		233	36	70	15	55	0	300			$12	405	536	942	15	81	32	0.91	295	136	17		7.92	21.1
2nd Half		264	36	76	9	43	0	288			$8	403	447	850	16	81	33	1.02	275	102	20		6.37	13.0
04	Proj	450	66	128	16	80	1	284			$15	398	456	854	16	80	32	0.96	281	109	33		6.43	18.3

As I write this, it's still unknown whether he will retire, but I'm going to err on the side of reality and give him a projection for 2004. After all, there are still about 1000 younger players who would kill for this skill set.

Martinez,Ramon

Pos 2B 3B SS
Age 31 Past Peak
Bats R

RISK		
R	High	
I		CON
S	PT	stb
K		

LIMA F BA: 40%

	Tm	AB	R	H	HR	RBI	SB	Avg	vL	vR	R$	OB	Slg	OPS	bb%	ct%	h%	Eye	xBA	PX	SX	G/F	RC/G	RAR
99	SF	* 258	31	70	6	32	3	271	259	267	$5	329	395	724	8	88	29	0.73	283	80	63	0.98	4.47	1.9
00	SF	189	30	57	6	25	3	302	297	304	$7	353	487	840	7	88	32	0.68	283	115	101	1.01	6.12	9.2
01	SF	391	48	99	5	37	1	253	293	243	$3	319	353	672	9	87	28	0.73	246	65	69	1.16	3.78	-0.9
02	SF	181	26	49	4	25	2	271	254	279	$5	323	414	737	7	86	30	0.54	276	97	108	0.72	4.75	1.7
03	CHC	293	30	83	3	34	0	283	346	259	$6	338	375	713	8	83	33	0.48	261	68	39	1.30	4.45	0.3
1st Half		143	15	39	3	20	0	273			$3	338	399	736	9	87	30	0.78	286	89	21		4.72	1.3
2nd Half		150	15	44	0	14	0	293			$2	337	353	691	6	79	37	0.31	239	48	58		4.18	-0.9
04	Proj	250	30	69	4	29	1	276			$5	331	387	718	8	84	32	0.52	269	76	74		4.47	1.1

Soft skill set retains some marginal value by keeping his OB in acceptable territory. But there is little production behind it, which means his ceiling will always be low. End-gamer if you're desperate.

Martinez,Tino

Pos 1B
Age 36 Decline
Bats L

RISK		
R	Low	
I		con
S		stb
K	AGE	

LIMA C+ BA: 60%

	Tm	AB	R	H	HR	RBI	SB	Avg	vL	vR	R$	OB	Slg	OPS	bb%	ct%	h%	Eye	xBA	PX	SX	G/F	RC/G	RAR
99	NYY	589	95	155	28	105	3	263	261	264	$17	340	458	799	10	85	27	0.80	291	113	60	1.08	5.29	-8.5
00	NYY	569	69	147	16	91	4	258	281	249	$11	320	422	742	8	87	27	0.70	277	101	81	0.90	4.66	-21.4
01	NYY	589	89	165	34	113	1	280	257	290	$24	328	501	829	7	85	28	0.47	296	126	48	1.14	5.75	-6.6
02	STL	511	63	134	21	75	3	262	207	278	$15	337	438	776	10	86	27	0.82	285	113	50	1.05	5.07	-7.9
03	STL	476	66	130	15	69	1	273	235	281	$13	346	429	775	10	85	29	0.75	286	100	55	1.22	5.17	-4.6
1st Half		253	36	70	9	38	0	277			$7	335	466	801	8	84	30	0.55	297	123	63		5.50	-0.1
2nd Half		223	30	60	6	31	1	269			$5	358	386	744	12	86	29	1.00	273	74	39		4.77	-4.8
04	Proj	500	68	140	19	77	2	280			$16	351	450	800	10	86	30	0.75	289	106	56		5.54	-1.3

HIdden behind this disappointing season was the fact that he hit over .300 for three of the six months, and was hurt for two of the other three. Skills are still there, opinion is low, which makes for profit opportunity.

Martinez,Victor

Pos CA
Age 25 Pre-Peak
Bats S

RISK		
R	High	
I	EXP	con
S		stb
K	age	

LIMA D BA: 50%

	Tm	AB	R	H	HR	RBI	SB	Avg	vL	vR	R$	OB	Slg	OPS	bb%	ct%	h%	Eye	xBA	PX	SX	G/F	RC/G	RAR
99		0	0	0	0	0	0	0								0								
00		0	0	0	0	0	0	0								0								
01		0	0	0	0	0	0	0								0								
02	aa	443	73	139	20	74	3	314			$21	383	535	918	10	87	33	0.86	311	148	49		7.48	43.5
03	CLE	* 445	53	133	8	58	4	299	271	300	$13	350	407	757	7	88	33	0.66	268	74	42	1.67	4.96	10.8
1st Half		286	39	90	7	42	3	315			$11	366	462	827	7	89	34	0.72	289	101	46		5.93	14.5
2nd Half		159	14	43	1	16	1	270			$2	322	308	630	7	87	31	0.57	232	26	35		3.41	-3.1
04	Proj	350	46	100	9	49	3	286			$10	346	425	771	8	87	31	0.72	273	92	45		5.10	11.5

1-16-.289 in 159 AB at CLE. An exiciting young skill set, but hope for a .300 hitter out of the gate is a bit optimistic. He's on the right path; consider him a long-term investment with a high ceiling.

Martin,Al

Pos DH
Age 36 Decline
Bats L

RISK		
R	X HIGH	
I		CON
S	pt	STB
K	AGE	

LIMA F BA: 40%

	Tm	AB	R	H	HR	RBI	SB	Avg	vL	vR	R$	OB	Slg	OPS	bb%	ct%	h%	Eye	xBA	PX	SX	G/F	RC/G	RAR
99	PIT	541	97	150	24	63	20	277	242	287	$20	337	506	844	8	78	32	0.41	285	139	160	0.99	6.13	14.4
00	2TM	480	81	137	15	36	10	285	156	310	$13	335	452	787	7	82	32	0.42	292	90	156	1.85	5.12	0.5
01	SEA	283	41	68	7	42	9	240	100	245	$7	328	382	710	12	79	28	0.63	257	89	104	1.23	4.21	-8.7
02		0	0	0	0	0	0	0								0								
03	TAM	238	19	60	3	26	2	252	333	250	$3	302	357	659	7	79	31	0.33	243	70	71	1.55	3.59	-7.3
1st Half		139	11	37	0	9	2	266			$1	306	331	637	5	82	32	0.32	241	50	73		3.38	-5.0
2nd Half		99	8	23	3	17	0	232			$1	296	394	690	8	74	29	0.35	244	99	55		3.88	-2.2
04	Proj	150	18	36	4	19	3	240			$2	295	387	682	7	78	28	0.36	250	89	116		3.77	-5.5

Declining skill set left him without a job for the 2002 season. He came back in '03 with an even lesser skill set... but got a job in TAM... which is more of an indictment of TAM than Martin.

Mateo,Henry

Pos 2B
Age 27 Peak
Bats S

RISK		
R	X HIGH	
I	EXP	CON
S	pt	stb
K		

LIMA F BA: 35%

	Tm	AB	R	H	HR	RBI	SB	Avg	vL	vR	R$	OB	Slg	OPS	bb%	ct%	h%	Eye	xBA	PX	SX	G/F	RC/G	RAR
99		0	0	0	0	0	0	0								0								
00	aa	530	74	132	5	51	39	249			$15	309	351	660	8	83	29	0.52	262	63	163		3.56	-9.0
01	aaa	509	66	129	5	39	43	253			$17	294	348	641	5	84	29	0.35	260	55	178	5.00	3.44	-9.1
02	aaa	308	32	71	4	22	15	231			$5	271	334	605	5	83	26	0.33	256	64	155	1.17	2.90	-12.7
03	MON	154	29	37	0	7	11	240	241	240	$3	291	273	564	7	75	32	0.29	223	23	164	2.50	2.96	-6.7
1st Half		76	15	21	0	3	6	276			$3	295	303	598	3	82	34	0.14	239	24	137		3.38	-2.3
2nd Half		78	14	16	0	4	5	205			$0	287	244	531	10	69	30	0.38	206	23	178		2.57	-4.5
04	Proj	150	23	35	1	9	10	233			$3	284	304	588	7	79	29	0.34	235	45	172		2.99	-6.1

April performance is self-perpetuating. Was batting .474 on May 1, then took five full months of .213 ball to get his BA back down to normal. And they actually gave him those ABs.

Mateo,Ruben

Pos RF
Age 26 Pre-Peak
Bats R

RISK		
R	Very High	
I	exp	con
S	PT	stb
K		

LIMA F BA: 45%

	Tm	AB	R	H	HR	RBI	SB	Avg	vL	vR	R$	OB	Slg	OPS	bb%	ct%	h%	Eye	xBA	PX	SX	G/F	RC/G	RAR
99	TEX	* 375	61	109	21	71	8	291	350	216	$17	320	517	837	4	85	30	0.28	303	131	93	0.79	5.87	9.5
00	TEX	206	32	60	7	19	6	291	318	284	$7	324	447	771	5	83	32	0.29	283	94	90	1.24	5.39	2.7
01	TEX	* 431	49	101	4	40	3	234	412	189	$1	270	339	609	5	84	27	0.30	259	70	100	1.47	3.01	-25.6
02	CIN	* 295	40	79	9	25	5	268	161	309	$7	301	427	728	5	83	30	0.29	278	112	76	0.65	4.44	-7.4
03	CIN	* 424	45	117	11	59	2	276	257	233	$11	328	415	743	7	81	32	0.41	259	93	50	1.09	4.78	-10.0
1st Half		214	22	59	7	37	2	276			$7	323	421	744	7	83	30	0.42	264	93	45		4.84	-4.7
2nd Half		210	23	58	4	22	0	276			$4	333	410	743	8	79	33	0.41	252	94	48		4.71	-5.4
04	Proj	250	30	67	6	29	2	268			$6	312	413	725	6	82	30	0.36	263	97	71		4.46	-7.3

3-18-.242 in 207 AB at CIN. Was a Grade A- prospect in 2000 based on his performance in AAA at age 21. But even then his strike zone judgment was questioned, and that has only improved marginally in 4 years.

Matheny,Mike

Pos CA | Age 33 Decline | Bats R | R: High | I: CON | S: pt, stb | K: age | LIMA D | BA: 50%

Yr	Tm	AB	R	H	HR	RBI	SB	Avg	vL	vR	R$	OB	Slg	OPS	bb%	ct%	h%	Eye	xBA	PX	SX	G/F	RC/G	RAR
99	TOR	163	16	35	3	17	0	215	164	241	($1)	269	307	575	7	77	26	0.32	201	59	27	1.30	2.68	-7.0
00	STL	417	43	109	6	47	0	261	250	265	$4	314	362	676	7	77	33	0.33	250	68	33	1.54	3.93	-0.8
01	STL	381	40	83	7	42	0	218	184	226	$0	271	304	576	7	80	26	0.37	233	55	33	1.12	2.66	-10.1
02	STL	315	31	77	3	35	1	244	265	239	$3	314	317	632	9	84	28	0.65	220	53	44	1.48	3.25	-8.2
03	STL	441	43	111	8	47	1	252	340	226	$5	320	356	676	9	82	29	0.54	255	69	49	1.10	3.85	-5.7
1st Half		253	26	69	4	26	0	273			$4	328	383	712	8	82	32	0.47	261	74	57		4.34	0.4
2nd Half		188	17	42	4	21	1	223			$1	308	319	627	11	81	26	0.64	247	62	34		3.26	-5.9
04	**Proj**	**350**	**34**	**84**	**6**	**38**	**1**	**240**			**$3**	**307**	**332**	**639**	**9**	**82**	**28**	**0.53**	**253**	**61**	**44**		**3.38**	**-7.5**

Coming into 2003, LaRussa said he'd start 2 out of every 3 gms for STL. Instead, he appeared in 141 gms, batted .216 from May 1 through Aug 31, and ate up a lot valuable at bats. Bet they'd like some of those back.

Matos,Julius

Pos 3B | Age 29 Past Peak | Bats R | R: X HIGH | I: EXP, CON | S: pt, STB | K: | LIMA F | BA: 55%

Yr	Tm	AB	R	H	HR	RBI	SB	Avg	vL	vR	R$	OB	Slg	OPS	bb%	ct%	h%	Eye	xBA	PX	SX	G/F	RC/G	RAR
99	aa	425	40	103	4	30	4	242			$1	260	327	587	2	93	25	0.36	284	53	98		2.84	-19.8
00	aa	546	43	111	4	25	8	203			($6)	233	267	500	4	90	22	0.40	267	46	58		1.85	-43.7
01	a/a	450	47	113	6	31	6	251			$4	272	331	603	3	88	27	0.25	261	53	63		2.77	-23.2
02	SD	* 371	36	93	5	41	2	251	200	264	$5	284	337	620	4	86	28	0.33	257	64	44	1.59	3.16	-15.8
03	KC	* 428	40	108	8	43	8	252	421	184	$7	269	350	620	2	91	26	0.26	272	65	63	0.84	3.09	-18.2
1st Half		320	29	80	5	31	7	250			$5	268	344	612	2	93	26	0.35	277	65	65		3.00	-14.5
2nd Half		108	11	28	3	12	1	259			$2	273	370	643	2	86	28	0.13	257	67	48		3.37	-3.6
04	**Proj**	**100**	**10**	**26**	**2**	**10**	**1**	**260**			**$2**	**281**	**353**	**634**	**3**	**88**	**28**	**0.25**	**266**	**61**	**50**		**3.27**	**-3.5**

2-7-.263 in 57 AB at KC. At face value, a consistent yet mediocre performer. But in '03, his contact rate topped out over 90% and his xBA was 20 points higher than his BA. Ha! Not JUST mediocre any more.

Matos,Luis

Pos CF | Age 25 Pre-Peak | Bats R | R: X HIGH | I: EXP, CON | S: PT, STB | K: age | LIMA C+ | BA: 30%

Yr	Tm	AB	R	H	HR	RBI	SB	Avg	vL	vR	R$	OB	Slg	OPS	bb%	ct%	h%	Eye	xBA	PX	SX	G/F	RC/G	RAR
99	aa	283	36	61	8	32	12	216			$4	247	339	587	4	88	22	0.34	279	73	111		2.61	-17.0
00	BAL	* 398	47	90	3	47	28	226	259	210	$8	282	312	594	7	85	26	0.53	258	51	160	1.45	2.79	-23.5
01	BAL	* 144	21	34	5	19	7	236	87	253	$4	313	417	729	10	75	28	0.44	256	119	88	0.80	4.49	-1.6
02	aa	249	28	56	8	35	13	225			$8	301	382	682	10	81	25	0.57	267	101	101		3.72	-8.6
03	BAL	* 614	96	181	14	68	21	295	269	314	$22	338	440	778	6	80	35	0.33	260	94	123	1.11	5.30	9.7
1st Half		313	54	96	6	40	15	307			$14	346	463	810	6	82	36	0.35	275	104	154		5.99	10.8
2nd Half		301	42	85	8	28	6	282			$8	329	415	744	7	78	34	0.32	245	84	79		4.64	-0.8
04	**Proj**	**550**	**76**	**143**	**15**	**66**	**23**	**260**			**$17**	**317**	**408**	**724**	**8**	**80**	**30**	**0.42**	**260**	**94**	**112**		**4.39**	**-6.0**

13-45-15-.303 in 439 AB at BAL, a huge jump up from past performance... but not really. BPIs were not all that different, and the one that was -- hit rate -- indicates his BA won't hold up. Let others overbid.

Matsui,Hideki

Pos LF CF | Age 29 Past Peak | Bats L | R: Very Low | I: con | S: stb | K: | LIMA C+ | BA: 55%

Yr	Tm	AB	R	H	HR	RBI	SB	Avg	vL	vR	R$	OB	Slg	OPS	bb%	ct%	h%	Eye	xBA	PX	SX	G/F	RC/G	RAR
99	JPN	471	95	133	25	90	0	283			$17	381	508	889	14	79	31	0.76	278	130	60		6.68	21.7
00	JPN	474	110	140	25	103	5	295			$22	402	528	931	15	77	34	0.79	282	138	85		7.66	33.1
01	JPN	481	102	149	22	99	3	310			$23	425	512	938	17	80	35	1.01	275	117	89		7.94	36.5
02	JPN	500	106	156	30	102	3	311			$28	418	552	970	16	79	34	0.88	283	145	67		8.47	38.9
03	NYY	623	82	179	16	106	2	287	287	287	$19	353	435	788	9	86	31	0.73	296	99	45	2.30	5.44	1.9
1st Half		333	44	100	9	62	0	300			$12	362	459	821	9	86	33	0.67	300	109	25		6.06	6.6
2nd Half		290	38	79	7	44	2	272			$7	343	407	750	10	87	29	0.82	291	88	57		4.80	-4.5
04	**Proj**	**625**	**108**	**184**	**15**	**95**	**3**	**294**			**$19**	**383**	**430**	**813**	**13**	**83**	**34**	**0.84**	**287**	**89**	**62**		**5.89**	**14.3**

Japan's premier power hitter has been more aggressive at the plate but it has not converted into HRs. 2nd half drop-off and very high G/F ratio forces us to continue to temper our expectations.

Matthews Jr.,Gary

Pos CF RF LF | Age 29 Past Peak | Bats S | R: Very High | I: exp, CON | S: pt, STB | K: | LIMA D | BA: 50%

Yr	Tm	AB	R	H	HR	RBI	SB	Avg	vL	vR	R$	OB	Slg	OPS	bb%	ct%	h%	Eye	xBA	PX	SX	G/F	RC/G	RAR
99	aaa	422	49	93	8	44	15	220			$4	299	329	628	10	77	27	0.48	242	70	97	3.60	3.17	-17.6
00	CHC	* 369	47	74	8	33	8	201	250	169	($0)	261	314	575	8	83	22	0.48	262	65	128	1.60	2.68	-19.1
01	2NL	405	63	92	14	44	8	227	241	222	$6	327	378	705	13	75	27	0.60	234	88	93	1.44	3.99	1.7
02	2TM	345	54	95	7	38	15	275	239	292	$12	356	426	782	11	80	33	0.62	284	105	126	1.96	5.32	5.0
03	2TM	468	71	116	6	42	12	248	287	233	$7	311	359	670	8	80	30	0.45	257	80	102	1.69	3.65	-17.0
1st Half		272	37	63	3	29	4	232			$2	279	335	614	6	81	28	0.34	256	76	88		2.91	-16.4
2nd Half		196	34	53	3	13	8	270			$5	353	393	746	11	79	33	0.60	258	87	111		4.82	-0.2
04	**Proj**	**350**	**54**	**92**	**7**	**33**	**11**	**263**			**$8**	**339**	**392**	**730**	**10**	**79**	**32**	**0.54**	**261**	**87**	**106**		**4.51**	**-2.3**

Got off to a horrible start in BAL, recovered after the trade to SD, but still netted out with a poor season. If he can ride his 2nd half into '04, he'll have some value, but don't go nuts at the draft table.

Mayne,Brent

Pos CA | Age 36 Decline | Bats L | R: High | I: CON | S: STB | K: AGE | LIMA D | BA: 55%

Yr	Tm	AB	R	H	HR	RBI	SB	Avg	vL	vR	R$	OB	Slg	OPS	bb%	ct%	h%	Eye	xBA	PX	SX	G/F	RC/G	RAR
99	SF	322	39	97	2	39	2	301	286	305	$7	384	419	803	12	80	37	0.66	261	96	38	1.41	5.78	16.2
00	COL	335	36	101	6	64	1	301	196	318	$11	387	418	805	12	86	34	0.98	288	80	22	1.31	5.74	16.2
01	2TM	326	28	93	2	40	1	285	206	295	$6	338	344	682	7	87	32	0.63	257	41	37	1.99	4.06	3.4
02	KC	330	35	78	4	31	4	236	162	256	$2	310	309	619	10	84	27	0.65	275	45	73	1.46	3.10	-5.2
03	KC	372	39	91	6	36	0	245	236	248	$2	304	344	649	8	84	28	0.54	262	67	36	1.43	3.45	-7.1
1st Half		184	16	46	4	20	0	250			$2	307	364	671	8	86	27	0.60	273	71	36		3.80	-1.6
2nd Half		188	23	45	2	16	0	239			$0	302	324	627	8	82	28	0.50	253	63	38		3.14	-5.4
04	**Proj**	**350**	**37**	**89**	**4**	**37**	**1**	**254**			**$4**	**319**	**341**	**660**	**9**	**84**	**29**	**0.60**	**260**	**59**	**45**		**3.62**	**-3.3**

With his BPIs, and playing in a hitter's park, you would expect at least BAs closer to pre-2002 levels. Instead, we're left with a 5-year down trend and little hope for future value.

McCarty,Dave

Pos LF | Age 34 Decline | Bats R | R: Very High | I: exp, con | S: pt, STB | K: age | LIMA F | BA: 60%

Yr	Tm	AB	R	H	HR	RBI	SB	Avg	vL	vR	R$	OB	Slg	OPS	bb%	ct%	h%	Eye	xBA	PX	SX	G/F	RC/G	RAR
99	aaa	466	54	89	22	49	4	191			$1	264	376	639	9	76	20	0.41	255	105	64		2.97	-31.3
00	KC	270	34	75	12	53	0	278	365	223	$8	332	478	810	8	75	33	0.32	262	115	55	1.19	5.60	3.9
01	KC	200	26	50	7	26	0	250	202	314	$3	330	405	735	11	78	29	0.53	235	96	24	1.65	4.55	-0.5
02	TAM	* 180	25	41	8	21	0	228	188	88	$2	294	411	706	9	72	27	0.33	236	106	64	1.56	3.90	-5.1
03	2AL	* 405	56	93	12	59	3	230	400	286	$6	291	380	671	8	81	26	0.45	261	97	73	1.00	3.66	-20.5
1st Half		324	43	68	10	48	2	210			$3	273	358	631	8	81	23	0.46	260	93	71		3.14	-22.1
2nd Half		81	13	25	2	11	1	309			$3	364	469	833	8	79	37	0.41	265	113	57		6.38	2.3
04	**Proj**	**100**	**14**	**25**	**3**	**13**	**1**	**250**			**$2**	**314**	**414**	**728**	**9**	**77**	**29**	**0.41**	**257**	**104**	**48**		**4.40**	**-2.0**

1-8-.340 in 53 AB at OAK and BOS but he's done that in brief stops in certain cities 8 times during his career. At 34, it's become fun to watch but never to bank on.

McCracken,Quinton

Pos RF | Age 34 Decline | Bats S | R: X HIGH | I: exp, CON | S: pt, STB | K: age | LIMA F | BA: 50%

Yr	Tm	AB	R	H	HR	RBI	SB	Avg	vL	vR	R$	OB	Slg	OPS	bb%	ct%	h%	Eye	xBA	PX	SX	G/F	RC/G	RAR
99	TAM	148	20	37	1	18	6	250	257	248	$3	315	324	639	9	84	29	0.61	240	50	110	2.39	3.50	-6.5
00	aaa	334	35	68	2	18	8	204			($3)	255	269	524	6	86	23	0.50	257	47	84		2.04	-32.1
01	MIN	* 425	45	115	3	35	5	271	143	240	$6	302	374	676	4	86	31	0.32	265	72	88	1.69	3.52	-18.4
02	ARI	349	60	108	3	40	5	309	306	312	$11	367	458	826	8	81	38	0.47	272	106	164	1.09	6.05	7.2
03	ARI	203	17	46	0	18	5	227	215	234	$1	280	271	551	7	83	27	0.44	229	31	106	2.27	2.57	-18.9
1st Half		105	8	21	0	11	3	200			($0)	257	248	504	7	84	24	0.47	232	34	104		2.15	-11.4
2nd Half		98	9	25	0	7	2	255			$1	305	296	601	7	83	31	0.41	224	27	96		3.06	-7.4
04	**Proj**	**150**	**17**	**38**	**1**	**14**	**3**	**253**			**$2**	**305**	**338**	**643**	**7**	**83**	**30**	**0.44**	**237**	**60**	**118**		**3.45**	**-9.0**

He was over his head with a .309 BA in 2002, but came crashing way down in '03. There will be some small rebound in '04, but his stock is low and not worth investing in any more.

McDonald,John

Pos 2B SS 3B | Age 29 Past Peak | Bats R | R: X HIGH | I: EXP, CON | S: PT, stb | K: | LIMA F | BA: 65%

Yr	Tm	AB	R	H	HR	RBI	SB	Avg	vL	vR	R$	OB	Slg	OPS	bb%	ct%	h%	Eye	xBA	PX	SX	G/F	RC/G	RAR
99	a/a	463	48	126	1	41	10	272			$6	308	330	638	5	91	30	0.56	269	46	72	1.50	3.45	-8.7
00	aaa	286	31	70	1	30	3	245			$1	287	318	605	6	91	27	0.68	277	55	69	0.20	2.99	-9.6
01	aaa	410	44	89	2	28	14	217			$1	267	273	540	6	84	25	0.44	245	41	90		2.25	-23.1
02	CLE	264	35	66	1	12	3	250	232	256	$1	277	326	603	4	81	31	0.20	254	52	124	1.38	3.13	-7.0
03	CLE	214	21	46	1	14	3	215	215	215	($1)	253	280	534	5	86	25	0.35	246	48	79	1.04	2.21	-13.0
1st Half		123	10	31	1	9	1	252			$1	287	341	628	5	86	29	0.35	257	62	70		3.13	-3.7
2nd Half		91	11	15	0	5	2	165			($2)	208	198	406	5	85	19	0.36	231	29	94		1.25	-8.7
04	**Proj**	**250**	**28**	**55**	**1**	**16**	**4**	**220**			**($1)**	**258**	**279**	**537**	**5**	**85**	**26**	**0.34**	**244**	**44**	**89**		**2.30**	**-14.0**

Back problems are at least partially responsible for his offensive struggles. A general lack of talent is responsible for the rest.

McEwing,Joe

		Tm	AB	R	H	HR	RBI	SB	Avg	vL	vR	R$	OB	Slg	OPS	bb%	ct%	h%	Eye	xBA	PX	SX	G/F	RC/G	RAR
Pos 2B SS	99	STL	513	65	141	9	44	7	275	292	267	$9	329	398	726	7	83	32	0.47	293	81	88	1.77	4.53	4.6
Age 31 Past Peak	00	NYM	* 324	44	73	6	34	9	225	163	250	$3	266	364	630	5	82	26	0.31	274	93	117	0.96	3.13	-12.4
Bats R	01	NYM	283	41	80	8	30	8	283	250	298	$9	323	449	772	6	80	33	0.30	271	103	125	1.01	4.94	8.8
R High	02	NYM	201	22	39	3	26	4	194	204	194	$0	229	289	517	4	75	24	0.18	230	65	104	0.93	1.94	-16.1
I CON	03	NYM	278	31	67	1	16	3	241	247	239	$0	304	291	595	8	79	30	0.44	238	41	64	1.17	3.03	-11.4
S PT stb	1st Half		111	10	24	0	6	0	216			($1)	269	252	521	7	77	28	0.31	222	32	30		2.21	-7.5
K	2nd Half		167	21	43	1	10	3	257			$2	326	317	643	9	81	31	0.55	248	47	68		3.66	-3.6
LIMA F BA: 45%	04	Proj	**250**	**29**	**59**	**3**	**22**	**4**	**236**			**$2**	**287**	**323**	**610**	**7**	**79**	**29**	**0.34**	**244**	**61**	**86**		**3.06**	**-9.5**

A batter who fares better with consistent playing time, but that's not something you can count on... or would really want to commit to anyway.

McGriff,Fred

		Tm	AB	R	H	HR	RBI	SB	Avg	vL	vR	R$	OB	Slg	OPS	bb%	ct%	h%	Eye	xBA	PX	SX	G/F	RC/G	RAR
Pos 1B	99	TAM	529	75	164	32	104	1	310	236	339	$25	407	552	958	14	80	34	0.80	311	140	35	1.28	8.31	36.2
Age 40 Decline	00	TAM	566	82	157	27	106	2	277	273	279	$18	377	452	830	14	79	31	0.76	247	96	41	1.15	6.05	1.7
Bats L	01	2TM	513	67	157	31	102	1	306	295	310	$26	385	544	929	11	79	34	0.62	281	136	36	1.30	7.60	19.7
R Very High	02	CHC	523	67	143	30	103	1	273	213	296	$23	352	505	856	11	81	29	0.64	277	144	41	0.89	6.15	8.2
I CON	03	LA	297	32	74	13	40	0	249	194	275	$6	320	428	748	9	78	28	0.47	286	111	16	1.14	4.65	-7.6
S pt STB	1st Half		227	23	55	10	35	0	242			$5	315	427	742	10	79	26	0.51	294	116	14		4.53	-6.7
K AGE	2nd Half		70	9	19	3	5	0	271			$2	338	429	766	9	73	33	0.37	259	93	23		5.06	-0.9
LIMA D BA: 55%	04	Proj	**350**	**39**	**91**	**13**	**48**	**0**	**260**			**$8**	**337**	**411**	**749**	**10**	**78**	**30**	**0.53**	**283**	**95**	**24**		**4.76**	**-8.8**

Injury-shortened season, but the writing is on the wall for this career anyway. BA vs LH has made him a straight platoon player, and bb%, h%, eye and OB are all charting his path to retirement.

McLemore,Mark

		Tm	AB	R	H	HR	RBI	SB	Avg	vL	vR	R$	OB	Slg	OPS	bb%	ct%	h%	Eye	xBA	PX	SX	G/F	RC/G	RAR
Pos SS 3B	99	TEX	566	105	155	6	45	16	274	163	299	$10	367	366	732	13	86	31	1.05	262	57	131	1.27	4.65	8.0
Age 39 Decline	00	SEA	481	72	118	3	46	30	245	293	236	$10	354	316	670	14	84	29	1.04	252	51	100	1.54	3.75	-9.8
Bats S	01	SEA	409	78	117	5	57	39	286	169	311	$22	389	406	795	14	79	35	0.82	253	71	192	1.27	5.99	18.9
R Moderate	02	SEA	337	54	91	7	41	18	270	152	283	$13	382	395	777	15	81	31	0.97	265	80	105	1.12	5.08	5.0
I CON	03	SEA	309	34	72	2	37	5	233	433	211	$2	317	314	631	11	77	30	0.54	242	58	80	1.25	3.18	-11.8
S stb	1st Half		155	20	33	2	19	3	213			$1	311	329	640	12	74	27	0.55	245	76	117		3.24	-5.8
K AGE	2nd Half		154	14	39	0	18	2	253			$1	324	299	622	9	80	32	0.52	237	40	43		3.11	-6.1
LIMA F BA: 50%	04	Proj	**250**	**30**	**61**	**1**	**30**	**5**	**244**			**$3**	**329**	**315**	**644**	**11**	**80**	**30**	**0.62**	**245**	**52**	**89**		**3.32**	**-8.5**

BPI decline is evident, and with his loss of speed, any remaining fanalytic value is pretty much gone.

McMillon,Billy

		Tm	AB	R	H	HR	RBI	SB	Avg	vL	vR	R$	OB	Slg	OPS	bb%	ct%	h%	Eye	xBA	PX	SX	G/F	RC/G	RAR
Pos LF	99	aaa	464	69	114	11	60	8	246			$7	316	399	715	9	83	27	0.62	281	101	103		4.29	-10.6
Age 32 Past Peak	00	DET	* 503	69	157	13	65	3	312	267	306	$15	402	469	872	13	86	34	1.12	289	101	59	0.95	7.00	26.0
Bats L	01	2AL	92	7	20	1	14	1	217	250	213	$0	273	359	631	7	73	29	0.28	227	101	86	1.00	3.24	-3.9
R X HIGH	02	aaa	442	53	106	6	33	2	240			$2	309	348	657	9	86	27	0.69	264	78	59		3.46	-28.7
I EXP CON	03	OAK	* 306	38	82	12	51	1	268	118	287	$9	337	448	785	9	79	30	0.50	264	114	34	0.65	5.21	-1.1
S PT STB	1st Half		186	25	50	6	27	1	269			$5	333	430	763	9	81	30	0.51	267	105	43		4.92	-2.2
K	2nd Half		120	13	32	6	24	0	267			$4	343	475	818	10	76	31	0.48	260	127	12		5.67	1.2
LIMA F BA: 45%	04	Proj	**150**	**19**	**40**	**7**	**21**	**1**	**267**			**$4**	**341**	**460**	**801**	**10**	**82**	**29**	**0.61**	**270**	**119**	**34**		**5.38**	**1.3**

6-26-.268 in 153 AB at OAK, a member of the Beane On Base Avg Reserve Corps at AAA. The Sacramento roster contained 9 hitters between 26 and 32 with OB avgs over .370. All cheap, productive talent.

Melhuse,Adam

		Tm	AB	R	H	HR	RBI	SB	Avg	vL	vR	R$	OB	Slg	OPS	bb%	ct%	h%	Eye	xBA	PX	SX	G/F	RC/G	RAR
Pos CA	99	a/a	445	65	100	14	58	4	225			$4	347	375	722	16	80	25	0.95	263	96	42		4.09	1.0
Age 32 Past Peak	00	a/a	306	46	79	5	34	7	258			$5	344	366	710	12	81	31	0.68	255	71	80	2.25	4.14	0.6
Bats S	01	COL	* 255	21	54	6	28	1	212	375	159	$0	285	329	614	9	81	24	0.54	253	72	46	1.93	3.00	-4.1
R X HIGH	02	aaa	341	33	87	10	34	3	255			$6	306	416	722	7	86	27	0.53	285	109	50		4.13	2.7
I EXP con	03	OAK	* 224	32	56	7	27	0	250	333	283	$3	333	406	740	11	79	29	0.58	256	102	34	0.68	4.52	2.9
S PT STB	1st Half		172	23	37	3	15	0	215			($1)	301	320	620	11	78	26	0.55	236	72	40		3.05	-5.6
K	2nd Half		52	9	19	4	12	0	365			$4	441	692	1133	12	81	39	0.70	323	201			12.26	10.6
LIMA F BA: 50%	04	Proj	**150**	**20**	**41**	**6**	**21**	**1**	**273**			**$4**	**348**	**459**	**807**	**10**	**82**	**30**	**0.62**	**265**	**118**	**35**		**5.48**	**6.6**

5-14-.299 in 77 AB at OAK. From Aug 2 on, batted a robust .441 with 4 HRs... though it was only in 34 AB. Despite the small data set, there are BPI signs that he could provide some profit on an end-game pick.

Mench,Kevin

		Tm	AB	R	H	HR	RBI	SB	Avg	vL	vR	R$	OB	Slg	OPS	bb%	ct%	h%	Eye	xBA	PX	SX	G/F	RC/G	RAR
Pos LF	99	0	0	0	0	0	0	0	0								0								
Age 26 Pre-Peak	00	0	0	0	0	0	0	0	0								0								
Bats R	01	aa	475	63	114	23	67	3	240			$11	282	457	739	6	87	23	0.46	305	133	56		4.07	-15.8
R High	02	TEX	* 464	65	113	20	71	1	244	269	256	$11	309	440	749	9	77	28	0.41	262	120	61	0.79	4.55	-3.9
I EXP con	03	TEX	* 241	29	67	6	28	3	278	346	301	$6	351	436	786	10	87	30	0.84	288	110	51	0.98	5.39	0.4
S pt stb	1st Half		219	26	58	6	26	3	265			$5	340	425	765	10	86	28	0.83	287	109	55		5.10	-1.5
K	2nd Half		22	3	9	0	2	0	409			$1	458	545	1004	8	91	45	1.00	308	119	43		9.11	2.1
LIMA C+ BA: 60%	04	Proj	**500**	**65**	**135**	**20**	**68**	**4**	**270**			**$14**	**341**	**461**	**802**	**10**	**84**	**29**	**0.68**	**288**	**121**	**53**		**5.40**	**4.7**

2-11-.320 in 125 AB at TEX. The seeds are here for a very productive career. As he recovers from his broken wrist, watch the recovery of his power. He could be looking at a breakout in 2004 or 2005.

Mendez,Donaldo

		Tm	AB	R	H	HR	RBI	SB	Avg	vL	vR	R$	OB	Slg	OPS	bb%	ct%	h%	Eye	xBA	PX	SX	G/F	RC/G	RAR
Pos SS	99		0	0	0	0	0	0	0								0								
Age 25 Pre-Peak	00		0	0	0	0	0	0	0								0								
Bats R	01	SD	118	11	18	1	5	1	153	231	114	($3)	187	212	399	4	69	21	0.14	190	35	113	1.46	1.09	-9.9
R Very High	02	a/a	441	58	82	8	31	22	186			$3	233	293	525	6	75	23	0.25	234	73	130		2.06	-31.5
I EXP con	03	SD	* 442	50	87	6	38	9	197	176	239	($1)	243	283	526	6	77	24	0.26	232	62	81	1.77	2.06	-29.1
S pt stb	1st Half		252	27	57	4	19	2	226			$0	270	325	595	6	74	29	0.23	225	71	51		2.61	-11.9
K age	2nd Half		190	23	30	2	19	7	158			($2)	208	226	434	6	81	18	0.33	241	49	115		1.46	-16.8
LIMA F BA: 55%	04	Proj	**100**	**12**	**21**	**1**	**8**	**3**	**210**			**$0**	**254**	**292**	**546**	**6**	**76**	**26**	**0.24**	**230**	**57**	**85**		**2.30**	**-5.1**

2-9-.226 in 84 AB at SD. It is impossible to imagine that any level of superb defense could possibly offset the damage done by these offensive (TRULY offensive) numbers.

Menechino,Frank

		Tm	AB	R	H	HR	RBI	SB	Avg	vL	vR	R$	OB	Slg	OPS	bb%	ct%	h%	Eye	xBA	PX	SX	G/F	RC/G	RAR
Pos 2B	99	aaa	501	81	125	11	70	3	250			$7	325	385	710	10	81	29	0.58	262	85	93	4.00	4.12	0.4
Age 33 Decline	00	OAK	* 183	38	48	8	28	2	262	224	271	$5	351	464	815	12	73	32	0.51	257	119	92	0.93	5.24	7.5
Bats R	01	OAK	471	82	114	12	60	2	242	317	203	$6	351	374	725	14	79	28	0.81	237	83	64	1.02	4.33	1.8
R X HIGH	02	OAK	* 446	55	86	7	48	6	193	185	218	($1)	276	276	551	10	82	22	0.64	239	55	68	0.95	2.37	-23.8
I exp CON	03	OAK	83	10	16	2	9	0	193	250	149	($1)	343	265	608	19	81	22	1.19	208	37	20	1.35	2.87	-3.3
S PT stb	1st Half		45	8	11	2	5	0	244			$1	346	378	724	13	78	27	0.70	219	68	36		4.41	0.4
K age	2nd Half		38	2	5	0	4	0	132			($1)	340	132	472	24	84	16	2.00	194	0	5		1.31	-3.7
LIMA F BA: 70%	04	Proj	**150**	**25**	**35**	**4**	**20**	**1**	**233**			**$2**	**323**	**379**	**702**	**12**	**78**	**27**	**0.61**	**222**	**89**	**88**		**3.91**	**-0.9**

PX charts the decline of his power skills, and with them, any other semblance of productivity. (Note that a 37 PX represents a level 63% below league avg skill.) That deficiency filters into everything else.

Merced,Orlando

		Tm	AB	R	H	HR	RBI	SB	Avg	vL	vR	R$	OB	Slg	OPS	bb%	ct%	h%	Eye	xBA	PX	SX	G/F	RC/G	RAR
Pos RF	99	MON	194	25	52	8	26	2	268	300	266	$5	355	464	818	12	86	28	0.96	302	122	60	1.13	5.69	3.9
Age 37 Decline	00	JPN	202	19	42	1	29	2	208			($1)	247	265	512	5	84	24	0.33	535	36	87		2.10	-18.5
Bats S	01	HOU	137	19	36	6	29	5	263	600	250	$6	331	453	784	9	77	30	0.44	244	110	108	1.35	5.25	-1.2
R Very High	02	HOU	251	35	72	6	30	4	287	231	297	$8	354	434	788	9	80	34	0.52	259	97	117	1.61	5.60	2.1
I CON	03	HOU	212	20	49	3	26	3	231	296	222	$2	282	373	655	7	84	26	0.45	278	102	94	1.50	3.40	-14.3
S pt stb	1st Half		140	14	35	1	19	3	250			$2	300	379	679	7	86	29	0.50	280	94	118		3.73	-7.9
K AGE	2nd Half		72	6	14	2	7	0	194			($0)	247	361	608	6	82	21	0.38	271	118	20		2.82	-6.3
LIMA F BA: 60%	04	Proj	**150**	**17**	**36**	**2**	**20**	**1**	**240**			**$1**	**300**	**354**	**654**	**8**	**82**	**28**	**0.47**	**268**	**83**	**78**		**3.54**	**-8.7**

Maintained some limited bench value upon his return from JPN, but that ended in '03. Pass.

Merloni,Lou

	Yr	Tm	AB	R	H	HR	RBI	SB	Avg	vL	vR	R$	OB	Slg	OPS	bb%	ct%	h%	Eye	xBA	PX	SX	G/F	RC/G	RAR
Pos 3B SS	99	BOS	* 355	56	93	7	44	1	262	184	299	$5	325	389	713	9	86	29	0.69	276	85	64	1.71	4.33	-0.9
Age 33 Decline	00	BOS	* 222	20	61	1	21	1	275	294	330	$2	309	374	683	5	83	33	0.30	259	71	74	2.42	4.09	-2.0
Bats R	01	BOS	* 341	44	82	6	28	4	240	303	257	$3	277	355	631	5	81	28	0.26	252	80	71	1.27	3.31	-10.7
R Very High	02	BOS	* 219	29	53	4	20	1	242	321	217	$2	308	379	687	9	83	28	0.55	264	91	84	0.87	3.80	-4.4
I exp con	03	2TM	181	24	48	1	18	2	265	196	337	$2	357	348	706	13	77	34	0.63	227	57	93	1.38	4.12	-1.4
S PT stb	1st Half		93	11	25	0	7	1	269			$1	376	333	709	15	77	35	0.76	221	47	85		4.11	-0.7
K age	2nd Half		88	13	23	1	11	1	261			$1	337	364	700	10	77	33	0.50	233	68	105		4.11	-0.7
LIMA F BA: 40%	04	Proj	**150**	**20**	**38**	**2**	**15**	**1**	**253**			**$2**	**326**	**355**	**681**	**10**	**80**	**31**	**0.53**	**237**	**71**	**79**		**3.83**	**-2.7**

Why 2003 was so odd...
- Reversed his platoon splits
- Gained plate patience, posted career high OB Avg
- Lost contact ability, xBA fell 40 points
- Power went MIA

Michaels,Jason

	Yr	Tm	AB	R	H	HR	RBI	SB	Avg	vL	vR	R$	OB	Slg	OPS	bb%	ct%	h%	Eye	xBA	PX	SX	G/F	RC/G	RAR
Pos LF	99	0	0	0	0	0	0	0	0								0								
Age 27 Peak	00	aa	437	55	114	7	57	6	261			$7	298	394	691	5	81	31	0.28	269	89	93		3.91	-16.0
Bats R	01	aaa	418	53	105	15	63	10	251			$12	311	426	736	8	69	33	0.28	233	106	107		4.50	-8.2
R High	02	PHI	* 137	19	36	2	17	2	263	242	302	$3	344	438	782	11	73	35	0.46	257	125	155	0.87	4.72	-6.8
I EXP con	03	PHI	109	20	36	5	17	0	330	382	278	$6	411	569	980	12	80	38	0.68	323	162	32	1.20	8.91	9.5
S pt stb	1st Half		53	9	16	3	9	0	302			$2	383	566	949	12	79	33	0.64	326	173	28		7.93	3.4
K	2nd Half		56	11	20	2	8	0	357			$3	437	571	1009	12	80	42	0.73	319	152	34		9.92	6.1
LIMA D BA: 40%	04	Proj	**250**	**40**	**74**	**8**	**36**	**1**	**296**			**$9**	**371**	**498**	**869**	**11**	**77**	**36**	**0.51**	**313**	**137**	**81**		**6.58**	**5.7**

Stats of PHI outfielders:

	AB	OB	PX
Abreu	577	.411	105
Burrell	522	.305	118
Byrd	495	.360	77
Ledee	255	.336	133
Michaels	109	.411	162

Mientkiewicz,Doug

	Yr	Tm	AB	R	H	HR	RBI	SB	Avg	vL	vR	R$	OB	Slg	OPS	bb%	ct%	h%	Eye	xBA	PX	SX	G/F	RC/G	RAR
Pos 1B	99	MIN	327	34	75	2	32	1	229	256	226	($1)	319	330	649	12	84	27	0.84	236	72	71	0.89	3.46	-23.0
Age 29 Past Peak	00	aaa	485	72	143	14	72	7	295			$16	355	449	804	8	89	31	0.83	297	97	74	1.50	5.58	-0.9
Bats L	01	MIN	543	77	166	15	74	2	306	322	300	$18	382	464	846	11	83	35	0.73	278	106	36	1.08	6.27	1.9
R Moderate	02	MIN	467	60	122	10	64	1	261	257	263	$9	362	392	754	14	85	29	1.07	260	88	39	0.86	4.84	-13.9
I con	03	MIN	487	67	146	11	65	4	300	300	310	$15	392	450	842	13	89	32	1.35	316	104	58	1.03	6.44	14.2
S pt stb	1st Half		242	32	73	7	32	3	302			$9	360	479	839	8	88	32	0.76	326	120	72		6.39	6.7
K	2nd Half		245	35	73	4	33	1	298			$7	421	420	841	18	89	32	2.00	306	89	33		6.37	6.7
LIMA B+ BA: 65%	04	Proj	**500**	**68**	**154**	**11**	**67**	**3**	**308**			**$16**	**404**	**450**	**854**	**14**	**88**	**33**	**1.33**	**312**	**97**	**45**		**6.63**	**13.2**

Excellent, pure hitter but with little power, a single flaw that makes him "less of a 1Bman" and probably costs him 100 AB per year. Someone should go blow up the Old School.

Millar,Kevin

	Yr	Tm	AB	R	H	HR	RBI	SB	Avg	vL	vR	R$	OB	Slg	OPS	bb%	ct%	h%	Eye	xBA	PX	SX	G/F	RC/G	RAR
Pos 1B	99	FLA	* 494	66	136	14	86	2	275	290	283	$13	339	433	773	9	84	30	0.62	280	98	84	0.72	5.20	-1.4
Age 32 Past Peak	00	FLA	259	36	67	14	42	0	259	254	261	$7	349	498	847	12	82	27	0.77	278	136	66	0.77	5.98	4.8
Bats R	01	FLA	449	62	141	20	85	0	314	351	304	$21	369	557	926	8	84	34	0.56	305	151	68	0.70	7.63	16.7
R Moderate	02	FLA	* 450	59	135	17	58	0	300	317	302	$16	357	504	862	8	82	33	0.50	287	145	24	0.71	6.45	10.5
I con	03	BOS	544	83	150	25	96	3	276	289	271	$19	348	472	820	10	80	30	0.56	279	120	56	0.81	5.74	5.5
S pt stb	1st Half		254	42	81	12	57	1	319			$13	389	555	944	10	81	36	0.60	302	151	57		7.99	17.8
K	2nd Half		290	41	69	13	39	2	238			$6	312	400	712	10	79	26	0.52	258	92	50		4.15	-10.7
LIMA C BA: 50%	04	Proj	**550**	**78**	**156**	**27**	**104**	**2**	**284**			**$21**	**350**	**504**	**854**	**9**	**82**	**31**	**0.55**	**286**	**135**	**52**		**6.23**	**8.7**

A Clemens HBP bruised his hand on 7/5, and he pulled a quad muscle on 8/3, yet insisted that the injuries were not the cause of his 2nd half slump. Maybe he believes his own noise, but we don't have to.

Miller,Corky

	Yr	Tm	AB	R	H	HR	RBI	SB	Avg	vL	vR	R$	OB	Slg	OPS	bb%	ct%	h%	Eye	xBA	PX	SX	G/F	RC/G	RAR
Pos CA	99	aa	104	16	20	3	13	0	192			($1)	257	365	622	8	76	22	0.36	260	118	51		2.96	-3.5
Age 28 Peak	00	aa	317	30	65	7	33	4	205			($0)	278	322	600	9	87	22	0.76	275	75	43		2.57	-15.4
Bats R	01	a/a	363	49	98	17	62	3	270			$13	331	477	807	8	85	28	0.59	292	128	48	0.71	5.43	18.3
R X HIGH	02	CIN	* 248	20	56	8	31	1	226	412	227	$3	286	383	669	8	86	23	0.60	279	108	27	0.97	3.50	-4.6
I EXP con	03	CIN	* 384	42	88	10	34	0	229	250	269	$2	288	380	669	8	86	24	0.59	279	106	27	2.60	3.63	-7.7
S PT stb	1st Half		226	27	54	8	23	0	239			$3	292	425	717	7	86	25	0.53	290	127	29		4.16	-0.9
K	2nd Half		158	15	34	2	11	0	215			($1)	283	316	600	9	86	24	0.68	260	76			2.91	-6.7
LIMA F BA: 70%	04	Proj	**150**	**16**	**39**	**4**	**16**	**0**	**260**			**$3**	**320**	**412**	**732**	**8**	**85**	**28**	**0.60**	**278**	**104**	**32**		**4.48**	**1.7**

0-1-.267 in 30 AB at CIN. Sent back to AAA in '03 to hasten his development, but BPIs finished nearly identical to '02. At 28, expectations for further growth have to be tempered, though xBA says there is some upside.

Miller,Damian

	Yr	Tm	AB	R	H	HR	RBI	SB	Avg	vL	vR	R$	OB	Slg	OPS	bb%	ct%	h%	Eye	xBA	PX	SX	G/F	RC/G	RAR
Pos CA	99	ARI	296	35	80	11	47	0	270	320	244	$7	314	446	760	6	74	33	0.24	219	113	23	1.15	4.90	7.9
Age 34 Decline	00	ARI	324	43	89	10	44	2	275	269	277	$8	347	441	789	10	77	33	0.49	249	109	42	1.09	5.30	12.1
Bats R	01	ARI	380	45	103	13	47	0	271	301	264	$9	333	424	756	8	79	31	0.44	266	94	24	1.11	4.88	14.8
R Low	02	ARI	306	41	77	11	42	0	252	275	238	$7	334	435	769	11	71	32	0.43	261	127	27	1.87	4.95	7.5
I con	03	CHC	352	34	82	9	36	1	233	248	226	$3	309	369	679	10	74	29	0.43	250	91	46	1.66	3.82	-5.0
S stb	1st Half		185	20	42	5	24	0	227			$2	309	368	677	11	71	29	0.42	241	91	48		3.75	-3.0
K age	2nd Half		167	14	40	4	12	1	240			$1	310	371	681	9	77	29	0.45	259	91	33		3.89	-2.0
LIMA D BA: 45%	04	Proj	**350**	**39**	**87**	**11**	**40**	**1**	**249**			**$5**	**322**	**399**	**721**	**10**	**75**	**31**	**0.42**	**254**	**101**	**33**		**4.36**	**2.6**

Back problems halted a potential career year in 2002, and it's possible that residual nagging injuries in '03 have begun to erode his skills. End-gamer at best.

Mirabelli,Doug

	Yr	Tm	AB	R	H	HR	RBI	SB	Avg	vL	vR	R$	OB	Slg	OPS	bb%	ct%	h%	Eye	xBA	PX	SX	G/F	RC/G	RAR
Pos CA	99	SF	* 407	58	107	11	49	6	263	240	258	$8	338	415	753	10	83	29	0.67	278	101	73	0.79	4.85	10.5
Age 33 Decline	00	SF	230	23	53	6	28	1	230	229	231	$2	335	370	704	14	75	28	0.63	225	83	67	0.91	4.12	0.9
Bats R	01	BOS	190	20	43	11	29	0	226	283	204	$4	323	453	775	12	70	26	0.47	233	133		0.85	4.81	5.5
R Moderate	02	BOS	151	17	34	7	25	0	225	364	168	$3	304	411	714	10	78	24	0.52	220	111		0.94	4.10	2.2
I CON	03	BOS	163	23	42	6	18	0	258	250	261	$3	305	448	752	6	78	30	0.31	283	126	35	1.30	4.69	2.8
S pt stb	1st Half		96	14	25	2	9	0	260			$1	283	396	679	3	79	31	0.15	268	95	47		3.86	-0.6
K age	2nd Half		67	9	17	4	9	0	254			$2	333	522	856	11	76	28	0.50	303	169	20		5.95	3.6
LIMA F BA: 45%	04	Proj	**150**	**19**	**36**	**7**	**20**	**0**	**240**			**$3**	**312**	**442**	**754**	**10**	**77**	**27**	**0.45**	**280**	**126**	**29**		**4.63**	**3.1**

Declining plate patience bottomed out in the 1st half, but 2nd half revealed a new player: patient, and powerful. Powerful? Well, he hit three of his four 2nd half HRs off of Rick Helling (2) and Rob Bell.

Moeller,Chad

	Yr	Tm	AB	R	H	HR	RBI	SB	Avg	vL	vR	R$	OB	Slg	OPS	bb%	ct%	h%	Eye	xBA	PX	SX	G/F	RC/G	RAR
Pos CA	99	aa	250	24	56	3	20	0	224			($1)	273	316	589	6	84	26	0.41	254	60	56		2.84	-8.9
Age 29 Past Peak	00	MIN	* 295	36	70	5	24	1	237	200	217	$0	277	353	629	5	77	29	0.24	241	73	80	1.96	3.22	-8.2
Bats R	01	ARI	* 330	39	79	7	29	1	239	77	279	$2	293	364	657	7	83	27	0.45	265	81	52	2.90	3.35	-1.7
R High	02	ARI	* 316	37	88	10	50	1	278	120	338	$10	354	449	803	10	81	32	0.63	271	112	71	1.21	5.58	13.1
I EXP CON	03	ARI	239	29	64	7	29	1	268	284	259	$5	332	435	767	9	75	33	0.39	299	113	57	1.80	4.89	4.1
S pt stb	1st Half		154	22	48	5	17	1	312			$6	365	487	852	8	79	37	0.39	315	121	45		6.30	8.5
K	2nd Half		85	7	16	2	12	0	188			($0)	274	341	615	11	69	25	0.38	270	100	72		2.93	-3.7
LIMA F BA: 45%	04	Proj	**250**	**28**	**68**	**9**	**31**	**1**	**272**			**$6**	**338**	**450**	**788**	**9**	**77**	**32**	**0.44**	**305**	**114**	**64**		**5.22**	**8.0**

Rising power trend is the only notable sign, but opportunity will determine whether we get to see the fruits of that developing skill. G/F limits his upside, but there is 15 HR potential here.

Mohr,Dustan

	Yr	Tm	AB	R	H	HR	RBI	SB	Avg	vL	vR	R$	OB	Slg	OPS	bb%	ct%	h%	Eye	xBA	PX	SX	G/F	RC/G	RAR
Pos RF LF	99	aa	42	3	6	0	2	0	143			($2)	217	214	432	9	81	18	0.50	241	41	116		1.39	-5.1
Age 27 Peak	00		0	0	0	0	0	0	0								0								
Bats R	01	MIN	51	6	12	0	4	1	235			$0	304	275	578	9	67	35	0.29	200	34	58	0.92	2.65	-3.7
R High	02	MIN	383	55	103	12	45	6	269	203	304	$10	324	433	757	7	78	32	0.36	257	104	91	1.13	4.83	-2.1
I exp con	03	MIN	348	50	87	10	36	5	250	250	242	$6	315	399	714	9	70	33	0.31	237	99	69	0.95	4.26	-9.2
S pt stb	1st Half		206	33	58	8	22	3	282			$6	327	461	788	6	70	37	0.23	247	114	72		5.45	1.7
K	2nd Half		142	17	29	2	14	2	204			($0)	298	310	608	12	69	28	0.43	222	77	56		2.86	-10.3
LIMA F BA: 30%	04	Proj	**250**	**35**	**62**	**7**	**27**	**4**	**248**			**$4**	**314**	**398**	**712**	**9**	**73**	**32**	**0.35**	**242**	**97**	**82**		**4.17**	**-6.7**

Got off to a solid start for the second straight year, but once again tanked in the 2nd half. In reality, 1st half BPIs were soft anyway. There's nothing here that points to much of a future.

Molina,Ben

Pos CA
Age 29 Past Peak
Bats R

R	Moderate	
I		con
S	PT	
K		

LIMA D+ BA: 65%

Yr	Tm	AB	R	H	HR	RBI	SB	Avg	vL	vR	R$	OB	Slg	OPS	bb%	ct%	h%	Eye	xBA	PX	SX	G/F	RC/G	RAR
99	ANA	* 342	38	93	8	54	1	272	143	314	$7	316	401	717	6	93	28	0.88	292	85	34	1.28	4.28	2.1
00	ANA	473	59	133	14	71	1	281	293	277	$11	315	421	735	5	93	28	0.70	288	82	58	0.94	4.71	7.4
01	ANA	325	31	85	6	40	0	262	218	281	$5	296	351	647	5	84	29	0.31	243	57	24	1.13	3.54	-3.1
02	ANA	428	34	105	5	47	0	245	248	244	$3	271	322	593	3	92	26	0.44	251	54	22	1.22	2.95	-8.4
03	ANA	409	37	115	14	71	1	281	289	278	$13	303	443	746	3	92	28	0.42	317	103	27	0.95	4.72	7.3
1st Half		238	23	69	6	40	1	290			$7	321	420	741	4	94	29	0.73	309	86	35		4.87	5.2
2nd Half		171	14	46	8	31	0	269			$6	277	474	751	1	91	26	0.13	328	127	17		4.45	1.8
04	Proj	450	40	132	17	67	0	293			$15	317	460	777	3	91	29	0.38	314	103	18		5.21	15.8

Opened up his swing in the 2nd half and started popping out HRs. The amazing part of that is he was able to maintain a 90%-plus contact rate. That bodes well for both his power and his BA. 15-20 HRs in 2004.

Molina,Jose

Pos CA
Age 28 Peak
Bats R

R	X HIGH	
I	EXP	CON
S	pt	stb
K		

LIMA F BA: 60%

Yr	Tm	AB	R	H	HR	RBI	SB	Avg	vL	vR	R$	OB	Slg	OPS	bb%	ct%	h%	Eye	xBA	PX	SX	G/F	RC/G	RAR
99	a/a	275	22	63	4	26	0	229			($1)	279	327	606	6	77	28	0.31	237	66	36	3.33	2.97	-8.7
00	aaa	248	18	50	1	14	1	202			($4)	258	246	504	7	79	25	0.36	224	33	31		1.85	-17.7
01	aaa	250	29	65	6	27	1	260			$4	299	392	691	5	82	30	0.31	260	84	57	2.60	3.92	1.7
02	ANA	* 360	27	94	3	36	0	261	100	340	$4	289	331	619	4	83	31	0.23	235	49	28	1.00	3.04	-6.1
03	ANA	114	12	21	0	6	0	184	240	141	($3)	191	219	411	1	77	24	0.04	256	31	57	1.81	1.31	-10.1
1st Half		49	5	10	0	2	0	204			($1)	204	245	449	0	80	26	0.00	267	36	52		1.60	-3.8
2nd Half		65	7	11	0	4	0	169			($2)	182	200	382	2	75	22	0.06	247	27	62		1.12	-6.3
04	Proj	150	14	38	1	13	0	253			$1	285	323	608	4	79	31	0.22	266	49	36		3.02	-4.1

The occasion was momentous... Sept 12 in Seattle, 9th inning, his team down 7-2 and facing Arthur Rhodes. He WALKED, and scored, but ANA still lost 7-4

It was his only walk of the year.

Mondesi,Raul

Pos RF
Age 33 Decline
Bats R

R	High	
I		con
S	pt	STB
K	age	

LIMA B BA: 55%

Yr	Tm	AB	R	H	HR	RBI	SB	Avg	vL	vR	R$	OB	Slg	OPS	bb%	ct%	h%	Eye	xBA	PX	SX	G/F	RC/G	RAR
99	LA	601	98	152	33	99	36	253	273	247	$28	332	483	814	11	78	27	0.53	276	133	132	1.06	5.49	8.9
00	TOR	388	78	105	24	67	22	271	311	261	$20	326	523	849	8	81	28	0.44	301	142	140	1.24	5.92	11.4
01	TOR	572	88	144	27	84	30	252	299	241	$24	336	453	789	11	78	28	0.57	260	117	115	1.00	5.11	2.3
02	2AL	569	90	132	26	88	15	232	244	228	$17	304	432	736	9	82	24	0.57	267	123	96	0.95	4.31	-12.3
03	2TM	523	83	142	24	71	22	272	262	274	$23	342	484	826	10	81	29	0.58	286	130	118	0.87	5.57	2.9
1st Half		314	48	84	14	43	15	268			$14	337	487	824	10	83	28	0.61	296	136	128		5.57	1.8
2nd Half		209	35	58	10	28	7	278			$9	349	478	828	10	79	31	0.53	272	120	96		5.56	1.1
04	Proj	550	89	152	31	90	17	276			$26	348	512	859	10	80	29	0.56	290	140	103		6.16	14.1

A rising PX trend in tandem with a falling G/F ratio = the ingredients for a HR spike. It might not seem outwardly possible, especially at age 33, but don't be surprised to see a return to the 30-HR level in '04.

Monroe,Craig

Pos LF RF
Age 27 Peak
Bats R

R	Moderate	
I	EXP	
S		stb
K		

LIMA B BA: 50%

Yr	Tm	AB	R	H	HR	RBI	SB	Avg	vL	vR	R$	OB	Slg	OPS	bb%	ct%	h%	Eye	xBA	PX	SX	G/F	RC/G	RAR
99		0	0	0	0	0	0	0								0								
00	aa	464	76	121	19	76	11	261			$15	340	470	810	11	83	28	0.73	298	126	101		5.02	-1.9
01	aaa	462	58	119	21	68	10	258			$15	325	465	790	9	82	28	0.54	283	123	92	1.73	4.91	-3.5
02	aaa	383	58	108	8	46	6	282			$11	341	444	784	8	86	31	0.63	289	110	117		5.19	-4.6
03	DET	* 472	64	119	25	76	5	252	293	209	$15	298	466	764	6	79	27	0.32	274	125	78	1.29	4.71	-8.7
1st Half		227	29	54	8	31	3	238			$4	300	405	705	8	76	28	0.36	248	100	97		4.06	-8.7
2nd Half		245	35	65	17	45	2	265			$10	297	522	819	4	82	26	0.26	298	149	52		5.33	-0.0
04	Proj	500	71	131	27	85	7	262			$18	317	496	813	7	82	27	0.44	283	137	92		5.26	2.6

23-70-.240 in 425 AB at DET, which was both good and bad news. The good news was the power skill, especially in the 2nd half. The bad news was the sub-.300 OB and poor eye which will limit any BA upside.

Mora,Melvin

Pos LF
Age 32 Past Peak
Bats R

R	Very High	
I		CON
S	PT	stb
K		

LIMA C+ BA: 40%

Yr	Tm	AB	R	H	HR	RBI	SB	Avg	vL	vR	R$	OB	Slg	OPS	bb%	ct%	h%	Eye	xBA	PX	SX	G/F	RC/G	RAR
99	NYM	* 335	48	80	5	29	16	239	118	214	$6	313	331	644	10	83	28	0.62	258	62	98	2.50	3.34	-17.7
00	2TM	* 441	66	122	8	53	14	277	280	274	$12	340	408	748	9	81	33	0.51	265	82	121	0.98	4.59	-7.2
01	BAL	436	49	109	7	48	11	250	308	231	$8	314	362	677	9	79	30	0.45	260	80	69	0.79	3.87	-9.8
02	BAL	557	86	130	19	64	16	233	240	231	$13	319	404	723	11	81	26	0.65	260	105	110	0.75	4.13	-12.0
03	BAL	344	68	109	15	48	6	317	324	315	$16	402	503	905	12	79	36	0.69	290	112	79	1.16	7.45	19.8
1st Half		230	48	81	11	38	5	352			$15	446	574	1020	14	80	41	0.83	308	137	81		9.83	26.8
2nd Half		114	20	28	4	10	1	246			$2	306	360	666	8	79	28	0.42	254	61	67		3.78	-5.2
04	Proj	550	90	146	18	63	12	265			$15	342	414	756	10	80	30	0.57	284	91	91		4.84	-3.8

Where did that 1st half come from? Well, an inflated 41% hit rate might have had something to do with it. And just as that regressed to the mean in the 2nd half, so will his BA in 2004.

Morban,Jose

Pos SS DH
Age 24 Growth
Bats R

R	Moderate	
I	EXP	
S		
K	age	

LIMA F BA: 55%

Yr	Tm	AB	R	H	HR	RBI	SB	Avg	vL	vR	R$	OB	Slg	OPS	bb%	ct%	h%	Eye	xBA	PX	SX	G/F	RC/G	RAR
99		0	0	0	0	0	0	0								0								
00		0	0	0	0	0	0	0								0								
01		0	0	0	0	0	0	0								0								
02		0	0	0	0	0	0	0								0								
03	BAL	71	14	10	2	5	8	141	100	157	$1	176	225	401	4	70	17	0.14	217	43	213	2.00	1.50	-7.0
1st Half		12	7	1	1	1	5	83			$1	214	333	548	14	25	0	0.22	98	127	490		3.35	-0.5
2nd Half		59	7	9	1	4	3	153			($0)	167	203	370	2	80	17	0.08	231	26	129		1.16	-6.4
04	Proj	50	7	10	1	4	3	200			$0	215	256	471	2	78	24	0.08	223	28	112		1.96	-3.9

"Morban shouldn't be in the major leagues as far as his development is concerned," said BAL's Jim Beattie. But there he was, granted by the wonders of Rule 5, to lose a precious year of development time.

Mordecai,Mike

Pos SS
Age 36 Decline
Bats S

R	X HIGH	
I		CON
S	PT	stb
K	AGE	

LIMA F BA: 45%

Yr	Tm	AB	R	H	HR	RBI	SB	Avg	vL	vR	R$	OB	Slg	OPS	bb%	ct%	h%	Eye	xBA	PX	SX	G/F	RC/G	RAR
99	MON	226	29	53	5	25	2	235	254	226	$2	297	363	660	8	86	25	0.65	270	80	81	1.18	3.29	-1.7
00	MON	169	20	48	4	16	2	284	309	267	$4	331	450	781	7	80	34	0.35	285	116	49	1.21	5.12	8.0
01	MON	254	28	71	3	32	2	280	313	252	$6	330	398	727	7	79	34	0.36	229	82	79	1.14	4.54	7.1
02	2NL	151	19	37	0	11	2	245	282	205	$1	305	298	603	8	82	30	0.48	202	49	64	1.92	2.97	-4.2
03	FLA	89	11	19	2	8	3	213	263	176	$1	278	326	604	8	76	26	0.38	209	75	81	0.76	3.11	-2.8
1st Half		42	5	9	0	3	2	214			$0	313	262	574	13	79	27	0.67	199	43	74		2.92	-1.5
2nd Half		47	6	10	2	5	1	213			$1	245	383	628	4	74	24	0.17	215	105	74		3.13	-1.4
04	Proj	100	12	22	1	10	1	220			$0	277	332	609	7	81	26	0.42	218	84	62		2.88	-3.2

Why he gets more undraftable every year:
- Batting under .200 vs RHers
- Mendoza Line xBAs
- Sub-.300 OB
And this year, has now lost his multi-positional advantage.

Morris,Warren

Pos 2B
Age 30 Past Peak
Bats L

R	High	
I	exp	con
S	pt	stb
K		

LIMA D BA: 55%

Yr	Tm	AB	R	H	HR	RBI	SB	Avg	vL	vR	R$	OB	Slg	OPS	bb%	ct%	h%	Eye	xBA	PX	SX	G/F	RC/G	RAR
99	PIT	511	65	147	15	73	3	288	336	274	$14	361	427	788	10	83	32	0.67	254	84	53	1.23	5.27	15.4
00	PIT	528	68	137	3	43	7	259	230	265	$5	341	343	683	11	85	30	0.83	257	62	65	1.26	3.81	-8.8
01	PIT	* 326	26	79	6	41	4	242	300	194	$5	271	365	636	4	92	25	0.48	293	83	56	1.53	3.00	-8.6
02	aaa	363	41	86	5	35	3	237			$3	271	355	626	4	87	26	0.36	274	81	101		3.13	-12.0
03	DET	* 552	60	143	8	53	8	259	286	268	$8	306	370	675	6	88	28	0.55	267	69	110	1.54	3.88	-4.3
1st Half		281	32	70	5	25	4	249			$3	297	384	681	6	89	27	0.59	278	80	134		3.76	-3.1
2nd Half		271	28	73	3	28	4	269			$5	315	354	669	6	87	30	0.51	256	59	75		3.98	-1.2
04	Proj	350	37	94	5	36	4	269			$6	312	379	691	6	88	29	0.52	268	72	83		4.02	-0.8

6-37-4-.272 in 346 AB at DET, his best numbers in four years and first signs of life since his 1999 rookie season. He might get a chance to build on that, but the window of opportunity is very small.

Mueller,Bill

Pos 3B
Age 33 Decline
Bats S

R	X HIGH	
I		CON
S	PT	STB
K	age	

LIMA B BA: 50%

Yr	Tm	AB	R	H	HR	RBI	SB	Avg	vL	vR	R$	OB	Slg	OPS	bb%	ct%	h%	Eye	xBA	PX	SX	G/F	RC/G	RAR
99	SF	414	61	120	2	36	4	290	248	306	$7	386	362	749	14	87	33	1.25	265	58	53	1.50	5.01	7.5
00	SF	560	97	150	10	55	4	268	306	259	$8	330	388	718	8	89	29	0.84	273	77	94	1.28	4.43	1.9
01	CHC	210	38	62	6	23	1	295	391	268	$6	401	448	848	15	91	30	1.95	308	96	64	1.48	6.42	10.7
02	2NL	382	52	101	8	42	0	264	221	272	$7	356	401	756	12	89	28	1.26	314	92	68	1.30	4.89	3.3
03	BOS	524	85	171	19	85	1	326	295	342	$23	395	540	935	10	85	36	0.77	330	138	67	1.10	7.85	46.8
1st Half		244	39	80	5	34	1	328			$9	386	537	923	9	85	37	0.62	336	149	89		7.52	19.7
2nd Half		280	46	91	14	51	0	325			$14	402	543	945	11	86	34	0.90	324	129	54		8.13	27.0
04	Proj	550	87	176	16	75	1	320			$20	399	495	894	12	87	34	1.04	324	111	67		7.28	41.6

We've been projecting this .300 season for a long time but the power was a surprise. There's little in his BPIs to suggest he'll maintain that pop, but the rest of the package still makes him worth owning.

Munson,Eric

	Yr	Tm	AB	R	H	HR	RBI	SB	Avg	vL	vR	R$	OB	Slg	OPS	bb%	ct%	h%	Eye	xBA	PX	SX	G/F	RC/G	RAR
Pos 3B	99		0	0	0	0	0	0	0								0								
Age 26 Pre-Peak	00	aa	365	42	81	10	54	4	222			$3	283	373	655	8	80	25	0.42	264	91	92		3.42	-10.5
Bats L	01	aa	519	70	117	17	81	0	225			$7	313	389	702	11	78	26	0.57	255	104	35	0.64	3.91	-8.9
R High	02	DET	* 536	72	123	20	81	1	229	200	182	$9	328	410	739	13	79	25	0.72	264	108	70	1.47	4.37	-1.5
I EXP con	03	DET	313	28	75	18	50	3	240	208	250	$9	316	441	757	10	81	24	0.57	253	113	34	1.05	4.73	2.0
S pt stb	1st Half		217	17	53	10	31	3	244			$6	317	424	741	10	82	25	0.61	256	106	36		4.61	0.6
K	2nd Half		96	11	22	8	19	0	229			$3	315	479	794	11	76	22	0.52	246	127	5		4.99	1.4
LIMA C BA: 60%	**04**	**Proj**	**500**	**58**	**125**	**23**	**82**	**2**	**250**			**$13**	**332**	**430**	**762**	**11**	**79**	**28**	**0.58**	**248**	**103**	**50**		**4.82**	**5.3**

Power skills have been rising, and his contact rate has been edging upward, but these BPIs still only paint the picture of a 20-25 HR, .250-.260 hitter at best. Okay on DET, I guess, but other teams will want more.

Myers,Greg

	Yr	Tm	AB	R	H	HR	RBI	SB	Avg	vL	vR	R$	OB	Slg	OPS	bb%	ct%	h%	Eye	xBA	PX	SX	G/F	RC/G	RAR
Pos CA DH	99	2NL	200	19	53	5	24	0	265	241	269	$3	350	370	720	12	85	29	0.87	247	64		1.33	4.49	3.0
Age 38 Decline	00	BAL	125	9	28	3	12	0	224		239	($0)	271	344	615	6	77	27	0.28	206	75		1.79	3.06	-4.1
Bats L	01	OAK	161	24	36	11	31	0	224	316	211	$4	313	447	760	12	76	22	0.55	226	120	24	1.18	4.60	3.6
R X HIGH	02	OAK	144	15	32	6	21	0	222	200	227	$2	341	382	723	15	75	25	0.72	224	93		2.10	4.27	2.9
I CON	03	TOR	329	51	101	15	52	0	307	333	303	$13	377	502	879	10	83	33	0.65	326	120	26	2.39	6.72	23.8
S PT STB	1st Half		173	29	61	8	31	0	353			$10	440	566	1006	14	82	40	0.87	336	136	26		9.62	24.5
K AGE	2nd Half		156	22	40	7	21	0	256			$4	301	429	731	6	83	27	0.38	316	102	40		4.19	0.4
LIMA F BA: 55%	**04**	**Proj**	**250**	**33**	**65**	**9**	**38**	**0**	**260**			**$6**	**342**	**413**	**756**	**11**	**80**	**29**	**0.62**	**310**	**92**	**26**		**4.78**	**6.1**

Plot the course of his OB and eye trends, and this .300 season is not a total surprise. Still, a 2.0-plus G/F ratio with this power spike is an anomaly, and when that comes down, everything else will follow.

Nady,Xavier

	Yr	Tm	AB	R	H	HR	RBI	SB	Avg	vL	vR	R$	OB	Slg	OPS	bb%	ct%	h%	Eye	xBA	PX	SX	G/F	RC/G	RAR
Pos RF	99		0	0	0	0	0	0	0								0								
Age 25 Pre-Peak	00		0	0	0	0	0	0	0								0								
Bats R	01		0	0	0	0	0	0	0								0								
R High	02	aaa	315	40	79	8	37	0	251			$5	289	368	657	5	83	28	0.31	253	74	51		3.57	-14.8
I EXP con	03	SD	* 507	66	130	14	58	6	256	311	249	$11	302	389	690	6	81	29	0.34	256	86	78	1.48	4.02	-23.6
S pt stb	1st Half		285	38	78	7	29	3	274			$7	317	407	724	6	82	31	0.35	260	89	75		4.45	-9.5
K age	2nd Half		222	28	52	7	29	3	234			$4	283	365	648	6	80	26	0.33	250	82	70		3.50	-14.0
LIMA D+ BA: 45%	**04**	**Proj**	**450**	**58**	**118**	**16**	**63**	**3**	**262**			**$12**	**305**	**415**	**720**	**6**	**81**	**29**	**0.33**	**260**	**94**	**66**		**4.36**	**-14.5**

9-39-6-.267 in 371 AB at SD. Some minor growth from 2002, but this is still a light hitter with marginal skills... which is odd considering he hit .373 with 26 HRs in A-ball in 2000. Patience, I suppose.

Nevin,Phil

	Yr	Tm	AB	R	H	HR	RBI	SB	Avg	vL	vR	R$	OB	Slg	OPS	bb%	ct%	h%	Eye	xBA	PX	SX	G/F	RC/G	RAR
Pos 1B RF	99	2TM	383	52	103	24	85	1	269	270	268	$15	355	527	882	12	79	29	0.62	283	156	30	0.95	6.55	11.0
Age 33 Decline	00	SD	538	87	163	31	107	2	303	342	288	$25	372	543	915	10	78	34	0.49	308	141	54	1.48	7.41	30.4
Bats R	01	SD	546	97	167	41	126	4	306	329	297	$33	386	588	974	12	73	35	0.48	294	161	46	1.23	8.16	28.7
R High	02	SD	407	53	116	12	57	4	285	337	268	$14	346	413	759	9	79	34	0.44	244	84	61	1.39	5.16	-5.0
I con	03	SD	226	30	63	13	46	2	279	349	252	$10	340	487	827	9	81	30	0.48	300	122	47	1.42	5.91	2.5
S PT stb	1st Half		0	0	0	0	0	0	0			($0)					0				0	0			
K age	2nd Half		226	30	63	13	46	2	279			$10	340	487	827	9	81	30	0.48	300	122	47		5.91	2.5
LIMA C BA: 55%	**04**	**Proj**	**550**	**81**	**159**	**31**	**109**	**4**	**289**			**$26**	**359**	**509**	**868**	**10**	**78**	**32**	**0.49**	**299**	**133**	**52**		**6.55**	**14.2**

Two injury-shortened seasons, with BPIs that took a departure from his 2001 levels. We'll project a rebound - as we did last year - but much will depend upon him pushing those BPIs back up.

Nixon,Trot

	Yr	Tm	AB	R	H	HR	RBI	SB	Avg	vL	vR	R$	OB	Slg	OPS	bb%	ct%	h%	Eye	xBA	PX	SX	G/F	RC/G	RAR
Pos RF	99	BOS	381	67	103	15	52	3	270	116	290	$10	359	472	832	12	80	30	0.71	278	119	114	1.07	5.93	10.5
Age 30 Past Peak	00	BOS	427	66	118	12	60	8	276	264	278	$11	369	461	831	13	80	32	0.74	274	110	150	1.02	6.09	14.2
Bats L	01	BOS	535	100	150	27	88	7	280	210	298	$21	373	505	878	13	79	31	0.70	285	133	92	0.89	6.58	24.4
R Very Low	02	BOS	532	81	136	24	94	4	256	233	262	$17	337	470	807	11	80	28	0.60	270	132	80	0.85	5.39	5.7
I con	03	BOS	441	81	135	28	87	4	306	219	330	$24	395	578	973	13	78	34	0.68	277	156	111	0.60	8.33	38.4
S pt	1st Half		231	43	73	10	47	3	316			$12	406	537	943	13	79	36	0.73	266	130	132		8.23	19.1
K	2nd Half		210	38	62	18	40	1	295			$12	383	624	1007	12	77	31	0.63	288	185	79		8.39	19.0
LIMA B+ BA: 40%	**04**	**Proj**	**550**	**96**	**157**	**36**	**114**	**5**	**285**			**$27**	**373**	**563**	**936**	**12**	**79**	**30**	**0.66**	**279**	**160**	**100**		**7.42**	**36.4**

The rising PX and falling G/F continues, which is good news for his power numbers. He would have hit 30 HRs had he not gotten hurt. He reaches that milestone, and more, in 2004.

Nix,Laynce

	Yr	Tm	AB	R	H	HR	RBI	SB	Avg	vL	vR	R$	OB	Slg	OPS	bb%	ct%	h%	Eye	xBA	PX	SX	G/F	RC/G	RAR
Pos RF CF	99		0	0	0	0	0	0	0								0								
Age 23 Growth	00		0	0	0	0	0	0	0								0								
Bats L	01		0	0	0	0	0	0	0								0								
R Moderate	02		0	0	0	0	0	0	0								0								
I EXP	03	TEX	* 519	70	138	22	85	11	266	150	268	$18	317	455	772	7	79	30	0.35	268	118	78	1.18	5.05	-1.4
S	1st Half		303	40	80	12	50	6	264			$10	322	446	768	8	82	29	0.42	276	115	66		4.95	-1.7
K AGE	2nd Half		216	30	58	10	35	5	269			$8	310	468	778	6	75	32	0.24	256	123	76		5.19	0.3
LIMA D+ BA: 45%	**04**	**Proj**	**450**	**61**	**118**	**17**	**63**	**7**	**262**			**$13**	**311**	**435**	**746**	**7**	**77**	**31**	**0.31**	**263**	**110**	**70**		**4.66**	**-5.3**

8-30-.255 in 184 AB at TEX. There are signs of a productive hitter coming, eventually. Slightly elevated G/F will limit his short-term power upside. Low OB limits his overall value. Patience is needed here.

Norton,Greg

	Yr	Tm	AB	R	H	HR	RBI	SB	Avg	vL	vR	R$	OB	Slg	OPS	bb%	ct%	h%	Eye	xBA	PX	SX	G/F	RC/G	RAR
Pos 3B	99	CHW	436	62	111	16	50	4	255	203	265	$8	356	424	781	14	79	29	0.74	266	106	46	1.49	5.06	8.2
Age 31 Past Peak	00	CHW	* 298	39	74	10	41	2	248	125	254	$5	347	389	736	13	78	29	0.69	248	80	60	1.80	4.62	2.0
Bats S	01	COL	225	30	60	13	40	1	267	271	265	$8	324	516	839	8	71	32	0.29	257	144	83	1.02	5.83	8.1
R High	02	COL	180	20	38	7	37	2	211	167	232	$4	311	383	694	13	69	26	0.47	247	109	68	1.14	3.65	-5.3
I CON	03	COL	179	19	47	6	31	2	263	273	261	$5	323	447	770	8	74	33	0.34	277	127	46	1.33	4.94	3.6
S pt stb	1st Half		117	11	29	2	15	1	248			$2	307	376	683	8	82	29	0.48	289	96	42		3.82	-1.5
K	2nd Half		62	8	18	4	16	1	290			$4	353	581	934	9	58	44	0.23	243	188	42		7.48	5.6
LIMA F BA: 40%	**04**	**Proj**	**150**	**18**	**40**	**7**	**29**	**2**	**267**			**$6**	**336**	**467**	**803**	**9**	**70**	**34**	**0.34**	**271**	**129**	**43**		**5.38**	**4.3**

Was hurt in 2002, and did rebound, to a season virtually identical to 2001. That's his productivity plateau -- he has it, he likes it, he owns it. And if COL will have him, he'll live there again in 2004.

Nunez,Abraham

	Yr	Tm	AB	R	H	HR	RBI	SB	Avg	vL	vR	R$	OB	Slg	OPS	bb%	ct%	h%	Eye	xBA	PX	SX	G/F	RC/G	RAR
Pos 2B SS	99	PIT	* 317	34	73	0	19	10	230	235	213	$0	301	256	556	9	81	28	0.53	233	22	80	3.08	2.68	-14.7
Age 28 Peak	00	PIT	* 442	49	105	3	31	16	238	200	222	$4	295	287	582	8	88	26	0.68	259	33	88	1.95	2.82	-20.8
Bats S	01	PIT	301	30	79	1	21	8	262	297	258	$4	325	336	661	9	82	32	0.53	264	48	122	2.81	3.83	-0.3
R Moderate	02	PIT	253	28	59	2	15	3	233	176	242	$0	307	320	627	10	83	28	0.61	249	67	68	2.33	3.12	-10.1
I con	03	PIT	311	37	77	4	35	9	248	163	261	$6	306	357	663	8	83	29	0.49	278	63	168	2.47	3.70	-6.5
S pt	1st Half		130	11	27	0	11	3	208			($1)	259	238	497	6	79	26	0.33	235	21	97		2.02	-9.7
K	2nd Half		181	26	50	4	24	6	276			$6	338	442	780	9	86	30	0.65	310	94	207		5.24	4.4
LIMA D BA: 55%	**04**	**Proj**	**300**	**34**	**74**	**3**	**27**	**7**	**247**			**$4**	**310**	**335**	**645**	**8**	**83**	**29**	**0.54**	**275**	**56**	**124**		**3.49**	**-7.4**

Extreme ground-ball hitter, but by the looks of it, rarely gets the ball out of the infield. A drag on the offense no matter how you look at him.

O'Leary,Troy

	Yr	Tm	AB	R	H	HR	RBI	SB	Avg	vL	vR	R$	OB	Slg	OPS	bb%	ct%	h%	Eye	xBA	PX	SX	G/F	RC/G	RAR
Pos LF RF	99	BOS	596	84	167	28	103	1	280	346	257	$19	342	495	837	9	85	29	0.62	310	127	59	1.10	5.93	14.5
Age 34 Decline	00	BOS	513	68	134	13	70	0	261	252	265	$7	320	411	731	8	85	29	0.58	275	93	61	0.96	4.46	-9.4
Bats L	01	BOS	341	50	82	13	50	1	240	154	261	$6	292	437	729	7	79	27	0.34	264	114	116	1.17	4.14	-5.0
R High	02	MON	* 359	36	103	6	50	1	287	351	275	$10	357	396	752	10	83	33	0.64	255	76	47	1.45	4.90	-15.1
I con	03	CHC	174	18	38	5	28	3	218	214	219	$3	277	356	633	7	82	24	0.45	262	91	63	1.42	3.30	-12.2
S pt stb	1st Half		121	15	28	3	19	1	231			$2	285	347	632	7	85	25	0.50	262	76	56		3.32	-8.3
K age	2nd Half		53	3	10	2	9	2	189			$1	259	377	636	9	75	21	0.38	257	127	47		3.24	-4.0
LIMA F BA: 65%	**04**	**Proj**	**150**	**15**	**36**	**4**	**23**	**2**	**240**			**$3**	**303**	**396**	**699**	**8**	**81**	**27**	**0.47**	**264**	**100**	**78**		**4.04**	**-7.7**

He'll likely rebound from a .218 BA, given the chance, based on better xBA levels. But G/F trends show that the power is not coming back.

Ojeda,Miguel

Pos CA | Age 29 Past Peak | Bats R
R: High | I: CON | S: pt, stb | K:
LIMA D+ | BA: 55%

	Tm	AB	R	H	HR	RBI	SB	Avg	vL	vR	R$	OB	Slg	OPS	bb%	ct%	h%	Eye	xBA	PX	SX	G/F	RC/G	RAR
99		0	0	0	0	0	0	0								0								
00	MEX	330	56	98	15	69	1	297			$14	386	546	933	13	85	31	0.95	315	146	113		7.59	32.2
01	MEX	422	74	122	10	62	4	289			$13	373	420	793	12	85	32	0.91	271	78	103		5.59	22.5
02	MEX	341	75	112	11	76	8	328			$21	419	501	920	13	86	36	1.08	289	114	95		7.75	35.7
03	SD	141	13	33	4	22	1	234	233	235	$2	321	362	682	11	82	26	0.69	243	82	32	1.14	3.79	-2.1
1st Half		42	2	8	1	10	0	190			$0	190	286	476	0	88	19	0.00	247	59	8		1.71	-3.4
2nd Half		99	11	25	3	12	1	253			$2	368	394	761	15	79	29	0.86	240	93	35		4.83	1.6
04	Proj	**200**	**33**	**52**	**6**	**33**	**2**	**260**			**$6**	**345**	**427**	**772**	**11**	**83**	**29**	**0.77**	**256**	**106**	**101**		**4.99**	**5.2**

Took a half season to start adapting to American baseball. 2nd half is more indicative of what he might do... It still pales in comparison to Mexico but at least you can begin to see that it's the same player.

Olerud,John

Pos 1B | Age 35 Decline | Bats L
R: Low | I: con | S: stb | K: age
LIMA B | BA: 65%

	Tm	AB	R	H	HR	RBI	SB	Avg	vL	vR	R$	OB	Slg	OPS	bb%	ct%	h%	Eye	xBA	PX	SX	G/F	RC/G	RAR
99	NYM	581	107	173	19	96	3	298	247	318	$20	422	463	885	18	89	31	1.89	313	109	52	1.44	7.14	29.4
00	SEA	565	84	161	14	103	0	285	242	297	$14	394	439	833	15	83	32	1.06	276	103	23	1.44	6.10	2.4
01	SEA	572	91	173	21	95	3	302	246	321	$22	401	472	873	14	88	32	1.34	295	106	51	1.21	6.92	12.1
02	SEA	553	85	166	22	102	0	300	287	306	$22	406	490	896	15	88	31	1.48	287	122	23	1.16	7.24	21.0
03	SEA	539	64	145	10	83	0	269	239	281	$11	368	390	757	13	88	29	1.25	286	85	21	1.23	4.96	-6.5
1st Half		268	33	77	4	39	0	287			$6	384	403	787	14	90	31	1.56	294	85	21		5.53	1.2
2nd Half		271	31	68	6	44	0	251			$4	351	376	728	13	85	28	1.05	279	85	22		4.44	-7.5
04	Proj	**550**	**76**	**160**	**14**	**91**	**1**	**291**			**$17**	**392**	**435**	**827**	**14**	**87**	**31**	**1.31**	**290**	**96**	**28**		**6.11**	**6.8**

Batted .300 in '02 and .269 in '03 but xBA says the seasons are identical from a skills perspective. That's good news for a BA rebound. As for power, with his high G/F ratios and at age 35, that might not return.

Olivo,Miguel

Pos CA | Age 25 Pre-Peak | Bats R
R: High | I: EXP, con | S: stb | K: age
LIMA D | BA: 40%

	Tm	AB	R	H	HR	RBI	SB	Avg	vL	vR	R$	OB	Slg	OPS	bb%	ct%	h%	Eye	xBA	PX	SX	G/F	RC/G	RAR
99		0	0	0	0	0	0	0								0								
00		0	0	0	0	0	0	0								0								
01	aa	316	36	74	13	45	5	234			$7	301	427	728	9	83	24	0.57	285	119	67		4.19	4.8
02	aa	359	44	98	6	43	25	273			$16	341	423	764	9	82	32	0.58	273	99	168		4.75	9.5
03	CHW	317	37	75	6	27	6	237	302	212	$3	280	360	639	6	75	30	0.24	255	84	83	1.24	3.26	-8.1
1st Half		172	21	39	5	16	1	227			$1	277	378	655	7	82	25	0.39	289	100	51		3.30	-4.2
2nd Half		145	16	36	1	11	5	248			$2	283	338	621	5	66	37	0.14	216	65	112		3.21	-3.9
04	Proj	**350**	**41**	**88**	**4**	**37**	**8**	**251**			**$5**	**306**	**363**	**669**	**7**	**78**	**31**	**0.35**	**259**	**77**	**107**		**3.72**	**-2.3**

Skills fell upon promotion and might take awhile to return. Many catchers have minor lg stats that get folks all hopped up, but spend the first 10 years of their career as an end-gamer, before breaking out at age 33.

Olmedo,Ranier

Pos SS | Age 22 Growth | Bats S
R: High | I: EXP, con | S: stb | K: AGE
LIMA F | BA: 40%

	Tm	AB	R	H	HR	RBI	SB	Avg	vL	vR	R$	OB	Slg	OPS	bb%	ct%	h%	Eye	xBA	PX	SX	G/F	RC/G	RAR
99		0	0	0	0	0	0	0								0								
00		0	0	0	0	0	0	0								0								
01		0	0	0	0	0	0	0								0								
02	aa	478	50	108	3	24	12	226			$1	288	293	581	8	86	26	0.64	251	51	71		2.42	-27.7
03	CIN	* 415	46	105	3	32	3	253	215	248	$3	297	323	620	6	82	30	0.36	242	52	61	3.27	3.17	-11.6
1st Half		202	27	57	2	16	2	282			$4	319	371	691	5	86	32	0.39	262	69	59		4.00	-0.6
2nd Half		213	19	48	1	16	1	225			($1)	276	277	553	7	79	28	0.33	223	37	62		2.49	-10.6
04	Proj	**250**	**27**	**60**	**2**	**17**	**4**	**240**			**$1**	**292**	**312**	**604**	**7**	**84**	**28**	**0.45**	**245**	**53**	**72**		**2.84**	**-8.2**

0-17-.239 in 230 AB at CIN. Only 22, but has a ways to go before his batting provides any benefit. Minor growth in '03, though 2nd half shows short-term struggles are ahead. Might be draftable by 2008.

Ordonez,Magglio

Pos RF | Age 30 Past Peak | Bats R
R: Very Low | I: | S: | K:
LIMA D+ | BA: 60%

	Tm	AB	R	H	HR	RBI	SB	Avg	vL	vR	R$	OB	Slg	OPS	bb%	ct%	h%	Eye	xBA	PX	SX	G/F	RC/G	RAR
99	CHW	624	100	188	30	117	13	301	320	298	$29	350	510	860	7	90	30	0.73	323	122	93	1.57	6.40	24.8
00	CHW	588	102	185	32	126	18	315	337	310	$33	378	546	924	9	89	31	0.94	324	132	105	1.26	7.71	44.6
01	CHW	593	97	181	31	113	25	305	325	300	$35	379	533	911	11	88	30	1.00	332	139	88	1.37	7.39	39.6
02	CHW	590	116	189	38	135	7	320	288	329	$37	376	597	973	8	87	32	0.69	344	168	74	1.12	8.24	51.2
03	CHW	606	95	192	29	99	9	317	317	317	$30	376	546	922	9	88	32	0.78	332	143	79	1.18	7.52	39.0
1st Half		298	45	85	14	46	6	285			$12	353	503	856	9	87	29	0.82	322	133	91		6.30	9.7
2nd Half		308	50	107	15	53	3	347			$18	398	588	986	8	89	36	0.74	341	153	60		8.89	29.9
04	Proj	**600**	**102**	**193**	**35**	**113**	**11**	**322**			**$35**	**381**	**578**	**958**	**9**	**88**	**32**	**0.79**	**336**	**156**	**80**		**8.12**	**49.4**

At face value, an off-year, but his BPIs barely budged and his 2nd half was nearly back to par. Expect vintage production in 2004, and perhaps a bit more..

Ordonez,Rey

Pos SS | Age 33 Decline | Bats S
R: Very High | I: CON | S: PT, stb | K: age
LIMA D | BA: 40%

	Tm	AB	R	H	HR	RBI	SB	Avg	vL	vR	R$	OB	Slg	OPS	bb%	ct%	h%	Eye	xBA	PX	SX	G/F	RC/G	RAR
99	NYM	520	49	134	1	60	8	258	231	267	$5	322	317	639	9	89	29	0.83	255	47	68	1.78	3.48	-0.7
00	NYM	133	10	25	0	9	0	188	192	187	($3)	280	226	506	11	88	21	1.06	198	32	19	1.41	1.98	-6.2
01	NYM	461	31	114	3	44	3	247	264	244	$3	299	336	635	7	91	27	0.79	262	62	67	2.15	3.38	-2.5
02	NYM	460	53	117	1	42	2	254	193	276	$3	291	324	615	5	90	28	0.52	268	58	69	2.23	3.19	-9.6
03	TAM	117	14	37	3	22	0	316	308	319	$5	328	487	815	2	90	33	0.17	293	121	38	1.20	5.51	3.5
1st Half		117	14	37	3	22	0	316			$5	328	487	815	2	90	33	0.17	293	121	38		5.51	3.5
2nd Half		0	0	0	0	0	0	0			($0)					0			0					
04	Proj	**450**	**43**	**123**	**8**	**54**	**2**	**273**			**$9**	**316**	**401**	**717**	**6**	**90**	**29**	**0.60**	**282**	**86**	**47**		**4.32**	**-1.6**

Oddly enough, the part of this abbreviated display that might be for real is the power surge. Sharply lower G/F shows more lift in his swing. The BA spike can be more easily explained away and should fade.

Ortiz,David

Pos 1B | Age 28 Peak | Bats L
R: Moderate | I: con | S: pt, stb | K:
LIMA B | BA: 60%

	Tm	AB	R	H	HR	RBI	SB	Avg	vL	vR	R$	OB	Slg	OPS	bb%	ct%	h%	Eye	xBA	PX	SX	G/F	RC/G	RAR
99	aaa	496	65	135	22	83	2	272			$15	358	480	837	12	81	30	0.71	283	128	50		5.95	5.8
00	MIN	415	59	117	10	63	1	282	423	249	$9	369	446	814	12	80	33	0.70	259	110	51	1.16	5.85	-1.1
01	MIN	303	46	71	18	48	1	234	221	240	$8	324	475	799	12	78	24	0.59	258	141	54	0.74	5.14	-9.1
02	MIN	412	52	112	20	75	1	272	203	299	$15	341	500	841	9	79	30	0.49	258	143	40	0.73	5.86	0.0
03	BOS	448	79	129	31	101	0	288	216	313	$22	370	592	961	11	81	29	0.70	318	185	46	0.87	7.83	30.6
1st Half		177	31	52	4	36	0	294			$6	381	486	867	12	82	34	0.81	294	143	36		6.69	6.4
2nd Half		271	48	77	27	65	0	284			$16	362	661	1022	11	81	26	0.63	333	213	53		8.51	23.8
04	Proj	**550**	**86**	**161**	**42**	**119**	**0**	**293**			**$29**	**371**	**611**	**982**	**11**	**80**	**30**	**0.63**	**314**	**189**	**38**		**8.13**	**37.7**

Healthy, productive, appreciated and peaking... and not even in 500 AB. He should get that F/T opportunity in 2004, and with these BPIs, his numbers could go through the roof.

Osik,Keith

Pos CA | Age 35 Decline | Bats R
R: High | I: CON | S: pt, stb | K: age
LIMA F | BA: 55%

	Tm	AB	R	H	HR	RBI	SB	Avg	vL	vR	R$	OB	Slg	OPS	bb%	ct%	h%	Eye	xBA	PX	SX	G/F	RC/G	RAR
99	PIT	167	12	31	2	13	0	186	213	170	($3)	236	251	487	6	82	21	0.37	194	39	42	0.98	1.86	-11.2
00	PIT	123	11	36	4	22	3	293	371	261	$5	365	455	820	10	91	30	1.27	302	97	73	1.76	6.17	7.4
01	PIT	120	9	25	2	13	1	208	119	256	($0)	286	292	577	10	80	24	0.54	204	54	35	0.98	2.73	-2.9
02	PIT	100	6	16	2	11	0	160	91	179	($2)	208	250	458	6	75	19	0.24	205	60		1.26	1.58	-8.4
03	MIL	241	22	60	2	21	0	249	378	225	$1	335	324	658	11	82	30	0.70	249	58	22	1.29	3.62	-4.8
1st Half		119	7	28	1	8	0	235			($0)	321	303	623	11	79	29	0.60	235	51	8		3.24	-3.8
2nd Half		122	15	32	1	13	0	262			$1	348	344	692	12	84	30	0.84	262	64	34		4.01	-1.0
04	Proj	**150**	**12**	**33**	**2**	**15**	**0**	**220**			**($0)**	**294**	**302**	**596**	**9**	**81**	**26**	**0.54**	**248**	**57**	**29**		**2.88**	**-5.6**

The Ultimate Back Door Slam... On April 3, Mgr Ned Yost said: I am going to make you the personal catcher for... Glendon Rusch and Todd Ritchie."

Overbay,Lyle

Pos 1B | Age 27 Peak | Bats L
R: High | I: EXP | S: pt, stb | K:
LIMA D | BA: 45%

	Tm	AB	R	H	HR	RBI	SB	Avg	vL	vR	R$	OB	Slg	OPS	bb%	ct%	h%	Eye	xBA	PX	SX	G/F	RC/G	RAR
99		0	0	0	0	0	0	0								0								
00	aa	244	33	76	6	38	2	311			$9	366	455	821	8	87	34	0.68	288	92	60		6.03	2.5
01	aa	534	60	161	9	73	5	301			$16	359	440	799	8	86	34	0.65	281	98	57		5.62	-8.5
02	aaa	525	62	161	15	82	0	307			$19	345	463	808	6	88	33	0.48	287	108	24		5.88	2.1
03	ARI	* 373	41	100	7	40	1	268	291	268	$6	364	405	768	13	78	33	0.69	252	101	33	1.48	5.15	-3.9
1st Half		196	18	56	4	22	0	286			$4	364	429	792	11	73	37	0.46	236	105	14		5.56	0.3
2nd Half		177	23	44	3	18	1	249			$2	364	379	742	15	84	28	1.10	265	97	42		4.71	-4.2
04	Proj	**350**	**41**	**92**	**7**	**45**	**1**	**263**			**$7**	**339**	**404**	**743**	**10**	**83**	**30**	**0.70**	**262**	**102**	**40**		**4.72**	**-9.2**

4-28-.276 in 254 AB at ARI. Was batting .286 on July 1 when he went into a sub-Mendoza funk resulting in a demotion. There are still small signs of growth but may not hit enough to hold down a regular 1B job.

Owens,Eric

Pos CF RF
Age 33 Decline
Bats R
R: Very High
I: CON
S: PT stb
K: age
LIMA F BA: 60%

Yr	Tm	AB	R	H	HR	RBI	SB	Avg	vL	vR	R$	OB	Slg	OPS	bb%	ct%	h%	Eye	xBA	PX	SX	G/F	RC/G	RAR
99	SD	440	55	117	9	61	33	266	231	281	$18	324	391	715	8	89	28	0.76	290	81	122	2.04	4.55	3.1
00	SD	583	87	171	6	51	29	293	307	287	$19	344	381	725	7	89	32	0.71	275	53	132	2.82	4.58	4.3
01	FLA	400	51	101	5	28	8	253	274	244	$5	303	335	638	7	85	29	0.49	254	55	82	2.53	3.34	-6.1
02	FLA	385	44	104	4	37	26	270	266	271	$15	325	366	691	7	91	29	0.94	296	65	142	2.74	4.14	-8.3
03	ANA	241	29	65	1	20	11	270	308	214	$6	299	307	606	4	90	30	0.42	277	28	84	1.89	2.96	-12.8
1st Half		125	15	29	1	12	8	232			$3	262	280	542	4	90	25	0.42	283	33	99		2.12	-10.5
2nd Half		116	14	36	0	8	3	310			$3	339	336	675	4	90	35	0.42	270	23	65		4.07	-2.1
04	**Proj**	**250**	**30**	**68**	**2**	**21**	**9**	**272**			**$6**	**313**	**335**	**648**	**6**	**90**	**30**	**0.57**	**283**	**43**	**92**		**3.60**	**-8.4**

Terrific contact hitter, but had nothing behind those swings in '03. Only 7 extra base hits all season, combined with declining speed skills, leaves him to the end-game scrap heap.

Palmeiro,Orlando

Pos RF LF
Age 35 Decline
Bats L
R: Moderate
I: CON
S: stb
K: age
LIMA D BA: 70%

Yr	Tm	AB	R	H	HR	RBI	SB	Avg	vL	vR	R$	OB	Slg	OPS	bb%	ct%	h%	Eye	xBA	PX	SX	G/F	RC/G	RAR
99	ANA	317	46	88	1	23	5	278	200	287	$4	357	331	688	11	91	30	1.30	235	40	71	1.49	4.02	-8.7
00	ANA	243	38	73	0	25	4	300	258	307	$5	395	399	794	14	92	33	1.90	304	76	93	1.35	5.79	5.9
01	ANA	230	29	56	2	23	6	243	67	256	$3	318	322	639	10	90	26	1.04	262	55	78	1.43	3.22	-12.4
02	ANA	263	35	79	0	31	7	300	412	284	$8	372	354	726	10	92	33	1.36	256	43	85	1.25	4.85	-1.2
03	STL	317	37	86	3	33	3	271	182	290	$5	338	347	685	9	90	29	1.03	283	54	60	1.45	4.01	-14.7
1st Half		175	22	49	1	18	1	280			$3	351	354	705	10	91	30	1.19	286	55	65		4.34	-6.3
2nd Half		142	15	37	2	15	2	261			$2	323	338	661	8	89	28	0.87	279	54	49		3.62	-8.3
04	**Proj**	**250**	**31**	**71**	**2**	**26**	**4**	**284**			**$6**	**354**	**356**	**710**	**10**	**90**	**31**	**1.13**	**285**	**53**	**73**		**4.40**	**-7.7**

Another great contact hitter, and incredibly consistent, whose BPIs will probably remain stable going into '04. Normally we'd project some skills erosion at 35, but this particular type of skill set tends to hold up well.

Palmeiro,Rafael

Pos 1B
Age 39 Decline
Bats L
R: Very Low
I:
S:
K: AGE
LIMA B BA: 75%

Yr	Tm	AB	R	H	HR	RBI	SB	Avg	vL	vR	R$	OB	Slg	OPS	bb%	ct%	h%	Eye	xBA	PX	SX	G/F	RC/G	RAR
99	TEX	565	96	183	47	148	2	324	274	341	$37	423	630	1053	15	88	30	1.41	334	171	31	0.61	9.84	61.4
00	TEX	565	102	163	39	120	2	288	326	276	$25	398	558	956	15	86	28	1.34	300	148	62	0.69	7.93	31.4
01	TEX	600	98	164	47	123	1	273	272	274	$28	378	563	941	14	85	25	1.12	301	166	27	0.64	7.44	22.2
02	TEX	546	99	149	43	105	2	273	220	295	$26	389	571	961	16	83	26	1.11	284	174	44	0.48	7.83	30.6
03	TEX	561	92	146	38	112	2	260	282	251	$22	357	508	865	13	86	24	1.09	287	139	59	0.71	6.27	14.5
1st Half		267	50	70	19	52	1	262			$11	375	521	895	15	87	24	1.33	292	148	43		6.77	10.7
2nd Half		294	42	76	19	60	1	259			$11	339	497	836	11	86	24	0.88	281	131	62		5.82	3.8
04	**Proj**	**550**	**92**	**153**	**35**	**101**	**1**	**278**			**$23**	**377**	**514**	**891**	**14**	**85**	**27**	**1.03**	**282**	**134**	**41**		**6.84**	**18.3**

At face value, an overall decline, but at 39, only power is not likely to rebound. Low hit rate, high contact rate and xBA all point to a better BA in 2004.

Palmer,Dean

Pos DH
Age 35 Decline
Bats R
R: High
I: CON
S: PT
K: age
LIMA F BA: 45%

Yr	Tm	AB	R	H	HR	RBI	SB	Avg	vL	vR	R$	OB	Slg	OPS	bb%	ct%	h%	Eye	xBA	PX	SX	G/F	RC/G	RAR
99	DET	560	92	147	38	100	3	263	390	235	$20	331	518	848	9	73	30	0.37	260	143	66	0.84	5.82	10.3
00	DET	524	73	134	29	102	4	256	228	264	$16	339	471	810	11	72	30	0.45	230	119	66	0.82	5.44	5.5
01	DET	216	34	48	11	40	4	222	340	184	$6	309	426	735	11	73	25	0.46	238	121	68	0.76	4.33	-6.0
02	DET	12	0	0	0	0	0	0			($1)	77	0	77	8	58	0	0.20	487				0.00	-2.6
03	DET	86	3	12	0	6	0	140	189	102	($3)	221	163	384	9	67	21	0.32	139	20	8	1.00	1.07	-10.3
1st Half		86	3	12	0	6	0	140			($3)	221	163	384	9	67	21	0.32	139	20	8		1.07	-10.3
2nd Half		0	0	0	0	0	0	0			($0)					0			0					
04	**Proj**	**150**	**17**	**35**	**6**	**23**	**1**	**233**			**$3**	**313**	**393**	**705**	**10**	**71**	**29**	**0.40**	**159**	**95**	**39**		**4.07**	**-4.1**

This projection is a gift, and is probably a 20% percentage play at this point. He'll make his retirement decision this winter, and odds are in favor of zeroing out that bottom line.

Patterson,Corey

Pos CF
Age 24 Growth
Bats L
R: High
I: exp CON
S: pt
K: age
LIMA C+ BA: 30%

Yr	Tm	AB	R	H	HR	RBI	SB	Avg	vL	vR	R$	OB	Slg	OPS	bb%	ct%	h%	Eye	xBA	PX	SX	G/F	RC/G	RAR
99		0	0	0	0	0	0	0								0								
00	CHC	* 486	78	113	21	80	27	233		194	$17	299	428	727	9	74	27	0.37	259	113	136	1.30	3.93	-6.1
01	CHC	* 498	83	114	10	42	21	229	267	208	$9	275	343	619	6	83	26	0.37	263	73	134	0.91	3.06	-12.2
02	CHC	592	71	150	14	54	18	253	188	275	$14	277	392	668	3	76	31	0.13	258	93	137	1.54	3.77	-19.3
03	CHC	329	49	98	13	55	16	298	289	301	$19	328	511	839	4	77	36	0.19	283	127	193	1.20	6.00	9.4
1st Half		312	48	94	13	55	15	301			$18	331	522	854	4	76	36	0.19	285	131	200		6.28	11.3
2nd Half		17	1	4	0	0	1	235			$0	278	294	572	6	82	29	0.33	251	53	69		2.25	-1.5
04	**Proj**	**550**	**84**	**146**	**22**	**79**	**24**	**265**			**$23**	**305**	**456**	**761**	**5**	**78**	**30**	**0.26**	**282**	**116**	**150**		**4.72**	**0.0**

Partial ACL tear ended it early, but was this breakout season for real? Thumbs up on the power, but low ct%, elevated hit rate, and monthly BAs of .277, .333, .269 give thumbs down on any idea of a .300 BA.

Payton,Jay

Pos LF
Age 31 Past Peak
Bats R
R: X HIGH
I: CON
S: PT STB
K:
LIMA C+ BA: 55%

Yr	Tm	AB	R	H	HR	RBI	SB	Avg	vL	vR	R$	OB	Slg	OPS	bb%	ct%	h%	Eye	xBA	PX	SX	G/F	RC/G	RAR
99	aaa	152	22	48	6	27	3	316			$7	354	526	880	6	91	32	0.64	323	134	83	0.67	6.71	6.9
00	NYM	488	63	142	17	62	5	291	365	271	$15	332	447	779	6	88	30	0.50	269	94	50	1.32	4.90	-4.4
01	NYM	361	44	92	8	34	4	255	261	253	$6	290	371	661	5	86	28	0.35	273	74	73	1.59	3.60	-22.3
02	2NL	445	69	135	16	59	7	303	252	326	$19	346	488	834	6	88	32	0.54	312	114	130	1.52	6.05	-4.1
03	COL	600	93	181	28	89	6	302	288	307	$26	348	512	860	7	87	31	0.56	327	128	93	1.38	6.40	13.5
1st Half		306	57	90	11	33	3	294			$10	343	464	808	7	87	31	0.58	312	100	122		5.67	0.7
2nd Half		294	36	91	17	56	3	310			$16	354	561	915	6	87	31	0.54	341	157	56		7.20	12.9
04	**Proj**	**550**	**80**	**168**	**22**	**78**	**5**	**305**			**$23**	**348**	**498**	**846**	**6**	**87**	**32**	**0.52**	**325**	**118**	**91**		**6.29**	**8.1**

Coors advantage? Hit 15 of his 28 HRs in August/Sept, and 9 of them on the road. G/F does not indicate any more power upside, so at 31, this is probably the best that we're going to see.

Pena,Carlos

Pos 1B
Age 25 Pre-Peak
Bats L
R: Very High
I: EXP con
S: pt STB
K: age
LIMA B BA: 40%

Yr	Tm	AB	R	H	HR	RBI	SB	Avg	vL	vR	R$	OB	Slg	OPS	bb%	ct%	h%	Eye	xBA	PX	SX	G/F	RC/G	RAR
99	0	0	0	0	0	0	0	0								0								
00	aa	529	103	151	27	92	11	285			$22	391	512	904	15	83	30	1.03	302	134	100		7.31	24.7
01	aaa	431	59	117	21	62	9	271			$16	372	513	885	14	77	31	0.69	281	151	80	1.43	6.65	5.6
02	2AL	* 572	65	131	26	76	4	229	265	230	$11	301	427	728	9	74	26	0.40	251	115	85	0.85	4.22	-28.5
03	DET	452	51	112	18	50	4	248	208	267	$9	327	440	767	10	73	30	0.43	243	113	97	0.88	4.71	-9.0
1st Half		175	15	44	6	20	3	251			$4	321	406	727	9	75	30	0.42	243	97	40		4.33	-5.5
2nd Half		277	36	68	12	30	1	245			$5	330	462	792	11	71	30	0.44	244	123	132		4.96	-3.5
04	**Proj**	**550**	**68**	**138**	**24**	**70**	**6**	**251**			**$14**	**335**	**455**	**789**	**11**	**75**	**29**	**0.50**	**257**	**121**	**89**		**5.09**	**-9.3**

Only very minor growth, and you'd have to think that a losing environment has to play at least a small part. 2nd half showed a bit more life, but his low BA is the biggest concern right now.

Pena,Wily Mo

Pos CF
Age 22 Growth
Bats R
R: Very High
I: EXP con
S: pt stb
K: AGE
LIMA F BA: 30%

Yr	Tm	AB	R	H	HR	RBI	SB	Avg	vL	vR	R$	OB	Slg	OPS	bb%	ct%	h%	Eye	xBA	PX	SX	G/F	RC/G	RAR
99		0	0	0	0	0	0	0								0								
00		0	0	0	0	0	0	0								0								
01		0	0	0	0	0	0	0								0								
02	aa	388	40	96	9	40	6	247			$7	300	384	684	7	76	30	0.32	246	94	80		3.99	-9.6
03	CIN	* 216	34	56	9	28	3	259	204	225	$6	310	435	746	7	71	32	0.26	237	107	92	1.44	4.54	-2.8
1st Half		34	8	3	0	2	1	88			($1)	114	147	261	3	56	16	0.07	180	53	303		0.52	-5.4
2nd Half		182	26	53	9	26	2	291			$8	345	489	834	8	74	35	0.32	250	117	75		5.88	4.6
04	**Proj**	**250**	**32**	**63**	**10**	**32**	**3**	**252**			**$6**	**307**	**425**	**732**	**7**	**75**	**30**	**0.32**	**243**	**107**	**76**		**4.39**	**-2.4**

5-16-.218 in 165 AB at CIN, but was 0-4-.156 in 77 AB coming into Sept. Late impressions can be good, but a free-swinging power hitter with a ground ball tendency is not a good combination.

Peralta,Jhonny

Pos SS
Age 21 Growth
Bats R
R: High
I: EXP con
S: stb
K: AGE
LIMA F BA: 35%

Yr	Tm	AB	R	H	HR	RBI	SB	Avg	vL	vR	R$	OB	Slg	OPS	bb%	ct%	h%	Eye	xBA	PX	SX	G/F	RC/G	RAR
99		0	0	0	0	0	0	0								0								
00		0	0	0	0	0	0	0								0								
01		0	0	0	0	0	0	0								0								
02	aa	470	58	132	15	58	4	281			$14	340	449	789	8	82	32	0.50	273	109	77		5.37	15.1
03	CLE	* 479	49	119	5	42	2	248	260	213	$3	298	336	634	7	78	31	0.33	231	61	52	1.76	3.24	-17.1
1st Half		261	27	68	1	22	1	261			$2	303	330	633	6	83	31	0.36	238	53	53		3.29	-8.7
2nd Half		218	22	51	4	20	1	234			$1	292	344	636	8	73	30	0.31	223	72	57		3.17	-8.4
04	**Proj**	**250**	**28**	**60**	**5**	**26**	**1**	**240**			**$2**	**296**	**360**	**657**	**7**	**79**	**28**	**0.39**	**238**	**79**	**59**		**3.47**	**-7.4**

4-21-.227 in 242 AB at CLE. Slated to go through the Jody Gerut School of Body-Building this winter. That'll work just fine so long as they also teach him how to get on base and hit RHers better.

Perez,Antonio

Pos 2B | Age 20 Green | Bats R
R: X HIGH | I: EXP con | S: pt stb | K: AGE
LIMA D | BA: 40%

Yr	Tm	AB	R	H	HR	RBI	SB	Avg	vL	vR	R$	OB	Slg	OPS	bb%	ct%	h%	Eye	xBA	PX	SX	G/F	RC/G	RAR
99		0	0	0	0	0	0	0								0								
00		0	0	0	0	0	0	0								0								
01	aa	21	3	3	0	0	0	143			($1)	143	143	286	0	67	21	0.00	168				0.61	-2.4
02	aa	240	30	59	2	24	15	246			$7	279	313	591	4	74	33	0.17	215	47	121		2.72	-11.2
03	TAM	*340	58	88	9	39	9	259	237	258	$8	342	429	771	11	75	32	0.50	251	110	134	1.00	5.04	9.1
1st Half		229	41	61	7	27	5	266			$6	339	463	801	10	75	33	0.43	261	127	137		5.39	8.4
2nd Half		111	17	27	2	12	4	243			$2	349	360	709	14	75	31	0.64	230	75	112		4.32	0.6
04	Proj	250	37	61	4	27	9	244			$5	314	360	674	9	74	31	0.40	241	75	119		3.75	-2.7

2-12-4-.248 in 125 AB at TAM, not bad for a 20-year-old. But 2nd half drop-off shows that there's still work to be done.

Perez,Eddie

Pos CA | Age 35 Decline | Bats R
R: X HIGH | I: CON | S: PT stb | K: age
LIMA F | BA: 50%

Yr	Tm	AB	R	H	HR	RBI	SB	Avg	vL	vR	R$	OB	Slg	OPS	bb%	ct%	h%	Eye	xBA	PX	SX	G/F	RC/G	RAR
99	ATL	309	30	77	7	30	0	249			$2	288	372	661	5	87	27	0.43	273	83	22	1.37	3.64	-2.9
00	ATL	22	0	4	0	3	0	182			($0)	182	227	409	0	91	20	0.00	238	39		1.29	1.29	-1.9
01	ATL	*48	6	15	3	4	0	313			$2	313	521	833	0	75	36	0.00	251	112		1.33	6.04	3.3
02	CLE	117	6	25	0	4	0	214	222	208	($2)	246	291	536	4	79	27	0.20	231	67		1.28	2.32	-4.7
03	MIL	350	26	95	12	45	0	271	342	252	$9	305	429	734	5	87	29	0.36	278	100	21	1.54	4.52	2.3
1st Half		180	18	54	8	34	0	300			$8	326	467	793	4	87	31	0.29	277	94	41		5.41	5.6
2nd Half		170	8	41	4	11	0	241			$1	283	388	672	6	86	26	0.43	279	105	1		3.70	-3.0
04	Proj	250	17	61	5	21	0	244			$2	279	366	645	5	84	27	0.30	271	87	16		3.43	-5.0

We estimate that fantasy league success is about 30% luck -- our job is to maximize the other 70%. This season falls well into the 30%. There's no way we could have projected it, and at 35, odds of a repeat are slim.

Perez,Eduardo

Pos RF | Age 34 Decline | Bats R
R: X HIGH | I: exp CON | S: pt STB | K: age
LIMA F | BA: 45%

Yr	Tm	AB	R	H	HR	RBI	SB	Avg	vL	vR	R$	OB	Slg	OPS	bb%	ct%	h%	Eye	xBA	PX	SX	G/F	RC/G	RAR
99	aaa	416	42	94	12	52	5	226			$4	276	365	642	7	79	26	0.33	255	89	47	1.63	3.09	-24.5
00	STL	*368	54	98	19	62	9	266	200	344	$14	341	473	814	10	84	27	0.72	294	116	85	1.46	5.46	3.5
01	JPN	167	19	34	2	18	3	206			($0)	279	304	583	9	71	28	0.35	220	72	67		2.74	-13.2
02	STL	154	22	31	10	26	0	201	271	143	$3	281	455	735	10	77	19	0.47	268	159	30	0.90	4.07	-5.9
03	STL	253	47	72	10	41	5	285	353	238	$10	358	466	825	10	79	33	0.55	283	118	79	1.10	5.91	2.1
1st Half		135	26	39	4	17	1	289			$4	360	437	797	10	76	35	0.47	261	99	64		5.53	-0.3
2nd Half		118	21	33	6	24	4	280			$6	356	500	856	11	82	30	0.67	307	140	81		6.32	2.4
04	Proj	150	24	37	6	24	2	247			$4	321	436	757	10	78	28	0.50	282	121	67		4.71	-3.4

A season pretty much on par with his BPIs, but he's essentially an interchangeable part. Some years better, some years worse, all years about $1 on draft day.

Perez,Neifi

Pos 2B SS | Age 30 Past Peak | Bats S
R: High | I: CON | S: pt STB | K:
LIMA D | BA: 70%

Yr	Tm	AB	R	H	HR	RBI	SB	Avg	vL	vR	R$	OB	Slg	OPS	bb%	ct%	h%	Eye	xBA	PX	SX	G/F	RC/G	RAR
99	COL	690	108	193	12	70	13	280	230	301	$15	308	403	711	4	92	29	0.52	286	75	139	1.09	4.36	2.8
00	COL	651	92	187	10	71	3	287	357	266	$13	319	427	746	4	90	31	0.48	291	88	107	0.98	4.70	6.2
01	2TM	581	83	162	8	59	9	279	266	284	$13	310	396	706	4	88	30	0.38	279	73	130	0.83	4.23	3.2
02	KC	554	65	131	3	37	8	236	227	240	$2	263	303	566	3	90	26	0.38	266	46	97	1.05	2.52	-25.8
03	SF	328	27	84	1	31	3	256	253	257	$3	287	348	634	4	93	27	0.61	303	67	92	1.36	3.37	-10.0
1st Half		182	21	51	0	18	3	280			$3	303	374	677	3	93	30	0.46	307	69	126		3.91	-2.6
2nd Half		146	6	33	1	13	0	226			($1)	266	315	581	5	93	24	0.80	295	66	30		2.76	-7.3
04	Proj	300	30	80	2	27	3	267			$4	297	358	655	4	91	29	0.51	300	65	90		3.61	-6.2

A true oddity of a season. At face value, as valueless as always, but 93% contact rate and large number of line drives helped boost his xBA over .300. For real? Doubtful. But if he hits .300 in '04, you read it here first.

Perez,Timo

Pos LF CF | Age 29 Past Peak | Bats L
R: High | I: CON | S: pt stb | K:
LIMA D | BA: 65%

Yr	Tm	AB	R	H	HR	RBI	SB	Avg	vL	vR	R$	OB	Slg	OPS	bb%	ct%	h%	Eye	xBA	PX	SX	G/F	RC/G	RAR
99	JPN	23	2	4	0	2	0	162			($1)	242	162	404	10	87	19	0.81	227		28		1.19	-2.9
00	NYM	*340	50	108	6	35	12	318	125	317	$14	348	453	801	4	92	33	0.59	304	86	118	1.06	5.49	2.6
01	NYM	*431	61	124	10	40	15	288	154	258	$15	324	415	739	5	90	30	0.53	289	79	112	1.14	4.64	-13.0
02	NYM	444	52	131	8	47	10	295	156	318	$15	330	437	767	5	92	31	0.64	305	98	118	1.06	5.05	-16.6
03	NYM	346	32	93	4	42	5	269	172	278	$7	305	367	672	5	92	28	0.62	297	75	51	1.21	3.68	-19.3
1st Half		119	11	30	1	14	0	252			$1	299	319	619	6	87	28	0.50	264	51	34		2.90	-9.7
2nd Half		227	21	63	3	28	5	278			$6	308	392	700	4	94	28	0.77	315	88	62		4.14	-9.5
04	Proj	300	33	85	5	33	6	283			$8	319	403	722	5	91	30	0.60	302	84	87		4.35	-12.2

Great contact hitter, but keep him far, far away from LHers. BPIs were off a bit in '03, and by all rights, he should not be seeing more than about 250 AB per year, for the value of his contribution.

Perez,Tomas

Pos 3B 2B | Age 30 Past Peak | Bats R
R: High | I: exp con | S: PT stb | K:
LIMA F | BA: 50%

Yr	Tm	AB	R	H	HR	RBI	SB	Avg	vL	vR	R$	OB	Slg	OPS	bb%	ct%	h%	Eye	xBA	PX	SX	G/F	RC/G	RAR
99	aaa	296	24	67	3	32	2	226			($0)	266	314	580	5	88	25	0.44	268	62	54		2.70	-15.3
00	PHI	*419	53	107	8	59	4	255	304	205	$7	297	387	684	6	83	29	0.35	272	85	89	1.50	3.90	-5.1
01	PHI	135	11	41	3	19	0	304	354	276	$4	338	437	775	5	84	35	0.32	276	84	48	1.10	5.24	2.4
02	PHI	221	24	56	5	21	1	253	250	250	$3	318	389	707	9	81	29	0.51	284	95	59	1.05	4.26	-2.2
03	PHI	298	39	79	5	33	0	265	266	265	$4	318	379	697	7	82	31	0.43	267	80	51	1.41	4.12	-1.1
1st Half		103	13	34	1	12	0	330			$3	367	427	794	6	84	38	0.38	269	67	66		5.97	4.6
2nd Half		195	26	45	4	21	0	231			$1	292	354	646	8	81	27	0.45	265	87	44		3.35	-5.3
04	Proj	250	29	67	5	28	0	268			$4	319	388	707	7	82	31	0.43	269	82	53		4.26	-1.0

Consistent mediocrity, any time his name comes up at the draft table, it's always with a muffled choking sound, and usually when the beer is all gone.

Perry,Herbert

Pos 1B | Age 34 Decline | Bats R
R: X HIGH | I: CON | S: PT STB | K: age
LIMA F | BA: 65%

Yr	Tm	AB	R	H	HR	RBI	SB	Avg	vL	vR	R$	OB	Slg	OPS	bb%	ct%	h%	Eye	xBA	PX	SX	G/F	RC/G	RAR
99	TAM	*312	47	83	11	49	0	266		259	$7	312	436	748	6	81	30	0.36	269	105	51	1.53	4.73	-9.5
00	2AL	411	71	124	12	62	4	302	296	303	$13	340	467	807	6	82	35	0.32	290	106	85	1.35	5.81	-1.5
01	CHW	285	38	73	7	32	2	256	256	256	$5	312	411	722	7	81	30	0.42	276	104	64	1.35	4.29	-15.5
02	TEX	450	64	124	22	77	4	276	260	282	$17	326	480	806	7	85	28	0.52	298	122	65	1.26	5.47	-5.1
03	TEX	*58	4	11	1	6	0	190	154	182	($1)	217	276	493	3	88	20	0.29	255	56	21	1.13	1.88	-6.4
1st Half		58	4	11	1	6	0	190			($1)	217	276	493	3	88	20	0.29	255	56	21		1.88	-6.4
2nd Half		0	0	0	0	0	0	0			($0)					0			0					
04	Proj	250	31	67	7	33	1	268			$6	310	419	729	6	84	29	0.38	271	96	61		4.50	-8.4

Some of your fellow owners will gaze longingly over the promise of his 2002 season and cough up an extra buck. You need to say to yourself, "34 years old, has seen 400 AB only twice in his career, is it worth the risk?"

Petrick,Ben

Pos LF | Age 27 Peak | Bats R
R: Moderate | I: EXP CON | S: stb | K:
LIMA F | BA: 55%

Yr	Tm	AB	R	H	HR	RBI	SB	Avg	vL	vR	R$	OB	Slg	OPS	bb%	ct%	h%	Eye	xBA	PX	SX	G/F	RC/G	RAR
99	COL	*412	66	128	25	74	10	311	333	320	$23	383	573	955	10	85	32	0.79	312	152	104	1.29	7.77	31.1
00	COL	*394	59	120	11	53	6	305	354	306	$14	373	480	853	10	85	34	0.72	294	113	87	1.12	6.42	13.1
01	COL	*273	48	73	12	45	4	237	213	250	$7	325	429	753	11	74	28	0.49	255	114	108	0.97	4.54	-10.7
02	COL	*360	43	97	18	46	6	269	250	163	$13	334	494	829	9	78	30	0.44	276	140	94	1.35	5.29	-11.6
03	2TM	*350	45	82	14	41	3	234	259	188	$6	287	426	713	7	80	25	0.38	273	120	76	1.03	3.85	-17.2
1st Half		211	24	53	10	26	2	251			$5	295	483	778	6	84	26	0.38	300	144	82		4.49	-6.2
2nd Half		139	21	29	4	15	1	209			$0	276	338	614	9	75	25	0.37	234	83	66		2.95	-10.9
04	Proj	150	21	37	6	19	2	247			$3	312	436	748	9	78	28	0.44	272	116	82		4.39	-4.7

4-12-.221 in 122 AB at COL and DET. Declined a suggestion to go to winter ball because, apparently, he's too good for that. If you can't make it in COL and bat under .230 in DET, isn't that enough of a message?

Phelps,Josh

Pos DH | Age 25 Pre-Peak | Bats R
R: High | I: EXP con | S: pt stb | K: age
LIMA C | BA: 35%

Yr	Tm	AB	R	H	HR	RBI	SB	Avg	vL	vR	R$	OB	Slg	OPS	bb%	ct%	h%	Eye	xBA	PX	SX	G/F	RC/G	RAR
99		0	0	0	0	0	0	0								0								
00	aa	184	18	38	7	22	1	207			$1	251	380	632	6	73	24	0.22	248	102	66		3.10	-11.4
01	aa	498	82	130	26	82	4	261			$17	349	492	841	12	77	29	0.59	275	141	62		5.83	8.7
02	TOR	*522	81	150	34	109	0	287	286	315	$25	344	567	911	8	72	34	0.30	270	169	45	0.97	6.98	21.2
03	TOR	396	57	106	20	66	1	268	317	239	$13	333	470	803	9	71	33	0.34	264	119	47	1.37	5.36	8.5
1st Half		240	38	65	10	32	0	271			$6	332	454	786	8	70	35	0.31	258	111	57		5.09	3.3
2nd Half		156	19	41	10	34	1	263			$7	335	494	829	10	72	30	0.39	274	131	31		5.77	5.2
04	Proj	500	71	132	25	85	1	264			$16	330	472	803	9	72	32	0.36	269	125	44		5.36	5.3

Bad things about 2003:
- Only minor improvement in batting eye and plate patience.
- No improvement in contact rate
- Increased GB tendency may hurt his power numbers.
- Only real skilll he has is power

Phillips,Brandon

Pos 2B
Age 22 Growth
Bats R
R X HIGH | I EXP con | S pt stb | K AGE
LIMA D BA: 60%

	Tm	AB	R	H	HR	RBI	SB	Avg	vL	vR	R$	OB	Slg	OPS	bb%	ct%	h%	Eye	xBA	PX	SX	G/F	RC/G	RAR
99		0	0	0	0	0	0	0								0								
00		0	0	0	0	0	0	0								0								
01	aa	265	32	77	6	33	12	291			$11	319	430	749	4	87	32	0.31	284	96	82		4.63	4.6
02	a/a	503	67	153	18	64	14	304			$23	343	479	822	6	86	32	0.44	292	115	85		5.97	24.2
03	CLE	* 524	50	104	9	46	10	198	179	218	($0)	236	302	538	5	82	23	0.27	247	69	79	1.26	2.16	-33.2
1st Half		261	26	55	4	22	4	211			($0)	243	310	553	4	82	24	0.23	246	67	84		2.40	-14.2
2nd Half		263	24	49	5	24	6	186			($1)	230	293	523	5	81	21	0.31	247	72	70		1.94	-19.0
04	Proj	**400**	**45**	**99**	**10**	**43**	**11**	**248**			**$8**	**285**	**384**	**669**	**5**	**84**	**27**	**0.33**	**258**	**89**	**83**		**3.57**	**-6.4**

6-33-4-.208 in 370 AB at CLE, and no better at AAA. Low hit rate says that some of this was bad luck, but BPIs were off across the board anyway. He'll bounce back, but don't bet on a Blalock level rebound in '04.

Phillips,Jason L.

Pos 1B CA
Age 27 Peak
Bats R
R X HIGH | I EXP con | S PT STB | K
LIMA D+ BA: 55%

	Tm	AB	R	H	HR	RBI	SB	Avg	vL	vR	R$	OB	Slg	OPS	bb%	ct%	h%	Eye	xBA	PX	SX	G/F	RC/G	RAR
99	aa	141	11	28	6	19	0	199			$0	257	362	618	7	87	19	0.61	281	95		0.83	2.95	-11.5
00	aa	98	15	36	0	12	0	367			$4	404	398	802	6	90	41	0.60	251	26	34	0.83	6.48	2.0
01	a/a	383	44	102	11	60	0	266			$9	325	410	734	8	92	27	1.06	293	93	25	1.50	4.57	-18.0
02	aaa	342	34	87	12	59	1	254			$9	298	421	719	6	92	25	0.72	301	107	45	1.50	4.30	-14.3
03	NYM	* 481	56	144	15	75	0	299	308	294	$17	364	455	819	9	88	32	0.83	283	105	20	1.14	5.99	6.3
1st Half		218	26	67	7	31	0	307			$8	386	463	849	11	88	32	1.08	283	104	18		6.59	6.4
2nd Half		263	30	77	8	44	0	293			$9	345	449	794	7	87	31	0.64	283	105	24		5.50	-0.1
04	Proj	**450**	**49**	**130**	**17**	**71**	**0**	**289**			**$16**	**345**	**459**	**804**	**8**	**89**	**29**	**0.80**	**288**	**110**	**22**		**5.64**	**0.2**

11-58-.298 in 403 AB at NYM. Solid BPIs with little drop-off in his first season in the majors. Growth should continue so long as he keeps getting regular ABs. Upside: 20 HRs, .300 BA.

Piatt,Adam

Pos LF
Age 28 Peak
Bats R
R X HIGH | I EXP CON | S PT stb | K
LIMA F BA: 40%

	Tm	AB	R	H	HR	RBI	SB	Avg	vL	vR	R$	OB	Slg	OPS	bb%	ct%	h%	Eye	xBA	PX	SX	G/F	RC/G	RAR
99	a/a	494	101	147	29	108	6	298			$24	390	569	959	13	84	30	0.96	318	167	79		7.91	39.3
00	OAK	* 411	57	113	12	62	3	275	369	219	$10	349	433	782	10	76	33	0.48	252	92	99	1.10	5.22	1.5
01	OAK	* 204	20	44	1	18	2	216	245	167	($1)	292	304	596	10	77	28	0.47	233	67	69	1.24	2.94	-10.6
02	OAK	* 371	51	88	11	50	5	237	233	234	$7	306	383	689	9	85	25	0.66	272	94	62	1.18	3.77	-12.0
03	2AL	132	11	30	6	18	1	227	263	135	$2	277	462	739	6	65	30	0.20	259	155	33	1.17	3.96	-5.6
1st Half		60	2	13	2	8	0	217			$0	288	400	688	9	80	24	0.50	295	123	-9		3.75	-2.9
2nd Half		72	9	17	4	10	1	236			$2	267	514	781	4	53	38	0.09	223	182	69		4.03	-2.9
04	Proj	**250**	**28**	**65**	**9**	**33**	**2**	**260**			**$6**	**319**	**448**	**767**	**8**	**73**	**32**	**0.32**	**265**	**124**	**42**		**4.72**	**-2.6**

The aura of his 1999 line hovers over these stats like a tease. Is this a dormant skill set lying in wait, ready to break out? After all, "once you display a skill..." Or are 3 poor years too much to discount? Never give up hope...

Piazza,Mike

Pos CA
Age 35 Decline
Bats R
R Very Low | I | S pt | K age
LIMA C BA: 50%

	Tm	AB	R	H	HR	RBI	SB	Avg	vL	vR	R$	OB	Slg	OPS	bb%	ct%	h%	Eye	xBA	PX	SX	G/F	RC/G	RAR
99	NYM	534	100	162	40	124	2	303	298	305	$30	364	575	939	9	87	29	0.73	321	155	45	1.07	7.58	53.1
00	NYM	482	90	156	38	113	4	324	354	318	$32	396	614	1010	11	86	31	0.84	329	163	51	0.99	9.10	65.7
01	NYM	503	81	151	36	94	0	300	323	295	$26	382	573	955	12	83	30	0.77	307	157		1.06	7.86	60.3
02	NYM	478	69	134	33	98	0	280	286	278	$24	357	544	901	11	83	28	0.70	311	160	35	1.03	6.71	35.4
03	NYM	234	37	67	11	34	0	286	265	292	$8	379	483	862	13	83	31	0.88	275	123	27	1.13	6.54	14.7
1st Half		111	21	37	7	15	0	333			$6	417	613	1030	13	86	34	1.07	318	179	29		9.78	15.9
2nd Half		123	16	30	4	19	0	244			$2	345	366	711	13	80	28	0.76	238	73	24		4.26	-0.1
04	Proj	**400**	**62**	**115**	**23**	**70**	**0**	**288**			**$17**	**373**	**512**	**884**	**12**	**83**	**30**	**0.80**	**280**	**135**	**28**		**6.76**	**29.9**

HQ readers were all over us last March when we projected only 396 AB. Though that was STILL an overestimate, the point is, the breakdown was coming. And unless he moves to 1B, the risk will remain.

Pierre,Juan

Pos CF
Age 26 Pre-Peak
Bats L
R Moderate | I exp CON | S stb | K
LIMA C BA: 70%

	Tm	AB	R	H	HR	RBI	SB	Avg	vL	vR	R$	OB	Slg	OPS	bb%	ct%	h%	Eye	xBA	PX	SX	G/F	RC/G	RAR
99		0	0	0	0	0	0	0								0								
00	COL	* 656	83	215	0	49	48	328	500	284	$31	368	367	736	6	94	35	1.14	275	29	111	3.03	5.02	12.6
01	COL	617	108	202	2	55	46	327	289	337	$33	369	415	784	6	95	34	1.41	320	56	173	2.77	5.70	31.4
02	COL	592	90	170	1	35	47	287	294	285	$24	323	343	666	5	91	31	0.60	290	42	152	3.20	4.08	-13.5
03	FLA	668	100	204	1	41	65	305	311	303	$34	358	373	731	8	95	32	1.57	319	49	151	2.96	4.96	-0.4
1st Half		348	49	104	0	22	38	299			$19	351	362	713	7	95	32	1.47	317	46	155		4.79	-1.9
2nd Half		320	51	100	1	19	27	312			$16	366	384	750	8	95	33	1.69	321	52	140		5.15	1.6
04	Proj	**650**	**99**	**205**	**1**	**43**	**56**	**315**			**$33**	**370**	**381**	**751**	**8**	**94**	**33**	**1.42**	**317**	**47**	**146**		**5.28**	**10.2**

If you think it can't get better, think again. Extreme contact hitter, extreme speed, and only 26. He could bat .350 one day, and just imagine what that would do to his SB totals... Frightening.

Pierzynski,A.J.

Pos CA
Age 27 Peak
Bats L
R Moderate | I exp con | S pt stb | K
LIMA D+ BA: 50%

	Tm	AB	R	H	HR	RBI	SB	Avg	vL	vR	R$	OB	Slg	OPS	bb%	ct%	h%	Eye	xBA	PX	SX	G/F	RC/G	RAR
99	aaa	228	23	56	1	20	0	246			($0)	286	298	585	5	91	27	0.62	262	41	30	5.00	2.89	-7.6
00	MIN	* 471	61	139	8	60	2	295		321	$10	318	437	756	3	89	32	0.32	296	94	84	1.77	5.01	11.3
01	MIN	381	51	110	7	55	1	289	167	312	$10	317	441	758	4	85	32	0.28	297	107	58	1.20	4.63	8.4
02	MIN	440	54	132	6	49	1	300	270	308	$11	320	439	759	3	86	34	0.21	301	94	93	1.64	5.03	17.1
03	MIN	487	63	152	11	74	3	312	312	324	$17	344	464	808	5	89	33	0.44	314	102	75	1.59	5.92	24.0
1st Half		234	26	68	9	47	1	291			$9	320	483	803	4	90	29	0.43	328	115	81		5.47	9.0
2nd Half		253	37	84	2	27	2	332			$8	367	447	814	5	87	37	0.44	300	91	59		6.32	14.8
04	Proj	**450**	**58**	**136**	**11**	**60**	**2**	**302**			**$14**	**331**	**461**	**792**	**4**	**88**	**33**	**0.35**	**313**	**106**	**70**		**5.49**	**19.2**

Naggy injuries, including a bruised shoulder, ate into his power output in the 2nd half. Those power skills are on an upswing, but as a catcher, the iniury risk tempers continuation of that trend.

Podsednik,Scott

Pos CF
Age 28 Peak
Bats L
R X HIGH | I EXP CON | S PT stb | K
LIMA C+ BA: 40%

	Tm	AB	R	H	HR	RBI	SB	Avg	vL	vR	R$	OB	Slg	OPS	bb%	ct%	h%	Eye	xBA	PX	SX	G/F	RC/G	RAR
99	aa	116	9	16	0	1	5	138			($3)	167	172	339	3	91	15	0.36	262	30	105		0.85	-14.6
00	aa	169	17	38	2	10	16	225			$4	328	325	654	13	83	26	0.93	260	62	134		3.71	-4.1
01	aaa	276	41	69	2	29	11	250			$5	281	348	629	4	84	29	0.27	264	64	156	2.00	3.18	-9.8
02	aaa	458	56	111	8	57	30	242			$15	305	360	665	8	85	27	0.59	267	78	131	1.60	3.51	-18.6
03	MIL	558	100	174	9	58	43	312	270	329	$31	375	441	815	9	84	36	0.62	287	85	171	1.42	6.25	19.7
1st Half		228	42	75	3	24	16	329			$13	398	447	845	10	82	39	0.63	263	72	189		6.76	11.0
2nd Half		330	58	99	6	34	27	300			$18	358	436	795	8	85	34	0.60	295	94	155		5.91	8.6
04	Proj	**600**	**91**	**159**	**8**	**61**	**36**	**265**			**$21**	**325**	**374**	**699**	**8**	**84**	**30**	**0.56**	**268**	**71**	**151**		**4.16**	**-9.8**

There is no question that he will be overbid in 2004. Why? High 36% hit rate means his BA will come down, perhaps close to historical levels. That will take a cut out of his SB output, and hence, his value.

Polanco,Placido

Pos 2B 3B
Age 28 Peak
Bats R
R Moderate | I con | S pt stb | K
LIMA B BA: 75%

	Tm	AB	R	H	HR	RBI	SB	Avg	vL	vR	R$	OB	Slg	OPS	bb%	ct%	h%	Eye	xBA	PX	SX	G/F	RC/G	RAR
99	STL	* 340	40	91	1	28	3	268	346	237	$3	304	338	643	5	90	30	0.53	273	48	93	1.67	3.50	-7.1
00	STL	323	50	102	5	39	4	316	333	309	$11	348	418	766	5	92	33	0.62	293	63	93	2.04	5.23	7.6
01	STL	564	87	173	3	38	12	307	350	292	$15	336	383	719	4	92	33	0.58	291	54	117	2.31	4.77	14.0
02	2NL	548	75	158	9	49	5	288	338	270	$13	321	403	724	5	93	30	0.63	309	84	79	1.86	4.58	2.6
03	PHI	492	87	142	14	63	14	289	292	288	$19	345	447	792	8	92	29	1.11	331	105	123	1.75	5.62	16.8
1st Half		248	38	64	6	26	9	258			$7	321	407	728	8	90	27	0.96	323	106	101		4.71	2.2
2nd Half		244	49	78	8	37	5	320			$12	369	488	857	7	94	32	1.36	338	103	128		6.68	14.9
04	Proj	**500**	**81**	**152**	**15**	**55**	**15**	**304**			**$21**	**347**	**461**	**808**	**6**	**92**	**31**	**0.87**	**331**	**101**	**116**		**5.93**	**22.2**

Consistently high contact rate has helped build him into a more productive hitter overall. You needed to be patient with this one, which, admittedly, I was not. I don't mind being proven wrong when the BPIs are there.

Posada,Jorge

Pos CA
Age 32 Past Peak
Bats S
R Low | I con | S pt | K
LIMA C BA: 55%

	Tm	AB	R	H	HR	RBI	SB	Avg	vL	vR	R$	OB	Slg	OPS	bb%	ct%	h%	Eye	xBA	PX	SX	G/F	RC/G	RAR
99	NYY	379	50	93	12	57	1	245	303	225	$6	338	401	739	12	76	29	0.58	249	95	62	1.61	4.60	5.9
00	NYY	505	92	145	28	86	2	287	321	272	$18	412	527	938	17	70	36	0.71	269	141	48	1.20	7.69	50.2
01	NYY	484	59	134	22	95	2	277	272	279	$18	359	475	834	11	73	34	0.47	259	121	32	1.12	5.76	26.5
02	NYY	511	79	137	20	99	1	268	326	247	$17	368	468	836	14	72	34	0.57	257	129	49	1.14	6.01	35.2
03	NYY	481	83	135	30	101	1	281	295	276	$21	397	518	915	16	77	31	0.85	281	139	24	1.18	7.04	40.6
1st Half		243	45	60	16	49	1	247			$9	386	494	880	18	77	26	0.98	284	143	38		6.39	16.6
2nd Half		238	38	75	14	52	0	315			$13	409	542	951	14	77	36	0.70	279	134	20		7.78	24.1
04	Proj	**450**	**71**	**124**	**23**	**90**	**1**	**276**			**$17**	**381**	**495**	**876**	**15**	**75**	**32**	**0.67**	**275**	**132**	**37**		**6.46**	**32.6**

Excellent season, apex of a 3-year trend, and second overall to his 2000 campaign. However, at 32 and with the rigors of catching, this is probably the peak. Expect a slight drop-off in 2004.

Pratt,Todd

Pos CA | Age 37 Decline | Bats R
R: Very High | I: CON | S: pt, stb | K: AGE
LIMA F | BA: 30%

Yr	Tm	AB	R	H	HR	RBI	SB	Avg	vL	vR	R$	OB	Slg	OPS	bb%	ct%	h%	Eye	xBA	PX	SX	G/F	RC/G	RAR
99	NYM	140	18	41	3	21	2	293	279	299	$4	361	386	747	10	77	36	0.47	233	58	50	0.93	5.13	4.5
00	NYM	160	33	44	8	25	0	275	256	282	$5	363	463	825	12	81	30	0.71	250	106	43	1.39	5.90	8.7
01	2NL	173	18	32	4	11	1	185	250	165	($2)	319	301	619	16	65	26	0.56	176	74	36	0.98	3.03	-2.7
02	PHI	106	14	33	3	16	2	311	417	280	$5	438	500	938	18	74	40	0.86	258	142	45	0.91	8.29	11.9
03	PHI	125	16	34	4	20	0	272	267	274	$3	381	464	845	15	70	36	0.58	260	129	58	1.20	6.19	6.8
1st Half		53	5	14	1	13	0	264			$2	381	472	853	16	74	34	0.71	288	148	96		6.23	3.0
2nd Half		72	11	20	3	7	0	278			$2	381	458	839	14	67	38	0.50	240	115	25		6.16	3.8
04	**Proj**	**100**	**13**	**26**	**3**	**14**	**1**	**260**			**$2**	**376**	**431**	**807**	**16**	**71**	**34**	**0.64**	**259**	**119**	**35**		**5.63**	**4.4**

BPIs were on a late career upswing coming into 2003, and really had no place else to go but down. Still, "down" was not such a bad place... better this for a buck than 250 AB with a .220 BA.

Pujols,Albert

Pos RF 1B | Age 24 Growth | Bats R
R: Low | I: exp, con | S: | K: age
LIMA C | BA: 60%

Yr	Tm	AB	R	H	HR	RBI	SB	Avg	vL	vR	R$	OB	Slg	OPS	bb%	ct%	h%	Eye	xBA	PX	SX	G/F	RC/G	RAR
99		0	0	0	0	0	0	0								0								
00		0	0	0	0	0	0	0								0								
01	STL	590	112	194	37	130	1	329	279	342	$36	399	610	1009	10	84	34	0.74	326	168	64	1.09	9.09	55.3
02	STL	590	118	185	34	127	2	314	309	315	$34	388	561	949	11	88	31	1.04	343	159	60	1.27	7.91	41.9
03	STL	591	137	212	43	124	5	359	387	350	$45	434	667	1101	12	89	35	1.22	375	193	77	1.15	11.52	88.2
1st Half		303	74	117	23	72	0	386			$26	445	710	1154	10	91	37	1.23	389	204	44		12.95	53.9
2nd Half		288	63	95	20	52	5	330			$19	424	622	1045	14	86	33	1.21	358	180	89		10.18	34.6
04	**Proj**	**600**	**128**	**206**	**44**	**126**	**4**	**343**			**$42**	**419**	**650**	**1069**	**12**	**88**	**34**	**1.07**	**372**	**188**	**70**		**10.49**	**78.1**

The good things...
- Incredible stats fully supported by BPIs
- Consistent upward trend
- He might really be only 24

The bad thing...
- He's not on my team.

Punto,Nick

Pos SS | Age 26 Pre-Peak | Bats S
R: Very High | I: EXP, con | S: pt, STB | K:
LIMA F | BA: 40%

Yr	Tm	AB	R	H	HR	RBI	SB	Avg	vL	vR	R$	OB	Slg	OPS	bb%	ct%	h%	Eye	xBA	PX	SX	G/F	RC/G	RAR
99		0	0	0	0	0	0	0								0			0					
00	aa	456	61	103	4	37	26	226			$7	312	300	612	11	86	26	0.88	258	48	117		3.05	-12.7
01	aaa	468	53	106	1	36	31	226			$8	322	301	623	12	75	30	0.57	230	53	137	4.00	3.32	-9.4
02	aaa	449	62	111	1	24	35	247			$12	346	298	645	13	82	30	0.86	235	35	137		3.70	-7.3
03	PHI	* 203	31	53	1	12	8	261	278	179	$4	306	330	636	6	83	31	0.38	250	52	121	2.79	3.55	-3.3
1st Half		84	12	25	0	6	5	298			$3	322	381	703	3	82	36	0.20	256	64	150		4.83	1.7
2nd Half		119	19	28	1	6	3	235			$1	295	294	589	8	84	27	0.53	244	43	88		2.80	-4.8
04	**Proj**	**150**	**21**	**37**	**1**	**9**	**8**	**247**			**$3**	**318**	**313**	**630**	**9**	**82**	**30**	**0.58**	**248**	**48**	**122**		**3.45**	**-2.1**

1-4-.217 in 92 AB at PHI. Weak hitter but with decent on base skills, and burns the basepaths once he gets on. But did not make the jump well to the bigs and now it's questionable whether he ever will.

Quinlan,Robb

Pos 1B | Age 27 Peak | Bats R
R: High | I: EXP, con | S: stb | K:
LIMA D | BA: 45%

Yr	Tm	AB	R	H	HR	RBI	SB	Avg	vL	vR	R$	OB	Slg	OPS	bb%	ct%	h%	Eye	xBA	PX	SX	G/F	RC/G	RAR
99		0	0	0	0	0	0	0								0								
00		0	0	0	0	0	0	0								0								
01	aa	492	62	124	11	59	0	253			$7	309	400	709	8	86	27	0.59	279	93	63		4.04	-31.5
02	aaa	528	72	154	17	85	6	292			$20	331	468	799	6	87	31	0.44	291	110	117		5.56	-2.5
03	ANA	* 487	56	133	7	56	9	273	286	288	$11	309	374	682	5	87	30	0.40	261	65	95	1.81	3.93	-20.4
1st Half		303	32	82	4	42	6	271			$7	305	363	668	5	89	29	0.45	264	60	89		3.87	-13.2
2nd Half		184	24	51	3	14	3	277			$4	314	391	706	5	84	32	0.33	256	72	102		4.03	-7.3
04	**Proj**	**300**	**38**	**83**	**7**	**37**	**4**	**277**			**$7**	**317**	**410**	**727**	**6**	**86**	**30**	**0.43**	**266**	**83**	**95**		**4.45**	**-10.5**

0-4-.287 in 94 AB at ANA. Solid contact hitter was PCL MVP in 2002. BPIs are just "okay" for a 27-year-old, despite optimism in ANA. Don't get taken in.

Ramirez,Aramis

Pos 3B | Age 25 Pre-Peak | Bats R
R: High | I: CON | S: pt, stb | K: age
LIMA D+ | BA: 50%

Yr	Tm	AB	R	H	HR	RBI	SB	Avg	vL	vR	R$	OB	Slg	OPS	bb%	ct%	h%	Eye	xBA	PX	SX	G/F	RC/G	RAR
99	PIT	* 516	72	146	17	63	4	283	200	174	$14	361	459	820	11	90	29	1.19	306	115	59	1.15	5.82	21.3
00	PIT	* 421	44	120	9	57	2	285	238	262	$10	317	425	743	5	85	32	0.31	280	86	65	1.16	4.74	5.1
01	PIT	603	83	181	34	112	5	300	297	301	$30	344	536	879	6	83	31	0.40	283	142	49	0.88	6.58	33.3
02	PIT	522	51	122	18	71	2	234	260	226	$9	274	387	661	5	82	25	0.31	245	102	45	0.80	3.55	-16.3
03	2NL	607	75	165	27	106	2	272	285	268	$21	319	465	784	6	84	29	0.42	271	120	52	0.78	5.14	15.4
1st Half		299	36	86	7	47	1	288			$9	339	431	770	7	83	33	0.44	257	99	53		5.18	7.8
2nd Half		308	39	79	20	59	1	256			$12	300	497	796	6	85	24	0.40	284	139	49		5.05	7.2
04	**Proj**	**600**	**72**	**170**	**36**	**108**	**3**	**283**			**$27**	**328**	**522**	**850**	**6**	**84**	**29**	**0.40**	**278**	**144**	**42**		**6.03**	**27.7**

2nd half outburst shows what he is capable of. At 25, he's probably not ready to annualize that rate of productivity, but PX and G/F trends say it's coming, and soon.

Ramirez,Manny

Pos LF DH | Age 31 Past Peak | Bats R
R: Very Low | I: con | S: stb | K:
LIMA D+ | BA: 55%

Yr	Tm	AB	R	H	HR	RBI	SB	Avg	vL	vR	R$	OB	Slg	OPS	bb%	ct%	h%	Eye	xBA	PX	SX	G/F	RC/G	RAR
99	CLE	522	131	174	44	165	2	333	383	319	$38	437	663	1100	16	75	37	0.73	292	186	73	0.80	10.82	79.5
00	CLE	439	92	154	38	122	1	351	396	339	$32	457	697	1154	16	73	41	0.74	302	195	55	0.89	12.44	82.5
01	BOS	529	93	162	41	125	0	306	342	296	$31	398	609	1007	13	72	35	0.55	295	175	39	0.87	8.85	61.0
02	BOS	* 466	86	155	34	109	0	333	438	331	$31	429	620	1050	14	80	36	0.84	301	170	23	1.49	10.17	65.1
03	BOS	569	117	185	37	104	3	325	385	305	$32	423	587	1010	15	83	34	1.03	321	156	59	0.89	9.38	61.1
1st Half		294	66	94	17	61	1	320			$16	415	558	973	14	88	32	1.33	329	145	52		8.71	26.5
2nd Half		275	51	91	20	43	2	331			$16	432	618	1050	15	79	36	0.84	311	168	57		10.12	34.7
04	**Proj**	**550**	**108**	**180**	**36**	**117**	**2**	**327**			**$33**	**425**	**595**	**1021**	**15**	**79**	**36**	**0.83**	**313**	**159**	**49**		**9.56**	**65.3**

PX trend is pessimistic about him returning to the 40-HR level, but everything else supports these heavy duty batting averages. Keep riding him.

Randa,Joe

Pos 3B | Age 34 Decline | Bats R
R: Low | I: con | S: | K: age
LIMA C+ | BA: 60%

Yr	Tm	AB	R	H	HR	RBI	SB	Avg	vL	vR	R$	OB	Slg	OPS	bb%	ct%	h%	Eye	xBA	PX	SX	G/F	RC/G	RAR
99	KC	628	92	197	16	84	5	314		306	$21	364	473	837	7	87	34	0.63	304	98	101	1.08	6.30	32.0
00	KC	612	88	186	15	106	6	304	310	302	$20	343	438	781	6	89	32	0.55	290	81	87	1.24	5.45	17.7
01	KC	581	59	147	13	83	3	253	261	250	$10	303	386	689	7	86	27	0.53	280	88	53	1.27	3.96	-6.8
02	KC	549	63	155	11	80	2	282	321	270	$14	338	426	764	8	87	31	0.67	299	95	75	1.28	5.10	9.8
03	KC	502	80	146	16	72	1	291	311	282	$15	344	452	797	8	88	31	0.67	306	104	56	0.89	5.61	15.4
1st Half		274	42	67	9	30	1	245			$4	298	398	696	7	88	25	0.62	283	98	57		4.03	-3.9
2nd Half		228	38	79	7	42	0	346			$11	399	518	917	8	88	37	0.74	312	112	47		8.06	20.7
04	**Proj**	**550**	**77**	**164**	**19**	**88**	**1**	**298**			**$19**	**350**	**473**	**823**	**7**	**88**	**31**	**0.65**	**291**	**110**	**58**		**6.01**	**23.4**

Perennially underappreciated and always turns a profit. That will happen again in '04. Owners will see his age and low RBI total, and max their bidding at $10. You see his PX, G/F and xBA trends, and say $11.

Reboulet,Jeff

Pos 2B | Age 40 Decline | Bats R
R: X HIGH | I: CON | S: pt, STB | K: AGE
LIMA F | BA: 50%

Yr	Tm	AB	R	H	HR	RBI	SB	Avg	vL	vR	R$	OB	Slg	OPS	bb%	ct%	h%	Eye	xBA	PX	SX	G/F	RC/G	RAR
99	BAL	154	25	25	0	4	1	162	235	126	($5)	310	188	498	18	81	20	1.14	202	22	61	1.30	1.81	-10.9
00	KC	182	29	44	0	14	3	242	297	228	$0	327	280	607	11	82	29	0.72	229	32	74	2.05	3.11	-4.1
01	LA	214	35	57	3	22	0	266	290	246	$3	364	397	762	13	78	33	0.69	263	89	79	1.33	4.94	6.7
02	LA	* 111	12	25	1	4	1	225			($0)	295	288	583	9	78	28	0.46	227	48	51	0.72	2.85	-5.3
03	PIT	* 310	42	72	3	27	2	232	220	255	$1	308	310	618	10	82	28	0.60	241	53	78	1.84	3.03	-13.0
1st Half		139	19	36	1	13	2	259			$2	352	331	683	13	80	32	0.71	235	50	82		3.67	-3.1
2nd Half		171	23	36	2	14	0	211			($1)	270	292	563	8	83	24	0.48	246	55	69		2.55	-9.8
04	**Proj**	**150**	**20**	**35**	**1**	**11**	**1**	**233**			**$0**	**314**	**315**	**629**	**11**	**80**	**28**	**0.60**	**241**	**56**	**80**		**3.23**	**-4.9**

3-25-.241 in 261 AB at PIT. There is a small group of players who toil in obscurity, year after year, grabbing that 25th spot on an MLB roster but never become an opening bid at a fantasy draft. Sad, but true.

Redman,Tike

Pos CF | Age 27 Peak | Bats L
R: X HIGH | I: EXP, CON | S: pt, STB | K:
LIMA B+ | BA: 65%

Yr	Tm	AB	R	H	HR	RBI	SB	Avg	vL	vR	R$	OB	Slg	OPS	bb%	ct%	h%	Eye	xBA	PX	SX	G/F	RC/G	RAR
99	aa	532	72	132	3	51	25	248			$9	306	336	642	8	91	27	0.96	284	56	146		3.23	-21.0
00	aaa	506	49	116	3	40	19	229			$4	266	324	590	5	88	26	0.41	273	60	133	0.50	2.42	-33.4
01	PIT	* 523	51	137	3	38	20	262	83	239	$10	293	348	641	4	89	29	0.42	274	55	135	1.00	3.32	-8.3
02	aaa	311	33	76	2	17	13	244			$5	284	305	589	5	94	26	0.89	270	42	106		2.78	-19.5
03	PIT	* 590	86	171	6	43	42	290	329	331	$25	339	397	736	7	92	31	0.98	293	70	163	1.93	4.84	-2.4
1st Half		276	42	75	3	18	27	272			$12	328	377	705	8	92	29	1.10	294	69	175		4.65	-2.7
2nd Half		314	44	96	3	25	15	306			$12	349	414	763	6	92	32	0.88	292	72	144		5.01	0.3
04	**Proj**	**500**	**63**	**140**	**4**	**35**	**27**	**280**			**$16**	**323**	**372**	**695**	**6**	**92**	**30**	**0.80**	**289**	**61**	**143**		**4.11**	**-8.8**

3-19-7-.326 in 230 AB at PIT, which is slightly over his head, but not by much. Solid contact, good eye and speed make for a legitimate lead-off hitter. Next step up is if he can add 20-30 points to his OB avg.

Redmond,Mike

	Tm	AB	R	H	HR	RBI	SB	Avg	vL	vR	R$	OB	Slg	OPS	bb%	ct%	h%	Eye	xBA	PX	SX	G/F	RC/G	RAR
Pos CA	99 FLA	242	22	73	1	27	0	302	304	300	$5	369	351	721	10	86	35	0.76	274	39		1.61	4.74	5.2
Age 32 Past Peak	00 FLA	210	17	53	0	15	0	252	321	209	($0)	296	300	596	6	91	28	0.68	262	36	38	1.54	3.03	-5.9
Bats R	01 FLA	141	19	44	4	14	0	312	375	271	$5	370	426	796	8	91	32	1.00	269	67	26	1.68	5.84	8.8
R Moderate	02 FLA	256	19	78	2	28	0	305	286	312	$7	357	387	744	8	87	35	0.62	281	67		2.25	4.91	5.6
I CON	03 FLA	125	12	30	0	11	0	240	314	211	($0)	280	312	592	5	87	28	0.44	266	57	61	1.71	2.93	-5.1
S PT	1st Half	80	5	19	0	9	0	238			$0	274	325	599	5	88	27	0.40	273	67	63		2.98	-3.1
K	2nd Half	45	7	11	0	2	0	244			($0)	292	289	581	6	87	28	0.50	253	40	54		2.84	-1.9
LIMA F BA: 60%	**04 Proj**	**150**	**13**	**42**	**1**	**15**	**0**	**280**			**$2**	**330**	**367**	**697**	**7**	**89**	**31**	**0.65**	**270**	**62**	**47**		**4.26**	**0.7**

After two .300 seasons, it must have been discouraging to end up as I-Rod's backup. 7% drop in hit rate was at least partially responsible for the 65 point drop in BA, but playing time is always the great motivator.

Reese,Pokey

	Tm	AB	R	H	HR	RBI	SB	Avg	vL	vR	R$	OB	Slg	OPS	bb%	ct%	h%	Eye	xBA	PX	SX	G/F	RC/G	RAR
Pos 2B	99 CIN	585	85	167	10	52	38	285	295	282	$22	326	417	743	6	86	32	0.43	280	89	138	1.07	5.00	13.1
Age 30 Past Peak	00 CIN	518	76	132	12	46	29	255	257	254	$15	314	386	700	8	83	29	0.52	253	77	152	0.90	4.38	0.2
Bats R	01 CIN	428	50	96	9	40	25	224	226	224	$10	281	343	625	7	81	26	0.41	240	76	127	0.86	3.33	-7.0
R Moderate	02 PIT	421	46	111	4	50	12	264	282	259	$10	329	352	681	9	81	32	0.51	261	70	83	1.16	4.14	-3.3
I CON	03 PIT	107	9	23	1	12	6	215	161	237	$2	276	262	538	8	71	29	0.29	209	31	83	0.93	2.62	-5.9
S pt stb	1st Half	107	9	23	1	12	6	215			$2	276	262	538	8	71	29	0.29	209	31	83		2.62	-5.9
K	2nd Half	0	0	0	0	0	0	0			($0)					0			0					
LIMA D BA: 40%	**04 Proj**	**350**	**39**	**84**	**5**	**36**	**10**	**240**			**$6**	**299**	**331**	**630**	**8**	**79**	**29**	**0.39**	**230**	**62**	**95**		**3.40**	**-9.6**

What little was here has been slowly slipping away. An injury-shortened year for a player like this helps teams focus and makes them realize how easy it is to get along without. Next!

Relaford,Desi

	Tm	AB	R	H	HR	RBI	SB	Avg	vL	vR	R$	OB	Slg	OPS	bb%	ct%	h%	Eye	xBA	PX	SX	G/F	RC/G	RAR
Pos 2B 3B	99 PHI	211	31	51	1	26	4	242	250	240	$2	304	327	631	8	84	28	0.56	254	61	107	1.16	3.24	-6.2
Age 30 Past Peak	00 2NL	410	55	88	5	46	13	215	194	221	$3	336	300	636	15	83	25	1.06	253	53	113	1.25	3.46	-11.4
Bats S	01 NYM	301	43	91	8	36	13	302	240	315	$14	360	472	832	8	78	36	0.42	271	117	86	1.01	6.09	18.8
R Very High	02 SEA	329	55	88	6	43	10	267	202	292	$10	334	374	708	9	84	30	0.65	254	67	114	1.00	4.38	3.2
I con	03 KC	500	70	127	8	59	20	254	300	238	$12	309	376	685	7	86	28	0.57	281	80	135	1.12	4.06	-1.1
S PT STB	1st Half	250	40	72	6	33	11	288			$10	343	440	783	8	86	31	0.62	293	96	138		5.52	9.7
K	2nd Half	250	30	55	2	26	9	220			$2	275	312	587	7	86	25	0.53	268	64	121		2.87	-9.8
LIMA D+ BA: 60%	**04 Proj**	**350**	**51**	**91**	**6**	**42**	**13**	**260**			**$9**	**322**	**381**	**703**	**8**	**84**	**29**	**0.58**	**278**	**80**	**123**		**4.28**	**1.8**

One of the anomalies of KC's surprise season is that they could give 500 ABs to a player with a .309 OB (only .275 in the 2nd half) and sub-zero RAR... and still contend. Odds are he'll never see 500 AB again.

Renteria,Edgar

	Tm	AB	R	H	HR	RBI	SB	Avg	vL	vR	R$	OB	Slg	OPS	bb%	ct%	h%	Eye	xBA	PX	SX	G/F	RC/G	RAR
Pos SS	99 STL	585	92	161	11	63	37	275	250	283	$21	335	400	735	8	86	30	0.65	284	85	118	1.16	4.85	22.4
Age 28 Peak	00 STL	562	94	156	16	76	21	278	259	284	$20	350	423	774	10	86	30	0.82	283	92	89	1.38	5.01	25.4
Bats R	01 STL	493	54	128	10	57	17	260	327	243	$13	314	371	685	7	85	29	0.53	261	69	106	1.37	4.07	7.5
R Low	02 STL	544	77	166	11	83	22	305	288	310	$26	363	439	802	8	90	33	0.86	311	97	102	1.56	5.83	29.2
I CON	03 STL	587	96	194	13	100	34	330	391	316	$37	397	480	878	10	91	35	1.20	324	108	107	1.37	7.41	51.7
S	1st Half	307	48	104	7	56	17	339			$21	396	498	894	9	92	35	1.21	333	114	108		7.78	29.6
K	2nd Half	280	48	90	6	44	17	321			$17	399	461	859	11	89	34	1.20	313	101	97		7.02	22.1
LIMA D+ BA: 60%	**04 Proj**	**550**	**93**	**174**	**17**	**93**	**32**	**316**			**$34**	**385**	**492**	**876**	**10**	**89**	**33**	**1.01**	**325**	**119**	**113**		**7.07**	**47.6**

Exciting BPIs and trends here. A .330 BA was probably a bit over his head, thanks to a 35% hit rate, but he should post a strong follow-up, and perhaps start pumping up his power numbers a bit as well.

Restovich,Mike

	Tm	AB	R	H	HR	RBI	SB	Avg	vL	vR	R$	OB	Slg	OPS	bb%	ct%	h%	Eye	xBA	PX	SX	G/F	RC/G	RAR
Pos RF	99	0	0	0	0	0	0	0								0								
Age 25 Pre-Peak	00	0	0	0	0	0	0	0								0								
Bats R	01 aa	501	69	136	22	84	15	271			$21	341	487	828	10	75	32	0.43	267	132	107		5.68	6.0
R High	02 aaa	518	69	130	20	71	8	251			$14	302	444	746	7	78	29	0.34	268	121	104		4.31	-13.3
I EXP con	03 MIN	* 507	77	134	13	69	9	264	283	323	$13	332	432	763	9	76	32	0.43	257	111	110	2.78	4.95	-2.9
S stb	1st Half	309	42	76	8	42	8	246			$7	307	398	705	8	77	30	0.38	252	102	95		4.16	-9.2
K age	2nd Half	198	35	58	5	27	1	293			$6	369	485	854	11	76	37	0.50	264	127	116		6.37	6.7
LIMA F BA: 45%	**04 Proj**	**150**	**22**	**40**	**5**	**21**	**2**	**267**			**$4**	**331**	**445**	**776**	**9**	**77**	**32**	**0.41**	**258**	**113**	**90**		**4.99**	**-0.4**

0-4-.283 in 53 AB at MIN. Despite a decent 2nd half, his BPIs have declined as he's been promoted from level to level. More consistent playing time will help, so keep tabs on his place in the depth chart.

Reyes,Jose

	Tm	AB	R	H	HR	RBI	SB	Avg	vL	vR	R$	OB	Slg	OPS	bb%	ct%	h%	Eye	xBA	PX	SX	G/F	RC/G	RAR
Pos SS	99	0	0	0	0	0	0	0								0								
Age 20 Green	00	0	0	0	0	0	0	0								0								
Bats S	01	0	0	0	0	0	0	0								0								
R High	02 aa	275	44	79	2	23	25	287			$13	324	411	735	5	89	32	0.48	288	83	197		4.17	-0.5
I EXP	03 NYM	* 434	77	129	5	46	41	297	225	340	$24	340	406	745	6	87	33	0.50	279	70	191	1.63	5.17	13.0
S pt stb	1st Half	233	39	60	1	29	29	258			$13	305	352	657	6	86	30	0.50	274	60	221		3.77	-2.4
K AGE	2nd Half	201	38	69	4	17	12	343			$12	380	468	848	6	88	38	0.50	283	80	148		7.24	16.3
LIMA A BA: 45%	**04 Proj**	**550**	**95**	**150**	**6**	**52**	**29**	**273**			**$18**	**320**	**391**	**711**	**6**	**88**	**30**	**0.57**	**282**	**77**	**184**		**4.43**	**8.2**

5-32-13-.307 in 274 AB at NYM. The true test will come next spring when opposing pitchers get to face him for the second time. At 20, there may still be some growing pains, but early indicators are exciting.

Reyes,Rene

	Tm	AB	R	H	HR	RBI	SB	Avg	vL	vR	R$	OB	Slg	OPS	bb%	ct%	h%	Eye	xBA	PX	SX	G/F	RC/G	RAR
Pos RF	99	0	0	0	0	0	0	0								0								
Age 26 Pre-Peak	00	0	0	0	0	0	0	0								0								
Bats S	01	0	0	0	0	0	0	0								0								
R Moderate	02 aa	455	44	121	12	37	7	266			$10	297	422	719	4	89	28	0.42	294	104	73		3.92	-16.8
I EXP	03 COL	* 486	58	150	8	44	11	309	289	244	$17	339	430	769	4	88	34	0.38	280	85	87	2.28	5.01	-8.2
S stb	1st Half	315	38	101	3	30	7	321			$11	350	425	775	4	90	35	0.45	282	77	86		5.22	-3.4
K	2nd Half	171	20	49	5	14	4	287			$5	318	439	757	4	84	32	0.30	275	98	85		4.63	-4.9
LIMA F BA: 40%	**04 Proj**	**150**	**16**	**43**	**3**	**13**	**3**	**287**			**$4**	**317**	**429**	**747**	**4**	**88**	**31**	**0.37**	**286**	**96**	**82**		**4.48**	**-4.3**

2-7-2-.259 in 116 AB at COL and just .250 in Coors Field. Not ready offensively or defensively, according to COL mgt, and that just about takes care of any positive projection for '04.

Richard,Chris

	Tm	AB	R	H	HR	RBI	SB	Avg	vL	vR	R$	OB	Slg	OPS	bb%	ct%	h%	Eye	xBA	PX	SX	G/F	RC/G	RAR
Pos LF	99 a/a	459	65	119	25	78	6	259			$15	313	486	799	7	86	25	0.55	304	133	70		4.92	-1.8
Age 29 Past Peak	00 2TM	* 590	96	151	29	104	15	256	237	286	$20	328	468	796	10	83	27	0.61	293	124	93	0.93	5.12	-0.7
Bats L	01 BAL	483	74	128	15	61	11	265	208	281	$13	328	435	762	9	79	31	0.45	259	108	94	1.19	4.70	1.1
R High	02 BAL	* 214	23	50	8	35	0	234	250	230	$4	290	421	711	7	79	26	0.37	267	122	28	0.89	3.81	-6.7
I exp	03 COL	27	3	6	1	3	0	222	500	200	$0	300	444	744	10	78	25	0.50	254	124	205	0.70	3.71	-1.6
S PT STB	1st Half	27	3	6	1	3	0	222			$0	300	444	744	10	78	25	0.50	254	124	205		3.71	-1.6
K	2nd Half	0	0	0	0	0	0	0			($0)					0			0					
LIMA F BA: 60%	**04 Proj**	**100**	**14**	**25**	**4**	**16**	**2**	**250**			**$3**	**313**	**438**	**751**	**8**	**81**	**27**	**0.49**	**253**	**120**	**60**		**4.45**	**-3.9**

Was cut loose by COL and then had a setback in the rehab to his injured shoulder.

Man, was that a bad day.

Riggs,Adam

	Tm	AB	R	H	HR	RBI	SB	Avg	vL	vR	R$	OB	Slg	OPS	bb%	ct%	h%	Eye	xBA	PX	SX	G/F	RC/G	RAR
Pos 1B	99 aaa	513	60	114	9	57	17	222			$5	273	329	603	7	82	26	0.38	257	69	99		2.60	-48.3
Age 31 Past Peak	00 aaa	348	51	86	8	41	8	247			$6	298	382	680	7	83	28	0.42	271	85	99		3.58	-21.8
Bats R	01 aaa	430	35	91	15	52	7	212			$5	231	358	589	2	80	23	0.13	255	87	68		2.61	-48.3
R X HIGH	02 aaa	122	20	23	2	8	4	189			($0)	293	295	588	13	79	22	0.69	245	77	93		2.78	-11.6
I EXP CON	03 ANA	* 455	53	109	13	64	8	240	350	195	$9	294	402	696	7	85	26	0.52	284	109	77	0.63	3.94	-19.7
S PT stb	1st Half	267	29	62	8	39	5	232			$5	276	386	661	6	87	24	0.44	282	101	67		3.50	-15.3
K	2nd Half	188	24	47	5	25	3	250			$4	319	426	744	9	84	28	0.61	285	119	81		4.60	-4.3
LIMA F BA: 65%	**04 Proj**	**100**	**13**	**25**	**4**	**12**	**2**	**250**			**$2**	**312**	**426**	**738**	**8**	**82**	**27**	**0.51**	**280**	**114**	**61**		**4.46**	**-3.6**

3-5-3-.246 in 61 AB at ANA. Take a look at his PX trend, including his 2nd half, and you'll see that his power peak is probably coming in 2004. We hope he enjoys it in Salt Lake.

Rios,Armando

Pos CF
Age 32 Past Peak
Bats L
R High
I exp CON
S pt STB
K
LIMA F BA: 55%

	Tm	AB	R	H	HR	RBI	SB	Avg	vL	vR	R$	OB	Slg	OPS	bb%	ct%	h%	Eye	xBA	PX	SX	G/F	RC/G	RAR
99	SF	* 259	50	74	10	45	9	286	269	339	$11	364	448	812	11	80	32	0.62	267	99	81	1.30	5.63	9.9
00	SF	233	38	62	10	50	3	266	167	288	$8	352	502	854	12	82	29	0.72	289	137	142	1.04	6.03	11.6
01	2NL	319	38	83	14	50	3	260	326	249	$10	335	464	799	10	77	30	0.49	258	120	85	0.94	5.28	13.4
02	PIT	* 262	24	65	1	28	2	248	300	258	$2	301	309	611	7	81	30	0.41	237	52	43	0.89	3.04	-14.3
03	CHW	* 259	22	64	7	34	4	247	214	211	$5	293	375	668	6	84	27	0.40	258	78	55	1.85	3.36	-11.0
1st Half		99	4	22	2	11	0	222			$0	260	313	573	5	89	23	0.45	257	57	10		2.53	-6.7
2nd Half		160	18	42	5	23	4	262			$5	314	412	726	7	81	30	0.39	257	91	80		3.91	-4.0
04	Proj	150	15	38	4	20	2	253			$3	310	388	698	8	82	29	0.45	258	84	70		3.86	-4.1

2-11-.212 in 104 AB at CHW. Has graduated from prospect to suspect, and I mean no disrespect, but in effect, he became a reject when he wrecked his pecs. No, wait. It was his knee.

Rivas,Luis

Pos 2B
Age 24 Growth
Bats R
R High
I exp CON
S pt stb
K age
LIMA B BA: 60%

	Tm	AB	R	H	HR	RBI	SB	Avg	vL	vR	R$	OB	Slg	OPS	bb%	ct%	h%	Eye	xBA	PX	SX	G/F	RC/G	RAR
99	aa	527	70	133	6	44	28	252			$11	303	370	673	7	85	29	0.49	278	80	136		3.56	-8.6
00	MIN	* 543	82	142	5	60	17	262	316	308	$10	316	389	704	7	90	28	0.77	295	86	138	1.65	4.12	4.0
01	MIN	563	70	150	7	47	31	266	241	275	$16	315	362	677	7	82	31	0.40	256	60	130	1.86	3.95	-4.3
02	MIN	316	46	81	4	35	9	256	234	268	$7	299	392	691	6	84	30	0.37	281	93	141	1.42	3.94	-0.9
03	MIN	475	69	123	8	43	17	259	259	281	$11	303	381	684	6	86	29	0.46	290	72	163	2.34	3.91	-3.2
1st Half		210	27	56	1	14	6	267			$3	322	357	679	7	85	31	0.53	274	57	142		3.84	-1.8
2nd Half		265	42	67	7	29	11	253			$7	288	400	688	5	88	27	0.39	304	83	174		3.94	-1.6
04	Proj	500	71	139	7	48	19	278			$14	322	403	724	6	85	31	0.44	292	78	149		4.49	5.6

Ground balls have a higher likelihood of becoming hits, so his spike in G/F ratio -- and increased ct% -- helped to boost his xBA, despite decline in PX. .300 potential? Not yet, but possibly within a few years.

Rivera,Carlos

Pos 1B
Age 25 Pre-Peak
Bats L
R Very High
I EXP con
S pt stb
K age
LIMA F BA: 55%

	Tm	AB	R	H	HR	RBI	SB	Avg	vL	vR	R$	OB	Slg	OPS	bb%	ct%	h%	Eye	xBA	PX	SX	G/F	RC/G	RAR
99		0	0	0	0	0	0	0								0								
00		0	0	0	0	0	0	0								0								
01	aa	389	40	84	9	45	0	216			$1	239	357	597	3	83	24	0.18	266	97	38		2.71	-42.0
02	aa	494	52	129	16	66	1	261			$11	291	415	706	4	88	27	0.34	283	100	43		4.14	-22.8
03	PIT	* 357	36	84	10	37	3	235	188	228	$4	274	384	658	5	83	26	0.32	271	101	55	1.80	3.50	-21.6
1st Half		274	26	66	7	28	3	241			$4	275	394	669	5	88	25	0.38	288	109	56		3.64	-15.4
2nd Half		83	10	18	3	9	0	217			$0	270	349	619	7	70	27	0.24	214	78	33		3.07	-6.2
04	Proj	150	16	37	5	18	0	247			$2	292	392	684	6	82	28	0.35	266	96	37		3.85	-7.9

3-10-.221 in 95 AB at PIT. Despite consistent growth in walk rate (though, when you start at 3%, there's really only one way to go), until he starts cracking a .300 OB with regularity, I'm not interested.

Rivera,Juan

Pos CF
Age 25 Pre-Peak
Bats R
R Very High
I EXP con
S pt stb
K age
LIMA D+ BA: 50%

	Tm	AB	R	H	HR	RBI	SB	Avg	vL	vR	R$	OB	Slg	OPS	bb%	ct%	h%	Eye	xBA	PX	SX	G/F	RC/G	RAR
99		0	0	0	0	0	0	0								0								
00		0	0	0	0	0	0	0								0								
01	a/a	519	79	157	27	86	8	303			$25	337	522	859	5	86	31	0.38	302	128	78		5.87	22.3
02	NYY	* 348	42	99	8	44	5	284	200	274	$10	318	428	746	5	88	31	0.40	285	97	75	1.14	4.82	0.4
03	NYY	* 481	62	136	13	58	1	283	340	236	$12	327	432	760	6	88	30	0.54	285	101	35	1.55	4.92	2.4
1st Half		275	28	75	3	25	0	273			$3	317	371	688	6	89	30	0.58	269	74	27		4.00	-5.9
2nd Half		206	34	61	10	33	1	296			$8	341	515	855	6	86	30	0.50	305	137	51		6.26	8.7
04	Proj	400	54	115	13	54	4	288			$12	327	458	785	6	87	30	0.46	288	110	62		5.21	5.1

7-26-.266 in 173 AB at NYY. Solid 2nd half bodes well for him claiming some more playing time in '04. BPIs are showing good growth and 2001 tells you the upside.

Rivera,Mike

Pos CA
Age 27 Peak
Bats R
R X HIGH
I EXP CON
S pt STB
K
LIMA F BA: 45%

	Tm	AB	R	H	HR	RBI	SB	Avg	vL	vR	R$	OB	Slg	OPS	bb%	ct%	h%	Eye	xBA	PX	SX	G/F	RC/G	RAR
99	aa	23	3	4	2	6	0	174			$0	240	478	718	8	78	13	0.40	292	169	21		3.54	-0.4
00	a/a	163	8	29	1	8	0	178			($4)	207	276	483	4	85	20	0.25	267	71	38		1.77	-12.1
01	aa	427	60	101	21	78	2	237			$11	291	433	725	7	80	25	0.39	270	115	59		4.15	5.9
02	DET	* 397	49	86	16	59	0	217	273	212	$5	283	393	676	9	77	24	0.40	252	105	53	1.23	3.58	-0.4
03	2TM	* 348	32	83	12	46	0	239		205	$5	278	374	651	5	79	27	0.26	243	81	20	1.35	3.38	-8.5
1st Half		152	9	29	4	12	0	191			($1)	241	289	530	6	74	23	0.25	214	58	15		2.12	-10.1
2nd Half		196	23	54	8	34	0	276			$6	307	439	746	4	83	30	0.27	265	99			4.64	2.5
04	Proj	100	10	23	4	14	0	230			$1	277	377	654	6	79	26	0.32	250	90	32		3.40	-1.9

1-2-.170 in 53 AB at CHW. History shows his pop potential. This will provide value so long as he figures out how to make solid contact with the ball, which has been an elusive element of his skill set.

Roberts,Brian

Pos 2B
Age 26 Pre-Peak
Bats S
R Moderate
I EXP con
S pt
K
LIMA B+ BA: 60%

	Tm	AB	R	H	HR	RBI	SB	Avg	vL	vR	R$	OB	Slg	OPS	bb%	ct%	h%	Eye	xBA	PX	SX	G/F	RC/G	RAR
99		0	0	0	0	0	0	0								0								
00		0	0	0	0	0	0	0								0								
01	BAL	* 515	68	130	4	34	42	252	247	255	$15	316	332	648	9	87	28	0.72	265	54	136	1.26	3.87	-5.2
02	BAL	* 441	61	106	4	37	28	240	146	264	$11	316	322	638	10	86	27	0.79	251	51	148	0.80	3.58	-6.1
03	BAL	* 638	99	174	5	55	41	273	264	272	$21	346	364	709	10	89	30	1.03	268	64	130	1.43	4.45	5.9
1st Half		336	61	95	3	31	27	283			$14	361	381	742	11	91	30	1.41	278	68	141		4.97	8.1
2nd Half		302	38	79	2	24	14	262			$7	328	344	673	9	87	30	0.75	257	59	109		3.91	-2.0
04	Proj	500	71	129	4	41	32	258			$14	336	340	676	10	87	29	0.93	264	56	129		4.06	-0.6

5-41-23-.270 in 460 AB at BAL. A strong season in his first exposure to full time play in the bigs. 2nd half decline will temper short-term growth, but 1st half shows you the longer-term potential.

Roberts,Dave

Pos CF
Age 31 Past Peak
Bats L
R X HIGH
I EXP CON
S pt STB
K
LIMA B BA: 65%

	Tm	AB	R	H	HR	RBI	SB	Avg	vL	vR	R$	OB	Slg	OPS	bb%	ct%	h%	Eye	xBA	PX	SX	G/F	RC/G	RAR
99	CLE	* 493	76	114	2	41	41	231			$12	292	304	596	8	87	26	0.65	268	48	174	1.89	3.17	-23.1
00	aaa	472	76	120	11	45	33	254			$16	324	362	687	9	87	27	0.78	270	63	122	5.00	4.03	-6.5
01	a/a	317	38	79	0	22	17	249			$6	300	319	619	7	84	30	0.45	254	52	129	2.00	3.21	-11.0
02	LA	422	63	117	3	34	45	277	400	270	$22	351	365	716	10	88	31	0.94	291	57	179	2.10	4.77	-1.2
03	LA	388	56	97	2	16	40	250	265	246	$14	325	307	632	10	90	27	1.10	277	33	161	2.25	3.45	-18.3
1st Half		218	32	55	1	10	24	252			$9	315	303	618	8	91	27	1.00	265	32	156		3.54	-9.5
2nd Half		170	24	42	1	6	16	247			$5	337	312	649	12	89	27	1.21	275	36	164		3.34	-8.8
04	Proj	400	57	107	2	24	37	268			$16	339	337	676	10	88	30	0.90	264	45	155		4.02	-8.3

The big problem with 2003's decline is that, in some ways, 2002 now looks more like an aberration than a step along the growth curve. Some trends are still positive, but the overall package is not as strong.

Robinson,Kerry

Pos RF LF CF
Age 30 Past Peak
Bats L
R High
I EXP con
S pt stb
K
LIMA D BA: 50%

	Tm	AB	R	H	HR	RBI	SB	Avg	vL	vR	R$	OB	Slg	OPS	bb%	ct%	h%	Eye	xBA	PX	SX	G/F	RC/G	RAR
99	aaa	464	72	117	1	45	41	252			$15	279	323	602	4	87	29	0.28	269	46	186		3.14	-25.8
00	aaa	437	52	118	0	24	28	270			$11	317	330	646	6	92	29	0.91	272	39	135		3.25	-23.7
01	STL	* 226	37	63	1	17	14	279	267	287	$7	324	332	656	6	87	32	0.52	256	37	130	2.15	3.95	-10.4
02	STL	181	27	47	1	15	7	260	222	262	$4	302	359	661	6	84	30	0.38	281	65	181	2.00	3.58	-9.3
03	STL	* 269	31	70	1	19	11	260	238	251	$5	284	331	615	3	87	30	0.26	261	46	156	2.38	3.40	-17.3
1st Half		138	20	35	0	8	7	254			$2	270	297	567	2	88	29	0.18	255	32	143		2.89	-11.1
2nd Half		131	11	35	1	11	4	267			$3	299	366	666	4	86	30	0.33	267	60	154		3.99	-6.1
04	Proj	200	26	53	1	15	9	265			$5	299	343	642	5	86	30	0.36	262	52	153		3.61	-10.9

1-16-6-.250 in 208 AB at STL. Skills are not horrible for a back-of-the-roster filler who can chip in with a few SBs. In this time of reduced emphasis on SBs, players like this become more valuable.

Rodriguez,Alex

Pos SS
Age 28 Peak
Bats R
R Very Low
I
S stb
K
LIMA C BA: 50%

	Tm	AB	R	H	HR	RBI	SB	Avg	vL	vR	R$	OB	Slg	OPS	bb%	ct%	h%	Eye	xBA	PX	SX	G/F	RC/G	RAR
99	SEA	502	110	143	42	111	21	285	277	287	$32	357	586	942	10	78	29	0.51	288	168	102	0.98	7.33	45.4
00	SEA	554	134	175	41	132	15	316	366	306	$36	420	606	1027	15	78	34	0.83	291	163	104	1.01	9.50	76.3
01	TEX	632	133	201	52	135	18	318	295	324	$45	390	622	1012	11	79	33	0.57	309	173	93	1.00	9.14	81.2
02	TEX	624	125	187	57	142	9	300	239	320	$42	385	623	1009	12	80	29	0.71	301	179	79	0.92	8.65	70.4
03	TEX	607	124	181	47	118	17	298	305	295	$38	386	600	986	13	79	31	0.69	311	170	129	1.01	8.47	68.1
1st Half		311	54	92	20	51	7	296			$16	371	559	930	11	78	32	0.54	296	154	97		7.49	26.6
2nd Half		296	70	89	27	67	10	301			$22	402	642	1044	14	80	29	0.86	327	186	148		9.56	41.9
04	Proj	625	131	189	55	133	16	302			$42	389	627	1016	12	80	30	0.69	315	181	111		8.94	77.5

He's just now entering his peak performance years, which is scary. Last year in this space, I projected 61 HRs. I'll hedge a little this year, but wouldn't be surprised to see him take that spike.

Rodriguez,Ivan

Pos CA
Age 32 Past Peak
Bats R
R Moderate
I con
S pt stb
K
LIMA C+ BA: 50%

Yr	Tm	AB	R	H	HR	RBI	SB	Avg	vL	vR	R$	OB	Slg	OPS	bb%	ct%	h%	Eye	xBA	PX	SX	G/F	RC/G	RAR
99	TEX	600	116	199	35	113	25	332	325	333	$39	357	558	916	4	89	33	0.38	351	130	105	1.96	7.28	52.1
00	TEX	363	66	126	27	83	5	347	342	349	$25	380	667	1046	5	87	34	0.40	365	180	103	1.42	9.45	50.3
01	TEX	442	70	136	25	65	10	308	289	312	$23	342	541	883	5	83	32	0.32	309	137	92	1.19	6.77	35.2
02	TEX	408	67	128	19	60	5	314	306	317	$19	353	542	895	6	83	34	0.35	314	143	83	1.08	6.91	36.7
03	FLA	511	90	152	16	85	10	297	376	274	$22	366	474	839	10	82	34	0.60	317	117	101	1.76	6.14	26.5
1st Half		248	44	72	10	44	9	290			$13	376	488	864	12	82	32	0.77	324	124	119		6.65	16.5
2nd Half		263	46	80	6	41	1	304			$9	356	460	816	7	82	35	0.44	308	111	68		5.66	10.0
04	Proj	**500**	**86**	**154**	**15**	**81**	**5**	**308**			**$22**	**370**	**481**	**851**	**9**	**83**	**35**	**0.58**	**319**	**116**	**96**		**6.41**	**31.8**

This was a different player who came over to the NL...
- Improved plate patience
- Less power
- Wider platoon splits
- Healthy
This new model could do well.

Rolen,Scott

Pos 3B
Age 29 Past Peak
Bats R
R Low
I con
S stb
K
LIMA D+ BA: 55%

Yr	Tm	AB	R	H	HR	RBI	SB	Avg	vL	vR	R$	OB	Slg	OPS	bb%	ct%	h%	Eye	xBA	PX	SX	G/F	RC/G	RAR
99	PHI	421	74	113	26	77	12	268	330	252	$19	369	525	894	14	73	31	0.59	258	155	88	0.64	6.83	30.0
00	PHI	483	88	144	26	89	8	298	283	302	$23	365	551	916	10	80	33	0.52	283	147	129	0.79	7.37	40.7
01	PHI	554	96	160	25	107	16	289	283	290	$28	373	498	871	12	77	34	0.58	271	130	92	0.68	6.64	32.1
02	2NL	580	89	154	31	110	8	266	288	260	$25	347	503	850	11	82	28	0.71	292	145	120	0.84	5.98	23.5
03	STL	559	98	160	28	104	13	286	283	287	$27	378	528	905	13	81	31	0.79	309	158	89	0.79	7.15	45.6
1st Half		273	50	79	15	56	5	289			$14	394	542	936	15	81	31	0.92	310	165	65		7.60	25.7
2nd Half		286	48	81	13	48	8	283			$13	361	514	875	11	81	31	0.66	307	152	99		6.71	19.9
04	Proj	**550**	**93**	**164**	**36**	**102**	**12**	**298**			**$32**	**382**	**572**	**954**	**12**	**80**	**32**	**0.69**	**311**	**167**	**96**		**7.92**	**53.8**

With 49 doubles, it was his second best power year ever, behind 1998. Odds are some of those hits will clear the fences in 2004, so a HR spike is a possibility.

Rollins,Jimmy

Pos SS
Age 25 Pre-Peak
Bats S
R Low
I exp
S stb
K age
LIMA B BA: 50%

Yr	Tm	AB	R	H	HR	RBI	SB	Avg	vL	vR	R$	OB	Slg	OPS	bb%	ct%	h%	Eye	xBA	PX	SX	G/F	RC/G	RAR
99	a/a	545	73	149	10	51	22	273			$15	332	398	730	8	93	28	1.30	300	77	120		4.29	7.2
00	PHI	* 523	59	137	9	61	23	262	333	317	$14	319	413	732	8	89	28	0.79	300	94	150	1.19	4.52	16.3
01	PHI	656	97	180	14	54	46	274	318	262	$27	324	419	743	7	84	31	0.44	274	86	189	1.06	4.94	26.3
02	PHI	637	82	156	11	60	31	245	243	246	$17	304	380	684	8	84	28	0.52	277	90	159	1.19	3.81	-1.7
03	PHI	628	85	165	8	62	20	263	262	263	$14	321	387	708	8	82	31	0.48	281	88	123	1.15	4.14	0.5
1st Half		342	48	91	4	35	9	266			$8	310	383	693	6	82	31	0.37	279	81	128		3.91	-2.0
2nd Half		286	37	74	4	27	11	259			$7	333	392	725	10	81	31	0.60	282	97	110		4.41	2.5
04	Proj	**650**	**87**	**174**	**10**	**62**	**23**	**268**			**$17**	**326**	**400**	**726**	**8**	**84**	**31**	**0.53**	**285**	**89**	**137**		**4.50**	**11.1**

Mostly stable skills set, though speed is in decline. No signs of any real growth here, but at 25 that still may come.

Rolls,Damian

Pos 3B RF
Age 26 Pre-Peak
Bats R
R High
I EXP con
S PT stb
K
LIMA D BA: 40%

Yr	Tm	AB	R	H	HR	RBI	SB	Avg	vL	vR	R$	OB	Slg	OPS	bb%	ct%	h%	Eye	xBA	PX	SX	G/F	RC/G	RAR
99		0	0	0	0	0	0	0								0								
00	aa	51	5	11	0	2	0	216			($1)	298	294	592	11	86	25	0.86	267	66	41		2.62	-2.8
01	TAM	237	33	62	2	12	12	262	225	280	$5	291	342	633	4	80	32	0.21	218	57	115	1.04	3.44	-6.5
02	TAM	* 367	49	87	5	35	14	256	500	260	$9	299	365	664	6	84	29	0.38	253	66	154	3.15	3.66	-8.2
03	TAM	* 450	53	112	7	54	15	249	273	246	$10	285	353	639	5	78	30	0.23	239	72	97	1.50	3.42	-14.7
1st Half		166	25	41	3	21	8	247			$4	302	367	669	7	80	29	0.38	249	80	121		3.71	-4.0
2nd Half		284	28	71	4	33	7	250			$5	276	345	621	3	77	31	0.16	233	68	74		3.25	-10.7
04	Proj	**350**	**46**	**84**	**5**	**36**	**11**	**240**			**$5**	**279**	**340**	**619**	**5**	**80**	**29**	**0.28**	**242**	**66**	**115**		**3.20**	**-13.3**

7-46-11-.255 in 373 AB at TAM. BPIs have been in a fairly consistent decline, except for his little power. There's not much value here except for those who need SBs, but those will come with a price -- low BA.

Ross,David

Pos CA
Age 27 Peak
Bats R
R High
I EXP con
S pt stb
K
LIMA F BA: 45%

Yr	Tm	AB	R	H	HR	RBI	SB	Avg	vL	vR	R$	OB	Slg	OPS	bb%	ct%	h%	Eye	xBA	PX	SX	G/F	RC/G	RAR
99		0	0	0	0	0	0	0								0								
00		0	0	0	0	0	0	0								0								
01	aa	246	31	57	10	40	1	232			$5	315	402	718	11	70	29	0.40	227	100	57		4.16	3.5
02	aaa	303	36	72	12	50	1	238			$7	300	409	709	8	78	27	0.40	256	106	53		4.07	1.8
03	LA	* 210	28	48	14	30	0	229	258	258	$5	302	476	778	9	69	26	0.34	242	147	27	0.68	4.56	1.7
1st Half		121	16	27	7	19	0	223			$2	282	430	712	8	73	25	0.30	243	120	39		3.69	-2.3
2nd Half		89	12	21	7	11	0	236			$3	327	539	866	12	64	28	0.38	238	183			5.88	4.2
04	Proj	**250**	**32**	**59**	**15**	**38**	**0**	**236**			**$6**	**310**	**473**	**783**	**10**	**71**	**27**	**0.37**	**247**	**146**	**30**		**4.80**	**5.3**

10-18-.258 in 124 AB at LA, a full season pace of 45 HRs. The power is very real, and getting more potent, but he's becoming more and more indiscriminate with the pitches he swings at. High risk, high reward here.

Rowand,Aaron

Pos CF LF
Age 26 Pre-Peak
Bats R
R High
I EXP CON
S pt stb
K
LIMA F BA: 60%

Yr	Tm	AB	R	H	HR	RBI	SB	Avg	vL	vR	R$	OB	Slg	OPS	bb%	ct%	h%	Eye	xBA	PX	SX	G/F	RC/G	RAR
99		0	0	0	0	0	0	0								0								
00	aa	532	72	129	20	88	19	242			$16	289	415	705	6	79	27	0.32	269	100	122		3.99	-8.1
01	CHW	* 452	70	129	21	64	12	285	309	279	$19	337	493	830	7	85	30	0.50	293	130	80	2.13	5.94	13.9
02	CHW	302	41	78	7	29	0	258	265	255	$4	287	394	681	4	82	29	0.22	265	87	71	1.65	3.82	-8.4
03	CHW	* 277	35	71	9	35	0	256	338	250	$5	299	412	711	6	89	26	0.55	287	100	31	1.32	4.22	-4.2
1st Half		212	22	46	6	24	0	217			$1	269	358	627	7	89	22	0.63	282	92	26		3.14	-10.4
2nd Half		65	13	25	3	11	0	385			$4	403	585	988	3	89	40	0.29	306	124	41		9.76	7.9
04	Proj	**200**	**30**	**54**	**7**	**27**	**2**	**270**			**$5**	**312**	**438**	**750**	**6**	**86**	**29**	**0.43**	**285**	**107**	**60**		**4.76**	**-0.0**

6-24-.287 in 157 AB at CHW. Hit into a lot of bad luck in the 1st half (22% hit rate) but didn't get enough 2nd half ABs to offset it. Despite outward appearances, this was a growth year, but there's still a ways to go.

Sadler,Donnie

Pos 3B CF
Age 28 Peak
Bats R
R Very High
I exp CON
S pt stb
K
LIMA F BA: 50%

Yr	Tm	AB	R	H	HR	RBI	SB	Avg	vL	vR	R$	OB	Slg	OPS	bb%	ct%	h%	Eye	xBA	PX	SX	G/F	RC/G	RAR
99	BOS	* 279	38	78	1	18	5	280		321	$4	323	380	703	6	82	34	0.36	261	70	127	1.87	4.26	-1.3
00	BOS	* 412	53	82	5	30	12	199	80	270	($1)	275	282	556	9	83	23	0.61	247	48	132	1.33	2.55	-24.1
01	KC	185	28	30	1	5	7	162	88	195	($3)	236	211	447	9	80	20	0.49	204	36	105	1.36	1.49	-17.9
02	TEX	* 162	26	30	0	10	7	185	71	200	($1)	246	241	486	7	84	22	0.50	237	38	161	1.32	1.62	-15.5
03	TEX	* 197	38	44	2	10	9	223	203	194	$2	298	330	628	10	78	28	0.49	240	69	173	1.38	3.18	-8.2
1st Half		124	22	32	1	8	7	258			$3	333	387	720	10	81	31	0.61	259	83	191		4.19	-1.2
2nd Half		73	16	12	1	2	2	164			($1)	237	233	470	9	73	21	0.35	208	45	129		1.80	-6.5
04	Proj	**100**	**18**	**20**	**1**	**5**	**4**	**200**			**($0)**	**269**	**282**	**551**	**9**	**79**	**25**	**0.46**	**236**	**54**	**146**		**2.35**	**-6.8**

1-5-4-.198 in 131 AB at TEX. Showed some marginal skills in the 1st half, but then gave back all those gains after the Break. Over the past 5 years, his bat has cost his teams almost 7 games, all by himself.

Salmon,Tim

Pos RF DH
Age 35 Decline
Bats R
R Low
I con
S pt
K age
LIMA B BA: 55%

Yr	Tm	AB	R	H	HR	RBI	SB	Avg	vL	vR	R$	OB	Slg	OPS	bb%	ct%	h%	Eye	xBA	PX	SX	G/F	RC/G	RAR
99	ANA	353	60	94	17	69	4	266	301	257	$12	377	490	867	15	77	30	0.77	260	135	83	0.81	6.44	15.0
00	ANA	568	108	165	34	97	0	290	226	315	$21	400	540	941	15	76	33	0.75	283	144	43	0.96	7.68	43.9
01	ANA	475	63	108	17	49	9	227	232	226	$7	357	383	740	17	75	27	0.79	236	94	66	0.73	4.54	-6.4
02	ANA	483	84	138	22	88	6	286	299	280	$20	377	503	880	13	79	32	0.70	271	137	71	0.76	6.71	23.1
03	ANA	528	78	145	19	72	3	275	274	275	$15	367	464	831	13	82	30	0.83	284	119	78	0.80	5.98	12.5
1st Half		278	39	76	10	36	2	273			$8	350	453	804	11	82	30	0.66	276	108	89		5.54	3.1
2nd Half		250	39	69	9	36	1	276			$7	384	476	860	15	83	30	1.02	293	132	56		6.47	9.4
04	Proj	**500**	**78**	**135**	**20**	**74**	**5**	**270**			**$15**	**372**	**466**	**838**	**14**	**80**	**30**	**0.80**	**281**	**123**	**70**		**6.04**	**13.9**

Posted the highest contact rate of his entire professional career, but it didn't translate into any other appreciable gains. At 35, and with his injury history, it's tough to see his stats getting any better.

Sanchez,Alex

Pos CF
Age 27 Peak
Bats L
R High
I EXP con
S pt STB
K
LIMA C BA: 45%

Yr	Tm	AB	R	H	HR	RBI	SB	Avg	vL	vR	R$	OB	Slg	OPS	bb%	ct%	h%	Eye	xBA	PX	SX	G/F	RC/G	RAR
99	aa	510	54	114	2	22	37	224			$7	253	267	519	4	87	25	0.30	252	30	114		1.77	-46.0
00	a/a	532	69	138	2	29	42	259			$15	291	318	609	4	89	29	0.39	261	40	125		2.72	-29.6
01	MIL	* 403	50	108	1	25	28	268	200	206	$12	308	340	647	5	88	30	0.48	267	48	151	2.42	3.58	-3.3
02	MIL	394	55	114	1	33	37	289	267	292	$19	341	358	699	7	84	34	0.50	268	44	178	2.40	4.31	-6.4
03	2TM	557	58	160	1	32	52	287	309	279	$24	318	363	681	4	87	33	0.34	286	52	154	1.80	3.86	-16.4
1st Half		286	25	78	0	15	22	273			$9	300	353	653	4	85	32	0.26	284	56	156		3.34	-13.2
2nd Half		271	33	82	1	17	30	303			$15	337	373	710	5	88	34	0.44	288	48	148		4.47	-3.1
04	Proj	**550**	**66**	**155**	**1**	**35**	**50**	**282**			**$23**	**320**	**349**	**669**	**5**	**87**	**32**	**0.41**	**287**	**45**	**151**		**3.77**	**-15.8**

It's quite a feat to steal 50-plus bases with a .318 OBA. That means he attempted a SB every other time he reached first base. Add in a marginal 68% success rate and you get an offensively detrimental speedster.

Sanchez,Rey

Pos SS
Age 36 Decline
Bats R

R	Very High
I	CON
S	pt STB
K	AGE

LIMA D BA: 55%

	Tm	AB	R	H	HR	RBI	SB	Avg	vL	vR	R$	OB	Slg	OPS	bb%	ct%	h%	Eye	xBA	PX	SX	G/F	RC/G	RAR
99	KC	479	66	141	2	56	11	294	326	286	$11	325	370	695	4	90	32	0.46	285	49	125	2.34	4.29	1.7
00	KC	509	68	139	1	38	7	273	290	267	$5	311	322	633	5	89	30	0.51	255	36	89	3.35	3.50	-13.3
01	2TM	544	56	153	0	37	11	281	256	290	$9	301	336	637	3	91	31	0.31	275	38	118	2.81	3.67	-4.5
02	BOS	357	46	102	1	38	2	286	273	289	$6	318	345	663	5	91	31	0.55	241	41	83	1.84	3.85	-7.3
03	2TM	344	33	86	0	23	2	250	292	235	$1	283	285	568	4	89	28	0.41	257	26	71	2.67	2.74	-15.5
1st Half		129	10	29	0	10	1	225			($1)	265	264	528	5	88	25	0.47	258	27	72		2.24	-8.0
2nd Half		215	23	57	0	13	1	265			$1	295	298	592	4	89	30	0.38	257	25	66		3.07	-7.4
04	Proj	300	33	80	0	24	2	267			$3	298	313	611	4	90	30	0.43	265	34	75		3.22	-8.3

Batted nearly 90 points higher in SEA than NYM and almost gave the perception that he was making a positive contribution. But a 26 PX means his power skills were 74% below league average. That's very bad.

Sandberg,Jared

Pos 3B
Age 26 Pre-Peak
Bats R

R	High
I	EXP con
S	pt stb
K	

LIMA D BA: 40%

	Tm	AB	R	H	HR	RBI	SB	Avg	vL	vR	R$	OB	Slg	OPS	bb%	ct%	h%	Eye	xBA	PX	SX	G/F	RC/G	RAR
99		0	0	0	0	0	0	0								0								
00	a/a	259	26	65	6	35	4	251			$4	322	398	719	9	83	28	0.60	275	96	62		4.17	-1.5
01	TAM	* 486	53	109	17	65	1	224	195	211	$6	298	381	679	9	74	27	0.40	234	98	31	1.88	3.71	-9.7
02	TAM	* 472	72	112	21	72	4	237	209	235	$11	312	439	750	10	63	33	0.29	216	125	74	1.28	4.54	1.0
03	TAM	* 408	50	87	16	56	1	213	209	217	$4	287	407	694	9	66	28	0.30	226	122	66	0.97	3.79	-9.0
1st Half		235	29	54	10	33	0	230			$4	307	447	753	10	65	31	0.31	228	135	67		4.53	0.2
2nd Half		173	21	33	6	23	1	191			$0	259	353	612	8	68	24	0.29	221	103	52		2.91	-8.8
04	Proj	350	44	82	13	49	2	234			$6	306	416	721	9	68	31	0.32	227	114	60		4.21	-2.7

6-23-.213 in 136 AB at TAM, and then another .213 MLE BA for 272 AB in AAA. His power skills are improving in tandem with the decline in his BA. At this rate, he'll soon hit 50 HRs and bat .125.

Sanders,Reggie

Pos RF LF
Age 36 Decline
Bats R

R	X HIGH
I	CON
S	pt STB
K	AGE

LIMA C+ BA: 40%

	Tm	AB	R	H	HR	RBI	SB	Avg	vL	vR	R$	OB	Slg	OPS	bb%	ct%	h%	Eye	xBA	PX	SX	G/F	RC/G	RAR
99	SD	478	92	136	26	72	36	285	303	277	$28	370	527	897	12	77	32	0.60	289	140	160	1.12	6.76	24.5
00	ATL	340	43	79	11	37	21	232	264	224	$10	298	403	701	9	77	27	0.41	267	108	112	1.24	4.11	-10.7
01	ARI	441	84	116	33	90	14	263	256	266	$24	333	549	881	9	71	29	0.37	258	159	121	0.95	5.93	4.9
02	SF	505	75	126	23	85	18	250	289	237	$21	313	455	769	9	76	29	0.39	255	127	145	0.91	4.81	-7.4
03	PIT	453	74	129	31	87	15	285	301	278	$27	340	567	907	8	76	31	0.35	293	168	127	0.92	6.78	15.2
1st Half		214	31	56	12	34	6	262			$9	313	486	799	7	71	32	0.25	254	134	103		5.31	-1.8
2nd Half		239	43	73	19	53	9	305			$18	364	640	1004	8	80	31	0.47	328	199	138		8.26	17.7
04	Proj	450	74	122	28	83	14	271			$23	333	530	864	9	76	30	0.38	290	154	124		6.01	7.1

Six teams in six seasons, but his 3-year streak of post-season appearances ends. There is never a question about his talent, only his health. Even at 36, he can put up the numbers. Check out that 2nd half!

Santiago,Benito

Pos CA
Age 39 Decline
Bats R

R	Very High
I	CON
S	pt stb
K	AGE

LIMA D BA: 50%

	Tm	AB	R	H	HR	RBI	SB	Avg	vL	vR	R$	OB	Slg	OPS	bb%	ct%	h%	Eye	xBA	PX	SX	G/F	RC/G	RAR
99	CHC	350	28	87	7	36	1	249	250	248	$3	312	377	689	8	80	29	0.45	255	83	57	1.16	3.95	-0.0
00	CIN	252	22	66	8	45	2	262	268	259	$6	314	409	722	7	82	29	0.42	242	88	47	1.11	4.32	2.4
01	SF	477	39	125	6	45	5	262	256	264	$7	296	369	665	5	84	30	0.29	257	71	80	1.37	3.69	2.4
02	SF	478	56	133	16	74	4	278	276	279	$16	317	450	767	5	85	30	0.37	283	110	94	1.41	4.99	12.0
03	SF	401	53	112	11	56	0	279	290	276	$10	328	424	752	7	83	31	0.42	280	94	53	1.33	4.87	6.5
1st Half		243	31	71	10	40	0	292			$9	336	457	793	6	84	31	0.41	285	98	45		5.43	7.7
2nd Half		158	22	41	1	16	0	259			$1	316	373	689	8	81	31	0.43	272	89	66		4.06	-1.1
04	Proj	400	47	108	9	57	0	270			$9	316	411	728	6	83	31	0.40	282	94	62		4.52	4.9

Dislocated finger derailed his 2nd half, but he was able to maintain most of his BPIs. Might hang on to double digit dollar value for one more year.

Santiago,Ramon

Pos SS 2B
Age 22 Growth
Bats S

R	High
I	EXP con
S	pt
K	AGE

LIMA D+ BA: 65%

	Tm	AB	R	H	HR	RBI	SB	Avg	vL	vR	R$	OB	Slg	OPS	bb%	ct%	h%	Eye	xBA	PX	SX	G/F	RC/G	RAR
99		0	0	0	0	0	0	0								0								
00		0	0	0	0	0	0	0								0								
01		0	0	0	0	0	0	0								0								
02	DET	* 325	48	84	6	31	13	258	222	250	$8	297	375	673	5	81	30	0.30	246	63	181	1.74	3.68	-8.8
03	DET	444	41	100	2	29	10	225	187	242	$1	279	284	563	7	85	26	0.50	274	44	78	1.73	2.61	-24.8
1st Half		202	19	46	0	6	4	228			($1)	288	277	565	8	84	27	0.52	268	43	62		2.62	-11.2
2nd Half		242	22	54	2	23	6	223			$1	271	289	561	6	86	25	0.48	279	45	84		2.59	-13.7
04	Proj	500	57	119	5	39	15	238			$6	285	321	606	6	84	28	0.41	277	52	118		3.02	-21.7

Good things about this season:
- Improved bb%, ct% and eye
- Improved in 2nd half, sort of
- Played enough to get rid of the rookie heebie jeebies
- Nice, fairly new ballpark
- Left town before winter hit

Santos,Angel

Pos 2B
Age 24 Growth
Bats S

R	X HIGH
I	EXP CON
S	pt STB
K	age

LIMA F BA: 55%

	Tm	AB	R	H	HR	RBI	SB	Avg	vL	vR	R$	OB	Slg	OPS	bb%	ct%	h%	Eye	xBA	PX	SX	G/F	RC/G	RAR
99		0	0	0	0	0	0	0								0								
00	aa	275	28	68	2	28	16	247			$6	315	342	656	9	81	30	0.52	254	66	109		3.46	-5.6
01	a/a	541	70	142	12	49	24	262			$15	324	394	717	8	82	30	0.51	266	89	85		4.29	4.2
02	aaa	350	34	84	8	42	10	240			$7	304	363	667	8	83	27	0.53	258	79	83		3.44	-8.4
03	CLE	* 336	40	75	9	31	13	223	231	222	$6	296	348	645	9	79	26	0.50	245	77	92	0.71	3.37	-8.0
1st Half		213	22	48	4	17	8	225			$3	319	319	632	11	79	27	0.60	233	61	67		3.23	-6.0
2nd Half		123	18	27	5	14	5	220			$3	267	398	666	6	80	24	0.32	264	105	129		3.53	-2.3
04	Proj	100	12	24	3	10	4	240			$2	303	367	671	8	81	27	0.48	249	82	72		3.64	-1.4

3-6-.224 in 76 AB at CLE. Soft skills and declining trends yielded a ticket to Buffalo.

Schneider,Brian

Pos CA
Age 27 Peak
Bats L

R	Very High
I	exp CON
S	PT stb
K	

LIMA D BA: 55%

	Tm	AB	R	H	HR	RBI	SB	Avg	vL	vR	R$	OB	Slg	OPS	bb%	ct%	h%	Eye	xBA	PX	SX	G/F	RC/G	RAR
99	aa	421	41	101	13	56	2	240			$5	286	380	666	6	89	24	0.57	284	86	45		3.59	-5.4
00	MON	* 353	25	82	4	38	1	232	364	204	$0	273	334	608	5	83	27	0.33	263	70	50	1.59	3.01	-10.5
01	MON	41	4	13	1	6	0	317			$2	404	463	868	13	93	32	2.00	317	99		0.93	7.00	3.8
02	MON	207	21	57	5	29	1	275	280	275	$6	342	459	801	9	80	32	0.51	290	133	72	1.31	5.34	7.3
03	MON	335	34	77	9	46	0	230	179	243	$3	306	394	700	10	78	27	0.50	260	114	35	1.59	3.90	-4.0
1st Half		140	18	35	6	21	0	250			$3	356	450	806	14	78	28	0.74	265	131	25		5.30	4.2
2nd Half		195	16	42	3	25	0	215			$0	268	354	622	7	78	26	0.33	256	102	49		3.01	-7.8
04	Proj	350	34	93	10	52	0	266			$8	329	441	770	9	80	31	0.48	270	118	44		4.97	8.8

Got off to a solid start but collapsed in the 2nd half after getting hit in the head by a bat in the follow-through of an Aramis Ramirez swing. He claimed he was okay, but the numbers say otherwise.

Scutaro,Marcos

Pos 2B
Age 28 Peak
Bats R

R	High
I	EXP con
S	stb
K	

LIMA D BA: 60%

	Tm	AB	R	H	HR	RBI	SB	Avg	vL	vR	R$	OB	Slg	OPS	bb%	ct%	h%	Eye	xBA	PX	SX	G/F	RC/G	RAR
99	aaa	462	65	118	7	43	18	255			$9	331	355	686	10	87	28	0.88	273	68	93		4.01	-1.2
00	aaa	438	54	105	4	44	8	240			$3	315	326	641	10	91	26	1.17	276	56	94		3.32	-10.6
01	aaa	495	70	131	9	41	9	265			$9	332	382	714	9	86	29	0.75	272	78	74		4.04	0.2
02	aaa	390	44	108	7	30	6	277			$8	320	405	726	6	82	32	0.36	260	83	102	1.20	4.17	-0.6
03	NYM	* 319	46	83	10	34	12	260	95	259	$10	344	426	771	11	85	28	0.85	284	108	103	1.04	4.86	4.4
1st Half		190	27	48	5	18	8	253			$5	321	405	726	9	86	27	0.73	286	102	104		4.09	-1.8
2nd Half		129	19	35	5	16	4	271			$5	377	457	835	15	83	29	1.00	281	116	96		6.09	6.3
04	Proj	150	20	40	4	15	4	267			$4	341	409	751	10	85	29	0.74	280	93	91		4.63	1.4

2-6-2-.213 in 75 AB at NYM, and was placed on waivers. But wait! He had a .401 OB at Norfolk, so that might....

Oops, too late. OAK has already picked him up. Figures.

Segui,David

Pos DH
Age 37 Decline
Bats S

R	Very High
I	con
S	PT stb
K	AGE

LIMA D+ BA: 40%

	Tm	AB	R	H	HR	RBI	SB	Avg	vL	vR	R$	OB	Slg	OPS	bb%	ct%	h%	Eye	xBA	PX	SX	G/F	RC/G	RAR
99	2AL	440	57	131	14	52	1	298	271	303	$12	356	468	824	8	86	32	0.67	284	106	58	1.13	5.96	9.4
00	2AL	574	93	192	19	103	0	334	310	344	$24	391	510	901	8	85	37	0.63	311	111	38	1.62	7.59	37.7
01	BAL	292	48	88	10	46	1	301	338	288	$11	402	473	874	14	79	35	0.80	296	108	50	1.21	6.87	13.2
02	BAL	95	10	25	2	16	0	263	192	290	$2	340	368	708	10	77	32	0.50	220	69		1.19	4.33	-3.3
03	BAL	224	26	59	5	25	1	263	200	282	$4	340	384	724	10	79	31	0.55	251	77	56	1.62	4.55	-0.4
1st Half		185	21	49	3	19	1	265			$3	343	368	711	11	78	33	0.54	241	67	61		4.41	-1.1
2nd Half		39	5	10	2	6	0	256			$1	326	462	787	9	85	26	0.67	298	123	21		5.15	0.6
04	Proj	350	50	106	10	50	1	303			$12	375	453	828	10	82	35	0.64	262	97	49		6.18	11.4

After three injury-shortened years and yet another statement out of BAL saying that "he'll be ready for spring training," it's time to start reading the noise for what it is. He's 37 now anyway. Play it risk averse here.

Sexson,Richie

	Yr	Tm	AB	R	H	HR	RBI	SB	Avg	vL	vR	R$	OB	Slg	OPS	bb%	ct%	h%	Eye	xBA	PX	SX	G/F	RC/G	RAR
Pos 1B	99	CLE	479	72	122	31	116	3	255	277	246	$18	304	514	818	7	76	27	0.29	273	139	117	1.26	5.23	-7.8
Age 29 Past Peak	00	2TM	537	89	146	30	91	2	272	220	286	$18	344	499	843	10	70	33	0.37	257	131	61	1.27	6.04	6.0
Bats R	01	MIL	598	94	162	45	125	2	271	295	264	$28	337	547	884	9	70	31	0.34	260	152	61	1.15	6.30	0.8
R Very Low	02	MIL	570	86	159	29	102	0	279	238	288	$23	358	504	861	11	76	32	0.51	289	145	42	1.33	6.37	12.5
I	03	MIL	606	97	165	45	124	2	272	279	271	$29	374	548	921	14	75	29	0.65	292	160	47	1.41	7.07	27.0
S stb	1st Half		305	52	79	22	55	2	259			$13	360	502	861	14	74	28	0.60	274	136	42		6.03	4.6
K	2nd Half		301	45	86	23	69	0	286			$16	387	595	982	14	76	30	0.70	310	185	46		8.23	22.9
LIMA D BA: 55%	04	Proj	600	94	170	46	121	1	283			$31	369	577	946	12	75	31	0.53	295	171	53		7.50	31.8

A powerful lesson in how this is such a game of inches... His HR output has fluctuated wildly over the past three years, but his (HR+2B) were 69, 66 73 -- not nearly as deviant a trend. He's peaking now -- ride it.

Sheffield,Gary

	Yr	Tm	AB	R	H	HR	RBI	SB	Avg	vL	vR	R$	OB	Slg	OPS	bb%	ct%	h%	Eye	xBA	PX	SX	G/F	RC/G	RAR
Pos RF	99	LA	549	103	165	34	101	11	301	336	288	$28	409	523	932	16	88	29	1.58	293	126	62	0.81	7.71	41.4
Age 35 Decline	00	LA	501	105	163	43	109	4	325	285	339	$33	439	643	1081	17	86	31	1.42	317	174	62	0.84	10.30	69.6
Bats R	01	LA	515	98	160	36	100	10	311	374	294	$32	417	583	1000	15	87	30	1.40	321	155	81	0.91	8.91	47.2
R Low	02	ATL	492	82	151	25	84	12	307	293	310	$28	395	512	908	13	89	30	1.36	306	131	77	1.04	7.53	30.0
I con	03	ATL	576	126	190	39	132	18	330	341	327	$44	417	604	1021	13	90	31	1.56	363	167	104	1.36	9.61	61.3
S stb	1st Half		282	66	91	22	64	11	323			$23	409	621	1029	13	91	29	1.71	374	179	94		9.50	29.6
K age	2nd Half		294	60	99	17	68	7	337			$21	425	588	1013	13	89	33	1.45	351	154	103		9.71	31.5
LIMA C BA: 75%	04	Proj	550	109	176	31	114	14	320			$35	413	554	967	14	89	32	1.46	354	143	95		8.60	46.3

Rising power trend with increased groundball frequency is an anomaly that will likely end, taking a bite out of his HR total. But superior skill will keep him valuable; just hold back if bidding hits $40.

Shinjo,Tsuyoshi

	Yr	Tm	AB	R	H	HR	RBI	SB	Avg	vL	vR	R$	OB	Slg	OPS	bb%	ct%	h%	Eye	xBA	PX	SX	G/F	RC/G	RAR
Pos CF	99	JPN	471	50	112	8	55	8	237			$5	266	382	648	4	85	26	0.26	281	85	162		3.41	-15.5
Age 32 Past Peak	00	JPN	511	67	132	17	81	15	259			$15	295	409	703	5	82	29	0.28	269	89	94		4.00	-7.4
Bats R	01	NYM	400	46	107	10	56	4	268	305	258	$10	311	405	716	6	83	30	0.36	266	89	60	1.03	4.20	4.1
R High	02	SF	369	42	86	9	37	5	233	291	214	$5	282	363	645	6	87	25	0.53	283	84	104	1.42	3.47	-15.5
I CON	03	NYM	* 225	20	52	4	14	0	231	247	61	($0)	273	329	602	5	87	25	0.43	259	64	45	1.19	2.85	-14.6
S pt STB	1st Half		114	10	22	1	7	0	193			($2)	233	246	479	5	89	21	0.50	252	37	42		1.73	-11.9
K	2nd Half		111	10	30	3	7	0	270			$2	314	414	728	6	84	30	0.39	267	91	60		4.36	-2.0
LIMA F BA: 60%	04	Proj	150	15	36	3	14	1	240			$1	283	360	643	6	86	26	0.42	263	76	72		3.34	-6.2

1-7-.193 in 114 AB at NYM, and not much better at AAA. Not one of the better talents to cross the Pacific, and his time may have just run out.

Shumpert,Terry

	Yr	Tm	AB	R	H	HR	RBI	SB	Avg	vL	vR	R$	OB	Slg	OPS	bb%	ct%	h%	Eye	xBA	PX	SX	G/F	RC/G	RAR
Pos DH	99	COL	* 341	68	119	15	48	16	349	395	324	$22	408	601	1009	9	87	37	0.74	324	162	141	0.61	9.91	41.2
Age 37 Decline	00	COL	263	52	68	9	40	8	259	277	249	$8	330	456	786	10	85	28	0.70	280	109	192	0.87	5.04	-0.4
Bats R	01	COL	242	37	70	4	24	14	289	233	322	$10	331	438	769	6	82	34	0.34	275	92	190	1.17	5.29	0.4
R Moderate	02	COL	234	30	55	6	21	4	235	294	201	$3	298	372	670	8	82	26	0.51	265	93	88	1.05	3.72	-12.8
I con	03	TAM	84	14	16	2	7	1	190	203	133	($0)	277	369	646	11	80	22	0.59	262	109	169	0.93	3.27	-3.6
S pt stb	1st Half		69	10	15	2	7	1	217			$1	280	406	686	8	83	24	0.50	276	120	124		3.77	-1.8
K AGE	2nd Half		15	4	1	0	0	0	67			($1)	263	200	463	21	67	10	0.80	201	58	393		1.44	-1.7
LIMA D+ BA: 65%	04	Proj	100	16	26	3	11	3	260			$3	318	442	761	8	83	29	0.51	269	111	158		4.90	-0.2

A token 100 AB projection should he decide not to retire. His value ended two years ago anyway.

Sierra,Ruben

	Yr	Tm	AB	R	H	HR	RBI	SB	Avg	vL	vR	R$	OB	Slg	OPS	bb%	ct%	h%	Eye	xBA	PX	SX	G/F	RC/G	RAR
Pos LF DH	99	ind	422	72	116	17	78	3	274			$13	347	460	807	10	85	29	0.75	291	111	88		5.61	6.6
Age 38 Decline	00	TEX	* 499	57	134	16	68	5	269	400	178	$11	330	419	749	8	87	28	0.73	284	89	67	1.05	4.81	-4.1
Bats S	01	TEX	* 438	66	121	26	76	4	276	321	281	$18	318	518	837	6	85	27	0.42	303	141	80	0.96	5.87	15.4
R Very High	02	SEA	419	47	113	13	60	4	270	266	272	$12	320	418	738	7	84	29	0.47	270	95	57	1.39	4.73	-1.3
I con	03	2AL	307	33	83	9	43	2	270	236	284	$8	329	420	750	8	85	29	0.57	299	96	52	1.50	4.81	-4.6
S pt STB	1st Half		182	21	54	6	25	1	297			$6	359	467	836	10	82	34	0.64	299	113	32		6.16	4.2
K AGE	2nd Half		125	12	29	3	18	1	232			$2	267	352	619	5	89	24	0.43	296	71	74		3.16	-8.2
LIMA F BA: 55%	04	Proj	250	29	66	7	37	1	264			$5	316	402	718	7	86	29	0.52	298	88	56		4.40	-4.9

From a skills perspective, our BPIs say that '02 and '03 were carbon copy seasons. Then why the 29-point jump in xBA? In '02, 19% of his batted balls were line drives; 25% in '03. Also helped: slightly higher ct%, PX and G/F.

Simon,Randall

	Yr	Tm	AB	R	H	HR	RBI	SB	Avg	vL	vR	R$	OB	Slg	OPS	bb%	ct%	h%	Eye	xBA	PX	SX	G/F	RC/G	RAR
Pos 1B	99	ATL	* 277	34	83	6	32	2	300	222	325	$7	345	433	778	6	90	32	0.68	294	93	41	2.38	5.24	-0.5
Age 28 Peak	00	aaa	432	44	103	15	65	5	238			$8	283	403	686	6	92	23	0.79	307	96	71		3.63	-26.4
Bats L	01	DET	* 478	50	145	13	62	0	303	233	319	$15	346	450	796	6	91	31	0.70	285	94	29	2.12	5.50	-8.6
R High	02	DET	482	51	145	19	82	0	301	255	320	$19	319	459	778	3	94	29	0.43	303	92	27	1.81	5.29	-7.6
I exp con	03	2NL	410	47	113	16	72	0	276	269	277	$13	303	434	737	4	91	27	0.43	292	98	25	1.76	4.63	-10.3
S pt STB	1st Half		222	23	62	7	40	0	279			$7	304	428	732	3	91	28	0.38	290	98	22		4.61	-5.7
K	2nd Half		188	24	51	9	32	0	271			$6	301	441	743	4	91	26	0.50	294	99	28		4.65	-4.6
LIMA D+ BA: 60%	04	Proj	400	45	113	15	65	0	283			$13	312	442	754	4	92	28	0.52	295	99	38		4.85	-8.8

List of trends in steady decline:
1. Batting average / hit rate
2. OBA / walk rate
3. Speed index
4. Runs created per game
5. Runs above replacement
6. My patience

Singleton,Chris

	Yr	Tm	AB	R	H	HR	RBI	SB	Avg	vL	vR	R$	OB	Slg	OPS	bb%	ct%	h%	Eye	xBA	PX	SX	G/F	RC/G	RAR
Pos CF	99	CHW	496	72	149	17	72	20	300		281	$22	330	490	820	4	91	30	0.49	333	115	139	1.36	5.90	16.5
Age 32 Past Peak	00	CHW	511	83	130	11	62	22	254	206	262	$13	302	382	684	6	83	29	0.41	261	76	147	1.29	3.94	-10.9
Bats L	01	CHW	392	57	117	7	45	12	298	300	298	$14	333	431	764	5	84	34	0.33	295	84	120	1.33	4.79	-0.7
R Moderate	02	BAL	466	67	122	9	50	20	262	208	272	$14	294	410	704	4	82	30	0.25	282	96	164	1.33	4.31	-6.3
I CON	03	OAK	306	38	75	1	36	7	245	167	260	$4	304	340	644	8	82	30	0.47	282	76	91	1.41	3.52	-11.2
S pt stb	1st Half		169	26	51	1	21	1	302			$4	348	420	768	7	83	36	0.43	266	92	77		5.12	1.8
K	2nd Half		137	12	24	0	15	6	175			($1)	252	241	493	9	80	22	0.52	262	57	87		2.06	-11.9
LIMA D BA: 55%	04	Proj	250	33	63	3	29	5	252			$4	301	370	671	6	83	29	0.40	262	83	107		3.77	-7.4

Officially announced that he has no intentions of coming back to OAK. After all, they treated him so poorly, giving him AB that could have otherwise gone to a player with talent. Beane must be clicking his heels.

Smitherman,Steve

	Yr	Tm	AB	R	H	HR	RBI	SB	Avg	vL	vR	R$	OB	Slg	OPS	bb%	ct%	h%	Eye	xBA	PX	SX	G/F	RC/G	RAR
Pos LF	99		0	0	0	0	0	0	0								0								
Age 25 Pre-Peak	00		0	0	0	0	0	0	0								0								
Bats R	01		0	0	0	0	0	0	0								0								
R Moderate	02		0	0	0	0	0	0	0								0								
I EXP	03	CIN	* 472	50	115	17	66	10	244	190	130	$12	312	405	717	9	78	28	0.46	256	102	74	0.75	4.26	-18.7
S	1st Half		274	31	74	13	39	5	270			$10	329	474	803	8	79	30	0.42	271	126	70		5.40	-1.5
K age	2nd Half		198	19	41	4	27	5	207			$2	290	308	598	10	77	25	0.51	235	68	66		2.93	-16.5
LIMA F BA: 50%	04	Proj	150	15	38	5	21	3	253			$4	324	393	717	9	78	30	0.48	253	90	55		4.38	-6.1

1-6-.159 in 44 AB at CIN. Small signs of potential but two strikes against him coming into '04...
1. Horrible 2nd half offset some nice numbers he posted earlier.
2. At 25, he's behind the curve and losing ground every day.

Smith,Mark

	Yr	Tm	AB	R	H	HR	RBI	SB	Avg	vL	vR	R$	OB	Slg	OPS	bb%	ct%	h%	Eye	xBA	PX	SX	G/F	RC/G	RAR
Pos LF	99	JPN	307	38	75	13	57	3	246			$8	294	424	718	6	73	30	0.25	243	103	75		4.15	-8.3
Age 33 Decline	00	FLA	192	22	47	5	27	2	245	173	291	$3	306	375	681	8	72	32	0.31	212	79	74	1.04	3.94	-7.3
Bats R	01	MON	* 339	44	72	11	32	4	212	275	214	$2	286	375	661	9	77	24	0.45	258	102	74	1.17	3.35	-24.9
R X HIGH	02	aaa	389	40	86	7	36	4	221			$2	272	334	606	6	83	25	0.40	257	81	58		2.91	-32.3
I exp CON	03	MIL	* 451	46	111	16	60	3	246	241	235	$9	280	415	694	4	84	26	0.29	277	109	56	1.15	3.87	-23.0
S pt STB	1st Half		262	27	69	7	35	3	263			$6	296	416	712	4	85	29	0.30	277	103	68		4.17	-10.8
K age	2nd Half		189	19	42	9	25	0	222			$3	258	413	670	5	83	22	0.28	275	117	20		3.49	-12.1
LIMA F BA: 55%	04	Proj	100	11	25	3	12	1	250			$2	295	397	693	6	81	28	0.34	269	95	44		3.93	-5.4

3-10-.238 in 63 AB at MIL. In his 12 year pro career, he has played in home ballparks in 16 different cities in three different countries. Has never once seen 500 ABs in a single season but did hit 19 HRs in Rochester.

Snow,J.T.

Pos 1B | Age 36 Decline | Bats L | R: Moderate | I: con | S: pt | K: AGE | LIMA D | BA: 55%

Yr	Tm	AB	R	H	HR	RBI	SB	Avg	vL	vR	R$	OB	Slg	OPS	bb%	ct%	h%	Eye	xBA	PX	SX	G/F	RC/G	RAR
99	SF	570	93	156	24	98	0	274	231	292	$17	369	451	820	13	79	31	0.71	250	106	37	0.83	5.69	6.3
00	SF	536	82	152	19	96	1	284	256	292	$17	362	459	821	11	76	34	0.51	249	108	49	0.95	5.80	6.9
01	SF	285	43	70	8	34	0	246	306	233	$4	368	379	747	16	72	32	0.68	231	81	44	1.09	4.71	-13.0
02	SF	422	47	104	6	53	0	246	229	250	$5	339	360	699	12	79	30	0.66	253	84	43	1.30	4.13	-18.3
03	SF	330	48	90	8	51	1	273	208	284	$8	377	418	795	14	83	31	1.00	264	95	72	0.90	5.42	-0.9
1st Half		188	18	52	3	30	0	277			$4	373	426	799	13	85	31	1.00	272	101	80		5.49	-0.1
2nd Half		142	30	38	5	21	1	268			$4	381	408	789	15	82	30	1.00	253	87	60		5.33	-0.7
04	Proj	**350**	**52**	**92**	**9**	**50**	**1**	**263**			**$7**	**366**	**402**	**768**	**14**	**80**	**31**	**0.80**	**257**	**91**	**61**		**5.04**	**-6.0**

Bothered by a strained groin for most of the season, he posted better BPIs than either of the previous two years. But while his skill set still shows small signs of life, it is not nearly rebust enough for a 1Bman.

Soriano,Alfonso

Pos 2B | Age 26 Pre-Peak | Bats R | R: Low | I: exp con | S: stb | K: | LIMA D | BA: 40%

Yr	Tm	AB	R	H	HR	RBI	SB	Avg	vL	vR	R$	OB	Slg	OPS	bb%	ct%	h%	Eye	xBA	PX	SX	G/F	RC/G	RAR
99	a/a	443	56	116	14	68	21	262			$16	312	424	736	7	85	28	0.47	285	100	103	1.50	3.91	-2.5
00	NYY	* 509	79	129	13	57	14	253	150	200	$10	284	409	693	4	85	28	0.29	285	97	127	0.76	3.78	-1.3
01	NYY	574	77	154	18	73	43	268	255	271	$27	303	432	736	5	78	32	0.23	261	103	126	0.97	4.47	4.6
02	NYY	696	128	209	39	102	41	300	316	297	$44	323	547	870	3	77	34	0.15	277	151	134	0.78	6.27	43.7
03	NYY	682	114	198	38	91	35	290	312	285	$37	328	525	853	5	81	31	0.29	281	137	136	0.75	6.19	39.6
1st Half		365	68	106	21	48	24	290			$22	334	512	847	6	81	31	0.35	273	124	148		6.29	22.2
2nd Half		317	46	92	17	43	11	290			$15	320	539	860	4	81	31	0.23	289	153	110		6.08	17.4
04	Proj	**675**	**109**	**193**	**36**	**97**	**36**	**286**			**$36**	**319**	**521**	**839**	**5**	**80**	**31**	**0.24**	**281**	**140**	**130**		**5.79**	**32.7**

Despite the slight drop in his face stats, there was skills growth here. At 26, he's at the age when some might expect a breakout year, but it's tough to think that these levels can get much better without a BPI spike.

Sosa,Sammy

Pos RF | Age 35 Decline | Bats R | R: Low | I: con | S: | K: age | LIMA D | BA: 40%

Yr	Tm	AB	R	H	HR	RBI	SB	Avg	vL	vR	R$	OB	Slg	OPS	bb%	ct%	h%	Eye	xBA	PX	SX	G/F	RC/G	RAR
99	CHC	625	114	180	63	141	7	288	313	279	$39	367	635	1002	11	73	30	0.46	286	190	60	0.90	8.02	53.8
00	CHC	604	106	193	50	138	7	320	347	313	$40	409	634	1043	13	72	37	0.54	291	178	56	1.01	9.58	72.2
01	CHC	577	146	189	64	160	0	328	387	316	$47	440	737	1177	17	73	35	0.76	304	225	75	0.92	12.15	100.8
02	CHC	556	122	160	49	108	2	288	366	270	$33	399	594	993	16	74	31	0.72	288	177	72	1.12	8.51	49.8
03	CHC	517	99	144	40	103	0	279	333	265	$26	356	553	909	11	72	31	0.43	270	159	36	1.09	6.90	19.0
1st Half		205	42	61	10	36	0	298			$9	407	512	920	16	67	40	0.57	241	137	39		7.45	10.5
2nd Half		312	57	83	30	67	0	266			$17	318	580	899	7	76	26	0.32	289	173	35		6.42	7.3
04	Proj	**550**	**114**	**160**	**48**	**117**	**1**	**291**			**$32**	**384**	**598**	**981**	**13**	**73**	**32**	**0.56**	**277**	**176**	**51**		**8.18**	**41.7**

To offset his poor 1st half, he opened up his swing and started cranking them. The result... Mega-HRs, but a huge drop in bb% and a horrible .318 OB. The line on his baseball card will hide the damage he did to CHC.

Spencer,Shane

Pos LF RF | Age 32 Past Peak | Bats R | R: High | I: con | S: PT stb | K: | LIMA D | BA: 45%

Yr	Tm	AB	R	H	HR	RBI	SB	Avg	vL	vR	R$	OB	Slg	OPS	bb%	ct%	h%	Eye	xBA	PX	SX	G/F	RC/G	RAR
99	NYY	* 255	40	65	10	29	0	255	289	197	$4	324	412	736	9	77	29	0.45	248	92	38	0.71	4.27	-6.0
00	NYY	248	33	70	9	40	1	282	312	269	$7	333	460	793	7	82	31	0.42	252	100	88	0.78	5.29	1.4
01	NYY	* 456	53	107	13	57	7	235	313	242	$7	295	382	677	8	83	26	0.50	267	91	88	1.03	3.76	-11.9
02	NYY	288	32	71	6	34	0	247	267	239	$3	320	375	695	10	78	30	0.50	231	83	54	1.01	3.88	-8.2
03	TEX	395	39	99	12	49	2	251	277	231	$7	327	392	720	10	77	30	0.49	250	90	37	0.94	4.40	-10.8
1st Half		174	15	43	3	16	2	247			$2	311	345	655	8	76	31	0.38	233	66	43		3.69	-8.4
2nd Half		221	24	56	9	33	0	253			$5	340	430	770	12	77	29	0.58	263	109	15		4.99	-2.2
04	Proj	**350**	**38**	**89**	**10**	**44**	**2**	**254**			**$6**	**326**	**395**	**721**	**10**	**78**	**30**	**0.49**	**252**	**88**	**47**		**4.36**	**-7.4**

Stable skill set, though he does have some hidden pop potential as demonstrated in the 2nd half. That's not something you can count on from him, as it's based on getting regular playing time, which he rarely gets.

Spiezio,Scott

Pos 1B 3B | Age 31 Past Peak | Bats S | R: Low | I: con | S: pt stb | K: | LIMA B | BA: 65%

Yr	Tm	AB	R	H	HR	RBI	SB	Avg	vL	vR	R$	OB	Slg	OPS	bb%	ct%	h%	Eye	xBA	PX	SX	G/F	RC/G	RAR
99	OAK	* 352	55	99	13	57	0	281	229	249	$10	358	486	844	11	86	30	0.86	302	133	42	0.65	6.17	3.8
00	ANA	297	47	72	17	49	1	242	250	241	$7	332	465	797	12	81	25	0.71	262	120	68	0.78	5.08	-7.7
01	ANA	457	57	124	13	54	5	271	239	282	$11	322	438	759	7	86	29	0.52	265	106	88	0.65	4.90	-16.3
02	ANA	491	80	140	12	82	6	285	368	248	$16	371	436	807	12	89	30	1.29	283	101	71	0.69	5.55	-4.4
03	ANA	521	69	138	16	83	6	265	223	282	$14	325	453	777	8	87	28	0.70	306	119	110	0.99	5.05	-5.0
1st Half		237	34	60	7	24	1	253			$4	332	426	758	11	87	27	0.93	297	108	89		4.69	-4.8
2nd Half		284	35	78	9	59	5	275			$11	318	475	793	6	87	29	0.50	312	128	118		5.34	-0.3
04	Proj	**550**	**77**	**164**	**22**	**97**	**6**	**298**			**$23**	**362**	**502**	**865**	**9**	**87**	**31**	**0.79**	**308**	**126**	**86**		**6.50**	**12.9**

In an analysis elsewhere in this book, he is tabbed for a 2004 breakout season. Look closely and you'll see the signs. This projection hedges a little, the reality could be better.

Spivey,Junior

Pos 2B | Age 29 Past Peak | Bats R | R: X HIGH | I: EXP CON | S: PT stb | K: | LIMA C | BA: 40%

Yr	Tm	AB	R	H	HR	RBI	SB	Avg	vL	vR	R$	OB	Slg	OPS	bb%	ct%	h%	Eye	xBA	PX	SX	G/F	RC/G	RAR
99	aa	164	29	42	2	14	10	256			$4	354	396	751	13	87	28	1.19	292	87	174		4.01	-0.5
00	a/a	136	20	37	3	14	2	272			$3	313	471	783	6	88	29	0.47	315	126	150		5.07	3.8
01	ARI	* 357	52	81	9	41	10	227	323	214	$6	310	353	663	11	80	26	0.59	253	74	113	1.56	3.47	-4.4
02	ARI	538	103	162	16	78	11	301	324	291	$23	376	476	852	11	81	35	0.65	278	117	127	1.22	6.41	30.0
03	ARI	* 391	55	100	13	52	6	256	288	238	$10	317	430	747	8	75	31	0.36	254	114	93	1.08	4.60	2.3
1st Half		204	30	52	9	30	1	255			$5	309	441	750	7	75	30	0.31	249	117	52		4.60	1.1
2nd Half		187	25	48	4	22	5	257			$4	325	417	742	9	76	32	0.43	258	110	121		4.61	1.1
04	Proj	**450**	**70**	**119**	**13**	**57**	**5**	**264**			**$11**	**328**	**429**	**757**	**9**	**79**	**31**	**0.44**	**260**	**107**	**105**		**4.80**	**6.3**

A torn ankle ligament and a neck strain might be the excuses used to explain away this season, but we see non-injury-related BPIs that show a more aggressive hacker swinging for the fences.

Stairs,Matt

Pos RF 1B | Age 36 Decline | Bats L | R: Very High | I: CON | S: pt STB | K: AGE | LIMA C | BA: 50%

Yr	Tm	AB	R	H	HR	RBI	SB	Avg	vL	vR	R$	OB	Slg	OPS	bb%	ct%	h%	Eye	xBA	PX	SX	G/F	RC/G	RAR
99	OAK	531	94	137	38	102	2	258		268	$19	365	533	897	14	77	27	0.72	259	154	58	0.87	6.38	22.2
00	OAK	476	74	108	21	81	5	227	202	235	$8	336	414	750	14	74	26	0.64	232	110	61	0.95	4.57	-5.0
01	CHC	340	48	85	17	61	2	250	172	257	$10	349	462	811	13	78	28	0.68	260	128	38	0.93	5.34	-2.2
02	MIL	270	41	66	16	41	2	244	154	249	$9	333	478	811	12	81	25	0.72	272	147	52	0.99	5.42	1.0
03	PIT	305	49	89	20	57	0	292	188	304	$15	383	561	944	13	79	31	0.70	289	164	39	0.79	7.64	17.3
1st Half		127	12	34	6	17	0	268			$4	340	472	813	10	81	29	0.58	274	130	8		5.60	-0.0
2nd Half		178	37	55	14	40	0	309			$11	411	624	1035	15	78	33	0.78	298	188	60		9.28	17.9
04	Proj	**350**	**55**	**94**	**21**	**62**	**1**	**269**			**$14**	**362**	**518**	**880**	**13**	**79**	**28**	**0.70**	**284**	**152**	**49**		**6.47**	**10.1**

With solid BPIs, primarily vs RHers, he could squeeze out another productive season. PIT would be a good place, a team with few other options, limited short-term upside, and a need to put bodies into the seats.

Stenson,Dernell

Pos LF | Age 25 Pre-Peak | Bats L | R: | I: | S: | K: | LIMA: | BA:

Yr	Tm	AB	R	H	HR	RBI	SB	Avg	vL	vR	R$	OB	Slg	OPS	bb%	ct%	h%	Eye	xBA	PX	SX	G/F	RC/G	RAR
99	aaa	440	61	123	15	78	2	280			$13	356	457	813	11	78	33	0.55	267	114	52		5.73	8.4
00	aaa	380	55	101	19	66	0	266			$11	336	455	791	10	78	29	0.48	265	107	27		5.31	1.7
01	aaa	464	45	102	12	59	0	220			$3	275	338	613	7	79	25	0.36	241	72	31		3.04	-30.1
02	aaa	368	37	85	7	30	3	231			$2	291	348	639	7	78	28	0.38	242	81	58		3.27	-26.2
03	CIN	* 496	60	131	19	81	3	264	200	250	$15	324	450	774	8	81	29	0.48	274	123	38	1.50	4.83	-11.0
1st Half		280	29	71	8	42	3	254			$7	310	400	710	8	81	29	0.44	262	99	46		4.11	-12.3
2nd Half		216	31	60	11	39	0	278			$8	342	514	856	9	81	30	0.53	290	154	31		5.86	1.7
04	Proj																							

3-13-.247 in 81 AB at CIN. Stenson tragically lost his life on November 4. His BPIs had been showing some growth and he probably would have made the CIN roster. May he rest in peace.

Stewart,Shannon

Pos LF | Age 30 Past Peak | Bats R | R: Very Low | I: con | S: stb | K: | LIMA C+ | BA: 55%

Yr	Tm	AB	R	H	HR	RBI	SB	Avg	vL	vR	R$	OB	Slg	OPS	bb%	ct%	h%	Eye	xBA	PX	SX	G/F	RC/G	RAR
99	TOR	608	102	185	11	67	37	304	369	291	$27	366	411	777	9	86	34	0.71	274	69	113	1.77	5.44	6.4
00	TOR	583	107	186	21	69	20	319	309	322	$26	360	518	878	6	86	34	0.47	321	122	133	1.34	6.98	29.8
01	TOR	640	103	202	12	60	27	316	333	312	$26	362	463	824	7	89	34	0.64	316	97	127	1.56	6.14	26.6
02	TOR	577	103	175	10	45	14	303	302	304	$18	363	442	805	9	90	33	0.90	303	93	133	1.52	5.97	17.9
03	2AL	573	90	176	13	73	4	307	331	300	$18	365	459	824	8	88	33	0.79	309	105	62	1.36	5.96	9.9
1st Half		253	42	77	5	31	1	304			$7	365	462	827	9	91	32	1.00	320	109	76		6.02	4.8
2nd Half		320	48	99	8	42	3	309			$11	365	456	821	8	87	34	0.67	300	101	50		5.91	5.1
04	Proj	**600**	**99**	**185**	**18**	**65**	**7**	**308**			**$21**	**364**	**482**	**846**	**8**	**89**	**33**	**0.76**	**313**	**113**	**91**		**6.39**	**21.6**

Three virtually identical seasons except for the red light on the basepaths. Outside possibility of a minor power spike, but otherwise you can probably bank on these levels for 2004.

Stinnett,Kelly

Pos CA | Age 34 Decline | Bats R
RISK: R High; I CON; S stb; K age
LIMA F | BA: 30%

Yr	Tm	AB	R	H	HR	RBI	SB	Avg	vL	vR	R$	OB	Slg	OPS	bb%	ct%	h%	Eye	xBA	PX	SX	G/F	RC/G	RAR
99	ARI	284	36	66	14	38	2	232	303	211	$5	292	426	718	8	71	28	0.29	222	115	47	1.02	4.11	1.3
00	ARI	240	22	52	8	33	0	217	250	208	$1	274	346	620	7	77	25	0.34	184	74	22	1.09	3.03	-7.2
01	CIN	187	27	48	9	25	2	257	325	238	$5	319	460	779	8	67	33	0.28	226	123	55	0.84	4.86	7.4
02	CIN	* 179	15	35	3	17	2	196	286	208	($1)	265	302	567	9	75	24	0.39	233	79	51	0.83	2.59	-8.6
03	2NL	186	14	44	3	19	0	237	193	256	$1	290	355	645	7	72	31	0.27	216	88	16	0.82	3.44	-4.8
1st Half		83	9	22	2	13	0	265			$2	307	434	741	6	75	33	0.24	241	124	26		4.62	0.8
2nd Half		103	5	22	1	6	0	214			($1)	277	291	568	8	70	30	0.29	196	59	7		2.61	-5.3
04	**Proj**	**150**	**13**	**34**	**3**	**16**	**1**	**227**			**$1**	**286**	**356**	**643**	**8**	**72**	**29**	**0.30**	**218**	**90**	**35**		**3.36**	**-3.4**

Nothing worthwhile left in this tank. An appropriate end-game pick only if you are 100% certain that one or two HRs will mean the difference between 1st and 2nd place come next October.

Stynes,Chris

Pos 3B | Age 31 Past Peak | Bats R
RISK: R Very High; I CON; S PT STB; K
LIMA D | BA: 60%

Yr	Tm	AB	R	H	HR	RBI	SB	Avg	vL	vR	R$	OB	Slg	OPS	bb%	ct%	h%	Eye	xBA	PX	SX	G/F	RC/G	RAR
99	CIN	113	18	27	2	14	5	239	292	225	$2	312	301	613	10	88	26	0.92	218	35	85	1.58	3.15	-4.2
00	CIN	380	71	127	12	40	5	334	398	315	$16	386	497	883	8	86	37	0.59	287	103	79	1.57	7.31	29.9
01	BOS	361	52	101	8	33	4	280	349	251	$8	318	410	728	5	84	31	0.36	285	84	78	1.99	4.40	0.4
02	CHC	195	25	47	5	26	1	241	240	242	$3	315	374	689	10	85	26	0.72	264	89	66	0.87	3.90	-4.0
03	COL	443	71	113	11	73	3	255	284	243	$10	328	413	741	10	83	29	0.63	294	108	93	1.83	4.64	5.0
1st Half		226	36	63	8	49	2	279			$9	358	473	832	11	85	30	0.85	314	127	90		5.96	10.9
2nd Half		217	35	50	3	24	1	230			$1	295	350	646	8	80	27	0.47	272	88	87		3.45	-5.2
04	**Proj**	**400**	**60**	**105**	**8**	**54**	**2**	**263**			**$8**	**328**	**393**	**721**	**9**	**84**	**30**	**0.60**	**290**	**88**	**74**		**4.42**	**0.3**

At face value, it doesn't look like Coors did much to help his game. However...

	AB	HR	BA
Home	227	10	.291
Road	216	1	.218

1H/2H splits are a concern too.

Surhoff,B.J.

Pos LF 1B | Age 39 Decline | Bats L
RISK: R High; I con; S pt STB; K AGE
LIMA F | BA: 65%

Yr	Tm	AB	R	H	HR	RBI	SB	Avg	vL	vR	R$	OB	Slg	OPS	bb%	ct%	h%	Eye	xBA	PX	SX	G/F	RC/G	RAR
99	BAL	673	104	207	28	107	5	308	327	302	$26	349	492	841	6	88	32	0.55	312	112	70	1.01	6.34	23.3
00	2TM	539	69	157	14	68	10	291	395	290	$16	341	443	785	7	89	31	0.71	280	98	85	0.98	5.49	5.0
01	ATL	484	68	131	10	58	9	271	219	280	$12	324	405	729	7	90	28	0.79	282	91	87	1.10	4.58	-15.6
02	ATL	75	5	22	0	9	1	293	1000	284	$2	369	360	729	11	93	31	1.80	309	62	33	1.43	4.18	-4.8
03	BAL	319	32	94	5	41	2	295	284	298	$8	353	404	758	8	91	31	1.00	302	79	35	1.82	5.08	-2.2
1st Half		155	16	51	2	23	2	329			$6	377	432	810	7	95	34	1.71	316	76	41		5.98	2.7
2nd Half		164	16	43	3	18	0	262			$2	331	378	710	9	87	29	0.77	289	81	18		4.33	-4.7
04	**Proj**	**250**	**30**	**72**	**3**	**32**	**2**	**288**			**$6**	**343**	**392**	**735**	**8**	**90**	**31**	**0.83**	**300**	**76**	**45**		**4.77**	**-2.2**

Even as he pushes 40, he's cultivated some solid BPIs; contact rate, batting eye, and reflected in his xBA. Power is completely gone, but he's a worthwhile end-gamer to fill that last $1 slot.

Suzuki,Ichiro

Pos RF | Age 30 Past Peak | Bats L
RISK: R Low; I con; S pt stb; K
LIMA B | BA: 50%

Yr	Tm	AB	R	H	HR	RBI	SB	Avg	vL	vR	R$	OB	Slg	OPS	bb%	ct%	h%	Eye	xBA	PX	SX	G/F	RC/G	RAR
99	JPN	411	76	131	13	65	12	320			$19	375	492	867	8	89	34	0.79	304	109	112		6.80	20.3
00	JPN	395	69	143	7	69	21	361			$26	424	479	903	10	91	38	1.21	291	77	100		7.98	30.1
01	SEA	692	127	242	8	69	56	350	318	362	$43	377	457	833	4	92	37	0.57	307	70	151	2.63	6.81	33.3
02	SEA	647	111	208	8	51	31	321	356	308	$28	386	425	811	10	90	35	1.10	298	66	134	2.48	5.99	17.2
03	SEA	679	111	212	13	62	34	312	359	291	$29	347	436	783	5	90	33	0.52	306	77	146	1.85	5.67	9.7
1st Half		338	59	115	7	26	21	340			$19	377	464	842	6	90	36	0.61	308	78	136		6.93	15.8
2nd Half		341	52	97	6	36	13	284			$11	317	408	724	4	89	30	0.44	303	75	148		4.59	-5.5
04	**Proj**	**650**	**110**	**198**	**11**	**64**	**29**	**305**			**$25**	**349**	**424**	**773**	**6**	**90**	**32**	**0.71**	**307**	**75**	**144**		**5.43**	**6.6**

Lots of warning signs, including batting eye that could not hold gains from '02, drop in OB, OPS, RAR, and stamina:

	1st half	2nd half
2002	.359	.284
2003	.340	.284

Sweeney,Mark

Pos RF | Age 34 Decline | Bats L
RISK: R X HIGH; I EXP CON; S PT STB; K age
LIMA F | BA: 55%

Yr	Tm	AB	R	H	HR	RBI	SB	Avg	vL	vR	R$	OB	Slg	OPS	bb%	ct%	h%	Eye	xBA	PX	SX	G/F	RC/G	RAR
99	aaa	342	47	81	10	39	2	237			$3	320	377	698	11	77	28	0.54	249	87	59	2.00	3.97	-10.4
00	MIL	* 128	21	41	2	18	0	320		222	$4	412	469	881	14	78	40	0.71	268	110	30	0.83	7.25	7.2
01	MIL	* 493	57	118	8	61	4	239	200	262	$5	313	359	672	10	83	28	0.62	265	82	71	0.92	3.75	-26.7
02	SD	65	3	11	1	4	0	169	89	189	($1)	217	262	479	6	71	22	0.21	215	67		0.71	1.75	-7.5
03	COL	* 262	29	67	7	37	1	256		275	$5	337	408	745	11	81	29	0.63	261	103	44	0.55	4.32	-10.2
1st Half		115	11	25	4	17	0	217			$1	297	391	688	10	75	26	0.45	248	117	28		3.37	-8.1
2nd Half		147	18	42	3	20	1	286			$4	367	422	789	11	85	32	0.86	272	93	64		5.16	-1.9
04	**Proj**	**100**	**12**	**26**	**2**	**13**	**0**	**260**			**$2**	**342**	**397**	**739**	**11**	**81**	**30**	**0.64**	**261**	**97**	**40**		**4.47**	**-3.0**

2-14-.258 in 97 AB at COL. Even bench players love those Coors splits:

	AB	BA	OB	Slg
Home	44	.364	.417	.523
Road	53	170	.241	.321

Sweeney,Mike

Pos 1B | Age 30 Past Peak | Bats R
RISK: R Very Low; I con; S; K
LIMA C+ | BA: 60%

Yr	Tm	AB	R	H	HR	RBI	SB	Avg	vL	vR	R$	OB	Slg	OPS	bb%	ct%	h%	Eye	xBA	PX	SX	G/F	RC/G	RAR
99	KC	575	101	185	22	102	6	322	350	316	$25	380	520	900	9	92	32	1.13	338	125	84	1.45	7.46	25.7
00	KC	618	105	206	29	144	8	333	374	322	$34	402	523	925	10	89	34	1.06	307	109	63	1.15	8.00	33.4
01	KC	559	97	170	29	99	10	304	268	317	$28	376	542	918	10	89	30	1.00	336	150	70	1.04	7.44	19.9
02	KC	483	83	163	25	89	9	337	357	334	$30	413	563	976	11	90	34	1.29	343	138	65	1.21	8.64	35.6
03	KC	392	62	115	16	83	3	293	277	300	$17	393	467	859	14	86	31	1.14	289	104	55	1.13	6.55	12.8
1st Half		215	40	69	12	50	2	321			$13	443	540	982	18	87	33	1.62	308	130	40		8.78	19.7
2nd Half		177	22	46	4	33	1	260			$4	325	379	703	9	85	29	0.63	265	74	65		4.27	-5.7
04	**Proj**	**450**	**72**	**137**	**19**	**88**	**5**	**304**			**$21**	**386**	**495**	**881**	**12**	**88**	**31**	**1.06**	**297**	**117**	**63**		**6.93**	**15.6**

Injuries shortened his season again, but this time started to chip away at his previously superb BPIs. For someone who was so consistent, 2002-2003 is only starting to register on the risk table, but be careful.

Taguchi,So

Pos CF | Age 34 Decline | Bats R
RISK: R High; I exp CON; S stb; K age
LIMA F | BA: 60%

Yr	Tm	AB	R	H	HR	RBI	SB	Avg	vL	vR	R$	OB	Slg	OPS	bb%	ct%	h%	Eye	xBA	PX	SX	G/F	RC/G	RAR
99	JPN	524	73	131	5	53	11	251			$6	283	327	610	4	83	29	0.26	251	52	97		3.09	-22.2
00	JPN	509	73	132	5	47	9	260			$6	319	357	676	8	84	30	0.55	263	64	116		3.97	-7.7
01	JPN	453	67	118	5	40	6	261			$6	314	380	694	7	81	32	0.39	258	73	148		3.96	-5.2
02	a/a	426	42	84	4	36	7	197			($2)	228	270	498	4	86	22	0.28	252	55	80	2.67	1.92	-39.4
03	STL	* 312	35	70	5	33	12	224	259	259	$5	280	317	597	7	84	25	0.49	256	59	112	2.09	2.89	-20.3
1st Half		153	17	31	1	11	5	203			($0)	265	261	526	8	84	23	0.54	245	45	81		2.08	-14.3
2nd Half		159	18	39	4	22	7	245			$5	294	371	665	6	84	27	0.44	266	73	135		3.82	-5.5
04	**Proj**	**100**	**12**	**23**	**1**	**10**	**3**	**230**			**$1**	**278**	**331**	**609**	**6**	**84**	**26**	**0.41**	**260**	**66**	**114**		**3.01**	**-5.2**

3-13-.259 in 54 AB at STL. 34-year-old "rookie" and it shows. Very weak hitter, as indicated by painfully low h% and PX levels. This is not one you want to chase.

Tatis,Fernando

Pos 3B | Age 29 Past Peak | Bats S
RISK: R High; I con; S PT stb; K
LIMA F | BA: 60%

Yr	Tm	AB	R	H	HR	RBI	SB	Avg	vL	vR	R$	OB	Slg	OPS	bb%	ct%	h%	Eye	xBA	PX	SX	G/F	RC/G	RAR
99	STL	537	104	160	34	107	21	298	290	301	$32	391	553	944	13	76	34	0.64	271	150	95	0.80	7.67	50.1
00	STL	324	59	82	18	64	2	253	261	250	$10	365	491	856	15	71	30	0.61	246	141	60	0.66	5.95	15.7
01	MON	145	20	37	2	11	0	255	235	261	$1	329	359	688	10	70	35	0.37	206	74	35	1.24	4.04	-2.3
02	MON	381	43	87	15	55	2	228	230	228	$7	293	399	692	8	76	26	0.39	247	110	53	1.21	3.80	-9.1
03	MON	175	15	34	2	15	2	194	240	176	($1)	269	263	532	9	77	24	0.45	212	49	49	1.79	2.24	-11.2
1st Half		175	15	34	2	15	2	194			($1)	269	263	532	9	77	24	0.45	212	49	49		2.24	-11.2
2nd Half		0	0	0	0	0	0	0			($0)					0			0					
04	**Proj**	**250**	**32**	**59**	**5**	**31**	**2**	**236**			**$3**	**304**	**352**	**657**	**9**	**74**	**30**	**0.38**	**216**	**80**	**58**		**3.54**	**-6.4**

Since 2001, this has been a different player. This one has less plate patience, less power. In fact, if all we had to go on was his 2001-03 stats, he would not be a draft day consideration at all. Best to leave it that way.

Taylor,Reggie

Pos CF | Age 27 Peak | Bats L
RISK: R Very High; I EXP con; S pt stb; K
LIMA F | BA: 30%

Yr	Tm	AB	R	H	HR	RBI	SB	Avg	vL	vR	R$	OB	Slg	OPS	bb%	ct%	h%	Eye	xBA	PX	SX	G/F	RC/G	RAR
99	aa	526	61	129	13	50	31	245			$14	266	378	645	3	87	26	0.22	283	77	143		2.87	-27.1
00	aaa	422	49	106	11	35	19	251			$10	282	389	670	4	82	29	0.23	262	75	149		3.37	-14.5
01	aaa	464	52	120	6	46	29	259			$15	294	386	679	5	80	31	0.24	260	79	171		3.60	-10.6
02	CIN	287	41	73	9	38	11	254	184	265	$10	289	429	718	5	72	32	0.18	256	112	159	1.11	3.89	-8.5
03	CIN	180	17	39	5	19	8	217	167	227	$3	262	350	612	6	62	32	0.16	211	78	144	1.00	3.16	-10.0
1st Half		87	8	19	2	9	6	218			$2	253	345	598	4	55	37	0.10	189	67	234		3.16	-4.9
2nd Half		93	9	20	3	10	1	215			$1	270	355	625	7	69	28	0.24	230	89	46		3.16	-5.2
04	**Proj**	**150**	**17**	**34**	**4**	**16**	**6**	**227**			**$3**	**267**	**373**	**640**	**5**	**70**	**30**	**0.18**	**227**	**89**	**149**		**3.22**	**-7.0**

A brutal season, characterized by a dreadful 62% contact rate. The only thing that managed to put a stop to his plummeting trends was a merciful August shoulder injury. Bottom line was, he HAD to be stopped.

Teixeira,Mark

Pos 1B
Age 23 Growth
Bats S
R: Very High | I: EXP, con | S: pt, stb | K: AGE
LIMA C+ | BA: 50%

Yr	Tm	AB	R	H	HR	RBI	SB	Avg	vL	vR	R$	OB	Slg	OPS	bb%	ct%	h%	Eye	xBA	PX	SX	G/F	RC/G	RAR
99		0	0	0	0	0	0	0								0								
00		0	0	0	0	0	0	0								0								
01		0	0	0	0	0	0	0								0								
02	aa	171	28	52	9	25	3	304			$9	387	556	942	12	82	33	0.74	300	151	128		7.66	9.2
03	TEX	529	66	137	26	84	1	259	295	242	$15	316	480	796	8	77	29	0.37	297	131	70	1.02	5.15	-3.6
1st Half		222	27	55	11	39	0	248			$6	321	468	790	10	75	28	0.44	286	127	82		5.01	-2.5
2nd Half		307	39	82	15	45	1	267			$9	312	489	801	6	79	30	0.31	304	134	65		5.25	-1.2
04	**Proj**	**550**	**77**	**152**	**31**	**95**	**2**	**276**			**$21**	**344**	**526**	**870**	**9**	**79**	**30**	**0.50**	**305**	**145**	**93**		**6.33**	**10.5**

The mark of true talent is a one who improves over the course of his rookie year, even after opposing pitchers have adjusted. The BPIs themselves are not yet star-caliber, but you can see it coming.

Tejada,Miguel

Pos SS
Age 27 Peak
Bats R
R: Very Low | I: con | S: | K:
LIMA D | BA: 65%

Yr	Tm	AB	R	H	HR	RBI	SB	Avg	vL	vR	R$	OB	Slg	OPS	bb%	ct%	h%	Eye	xBA	PX	SX	G/F	RC/G	RAR
99	OAK	593	93	149	21	84	8	251	271	245	$13	317	427	744	9	84	27	0.61	277	106	94	1.35	4.46	5.1
00	OAK	607	105	167	30	115	6	275	220	296	$21	346	479	826	10	83	29	0.65	279	118	83	1.10	5.90	25.7
01	OAK	622	107	166	31	113	11	267	273	264	$24	314	476	790	6	86	27	0.48	291	123	98	1.00	5.13	13.6
02	OAK	662	108	204	34	131	7	308	285	314	$34	346	508	853	5	87	31	0.45	284	117	70	1.25	6.46	33.9
03	OAK	636	98	177	27	106	10	278	269	281	$24	334	472	806	8	90	28	0.82	317	122	83	1.26	5.67	22.3
1st Half		328	44	81	15	55	3	247			$9	300	442	742	7	90	24	0.76	315	120	60		4.55	1.2
2nd Half		308	54	96	12	51	7	312			$15	369	503	872	8	90	32	0.88	318	124	84		7.05	21.8
04	**Proj**	**650**	**106**	**206**	**32**	**135**	**10**	**317**			**$35**	**366**	**521**	**887**	**7**	**88**	**32**	**0.64**	**314**	**124**	**74**		**7.16**	**47.4**

His 1st half 24% hit rate shows he was hitting into bad luck, as most of his other BPIs were still solid. 2nd half levels were better than his 2002 MVP season, so don't be surprised to see a monster year in 2004.

Thames,Marcus

Pos RF
Age 27 Peak
Bats R
R: X HIGH | I: EXP, CON | S: pt, stb | K:
LIMA F | BA: 45%

Yr	Tm	AB	R	H	HR	RBI	SB	Avg	vL	vR	R$	OB	Slg	OPS	bb%	ct%	h%	Eye	xBA	PX	SX	G/F	RC/G	RAR
99	aa	182	22	37	3	23	0	203			($1)	279	297	575	9	81	24	0.54	245	58	60		2.58	-13.8
00	aa	474	61	104	15	67	1	219			$3	284	376	660	8	83	23	0.54	277	97	46		3.33	-24.9
01	aa	520	99	153	29	85	9	294			$25	372	548	920	11	82	31	0.67	301	154	97		7.27	29.1
02	aaa	399	43	72	12	38	4	180			($1)	247	331	577	8	84	18	0.56	273	97	77	0.40	2.42	-35.6
03	TEX	* 333	42	78	5	34	4	234	250	95	$2	296	342	638	8	78	29	0.39	238	75	71	1.05	3.21	-19.8
1st Half		249	29	61	4	30	4	245			$4	301	365	667	7	78	30	0.37	245	84	75		3.54	-12.1
2nd Half		84	13	17	1	4	0	202			($1)	280	274	553	10	76	25	0.45	218	49	59		2.32	-7.6
04	**Proj**	**100**	**14**	**22**	**3**	**10**	**1**	**220**			**$0**	**290**	**345**	**635**	**9**	**80**	**25**	**0.49**	**244**	**81**	**57**		**3.14**	**-6.0**

1-4-.205 in 73 AB at TEX. It sure looks like 2001 was a brief, shining aberration. He had done nothing before, and has done nothing since. Does he still own those skills? Possibly. But we've seen no sign of them in 2 years.

Thomas,Frank

Pos 1B DH
Age 35 Decline
Bats R
R: Moderate | I: CON | S: pt | K: age
LIMA B | BA: 55%

Yr	Tm	AB	R	H	HR	RBI	SB	Avg	vL	vR	R$	OB	Slg	OPS	bb%	ct%	h%	Eye	xBA	PX	SX	G/F	RC/G	RAR
99	CHW	486	74	148	15	77	3	305	253	314	$16	410	471	881	15	86	33	1.32	284	109	40	0.88	6.98	16.1
00	CHW	582	115	191	43	143	1	328	407	314	$35	437	625	1062	16	84	33	1.19	312	171	28	0.79	10.20	65.7
01	CHW	68	8	15	4	10	0	221	313	192	$1	321	441	762	13	82	21	0.83	262	127		0.59	4.63	-3.2
02	CHW	523	77	132	28	92	3	252	214	264	$17	360	472	832	14	78	27	0.77	240	131	57	0.40	5.84	-0.3
03	CHW	546	87	146	42	105	0	267	315	249	$24	381	562	943	15	79	27	0.87	276	173	18	0.44	7.45	32.5
1st Half		256	41	72	17	39	0	281			$10	414	555	969	18	78	30	1.04	269	166	17		8.15	20.0
2nd Half		290	46	74	25	66	0	255			$13	349	569	918	13	80	24	0.71	282	180	19		6.81	12.1
04	**Proj**	**550**	**89**	**152**	**37**	**107**	**1**	**276**			**$24**	**385**	**540**	**926**	**15**	**80**	**28**	**0.90**	**273**	**156**	**32**		**7.32**	**25.9**

Despite the production, his BPIs are not at the same level as they were in 2000 and prior. He has become streaky, struggles vs RHers, and is always hitting for the fences. Odds of him turning a profit on $25 is slim.

Thome,Jim

Pos 1B
Age 33 Decline
Bats L
R: Low | I: con | S: stb | K: age
LIMA D+ | BA: 45%

Yr	Tm	AB	R	H	HR	RBI	SB	Avg	vL	vR	R$	OB	Slg	OPS	bb%	ct%	h%	Eye	xBA	PX	SX	G/F	RC/G	RAR
99	CLE	494	101	137	33	108	0	277	239	292	$20	425	540	966	20	65	36	0.74	253	150	48	1.23	8.11	32.6
00	CLE	557	106	150	37	106	1	269	250	277	$20	397	531	928	17	69	32	0.69	258	148	49	1.00	7.38	22.8
01	CLE	526	101	153	49	124	0	291	232	313	$31	414	624	1038	17	65	36	0.60	274	186	29	0.97	9.23	45.3
02	CLE	480	101	146	52	118	1	304	245	333	$34	445	677	1122	20	71	33	0.88	278	203	46	0.78	10.92	66.6
03	PHI	578	111	154	47	131	0	266	254	272	$29	385	573	957	16	69	31	0.61	274	178	51	0.98	7.52	33.6
1st Half		286	54	75	21	58	0	262			$12	387	542	929	17	70	30	0.68	274	162	63		6.98	12.3
2nd Half		292	57	79	26	73	0	271			$16	383	603	985	15	67	31	0.55	271	194			8.06	21.3
04	**Proj**	**550**	**109**	**154**	**51**	**128**	**0**	**280**			**$32**	**407**	**615**	**1021**	**18**	**68**	**32**	**0.67**	**278**	**192**	**44**		**8.76**	**48.8**

At face value, a 38-point drop in BA, but xBA says NO. There are some down indicators from '02, but they are not significant. If he regains just a tad more patience with NL pitchers, his numbers should bounce right back.

Torrealba,Yorvit

Pos CA
Age 25 Pre-Peak
Bats R
R: X HIGH | I: EXP, CON | S: PT, STB | K: age
LIMA D | BA: 45%

Yr	Tm	AB	R	H	HR	RBI	SB	Avg	vL	vR	R$	OB	Slg	OPS	bb%	ct%	h%	Eye	xBA	PX	SX	G/F	RC/G	RAR
99	a/a	280	30	64	5	25	0	229			($0)	260	332	592	4	86	25	0.32	266	67	49		2.71	-11.2
00	aa	398	47	108	4	30	2	271			$4	324	357	681	7	87	30	0.61	266	59	52		3.95	-1.4
01	aaa	398	42	94	6	29	1	236			$1	262	347	609	3	88	26	0.30	273	73	68		2.90	-9.6
02	SF	136	17	38	2	14	0	279	385	255	$3	347	397	744	9	85	32	0.70	280	92	28	2.07	4.87	2.9
03	SF	200	22	52	4	29	1	260	212	269	$4	308	390	698	7	81	31	0.36	276	85	85	2.38	4.17	-0.7
1st Half		78	7	20	1	14	0	256			$1	293	397	690	5	85	29	0.33	298	100	72		3.99	-0.7
2nd Half		122	15	32	3	15	1	262			$3	318	385	703	8	78	32	0.37	261	75	84		4.29	-0.0
04	**Proj**	**350**	**40**	**91**	**6**	**41**	**1**	**260**			**$5**	**310**	**380**	**690**	**7**	**84**	**30**	**0.44**	**280**	**83**	**64**		**4.03**	**-0.7**

A step back from 2002, but still not a bad skill set. This is the type of $1 end-gamer that could net you $5, and in a few years might surprise with a 10-HR season.

Torres,Andres

Pos CF
Age 26 Pre-Peak
Bats S
R: Very High | I: EXP, CON | S: pt, stb | K:
LIMA F | BA: 45%

Yr	Tm	AB	R	H	HR	RBI	SB	Avg	vL	vR	R$	OB	Slg	OPS	bb%	ct%	h%	Eye	xBA	PX	SX	G/F	RC/G	RAR
99		0	0	0	0	0	0	0								0								
00	aa	54	3	7	0	0	2	130			($2)	203	130	333	8	72	18	0.33	189		63		0.80	-6.9
01	aa	252	44	67	1	18	16	266			$7	342	357	699	10	85	31	0.74	265	68	127		3.76	-4.6
02	DET	* 532	79	129	3	41	40	242	235	189	$15	315	327	642	10	78	30	0.49	230	51	186	2.00	3.46	-21.6
03	DET	* 439	57	101	3	24	31	230	258	198	$8	275	317	591	6	79	28	0.30	235	54	171	1.81	2.67	-28.8
1st Half		265	36	69	1	14	21	260			$8	307	358	666	6	80	32	0.33	241	62	192		3.46	-10.4
2nd Half		174	21	32	2	10	10	184			$0	224	253	477	5	79	22	0.25	226	43	135		1.69	-17.6
04	**Proj**	**150**	**21**	**35**	**1**	**10**	**10**	**233**			**$3**	**292**	**314**	**606**	**8**	**80**	**29**	**0.41**	**236**	**51**	**155**		**2.90**	**-8.8**

1-9-5-.220 in 168 AB at DET. Took a step back in 2003 after a poor 2nd half, which can be at least partially attributed to a low 22% hit rate. He's still a long way from being able to make good use of his speed skills.

Trammell,Bubba

Pos DH
Age 32 Past Peak
Bats R
R: High | I: con | S: PT, STB | K:
LIMA F | BA: 70%

Yr	Tm	AB	R	H	HR	RBI	SB	Avg	vL	vR	R$	OB	Slg	OPS	bb%	ct%	h%	Eye	xBA	PX	SX	G/F	RC/G	RAR
99	TAM	* 469	70	129	21	65	0	275	227	309	$12	351	475	827	10	86	28	0.83	294	123	27	0.66	5.78	7.8
00	2TM	245	28	65	10	45	4	265	305	245	$8	343	457	800	11	80	30	0.59	247	112	87	0.80	5.55	3.3
01	SD	490	66	128	25	92	2	261	279	255	$17	327	467	794	9	84	27	0.62	280	117	65	0.84	5.21	-0.3
02	SD	403	54	98	17	56	1	243	305	213	$9	331	414	746	12	82	26	0.75	254	107	42	0.90	4.50	-12.4
03	NYY	55	4	11	0	5	0	200	188	217	($1)	279	291	570	10	82	24	0.60	269	79	19	0.89	2.58	-3.5
1st Half		55	4	11	0	5	0	200			($1)	279	291	570	10	82	24	0.60	269	79	19		2.58	-3.5
2nd Half		0	0	0	0	0	0	0			($0)					0			0					
04	**Proj**	**50**	**6**	**12**	**2**	**7**	**0**	**240**			**$1**	**317**	**395**	**713**	**10**	**83**	**26**	**0.65**	**278**	**100**	**34**		**4.18**	**-1.2**

MIA? He's claiming "depression" and wants NYY to pay the remainder of his salary. But he also threatened to kill a friend of his estranged wife, according to police reports, and says he left NYY for "good reason." Good.

Tucker,Michael

Pos RF CF LF
Age 32 Past Peak
Bats L
R: Moderate | I: con | S: pt, stb | K:
LIMA B | BA: 50%

Yr	Tm	AB	R	H	HR	RBI	SB	Avg	vL	vR	R$	OB	Slg	OPS	bb%	ct%	h%	Eye	xBA	PX	SX	G/F	RC/G	RAR
99	CIN	296	55	75	11	44	11	253	154	268	$9	336	426	762	11	73	31	0.46	239	95	162	1.17	4.85	-1.3
00	CIN	270	55	72	15	36	13	267	167	276	$12	369	511	881	14	76	30	0.69	271	136	153	0.88	6.36	9.7
01	2NL	436	62	110	12	61	16	252	211	263	$13	324	415	739	10	77	30	0.45	261	94	164	1.31	4.45	-14.5
02	KC	475	65	118	12	56	23	248	208	256	$15	328	406	734	11	78	30	0.53	270	99	143	1.14	4.45	-8.1
03	KC	389	61	102	13	55	8	262	236	274	$11	329	440	769	9	77	31	0.44	279	107	120	1.28	4.61	-6.3
1st Half		273	44	75	10	41	7	275			$10	340	469	809	9	77	33	0.42	284	120	116		5.11	-0.3
2nd Half		116	17	27	3	14	1	233			$1	305	371	675	9	79	27	0.50	266	77	126		3.53	-5.8
04	**Proj**	**500**	**76**	**125**	**15**	**65**	**15**	**250**			**$13**	**325**	**412**	**737**	**10**	**78**	**30**	**0.49**	**277**	**96**	**135**		**4.35**	**-10.9**

Broken leg cut short his first 500 AB season. It would have been another unremarkable season, except for a career-high .236 BA vs LHers. Every year continues to pale to his 2000 campaign and that probably won't change.

Tyner,Jason

		Tm	AB	R	H	HR	RBI	SB	Avg	vL	vR	R$	OB	Slg	OPS	bb%	ct%	h%	Eye	xBA	PX	SX	G/F	RC/G	RAR
Pos RF	99	a/a	526	78	147	0	28	42	279			$17	345	327	672	9	92	30	1.20	270	34	126		3.94	-16.3
Age 27 Peak	00	2TM	* 451	49	119	0	34	31	264	150	240	$12	305	288	594	6	91	29	0.69	254	19	97	2.71	2.81	-30.7
Bats L	01	TAM	* 553	73	157	0	32	41	284	321	270	$18	318	324	642	5	91	31	0.55	259	25	139	2.69	3.75	-19.6
R Very High	02	TAM	* 519	67	131	0	32	24	252	189	221	$9	301	299	600	6	92	28	0.84	253	32	131	2.56	3.08	-30.3
I EXP CON	03	TAM	* 365	41	107	0	26	11	293	167	295	$8	344	370	713	7	90	33	0.78	264	55	112	3.92	4.32	-8.7
S pt stb	1st Half		190	25	61	0	16	6	321			$6	371	426	797	7	93	35	1.07	286	73	138		5.68	2.7
K	2nd Half		175	16	46	0	10	5	263			$2	314	309	622	7	87	30	0.59	241	35	78		3.10	-10.8
LIMA D BA: 55%	04	Proj	**200**	**24**	**55**	**0**	**13**	**13**	**275**			**$6**	**323**	**330**	**653**	**7**	**90**	**30**	**0.74**	**261**	**39**	**129**		**3.91**	**-6.7**

0-6-2-.278 in 90 AB at TAM. There are BPIs here that always make me want to tuck him away on my roster... high contact rate, speed, and now a glimmer of on base ability. Yes, he's weak and can't hit LHers, but one day...

Uribe,Juan

		Tm	AB	R	H	HR	RBI	SB	Avg	vL	vR	R$	OB	Slg	OPS	bb%	ct%	h%	Eye	xBA	PX	SX	G/F	RC/G	RAR
Pos SS	99		0	0	0	0	0	0	0								0								
Age 24 Growth	00		0	0	0	0	0	0	0								0								
Bats R	01	COL	* 567	65	173	15	92	12	305	311	298	$24	325	517	842	3	85	34	0.20	306	129	177	1.00	5.88	36.6
R Moderate	02	COL	566	69	136	6	49	9	240	241	240	$6	283	341	624	6	79	30	0.28	245	69	135	1.34	3.27	-10.6
I EXP con	03	COL	316	45	80	10	33	7	253	301	236	$7	291	427	719	5	81	28	0.28	285	112	127	1.00	4.24	1.2
S pt	1st Half		116	18	30	4	13	0	259			$2	295	405	700	5	85	27	0.35	281	93	46		4.11	0.0
K age	2nd Half		200	27	50	6	20	7	250			$5	289	440	729	5	79	29	0.26	285	123	157		4.31	1.2
LIMA D+ BA: 50%	04	Proj	**350**	**46**	**94**	**11**	**37**	**7**	**269**			**$10**	**305**	**451**	**756**	**5**	**81**	**30**	**0.27**	**287**	**114**	**135**		**4.76**	**8.6**

Each data point seems to show some small sign of progress, which then disappears in the next data point in lieu of other short-lived positive signs. There's no coordinated positive trend, and that's a concern.

Utley,Chase

		Tm	AB	R	H	HR	RBI	SB	Avg	vL	vR	R$	OB	Slg	OPS	bb%	ct%	h%	Eye	xBA	PX	SX	G/F	RC/G	RAR
Pos 2B	99		0	0	0	0	0	0	0								0								
Age 25 Pre-Peak	00		0	0	0	0	0	0	0								0								
Bats L	01		0	0	0	0	0	0	0								0								
R Moderate	02	aaa	464	64	119	15	61	7	256			$12	320	446	766	8	84	28	0.57	292	132	79		4.85	8.5
I EXP	03	PHI	* 565	85	162	18	90	11	287	333	230	$22	344	457	800	8	83	32	0.52	280	112	99	1.10	5.58	18.7
S stb	1st Half		300	44	88	11	48	4	293			$12	335	473	809	6	83	32	0.37	280	117	85		5.82	11.7
K age	2nd Half		265	41	74	7	42	7	279			$10	353	438	790	10	84	31	0.71	280	105	104		5.31	6.9
LIMA C+ BA: 45%	04	Proj	**400**	**58**	**109**	**10**	**59**	**7**	**273**			**$12**	**334**	**427**	**761**	**8**	**84**	**31**	**0.56**	**280**	**106**	**94**		**4.95**	**7.3**

2-21-.239 in 134 AB at PHI. Some small signs of growth from '02 to '03, but his performance in the bigs shows there's still work to be done. This projection may be a slight leap of faith.

Valentin,Javier

		Tm	AB	R	H	HR	RBI	SB	Avg	vL	vR	R$	OB	Slg	OPS	bb%	ct%	h%	Eye	xBA	PX	SX	G/F	RC/G	RAR
Pos CA	99	MIN	218	22	54	5	28	0	248			$2	317	381	697	9	82	28	0.56	614	85	38		4.09	0.1
Age 28 Peak	00	aaa	140	19	46	5	27	1	325			$7	357	552	909	5	85	36	0.33	315	148	72		7.50	12.7
Bats S	01	aaa	431	40	107	13	53	0	248			$6	305	404	708	8	80	28	0.40	258	99	27		4.13	5.6
R X HIGH	02	aaa	455	48	108	14	55	0	237			$6	283	398	681	6	83	26	0.38	273	107	36		3.73	-1.9
I EXP CON	03	TAM	135	13	30	3	15	0	222	231	221	$0	250	356	606	4	77	27	0.16	234	86	59	0.87	2.91	-4.8
S PT stb	1st Half		84	8	21	1	11	0	250			$1	267	369	636	2	79	31	0.11	236	80	76		3.36	-1.8
K	2nd Half		51	5	9	2	4	0	176			($0)	222	333	556	6	75	19	0.23	230	94	27		2.29	-3.0
LIMA F BA: 45%	04	Proj	**100**	**10**	**23**	**3**	**11**	**0**	**230**			**$1**	**272**	**378**	**650**	**5**	**79**	**26**	**0.28**	**240**	**96**	**29**		**3.39**	**-1.7**

Trends that tell you all you need to know: BA, OB, bb%, ct%, batting eye, xBA, RC/G and RAR. Some will be enamored by the potential of a power hitting catcher, but PX tells us those skills are not real.

Valentin,Jose

		Tm	AB	R	H	HR	RBI	SB	Avg	vL	vR	R$	OB	Slg	OPS	bb%	ct%	h%	Eye	xBA	PX	SX	G/F	RC/G	RAR
Pos SS	99	MIL	256	45	58	10	38	3	227	253	215	$4	349	418	767	16	80	25	0.92	238	107	134	0.56	4.74	9.5
Age 34 Decline	00	CHW	568	107	155	25	92	19	273	215	282	$22	341	491	833	9	81	30	0.56	269	128	150	0.69	6.01	26.0
Bats S	01	CHW	438	74	113	28	68	9	258	203	267	$17	334	509	843	10	74	29	0.44	257	144	87	0.74	5.65	16.6
R Low	02	CHW	474	70	118	25	75	3	249	152	259	$14	311	479	790	8	79	27	0.43	274	135	87	0.79	4.96	5.4
I con	03	CHW	503	79	119	28	74	8	237	131	265	$14	311	463	774	10	77	25	0.47	265	133	90	0.68	4.77	5.3
S pt stb	1st Half		262	38	63	12	35	4	240			$6	328	458	786	11	78	27	0.59	267	133	91		4.98	4.3
K age	2nd Half		241	41	56	16	39	4	232			$8	291	469	760	8	77	24	0.36	263	134	78		4.54	0.8
LIMA B BA: 55%	04	Proj	**500**	**80**	**117**	**26**	**72**	**7**	**234**			**$13**	**307**	**452**	**759**	**10**	**77**	**26**	**0.45**	**263**	**127**	**99**		**4.56**	**1.8**

Declining trends abound, the most critical being his complete ineptitude vs LHers. CHW is doing all it can to limit his exposure to southpaws, but he's still amassed 217 sub-Mendoza ABs since 2001.

Vander Wal,John

		Tm	AB	R	H	HR	RBI	SB	Avg	vL	vR	R$	OB	Slg	OPS	bb%	ct%	h%	Eye	xBA	PX	SX	G/F	RC/G	RAR
Pos RF	99	SD	246	26	67	6	41	2	272	111	285	$6	367	419	786	13	76	34	0.63	257	101	35	1.64	5.37	2.6
Age 38 Decline	00	PIT	384	74	115	24	94	11	299	200	314	$23	410	563	973	16	76	34	0.78	279	157	75	0.89	8.48	35.4
Bats L	01	2NL	452	58	122	14	70	8	270	296	266	$14	365	442	808	13	73	34	0.56	243	107	94	0.94	5.49	-0.9
R X HIGH	02	NYY	219	30	57	6	20	1	260	238	263	$4	331	429	760	10	74	33	0.40	242	113	66	0.94	4.83	-1.2
I con	03	MIL	327	50	84	14	45	1	257	158	270	$8	349	468	816	12	68	33	0.44	251	138	55	1.11	5.48	-1.2
S PT STB	1st Half		181	33	52	8	25	1	287			$7	371	503	873	12	68	38	0.41	252	143	53		6.57	4.9
K AGE	2nd Half		146	17	32	6	20	0	219			$2	321	425	746	13	68	28	0.48	249	132	60		4.34	-5.7
LIMA F BA: 35%	04	Proj	**250**	**35**	**60**	**6**	**34**	**1**	**240**			**$3**	**332**	**395**	**727**	**12**	**68**	**33**	**0.43**	**244**	**107**	**61**		**4.30**	**-8.8**

An inflamed elbow, the flu and a strained groin led to him batting just .205 over his final 73 ABs. Still, the significant drop in his contact rate may be an early warning that his overall numbers are about to take a dive.

Varitek,Jason

		Tm	AB	R	H	HR	RBI	SB	Avg	vL	vR	R$	OB	Slg	OPS	bb%	ct%	h%	Eye	xBA	PX	SX	G/F	RC/G	RAR
Pos CA	99	BOS	483	70	130	20	76	1	269	282	266	$12	333	482	815	9	82	29	0.54	295	134	55	1.07	5.52	20.2
Age 32 Past Peak	00	BOS	448	55	111	10	65	1	248	254	245	$5	337	388	725	12	81	29	0.71	257	92	44	1.20	4.41	3.4
Bats S	01	BOS	174	19	51	7	25	0	293	283	298	$6	369	489	858	11	80	33	0.60	273	121	35	1.48	6.51	12.8
R Moderate	02	BOS	467	58	124	10	61	4	266	263	266	$10	325	392	717	8	80	31	0.43	256	85	61	1.20	4.35	10.0
I CON	03	BOS	451	63	123	25	85	3	273	309	257	$18	347	512	859	10	76	31	0.48	293	146	53	1.19	6.16	26.8
S pt	1st Half		216	39	62	13	45	2	287			$10	353	551	904	9	80	31	0.50	296	160	76		6.76	16.3
K	2nd Half		235	24	61	12	40	1	260			$7	341	477	818	11	74	30	0.47	273	133	25		5.62	10.4
LIMA D+ BA: 50%	04	Proj	**450**	**57**	**122**	**19**	**73**	**2**	**271**			**$14**	**343**	**466**	**808**	**10**	**78**	**31**	**0.50**	**266**	**121**	**50**		**5.54**	**20.6**

Last year, in this space, I reminded you that his dormant power was still a part of his skill set. While he obliged, his BPIs are slightly weaker now at age 32, and the odds are down for him maintaining these levels.

Vaughn,Mo

		Tm	AB	R	H	HR	RBI	SB	Avg	vL	vR	R$	OB	Slg	OPS	bb%	ct%	h%	Eye	xBA	PX	SX	G/F	RC/G	RAR
Pos 1B	99	ANA	524	63	147	33	108	0	281	336	258	$21	348	508	855	9	76	31	0.43	289	127		1.10	6.26	7.0
Age 36 Decline	00	ANA	614	93	167	36	117	2	272	204	303	$21	355	498	853	11	71	33	0.44	256	128	44	0.96	6.22	4.8
Bats L	01	ANA	0	0	0	0	0	0	0								0			0					
R High	02	NYM	487	67	126	26	72	0	259	272	254	$15	339	456	795	11	70	32	0.41	253	120	24	1.02	5.27	-4.7
I con	03	NYM	79	10	15	3	15	0	190	133	203	$0	312	329	641	15	72	22	0.64	202	82	24	1.00	3.23	-5.7
S pt stb	1st Half		79	10	15	3	15	0	190			$0	312	329	641	15	72	22	0.64	202	82	24		3.23	-5.7
K AGE	2nd Half		0	0	0	0	0	0	0			($0)					0			0					
LIMA F BA: 60%	04	Proj	**150**	**20**	**33**	**5**	**28**	**0**	**220**			**$2**	**315**	**356**	**671**	**12**	**72**	**27**	**0.49**	**204**	**86**	**37**		**3.66**	**-9.0**

This 150 AB projection is a token gift on the remote chance that he is able to return to baseball. You don't want to be investing anything in that chance.

Vazquez,Ramon

		Tm	AB	R	H	HR	RBI	SB	Avg	vL	vR	R$	OB	Slg	OPS	bb%	ct%	h%	Eye	xBA	PX	SX	G/F	RC/G	RAR
Pos SS	99	aa	438	56	96	5	44	8	219			$1	313	317	631	12	82	26	0.74	256	69	92		3.32	-7.1
Age 27 Peak	00	aa	405	55	103	7	56	1	254			$5	339	375	714	11	79	31	0.61	252	78	62		4.12	2.2
Bats L	01	aaa	501	79	130	8	72	8	259			$11	349	361	710	12	84	30	0.84	257	69	70	1.64	4.18	3.2
R Moderate	02	SD	423	50	116	2	32	7	274	157	297	$7	344	362	706	10	81	33	0.57	269	64	114	2.17	4.40	6.1
I EXP con	03	SD	422	56	110	3	30	10	261	224	275	$6	342	341	683	11	79	32	0.59	250	56	116	1.59	4.06	-0.6
S stb	1st Half		210	29	56	3	20	7	267			$5	353	367	720	12	83	31	0.80	269	65	114		4.55	2.7
K	2nd Half		212	27	54	0	10	3	255			$1	331	316	647	10	75	34	0.45	231	46	104		3.59	-3.2
LIMA D+ BA: 40%	04	Proj	**400**	**53**	**104**	**3**	**34**	**12**	**260**			**$7**	**340**	**344**	**684**	**11**	**80**	**32**	**0.61**	**253**	**59**	**109**		**4.01**	**1.2**

Stable, unremarkable skill set showing little sign of growth. Might steal 15 bases one day, and bat .280, but that's about his ceiling.

Velandia,Jorge

Pos SS
Age 29 Past Peak
Bats R
R X HIGH
I EXP CON
S PT stb
K
LIMA F BA: 60%

Yr	Tm	AB	R	H	HR	RBI	SB	Avg	vL	vR	R$	OB	Slg	OPS	bb%	ct%	h%	Eye	xBA	PX	SX	G/F	RC/G	RAR
99	OAK	48	4	9	0	2	2	188			($1)	220	208	428	4	73	26	0.15	472	18	82		1.42	-4.3
00	aaa	336	52	80	8	53	5	238			$5	304	372	676	9	84	26	0.58	273	85	85		3.73	-2.2
01	aaa	260	22	58	4	33	8	223			$3	263	342	605	5	82	26	0.30	262	86	72		2.87	-8.8
02	aaa	407	36	69	5	31	4	170			($6)	218	253	471	6	81	20	0.33	241	59	76		1.68	-34.1
03	NYM	* 432	44	85	9	49	2	197	250	180	($1)	266	319	586	9	76	24	0.39	237	82	61	1.47	2.58	-21.2
1st Half		208	24	41	6	23	2	197			$0	261	356	617	8	75	23	0.35	247	105	78		2.66	-9.8
2nd Half		224	20	44	3	26	0	196			($2)	271	286	557	9	76	24	0.43	227	61	43		2.46	-11.7
04	Proj	100	10	20	2	11	1	200			($0)	260	303	563	7	79	24	0.38	240	72	54		2.44	-4.7

0-8-.190 in 58 AB at NYM. Was a Grade C- prospect in the 1998 Minor League Scouting Notebook because he was all glove, no bat.

Ventura,Robin

Pos 1B 3B
Age 36 Decline
Bats L
R Moderate
I con
S stb
K AGE
LIMA F BA: 50%

Yr	Tm	AB	R	H	HR	RBI	SB	Avg	vL	vR	R$	OB	Slg	OPS	bb%	ct%	h%	Eye	xBA	PX	SX	G/F	RC/G	RAR
99	NYM	588	88	177	32	120	1	301	271	314	$26	379	529	908	11	81	32	0.68	301	140	30	0.83	7.28	32.0
00	NYM	469	61	109	24	84	3	232	225	234	$11	338	439	777	14	81	24	0.82	262	120	41	1.07	4.77	-8.2
01	NYM	456	70	108	21	61	2	237	271	228	$9	360	419	779	16	78	26	0.95	243	107	34	0.95	4.87	-19.1
02	NYY	465	68	115	27	93	3	247	218	255	$16	369	458	827	16	78	26	0.89	244	120	42	0.86	5.73	-1.8
03	2TM	392	42	95	14	55	0	242	216	246	$7	340	401	741	13	78	28	0.67	245	98	26	0.95	4.58	-10.0
1st Half		231	26	59	9	36	0	255			$5	344	420	763	12	78	29	0.61	247	102	17		4.94	-3.4
2nd Half		161	16	36	5	19	0	224			$1	335	373	708	14	78	26	0.75	242	92	40		4.10	-6.6
04	Proj	250	31	60	9	39	0	240			$5	338	391	730	13	75	29	0.60	242	94	27		4.44	-9.0

Has not seen a .250 BA since the last century. Prior to '03, there were some BPIs that made him worth keeping around, but those reasons are slowly dwindling away.

Vidro,Jose

Pos 2B
Age 29 Past Peak
Bats S
R Low
I con
S pt
K
LIMA B BA: 65%

Yr	Tm	AB	R	H	HR	RBI	SB	Avg	vL	vR	R$	OB	Slg	OPS	bb%	ct%	h%	Eye	xBA	PX	SX	G/F	RC/G	RAR
99	MON	494	67	150	12	59	0	304	260	315	$13	342	476	818	6	90	32	0.57	309	120	41	1.36	5.76	21.1
00	MON	606	101	200	24	97	5	330	373	315	$28	380	540	920	7	89	34	0.71	347	133	66	1.74	7.67	53.2
01	MON	486	82	155	15	59	4	319	348	308	$19	360	486	845	6	90	33	0.63	306	108	77	1.44	6.55	35.0
02	MON	604	103	190	19	96	2	315	297	321	$26	377	490	867	9	88	33	0.86	313	121	72	1.67	6.85	39.6
03	MON	509	77	158	15	65	3	310	315	309	$19	393	470	862	12	90	32	1.38	315	109	47	1.85	6.77	32.7
1st Half		275	43	89	8	38	2	324			$12	411	495	906	13	91	34	1.58	323	120	47		7.63	23.7
2nd Half		234	34	69	7	27	1	295			$7	370	440	810	11	90	31	1.17	305	97	42		5.83	9.3
04	Proj	600	105	197	19	91	3	328			$27	393	498	891	10	90	34	1.02	317	114	60		7.38	48.7

Despite a knee injury that slowed him down in the 2nd half, this was clearly a growth year. PX and G/F trends indicate that he won't likely become a power threat, but a batting title could be coming very soon.

Vina,Fernando

Pos 2B
Age 35 Decline
Bats L
R Moderate
I con
S PT stb
K age
LIMA C BA: 70%

Yr	Tm	AB	R	H	HR	RBI	SB	Avg	vL	vR	R$	OB	Slg	OPS	bb%	ct%	h%	Eye	xBA	PX	SX	G/F	RC/G	RAR
99	MIL	154	17	41	1	16	5	266	333	236	$3	327	331	659	8	96	27	2.33	285	50	66	1.53	3.76	-2.0
00	STL	487	81	146	4	31	10	300	267	311	$11	348	398	746	7	93	32	1.00	304	65	116	1.38	4.85	6.7
01	STL	631	95	191	9	56	17	303	315	299	$20	336	418	755	5	94	31	0.91	313	73	133	1.43	5.08	21.4
02	STL	622	75	168	1	54	17	270	238	280	$12	318	338	656	7	94	29	1.22	286	53	106	1.55	3.63	-14.2
03	STL	259	35	65	4	23	4	251	163	271	$3	281	382	664	4	91	26	0.46	309	86	132	1.25	3.48	-7.2
1st Half		172	23	45	4	19	3	262			$4	287	430	717	3	91	27	0.38	324	109	138		3.89	-2.7
2nd Half		87	12	20	0	4	1	230			($0)	272	287	559	5	91	25	0.63	279	41	115		2.64	-4.6
04	Proj	550	74	144	4	44	11	262			$8	302	355	657	5	93	28	0.77	305	64	119		3.61	-11.3

Torn hamstring derailed his season, but there were BPI warning signs even before that happened. Plate patience, BA vs LH, batting eye all point to a 35-year-old experiencing some skills erosion. Bid cautiously.

Vitiello,Joe

Pos LF
Age 34 Decline
Bats R
R X HIGH
I EXP CON
S pt STB
K age
LIMA F BA: 60%

Yr	Tm	AB	R	H	HR	RBI	SB	Avg	vL	vR	R$	OB	Slg	OPS	bb%	ct%	h%	Eye	xBA	PX	SX	G/F	RC/G	RAR
99	aaa	487	50	112	20	69	2	230			$7	294	402	696	8	83	24	0.52	273	105	29		3.80	-18.7
00	aaa	326	41	91	10	45	2	279			$8	340	457	797	8	79	33	0.43	274	118	48		5.54	3.5
01	JPN	407	49	104	13	79	0	256			$10	306	405	711	7	69	34	0.23	221	93	27		4.25	-10.8
02	aaa	431	45	122	13	65	1	283			$13	330	448	778	7	87	30	0.54	289	114	33		5.27	-4.1
03	MON	* 247	26	60	5	25	0	243	375	250	$2	300	372	672	7	85	27	0.56	270	93	26	1.56	3.76	-13.4
1st Half		177	15	37	2	13	0	209			($2)	267	311	578	7	86	23	0.58	264	78	24		2.67	-16.0
2nd Half		70	11	23	3	12	0	329			$4	382	529	910	8	83	36	0.50	279	131			7.66	3.8
04	Proj	100	12	28	3	15	0	280			$3	333	443	776	7	82	31	0.45	271	111	31		5.22	-1.5

3-13-.342 in 76 AB at MON. Spent most of his career in the minors and Japan, yet made a minor statement in '03. You'd think, if you caught lightning in a bottle, you'd find a way to get him more than 76 AB.

Vizcaino,Jose

Pos SS 2B
Age 36 Decline
Bats S
R Very High
I CON
S pt stb
K AGE
LIMA F BA: 55%

Yr	Tm	AB	R	H	HR	RBI	SB	Avg	vL	vR	R$	OB	Slg	OPS	bb%	ct%	h%	Eye	xBA	PX	SX	G/F	RC/G	RAR
99	LA	266	27	67	1	29	2	252	329	224	$1	304	297	601	7	91	27	0.87	253	35	47	2.69	3.07	-3.6
00	2TM	267	32	67	0	14	6	251	233	258	$1	308	303	611	8	84	30	0.51	242	38	93	1.57	2.95	-8.0
01	HOU	256	38	71	1	14	3	277	250	282	$3	317	344	661	6	87	32	0.45	254	43	114	1.51	3.79	1.7
02	HOU	406	53	123	5	37	3	303	337	292	$11	342	397	738	6	90	33	0.60	272	68	67	1.11	4.76	9.7
03	HOU	189	14	47	3	26	0	249	222	255	$2	279	365	644	4	88	27	0.36	278	72	81	1.75	3.37	-4.1
1st Half		143	11	35	2	19	0	245			$1	270	371	641	3	87	27	0.26	279	78	107		3.27	-3.6
2nd Half		46	3	12	1	7	0	261			$1	306	348	654	6	93	26	1.00	275	53	8		3.67	-0.6
04	Proj	250	29	65	2	23	0	260			$2	300	348	648	5	88	29	0.46	274	59	83		3.55	-2.6

Opened the season with a sprained ankle, then a broken wrist took a bite out of his 2nd half. In all, a lost year from a BPI perspective, and at 36, long odds on much of a rebound.

Vizquel,Omar

Pos SS
Age 37 Decline
Bats S
R Moderate
I CON
S pt
K AGE
LIMA C BA: 85%

Yr	Tm	AB	R	H	HR	RBI	SB	Avg	vL	vR	R$	OB	Slg	OPS	bb%	ct%	h%	Eye	xBA	PX	SX	G/F	RC/G	RAR
99	CLE	574	112	191	5	66	42	333	333	333	$31	401	436	836	10	91	36	1.30	291	73	137	0.99	6.87	41.5
00	CLE	613	101	176	7	66	22	287	218	311	$17	376	375	751	12	88	32	1.21	275	58	102	1.23	4.99	10.1
01	CLE	611	84	156	2	50	13	255	228	266	$7	323	334	657	9	88	29	0.85	269	53	115	1.27	3.59	-14.2
02	CLE	582	85	160	14	72	18	275	281	273	$19	339	418	756	9	89	29	0.88	281	90	111	0.85	4.82	4.1
03	CLE	250	43	61	2	19	8	244	224	251	$3	323	336	659	10	92	26	1.45	294	64	119	1.22	3.66	-5.8
1st Half		231	40	59	2	18	8	255			$4	333	351	684	10	92	27	1.42	277	66	123		4.07	-2.4
2nd Half		19	3	2	0	1	0	105			($1)	190	158	348	10	95	11	2.00	288	46	117		0.61	-2.7
04	Proj	400	64	109	4	38	9	273			$8	346	375	721	10	90	30	1.09	274	68	112		4.48	0.5

Two knee surgeries... hmm... Y'know, it's getting tiring writing the same thing over and over in these commentaries... Injured this, lost time, hurt his BPIs, he's old, he's not, he'll come back, he won't. This is ridiculous.

Walbeck,Matt

Pos CA
Age 34 Decline
Bats S
R X HIGH
I exp CON
S PT stb
K age
LIMA F BA: 60%

Yr	Tm	AB	R	H	HR	RBI	SB	Avg	vL	vR	R$	OB	Slg	OPS	bb%	ct%	h%	Eye	xBA	PX	SX	G/F	RC/G	RAR
99	ANA	288	26	69	3	22	2	240	266	232	$0	303	306	608	8	84	28	0.57	229	42	51	1.38	3.00	-9.3
00	ANA	146	17	29	6	12	0	199	276	179	($1)	235	356	591	5	85	19	0.32	245	89	45	1.55	2.57	-7.3
01	aaa	339	32	78	4	39	1	230			$1	293	322	614	8	85	26	0.58	255	66	34		3.05	-6.6
02	DET	* 160	8	33	1	8	0	206	286	219	($2)	240	256	496	4	85	24	0.29	232	37		1.42	1.97	-8.2
03	DET	138	11	24	1	6	0	174	269	152	($3)	191	239	431	2	81	21	0.12	246	43	75	1.18	1.35	-12.4
1st Half		70	5	10	0	2	0	143			($3)	143	200	343	0	77	19	0.00	232	37	108		0.85	-7.6
2nd Half		68	6	14	1	4	0	206			($1)	239	279	519	4	85	23	0.30	261	48	42		1.99	-4.5
04	Proj	100	8	20	1	6	0	200			($1)	234	261	495	4	83	23	0.27	249	42	36		1.89	-6.5

The designated hitter rule was designed so that teams could avoid the automatic outs generated by most pitchers, but it was short-sighted in that it did not address ALL automatic outs. Why discriminate against others?

Walker,Larry

Pos RF
Age 37 Decline
Bats L
R High
I CON
S pt
K AGE
LIMA B BA: 60%

Yr	Tm	AB	R	H	HR	RBI	SB	Avg	vL	vR	R$	OB	Slg	OPS	bb%	ct%	h%	Eye	xBA	PX	SX	G/F	RC/G	RAR
99	COL	438	108	166	37	115	11	379	345	395	$40	451	710	1161	12	88	37	1.10	379	189	111	1.40	12.96	86.2
00	COL	314	64	97	9	51	5	309	341	297	$13	397	506	904	13	87	33	1.15	326	119	145	1.54	7.12	17.2
01	COL	497	107	174	38	123	14	350	378	338	$42	442	662	1104	14	79	38	0.80	345	180	103	1.61	11.35	74.5
02	COL	477	95	161	26	104	6	338	337	338	$32	417	602	1019	12	85	36	0.89	355	173	94	1.46	9.40	51.7
03	COL	454	86	129	15	79	7	284	321	265	$17	411	469	880	18	81	32	1.13	299	115	127	1.74	6.79	15.2
1st Half		247	52	74	8	50	5	300			$12	429	502	931	18	81	34	1.19	308	119	183		7.70	14.4
2nd Half		207	34	55	7	29	2	266			$6	390	430	820	17	81	30	1.05	287	109	50		5.79	1.1
04	Proj	350	69	97	12	68	5	277			$13	387	465	852	15	82	31	1.01	303	120	112		6.24	7.7

Shoulder and knee surgeries (here we go again) could delay his start to 2004. At 37, the odds are slim that we'll ever see vintage productivity levels from him again.

Walker,Todd

Pos 2B | Age 30 Past Peak | Bats L | R: Moderate | I: con | S: STB | K: | LIMA B | BA: 65%

	Tm	AB	R	H	HR	RBI	SB	Avg	vL	vR	R$	OB	Slg	OPS	bb%	ct%	h%	Eye	xBA	PX	SX	G/F	RC/G	RAR
99	MIN	531	62	148	6	46	18	279	178	302	$12	343	397	740	9	84	32	0.63	280	83	102	1.75	4.67	10.8
00	2TM	* 497	78	148	11	70	13	298	357	286	$17	362	433	795	9	90	31	0.98	292	82	114	1.39	5.65	21.3
01	2NL	551	93	163	17	75	1	296	269	302	$18	355	459	815	8	85	32	0.62	295	104	52	1.15	5.59	26.8
02	CIN	612	79	183	11	64	8	299	278	306	$19	352	431	783	8	87	33	0.62	293	97	80	1.25	5.43	17.4
03	BOS	587	92	166	13	85	1	283	234	301	$15	337	428	765	8	91	29	0.89	300	96	71	0.91	5.10	15.9
1st Half		312	58	98	8	46	1	314			$11	369	465	833	8	91	32	1.00	303	98	76		6.31	18.3
2nd Half		275	34	68	5	39	0	247			$3	301	385	686	7	90	26	0.78	296	94	58		3.93	-1.7
04	**Proj**	**550**	**80**	**164**	**16**	**81**	**2**	**298**			**$18**	**353**	**460**	**813**	**8**	**90**	**31**	**0.81**	**301**	**105**	**65**		**5.86**	**26.8**

2nd half slump erased a potential career year, but post-season heroics helped him save face somewhat. BPI trends are very positive, and point to bigger things ahead, but can defensive woes be overlooked?

Ward,Daryle

Pos 1B | Age 28 Peak | Bats L | R: Moderate | I: con | S: PT stb | K: | LIMA F | BA: 60%

	Tm	AB	R	H	HR	RBI	SB	Avg	vL	vR	R$	OB	Slg	OPS	bb%	ct%	h%	Eye	xBA	PX	SX	G/F	RC/G	RAR
99	HOU	* 391	54	113	27	80	1	289	250	275	$18	333	552	886	6	83	29	0.39	302	152	41	0.96	6.55	13.7
00	HOU	264	36	68	20	47	0	258	304	253	$10	297	538	835	5	77	26	0.25	263	152	54	0.78	5.50	1.2
01	HOU	213	21	56	9	39	0	263	308	257	$6	323	460	783	8	77	30	0.40	260	124		1.09	5.15	-6.8
02	HOU	453	41	125	12	72	1	276	204	286	$13	325	424	749	7	82	31	0.40	269	106	22	0.88	4.73	-11.3
03	LA	* 253	18	50	3	28	0	198	400	173	($2)	231	265	496	4	82	23	0.24	234	47	23	1.34	1.94	-28.4
1st Half		111	6	20	0	7	0	180			($3)	195	189	384	2	84	22	0.11	218	8	25		1.15	-15.6
2nd Half		142	12	30	3	21	0	211			$0	258	324	582	6	81	24	0.33	247	77	22		2.70	-12.3
04	**Proj**	**150**	**13**	**40**	**6**	**21**	**0**	**267**			**$4**	**308**	**433**	**741**	**6**	**81**	**29**	**0.32**	**249**	**104**	**18**		**4.61**	**-4.4**

0-9-.183 in 109 AB at LA. This is a player who once owned a set of decent skills, but has fallen off the map due to injury, circumstance and an ill-timed off year. Don't bid on him, not now, but do follow his whereabouts.

Wells,Vernon

Pos CF | Age 25 Pre-Peak | Bats R | R: High | I: exp con | S: pt stb | K: age | LIMA D | BA: 50%

	Tm	AB	R	H	HR	RBI	SB	Avg	vL	vR	R$	OB	Slg	OPS	bb%	ct%	h%	Eye	xBA	PX	SX	G/F	RC/G	RAR
99	TOR	* 323	41	98	7	41	11	303	412	225	$12	352	443	794	7	86	34	0.53	283	91	97	1.04	5.57	7.8
00	aaa	493	69	122	15	59	21	247			$13	308	432	740	8	87	26	0.67	305	113	141		4.51	0.2
01	TOR	* 509	64	144	13	52	19	283	372	264	$17	323	442	765	6	87	31	0.44	288	105	96	1.30	4.74	-1.6
02	TOR	608	87	167	23	100	9	275	260	280	$22	306	457	763	4	86	29	0.32	299	112	101	1.13	4.85	1.3
03	TOR	678	118	215	33	117	4	317	347	307	$32	357	550	907	6	88	32	0.53	321	144	91	0.97	7.33	47.2
1st Half		352	66	109	20	76	1	310			$18	350	568	918	6	88	31	0.54	331	158	75		7.29	24.4
2nd Half		326	52	106	13	41	3	325			$14	364	531	895	6	88	34	0.51	309	128	96		7.37	22.7
04	**Proj**	**650**	**100**	**204**	**35**	**112**	**6**	**314**			**$32**	**352**	**559**	**911**	**6**	**88**	**31**	**0.49**	**322**	**147**	**89**		**7.29**	**44.5**

Breakout year, fully supported by his BPIs. At 25, he could still grow some more. A keeper.

Werth,Jayson

Pos RF | Age 24 Growth | Bats R | R: X HIGH | I: EXP con | S: PT stb | K: age | LIMA D | BA: 45%

	Tm	AB	R	H	HR	RBI	SB	Avg	vL	vR	R$	OB	Slg	OPS	bb%	ct%	h%	Eye	xBA	PX	SX	G/F	RC/G	RAR
99	aa	121	17	32	1	11	6	264			$3	346	339	684	11	82	32	0.68	247	48	113		4.25	-2.6
00	aa	276	42	57	5	23	8	207			$0	328	315	643	15	84	23	1.11	264	70	91		3.35	-14.6
01	aa	369	43	99	16	59	10	268			$14	360	466	826	13	79	30	0.69	272	121	71		5.85	6.3
02	aaa	489	56	115	14	71	20	235			$14	318	384	702	11	78	28	0.54	254	98	97	1.30	4.02	-17.0
03	TOR	* 284	39	64	10	40	11	225	56	300	$7	267	419	686	5	71	28	0.20	250	127	123	1.10	3.80	-11.7
1st Half		114	16	25	4	19	3	219			$2	276	421	697	7	68	28	0.25	243	138	83		3.77	-4.9
2nd Half		170	23	39	6	21	8	229			$5	260	418	678	4	74	28	0.16	253	120	136		3.81	-6.9
04	**Proj**	**150**	**19**	**37**	**6**	**21**	**6**	**247**			**$5**	**312**	**444**	**757**	**9**	**75**	**29**	**0.39**	**255**	**123**	**106**		**4.75**	**-1.4**

2-10-.208 in 48 AB at TOR. Players all have their individual skills ceilings, above which they simply can not succeed. For him, AA looks like his ceiling.

White,Rondell

Pos LF | Age 32 Past Peak | Bats R | R: High | I: con | S: pt STB | K: | LIMA D+ | BA: 45%

	Tm	AB	R	H	HR	RBI	SB	Avg	vL	vR	R$	OB	Slg	OPS	bb%	ct%	h%	Eye	xBA	PX	SX	G/F	RC/G	RAR
99	MON	539	83	168	22	64	10	312	374	293	$22	350	505	855	6	84	34	0.38	295	114	108	1.48	6.38	19.7
00	2NL	357	59	111	13	61	5	311	338	304	$16	369	493	862	8	78	37	0.42	282	116	62	2.25	6.62	13.7
01	CHC	323	43	99	17	50	1	307	268	317	$15	358	529	888	7	83	33	0.46	297	132	48	1.47	6.99	11.4
02	NYY	455	59	109	14	62	1	240	286	226	$7	279	378	657	5	81	27	0.29	250	87	47	1.57	3.48	-18.5
03	2TM	488	62	141	22	87	1	289	299	285	$19	331	488	819	6	84	31	0.39	291	119	61	1.26	5.61	2.1
1st Half		268	37	78	15	46	1	291			$12	340	500	840	7	85	29	0.51	296	119	47		5.77	2.4
2nd Half		220	25	63	7	41	0	286			$7	320	473	793	5	82	32	0.28	279	117			5.41	-0.3
04	**Proj**	**450**	**59**	**131**	**18**	**73**	**2**	**291**			**$16**	**333**	**478**	**812**	**6**	**82**	**32**	**0.36**	**290**	**115**	**64**		**5.64**	**2.8**

He's performing in his comfort zone right now. 20ish HRs, BA around .300, and 500 ABs representing a level of health and stamina in his distant past. A decent, albeit always slightly risky investment.

Widger,Chris

Pos CA | Age 32 Past Peak | Bats R | R: High | I: con | S: pt STB | K: | LIMA F | BA: 60%

	Tm	AB	R	H	HR	RBI	SB	Avg	vL	vR	R$	OB	Slg	OPS	bb%	ct%	h%	Eye	xBA	PX	SX	G/F	RC/G	RAR
99	MON	383	42	101	14	56	1	264	350	233	$9	314	441	755	7	78	31	0.33	265	113	37	1.16	4.60	7.2
00	2TM	292	32	68	13	35	1	233	260	223	$4	304	438	743	9	78	25	0.48	267	121	58	1.14	4.32	2.2
01	SEA	0	0	0	0	0	0	0								0			0					
02	NYY	* 281	23	61	7	33	0	217	294	298	$1	257	356	613	5	87	23	0.41	275	90	37	1.00	2.77	-7.5
03	STL	* 173	15	38	2	22	1	220	227	238	$0	270	341	611	6	82	26	0.38	260	96	45	1.78	3.04	-6.6
1st Half		89	7	16	2	11	1	180			($0)	247	326	573	8	83	19	0.53	271	106	45		2.55	-5.0
2nd Half		84	8	22	0	11	0	262			$1	295	357	653	5	80	33	0.24	248	85	29		3.65	-1.6
04	**Proj**	**100**	**9**	**23**	**2**	**13**	**0**	**230**			**$1**	**279**	**363**	**642**	**6**	**82**	**26**	**0.38**	**261**	**95**	**37**		**3.29**	**-2.5**

0-14-.235 in 102 AB at STL. He said: "I've had enough of AAA. I just don't believe I should be there and I'm not going to put my family through that stuff." Okay, but there are other alternatives besides the majors.

Wigginton,Ty

Pos 3B | Age 26 Pre-Peak | Bats R | R: Very High | I: EXP CON | S: pt stb | K: | LIMA D+ | BA: 40%

	Tm	AB	R	H	HR	RBI	SB	Avg	vL	vR	R$	OB	Slg	OPS	bb%	ct%	h%	Eye	xBA	PX	SX	G/F	RC/G	RAR
99		0	0	0	0	0	0	0								0								
00	aa	453	53	113	16	64	4	249			$9	280	417	697	4	78	29	0.19	263	101	69		3.76	-8.1
01	a/a	288	30	66	6	21	4	229			$2	297	340	638	9	77	28	0.42	238	73	52		3.27	-10.6
02	NYM	* 499	62	139	11	61	6	279	314	296	$14	339	417	756	8	87	30	0.71	282	99	72	1.07	4.92	4.7
03	NYM	573	73	146	11	71	12	255	297	239	$12	310	396	706	7	78	31	0.37	264	96	129	1.33	4.26	0.1
1st Half		299	46	82	6	38	5	274			$8	326	431	758	7	80	33	0.38	268	100	160		4.91	5.6
2nd Half		274	27	64	5	33	7	234			$4	293	358	651	8	77	29	0.37	252	91	78		3.62	-5.2
04	**Proj**	**550**	**65**	**135**	**12**	**64**	**9**	**245**			**$10**	**303**	**381**	**684**	**8**	**80**	**29**	**0.41**	**260**	**92**	**95**		**3.89**	**-8.3**

Started out performing pretty much how we'd expected, but after the scouting reports made their rounds, he tanked. These 2nd half numbers are where you need to set the bar for 2004.

Wilkerson,Brad

Pos LF CF 1B | Age 26 Pre-Peak | Bats L | R: High | I: EXP CON | S: pt stb | K: | LIMA B+ | BA: 30%

	Tm	AB	R	H	HR	RBI	SB	Avg	vL	vR	R$	OB	Slg	OPS	bb%	ct%	h%	Eye	xBA	PX	SX	G/F	RC/G	RAR
99	aa	422	56	91	6	42	3	216			($1)	333	315	648	15	80	26	0.88	247	67	59		3.27	-23.7
00	a/a	441	80	121	17	68	11	274			$15	377	501	879	14	80	31	0.85	300	147	89		6.33	15.2
01	MON	* 350	50	84	13	49	13	240			$10	367	411	778	17	70	30	0.67	237	102	98	0.81	4.99	-7.5
02	MON	507	92	135	20	59	7	266	230	274	$15	367	469	837	14	68	35	0.50	239	127	140	1.00	5.74	-9.6
03	MON	504	78	135	19	77	13	268	281	263	$19	378	464	842	15	69	35	0.57	254	126	103	1.10	5.86	4.0
1st Half		232	35	69	9	43	7	297			$12	416	513	929	17	67	41	0.62	253	142	101		7.42	12.1
2nd Half		272	43	66	10	34	6	243			$7	344	423	767	13	71	31	0.53	253	113	102		4.69	-7.4
04	**Proj**	**500**	**80**	**130**	**22**	**79**	**12**	**260**			**$18**	**370**	**475**	**844**	**15**	**70**	**33**	**0.59**	**258**	**133**	**112**		**5.81**	**0.7**

The only area of REAL growth this season was in his ability to hit LHers. Zero growth otherwise and 2nd half fade are bad signs for a 26-year-old who should be taking forward steps right now. Maybe in '04, but risk is higher.

Williams,Bernie

Pos CF | Age 35 Decline | Bats S | R: Low | I: con | S: pt | K: age | LIMA B | BA: 65%

	Tm	AB	R	H	HR	RBI	SB	Avg	vL	vR	R$	OB	Slg	OPS	bb%	ct%	h%	Eye	xBA	PX	SX	G/F	RC/G	RAR
99	NYY	591	116	202	25	115	9	342	297	359	$32	437	536	973	14	84	38	1.05	299	112	94	1.78	8.69	62.4
00	NYY	537	108	165	30	121	13	307	289	315	$29	388	566	954	12	84	32	0.85	344	149	126	1.83	8.00	49.4
01	NYY	540	102	166	26	94	11	307	311	306	$27	395	522	917	13	88	31	1.16	310	134	69	1.33	7.50	39.3
02	NYY	612	102	204	19	102	8	333	354	326	$30	413	493	906	12	84	37	0.86	301	102	73	1.87	7.72	47.6
03	NYY	445	77	117	15	64	5	263	280	256	$12	364	411	776	14	86	28	1.16	274	91	78	1.58	5.26	6.7
1st Half		175	32	50	7	31	2	286			$7	396	457	853	15	89	29	1.68	290	101	76		6.55	8.9
2nd Half		270	45	67	8	33	3	248			$5	343	381	725	13	84	27	0.93	264	84	66		4.51	-1.8
04	**Proj**	**500**	**88**	**142**	**17**	**80**	**4**	**284**			**$17**	**378**	**448**	**826**	**13**	**85**	**31**	**1.00**	**276**	**101**	**72**		**5.99**	**17.4**

Negative signs at age 35:
- Declining PX trend
- 70 point drop in BA vs RH
- Lowest OB avg since 1993
- Injuries = fewest AB since '94.
- Negatives tend to snowball as you age.

Williams,Matt

Pos 3B
Age 38 Decline
Bats R

R: Moderate
I: con
S: PT
K: AGE

LIMA F BA: 55%

Yr	Tm	AB	R	H	HR	RBI	SB	Avg	vL	vR	R$	OB	Slg	OPS	bb%	ct%	h%	Eye	xBA	PX	SX	G/F	RC/G	RAR
99	ARI	627	98	190	35	142	2	303	333	291	$30	346	536	882	6	85	31	0.44	301	140	60	1.02	6.80	41.8
00	ARI	371	43	102	12	47	1	275	311	260	$9	312	431	743	5	86	29	0.39	274	94	54	1.19	4.64	3.4
01	ARI	408	58	112	16	65	1	275	313	259	$13	312	466	777	5	83	30	0.31	255	122	50	0.85	5.12	6.1
02	ARI	226	30	57	13	41	3	252	289	242	$9	316	473	789	9	82	26	0.51	293	130	92	1.10	5.08	3.3
03	ARI	134	17	33	4	16	0	246	302	220	$2	327	403	730	11	81	28	0.62	255	107	27	0.91	4.45	0.8
1st Half		134	17	33	4	16	0	246			$2	327	403	730	11	81	28	0.62	255	107	27		4.45	0.8
2nd Half		0	0	0	0	0	0	0			($0)					0			0					
04	Proj	0	0	0	0	0	0	0			$0					0			128	0	0			

Biggest regret of his career... Having the 1994 strike shut down his power display at 43 HRs, a pace that put him on dead target for breaking Roger Maris' record four years before Mark McGwire did.

Wilson,Craig

Pos RF 1B CA
Age 27 Peak
Bats R

R: Very High
I: EXP CON
S: pt stb
K:

LIMA C+ BA: 35%

Yr	Tm	AB	R	H	HR	RBI	SB	Avg	vL	vR	R$	OB	Slg	OPS	bb%	ct%	h%	Eye	xBA	PX	SX	G/F	RC/G	RAR
99	aa	362	49	91	18	59	1	251			$9	316	470	785	9	75	29	0.37	263	130	58		4.89	-1.0
00	aaa	396	66	100	27	68	1	253			$12	312	520	832	8	74	27	0.33	278	152	57		5.43	4.6
01	PIT	* 203	30	61	14	34	3	300	378	283	$11	355	552	906	8	68	38	0.27	245	133	104	1.23	7.09	8.6
02	PIT	368	48	97	16	57	2	264	313	242	$12	323	443	765	8	68	34	0.28	238	113	55	0.98	4.81	-5.3
03	PIT	309	49	81	18	49	3	262	308	238	$11	337	505	842	10	71	31	0.39	261	143	106	1.15	5.87	2.3
1st Half		112	12	28	3	15	2	250			$2	333	402	735	11	68	34	0.39	227	106	51		4.66	-3.1
2nd Half		197	37	53	15	34	1	269			$9	339	563	903	10	73	29	0.40	280	165	128		6.57	5.5
04	Proj	400	59	107	25	64	4	268			$16	334	516	850	9	70	32	0.34	259	145	89		5.94	5.4

Does he merit more regular playing time? He doesn't have the best platoon splits, and he might never hit better than .265, but his position versatility alone should certainly find 500 AB, which could mean 30 HRs.

Wilson,Dan

Pos CA
Age 35 Decline
Bats R

R: Moderate
I: CON
S: pt
K: age

LIMA D BA: 45%

Yr	Tm	AB	R	H	HR	RBI	SB	Avg	vL	vR	R$	OB	Slg	OPS	bb%	ct%	h%	Eye	xBA	PX	SX	G/F	RC/G	RAR
99	SEA	414	46	110	7	38	5	266	255	269	$6	314	382	695	7	80	32	0.35	257	77	85	0.95	4.23	2.0
00	SEA	268	31	63	5	27	1	235	234	235	$1	293	336	629	8	81	27	0.43	223	65	43	1.12	3.19	-7.8
01	SEA	377	44	100	10	42	3	265	290	252	$8	302	403	705	5	82	30	0.29	244	88	60	0.83	4.17	3.4
02	SEA	359	35	106	6	44	1	295	288	298	$9	329	396	724	5	77	37	0.22	232	66	47	0.96	4.73	11.0
03	SEA	316	32	76	4	43	0	241	264	229	$2	275	339	614	5	84	28	0.29	247	66	53	1.29	3.13	-9.1
1st Half		152	11	35	1	20	0	230			$0	269	296	565	5	80	28	0.27	224	44	45		2.64	-6.7
2nd Half		164	21	41	3	23	0	250			$2	281	378	659	4	87	27	0.32	270	86	61		3.61	-2.3
04	Proj	300	32	78	5	38	1	260			$4	296	367	663	5	82	30	0.28	247	72	53		3.74	-1.7

xBA says that this year's .241 BA is a better reflection of his skills than the more inflated BAs he posted in 2001 and 2002. But on draft day, keep talking up 2002's .295 BA and how 2003 was just an off-year.

Wilson,Enrique

Pos SS
Age 30 Past Peak
Bats S

R: Very High
I: CON
S: PT stb
K:

LIMA F BA: 70%

Yr	Tm	AB	R	H	HR	RBI	SB	Avg	vL	vR	R$	OB	Slg	OPS	bb%	ct%	h%	Eye	xBA	PX	SX	G/F	RC/G	RAR
99	CLE	332	41	87	2	24	5	262	255	266	$3	314	352	666	7	88	29	0.61	253	68	75	1.52	3.71	-4.4
00	2TM	239	27	70	5	27	2	293	349	273	$6	342	427	769	7	90	31	0.75	288	87	57	1.62	5.14	8.1
01	2TM	228	17	48	2	20	0	211	188	217	($2)	241	281	521	4	84	24	0.24	211	47	46	2.10	1.94	-14.7
02	NYY	105	17	19	2	11	1	181	105	224	($1)	239	295	534	7	79	21	0.36	225	62	166	1.06	2.13	-8.4
03	NYY	135	18	31	3	15	3	230	133	257	$2	268	363	631	5	90	24	0.50	307	92	82	1.09	3.21	-5.0
1st Half		53	4	10	1	6	0	189			($0)	218	302	520	4	91	19	0.40	298	78	43		1.85	-4.4
2nd Half		82	14	21	2	9	3	256			$2	299	402	701	6	89	27	0.56	313	101	97		4.33	-0.2
04	Proj	150	19	36	3	16	2	240			$2	282	356	637	6	86	26	0.42	296	74	92		3.27	-5.3

Hilarity of the Day, from Rotowire.com: "The career .252 hitter is now 10-for-20 against Pedro Martinez. There has been speculation that Pedro has been reluctant to come inside on his fellow Dominican."

Wilson,Jack

Pos SS
Age 26 Pre-Peak
Bats R

R: Moderate
I: EXP CON
S: stb
K:

LIMA D+ BA: 60%

Yr	Tm	AB	R	H	HR	RBI	SB	Avg	vL	vR	R$	OB	Slg	OPS	bb%	ct%	h%	Eye	xBA	PX	SX	G/F	RC/G	RAR
99		0	0	0	0	0	0	0								0								
00	aa	482	74	126	7	45	3	261			$5	330	392	722	9	85	29	0.70	277	81	112		4.24	4.3
01	PIT	* 493	60	121	4	30	3	245	220	224	$1	279	325	604	4	84	29	0.28	252	56	73	1.23	2.95	-9.0
02	PIT	527	77	133	4	47	5	252	360	223	$5	301	332	633	7	86	29	0.50	246	58	105	1.16	3.41	-7.6
03	PIT	558	58	143	9	62	5	256	261	255	$9	301	357	658	6	87	28	0.49	278	65	77	1.27	3.59	-8.6
1st Half		277	28	67	4	28	3	242			$3	283	343	626	5	86	27	0.40	276	68	86		3.27	-7.0
2nd Half		281	30	76	5	34	2	270			$6	319	370	689	7	88	29	0.59	279	63	67		3.92	-1.6
04	Proj	550	67	144	7	54	5	262			$8	309	357	665	6	86	29	0.48	277	64	82		3.70	-3.4

Carbon copy seasons, except for slight power bump. But that power bump means nothing because his PX and G/F levels paint the picture of a hitter not likely to break into double digit HRs with any regularity.

Wilson,Preston

Pos CF
Age 29 Past Peak
Bats R

R: Low
I: con
S: stb
K:

LIMA D BA: 45%

Yr	Tm	AB	R	H	HR	RBI	SB	Avg	vL	vR	R$	OB	Slg	OPS	bb%	ct%	h%	Eye	xBA	PX	SX	G/F	RC/G	RAR
99	FLA	482	67	135	26	71	11	280	285	279	$19	343	502	845	9	68	36	0.29	240	128	104	1.13	6.04	23.8
00	FLA	605	94	160	31	121	36	264	250	269	$32	326	486	812	8	69	33	0.29	251	130	120	1.27	5.31	17.7
01	FLA	468	70	128	23	71	20	274	208	293	$22	325	494	819	7	77	31	0.34	267	132	111	0.99	5.49	22.3
02	FLA	510	80	124	23	65	20	243	242	244	$18	320	429	750	10	73	29	0.41	250	116	107	1.40	4.45	-6.6
03	COL	600	94	169	36	141	14	282	274	285	$34	341	537	878	8	77	31	0.39	299	159	83	1.11	6.34	23.4
1st Half		322	50	97	17	70	6	301			$18	357	550	907	8	78	34	0.40	304	160	77		6.85	16.9
2nd Half		278	44	72	19	71	8	259			$16	322	522	844	9	75	28	0.38	292	158	82		5.78	6.6
04	Proj	600	93	175	38	130	15	292			$35	353	557	910	9	75	33	0.38	297	163	86		6.87	36.5

When he was dealt to COL, we revised our original projection of 26 HR/.260 to 37/.291, but the HQ's reader boards rejected it as being beyond the limits of reality. Well, they were correct... by 1 HR and 9 points of BA.

Wilson,Tom

Pos CA
Age 33 Decline
Bats R

R: Very High
I: EXP CON
S: stb
K: age

LIMA F BA: 25%

Yr	Tm	AB	R	H	HR	RBI	SB	Avg	vL	vR	R$	OB	Slg	OPS	bb%	ct%	h%	Eye	xBA	PX	SX	G/F	RC/G	RAR
99	a/a	319	34	66	15	42	0	207			$2	299	398	697	12	73	23	0.49	244	114			3.73	-2.8
00	aaa	330	45	75	15	50	2	227			$5	332	412	745	14	71	27	0.54	242	108	40		4.45	3.8
01	aaa	280	35	61	7	38	0	218			$1	307	343	650	11	79	25	0.61	245	78	46	0.40	3.38	-2.7
02	TOR	265	33	68	8	37	0	257	337	220	$5	328	385	713	10	70	34	0.35	220	79	26	0.96	4.33	5.5
03	TOR	256	37	66	5	35	0	258	299	228	$4	331	391	722	10	69	36	0.35	250	94	34	1.03	4.44	2.6
1st Half		148	25	46	5	24	0	311			$6	382	500	882	10	67	44	0.35	231	128	33		7.06	11.9
2nd Half		108	12	20	0	11	0	185			($2)	261	241	501	9	71	26	0.35	230	48	38		1.96	-7.3
04	Proj	250	32	59	6	33	0	236			$2	314	360	674	10	71	31	0.40	222	83	34		3.76	-1.4

The wonders of statistics... His .311 1st half BA hid his horrific 2nd half. His monthly running BAs softened the reality...

APRIL: .269 JULY: .281
MAY: .309 AUG: .262
JUNE: .311 SEP: .258

Wilson,Vance

Pos CA
Age 31 Past Peak
Bats R

R: Very High
I: EXP con
S: PT stb
K:

LIMA F BA: 45%

Yr	Tm	AB	R	H	HR	RBI	SB	Avg	vL	vR	R$	OB	Slg	OPS	bb%	ct%	h%	Eye	xBA	PX	SX	G/F	RC/G	RAR
99	aaa	53	9	12	2	4	1	226			$1	268	377	645	5	83	24	0.33	272	90	87		3.12	-1.5
00	aaa	404	38	88	12	49	9	218			$4	253	361	614	4	84	23	0.30	276	88	75		2.82	-15.9
01	NYM	* 285	23	65	5	33	0	228	286	300	$1	259	333	593	4	82	26	0.24	254	72	26	1.31	2.76	-6.6
02	NYM	163	19	40	5	26	0	245	125	275	$3	268	380	648	3	80	28	0.16	248	89	42	1.04	3.34	-3.6
03	NYM	268	28	65	8	39	1	243	243	242	$5	283	373	656	5	79	28	0.27	257	80	54	1.26	3.45	-6.8
1st Half		155	20	42	7	26	1	271			$5	307	432	739	5	79	30	0.25	264	94	48		4.68	1.7
2nd Half		113	8	23	1	13	0	204			($1)	250	292	542	6	79	25	0.29	247	61	69		2.13	-7.8
04	Proj	200	20	50	5	27	1	250			$3	284	375	659	5	80	29	0.24	260	79	57		3.48	-3.7

Almost looked like he would break beyond his soft skills set, the 2nd half brought him back to career levels. So it looks like '04 will be yet another year on his endless quest for positive replacement value.

Winn,Randy

Pos LF CF
Age 29 Past Peak
Bats S

R: Low
I: con
S: pt stb
K:

LIMA C+ BA: 35%

Yr	Tm	AB	R	H	HR	RBI	SB	Avg	vL	vR	R$	OB	Slg	OPS	bb%	ct%	h%	Eye	xBA	PX	SX	G/F	RC/G	RAR
99	TAM	* 510	77	150	5	50	17	294	238	278	$14	333	416	749	6	83	35	0.35	273	83	129	2.65	4.60	-6.9
00	TAM	* 462	77	128	6	46	19	277	256	250	$12	363	387	750	12	86	31	0.98	273	73	108	1.73	4.70	-5.3
01	TAM	429	54	117	6	50	12	273	306	259	$11	332	401	733	8	81	32	0.47	273	84	118	1.91	4.39	-3.0
02	TAM	607	87	181	14	75	27	298	347	283	$26	356	461	818	8	82	35	0.50	290	104	150	1.46	5.97	19.3
03	SEA	600	103	177	11	75	23	295	314	288	$23	340	425	765	6	82	35	0.38	278	88	130	1.76	5.30	-0.5
1st Half		294	45	76	2	28	14	259			$7	308	350	658	7	83	31	0.41	266	67	134		3.87	-12.6
2nd Half		306	58	101	9	47	9	330			$16	371	497	868	6	81	38	0.35	289	108	115		6.96	13.3
04	Proj	600	95	174	14	74	22	290			$22	342	444	787	7	82	33	0.44	284	101	131		5.39	5.4

Solid 2nd half salvaged a slow start, but the net result was still off from 2002. Safeco was part of the problem, where he batted only .284 (as opposed to .325 in TAM in '02). BPIs do not support further growth in 2004.

Witt,Kevin

		Yr	Tm	AB	R	H	HR	RBI	SB	Avg	vL	vR	R$	OB	Slg	OPS	bb%	ct%	h%	Eye	xBA	PX	SX	G/F	RC/G	RAR
Pos	1B	99	aaa	421	59	105	18	58	0	249			$8	333	444	778	11	79	28	0.60	269	118	45		5.03	-6.3
Age	28 Peak	00	aaa	489	48	112	22	59	1	229			$6	283	429	713	7	78	25	0.35	272	115	61		4.00	-24.4
Bats	L	01	aaa	483	53	122	24	80	1	253			$14	282	466	748	4	74	29	0.16	256	125	60		4.45	-24.8
R	High	02	aaa	509	57	118	19	81	0	232			$9	266	407	673	5	79	26	0.23	263	113	40		3.56	-33.3
I	EXP con	03	DET	* 403	45	107	17	52	1	266	241	266	$10	316	437	753	7	74	32	0.29	243	103	30	1.38	4.76	-7.2
S	stb	1st Half		243	28	67	12	40	0	276			$8	333	477	811	8	76	32	0.36	259	122	16		5.60	1.5
K		2nd Half		160	17	40	5	12	1	250			$2	290	375	665	5	72	32	0.20	219	75	41		3.62	-8.3
LIMA	D BA: 30%	04	Proj	**450**	**50**	**112**	**17**	**60**	**1**	**249**			**$9**	**293**	**417**	**710**	**6**	**76**	**29**	**0.25**	**245**	**102**	**44**		**4.11**	**-20.7**

10-26-.263 in 270 AB at DET. Elevated hit rate in comparison to his history, and xBA, paint a clearer pitcure about his BA. PX trend and G/F discount his power potential. He'll hit some HRs, but might not bat .250.

Womack,Tony

		Yr	Tm	AB	R	H	HR	RBI	SB	Avg	vL	vR	R$	OB	Slg	OPS	bb%	ct%	h%	Eye	xBA	PX	SX	G/F	RC/G	RAR
Pos	SS 2B	99	ARI	614	111	170	4	41	72	277	290	272	$29	333	370	703	8	89	31	0.76	273	60	186	1.31	4.67	20.4
Age	34 Decline	00	ARI	617	95	167	7	57	45	271	276	269	$22	304	384	689	5	88	30	0.41	282	65	199	1.52	4.16	12.7
Bats	L	01	ARI	481	66	128	3	30	28	266	188	286	$13	300	345	645	5	89	29	0.43	269	52	151	1.66	3.67	1.6
R	High	02	ARI	590	90	160	5	57	29	271	214	297	$18	324	353	676	7	86	31	0.58	260	57	135	1.58	3.94	0.8
I	CON	03	2NL	349	43	79	2	22	13	226	268	218	$3	246	307	552	3	87	26	0.19	277	55	152	1.90	2.45	-17.9
S	pt stb	1st Half		219	30	52	2	15	8	237			$3	264	338	602	4	88	26	0.30	288	67	156		2.95	-7.7
K	age	2nd Half		130	13	27	0	7	5	208			($0)	214	254	468	1	85	25	0.05	257	34	133		1.72	-9.8
LIMA	D BA: 60%	04	Proj	**350**	**46**	**91**	**2**	**25**	**15**	**260**			**$7**	**300**	**337**	**637**	**5**	**87**	**30**	**0.43**	**276**	**52**	**139**		**3.42**	**-5.2**

Could get off to a slow start in 2004 due to off-season Tommy John surgery. Players who open the season on the DL tend to get discounted at the draft table, and while he is no great prize, don't ignore valuable SBs.

Woodward,Chris

		Yr	Tm	AB	R	H	HR	RBI	SB	Avg	vL	vR	R$	OB	Slg	OPS	bb%	ct%	h%	Eye	xBA	PX	SX	G/F	RC/G	RAR
Pos	SS	99	aaa	281	38	74	1	16	3	263			$1	337	359	696	10	86	30	0.78	271	73	85	1.33	4.19	2.8
Age	27 Peak	00	TOR	* 247	35	62	7	35	3	251	235	172	$4	305	433	738	7	79	29	0.37	277	116	105	0.93	4.56	1.0
Bats	R	01	TOR	* 256	34	67	12	31	0	262	77	220	$6	300	500	800	5	82	28	0.30	292	142	93	1.18	5.09	5.4
R	High	02	TOR	312	48	86	13	45	3	276	149	315	$10	331	468	799	8	77	32	0.36	256	111	120	0.82	5.52	8.3
I	exp CON	03	TOR	349	49	91	7	45	1	261	307	242	$6	316	395	711	7	79	31	0.39	256	91	69	0.70	4.22	-2.1
S	pt stb	1st Half		232	36	62	5	30	1	267			$5	328	405	733	8	80	31	0.46	258	89	89		4.65	1.5
K		2nd Half		117	13	29	2	15	0	248			$1	290	376	666	6	78	30	0.27	251	93	41		3.42	-3.6
LIMA	D BA: 40%	04	Proj	**450**	**61**	**118**	**13**	**58**	**2**	**262**			**$9**	**313**	**428**	**741**	**7**	**79**	**31**	**0.36**	**260**	**105**	**84**		**4.54**	**1.3**

Lost his starting job because of defense, but he committed just 4 more errors than 2002, in 24 more games, and posted a fielding pct and range rating nearly identical to '02. Offense tanked only after he lost his job.

Wooten,Shawn

		Yr	Tm	AB	R	H	HR	RBI	SB	Avg	vL	vR	R$	OB	Slg	OPS	bb%	ct%	h%	Eye	xBA	PX	SX	G/F	RC/G	RAR
Pos	1B DH	99	aa	518	55	119	15	69	2	230			$5	285	361	646	7	77	27	0.34	246	80	50		3.40	-33.7
Age	31 Past Peak	00	a/a	443	61	128	18	63	4	289			$14	333	494	827	6	86	30	0.47	305	123	93		5.90	3.1
Bats	R	01	ANA	221	24	69	8	32	2	312	304	321	$9	327	466	793	2	81	36	0.12	257	90	61	0.67	5.72	-2.5
R	Very High	02	ANA	* 155	15	42	3	24	2	271	282	310	$4	298	394	692	4	79	33	0.18	247	85	53	0.89	4.18	-7.5
I	EXP CON	03	ANA	272	25	66	7	32	0	243	238	248	$3	304	349	653	8	83	27	0.53	248	65	18	1.03	3.35	-16.7
S	PT stb	1st Half		99	11	32	4	16	0	323			$4	380	485	864	8	85	35	0.60	273	97	22		6.15	2.1
K		2nd Half		173	14	34	3	16	0	197			($1)	261	272	532	8	83	22	0.50	234	47	25		2.19	-17.5
LIMA	D BA: 55%	04	Proj	**400**	**40**	**106**	**11**	**54**	**2**	**265**			**$9**	**309**	**389**	**698**	**6**	**82**	**30**	**0.35**	**250**	**78**	**34**		**4.06**	**-18.7**

The peak is passing, and so are his chances. BPIs are in decline, others are taking away potential playing time, and he didn't help his cause by flirting with the Mendoza Line in the 2nd half. 2004 could be his last shot.

Young,Dmitri

		Yr	Tm	AB	R	H	HR	RBI	SB	Avg	vL	vR	R$	OB	Slg	OPS	bb%	ct%	h%	Eye	xBA	PX	SX	G/F	RC/G	RAR
Pos	LF	99	CIN	373	63	112	14	56	3	300	266	314	$13	352	504	856	7	81	34	0.42	298	132	82	1.80	6.46	14.5
Age	30 Past Peak	00	CIN	548	68	166	18	88	0	303	333	292	$19	346	491	837	6	85	33	0.45	309	116	61	1.85	6.07	12.9
Bats	S	01	CIN	540	68	163	21	69	8	302	280	311	$22	347	481	828	6	86	32	0.48	283	108	79	1.61	5.96	4.1
R	Moderate	02	DET	201	25	57	7	27	2	284	296	279	$7	324	458	782	6	81	32	0.31	281	113	54	1.79	5.34	2.9
I	con	03	DET	562	78	167	29	85	2	297	293	299	$23	363	537	900	9	77	34	0.45	311	142	91	1.52	7.05	26.7
S	PT stb	1st Half		282	37	83	15	45	1	294			$12	360	546	906	9	79	33	0.48	322	146	107		7.13	14.1
K		2nd Half		280	41	84	14	40	1	300			$11	366	529	894	9	75	36	0.41	300	138	68		6.97	12.7
LIMA	C+ BA: 45%	04	Proj	**550**	**74**	**160**	**23**	**79**	**2**	**291**			**$19**	**346**	**491**	**837**	**8**	**80**	**33**	**0.41**	**309**	**122**	**69**		**6.08**	**15.5**

A healthy year, a breakout year, but not without a little outside help. Drop in contact rate and high G/F ratio show some downside. He won't repeat, but he'll do all right.

Young,Eric

		Yr	Tm	AB	R	H	HR	RBI	SB	Avg	vL	vR	R$	OB	Slg	OPS	bb%	ct%	h%	Eye	xBA	PX	SX	G/F	RC/G	RAR
Pos	2B	99	LA	456	73	128	2	41	51	281	295	275	$22	368	355	723	12	94	29	2.42	283	56	118	1.29	4.51	4.0
Age	36 Decline	00	CHC	607	98	180	6	47	54	297	341	284	$28	363	399	761	9	94	31	1.62	309	74	126	1.40	5.62	21.4
Bats	R	01	CHC	603	98	168	6	42	31	279	308	271	$18	326	393	719	7	93	29	0.93	302	82	132	1.27	4.38	9.2
R	High	02	MIL	496	57	139	3	28	31	280	292	278	$17	333	369	702	7	92	30	1.03	289	69	117	1.43	4.33	-1.2
I	con	03	2NL	475	80	119	15	34	28	251	246	252	$16	331	392	722	11	91	25	1.30	303	89	112	1.21	4.30	-1.5
S	pt STB	1st Half		260	49	67	9	20	17	258			$10	330	427	757	10	92	25	1.33	322	109	136		5.08	5.2
K	AGE	2nd Half		215	31	52	6	14	11	242			$5	332	349	681	12	89	25	1.26	280	64	80		3.48	-6.3
LIMA	B+ BA: 80%	04	Proj	**450**	**68**	**124**	**8**	**31**	**25**	**276**			**$15**	**344**	**384**	**728**	**9**	**92**	**29**	**1.23**	**300**	**74**	**113**		**4.60**	**3.8**

The lowest BA of his career, his fewest SB since 1994... and nearly twice as many HRs as any previous season. This is not a typical skills progression, and if you look at his 1H/2H PX split, it only lasted 3 months anyway.

Young,Mike

		Yr	Tm	AB	R	H	HR	RBI	SB	Avg	vL	vR	R$	OB	Slg	OPS	bb%	ct%	h%	Eye	xBA	PX	SX	G/F	RC/G	RAR
Pos	2B	99		0	0	0	0	0	0	0								0								
Age	27 Peak	00	aa	533	60	133	6	58	18	250			$9	301	373	674	7	85	28	0.49	277	82	128		3.68	-7.0
Bats	R	01	TEX	* 575	80	147	18	72	6	256	255	247	$12	307	409	716	7	79	29	0.36	257	93	87	1.44	4.23	0.5
R	Low	02	TEX	573	77	150	9	62	6	262	290	251	$10	311	382	693	7	80	31	0.37	257	75	115	1.64	3.95	-1.5
I	EXP con	03	TEX	666	106	204	14	72	13	306	308	306	$22	342	446	788	5	85	35	0.35	297	87	139	1.55	5.67	27.8
S	stb	1st Half		316	47	100	5	32	6	316			$11	357	437	794	6	83	37	0.36	255	74	134		5.88	14.8
K		2nd Half		350	59	104	9	40	7	297			$12	328	454	782	4	86	32	0.33	311	99	132		5.47	12.9
LIMA	C+ BA: 40%	04	Proj	**650**	**95**	**183**	**13**	**72**	**11**	**282**			**$17**	**324**	**417**	**741**	**6**	**83**	**32**	**0.37**	**264**	**85**	**124**		**4.75**	**12.0**

A huge step up, but somewhat over his head. Low PX and high G/F show no power upside. Plate patience and batting eye are weak though contact rate improved. If he hasn't already reached his ceiling, he's close.

Zaun,Gregg

		Yr	Tm	AB	R	H	HR	RBI	SB	Avg	vL	vR	R$	OB	Slg	OPS	bb%	ct%	h%	Eye	xBA	PX	SX	G/F	RC/G	RAR
Pos	CA	99	TEX	93	12	23	1	12	1	247	211	257	$1	320	323	643	10	92	26	1.43	263	44	90	1.62	3.57	-1.4
Age	32 Past Peak	00	2AL	234	36	64	7	33	7	274	324	265	$7	386	410	797	16	85	30	1.26	281	83	66	1.08	5.53	9.3
Bats	S	01	KC	125	15	40	6	18	1	320	264	361	$6	380	536	916	9	87	33	0.75	309	135	30	1.20	7.23	11.5
R	X HIGH	02	HOU	185	18	41	3	24	1	222	316	197	$1	269	319	588	6	81	26	0.33	236	66	69	1.11	2.84	-7.2
I	CON	03	2NL	166	15	38	4	21	1	229	308	205	$2	308	349	658	10	87	24	0.90	275	81	34	1.24	3.50	-4.0
S	PT STB	1st Half		81	6	20	0	9	1	247			$1	315	321	636	9	93	27	1.33	283	66	40		3.49	-1.9
K		2nd Half		85	9	18	4	12	0	212			$1	302	376	679	11	82	21	0.73	266	95	25		3.50	-2.1
LIMA	F BA: 75%	04	Proj	**150**	**16**	**40**	**4**	**20**	**1**	**267**			**$4**	**338**	**398**	**736**	**10**	**85**	**29**	**0.72**	**274**	**86**	**37**		**4.60**	**2.2**

The good things...
- Contact rate, walk rate, eye
- Consistently better xBAs
- On COL, for now anyway

The bad things...
- Poor BA vs RHers
- Not enough ABs to air out BPIs

Zeile,Todd

		Yr	Tm	AB	R	H	HR	RBI	SB	Avg	vL	vR	R$	OB	Slg	OPS	bb%	ct%	h%	Eye	xBA	PX	SX	G/F	RC/G	RAR
Pos	3B 1B	99	TEX	588	80	172	24	98	1	293	291	293	$19	354	488	842	9	84	31	0.60	274	122	38	1.18	6.16	28.5
Age	38 Decline	00	NYM	544	67	146	22	79	3	268	248	274	$14	356	467	823	12	84	28	0.87	292	121	53	1.22	5.67	21.3
Bats	R	01	NYM	531	66	141	10	62	1	266	288	260	$9	354	373	727	12	81	31	0.72	254	70	45	1.38	4.60	0.2
R	Very High	02	COL	506	61	138	18	87	1	273	274	272	$17	357	425	782	12	82	30	0.72	264	99	29	1.79	5.29	10.1
I	CON	03	2TM	299	40	68	11	42	1	227	235	224	$4	306	385	691	10	82	24	0.63	249	92	72	1.17	3.91	-4.3
S	pt STB	1st Half		157	25	32	6	22	0	204			$1	298	363	661	12	82	21	0.72	249	98	41		3.46	-4.5
K	AGE	2nd Half		142	15	36	5	20	1	254			$3	316	408	725	8	82	28	0.52	248	86	93		4.45	0.3
LIMA	D BA: 65%	04	Proj	**350**	**42**	**87**	**10**	**41**	**1**	**249**			**$5**	**323**	**385**	**708**	**10**	**82**	**28**	**0.61**	**249**	**84**	**62**		**4.22**	**-2.2**

BPIs took a big drop, and now he'll have to cling desperately onto gainful employment. The fact that he now holds the record for homering for the most teams (11) doesn't buy ABs, just a few media bites.

The Pitchers

QUALIFICATION: All pitchers who accumulated at least 40 IP in the majors in 2003 are included. Some select players with fewer than 40 IP are included if we believe they will have an impact in 2004.

This book is designed to be an historical analysis, so players who will likely have a vital role in 2004, but spent the better part of 2003 on the sidelines or in the minors, are not included. We cover some of them briefly on page 145 and others in the Top Prospects section. All of these players will appear on BaseballHQ.com over the winter as their 2004 roles and projected impacts become clearer.

THROWS: The side from which he throws — right (RH) or left (LH).

ROLE: Pitchers are classified as Starters (20 or more batters faced per game projected for 2004) or Relievers (under 20 BF/G).

AGE: Each pitcher's current age is shown, along with a description of the associated stage in his career.

TYPE evaluates the extent to which a pitcher allows the ball to be put into play. FINESSE represents those pitchers who allow the ball to be put into play a great deal. POWER represents those with high strikeout and/or walk totals who keep the ball out of play.

RISK TABLE: An analysis of each player's forecast risk, the variables that impact the viability of his projection. Atop the table is an overall risk level. In the grid below are six variables that contribute to the overall rating – experience (EXP), consistency (CON), playing time (PT), stability (STB), age (AGE) and burnout potential (BRN). (A full description of these variables appears in the Forecasters Toolbox.) If the variable appears in lower case, then it represents a small or moderate risk factor; UPPER CASE represents a significant risk factor.

LIMA GRADE: Rating that evaluates how well that pitcher would be a good fit for a team employing the LIMA Plan. Best grades will go to pitchers who have excellent base skills (BPV) and had a 2003 Rotisserie value under $20. Lowest grades will go to poor skills and values over $20.

ERA PERCENTAGE PLAY (EP): The probability that a pitcher will improve his ERA in 2004 over 2003, based on an evaluation of strand rate, hit rate, xERA variance and base performance value. These percentages are in 5% increments, ranging from 10% to 90%, though most will be centered closer to the mean. If a pitcher's EP says 60%, for instance, it means that he has a 60% chance of improving his ERA in 2004. It also means that he has a 40% of seeing no change, or a drop-off.

PLAYER STAT LINES: The past five year's statistics represent the total accumulated in the majors as well as in Triple-A, Double-A ball and various foreign leagues during each year. All non-major league stats used have been converted to their equivalent major league performance level. Minor league levels below AA are not included.

Nearly all baseball publications separate a player's statistical experiences in the major leagues from the minor leagues and outside leagues. While this may be an appropriate approach for the sake of official record-keeping, it is not an accurate measure of a player's complete performance for the year.

Bill James has proven that minor league statistics, at Double-A level or above, are accurate indicators of future potential. Other researchers have also devised conversion factors for foreign leagues that place them on a comparable playing field as MLB stats. If we can agree that these conversions are accurate barometers of potential performance, then we should be including them in the pool of historical data.

By limiting an analysis of a player's performance trends to major league numbers only, we ignore a wealth of valuable data. This data adds more depth to a player's historical trends, especially those with limited major league experience. So we include major league equivalencies as a part of each batter's and pitcher's yearly stats in this book.

TEAM DESIGNATIONS: An asterisk (*) appearing with a team name means that major league equivalent Triple-A and/or Double-A numbers are included in that year's stat line. A designation of "a/a" means the stats were accumulated at both Triple-A and Double-A levels that year. "JPN" means Japan, "MEX" means Mexico, "KOR" means Korea, "TWN" means Taiwan, "CUB" means Cuba and "ind" means independent league.

The designation "2TM" appears whenever a player was on more than one major league team, crossing leagues, in a season. "2AL" and "2NL" represent more than one team in the same league. Complete season stats are presented for players who crossed leagues during the season.

SABERMETRIC CATEGORIES: Descriptions of all the sabermetric categories appear in the glossary. The decimal point has been suppressed on several categories to conserve space.

2004 FORECASTS: It is far too early to be making definitive projections for 2004, especially on playing time. Focus on the skill levels and trends, then consult Baseball HQ for playing time revisions as players change teams and roles become finalized. A free projections update will also be available online at BaseballForecaster.com in March.

Forecasts are computed from a player's trends over the past five years. Adjustments were made for leading indicators and variances between skill and output. After reviewing the leading indicators, you might opt to make further adjustments.

Although each year's numbers include all playing time at the Double-A level or above, the 2004 forecast only represents potential playing time at the major league level, and again is highly preliminary.

CAPSULE COMMENTARIES: For each player, a brief analysis of their BPIs and the potential impact on performance in 2004 is provided. For those who played only a portion of 2003 at the major league level, and whose isolated MLB stats are significantly different from their full-season total, their MLB stats are listed here. Note that these commentaries generally look at performance related issues only. Playing time expectations may impact these analyses, so you will have to adjust accordingly, especially as we get closer to Opening Day. Upside and downside statistical potential appears for some players. These are less grounded in hard data and more speculative of longer-term potential.

Abbott,Paul

RH Starter
AGE 36 Decline
TYPE Power
R Very High
I exp CON
S PT stb
K AGE
LIMA D EP: 55%

	Tm	W	L	Sv	IP	K	ERA	Br/IP	R$	BF/G	OBA	vL	vR	H%	xERA	RAR	Ctl	Dom	Cmd	hr/9	G/F	S%	BPV	BPX
99	SEA *	7	3	0	86	77	3.98	1.29	$10	13.4	236	159	231	28%	3.73	21.8	3.8	8.1	**2.1**	1.0	1.10	72%	70	175
00	SEA	9	7	0	179	100	4.22	1.36	$13	21.9	245	259	222	26%	4.12	40.5	4.0	5.0	**1.3**	1.2	0.90	72%	28	72
01	SEA	17	4	0	163	118	4.25	1.42	$13	25.3	240	243	232	27%	4.23	26.9	4.8	6.5	**1.4**	1.2	0.76	73%	40	80
02	SEA *	1	4	0	34	29	11.12	2.32	($11)	19.8	369	383	315	42%	9.45 +	-25.8	6.1	7.7	**1.3**	2.1	0.87	52%	-10	-20
03	2TM *	4	6	0	101	74	5.06	1.58	($2)	21.7	299	305	192	34%	5.28	4.5	3.4	6.6	**1.9**	1.0	0.95	69%	46	94
1st Half		1	4	0	26	10	7.56	1.87	($4)	25.1	362			39%	6.51 +	-7.6	2.4	3.4	**1.4**	0.3		56%	23	46
2nd Half		3	2	0	75	64	4.19	1.48	$1	20.7	274			32%	4.85 -	12.1	3.7	7.7	**2.1**	1.2		75%	54	109
04	**Proj**	**4**	**6**	**0**	**80**	**58**	**5.51**	**1.63**	**($3)**	**20.2**	**290**			**33%**	**5.48**	**-1.3**	**4.3**	**6.5**	**1.5**	**1.2**	**--**	**68%**	**31**	**63**

1-2, 5.36 ERA in 47 IP at KC. Control had completely abandoned him until this year... apparently. However, those 47 major league IP generated 5 walks per game, so he's not out of the woods yet. If ever.

Acevedo,Jose

RH Starter
AGE 26 Growth
TYPE
R Low
I EXP con
S pt
K
LIMA C+ EP: 50%

	Tm	W	L	Sv	IP	K	ERA	Br/IP	R$	BF/G	OBA	vL	vR	H%	xERA	RAR	Ctl	Dom	Cmd	hr/9	G/F	S%	BPV	BPX
99		0	0	0	0	0	0.00	0.00																
00		0	0	0	0	0	0.00	0.00																
01	CIN *	9	11	0	174	139	5.07	1.39	$3	22.0	269	249	292	31%	4.60	6.9	3.1	7.2	**2.3**	1.2	1.05	66%	56	103
02	CIN *	16	9	0	177	121	4.02	1.29	$15	25.7	271			30%	4.34	25.8	2.2	6.2	**2.8**	1.3	0.71	74%	59	111
03	CIN *	8	2	0	87	72	3.93	1.27	$9	10.7	257	136	224	30%	3.93	15.8	2.7	7.4	**2.8**	1.0	0.78	72%	75	145
1st Half		6	2	0	51	43	4.58	1.45	$4	8.3	283			34%	4.59	4.8	3.0	7.6	**2.5**	0.9		70%	70	136
2nd Half		2	0	0	36	29	3.00	1.03	$5	20.3	216			24%	2.99	11.0	2.2	7.2	**3.2**	1.2		78%	85	164
04	**Proj**	**11**	**8**	**0**	**160**	**123**	**3.99**	**1.26**	**$12**	**23.9**	**258**			**29%**	**4.03**	**27.2**	**2.5**	**6.9**	**2.7**	**1.2**	**F**	**72%**	**67**	**129**

2-0, 2.67 ERA in 27 IP at CIN, which was three PQS-5 starts prior to getting hurt. Excellent potential here, and rising trends. As a flyball pitcher, he'll hit his occasional rough spots, but this is one you want to tuck away.

Acevedo,Juan

RH Reliever
AGE 33 Past
TYPE
R Very High
I CON
S PT STB
K age
LIMA D EP: 55%

	Tm	W	L	Sv	IP	K	ERA	Br/IP	R$	BF/G	OBA	vL	vR	H%	xERA	RAR	Ctl	Dom	Cmd	hr/9	G/F	S%	BPV	BPX
99	STL	6	8	4	102	52	5.91	1.60	($1)	9.2	286	275	301	29%	5.27 +	-9.2	4.2	4.6	**1.1**	1.5	1.14	66%	3	7
00	MIL	3	7	0	82	51	3.83	1.31	$5	5.6	249	287	220	27%	4.12	19.8	3.4	5.6	**1.6**	1.2	0.98	75%	37	82
01	2NL	2	5	0	60	47	4.19	1.71	($2)	4.8	286	319	264	34%	5.35 -	9.4	5.2	7.0	**1.3**	0.9	1.28	77%	41	76
02	DET	1	5	28	74	43	2.68	1.23	$22	4.7	246	264	228	28%	3.25 -	27.6	2.8	5.2	**1.9**	0.5	1.32	79%	62	127
03	TOR	1	5	6	38	28	6.61	1.84	($1)	4.6	326	292	341	37%	6.80	-5.6	4.3	6.6	**1.6**	1.4	0.81	66%	20	42
1st Half		0	3	6	28	20	7.05	1.74	($0)	4.7	324			36%	6.71	-5.7	3.5	6.4	**1.8**	1.6	0.76	61%	19	40
2nd Half		1	2	0	10	8	5.40	2.10	($1)	4.6	332			39%	7.07 -	0.2	6.3	7.2	**1.1**	0.9	1.00	75%	29	62
04	**Proj**	**1**	**5**	**2**	**60**	**40**	**4.80**	**1.57**	**($1)**	**5.1**	**287**			**32%**	**5.31 -**	**5.9**	**3.9**	**6.0**	**1.5**	**1.2**	**--**	**72%**	**30**	**64**

Closers need a minimum level of BPIs in order to be successful, and he never had it. Opportunity will get you just so far. On the flipside, 37/66% hit/strand rates mean his ERA will rebound, but it's still a lack of skills issue here.

Adams,Terry

RH Reliever
AGE 31 Peak
TYPE Power
R High
I CON
S PT stb
K
LIMA B+ EP: 50%

	Tm	W	L	Sv	IP	K	ERA	Br/IP	R$	BF/G	OBA	vL	vR	H%	xERA	RAR	Ctl	Dom	Cmd	hr/9	G/F	S%	BPV	BPX
99	CHC	6	3	13	65	57	4.02	1.35	$14	5.3	247	184	289	29%	3.84	10.6	3.9	7.9	**2.0**	1.2	2.41	75%	58	127
00	LA	6	9	2	84	56	3.53	1.41	$9	5.5	252	220	268	29%	3.88	23.6	4.2	6.0	**1.4**	0.6	2.68	76%	51	113
01	LA	12	8	0	166	141	4.33	1.36	$10	16.5	269	232	295	33%	3.81 +	22.9	2.9	7.6	**2.6**	0.5	2.29	67%	87	162
02	PHI	7	9	0	136	96	4.37	1.40	$4	12.8	256	246	263	30%	3.75 +	13.5	3.8	6.4	**1.7**	0.6	2.70	69%	59	111
03	PHI	1	4	0	68	51	2.65	1.34	$4	4.4	262	264	271	32%	3.31 -	24.0	3.0	6.8	**2.2**	0.1	1.96	79%	86	165
1st Half		0	2	0	41	28	2.85	1.34	$2	4.6	271			32%	3.52 -	13.4	2.6	6.1	**2.3**	0.2	2.00	78%	80	154
2nd Half		1	2	0	27	23	2.34	1.34	$2	4.1	248			32%	2.99 -	10.6	3.7	7.7	**2.1**	0.0	1.89	81%	96	184
04	**Proj**	**5**	**3**	**1**	**80**	**62**	**3.38**	**1.35**	**$7**	**5.2**	**257**			**31%**	**3.44**	**20.2**	**3.4**	**7.0**	**2.1**	**0.3**	**G**	**74%**	**79**	**152**

The outlier here is 2002, an off-year which looks like the fallout from his 2000-2001 workload increase. That being the case, the bullpen is where he should call home, as 2003 shows.

Affeldt,Jeremy

LH Starter
AGE 24 Growth
TYPE Power
R High
I EXP con
S pt stb
K age
LIMA C+ EP: 50%

	Tm	W	L	Sv	IP	K	ERA	Br/IP	R$	BF/G	OBA	vL	vR	H%	xERA	RAR	Ctl	Dom	Cmd	hr/9	G/F	S%	BPV	BPX
99		0	0	0	0	0	0.00	0.00																
00		0	0	0	0	0	0.00	0.00																
01	aa	10	6	0	145	106	4.53	1.47	$5	25.5	295			35%	4.61	17.3	2.6	6.6	**2.5**	0.6		69%	70	134
02	KC	3	4	0	77	67	4.68	1.58	($1)	10.2	281	283	271	34%	5.03	8.1	4.3	7.8	**1.8**	0.9	1.24	72%	56	114
03	KC	7	6	4	126	98	3.93	1.30	$11	14.8	262	223	272	31%	3.96	26.9	2.7	7.0	**2.6**	0.9	1.04	72%	73	158
1st Half		4	4	0	71	52	4.82	1.52	$1	22.5	296			34%	4.91	6.7	3.0	6.6	**2.2**	0.8	0.89	69%	58	126
2nd Half		3	2	4	55	46	2.78	1.02	$10	9.8	213			25%	2.73	20.2	2.3	7.5	**3.3**	1.0	1.27	78%	97	210
04	**Proj**	**8**	**7**	**0**	**160**	**130**	**4.11**	**1.39**	**$7**	**23.8**	**268**			**32%**	**4.24**	**30.7**	**3.2**	**7.3**	**2.3**	**0.8**	**--**	**72%**	**68**	**146**

Starter or reliever? You pick:

	IP	ERA	Ctl	Dom
SP	94	4.39	2.8	6.0
RP	32	2.56	2.5	9.8

Tony Pena: "Long-term, Affeldt is not a bullpen guy."
Shandler: "Go Yankees."

Ainsworth,Kurt

RH Starter
AGE 25 Growth
TYPE Power
R High
I EXP con
S pt stb
K
LIMA B+ EP: 50%

	Tm	W	L	Sv	IP	K	ERA	Br/IP	R$	BF/G	OBA	vL	vR	H%	xERA	RAR	Ctl	Dom	Cmd	hr/9	G/F	S%	BPV	BPX
99		0	0	0	0	0	0.00	0.00																
00	aa	10	9	0	158	108	4.22	1.42	$11	24.5	267			31%	4.18	32.7	3.6	6.2	**1.7**	0.7		71%	52	124
01	aaa	10	9	0	149	130	4.89	1.27	$8	23.1	253			30%	3.93 +	10.6	2.8	7.9	**2.8**	1.1		63%	77	148
02	aaa	9	8	0	141	117	3.64	1.33	$10	23.1	253			31%	3.47	30.8	3.4	7.5	**2.2**	0.4	1.37	72%	82	161
03	2TM	5	5	0	68	52	4.10	1.45	$4	21.3	273	286	261	31%	4.65 -	11.8	3.6	6.9	**1.9**	1.1	1.21	75%	50	102
1st Half		5	4	0	66	48	3.82	1.39	$5	25.9	262			30%	4.26	13.9	3.5	6.5	**1.8**	1.0	1.23	75%	52	106
2nd Half		0	1	0	2	4	12.85	3.33	($1)	4.4	503			72%	17.09 -	-2.1	4.3	17.1	**4.0**	4.3	0.50	67%	13	26
04	**Proj**	**9**	**11**	**0**	**160**	**127**	**4.22**	**1.34**	**$8**	**24.4**	**258**			**30%**	**3.95**	**25.2**	**3.3**	**7.1**	**2.2**	**0.8**	**--**	**70%**	**67**	**135**

You can see the talent here, but you'd also like to see trends that were more positive. Note that, in moving from SF to BAL, any longball lapses will be exploited, so expect the occasional blowout. A keeper, though.

Alfonseca,Antonio

RH Reliever
AGE 32 Peak
TYPE Power
R Very Low
I con
S stb
K
LIMA D+ EP: 60%

	Tm	W	L	Sv	IP	K	ERA	Br/IP	R$	BF/G	OBA	vL	vR	H%	xERA	RAR	Ctl	Dom	Cmd	hr/9	G/F	S%	BPV	BPX
99	FLA	4	5	21	77	46	3.27	1.40	$17	4.6	267	270	278	30%	3.53	20.2	3.4	5.4	**1.6**	0.5	1.59	77%	53	116
00	FLA	5	6	45	70	47	4.24	1.51	$30	4.6	293	277	303	33%	4.96 -	13.0	3.1	6.0	**2.0**	0.9	1.91	74%	47	103
01	FLA	4	4	28	61	40	3.09	1.36	$22	4.5	283	302	259	32%	4.39 -	18.7	2.2	5.9	**2.7**	0.9	2.02	81%	63	117
02	CHC	2	5	19	74	61	4.01	1.47	$11	4.9	259	304	220	32%	3.98	10.8	4.4	7.4	**1.7**	0.6	2.23	73%	65	123
03	CHC	3	1	0	66	51	5.85	1.56	($3)	4.9	290	340	259	34%	5.04 +	-5.1	3.7	6.9	**1.9**	1.0	2.11	63%	50	96
1st Half		0	1	0	28	18	4.16	1.14	$1	4.1	217			23%	3.32 +	4.2	3.2	5.8	**1.8**	1.3	1.44	68%	45	88
2nd Half		3	0	0	38	33	7.11	1.87	($4)	5.7	335			41%	6.30 +	-9.3	4.0	7.8	**1.9**	0.7	3.00	60%	54	105
04	**Proj**	**3**	**3**	**0**	**65**	**49**	**4.85**	**1.51**	**($0)**	**4.9**	**282**			**33%**	**4.65**	**3.6**	**3.6**	**6.8**	**1.9**	**0.8**	**G**	**68%**	**54**	**104**

34/63% hit/strand rates inflated his ERA a bit, but his BPI trends still paint a pessimistic picture. LHers have been progressively killing him. Little chance of returning to a closer's role with his current BPIs.

Almanza,Armando

LH Reliever
AGE 31 Peak
TYPE Power
R Low
I con
S pt
K
LIMA D+ EP: 60%

	Tm	W	L	Sv	IP	K	ERA	Br/IP	R$	BF/G	OBA	vL	vR	H%	xERA	RAR	Ctl	Dom	Cmd	hr/9	G/F	S%	BPV	BPX
99	FLA *	2	4	3	44	55	6.14	1.68	($1)	5.2	262	63	194	36%	4.63 +	-5.3	6.1	11.3	**1.8**	1.0	0.64	64%	78	169
00	FLA	4	2	0	46	46	4.88	1.76	$0	3.2	226	191	253	29%	4.33 +	4.6	8.4	9.0	**1.1**	0.6	0.63	72%	69	151
01	FLA	2	2	0	41	45	4.83	1.46	$0	3.5	227	210	244	27%	4.70	2.9	5.7	9.9	**1.7**	1.8	0.51	73%	52	97
02	FLA	3	2	2	45	57	4.40	1.31	$3	3.7	221	255	208	29%	3.97	4.3	4.6	11.4	**2.5**	1.6	0.61	73%	83	157
03	FLA	4	5	0	50	49	6.11	1.68	($2)	4.5	295	277	306	35%	6.18	-5.6	4.5	8.8	**2.0**	1.8	0.98	68%	36	70
1st Half		4	4	0	36	38	4.97	1.57	$1	4.2	282			35%	5.44	1.5	4.2	9.4	**2.2**	1.5	0.97	73%	58	111
2nd Half		0	1	0	14	11	9.06	1.94	($4)	5.6	326			35%	8.12 +	-7.0	5.2	7.1	**1.4**	2.6	1.00	57%	-16	-32
04	**Proj**	**4**	**3**	**1**	**50**	**56**	**4.86**	**1.52**	**$2**	**3.8**	**246**			**31%**	**4.72**	**2.7**	**5.4**	**10.1**	**1.9**	**1.4**	**--**	**72%**	**62**	**120**

As a situational LH specialist, one has to be concerned about his BA vs LH trend. A hard thrower, but inconsistent control and gopheritis makes him a risky pick.

Almonte,Hector

RH Reliever
AGE 28 Pre-Peak
TYPE Power
R X HIGH
I EXP CON
S pt STB
K
LIMA D+ EP: 55%

	Tm	W	L	Sv	IP	K	ERA	Br/IP	R$	BF/G	OBA	vL	vR	H%	xERA	RAR	Ctl	Dom	Cmd	hr/9	G/F	S%	BPV	BPX
99	aa	1	6	23	59	45	3.36	1.63	$14	4.3	275			32%	4.64 -	17.2	5.0	6.9	**1.4**	0.8		81%	47	109
00	a/a	0	5	6	24	20	10.50	2.42	($5)	5.8	389			46%	9.06 +	-15.2	5.6	7.5	**1.3**	1.1		55%	17	39
01	aaa	0	0	0	24	18	7.88	2.08	($6)	6.7	347			38%	8.18	-7.9	5.3	6.8	**1.3**	1.9		64%	-3	-6
02	JPN	0	0	0	24	18	1.50	1.04	$3	3.5	210			24%	2.48 -	12.1	2.6	6.8	**2.6**	0.8		91%	85	167
03	MON *	4	2	9	62	55	5.06	1.50	$5	4.9	264	326	280	32%	4.56 +	1.8	4.3	8.0	**1.8**	1.0	0.92	67%	58	112
1st Half		3	1	9	33	29	3.52	1.27	$9	5.0	236			29%	3.42	7.8	3.5	7.9	**2.2**	0.8	0.55	74%	77	149
2nd Half		1	1	0	29	26	6.83	1.76	($3)	4.8	294			35%	5.86 +	-6.0	5.3	8.1	**1.5**	1.2	1.07	62%	40	76
04	**Proj**	**2**	**4**	**0**	**60**	**50**	**4.65**	**1.58**	**($1)**	**4.7**	**271**			**32%**	**4.75**	**4.9**	**4.8**	**7.5**	**1.6**	**0.9**	**--**	**72%**	**52**	**99**

1-2, 7.25 ERA in 36 IP at MON. Looked like he carred over the BPIs from Japan early in the year, but then got hit hard, at least some of it due to bad luck. Seeds of something good here, but not enough to bid on.

Alvarez,Wilson

LH Starter
AGE 33 Past
TYPE
R X HIGH
I exp CON
S PT STB
K age brn
LIMA C+ EP: 45%

	Tm	W	L	Sv	IP	K	ERA	Br/IP	R$	BF/G	OBA	vL	vR	H%	xERA	RAR	Ctl	Dom	Cmd	hr/9	G/F	S%	BPV	BPX
99	TAM	9	9	0	160	128	4.22	1.49	$9	25.2	261			30%	4.73 -	35.4	4.4	7.2	**1.6**	1.2	1.29	75%	43	108
00	TAM	0	0	0	0	0	0.00	0.00																
01	a/a	2	4	0	38	32	4.26	1.32	$2	17.9	251			32%	3.01 +	5.9	3.3	7.6	**2.3**	0.0		64%	98	188
02	TAM	* 3	3	1	83	61	4.88	1.52	($1)	14.7	273	299	263	30%	5.21	6.4	4.1	6.6	**1.6**	1.4	0.55	72%	31	65
03	LA	* 11	3	1	142	110	2.03	1.04	$25	19.4	229	235	360	28%	2.37	61.8	1.8	7.0	**3.8**	0.4	0.90	82%	119	229
1st Half		5	1	1	60	42	1.35	0.95	$14	19.4	220			26%	2.09 -	31.7	1.3	6.3	**4.7**	0.4	1.08	89%	133	256
2nd Half		6	2	0	82	68	2.53	1.11	$12	19.4	235			29%	2.57	30.1	2.2	7.5	**3.4**	0.3	0.88	77%	114	220
04	**Proj**	**10**	**7**	**0**	**160**	**125**	**3.32**	**1.25**	**$15**	**24.7**	**247**			**29%**	**3.37**	**41.7**	**2.9**	**7.0**	**2.4**	**0.7**	**--**	**75%**	**78**	**151**

6-2, 2.37 ERA in 95 IP at LA Rediscovered control hiked his BPIs, but strand rate will come down some to temper these results. Health is a big risk at this point, but solid starter if he can throw enough innings.

Anderson,Brian

LH Starter
AGE 32 Peak
TYPE Finesse
R High
I CON
S PT stb
K
LIMA D EP: 35%

	Tm	W	L	Sv	IP	K	ERA	Br/IP	R$	BF/G	OBA	vL	vR	H%	xERA	RAR	Ctl	Dom	Cmd	hr/9	G/F	S%	BPV	BPX
99	ARI	8	2	1	130	75	4.57	1.32	$8	17.8	282	295	275	30%	4.28	11.6	1.9	5.2	**2.7**	1.2	1.02	69%	49	106
00	ARI	11	7	0	213	104	4.05	1.24	$17	26.9	273	266	278	27%	4.66 -	44.9	1.6	4.4	**2.7**	1.6	1.02	74%	35	76
01	ARI	4	9	0	133	55	5.21	1.40	($1)	19.8	294	272	304	29%	5.44	2.8	2.0	3.7	**1.8**	1.7	0.96	68%	6	12
02	ARI	6	11	0	156	81	4.79	1.32	$2	18.9	283	302	278	30%	4.64	6.6	1.8	4.7	**2.5**	1.3	1.18	67%	40	75
03	2AL	14	11	0	197	87	3.79	1.29	$17	26.0	276	258	286	28%	4.52 -	45.9	2.0	4.0	**2.0**	1.2	1.06	75%	29	63
1st Half		5	6	0	92	32	4.30	1.38	$4	24.8	293			29%	5.12 -	15.2	1.9	3.1	**1.7**	1.4	1.00	73%	9	20
2nd Half		9	5	0	105	55	3.34	1.22	$13	27.2	260			27%	3.99 -	30.7	2.1	4.7	**2.3**	1.1	1.12	77%	46	99
04	**Proj**	**10**	**10**	**0**	**180**	**85**	**4.45**	**1.31**	**$10**	**22.4**	**280**			**29%**	**4.72**	**26.2**	**2.0**	**4.3**	**2.2**	**1.4**	**--**	**70%**	**30**	**64**

Extreme soft tosser with high hr/9. xERA is in line with prior BPIs -- 2003 was not a breakout year. Second half gives some hope, but more likely result is regression to 4.20-4.50 ERA.

Anderson,Jason

RH Reliever
AGE 24 Growth
TYPE
R High
I EXP con
S stb
K age
LIMA B EP: 40%

	Tm	W	L	Sv	IP	K	ERA	Br/IP	R$	BF/G	OBA	vL	vR	H%	xERA	RAR	Ctl	Dom	Cmd	hr/9	G/F	S%	BPV	BPX
99		0	0	0	0	0	0.00	0.00																
00		0	0	0	0	0	0.00	0.00																
01		0	0	0	0	0	0.00	0.00																
02	a/a	6	2	9	53	44	2.72	1.15	$14	5.1	231			28%	2.94	18.1	2.7	7.5	**2.8**	0.7		79%	91	179
03	2TM	* 2	3	7	62	34	3.62	1.35	$7	6.0	242	354	219	25%	4.10	14.7	4.1	4.9	**1.2**	1.2	0.40	78%	27	54
1st Half		1	0	3	25	20	2.86	1.35	$4	4.3	236			29%	3.24	8.6	4.3	7.1	**1.7**	0.4	0.45	79%	75	152
2nd Half		1	3	4	37	14	4.15	1.35	$3	8.3	246			23%	4.69 -	6.2	3.9	3.4	**0.9**	1.7	0.33	77%	-7	-13
04	**Proj**	**4**	**3**	**0**	**65**	**43**	**4.57**	**1.26**	**$4**	**5.7**	**237**			**26%**	**3.60 +**	**7.2**	**3.5**	**6.0**	**1.7**	**1.0**	**F**	**65%**	**50**	**102**

1-0, 4.88 ERA in 31.1 IP at NYM and NYY. Soft-tosser with poor control and gopheritis in the 2nd half. 2002 BPIs point to possible rebound, but not enough to make him rosterable.

Anderson,Jimmy

LH Starter
AGE 28 Pre-Peak
TYPE Finesse
R Moderate
I exp CON
S pt stb
K brn
LIMA F EP: 50%

	Tm	W	L	Sv	IP	K	ERA	Br/IP	R$	BF/G	OBA	vL	vR	H%	xERA	RAR	Ctl	Dom	Cmd	hr/9	G/F	S%	BPV	BPX
99	PIT	* 13	3	0	162	96	4.28	1.54	$8	21.3	297	231	235	34%	4.25	20.8	3.2	5.3	**1.7**	0.4	2.76	71%	51	111
00	PIT	* 6	11	0	166	84	4.93	1.57	($1)	24.8	296	303	292	32%	4.96	15.5	3.4	4.6	**1.3**	0.7	2.96	68%	30	66
01	PIT	9	17	0	206	89	5.11	1.53	($2)	27.0	285	324	279	31%	4.67	7.1	3.6	3.9	**1.1**	0.7	2.53	66%	24	45
02	PIT	8	13	0	140	47	5.46	1.64	($5)	22.8	297	273	306	30%	5.64	-6.7	4.1	3.0	**0.7**	1.3	2.66	69%	-9	-17
03	CIN	* 8	10	0	142	51	6.14	1.72	($9)	26.4	335	357	360	35%	6.07	-16.4	2.7	3.2	**1.2**	0.8	1.91	64%	8	16
1st Half		7	6	0	98	38	6.13	1.69	($5)	26.7	331			34%	6.09	-11.2	2.7	3.5	**1.3**	1.0	1.91	64%	7	14
2nd Half		1	4	0	44	13	6.16	1.78	($5)	25.7	345			36%	6.02	-5.2	2.7	2.7	**1.0**	0.4		63%	11	21
04	**Proj**	**5**	**8**	**0**	**100**	**37**	**5.67**	**1.67**	**($5)**	**25.5**	**317**			**33%**	**5.61**	**-5.4**	**3.2**	**3.3**	**1.0**	**0.8**	**G**	**66%**	**9**	**17**

1-5, 8.84 ERA in 38.2 IP at CIN. Extreme groundball LHer was hit like a batting practice pitcher.

Past 5 yrs Br/IP over 1.50

Pass.

Anderson,Matt

RH Reliever
AGE 27 Pre-Peak
TYPE
R High
I CON
S pt
K brn
LIMA C+ EP: 50%

	Tm	W	L	Sv	IP	K	ERA	Br/IP	R$	BF/G	OBA	vL	vR	H%	xERA	RAR	Ctl	Dom	Cmd	hr/9	G/F	S%	BPV	BPX
99	DET	* 2	5	5	76	65	6.99	1.83	($5)	5.9	249	246	224	25%	6.49 +	-11.3	8.1	7.7	**1.0**	2.4	0.61	67%	0	1
00	DET	3	2	1	74	71	4.74	1.43	$3	4.7	226	200	247	28%	3.84 +	11.7	5.5	8.6	**1.6**	1.0	1.41	68%	66	170
01	DET	3	1	22	56	52	4.82	1.32	$14	3.8	262	291	222	34%	3.46 +	5.0	2.9	8.4	**2.9**	0.3	0.92	61%	104	208
02	DET	2	1	0	11	8	9.00	2.27	($2)	4.8	354			41%	7.84 +	-5.2	6.5	6.5	**1.0**	0.8		58%	20	41
03	DET	* 1	4	6	61	39	5.30	1.70	($1)	6.1	336	286	263	37%	6.54 -	1.8	2.5	5.7	**2.3**	1.3	1.12	72%	31	66
1st Half		0	3	4	42	27	5.09	1.79	($2)	7.1	359			40%	7.14 -	2.4	1.9	5.7	**3.0**	1.3	1.13	74%	42	91
2nd Half		1	1	2	19	12	5.78	1.50	$1	4.6	275			29%	5.20 +	-0.6	3.9	5.8	**1.5**	1.4	1.09	64%	23	49
04	**Proj**	**2**	**3**	**9**	**60**	**43**	**5.25**	**1.45**	**$5**	**4.8**	**281**			**31%**	**4.92**	**2.3**	**3.2**	**6.5**	**2.0**	**1.2**	**--**	**66%**	**45**	**96**

3 Sv, 5.40 ERA in 23 IP at DET. Pitched through a shoulder problem most of the year after a lost 2002. Career is at crossroads and will have to show velocity returned in 2004.

Appier,Kevin

RH Starter
AGE 36 Decline
TYPE
R Very High
I CON
S pt STB
K age
LIMA C EP: 45%

	Tm	W	L	Sv	IP	K	ERA	Br/IP	R$	BF/G	OBA	vL	vR	H%	xERA	RAR	Ctl	Dom	Cmd	hr/9	G/F	S%	BPV	BPX
99	2AL	16	14	0	209	131	5.17	1.50	$9	27.2	281	297	262	31%	5.00	19.7	3.6	5.6	**1.6**	1.2	1.25	68%	31	77
00	OAK	15	11	0	195	129	4.52	1.55	$11	28.1	267	296	224	30%	4.78	36.3	4.7	6.0	**1.3**	1.1	0.93	73%	32	83
01	NYM	11	10	0	206	172	3.58	1.19	$18	25.7	237	242	233	28%	3.41	49.4	2.8	7.5	**2.7**	1.0	1.19	73%	80	149
02	ANA	14	12	0	188	132	3.93	1.36	$14	25.1	265	250	286	30%	4.39	38.6	3.1	6.3	**2.1**	1.1	0.83	75%	50	103
03	2AL	8	9	0	111	55	5.42	1.47	$2	21.2	277	253	289	28%	5.40	1.5	3.5	4.5	**1.3**	1.7	0.58	68%	2	5
1st Half		6	4	0	77	44	4.56	1.42	$4	23.8	264			27%	5.03	10.0	3.6	5.1	**1.4**	1.6	0.61	74%	14	30
2nd Half		2	5	0	34	11	7.37	1.58	($3)	17.1	303			29%	6.23 +	-8.4	3.2	2.9	**0.9**	1.8	0.52	55%	-24	-53
04	**Proj**	**9**	**12**	**0**	**140**	**81**	**4.95**	**1.43**	**$4**	**21.7**	**274**			**29%**	**4.98**	**11.0**	**3.3**	**5.2**	**1.6**	**1.4**	**F**	**69%**	**22**	**48**

Losing ground on all BPIs until he was done in by injury but some team will take him. Bad elbow bothered him all season, but at age 36, the decline is evident anyway.

Armas Jr.,Tony

RH Starter
AGE 26 Growth
TYPE Power
R High
I exp CON
S pt stb
K
LIMA B EP: 30%

	Tm	W	L	Sv	IP	K	ERA	Br/IP	R$	BF/G	OBA	vL	vR	H%	xERA	RAR	Ctl	Dom	Cmd	hr/9	G/F	S%	BPV	BPX
99	aa	9	7	0	149	93	3.38	1.28	$15	26.0	246			28%	3.22	42.9	3.2	5.6	**1.8**	0.6	0.43	74%	58	135
00	MON	* 8	11	0	114	69	4.42	1.35	$8	23.2	237	266	183	25%	3.97	18.4	4.3	5.4	**1.3**	1.1	1.30	70%	34	75
01	MON	9	14	0	196	176	4.04	1.38	$8	24.8	245	275	225	30%	3.87	34.9	4.2	8.1	**1.9**	0.8	1.04	72%	70	130
02	MON	12	12	0	164	131	4.45	1.38	$8	24.3	244	309	190	28%	4.12	14.5	4.3	7.2	**1.7**	1.2	1.42	71%	48	92
03	MON	2	1	0	31	23	2.61	1.06	$5	24.7	222	250	209	25%	3.08	11.1	2.3	6.7	**2.9**	1.2	0.59	83%	76	146
1st Half		2	1	0	31	23	2.61	1.06	$5	24.7	222			25%	3.08	11.1	2.3	6.7	**2.9**	1.2	0.59	83%	76	146
2nd Half		0	0	0	0	0	0.00	0.00																
04	**Proj**	**10**	**10**	**0**	**160**	**122**	**3.66**	**1.26**	**$13**	**24.8**	**237**			**27%**	**3.59**	**34.4**	**3.5**	**6.9**	**2.0**	**1.0**	**F**	**74%**	**60**	**115**

Bum rotator cuff made 2003 a lost season. BPIs intact and growing, and if he can harness bb/9, he could be ready to take the next step up. Sleeper potential.

Asencio,Miguel

RH Starter
AGE 23 Growth
TYPE
R Moderate
I EXP con
S pt
K age
LIMA D EP: 50%

	Tm	W	L	Sv	IP	K	ERA	Br/IP	R$	BF/G	OBA	vL	vR	H%	xERA	RAR	Ctl	Dom	Cmd	hr/9	G/F	S%	BPV	BPX
99		0	0	0	0	0	0.00	0.00																
00		0	0	0	0	0	0.00	0.00																
01		0	0	0	0	0	0.00	0.00																
02	KC	4	7	0	123	58	5.12	1.63	($5)	18.0	282	264	302	29%	5.47	5.6	4.7	4.2	**0.9**	1.2	1.41	71%	6	12
03	KC	2	1	0	48	27	5.24	1.56	($1)	26.9	285	344	241	32%	4.85	1.8	3.9	5.1	**1.3**	0.7	1.05	66%	33	71
1st Half		2	1	0	48	27	5.24	1.56	($1)	26.9	285			32%	4.85	1.8	3.9	5.1	**1.3**	0.7	1.05	66%	33	71
2nd Half		0	0	0	0	0	0.00	0.00																
04	**Proj**	**5**	**5**	**0**	**140**	**78**	**5.21**	**1.56**	**($3)**	**22.4**	**283**			**31%**	**5.04**	**6.2**	**4.1**	**5.0**	**1.2**	**1.0**	**--**	**68%**	**26**	**55**

Rushed and now just consistently bad. BPIs indicate that he lacks command of the strike zone, and until he figures it out, forget it.

Ashby,Andy

RH Reliever
AGE 36 Decline
TYPE Finesse
R Very High
I CON
S PT stb
K AGE
LIMA D EP: 50%

	Tm	W	L	Sv	IP	K	ERA	Br/IP	R$	BF/G	OBA	vL	vR	H%	xERA	RAR	Ctl	Dom	Cmd	hr/9	G/F	S%	BPV	BPX
99	SD	14	10	0	206	132	3.80	1.25	$19	27.7	260	281	240	28%	3.68	39.6	2.4	5.8	**2.4**	1.1	2.01	74%	55	119
00	2NL	12	13	0	199	106	4.93	1.39	$9	27.7	278	312	251	29%	4.82	18.7	2.8	4.8	**1.7**	1.3	1.55	68%	25	56
01	LA	2	0	0	11	7	4.02	1.34	$2	23.9	307			33%	5.40 -	2.0	0.8	5.6	**7.0**	1.6	2.60	77%	126	234
02	LA	9	13	0	181	107	3.93	1.35	$8	25.8	260	285	233	28%	4.06	28.6	3.2	5.3	**1.6**	1.0	1.49	74%	40	75
03	LA	3	10	0	73	41	5.18	1.47	($1)	15.2	304	336	291	33%	5.07	1.0	2.1	5.1	**2.4**	1.0	1.12	66%	46	88
1st Half		2	4	0	27	17	5.00	1.37	$1	10.5	276			31%	4.42 +	1.0	2.7	5.7	**2.1**	1.0	0.73	65%	48	93
2nd Half		1	6	0	46	24	5.28	1.52	($2)	20.4	320			35%	5.46	-0.0	1.8	4.7	**2.7**	1.0	1.45	66%	46	88
04	**Proj**	**0**	**0**	**0**	**0**	**0**	**0.00**	**0.00**	**$0**	**0.0**	**0**			**0%**	**0.00**	**0.0**	**0.0**	**0.0**	**0.0**	**0.0**	**--**	**0%**	**0**	**0**

His last good season was 1999. K/9 has been dropping, xERA rising, this skill set is in full decline. Tommy John surgery will put him on the shelf until '05.

DOUG DENNIS

Astacio,Pedro

	Yr	Tm	W	L	Sv	IP	K	ERA	Br/IP	R$	BF/G	OBA	vL	vR	H%	xERA	RAR	Ctl	Dom	Cmd	hr/9	G/F	S%	BPV	BPX
RH Starter	99	COL	17	11	0	232	210	5.04	1.44	$9	29.7	283	306	268	33%	4.76	6.0	2.9	8.1	2.8	1.5	1.26	69%	62	135
AGE 34 Past	00	COL	12	9	0	196	193	5.28	1.50	$4	27.1	282	290	274	34%	5.26	9.2	3.5	8.9	2.5	1.5	1.63	68%	60	133
TYPE	01	2NL	8	14	0	169	144	5.11	1.39	$2	28.0	275	286	268	32%	4.62	5.9	2.9	7.7	2.7	1.2	1.18	65%	67	124
R High	02	NYM	12	11	0	191	152	4.81	1.34	$7	26.2	263	237	283	29%	4.53	7.7	3.0	7.2	2.4	1.5	1.03	69%	51	96
I con	03	NYM	3	2	0	36	20	7.46	1.80	($4)	24.4	315	324	300	32%	7.02	-10.6	4.5	5.0	1.1	2.0	0.74	61%	-15	-28
S pt stb	1st Half		3	2	0	36	20	7.46	1.80	($4)	24.4	315			32%	7.02	-10.6	4.5	5.0	1.1	2.0	0.74	61%	-15	-28
K age	2nd Half		0	0	0	0	0	0.00	0.00																
LIMA D EP: 50%	04	Proj	7	6	0	100	73	4.95	1.51	$1	24.6	288			32%	5.40	4.2	3.3	6.6	2.0	1.5	F	72%	32	62

Torn labrum ruined his season and probably August/Sept. '02 as well. Question now is can he come back and be effective: HR/9 and xERAs no better for the Mets than COL -- age is a factor as well.

Ayala,Luis

	Yr	Tm	W	L	Sv	IP	K	ERA	Br/IP	R$	BF/G	OBA	vL	vR	H%	xERA	RAR	Ctl	Dom	Cmd	hr/9	G/F	S%	BPV	BPX
RH Reliever	99	MEX	2	0	3	20	7	0.90	0.90	$7	8.5	199			22%	1.15	12.4	1.8	3.2	1.8	0.0		89%	71	164
AGE 26 Growth	00	MEX	0	0	1	7	5	2.57	1.86	$1	11.1	313			35%	6.47 -	3.0	5.1	6.4	1.3	1.3		92%	19	44
TYPE	01	MEX	0	0	0	9	8	0.00	1.22	$1	12.4	191			26%	2.03 -	6.5	5.0	8.0	1.6	0.0		100%	98	189
R Very High	02	MEX *	0	0	1	11	11	6.55	1.55	($1)	5.5	295			35%	5.70 +	-1.9	3.3	9.0	2.8	1.6		60%	59	115
I CON	03	MON	10	3	5	71	46	2.92	1.10	$17	4.4	245	337	188	27%	3.32	22.5	1.6	5.8	3.5	1.0	2.08	79%	85	163
S PT stb	1st Half		6	2	2	35	17	3.09	0.83	$11	3.9	209			20%	2.70	10.3	0.8	4.4	5.7	1.5	2.78	74%	112	216
K brn	2nd Half		4	1	3	36	29	2.75	1.36	$7	5.0	278			34%	3.93 -	12.2	2.5	7.2	2.9	0.5	1.53	81%	89	171
LIMA C EP: 45%	04	Proj	7	5	5	70	50	3.47	1.21	$12	4.6	251			28%	3.66	16.8	2.4	6.4	2.6	1.0	G	75%	68	131

Arrived out of nowhere in March -- soft-tossing control ground ball pitcher dialed up K/9 in the second half and looks like a decent target for saves speculators -- beware his low hit rate and erratic BPIs.

Backe,Brandon

	Yr	Tm	W	L	Sv	IP	K	ERA	Br/IP	R$	BF/G	OBA	vL	vR	H%	xERA	RAR	Ctl	Dom	Cmd	hr/9	G/F	S%	BPV	BPX
RH Reliever	99		0	0	0	0	0	0.00	0.00																
AGE 26 Growth	00		0	0	0	0	0	0.00	0.00																
TYPE	01	aa	1	0	0	22	16	8.59	1.73	($3)	7.3	295			35%	5.07 +	-9.3	4.9	6.5	1.3	0.4		46%	51	98
R High	02	TAM	4	6	2	105	42	6.26	1.65	($6)	16.5	299			31%	5.74 +	-11.2	4.0	3.6	0.9	1.2	0.67	63%	-0	
I EXP con	03	TAM	3	2	0	77	59	5.71	1.53	($3)	7.8	266	302	220	31%	4.55 +	-1.9	4.5	6.9	1.5	0.8	0.75	62%	50	109
S pt stb	1st Half		2	1	0	41	29	5.91	1.63	($2)	9.4	297			35%	4.91 +	-2.1	3.9	6.4	1.6	0.4	0.90	62%	54	117
K	2nd Half		1	1	0	36	30	5.48	1.41	($1)	6.5	228			26%	4.15 +	0.2	5.2	7.5	1.4	1.2	0.72	63%	47	101
LIMA D EP: 60%	04	Proj	3	3	1	80	50	5.85	1.56	($3)	9.7	276			30%	4.97 +	-3.3	4.4	5.6	1.3	1.0	F	63%	30	64

Consistently above 4.0 BB/9, erratic K/9, low strand and high xERA makes him a bad bet. Pass.

Baez,Danys

	Yr	Tm	W	L	Sv	IP	K	ERA	Br/IP	R$	BF/G	OBA	vL	vR	H%	xERA	RAR	Ctl	Dom	Cmd	hr/9	G/F	S%	BPV	BPX
RH Reliever	99		0	0	0	0	0	0.00	0.00																
AGE 26 Growth	00	aa	4	9	0	102	64	4.68	1.45	$3	24.8	287			33%	4.43	14.8	2.8	5.6	2.0	0.6		67%	55	130
TYPE Power	01	CLE	5	3	0	50	52	2.51	1.08	$9	4.7	194	188	193	25%	2.53	19.9	3.6	9.3	2.6	0.9	0.82	82%	100	200
R High	02	CLE	10	11	6	165	130	4.42	1.47	$9	18.6	256	278	233	30%	4.22	23.0	4.5	7.1	1.6	0.8	1.06	71%	57	116
I exp CON	03	CLE	2	9	25	75	66	3.83	1.17	$20	4.2	235	285	165	28%	3.46	17.1	2.8	7.9	2.9	1.1	1.12	71%	83	180
S PT stb	1st Half		0	6	19	41	33	3.51	1.07	$14	4.1	211			25%	2.75 +	11.1	2.9	7.2	2.5	0.9	1.25	70%	83	180
K	2nd Half		2	3	6	34	33	4.21	1.29	$6	4.4	261			31%	4.32	6.0	2.6	8.7	3.3	1.3	0.97	72%	85	183
LIMA C+ EP: 55%	04	Proj	4	6	11	70	61	3.99	1.24	$12	6.1	245			29%	3.61	14.6	3.0	7.8	2.7	0.9	--	70%	82	175

Did a lot early to earn the closer role, pumping up his K/9 and lowering bb/9 at the same time. Gave way late in the year as his hr/9 crept upwards -- 2nd half might be what to expect over a full season in 2004.

Bale,John

	Yr	Tm	W	L	Sv	IP	K	ERA	Br/IP	R$	BF/G	OBA	vL	vR	H%	xERA	RAR	Ctl	Dom	Cmd	hr/9	G/F	S%	BPV	BPX
LH Reliever	99	a/a	2	5	1	85	88	4.24	1.32	$4	9.2	266			34%	3.80	14.7	2.6	9.3	3.5	0.8	3.00	69%	106	246
AGE 29 Peak	00	aaa	3	4	0	79	58	3.99	1.53	$3	16.7	264			31%	4.25	18.8	4.7	6.6	1.4	0.6	0.33	74%	54	129
TYPE	01	2AL *	2	1	0	56	56	2.89	1.41	$3	10.5	265	138	219	35%	3.88 -	19.4	3.5	9.0	2.5	0.5	1.21	80%	95	190
R X HIGH	02	aaa	2	2	0	28	21	4.50	1.25	$2	9.7	255			30%	3.47 +	2.9	2.6	6.8	2.6	0.6		64%	80	158
I EXP con	03	CIN *	5	4	4	103	83	4.97	1.41	$3	10.2	283	103	315	34%	4.34 +	4.2	2.7	7.2	2.7	0.7	1.18	64%	77	148
S PT STB	1st Half		0	2	0	42	33	5.13	1.47	($2)	8.4	292			36%	4.16 +	0.8	2.8	7.1	2.5	0.2		62%	86	165
K BRN	2nd Half		5	2	4	61	50	4.86	1.37	$5	11.9	277			33%	4.46	3.4	2.7	7.4	2.8	1.0		66%	71	137
LIMA B+ EP: 60%	04	Proj	3	3	2	80	61	4.28	1.41	$3	9.4	274			32%	4.14	10.6	3.2	6.9	2.2	0.7	--	70%	67	129

1-2, 4.47 ERA in 46 IP at CIN. Solid LH with decent control, but too hittable by RHers, which could relegate him to specialist role against LHers.

Batista,Miguel

	Yr	Tm	W	L	Sv	IP	K	ERA	Br/IP	R$	BF/G	OBA	vL	vR	H%	xERA	RAR	Ctl	Dom	Cmd	hr/9	G/F	S%	BPV	BPX
RH Starter	99	MON	8	7	1	134	95	4.90	1.52	$2	15.3	279	339	230	32%	4.19 +	6.0	3.9	6.4	1.6	0.7	1.40	68%	52	113
AGE 33 Past	00	KC *	4	9	3	93	59	8.03	1.83	($9)	12.3	321	298	333	33%	7.67	-26.4	4.5	5.7	1.3	2.5	1.11	60%	-23	
TYPE	01	ARI	11	8	0	139	90	3.36	1.24	$15	12.1	224	218	232	25%	3.28	37.3	3.9	5.8	1.5	0.8	1.35	76%	51	95
R High	02	ARI	8	9	0	184	112	4.30	1.32	$6	21.6	249	269	223	28%	3.45 +	19.8	3.4	5.5	1.6	0.6	1.74	67%	54	102
I CON	03	ARI	10	9	0	193	142	3.54	1.33	$12	22.8	266	297	241	31%	3.80	44.9	2.8	6.6	2.4	0.6	1.77	74%	73	141
S PT stb	1st Half		6	3	0	96	67	2.91	1.27	$10	20.1	258			31%	3.32	30.5	2.6	6.3	2.4	0.4	1.56	77%	80	154
K	2nd Half		4	6	0	97	75	4.17	1.39	$3	26.2	273			32%	4.26	14.4	3.0	7.0	2.3	0.8	2.01	71%	66	127
LIMA C EP: 50%	04	Proj	9	10	0	180	124	4.05	1.35	$8	22.0	260			30%	3.87	29.3	3.3	6.2	1.9	0.8	G	71%	58	112

As k/bb improves, xERA gets worse -- hit rate has a lot to do with it. No reason that he cannot maintain this level in 2004, but it would be a lot easier on him if put in a role and left there.

Bauer,Rick

	Yr	Tm	W	L	Sv	IP	K	ERA	Br/IP	R$	BF/G	OBA	vL	vR	H%	xERA	RAR	Ctl	Dom	Cmd	hr/9	G/F	S%	BPV	BPX
RH Reliever	99		0	0	0	0	0	0.00	0.00																
AGE 27 Growth	00	aa	6	8	1	129	76	6.84	1.75	($8)	23.2	337			36%	6.72	-18.6	2.9	5.3	1.9	1.4		62%	16	39
TYPE	01	BAL *	12	15	0	207	123	4.87	1.40	$6	26.3	292	274	254	31%	5.05	17.1	2.1	5.3	2.5	1.3	1.54	68%	42	85
R X HIGH	02	BAL	6	8	1	87	46	4.24	1.46	$4	6.7	266	288	253	27%	5.01 -	14.2	3.9	4.8	1.2	1.4	1.67	76%	12	25
I EXP CON	03	BAL *	3	1	0	97	60	4.07	1.36	$3	9.9	257	247	261	29%	3.76	19.0	3.4	5.5	1.6	0.6	1.16	70%	54	117
S PT stb	1st Half		1	1	0	53	32	4.73	1.44	($1)	8.9	282			32%	4.45	5.7	3.0	5.4	1.8	0.7	1.42	67%	48	104
K BRN	2nd Half		2	0	0	44	28	3.27	1.25	$4	11.5	225			26%	2.93	13.3	3.9	5.7	1.5	0.4	0.77	74%	63	136
LIMA C+ EP: 50%	04	Proj	4	4	0	80	47	4.50	1.41	$2	10.5	269			30%	4.39	11.1	3.4	5.3	1.6	0.9	--	70%	39	83

0-0, 4.55 ERA in 61 IP at BAL. 2nd half improvement due to drop in hit rate, not a change in BPIs. Marginal BPIs makes him a poor bet for 2004.

Beckett,Josh

	Yr	Tm	W	L	Sv	IP	K	ERA	Br/IP	R$	BF/G	OBA	vL	vR	H%	xERA	RAR	Ctl	Dom	Cmd	hr/9	G/F	S%	BPV	BPX
RH Starter	99		0	0	0	0	0	0.00	0.00																
AGE 23 Growth	00		0	0	0	0	0	0.00	0.00																
TYPE Power	01	FLA *	10	3	0	98	113	2.20	1.08	$19	23.1	211	231	104	28%	2.92 -	41.5	2.9	10.4	3.5	1.1	0.60	87%	116	215
R Moderate	02	FLA	6	7	0	107	113	4.12	1.28	$6	19.5	236	246	218	30%	3.62 +	14.1	3.7	9.5	2.6	1.1	0.82	71%	86	163
I EXP con	03	FLA	9	8	0	142	152	3.04	1.32	$13	25.1	248	220	267	33%	3.47	42.5	3.5	9.6	2.7	0.6	1.23	78%	103	198
S pt	1st Half		2	3	0	40	45	3.81	1.57	$1	22.5	275			37%	4.55 -	7.9	4.5	10.1	2.3	0.7	1.20	77%	88	168
K age	2nd Half		7	5	0	102	107	2.74	1.23	$12	26.4	237			32%	3.05	34.6	3.2	9.5	3.0	0.5	1.25	79%	111	213
LIMA B+ EP: 60%	04	Proj	16	7	0	180	195	3.10	1.27	$22	22.2	241			32%	3.47	52.2	3.4	9.8	2.9	0.9	--	79%	101	195

BPIs are dominant; needs to put together a 200-inning season.

Upside: 20 wins, 2.80 ERA.

Beck,Rod

	Yr	Tm	W	L	Sv	IP	K	ERA	Br/IP	R$	BF/G	OBA	vL	vR	H%	xERA	RAR	Ctl	Dom	Cmd	hr/9	G/F	S%	BPV	BPX
RH Reliever	99	2TM	2	5	10	44	25	5.93	1.55	$5	4.6	287	115	261	31%	4.88 +	-2.4	3.7	5.1	1.4	1.0	0.98	62%	27	62
AGE 35 Decline	00	BOS	3	0	0	40	35	3.13	1.14	$7	4.8	231	246	202	29%	2.69	15.0	2.7	7.8	2.9	0.4	1.56	73%	104	269
TYPE Power	01	BOS	6	4	6	80	63	3.93	1.31	$10	5.0	254	213	285	28%	4.62 -	16.7	3.1	7.1	2.3	1.7	1.28	78%	43	87
R Very High	02		0	0	0	0	0	0.00	0.00																
I exp CON	03	SD *	4	3	24	65	54	1.24	1.10	$25	4.6	227	159	241	27%	2.91 -	35.3	2.5	7.4	3.0	0.8	1.18	95%	92	178
S pt stb	1st Half		2	2	8	40	32	1.12	1.12	$11	5.2	236			28%	2.92 -	22.4	2.2	7.2	3.2	0.7	1.22	95%	98	188
K age brn	2nd Half		2	1	16	25	22	1.43	1.08	$14	3.9	212			25%	2.88 -	12.9	2.9	7.9	2.8	1.1	1.16	96%	85	164
LIMA C EP: 25%	04	Proj	4	3	16	60	48	3.00	1.22	$16	4.6	239			28%	3.52 -	18.2	3.0	7.2	2.4	1.1	--	80%	69	134

From an Iowa trailer to Padres closer -- great BPIs at age 35; tough to repeat them (95% strand rate!), but even with a decline he should be a serviceable RP for someone.

DOUG DENNIS

Beimel,Joe

LH Reliever
AGE 27 Growth
TYPE
R High
I exp con
S PT stb
K brn
LIMA F EP: 40%

Yr	Tm	W	L	Sv	IP	K	ERA	Br/IP	R$	BF/G	OBA	vL	vR	H%	xERA	RAR	Ctl	Dom	Cmd	hr/9	G/F	S%	BPV	BPX
99		0	0	0	0	0	0.00	0.00																
00	aa	1	6	0	62	23	5.23	1.74	($3)	28.9	327			33%	6.46 -	4.4	3.3	3.3	**1.0**	1.3		73%	-9	-20
01	PIT	7	11	0	115	58	5.24	1.56	($1)	12.3	288	268	298	31%	5.05	2.0	3.8	4.5	**1.2**	0.9	1.67	67%	21	40
02	PIT	2	5	0	85	53	4.66	1.56	($3)	7.2	269	262	269	30%	4.68	5.1	4.8	5.6	**1.2**	1.0	1.77	72%	31	59
03	PIT	1	3	0	62	42	5.07	1.64	($4)	4.1	283	311	288	32%	5.21	1.7	4.8	6.1	**1.3**	1.0	1.23	71%	31	60
1st Half		1	1	0	38	30	3.07	1.44	$1	4.5	261			31%	4.11 -	11.3	4.0	7.1	**1.8**	0.7	1.50	81%	61	117
2nd Half		0	2	0	24	12	8.25	1.96	($5)	3.7	314			33%	6.96 +	-9.6	6.0	4.5	**0.8**	1.5	0.93	58%	-10	-19
04	**Proj**	**1**	**4**	**0**	**65**	**37**	**5.54**	**1.68**	**($5)**	**5.6**	**290**			**31%**	**5.48**	**-2.4**	**4.7**	**5.1**	**1.1**	**1.1**	**--**	**68%**	**17**	**33**

Splits indicate some potential as a lefty specialist.

	IP	ERA	K	BB
vs. LH	28	3.49	28	16
vs. RH	35	6.35	14	17

Even so, Ctl ratios don't bode well for future success.

Bell,Rob

RH Starter
AGE 27 Growth
TYPE
R X HIGH
I EXP CON
S pt STB
K
LIMA F EP: 50%

Yr	Tm	W	L	Sv	IP	K	ERA	Br/IP	R$	BF/G	OBA	vL	vR	H%	xERA	RAR	Ctl	Dom	Cmd	hr/9	G/F	S%	BPV	BPX
99	aa	3	6	0	72	62	3.63	1.40	$4	25.9	293			35%	4.55 -	18.4	2.1	7.8	**3.6**	1.0		77%	90	208
00	CIN	* 11	8	0	181	154	4.87	1.40	$8	24.5	249	226	257	27%	5.01	18.4	4.2	7.7	**1.8**	1.9	0.86	73%	31	69
01	2TM	* 7	12	0	176	120	6.34	1.60	($10)	24.8	300	308	290	32%	6.21	-21.7	3.5	6.1	**1.8**	1.9	0.84	64%	12	23
02	TEX	* 10	3	0	177	119	5.54	1.48	($1)	26.0	288	307	282	31%	5.34	-2.0	3.1	6.1	**2.0**	1.4	1.14	65%	33	67
03	TAM	* 11	8	0	172	84	5.44	1.43	$3	24.2	282	247	282	29%	5.06	2.1	2.9	4.4	**1.5**	1.4	1.07	65%	16	35
1st Half		6	6	0	84	47	5.99	1.48	($0)	24.7	292			31%	5.17 +	-5.2	2.9	5.0	**1.7**	1.2	1.13	61%	28	60
2nd Half		5	2	0	88	37	4.91	1.37	$3	23.6	273			27%	4.96	7.3	2.9	3.8	**1.3**	1.5	1.06	69%	5	11
04	**Proj**	**4**	**6**	**0**	**100**	**59**	**5.40**	**1.46**	**($1)**	**24.3**	**284**			**30%**	**5.24**	**1.9**	**3.1**	**5.3**	**1.7**	**1.4**	**--**	**66%**	**23**	**50**

5-4, 5.52 ERA in 101 IP at TAM. Continues to improve his Ctl, but these gains are outstripped by a Dom ratio that is plummeting southward. Not much hope for a sub-5 ERA here.

Benitez,Armando

RH Reliever
AGE 31 Peak
TYPE Power
R Low
I CON
S stb
K
LIMA C+ EP: 45%

Yr	Tm	W	L	Sv	IP	K	ERA	Br/IP	R$	BF/G	OBA	vL	vR	H%	xERA	RAR	Ctl	Dom	Cmd	hr/9	G/F	S%	BPV	BPX
99	NYM	4	3	22	78	128	1.85	1.04	$26	4.0	154	177	127	28%	1.15 +	35.4	4.7	14.8	**3.1**	0.5	0.43	84%	165	358
00	NYM	4	4	41	76	106	2.61	1.01	$36	3.9	154	136	159	21%	2.15	30.8	4.5	12.6	**2.8**	1.2	0.66	82%	123	270
01	NYM	6	4	43	76	93	3.78	1.30	$32	4.4	216	212	215	28%	3.81	16.1	4.7	11.0	**2.3**	1.4	0.74	77%	84	156
02	NYM	1	0	33	67	79	2.28	1.06	$25	4.3	196	160	220	26%	2.55	25.3	3.4	10.6	**3.2**	1.1	0.65	86%	114	215
03	2TM	4	4	21	73	75	2.96	1.37	$18	4.5	223	214	221	29%	3.46 -	23.8	5.1	9.2	**1.8**	0.7	0.74	81%	82	167
1st Half		1	3	19	43	43	3.13	1.37	$13	4.6	228			29%	3.60	13.1	4.8	9.0	**1.9**	0.8	0.89	80%	77	157
2nd Half		3	1	2	30	32	2.72	1.38	$5	4.4	215			29%	3.24 -	10.7	5.4	9.7	**1.8**	0.6	0.56	82%	89	181
04	**Proj**	**4**	**3**	**5**	**70**	**77**	**2.83**	**1.26**	**$10**	**4.4**	**209**			**27%**	**3.24**	**24.1**	**4.6**	**9.9**	**2.1**	**1.0**	**F**	**83%**	**87**	**176**

For years, has been tagged unfairly as overrated. In '03, he earned the distinction, with skills declining in every area except hr/9 (a likely artifact of Safeco Field). He is now a borderline closer candidate at best.

Benoit,Joaquin

RH Starter
AGE 26 Growth
TYPE Power
R High
I EXP con
S pt stb
K
LIMA B EP: 50%

Yr	Tm	W	L	Sv	IP	K	ERA	Br/IP	R$	BF/G	OBA	vL	vR	H%	xERA	RAR	Ctl	Dom	Cmd	hr/9	G/F	S%	BPV	BPX
99		0	0	0	0	0	0.00	0.00																
00	aa	4	4	0	82	64	5.16	1.43	$2	22.3	273			32%	4.40 +	6.6	3.3	7.0	**2.1**	0.9		64%	61	144
01	a/a	10	5	0	153	148	5.12	1.53	$1	24.3	268			33%	4.82	6.2	4.5	8.7	**1.9**	1.1	0.78	68%	61	117
02	TEX	* 12	9	1	182	148	4.65	1.46	$6	24.2	252	275	268	30%	4.09 +	19.8	4.6	7.3	**1.6**	0.7	0.90	68%	61	125
03	TEX	* 10	6	0	138	113	5.48	1.42	$3	19.3	256	222	272	28%	5.02	0.9	4.0	7.4	**1.8**	1.8	0.72	66%	33	72
1st Half		5	4	0	76	67	5.45	1.32	$2	21.5	249			28%	4.67 +	0.8	3.4	7.9	**2.3**	1.8	0.91	64%	48	104
2nd Half		5	2	0	62	46	5.52	1.55	$0	17.3	265			28%	5.46	0.1	4.8	6.7	**1.4**	1.7	0.62	69%	19	41
04	**Proj**	**8**	**5**	**0**	**120**	**103**	**4.95**	**1.44**	**$4**	**20.9**	**260**			**30%**	**4.67**	**9.5**	**4.1**	**7.7**	**1.9**	**1.3**	**F**	**69%**	**51**	**110**

8-5, 5.49 ERA in 105 IP at TEX. Coughed up a lot of homers in '03, even by TEX standards. HR/9 aside, 1st half BPIs were solid, so there could be a consolidation of skills in the near future.

Benson,Kris

RH Starter
AGE 29 Pre-Peak
TYPE
R Low
I con
S pt
K brn
LIMA D EP: 50%

Yr	Tm	W	L	Sv	IP	K	ERA	Br/IP	R$	BF/G	OBA	vL	vR	H%	xERA	RAR	Ctl	Dom	Cmd	hr/9	G/F	S%	BPV	BPX
99	PIT	11	14	0	196	139	4.09	1.36	$11	27.1	250	279	225	29%	3.44 +	30.2	3.8	6.4	**1.7**	0.7	1.64	71%	56	123
00	PIT	10	12	0	217	184	3.85	1.34	$14	28.9	252	276	225	30%	4.01	51.6	3.6	7.6	**2.1**	1.0	1.76	74%	66	144
01	PIT	0	0	0	0	0	0.00	0.00																
02	PIT	* 10	8	0	154	102	4.32	1.48	$4	22.6	280	313	281	31%	4.84 -	16.1	3.4	6.0	**1.7**	1.2	1.05	74%	36	68
03	PIT	5	9	0	105	68	4.97	1.55	($1)	26.1	300	339	260	33%	5.42	4.3	3.1	5.8	**1.9**	1.2	0.66	70%	34	65
1st Half		5	8	0	91	58	5.04	1.55	($1)	27.1	304			33%	5.46	2.9	2.9	5.7	**2.0**	1.2	0.66	70%	35	67
2nd Half		0	1	0	14	10	4.50	1.57	($1)	21.0	275			31%	5.18 -	1.5	4.5	6.4	**1.4**	1.3	0.68	75%	30	58
04	**Proj**	**9**	**11**	**0**	**160**	**116**	**4.33**	**1.44**	**$5**	**26.8**	**274**			**31%**	**4.58**	**20.0**	**3.4**	**6.5**	**1.9**	**1.1**	**F**	**73%**	**48**	**93**

Dom is down compared to pre-TJ surgery levels, but Cmd is roughly the same. The bigger concern is his health. Until his shoulder is sound and he shows some consistency, bid cautiously.

Bernero,Adam

RH Reliever
AGE 27 Growth
TYPE
R Moderate
I EXP CON
S pt stb
K
LIMA D EP: 55%

Yr	Tm	W	L	Sv	IP	K	ERA	Br/IP	R$	BF/G	OBA	vL	vR	H%	xERA	RAR	Ctl	Dom	Cmd	hr/9	G/F	S%	BPV	BPX
99		0	0	0	0	0	0.00	0.00																
00	DET	* 5	7	0	142	91	3.36	1.23	$14	20.3	245	242	300	28%	3.39	48.5	2.8	5.8	**2.1**	0.8	1.59	75%	61	159
01	DET	* 6	11	0	152	92	6.10	1.70	($10)	22.7	325	185	348	36%	5.99	-12.5	3.1	5.4	**1.7**	0.9	1.58	64%	31	62
02	DET	* 6	9	0	158	113	4.67	1.42	$2	18.6	290	321	295	33%	4.91	16.7	2.4	6.4	**2.6**	1.1	1.18	69%	58	120
03	2TM	1	14	0	133	80	5.88	1.44	($7)	11.8	267	306	225	29%	4.76 +	-8.7	3.7	5.4	**1.5**	1.3	1.07	60%	27	54
1st Half		1	11	0	96	54	5.81	1.42	($4)	26.0	264			28%	4.51 +	-5.3	3.7	5.1	**1.4**	1.1	0.97	60%	28	57
2nd Half		0	3	0	37	26	6.08	1.49	($3)	4.9	277			30%	5.41 +	-3.4	3.6	6.3	**1.7**	1.7	1.40	63%	23	46
04	**Proj**	**2**	**8**	**0**	**100**	**66**	**5.40**	**1.46**	**($3)**	**10.7**	**282**			**31%**	**4.99**	**-0.1**	**3.2**	**5.9**	**1.9**	**1.3**	**--**	**65%**	**36**	**73**

Predictably, the long ball was a problem in COL, but other BPIs returned to career norms after leaving dismal DET. Not much Roto value while he remains a reliever, but could be useful as bullpen filler in a sim format.

Betancourt,Rafael

RH Reliever
AGE 29 Pre-Peak
TYPE Power
R X HIGH
I EXP CON
S pt STB
K BRN
LIMA A EP: 45%

Yr	Tm	W	L	Sv	IP	K	ERA	Br/IP	R$	BF/G	OBA	vL	vR	H%	xERA	RAR	Ctl	Dom	Cmd	hr/9	G/F	S%	BPV	BPX
99	aa	6	2	13	54	48	4.67	1.30	$13	5.8	283			34%	4.29	6.2	1.7	8.0	**4.8**	1.2		67%	112	260
00	JPN	2	2	0	52	45	2.77	1.23	$6	7.0	243			29%	3.47 -	20.8	2.9	7.8	**2.6**	0.9		81%	83	196
01	aa	0	1	4	24	19	8.25	1.71	($2)	6.9	360			44%	5.69 +	-9.1	1.1	7.1	**6.3**	0.0		46%	159	305
02		0	0	0	0	0	0.00	0.00																
03	CLE	* 2	2	18	90	95	2.40	1.27	$19	5.5	244	270	133	32%	3.37 -	37.7	3.2	9.5	**3.0**	0.6	0.32	83%	108	232
1st Half		0	0	16	45	51	2.20	1.51	$11	6.4	282			40%	3.93 -	20.1	3.6	10.2	**2.8**	0.0		84%	119	257
2nd Half		2	2	2	45	44	2.61	1.02	$8	4.8	202			24%	2.80	17.6	2.8	8.8	**3.1**	1.2		83%	97	211
04	**Proj**	**3**	**3**	**2**	**80**	**77**	**2.93**	**1.23**	**$9**	**5.9**	**244**			**31%**	**3.45 -**	**28.0**	**2.8**	**8.7**	**3.1**	**0.8**	**F**	**79%**	**99**	**212**

2-2, 2.13 ERA in 38 IP at CLE. Closerworthy BPIs. Talent is clearly there, but Opportunity and Guile are question marks. Low ERA and WHIP make him a strong LIMA candidate.

Biddle,Rocky

RH Reliever
AGE 27 Pre-Peak
TYPE Power
R High
I exp con
S pt stb
K brn
LIMA D EP: 40%

Yr	Tm	W	L	Sv	IP	K	ERA	Br/IP	R$	BF/G	OBA	vL	vR	H%	xERA	RAR	Ctl	Dom	Cmd	hr/9	G/F	S%	BPV	BPX
99		0	0	0	0	0	0.00	0.00																
00	aa	11	6	0	146	99	4.68	1.66	$4	29.1	305			35%	5.57 -	21.0	3.8	6.1	**1.6**	1.0	0.97	73%	35	83
01	CHW	7	8	0	128	85	5.41	1.47	($0)	18.8	275	270	274	30%	4.81 +	1.4	3.7	6.0	**1.6**	1.1	1.19	65%	36	73
02	CHW	3	4	1	84	72	3.86	1.39	$4	7.9	245	287	205	28%	4.48 -	18.0	4.3	7.7	**1.8**	1.4	1.67	78%	48	99
03	MON	5	8	34	71	54	4.68	1.56	$20	4.4	261	242	264	29%	4.93	5.7	5.1	6.8	**1.4**	1.3	1.52	73%	34	66
1st Half		3	2	22	40	39	3.59	1.30	$16	4.4	221			29%	2.95 +	9.1	4.5	8.8	**2.0**	0.4	1.45	72%	91	175
2nd Half		2	6	12	31	15	6.08	1.90	$4	4.3	308			30%	7.47 -	-3.3	5.8	4.3	**0.8**	2.3	1.60	75%	-34	-66
04	**Proj**	**4**	**7**	**9**	**75**	**54**	**4.80**	**1.57**	**$4**	**4.9**	**272**			**30%**	**5.25**	**4.7**	**4.7**	**6.5**	**1.4**	**1.4**	**G**	**74%**	**25**	**49**

Like the cinematic Rocky, the debut of Rocky the Closer was more satisfying than the sequel. He has never had closer-worthy BPIs, so while he's not as bad as the 2nd half collapse seems, he's a poor bet for saves.

Bierbrodt,Nick

LH Reliever
AGE 25 Growth
TYPE Power
R X HIGH
I EXP con
S PT STB
K brn
LIMA D EP: 60%

Yr	Tm	W	L	Sv	IP	K	ERA	Br/IP	R$	BF/G	OBA	vL	vR	H%	xERA	RAR	Ctl	Dom	Cmd	hr/9	G/F	S%	BPV	BPX
99	a/a	6	10	0	119	88	5.52	1.58	($1)	21.4	284			33%	4.65 +	0.2	4.2	6.7	**1.6**	0.8		65%	49	114
00	aa	3	4	0	54	40	7.17	1.69	($4)	22.6	265			31%	4.75 +	-10.2	6.0	6.7	**1.1**	0.7		55%	45	107
01	2TM	* 11	8	0	149	137	4.11	1.48	$7	24.3	284	297	289	34%	4.89 -	26.2	3.2	8.3	**2.6**	1.1	0.96	75%	69	133
02		0	0	0	0	0	0.00	0.00																
03	2AL	* 2	4	0	70	56	7.19	1.94	($11)	10.0	313	393	328	36%	6.72	-15.6	5.9	7.2	**1.2**	1.3	0.92	63%	23	49
1st Half		0	2	0	39	26	9.44	2.28	($11)	12.5	360			39%	8.93 +	-20.5	5.5	6.0	**1.1**	2.1	1.02	58%	-20	-44
2nd Half		2	2	0	31	30	4.35	1.61	$0	7.8	243			32%	3.93	4.9	6.4	8.7	**1.4**	0.3	0.29	71%	79	170
04	**Proj**	**4**	**5**	**0**	**80**	**67**	**5.29**	**1.65**	**($2)**	**13.1**	**276**			**33%**	**5.06**	**2.7**	**5.2**	**7.5**	**1.5**	**0.9**	**--**	**69%**	**49**	**104**

0-2, 9.14 ERA in 43 IP at TAM and CLE. Despite bouts with wildness, he seemed poised for big things before getting shot in his non-pitching arm in '01. Still has long-term potential, but decent Ctl won't come overnight.

AL MELCHIOR

Boehringer,Brian

	Yr	Tm	W	L	Sv	IP	K	ERA	Br/IP	R$	BF/G	OBA	vL	vR	H%	xERA	RAR	Ctl	Dom	Cmd	hr/9	G/F	S%	BPV	BPX
RH Reliever	99	SD	6	5	0	94	64	3.26	1.40	$8	12.3	268	223	298	30%	4.01 -	24.9	3.4	6.1	**1.8**	1.0	1.21	80%	48	104
AGE 34 Past	00	SD	0	3	0	16	9	5.63	1.75	($2)	10.7	285	280	289	28%	6.71 -	0.0	5.6	5.1	**0.9**	2.3	1.60	75%	-20	-45
TYPE Power	01	2TM	0	4	2	69	60	3.65	1.39	$2	5.8	256	316	208	31%	4.12	16.4	3.8	7.8	**2.1**	0.9	0.87	76%	67	128
R Moderate	02	PIT	4	4	1	79	65	3.42	1.24	$7	4.7	226	250	218	28%	2.92 +	17.9	3.8	7.4	**2.0**	0.6	0.69	73%	79	148
I CON	03	PIT	5	4	0	62	47	5.51	1.51	$0	4.4	268	193	309	29%	5.21	-1.9	4.3	6.8	**1.6**	1.6	0.77	67%	27	53
S pt stb	1st Half		3	2	0	30	19	7.48	1.69	($2)	4.0	298			30%	6.87 +	-8.9	4.5	5.7	**1.3**	2.4	0.61	60%	-16	-30
K age	2nd Half		2	2	0	32	28	3.66	1.34	$2	5.1	237			29%	3.65	7.0	4.2	7.9	**1.9**	0.8	0.97	75%	69	132
LIMA B EP: 50%	04	Proj	**4**	**4**	**0**	**65**	**52**	**4.29**	**1.40**	**$3**	**5.1**	**253**			**29%**	**4.23**	**8.5**	**4.0**	**7.2**	**1.8**	**1.1**	**F**	**72%**	**52**	**101**

2nd half BPIs show he is still a solid middle reliever. While not really closer material, he has better skills than a few actual closers. Not much Roto value, but a valuable arm to have for simulation games.

Bonderman,Jeremy

	Yr	Tm	W	L	Sv	IP	K	ERA	Br/IP	R$	BF/G	OBA	vL	vR	H%	xERA	RAR	Ctl	Dom	Cmd	hr/9	G/F	S%	BPV	BPX
RH Starter	99		0	0	0	0	0	0.00	0.00																
AGE 21 Green	00		0	0	0	0	0	0.00	0.00																
TYPE	01		0	0	0	0	0	0.00	0.00																
R Moderate	02		0	0	0	0	0	0.00	0.00																
I EXP	03	DET	6	19	0	162	108	5.56	1.55	($5)	21.9	297	306	277	33%	5.49	-0.7	3.2	6.0	**1.9**	1.3	1.17	66%	32	70
S	1st Half		2	12	0	90	68	5.09	1.47	($2)	24.8	292			34%	4.77	5.3	2.8	6.8	**2.4**	0.8	1.18	66%	64	139
K AGE	2nd Half		4	7	0	72	40	6.14	1.64	($4)	19.3	303			31%	6.40	-5.9	3.8	5.0	**1.3**	1.9	1.17	67%	-4	-8
LIMA D EP: 50%	04	Proj	**8**	**18**	**0**	**180**	**117**	**5.20**	**1.49**	**($0)**	**20.9**	**284**			**31%**	**5.07**	**8.2**	**3.4**	**5.9**	**1.7**	**1.2**	**--**	**67%**	**34**	**73**

DET Mgr Trammell did the right thing by cutting back his workload late in the year. 1st half indicators were very impressive, and he was clearly wearing down. Great keeper pick.

Bong,Jung

	Yr	Tm	W	L	Sv	IP	K	ERA	Br/IP	R$	BF/G	OBA	vL	vR	H%	xERA	RAR	Ctl	Dom	Cmd	hr/9	G/F	S%	BPV	BPX
LH Reliever	99		0	0	0	0	0	0.00	0.00																
AGE 23 Growth	00		0	0	0	0	0	0.00	0.00																
TYPE Power	01		0	0	0	0	0	0.00	0.00																
R High	02	aa	7	9	2	128	94	3.94	1.60	$3	20.7	307			37%	4.91 -	22.9	3.2	6.6	**2.1**	0.4	0.88	75%	64	127
I EXP	03	ATL	* 7	4	1	68	60	5.55	1.51	$2	6.4	264	264	268	31%	4.77 +	-2.5	4.5	7.9	**1.8**	1.2	1.71	65%	51	98
S pt stb	1st Half		5	1	1	40	36	3.37	1.27	$7	5.8	231			28%	3.45	10.3	3.8	8.1	**2.1**	0.9	1.59	77%	75	144
K age	2nd Half		2	3	0	28	24	8.68	1.86	($4)	7.4	307			35%	6.66 +	-12.7	5.5	7.7	**1.4**	1.6	2.00	53%	21	41
LIMA B EP: 60%	04	Proj	**6**	**5**	**1**	**75**	**62**	**4.80**	**1.51**	**$3**	**9.0**	**277**			**33%**	**4.69**	**4.7**	**3.8**	**7.4**	**1.9**	**1.0**	**G**	**70%**	**56**	**108**

6-2, 5.05 ERA in 57 IP at ATL. 2nd half meltdown was no joke to Bong owners. The 35% hit rate suggests a rebound in '04, but rough times lie ahead until he can demonstrate consistent control.

Borowski,Joe

	Yr	Tm	W	L	Sv	IP	K	ERA	Br/IP	R$	BF/G	OBA	vL	vR	H%	xERA	RAR	Ctl	Dom	Cmd	hr/9	G/F	S%	BPV	BPX
RH Reliever	99	aaa	6	2	4	89	56	6.38	1.73	($2)	7.1	306			35%	5.40 +	-10.1	4.4	5.7	**1.3**	0.8		62%	32	74
AGE 32 Past	00	ind	10	5	1	80	83	4.28	1.38	$11	8.6	250			32%	3.94	15.9	3.9	9.3	**2.4**	0.9		71%	84	199
TYPE Power	01	aaa	8	8	1	112	102	3.62	1.26	$11	11.7	258			32%	3.79	27.1	2.5	8.2	**3.3**	0.9	3.00	74%	95	183
R High	02	CHC	4	4	2	95	97	2.75	1.19	$10	5.3	239	209	260	30%	3.30 -	30.0	2.7	9.2	**3.3**	0.9	1.02	82%	104	197
I exp con	03	CHC	2	2	33	68	66	2.64	1.06	$26	4.0	216	212	204	28%	2.49	24.0	2.5	8.7	**3.5**	0.7	0.84	78%	117	225
S PT STB	1st Half		1	1	15	38	40	2.59	1.05	$13	4.1	206			27%	2.38	13.7	2.8	9.4	**3.3**	0.7	0.74	78%	119	229
K	2nd Half		1	1	18	30	26	2.71	1.07	$14	3.8	229			28%	2.63	10.3	2.1	7.8	**3.7**	0.6	0.97	77%	116	223
LIMA C+ EP: 55%	04	Proj	**3**	**3**	**39**	**70**	**66**	**3.09**	**1.17**	**$29**	**4.3**	**236**			**30%**	**3.10**	**20.4**	**2.7**	**8.5**	**3.1**	**0.8**	**--**	**76%**	**102**	**196**

Other than a slight slip in Dom, all indicators rose from his surprisingly good '02 levels. Should be a good bet for saves and WHIP in '04.

Boyd,Jason

	Yr	Tm	W	L	Sv	IP	K	ERA	Br/IP	R$	BF/G	OBA	vL	vR	H%	xERA	RAR	Ctl	Dom	Cmd	hr/9	G/F	S%	BPV	BPX
RH Reliever	99	aaa	6	5	5	80	49	4.73	1.40	$8	7.1	278			31%	4.05 +	8.6	2.8	5.5	**2.0**	0.7	0.22	66%	53	124
AGE 31 Peak	00	PHI	* 1	1	0	49	41	5.29	1.76	($3)	5.6	257	283	299	32%	4.55 +	2.2	7.1	7.5	**1.1**	0.4	1.50	68%	60	132
TYPE Power	01	aaa	2	7	12	59	56	2.90	1.46	$10	5.0	258			32%	4.17 -	19.9	4.3	8.5	**2.0**	0.8		83%	74	141
R Very High	02	SD	* 2	1	5	70	46	4.76	1.49	$1	6.0	265			28%	4.86	3.3	4.2	5.9	**1.4**	1.4	1.66	72%	24	46
I EXP con	03	CLE	* 4	1	3	66	42	3.80	1.24	$8	5.2	224	232	176	26%	3.02 +	15.3	3.8	5.7	**1.5**	0.5	1.27	69%	60	129
S pt STB	1st Half		2	1	3	43	32	3.33	1.15	$6	5.3	228			27%	2.92	12.8	2.9	6.7	**2.3**	0.6		72%	79	170
K	2nd Half		2	0	0	23	10	4.70	1.39	$1	5.0	217			24%	3.20 +	2.6	5.5	3.9	**0.7**	0.4		65%	38	83
LIMA C EP: 50%	04	Proj	**4**	**2**	**5**	**70**	**46**	**4.24**	**1.39**	**$6**	**5.4**	**242**			**27%**	**3.83**	**12.1**	**4.4**	**5.9**	**1.4**	**0.8**	**--**	**70%**	**47**	**101**

3-1, 4.30 ERA in 52 IP at CLE. Has potential to earn a set-up role, but has not lived up to it over an extended period of time.
UPSIDE: 3.50 ERA
DOWNSIDE: 5.00+ ERA

Bradford,Chad

	Yr	Tm	W	L	Sv	IP	K	ERA	Br/IP	R$	BF/G	OBA	vL	vR	H%	xERA	RAR	Ctl	Dom	Cmd	hr/9	G/F	S%	BPV	BPX
RH Reliever	99	aaa	9	3	5	74	48	2.07	1.09	$20	6.3	243			29%	2.39	34.3	1.7	5.8	**3.4**	0.2		81%	106	246
AGE 29 Peak	00	aaa	2	4	10	53	36	1.87	1.06	$15	3.8	227			27%	2.36 -	27.6	2.0	6.1	**3.0**	0.3	17.00	83%	99	235
TYPE	01	OAK	* 2	1	3	59	54	1.83	1.12	$10	5.1	258	300	274	32%	3.47 -	28.9	1.2	8.2	**6.8**	0.9	3.13	90%	167	334
R High	02	OAK	4	2	2	75	56	3.12	1.16	$9	4.1	257	267	247	31%	2.97	23.5	1.7	6.7	**4.0**	0.2	3.28	72%	121	248
I EXP CON	03	OAK	7	4	2	77	62	3.04	1.26	$11	4.5	236	326	190	28%	3.47	25.6	3.5	7.2	**2.1**	0.8	3.46	79%	70	152
S pt stb	1st Half		5	3	1	41	34	3.95	1.27	$6	4.6	232			27%	3.70	8.6	3.7	7.5	**2.0**	1.1	3.00	72%	62	135
K	2nd Half		2	1	1	36	28	2.00	1.25	$5	4.3	240			29%	3.20 -	17.0	3.2	7.0	**2.2**	0.5	4.13	86%	79	171
LIMA B EP: 50%	04	Proj	**5**	**3**	**3**	**75**	**59**	**2.88**	**1.20**	**$11**	**4.5**	**246**			**30%**	**3.24**	**26.7**	**2.5**	**7.1**	**2.8**	**0.6**	**G**	**78%**	**89**	**191**

Favorable hit and strand rates disguised the fact that his skills were not as sharp in '03. Assuming he regains pinpoint control, expect an ERA under 3.00. Otherwise, the mid-3s may be more realistic.

Brazelton,Dewan

	Yr	Tm	W	L	Sv	IP	K	ERA	Br/IP	R$	BF/G	OBA	vL	vR	H%	xERA	RAR	Ctl	Dom	Cmd	hr/9	G/F	S%	BPV	BPX
RH Starter	99		0	0	0	0	0	0.00	0.00																
AGE 23 Growth	00		0	0	0	0	0	0.00	0.00																
TYPE	01		0	0	0	0	0	0.00	0.00																
R High	02	a/a	6	9	0	151	97	3.99	1.49	$2	24.7	267			31%	4.09	25.8	4.2	5.8	**1.4**	0.5		73%	51	100
I EXP con	03	TAM	* 5	8	0	84	44	6.11	1.63	($3)	22.5	284	287	299	30%	5.33 +	-6.6	4.6	4.7	**1.0**	1.1	1.69	63%	16	34
S pt stb	1st Half		3	8	0	74	39	6.32	1.61	($5)	22.3	287			30%	5.45 +	-7.9	4.3	4.7	**1.1**	1.2	1.69	61%	13	28
K age	2nd Half		2	0	0	10	5	4.50	1.80	$1	23.6	262			30%	4.43	1.4	7.2	4.5	**0.6**	0.0		72%	43	92
LIMA D EP: 55%	04	Proj	**2**	**5**	**0**	**60**	**34**	**5.40**	**1.57**	**($2)**	**22.4**	**281**			**31%**	**4.95**	**1.1**	**4.2**	**5.1**	**1.2**	**0.9**	**G**	**66%**	**28**	**60**

1-6, 6.89 ERA in 48 IP at TAM. Rough start earned him a demotion all the way to Single-A. He worked his way back to AA, but not without some serious Ctl problems. Definitely a work in progress.

Brower,Jim

	Yr	Tm	W	L	Sv	IP	K	ERA	Br/IP	R$	BF/G	OBA	vL	vR	H%	xERA	RAR	Ctl	Dom	Cmd	hr/9	G/F	S%	BPV	BPX
RH Reliever	99	CLE	* 14	12	0	185	84	5.25	1.49	$8	22.7	285	286	259	29%	5.33	15.3	3.3	4.1	**1.2**	1.5	0.82	68%	5	12
AGE 31 Peak	00	CLE	* 11	7	0	163	90	4.86	1.54	$7	22.0	299	292	324	32%	5.27	23.1	3.0	5.0	**1.6**	1.1	1.32	71%	26	68
TYPE	01	CIN	* 8	10	1	140	103	4.05	1.40	$7	12.6	253	273	227	28%	4.34	24.7	4.0	6.6	**1.7**	1.2	1.40	75%	44	82
R X HIGH	02	2NL	3	2	0	80	57	4.39	1.36	$1	6.6	254	254	251	30%	3.61 +	7.7	3.6	6.4	**1.8**	0.6	1.86	67%	63	119
I exp CON	03	SF	8	5	2	100	65	3.96	1.29	$10	8.3	242	291	220	27%	3.49	17.7	3.5	5.9	**1.7**	0.7	2.21	70%	55	106
S pt STB	1st Half		3	1	2	43	30	4.18	1.51	$3	7.1	261			29%	4.60	6.4	4.6	6.3	**1.4**	1.0	2.20	75%	38	72
K BRN	2nd Half		5	4	0	57	35	3.80	1.12	$7	9.6	227			26%	2.65 +	11.3	2.7	5.5	**2.1**	0.5	2.22	66%	72	138
LIMA C+ EP: 50%	04	Proj	**5**	**4**	**1**	**80**	**53**	**4.16**	**1.34**	**$5**	**8.7**	**252**			**29%**	**3.77**	**11.8**	**3.5**	**6.0**	**1.7**	**0.8**	**G**	**70%**	**53**	**102**

Could be the prototypical anonymous swingman, pitching with moderate success in both starting and relief roles. It may surprise some that he produces well above replacement level.

Brown,Kevin

	Yr	Tm	W	L	Sv	IP	K	ERA	Br/IP	R$	BF/G	OBA	vL	vR	H%	xERA	RAR	Ctl	Dom	Cmd	hr/9	G/F	S%	BPV	BPX
RH Starter	99	LA	18	9	0	252	221	3.00	1.07	$35	28.7	228	255	189	28%	2.35 +	75.4	2.1	7.9	**3.7**	0.7	2.20	74%	115	250
AGE 39 Decline	00	LA	13	6	0	230	216	2.58	0.99	$36	27.3	218	221	206	27%	2.52	93.8	1.8	8.5	**4.6**	0.8	2.11	78%	134	295
TYPE Power	01	LA	10	4	0	115	104	2.66	1.15	$17	23.4	224	263	184	28%	2.81	41.8	3.0	8.1	**2.7**	0.6	2.57	79%	98	181
R Very High	02	LA	4	4	0	73	64	4.44	1.37	$2	16.5	264	245	296	31%	4.26	6.5	3.2	7.9	**2.5**	1.1	1.53	70%	68	128
I CON	03	LA	14	9	0	211	185	2.39	1.14	$28	26.8	236	254	219	30%	2.77	81.7	2.4	7.9	**3.3**	0.5	3.04	80%	110	212
S PT	1st Half		10	3	0	112	97	2.25	1.07	$20	26.3	229			29%	2.45	45.5	2.1	7.8	**3.7**	0.4	3.27	80%	122	235
K AGE BRN	2nd Half		4	6	0	99	88	2.55	1.21	$10	27.3	244			31%	3.14 -	36.2	2.7	8.0	**2.9**	0.5	2.79	81%	99	191
LIMA C+ EP: 45%	04	Proj	**12**	**8**	**0**	**180**	**159**	**3.00**	**1.20**	**$20**	**22.5**	**242**			**30%**	**3.19**	**54.6**	**2.7**	**8.0**	**2.9**	**0.7**	**G**	**77%**	**95**	**184**

Fantasy owners questioned whether he could rebound from back surgery at age 38. Brown's response: a DOM/DIS ratio of 75/0% in 32 starts. Despite the ongoing health risks, he has re-emerged as one of the Elite.

AL MELCHIOR

Buehrle,Mark

	Yr	Tm	W	L	Sv	IP	K	ERA	Br/IP	R$	BF/G	OBA	vL	vR	H%	xERA	RAR	Ctl	Dom	Cmd	hr/9	G/F	S%	BPV	BPX
LH Starter	99		0	0	0	0	0	0.00	0.00																
AGE 25 Growth	00	CHW	* 12	5	0	169	97	3.56	1.25	$21	16.0	267	260	279	29%	3.89	53.3	2.0	5.2	2.6	0.9	1.15	74%	60	157
TYPE Finesse	01	CHW	16	8	0	221	126	3.30	1.07	$28	27.6	232	208	236	25%	3.07	64.8	2.0	5.1	2.6	1.0	1.10	73%	65	131
R Moderate	02	CHW	19	12	0	239	134	3.58	1.24	$24	29.3	259	228	271	28%	3.89	60.2	2.3	5.0	2.2	0.9	1.50	74%	51	105
I exp	03	CHW	14	14	0	230	119	4.15	1.35	$13	28.1	278	263	285	30%	4.34	42.5	2.4	4.7	2.0	0.9	1.13	71%	42	92
S pt	1st Half		5	10	0	113	58	4.61	1.42	$2	27.3	277			29%	4.73	13.8	3.1	4.6	1.5	1.1	1.25	70%	25	54
K age BRN	2nd Half		9	4	0	117	61	3.70	1.28	$11	28.9	280			31%	3.96	28.6	1.7	4.7	2.8	0.6	1.02	72%	67	145
LIMA C EP: 50%	04	Proj	16	11	0	225	122	3.96	1.27	$19	26.2	266			29%	3.97	47.6	2.2	4.9	2.2	0.9	--	71%	51	110

29.3 BF/G and 239 IP at age 23 likely led to dropoff. Three-year declines in Ctl and Dom, along with high burnout potential make him risky. However, strong 2nd half overshadowed slow start, leaving a possible bargain.

Bump,Nate

	Yr	Tm	W	L	Sv	IP	K	ERA	Br/IP	R$	BF/G	OBA	vL	vR	H%	xERA	RAR	Ctl	Dom	Cmd	hr/9	G/F	S%	BPV	BPX
RH Reliever	99	aa	6	16	0	135	80	5.40	1.59	($2)	24.4	305			34%	5.18	2.4	3.2	5.3	1.7	0.9		67%	33	77
AGE 27 Pre-Peak	00	aa	8	9	0	149	81	5.80	1.72	($4)	26.6	325			35%	6.08	-0.8	3.3	4.9	1.5	1.0		67%	20	48
TYPE Finesse	01	aa	4	5	0	54	32	8.00	1.57	($4)	22.1	324			34%	6.64 +	-18.6	2.0	5.3	2.7	2.0		51%	18	35
R Very High	02	aa	7	6	0	127	62	4.32	1.35	$5	27.1	278			31%	3.86	16.1	2.3	4.4	1.9	0.4		67%	52	103
I EXP con	03	FLA	* 10	5	0	121	62	4.75	1.44	$5	11.3	279	229	258	31%	4.13 +	8.5	3.2	4.6	1.4	0.4	1.81	66%	44	84
S PT stb	1st Half		7	5	0	87	46	4.85	1.47	$3	23.9	291			33%	4.25 +	5.0	2.8	4.7	1.7	0.3	4.00	65%	52	100
K	2nd Half		3	0	0	34	16	4.50	1.38	$2	4.7	244			26%	3.84 +	3.5	4.2	4.2	1.0	0.8	1.74	68%	29	55
LIMA D EP: 50%	04	Proj	3	1	0	80	41	4.95	1.45	($1)	10.9	283			31%	4.50	3.4	3.0	4.6	1.5	0.8	G	66%	34	66

4-0, 4.71 ERA in 36 IP at FLA. Mediocre BPIs, other than low hr/9 caused by extreme GB tendency. A 27-year-old rookie needs better than a 1.4 Cmd (0.9 with FLA) to get anything more than mop-up duty.

Burba,Dave

	Yr	Tm	W	L	Sv	IP	K	ERA	Br/IP	R$	BF/G	OBA	vL	vR	H%	xERA	RAR	Ctl	Dom	Cmd	hr/9	G/F	S%	BPV	BPX
RH Reliever	99	CLE	15	9	0	220	174	4.25	1.40	$17	27.9	254	224	279	29%	4.40	47.6	3.9	7.1	1.8	1.2	1.04	73%	48	121
AGE 37 Decline	00	CLE	16	6	0	191	180	4.47	1.52	$13	26.5	270	259	274	33%	4.56	36.8	4.3	8.5	2.0	0.9	1.40	72%	67	173
TYPE	01	CLE	10	10	0	150	118	6.23	1.61	($5)	21.3	307	359	255	36%	5.47 +	-15.0	3.2	7.1	2.2	1.0	1.11	61%	53	106
R Low	02	2AL	5	5	0	149	96	5.07	1.44	($1)	18.1	272	247	293	30%	4.59	7.7	3.5	5.8	1.7	1.0	0.97	66%	41	84
I con	03	MIL	* 7	8	0	115	70	4.84	1.59	($0)	16.8	304	219	269	34%	5.33	6.8	3.2	5.5	1.7	0.9	1.14	71%	35	67
S stb	1st Half		6	8	0	77	38	5.58	1.71	($2)	23.9	333			36%	6.21 -	-3.1	2.7	4.4	1.7	1.0	1.33	68%	18	35
K AGE	2nd Half		1	0	0	38	32	3.32	1.35	$2	10.1	236			29%	3.53	9.9	4.3	7.6	1.8	0.7	1.11	77%	69	133
LIMA C+ EP: 50%	04	Proj	5	4	0	100	62	4.77	1.49	$0	16.3	279			31%	4.64	6.6	3.6	5.6	1.6	0.9	--	69%	38	74

1-1, 3.53 ERA in 43 IP at MIL. BPIs held steady from 2002, but nowhere to go but down as xERA will attest.

Burkett,John

	Yr	Tm	W	L	Sv	IP	K	ERA	Br/IP	R$	BF/G	OBA	vL	vR	H%	xERA	RAR	Ctl	Dom	Cmd	hr/9	G/F	S%	BPV	BPX
RH Starter	99	TEX	9	8	0	147	96	5.63	1.56	$1	22.0	307	279	337	34%	5.50	4.7	2.8	5.9	2.1	1.1	1.59	65%	40	99
AGE 39 Decline	00	ATL	10	6	0	134	110	4.90	1.59	$4	19.5	300	294	309	36%	5.21	13.1	3.4	7.4	2.2	0.9	1.53	70%	58	129
TYPE	01	ATL	12	12	0	219	187	3.04	1.17	$22	26.4	232	223	235	28%	3.06	68.3	2.9	7.7	2.7	0.7	1.19	76%	90	166
R High	02	BOS	13	8	0	173	124	4.53	1.44	$8	26.0	290	278	296	32%	5.15 -	21.6	2.6	6.5	2.5	1.3	1.20	72%	49	100
I CON	03	BOS	12	9	0	181	107	5.17	1.37	$6	24.3	283	273	290	31%	4.59 +	8.7	2.3	5.3	2.3	1.0	1.04	63%	48	104
S pt stb	1st Half		6	3	0	86	55	5.33	1.43	$2	25.0	283			32%	4.67 +	2.2	2.8	5.7	2.0	0.9	0.89	63%	47	102
K AGE	2nd Half		6	6	0	95	52	5.02	1.32	$4	23.7	283			31%	4.51 +	6.5	1.9	4.9	2.6	1.0	1.19	63%	51	111
LIMA C+ EP: 60%	04	Proj	11	8	0	160	108	4.67	1.38	$8	24.5	279			31%	4.54	18.6	2.5	6.1	2.4	1.0	--	68%	56	119

Contemplating retirement, but could still have decent value especially in NL. 63% strand rate helped drive his ERA over 5.00, so 4.50 isn't out of the question if he returns.

Burnett,A.J.

	Yr	Tm	W	L	Sv	IP	K	ERA	Br/IP	R$	BF/G	OBA	vL	vR	H%	xERA	RAR	Ctl	Dom	Cmd	hr/9	G/F	S%	BPV	BPX
RH Starter	99	FLA	* 10	14	0	161	140	5.53	1.71	($5)	22.6	286	269	221	34%	5.02 +	-6.4	5.3	7.8	1.5	1.0	1.78	68%	47	103
AGE 27 Growth	00	FLA	3	7	0	82	57	4.82	1.51	$0	28.0	257	302	219	29%	4.40	8.9	4.8	6.2	1.3	0.9	1.17	69%	42	93
TYPE Power	01	FLA	11	12	0	173	128	4.06	1.32	$11	27.2	229	247	213	26%	3.71	30.4	4.3	6.7	1.5	1.0	1.13	72%	50	93
R Moderate	02	FLA	12	9	0	204	203	3.31	1.19	$19	27.1	210	242	177	27%	2.55 +	49.1	4.0	9.0	2.3	0.5	1.10	73%	98	186
I con	03	FLA	0	2	0	23	21	4.70	1.57	($1)	25.8	217	234	194	27%	3.91 +	1.8	7.0	8.2	1.2	0.8	1.35	71%	62	119
S PT	1st Half		0	2	0	23	21	4.70	1.57	($1)	25.8	217			27%	3.91 +	1.8	7.0	8.2	1.2	0.8	1.35	71%	62	119
K brn	2nd Half		0	0	0	0	0	0.00	0.00																
LIMA D EP: 50%	04	Proj	5	9	0	120	87	4.35	1.43	$2	26.1	232			27%	3.78 +	14.7	5.3	6.5	1.2	0.8	--	71%	49	95

Underwent TJ surgery in April and should miss at least the beginning of 2004. Think of Kris Benson in 2002 when projecting his 2004 effectiveness -- i.e., big drop-off in Dom and Cmd while he tries to regain his stuff.

Bynum,Mike

	Yr	Tm	W	L	Sv	IP	K	ERA	Br/IP	R$	BF/G	OBA	vL	vR	H%	xERA	RAR	Ctl	Dom	Cmd	hr/9	G/F	S%	BPV	BPX
LH Reliever	99		0	0	0	0	0	0.00	0.00																
AGE 26 Growth	00	aa	3	1	0	34	22	2.91	1.38	$5	24.4	250			29%	3.66 -	13.0	4.0	5.8	1.5	0.5		80%	55	130
TYPE	01	aa	2	7	0	84	53	6.32	1.71	($8)	24.3	309			33%	6.38	-10.1	4.1	5.7	1.4	1.6		66%	8	16
R Very High	02	SD	* 8	2	0	101	69	3.48	1.22	$11	15.5	248			28%	3.38	22.1	2.6	6.1	2.4	0.8	1.42	74%	68	129
I EXP CON	03	SD	* 8	16	0	161	122	5.92	1.59	($6)	19.6	287	278	304	32%	5.44	-13.9	4.1	6.8	1.7	1.3	1.69	65%	33	64
S pt stb	1st Half		4	5	0	69	54	7.14	1.62	($5)	17.5	285			31%	5.93 +	-17.3	4.4	7.0	1.6	1.8	1.57	58%	19	36
K brn	2nd Half		4	11	0	92	68	5.00	1.57	($2)	21.7	289			33%	5.07	3.4	3.8	6.7	1.7	1.0	1.83	69%	44	86
LIMA C+ EP: 55%	04	Proj	5	6	0	80	57	5.06	1.50	$0	19.6	278			31%	4.86	2.2	3.7	6.4	1.7	1.1	G	68%	40	78

1-4, 8.75 ERA in 36 IP at SD. Looks like his 2002 BPIs were the exception, as evidenced by Ctl rate jump back to pre-2002 levels. Plus, he's a GB pitcher giving up 1.3 HR/9 - don't expect much improvement.

Calero,Kiko

	Yr	Tm	W	L	Sv	IP	K	ERA	Br/IP	R$	BF/G	OBA	vL	vR	H%	xERA	RAR	Ctl	Dom	Cmd	hr/9	G/F	S%	BPV	BPX
RH Reliever	99	aa	9	3	1	129	76	5.09	1.74	($0)	23.1	316			35%	5.89 -	7.6	3.9	5.3	1.4	1.1		73%	19	43
AGE 29 Pre-Peak	00	aa	10	7	0	153	81	6.12	1.98	($10)	26.8	337			36%	7.36 -	-7.3	4.9	4.8	1.0	1.5		72%	-8	-18
TYPE Power	01	aa	14	5	0	124	68	4.43	1.57	$8	20.6	287			31%	5.08 -	16.5	3.9	4.9	1.3	0.9		74%	25	49
R Very High	02	a/a	8	7	0	141	90	4.85	1.48	$1	24.8	292			32%	5.01	7.9	2.9	5.7	2.0	1.1		69%	41	80
I EXP CON	03	STL	1	1	1	38	51	2.83	1.29	$3	6.2	213	222	205	30%	3.48 -	12.5	4.7	12.0	2.6	1.2	0.48	84%	103	198
S pt stb	1st Half		1	1	1	38	51	2.83	1.29	$3	6.2	213			30%	3.48 -	12.5	4.7	12.0	2.6	1.2	0.48	84%	103	198
K	2nd Half		0	0	0	0	0	0.00	0.00																
LIMA C+ EP: 35%	04	Proj	4	2	1	60	48	4.35	1.53	$2	12.7	278			32%	4.99 -	7.3	4.1	7.2	1.8	1.2	F	75%	44	85

Six-year minor league free agent. Two reasons why he won't repeat success:
- Dom more than DOUBLE previous high rate;
- 84% strand signals big ERA jump in 2004.

Callaway,Mickey

	Yr	Tm	W	L	Sv	IP	K	ERA	Br/IP	R$	BF/G	OBA	vL	vR	H%	xERA	RAR	Ctl	Dom	Cmd	hr/9	G/F	S%	BPV	BPX
RH Reliever	99	a/a	8	2	0	91	53	4.75	1.52	$5	23.7	300			34%	4.60	9.5	2.8	5.2	1.9	0.6		68%	48	112
AGE 28 Pre-Peak	00	aaa	11	6	0	117	54	5.54	1.76	$1	21.1	328			35%	6.08 -	3.5	3.5	4.2	1.2	0.8		69%	14	34
TYPE Finesse	01	TAM	0	0	0	5	2	7.20	1.00	($0)	9.8	175			8%	4.72 +	-1.1	3.6	3.6	1.0	3.6	1.00	33%	-45	-91
R X HIGH	02	ANA	* 11	3	0	125	84	2.59	1.23	$17	22.6	257	215	254	29%	3.75 -	48.0	2.3	6.0	2.6	0.9	3.00	83%	69	142
I EXP CON	03	TEX	* 4	7	0	98	57	5.22	1.68	($4)	13.3	318	358	307	35%	5.64	4.0	3.3	5.2	1.6	0.7	1.64	69%	34	74
S PT STB	1st Half		1	4	0	41	22	5.26	1.65	($2)	11.1	306			32%	5.94 -	1.5	3.7	4.8	1.3	1.3	2.11	71%	11	23
K	2nd Half		3	3	0	57	35	5.19	1.70	($2)	15.5	326			38%	5.42	2.5	3.0	5.5	1.8	0.3	1.12	67%	52	113
LIMA C+ EP: 55%	04	Proj	5	4	0	80	47	4.61	1.56	$1	16.3	303			34%	5.16 -	9.9	3.0	5.3	1.7	0.8	G	71%	39	84

1-7, 6.68 ERA in 60 IP at ANA and TEX. Took a major step back from the promise of 2002 at age 28. 35% hit rate could indicate that luck will change again, but at a very high risk.

Carrasco,D.J.

	Yr	Tm	W	L	Sv	IP	K	ERA	Br/IP	R$	BF/G	OBA	vL	vR	H%	xERA	RAR	Ctl	Dom	Cmd	hr/9	G/F	S%	BPV	BPX
RH Reliever	99		0	0	0	0	0	0.00	0.00																
AGE 27 Growth	00		0	0	0	0	0	0.00	0.00																
TYPE Power	01	aa	2	2	1	37	29	5.84	1.95	($3)	6.7	292			35%	5.63	-2.1	7.1	7.1	1.0	0.5		69%	45	87
R Very High	02		0	0	0	0	0	0.00	0.00																
I EXP con	03	KC	6	5	2	80	57	4.83	1.52	$3	7.1	266	290	255	30%	4.62	7.4	4.5	6.4	1.4	0.9	1.66	69%	43	93
S pt stb	1st Half		3	4	2	42	35	3.63	1.35	$4	6.4	223			26%	3.57	10.7	4.9	7.5	1.5	0.9	1.37	75%	62	133
K BRN	2nd Half		3	1	0	38	22	6.16	1.71	($2)	8.0	309			34%	5.79	-3.2	4.0	5.2	1.3	0.9	2.03	64%	23	50
LIMA C+ EP: 50%	04	Proj	5	4	0	80	58	5.40	1.73	($3)	7.0	283			33%	5.26	1.5	5.5	6.5	1.2	0.8	G	69%	39	83

Rule 5 pick without much of a track record before this season. Too many walks and lack of effectiveness against LH hitters are two reasons not to bid.

SCOTT MONROE

Carrasco,Hector

		Tm	W	L	Sv	IP	K	ERA	Br/IP	R$	BF/G	OBA	vL	vR	H%	xERA	RAR	Ctl	Dom	Cmd	hr/9	G/F	S%	BPV	BPX
RH Reliever	99	MIN	2	3	1	49	35	4.78	1.35	$3	5.4	258	297	242	30%	3.70 +	7.2	3.3	6.4	1.9	0.6	1.29	63%	66	166
AGE 34 Decline	00	2AL	5	4	1	78	64	4.72	1.64	$3	5.2	290	281	297	34%	5.19	12.5	4.4	7.4	1.7	0.9	1.60	73%	49	127
TYPE Power	01	MIN	4	3	1	73	70	4.67	1.46	$2	5.7	272	318	251	34%	4.57	8.0	3.7	8.6	2.3	1.0	1.29	70%	72	144
R X HIGH	02	TEX	0	0	0	0	0	0.00	0.00																
I CON	03	BAL *	6	8	5	82	66	3.94	1.47	$8	4.9	256	288	256	30%	4.32	17.5	4.5	7.2	1.6	0.9	1.49	75%	55	118
S pt STB	1st Half		4	2	4	46	41	2.91	1.36	$8	5.8	234			29%	3.46 -	16.3	4.5	8.0	1.8	0.6	0.50	80%	76	164
K age BRN	2nd Half		2	6	1	36	25	5.26	1.62	($0)	4.2	283			31%	5.43	1.3	4.5	6.3	1.4	1.3	1.61	70%	28	59
LIMA B EP: 45%	04	Proj	4	5	2	65	53	4.57	1.51	$3	5.0	271			32%	4.70	8.4	4.2	7.3	1.8	1.0	--	71%	53	113

2-6, 1 Sv, 4.93 ERA in 38 IP at BAL. Continues to stick around because he can still get RH hitters out with some success. But rising Ctl and falling Dom indicate that the end is near.

Carter,Lance

		Tm	W	L	Sv	IP	K	ERA	Br/IP	R$	BF/G	OBA	vL	vR	H%	xERA	RAR	Ctl	Dom	Cmd	hr/9	G/F	S%	BPV	BPX
RH Reliever	99	aa	5	3	13	74	66	1.22	1.23	$21	6.1	226			29%	2.61 -	42.8	3.6	8.0	2.2	0.4		92%	93	216
AGE 29 Pre-Peak	00	aaa	2	8	5	76	42	6.04	1.55	$0	10.0	320			34%	6.18	-2.8	2.0	5.0	2.5	1.7		64%	23	54
TYPE Finesse	01		0	0	0	0	0	0.00	0.00																
R X HIGH	02	aaa	14	2	3	152	86	3.38	1.11	$22	14.9	261			28%	3.73	38.6	1.1	5.1	4.8	1.2		75%	98	193
I EXP CON	03	TAM	7	5	26	79	47	4.33	1.15	$24	5.2	244	222	265	25%	3.84	12.6	2.2	5.4	2.5	1.4	0.61	67%	49	106
S PT STB	1st Half		4	3	13	41	26	3.72	1.22	$13	5.5	247			27%	3.78	9.9	2.6	5.7	2.2	1.1	0.63	73%	52	113
K	2nd Half		3	2	13	38	21	4.99	1.08	$11	4.9	241			24%	3.91 +	2.7	1.7	5.0	3.0	1.7	0.59	59%	50	108
LIMA D EP: 50%	04	Proj	6	4	28	80	49	4.16	1.20	$24	6.9	259			28%	4.14	14.7	1.9	5.5	2.9	1.4	F	70%	56	120

Not dominant, but managed to guile out 26 Svs in 33 chances. Borderline acceptable save pct. (79%) and relief effectiveness (74%). Low H% and fly ball tendency could be a problem, so ERA should stay above 4.00.

Cerda,Jaime

		Tm	W	L	Sv	IP	K	ERA	Br/IP	R$	BF/G	OBA	vL	vR	H%	xERA	RAR	Ctl	Dom	Cmd	hr/9	G/F	S%	BPV	BPX
LH Reliever	99		0	0	0	0	0	0.00	0.00																
AGE 25 Growth	00		0	0	0	0	0	0.00	0.00																
TYPE Power	01	a/a	1	0	3	25	22	3.96	1.20	$3	6.9	238			30%	2.88 +	4.9	2.9	7.9	2.8	0.4		66%	102	196
R Moderate	02	NYM *	5	1	1	77	63	1.99	1.13	$12	5.4	205			27%	1.86	32.2	3.6	7.4	2.0	0.0	0.90	80%	101	191
I EXP con	03	NYM *	4	1	0	64	48	3.93	1.48	$3	5.8	264	242	276	30%	4.50 -	11.6	4.2	6.7	1.6	1.0	0.80	76%	47	90
S pt stb	1st Half		1	1	0	38	30	4.96	1.52	($1)	6.0	291			33%	5.39	1.6	3.3	7.1	2.1	1.4	0.57	71%	42	81
K	2nd Half		3	0	0	26	18	2.41	1.42	$4	5.4	222			26%	3.20 -	10.0	5.5	6.2	1.1	0.3	1.11	83%	61	118
LIMA B EP: 45%	04	Proj	5	1	0	65	50	4.29	1.32	$4	5.5	234			27%	3.66 +	8.5	4.2	6.9	1.7	1.0	--	70%	56	107

1-1, 5.85 ERA in 32 IP at NYM. Still good skills but a lost year in terms of growth. Despite overall struggles, was solid vs. LH batters, so could fill that role in bullpen.

Chacon,Shawn

		Tm	W	L	Sv	IP	K	ERA	Br/IP	R$	BF/G	OBA	vL	vR	H%	xERA	RAR	Ctl	Dom	Cmd	hr/9	G/F	S%	BPV	BPX
RH Starter	99		0	0	0	0	0	0.00	0.00																
AGE 26 Growth	00	aa	10	10	0	173	152	5.36	1.73	($2)	29.8	295			35%	5.63	9.3	5.0	7.9	1.6	1.0		70%	46	108
TYPE Power	01	COL *	8	10	0	184	159	4.79	1.48	$0	26.1	255	261	259	29%	4.90	14.1	4.6	7.8	1.7	1.5	1.20	72%	41	75
R Moderate	02	COL *	7	11	0	139	80	5.76	1.56	($5)	24.9	274	319	220	28%	5.63	-12.2	4.5	5.2	1.2	1.9	1.18	68%	-1	-1
I EXP con	03	COL	11	8	0	137	93	4.60	1.33	$9	25.3	243	254	230	28%	3.66 +	12.5	3.8	6.1	1.6	0.8	0.85	66%	53	102
S stb	1st Half		11	4	0	105	72	4.28	1.31	$10	26.2	248			29%	3.60 +	14.0	3.4	6.2	1.8	0.7	0.95	68%	60	115
K brn	2nd Half		0	4	0	32	21	5.64	1.38	($2)	22.9	224			24%	3.87 +	-1.6	5.1	5.9	1.2	1.1	0.59	60%	36	70
LIMA D+ EP: 50%	04	Proj	6	11	0	140	97	5.27	1.46	($1)	25.5	253			27%	4.80	-0.1	4.5	6.2	1.4	1.5	--	68%	25	47

One reason why you shouldn't expect his value to continue going up is his increasing fly ball tendency. Despite this shift, his hr/9 dropped by more than half, which should not happen again in Coors.

Christiansen,Jason

		Tm	W	L	Sv	IP	K	ERA	Br/IP	R$	BF/G	OBA	vL	vR	H%	xERA	RAR	Ctl	Dom	Cmd	hr/9	G/F	S%	BPV	BPX
LH Reliever	99	PIT	2	3	3	37	35	4.14	1.30	$4	4.0	199	205	195	26%	2.40 +	5.5	5.4	8.5	1.6	0.5	1.66	67%	85	185
AGE 34 Decline	00	STL	3	8	1	48	53	5.06	1.42	$2	3.2	232	246	225	32%	3.52 +	3.6	5.1	9.9	2.0	0.6	1.06	63%	92	204
TYPE Power	01	2NL *	2	1	3	44	39	3.07	1.25	$6	3.0	244	254	200	29%	3.70 -	13.5	3.1	8.0	2.6	1.0	1.41	80%	78	145
R High	02	SF	0	1	0	5	1	5.40	1.60	($0)	3.8	299			28%	6.04 -	-0.2	3.6	1.8	0.5	1.8	0.88	71%	-37	
I con	03	SF	0	0	0	26	22	5.19	1.38	($1)	2.8	254	208	273	30%	4.17 +	0.3	3.8	7.6	2.0	1.0	0.87	64%	61	117
S PT STB	1st Half		0	0	0	12	5	5.25	1.42	($1)	3.7	293			33%	3.86 +	0.0	2.3	3.8	1.7	0.0		59%	54	104
K age	2nd Half		0	0	0	14	17	5.14	1.36	($0)	2.3	218			26%	4.44 +	0.3	5.1	10.9	2.1	1.9		69%	64	123
LIMA C+ EP: 70%	04	Proj	3	4	3	50	48	3.96	1.32	$5	3.4	225			28%	3.29 +	8.7	4.5	8.6	1.9	0.7	--	71%	81	155

xERA indicates that he pitched better than ERA shows after coming off of TJ surgery – low strand rate appears to be main culprit. Regained dominance against LH batters, and should be worth a flier come draft day.

Clemens,Roger

		Tm	W	L	Sv	IP	K	ERA	Br/IP	R$	BF/G	OBA	vL	vR	H%	xERA	RAR	Ctl	Dom	Cmd	hr/9	G/F	S%	BPV	BPX
RH Reliever	99	NYY	14	10	0	187	163	4.62	1.47	$12	27.4	260	263	259	31%	4.41	31.3	4.3	7.8	1.8	1.0	1.37	70%	59	149
AGE 41 Decline	00	NYY	13	8	0	204	188	3.70	1.31	$21	27.0	242	206	267	29%	3.92	60.3	3.7	8.3	2.2	1.1	1.08	76%	69	179
TYPE	01	NYY	20	3	0	220	213	3.52	1.26	$25	27.9	248	235	258	31%	3.55	58.0	2.9	8.7	3.0	0.8	1.48	74%	96	193
R Low	02	NYY	13	7	0	187	197	4.24	1.29	$13	26.3	253	220	283	33%	3.83	30.6	3.0	9.5	3.1	0.9	1.26	69%	101	207
I con	03	NYY	17	9	0	211	190	3.92	1.22	$21	26.5	250	215	288	30%	3.73	45.4	2.5	8.1	3.3	1.0	1.05	71%	92	198
S	1st Half		8	5	0	112	119	3.37	1.15	$13	26.8	237			31%	3.24	32.3	2.5	9.6	3.8	0.9	1.05	74%	119	257
K AGE	2nd Half		9	4	0	99	71	4.54	1.29	$8	26.1	265			30%	4.29	13.1	2.5	6.4	2.6	1.2	1.06	68%	60	130
LIMA EP:	04	Proj	0	0	0	0	0	0.00	0.00													--			

Showed no signs of decline at age 40, and if he does retire for good he is certainly walking out on top. Looks like he could go for at least a couple more years at this level.

Clement,Matt

		Tm	W	L	Sv	IP	K	ERA	Br/IP	R$	BF/G	OBA	vL	vR	H%	xERA	RAR	Ctl	Dom	Cmd	hr/9	G/F	S%	BPV	BPX
RH Starter	99	SD	10	12	0	180	135	4.50	1.53	$4	25.9	272	319	235	32%	4.33	17.7	4.3	6.8	1.6	0.9	1.92	72%	47	102
AGE 29 Peak	00	SD	13	17	0	205	170	5.14	1.56	$4	27.0	251	267	227	30%	4.52 +	13.5	5.5	7.5	1.4	1.0	2.06	68%	49	108
TYPE Power	01	FLA	9	10	0	169	134	5.06	1.52	($0)	24.2	265	286	248	31%	4.46 +	7.0	4.5	7.1	1.6	0.8	1.36	67%	54	100
R Low	02	CHC	12	11	0	205	215	3.60	1.20	$17	26.4	219	219	212	28%	2.94 +	41.4	3.7	9.4	2.5	0.8	1.62	72%	97	184
I con	03	CHC	14	12	0	201	171	4.12	1.23	$16	26.1	229	246	209	27%	3.41 +	31.3	3.5	7.6	2.2	1.0	1.75	69%	71	136
S stb	1st Half		5	7	0	91	77	4.94	1.35	$2	25.9	259			30%	4.29 +	4.1	3.3	7.6	2.3	1.2	1.87	66%	62	120
K	2nd Half		9	5	0	110	94	3.43	1.14	$14	26.3	203			24%	2.69 +	27.2	3.8	7.7	2.0	0.8	1.67	72%	79	152
LIMA C EP: 60%	04	Proj	13	12	0	200	177	3.92	1.30	$14	25.5	235			28%	3.52	36.1	3.9	8.0	2.1	0.9	G	72%	72	139

Dom rate tracked back to previous levels, but continued decline in walk rate which bodes well for 2004. With a little luck, will post sub-4 ERA again.

Colome,Jesus

		Tm	W	L	Sv	IP	K	ERA	Br/IP	R$	BF/G	OBA	vL	vR	H%	xERA	RAR	Ctl	Dom	Cmd	hr/9	G/F	S%	BPV	BPX
RH Reliever	99		0	0	0	0	0	0.00	0.00																
AGE 26 Growth	00	aa	10	6	0	125	90	3.67	1.34	$14	23.1	249			29%	3.70	35.0	3.6	6.5	1.8	0.7		74%	60	143
TYPE Power	01	TAM *	2	6	0	65	49	4.43	1.40	$1	6.5	250	186	222	28%	4.38	9.2	4.2	6.8	1.6	1.2	1.37	72%	43	85
R Moderate	02	TAM *	4	9	1	70	58	6.04	1.76	($4)	6.5	281	414	287	33%	5.43 +	-5.5	5.9	7.5	1.3	0.9	1.15	66%	43	88
I EXP con	03	TAM	3	7	2	74	69	4.50	1.55	$1	6.1	248	218	269	30%	4.62	10.2	5.6	8.4	1.5	1.1	0.58	74%	54	117
S pt stb	1st Half		1	3	0	44	42	3.48	1.39	$2	6.8	215			27%	3.51	12.1	5.5	8.6	1.6	0.8	0.42	77%	72	155
K	2nd Half		2	4	2	30	27	6.00	1.80	($1)	5.4	293			34%	6.25	-1.9	5.7	8.1	1.4	1.5	0.88	69%	30	65
LIMA C+ EP: 50%	04	Proj	4	8	2	75	64	5.04	1.60	$0	6.6	264			31%	4.94	5.0	5.3	7.7	1.5	1.1	F	70%	46	99

G/F ratio dropped by half, and this increased FB tendency combined with a high walk rate has some very incendiary possibilities. Until Ctl drops back to '00-01 levels, his role won't expand and you don't want him.

Colon,Bartolo

		Tm	W	L	Sv	IP	K	ERA	Br/IP	R$	BF/G	OBA	vL	vR	H%	xERA	RAR	Ctl	Dom	Cmd	hr/9	G/F	S%	BPV	BPX
RH Starter	99	CLE	18	5	0	205	161	3.95	1.27	$24	26.9	242	255	229	28%	3.78	52.7	3.3	7.1	2.1	1.1	1.52	72%	62	155
AGE 30 Peak	00	CLE	15	8	0	188	212	3.88	1.39	$19	27.0	235	242	225	31%	3.86	51.2	4.7	10.1	2.2	1.0	1.13	75%	84	218
TYPE	01	CLE	14	12	0	222	201	4.09	1.40	$12	28.2	260	278	242	31%	4.32	41.4	3.6	8.1	2.2	1.1	1.15	74%	67	134
R Low	02	2TM	20	8	0	233	149	2.94	1.24	$28	29.4	250	242	261	28%	3.51 -	72.9	2.7	5.8	2.1	0.8	1.37	79%	61	120
I con	03	CHW	15	13	0	242	173	3.87	1.20	$21	29.3	246	250	246	27%	3.74	53.7	2.5	6.4	2.6	1.1	0.81	72%	65	141
S stb	1st Half		6	7	0	122	87	4.20	1.22	$8	29.7	242			27%	3.66 +	21.6	2.9	6.4	2.2	1.0	0.96	68%	61	132
K brn	2nd Half		9	6	0	120	86	3.52	1.17	$14	28.9	250			28%	3.81	32.1	2.1	6.4	3.1	1.2	0.68	75%	72	156
LIMA D EP: 50%	04	Proj	16	10	0	225	169	3.64	1.25	$22	28.4	249			28%	3.82	57.2	2.8	6.8	2.4	1.0	--	75%	65	138

Regained some of the lost dominance of '02 and continued to improve his walk rate. The luck (i.e., inflated strand rate) wasn't there, but the skills were. Only downside is burnout risk – 242 IP is getting up there.

SCOTT MONROE

Condrey,Clayton

Condrey,Clayton	Yr	Tm	W	L	Sv	IP	K	ERA	Br/IP	R$	BF/G	OBA	vL	vR	H%	xERA	RAR	Ctl	Dom	Cmd	hr/9	G/F	S%	BPV	BPX
RH Reliever	99		0	0	0	0	0	0.00	0.00																
AGE 28 Pre-Peak	00	aa	2	2	6	43	19	5.65	1.51	$3	5.4	271			29%	4.37 +	0.6	4.2	4.0	**1.0**	0.6		61%	26	61
TYPE Finesse	01	a/a	3	5	14	87	50	5.79	1.67	$2	6.0	317			35%	5.66	-4.3	3.2	5.2	**1.6**	0.8		65%	32	61
R Very High	02	aaa	11	6	0	159	76	3.74	1.35	$11	19.9	269			29%	3.97	32.7	2.8	4.3	**1.6**	0.7	1.34	73%	39	77
I EXP	03	SD *	4	5	0	97	61	5.94	1.53	($4)	21.6	296	309	302	32%	5.30 +	-8.6	3.1	5.7	**1.8**	1.2	2.17	62%	32	62
S PT STB	1st Half		1	2	0	39	28	7.38	1.69	($5)	18.0	290			32%	6.01 +	-11.0	4.8	6.5	**1.3**	1.6	2.17	58%	15	29
K	2nd Half		3	3	0	58	33	4.97	1.41	$1	25.1	300			33%	4.82	2.4	1.9	5.1	**2.8**	0.9		66%	56	107
LIMA D EP: 55%	04	Proj	**4**	**4**	**0**	**80**	**45**	**5.29**	**1.50**	**($1)**	**12.6**	**290**			**31%**	**4.93**	**-0.3**	**3.2**	**5.1**	**1.6**	**1.0**	**G**	**66%**	**31**	**59**

1-2, 8.47 ERA in 34 IP at SD. Made some gains in 2nd half, but further upside is limited for this soft-tosser. Could make a living as a reliever if he can sustain the Cmd trend. No fantasy value, though.

Contreras,Jose

Contreras,Jose	Yr	Tm	W	L	Sv	IP	K	ERA	Br/IP	R$	BF/G	OBA	vL	vR	H%	xERA	RAR	Ctl	Dom	Cmd	hr/9	G/F	S%	BPV	BPX
RH Starter	99	CUB	0	0	0	0	0	0.00																	
AGE 32 Peak	00	CUB	13	2	0	167	146	1.24										2.8	7.9	**2.8**					
TYPE Power	01	CUB	14	6	0	159	188	3.51										2.5	10.6	**4.2**					
R Low	02	CUB	13	4	0	143	149	1.76										2.6	9.4	**3.6**					
I con	03	NYY *	9	2	0	87	88	2.89	1.14	$14	16.1	209	203	202	28%	2.52	30.8	3.5	9.1	**2.6**	0.5	1.36	76%	107	230
S pt stb	1st Half		5	1	0	41	42	3.27	1.26	$6	12.3	226			30%	2.96	12.5	3.9	9.2	**2.3**	0.4	1.78	74%	101	217
K	2nd Half		4	1	0	46	46	2.55	1.02	$8	22.6	193			25%	2.12	18.3	3.1	9.0	**2.9**	0.6	1.17	77%	113	244
LIMA C+ EP: 55%	04	Proj	**15**	**9**	**0**	**160**	**165**	**3.09**	**1.21**	**$22**	**22.0**	**236**			**31%**	**3.06**	**52.4**	**3.0**	**9.3**	**3.1**	**0.6**	**--**	**75%**	**111**	**238**

From a skills perspective, this debut justified last winter's bidding war. Cuban BPIs held up well in his first exposure to MLB hitters. Assuming good health, he will emerge as an elite-level SP.

Cook,Aaron

Cook,Aaron	Yr	Tm	W	L	Sv	IP	K	ERA	Br/IP	R$	BF/G	OBA	vL	vR	H%	xERA	RAR	Ctl	Dom	Cmd	hr/9	G/F	S%	BPV	BPX
RH Reliever	99		0	0	0	0	0	0.00	0.00																
AGE 25 Growth	00		0	0	0	0	0	0.00	0.00																
TYPE Finesse	01		0	0	0	0	0	0.00	0.00																
R High	02	a/a	13	7	0	194	93	3.29	1.28	$17	24.7	269	295	295	29%	3.99 -	51.4	2.2	4.3	**1.9**	0.9	3.00	77%	41	81
I EXP con	03	COL *	5	7	0	140	53	5.66	1.66	($8)	14.3	303	342	298	32%	5.32	-7.1	3.9	3.4	**0.9**	0.7	2.12	65%	12	23
S pt stb	1st Half		3	7	0	92	37	5.17	1.63	($4)	26.2	295			31%	5.17	1.3	4.0	3.6	**0.9**	0.8	1.88	68%	13	25
K age	2nd Half		2	0	0	48	16	6.59	1.74	($5)	7.7	319			34%	5.61 +	-8.4	3.8	3.0	**0.8**	0.6	2.57	60%	9	18
LIMA C EP: 50%	04	Proj	**9**	**8**	**0**	**160**	**65**	**5.01**	**1.53**	**$0**	**13.7**	**293**			**31%**	**4.79**	**5.5**	**3.2**	**3.7**	**1.1**	**0.7**	**G**	**67%**	**20**	**39**

4-6, 6.02 ERA in 124 IP at COL. Ground-ball pitcher had some success in Triple-A in 2002, but couldn't bring it to COL. Managed to keep his HR total down, but sub-1.0 Cmd is all you need to see.

Cordero,Francisco

Cordero,Francisco	Yr	Tm	W	L	Sv	IP	K	ERA	Br/IP	R$	BF/G	OBA	vL	vR	H%	xERA	RAR	Ctl	Dom	Cmd	hr/9	G/F	S%	BPV	BPX
RH Reliever	99	DET *	6	3	27	71	73	2.03	1.38	$27	4.6	225	133	405	29%	3.41 -	36.5	5.1	9.3	**1.8**	0.6	1.12	88%	85	213
AGE 28 Pre-Peak	00	TEX	1	2	0	77	49	5.37	1.75	($4)	6.4	286	310	271	31%	5.78	5.6	5.6	5.7	**1.0**	1.3	0.79	72%	15	39
TYPE Power	01	TEX	0	1	0	2	1	4.29	2.38	($0)	3.7	336			38%	7.01 -	0.3	8.6	4.3	**0.5**	0.0	0.75	80%	24	48
R High	02	TEX *	2	2	12	57	58	2.84	1.23	$12	4.7	237	189	216	31%	3.23	20.0	3.2	9.2	**2.9**	0.6	1.00	79%	104	214
I CON	03	TEX	5	8	15	82	90	2.96	1.31	$17	4.8	232	236	223	32%	3.17	28.3	4.2	9.9	**2.4**	0.4	1.49	78%	104	225
S PT stb	1st Half		3	6	2	44	47	3.87	1.49	$3	4.9	252			35%	3.67	9.8	4.9	9.6	**2.0**	0.2	1.53	72%	97	210
K	2nd Half		2	2	13	38	43	1.89	1.11	$14	4.6	207			28%	2.59 -	18.5	3.3	10.2	**3.1**	0.7	1.44	87%	118	255
LIMA B EP: 55%	04	Proj	**4**	**4**	**35**	**75**	**80**	**2.88**	**1.28**	**$28**	**4.8**	**238**			**31%**	**3.42 -**	**26.7**	**3.6**	**9.6**	**2.7**	**0.7**	**--**	**80%**	**99**	**213**

TEX could have handed him the closer role last winter, but instead brought in Urbina for half a season. BPIs are clearly closer-worthy, and he only got better when he resumed closer role in 2nd half. This is a stud.

Corey,Mark

Corey,Mark	Yr	Tm	W	L	Sv	IP	K	ERA	Br/IP	R$	BF/G	OBA	vL	vR	H%	xERA	RAR	Ctl	Dom	Cmd	hr/9	G/F	S%	BPV	BPX
RH Reliever	99	aa	7	13	0	155	91	6.74	1.77	($12)	25.1	322			35%	6.08 +	-25.0	3.9	5.3	**1.4**	1.1		62%	18	41
AGE 29 Pre-Peak	00	a/a	3	7	1	89	49	6.17	1.73	($5)	12.2	307			33%	6.00	-4.9	4.3	5.0	**1.1**	1.2		65%	11	26
TYPE Power	01	a/a	9	4	27	73	73	2.47	1.45	$26	5.8	237			32%	3.39 -	28.9	5.2	9.0	**1.7**	0.2	1.50	83%	91	174
R X HIGH	02	COL *	3	4	7	48	50	4.69	1.50	$4	4.2	266			32%	4.96	2.7	4.3	9.4	**2.2**	1.5	0.96	73%	59	111
I EXP CON	03	PIT *	2	5	30	75	77	5.86	1.41	$14	4.8	264	316	221	33%	4.26 +	-5.8	3.6	9.2	**2.6**	1.0	0.75	58%	83	159
S PT STB	1st Half		1	3	23	34	36	7.13	1.67	$9	4.5	299			38%	5.53 +	-8.4	4.2	9.5	**2.3**	1.1		57%	68	130
K	2nd Half		1	2	7	41	41	4.81	1.19	$5	5.1	232			29%	3.21 +	2.6	3.1	9.0	**2.9**	0.9		60%	98	188
LIMA B EP: 75%	04	Proj	**4**	**5**	**6**	**75**	**73**	**4.08**	**1.47**	**$6**	**5.1**	**264**			**33%**	**4.40**	**11.9**	**4.1**	**8.8**	**2.1**	**1.0**	**F**	**75%**	**71**	**137**

1-2, 5.34 ERA in 30 IP at PIT. Consistently high Dom level, improving Ctl is driving Cmd growth. Would be on everyone's sleeper list if not for the ridiculously low S%. Note 2nd-half xERA..

Cormier,Rheal

Cormier,Rheal	Yr	Tm	W	L	Sv	IP	K	ERA	Br/IP	R$	BF/G	OBA	vL	vR	H%	xERA	RAR	Ctl	Dom	Cmd	hr/9	G/F	S%	BPV	BPX
LH Reliever	99	BOS	2	0	0	63	39	3.71	1.25	$5	4.4	256	198	276	29%	3.47	18.2	2.6	5.6	**2.2**	0.6	1.61	71%	66	165
AGE 37 Decline	00	BOS	3	3	0	68	43	4.63	1.34	$4	4.5	278	264	280	31%	4.28	11.7	2.2	5.7	**2.5**	0.9	1.49	67%	59	153
TYPE	01	PHI	5	6	1	51	37	4.23	1.29	$5	3.6	254	294	223	29%	3.82	7.8	3.0	6.5	**2.2**	0.9	2.05	69%	63	116
R Low	02	PHI	5	6	0	60	49	5.25	1.55	$0	5.0	265	291	253	31%	4.53 +	-1.2	4.8	7.4	**1.5**	0.9	2.63	67%	51	97
I con	03	PHI	8	0	1	84	67	1.82	0.95	$19	5.0	188	119	207	23%	1.69	39.0	2.7	7.2	**2.7**	0.4	1.79	83%	104	200
S pt stb	1st Half		2	0	0	38	33	1.65	0.97	$7	4.6	176			23%	1.41	18.6	3.3	7.8	**2.4**	0.2	2.28	83%	109	210
K AGE	2nd Half		6	0	1	46	34	1.96	0.93	$12	5.4	198			23%	1.92	20.5	2.2	6.7	**3.1**	0.6	1.49	83%	103	197
LIMA C EP: 35%	04	Proj	**6**	**3**	**1**	**70**	**54**	**3.34**	**1.19**	**$9**	**4.7**	**227**			**27%**	**2.92**	**18.0**	**3.2**	**6.9**	**2.2**	**0.6**	**G**	**73%**	**77**	**149**

Sure, some of this surge was rooted in improved BPIs, specifically better Ctl and hr/9. But the anomalous H% and S% had an awful lot to do with it as well. He'll never see these ERA or WHIP levels again.

Cornejo,Nate

Cornejo,Nate	Yr	Tm	W	L	Sv	IP	K	ERA	Br/IP	R$	BF/G	OBA	vL	vR	H%	xERA	RAR	Ctl	Dom	Cmd	hr/9	G/F	S%	BPV	BPX
RH Starter	99		0	0	0	0	0	0.00	0.00																
AGE 24 Growth	00	aa	5	7	0	91	51	5.34	1.54	$1	25.4	282			32%	4.47 +	5.1	3.9	5.0	**1.3**	0.5		64%	41	98
TYPE Finesse	01	a/a	16	3	0	154	108	2.98	1.23	$22	27.8	253			29%	3.50 -	50.3	2.5	6.3	**2.5**	0.7	1.79	78%	74	142
R Very High	02	DET *	10	13	0	182	101	5.34	1.64	($4)	27.6	328	273	337	36%	5.79	2.9	2.3	5.0	**2.1**	0.8	2.23	67%	41	83
I EXP CON	03	DET	6	17	0	194	46	4.63	1.51	($1)	26.9	301	309	305	30%	5.09	23.2	2.7	2.1	**0.8**	0.8	1.43	70%	-1	-2
S pt stb	1st Half		3	6	0	92	17	4.40	1.51	$0	25.5	301			29%	5.31 -	13.9	2.6	1.7	**0.6**	1.1	1.36	73%	-14	-31
K age	2nd Half		3	11	0	102	29	4.85	1.52	($1)	28.3	301			31%	4.89	9.3	2.7	2.6	**0.9**	0.6	1.51	68%	11	24
LIMA F EP: 45%	04	Proj	**10**	**15**	**0**	**200**	**84**	**4.64**	**1.51**	**$3**	**26.8**	**299**			**32%**	**4.95**	**24.2**	**2.7**	**3.8**	**1.4**	**0.8**	**--**	**70%**	**24**	**52**

The three-year deterioration of his Dom is fascinating for a (reportedly healthy) pitcher of his age. Two years ago, this was an intriguing skill set. Now, the plummeting Dom and sub-1.0 Cmd send a clear message.

Cressend,Jack

Cressend,Jack	Yr	Tm	W	L	Sv	IP	K	ERA	Br/IP	R$	BF/G	OBA	vL	vR	H%	xERA	RAR	Ctl	Dom	Cmd	hr/9	G/F	S%	BPV	BPX
RH Reliever	99	aa	8	10	0	160	116	6.02	1.68	($6)	26.3	313			36%	5.37 +	-10.5	3.5	6.5	**1.9**	0.8		63%	47	109
AGE 28 Pre-Peak	00	MIN *	4	4	8	100	79	4.32	1.63	$6	7.0	297			36%	4.84 -	21.3	4.0	7.1	**1.8**	0.5	1.83	73%	63	162
TYPE	01	MIN *	5	4	1	74	48	3.77	1.30	$7	5.6	259	294	198	29%	4.00	17.0	2.8	5.8	**2.1**	1.0	1.56	74%	53	106
R Very High	02	MIN	0	1	0	32	22	5.91	1.84	($4)	6.6	307	355	261	33%	6.80 -	-1.9	5.3	6.2	**1.2**	1.7	0.79	72%	4	9
I EXP CON	03	CLE *	5	1	1	73	44	1.97	1.24	$11	6.2	256	253	250	30%	3.05 -	34.9	2.5	5.4	**2.2**	0.1	0.64	83%	79	170
S PT stb	1st Half		3	0	1	30	16	1.19	1.39	$6	8.1	267			31%	3.47 -	17.5	3.3	4.8	**1.5**	0.0		90%	61	131
K	2nd Half		2	1	0	43	28	2.51	1.14	$6	5.3	248			29%	2.76	17.4	1.9	5.9	**3.1**	0.2		77%	100	215
LIMA C+ EP: 35%	04	Proj	**3**	**2**	**1**	**70**	**45**	**3.60**	**1.31**	**$5**	**6.3**	**265**			**30%**	**3.83**	**18.2**	**2.7**	**5.8**	**2.1**	**0.6**	**F**	**74%**	**63**	**134**

2-1-2.51 in 43 IP at CLE. Nice comeback from shoulder surgery. BPIs are similar to '01, which implies that '02 was tainted by injury. Gains in S% and hr/9 saved ERA. Set your expectations against 2001.

Cruz,Juan

Cruz,Juan	Yr	Tm	W	L	Sv	IP	K	ERA	Br/IP	R$	BF/G	OBA	vL	vR	H%	xERA	RAR	Ctl	Dom	Cmd	hr/9	G/F	S%	BPV	BPX
RH Reliever	99		0	0	0	0	0	0.00	0.00																
AGE 25 Growth	00		0	0	0	0	0	0.00	0.00																
TYPE Power	01	CHC *	12	7	0	166	163	3.90	1.34	$12	22.8	243			31%	3.51	32.5	4.0	8.8	**2.2**	0.6		71%	88	164
R Moderate	02	CHC	3	11	1	97	81	3.99	1.47	$1	9.5	235	250	234	27%	4.05	14.5	5.5	7.5	**1.4**	1.0	1.16	76%	51	97
I EXP con	03	CHC *	6	7	0	111	106	4.37	1.31	$5	13.8	254	292	265	32%	3.62 +	13.5	3.2	8.6	**2.7**	0.6	1.17	67%	93	179
S pt	1st Half		3	3	0	46	48	4.66	1.27	$3	9.3	234			31%	3.18 +	3.9	3.7	9.3	**2.5**	0.6		63%	100	192
K	2nd Half		3	4	0	65	58	4.17	1.34	$3	21.2	268			33%	3.93	9.6	2.8	8.1	**2.9**	0.7		70%	90	173
LIMA C+ EP: 65%	04	Proj	**10**	**8**	**1**	**140**	**128**	**3.92**	**1.33**	**$11**	**12.4**	**242**			**30%**	**3.58**	**25.2**	**3.9**	**8.2**	**2.1**	**0.8**	**--**	**72%**	**78**	**150**

2-7-6.05 in 61 IP at CHC. Was lights-out in Triple-A (1.95 ERA, 4.3 Cmd) after getting sent down in June, and brought that improvement back to Chicago when recalled.
UP: 14 wins, 3.60 ERA.

RAY MURPHY

Cruz,Nelson

Profile	Yr	Tm	W	L	Sv	IP	K	ERA	Br/IP	R$	BF/G	OBA	vL	vR	H%	xERA	RAR	Ctl	Dom	Cmd	hr/9	G/F	S%	BPV	BPX
RH Reliever	99	DET	* 9	6	0	128	84	4.71	1.37	$9	14.1	265	302	263	29%	4.46	19.9	3.2	5.9	**1.9**	1.2		68%	41	102
AGE 31 Peak	00	DET	* 7	6	0	93	67	4.35	1.35	$9	10.5	272	236	268	31%	4.45	19.5	2.7	6.5	**2.4**	1.2	1.32	71%	55	143
TYPE	01	HOU	3	3	2	82	75	4.17	1.17	$6	5.1	237	273	209	28%	3.58 +	13.2	2.6	8.2	**3.1**	1.2	0.82	68%	86	160
R X HIGH	02	HOU	* 2	7	1	86	67	4.81	1.50	($2)	7.8	284	299	272	32%	5.30	3.4	3.5	7.0	**2.0**	1.6	1.02	73%	36	68
I exp CON	03	COL	* 4	7	0	68	47	7.92	1.61	($7)	12.9	333	308	295	34%	7.45	-24.1	1.8	6.2	**3.4**	2.6	1.16	56%	17	33
S PT stb	1st Half		3	4	0	50	33	6.48	1.38	($1)	14.3	295			30%	5.81 +	-8.0	1.8	5.9	**3.3**	2.2	1.09	58%	36	70
K	2nd Half		1	3	0	18	14	11.87	2.25	($6)	10.5	419			44%	11.95	-16.1	2.0	6.9	**3.5**	4.0	5.00	52%	-32	-62
LIMA C+ EP: 60%	04	Proj	**4**	**7**	**0**	**75**	**57**	**4.92**	**1.44**	**$1**	**8.6**	**291**			**32%**	**5.42 -**	**3.5**	**2.5**	**6.8**	**2.7**	**1.7**	**--**	**71%**	**44**	**86**

3-5, 7.21 in 54 IP at COL. Has always had problems with hr/9, but 2003 was ridiculous. Makes you wonder why COL ever thought he would be good for them. Would be serviceable in a low-altitude park.

Cunnane,Will

Profile	Yr	Tm	W	L	Sv	IP	K	ERA	Br/IP	R$	BF/G	OBA	vL	vR	H%	xERA	RAR	Ctl	Dom	Cmd	hr/9	G/F	S%	BPV	BPX
RH Reliever	99	SD	* 4	2	11	67	66	2.96	1.36	$13	5.5	256	421	231	32%	3.81 -	20.5	3.5	8.9	**2.5**	1.1	1.09	83%	78	170
AGE 30 Peak	00	SD	* 8	5	0	135	112	4.39	1.40	$8	13.3	270	243	239	33%	4.03	22.4	3.2	7.5	**2.3**	0.6	1.46	68%	77	169
TYPE Power	01	MIL	* 0	4	1	74	58	5.35	1.66	($6)	8.9	313	295	336	37%	5.70	0.1	3.4	7.1	**2.1**	1.0	1.29	69%	49	91
R X HIGH	02	CHC	* 5	2	2	99	87	3.09	1.37	$7	7.2	264			32%	3.90 -	26.7	3.3	7.9	**2.4**	0.7	1.22	80%	79	149
I EXP CON	03	ATL	* 3	3	5	57	47	1.73	1.16	$11	5.0	233	200	182	29%	2.64 -	27.1	2.7	7.4	**2.8**	0.3	1.11	86%	101	195
S PT STB	1st Half		0	1	0	16	13	2.80	1.86	($1)	6.4	316			39%	5.32 -	5.4	5.0	7.3	**1.4**	0.0		83%	66	126
K	2nd Half		3	2	5	41	34	1.32	0.88	$12	4.4	195			24%	1.59	21.8	1.8	7.5	**4.3**	0.4		88%	137	263
LIMA B+ EP: 35%	04	Proj	**2**	**3**	**3**	**60**	**50**	**3.45**	**1.37**	**$4**	**6.3**	**265**			**32%**	**3.83**	**14.6**	**3.2**	**7.5**	**2.4**	**0.6**	**--**	**76%**	**79**	**152**

2-2, 2.70 ERA, 3 Sv in 20 IP at ATL. Seemed like ATL's latest successful bullpen reclamation project. In fact, he's shown a nice skill set for the last 5 years. It's just that most of that work has been in the minors.

D'Amico,Jeff

Profile	Yr	Tm	W	L	Sv	IP	K	ERA	Br/IP	R$	BF/G	OBA	vL	vR	H%	xERA	RAR	Ctl	Dom	Cmd	hr/9	G/F	S%	BPV	BPX
RH Starter	99	MIL	* 0	0	0	6	4	19.50	2.67	($4)	11.2	434			48%	10.71 +	-11.5	4.5	6.0	**1.3**	1.5	1.00	20%	-13	-28
AGE 28 Pre-Peak	00	MIL	* 13	8	0	193	118	2.75	1.16	$27	27.2	237	242	234	26%	3.28 -	74.5	2.6	5.5	**2.1**	0.9	1.03	81%	58	129
TYPE Finesse	01	MIL	2	4	0	47	32	6.11	1.61	($3)	21.4	311	333	289	33%	6.62 -	-4.7	3.1	6.1	**2.0**	2.1	0.60	68%	8	16
R Very High	02	NYM	6	10	0	145	101	4.97	1.30	$2	21.1	271	249	283	30%	4.32 +	2.7	2.3	6.3	**2.7**	1.2	0.82	64%	58	111
I CON	03	PIT	9	16	0	175	100	4.78	1.40	$3	26.1	292	293	290	31%	4.92	11.7	2.2	5.1	**2.4**	1.2	0.85	69%	42	81
S PT stb	1st Half		5	8	0	83	45	4.22	1.30	$5	25.1	277			30%	4.34	11.8	1.9	4.9	**2.5**	1.1	1.01	70%	49	94
K	2nd Half		4	8	0	92	55	5.29	1.50	($2)	27.1	305			33%	5.45	-0.1	2.4	5.4	**2.3**	1.3	0.72	67%	36	70
LIMA C+ EP: 50%	04	Proj	**8**	**13**	**0**	**160**	**100**	**4.56**	**1.39**	**$4**	**23.8**	**286**			**31%**	**4.87**	**15.2**	**2.4**	**5.6**	**2.4**	**1.3**	**--**	**71%**	**43**	**82**

Continues to display solid Cmd levels. Luck had a lot to do with his 2000 "breakout". A repeat of those H% and S% numbers is the only way he can be league-average or better. Don't bet on that.

Daal,Omar

Profile	Yr	Tm	W	L	Sv	IP	K	ERA	Br/IP	R$	BF/G	OBA	vL	vR	H%	xERA	RAR	Ctl	Dom	Cmd	hr/9	G/F	S%	BPV	BPX
LH Starter	99	ARI	16	9	0	214	148	3.66	1.25	$22	27.9	238	204	242	27%	3.13 +	45.2	3.3	6.2	**1.9**	0.9	1.26	73%	58	125
AGE 32 Peak	00	2NL	4	19	0	167	96	6.14	1.68	($11)	24.0	306	298	307	33%	6.05	-11.5	3.9	5.2	**1.3**	1.4	1.33	65%	11	24
TYPE	01	PHI	13	7	0	185	107	4.47	1.38	$9	24.9	276	214	286	29%	4.71	22.2	2.7	5.2	**1.9**	1.3	1.17	71%	33	62
R High	02	LA	11	9	0	161	105	3.91	1.22	$13	17.1	238	243	237	26%	3.55	25.7	3.0	5.9	**1.9**	1.1	1.08	72%	50	94
I CON	03	BAL	4	11	0	93	53	6.37	1.76	($8)	23.0	338	312	350	37%	6.48	-10.6	2.9	5.1	**1.8**	1.1	1.28	64%	23	51
S pt STB	1st Half		4	10	0	86	49	5.86	1.67	($5)	24.7	327			36%	5.98	-3.9	2.7	5.1	**1.9**	0.9	1.22	65%	32	68
K	2nd Half		0	1	0	7	4	12.50	2.78	($4)	13.7	441			46%	12.48	-6.7	5.0	5.0	**1.0**	2.5	2.17	56%	-57	-123
LIMA D EP: 60%	04	Proj	**8**	**11**	**0**	**140**	**84**	**4.95**	**1.46**	**$3**	**22.7**	**286**			**31%**	**4.94**	**11.0**	**3.0**	**5.4**	**1.8**	**1.1**	**--**	**68%**	**35**	**75**

Abnormally low H% kept 2002 ERA down, but gave that back, and more, in '03. Looking at the BPIs, we wouldn't expect an ERA difference of 2.54 between '02 and '03. Reality, of course, lies somewhere in between.

Davis,Doug

Profile	Yr	Tm	W	L	Sv	IP	K	ERA	Br/IP	R$	BF/G	OBA	vL	vR	H%	xERA	RAR	Ctl	Dom	Cmd	hr/9	G/F	S%	BPV	BPX
LH Starter	99	a/a	11	4	0	152	129	3.43	1.45	$13	26.6	279			33%	4.44 -	42.7	3.3	7.6	**2.3**	0.9	0.75	80%	66	153
AGE 28 Pre-Peak	00	TEX	* 15	9	0	167	113	4.62	1.62	$9	18.1	277	314	280	30%	5.34 -	28.9	4.9	6.1	**1.2**	1.3	1.22	75%	23	61
TYPE	01	TEX	* 13	10	0	201	128	4.39	1.52	$6	27.9	290	307	291	33%	4.72	29.5	3.3	5.7	**1.8**	0.7	1.25	71%	48	96
R X HIGH	02	TEX	* 7	8	0	120	68	5.48	1.51	($1)	28.0	304	243	312	33%	5.32	-0.3	2.5	5.1	**2.1**	1.1	0.95	65%	37	75
I EXP CON	03	MIL	* 12	10	0	177	93	4.47	1.57	$3	25.7	297	293	283	32%	5.40 -	19.2	3.4	4.7	**1.4**	1.2	0.96	75%	18	35
S PT stb	1st Half		7	5	0	80	38	5.05	1.66	$0	22.9	313			33%	6.04 -	2.5	3.4	4.3	**1.3**	1.3	0.96	73%	4	8
K brn	2nd Half		5	5	0	97	55	3.99	1.49	$3	28.5	283			31%	4.86 -	16.7	3.4	5.1	**1.5**	1.0	0.97	76%	30	57
LIMA C+ EP: 40%	04	Proj	**8**	**10**	**0**	**140**	**81**	**4.63**	**1.54**	**$1**	**26.0**	**295**			**32%**	**5.11**	**11.9**	**3.2**	**5.2**	**1.6**	**1.0**	**--**	**72%**	**30**	**59**

7-8, 4.03 ERA in 109 IP at TEX/MIL/TOR. He may have figured something out in MIL:

	ERA	Ctl	Dom	Cmd	hr/9
AL	5.37	4.7	4.2	0.9	1.3
MIL	2.58	3.6	6.0	1.7	1.4

But 1.7 Cmd isn't overwhelming.

Davis,Jason

Profile	Yr	Tm	W	L	Sv	IP	K	ERA	Br/IP	R$	BF/G	OBA	vL	vR	H%	xERA	RAR	Ctl	Dom	Cmd	hr/9	G/F	S%	BPV	BPX
RH Starter	99		0	0	0	0	0	0.00	0.00																
AGE 23 Growth	00		0	0	0	0	0	0.00	0.00																
TYPE Finesse	01		0	0	0	0	0	0.00	0.00																
R X HIGH	02	aa	6	2	0	59	39	4.58	1.56	$2	26.4	311			36%	4.90	5.5	2.6	5.9	**2.3**	0.5		70%	63	124
I EXP con	03	CLE	8	11	0	165	85	4.69	1.33	$6	26.0	270	259	289	28%	4.63	18.5	2.6	4.6	**1.8**	1.4	1.28	69%	26	56
S pt stb	1st Half		7	6	0	97	52	4.54	1.34	$6	25.8	273			29%	4.65	12.8	2.5	4.8	**1.9**	1.3	1.24	70%	31	66
K age BRN	2nd Half		1	5	0	68	33	4.90	1.31	$0	26.1	265			27%	4.60	5.7	2.6	4.4	**1.7**	1.5	1.33	67%	19	42
LIMA C EP: 50%	04	Proj	**8**	**13**	**0**	**180**	**102**	**4.70**	**1.42**	**$4**	**26.0**	**286**			**31%**	**4.73**	**20.2**	**2.6**	**5.1**	**2.0**	**1.0**	**--**	**69%**	**40**	**85**

BPIs suffered predictably as he made the jump from Double-A to CLE. 2nd half was marginally worse than the first, so chances are good that there are more struggles to come.

Day,Zach

Profile	Yr	Tm	W	L	Sv	IP	K	ERA	Br/IP	R$	BF/G	OBA	vL	vR	H%	xERA	RAR	Ctl	Dom	Cmd	hr/9	G/F	S%	BPV	BPX
RH Starter	99		0	0	0	0	0	0.00	0.00																
AGE 25 Growth	00	aa	4	2	0	46	37	4.30	1.39	$4	24.8	253			32%	3.39 +	9.0	3.9	7.2	**1.9**	0.2		67%	81	191
TYPE	01	a/a	12	12	0	169	94	4.74	1.47	$5	25.6	287			32%	4.52	15.4	3.0	5.0	**1.7**	0.6		67%	44	84
R Very High	02	MON	* 9	7	1	127	83	4.32	1.31	$8	14.9	249	158	244	29%	3.49 +	13.3	3.4	5.9	**1.7**	0.6	3.14	67%	58	109
I EXP CON	03	MON	9	8	0	131	61	4.19	1.46	$6	24.9	263	282	244	29%	4.05	19.2	4.1	4.2	**1.0**	0.5	2.58	71%	33	63
S PT stb	1st Half		4	3	0	65	30	3.46	1.40	$4	25.6	243			27%	3.51	15.9	4.4	4.1	**0.9**	0.4	3.21	75%	38	74
K	2nd Half		5	5	0	66	31	4.91	1.52	$1	24.4	282			30%	4.58	3.3	3.7	4.2	**1.1**	0.7	2.11	67%	28	53
LIMA C EP: 45%	04	Proj	**12**	**10**	**0**	**160**	**90**	**4.39**	**1.42**	**$8**	**21.7**	**264**			**30%**	**3.94**	**18.8**	**3.7**	**5.1**	**1.4**	**0.6**	**G**	**69%**	**45**	**86**

Battled blisters, bad knee, and partial rotator cuff tear in 2003. It's a reasonable hypothesis that Dom decline was injury-related. If he can get the Dom back up and maintain the G/F ratio, he'd be on to something.

de los Santos,Valerio

Profile	Yr	Tm	W	L	Sv	IP	K	ERA	Br/IP	R$	BF/G	OBA	vL	vR	H%	xERA	RAR	Ctl	Dom	Cmd	hr/9	G/F	S%	BPV	BPX
LH Reliever	99	MIL	0	1	0	8	5	6.75	2.38	($2)	6.1	347			39%	7.86 -	-1.6	7.9	5.6	**0.7**	1.1	0.43	72%	1	1
AGE 31 Peak	00	MIL	2	3	0	73	70	5.16	1.43	($0)	4.8	259	273	243	29%	5.12	4.6	4.1	8.6	**2.1**	1.8	0.73	70%	44	97
TYPE Power	01	MIL	0	0	0	1	1	9.00	2.00	($0)	4.9	262			35%	4.86 +	-0.5	9.0	9.0	**1.0**	0.0		50%	78	144
R Moderate	02	MIL	2	3	0	57	38	3.16	1.19	$4	4.6	207			24%	2.65 +	14.9	4.1	6.0	**1.5**	0.6	0.57	75%	61	116
I CON	03	2NL	4	3	1	52	39	4.50	1.35	$4	4.3	235	267	228	26%	4.15	5.4	4.3	6.8	**1.6**	1.4	1.09	71%	40	76
S PT stb	1st Half		0	2	1	23	15	4.30	1.26	$1	4.4	253			24%	5.09 -	3.0	2.7	5.9	**2.1**	2.3	0.93	78%	14	27
K	2nd Half		4	1	0	29	24	4.66	1.41	$3	4.3	220			27%	3.41 +	2.4	5.6	7.4	**1.3**	0.6	1.26	67%	65	125
LIMA B EP: 45%	04	Proj	**3**	**3**	**1**	**60**	**45**	**3.90**	**1.30**	**$4**	**4.5**	**228**			**27%**	**3.32 +**	**11.0**	**4.2**	**6.8**	**1.6**	**0.8**	**--**	**71%**	**61**	**118**

Elevated hr/9 was almost entirely due to 5 HR allowed in April, before he hit the DL with shoulder tendonitis. Upon his return, gopheritis was cured, but his Cmd fell apart. Should bounce back if healthy.

DeJean,Mike

Profile	Yr	Tm	W	L	Sv	IP	K	ERA	Br/IP	R$	BF/G	OBA	vL	vR	H%	xERA	RAR	Ctl	Dom	Cmd	hr/9	G/F	S%	BPV	BPX
RH Reliever	99	COL	2	4	0	61	31	8.41	1.89	($11)	5.2	325	376	310	33%	7.01 +	-25.9	4.7	4.6	**1.0**	1.9	1.42	57%	-20	-43
AGE 33 Past	00	COL	4	4	0	53	34	4.92	1.58	$1	4.4	265	293	254	28%	5.31	5.1	5.1	5.8	**1.1**	1.5	1.10	73%	15	32
TYPE Power	01	MIL	4	2	2	84	68	2.78	1.36	$8	4.8	240	227	242	30%	3.37 -	29.1	4.2	7.3	**1.7**	0.4	1.41	80%	74	138
R Moderate	02	MIL	1	5	27	75	65	3.12	1.40	$17	4.8	238	259	213	29%	3.73 -	20.0	4.7	7.8	**1.7**	0.8	1.71	81%	64	121
I CON	03	2NL	5	8	19	82	71	4.71	1.52	$11	4.8	271	329	216	31%	5.10	6.3	4.3	7.8	**1.8**	1.4	1.58	73%	43	83
S pt stb	1st Half		2	5	16	40	32	4.50	1.50	$9	4.8	281			32%	5.13 -	4.2	3.6	7.2	**2.0**	1.4	1.93	74%	44	84
K age	2nd Half		3	3	3	42	39	4.91	1.54	$2	4.8	261			30%	5.07	2.1	4.9	8.3	**1.7**	1.5	1.30	72%	44	84
LIMA D+ EP: 50%	04	Proj	**4**	**6**	**5**	**75**	**62**	**4.20**	**1.48**	**$5**	**4.8**	**259**			**30%**	**4.60**	**10.7**	**4.4**	**7.4**	**1.7**	**1.2**	**G**	**75%**	**47**	**91**

Suddenly developed a complete an utter inability to retire LH batters (984 OPS allowed, vs. 636 OPS to RH batters). If this continues, will likely relegate him to situational roles for the rest of his career.

RAY MURPHY

Dempster,Ryan

RH Starter | AGE 26 Growth | TYPE Power
R: High | I: con | S: pt, stb | K: BRN
LIMA D | EP: 60%

Yr	Tm	W	L	Sv	IP	K	ERA	Br/IP	R$	BF/G	OBA	vL	vR	H%	xERA	RAR	Ctl	Dom	Cmd	hr/9	G/F	S%	BPV	BPX
99	FLA	* 8	9	0	177	152	4.78	1.58	($1)	26.5	262	282	243	30%	4.68	10.8	5.2	7.7	1.5	1.3	1.15	73%	41	88
00	FLA	14	10	0	226	209	3.66	1.36	$19	29.3	248	249	239	30%	4.18 -	59.5	3.9	8.3	2.2	1.2	1.08	78%	65	143
01	FLA	15	12	0	211	171	4.95	1.56	$3	27.8	268	270	269	32%	4.70	11.9	4.8	7.3	1.5	0.9	1.22	69%	50	93
02	2NL	10	13	0	209	153	5.38	1.54	($5)	28.2	279	332	248	33%	4.50 +	-7.7	4.0	6.6	1.6	0.7	1.10	64%	53	99
03	CIN	3	7	0	115	84	6.56	1.77	($13)	24.6	292	300	288	33%	5.74 +	-19.8	5.5	6.6	1.2	1.1	1.10	63%	28	55
1st Half		2	4	0	84	59	6.21	1.70	($8)	24.3	266			31%	4.88 +	-10.5	6.1	6.3	1.0	0.8	1.02	63%	39	75
2nd Half		1	3	0	31	25	7.50	1.96	($5)	25.4	353			39%	8.07 -	-9.3	3.7	7.2	1.9	2.0	1.33	65%	7	14
04	Proj	2	3	0	40	31	5.85	1.70	($3)	23.1	299			34%	5.66	-3.1	4.5	7.0	1.6	1.1	--	67%	36	69

Early career workload abuse led to Tommy John surgery, which will cause him to miss most of 2004. Four year trend of declining control and dominance casts doubt upon his effectiveness when he returns.

Dessens,Elmer

RH Starter | AGE 32 Peak | TYPE Finesse
R: Low | I: con | S: pt, stb | K:
LIMA D | EP: 55%

Yr	Tm	W	L	Sv	IP	K	ERA	Br/IP	R$	BF/G	OBA	vL	vR	H%	xERA	RAR	Ctl	Dom	Cmd	hr/9	G/F	S%	BPV	BPX
99	JPN	0	1	0	16	6	3.94	1.75	($1)	9.3	347			36%	6.47 -	3.4	2.3	3.4	1.5	1.1		81%	4	8
00	CIN	* 13	5	1	169	97	4.20	1.46	$12	16.8	292	328	269	33%	4.51	32.4	2.7	5.2	1.9	0.6	1.84	71%	51	112
01	CIN	10	14	0	205	128	4.48	1.35	$7	25.8	277	325	239	30%	4.79	24.4	2.5	5.6	2.3	1.4	1.27	71%	39	73
02	CIN	7	8	0	178	93	3.03	1.25	$13	24.7	256	244	268	27%	3.97 -	49.4	2.5	4.7	1.9	1.2	1.48	82%	35	67
03	ARI	8	8	0	175	113	5.09	1.54	($2)	23.0	300	364	242	33%	5.32	4.5	2.9	5.8	2.0	1.1	1.39	69%	38	72
1st Half		5	4	0	101	60	5.08	1.56	($2)	25.2	300			32%	5.75 -	2.7	3.2	5.3	1.7	1.5	1.26	72%	17	32
2nd Half		3	4	0	74	53	5.09	1.50	($1)	20.5	301			35%	4.73	1.8	2.5	6.4	2.5	0.6	1.58	65%	68	131
04	Proj	7	8	0	160	98	4.39	1.42	$3	23.1	285			31%	4.71	18.8	2.6	5.5	2.1	1.1	--	72%	43	83

65% strand rate and 35% hit rate masked second half growth. Note the rising Dom and Cmd and improved hr/9. Should rebound, although won't repeat his fine 2002.

Dickey,R.A.

RH Reliever | AGE 29 Peak | TYPE
R: High | I: EXP, con | S: pt, stb | K:
LIMA C+ | EP: 50%

Yr	Tm	W	L	Sv	IP	K	ERA	Br/IP	R$	BF/G	OBA	vL	vR	H%	xERA	RAR	Ctl	Dom	Cmd	hr/9	G/F	S%	BPV	BPX
99	a/a	8	9	10	118	64	5.64	1.65	$5	13.2	309			33%	5.75	-1.8	3.5	4.9	1.4	1.3		68%	13	30
00	aaa	8	9	1	158	74	5.75	1.67	($3)	24.2	310			33%	5.62	0.2	3.6	4.2	1.2	0.9		66%	15	36
01	aaa	11	7	0	163	104	4.91	1.48	$4	29.9	300			33%	5.12	11.1	2.4	5.7	2.4	1.0	0.88	68%	48	91
02	aaa	8	7	0	154	90	4.79	1.62	($2)	18.9	319			36%	5.19	9.9	2.7	5.3	2.0	0.5		69%	50	98
03	TEX	* 10	9	1	131	97	4.73	1.48	$5	14.1	293	279	307	33%	5.14	13.9	2.8	6.7	2.4	1.2	0.96	71%	51	110
1st Half		4	4	0	51	35	4.24	1.67	$1	9.7	308			36%	5.42 -	8.8	3.7	6.2	1.7	0.7	1.12	75%	44	96
2nd Half		6	5	1	80	62	5.05	1.36	$4	20.2	282			32%	4.96	5.1	2.2	7.0	3.1	1.5	0.90	67%	62	133
04	Proj	5	5	1	80	53	4.84	1.54	$2	17.0	303			34%	5.30	7.5	2.8	6.0	2.1	1.0	--	70%	44	95

9-8, 5.09 ERA in 117 IP at TEX. Excellent Cmd could eventually lead to success but must keep the ball in the park. G/F ratio got worse in second half, so don't bet on improvement in 2004.

Donnelly,Brendan

RH Reliever | AGE 32 Past | TYPE Power
R: High | I: EXP, CON | S: STB | K:
LIMA B+ | EP: 45%

Yr	Tm	W	L	Sv	IP	K	ERA	Br/IP	R$	BF/G	OBA	vL	vR	H%	xERA	RAR	Ctl	Dom	Cmd	hr/9	G/F	S%	BPV	BPX
99	a/a	5	6	3	74	56	3.89	1.38	$8	7.2	270			31%	4.03	16.2	3.0	6.8	2.2	0.9		74%	63	147
00	aaa	4	9	1	59	37	8.24	2.12	($9)	6.5	351			38%	8.00	-19.6	5.3	5.6	1.1	1.5		62%	-5	-12
01	a/a	9	2	13	70	60	3.34	1.51	$15	5.5	291			34%	5.16 -	19.5	3.2	7.7	2.4	1.2		82%	59	113
02	ANA	* 5	1	7	82	88	2.96	1.13	$14	4.7	214	242	148	28%	2.83	27.4	3.3	9.7	2.9	0.8	0.98	77%	109	223
03	ANA	2	2	3	74	79	1.58	1.07	$13	4.7	209	199	202	29%	2.08 -	39.1	2.9	9.6	3.3	0.2	0.52	86%	133	287
1st Half		0	0	1	41	49	0.44	0.85	$9	4.6	171			26%	0.87	28.1	2.4	10.7	4.5	0.0	0.41	94%	179	386
2nd Half		2	2	2	33	30	3.02	1.34	$4	4.8	251			32%	3.61 -	11.0	3.6	8.2	2.3	0.5	0.68	79%	86	186
04	Proj	4	3	6	75	73	3.00	1.25	$11	5.0	241			31%	3.29	25.5	3.2	8.8	2.7	0.6	F	78%	98	210

Reasons he won't see a sub-2.00 ERA again: 94% strand rate in first half, hr/9 rate only 0.2 with many fly balls, Dom regressed in 2nd half, xERA 3.61 in 2nd half. 2nd half line is a reasonable expectation.

Dotel,Octavio

RH Reliever | AGE 30 Peak | TYPE Power
R: Low | I: con | S: pt, stb | K:
LIMA B | EP: 40%

Yr	Tm	W	L	Sv	IP	K	ERA	Br/IP	R$	BF/G	OBA	vL	vR	H%	xERA	RAR	Ctl	Dom	Cmd	hr/9	G/F	S%	BPV	BPX
99	NYM	* 13	5	0	155	161	4.94	1.34	$10	20.6	224	210	240	28%	3.48 +	6.2	4.8	9.3	2.0	1.2	0.80	66%	71	154
00	HOU	3	7	16	125	142	5.40	1.50	$7	11.1	265	282	250	32%	5.39	3.8	4.4	10.2	2.3	1.9	0.51	70%	56	124
01	HOU	7	5	2	105	145	2.66	1.20	$14	7.1	211	238	178	33%	2.55	38.1	4.0	12.4	3.1	0.4	0.79	79%	139	259
02	HOU	6	4	6	97	118	1.86	0.88	$22	4.4	175	190	159	25%	1.45	42.2	2.5	10.9	4.4	0.6	0.53	83%	158	299
03	HOU	6	4	4	87	97	2.48	0.97	$17	4.4	178	152	186	23%	2.06	32.6	3.2	10.0	3.1	0.9	0.75	80%	117	226
1st Half		6	3	2	47	55	2.11	0.91	$13	4.4	164			23%	1.44 +	20.0	3.3	10.5	3.2	0.6	0.74	80%	136	262
2nd Half		0	1	2	40	42	2.92	1.02	$5	4.5	193			23%	2.78	12.6	3.1	9.4	3.0	1.3	0.77	80%	96	184
04	Proj	5	3	4	80	89	2.70	1.03	$14	5.2	190			25%	2.29	27.5	3.3	10.0	3.1	0.9	F	78%	114	221

Third consecutive year of 100+ BPV. Two small reasons for caution... Three year trend of falling Dom and rising hr/9. Should be strong but don't go overboard.

Dreifort,Darren

RH Starter | AGE 31 Peak | TYPE Power
R: Low | I: con | S: pt | K: brn
LIMA B+ | EP: 55%

Yr	Tm	W	L	Sv	IP	K	ERA	Br/IP	R$	BF/G	OBA	vL	vR	H%	xERA	RAR	Ctl	Dom	Cmd	hr/9	G/F	S%	BPV	BPX
99	LA	13	13	0	178	140	4.80	1.42	$8	25.8	261	274	249	30%	3.99 +	10.3	3.8	7.1	1.8	1.0	1.84	68%	54	117
00	LA	12	9	0	192	164	4.17	1.36	$14	25.7	244	268	211	28%	4.39	37.6	4.1	7.7	1.9	1.5	1.76	75%	48	106
01	LA	4	7	0	94	91	5.16	1.44	($1)	25.7	251	294	215	31%	4.30 +	2.6	4.5	8.7	1.9	1.1	1.53	66%	66	123
02	LA	0	0	0	0	0	0.00	0.00																
03	LA	4	4	0	60	67	4.04	1.38	$3	25.8	255	306	202	34%	4.02	9.9	3.7	10.0	2.7	0.9	1.90	73%	94	180
1st Half		4	4	0	60	67	4.04	1.38	$3	25.8	255			34%	4.02	9.9	3.7	10.0	2.7	0.9	1.90	73%	94	180
2nd Half		0	0	0	0	0	0.00	0.00																
04	Proj	5	5	0	80	76	3.94	1.40	$4	26.6	252			31%	4.22	14.2	4.1	8.6	2.1	1.1	G	75%	66	128

Knee surgery ended his comeback in June. Showed growth in Ctl, Dom, Cmd. HR/9 fell and G/F rose. DOM/DIS of 60/10. Could improve even more if healthy, but that's a large IF given his track record.

Drese,Ryan

RH Starter | AGE 28 Pre-Peak | TYPE
R: Moderate | I: EXP, con | S: stb | K:
LIMA D | EP: 55%

Yr	Tm	W	L	Sv	IP	K	ERA	Br/IP	R$	BF/G	OBA	vL	vR	H%	xERA	RAR	Ctl	Dom	Cmd	hr/9	G/F	S%	BPV	BPX
99		0	0	0	0	0	0.00	0.00																
00		0	0	0	0	0	0.00	0.00																
01	a/a	11	10	0	184	126	4.70	1.36	$7	23.2	266	205	288	30%	4.13 +	17.9	3.1	6.2	2.0	0.8	2.64	66%	56	107
02	CLE	* 11	9	0	159	116	5.94	1.65	($5)	25.0	304	333	297	35%	5.52	-10.3	3.7	6.6	1.8	0.9	1.25	64%	43	89
03	TEX	* 11	11	0	177	83	7.02	1.93	($18)	26.0	353	438	210	38%	7.24	-35.4	3.6	4.2	1.2	1.1	1.27	64%	1	2
1st Half		5	7	0	81	51	8.55	2.26	($17)	26.2	385			42%	8.85	-32.8	4.4	5.7	1.3	1.3	1.38	62%	-1	-3
2nd Half		6	4	0	96	32	5.72	1.66	($3)	25.8	323			33%	5.89	-2.6	2.8	3.0	1.1	0.9	1.21	66%	3	6
04	Proj	5	5	0	80	47	5.96	1.66	($3)	24.4	311			34%	5.76	-4.5	3.5	5.3	1.5	1.0	--	65%	26	56

2-4, 6.85 ERA in 46 IP at TEX. To give him credit, 38% hit rate and 64% strand rate elevated his ERA. But BPIs regressed. Young enough that he may get another opportunity, but his window is closing.

Driskill,Travis

RH Reliever | AGE 32 Past | TYPE Finesse
R: Very High | I: EXP, CON | S: pt, stb | K:
LIMA C | EP: 40%

Yr	Tm	W	L	Sv	IP	K	ERA	Br/IP	R$	BF/G	OBA	vL	vR	H%	xERA	RAR	Ctl	Dom	Cmd	hr/9	G/F	S%	BPV	BPX
99	aaa	9	8	0	132	73	6.68	1.67	($5)	19.6	332			35%	6.62	-20.4	2.5	5.0	2.0	1.8		63%	8	18
00	aaa	12	11	0	179	88	5.93	1.78	($5)	30.0	344			37%	6.64 -	-4.1	2.7	4.4	1.7	1.1		68%	14	34
01	aaa	11	5	0	178	113	5.51	1.51	($0)	28.2	314			34%	5.86	-2.1	2.0	5.7	2.9	1.5		67%	42	80
02	BAL	* 10	10	0	154	90	4.56	1.42	$6	20.3	281	289	277	30%	4.98	18.6	2.9	5.3	1.8	1.3	1.48	72%	30	62
03	BAL	* 7	5	1	98	62	4.86	1.36	$5	14.5	301	313	308	32%	5.52 -	8.8	1.4	5.7	4.1	1.7	1.04	70%	64	137
1st Half		3	3	1	68	47	4.24	1.25	$5	15.8	287			32%	4.62	11.7	1.1	6.2	5.9	1.3	1.02	71%	119	256
2nd Half		4	2	0	30	15	6.26	1.62	$0	12.5	330			32%	7.54 -	-3.0	2.1	4.5	2.1	2.7	1.08	70%	-20	-43
04	Proj	5	3	0	60	35	5.10	1.48	$2	12.6	307			32%	5.98 -	3.5	2.1	5.3	2.5	1.8	--	71%	24	51

3-5, 6.00 ERA in 48 IP at BAL. Good command ruined by too many hits and home runs allowed. And with a 7.54 xERA in the second half, there is no sign that he's going to improve soon.

DuBose,Eric

LH Starter | AGE 27 Pre-Peak | TYPE
R: Very High | I: EXP, con | S: PT, stb | K:
LIMA C+ | EP: 50%

Yr	Tm	W	L	Sv	IP	K	ERA	Br/IP	R$	BF/G	OBA	vL	vR	H%	xERA	RAR	Ctl	Dom	Cmd	hr/9	G/F	S%	BPV	BPX
99	aa	4	2	1	77	57	5.03	1.62	$0	16.7	288			33%	5.00	5.2	4.3	6.7	1.5	0.9		70%	42	96
00	aa	5	1	0	28	19	5.14	1.68	$3	7.2	255			29%	4.57 +	2.3	6.4	6.1	1.0	0.6		69%	41	98
01		0	0	0	0	0	0.00	0.00																
02	a/a	5	3	3	65	50	3.32	1.31	$8	6.5	243			30%	3.12	17.0	3.6	6.9	1.9	0.3		73%	80	157
03	BAL	3	6	0	73	44	3.81	1.16	$6	17.6	225	305	186	25%	3.03 +	16.8	3.1	5.4	1.8	0.7	1.63	68%	57	124
1st Half		0	1	0	6	5	2.95	0.82	$1	22.8	149			14%	1.97 +	2.1	3.0	7.4	2.5	1.5	1.17	75%	78	168
2nd Half		3	5	0	67	39	3.89	1.19	$5	17.2	231			26%	3.12 +	14.7	3.1	5.2	1.7	0.7	1.68	68%	56	120
04	Proj	6	7	0	120	83	4.35	1.39	$5	23.5	259			30%	3.97	19.1	3.7	6.2	1.7	0.7	G	69%	56	120

Succeeded by keeping ball on the ground and dominating right-handed hitters. With his low Dom, he has little margin for error. 25% hit rate suggests that keeping ERA under 4.00 could be a stretch.

HAROLD NICHOLS

Duckworth,Brandon

Info	Yr	Tm	W	L	Sv	IP	K	ERA	Br/IP	R$	BF/G	OBA	vL	vR	H%	xERA	RAR	Ctl	Dom	Cmd	hr/9	G/F	S%	BPV	BPX
RH Starter	99		0	0	0	0	0	0.00	0.00																
AGE 28 Pre-Peak	00	aa	13	7	0	165	154	3.98	1.41	$15	26.4	271			33%	4.40	39.3	3.2	8.4	**2.6**	1.0		74%	77	181
TYPE Power	01	PHI	* 16	4	0	216	175	3.63	1.29	$19	27.6	255	256	221	30%	3.70	50.4	3.0	7.3	**2.5**	0.8	1.75	74%	77	143
R High	02	PHI	8	9	0	163	167	5.41	1.45	($2)	23.7	266	248	273	33%	4.78 +	-6.6	3.8	9.2	**2.4**	1.4	0.85	66%	65	122
I EXP con	03	PHI	* 6	8	0	113	80	4.85	1.55	($1)	18.1	285	246	297	31%	5.33	6.5	3.9	6.4	**1.6**	1.4	1.05	72%	30	58
S pt	1st Half		4	2	0	51	35	5.26	1.58	($0)	19.2	290			32%	5.36	0.1	3.9	6.1	**1.6**	1.2	1.02	69%	30	59
K brn	2nd Half		2	6	0	62	45	4.51	1.53	($1)	17.2	280			31%	5.32 -	6.4	3.9	6.5	**1.7**	1.5	1.08	75%	30	57
LIMA C+ EP: 50%	04	Proj	**8**	**8**	**0**	**140**	**109**	**4.69**	**1.47**	**$2**	**21.2**	**274**			**31%**	**4.81**	**10.7**	**3.7**	**7.0**	**1.9**	**1.2**	**--**	**71%**	**46**	**88**

4-7, 4.94 ERA in 93 IP at PHI. Disappointing season led to his demotion in August. The real difference between 2002 and 2003 was loss of Dom. Must regain that if he is to fulfill his potential.

Eaton,Adam

Info	Yr	Tm	W	L	Sv	IP	K	ERA	Br/IP	R$	BF/G	OBA	vL	vR	H%	xERA	RAR	Ctl	Dom	Cmd	hr/9	G/F	S%	BPV	BPX
RH Starter	99	a/a	6	5	0	98	75	3.21	1.14	$13	26.5	224			26%	2.90	30.4	2.9	6.9	**2.3**	0.9		75%	73	169
AGE 26 Growth	00	SD	* 11	5	0	192	137	3.70	1.36	$15	25.7	253	302	215	29%	3.89	49.5	3.7	6.4	**1.8**	0.8	1.31	75%	56	123
TYPE Power	01	SD	8	5	0	116	109	4.34	1.27	$8	28.7	248	260	220	29%	4.30	16.0	3.1	8.4	**2.7**	1.5	0.98	72%	67	124
R X HIGH	02	SD	* 2	2	0	45	30	5.00	1.29	$1	23.7	230	333	162	24%	4.09 +	0.6	4.0	6.0	**1.5**	1.6	0.83	66%	28	54
I exp con	03	SD	9	12	0	183	146	4.08	1.32	$9	25.0	251	276	222	29%	3.91	29.3	3.3	7.2	**2.1**	1.0	1.12	71%	63	122
S PT	1st Half		2	7	0	89	79	4.65	1.40	($0)	25.7	257			32%	3.94 +	7.5	3.8	8.0	**2.1**	0.7	1.42	67%	74	142
K BRN	2nd Half		7	5	0	94	67	3.55	1.24	$9	24.4	245			27%	3.88	21.8	2.9	6.4	**2.2**	1.2	0.92	77%	54	104
LIMA C+ EP: 50%	04	Proj	**11**	**11**	**0**	**200**	**155**	**4.23**	**1.29**	**$11**	**25.5**	**244**			**27%**	**3.94**	**27.7**	**3.4**	**7.0**	**2.0**	**1.2**	**--**	**71%**	**54**	**105**

Continued to rebound from 2001 elbow surgery. BPIs almost back to 2001 level. 2nd half ERA was strong, but Dom faded and hr/9 rose. 183 IP and 2nd half fade now make a letdown a strong possibility.

Eischen,Joey

Info	Yr	Tm	W	L	Sv	IP	K	ERA	Br/IP	R$	BF/G	OBA	vL	vR	H%	xERA	RAR	Ctl	Dom	Cmd	hr/9	G/F	S%	BPV	BPX
LH Reliever	99	aaa	1	3	1	41	26	10.98	2.49	($14)	8.2	397			44%	9.64 +	-29.9	5.7	5.7	**1.0**	1.5		55%	-15	-35
AGE 33 Past	00	aaa	0	4	0	60	25	5.70	1.72	($5)	25.3	313			31%	6.48 -	0.5	3.9	3.8	**1.0**	1.7		71%	-14	-34
TYPE	01	MON	* 2	4	7	81	62	3.78	1.37	$6	6.0	264	231	270	30%	4.58 -	17.2	3.2	6.9	**2.1**	1.3	1.89	78%	48	90
R High	02	MON	* 7	1	6	67	63	1.07	1.12	$18	3.9	222	173	261	30%	2.15 -	36.2	2.8	8.5	**3.0**	0.1	3.64	91%	120	227
I EXP CON	03	MON	2	2	1	53	40	3.06	1.32	$4	3.2	276	255	308	31%	4.46 -	15.8	2.2	6.8	**3.1**	1.2	1.69	83%	69	134
S pt	1st Half		1	1	0	31	24	2.61	1.61	$1	3.4	314			37%	5.47 -	11.1	2.9	7.0	**2.4**	0.9	1.64	87%	58	112
K age	2nd Half		1	1	1	22	16	3.68	0.91	$3	2.9	215			22%	3.04 +	4.7	1.2	6.5	**5.3**	1.6	1.76	69%	114	220
LIMA B+ EP: 35%	04	Proj	**3**	**2**	**3**	**60**	**47**	**3.45**	**1.28**	**$6**	**3.9**	**262**			**30%**	**4.00 -**	**14.6**	**2.6**	**7.1**	**2.8**	**1.1**	**G**	**77%**	**72**	**138**

ERA will continue rising because:
- 83% strand rate
- Falling Dom and rising hr/9 in 2nd half
- 4.46 xERA

We're on downhill side of a bell curve that peaked in 2002.

Elarton,Scott

Info	Yr	Tm	W	L	Sv	IP	K	ERA	Br/IP	R$	BF/G	OBA	vL	vR	H%	xERA	RAR	Ctl	Dom	Cmd	hr/9	G/F	S%	BPV	BPX
RH Starter	99	HOU	9	5	1	124	121	3.48	1.24	$14	12.3	241	251	227	31%	2.85 +	29.1	3.1	8.8	**2.8**	0.6	0.81	73%	101	220
AGE 28 Pre-Peak	00	HOU	17	7	0	192	131	4.82	1.47	$12	28.1	268	264	262	29%	4.90	20.7	3.9	6.1	**1.6**	1.4	0.77	71%	30	67
TYPE	01	2NL	4	10	0	132	87	7.08	1.55	($11)	24.6	281	252	310	28%	6.21 +	-30.3	4.0	5.9	**1.5**	2.3	0.98	59%	-4	-8
R Very High	02	COL	0	0	0	0	0	0.00	0.00																
I CON	03	COL	* 10	12	0	169	96	7.23	1.88	($18)	26.2	351	318	344	37%	7.80 -	-44.2	3.2	5.1	**1.6**	2.0	0.84	65%	-10	-19
S PT stb	1st Half		4	6	0	92	50	5.97	1.85	($9)	27.4	342			36%	7.39 -	-8.5	3.4	4.9	**1.4**	1.8	0.88	72%	-7	-13
K BRN	2nd Half		6	6	0	77	46	8.72	1.91	($12)	24.9	360			38%	8.29	-35.7	2.9	5.3	**1.8**	2.2	0.73	57%	-13	-24
LIMA F EP: 50%	04	Proj	**7**	**8**	**0**	**120**	**78**	**6.00**	**1.68**	**($6)**	**24.0**	**314**			**33%**	**6.55 -**	**-11.8**	**3.5**	**5.9**	**1.7**	**1.9**	**--**	**69%**	**7**	**13**

4-4, 6.27 ERA in 52 IP at COL. Tempting to blame COL pitching hell for this, but he was better at home (1.9 HR/9) than on the road (3.3 HR/9). Must keep ball in park to have chance for success.

Eldred,Cal

Info	Yr	Tm	W	L	Sv	IP	K	ERA	Br/IP	R$	BF/G	OBA	vL	vR	H%	xERA	RAR	Ctl	Dom	Cmd	hr/9	G/F	S%	BPV	BPX
RH Reliever	99	MIL	* 2	10	0	113	88	7.33	1.69	($13)	20.0	296	354	247	32%	6.02 +	-31.7	4.5	7.0	**1.5**	1.9	0.98	59%	13	28
AGE 36 Decline	00	CHW	10	2	0	112	97	4.58	1.45	$9	24.5	246	234	252	29%	4.13	20.0	4.7	7.8	**1.6**	1.0	1.10	70%	58	151
TYPE Power	01	CHW	0	1	0	6	6	13.50	2.50	($3)	16.3	415			50%	10.19 +	-6.4	4.5	9.0	**2.0**	1.5	1.29	43%	23	46
R Very High	02		0	0	0	0	0	0.00	0.00																
I exp CON	03	STL	7	4	8	67	67	3.76	1.39	$11	4.7	247	295	227	30%	4.22	13.7	4.2	9.0	**2.2**	1.2	0.91	77%	69	132
S pt stb	1st Half		3	2	8	32	31	4.77	1.56	$5	5.0	279			33%	5.54 -	2.2	4.2	8.7	**2.1**	1.7	0.86	75%	44	85
K age brn	2nd Half		4	2	0	35	36	2.83	1.23	$6	4.4	215			28%	3.01	11.5	4.1	9.3	**2.3**	0.8	0.97	80%	92	176
LIMA C EP: 45%	04	Proj	**5**	**3**	**3**	**60**	**55**	**4.50**	**1.43**	**$5**	**7.7**	**252**			**30%**	**4.38**	**6.1**	**4.4**	**8.3**	**1.9**	**1.2**	**--**	**72%**	**58**	**112**

The Phoenix rises! Conversion to relief revived his career. Was better in the 2nd half, aided by an 80% strand rate. Increased Dom and falling hr/9 say he might repeat, but at age 36 don't count on it.

Embree,Alan

Info	Yr	Tm	W	L	Sv	IP	K	ERA	Br/IP	R$	BF/G	OBA	vL	vR	H%	xERA	RAR	Ctl	Dom	Cmd	hr/9	G/F	S%	BPV	BPX
LH Reliever	99	SF	3	2	0	58	53	3.41	1.17	$6	3.5	204	200	200	25%	2.56 +	14.2	4.0	8.2	**2.0**	0.9	0.56	74%	78	170
AGE 34 Past	00	SF	3	5	2	60	49	4.95	1.45	$3	4.2	268	286	267	33%	4.14 +	5.5	3.8	7.4	**2.0**	0.6	0.74	65%	69	151
TYPE Power	01	2TM	1	4	0	54	59	7.33	1.52	($6)	3.9	299	180	299	35%	6.37 +	-13.8	2.8	9.8	**3.5**	2.3	0.85	56%	57	110
R Low	02	2TM	4	6	2	62	81	2.03	1.08	$11	3.6	212	156	244	30%	2.66 -	26.9	2.9	11.8	**4.1**	0.9	1.45	87%	142	279
I con	03	BOS	4	1	1	55	45	4.25	1.18	$6	3.5	240	263	221	29%	3.32 +	9.4	2.6	7.4	**2.8**	0.8	1.09	65%	86	185
S stb	1st Half		3	1	0	30	24	3.89	1.13	$4	3.9	213			24%	3.21 +	6.6	3.3	7.2	**2.2**	1.2	0.83	70%	65	141
K age	2nd Half		1	0	1	25	21	4.70	1.24	$2	3.1	270			34%	3.46 +	2.8	1.8	7.6	**4.2**	0.4	1.52	60%	124	267
LIMA B+ EP: 65%	04	Proj	**3**	**3**	**1**	**60**	**52**	**3.90**	**1.22**	**$5**	**3.5**	**245**			**29%**	**3.69**	**13.2**	**2.7**	**7.8**	**2.9**	**1.1**	**--**	**71%**	**82**	**176**

60% strand rate and 34% hit rate in the second half pushed his season ERA over 4.00. Posted a 124 second half BPV, with improved Cmd and a falling hr/9. Good chance he'll post a sub-4.00 ERA once again.

Escobar,Kelvim

Info	Yr	Tm	W	L	Sv	IP	K	ERA	Br/IP	R$	BF/G	OBA	vL	vR	H%	xERA	RAR	Ctl	Dom	Cmd	hr/9	G/F	S%	BPV	BPX
RH Reliever	99	TOR	14	11	0	174	129	5.69	1.63	$3	24.0	293	279	306	34%	5.32	4.2	4.2	6.7	**1.6**	1.0	1.11	66%	40	101
AGE 28 Pre-Peak	00	TOR	10	15	2	180	142	5.35	1.51	$6	18.5	268	282	253	30%	4.91	13.5	4.3	7.1	**1.7**	1.3	1.04	67%	40	104
TYPE Power	01	TOR	6	8	0	126	121	3.50	1.15	$12	8.7	207	203	206	27%	2.57 +	33.5	3.7	8.6	**2.3**	0.6	1.36	70%	97	194
R High	02	TOR	5	7	38	78	85	4.27	1.53	$24	4.6	254	245	246	33%	4.69	12.4	5.1	9.8	**1.9**	1.2	1.03	75%	69	141
I con	03	TOR	13	9	4	180	159	4.30	1.48	$11	19.3	271	233	308	33%	4.43	29.6	3.9	7.9	**2.0**	0.7	1.37	72%	69	148
S PT	1st Half		5	5	4	71	77	4.30	1.49	$5	13.1	275			36%	4.49	11.7	3.8	9.7	**2.6**	0.8	1.45	72%	90	194
K BRN	2nd Half		8	4	0	109	82	4.30	1.48	$5	28.2	269			32%	4.40	17.9	4.0	6.8	**1.7**	0.7	1.32	72%	55	120
LIMA C+ EP: 55%	04	Proj	**12**	**12**	**24**	**180**	**163**	**4.55**	**1.45**	**$21**	**9.7**	**259**			**32%**	**4.26**	**23.8**	**4.2**	**8.2**	**1.9**	**0.9**	**--**	**70%**	**67**	**145**

After a rough April, moved to the rotation in May. Although outwardly successful, Dom and Cmd faded in 2nd half. With increase in IP, burnout becomes a strong possibility.

Estes,Shawn

Info	Yr	Tm	W	L	Sv	IP	K	ERA	Br/IP	R$	BF/G	OBA	vL	vR	H%	xERA	RAR	Ctl	Dom	Cmd	hr/9	G/F	S%	BPV	BPX
LH Starter	99	SF	11	11	0	203	159	4.92	1.58	$0	28.6	267	270	267	31%	4.41 +	8.5	5.0	7.0	**1.4**	0.9	1.53	70%	46	99
AGE 31 Peak	00	SF	15	6	0	190	136	4.26	1.59	$10	28.6	266	216	285	31%	4.39	34.8	5.1	6.4	**1.3**	0.5	2.06	73%	51	113
TYPE Power	01	SF	9	8	0	159	109	4.02	1.43	$7	25.6	252	227	262	29%	3.91	28.7	4.4	6.2	**1.4**	0.6	1.64	72%	53	98
R Low	02	2NL	5	12	0	160	109	5.12	1.59	($7)	24.9	275	302	276	33%	3.98 +	-0.3	4.7	6.1	**1.3**	0.1	1.72	64%	63	119
I con	03	CHC	8	11	0	152	103	5.74	1.74	($9)	24.5	298	276	312	33%	5.85	-9.4	4.9	6.1	**1.2**	1.2	1.81	69%	23	43
S stb	1st Half		6	7	0	93	55	5.41	1.73	($4)	25.5	299			34%	5.36	-1.6	4.7	5.3	**1.1**	0.7	2.04	68%	30	58
K	2nd Half		2	4	0	59	48	6.26	1.77	($6)	23.0	296			33%	6.63	-7.8	5.2	7.3	**1.4**	2.0	1.47	69%	10	19
LIMA D EP: 50%	04	Proj	**6**	**9**	**0**	**140**	**99**	**5.27**	**1.64**	**($5)**	**24.6**	**282**			**32%**	**5.06**	**-0.1**	**4.8**	**6.4**	**1.3**	**0.9**	**G**	**69%**	**38**	**72**

BPI remained consistent, except for rise in hr/9. Given these mediocre BPIs, that was disastrous. Stable G/F says that hr/9 will come back down, but he's been below replacement value for past two seasons.

Estrella,Leo

Info	Yr	Tm	W	L	Sv	IP	K	ERA	Br/IP	R$	BF/G	OBA	vL	vR	H%	xERA	RAR	Ctl	Dom	Cmd	hr/9	G/F	S%	BPV	BPX
RH Reliever	99		0	0	0	0	0	0.00	0.00																
AGE 29 Pre-Peak	00	a/a	10	9	0	166	90	4.72	1.40	$9	25.6	256			28%	4.10 +	23.2	3.8	4.9	**1.3**	0.9		67%	34	80
TYPE Finesse	01	a/a	3	2	1	95	47	5.78	1.85	($8)	10.1	327			35%	6.40 -	-4.5	4.4	4.5	**1.0**	0.9		69%	9	18
R Very High	02	a/a	4	4	1	74	38	5.59	1.85	($5)	11.0	320			35%	5.93	-3.2	4.7	4.6	**1.0**	0.6		69%	21	41
I EXP CON	03	MIL	* 8	3	3	81	34	3.89	1.41	$9	5.4	276	290	289	28%	4.74 -	15.1	3.0	3.8	**1.3**	1.2	1.59	77%	12	24
S pt	1st Half		3	0	0	42	23	1.49	1.09	$8	5.6	232			25%	2.99 -	21.4	2.1	4.9	**2.3**	0.9	1.68	93%	61	117
K	2nd Half		5	3	3	39	11	6.49	1.75	$1	5.2	318			31%	6.64	-6.3	3.9	2.6	**0.6**	1.6	1.54	66%	-28	-55
LIMA F EP: 30%	04	Proj	**6**	**4**	**0**	**80**	**36**	**5.06**	**1.63**	**($0)**	**7.4**	**299**			**31%**	**5.39**	**2.2**	**3.8**	**4.1**	**1.1**	**1.0**	**G**	**70%**	**11**	**22**

7-3, 4.36 ERA in 66 IP at MIL. His early success was driven by a 93% strand rate. Faded strongly in second half, with Cmd 0.6, BPV -28, and xERA 6.64. Won't repeat 2003's success.

HAROLD NICHOLS

Eyre,Scott

LH Reliever
AGE 31 Peak
TYPE Power
R High
I exp con
S pt STB
K
LIMA C+ EP: 40%

Yr	Tm	W	L	Sv	IP	K	ERA	Br/IP	R$	BF/G	OBA	vL	vR	H%	xERA	RAR	Ctl	Dom	Cmd	hr/9	G/F	S%	BPV	BPX
99	CHW *	7	5	0	93	68	5.13	1.71	$1	13.0	317			37%	5.80 -	9.3	3.6	6.6	**1.8**	0.9	0.85	71%	43	109
00	CHW *	4	3	12	67	54	4.57	1.54	$10	5.0	268			33%	4.26	12.1	4.6	7.3	**1.6**	0.5	1.33	70%	62	162
01	TOR *	5	8	2	95	91	4.17	1.44	$4	5.2	274	323	192	34%	4.61	16.7	3.4	8.6	**2.5**	1.0	0.58	74%	74	148
02	2TM	2	4	0	74	58	4.50	1.57	($2)	4.7	277	233	317	34%	4.43	7.6	4.4	7.1	**1.6**	0.5	1.35	71%	61	120
03	SF	2	1	1	57	35	3.32	1.51	$2	3.4	272	219	305	31%	4.36 -	15.0	4.1	5.5	**1.3**	0.6	1.06	79%	43	83
1st Half		0	1	1	32	20	3.38	1.28	$2	3.4	256			29%	3.77	8.2	2.8	5.6	**2.0**	0.8	0.81	76%	54	104
2nd Half		2	0	0	25	15	3.24	1.80	$1	3.4	291			34%	5.13 -	6.8	5.8	5.4	**0.9**	0.4	1.52	82%	38	73
04	**Proj**	**3**	**2**	**1**	**60**	**39**	**4.05**	**1.57**	**$1**	**4.1**	**278**			**32%**	**4.53**	**9.8**	**4.4**	**5.9**	**1.3**	**0.6**	**--**	**74%**	**45**	**87**

Rapidly declining Dom leaves little wiggle room for this soft-tosser. Has potential to be effective LH specialist but allows too many baserunners to be effective over the long haul. Struggles vs RHers limit growth.

Farnsworth,Kyle

RH Reliever
AGE 28 Pre-Peak
TYPE Power
R High
I CON
S PT
K
LIMA B+ EP: 60%

Yr	Tm	W	L	Sv	IP	K	ERA	Br/IP	R$	BF/G	OBA	vL	vR	H%	xERA	RAR	Ctl	Dom	Cmd	hr/9	G/F	S%	BPV	BPX
99	CHC *	7	11	0	169	96	4.63	1.42	$3	22.2	274	277	267	28%	4.90	13.6	3.2	5.1	**1.6**	1.8	0.91	74%	12	25
00	CHC *	2	11	10	102	93	5.73	1.79	($2)	7.1	287	258	314	34%	5.94	-1.4	5.9	8.2	**1.4**	1.3	1.03	70%	36	80
01	CHC	4	6	2	82	107	2.74	1.15	$11	4.4	219	223	207	31%	2.96	28.8	3.2	11.7	**3.7**	0.9	0.74	80%	133	246
02	CHC	4	7	1	49	48	7.35	1.63	($3)	4.7	288	392	216	34%	5.94 +	-14.7	4.4	8.8	**2.0**	1.8	0.85	57%	37	70
03	CHC	3	2	0	76	92	3.31	1.17	$7	4.0	198	189	199	28%	2.58 +	20.0	4.3	10.9	**2.6**	0.7	1.29	73%	113	217
1st Half		2	0	0	37	44	2.43	1.11	$5	4.0	181			26%	2.02	14.1	4.4	10.7	**2.4**	0.5	1.00	79%	120	231
2nd Half		1	2	0	39	48	4.14	1.23	$2	4.1	214			29%	3.12 +	5.9	4.1	11.0	**2.7**	0.9	1.68	68%	107	206
04	**Proj**	**3**	**5**	**1**	**70**	**78**	**3.21**	**1.33**	**$5**	**4.6**	**236**			**31%**	**3.61**	**19.2**	**4.1**	**10.0**	**2.4**	**0.9**	**--**	**79%**	**92**	**178**

Once plagued my gopheritis, G/F trend is encouraging and is making him more reliable in key situations. Hit and strand rates suggest he pitched even better than his 3.31 ERA indicates. Improving control is final step.

Fassero,Jeff

LH Reliever
AGE 41 Decline
TYPE Power
R Very High
I CON
S pt STB
K AGE
LIMA F EP: 40%

Yr	Tm	W	L	Sv	IP	K	ERA	Br/IP	R$	BF/G	OBA	vL	vR	H%	xERA	RAR	Ctl	Dom	Cmd	hr/9	G/F	S%	BPV	BPX
99	2AL	5	14	0	156	114	7.21	1.87	($16)	20.2	321	271	330	35%	7.33	-28.0	4.8	6.6	**1.4**	2.0	1.27	65%	-1	-4
00	BOS	8	8	0	130	97	4.78	1.56	$5	15.3	294	255	307	34%	5.25	19.8	3.5	6.7	**1.9**	1.1	1.68	72%	44	114
01	CHC	4	4	12	73	79	3.44	1.22	$14	3.7	242	247	228	32%	3.31	18.9	2.8	9.7	**3.4**	0.7	1.49	73%	115	213
02	2NL	8	6	0	69	56	5.35	1.57	$2	4.2	294	318	275	36%	4.63 +	-2.2	3.5	7.3	**2.1**	0.5	2.32	64%	68	128
03	STL	1	7	3	77	55	5.71	1.65	($5)	5.7	299	337	278	32%	6.37 -	-4.5	4.0	6.4	**1.6**	2.0	0.96	71%	8	16
1st Half		1	3	3	29	16	7.14	1.66	($2)	3.6	294			30%	6.21 +	-7.2	4.3	5.0	**1.1**	1.9	1.26	60%	-6	-11
2nd Half		0	4	0	48	39	4.85	1.64	($3)	8.8	303			33%	6.47 -	2.7	3.7	7.3	**2.0**	2.1	0.79	78%	17	34
04	**Proj**	**2**	**3**	**1**	**40**	**27**	**5.40**	**1.63**	**($1)**	**5.2**	**290**			**32%**	**5.55**	**-0.7**	**4.3**	**6.1**	**1.4**	**1.4**	**--**	**69%**	**23**	**44**

Increasing control rate and declining dominance rate suggest end is near for this 41 year-old. Chronic struggles against LHers last two seasons seal his fate.

Feliciano,Pedro

LH Reliever
AGE 27 Pre-Peak
TYPE
R Moderate
I EXP con
S
K
LIMA B EP: 45%

Yr	Tm	W	L	Sv	IP	K	ERA	Br/IP	R$	BF/G	OBA	vL	vR	H%	xERA	RAR	Ctl	Dom	Cmd	hr/9	G/F	S%	BPV	BPX
99		0	0	0	0	0	0.00	0.00																
00		0	0	0	0	0	0.00	0.00																
01	a/a	5	5	17	69	48	3.00	1.19	$18	4.7	250			29%	3.30	22.4	2.2	6.3	**2.8**	0.7		77%	82	158
02	a/a	3	2	6	74	42	4.01	1.58	$3	6.3	324			36%	5.43 -	12.5	2.1	5.1	**2.5**	0.7		76%	51	100
03	NYM *	3	2	1	70	57	3.97	1.47	$2	8.1	277	304	259	32%	4.68 -	12.3	3.5	7.3	**2.1**	1.0	1.15	76%	57	110
1st Half		3	2	1	42	33	4.05	1.40	$3	7.3	265			31%	4.39	6.9	3.4	7.0	**2.1**	1.1		74%	55	107
2nd Half		0	0	0	28	24	3.84	1.57	($1)	9.7	294			35%	5.12 -	5.4	3.5	7.7	**2.2**	1.0		78%	59	114
04	**Proj**	**3**	**2**	**5**	**70**	**50**	**3.86**	**1.49**	**$4**	**6.9**	**293**			**34%**	**4.83 -**	**13.2**	**2.8**	**6.4**	**2.3**	**0.9**	**--**	**76%**	**56**	**107**

0-0, 3.35 ERA in 48 IP at NYM. LH specialist who allowed a .304 OBA against them in 2003. Skills show potential for upside, but declining command ratio suggests he has more work to do before making an impact.

Fernandez,Jared

RH Starter
AGE 32 Peak
TYPE Finesse
R X HIGH
I EXP CON
S pt STB
K
LIMA F EP: 45%

Yr	Tm	W	L	Sv	IP	K	ERA	Br/IP	R$	BF/G	OBA	vL	vR	H%	xERA	RAR	Ctl	Dom	Cmd	hr/9	G/F	S%	BPV	BPX
99	a/a	15	9	1	182	70	5.49	1.57	$5	24.0	312			32%	5.58	1.0	2.6	3.5	**1.3**	1.3		67%	3	7
00	aaa	10	4	4	113	50	4.30	1.51	$11	16.2	291			31%	4.91 -	22.1	3.2	4.0	**1.3**	0.9		73%	21	49
01	aaa	10	10	0	208	101	5.63	1.72	($10)	29.2	332			35%	6.61 -	-5.7	2.8	4.4	**1.6**	1.4	1.33	70%	5	9
02	CIN *	13	8	1	178	96	4.70	1.66	$0	20.4	324	191	346	35%	5.93 -	9.6	2.8	4.9	**1.7**	1.1	1.63	74%	23	43
03	HOU *	10	13	0	194	60	5.33	1.57	($3)	22.9	314	311	220	32%	5.66	-1.4	2.5	2.8	**1.1**	1.2	1.19	68%	-2	-5
1st Half		5	7	0	110	26	6.29	1.77	($10)	25.8	341			33%	7.01 -	-14.9	2.8	2.1	**0.8**	1.6		67%	-31	-60
2nd Half		5	6	0	84	34	4.08	1.30	$5	19.7	273			29%	3.89	13.5	2.1	3.6	**1.7**	0.6		69%	39	74
04	**Proj**	**2**	**5**	**0**	**60**	**25**	**5.10**	**1.57**	**($2)**	**22.4**	**313**			**33%**	**5.50**	**1.3**	**2.6**	**3.8**	**1.5**	**1.1**	**--**	**69%**	**14**	**28**

3-3, 3.99 ERA in 38 IP at HOU. Sub-4.00 ERA is nice but will not last with these skills. Miniscule dominance rate and struggles against LHers will expose him over the long run. High risk/low upside.

Figueroa,Nelson

RH Starter
AGE 29 Peak
TYPE
R X HIGH
I EXP con
S pt STB
K brn
LIMA C+ EP: 45%

Yr	Tm	W	L	Sv	IP	K	ERA	Br/IP	R$	BF/G	OBA	vL	vR	H%	xERA	RAR	Ctl	Dom	Cmd	hr/9	G/F	S%	BPV	BPX
99	aaa	11	6	0	128	86	4.22	1.36	$12	22.8	277			31%	4.28	22.5	2.5	6.0	**2.4**	1.1		72%	54	126
00	ARI *	13	8	0	178	101	3.89	1.29	$18	26.7	271			30%	4.13	41.4	2.1	5.1	**2.4**	1.0	1.20	72%	53	117
01	PHI *	8	7	0	176	125	3.78	1.41	$7	23.8	277	333	241	32%	4.34 -	37.3	3.0	6.4	**2.1**	0.8	1.43	75%	59	110
02	MIL *	6	7	0	132	71	5.11	1.50	($2)	16.2	283	273	269	29%	5.19	-0.1	3.5	4.8	**1.4**	1.4	0.95	69%	14	26
03	PIT *	14	6	0	186	117	4.06	1.44	$10	23.2	291	190	235	32%	4.85 -	30.4	2.6	5.7	**2.2**	1.0	1.19	75%	47	90
1st Half		7	5	0	98	56	5.04	1.71	($2)	28.4	333			37%	5.91 -	3.1	2.7	5.1	**1.9**	0.7		71%	36	70
2nd Half		7	1	0	88	61	2.97	1.15	$12	18.8	239			26%	3.66 -	27.3	2.4	6.2	**2.7**	1.3		82%	60	116
04	**Proj**	**7**	**7**	**0**	**140**	**87**	**4.18**	**1.41**	**$5**	**20.9**	**279**			**31%**	**4.62**	**20.4**	**2.8**	**5.6**	**2.0**	**1.1**	**--**	**73%**	**41**	**80**

2-1, 3.31 ERA in 35 IP at PIT. Was one of PIT's best starters in Sept. Skills are consistent with previous norms, so keep your expectations reasonable for '04. Limited upside, but worthy of an end-game pick.

Fiore,Tony

RH Reliever
AGE 32 Past
TYPE
R Very High
I EXP CON
S PT
K
LIMA C+ EP: 55%

Yr	Tm	W	L	Sv	IP	K	ERA	Br/IP	R$	BF/G	OBA	vL	vR	H%	xERA	RAR	Ctl	Dom	Cmd	hr/9	G/F	S%	BPV	BPX
99	aaa	2	1	19	67	41	5.24	1.93	$5	6.1	313			36%	5.39	2.6	5.8	5.5	**1.0**	0.1		70%	41	96
00	aaa	9	6	8	90	39	3.50	1.53	$14	6.3	266	400	289	29%	4.24 -	27.2	4.6	3.9	**0.8**	0.5	1.88	77%	28	66
01	aaa	6	1	4	111	61	3.97	1.49	$6	9.1	285			32%	4.25	21.5	3.2	4.9	**1.5**	0.3	2.25	72%	50	96
02	MIN *	12	3	0	104	60	3.38	1.32	$13	8.8	239	247	203	26%	3.90 -	29.0	3.9	5.2	**1.3**	1.0	0.70	78%	35	72
03	MIN *	6	7	1	120	62	5.55	1.48	($0)	14.3	282	237	247	31%	4.69 +	-0.3	3.4	4.6	**1.4**	0.8	0.91	62%	31	66
1st Half		1	1	1	43	26	5.63	1.60	($2)	7.8	265			28%	5.14	-0.6	5.2	5.4	**1.0**	1.3	0.91	67%	19	41
2nd Half		5	6	0	77	36	5.50	1.42	$1	27.8	291			32%	4.44 +	0.2	2.3	4.2	**1.8**	0.6		60%	42	91
04	**Proj**	**3**	**2**	**0**	**50**	**27**	**4.68**	**1.48**	**$1**	**10.0**	**273**			**30%**	**4.45**	**5.8**	**3.8**	**4.9**	**1.3**	**0.7**	**--**	**69%**	**35**	**75**

1-1, 5.50 ERA in 36 IP at MIN. Palmball specialist with only a slight chance of improving his ERA. Low Dom ceiling and periodic Ctl problems place him in a large pool of mediocre pitchers looking for another shot.

Fogg,Josh

RH Starter
AGE 27 Growth
TYPE Finesse
R X HIGH
I EXP CON
S PT stb
K brn
LIMA C EP: 50%

Yr	Tm	W	L	Sv	IP	K	ERA	Br/IP	R$	BF/G	OBA	vL	vR	H%	xERA	RAR	Ctl	Dom	Cmd	hr/9	G/F	S%	BPV	BPX
99	aa	3	2	0	55	34	7.53	1.75	($5)	25.7	335			36%	6.55 +	-14.7	2.9	5.6	**1.9**	1.5		57%	17	39
00	aa	11	7	0	192	116	3.80	1.53	$11	31.6	311			35%	4.84 -	50.5	2.3	5.4	**2.4**	0.5		75%	61	145
01	aaa	4	7	5	127	96	6.31	1.61	($6)	14.0	321	206	214	35%	6.63	-15.1	2.5	6.8	**2.7**	2.0	1.27	65%	30	57
02	PIT	12	12	0	194	113	4.36	1.38	$8	25.3	267	292	243	28%	4.53	19.4	3.2	5.2	**1.6**	1.3	1.32	73%	29	54
03	PIT	10	9	0	142	71	5.26	1.45	$2	23.0	293	320	273	30%	5.25	0.3	2.5	4.5	**1.8**	1.4	1.16	67%	19	36
1st Half		4	3	0	60	29	4.35	1.33	$3	25.5	278			28%	4.97 -	7.5	2.3	4.4	**1.9**	1.7	0.99	74%	17	32
2nd Half		6	6	0	82	42	5.93	1.54	($1)	21.5	304			32%	5.46	-7.1	2.7	4.6	**1.7**	1.2	1.31	63%	21	40
04	**Proj**	**8**	**10**	**1**	**140**	**75**	**5.27**	**1.48**	**$1**	**22.0**	**295**			**31%**	**5.33**	**-0.1**	**2.7**	**4.8**	**1.8**	**1.4**	**--**	**68%**	**20**	**39**

Three-year Dom rate trend has turned this once prospect into a soft-tosser. Struggles against LHers last two seasons gives shaky skills even less room for error. Developing into a non-descript innings-eater.

Foppert,Jesse

RH Starter
AGE 23 Growth
TYPE Power
R High
I EXP con
S
K age
LIMA B+ EP: 55%

Yr	Tm	W	L	Sv	IP	K	ERA	Br/IP	R$	BF/G	OBA	vL	vR	H%	xERA	RAR	Ctl	Dom	Cmd	hr/9	G/F	S%	BPV	BPX
99		0	0	0	0	0	0.00	0.00																
00		0	0	0	0	0	0.00	0.00																
01		0	0	0	0	0	0.00	0.00																
02	a/a	6	9	0	140	156	3.92	1.29	$7	23.6	243			32%	3.56	25.3	3.4	10.0	**2.9**	0.8		71%	103	203
03	SF	8	9	0	111	101	5.03	1.55	$1	21.6	248	267	231	29%	4.74	3.7	5.6	8.2	**1.5**	1.3	0.70	71%	46	89
1st Half		4	7	0	71	60	4.94	1.55	($0)	21.2	242			29%	4.40 +	3.2	5.8	7.6	**1.3**	1.0	0.70	70%	49	95
2nd Half		4	2	0	40	41	5.17	1.55	$1	22.4	257			30%	5.32	0.6	5.2	9.2	**1.8**	1.8	0.70	72%	42	82
04	**Proj**	**1**	**1**	**0**	**10**	**10**	**4.50**	**1.40**	**$1**	**21.6**	**242**			**31%**	**3.87 +**	**1.0**	**4.5**	**9.0**	**2.0**	**0.9**	**F**	**69%**	**76**	**146**

Did not quite live up to the hype, and Tommy John surgery completed in September wipes out 2004.

STEPHEN NICKRAND

Ford,Matt

LH Reliever | AGE 23 Growth | TYPE
R: Moderate | I: EXP | S: | K: AGE
LIMA D | EP: 40%

Yr	Tm	W	L	Sv	IP	K	ERA	Br/IP	R$	BF/G	OBA	vL	vR	H%	xERA	RAR	Ctl	Dom	Cmd	hr/9	G/F	S%	BPV	BPX
99		0	0	0	0	0	0.00	0.00																
00		0	0	0	0	0	0.00	0.00																
01		0	0	0	0	0	0.00	0.00																
02		0	0	0	0	0	0.00	0.00																
03	MIL	0	3	0	43	26	4.38	1.55	($2)	7.7	274	304	250	30%	4.89 -	5.2	4.4	5.4	1.2	1.0	0.41	74%	27	53
1st Half		0	0	0	32	19	2.24	1.25	$2	6.1	223			27%	2.47	13.0	3.9	5.3	1.4	0.0	0.51	80%	71	136
2nd Half		0	3	0	11	7	10.54	2.43	($4)	19.8	390			38%	11.90 -	-7.8	5.7	5.7	1.0	4.1	0.18	64%	-90	-172
04	Proj	0	1	0	50	31	4.50	1.38	($1)	5.7	242			26%	4.02	5.1	4.3	5.6	1.3	1.1	F	70%	35	67

2.15 ERA as a starter, 8.79 ERA as a reliever, and as a soft-tossing LHer, has little room for error in either role. Has no experience above High-A and had bone fragments removed from throwing elbow in Sept.

Fossum,Casey

LH Starter | AGE 26 Growth | TYPE Power
R: Moderate | I: EXP con | S: pt | K:
LIMA B | EP: 65%

Yr	Tm	W	L	Sv	IP	K	ERA	Br/IP	R$	BF/G	OBA	vL	vR	H%	xERA	RAR	Ctl	Dom	Cmd	hr/9	G/F	S%	BPV	BPX
99		0	0	0	0	0	0.00	0.00																
00		0	0	0	0	0	0.00	0.00																
01	BOS	* 6	9	0	161	131	4.02	1.35	$6	20.9	270	188	275	33%	3.84	31.5	2.8	7.3	2.6	0.5	1.21	70%	85	170
02	BOS	* 5	7	1	131	125	3.78	1.44	$5	11.9	292	277	265	36%	4.76 -	29.5	2.5	8.6	3.5	0.9	1.14	76%	94	194
03	BOS	* 7	6	2	96	80	5.53	1.50	$2	15.7	274	230	286	32%	4.78 +	-0.1	3.9	7.5	1.9	1.0	0.65	64%	54	117
1st Half		4	4	0	59	50	5.79	1.44	$0	21.5	268			32%	4.43 +	-2.1	3.7	7.6	2.1	0.9	0.65	59%	63	137
2nd Half		3	2	2	37	30	5.12	1.60	$1	11.1	283			33%	5.34	2.0	4.4	7.3	1.7	1.2	0.64	70%	41	88
04	Proj	8	6	0	120	104	4.35	1.38	$7	21.5	265			32%	4.23	19.1	3.3	7.8	2.4	0.9	F	70%	71	153

6-5, 5.47 ERA in 79 IP at BOS. Skills suggested a breakout for 2003, but injuries negated that. Solid April turned into lost season after shoulder tendinitis. Upside remains, but so do injury risk and durability questions.

Foulke,Keith

RH Reliever | AGE 31 Peak | TYPE Power
R: Very Low | I: con | S: | K:
LIMA C | EP: 40%

Yr	Tm	W	L	Sv	IP	K	ERA	Br/IP	R$	BF/G	OBA	vL	vR	H%	xERA	RAR	Ctl	Dom	Cmd	hr/9	G/F	S%	BPV	BPX
99	CHW	3	3	9	105	123	2.23	0.89	$24	6.0	196	182	193	26%	2.09	51.2	1.8	10.5	5.9	0.9	0.72	82%	174	436
00	CHW	3	1	34	88	91	2.97	1.00	$33	4.8	210	221	192	27%	2.50	34.7	2.3	9.3	4.1	0.9	0.63	75%	128	332
01	CHW	4	9	42	81	75	2.33	0.98	$36	4.4	200	212	183	26%	1.82 +	34.2	2.4	8.3	3.4	0.3	0.66	76%	127	254
02	CHW	2	4	11	77	58	2.92	1.01	$15	4.7	230	266	185	27%	2.80	26.2	1.5	6.8	4.5	0.8	1.04	75%	119	244
03	OAK	9	1	43	86	88	2.09	0.89	$45	4.6	190	158	210	23%	2.18	39.7	2.1	9.2	4.4	1.0	0.46	85%	133	288
1st Half		4	1	21	42	45	2.57	1.02	$21	4.6	218			28%	2.85	16.7	2.1	9.6	4.5	1.1	0.42	82%	132	284
2nd Half		5	0	22	44	43	1.63	0.77	$25	4.5	162			19%	1.54	23.0	2.0	8.8	4.3	1.0	0.50	90%	135	292
04	Proj	6	3	41	80	76	2.93	0.99	$37	4.7	213			26%	2.56	28.0	2.0	8.6	4.2	0.9	F	75%	125	269

As steady as they come. Excellent control history and dominance rate peaked to highest level since 2000. Periodic struggles with HR ball and sharp G/F reduction could send ERA north a touch.

Fox,Chad

RH Reliever | AGE 33 Past | TYPE Power
R: High | I: CON | S: PT | K: age
LIMA A | EP: 45%

Yr	Tm	W	L	Sv	IP	K	ERA	Br/IP	R$	BF/G	OBA	vL	vR	H%	xERA	RAR	Ctl	Dom	Cmd	hr/9	G/F	S%	BPV	BPX
99	MIL	0	0	0	7	12	10.29	2.14	($2)	5.9	358	222	409	56%	7.52 +	-4.7	5.1	15.4	3.0	1.3	0.78	50%	100	218
00	MIL	0	0	0	0	0	0.00	0.00																
01	MIL	* 8	2	2	72	87	1.88	1.21	$15	4.3	191	158	197	27%	2.67 -	33.7	4.9	10.9	2.2	0.8	0.95	89%	106	197
02	MIL	* 1	1	0	9	8	3.00	2.22	($0)	7.7	339	182	500	43%	6.51 -	2.5	7.0	8.0	1.1	0.0	0.88	85%	59	112
03	2TM	3	3	3	43	46	3.13	1.53	$4	5.0	224	205	241	30%	3.76 -	13.1	6.5	9.6	1.5	0.6	0.75	81%	80	163
1st Half		1	2	3	9	9	3.96	1.98	$2	4.5	238			30%	5.41 -	1.8	9.9	8.9	0.9	1.0	1.11	82%	50	102
2nd Half		2	1	0	34	37	2.91	1.41	$3	5.3	220			30%	3.32	11.3	5.6	9.8	1.8	0.5	0.67	80%	91	184
04	Proj	4	2	1	60	65	3.30	1.33	$6	4.8	210			28%	3.05	16.8	5.3	9.8	1.9	0.6	F	76%	92	187

Perennial closer-in-waiting has never stayed healthy enough to grow into the role. Chronic control troubles remain and has thrown 50+ IP only twice in his career. G/F trend could spell trouble if it continues.

Franco,John

LH Reliever | AGE 43 Decline | TYPE
R: Low | I: con | S: pt | K: AGE
LIMA C | EP: 20%

Yr	Tm	W	L	Sv	IP	K	ERA	Br/IP	R$	BF/G	OBA	vL	vR	H%	xERA	RAR	Ctl	Dom	Cmd	hr/9	G/F	S%	BPV	BPX
99	NYM	0	2	19	40	41	2.93	1.48	$12	3.8	262	300	244	35%	3.38	12.4	4.3	9.2	2.2	0.2	2.29	79%	97	210
00	NYM	5	4	4	55	56	3.42	1.30	$10	3.8	228	209	227	29%	3.58	16.3	4.2	9.1	2.2	1.0	2.07	77%	80	176
01	NYM	6	2	2	53	50	4.07	1.39	$6	3.9	269	236	275	32%	4.71 -	9.2	3.2	8.5	2.6	1.4	1.61	76%	67	124
02	NYM	0	0	0	0	0	0.00	0.00																
03	NYM	0	3	2	34	16	2.64	1.41	$2	3.9	267	267	264	27%	4.70 -	12.1	3.4	4.2	1.2	1.3	2.86	88%	13	25
1st Half		0	0	0	9	3	1.96	1.30	$1	3.9	298			30%	4.58 -	4.1	1.0	2.9	3.0	1.0	1.78	91%	47	90
2nd Half		0	3	2	25	13	2.89	1.45	$2	3.9	255			26%	4.74 -	8.0	4.3	4.7	1.1	1.4	3.62	88%	12	22
04	Proj	2	2	2	30	15	4.20	1.40	$3	3.8	249			26%	4.29	4.3	4.2	4.5	1.1	1.2	G	74%	19	36

On surface, best season since 1997. But a closer look reveals that he did it with smoke and mirrors. He won't survive long with these K rates, and LHers increased their BA against him for the second straight season.

Franklin,Ryan

RH Starter | AGE 31 Peak | TYPE Finesse
R: Very High | I: exp con | S: PT | K: BRN
LIMA D | EP: 30%

Yr	Tm	W	L	Sv	IP	K	ERA	Br/IP	R$	BF/G	OBA	vL	vR	H%	xERA	RAR	Ctl	Dom	Cmd	hr/9	G/F	S%	BPV	BPX
99	aaa	6	9	2	135	80	6.47	1.56	($4)	20.9	314			34%	5.74 +	-16.0	2.5	5.3	2.2	1.5		60%	26	50
00	aaa	11	5	0	164	122	5.32	1.36	$8	22.6	284			31%	5.26	9.6	2.2	6.7	3.1	1.8		66%	48	114
01	SEA	5	1	0	78	60	3.57	1.28	$7	8.6	257	276	232	28%	4.41 -	20.0	2.8	6.9	2.5	1.5	0.62	79%	53	106
02	SEA	7	5	0	118	65	4.04	1.18	$10	11.8	260	265	247	28%	3.86	22.4	1.7	5.0	3.0	1.1	0.82	69%	63	129
03	SEA	11	13	0	212	99	3.57	1.23	$18	27.5	250	267	233	25%	4.18 -	55.6	2.6	4.2	1.6	1.4	0.62	78%	21	45
1st Half		6	6	0	105	51	3.51	1.17	$11	26.9	241			23%	4.25 -	28.4	2.5	4.4	1.8	1.8	0.55	80%	16	35
2nd Half		5	7	0	107	48	3.62	1.28	$8	28.1	259			27%	4.12 -	27.2	2.7	4.0	1.5	1.1	0.70	76%	26	57
04	Proj	11	10	0	200	110	4.14	1.26	$14	26.9	260			27%	4.29	37.5	2.4	5.0	2.1	1.4	F	72%	36	77

Workload, durability, and ERA suggest that '03 was one of his best. Poor Cmd due to lack of Dom indicates otherwise. Artificial hit and strand rates will help push ERA back over 4.00.

Franklin,Wayne

LH Reliever | AGE 30 Peak | TYPE
R: Very High | I: EXP CON | S: pt STB | K:
LIMA F | EP: 45%

Yr	Tm	W	L	Sv	IP	K	ERA	Br/IP	R$	BF/G	OBA	vL	vR	H%	xERA	RAR	Ctl	Dom	Cmd	hr/9	G/F	S%	BPV	BPX
99	aa	3	1	20	50	32	2.16	1.10	$20	4.4	208			24%	2.25	22.6	3.2	5.8	1.8	0.5		83%	69	160
00	HOU	* 3	3	4	65	53	5.10	1.79	($0)	4.2	316	256	304	37%	6.05 -	4.6	4.4	7.3	1.7	1.0	0.88	73%	42	91
01	HOU	* 2	1	0	61	51	5.46	1.72	($4)	5.4	306			35%	6.49 -	-0.8	4.3	7.5	1.8	1.8	0.79	73%	23	42
02	aaa	* 15	10	0	203	130	4.39	1.49	$7	27.1	275			30%	4.72	24.0	3.8	5.8	1.5	1.0	0.83	73%	36	70
03	MIL	10	13	0	194	116	5.51	1.52	($3)	23.9	268	255	271	28%	5.32	-6.2	4.4	5.4	1.2	1.7	0.74	68%	9	18
1st Half		4	5	0	100	65	5.03	1.42	($0)	22.9	248			26%	4.73	3.3	4.4	5.8	1.3	1.6	0.90	69%	20	38
2nd Half		6	8	0	94	51	6.03	1.63	($4)	25.2	289			30%	5.94	-9.4	4.3	4.9	1.1	1.7	0.60	67%	-1	-3
04	Proj	11	11	5	200	130	5.09	1.55	$2	12.2	278			30%	5.27	4.8	4.1	5.9	1.4	1.4	F	71%	21	41

First full season in MLB yielded mediocre results. Lack of command and sharply declining dominance rate leaves little room for error. ERA not likely to dip below 5.00 until his skills improve.

Fuentes,Brian

LH Reliever | AGE 28 Pre-Peak | TYPE Power
R: High | I: EXP con | S: pt stb | K:
LIMA B+ | EP: 45%

Yr	Tm	W	L	Sv	IP	K	ERA	Br/IP	R$	BF/G	OBA	vL	vR	H%	xERA	RAR	Ctl	Dom	Cmd	hr/9	G/F	S%	BPV	BPX
99	aa	3	3	0	60	56	6.90	1.98	($7)	19.6	281			35%	5.74 +	-11.0	8.0	8.4	1.1	0.9		65%	44	103
00	aa	7	12	0	139	124	6.67	1.84	($10)	25.5	301			37%	5.57 +	-16.9	5.6	8.0	1.4	0.6		62%	55	131
01	SEA	* 4	3	6	63	71	3.70	1.28	$9	5.9	205			27%	3.12 +	15.1	5.0	10.1	2.0	0.9	1.44	73%	92	183
02	COL	* 5	3	1	75	89	4.56	1.61	$0	4.7	267			37%	4.29	5.5	5.3	10.7	2.0	0.5	0.76	71%	94	177
03	COL	3	3	4	75	82	2.76	1.30	$8	4.2	232	238	227	31%	3.47 -	25.4	4.1	9.8	2.4	0.8	0.69	82%	93	179
1st Half		1	0	0	39	43	2.54	1.28	$3	4.6	214			29%	3.05 -	14.3	4.6	9.9	2.2	0.7	0.87	83%	96	185
2nd Half		2	3	4	36	39	2.99	1.33	$5	3.9	250			32%	3.92 -	11.1	3.5	9.7	2.8	1.0	0.53	82%	92	177
04	Proj	4	4	14	75	83	3.72	1.44	$11	4.6	246			33%	3.85	15.5	4.7	10.0	2.1	0.7	F	75%	89	171

Breakout season. Lefty handled both LH and RH batters well. Maintained strong Dom while reducing control, especially in second half. Has goods to close, but G/F trend in Coors will keep him on a short leash.

Fultz,Aaron

LH Reliever | AGE 30 Peak | TYPE Power
R: Moderate | I: exp CON | S: pt stb | K:
LIMA D | EP: 50%

Yr	Tm	W	L	Sv	IP	K	ERA	Br/IP	R$	BF/G	OBA	vL	vR	H%	xERA	RAR	Ctl	Dom	Cmd	hr/9	G/F	S%	BPV	BPX
99	aaa	9	8	0	137	128	5.06	1.47	$4	16.3	281			32%	5.47	8.7	3.4	8.4	2.5	2.0		73%	43	99
00	SF	5	2	1	69	62	4.69	1.37	$5	5.1	256	221	284	31%	4.19 +	8.7	3.6	8.1	2.2	1.0	1.57	68%	68	149
01	SF	3	1	1	71	67	4.56	1.28	$3	4.5	259	237	276	31%	4.09	7.6	2.7	8.5	3.2	1.1	1.12	67%	87	161
02	SF	* 3	5	3	63	48	4.57	1.59	$1	4.7	280	302	284	33%	4.66	4.5	4.4	6.9	1.5	0.7	1.04	72%	51	97
03	TEX	1	3	0	67	53	5.23	1.52	($3)	4.7	284	218	345	33%	5.15	2.6	3.6	7.1	2.0	1.2	1.32	68%	46	99
1st Half		1	1	0	39	32	3.67	1.22	$2	4.2	256			31%	3.52	9.7	2.3	7.3	3.2	0.7	1.24	71%	94	204
2nd Half		0	2	0	28	21	7.42	1.94	($5)	5.0	320			35%	7.43	-7.1	5.5	6.8	1.2	1.9	1.44	65%	-0	-1
04	Proj	2	3	0	65	53	4.85	1.52	($1)	4.9	285			33%	5.20	6.0	3.6	7.3	2.0	1.2	--	71%	47	102

Has shown LIMA-worthy skills like these before, but with better results. Lefty specialist should fare well if used carefully. First half skills show renewed promise but second half fade is worrisome.

STEPHEN NICKRAND

Gagne,Eric

RH Reliever
AGE 28 Pre-Peak
TYPE Power
R: Low
I: exp | CON
S: pt
K:
LIMA C | EP: 50%

Yr	Tm	W	L	Sv	IP	K	ERA	Br/IP	R$	BF/G	OBA	vL	vR	H%	xERA	RAR	Ctl	Dom	Cmd	hr/9	G/F	S%	BPV	BPX
99	LA	* 13	5	0	197	185	2.56	1.11	$28	25.6	207	196	154	26%	2.28	70.6	3.3	8.5	**2.5**	0.8	0.88	81%	94	205
00	LA	* 9	7	0	156	129	4.72	1.52	$4	23.9	271	263	276	31%	5.26 -	19.0	4.3	7.4	**1.7**	1.6	0.70	74%	35	78
01	LA	* 9	7	0	174	157	4.34	1.22	$11	19.5	245	256	247	28%	3.93	23.8	2.7	8.1	**3.0**	1.3	0.72	69%	77	142
02	LA	4	1	52	82	114	1.98	0.87	$43	4.0	192	213	163	29%	1.61	34.4	1.8	12.5	**7.1**	0.7	0.80	82%	222	419
03	LA	2	3	55	82	137	1.21	0.69	$48	3.9	138	130	135	27%	0.23 +	44.8	2.2	15.0	**6.9**	0.2	1.20	84%	255	490
1st Half		1	2	29	39	69	2.07	0.72	$23	3.6	147			30%	0.38 +	16.8	2.1	15.9	**7.7**	0.2	1.33	70%	275	529
2nd Half		1	1	26	43	68	0.42	0.67	$25	4.1	129			24%	0.09	28.0	2.3	14.2	**6.2**	0.2	1.11	96%	238	458
04	**Proj**	**3**	**2**	**50**	**80**	**112**	**2.03**	**0.88**	**$42**	**4.0**	**178**			**28%**	**1.43 +**	**34.7**	**2.4**	**12.6**	**5.3**	**0.6**	**--**	**80%**	**190**	**367**

Perhaps the most dominant relief relief season in history, Hank Blalock not withstanding. Another 50 save season? Nothing in his skills set suggests otherwise -- even if he's already the only pitcher with two of them.

Gallo,Mike

LH Reliever
AGE 26 Growth
TYPE Finesse
R: Low
I: EXP
S:
K:
LIMA C+ | EP: 35%

Yr	Tm	W	L	Sv	IP	K	ERA	Br/IP	R$	BF/G	OBA	vL	vR	H%	xERA	RAR	Ctl	Dom	Cmd	hr/9	G/F	S%	BPV	BPX
99		0	0	0	0	0	0.00	0.00																
00		0	0	0	0	0	0.00	0.00																
01		0	0	0	0	0	0.00	0.00																
02		0	0	0	0	0	0.00	0.00																
03	HOU	* 5	1	2	67	43	2.55	1.27	$9	4.3	259	227	295	30%	3.49 -	24.5	2.6	5.8	**2.3**	0.5	1.12	81%	69	133
1st Half		4	1	2	37	27	2.19	1.27	$7	4.7	267			32%	3.32 -	15.3	2.2	6.6	**3.0**	0.2		83%	97	186
2nd Half		1	0	0	30	16	3.00	1.27	$2	3.9	249			27%	3.70 -	9.2	3.0	4.8	**1.6**	0.9		80%	41	78
04	**Proj**	**4**	**1**	**2**	**70**	**43**	**3.34**	**1.27**	**$7**	**4.2**	**256**			**29%**	**3.53**	**18.0**	**2.7**	**5.5**	**2.0**	**0.6**	**--**	**75%**	**61**	**117**

1-0, 3.00 ERA in 30 IP at HOU. Fine rookie year, but the xERA is a better indication of his season, and true potential. Doesn't have the stuff to support an 80% strand rate consistently, so ERA goes up.

Garcia,Freddy

RH Starter
AGE 27 Pre-Peak
TYPE
R: Moderate
I: CON
S: pt
K: brn
LIMA C | EP: 50%

Yr	Tm	W	L	Sv	IP	K	ERA	Br/IP	R$	BF/G	OBA	vL	vR	H%	xERA	RAR	Ctl	Dom	Cmd	hr/9	G/F	S%	BPV	BPX
99	SEA	17	8	0	201	170	4.07	1.47	$17	26.7	266	255	273	32%	4.34	48.4	4.0	7.6	**1.9**	0.8	1.40	74%	63	158
00	SEA	9	5	0	124	79	3.92	1.42	$11	25.6	242	272	205	26%	4.22	33.2	4.6	5.7	**1.2**	1.2	1.15	76%	32	83
01	SEA	18	6	0	238	163	3.06	1.13	$31	28.3	229	242	205	26%	2.82	77.3	2.6	6.2	**2.4**	0.6	1.45	74%	78	156
02	SEA	16	10	0	223	181	4.40	1.30	$15	27.7	265	255	265	31%	4.35	31.7	2.5	7.3	**2.9**	1.2	1.13	70%	70	143
03	SEA	12	14	0	201	144	4.52	1.33	$10	25.9	257	281	223	28%	4.46	27.1	3.2	6.4	**2.0**	1.4	0.93	70%	43	93
1st Half		9	6	0	109	69	4.13	1.29	$10	27.0	249			26%	4.29	20.4	3.2	5.7	**1.8**	1.4	0.93	73%	34	74
2nd Half		3	8	0	92	75	4.98	1.37	$1	24.7	266			30%	4.66	6.7	3.1	7.3	**2.3**	1.4	0.92	67%	54	117
04	**Proj**	**13**	**11**	**0**	**200**	**150**	**4.28**	**1.31**	**$13**	**26.4**	**256**			**29%**	**4.19**	**33.9**	**3.1**	**6.8**	**2.2**	**1.2**	**--**	**71%**	**56**	**119**

Pros:
- Second-half k/9 surge
- Workload eased off a bit

Cons:
- BPIs trending down
- G/F, hr/9 going the wrong way

Upside? Another 2001.

Garcia,Rosman

RH Reliever
AGE 25 Growth
TYPE
R: High
I: EXP | con
S: pt
K: age
LIMA C+ | EP: 50%

Yr	Tm	W	L	Sv	IP	K	ERA	Br/IP	R$	BF/G	OBA	vL	vR	H%	xERA	RAR	Ctl	Dom	Cmd	hr/9	G/F	S%	BPV	BPX
99		0	0	0	0	0	0.00	0.00																
00		0	0	0	0	0	0.00	0.00																
01	aa	1	0	0	6	5	0.00	1.33	$2	25.5	262			33%	3.20 -	4.4	3.0	7.5	**2.5**	0.0		100%	100	192
02	aa	8	5	6	74	32	4.26	1.72	$6	6.5	308			34%	4.96 -	10.0	4.1	3.9	**0.9**	0.1		73%	33	64
03	TEX	* 2	4	10	74	43	4.74	1.57	$4	5.3	294	333	312	33%	4.87	7.8	3.5	5.2	**1.5**	0.6	1.37	69%	40	87
1st Half		1	0	10	41	22	3.28	1.21	$9	5.2	246			28%	2.95	12.4	2.6	4.8	**1.8**	0.2	1.46	71%	66	144
2nd Half		1	4	0	33	21	6.57	2.01	($5)	5.4	346			39%	7.27 -	-4.6	4.7	5.7	**1.2**	1.1	1.28	68%	13	29
04	**Proj**	**4**	**5**	**2**	**75**	**40**	**4.80**	**1.56**	**$1**	**5.6**	**284**			**32%**	**4.59**	**7.4**	**4.0**	**4.8**	**1.2**	**0.5**	**--**	**68%**	**38**	**81**

1-2, 6.02 ERA in 46 IP at TEX. Sinkerball specialist whose control deserted him in the second half. Ridiculously low hr/9 rates suggest the makings of a Ben Weber-type, HR-stingy middle man, given the time.

Garland,Jon

RH Starter
AGE 24 Growth
TYPE
R: High
I: exp | con
S: pt
K: age
LIMA C | EP: 40%

Yr	Tm	W	L	Sv	IP	K	ERA	Br/IP	R$	BF/G	OBA	vL	vR	H%	xERA	RAR	Ctl	Dom	Cmd	hr/9	G/F	S%	BPV	BPX
99	aa	3	1	0	39	24	5.31	1.56	$1	25.0	286			32%	4.81 +	1.2	3.9	5.5	**1.4**	0.9		67%	33	77
00	CHW	* 13	10	0	178	107	4.09	1.52	$13	24.7	283	304	278	32%	4.62 -	43.6	3.6	5.4	**1.5**	0.7	1.40	74%	41	106
01	CHW	* 6	10	1	150	85	3.66	1.50	$5	16.6	273	276	278	30%	4.76 -	36.7	4.0	5.1	**1.3**	1.0	1.49	79%	27	55
02	CHW	12	12	0	192	112	4.59	1.41	$7	25.2	258	287	220	28%	4.42	22.3	3.9	5.3	**1.3**	1.1	1.14	70%	31	63
03	CHW	12	13	0	191	108	4.52	1.37	$9	25.6	259	278	234	27%	4.54	25.8	3.5	5.1	**1.5**	1.3	1.22	71%	25	54
1st Half		6	6	0	93	54	4.65	1.37	$4	24.9	264			28%	4.72	11.0	3.2	5.2	**1.6**	1.5	1.21	71%	24	53
2nd Half		6	7	0	98	54	4.40	1.37	$5	26.4	253			27%	4.36	14.8	3.8	4.9	**1.3**	1.2	1.23	71%	26	56
04	**Proj**	**12**	**13**	**0**	**200**	**115**	**4.50**	**1.42**	**$8**	**25.5**	**263**			**28%**	**4.56**	**27.8**	**3.7**	**5.2**	**1.4**	**1.2**	**--**	**71%**	**28**	**60**

Threw it over the plate more, but they just hit more of 'em out. Yes, he's still young, but where is the skills growth? There's really nothing here to suggest a breakout anytime soon.

Gaudin,Chad

RH Reliever
AGE 21 Green
TYPE
R: Moderate
I: EXP
S:
K: AGE
LIMA C+ | EP: 40%

Yr	Tm	W	L	Sv	IP	K	ERA	Br/IP	R$	BF/G	OBA	vL	vR	H%	xERA	RAR	Ctl	Dom	Cmd	hr/9	G/F	S%	BPV	BPX
99		0	0	0	0	0	0.00	0.00																
00		0	0	0	0	0	0.00	0.00																
01		0	0	0	0	0	0.00	0.00																
02		0	0	0	0	0	0.00	0.00																
03	TAM	* 4	0	0	59	44	2.59	1.12	$9	13.2	220	269	218	26%	2.73	23.2	2.9	6.7	**2.3**	0.6	0.70	79%	82	176
1st Half		0	0	0	0	0	0.00	0.00																
2nd Half		4	0	0	59	44	2.59	1.12	$9	13.2	220			26%	2.73	23.2	2.9	6.7	**2.3**	0.6		79%	82	176
04	**Proj**	**2**	**3**	**0**	**60**	**39**	**4.35**	**1.45**	**$1**	**13.1**	**265**			**30%**	**4.42**	**9.6**	**3.9**	**5.9**	**1.5**	**0.9**	**F**	**72%**	**42**	**89**

2-0, 3.60 ERA in 40 IP at TAM. Solid BPIs across the board, but just 19 IP at Double-A? Cmd ratio 1.4 at TAM, so he didn't exactly come up and dominate. Real potential, but expect some growing pains.

George,Chris

LH Starter
AGE 24 Growth
TYPE
R: Very High
I: EXP | con
S: pt
K: age | brn
LIMA F | EP: 50%

Yr	Tm	W	L	Sv	IP	K	ERA	Br/IP	R$	BF/G	OBA	vL	vR	H%	xERA	RAR	Ctl	Dom	Cmd	hr/9	G/F	S%	BPV	BPX
99		0	0	0	0	0	0.00	0.00																
00	aa	11	7	0	142	89	4.63	1.61	$6	24.8	287			32%	5.15 -	21.6	4.3	5.6	**1.3**	1.0		73%	30	72
01	KC	* 15	11	0	191	106	4.62	1.35	$12	24.7	265	222	303	28%	4.59	22.2	3.0	5.0	**1.7**	1.4	0.86	70%	26	52
02	KC	* 6	16	0	154	91	6.90	1.78	($16)	25.8	319			35%	6.28 +	-29.6	4.1	5.3	**1.3**	1.1	1.06	61%	17	34
03	KC	* 12	11	0	147	62	7.88	1.82	($14)	24.9	328	280	319	33%	7.33 +	-46.5	4.0	3.8	**1.0**	2.0	1.22	59%	-27	-57
1st Half		9	5	0	84	37	6.86	1.75	($3)	24.5	317			32%	6.84	-15.0	4.0	4.0	**1.0**	1.8	1.18	64%	-18	-39
2nd Half		3	6	0	63	25	9.24	1.91	($12)	25.5	343			34%	7.97 +	-31.5	4.0	3.6	**0.9**	2.1	1.70	53%	-37	-81
04	**Proj**	**8**	**10**	**0**	**120**	**60**	**5.93**	**1.73**	**($5)**	**25.4**	**316**			**33%**	**6.54 -**	**-6.2**	**3.9**	**4.5**	**1.2**	**1.6**	**--**	**69%**	**-4**	**-9**

9-6, 7.16 ERA in 93 IP at KC. Just when you thought it couldn't get any uglier, it got uglier. If you're looking for silver linings, his S% has to improve -- although that would only take him from horrendous to just bad.

German,Franklyn

RH Reliever
AGE 24 Growth
TYPE Power
R: High
I: EXP | con
S:
K: age
LIMA B | EP: 55%

Yr	Tm	W	L	Sv	IP	K	ERA	Br/IP	R$	BF/G	OBA	vL	vR	H%	xERA	RAR	Ctl	Dom	Cmd	hr/9	G/F	S%	BPV	BPX
99		0	0	0	0	0	0.00	0.00																
00		0	0	0	0	0	0.00	0.00																
01		0	0	0	0	0	0.00	0.00																
02	a/a	2	2	29	64	82	2.95	1.23	$21	4.4	210			33%	2.21 +	19.9	4.4	11.5	**2.6**	0.0		73%	138	270
03	DET	* 3	8	9	73	69	4.91	1.72	$3	4.9	258	238	304	32%	4.95	6.0	6.6	8.5	**1.3**	0.9	1.24	72%	55	119
1st Half		2	3	5	32	34	3.93	1.81	$3	4.9	223			30%	4.42 -	6.9	9.0	9.5	**1.1**	0.6	1.10	79%	73	158
2nd Half		1	5	4	41	35	5.68	1.65	($0)	5.0	284			34%	5.36	-0.9	4.8	7.6	**1.6**	1.1	1.64	67%	45	97
04	**Proj**	**3**	**5**	**18**	**70**	**75**	**4.11**	**1.53**	**$12**	**4.7**	**242**			**33%**	**3.91**	**13.4**	**5.7**	**9.6**	**1.7**	**0.5**	**--**	**73%**	**85**	**182**

5 Sv, 6.04 ERA in 45 IP at DET. Came out firing but walked everybody, then eased up and got hit. Still, great stuff, and could put it together quickly if he can find the plate.
Upside: 3.00, 25 saves.

Glavine,Tom

LH Starter
AGE 38 Decline
TYPE Finesse
R: Moderate
I: CON
S:
K: AGE
LIMA C+ | EP: 45%

Yr	Tm	W	L	Sv	IP	K	ERA	Br/IP	R$	BF/G	OBA	vL	vR	H%	xERA	RAR	Ctl	Dom	Cmd	hr/9	G/F	S%	BPV	BPX
99	ATL	14	11	0	234	138	4.12	1.46	$11	29.3	282	267	292	32%	4.11	35.1	3.2	5.3	**1.7**	0.7	1.74	73%	45	97
00	ATL	21	9	0	241	152	3.40	1.19	$33	28.3	246	242	245	27%	3.48	72.0	2.4	5.7	**2.3**	0.9	1.45	75%	62	137
01	ATL	16	7	0	219	116	3.57	1.41	$16	27.1	256	251	263	27%	4.28 -	52.6	4.0	4.8	**1.2**	1.0	1.15	78%	28	52
02	ATL	18	11	0	224	127	2.97	1.29	$24	26.2	250	244	254	27%	3.62 -	64.0	3.1	5.1	**1.6**	0.8	1.06	80%	45	84
03	NYM	9	14	0	183	82	4.52	1.48	$2	25.2	284	285	289	30%	4.86	18.5	3.2	4.0	**1.2**	1.0	1.21	72%	17	34
1st Half		5	8	0	92	42	4.89	1.53	($0)	25.6	290			30%	5.40 -	4.8	3.4	4.1	**1.2**	1.4	1.47	72%	6	11
2nd Half		4	6	0	91	40	4.15	1.43	$2	24.8	278			30%	4.32	13.8	3.1	4.0	**1.3**	0.7	1.01	72%	29	57
04	**Proj**	**10**	**12**	**0**	**180**	**91**	**4.10**	**1.40**	**$8**	**25.9**	**269**			**29%**	**4.28**	**28.1**	**3.3**	**4.6**	**1.4**	**0.9**	**--**	**73%**	**31**	**60**

Not even the epitomé of the finesse lefty can get people out with 4 k/9. Things didn't get much better in the 2nd half. Beginning the Steve Carlton Path to Retirement, with a QuesTec twist.

ROD TRUESDELL

Glover,Gary

RH Reliever
AGE 27 Growth
TYPE
R Very High
I EXP CON
S pt STB
K
LIMA D EP: 45%

Tm	W	L	Sv	IP	K	ERA	Br/IP	R$	BF/G	OBA	vL	vR	H%	xERA	RAR	Ctl	Dom	Cmd	hr/9	G/F	S%	BPV	BPX
99 a/a	12	8	0	162	123	4.56	1.40	$11	25.9	271			32%	3.97 +	21.2	3.1	6.8	2.2	0.7		68%	66	153
00 aaa	9	9	0	166	101	6.13	1.61	($3)	27.8	307			33%	5.77	-8.1	3.3	5.5	1.7	1.3		63%	23	54
01 CHW *	7	6	0	138	89	4.30	1.17	$10	10.8	242	237	269	26%	3.75 +	21.8	2.4	5.8	2.4	1.3	1.15	67%	53	106
02 CHW	7	8	1	138	70	5.22	1.36	$3	14.4	259	280	219	26%	4.60 +	4.5	3.4	4.6	1.3	1.4	0.86	65%	18	36
03 2AL	2	0	0	62	37	4.77	1.59	($1)	6.7	305	360	258	34%	5.35 -	6.2	3.2	5.4	1.7	0.9	1.01	71%	35	76
1st Half	1	0	0	28	17	5.74	1.81	($2)	7.0	340			38%	6.55 -	-0.8	3.2	5.4	1.7	1.0	0.97	69%	26	57
2nd Half	1	0	0	34	20	3.97	1.41	$1	6.4	273			30%	4.35	7.1	3.2	5.3	1.7	0.8	1.05	73%	43	94
04 Proj	3	2	0	80	47	4.61	1.45	$1	9.0	281			30%	4.86	9.9	3.2	5.3	1.7	1.1	--	71%	32	69

Numbers were better with ANA, but that was mainly the hit rate returning to normal, and lefties ate him up again. He's shown better, but something to compliment the fastball/curve repertoire would help.

Gobble,Jimmy

LH Starter
AGE 22 Growth
TYPE Finesse
R X HIGH
I EXP con
S pt
K AGE BRN
LIMA C+ EP: 45%

Tm	W	L	Sv	IP	K	ERA	Br/IP	R$	BF/G	OBA	vL	vR	H%	xERA	RAR	Ctl	Dom	Cmd	hr/9	G/F	S%	BPV	BPX
99	0	0	0	0	0	0.00	0.00																
00	0	0	0	0	0	0.00	0.00																
01	0	0	0	0	0	0.00	0.00																
02 aa	5	7	0	69	43	4.57	1.52	$2	23.6	307			35%	4.80	6.5	2.5	5.6	2.3	0.5		69%	59	116
03 KC *	16	13	0	184	114	4.44	1.44	$11	25.9	289	263	273	32%	4.96 -	26.8	2.7	5.6	2.1	1.1	0.52	72%	41	87
1st Half	9	6	0	99	63	5.09	1.49	$4	25.7	295			32%	5.24	5.8	2.8	5.7	2.0	1.2		68%	38	81
2nd Half	7	7	0	85	51	3.69	1.38	$7	26.2	281			31%	4.63 -	21.0	2.5	5.4	2.1	1.1		77%	44	95
04 Proj	9	11	0	120	74	4.80	1.47	$4	25.1	296			33%	4.91	11.9	2.6	5.6	2.2	0.9	F	68%	48	103

4-5, 4.61 ERA in 53 IP at KC. Good - held his own despite limited experience, and even better in the second half. Bad - jump in IP at age 21 means a significant burnout risk. Looks better for '05.

Gonzalez,Jeremi

RH Reliever
AGE 29 Pre-Peak
TYPE
R X HIGH
I EXP con
S pt stb
K BRN
LIMA C EP: 45%

Tm	W	L	Sv	IP	K	ERA	Br/IP	R$	BF/G	OBA	vL	vR	H%	xERA	RAR	Ctl	Dom	Cmd	hr/9	G/F	S%	BPV	BPX
99 a/a	0	1	0	20	20	4.05	1.75	($1)	15.6	242			31%	4.61 -	4.0	7.7	9.0	1.2	0.9		79%	58	135
00	0	0	0	0	0	0.00	0.00																
01	0	0	0	0	0	0.00	0.00																
02 aaa	6	5	14	92	77	3.91	1.49	$12	8.8	276			33%	4.49 -	16.7	3.7	7.5	2.0	0.8		75%	64	126
03 TAM *	7	11	0	188	123	3.88	1.25	$11	24.5	233	235	220	26%	3.56	41.5	3.6	5.9	1.6	1.0	0.60	72%	49	107
1st Half	4	4	0	86	68	3.77	1.17	$7	22.0	216			25%	3.03 +	20.2	3.6	7.1	2.0	0.8	0.54	70%	71	154
2nd Half	3	7	0	102	55	3.97	1.32	$4	27.1	246			26%	4.01	21.3	3.6	4.8	1.3	1.1	0.63	73%	31	68
04 Proj	7	10	10	160	115	4.16	1.36	$13	14.3	252			29%	4.00	29.5	3.7	6.5	1.8	0.9	F	71%	54	115

6-11, 3.91 ERA in 156 IP at TAM. People asked where this came from, but he spent all of 2002 doing the same thing at Triple-A. Second-half k/9 drop appears fatigue related; low hit rate means an ERA jump.

Good,Andrew

RH Starter
AGE 24 Growth
TYPE Finesse
R Very High
I EXP con
S pt
K age
LIMA C+ EP: 50%

Tm	W	L	Sv	IP	K	ERA	Br/IP	R$	BF/G	OBA	vL	vR	H%	xERA	RAR	Ctl	Dom	Cmd	hr/9	G/F	S%	BPV	BPX
99	0	0	0	0	0	0.00	0.00																
00	0	0	0	0	0	0.00	0.00																
01 aa	2	3	0	56	40	6.43	1.88	($7)	26.9	353			42%	6.30	-7.6	3.1	6.4	2.1	0.3		63%	58	111
02 aa	13	6	0	178	103	4.15	1.24	$14	26.4	280			30%	4.29	26.8	1.3	5.2	4.1	1.2		70%	82	161
03 ARI *	8	6	0	129	82	5.58	1.47	($0)	21.0	308	337	245	32%	6.11 -	-5.2	2.0	5.7	2.9	2.0	1.01	68%	29	55
1st Half	3	2	0	71	44	4.94	1.29	$2	20.0	267			28%	4.59	3.3	2.4	5.6	2.3	1.5	0.76	66%	38	73
2nd Half	5	4	0	58	38	6.36	1.69	($3)	22.3	352			36%	7.98 -	-8.4	1.4	5.9	4.2	2.6	3.13	70%	29	57
04 Proj	8	6	0	120	76	4.58	1.44	$4	23.8	306			33%	5.55 -	11.1	1.8	5.7	3.2	1.6	--	74%	47	91

4-2, 5.29 ERA in 66 IP at ARI. Control artist who grooved a few too many pitches (2.0 hr/9). Consistently good Cmd ratios intriguing. Question: How did he combine a 3.13 G/F and 2.6 hr/9 in the second half?

Gordon,Tom

RH Reliever
AGE 36 Decline
TYPE Power
R High
I con
S pt STB
K age
LIMA B EP: 60%

Tm	W	L	Sv	IP	K	ERA	Br/IP	R$	BF/G	OBA	vL	vR	H%	xERA	RAR	Ctl	Dom	Cmd	hr/9	G/F	S%	BPV	BPX
99 BOS	0	2	11	18	24	5.50	1.61	$5	3.9	251	300	205	36%	4.64 +	0.9	6.0	12.0	2.0	1.0	0.56	67%	89	223
00 BOS	0	0	0	0	0	0.00	0.00																
01 CHC	1	2	27	45	67	3.39	1.06	$20	3.8	201	188	188	32%	2.44 +	11.9	3.2	13.4	4.2	0.8	1.05	70%	159	295
02 HOU	1	3	1	43	48	3.98	1.44	$1	5.2	262	269	255	36%	3.73	6.5	4.0	10.0	2.5	0.4	0.86	72%	103	196
03 CHW	7	6	12	74	91	3.16	1.19	$18	4.6	215	231	196	31%	2.67	23.4	3.8	11.1	2.9	0.5	1.05	74%	126	271
1st Half	4	5	1	39	50	3.90	1.40	$4	5.0	240			36%	3.29 +	8.5	4.6	11.5	2.5	0.2	0.91	70%	121	262
2nd Half	3	1	11	35	41	2.33	0.95	$14	4.2	183			25%	1.98	14.9	2.8	10.6	3.7	0.8	1.21	80%	137	296
04 Proj	4	5	15	75	92	3.36	1.24	$16	4.7	227			32%	3.05	21.9	3.7	11.0	3.0	0.6	--	74%	120	258

BPIs still rock-solid, but the specter of injury will always be there. It's pretty simple, really: if Gordon is healthy, he'll be darn good again. Last spring, though, he was a draft-day sleeper; he won't be this time.

Graves,Danny

RH Reliever
AGE 30 Peak
TYPE Finesse
R Low
I con
S pt
K brn
LIMA D EP: 50%

Tm	W	L	Sv	IP	K	ERA	Br/IP	R$	BF/G	OBA	vL	vR	H%	xERA	RAR	Ctl	Dom	Cmd	hr/9	G/F	S%	BPV	BPX
99 CIN	8	7	27	111	69	3.08	1.25	$28	6.2	223	220	233	25%	2.90	32.0	4.0	5.6	1.4	0.8	2.32	78%	49	107
00 CIN	10	5	30	91	53	2.57	1.35	$32	5.9	240	261	226	26%	3.70 -	37.3	4.1	5.2	1.3	0.8	2.21	84%	41	91
01 CIN	6	5	32	80	49	4.16	1.26	$25	5.1	269	301	243	30%	3.87	13.0	2.0	5.5	2.7	0.8	1.99	68%	68	126
02 CIN	7	3	32	98	58	3.21	1.27	$27	6.0	264	272	259	30%	3.57	24.8	2.3	5.3	2.3	0.6	2.20	76%	64	120
03 CIN	4	15	2	169	60	5.33	1.45	($4)	24.6	300	297	299	29%	5.56	-1.1	2.2	3.2	1.5	1.6	1.25	67%	-3	-6
1st Half	3	7	1	95	33	4.93	1.46	($1)	26.0	291			29%	5.38	4.5	2.7	3.1	1.1	1.5	1.34	71%	-6	-12
2nd Half	1	8	1	74	27	5.84	1.43	($3)	23.0	311			31%	5.78	-5.5	1.5	3.3	2.3	1.7	1.15	63%	9	17
04 Proj	4	6	14	80	44	4.50	1.35	$11	7.3	281			30%	4.53	8.2	2.3	5.0	2.2	1.1	--	69%	41	79

That starting thing didn't work out too well, did it? If his shoulder is okay, if he resumes closing, and if he can get the k/9 and G/F back up, 30 saves is again realistic. That's a lot of ifs.

Grimsley,Jason

RH Reliever
AGE 36 Decline
TYPE Power
R Moderate
I CON
S pt
K AGE
LIMA D+ EP: 60%

Tm	W	L	Sv	IP	K	ERA	Br/IP	R$	BF/G	OBA	vL	vR	H%	xERA	RAR	Ctl	Dom	Cmd	hr/9	G/F	S%	BPV	BPX
99 NYY	7	2	1	75	49	3.60	1.41	$9	5.9	238	165	275	27%	3.88	22.8	4.8	5.9	1.2	0.8	2.17	77%	43	108
00 NYY	3	2	1	96	53	5.06	1.48	$2	6.7	270	228	299	29%	4.54 +	11.0	3.9	5.0	1.3	0.9	1.82	67%	29	76
01 KC	1	5	0	80	61	3.03	1.24	$5	4.6	239	261	218	28%	3.50	26.3	3.1	6.9	2.2	0.9	3.30	79%	67	134
02 KC	4	7	1	72	59	4.00	1.43	$4	4.4	243	248	225	30%	3.70	14.1	4.8	7.4	1.6	0.5	3.27	72%	68	140
03 KC	2	6	0	75	58	5.16	1.65	($4)	4.5	294	316	282	35%	5.17	3.7	4.3	7.0	1.6	0.7	3.38	69%	50	108
1st Half	2	3	0	45	37	3.80	1.29	$3	4.4	262			32%	3.68	10.4	2.6	7.4	2.8	0.6	4.59	71%	89	192
2nd Half	0	3	0	30	21	7.20	2.20	($7)	4.7	337			39%	7.42	-6.7	6.9	6.3	0.9	0.9	2.35	67%	18	38
04 Proj	3	5	0	75	57	4.44	1.53	$0	4.6	264			31%	4.44	11.0	4.7	6.8	1.5	0.7	G	72%	52	112

His base skills were almost identical to '02, but the ERA was over a run higher. See what 5% more grounders missing a glove will do? That second-half fade is a little troubling for someone his age.

Groom,Buddy

LH Reliever
AGE 38 Decline
TYPE
R Moderate
I con
S pt
K AGE
LIMA C EP: 65%

Tm	W	L	Sv	IP	K	ERA	Br/IP	R$	BF/G	OBA	vL	vR	H%	xERA	RAR	Ctl	Dom	Cmd	hr/9	G/F	S%	BPV	BPX
99 OAK	3	2	0	46	32	5.09	1.43	$2	2.6	270	245	315	32%	3.76 +	4.8	3.5	6.3	1.8	0.2	2.34	62%	70	176
00 BAL	6	3	4	59	44	4.87	1.42	$8	3.7	274	193	326	32%	4.28 +	8.2	3.2	6.7	2.1	0.8	1.52	66%	61	160
01 BAL	1	4	11	66	54	3.55	1.11	$11	3.8	256	194	291	31%	3.06	17.1	1.2	7.4	6.0	0.5	1.70	68%	158	316
02 BAL	3	2	2	62	48	1.60	0.90	$13	3.4	201	181	208	24%	1.94	32.1	1.7	7.0	4.0	0.6	1.54	87%	123	253
03 BAL	1	3	1	45	34	5.39	1.60	($2)	3.4	313	270	343	35%	5.97 -	0.8	2.8	6.8	2.4	1.4	1.32	69%	42	91
1st Half	1	3	0	24	20	6.32	1.45	($1)	3.5	291			33%	5.33 +	-2.6	2.6	7.4	2.9	1.5	1.57	58%	57	123
2nd Half	0	0	1	21	14	4.31	1.77	($1)	3.3	337			38%	6.71 -	3.4	3.0	6.0	2.0	1.3	1.09	79%	27	58
04 Proj	2	2	3	50	38	3.96	1.36	$4	3.4	281			33%	4.41	10.6	2.3	6.8	2.9	0.9	--	73%	74	159

His base skills weren't much worse, but the ERA was 4 runs higher. That's what 11% more glove-misses will do -- and three more HR. Reality is somewhere between '02 and 03, but age isn't on Groom's side, either.

Gryboski,Kevin

RH Reliever
AGE 30 Peak
TYPE Power
R High
I EXP CON
S STB
K
LIMA C+ EP: 45%

Tm	W	L	Sv	IP	K	ERA	Br/IP	R$	BF/G	OBA	vL	vR	H%	xERA	RAR	Ctl	Dom	Cmd	hr/9	G/F	S%	BPV	BPX
99 aa	2	5	10	62	33	4.21	1.81	$4	6.2	335			36%	6.29 -	11.0	3.5	4.8	1.4	1.0		79%	15	35
00 a/a	3	3	11	59	45	5.95	1.98	$1	6.2	322			39%	6.15	-1.5	5.8	6.9	1.2	0.5		68%	43	102
01 aaa	2	5	22	60	43	4.80	1.60	$11	4.7	307			35%	5.67 -	5.0	3.2	6.5	2.0	1.2		73%	39	75
02 ATL *	3	1	3	58	37	3.26	1.67	$2	4.2	265	169	306	30%	4.89 -	14.4	5.9	5.7	1.0	0.9	2.09	84%	29	55
03 ATL	6	4	0	44	32	3.88	1.52	$5	3.1	261	227	288	31%	4.22	8.3	4.7	6.5	1.4	0.6	3.95	75%	53	102
1st Half	4	3	0	26	19	5.52	1.57	$2	3.1	276			31%	4.94 +	-0.8	4.5	6.6	1.5	1.0	4.80	66%	39	75
2nd Half	2	1	0	18	13	1.50	1.44	$3	3.0	240			30%	3.16 -	9.1	5.0	6.5	1.3	0.0	3.10	88%	73	141
04 Proj	4	3	1	50	35	4.14	1.58	$2	3.7	269			31%	4.55	7.5	4.9	6.3	1.3	0.7	G	75%	45	86

ERA again suppressed by an 88% strand rate in the second half. Threw more strikes, but still not enough to predict good things. His '03 first half is more likely than another sub-4 ERA.

ROD TRUESDELL

Guardado,Eddie

LH Reliever
AGE 32 Past
TYPE Power
R Low
I | | con
S | pt |
K | |
LIMA C EP: 50%

Yr	Tm	W	L	Sv	IP	K	ERA	Br/IP	R$	BF/G	OBA	vL	vR	H%	xERA	RAR	Ctl	Dom	Cmd	hr/9	G/F	S%	BPV	BPX
99	MIN	2	5	2	48	50	4.69	1.29	$4	3.2	215	176	258	27%	3.52 +	7.6	4.7	9.4	**2.0**	1.1	0.55	66%	77	192
00	MIN	7	4	9	61	52	3.97	1.31	$14	3.7	242	287	208	25%	4.76 -	15.9	3.7	7.6	**2.1**	2.1	0.46	80%	34	89
01	MIN	7	1	12	66	67	3.53	1.06	$17	3.9	201	167	216	26%	2.36 +	17.3	3.1	9.1	**2.9**	0.7	0.64	68%	110	221
02	MIN	1	3	45	67	70	2.96	1.06	$32	3.9	219	263	200	27%	3.12	22.5	2.4	9.4	**3.9**	1.2	0.61	79%	113	232
03	MIN	3	5	41	65	60	2.90	0.98	$34	3.8	214	175	219	26%	2.63	22.9	1.9	8.3	**4.3**	1.0	0.51	75%	123	265
1st Half		1	2	20	32	29	2.80	1.02	$16	3.8	229			28%	2.80	11.8	1.7	8.1	**4.8**	0.8	0.43	77%	134	290
2nd Half		2	3	21	33	31	3.01	0.94	$18	3.9	199			24%	2.46 +	11.1	2.2	8.5	**3.9**	1.1	0.60	74%	115	248
04	**Proj**	**3**	**4**	**39**	**65**	**63**	**3.18**	**1.05**	**$31**	**3.8**	**214**			**26%**	**2.91**	**20.5**	**2.5**	**8.7**	**3.5**	**1.1**	**F**	**75%**	**105**	**224**

Pinpoint control in the 1st half boosted an overall up-year. Flyball tendency always makes him more risky than others of the Elite, but should be good for another $30 year.

Guthrie,Mark

LH Reliever
AGE 38 Decline
TYPE Power
R Very High
I | | CON
S | pt | STB
K | AGE |
LIMA C+ EP: 20%

Yr	Tm	W	L	Sv	IP	K	ERA	Br/IP	R$	BF/G	OBA	vL	vR	H%	xERA	RAR	Ctl	Dom	Cmd	hr/9	G/F	S%	BPV	BPX
99	CHC	1	3	2	58	45	5.43	1.40	($0)	4.4	258	182	167	28%	4.41 +	-1.5	3.7	7.0	**1.9**	1.6	1.12	65%	38	83
00	TOR	3	6	0	71	63	4.68	1.50	$2	4.1	259	265	261	31%	4.50	11.7	4.7	8.0	**1.7**	1.0	1.25	71%	56	147
01	OAK	6	2	1	52	52	4.49	1.32	$6	4.1	250	259	241	31%	4.14	6.9	3.5	9.0	**2.6**	1.2	1.05	69%	77	155
02	NYM	5	3	1	48	44	2.44	1.13	$9	2.9	205	187	223	26%	2.37	17.2	3.6	8.3	**2.3**	0.6	2.28	80%	95	180
03	CHC	2	3	0	42	24	2.77	1.47	$3	2.8	252	280	241	26%	4.60 -	14.2	4.7	5.1	**1.1**	1.3	1.22	88%	20	38
1st Half		0	3	0	18	14	2.97	1.37	$1	2.6	249			26%	4.96 -	5.6	4.0	6.9	**1.8**	2.0	1.56	90%	24	47
2nd Half		2	0	0	24	10	2.62	1.54	$2	3.1	254			27%	4.33 -	8.5	5.2	3.7	**0.7**	0.7	1.03	86%	19	37
04	**Proj**	**2**	**3**	**0**	**40**	**26**	**4.50**	**1.48**	**$0**	**3.2**	**257**			**28%**	**4.50**	**4.1**	**4.5**	**5.9**	**1.3**	**1.1**	**--**	**72%**	**32**	**62**

By all rights, should have had an ERA closer to 4.50, but an 88% strand rate will do that. The regression to the mean, along with a rapidly deteriorating skill set make him a great bet to go SPLAT in 2004.

Hackman,Luther

RH Reliever
AGE 29 Peak
TYPE
R X HIGH
I | EXP | CON
S | PT | STB
K | | brn
LIMA D EP: 50%

Yr	Tm	W	L	Sv	IP	K	ERA	Br/IP	R$	BF/G	OBA	vL	vR	H%	xERA	RAR	Ctl	Dom	Cmd	hr/9	G/F	S%	BPV	BPX
99	a/a	11	9	0	163	117	5.52	1.65	($1)	28.7	301			34%	5.31	0.2	3.9	6.5	**1.6**	1.0		67%	38	89
00	aaa	8	9	0	119	60	5.45	1.59	$1	25.5	312			34%	5.44	5.0	2.8	4.5	**1.6**	0.9	0.75	66%	27	63
01	STL	* 1	4	1	62	38	4.06	1.19	$3	4.7	249	308	172	26%	3.92	10.8	2.3	5.5	**2.4**	1.3	0.79	71%	49	91
02	STL	5	4	0	81	46	4.11	1.59	$1	8.5	283	298	279	31%	4.80 -	10.8	4.3	5.1	**1.2**	0.8	1.11	75%	31	58
03	SD	2	2	0	74	46	5.09	1.46	($2)	5.1	261	238	277	29%	4.29 +	1.8	4.1	5.6	**1.4**	0.8	0.94	65%	39	75
1st Half		2	1	0	41	25	4.15	1.41	$1	5.0	261			29%	3.98	6.2	3.7	5.5	**1.5**	0.7	0.88	71%	47	90
2nd Half		0	1	0	33	21	6.27	1.52	($3)	5.2	262			29%	4.67 +	-4.4	4.6	5.7	**1.2**	1.1	1.03	59%	30	58
04	**Proj**	**2**	**4**	**0**	**75**	**46**	**4.68**	**1.48**	**($1)**	**6.2**	**269**			**30%**	**4.54**	**5.9**	**4.0**	**5.5**	**1.4**	**1.0**	**--**	**70%**	**35**	**67**

Soft-tosser without much command, his ERA will improve a bit just because of his depressed strand rate. But it won't be enough to make him draft-worthy.

Halama,John

LH Reliever
AGE 32 Peak
TYPE Finesse
R Moderate
I | | CON
S | |
K | |
LIMA C+ EP: 35%

Yr	Tm	W	L	Sv	IP	K	ERA	Br/IP	R$	BF/G	OBA	vL	vR	H%	xERA	RAR	Ctl	Dom	Cmd	hr/9	G/F	S%	BPV	BPX
99	SEA	11	10	0	179	105	4.22	1.39	$13	20.3	277	286	280	30%	4.52	39.5	2.8	5.3	**1.9**	1.0	1.31	72%	41	102
00	SEA	14	9	0	166	87	5.09	1.58	$8	24.9	305	343	297	33%	5.40	18.3	3.0	4.7	**1.6**	1.0	1.18	69%	24	62
01	SEA	* 12	7	0	129	68	4.12	1.31	$12	16.0	282	354	273	30%	4.70 -	23.6	1.8	4.7	**2.6**	1.3	1.29	73%	42	84
02	SEA	* 6	6	0	115	77	4.15	1.48	$3	15.3	295	246	298	34%	4.77 -	20.2	2.7	6.0	**2.3**	0.7	1.42	73%	58	120
03	OAK	3	5	0	108	51	4.24	1.41	$2	13.4	277	214	287	28%	5.08 -	18.6	3.0	4.2	**1.4**	1.5	1.39	76%	10	21
1st Half		2	4	0	60	32	4.19	1.45	$1	17.5	268			27%	5.02 -	10.8	3.7	4.8	**1.3**	1.5	1.10	77%	12	26
2nd Half		1	1	0	48	19	4.31	1.37	$1	10.3	289			29%	5.17 -	7.8	2.1	3.6	**1.7**	1.5	1.88	74%	10	21
04	**Proj**	**4**	**4**	**0**	**80**	**42**	**3.94**	**1.35**	**$5**	**7.8**	**274**			**29%**	**4.62 -**	**17.2**	**2.6**	**4.7**	**1.8**	**1.2**	**--**	**75%**	**30**	**64**

Starter or reliever? You pick:

	IP	ERA	Ctl	Dom
2003	IP	ERA	Ctl	Dom
SP	67	4.84	3.6	4.4
RP	42	3.24	1.9	3.8
4 Yrs	IP	ERA	Ctl	Dom
SP	265	5.13	3.1	4.7
RP	164	2.69	2.3	4.6

Halladay,Roy

RH Starter
AGE 26 Growth
TYPE
R High
I | | CON
S | PT |
K | | brn
LIMA C EP: 60%

Yr	Tm	W	L	Sv	IP	K	ERA	Br/IP	R$	BF/G	OBA	vL	vR	H%	xERA	RAR	Ctl	Dom	Cmd	hr/9	G/F	S%	BPV	BPX
99	TOR	8	7	1	149	82	3.93	1.58	$7	18.6	271	274	266	29%	5.04 -	38.8	4.8	5.0	**1.0**	1.1	1.36	79%	18	45
00	TOR	* 5	8	0	111	60	8.59	1.92	($15)	21.5	340	364	350	36%	7.38 +	-39.9	4.2	4.9	**1.2**	1.6	1.41	55%	-8	-21
01	TOR	* 8	4	0	153	131	3.12	1.12	$17	25.8	246	228	255	31%	2.90	48.5	1.8	7.7	**4.2**	0.5	2.56	73%	127	253
02	TOR	19	7	0	239	168	2.94	1.19	$30	28.9	249	259	228	30%	3.08	80.7	2.3	6.3	**2.7**	0.4	2.75	75%	89	182
03	TOR	22	7	0	266	204	3.25	1.07	$37	29.5	252	262	224	29%	3.27	81.1	1.1	6.9	**6.4**	0.9	2.32	73%	153	331
1st Half		11	2	0	129	100	3.70	1.19	$15	29.5	269			31%	4.10	31.6	1.4	7.0	**5.0**	1.2	1.84	74%	112	243
2nd Half		11	5	0	137	104	2.82	0.96	$23	29.5	235			28%	2.49	49.5	0.8	6.8	**8.7**	0.6	2.95	72%	213	460
04	**Proj**	**18**	**8**	**0**	**250**	**200**	**3.42**	**1.13**	**$30**	**27.4**	**255**			**30%**	**3.29**	**70.9**	**1.5**	**7.2**	**4.9**	**0.7**	**G**	**71%**	**128**	**274**

Not an overpowering pitcher, but when you allowed only 1 BB every 11 IP in the 2nd half, you must be doing something right. Pay full value.

Hammond,Chris

LH Reliever
AGE 38 Decline
TYPE
R High
I | EXP | con
S | | stb
K | AGE |
LIMA C EP: 40%

Yr	Tm	W	L	Sv	IP	K	ERA	Br/IP	R$	BF/G	OBA	vL	vR	H%	xERA	RAR	Ctl	Dom	Cmd	hr/9	G/F	S%	BPV	BPX
99		0	0	0	0	0	0.00	0.00																
00		0	0	0	0	0	0.00	0.00																
01	aaa	10	4	1	82	69	4.06	1.60	$7	7.6	312			38%	5.23 -	14.9	2.9	7.6	**2.7**	0.7		75%	74	142
02	ATL	7	2	0	76	63	0.95	1.11	$16	4.9	198	174	206	26%	1.83 -	42.3	3.7	7.5	**2.0**	0.1	1.67	92%	99	188
03	NYY	3	2	1	63	45	2.86	1.21	$7	4.2	268	292	257	31%	3.67 -	22.5	1.6	6.4	**4.1**	0.7	0.56	79%	104	226
1st Half		2	0	1	37	29	2.92	1.22	$5	4.1	272			34%	3.31	12.9	1.5	7.1	**4.8**	0.2	0.63	75%	137	296
2nd Half		1	2	0	26	16	2.77	1.19	$3	4.3	262			28%	4.19 -	9.6	1.7	5.5	**3.2**	1.4	0.49	85%	62	133
04	**Proj**	**2**	**2**	**0**	**60**	**39**	**3.90**	**1.38**	**$2**	**5.0**	**271**			**30%**	**4.48 -**	**13.2**	**3.0**	**5.9**	**2.0**	**1.1**	**F**	**75%**	**45**	**97**

Even with his hit and strand rates reverting to the mean, his BPIs still generated an excellent season. At age 38, however, the risk for a drop-off increases dramatically.

Hampton,Mike

LH Starter
AGE 31 Peak
TYPE
R Moderate
I | | CON
S | | STB
K | | brn
LIMA D+ EP: 45%

Yr	Tm	W	L	Sv	IP	K	ERA	Br/IP	R$	BF/G	OBA	vL	vR	H%	xERA	RAR	Ctl	Dom	Cmd	hr/9	G/F	S%	BPV	BPX
99	HOU	22	4	0	239	177	2.90	1.28	$31	29.6	234	149	259	28%	2.77	74.8	3.8	6.7	**1.8**	0.5	2.56	78%	71	155
00	NYM	15	10	0	217	151	3.15	1.35	$23	28.1	241	257	237	29%	3.35	72.1	4.1	6.3	**1.5**	0.4	2.51	77%	64	141
01	COL	14	13	0	203	122	5.41	1.58	($1)	28.6	292	346	284	31%	5.56	-1.2	3.8	5.4	**1.4**	1.4	1.75	69%	18	33
02	COL	7	15	0	178	74	6.17	1.79	($16)	28.0	312	376	293	32%	6.17	-25.3	4.6	3.7	**0.8**	1.2	1.67	67%	-4	-8
03	ATL	14	8	0	190	110	3.84	1.39	$13	26.4	258	164	278	29%	3.90	36.7	3.7	5.2	**1.4**	0.7	1.58	73%	44	86
1st Half		3	4	0	72	40	3.86	1.43	$2	24.1	233			27%	3.41	13.7	5.1	5.0	**1.0**	0.4	1.47	72%	47	91
2nd Half		11	4	0	118	70	3.82	1.37	$11	28.1	272			30%	4.21	23.0	2.8	5.3	**1.9**	0.8	1.65	74%	47	91
04	**Proj**	**13**	**11**	**0**	**200**	**111**	**4.14**	**1.44**	**$9**	**27.2**	**266**			**29%**	**4.32**	**30.1**	**3.7**	**5.0**	**1.3**	**0.9**	**G**	**73%**	**33**	**64**

His BPIs picked up from where they left off prior to Coors. That's not an endorsement of his 3.84 ERA; it's a statement of curiosity. This is still a soft skill set that succeeds in spite of itself. Too risky for me.

Harang,Aaron

RH Starter
AGE 25 Growth
TYPE
R Moderate
I | EXP |
S | | stb
K | |
LIMA C+ EP: 60%

Yr	Tm	W	L	Sv	IP	K	ERA	Br/IP	R$	BF/G	OBA	vL	vR	H%	xERA	RAR	Ctl	Dom	Cmd	hr/9	G/F	S%	BPV	BPX
99		0	0	0	0	0	0.00	0.00																
00		0	0	0	0	0	0.00	0.00																
01	aa	10	8	0	150	93	4.56	1.52	$4	24.7	312			36%	4.94	17.3	2.2	5.6	**2.6**	0.5		69%	64	123
02	OAK	* 10	7	0	133	113	4.06	1.48	$7	21.7	268	237	287	33%	4.21	24.9	4.1	7.6	**1.9**	0.5	0.67	72%	71	145
03	2TM	* 13	9	0	148	96	4.61	1.37	$10	21.9	284	272	322	31%	4.65	15.5	2.2	5.8	**2.6**	1.1	0.97	69%	55	111
1st Half		8	4	0	81	53	3.21	1.33	$10	23.0	275			31%	4.12 -	23.7	2.3	5.9	**2.5**	0.8	0.71	78%	65	132
2nd Half		5	5	0	67	43	6.30	1.42	($0)	20.8	295			32%	5.28 +	-8.2	2.1	5.8	**2.7**	1.5	1.17	57%	43	87
04	**Proj**	**11**	**8**	**0**	**140**	**100**	**4.24**	**1.29**	**$11**	**21.1**	**271**			**31%**	**4.06**	**21.6**	**2.2**	**6.4**	**2.9**	**0.9**	**--**	**69%**	**74**	**150**

5-5, 5.33 ERA in 76 IP at OAK and CIN. There are seeds of something very good here, and I suppose it's always good to acquire an OAK castoff. Might need a year to work out the bugs but a good long-term buy.

Harden,Rich

RH Starter
AGE 22 Green
TYPE Power
R Very High
I | EXP |
S | pt |
K | AGE | BRN
LIMA B EP: 55%

Yr	Tm	W	L	Sv	IP	K	ERA	Br/IP	R$	BF/G	OBA	vL	vR	H%	xERA	RAR	Ctl	Dom	Cmd	hr/9	G/F	S%	BPV	BPX
99		0	0	0	0	0	0.00	0.00																
00		0	0	0	0	0	0.00	0.00																
01		0	0	0	0	0	0.00	0.00																
02	aa	8	3	0	85	91	3.28	1.41	$8	23.0	229			32%	3.10	22.6	5.2	9.6	**1.9**	0.2		75%	100	196
03	OAK	* 16	8	0	175	164	3.54	1.24	$20	22.1	228	271	241	29%	3.07	46.6	3.7	8.4	**2.3**	0.6	1.48	72%	91	196
1st Half		11	2	0	88	84	2.66	1.00	$19	23.0	200			26%	2.07 +	33.8	2.7	8.6	**3.2**	0.5		75%	119	257
2nd Half		5	6	0	87	80	4.43	1.49	$2	21.4	254			32%	4.09	12.8	4.7	8.2	**1.7**	0.6		70%	72	155
04	**Proj**	**14**	**9**	**0**	**160**	**158**	**3.83**	**1.36**	**$14**	**22.8**	**237**			**31%**	**3.37**	**36.7**	**4.4**	**8.9**	**2.0**	**0.5**	**--**	**71%**	**90**	**193**

5-4, 4.50 ERA in 74 IP at OAK. One of the reasons they can afford to give up ones like Harang. Excellent skill set and could easily post a solid full-season debut in 2004.

Haren,Danny

RH Starter | AGE 23 Growth | TYPE Finesse
R: Moderate | I: EXP | S: | K: age
LIMA B | EP: 55%

Yr	Tm	W	L	Sv	IP	K	ERA	Br/IP	R$	BF/G	OBA	vL	vR	H%	xERA	RAR	Ctl	Dom	Cmd	hr/9	G/F	S%	BPV	BPX
99		0	0	0	0	0	0.00	0.00																
00		0	0	0	0	0	0.00	0.00																
01		0	0	0	0	0	0.00	0.00																
02		0	0	0	0	0	0.00	0.00																
03	STL	* 11	8	0	172	120	4.23	1.30	$11	24.2	278	278	304	31%	4.25	24.2	1.9	6.3	**3.2**	1.0	0.86	70%	75	145
1st Half		8	2	0	106	80	3.56	1.19	$12	25.7	269			31%	3.70	24.4	1.4	6.8	**5.0**	0.8	0.50	72%	122	234
2nd Half		3	6	0	66	40	5.30	1.48	($1)	22.4	292			32%	5.14	-0.2	2.9	5.4	**1.9**	1.2	0.90	66%	33	63
04	**Proj**	**8**	**9**	**0**	**140**	**93**	**4.63**	**1.36**	**$5**	**24.0**	**283**			**32%**	**4.56**	**11.9**	**2.3**	**6.0**	**2.7**	**1.1**	**--**	**68%**	**57**	**110**

3-7, 5.08 ERA in 72 IP at STL. The story of a rushed player:

	ERA	Ctl	Dom	Cmd
AA	0.82	0.9	8.0	8.2
AAA	4.93	1.6	6.9	4.4
STL	5.08	2.7	5.3	1.9

There's a future, but not just yet.

Harper,Travis

RH Reliever | AGE 27 Pre-Peak | TYPE
R: High | I: EXP con | S: PT | K:
LIMA C | EP: 45%

Yr	Tm	W	L	Sv	IP	K	ERA	Br/IP	R$	BF/G	OBA	vL	vR	H%	xERA	RAR	Ctl	Dom	Cmd	hr/9	G/F	S%	BPV	BPX
99	aa	6	3	0	72	57	6.50	1.51	$0	22.8	290			33%	5.16 +	-9.3	3.3	7.1	**2.2**	1.4		58%	45	103
00	TAM	* 11	7	0	187	85	4.09	1.27	$18	24.5	264	234	254	28%	3.97	45.7	2.4	4.1	**1.7**	1.0	0.72	70%	34	89
01	TAM	* 12	8	0	162	101	4.94	1.38	$7	25.8	285			29%	5.48 -	11.7	2.3	5.6	**2.5**	1.9	1.00	71%	25	50
02	TAM	* 6	11	1	104	74	6.23	1.62	($4)	11.5	320	301	280	35%	6.46	-10.7	2.6	6.4	**2.5**	1.7	1.15	65%	29	60
03	TAM	4	8	1	93	64	3.77	1.26	$7	6.4	247	287	223	28%	3.67	21.8	3.0	6.2	**2.1**	0.9	1.41	72%	60	130
1st Half		0	4	0	55	40	3.44	1.24	$2	6.9	244			29%	3.36	15.4	2.9	6.5	**2.2**	0.7	1.30	73%	73	157
2nd Half		4	4	1	38	24	4.26	1.29	$5	5.7	251			27%	4.11	6.4	3.1	5.7	**1.8**	1.2	1.59	70%	42	91
04	**Proj**	**5**	**7**	**0**	**80**	**53**	**4.28**	**1.33**	**$5**	**8.7**	**264**			**29%**	**4.31**	**13.5**	**2.8**	**6.0**	**2.1**	**1.1**	**--**	**71%**	**49**	**104**

There is growth here, but 2003's performance was probably as good as it will get. Not dominant enough for a 9th inning role, but should fare quite well in set-up.

Hasegawa,Shige

RH Reliever | AGE 35 Decline | TYPE Finesse
R: Moderate | I: con | S: pt | K: age
LIMA F | EP: 20%

Yr	Tm	W	L	Sv	IP	K	ERA	Br/IP	R$	BF/G	OBA	vL	vR	H%	xERA	RAR	Ctl	Dom	Cmd	hr/9	G/F	S%	BPV	BPX
99	ANA	4	6	2	77	44	4.91	1.48	$4	5.3	269	274	277	28%	5.23	9.9	4.0	5.1	**1.3**	1.6	0.74	72%	10	25
00	ANA	10	6	9	95	59	3.59	1.45	$17	6.3	271	246	291	30%	4.58 -	29.6	3.6	5.6	**1.6**	1.0	1.28	79%	36	92
01	ANA	5	6	0	55	41	4.08	1.30	$5	5.1	250	221	270	29%	3.75	10.4	3.3	6.7	**2.1**	0.8	1.29	70%	64	127
02	SEA	8	3	1	70	39	3.21	1.29	$10	5.6	233	284	199	26%	3.26	21.0	3.9	5.0	**1.3**	0.5	1.10	76%	50	103
03	SEA	2	4	16	73	32	1.48	1.10	$20	4.7	231	246	221	25%	2.84 -	39.5	2.2	3.9	**1.8**	0.6	1.33	91%	51	111
1st Half		1	0	2	41	20	0.88	0.97	$9	4.6	227			25%	2.30 -	25.6	1.3	4.4	**3.3**	0.4	1.17	95%	93	200
2nd Half		1	4	14	32	12	2.26	1.25	$12	4.8	237			24%	3.54 -	14.0	3.4	3.4	**1.0**	0.8	1.56	86%	23	51
04	**Proj**	**5**	**5**	**11**	**75**	**39**	**3.24**	**1.24**	**$15**	**5.0**	**241**			**26%**	**3.41**	**23.1**	**3.1**	**4.7**	**1.5**	**0.7**	**--**	**76%**	**45**	**96**

These are NOT the BPIs of a 1.48 ERA pitcher...
3.9 strikeouts per game??
91% strand rate??
25% hit rate??
Take this bet: He will not see 20 saves in 2004.

Hawkins,LaTroy

RH Reliever | AGE 31 Peak | TYPE
R: Moderate | I: CON | S: PT | K:
LIMA B | EP: 45%

Yr	Tm	W	L	Sv	IP	K	ERA	Br/IP	R$	BF/G	OBA	vL	vR	H%	xERA	RAR	Ctl	Dom	Cmd	hr/9	G/F	S%	BPV	BPX
99	MIN	10	14	0	174	103	6.67	1.71	($7)	24.4	327	310	335	35%	6.56	-18.7	3.1	5.3	**1.7**	1.5	1.10	63%	13	32
00	MIN	2	5	14	87	59	3.41	1.34	$15	5.6	257	238	267	29%	3.81	29.3	3.3	6.1	**1.8**	0.7	1.32	76%	57	149
01	MIN	1	5	28	51	36	5.99	1.92	$9	4.0	290	276	305	34%	5.59	-3.4	6.9	6.3	**0.9**	0.5	1.17	67%	38	77
02	MIN	6	0	0	80	63	2.14	0.98	$15	4.8	218			26%	2.31	35.6	1.7	7.1	**4.2**	0.6	1.34	81%	125	257
03	MIN	9	3	2	77	75	1.87	1.09	$18	4.2	241	205	263	31%	2.76 -	37.8	1.8	8.8	**5.0**	0.5	0.84	85%	150	325
1st Half		5	2	0	40	48	1.80	1.10	$9	4.2	236			34%	2.68 -	20.0	2.0	10.8	**5.3**	0.4	0.87	86%	171	369
2nd Half		4	1	2	37	27	1.95	1.08	$9	4.1	246			29%	2.84 -	17.7	1.5	6.6	**4.5**	0.5	0.82	84%	125	270
04	**Proj**	**7**	**3**	**9**	**80**	**71**	**2.59**	**1.16**	**$18**	**4.5**	**250**			**31%**	**3.15 -**	**31.6**	**2.0**	**8.0**	**3.9**	**0.6**	**--**	**80%**	**119**	**255**

This is a legitimate sub-2.00 ERA pitcher. More or less. Note:
- Superb control
- Excellent dominance
- 30% par hit rate

High strand rate might push his ERA up a bit, but this is for real.

Haynes,Jimmy

RH Starter | AGE 31 Peak | TYPE
R: Moderate | I: CON | S: pt stb | K:
LIMA F | EP: 50%

Yr	Tm	W	L	Sv	IP	K	ERA	Br/IP	R$	BF/G	OBA	vL	vR	H%	xERA	RAR	Ctl	Dom	Cmd	hr/9	G/F	S%	BPV	BPX
99	OAK	7	12	0	142	93	6.34	1.68	($5)	21.8	283	283	280	31%	5.63 +	-8.9	5.1	5.9	**1.2**	1.3	0.90	64%	18	46
00	MIL	12	13	0	199	88	5.33	1.65	($1)	27.6	289	319	276	30%	5.29	7.9	4.5	4.0	**0.9**	0.9	1.29	68%	11	24
01	MIL	8	17	0	172	112	4.86	1.51	($0)	24.6	273	259	291	30%	4.79	11.7	4.1	5.9	**1.4**	1.0	1.70	70%	34	64
02	CIN	15	10	0	196	126	4.13	1.48	$9	25.4	275	280	276	31%	4.59	25.6	3.7	5.8	**1.6**	1.0	1.34	74%	38	73
03	CIN	2	12	0	94	49	6.31	1.86	($12)	25.0	308	299	320	32%	6.46	-13.0	5.5	4.7	**0.9**	1.3	1.38	68%	-1	-1
1st Half		1	7	0	61	29	5.90	1.87	($8)	26.6	301			31%	6.37	-5.1	5.9	4.3	**0.7**	1.3	1.32	70%	-4	-8
2nd Half		1	5	0	33	20	7.07	1.84	($5)	22.5	320			35%	6.63	-7.9	4.6	5.4	**1.2**	1.4	1.52	63%	7	14
04	**Proj**	**4**	**8**	**0**	**80**	**47**	**4.84**	**1.56**	**($1)**	**23.9**	**283**			**30%**	**5.20**	**4.6**	**4.1**	**5.3**	**1.3**	**1.2**	**--**	**72%**	**20**	**39**

Back problem bothered him all season... There are some players you want to nurture back to health and others for which it really doesn't matter. Low ceiling here... whenever he comes back, he comes back.

Heilman,Aaron

RH Starter | AGE 25 Growth | TYPE Power
R: High | I: EXP con | S: | K: age
LIMA D | EP: 50%

Yr	Tm	W	L	Sv	IP	K	ERA	Br/IP	R$	BF/G	OBA	vL	vR	H%	xERA	RAR	Ctl	Dom	Cmd	hr/9	G/F	S%	BPV	BPX
99		0	0	0	0	0	0.00	0.00																
00		0	0	0	0	0	0.00	0.00																
01		0	0	0	0	0	0.00	0.00																
02	a/a	6	7	0	146	112	4.19	1.27	$7	22.6	255			30%	3.49 +	21.1	2.7	6.9	**2.5**	0.6		67%	80	158
03	NYM	* 8	11	0	159	110	5.14	1.68	($3)	24.4	301	299	301	34%	5.57	2.9	4.2	6.2	**1.5**	1.0	1.27	71%	33	63
1st Half		6	5	0	100	61	3.87	1.55	$3	26.3	298			34%	4.68 -	18.9	3.1	5.5	**1.7**	0.4	2.00	75%	51	99
2nd Half		2	6	0	59	49	7.31	1.90	($9)	21.9	305			34%	7.07	-16.1	5.9	7.5	**1.3**	2.0	1.21	65%	6	11
04	**Proj**	**5**	**8**	**0**	**120**	**90**	**4.95**	**1.56**	**($2)**	**23.4**	**284**			**33%**	**5.01**	**5.0**	**4.0**	**6.8**	**1.7**	**1.1**	**--**	**70%**	**43**	**83**

2-7, 6.78 ERA in 65 IP at NYM. Good skills potential but lost his control in the bigs (5.7 bb/9). He'll improve next year, but probably won't return solid value until 2005.

Helling,Rick

RH Reliever | AGE 33 Past | TYPE
R: Low | I: CON | S: stb | K:
LIMA B+ | EP: 55%

Yr	Tm	W	L	Sv	IP	K	ERA	Br/IP	R$	BF/G	OBA	vL	vR	H%	xERA	RAR	Ctl	Dom	Cmd	hr/9	G/F	S%	BPV	BPX
99	TEX	13	11	0	219	131	4.85	1.43	$11	27.2	270	263	281	28%	5.15	30.0	3.5	5.4	**1.5**	1.7	0.72	72%	15	38
00	TEX	16	13	0	217	146	4.48	1.43	$16	27.0	257	238	267	28%	4.49	41.6	4.1	6.1	**1.5**	1.2	0.56	72%	35	90
01	TEX	12	11	0	215	154	5.19	1.48	$2	27.9	297	296	298	32%	5.58	8.6	2.6	6.4	**2.4**	1.6	0.81	69%	38	76
02	ARI	11	12	0	182	126	4.40	1.28	$9	24.7	264	283	249	28%	4.44	17.2	2.4	6.2	**2.6**	1.5	0.71	71%	48	90
03	FLA	8	8	0	155	98	5.17	1.37	$2	19.0	276	281	273	29%	5.17	2.3	2.6	5.7	**2.2**	1.8	0.78	68%	26	49
1st Half		5	6	0	90	52	5.79	1.47	($2)	24.8	282			29%	5.43	-6.1	3.3	5.2	**1.6**	1.7	0.77	65%	12	23
2nd Half		3	2	0	65	46	4.31	1.22	$4	14.1	268			28%	4.81 -	8.4	1.7	6.4	**3.8**	1.9	0.79	74%	62	119
04	**Proj**	**4**	**4**	**0**	**80**	**59**	**4.05**	**1.23**	**$5**	**7.2**	**250**			**28%**	**3.77**	**13.0**	**2.6**	**6.6**	**2.6**	**1.1**	**F**	**70%**	**65**	**126**

Is this anything??

	IP	ERA	Ctl	Dom
SP	139	5.71	2.6	5.6
RP	16	0.55	2.8	6.6

Hard to tell. Small data set. But if you hear that he's going to be in the pen, take a chance.

Hendrickson,Mark

LH Reliever | AGE 29 Peak | TYPE Finesse
R: X HIGH | I: EXP CON | S: PT stb | K:
LIMA F | EP: 50%

Yr	Tm	W	L	Sv	IP	K	ERA	Br/IP	R$	BF/G	OBA	vL	vR	H%	xERA	RAR	Ctl	Dom	Cmd	hr/9	G/F	S%	BPV	BPX
99	aa	2	7	0	55	32	7.53	1.87	($7)	22.0	346			39%	6.30 +	-14.7	3.4	5.2	**1.5**	0.7		58%	30	69
00	aa	3	1	0	39	22	4.85	1.36	$3	27.8	267			28%	4.63	4.8	3.0	5.1	**1.7**	1.4		68%	26	62
01	aaa	2	9	0	73	27	6.29	1.60	($6)	8.7	323			31%	6.68	-8.5	2.3	3.3	**1.4**	2.0		65%	-19	-36
02	TOR	* 10	5	0	128	76	3.87	1.32	$11	15.5	271	194	204	30%	4.28	27.3	2.5	5.3	**2.2**	1.0	1.25	74%	49	100
03	TOR	9	9	0	158	76	5.52	1.56	($2)	23.6	317	269	333	33%	5.94	0.1	2.3	4.3	**1.9**	1.4	1.11	67%	16	36
1st Half		5	5	0	82	38	5.71	1.59	($2)	23.1	320			34%	5.90	-2.0	2.3	4.2	**1.8**	1.2	1.23	66%	18	38
2nd Half		4	4	0	76	38	5.32	1.54	($1)	24.2	313			32%	5.98 -	2.1	2.2	4.5	**2.0**	1.5	0.99	69%	15	33
04	**Proj**	**8**	**10**	**0**	**160**	**81**	**5.29**	**1.51**	**($1)**	**17.3**	**306**			**32%**	**5.62**	**5.4**	**2.4**	**4.6**	**1.9**	**1.4**	**--**	**68%**	**20**	**43**

Out of 30 starts, posted a PQS 4 or 5 in only five of them. Opposing batters had him for lunch this year, making 2002 look like the aberration. At 29, odds are against him suddenly becoming a rotation anchor.

Hentgen,Pat

RH Starter | AGE 35 Decline | TYPE
R: Very High | I: CON | S: PT stb | K: age BRN
LIMA C | EP: 40%

Yr	Tm	W	L	Sv	IP	K	ERA	Br/IP	R$	BF/G	OBA	vL	vR	H%	xERA	RAR	Ctl	Dom	Cmd	hr/9	G/F	S%	BPV	BPX
99	TOR	11	12	0	199	118	4.79	1.46	$8	25.6	286	306	265	30%	5.24	28.7	2.9	5.3	**1.8**	1.4	1.14	71%	24	61
00	STL	15	12	0	194	118	4.73	1.50	$10	26.0	270	252	295	29%	4.78	23.4	4.1	5.5	**1.3**	1.1	1.32	71%	28	63
01	BAL	2	3	0	62	33	3.48	1.13	$5	27.9	226	178	275	24%	3.19	16.7	2.8	4.8	**1.7**	1.0	1.15	73%	45	89
02	BAL	* 0	4	0	28	14	6.43	1.79	($4)	26.4	325	333	341	32%	7.48 -	-3.6	3.9	4.5	**1.2**	2.3	1.00	70%	-26	
03	BAL	7	8	1	160	100	4.10	1.30	$9	24.1	249	237	258	26%	4.31	30.5	3.3	5.6	**1.7**	1.4	0.80	74%	33	71
1st Half		1	5	1	66	40	5.44	1.63	($4)	21.5	295			31%	5.88	0.8	4.1	5.4	**1.3**	1.5	0.96	70%	12	26
2nd Half		6	3	0	94	60	3.16	1.06	$13	26.7	214			22%	3.20	29.8	2.7	5.7	**2.1**	1.3	0.70	78%	52	111
04	**Proj**	**4**	**8**	**0**	**120**	**71**	**5.25**	**1.38**	**$0**	**25.8**	**267**			**28%**	**4.63 +**	**4.6**	**3.2**	**5.3**	**1.7**	**1.3**	**F**	**64%**	**30**	**64**

Warning signs of a coming crash:
- BPIs as mediocre as ever
- Increasing flyball tendency in Camden Yards
- 26% hit rate ready to regress
- Huge increase in innings
- He ain't no spring chicken

Heredia,Felix

LH Reliever
AGE 28 Pre-Peak
TYPE
R Moderate
I con
S PT stb
K
LIMA D+ EP: 20%

	Tm	W	L	Sv	IP	K	ERA	Br/IP	R$	BF/G	OBA	vL	vR	H%	xERA	RAR	Ctl	Dom	Cmd	hr/9	G/F	S%	BPV	BPX
99	CHC	3	1	1	52	50	4.85	1.56	$1	3.4	276	247	292	34%	4.73	2.7	4.3	8.7	**2.0**	1.2	0.85	72%	57	125
00	CHC	7	3	2	58	52	4.79	1.36	$7	3.4	219	195	236	26%	3.56 +	6.5	5.1	8.0	**1.6**	0.9	1.11	66%	65	143
01	CHC	2	2	0	35	28	6.17	1.74	($3)	3.4	313	288	338	36%	6.44	-3.8	4.1	7.2	**1.8**	1.5	0.82	67%	26	48
02	TOR	1	2	0	52	31	3.63	1.48	$1	4.3	258	224	281	28%	4.40 -	12.7	4.5	5.4	**1.2**	0.9	1.16	78%	35	71
03	2TM	5	3	1	87	45	2.69	1.23	$10	5.2	232	233	225	24%	3.54 -	31.5	3.4	4.7	**1.4**	1.0	1.38	84%	34	69
1st Half		3	0	0	47	28	2.67	1.21	$6	6.1	231			25%	3.39 -	17.2	3.2	5.3	**1.6**	1.0	1.09	83%	47	95
2nd Half		2	3	1	40	17	2.71	1.26	$5	4.5	232			23%	3.71 -	14.3	3.6	3.8	**1.1**	1.1	1.81	84%	20	40
04	Proj	3	4	1	70	43	3.99	1.40	$3	4.3	253			28%	4.22	13.2	4.0	5.5	1.4	1.0	--	74%	36	72

A $10 player who might not be worth a plug nickel in 2004. His 2.69 ERA was a figment created out of a 24/84% hit/strand rate. That, along with a rapidly plummeting strikeout rate, could make a 4.00 ERA a longshot.

Herges,Matt

RH Reliever
AGE 34 Past
TYPE Power
R Moderate
I CON
S pt stb
K age
LIMA B EP: 50%

	Tm	W	L	Sv	IP	K	ERA	Br/IP	R$	BF/G	OBA	vL	vR	H%	xERA	RAR	Ctl	Dom	Cmd	hr/9	G/F	S%	BPV	BPX
99	LA	* 8	5	0	155	92	4.47	1.35	$7	17.4	269	250	259	29%	3.99	15.9	2.8	5.3	**1.9**	1.0	0.65	69%	41	90
00	LA	11	3	1	110	75	3.19	1.27	$17	7.8	243	268	235	28%	3.34	36.1	3.3	6.1	**1.9**	0.6	2.04	76%	65	144
01	LA	9	8	1	99	76	3.45	1.44	$9	5.8	258	280	243	30%	4.10 -	25.4	4.2	6.9	**1.7**	0.7	1.58	78%	58	107
02	MON	2	5	6	64	50	4.08	1.66	$2	4.7	307	315	300	35%	5.90 -	8.8	3.7	7.0	**1.9**	1.4	1.43	80%	34	64
03	2NL	3	2	3	79	68	2.62	1.23	$9	4.9	234	209	249	30%	2.85	28.1	3.3	7.7	**2.3**	0.3	1.02	79%	94	180
1st Half		1	1	3	38	34	2.83	1.44	$3	4.8	245			32%	3.43 -	12.5	4.7	8.0	**1.7**	0.2	0.80	80%	83	159
2nd Half		2	1	0	41	34	2.43	1.03	$6	5.0	223			28%	2.31	15.6	2.0	7.5	**3.8**	0.4	1.29	78%	122	234
04	Proj	4	4	3	80	64	3.26	1.36	$7	5.3	259			31%	3.82 -	21.4	3.4	7.2	2.1	0.7	--	78%	71	137

Got a short-lived shot at closer with SD, but became a new pitcher when he was traded to SF. It wasn't Pac Bell; he fared just as well at Qualcomm. But it helped him net the best Cmd ratio of his career.

Hermanson,Dustin

RH Starter
AGE 31 Peak
TYPE Finesse
R Very High
I CON
S pt STB
K brn
LIMA C+ EP: 50%

	Tm	W	L	Sv	IP	K	ERA	Br/IP	R$	BF/G	OBA	vL	vR	H%	xERA	RAR	Ctl	Dom	Cmd	hr/9	G/F	S%	BPV	BPX
99	MON	9	14	0	216	145	4.21	1.36	$9	27.2	270	272	271	31%	3.81	29.7	2.9	6.0	**2.1**	0.8	0.94	70%	56	123
00	MON	12	14	4	198	94	4.77	1.52	$8	23.1	288	317	272	30%	5.18	22.7	3.4	4.3	**1.3**	1.2	1.40	71%	14	31
01	STL	14	13	0	192	123	4.45	1.40	$10	25.1	265	276	255	28%	4.90	23.6	3.4	5.8	**1.7**	1.6	1.14	74%	24	45
02	BOS	* 1	2	0	35	21	6.17	1.74	($3)	9.6	318	325	373	36%	5.86	-3.3	3.9	5.4	**1.4**	0.8	0.90	64%	30	62
03	SF	* 3	4	1	94	52	4.49	1.39	$1	11.3	281	282	264	31%	4.51	9.9	2.6	5.0	**1.9**	1.0	1.08	69%	40	78
1st Half		1	2	1	29	12	5.55	1.68	($1)	5.8	298			31%	5.76	-1.1	4.3	3.7	**0.9**	1.2	1.40	69%	-1	-3
2nd Half		2	2	0	65	40	4.02	1.26	$3	20.9	273			31%	3.95	11.0	1.8	5.5	**3.1**	0.8	0.87	70%	73	141
04	Proj	5	6	0	120	68	4.20	1.43	$3	23.7	282			31%	4.67	17.1	2.9	5.1	1.8	1.1	--	73%	35	68

3-3, 4.10 ERA in 68 IP at SF. Six starts, on strict sub-100 pitch counts, generated a DOM/DIS split of 67/17 and the first sign of BPI life this century. While it's impressive, will he have the stamina over a full season?

Hernandez,Livan

RH Starter
AGE 29 Pre-Peak
TYPE
R High
I CON
S
K BRN
LIMA C EP: 50%

	Tm	W	L	Sv	IP	K	ERA	Br/IP	R$	BF/G	OBA	vL	vR	H%	xERA	RAR	Ctl	Dom	Cmd	hr/9	G/F	S%	BPV	BPX
99	SF	8	12	0	199	144	4.66	1.52	$1	29.5	288	292	280	33%	4.67	15.4	3.4	6.5	**1.9**	1.0	1.21	71%	45	98
00	SF	17	11	0	240	165	3.75	1.36	$21	31.1	273	273	272	31%	4.21	60.4	2.7	6.2	**2.3**	0.8	1.44	74%	60	133
01	SF	13	15	0	226	138	5.25	1.55	($1)	29.8	294	299	296	33%	5.13	3.5	3.4	5.5	**1.6**	1.0	1.29	67%	35	64
02	SF	12	16	0	216	134	4.38	1.41	$6	28.3	277	295	273	31%	4.25	21.2	3.0	5.6	**1.9**	0.8	1.36	70%	49	93
03	MON	15	10	0	233	178	3.20	1.21	$23	29.2	255	278	233	29%	3.75 -	64.7	2.2	6.9	**3.1**	1.0	1.24	78%	80	153
1st Half		6	6	0	103	63	4.19	1.41	$4	27.9	294			32%	4.91 -	15.0	2.1	5.5	**2.6**	1.1	1.30	73%	50	97
2nd Half		9	4	0	130	115	2.42	1.05	$20	30.4	221			26%	2.84	49.8	2.3	8.0	**3.5**	1.0	1.20	83%	103	198
04	Proj	16	9	0	220	175	3.27	1.19	$24	28.3	246			29%	3.45	58.7	2.5	7.2	2.9	0.9	--	76%	82	158

On July 2, he began pitching from a different arm angle and threw every pitch from the same spot. You can see the results. The question now is, how will batters adjust next spring? Expect some fall-off, but still...

Hernandez,Roberto

RH Reliever
AGE 39 Decline
TYPE Power
R High
I CON
S stb
K AGE
LIMA C+ EP: 30%

	Tm	W	L	Sv	IP	K	ERA	Br/IP	R$	BF/G	OBA	vL	vR	H%	xERA	RAR	Ctl	Dom	Cmd	hr/9	G/F	S%	BPV	BPX
99	TAM	2	3	43	73	69	3.08	1.38	$30	4.4	248	241	248	33%	3.25	27.3	4.1	8.5	**2.1**	0.1	1.95	76%	97	242
00	TAM	4	7	32	73	61	3.20	1.35	$26	4.6	269	328	223	32%	4.36 -	26.5	2.8	7.5	**2.7**	1.1	1.43	81%	69	178
01	KC	5	6	28	67	46	4.15	1.41	$19	4.6	267	299	230	30%	4.37	12.0	3.5	6.2	**1.8**	0.9	1.37	73%	48	95
02	KC	1	3	26	53	40	4.25	1.45	$15	4.3	293	282	317	34%	4.96 -	8.6	2.5	6.8	**2.7**	1.0	1.78	73%	63	128
03	ATL	5	3	0	60	45	4.35	1.73	$0	4.2	265	248	276	29%	5.64 -	7.5	6.5	6.8	**1.0**	1.5	2.02	80%	19	37
1st Half		5	2	0	32	26	4.47	1.68	$2	4.2	242			26%	5.35 -	3.5	7.0	7.3	**1.0**	1.7	2.14	79%	22	42
2nd Half		0	1	0	28	19	4.21	1.80	($2)	4.2	290			32%	5.97 -	4.0	5.8	6.2	**1.1**	1.3	1.90	80%	17	33
04	Proj	1	4	0	50	37	5.04	1.60	($3)	4.3	277			31%	5.22	1.5	4.7	6.7	1.4	1.3	G	71%	32	61

Only an 80% strand rate was able to hide the fact that he completely lost the plate in '03. Gone. Disappeared. At a more normal S%, his ERA would have been, well, his xERA. Do you want a 5.64 ERA on your team?

Hernandez,Runelvys

RH Starter
AGE 26 Growth
TYPE
R Low
I EXP con
S pt
K
LIMA C EP: 50%

	Tm	W	L	Sv	IP	K	ERA	Br/IP	R$	BF/G	OBA	vL	vR	H%	xERA	RAR	Ctl	Dom	Cmd	hr/9	G/F	S%	BPV	BPX
99		0	0	0	0	0	0.00	0.00																
00		0	0	0	0	0	0.00	0.00																
01		0	0	0	0	0	0.00	0.00																
02	KC	* 12	7	0	181	117	3.93	1.33	$12	26.5	276	302	236	32%	4.02	37.1	2.3	5.8	**2.5**	0.6	1.78	71%	70	144
03	KC	7	5	0	91	48	4.64	1.36	$5	24.4	253	267	231	27%	4.03 +	10.8	3.7	4.7	**1.3**	0.9	0.90	67%	33	72
1st Half		4	3	0	58	31	2.79	1.10	$8	25.9	204			22%	2.67	21.2	3.4	4.8	**1.4**	0.8	0.99	78%	49	107
2nd Half		3	2	0	33	17	7.86	1.81	($3)	22.4	325			35%	6.41 +	-10.4	4.1	4.6	**1.1**	1.1	0.76	55%	9	19
04	Proj	1	0	0	10	6	5.40	1.50	$0	22.1	281			31%	4.77 +	0.2	3.6	5.4	1.5	0.9	--	64%	36	77

Reconstructive elbow surgery will put him on the shelf for most, if not all, of 2004.

Hitchcock,Sterling

LH Starter
AGE 33 Past
TYPE
R Very High
I CON
S PT STB
K
LIMA B EP: 50%

	Tm	W	L	Sv	IP	K	ERA	Br/IP	R$	BF/G	OBA	vL	vR	H%	xERA	RAR	Ctl	Dom	Cmd	hr/9	G/F	S%	BPV	BPX
99	SD	12	14	0	205	194	4.13	1.36	$12	26.6	259	253	254	31%	4.03	30.4	3.3	8.5	**2.6**	1.3	0.90	74%	70	152
00	SD	1	6	0	65	61	4.97	1.46	($1)	25.9	273	220	279	32%	5.20	5.8	3.6	8.4	**2.3**	1.7	1.22	71%	51	111
01	2TM	* 8	5	0	87	51	5.48	1.56	$1	24.4	315	375	297	35%	5.27	-0.7	2.4	5.3	**2.2**	0.7	1.00	64%	48	93
02	NYY	* 1	2	0	46	34	7.24	2.11	($9)	10.5	378	316	331	43%	8.22 -	-11.0	3.5	6.7	**1.9**	1.2	0.86	66%	24	49
03	2TM	6	4	0	87	68	4.75	1.41	$3	10.8	270	202	291	30%	4.87	7.5	3.3	7.0	**2.1**	1.4	0.67	71%	44	90
1st Half		0	1	0	26	22	5.17	1.42	($1)	6.7	296			35%	4.88	0.8	2.1	7.6	**3.7**	1.0	0.93	65%	87	177
2nd Half		6	3	0	61	46	4.57	1.41	$4	14.7	258			28%	4.86	6.8	3.8	6.8	**1.8**	1.6	0.58	73%	33	66
04	Proj	7	7	0	140	107	4.50	1.39	$4	23.2	270			31%	4.59	16.8	3.2	6.9	2.2	1.2	F	71%	51	104

Sterling's comfort zone:

	--Amer Lg--	--Natl Lg--
	ERA/Cmd	ERA/Cmd
2003	5.44/2.0	3.79/2.3
Career	5.22/1.7	4.36/2.5

Just might surprise if he stays in the NL.

Hodges,Trey

RH Reliever
AGE 25 Growth
TYPE Power
R Moderate
I EXP
S pt
K
LIMA C EP: 55%

	Tm	W	L	Sv	IP	K	ERA	Br/IP	R$	BF/G	OBA	vL	vR	H%	xERA	RAR	Ctl	Dom	Cmd	hr/9	G/F	S%	BPV	BPX
99		0	0	0	0	0	0.00	0.00																
00		0	0	0	0	0	0.00	0.00																
01		0	0	0	0	0	0.00	0.00																
02	aaa	15	9	0	172	97	3.92	1.38	$13	26.4	273			31%	3.95	31.0	2.9	5.1	**1.8**	0.5		71%	52	103
03	ATL	3	3	0	65	66	4.69	1.53	($0)	5.6	273	269	268	33%	5.24 -	5.1	4.3	9.1	**2.1**	1.5	0.93	74%	54	104
1st Half		3	0	0	41	42	2.85	1.31	$4	6.0	232			30%	3.53 -	13.4	4.2	9.2	**2.2**	0.9	1.13	82%	84	161
2nd Half		0	3	0	24	24	7.84	1.91	($5)	5.1	333			38%	8.15	-8.3	4.5	9.0	**2.0**	2.6	0.66	64%	6	11
04	Proj	4	5	0	80	71	3.94	1.35	$4	7.4	250			30%	3.86	14.2	3.7	8.0	2.2	0.9	--	73%	71	137

Hard thrower, still learning the strike zone. 2nd half travesty was not likely due to "second time around the league" but to a balky elbow. Good sign is that his key BPIs held up even while he was hurt.

Hoffman,Trevor

RH Reliever
AGE 36 Decline
TYPE Power
R Moderate
I CON
S pt
K AGE
LIMA A+ EP: 40%

	Tm	W	L	Sv	IP	K	ERA	Br/IP	R$	BF/G	OBA	vL	vR	H%	xERA	RAR	Ctl	Dom	Cmd	hr/9	G/F	S%	BPV	BPX
99	SD	2	3	40	67	73	2.15	0.94	$33	4.0	203	215	182	27%	1.69	27.7	2.0	9.8	**4.9**	0.7	1.29	81%	155	338
00	SD	4	7	43	72	85	3.00	1.00	$37	4.0	231	200	246	31%	2.73	25.4	1.4	10.6	**7.7**	0.9	0.81	74%	209	459
01	SD	3	4	43	60	63	3.44	1.15	$31	3.9	221	214	218	26%	3.58	15.5	3.1	9.4	**3.0**	1.5	0.75	78%	86	159
02	SD	2	5	38	59	69	2.75	1.19	$26	4.0	238	186	275	34%	2.66	18.7	2.7	10.5	**3.8**	0.3	0.83	76%	142	268
03	SD	0	0	0	9	11	2.00	1.11	$1	4.0	216	182	273	29%	2.92 -	4.0	3.0	11.0	**3.7**	1.0	1.29	89%	125	240
1st Half		0	0	0	0	0	0.00	0.00																
2nd Half		0	0	0	9	11	2.00	1.11	$1	4.0	216			29%	2.93 -	3.9	3.0	11.0	**3.7**	1.0		89%	125	240
04	Proj	3	5	38	60	68	3.15	1.22	$27	4.1	239			31%	3.49	17.0	3.0	10.2	3.4	1.1	--	79%	108	209

Even in his short time back, his BPIs looked as good as ever. Stamina will be the key issue now, so while we're projecting a return to form, be aware of the increased risk of breakdown.

Holmes,Darren

RH Reliever | AGE 38 Decline | TYPE Power
R: High | I: exp, con | S: pt, stb | K: AGE
LIMA B+ | EP: 60%

Yr	Tm	W	L	Sv	IP	K	ERA	Br/IP	R$	BF/G	OBA	vL	vR	H%	xERA	RAR	Ctl	Dom	Cmd	hr/9	G/F	S%	BPV	BPX
99	ARI	4	3	0	49	35	3.67	1.53	$3	5.0	266			31%	3.91	10.3	4.6	6.4	1.4	0.6	1.65	76%	53	116
00	2TM *	1	2	2	38	26	7.82	1.76	($4)	5.9	322			36%	6.52 +	-10.5	3.8	6.2	1.6	1.4	0.78	56%	19	45
01		0	0	0	0	0	0.00	0.00																
02	ATL	2	2	1	54	47	1.83	0.98	$9	3.8	212	230	198	27%	2.03	23.7	2.0	7.8	3.9	0.5	0.97	84%	127	240
03	ATL	1	2	0	42	46	4.29	1.38	$0	3.8	284	355	236	37%	4.59	5.6	2.4	9.9	4.2	1.1	0.80	72%	113	217
1st Half		1	1	0	24	30	4.46	1.40	$0	3.5	283			38%	5.02 -	2.6	2.6	11.2	4.3	1.5	0.52	73%	111	213
2nd Half		0	1	0	18	16	4.04	1.35	($0)	4.2	285			36%	4.00	2.9	2.0	8.1	4.0	0.5	1.33	70%	115	222
04	Proj	1	2	0	40	36	3.60	1.35	$1	4.2	271			33%	4.36 -	8.9	2.7	8.1	3.0	1.1	F	78%	79	152

Amazing resurgence continues, despite higher ERA (which was inflated by 37% hit rate). Signs look good for another solid season, with a more realistic ERA.

Howard,Ben

RH Starter | AGE 25 Growth | TYPE
R: X HIGH | I: EXP, con | S: pt, stb | K: age, BRN
LIMA C | EP: 40%

Yr	Tm	W	L	Sv	IP	K	ERA	Br/IP	R$	BF/G	OBA	vL	vR	H%	xERA	RAR	Ctl	Dom	Cmd	hr/9	G/F	S%	BPV	BPX
99		0	0	0	0	0	0.00	0.00																
00		0	0	0	0	0	0.00	0.00																
01	aa	2	0	0	30	23	3.00	1.17	$4	17.5	183			21%	2.66	9.7	4.8	6.9	1.4	0.9		78%	63	121
02	a/a	3	6	0	88	57	5.73	1.60	($5)	19.9	277			29%	5.61	-5.4	4.7	5.8	1.2	1.6	0.39	68%	12	23
03	SD *	8	12	0	164	80	4.54	1.32	$6	24.9	252	227	242	25%	4.32	16.2	3.3	4.4	1.3	1.4	0.80	70%	17	33
1st Half		4	7	0	92	39	4.30	1.24	$5	25.5	242			25%	3.71 +	12.1	3.0	3.8	1.3	1.1		68%	24	46
2nd Half		4	5	0	72	41	4.86	1.43	$1	24.1	264			27%	5.10	4.0	3.7	5.1	1.4	1.7		72%	9	18
04	Proj	4	5	0	80	48	4.73	1.40	$1	21.6	252			26%	4.57	5.8	4.1	5.4	1.3	1.5	F	71%	21	41

1-3, 3.71 ERA in 34 IP at SD, but also a huge 10 HRs in those innings. Gopheritis has been somewhat of an undoing over the past two years. And, with an overall soft skill set, success does not look very close.

Hudson,Tim

RH Starter | AGE 28 Pre-Peak | TYPE
R: Low | I: con | S: | K: brn
LIMA C | EP: 50%

Yr	Tm	W	L	Sv	IP	K	ERA	Br/IP	R$	BF/G	OBA	vL	vR	H%	xERA	RAR	Ctl	Dom	Cmd	hr/9	G/F	S%	BPV	BPX
99	OAK *	18	2	0	203	197	2.84	1.28	$30	26.6	233	234	240	30%	3.08	82.5	3.8	8.7	2.3	0.4	2.27	78%	96	241
00	OAK	20	6	0	202	169	4.14	1.24	$27	26.3	229	231	221	27%	3.50 +	47.9	3.7	7.5	2.1	1.1	2.02	70%	66	170
01	OAK	18	9	0	235	181	3.37	1.22	$25	27.8	246	255	233	29%	3.43	66.5	2.7	6.9	2.5	0.8	2.26	75%	78	156
02	OAK	15	9	0	238	152	2.99	1.26	$24	29.2	261	283	239	30%	3.73 -	78.8	2.3	5.7	2.5	0.7	2.03	79%	67	138
03	OAK	16	7	0	240	162	2.70	1.08	$33	28.2	225	229	214	26%	2.64	90.8	2.3	6.1	2.7	0.6	2.03	77%	85	184
1st Half		6	3	0	119	70	3.10	1.14	$13	28.5	238			27%	3.02	38.7	2.3	5.3	2.3	0.6	1.90	74%	68	148
2nd Half		10	4	0	121	92	2.31	1.01	$22	27.9	213			25%	2.27	52.1	2.2	6.8	3.1	0.5	2.18	79%	102	221
04	Proj	20	8	0	240	181	2.93	1.13	$34	27.7	237			29%	2.79	84.0	2.3	6.8	3.0	0.5	G	74%	98	210

Excellent, stable skill set, he posted his highest BPV in the majors and could be en route to 100 very soon.

Ishii,Kazuhisa

LH Starter | AGE 30 Peak | TYPE Power
R: Low | I: con | S: pt | K:
LIMA B | EP: 45%

Yr	Tm	W	L	Sv	IP	K	ERA	Br/IP	R$	BF/G	OBA	vL	vR	H%	xERA	RAR	Ctl	Dom	Cmd	hr/9	G/F	S%	BPV	BPX
99	JPN	8	6	0	133	162	4.80	1.28	$9	24.3	219			30%	3.09 +	12.9	4.4	11.0	2.5	0.9		63%	103	239
00	JPN	10	9	0	173	210	2.76	1.21	$23	24.7	219			31%	3.02	69.6	3.8	10.9	2.9	0.8		81%	114	269
01	JPN	12	6	0	175	173	3.39	1.24	$17	27.0	215			27%	3.21	47.5	4.2	8.9	2.1	0.9		76%	82	157
02	LA	14	10	0	154	143	4.27	1.58	$6	24.7	240	223	245	29%	4.51	17.3	6.2	8.4	1.3	1.2	1.04	76%	50	95
03	LA	9	7	0	147	140	3.86	1.56	$4	24.4	237	192	252	29%	4.34	28.0	6.2	8.6	1.4	1.0	0.80	78%	59	113
1st Half		7	3	0	92	87	2.93	1.42	$8	25.0	214			27%	3.50 -	29.0	5.9	8.5	1.5	0.8	0.84	82%	70	135
2nd Half		2	4	0	55	53	5.42	1.81	($4)	23.5	273			33%	5.74	-1.0	6.7	8.7	1.3	1.3	0.75	73%	40	78
04	Proj	9	11	0	160	157	4.16	1.53	$3	24.6	239			29%	4.33	23.6	5.8	8.8	1.5	1.1	--	76%	60	116

Missed August with a strained left knee, then pitched very poorly upon his return. However, as long as home plate remains an elusive concept to him, it's not going to get much better than this.

Isringhausen,Jason

RH Reliever | AGE 31 Peak | TYPE Power
R: Moderate | I: CON | S: pt, stb | K:
LIMA B | EP: 50%

Yr	Tm	W	L	Sv	IP	K	ERA	Br/IP	R$	BF/G	OBA	vL	vR	H%	xERA	RAR	Ctl	Dom	Cmd	hr/9	G/F	S%	BPV	BPX
99	2TM *	4	5	9	115	93	3.91	1.37	$11	11.0	241	159	280	28%	3.83	24.9	4.2	7.3	1.7	1.1	1.18	75%	54	125
00	OAK	6	4	33	69	57	3.78	1.43	$27	4.6	256	242	265	31%	4.07	19.7	4.2	7.4	1.8	0.8	1.42	75%	62	162
01	OAK	4	3	34	71	74	2.66	1.08	$28	4.4	212	240	152	28%	2.51	26.9	2.9	9.4	3.2	0.6	1.07	78%	117	235
02	STL	3	2	32	65	68	2.49	0.98	$27	4.2	201	247	164	29%	1.42 +	22.8	2.5	9.4	3.8	0.0	1.48	72%	151	285
03	STL	0	1	22	42	41	2.36	1.17	$16	4.3	207	254	159	27%	2.44	16.4	3.9	8.8	2.3	0.4	1.39	81%	101	195
1st Half		0	0	2	7	6	0.00	0.85	$3	3.3	130			18%	0.41	5.0	3.8	7.6	2.0	0.0	2.20	100%	117	224
2nd Half		0	1	20	35	35	2.84	1.23	$13	4.5	221			29%	2.86	11.4	3.9	9.0	2.3	0.5	1.26	78%	98	189
04	Proj	3	3	37	70	68	2.96	1.20	$27	4.7	224			29%	2.78	21.6	3.5	8.7	2.5	0.5	--	76%	100	193

Returned from injury nearly as good as ever, with BPIs still closer-worthy. Continues to totally baffle RHers.

Jarvis,Kevin

RH Starter | AGE 34 Decline | TYPE Finesse
R: Very High | I: exp, CON | S: PT, stb | K: age, brn
LIMA D | EP: 50%

Yr	Tm	W	L	Sv	IP	K	ERA	Br/IP	R$	BF/G	OBA	vL	vR	H%	xERA	RAR	Ctl	Dom	Cmd	hr/9	G/F	S%	BPV	BPX
99	aaa	10	2	0	103	50	4.63	1.61	$5	27.5	324			34%	5.97 -	12.4	2.4	4.4	1.9	1.4	0.81	75%	13	31
00	COL *	6	6	0	154	76	4.68	1.34	$6	21.2	269	337	271	27%	4.87	19.7	2.7	4.4	1.7	1.6	1.30	71%	13	30
01	SD	12	11	0	193	133	4.80	1.23	$11	25.1	258	257	252	27%	4.52	14.6	2.3	6.2	2.7	1.7	1.11	67%	46	85
02	SD	2	4	0	38	27	4.03	1.26	$2	19.9	262	218	304	29%	4.04	5.5	2.4	6.4	2.7	1.2	0.91	72%	62	118
03	SD	4	8	0	92	49	5.87	1.58	($4)	25.9	303	288	316	32%	5.79	-7.3	3.1	4.8	1.5	1.5	1.42	65%	11	22
1st Half		0	2	0	22	14	6.14	1.68	($3)	25.3	319			34%	6.45	-2.5	3.3	5.7	1.8	1.6	1.23	67%	13	26
2nd Half		4	6	0	70	35	5.79	1.54	($2)	26.0	299			31%	5.59	-4.8	3.1	4.5	1.5	1.4	1.48	65%	10	20
04	Proj	4	7	0	80	49	4.95	1.39	$1	23.0	276			30%	4.76	3.4	2.8	5.5	2.0	1.4	--	68%	34	65

Finished his season with three gruesome PQS-0 starts (14 IP, 14 ER), but by the looks of the rest of the year, you'd hardly notice. It's the elbow, and its amazing he got through 92 IP. Hmm, maybe he shouldn't have.

Jennings,Jason

RH Starter | AGE 25 Growth | TYPE
R: Moderate | I: EXP, con | S: pt, stb | K:
LIMA D | EP: 45%

Yr	Tm	W	L	Sv	IP	K	ERA	Br/IP	R$	BF/G	OBA	vL	vR	H%	xERA	RAR	Ctl	Dom	Cmd	hr/9	G/F	S%	BPV	BPX
99		0	0	0	0	0	0.00	0.00																
00	aa	1	3	0	36	29	6.00	1.53	($1)	26.7	298			33%	6.06	-1.2	3.0	7.3	2.4	2.0		66%	30	70
01	a/a *	13	9	0	196	144	6.02	1.65	($6)	27.2	315	247	310	37%	5.62	-15.6	3.2	6.6	2.1	0.9	1.59	63%	49	94
02	COL	16	8	0	185	127	4.52	1.46	$8	25.4	278	299	267	31%	4.86	14.4	3.4	6.2	1.8	1.3	1.64	73%	37	69
03	COL	12	13	0	181	119	5.12	1.66	($2)	25.9	293	323	271	33%	5.39	3.9	4.4	5.9	1.4	1.0	1.36	70%	30	58
1st Half		7	6	0	97	78	4.72	1.65	$0	26.1	286			34%	5.18	7.2	4.6	7.2	1.6	0.9	1.39	73%	46	89
2nd Half		5	7	0	84	41	5.58	1.67	($3)	25.7	301			32%	5.63	-3.4	4.1	4.4	1.1	1.1	1.33	68%	12	22
04	Proj	12	11	0	180	121	5.25	1.60	($1)	26.2	295			33%	5.38	0.3	3.8	6.1	1.6	1.2	--	69%	31	60

If there's any place that has a curse, it's gotta be Denver. Look at how the mere aura of playing in Coors has slowly eaten into his BPIs, year by year, chewing up a perfectly good pitcher 'til nothing's left.

Jimenez,Jose

RH Reliever | AGE 30 Peak | TYPE Finesse
R: High | I: con | S: PT | K: BRN
LIMA B | EP: 60%

Yr	Tm	W	L	Sv	IP	K	ERA	Br/IP	R$	BF/G	OBA	vL	vR	H%	xERA	RAR	Ctl	Dom	Cmd	hr/9	G/F	S%	BPV	BPX
99	STL *	7	16	0	189	129	5.57	1.52	($4)	25.4	280	304	249	32%	4.28 +	-8.5	3.8	6.1	1.6	0.8	2.50	63%	47	102
00	COL	5	2	24	70	44	3.21	1.30	$22	4.1	241	245	234	28%	3.32	22.8	3.6	5.6	1.6	0.5	2.88	76%	58	128
01	COL	6	1	17	55	37	4.09	1.42	$15	4.3	265	255	271	30%	4.39	9.4	3.6	6.1	1.7	1.0	3.03	74%	44	82
02	COL	2	10	41	73	47	3.58	1.19	$27	4.1	270	266	264	30%	3.67	15.0	1.4	5.8	4.3	0.9	3.04	73%	100	188
03	COL	2	10	20	101	45	5.25	1.67	$4	7.4	324	382	266	35%	5.58	0.4	2.8	4.0	1.4	0.6	2.16	68%	25	48
1st Half		0	4	19	38	21	7.11	1.97	$3	4.6	355			39%	6.94	-9.3	3.8	5.0	1.3	0.7	1.82	63%	20	39
2nd Half		2	6	1	63	24	4.13	1.49	$1	12.1	304			32%	4.76 -	9.7	2.3	3.4	1.5	0.6	2.39	72%	29	56
04	Proj	5	5	5	80	49	3.49	1.34	$9	5.4	274			31%	4.07 -	19.0	2.5	5.5	2.2	0.8	G	76%	56	109

October 7. An exciting day when he was officially freed from COL. While he had his moments in thin air, it will be exciting to see whether he can rediscover his BPIs some place less, um.... cursed. I'm VERY optimistic.

Johnson,Jason

RH Starter | AGE 30 Peak | TYPE
R: High | I: CON | S: pt | K: brn
LIMA C+ | EP: 35%

Yr	Tm	W	L	Sv	IP	K	ERA	Br/IP	R$	BF/G	OBA	vL	vR	H%	xERA	RAR	Ctl	Dom	Cmd	hr/9	G/F	S%	BPV	BPX
99	BAL *	12	9	0	159	111	5.26	1.54	$6	23.6	264	242	289	29%	4.99	12.9	4.8	6.3	1.3	1.3	0.83	68%	29	72
00	BAL *	4	11	0	162	129	5.27	1.47	$1	21.6	254	267	288	29%	4.60 +	13.9	4.5	7.2	1.6	1.3	0.92	67%	42	109
01	BAL	10	12	0	196	114	4.09	1.38	$9	26.4	260	263	252	27%	4.53	36.7	3.5	5.2	1.5	1.3	1.09	75%	27	54
02	BAL	6	14	0	136	102	4.43	1.40	$4	25.5	274	261	290	31%	4.77	18.7	3.0	6.8	2.3	1.3	1.18	72%	51	104
03	BAL	10	10	0	189	118	4.19	1.56	$4	26.5	288	283	283	32%	5.19 -	33.9	3.8	5.6	1.5	1.0	1.08	76%	31	66
1st Half		6	3	0	83	50	3.80	1.43	$5	24.1	275			30%	4.71 -	19.2	3.3	5.4	1.7	1.1	1.26	77%	35	75
2nd Half		4	7	0	106	68	4.49	1.67	($2)	28.7	298			33%	5.56 -	14.7	4.2	5.8	1.4	1.0	0.96	75%	28	61
04	Proj	10	14	0	200	132	4.37	1.49	$5	25.9	278			31%	4.96 -	31.4	3.6	5.9	1.6	1.2	--	74%	34	73

The slight uptick in dominance he displayed in '02 was gone this year, leaving him wallowing back in his mediocrity. I always see him as the epitome of the O's -- constant, reliable, droning on, forever just below average.

Johnson,Randy

	Yr	Tm	W	L	Sv	IP	K	ERA	Br/IP	R$	BF/G	OBA	vL	vR	H%	xERA	RAR	Ctl	Dom	Cmd	hr/9	G/F	S%	BPV	BPX
LH Starter	99	ARI	17	9	0	271	364	2.49	1.02	$40	30.5	213	103	219	31%	2.31	99.6	2.3	12.1	**5.2**	1.0	1.25	82%	164	357
AGE 40 Decline	00	ARI	19	7	0	248	347	2.65	1.12	$39	28.6	224	226	224	34%	2.89	99.1	2.8	12.6	**4.6**	0.8	1.18	80%	157	345
TYPE Power	01	ARI	21	6	0	249	372	2.49	1.01	$41	28.0	205	196	204	33%	2.24	95.9	2.6	13.4	**5.2**	0.7	1.19	79%	184	341
R Low	02	ARI	24	5	0	260	334	2.32	1.03	$44	29.3	212	221	206	30%	2.49	97.0	2.5	11.6	**4.7**	0.9	1.42	83%	154	291
I	03	ARI	6	8	0	114	125	4.26	1.33	$5	26.9	280	303	276	36%	4.59	15.5	2.1	9.9	**4.6**	1.3	1.13	72%	118	226
S pt	1st Half		1	2	0	23	31	7.01	1.52	($2)	25.6	315			44%	5.47 +	-5.4	1.9	12.1	**6.2**	1.2	1.12	53%	160	307
K AGE brn	2nd Half		5	6	0	91	94	3.56	1.29	$7	27.3	270			34%	4.36 -	20.9	2.2	9.3	**4.3**	1.3	1.14	78%	108	208
LIMA A EP: 65%	**04**	**Proj**	**16**	**10**	**0**	**200**	**222**	**3.69**	**1.21**	**$21**	**27.5**	**252**			**33%**	**3.63**	**42.2**	**2.3**	**10.0**	**4.4**	**1.0**	**--**	**73%**	**125**	**241**

I don't think I've ever seen a 160 BPV with a 7.01 ERA, but thanks to ridiculously unlucky 44/53% hit/strand rates, that's what he did in the 1st half. After his DL stint, he was slightly less dominant but no less successful.

Jones,Todd

	Yr	Tm	W	L	Sv	IP	K	ERA	Br/IP	R$	BF/G	OBA	vL	vR	H%	xERA	RAR	Ctl	Dom	Cmd	hr/9	G/F	S%	BPV	BPX
RH Reliever	99	DET	4	4	30	66	64	3.82	1.50	$21	4.5	256	290	224	32%	4.42 -	18.2	4.8	8.7	**1.8**	1.0	1.41	77%	66	165
AGE 36 Decline	00	DET	2	4	42	64	67	3.52	1.44	$29	4.2	271	294	256	35%	4.32 -	20.5	3.5	9.4	**2.7**	0.8	1.94	78%	88	229
TYPE Power	01	2AL	5	5	13	68	54	4.24	1.71	$8	4.6	312	325	301	36%	6.00 -	11.4	3.8	7.1	**1.9**	1.2	2.20	79%	39	78
R High	02	COL	1	4	1	82	73	4.72	1.37	($1)	4.4	266	233	301	32%	4.27	4.2	3.1	8.0	**2.6**	1.1	1.42	68%	72	135
I CON	03	2TM	3	5	0	68	59	7.13	1.82	($8)	5.5	326	323	323	38%	6.62 +	-15.8	4.1	7.8	**1.9**	1.3	1.32	61%	37	75
S STB	1st Half		1	4	0	39	28	8.29	2.02	($8)	5.9	356			39%	8.16	-15.1	4.1	6.4	**1.6**	1.8	1.44	61%	-0	-0
K age	2nd Half		2	1	0	29	31	5.57	1.55	($0)	5.0	281			37%	4.56 +	-0.7	4.0	9.6	**2.4**	0.6	1.15	63%	88	178
LIMA C EP: 70%	**04**	**Proj**	**3**	**4**	**0**	**70**	**67**	**4.63**	**1.53**	**($0)**	**4.8**	**283**			**35%**	**4.81**	**7.2**	**3.7**	**8.6**	**2.3**	**0.9**	**--**	**71%**	**72**	**145**

Posted a horrible 8.24 ERA in COL, but then improved dramatically in BOS, posting a 5.52 ERA there. How often can you talk about a legitimate 2.72 improvement in ERA with tongue planted firmly in cheek?

Julio,Jorge

	Yr	Tm	W	L	Sv	IP	K	ERA	Br/IP	R$	BF/G	OBA	vL	vR	H%	xERA	RAR	Ctl	Dom	Cmd	hr/9	G/F	S%	BPV	BPX
RH Reliever	99		0	0	0	0	0	0.00	0.00																
AGE 25 Growth	00		0	0	0	0	0	0.00	0.00																
TYPE Power	01	a/a	2	3	19	77	77	3.86	1.39	$13	5.2	259	286	290	33%	4.06	16.1	3.6	9.0	**2.5**	0.8	1.19	74%	85	163
R Moderate	02	BAL	5	6	25	68	55	1.99	1.21	$25	4.2	223	213	214	27%	3.04 -	31.6	3.6	7.3	**2.0**	0.7	0.93	87%	77	158
I EXP con	03	BAL	0	7	36	61	52	4.41	1.54	$20	4.3	258	273	239	29%	5.06 -	9.1	5.0	7.6	**1.5**	1.5	1.06	76%	37	81
S	1st Half		0	4	16	31	28	4.06	1.48	$9	4.3	243			30%	3.89	6.1	5.2	8.1	**1.6**	0.6	1.25	73%	71	152
K age	2nd Half		0	3	20	30	24	4.77	1.59	$10	4.3	273			28%	6.27 -	3.1	4.8	7.2	**1.5**	2.4	0.92	80%	3	7
LIMA D+ EP: 40%	**04**	**Proj**	**2**	**6**	**30**	**65**	**55**	**3.46**	**1.37**	**$21**	**4.3**	**247**			**29%**	**4.15 -**	**18.1**	**4.0**	**7.6**	**1.9**	**1.1**	**--**	**79%**	**58**	**124**

His BPIs were off, but he still succeeded in closing out 82% of his save opps, the exact same percentage as '02. It's all about getting the job done, but you'd like to have more confidence in the skill set.

Kennedy,Joe

	Yr	Tm	W	L	Sv	IP	K	ERA	Br/IP	R$	BF/G	OBA	vL	vR	H%	xERA	RAR	Ctl	Dom	Cmd	hr/9	G/F	S%	BPV	BPX
LH Reliever	99		0	0	0	0	0	0.00	0.00																
AGE 24 Growth	00		0	0	0	0	0	0.00	0.00																
TYPE	01	TAM	* 13	8	0	190	143	3.27	1.21	$20	25.3	255	225	279	29%	3.63	56.4	2.2	6.8	**3.1**	0.9	0.97	76%	83	166
R High	02	TAM	8	11	0	196	109	4.55	1.32	$6	27.7	270	273	268	29%	4.34	24.0	2.5	5.0	**2.0**	1.1	0.87	68%	41	84
I EXP con	03	TAM	3	12	1	133	77	6.15	1.61	($8)	18.8	308	230	324	33%	5.82	-11.1	3.2	5.2	**1.6**	1.3	1.06	63%	21	44
S pt	1st Half		3	5	0	67	30	5.90	1.64	($3)	25.5	325			35%	5.73	-3.4	2.5	4.0	**1.6**	0.8	1.32	63%	23	50
K age brn	2nd Half		0	7	1	66	47	6.40	1.57	($6)	14.9	290			31%	5.90 +	-7.7	3.8	6.4	**1.7**	1.8	0.83	63%	18	38
LIMA D+ EP: 60%	**04**	**Proj**	**5**	**5**	**0**	**100**	**66**	**4.32**	**1.31**	**$5**	**8.5**	**266**			**29%**	**4.25**	**16.3**	**2.6**	**5.9**	**2.3**	**1.1**	**--**	**70%**	**53**	**113**

It's simple: the excessive innings have done him in. TAM may move him to the pen (2.40 ERA) because "he's failed as a starter," but the truth is, he'd do better with fewer IP because the poor guy needs a break.

Kershner,Jason

	Yr	Tm	W	L	Sv	IP	K	ERA	Br/IP	R$	BF/G	OBA	vL	vR	H%	xERA	RAR	Ctl	Dom	Cmd	hr/9	G/F	S%	BPV	BPX
LH Reliever	99	aa	4	4	8	92	77	6.95	1.68	($2)	7.4	303			35%	5.96 +	-17.4	4.1	7.5	**1.8**	1.6		60%	31	72
AGE 27 Growth	00	aa	9	2	1	119	71	4.46	1.46	$8	19.3	303			33%	5.19 -	20.7	2.1	5.4	**2.5**	1.1		72%	46	109
TYPE Finesse	01	a/a	6	10	0	139	68	6.15	1.62	($8)	19.7	329			34%	6.36	-13.6	2.1	4.4	**2.1**	1.5		64%	14	27
R X HIGH	02	2TM	* 7	3	1	110	87	3.76	1.21	$10	8.1	231			27%	3.29	22.2	3.3	7.1	**2.2**	0.9	1.12	71%	70	138
I EXP CON	03	TOR	* 9	4	0	99	57	3.18	1.20	$13	6.4	254	178	250	29%	3.31	31.2	2.2	5.2	**2.4**	0.5	0.76	74%	69	149
S pt STB	1st Half		6	2	0	50	27	3.94	1.41	$5	7.3	294			33%	4.24	10.7	2.1	4.8	**2.3**	0.4	1.00	71%	62	133
K BRN	2nd Half		3	2	0	49	30	2.39	0.98	$8	5.6	207			23%	2.35	20.5	2.2	5.5	**2.5**	0.7	0.73	80%	77	167
LIMA C+ EP: 50%	**04**	**Proj**	**6**	**3**	**0**	**80**	**51**	**3.60**	**1.23**	**$9**	**7.7**	**250**			**28%**	**3.65**	**20.8**	**2.6**	**5.7**	**2.2**	**0.9**	**F**	**73%**	**59**	**127**

3-3, 3.17 ERA in 54 IP at TOR. He's toiled in the minors for awhile, but despite his up and down ERA history, he's always managed a 2.0 command ratio. Expect a slight drop-off in '04, but still close to LIMA-worthy.

Kieschnick,Brooks

	Yr	Tm	W	L	Sv	IP	K	ERA	Br/IP	R$	BF/G	OBA	vL	vR	H%	xERA	RAR	Ctl	Dom	Cmd	hr/9	G/F	S%	BPV	BPX
LH Reliever	99		0	0	0	0	0	0.00	0.00																
AGE 31 Peak	00		0	0	0	0	0	0.00	0.00																
TYPE Power	01		0	0	0	0	0	0.00	0.00																
R Moderate	02	aaa	0	1	0	31	25	3.77	1.68	($1)	5.7	314			38%	5.08 -	6.2	3.5	7.3	**2.1**	0.3		76%	71	139
I EXP con	03	MIL	* 2	1	0	66	50	6.66	1.68	($7)	6.1	318	239	338	36%	6.03 +	-12.3	3.3	6.8	**2.1**	1.2	1.42	61%	39	76
S pt	1st Half		1	1	0	37	24	7.74	1.83	($6)	7.1	340			37%	7.22 +	-12.3	3.4	5.8	**1.7**	1.7	1.95	59%	7	14
K	2nd Half		1	0	0	29	26	5.28	1.48	($1)	5.1	287			36%	4.49 +	0.0	3.1	8.1	**2.6**	0.6	1.07	63%	82	158
LIMA C EP: 65%	**04**	**Proj**	**1**	**1**	**0**	**60**	**48**	**4.20**	**1.47**	**($0)**	**5.5**	**284**			**34%**	**4.49**	**8.5**	**3.2**	**7.2**	**2.3**	**0.8**	**--**	**72%**	**67**	**129**

1-1, 5.26 ERA in 53 IP at MIL but a solid 79 BPV. His 36/61% hit/strand rates wreaked havoc with his ERA, so it's better than it looks. 2nd half surge is also encouraging. Keep him on your radar.

Kim,Byung-Hyun

	Yr	Tm	W	L	Sv	IP	K	ERA	Br/IP	R$	BF/G	OBA	vL	vR	H%	xERA	RAR	Ctl	Dom	Cmd	hr/9	G/F	S%	BPV	BPX
RH Starter	99	ARI	* 7	2	2	78	87	3.23	1.15	$13	6.9	182	265	180	25%	1.80 +	20.9	4.7	10.0	**2.1**	0.5	1.41	72%	110	238
AGE 25 Growth	00	ARI	6	6	14	70	111	4.49	1.40	$14	5.0	208	237	171	33%	3.68 +	10.7	5.9	14.2	**2.4**	1.2	0.98	71%	115	253
TYPE Power	01	ARI	5	6	19	98	113	2.94	1.04	$24	5.0	173	199	151	23%	2.21 +	31.9	4.0	10.4	**2.6**	0.9	1.07	76%	109	202
R High	02	ARI	8	3	36	84	92	2.04	1.07	$35	4.7	213	220	198	29%	2.28	34.5	2.8	9.9	**3.5**	0.5	1.70	84%	130	245
I con	03	2TM	9	10	16	122	102	3.32	1.12	$25	8.8	232	221	227	28%	3.10	34.0	2.4	7.5	**3.1**	0.9	1.27	74%	92	187
S pt	1st Half		3	6	0	75	52	3.96	1.25	$4	22.4	251			28%	3.99	14.4	2.8	6.2	**2.3**	1.2	1.36	73%	54	109
K age BRN	2nd Half		6	4	16	47	50	2.29	0.91	$21	4.3	199			27%	1.68 +	19.6	1.9	9.6	**5.0**	0.4	1.12	76%	166	337
LIMA C EP: 55%	**04**	**Proj**	**14**	**10**	**0**	**160**	**136**	**3.77**	**1.27**	**$16**	**25.8**	**250**			**30%**	**3.53**	**34.8**	**3.0**	**7.7**	**2.6**	**0.7**	**--**	**72%**	**83**	**168**

Starter or reliever? You decide:

	IP	ERA	Ctl	Dom
SP	72	3.38	2.9	6.0
RP	50	3.22	1.8	9.7

But BOS plans to use him as a starter, at least as of today, so as long as his shoulder is okay...

King,Ray

	Yr	Tm	W	L	Sv	IP	K	ERA	Br/IP	R$	BF/G	OBA	vL	vR	H%	xERA	RAR	Ctl	Dom	Cmd	hr/9	G/F	S%	BPV	BPX
LH Reliever	99	CHC	* 4	4	2	54	41	3.17	1.46	$6	5.0	236			29%	3.13	15.0	5.3	6.8	**1.3**	0.3	2.71	78%	66	143
AGE 30 Peak	00	MIL	* 3	5	1	53	36	2.36	1.24	$8	3.4	230	204	157	27%	2.86 -	23.4	3.5	6.1	**1.7**	0.3	1.33	81%	71	157
TYPE Power	01	MIL	0	4	1	55	49	3.60	1.35	$1	2.9	240	210	276	29%	3.70	13.0	4.1	8.0	**2.0**	0.8	1.74	75%	72	133
R Low	02	MIL	3	2	0	66	51	3.00	1.32	$5	3.6	250	219	280	30%	3.54 -	18.6	3.4	7.0	**2.0**	0.7	1.90	79%	69	131
I	03	ATL	3	4	0	59	43	3.51	1.24	$5	3.1	217	200	223	26%	2.78 +	14.0	4.1	6.6	**1.6**	0.5	1.75	71%	71	136
S stb	1st Half		2	0	0	30	17	2.39	1.33	$3	2.9	220			25%	2.93 -	11.6	4.8	5.1	**1.1**	0.3	1.67	82%	55	105
K	2nd Half		1	4	0	29	26	4.67	1.14	$1	3.3	213			26%	2.63 +	2.4	3.4	8.1	**2.4**	0.6	1.86	58%	92	177
LIMA B+ EP: 50%	**04**	**Proj**	**2**	**4**	**0**	**60**	**47**	**3.45**	**1.23**	**$4**	**3.2**	**232**			**28%**	**3.06**	**14.6**	**3.5**	**7.1**	**2.0**	**0.6**	**G**	**73%**	**76**	**146**

Low 26% hit rate served to keep his OBA in check and that was the only thing that saved his ERA. BPIs have run hot and cold over time, but he does have the goods to put together strong stretches.

Kinney,Matt

	Yr	Tm	W	L	Sv	IP	K	ERA	Br/IP	R$	BF/G	OBA	vL	vR	H%	xERA	RAR	Ctl	Dom	Cmd	hr/9	G/F	S%	BPV	BPX
RH Starter	99	aa	4	7	0	60	44	9.15	1.98	($10)	21.0	324			37%	6.84 +	-29.1	5.7	6.6	**1.2**	1.4		53%	14	32
AGE 27 Growth	00	MIN	* 13	6	0	188	154	4.59	1.49	$11	25.1	263	305	194	31%	4.60	33.2	4.4	7.4	**1.7**	1.1	0.77	71%	49	128
TYPE Power	01	aaa	6	11	0	161	124	6.04	1.71	($11)	25.7	308			35%	6.19	-13.3	4.1	6.9	**1.7**	1.5		67%	27	52
R X HIGH	02	MIN	* 4	8	0	97	65	6.59	1.75	($9)	22.7	325	336	246	34%	7.37 -	-14.7	3.5	6.0	**1.7**	2.2	0.81	68%	-5	
I EXP CON	03	MIL	10	13	0	190	152	5.21	1.48	($0)	25.3	273	284	260	31%	4.89	1.9	3.8	7.2	**1.9**	1.3	0.77	67%	45	87
S PT STB	1st Half		6	6	0	99	79	4.27	1.28	$6	26.0	246			28%	3.85	13.4	3.3	7.2	**2.2**	1.1	1.05	70%	62	120
K BRN	2nd Half		4	7	0	91	73	6.22	1.69	($7)	24.7	300			34%	6.02	-11.5	4.3	7.2	**1.7**	1.5	0.54	65%	29	55
LIMA D EP: 50%	**04**	**Proj**	**9**	**13**	**0**	**180**	**137**	**5.45**	**1.52**	**($3)**	**23.5**	**278**			**31%**	**5.11**	**-4.5**	**4.0**	**6.9**	**1.7**	**1.4**	**F**	**67%**	**37**	**70**

Got off to a terrific start, but couldn't keep it up. 2nd half 34/65% hit/strand rates hurt his ERA, but BPIs were off too. For whatever potential there once was, a look at his risk table is enough to scare off the bravest.

Kline,Steve

LH Reliever | AGE 31 Peak | TYPE
RISK: R Low; I con; S stb; K
LIMA C+ | EP: 45%

Yr	Tm	W	L	Sv	IP	K	ERA	Br/IP	R$	BF/G	OBA	vL	vR	H%	xERA	RAR	Ctl	Dom	Cmd	hr/9	G/F	S%	BPV	BPX
99	MON	7	4	0	69	69	3.78	1.29	$8	3.5	223	194	232	28%	3.18 +	13.4	4.3	9.0	**2.1**	1.0	2.04	74%	77	167
00	MON	1	5	14	82	64	3.51	1.40	$11	4.3	275	243	297	32%	4.38 -	23.3	3.0	7.0	**2.4**	0.9	2.08	78%	65	144
01	2NL	3	3	9	75	54	1.80	1.09	$16	3.4	200	149	238	24%	2.16	35.8	3.5	6.5	**1.9**	0.4	1.70	85%	82	152
02	STL	2	1	6	60	42	3.30	1.27	$7	3.7	242	230	266	29%	3.09	14.5	3.3	6.3	**1.9**	0.5	1.56	74%	71	134
03	STL	5	5	3	63	31	3.84	1.36	$7	3.5	239	243	233	26%	3.64	12.1	4.3	4.4	**1.0**	0.7	1.36	73%	34	65
1st Half		3	4	3	31	12	3.75	1.60	$3	4.0	248			25%	4.51 -	6.4	6.1	3.5	**0.6**	0.9	1.18	79%	12	24
2nd Half		2	1	0	32	19	3.94	1.12	$3	3.0	230			26%	2.78 +	5.7	2.5	5.3	**2.1**	0.6	1.59	65%	68	132
04	**Proj**	**3**	**3**	**4**	**60**	**38**	**3.45**	**1.28**	**$7**	**3.5**	**235**			**27%**	**3.24**	**14.6**	**3.8**	**5.7**	**1.5**	**0.6**	**--**	**74%**	**56**	**108**

HIs saves percentages the past three years are 90%, 85%, 43%. While his BPIs have eroded into nothing, the fact is, once he was removed from any save opps in the 2nd half, his BPIs soared. Coincidence? You decide.

Knotts,Gary

RH Starter | AGE 27 Growth | TYPE
RISK: R X HIGH; I EXP CON; S PT STB; K BRN
LIMA D | EP: 50%

Yr	Tm	W	L	Sv	IP	K	ERA	Br/IP	R$	BF/G	OBA	vL	vR	H%	xERA	RAR	Ctl	Dom	Cmd	hr/9	G/F	S%	BPV	BPX
99	aa	6	3	0	81	57	4.44	1.51	$4	29.9	280			31%	4.96 -	11.8	3.7	6.3	**1.7**	1.3		75%	33	77
00	aa	9	8	0	156	95	5.77	1.65	($2)	26.4	301			34%	5.36	-0.2	3.9	5.5	**1.4**	0.9		65%	31	74
01	aaa	6	8	0	124	99	5.08	1.47	$0	23.7	289			34%	4.81	5.7	2.9	7.2	**2.5**	0.9	1.17	66%	64	123
02	FLA *	8	4	3	83	60	4.23	1.47	$7	5.2	245	191	194	28%	4.14	9.8	5.0	6.5	**1.3**	1.0	1.05	73%	43	82
03	DET *	7	14	0	174	104	6.41	1.76	($14)	24.7	320	323	249	34%	6.59	-20.6	3.9	5.4	**1.4**	1.5	1.00	66%	7	16
1st Half		3	5	0	81	39	4.67	1.52	($0)	22.5	269			28%	4.76	9.3	4.3	4.3	**1.0**	1.0	1.07	71%	18	39
2nd Half		4	9	0	93	65	7.93	1.97	($15)	26.8	359			39%	8.19	-30.0	3.5	6.3	**1.8**	1.9	0.76	62%	1	2
04	**Proj**	**5**	**10**	**0**	**120**	**81**	**5.25**	**1.61**	**($3)**	**24.7**	**299**			**33%**	**5.66**	**4.6**	**3.7**	**6.1**	**1.7**	**1.3**	**--**	**70%**	**28**	**60**

3-8, 6.06 ERA in 95 IP at DET. Ten of his 18 starts were PQS-0 disasters. Minor league BPIs have shown some promise, but skills development in DET is going to be slow and arduous.

Koch,Billy

RH Reliever | AGE 29 Pre-Peak | TYPE Power
RISK: R High; I CON; S pt stb; K
LIMA C+ | EP: 55%

Yr	Tm	W	L	Sv	IP	K	ERA	Br/IP	R$	BF/G	OBA	vL	vR	H%	xERA	RAR	Ctl	Dom	Cmd	hr/9	G/F	S%	BPV	BPX
99	TOR *	3	5	31	88	76	4.09	1.48	$21	6.3	264	209	261	32%	4.45	21.0	4.2	7.8	**1.9**	0.9	1.94	74%	60	151
00	TOR	9	3	33	78	60	2.65	1.23	$35	4.8	261	255	261	31%	3.54 -	34.2	2.1	6.9	**3.3**	0.7	1.63	81%	93	243
01	TOR	2	5	36	69	55	4.82	1.48	$19	4.4	262	292	243	31%	4.42	6.2	4.3	7.2	**1.7**	0.9	1.36	68%	53	107
02	OAK	11	4	44	93	93	3.29	1.28	$38	4.6	218	237	196	28%	3.16	27.0	4.5	9.0	**2.0**	0.7	1.29	76%	88	180
03	CHW	5	5	11	53	42	5.77	1.64	$6	4.4	283	294	267	31%	5.90	-1.8	4.8	7.1	**1.5**	1.7	0.98	69%	22	47
1st Half		4	4	11	35	26	4.63	1.43	$9	4.0	251			26%	5.01	4.2	4.4	6.7	**1.5**	1.8	1.08	74%	23	50
2nd Half		1	1	0	18	16	8.00	2.06	($3)	5.3	339			40%	7.63	-6.0	5.5	8.0	**1.5**	1.5	0.81	62%	21	45
04	**Proj**	**5**	**6**	**3**	**70**	**61**	**4.24**	**1.59**	**$4**	**4.7**	**275**			**33%**	**5.01 -**	**12.1**	**4.6**	**7.8**	**1.7**	**1.0**	**--**	**76%**	**52**	**111**

CHW was fooled into thinking they were trading for a "real" closer, but his BPIs were always suspect. Note how control has gotten worse each year. While 2nd half debacle was mostly bad luck, the skill is just not there.

Kolb,Danny

RH Reliever | AGE 29 Pre-Peak | TYPE Power
RISK: R Very High; I exp CON; S pt STB; K
LIMA C | EP: 35%

Yr	Tm	W	L	Sv	IP	K	ERA	Br/IP	R$	BF/G	OBA	vL	vR	H%	xERA	RAR	Ctl	Dom	Cmd	hr/9	G/F	S%	BPV	BPX
99	TEX *	8	6	0	130	60	5.12	1.72	($0)	17.7	309	280	260	34%	5.47	13.0	4.1	4.2	**1.0**	0.6	3.09	70%	21	52
00	aaa	4	1	4	19	17	3.79	1.53	$6	6.0	251			30%	4.41 -	5.0	5.2	8.1	**1.5**	0.9	2.00	78%	57	135
01	TEX *	1	1	0	36	35	3.00	1.28	$3	5.0	228	257	261	27%	3.78 -	12.0	4.0	8.8	**2.2**	1.3	2.56	83%	70	141
02	TEX	3	7	1	40	22	4.28	1.65	$1	4.7	262	291	172	30%	4.28	6.3	5.9	5.0	**0.8**	0.2	2.65	72%	43	89
03	MIL	1	2	21	41	39	1.97	1.29	$16	4.7	227	209	230	29%	3.00 -	18.2	4.2	8.5	**2.1**	0.4	2.46	86%	91	175
1st Half		0	0	0	6	9	2.95	1.97	($0)	7.5	225			38%	4.23 -	1.9	10.3	13.3	**1.3**	0.0	9.00	83%	117	224
2nd Half		1	2	21	35	30	1.80	1.17	$16	4.3	227			28%	2.79 -	16.3	3.1	7.7	**2.5**	0.5	2.17	87%	93	179
04	**Proj**	**3**	**4**	**26**	**60**	**52**	**3.15**	**1.37**	**$19**	**4.6**	**249**			**30%**	**3.75 -**	**17.0**	**3.9**	**7.8**	**2.0**	**0.8**	**G**	**79%**	**72**	**138**

A real closer? History shows little indication, but 2nd half BPIs are promising. Given his borderline control, a little more dominance would go a long way towards getting him into a closer-worthy comfort zone.

Koplove,Mike

RH Reliever | AGE 27 Pre-Peak | TYPE
RISK: R High; I EXP con; S pt stb; K
LIMA B+ | EP: 40%

Yr	Tm	W	L	Sv	IP	K	ERA	Br/IP	R$	BF/G	OBA	vL	vR	H%	xERA	RAR	Ctl	Dom	Cmd	hr/9	G/F	S%	BPV	BPX
99		0	0	0	0	0	0.00	0.00																
00	aa	4	3	6	46	38	4.70	1.37	$7	5.6	253			31%	3.52 +	6.6	3.7	7.4	**2.0**	0.4		64%	79	188
01	a/a	7	7	13	76	67	3.20	1.53	$14	5.6	269	192	250	33%	4.34 -	22.6	4.4	7.9	**1.8**	0.6	1.71	80%	69	132
02	ARI *	7	3	3	91	71	2.67	1.08	$15	4.7	217	174	230	27%	2.15 +	29.7	2.7	7.0	**2.6**	0.3	2.38	75%	100	189
03	ARI	3	0	0	37	27	2.18	1.10	$6	4.8	228	224	225	26%	2.84 -	15.4	2.4	6.5	**2.7**	0.7	2.00	84%	83	161
1st Half		3	0	0	37	27	2.18	1.10	$6	4.8	228			26%	2.84 -	15.4	2.4	6.5	**2.7**	0.7	2.00	84%	83	161
2nd Half		0	0	0	0	0	0.00	0.00																
04	**Proj**	**5**	**3**	**0**	**60**	**47**	**3.00**	**1.23**	**$8**	**4.9**	**245**			**29%**	**3.23**	**18.2**	**2.9**	**7.1**	**2.5**	**0.6**	**G**	**77%**	**82**	**159**

Shoulder surgery ended his season early, but that's good news for fantasy leaguers. He'll likely fly under the radar on draft day and you can grab this LIMA-worthy pick for your reserve list.

Lackey,John

RH Starter | AGE 25 Growth | TYPE
RISK: R Very High; I EXP con; S pt stb; K BRN
LIMA C+ | EP: 50%

Yr	Tm	W	L	Sv	IP	K	ERA	Br/IP	R$	BF/G	OBA	vL	vR	H%	xERA	RAR	Ctl	Dom	Cmd	hr/9	G/F	S%	BPV	BPX
99		0	0	0	0	0	0.00	0.00																
00	aa	6	1	0	57	37	4.74	1.42	$5	30.9	309			34%	5.30 -	7.8	1.4	5.8	**4.1**	1.3		70%	77	182
01	a/a	12	11	0	185	118	5.06	1.31	$8	27.9	277			31%	4.14 +	9.0	2.0	5.7	**2.8**	0.8		61%	68	131
02	ANA *	17	6	0	209	139	3.27	1.29	$22	25.9	263	208	317	30%	3.76 -	61.2	2.5	6.0	**2.4**	0.6	1.31	76%	68	140
03	ANA	10	16	0	204	151	4.63	1.42	$5	26.8	279	286	269	31%	4.98	24.4	2.9	6.7	**2.3**	1.4	0.95	71%	46	100
1st Half		5	7	0	97	74	5.47	1.52	($1)	25.3	300			34%	5.63	0.7	2.8	6.9	**2.5**	1.5	1.07	67%	44	94
2nd Half		5	9	0	107	77	3.87	1.33	$6	28.4	260			29%	4.38 -	23.7	3.0	6.5	**2.1**	1.3	0.86	76%	49	106
04	**Proj**	**13**	**12**	**0**	**200**	**149**	**4.23**	**1.32**	**$13**	**27.3**	**268**			**30%**	**4.28**	**35.1**	**2.6**	**6.7**	**2.6**	**1.1**	**--**	**71%**	**64**	**138**

BPIs didn't hold up well over a full season in the bigs, but there are still some positive signs here -- improved Dom and BA vs RHers. There's work to be done, but he should continue growth trend into 2004.

Lawrence,Brian

RH Starter | AGE 27 Pre-Peak | TYPE Finesse
RISK: R Moderate; I EXP con; S pt; K
LIMA C | EP: 50%

Yr	Tm	W	L	Sv	IP	K	ERA	Br/IP	R$	BF/G	OBA	vL	vR	H%	xERA	RAR	Ctl	Dom	Cmd	hr/9	G/F	S%	BPV	BPX
99		0	0	0	0	0	0.00	0.00																
00	a/a	11	6	0	173	129	2.50	1.14	$27	24.2	249			30%	3.08 -	75.6	1.9	6.7	**3.6**	0.6		80%	103	245
01	SD *	6	8	1	159	118	3.68	1.28	$9	18.6	254	281	215	30%	3.67	35.9	2.9	6.7	**2.3**	0.7	2.42	73%	71	131
02	SD	12	12	0	210	149	3.69	1.34	$12	25.6	280	324	236	33%	4.03	40.0	2.2	6.4	**2.9**	0.7	2.51	74%	77	146
03	SD	10	15	0	210	116	4.20	1.25	$11	26.6	258	275	244	27%	4.02	30.5	2.4	5.0	**2.0**	1.2	1.43	70%	41	79
1st Half		4	9	0	109	66	4.86	1.20	$4	26.5	247			26%	3.82 +	6.1	2.5	5.4	**2.2**	1.2	1.27	62%	47	91
2nd Half		6	6	0	101	50	3.48	1.31	$8	26.7	269			28%	4.24 -	24.4	2.4	4.5	**1.9**	1.1	1.63	78%	35	67
04	**Proj**	**10**	**12**	**0**	**200**	**122**	**3.74**	**1.28**	**$13**	**24.7**	**264**			**29%**	**3.88**	**41.0**	**2.4**	**5.5**	**2.3**	**0.9**	**--**	**73%**	**57**	**109**

A velocity issue? Didn't throw as hard (lower Dom), leading to more fly balls and more HRs. Improved his OBA so there is still something good here, but I had him at $10 in a keeper league and opted to let him go.

Ledezma,Wil

LH Reliever | AGE 23 Growth | TYPE
RISK: R Moderate; I EXP; S; K AGE
LIMA F | EP: 45%

Yr	Tm	W	L	Sv	IP	K	ERA	Br/IP	R$	BF/G	OBA	vL	vR	H%	xERA	RAR	Ctl	Dom	Cmd	hr/9	G/F	S%	BPV	BPX
99		0	0	0	0	0	0.00	0.00																
00		0	0	0	0	0	0.00	0.00																
01		0	0	0	0	0	0.00	0.00																
02		0	0	0	0	0	0.00	0.00																
03	DET	3	7	0	84	49	5.79	1.60	($4)	11.2	295	309	292	32%	5.59	-2.9	3.8	5.3	**1.4**	1.3	0.61	66%	18	40
1st Half		2	2	0	36	27	4.00	1.28	$3	8.0	240			27%	3.74	7.4	3.5	6.8	**1.9**	1.0	0.88	71%	58	125
2nd Half		1	5	0	48	22	7.12	1.83	($7)	15.2	331			34%	6.98	-10.3	3.9	4.1	**1.0**	1.5	0.47	63%	-9	-20
04	**Proj**	**1**	**3**	**0**	**40**	**23**	**5.85**	**1.63**	**($3)**	**11.4**	**299**			**32%**	**5.78**	**-1.7**	**3.8**	**5.2**	**1.4**	**1.4**	**F**	**66%**	**14**	**31**

His PQS scores looked like this: 4,4,0,3,0,0,0,0 -- and then he got kicked back to the bullpen... where he only got into 6 more games, allowing 10 runs in 8 IP. Clearly not ready for the bigs, but then again, it's just DET.

Lee,Cliff

LH Starter | AGE 25 Growth | TYPE Power
RISK: R High; I EXP con; S pt; K brn
LIMA C | EP: 40%

Yr	Tm	W	L	Sv	IP	K	ERA	Br/IP	R$	BF/G	OBA	vL	vR	H%	xERA	RAR	Ctl	Dom	Cmd	hr/9	G/F	S%	BPV	BPX
99		0	0	0	0	0	0.00	0.00																
00		0	0	0	0	0	0.00	0.00																
01		0	0	0	0	0	0.00	0.00																
02	a/a	5	3	0	59	40	5.80	1.58	($1)	24.1	258			28%	5.18 +	-4.2	5.3	6.1	**1.1**	1.5		66%	18	36
03	CLE *	10	4	0	127	104	3.96	1.47	$8	25.4	263	278	197	31%	4.52 -	26.6	4.2	7.4	**1.8**	1.0	0.77	76%	54	116
1st Half		4	0	0	34	28	2.12	1.44	$5	24.7	238			28%	3.93 -	15.5	5.0	7.4	**1.5**	0.8	0.86	89%	59	127
2nd Half		6	4	0	93	76	4.64	1.48	$3	25.6	272			32%	4.73	11.1	3.9	7.3	**1.9**	1.1	0.76	71%	53	114
04	**Proj**	**10**	**8**	**0**	**140**	**109**	**4.31**	**1.42**	**$8**	**24.3**	**258**			**29%**	**4.48**	**23.1**	**4.0**	**7.0**	**1.8**	**1.2**	**F**	**73%**	**48**	**102**

3-3, 3.63 ERA in 52 IP at CLE, with a 3.5 Ctl and 2.2 Cmd, better levels than his MLEs. There is potential here, but it will rest on his ability to own the strike zone, and he's not quite there yet.

Leiter,Al

LH Starter | AGE 38 Decline | TYPE Power | R: Low | I: con | S: | K: AGE | LIMA C+ | EP: 50%

Yr	Tm	W	L	Sv	IP	K	ERA	Br/IP	R$	BF/G	OBA	vL	vR	H%	xERA	RAR	Ctl	Dom	Cmd	hr/9	G/F	S%	BPV	BPX
99	NYM	13	12	0	213	162	4.23	1.42	$11	28.9	258	260	262	30%	3.75	28.8	3.9	6.8	**1.7**	0.8	1.13	71%	57	124
00	NYM	16	8	0	208	200	3.20	1.21	$27	27.7	231	118	248	29%	3.23	67.6	3.3	8.7	**2.6**	0.8	1.27	76%	91	201
01	NYM	11	11	0	187	142	3.32	1.20	$18	26.6	252	254	251	29%	3.54	51.3	2.2	6.8	**3.1**	0.9	1.05	75%	84	157
02	NYM	13	13	0	204	172	3.49	1.29	$16	26.0	252	221	257	30%	3.80	44.3	3.0	7.6	**2.5**	1.0	1.18	77%	72	136
03	NYM	15	9	0	180	139	4.00	1.50	$10	26.5	257	299	252	30%	4.23	31.0	4.7	6.9	**1.5**	0.7	0.80	75%	54	103
1st Half		8	5	0	97	71	5.57	1.77	($3)	26.8	285			33%	5.58	-3.7	5.8	6.6	**1.1**	1.0	0.97	70%	31	59
2nd Half		7	4	0	83	68	2.16	1.18	$13	26.2	222			27%	2.67 -	34.7	3.4	7.4	**2.2**	0.4	0.63	83%	88	169
04	**Proj**	**13**	**10**	**0**	**180**	**144**	**3.50**	**1.34**	**$15**	**26.5**	**250**			**30%**	**3.76**	**42.5**	**3.7**	**7.2**	**2.0**	**0.8**	**--**	**76%**	**66**	**127**

He denies it, but a sore knee is what hurt his 1st half. After a DL stint, he was golden. A 2.16 ERA in the 2nd half won't happen again (83% strand rate), but he's got at least one more $15-20 season left in him.

Leskanic,Curtis

RH Reliever | AGE 36 Decline | TYPE Power | R: High | I: con | S: pt STB | K: age | LIMA B | EP: 40%

Yr	Tm	W	L	Sv	IP	K	ERA	Br/IP	R$	BF/G	OBA	vL	vR	H%	xERA	RAR	Ctl	Dom	Cmd	hr/9	G/F	S%	BPV	BPX
99	COL	6	2	0	85	77	5.08	1.60	$0	6.1	266	300	257	33%	4.25 +	1.7	5.2	8.2	**1.6**	0.7	2.02	68%	61	133
00	MIL	9	3	12	77	75	2.57	1.41	$19	4.6	211	214	211	26%	3.49 -	31.6	6.0	8.8	**1.5**	0.8	1.60	85%	72	158
01	MIL	2	6	17	69	64	3.65	1.36	$13	4.2	244	275	220	28%	4.37 -	15.9	4.0	8.3	**2.1**	1.4	1.01	80%	57	105
02	a/a	0	0	0	10	8	2.70	1.40	$0	5.4	262			33%	3.34 -	3.4	3.6	7.2	**2.0**	0.0		79%	88	172
03	2TM	5	0	2	52	50	2.24	1.28	$9	4.1	205	176	228	27%	2.66	22.0	5.0	8.6	**1.7**	0.3	1.21	83%	92	186
1st Half		4	0	0	26	28	2.75	1.53	$4	4.5	229			31%	3.56 -	9.3	6.2	9.6	**1.6**	0.3	1.13	82%	89	181
2nd Half		1	0	2	26	22	1.73	1.04	$5	3.8	179			23%	1.76	12.8	3.8	7.6	**2.0**	0.3	1.29	85%	96	196
04	**Proj**	**3**	**3**	**1**	**60**	**53**	**3.60**	**1.42**	**$4**	**4.4**	**239**			**29%**	**3.78**	**14.4**	**4.8**	**8.0**	**1.7**	**0.8**	**--**	**76%**	**67**	**136**

Erratic control has followed him his entire career, which is what makes this year's performance so amazing. Eventually, it's going to come back to haunt him, and you don't want him on your roster when it does.

Levine,Al

RH Reliever | AGE 35 Decline | TYPE | R: Moderate | I: CON | S: pt | K: age | LIMA D+ | EP: 15%

Yr	Tm	W	L	Sv	IP	K	ERA	Br/IP	R$	BF/G	OBA	vL	vR	H%	xERA	RAR	Ctl	Dom	Cmd	hr/9	G/F	S%	BPV	BPX
99	ANA	1	1	0	85	37	3.39	1.24	$7	7.1	241	233	255	24%	4.00 -	28.3	3.1	3.9	**1.3**	1.4	1.37	79%	16	40
00	ANA	3	4	2	95	42	3.88	1.55	$5	8.3	268	261	269	28%	4.70 -	25.9	4.6	4.0	**0.9**	0.9	1.78	77%	15	39
01	ANA	8	10	2	75	40	2.39	1.32	$13	5.0	251	288	229	27%	3.82 -	31.1	3.4	4.8	**1.4**	0.8	1.82	86%	38	77
02	ANA	4	4	5	63	40	4.29	1.51	$5	5.4	256	240	263	28%	4.69	9.9	4.9	5.7	**1.2**	1.1	1.32	75%	29	59
03	2AL	3	6	1	71	30	2.79	1.35	$6	5.6	251	218	284	25%	4.23 -	26.0	3.7	3.8	**1.0**	1.1	1.35	85%	15	33
1st Half		2	5	0	39	21	1.84	1.15	$6	6.4	240			26%	3.36 -	19.4	2.3	4.8	**2.1**	0.9	1.19	90%	52	113
2nd Half		1	1	1	32	9	3.96	1.60	$0	5.0	263			25%	5.30 -	6.7	5.4	2.5	**0.5**	1.4	1.55	80%	-15	-32
04	**Proj**	**3**	**5**	**0**	**65**	**31**	**4.02**	**1.46**	**$2**	**5.6**	**262**			**27%**	**4.62 -**	**13.3**	**4.2**	**4.3**	**1.0**	**1.1**	**--**	**76%**	**17**	**36**

As his strand rate goes, so does his ERA. With little in the way of skills to support him, his fate ends up in the hands of his defense, the rest of his bullpen, managerial whim, and the wind.

Levrault,Allen

RH Reliever | AGE 26 Growth | TYPE | R: X HIGH | I: EXP con | S: PT STB | K: | LIMA D | EP: 25%

Yr	Tm	W	L	Sv	IP	K	ERA	Br/IP	R$	BF/G	OBA	vL	vR	H%	xERA	RAR	Ctl	Dom	Cmd	hr/9	G/F	S%	BPV	BPX
99	a/a	10	5	0	134	105	5.24	1.31	$8	22.7	259			29%	4.09 +	5.2	2.9	7.1	**2.4**	1.3		62%	59	136
00	aaa	6	8	0	108	67	4.33	1.33	$8	21.9	253			29%	3.62 +	20.6	3.4	5.6	**1.6**	0.6	1.00	67%	55	130
01	MIL *	8	11	0	160	106	5.51	1.49	($2)	19.1	275	270	289	29%	5.26	-3.1	3.8	6.0	**1.6**	1.6	1.01	67%	22	40
02	aaa	7	8	0	111	68	6.41	1.73	($8)	21.5	325			36%	6.13	-16.9	3.3	5.5	**1.7**	1.1		63%	26	51
03	FLA *	4	0	0	53	37	2.71	1.41	$5	5.8	254	383	299	29%	4.06 -	18.3	4.1	6.3	**1.5**	0.8	0.68	84%	49	94
1st Half		2	0	0	39	29	3.00	1.51	$2	6.4	281			33%	4.77 -	11.9	3.7	6.7	**1.8**	0.9	0.68	84%	49	95
2nd Half		2	0	0	14	8	1.90	1.13	$3	4.4	167			18%	2.11	6.4	5.1	5.1	**1.0**	0.6		87%	54	104
04	**Proj**	**1**	**3**	**0**	**40**	**27**	**4.73**	**1.50**	**($1)**	**6.1**	**281**			**31%**	**4.90**	**2.9**	**3.6**	**6.1**	**1.7**	**1.1**	**F**	**71%**	**37**	**71**

1-0, 3.86 ERA in 28 IP at FLA, and then apparently tore up AAA after his demotion... but not really. His 2nd half was a mirage built on 18/87% strand/hit rates. Take a scan of his 5-year Cmd trend for a dose of reality.

Lewis,Colby

RH Starter | AGE 24 Growth | TYPE Power | R: High | I: EXP con | S: pt | K: age | LIMA D | EP: 55%

Yr	Tm	W	L	Sv	IP	K	ERA	Br/IP	R$	BF/G	OBA	vL	vR	H%	xERA	RAR	Ctl	Dom	Cmd	hr/9	G/F	S%	BPV	BPX
99		0	0	0	0	0	0.00	0.00																
00		0	0	0	0	0	0.00	0.00																
01	aa	10	10	0	156	145	5.65	1.51	($1)	27.6	285			35%	4.98 +	-4.9	3.5	8.4	**2.4**	1.1		63%	66	127
02	TEX *	6	9	0	140	114	4.63	1.46	$1	17.5	278	320	286	34%	4.27	15.6	3.3	7.3	**2.2**	0.5	1.32	67%	74	152
03	TEX *	15	10	0	174	126	6.41	1.69	($5)	24.4	295	319	313	32%	6.13	-20.6	4.6	6.5	**1.4**	1.6	1.16	65%	17	36
1st Half		6	6	0	82	58	7.78	2.00	($11)	23.7	314			34%	7.33	-24.8	6.4	6.4	**1.0**	1.8	1.03	63%	-1	-3
2nd Half		9	4	0	92	68	5.18	1.42	$5	25.0	278			31%	5.06	4.3	3.0	6.6	**2.2**	1.5	1.29	67%	41	89
04	**Proj**	**6**	**10**	**0**	**120**	**94**	**5.55**	**1.57**	**($2)**	**24.5**	**287**			**33%**	**5.23**	**-0.2**	**3.9**	**7.1**	**1.8**	**1.1**	**--**	**66%**	**44**	**95**

10-9, 7.30 ERA in 127 IP at TEX, somewhat inflated by 34/62% strand/hit rates. There are small seeds of skill here, but tons of obstacles to overcome... pitch movement, gopheritis, control... at least 2 years away.

Lidge,Brad

RH Reliever | AGE 27 Growth | TYPE Power | R: Very High | I: EXP con | S: pt stb | K: | LIMA A | EP: 60%

Yr	Tm	W	L	Sv	IP	K	ERA	Br/IP	R$	BF/G	OBA	vL	vR	H%	xERA	RAR	Ctl	Dom	Cmd	hr/9	G/F	S%	BPV	BPX
99		0	0	0	0	0	0.00	0.00																
00		0	0	0	0	0	0.00	0.00																
01	aa	2	0	0	26	34	2.08	1.27	$4	21.8	262			39%	3.32 -	11.6	2.4	11.8	**4.9**	0.3		84%	165	316
02	a/a	7	6	0	130	117	4.64	1.48	$2	16.3	257			31%	4.30	11.0	4.5	8.1	**1.8**	0.9	1.00	70%	63	124
03	HOU	6	3	1	85	97	3.60	1.20	$9	4.5	200	230	179	27%	2.62 +	19.1	4.4	10.3	**2.3**	0.6	0.77	71%	106	204
1st Half		4	1	1	47	53	2.86	1.21	$7	4.9	199			29%	2.21 +	15.3	4.6	10.1	**2.2**	0.2	0.72	75%	117	224
2nd Half		2	2	0	38	44	4.52	1.19	$2	4.5	202			26%	3.14 +	3.8	4.3	10.5	**2.4**	1.2	0.83	65%	93	179
04	**Proj**	**5**	**3**	**0**	**80**	**89**	**3.38**	**1.26**	**$7**	**6.2**	**221**			**29%**	**3.14**	**20.2**	**4.2**	**10.0**	**2.4**	**0.8**	**F**	**76%**	**98**	**189**

Solid growth year, and great LIMA pick. Tough to find fauit with a 100+ BPV, but imagine how high he could go if he improved his control a tad, and reeled in his flyball tendency. There's more upside here.

Lidle,Cory

RH Starter | AGE 32 Peak | TYPE Finesse | R: Moderate | I: con | S: pt stb | K: | LIMA B | EP: 60%

Yr	Tm	W	L	Sv	IP	K	ERA	Br/IP	R$	BF/G	OBA	vL	vR	H%	xERA	RAR	Ctl	Dom	Cmd	hr/9	G/F	S%	BPV	BPX
99	TAM *	1	0	0	11	10	5.73	1.91	($0)	6.6	354			42%	7.63 -	0.2	3.3	8.2	**2.5**	1.6	1.40	74%	37	92
00	TAM *	10	8	0	146	100	4.19	1.40	$2	15.8	291	295	293	33%	4.69 -	33.8	2.2	6.2	**2.8**	1.0	2.76	72%	63	162
01	OAK	13	6	0	188	118	3.59	1.15	$20	26.4	243	213	276	26%	3.55	47.7	2.3	5.6	**2.5**	1.1	1.81	73%	60	120
02	OAK	8	10	0	196	114	3.86	1.20	$13	25.2	259	248	269	29%	3.62	42.0	1.9	5.2	**2.7**	0.8	1.42	69%	68	140
03	TOR	12	15	0	192	112	5.76	1.44	$1	27.0	285	265	305	31%	4.89 +	-6.0	2.8	5.2	**1.9**	1.1	1.52	61%	35	76
1st Half		10	6	0	116	75	5.34	1.33	$6	27.4	279			31%	4.27 +	2.8	2.1	5.8	**2.8**	0.9	1.38	59%	67	144
2nd Half		2	9	0	76	37	6.39	1.61	($6)	26.5	293			30%	5.84 +	-8.9	3.9	4.4	**1.1**	1.5	1.76	62%	-0	-0
04	**Proj**	**11**	**14**	**0**	**200**	**127**	**4.37**	**1.31**	**$11**	**24.1**	**269**			**30%**	**4.25**	**31.4**	**2.4**	**5.7**	**2.4**	**1.0**	**G**	**69%**	**55**	**117**

Some explanations... First, discount the 2nd half because he was struggling with a groin problem. His 1st half ERA was grossly inflated by a 59% strand rate. A more normal level would have yielded a 4.19 ERA.

Ligtenberg,Kerry

RH Reliever | AGE 32 Past | TYPE Power | R: Very Low | I: | S: | K: | LIMA C+ | EP: 35%

Yr	Tm	W	L	Sv	IP	K	ERA	Br/IP	R$	BF/G	OBA	vL	vR	H%	xERA	RAR	Ctl	Dom	Cmd	hr/9	G/F	S%	BPV	BPX
99		0	0	0	0	0	0.00	0.00																
00	ATL	2	3	12	52	51	3.63	1.29	$11	3.7	226	206	236	27%	3.73	14.0	4.1	8.8	**2.1**	1.2	0.67	77%	71	156
01	ATL	3	3	1	59	56	3.04	1.35	$5	4.8	230	241	216	29%	3.39	18.4	4.6	8.5	**1.9**	0.6	0.90	79%	81	150
02	ATL	3	4	0	66	51	3.00	1.29	$5	5.3	218	214	212	25%	3.19	18.6	4.5	7.0	**1.5**	0.8	0.72	80%	61	115
03	BAL	4	2	1	59	47	3.35	1.25	$7	3.6	265	356	206	30%	4.35 -	17.2	2.1	7.2	**3.4**	1.4	0.59	80%	74	161
1st Half		0	0	1	31	25	2.88	1.25	$2	4.2	261			31%	3.81 -	11.0	2.3	7.2	**3.1**	0.9	0.74	81%	86	185
2nd Half		4	2	0	28	22	3.87	1.25	$4	3.1	269			29%	4.95 -	6.2	1.9	7.1	**3.7**	1.9	0.46	79%	63	135
04	**Proj**	**4**	**3**	**2**	**60**	**50**	**3.60**	**1.28**	**$7**	**4.1**	**245**			**28%**	**4.00**	**15.6**	**3.3**	**7.5**	**2.3**	**1.2**	**F**	**77%**	**63**	**134**

Interesting 2nd half, where he allowed the same number of BBs as HRs (6). Solid BPIs but not without a few concerns, most notably his BA vs LHers.

Lilly,Ted

LH Starter | AGE 28 Pre-Peak | TYPE Power | R: X HIGH | I: exp | S: PT STB | K: BRN | LIMA C+ | EP: 50%

Yr	Tm	W	L	Sv	IP	K	ERA	Br/IP	R$	BF/G	OBA	vL	vR	H%	xERA	RAR	Ctl	Dom	Cmd	hr/9	G/F	S%	BPV	BPX
99	MON *	8	6	0	113	96	5.26	1.35	$4	19.3	275			32%	4.19 +	-0.3	2.5	7.6	**3.0**	1.2		63%	73	159
00	aaa	8	11	0	137	110	4.80	1.61	$3	28.2	311			36%	5.57 -	17.7	3.0	7.2	**2.4**	1.1	0.90	72%	55	130
01	NYY *	5	6	0	145	138	5.09	1.41	$0	20.2	262	229	278	31%	4.72	7.7	3.7	8.6	**2.3**	1.4	0.74	67%	60	121
02	2AL	5	7	0	100	77	3.69	1.11	$10	18.3	221	154	231	24%	3.43	23.7	2.8	6.9	**2.5**	1.4	0.68	73%	64	131
03	OAK	12	10	0	178	147	4.35	1.33	$11	23.7	263	235	261	30%	4.37	28.1	2.9	7.4	**2.5**	1.2	0.71	71%	64	138
1st Half		5	6	0	95	70	4.83	1.31	$4	25.1	256			27%	4.59	8.8	3.0	6.6	**2.2**	1.6	0.64	68%	41	89
2nd Half		7	4	0	83	77	3.79	1.36	$7	22.2	271			34%	4.12	19.3	2.8	8.3	**3.0**	0.8	0.79	74%	90	195
04	**Proj**	**11**	**10**	**0**	**180**	**152**	**4.05**	**1.28**	**$13**	**21.0**	**251**			**29%**	**4.06**	**35.9**	**3.0**	**7.6**	**2.5**	**1.2**	**F**	**72%**	**68**	**145**

Skills remain stable and not half bad if not for chronic gopheritis. 2nd half showed small sign of what his stat line might look like if he managed to harness the longball. But can he do that consistently? Possibly not.

Lima,Jose

RH Starter
AGE 31 Peak
TYPE Finesse

R	High	
I		CON
S	pt	STB
K		

LIMA C EP: 45%

Yr	Tm	W	L	Sv	IP	K	ERA	Br/IP	R$	BF/G	OBA	vL	vR	H%	xERA	RAR	Ctl	Dom	Cmd	hr/9	G/F	S%	BPV	BPX
99	HOU	21	10	0	246	187	3.59	1.22	$29	29.1	270	287	248	31%	3.69	54.4	1.6	6.8	**4.3**	1.1	1.33	75%	98	214
00	HOU	7	16	0	196	124	6.65	1.63	($11)	27.0	312	364	272	32%	6.76	-26.9	3.1	5.7	**1.8**	2.2	0.92	64%	-1	-2
01	2TM	6	12	0	165	84	5.56	1.42	($2)	22.4	297	301	298	30%	5.75	-3.0	2.1	4.6	**2.2**	1.9	1.04	67%	12	23
02	DET	4	6	0	68	33	7.81	1.57	($6)	15.3	310	319	308	32%	6.08 +	-21.4	2.8	4.4	**1.6**	1.6	0.74	51%	5	10
03	KC	8	3	0	73	32	4.92	1.45	$5	22.8	280	329	210	30%	4.62	5.9	3.2	3.9	**1.2**	0.9	0.76	67%	23	49
1st Half		2	0	0	18	5	3.48	1.22	$3	25.0	227			23%	2.99	5.0	3.5	2.5	**0.7**	0.5	0.92	71%	25	53
2nd Half		6	3	0	55	27	5.40	1.53	$2	22.2	295			32%	5.15	0.9	3.1	4.4	**1.4**	1.0	0.71	65%	23	49
04	**Proj**	**4**	**6**	**0**	**80**	**38**	**5.06**	**1.46**	**$1**	**23.4**	**287**			**30%**	**5.11**	**5.1**	**2.9**	**4.3**	**1.5**	**1.2**	**F**	**68%**	**17**	**36**

First 8 starts vs last 6 starts:

	IP	ERA	Ctl	Dom	Cmd
F8	50	2.16	3.1	4.0	1.3
L6	24	9.38	3.0	3.3	1.1

His 7 wins in those first 8 starts gave false hope. His skills have not returned, just 50 IP of luck.

Lincoln,Mike

RH Reliever
AGE 29 Pre-Peak
TYPE

R	High	
I	EXP	con
S	PT	
K		

LIMA B EP: 50%

Yr	Tm	W	L	Sv	IP	K	ERA	Br/IP	R$	BF/G	OBA	vL	vR	H%	xERA	RAR	Ctl	Dom	Cmd	hr/9	G/F	S%	BPV	BPX
99	MIN	* 8	12	0	135	61	7.53	1.76	($10)	23.4	334	358	282	35%	6.77 +	-30.0	3.1	4.1	**1.3**	1.5	1.36	58%	-4	-9
00	MIN	* 4	4	0	95	46	5.87	1.55	($1)	21.2	306	378	388	33%	5.00 +	0.5	2.7	4.4	**1.6**	0.7	1.46	61%	33	87
01	PIT	* 7	5	0	131	83	3.57	1.33	$9	11.4	269	196	240	30%	4.14 -	31.5	2.6	5.7	**2.2**	0.9	1.41	76%	54	101
02	PIT	* 2	4	2	86	62	2.83	1.47	$4	5.8	286	276	296	33%	4.46 -	26.3	3.0	6.5	**2.1**	0.7	1.82	83%	60	113
03	PIT	* 4	5	5	48	35	4.10	1.35	$6	4.7	261	333	250	29%	4.25	7.6	3.2	6.5	**2.1**	1.1	1.66	73%	52	99
1st Half		1	1	0	12	7	0.74	1.15	$3	6.2	225			25%	2.94 -	7.4	3.0	5.2	**1.8**	0.7		100%	56	107
2nd Half		3	4	5	36	28	5.24	1.41	$4	4.3	272			31%	4.69 +	0.2	3.2	7.0	**2.2**	1.2		65%	50	97
04	**Proj**	**3**	**3**	**2**	**50**	**34**	**4.32**	**1.40**	**$3**	**7.2**	**273**			**31%**	**4.33**	**6.3**	**3.1**	**6.1**	**2.0**	**0.9**	**G**	**71%**	**52**	**101**

5.25 ERA, 5 Sv in 36 IP at PIT. He got all his saves between July 20 and Aug 10. BPIs have shown promise from time to time, but this year's problems with LHers and the longball hurt his chances for more work.

Linebrink,Scott

RH Reliever
AGE 27 Pre-Peak
TYPE Power

R	X HIGH	
I	EXP	CON
S	PT	STB
K		brn

LIMA B+ EP: 45%

Yr	Tm	W	L	Sv	IP	K	ERA	Br/IP	R$	BF/G	OBA	vL	vR	H%	xERA	RAR	Ctl	Dom	Cmd	hr/9	G/F	S%	BPV	BPX
99	aa	1	8	0	43	29	8.37	1.67	($6)	19.8	320			35%	6.31 +	-16.4	3.1	6.1	**1.9**	1.7		50%	18	41
00	aaa	3	4	5	77	61	6.08	1.34	$3	8.4	277			31%	4.82 +	-3.3	2.3	7.1	**3.1**	1.5	0.75	57%	61	144
01	aaa	7	6	8	82	70	4.28	1.22	$12	5.8	230			28%	3.00 +	12.5	3.4	7.7	**2.3**	0.5	0.47	64%	86	165
02	HOU	* 1	1	0	41	38	7.24	2.05	($8)	5.5	322			40%	6.41 +	-11.7	6.4	8.3	**1.3**	0.7	0.61	63%	48	91
03	2NL	3	2	0	92	68	3.32	1.40	$4	7.7	264	275	265	30%	4.20 -	24.1	3.5	6.6	**1.9**	0.9	0.71	79%	55	107
1st Half		1	2	0	55	31	3.43	1.47	$1	12.1	279			30%	4.85 -	13.6	3.4	5.1	**1.5**	1.1	0.71	81%	26	51
2nd Half		2	0	0	37	37	3.16	1.30	$3	4.9	240			32%	3.23	10.5	3.6	9.0	**2.5**	0.5	0.71	76%	98	189
04	**Proj**	**3**	**3**	**0**	**80**	**68**	**3.71**	**1.34**	**$4**	**6.1**	**250**			**30%**	**3.62**	**16.6**	**3.6**	**7.7**	**2.1**	**0.7**	**F**	**73%**	**75**	**145**

Excellent 2nd half after comng over to SD. Knee surgery ended his season but he could be a good LIMA pick for 2004.

Lloyd,Graeme

LH Reliever
AGE 37 Decline
TYPE Finesse

R	High	
I		con
S	pt	STB
K	AGE	

LIMA D EP: 60%

Yr	Tm	W	L	Sv	IP	K	ERA	Br/IP	R$	BF/G	OBA	vL	vR	H%	xERA	RAR	Ctl	Dom	Cmd	hr/9	G/F	S%	BPV	BPX
99	TOR	5	3	3	72	47	3.63	1.26	$10	4.1	251	268	238	27%	4.18 -	21.7	2.9	5.9	**2.0**	1.4	1.38	78%	42	105
00	MON	0	0	0	0	0	0.00	0.00																
01	MON	9	5	1	70	44	4.37	1.36	$8	3.6	272	252	284	31%	4.14	9.4	2.7	5.6	**2.1**	0.8	2.03	69%	55	103
02	2NL	4	5	5	57	37	5.21	1.51	$3	3.8	294	326	281	35%	4.17 +	-0.8	3.0	5.8	**1.9**	0.2	1.57	62%	67	127
03	2TM	1	4	0	47	25	5.34	1.74	($4)	4.2	338	338	333	38%	5.77	0.3	2.7	4.8	**1.8**	0.4	1.21	68%	42	85
1st Half		1	2	0	27	12	2.65	1.21	$3	4.3	260			29%	3.22 -	10.0	2.0	4.0	**2.0**	0.3	1.63	78%	59	119
2nd Half		0	2	0	20	13	9.00	2.45	($7)	4.1	421			48%	9.24	-9.7	3.6	5.8	**1.6**	0.4	0.77	60%	27	54
04	**Proj**	**2**	**3**	**0**	**40**	**22**	**4.73**	**1.63**	**($1)**	**4.0**	**311**			**35%**	**5.09**	**3.6**	**3.2**	**5.0**	**1.6**	**0.5**	**--**	**70%**	**42**	**85**

Moved from NYM to KC in late July and immediately tripled his ERA. While there was minor BPI decline, the real culprits were 48/60% hit/strand rates. Still, after two years of .300+ OB vs LHers, his value is about shot.

Loaiza,Esteban

RH Starter
AGE 32 Peak
TYPE

R	Moderate	
I		con
S	pt	STB
K		brn

LIMA C EP: 55%

Yr	Tm	W	L	Sv	IP	K	ERA	Br/IP	R$	BF/G	OBA	vL	vR	H%	xERA	RAR	Ctl	Dom	Cmd	hr/9	G/F	S%	BPV	BPX
99	TEX	9	5	0	120	77	4.58	1.40	$9	17.3	274	257	290	31%	4.26	20.8	3.0	5.8	**1.9**	0.8	1.15	68%	53	132
00	2AL	10	13	1	199	137	4.57	1.43	$11	25.5	289	287	289	32%	5.04	35.9	2.6	6.2	**2.4**	1.3	1.18	72%	46	118
01	TOR	11	11	0	190	110	5.02	1.47	$3	23.2	308	329	286	33%	5.45	11.8	1.9	5.2	**2.8**	1.3	1.36	69%	44	88
02	TOR	* 11	10	0	169	99	5.43	1.49	$1	26.6	308	308	311	34%	5.23	0.6	2.1	5.3	**2.5**	1.0	1.32	64%	50	102
03	CHW	21	9	0	226	207	2.91	1.11	$34	26.8	235	259	191	29%	2.95	79.3	2.2	8.2	**3.7**	0.7	1.28	76%	115	248
1st Half		11	3	0	115	94	2.19	1.04	$22	26.8	223			27%	2.57	51.4	2.1	7.4	**3.5**	0.6	1.41	82%	109	235
2nd Half		10	6	0	111	113	3.65	1.19	$14	26.8	248			32%	3.34	27.9	2.4	9.2	**3.9**	0.7	1.14	71%	120	260
04	**Proj**	**17**	**11**	**0**	**225**	**198**	**3.32**	**1.14**	**$28**	**26.1**	**241**			**29%**	**3.29**	**66.9**	**2.2**	**7.9**	**3.6**	**0.9**	**--**	**74%**	**103**	**222**

His stats provided 2003's big surprise, but a scan of some of his BPIs shows a trend that is not so far out of line. Greatest impact was on his OBA and Dom. Since they held up well in the 2nd half, he'll be solid for '04.

Lohse,Kyle

RH Starter
AGE 25 Growth
TYPE

R	Very High	
I	EXP	CON
S	pt	
K		BRN

LIMA C EP: 50%

Yr	Tm	W	L	Sv	IP	K	ERA	Br/IP	R$	BF/G	OBA	vL	vR	H%	xERA	RAR	Ctl	Dom	Cmd	hr/9	G/F	S%	BPV	BPX
99	aa	3	4	0	70	37	7.33	1.77	($7)	29.9	336			36%	6.48 +	-16.9	3.1	4.8	**1.5**	1.3		59%	10	23
00	aa	3	18	0	167	106	8.25	1.77	($22)	28.0	336			37%	6.85 +	-55.6	3.1	5.7	**1.8**	1.5		53%	15	36
01	MIN	* 11	10	0	177	132	4.78	1.40	$6	23.2	287	348	219	32%	4.98	16.7	2.4	6.7	**2.8**	1.3	0.89	69%	57	114
02	MIN	13	8	0	180	124	4.25	1.39	$10	24.3	263	308	213	29%	4.65	29.1	3.5	6.2	**1.8**	1.3	0.83	74%	38	78
03	MIN	14	11	0	201	130	4.61	1.27	$13	25.5	271	283	249	30%	4.40	24.6	2.0	5.8	**2.9**	1.3	0.83	67%	59	127
1st Half		6	6	0	104	76	3.97	1.17	$9	26.6	252			28%	3.99	21.7	2.0	6.6	**3.3**	1.4	0.90	72%	72	155
2nd Half		8	5	0	97	54	5.30	1.38	$4	24.5	291			31%	4.84	2.9	2.0	5.0	**2.5**	1.1	0.76	63%	45	97
04	**Proj**	**12**	**10**	**0**	**180**	**123**	**4.45**	**1.30**	**$12**	**24.5**	**265**			**29%**	**4.37**	**26.2**	**2.6**	**6.2**	**2.4**	**1.3**	**--**	**69%**	**52**	**112**

You couldn't tell from his ERA, but there were some gains this season. Wore down in the 2nd half, most notably his Dom, and you can see why. If they can monitor his workload better, he could provide solid numbers.

Looper,Braden

RH Reliever
AGE 29 Peak
TYPE

R	Very Low	
I		con
S		
K		

LIMA D EP: 50%

Yr	Tm	W	L	Sv	IP	K	ERA	Br/IP	R$	BF/G	OBA	vL	vR	H%	xERA	RAR	Ctl	Dom	Cmd	hr/9	G/F	S%	BPV	BPX
99	FLA	3	3	0	83	50	3.80	1.53	$2	5.1	291	343	257	33%	4.47 -	16.0	3.4	5.4	**1.6**	0.8	1.89	77%	40	88
00	FLA	5	1	2	67	29	4.43	1.59	$4	4.1	273	359	230	30%	4.42	10.8	4.8	3.9	**0.8**	0.4	3.04	71%	29	63
01	FLA	3	3	3	71	52	3.55	1.31	$6	4.2	239	250	236	27%	3.80	17.3	3.8	6.6	**1.7**	1.0	1.69	76%	53	98
02	FLA	2	5	13	86	55	3.14	1.17	$13	4.5	231	278	191	26%	3.10	22.7	2.9	5.8	**2.0**	0.8	1.25	76%	59	112
03	FLA	6	4	28	80	56	3.70	1.38	$21	4.7	266	280	250	31%	3.79	16.9	3.3	6.3	**1.9**	0.4	1.64	73%	67	128
1st Half		3	2	14	43	31	2.29	1.27	$13	4.8	261			32%	3.21 -	17.3	2.5	6.5	**2.6**	0.2	1.83	81%	90	172
2nd Half		3	2	14	37	25	5.35	1.51	$8	4.6	272			31%	4.47 +	-0.4	4.1	6.1	**1.5**	0.7	1.46	64%	46	89
04	**Proj**	**4**	**4**	**28**	**80**	**53**	**3.83**	**1.30**	**$21**	**4.5**	**257**			**29%**	**3.64**	**15.4**	**2.9**	**6.0**	**2.0**	**0.7**	**G**	**71%**	**62**	**120**

Not the type of dominant skill set you'd want to see in your closer, but he managed to make it work again, closing out 82% of his save opps (81% in '02). BPIs tumbled when Urbina arrived, but he was hurt, or so he said.

Lopez,Aquilino

RH Reliever
AGE 29 Pre-Peak
TYPE Power

R	High	
I	EXP	
S	pt	stb
K		

LIMA C+ EP: 55%

Yr	Tm	W	L	Sv	IP	K	ERA	Br/IP	R$	BF/G	OBA	vL	vR	H%	xERA	RAR	Ctl	Dom	Cmd	hr/9	G/F	S%	BPV	BPX
99		0	0	0	0	0	0.00	0.00																
00		0	0	0	0	0	0.00	0.00																
01	aa	4	3	2	62	71	3.63	1.29	$6	6.2	236			33%	3.26	14.9	3.8	10.3	**2.7**	0.6		72%	110	210
02	aaa	4	4	5	109	84	3.06	1.23	$11	13.3	256			31%	3.30	32.3	2.3	6.9	**3.0**	0.5		76%	93	184
03	TOR	1	3	14	73	64	3.44	1.26	$12	4.2	219	250	186	27%	3.06	20.4	4.2	7.9	**1.9**	0.6	0.90	74%	79	172
1st Half		1	1	2	42	43	4.05	1.23	$3	4.6	212			28%	2.71 +	8.3	4.3	9.2	**2.2**	0.4	0.98	66%	100	216
2nd Half		0	2	12	31	21	2.61	1.29	$9	3.8	229			26%	3.52 -	12.1	4.1	6.1	**1.5**	0.9	0.82	84%	51	110
04	**Proj**	**2**	**3**	**25**	**70**	**59**	**3.21**	**1.26**	**$20**	**5.8**	**236**			**29%**	**3.29**	**21.8**	**3.5**	**7.6**	**2.2**	**0.6**	**--**	**76%**	**80**	**171**

Why he may not be the guy...
- 2.61 ERA, but 84% strand rate
- 51 BPV after started closing
- Didn't have a good sense of where home plate was all year.
However... he did convert 88% of his saves opps...

Lopez,Javier

LH Reliever
AGE 26 Growth
TYPE

R	High	
I	EXP	con
S	pt	
K		

LIMA C+ EP: 50%

Yr	Tm	W	L	Sv	IP	K	ERA	Br/IP	R$	BF/G	OBA	vL	vR	H%	xERA	RAR	Ctl	Dom	Cmd	hr/9	G/F	S%	BPV	BPX
99		0	0	0	0	0	0.00	0.00																
00		0	0	0	0	0	0.00	0.00																
01	aa	1	0	2	40	17	8.55	2.18	($9)	9.3	393			41%	8.81	-16.8	3.2	3.8	**1.2**	1.4		60%	-16	-30
02	aa	2	2	6	46	35	3.52	1.28	$6	3.2	245			29%	3.36	10.8	3.3	6.8	**2.1**	0.6		73%	73	143
03	COL	4	1	1	58	40	3.72	1.20	$6	3.2	261	250	266	30%	3.58	12.1	1.9	6.2	**3.3**	0.8	2.06	71%	87	167
1st Half		1	0	0	29	22	4.03	1.07	$2	3.1	241			29%	2.82 +	4.8	1.6	6.8	**4.4**	0.6	1.85	62%	121	234
2nd Half		3	1	1	29	18	3.40	1.34	$4	3.3	281			31%	4.34 -	7.3	2.2	5.6	**2.6**	0.9	2.35	78%	58	112
04	**Proj**	**3**	**2**	**4**	**60**	**40**	**4.35**	**1.38**	**$4**	**3.6**	**281**			**32%**	**4.25**	**7.3**	**2.6**	**6.0**	**2.4**	**0.8**	**G**	**69%**	**62**	**119**

Here's something... A Rule 5 pick gets bounced around and ends up in COL... where he posts a 3.72 ERA and 87 BPV. It gets worse... He posted a 1.71 ERA at home and 6.08 on the road! Who IS this guy?

Lopez,Rodrigo

RH Starter
AGE 28 Pre-Peak
TYPE
R Very High
I EXP con
S PT stb
K
LIMA D+ EP: 60%

	Tm	W	L	Sv	IP	K	ERA	Br/IP	R$	BF/G	OBA	vL	vR	H%	xERA	RAR	Ctl	Dom	Cmd	hr/9	G/F	S%	BPV	BPX
99	aa	10	8	0	169	114	4.79	1.54	$4	26.9	298			34%	4.75	16.7	3.1	6.1	2.0	0.7		69%	51	118
00	aaa	8	7	0	109	80	5.28	1.66	$1	25.0	305			36%	5.34	7.0	3.8	6.6	1.7	0.7	1.96	68%	48	113
01	aaa	2	2	0	52	30	3.81	1.27	$3	19.8	258			27%	4.15	11.2	2.6	5.2	2.0	1.2		75%	40	77
02	BAL	15	9	0	196	136	3.58	1.19	$21	24.4	237	228	241	26%	3.58	49.3	2.8	6.2	2.2	1.1	1.01	74%	59	122
03	BAL	7	10	0	147	103	5.82	1.57	($4)	25.4	312	308	319	34%	5.96	-5.7	2.6	6.3	2.4	1.5	1.09	66%	37	79
1st Half		1	4	0	43	23	7.71	1.76	($6)	22.5	334			35%	6.99 +	-12.6	3.1	4.8	1.5	1.7	1.15	57%	-1	-2
2nd Half		6	6	0	104	80	5.03	1.49	$1	26.9	303			34%	5.53 -	6.9	2.4	6.9	2.9	1.4	1.06	70%	54	118
04	Proj	12	11	0	200	138	4.14	1.32	$13	23.5	268			30%	4.41	37.5	2.6	6.2	2.4	1.2	--	72%	53	114

A strained oblique muscle may have contributed to his debacle, but wait... Aside from hr/9, his BPIs improved from 2002! His 34/66% hit/strand rates made this a somewhat unlucky season from which he should rebound.

Loux,Shane

RH Starter
AGE 24 Growth
TYPE Finesse
R Very High
I EXP CON
S stb
K age
LIMA D EP: 50%

	Tm	W	L	Sv	IP	K	ERA	Br/IP	R$	BF/G	OBA	vL	vR	H%	xERA	RAR	Ctl	Dom	Cmd	hr/9	G/F	S%	BPV	BPX
99		0	0	0	0	0	0.00	0.00																
00	aa	12	9	0	157	111	4.41	1.38	$13	25.9	274			32%	4.05	28.3	2.8	6.4	2.3	0.6		68%	67	159
01	aaa	10	11	0	151	64	6.44	1.85	($11)	25.7	337			35%	6.74	-20.5	3.8	3.8	1.0	1.1		66%	-2	-4
02	aaa	11	10	0	158	79	5.87	1.66	($5)	27.9	338			37%	5.72	-12.6	2.1	4.5	2.2	0.6		63%	43	85
03	DET	* 12	7	0	158	59	4.50	1.45	$7	21.6	298	352	235	32%	4.57	21.8	2.3	3.4	1.4	0.5	1.29	68%	30	66
1st Half		8	4	0	93	35	3.57	1.43	$8	25.3	293			31%	4.41 -	24.4	2.3	3.4	1.5	0.5		75%	33	71
2nd Half		4	3	0	65	24	5.82	1.49	($1)	17.9	304			32%	4.81 +	-2.6	2.4	3.3	1.4	0.6		59%	27	59
04	Proj	3	7	0	80	36	5.29	1.56	($2)	22.4	313			34%	5.23	2.7	2.5	4.1	1.6	0.7	--	66%	31	66

1-1, 7.20 ERA in 30 IP at DET. Good Ctl, but batters always put the ball into play. (In 30 IP, he had but 8 strikeouts!) As a result, H% and S% have to work overtime, not something you want to rely on in DET.

Lowe,Derek

RH Starter
AGE 30 Peak
TYPE Finesse
R Very Low
I con
S pt
K
LIMA D+ EP: 50%

	Tm	W	L	Sv	IP	K	ERA	Br/IP	R$	BF/G	OBA	vL	vR	H%	xERA	RAR	Ctl	Dom	Cmd	hr/9	G/F	S%	BPV	BPX
99	BOS	6	3	15	109	80	2.64	1.00	$27	5.8	215	232	188	25%	2.30	47.1	2.1	6.6	3.2	0.6	3.17	75%	102	255
00	BOS	4	4	42	91	79	2.57	1.23	$37	5.1	259	268	247	32%	3.42 -	40.8	2.2	7.8	3.6	0.6	3.45	81%	108	279
01	BOS	5	10	24	91	82	3.55	1.45	$18	5.9	286	317	250	35%	4.47 -	23.6	2.9	8.1	2.8	0.7	3.57	77%	85	170
02	BOS	21	8	0	219	127	2.59	0.98	$39	26.7	212	209	213	24%	2.19	84.2	2.0	5.2	2.6	0.5	3.46	75%	85	174
03	BOS	17	7	0	203	110	4.48	1.42	$12	26.7	274	276	266	30%	4.34	28.5	3.2	4.9	1.5	0.8	3.12	69%	39	84
1st Half		9	3	0	103	58	4.53	1.43	$6	26.4	272			30%	4.31	13.7	3.4	5.1	1.5	0.7	3.13	69%	41	89
2nd Half		8	4	0	100	52	4.41	1.40	$6	27.0	275			30%	4.38	14.9	3.0	4.7	1.6	0.8	3.10	69%	37	80
04	Proj	15	10	0	200	111	4.10	1.36	$15	26.7	268			30%	4.02	38.7	2.9	5.0	1.7	0.7	G	70%	47	101

A dangerous skill set, with dangerous trends. Declining Dom means more balls into play and more potential for damage. Even with a slight rebound, a return to a sub-4.00 ERA may be a stretch right now.

Lyon,Brandon

RH Reliever
AGE 24 Growth
TYPE
R Very High
I EXP con
S pt
K age brn
LIMA C+ EP: 50%

	Tm	W	L	Sv	IP	K	ERA	Br/IP	R$	BF/G	OBA	vL	vR	H%	xERA	RAR	Ctl	Dom	Cmd	hr/9	G/F	S%	BPV	BPX
99		0	0	0	0	0	0.00	0.00																
00		0	0	0	0	0	0.00	0.00																
01	TOR	* 15	7	0	190	118	4.50	1.27	$14	25.7	280	296	232	31%	4.34	25.1	1.6	5.6	3.5	1.1	1.14	67%	73	146
02	TOR	* 5	13	0	137	60	6.24	1.65	($9)	21.6	329	321	289	34%	6.20	-14.3	2.4	3.9	1.6	1.2	1.07	63%	12	24
03	2TM	4	6	9	59	50	4.12	1.56	$7	5.4	305	317	276	37%	5.25 -	10.1	2.9	7.6	2.6	0.9	0.74	76%	68	137
1st Half		3	4	9	43	39	3.98	1.37	$8	5.3	275			34%	4.06	8.2	2.7	8.2	3.0	0.6	0.61	71%	93	189
2nd Half		1	2	0	16	11	4.50	2.06	($1)	5.7	374			41%	8.46 -	1.9	3.4	6.2	1.8	1.7	1.18	83%	5	10
04	Proj	7	6	3	80	61	4.05	1.41	$8	5.6	283			33%	4.63 -	14.4	2.7	6.9	2.5	1.0	F	74%	63	127

For someone who claims he was battling elbow soreness all season, his BPIs certainly don't show it. 37% hit rate hurt his ERA, but everything else was solid. Potentially LIMA-worthy.

MacDougal,Mike

RH Reliever
AGE 27 Growth
TYPE Power
R X HIGH
I EXP CON
S PT STB
K brn
LIMA D+ EP: 50%

	Tm	W	L	Sv	IP	K	ERA	Br/IP	R$	BF/G	OBA	vL	vR	H%	xERA	RAR	Ctl	Dom	Cmd	hr/9	G/F	S%	BPV	BPX
99		0	0	0	0	0	0.00	0.00																
00	aa	0	1	0	12	8	8.25	2.00	($2)	29.5	321			38%	5.75 +	-4.0	6.0	6.0	1.0	0.0		54%	48	113
01	aaa	9	9	0	159	98	5.49	1.61	($4)	23.2	288			32%	5.19	-1.5	4.2	5.5	1.3	1.0	3.50	67%	29	56
02	a/a	4	7	0	79	44	6.61	2.18	($13)	18.3	271			30%	6.09 +	-14.1	10.1	5.0	0.5	0.7	7.00	69%	21	41
03	KC	3	5	27	64	57	4.08	1.50	$18	4.2	262	230	314	33%	4.17	12.4	4.5	8.0	1.8	0.6	2.17	73%	71	154
1st Half		3	3	20	36	30	2.98	1.46	$15	4.2	244			31%	3.55 -	12.3	5.0	7.5	1.5	0.2	1.75	79%	75	162
2nd Half		0	2	7	28	27	5.50	1.55	$2	4.1	283			35%	4.97 +	0.1	3.9	8.7	2.3	1.0	3.00	65%	69	149
04	Proj	3	5	11	60	52	4.65	1.58	$6	6.8	271			33%	4.69	7.1	4.8	7.8	1.6	0.8	G	71%	59	127

4 months in which at least 40% of his appearances were save situations: 4.71 ERA, 1.3 Cmd

2 months in which fewer than 40% were save situations: 1.35 ERA, 4.8 Cmd

Maddux,Greg

RH Starter
AGE 38 Decline
TYPE Finesse
R Low
I CON
S
K AGE
LIMA D+ EP: 55%

	Tm	W	L	Sv	IP	K	ERA	Br/IP	R$	BF/G	OBA	vL	vR	H%	xERA	RAR	Ctl	Dom	Cmd	hr/9	G/F	S%	BPV	BPX
99	ATL	19	9	0	219	136	3.58	1.35	$22	28.3	295	300	288	33%	3.97	48.7	1.5	5.6	3.7	0.7	2.22	75%	87	189
00	ATL	19	9	0	249	190	3.00	1.07	$38	28.4	243	269	214	29%	2.92	87.7	1.5	6.9	4.5	0.7	2.66	74%	122	269
01	ATL	17	11	0	233	173	3.05	1.06	$31	27.3	251	264	243	29%	3.09	72.2	1.0	6.7	6.4	0.8	1.84	74%	156	290
02	ATL	16	6	0	199	118	2.62	1.20	$25	24.1	257	232	276	29%	3.31 -	66.2	2.0	5.3	2.6	0.6	2.23	80%	72	136
03	ATL	16	11	0	218	123	3.96	1.18	$20	24.9	268	271	264	29%	3.83	38.5	1.4	5.1	3.7	1.0	1.66	69%	80	155
1st Half		6	8	0	113	69	4.85	1.28	$4	25.0	278			30%	4.34 +	6.4	1.8	5.5	3.1	1.1	1.40	64%	65	125
2nd Half		10	3	0	105	54	3.00	1.08	$17	24.7	256			28%	3.28	32.0	0.9	4.6	4.9	0.9	2.00	76%	109	210
04	Proj	14	9	0	200	118	3.56	1.19	$20	25.7	262			28%	3.76	45.8	1.7	5.3	3.2	1.0	G	74%	70	136

Despite ERA spike, there's little sign of skills erosion, other than the continuing decline in Dom. Most of the 1.34 run increase in ERA was due to an 11% drop in his strand rate, due at least in part to ATL's bullpen.

Mahay,Ron

LH Reliever
AGE 32 Past
TYPE Power
R X HIGH
I EXP con
S PT STB
K
LIMA B+ EP: 60%

	Tm	W	L	Sv	IP	K	ERA	Br/IP	R$	BF/G	OBA	vL	vR	H%	xERA	RAR	Ctl	Dom	Cmd	hr/9	G/F	S%	BPV	BPX
99	aaa	7	2	0	107	56	5.89	1.82	($5)	15.9	328			35%	6.36	-5.1	4.0	4.7	1.2	1.2	0.42	69%	7	16
00	FLA	* 1	2	0	54	45	6.65	1.77	($6)	8.2	296	262	357	33%	6.51	-7.4	5.3	7.5	1.4	1.8	0.71	66%	15	34
01	CHC	* 4	3	14	83	74	3.14	1.17	$17	5.1	217			25%	3.41	24.8	3.5	8.0	2.3	1.3	0.50	80%	69	128
02	CHC	* 2	1	2	60	56	3.75	1.17	$5	4.9	217			25%	3.36	10.9	3.5	8.4	2.4	1.4	0.75	74%	73	137
03	TEX	* 7	5	3	87	80	4.54	1.25	$9	6.0	241	208	190	29%	3.69 +	11.6	3.2	8.2	2.6	1.0	0.48	66%	80	172
1st Half		4	2	3	46	46	5.44	1.25	$5	6.9	261			32%	4.27 +	0.5	2.3	8.9	3.8	1.4		59%	96	208
2nd Half		3	3	0	41	34	3.51	1.24	$4	5.2	217			26%	3.04	11.1	4.2	7.5	1.8	0.7		73%	74	160
04	Proj	2	2	0	40	35	3.83	1.28	$3	5.8	237			28%	3.80	9.2	3.6	7.9	2.2	1.1	F	74%	67	144

3-3, 3.20 ERA in 45 IP at TEX. He's posted solid BPIs for the past three years, most of them in the minors because major league clubs often don't look past a player's birth certificate.

Mantei,Matt

RH Reliever
AGE 30 Peak
TYPE Power
R Moderate
I con
S PT
K
LIMA C+ EP: 50%

	Tm	W	L	Sv	IP	K	ERA	Br/IP	R$	BF/G	OBA	vL	vR	H%	xERA	RAR	Ctl	Dom	Cmd	hr/9	G/F	S%	BPV	BPX
99	2NL	1	3	32	65	99	2.77	1.35	$22	4.3	194	159	217	32%	2.61	21.5	6.1	13.7	2.3	0.7	0.63	82%	125	272
00	ARI	1	1	17	45	53	4.59	1.46	$10	4.2	196	183	200	27%	3.41 +	6.3	7.0	10.6	1.5	0.8	0.47	69%	87	192
01	ARI	0	0	2	7	12	2.57	1.43	$1	3.8	233	455	63	34%	5.39 -	2.6	5.1	15.4	3.0	2.6	0.33	100%	87	161
02	ARI	* 3	3	0	40	36	3.38	1.53	$2	4.0	276	250	260	34%	4.40 -	9.3	4.1	8.1	2.0	0.7	0.61	79%	70	133
03	ARI	5	4	29	55	68	2.62	1.00	$26	4.3	193	155	218	26%	2.35	19.6	2.9	11.1	3.8	1.0	0.78	80%	133	256
1st Half		4	3	7	23	30	4.29	1.26	$8	4.6	244			34%	3.79 +	3.1	3.1	11.7	3.8	1.2	1.00	69%	120	231
2nd Half		1	1	22	32	38	1.41	0.82	$18	4.1	151			20%	1.30	16.5	2.8	10.7	3.8	0.8	0.65	91%	144	276
04	Proj	4	4	32	60	70	3.00	1.15	$25	4.1	214			29%	2.87	18.2	3.5	10.5	3.0	0.9	F	78%	112	216

He's back.... and while some fantasy leaguers will hedge their bets against his injury history, you'll look far to find many 100 BPVs these days.

Maroth,Mike

LH Starter
AGE 26 Growth
TYPE Finesse
R Very High
I EXP CON
S pt stb
K brn
LIMA D EP: 50%

	Tm	W	L	Sv	IP	K	ERA	Br/IP	R$	BF/G	OBA	vL	vR	H%	xERA	RAR	Ctl	Dom	Cmd	hr/9	G/F	S%	BPV	BPX
99		0	0	0	0	0	0.00	0.00																
00	aa	9	14	0	164	70	4.72	1.56	$4	27.2	304			33%	5.02	22.9	3.0	3.8	1.3	0.7		70%	25	59
01	aaa	7	10	0	131	54	5.43	1.69	($5)	25.2	324			35%	5.72	-0.1	3.1	3.7	1.2	0.7		67%	17	33
02	DET	* 14	11	0	201	104	4.12	1.27	$15	26.3	259	252	284	29%	3.62 +	36.1	2.6	4.7	1.8	0.6	1.64	67%	52	107
03	DET	9	21	0	193	87	5.73	1.46	($2)	25.6	298	257	311	30%	5.58	-5.4	2.3	4.1	1.7	1.6	1.17	64%	9	19
1st Half		3	12	0	99	46	4.82	1.23	$3	24.2	266			28%	4.08 +	9.4	1.9	4.2	2.2	1.1	1.11	63%	40	87
2nd Half		6	9	0	94	41	6.69	1.69	($6)	27.1	329			32%	7.15	-14.7	2.8	3.9	1.4	2.1	1.24	65%	-21	-45
04	Proj	11	17	0	200	97	4.86	1.38	$6	25.3	279			29%	4.71	18.2	2.6	4.4	1.7	1.2	--	67%	25	55

BPIs crashed in the 2nd half, but it's got to take a toll after awhile, going out there each start with the result already written. Soft-tosser has a low upside anyway; "We might as well feed him to the wolves," said the Tigers.

Marquis,Jason

RH Starter
AGE 25 Growth
TYPE
R High
I exp CON
S pt
K
LIMA C+ EP: 55%

	Tm	W	L	Sv	IP	K	ERA	Br/IP	R$	BF/G	OBA	vL	vR	H%	xERA	RAR	Ctl	Dom	Cmd	hr/9	G/F	S%	BPV	BPX
99	aa	3	4	0	55	31	5.07	1.51	$1	20.3	265			28%	4.59	3.4	4.4	5.1	1.1	1.1		68%	22	51
00	ATL *	5	5	0	111	76	5.59	1.58	($2)	15.6	292	226	281	32%	5.48	0.6	3.8	6.2	1.6	1.3	1.48	67%	29	63
01	ATL	5	6	0	129	98	3.49	1.33	$7	14.4	237	220	243	27%	3.78	32.5	4.1	6.8	1.7	1.0	1.39	77%	54	101
02	ATL	8	10	0	119	89	4.99	1.54	$0	23.1	284	292	276	32%	5.28	1.8	3.8	6.7	1.8	1.4	1.10	71%	33	62
03	ATL *	8	4	1	134	82	4.96	1.57	($0)	16.7	295	250	287	33%	4.83	5.7	3.6	5.5	1.5	0.6	1.46	68%	43	84
1st Half		5	3	0	82	51	4.70	1.56	$0	21.7	279			32%	4.61	6.3	4.2	5.6	1.3	0.7	1.21	70%	41	79
2nd Half		3	1	1	52	31	5.38	1.60	($1)	12.3	317			36%	5.17	-0.7	2.6	5.4	2.1	0.5	1.68	65%	52	99
04	Proj	5	4	0	80	53	4.84	1.54	$0	22.3	287			32%	4.88	4.6	3.6	6.0	1.7	0.9	--	70%	41	79

0-0, 5.63 ERA in 40 IP at ATL. Shows signs of life in small doses but can't string together more than 2 good outings at a time. Velocity was down in '03, luck was often not with him, and time is running out.

Marte,Damaso

LH Reliever
AGE 29 Pre-Peak
TYPE Power
R X HIGH
I EXP CON
S PT STB
K
LIMA B EP: 40%

	Tm	W	L	Sv	IP	K	ERA	Br/IP	R$	BF/G	OBA	vL	vR	H%	xERA	RAR	Ctl	Dom	Cmd	hr/9	G/F	S%	BPV	BPX
99	aaa	3	3	0	73	51	6.78	1.88	($8)	11.3	313			33%	7.00	-12.2	5.3	6.3	1.2	2.0		68%	-4	-10
00	aa	0	0	0	6	3	3.00	1.67	$0	6.9	293			30%	5.90 -	2.2	4.5	4.5	1.0	1.5		89%	-1	-1
01	PIT *	3	2	1	77	70	4.68	1.23	$3	6.4	257	310	223	30%	4.19	7.1	2.3	8.2	3.5	1.4	0.71	66%	84	156
02	CHW	1	1	10	60	72	2.85	1.03	$12	3.5	206	149	252	29%	2.45	21.0	2.7	10.8	4.0	0.8	1.27	75%	140	287
03	CHW	4	2	11	79	87	1.59	1.06	$20	4.4	183	168	199	26%	1.86	41.7	3.9	9.9	2.6	0.3	0.77	86%	121	262
1st Half		2	1	4	34	36	2.11	1.14	$8	3.8	200			27%	2.44	15.6	4.0	9.5	2.4	0.5	0.43	84%	107	230
2nd Half		2	1	7	45	51	1.20	1.00	$13	5.0	170			25%	1.42	26.1	3.8	10.2	2.7	0.2	1.19	89%	132	286
04	Proj	3	2	9	80	85	2.93	1.16	$14	4.7	216			28%	2.91	28.0	3.5	9.6	2.7	0.8	F	78%	103	221

May or may not be the closer. Has the skills, for sure, but throws with the wrong hand. When a team has an option, the lefty usually won't get the nod. And CHW thinks they have options.

Martinez,Pedro

RH Starter
AGE 32 Past
TYPE Power
R Very Low
I
S pt
K
LIMA C EP: 55%

	Tm	W	L	Sv	IP	K	ERA	Br/IP	R$	BF/G	OBA	vL	vR	H%	xERA	RAR	Ctl	Dom	Cmd	hr/9	G/F	S%	BPV	BPX
99	BOS	23	4	0	213	313	2.07	0.92	$50	26.4	210	221	187	34%	1.81	108.4	1.6	13.2	8.5	0.4	1.30	79%	259	648
00	BOS	18	6	0	217	284	1.74	0.74	$54	27.4	173	150	184	25%	1.19 +	121.2	1.3	11.8	8.9	0.7	1.25	83%	256	665
01	BOS	7	3	0	116	163	2.40	0.94	$20	24.9	204	216	176	32%	1.78 +	48.0	1.9	12.6	6.5	0.4	1.44	75%	215	431
02	BOS	20	4	0	199	239	2.26	0.92	$40	25.5	204	203	191	29%	2.00	85.2	1.8	10.8	6.0	0.6	1.16	78%	187	383
03	BOS	14	4	0	186	206	2.22	1.04	$31	25.4	219	238	179	30%	2.23	82.3	2.3	10.0	4.4	0.3	1.03	79%	153	330
1st Half		5	2	0	82	86	2.74	1.06	$12	25.1	217			29%	2.35	30.5	2.5	9.4	3.7	0.4	0.87	75%	134	289
2nd Half		9	2	0	104	120	1.81	1.03	$20	25.7	220			32%	2.13	51.8	2.1	10.4	5.0	0.3	1.18	83%	170	368
04	Proj	15	6	0	180	202	2.70	1.06	$29	26.5	222			31%	2.36	68.4	2.3	10.1	4.5	0.4	--	75%	153	329

No question that we're looking at a trend of skills erosion here, but when you start out in such a high place, there's lots of room to erode without affecting your value too much.

Martin,Tom

LH Reliever
AGE 33 Past
TYPE Power
R Very High
I exp CON
S PT STB
K age
LIMA B+ EP: 45%

	Tm	W	L	Sv	IP	K	ERA	Br/IP	R$	BF/G	OBA	vL	vR	H%	xERA	RAR	Ctl	Dom	Cmd	hr/9	G/F	S%	BPV	BPX
99	CLE *	1	1	0	24	22	4.88	1.29	$1	7.2	254			30%	4.03 +	3.2	3.0	8.3	2.8	1.1	1.25	64%	78	195
00	CLE *	1	1	0	43	24	4.19	1.44	$2	4.7	271	281	232	30%	4.37	9.9	3.6	5.0	1.4	0.8	1.29	72%	36	92
01	NYM *	3	1	1	40	31	9.00	2.08	($7)	5.4	351			39%	8.15 +	-19.5	5.0	7.0	1.4	1.8	0.57	57%	2	4
02	TAM *	0	0	2	4	5	9.00	2.50	($0)	3.6	415			56%	8.80	-1.9	4.5	11.3	2.5	0.0		60%	92	189
03	LA	1	2	0	51	51	3.53	1.18	$3	2.6	200	189	211	24%	2.97 +	11.9	4.2	9.0	2.1	1.1	1.46	74%	82	157
1st Half		0	1	0	23	22	2.74	1.13	$2	2.7	198			25%	2.57	7.8	3.9	8.6	2.2	0.8	1.30	79%	90	173
2nd Half		1	1	0	28	29	4.18	1.21	$1	2.5	202			24%	3.30 +	4.1	4.5	9.3	2.1	1.3	1.62	70%	75	145
04	Proj	2	2	0	50	48	4.14	1.32	$2	3.4	230			27%	3.85	7.5	4.3	8.6	2.0	1.3	--	73%	65	126

Posted a 0.93 ERA in April and rode that all year, even through a couple of 5+ ERA months. Now, had he posted one of those 5+ ERA months in April, he likely would have spent the rest of the year in Las Vegas.

Mateo,Julio

RH Reliever
AGE 24 Growth
TYPE
R Moderate
I EXP con
S
K age
LIMA B EP: 45%

	Tm	W	L	Sv	IP	K	ERA	Br/IP	R$	BF/G	OBA	vL	vR	H%	xERA	RAR	Ctl	Dom	Cmd	hr/9	G/F	S%	BPV	BPX
99		0	0	0	0	0	0.00	0.00																
00		0	0	0	0	0	0.00	0.00																
01		0	0	0	0	0	0.00	0.00																
02	SEA *	5	2	6	69	48	3.91	1.45	$7	6.9	284			33%	4.59 -	14.3	3.0	6.3	2.1	0.8	0.96	74%	56	115
03	SEA	4	0	1	85	71	3.17	0.96	$12	6.6	223	220	219	25%	3.18	26.9	1.4	7.5	5.5	1.5	0.52	76%	126	271
1st Half		1	0	0	32	25	3.94	1.25	$2	6.7	256			27%	4.79 -	6.8	2.5	7.0	2.8	1.2	0.45	79%	45	98
2nd Half		3	0	1	53	46	2.71	0.79	$11	6.6	202			23%	2.21 +	20.1	0.7	7.8	11.5	1.2	0.56	74%	267	577
04	Proj	4	2	3	80	62	3.49	1.16	$10	6.7	250			28%	3.79	22.0	2.0	7.0	3.4	1.2	F	76%	82	176

Would you check out that 2nd half? 4 walks and 46 Ks is how you get an 11.5 Cmd ratio. Although this skill set isn't perfect, it WILL come cheap at the draft table, and the return on investment could be huge.

Matthews,Mike

LH Reliever
AGE 30 Peak
TYPE Power
R Very High
I exp con
S PT STB
K
LIMA B EP: 55%

	Tm	W	L	Sv	IP	K	ERA	Br/IP	R$	BF/G	OBA	vL	vR	H%	xERA	RAR	Ctl	Dom	Cmd	hr/9	G/F	S%	BPV	BPX
99	a/a	3	7	0	71	37	7.99	1.85	($9)	9.4	303			31%	6.34 +	-23.3	5.6	4.7	0.8	1.5		57%	-5	
00	aaa	3	1	0	52	45	3.63	1.38	$5	24.9	206			25%	3.24	14.8	5.9	7.8	1.3	0.7	0.86	75%	68	160
01	STL	3	4	1	89	72	3.24	1.20	$8	7.2	228	133	268	26%	3.46	25.4	3.3	7.3	2.2	1.1	0.77	78%	66	122
02	MIL	2	1	0	45	34	4.00	1.60	($0)	4.3	253	208	292	32%	3.65	6.7	5.8	6.8	1.2	0.0	1.00	72%	70	132
03	SD	6	4	0	64	44	4.49	1.46	$4	3.7	264	294	254	31%	4.07	6.8	4.1	6.2	1.5	0.6	1.31	69%	54	104
1st Half		3	3	0	41	29	4.17	1.44	$2	4.5	252			29%	3.94	6.1	4.4	6.4	1.5	0.7	1.51	71%	53	103
2nd Half		3	1	0	23	15	5.04	1.51	$1	2.8	284			33%	4.31 +	0.7	3.5	5.8	1.7	0.4	1.04	65%	56	109
04	Proj	4	3	0	60	43	4.35	1.48	$2	4.2	259			30%	4.05	7.3	4.5	6.5	1.4	0.6	--	71%	54	104

No real improvement over last year, and with his outwardly poor 2nd half (though really no worse than his 1st half), future opportunities could begin dwindling.

Mays,Joe

RH Reliever
AGE 28 Pre-Peak
TYPE
R High
I CON
S PT
K brn
LIMA EP:

	Tm	W	L	Sv	IP	K	ERA	Br/IP	R$	BF/G	OBA	vL	vR	H%	xERA	RAR	Ctl	Dom	Cmd	hr/9	G/F	S%	BPV	BPX
99	MIN	6	11	0	171	115	4.37	1.44	$7	15.2	271	255	284	30%	4.79	34.4	3.5	6.1	1.7	1.3	1.54	73%	35	89
00	MIN *	9	15	0	175	117	5.29	1.60	$2	23.3	299	300	298	34%	5.34	14.6	3.5	6.0	1.7	1.0	1.56	68%	36	93
01	MIN	17	13	0	233	123	3.16	1.15	$28	27.9	238	237	233	25%	3.36	72.5	2.5	4.7	1.9	1.0	1.28	77%	47	95
02	MIN	5	8	0	102	41	5.12	1.38	$1	24.4	286	275	315	29%	4.99	4.7	2.3	3.6	1.6	1.3	1.18	66%	13	27
03	MIN	8	8	0	130	50	6.30	1.52	($3)	18.6	303	346	246	30%	5.70 +	-13.5	2.7	3.5	1.3	1.5	1.28	60%	-1	-3
1st Half		8	5	0	94	38	6.31	1.47	$0	24.3	289			29%	5.43 +	-9.9	2.9	3.6	1.3	1.5	1.37	59%	-0	-1
2nd Half		0	3	0	36	12	6.27	1.67	($4)	11.8	335			34%	6.42	-3.6	2.3	3.0	1.3	1.3	1.07	64%	-4	-8
04	Proj	0	0	0	0	0	0.00	0.00													--			

Underwent Tommy John surgery and will miss the 2004 season.

26 seasons, 288 victories, and all he'll be remembered for is elbow ligament transplant surgery. Not Mays, John.

May,Darrell

LH Starter
AGE 31 Peak
TYPE Finesse
R Moderate
I CON
S pt
K brn
LIMA D EP: 40%

	Tm	W	L	Sv	IP	K	ERA	Br/IP	R$	BF/G	OBA	vL	vR	H%	xERA	RAR	Ctl	Dom	Cmd	hr/9	G/F	S%	BPV	BPX
99	JPN	7	7	0	122	125	3.91	1.19	$12	25.1	234			29%	3.43	26.5	3.0	9.2	3.1	1.3		72%	92	212
00	JPN	12	7	0	159	169	2.89	1.04	$27	25.2	218			28%	2.87	61.2	2.3	9.6	4.1	1.1		78%	123	292
01	JPN	10	8	0	159	168	4.13	1.29	$11	25.7	263			33%	4.36	27.5	2.5	9.5	3.7	1.4		73%	97	186
02	KC *	5	10	0	147	105	5.02	1.45	($1)	19.5	281	288	273	30%	5.43	8.6	3.1	6.4	2.1	1.7	0.78	71%	29	60
03	KC	10	8	0	210	115	3.77	1.19	$17	24.7	250	217	255	26%	3.98	49.3	2.3	4.9	2.2	1.3	0.60	74%	40	87
1st Half		1	4	0	91	53	4.05	1.27	$3	22.5	264			28%	4.24	17.9	2.4	5.2	2.2	1.2	0.67	72%	44	96
2nd Half		9	4	0	119	62	3.55	1.13	$15	26.7	238			24%	3.77	31.4	2.2	4.7	2.1	1.4	0.55	76%	37	80
04	Proj	10	10	0	200	123	4.10	1.26	$13	25.3	257			27%	4.30	38.7	2.6	5.5	2.2	1.4	F	73%	40	86

Pitched with more precision in '03, walking fewer batters but striking out fewer as well. He netted out with a better season at face value, but somewhat less of a step up from a skills perspective. Bid cautiously.

McClung,Seth

RH Reliever
AGE 23 Growth
TYPE Power
R High
I EXP con
S pt
K AGE
LIMA C EP: 40%

	Tm	W	L	Sv	IP	K	ERA	Br/IP	R$	BF/G	OBA	vL	vR	H%	xERA	RAR	Ctl	Dom	Cmd	hr/9	G/F	S%	BPV	BPX
99		0	0	0	0	0	0.00	0.00																
00		0	0	0	0	0	0.00	0.00																
01		0	0	0	0	0	0.00	0.00																
02	aa	5	7	0	114	54	6.71	1.88	($13)	27.3	332			35%	6.60	-22.0	4.3	4.3	1.0	1.0		64%	4	8
03	TAM	4	1	0	38	25	5.42	1.52	$1	14.1	235	281	205	25%	4.67 +	0.5	5.9	5.9	1.0	1.4	0.74	67%	22	48
1st Half		4	1	0	38	25	5.42	1.52	$1	14.1	235			25%	4.67 +	0.5	5.9	5.9	1.0	1.4	0.74	67%	22	48
2nd Half		0	0	0	0	0	0.00	0.00																
04	Proj	3	2	0	40	23	5.85	1.65	($1)	18.3	276			29%	5.51	-1.7	5.2	5.2	1.0	1.4	F	67%	11	24

Had Tommy John surgery in June and should be back some time later in the 2004 season.

Not that you will be holding your breath or anything.

Meadows,Brian

RH Reliever
AGE 28 Pre-Peak
TYPE Finesse
R High
I exp CON
S pt STB
K
LIMA B EP: 55%

	Tm	W	L	Sv	IP	K	ERA	Br/IP	R$	BF/G	OBA	vL	vR	H%	xERA	RAR	Ctl	Dom	Cmd	hr/9	G/F	S%	BPV	BPX
99	FLA	11	15	0	178	72	5.61	1.52	($0)	25.5	299	313	291	30%	5.35	-9.0	2.9	3.6	**1.3**	1.6	1.09	67%	-3	-7
00	2TM	13	10	0	196	79	5.14	1.52	$6	26.4	297	309	287	30%	5.58	16.3	2.9	3.6	**1.2**	1.5	1.22	70%	-1	-2
01	KC	* 7	11	0	155	81	7.32	1.73	($15)	25.7	352	350	352	36%	7.54	-38.0	1.8	4.7	**2.6**	2.0	1.03	61%	7	14
02	PIT	* 10	14	0	188	112	4.88	1.37	$4	23.7	291	267	248	32%	4.63	5.6	1.9	5.4	**2.8**	1.1	1.16	66%	56	106
03	PIT	* 9	1	1	127	70	3.61	1.12	$15	11.9	268	276	299	30%	3.40	28.4	0.8	5.0	**6.4**	0.7	1.42	69%	144	276
1st Half		4	1	0	57	29	4.42	1.19	$5	13.0	282			30%	4.16	6.5	0.8	4.6	**5.8**	1.1	1.06	66%	115	221
2nd Half		5	0	1	70	41	2.95	1.06	$11	11.1	256			29%	2.77	21.8	0.8	5.3	**6.8**	0.4	1.70	72%	167	322
04	**Proj**	**5**	**3**	**0**	**80**	**44**	**3.71**	**1.19**	**$7**	**6.4**	**267**			**29%**	**3.71**	**16.6**	**1.5**	**5.0**	**3.4**	**0.9**	**--**	**71%**	**75**	**146**

2-1, 4.74 ERA in 76 IP at PIT. Yes, he's a soft-tosser. Yes, he's too old to be a "real" prospect. Yes, his MLB history is unimpressive. But you CAN NOT ignore these BPIs. There is value here if used correctly.

Mears,Chris

RH Reliever
AGE 26 Growth
TYPE Finesse
R High
I EXP
S pt stb
K BRN
LIMA C+ EP: 45%

	Tm	W	L	Sv	IP	K	ERA	Br/IP	R$	BF/G	OBA	vL	vR	H%	xERA	RAR	Ctl	Dom	Cmd	hr/9	G/F	S%	BPV	BPX
99		0	0	0	0	0	0.00	0.00																
00		0	0	0	0	0	0.00	0.00																
01		0	0	0	0	0	0.00	0.00																
02	aa	6	9	0	143	84	4.47	1.52	($0)	21.2	304			33%	5.40 -	15.4	2.6	5.3	**2.0**	1.2		74%	32	63
03	DET	* 6	4	7	99	45	4.35	1.44	$8	8.0	290	395	230	31%	4.78	15.5	2.6	4.1	**1.6**	0.9	1.02	71%	27	58
1st Half		5	1	0	51	23	3.68	1.48	$4	10.3	290			31%	4.69 -	12.6	3.0	4.0	**1.4**	0.7		76%	29	62
2nd Half		1	3	7	48	22	5.07	1.40	$4	6.5	289			30%	4.88	2.9	2.3	4.1	**1.8**	1.1		66%	27	57
04	**Proj**	**4**	**4**	**4**	**80**	**41**	**4.61**	**1.48**	**$4**	**10.3**	**296**			**32%**	**5.06**	**9.9**	**2.6**	**4.6**	**1.8**	**1.0**	**--**	**71%**	**30**	**65**

1-3, 5.44 ERA in 41 IP at DET, including 5 saves and three PQS-0 starts. Another one who never really mastered AAA before his trial by fire in DET:
AA 3.14 ERA 2.7 Cmd
AAA 2.78 ERA 1.5 Cmd

Meche,Gil

RH Reliever
AGE 25 Growth
TYPE
R X HIGH
I exp CON
S PT stb
K BRN
LIMA D+ EP: 45%

	Tm	W	L	Sv	IP	K	ERA	Br/IP	R$	BF/G	OBA	vL	vR	H%	xERA	RAR	Ctl	Dom	Cmd	hr/9	G/F	S%	BPV	BPX
99	SEA	* 13	10	0	175	118	4.27	1.53	$11	24.3	254	240	233	29%	4.36	37.6	5.1	6.1	**1.2**	0.8	0.97	73%	41	103
00	SEA	* 5	5	0	99	74	3.99	1.39	$7	23.8	237	236	244	28%	3.67	25.5	4.6	6.7	**1.5**	0.7	0.95	72%	57	147
01	SEA	0	0	0	0	0	0.00	0.00																
02	aa	4	6	0	65	46	9.14	1.86	($11)	12.4	319			36%	6.54 +	-33.7	4.8	6.4	**1.3**	1.2		49%	20	38
03	SEA	15	13	0	186	130	4.59	1.34	$12	24.8	263	275	248	28%	4.64	23.2	3.0	6.3	**2.1**	1.5	0.81	70%	40	86
1st Half		10	3	0	96	70	3.28	1.20	$14	26.4	241			27%	3.67	28.9	2.7	6.6	**2.4**	1.1	0.83	78%	63	136
2nd Half		5	10	0	90	60	6.00	1.50	($2)	23.4	285			30%	5.68	-5.7	3.4	6.0	**1.8**	1.8	0.79	64%	17	37
04	**Proj**	**9**	**11**	**0**	**140**	**98**	**4.69**	**1.44**	**$5**	**19.1**	**275**			**31%**	**4.79**	**15.9**	**3.3**	**6.3**	**1.9**	**1.2**	**--**	**70%**	**43**	**91**

Few realize how bad his 2nd half burnout was. Putting him out there for more IP than he had in the past 3 years COMBINED was a crime. Anyone ever hear of the concept of protecting valuable commodities?

Mecir,Jim

RH Reliever
AGE 33 Past
TYPE Power
R Moderate
I con
S PT stb
K age
LIMA B EP: 60%

	Tm	W	L	Sv	IP	K	ERA	Br/IP	R$	BF/G	OBA	vL	vR	H%	xERA	RAR	Ctl	Dom	Cmd	hr/9	G/F	S%	BPV	BPX
99	TAM	0	1	0	20	15	2.70	1.45	$1	5.1	210	214	200	27%	2.83	8.5	6.3	6.8	**1.1**	0.0	1.45	79%	76	191
00	2AL	10	3	5	85	70	2.96	1.25	$19	5.6	226	204	245	28%	2.87	33.5	3.8	7.4	**1.9**	0.4	1.68	76%	82	214
01	OAK	2	8	3	63	61	3.43	1.27	$6	4.9	233	195	267	30%	3.18	17.3	3.7	8.7	**2.3**	0.6	1.56	74%	93	186
02	OAK	6	4	1	67	53	4.30	1.45	$5	4.8	265	204	297	32%	4.21	10.4	3.9	7.1	**1.8**	0.7	1.53	71%	63	129
03	OAK	2	3	1	37	25	5.59	1.51	$0	4.0	277	311	256	31%	4.82 +	-0.3	3.9	6.1	**1.6**	1.0	1.58	63%	40	86
1st Half		1	1	0	22	17	4.09	1.18	$2	4.3	253			30%	3.50 +	4.2	2.0	7.0	**3.4**	0.8	1.88	67%	93	201
2nd Half		1	2	1	15	8	7.80	2.00	($2)	3.7	310			33%	6.77 +	-4.6	6.6	4.8	**0.7**	1.2	1.25	61%	1	2
04	**Proj**	**4**	**5**	**2**	**60**	**46**	**4.35**	**1.43**	**$4**	**4.3**	**268**			**32%**	**4.27**	**9.6**	**3.6**	**6.9**	**1.9**	**0.8**	**G**	**70%**	**61**	**130**

I am starting to think that EVERY SINGLE incidence of a sharp drop in performance is caused by some type of injury, be it real, hidden, unreported or imagined. In this case, a "real" bum knee in the 2nd half.

Mendoza,Ramiro

RH Reliever
AGE 31 Peak
TYPE Finesse
R Moderate
I CON
S PT
K
LIMA D EP: 60%

	Tm	W	L	Sv	IP	K	ERA	Br/IP	R$	BF/G	OBA	vL	vR	H%	xERA	RAR	Ctl	Dom	Cmd	hr/9	G/F	S%	BPV	BPX
99	NYY	9	9	3	123	80	4.32	1.37	$12	9.9	289	283	285	32%	4.58	25.6	2.0	5.9	**3.0**	1.0	2.11	70%	66	166
00	NYY	7	4	0	65	30	4.28	1.32	$8	19.7	264	299	220	27%	4.36	14.3	2.8	4.1	**1.5**	1.2	1.21	71%	21	55
01	NYY	8	4	6	100	70	3.77	1.12	$15	7.2	240	248	236	27%	3.13 +	23.0	2.1	6.3	**3.0**	0.8	1.71	68%	84	169
02	NYY	8	4	4	91	61	3.46	1.30	$12	6.2	284	261	286	32%	4.23 -	24.3	1.6	6.0	**3.8**	0.8	2.04	75%	91	186
03	BOS	3	5	0	66	36	6.80	1.78	($7)	8.4	344	320	372	37%	6.94	-11.3	2.7	4.9	**1.8**	1.4	1.61	63%	13	27
1st Half		1	3	0	38	19	6.85	1.92	($5)	6.6	358			38%	7.36 -	-6.8	3.1	4.5	**1.5**	1.2	1.33	65%	6	12
2nd Half		2	2	0	28	17	6.73	1.60	($1)	14.1	324			35%	6.36	-4.5	2.2	5.4	**2.4**	1.6	2.14	60%	26	56
04	**Proj**	**4**	**4**	**1**	**60**	**37**	**4.50**	**1.38**	**$4**	**8.1**	**287**			**31%**	**4.85**	**8.3**	**2.3**	**5.6**	**2.5**	**1.2**	**G**	**71%**	**47**	**100**

Starter or reliever? You pick:

	IP	ERA	Ctl	Dom
SP	24	7.03	2.0	5.3
RP	42	6.59	1.7	4.7

If you picked SP, know that his PQS log read 1,4,2,0,0. If RP, his REff pct was only 50%.

Mercker,Kent

LH Reliever
AGE 36 Decline
TYPE Power
R Very High
I CON
S pt STB
K age
LIMA C+ EP: 20%

	Tm	W	L	Sv	IP	K	ERA	Br/IP	R$	BF/G	OBA	vL	vR	H%	xERA	RAR	Ctl	Dom	Cmd	hr/9	G/F	S%	BPV	BPX
99	2TM	8	5	0	129	81	4.81	1.64	$1	19.6	289	304	213	32%	5.24	12.4	4.5	5.7	**1.3**	1.1	1.11	73%	24	56
00	ANA	1	3	0	48	30	6.55	1.79	($4)	10.8	296	235	324	30%	6.92	-4.1	5.4	5.6	**1.0**	2.2	0.69	69%	-16	
01		0	0	0	0	0	0.00	0.00																
02	COL	3	1	0	48	37	7.00	1.82	($5)	3.6	314	209	350	32%	7.91 -	-11.4	4.8	7.4	**1.5**	3.0	0.97	70%	-21	-40
03	2NL	0	2	1	55	48	1.96	1.42	$3	3.6	228	222	230	27%	3.86 -	24.5	5.2	7.8	**1.5**	1.0	0.89	92%	58	112
1st Half		0	1	0	25	27	2.50	1.55	$0	3.1	220			29%	3.81 -	9.4	6.8	9.6	**1.4**	0.7	1.45	86%	77	149
2nd Half		0	1	1	30	21	1.50	1.30	$3	4.1	236			26%	3.89 -	15.1	3.9	6.3	**1.6**	1.2	0.62	97%	44	84
04	**Proj**	**1**	**1**	**0**	**40**	**31**	**4.50**	**1.58**	**($1)**	**4.4**	**267**			**30%**	**5.09 -**	**4.1**	**5.0**	**7.0**	**1.4**	**1.4**	**--**	**75%**	**33**	**63**

A sub-2.00 ERA driven by 27/92% hit/strand rates. At more normal levels, his ERA would have been 4.58. That's a better benchmark given all his other BPIs.

Mesa,Jose

RH Reliever
AGE 37 Decline
TYPE Power
R Moderate
I CON
S
K AGE
LIMA C EP: 60%

	Tm	W	L	Sv	IP	K	ERA	Br/IP	R$	BF/G	OBA	vL	vR	H%	xERA	RAR	Ctl	Dom	Cmd	hr/9	G/F	S%	BPV	BPX
99	SEA	3	6	33	68	42	5.03	1.82	$16	4.7	305	331	271	33%	6.44 -	7.7	5.3	5.6	**1.1**	1.5	1.17	76%	6	15
00	SEA	4	6	1	80	84	5.39	1.62	$0	5.5	282	257	300	35%	5.32	5.6	4.6	9.4	**2.0**	1.2	0.88	69%	61	159
01	PHI	3	3	42	69	59	2.34	1.23	$32	4.0	250	236	255	31%	3.26 -	28.0	2.6	7.7	**3.0**	0.5	1.30	83%	97	181
02	PHI	4	6	45	75	64	3.00	1.39	$30	4.4	235	225	237	29%	3.44	21.2	4.7	7.7	**1.6**	0.6	1.06	80%	71	133
03	PHI	5	7	24	58	45	6.52	1.76	$10	4.4	303	213	349	35%	5.86 +	-9.6	4.8	7.0	**1.5**	1.1	1.22	63%	34	66
1st Half		3	4	18	36	26	4.50	1.44	$12	4.6	278			33%	4.15	3.8	3.3	6.5	**2.0**	0.5	1.10	68%	65	126
2nd Half		2	3	6	22	19	9.82	2.27	($2)	4.2	340			39%	8.66 +	-13.4	7.4	7.8	**1.1**	2.0	1.47	58%	-6	-11
04	**Proj**	**3**	**6**	**2**	**60**	**48**	**4.95**	**1.60**	**($0)**	**4.3**	**271**			**32%**	**4.93**	**2.5**	**5.0**	**7.2**	**1.5**	**1.1**	**--**	**71%**	**43**	**83**

Ctl/Dom/Cmd were virtually the same as last year, but I warned you that those levels could not support his '02 performance. It came crashing down in '03, and exacerbated by 35/63% H/S%. Stick a fork in him; he's done.

Miceli,Dan

RH Reliever
AGE 33 Past
TYPE Power
R Very High
I CON
S PT STB
K age brn
LIMA C+ EP: 30%

	Tm	W	L	Sv	IP	K	ERA	Br/IP	R$	BF/G	OBA	vL	vR	H%	xERA	RAR	Ctl	Dom	Cmd	hr/9	G/F	S%	BPV	BPX
99	SD	4	5	2	68	59	4.50	1.51	$3	4.6	259	269	264	31%	4.11	6.7	4.8	7.8	**1.6**	0.9	1.35	72%	57	123
00	FLA	6	4	0	48	40	4.29	1.31	$7	4.5	249	270	216	30%	3.65 +	8.6	3.4	7.5	**2.2**	0.7	0.88	68%	74	164
01	COL	2	5	1	45	48	4.80	1.40	$1	3.8	270	361	196	34%	4.78	3.4	3.2	9.6	**3.0**	1.4	1.11	70%	80	148
02	TEX	0	2	0	8	5	9.00	2.00	($2)	4.4	366			41%	7.66 +	-3.8	3.4	5.6	**1.7**	1.1	3.14	53%	17	35
03	2TM	2	4	1	70	58	3.21	1.20	$6	5.1	230	194	244	25%	4.00 -	20.5	3.2	7.4	**2.3**	1.7	0.83	83%	52	106
1st Half		1	3	1	37	37	3.88	1.35	$2	5.3	240			27%	4.75 -	7.5	4.1	9.0	**2.2**	1.9	0.68	81%	48	98
2nd Half		1	1	0	33	21	2.45	1.03	$4	4.8	218			23%	3.17 -	13.0	2.2	5.7	**2.6**	1.4	1.00	86%	60	121
04	**Proj**	**4**	**5**	**1**	**70**	**61**	**3.99**	**1.27**	**$6**	**4.5**	**245**			**28%**	**4.12**	**13.2**	**3.2**	**7.8**	**2.4**	**1.4**	**--**	**74%**	**62**	**125**

Decent rebound season, but his ERA was artificially depressed by 25/83% hit/strand rates. That means his ERA in '04 will end up closer to last year's xERA.

Miller,Trever

LH Reliever
AGE 30 Peak
TYPE Power
R X HIGH
I EXP CON
S PT stb
K
LIMA C+ EP: 45%

	Tm	W	L	Sv	IP	K	ERA	Br/IP	R$	BF/G	OBA	vL	vR	H%	xERA	RAR	Ctl	Dom	Cmd	hr/9	G/F	S%	BPV	BPX
99	HOU	3	2	1	50	37	5.04	1.74	($1)	5.0	291			34%	5.13	1.3	5.2	6.7	**1.3**	0.9		72%	36	79
00	aaa	4	2	0	74	41	5.47	1.72	($2)	12.3	311			34%	5.68	2.9	4.0	5.0	**1.2**	0.9		68%	23	55
01	aaa	3	11	0	116	72	6.98	1.84	($15)	16.7	351			39%	7.14	-24.3	2.9	5.6	**1.9**	1.3		63%	20	38
02	aaa	9	5	0	82	61	3.84	1.38	$8	5.4	280			33%	4.27	15.7	2.5	6.7	**2.7**	0.8		74%	72	141
03	TOR	2	2	4	52	44	4.66	1.42	$3	2.9	238	226	237	27%	4.26	6.1	4.8	7.6	**1.6**	1.2	0.92	70%	50	107
1st Half		1	0	0	27	21	5.31	1.48	($0)	2.7	254			28%	4.73 +	0.8	4.6	7.0	**1.5**	1.3	1.07	67%	38	81
2nd Half		1	2	4	25	23	3.04	1.35	$4	3.1	220			26%	3.74	5.3	5.0	8.2	**1.6**	1.1	0.77	74%	63	135
04	**Proj**	**3**	**3**	**1**	**50**	**39**	**4.86**	**1.44**	**$2**	**4.2**	**262**			**30%**	**4.51**	**4.5**	**4.0**	**7.0**	**1.8**	**1.1**	**--**	**68%**	**50**	**106**

AAA-lifer had a solid '02 season, earning himself another shot in the bigs. But BPIs did not hold up, which is something you'd hope a 30-year-old would be better able to do. Not quite good enough for LIMA consideration.

Miller,Wade

RH Starter | AGE 27 Pre-Peak | TYPE Power | R Low | I exp | S pt | K brn | LIMA C+ EP: 60%

Yr	Tm	W	L	Sv	IP	K	ERA	Br/IP	R$	BF/G	OBA	vL	vR	H%	xERA	RAR	Ctl	Dom	Cmd	hr/9	G/F	S%	BPV	BPX
99	aaa	11	9	0	162	115	4.94	1.46	$6	27.3	272			31%	4.27 +	12.7	3.7	6.4	1.7	0.8		67%	50	117
00	HOU	* 10	11	0	210	159	5.01	1.43	$5	28.6	269	309	222	31%	4.43 +	17.4	3.6	6.8	1.9	0.9	1.39	66%	54	119
01	HOU	16	8	0	212	183	3.40	1.22	$22	27.4	234	216	250	27%	3.78	55.9	3.2	7.8	2.4	1.3	1.37	79%	66	122
02	HOU	* 15	4	0	172	152	3.30	1.31	$17	26.0	252	254	245	31%	3.59	41.7	3.3	8.0	2.4	0.7	1.24	77%	81	153
03	HOU	14	13	0	187	161	4.14	1.31	$14	24.0	242	258	227	29%	3.60 +	28.6	3.7	7.7	2.1	0.8	1.15	70%	73	140
1st Half		5	8	0	97	77	4.54	1.30	$4	24.1	249			30%	3.53 +	9.6	3.2	7.1	2.2	0.6	1.30	65%	75	144
2nd Half		9	5	0	90	84	3.70	1.32	$10	23.9	233			28%	3.69	19.0	4.2	8.4	2.0	1.0	1.00	75%	71	136
04	Proj	16	10	0	200	172	3.87	1.32	$17	25.7	245			29%	3.71	37.3	3.6	7.7	2.2	0.9	--	73%	71	136

Analysts wrote about his "great 2nd half" but that really did not happen. BPIs were inconsistent all year. He did post a terrific August (1.69 ERA, 3.6 Cmd), which lends hope that the upside still exists.

Millwood,Kevin

RH Starter | AGE 29 Pre-Peak | TYPE | R Moderate | I CON | S pt | K brn | LIMA C EP: 55%

Yr	Tm	W	L	Sv	IP	K	ERA	Br/IP	R$	BF/G	OBA	vL	vR	H%	xERA	RAR	Ctl	Dom	Cmd	hr/9	G/F	S%	BPV	BPX
99	ATL	18	7	0	228	205	2.68	1.00	$38	27.1	207	230	175	25%	2.16 +	77.9	2.3	8.1	3.5	0.9	0.88	78%	107	232
00	ATL	10	13	0	212	168	4.67	1.30	$11	24.9	263	289	235	30%	4.15 +	27.4	2.6	7.1	2.7	1.1	0.71	66%	69	152
01	ATL	7	7	0	121	84	4.31	1.33	$6	24.5	262	282	244	28%	4.60	17.1	3.0	6.2	2.1	1.5	0.88	73%	40	73
02	ATL	18	8	0	217	178	3.24	1.16	$26	25.3	233	246	215	28%	2.89	54.4	2.7	7.4	2.7	0.7	1.22	74%	90	171
03	PHI	14	12	0	222	169	4.01	1.25	$16	26.5	251	246	253	29%	3.55	37.6	2.8	6.9	2.5	0.8	0.88	69%	75	144
1st Half		9	6	0	111	93	4.05	1.26	$10	25.8	256			31%	3.67	18.3	2.6	7.5	2.9	0.8	0.90	69%	86	165
2nd Half		5	6	0	111	76	3.98	1.25	$7	27.1	246			28%	3.44 +	19.3	2.9	6.2	2.1	0.7	0.86	69%	65	125
04	Proj	17	9	0	225	173	3.56	1.23	$22	25.9	246			29%	3.49	51.3	2.8	6.9	2.5	0.9	--	74%	74	142

Didn't have the breakout year we were expecting, but his BPIs were still solid and should have generated a sub-4.00 ERA. PHI bullpen can be blamed for that. Could still see that breakout with more offense and pen support.

Milton,Eric

LH Starter | AGE 28 Pre-Peak | TYPE Finesse | R Low | I CON | S pt | K brn | LIMA B+ EP: 40%

Yr	Tm	W	L	Sv	IP	K	ERA	Br/IP	R$	BF/G	OBA	vL	vR	H%	xERA	RAR	Ctl	Dom	Cmd	hr/9	G/F	S%	BPV	BPX
99	MIN	7	11	0	206	163	4.50	1.23	$13	25.1	246	253	240	28%	3.88 +	37.8	2.8	7.1	2.6	1.2	0.58	67%	66	166
00	MIN	13	10	0	200	160	4.86	1.25	$17	25.2	267	242	265	30%	4.49	28.2	2.0	7.2	3.6	1.6	0.62	66%	74	192
01	MIN	15	7	0	220	157	4.33	1.29	$15	26.5	263	246	259	29%	4.46	34.0	2.5	6.4	2.6	1.4	0.59	71%	52	104
02	MIN	13	9	0	171	121	4.84	1.19	$13	24.2	264	306	249	29%	4.11 +	14.1	1.6	6.4	4.0	1.3	0.67	62%	87	179
03	MIN	1	0	0	17	7	2.65	0.94	$3	21.9	238	389	174	24%	2.96	6.6	0.5	3.7	7.0	1.1	0.45	79%	145	313
1st Half		0	0	0	0	0	0.00	0.00																
2nd Half		1	0	0	17	7	2.65	0.94	$3	21.9	238			24%	2.96	6.5	0.5	3.7	7.0	1.1		79%	145	313
04	Proj	11	6	0	180	116	4.05	1.15	$17	24.4	255			27%	3.91	35.9	1.7	5.8	3.5	1.3	F	70%	74	158

The high-precision approach sure looked good for those 17 IP, but lack of Dom likely won't yield the same results over a full season. MIN will be tempted to ride him, but they should take a lesson from STL and Matt Morris.

Morris,Matt

RH Starter | AGE 29 Peak | TYPE | R Low | I con | S pt | K | LIMA C+ EP: 55%

Yr	Tm	W	L	Sv	IP	K	ERA	Br/IP	R$	BF/G	OBA	vL	vR	H%	xERA	RAR	Ctl	Dom	Cmd	hr/9	G/F	S%	BPV	BPX
99		0	0	0	0	0	0.00	0.00																
00	STL	3	3	4	53	34	3.57	1.32	$7	7.3	262	255	266	30%	3.65	14.6	2.9	5.8	2.0	0.5	1.31	73%	64	141
01	STL	22	8	0	216	185	3.17	1.26	$28	26.6	263	237	286	33%	3.54	63.7	2.2	7.7	3.4	0.5	2.01	76%	104	193
02	STL	17	9	0	210	171	3.43	1.30	$19	27.7	262	267	255	32%	3.67	47.2	2.7	7.3	2.7	0.7	1.65	75%	82	155
03	STL	11	8	0	172	120	3.77	1.18	$16	26.1	253	255	249	28%	3.65	34.9	2.0	6.3	3.1	1.0	1.23	72%	75	145
1st Half		8	5	0	114	87	3.86	1.18	$11	27.6	253			29%	3.64	21.7	2.0	6.9	3.3	1.0	1.35	70%	85	164
2nd Half		3	3	0	58	33	3.58	1.17	$5	23.7	252			27%	3.68	13.2	2.0	5.1	2.5	1.1	1.04	74%	56	108
04	Proj	17	8	0	200	154	3.56	1.24	$22	26.0	257			30%	3.63	45.8	2.3	6.9	3.0	0.9	--	74%	82	158

Speaking of which... Eased back into heavier workload in 2000 and it has served him well. Dom was off a bit early in '03, then a hand injury cut into his 2nd half BPIs. Should be fine for 2004.

Moss,Damian

LH Starter | AGE 27 Growth | TYPE | R X HIGH | I EXP CON | S PT STB | K | LIMA F EP: 40%

Yr	Tm	W	L	Sv	IP	K	ERA	Br/IP	R$	BF/G	OBA	vL	vR	H%	xERA	RAR	Ctl	Dom	Cmd	hr/9	G/F	S%	BPV	BPX
99	aa	1	3	0	32	19	9.84	2.34	($9)	24.1	379			41%	9.06 +	-18.5	5.6	5.3	1.0	1.7		58%	-19	-45
00	aaa	9	6	0	160	108	3.83	1.59	$7	24.9	248			28%	4.44 -	41.5	5.9	6.1	1.0	0.8		78%	38	90
01	a/a	5	5	0	107	97	4.12	1.42	$4	18.6	254			30%	4.58	18.6	4.1	8.2	2.0	1.3	0.91	76%	54	104
02	ATL	12	6	0	179	111	3.42	1.28	$15	22.8	217	165	232	23%	3.34	40.5	4.5	5.6	1.2	1.0	1.02	77%	41	78
03	2TM	10	12	0	165	79	5.18	1.67	($3)	24.5	283	342	261	29%	5.61	4.8	5.0	4.3	0.9	1.3	1.05	72%	3	6
1st Half		7	6	0	89	44	4.94	1.67	($0)	25.6	280			30%	5.38	5.4	5.1	4.4	0.9	1.2	1.27	72%	10	21
2nd Half		3	6	0	76	35	5.45	1.67	($4)	23.3	286			29%	5.88	-0.5	4.9	4.1	0.9	1.5	0.84	71%	-6	-11
04	Proj	7	13	0	160	87	4.95	1.63	($3)	25.1	279			29%	5.46 -	9.5	4.8	4.9	1.0	1.4	--	73%	9	19

2002 BPIs had him targeted for a major fall even if his skill levels held up. They didn't, and the fall became more of a plummet. It was bad in SF, worse in BAL, where he posted a 1.9 hr/9 at home. Stay far away.

Mota,Guillermo

RH Reliever | AGE 30 Peak | TYPE Power | R Very High | I exp CON | S PT | K BRN | LIMA B EP: 45%

Yr	Tm	W	L	Sv	IP	K	ERA	Br/IP	R$	BF/G	OBA	vL	vR	H%	xERA	RAR	Ctl	Dom	Cmd	hr/9	G/F	S%	BPV	BPX
99	MON	* 4	4	5	74	42	2.80	1.39	$9	4.9	259	250	262	29%	3.54 -	24.2	3.6	5.1	1.4	0.6	1.33	82%	45	98
00	MON	* 5	6	7	93	53	3.87	1.38	$11	6.2	243	244	246	27%	3.79	21.9	4.3	5.1	1.2	0.8	0.86	73%	39	87
01	MON	1	3	0	49	31	5.30	1.40	($1)	4.0	269	310	248	28%	5.03	0.4	3.3	5.7	1.7	1.6	0.98	67%	22	41
02	LA	* 2	6	1	96	79	3.75	1.21	$5	6.3	230	188	213	28%	2.80 +	17.4	3.3	7.4	2.3	0.5	0.96	68%	87	164
03	LA	6	3	1	105	99	1.97	0.99	$18	5.4	209	181	220	26%	2.18	46.5	2.2	8.5	3.8	0.6	1.27	84%	126	243
1st Half		2	2	1	46	44	1.95	1.04	$8	5.5	216			28%	2.20	20.6	2.3	8.6	3.7	0.4	1.24	83%	128	247
2nd Half		4	1	0	59	55	1.99	0.95	$11	5.3	202			25%	2.16	25.9	2.1	8.4	3.9	0.8	1.29	84%	125	240
04	Proj	3	4	1	80	70	2.93	1.09	$9	5.3	226			28%	2.58	25.1	2.4	7.9	3.3	0.6	--	74%	110	213

This $18 season was better than that of 52 180-IP starters. Yes, some of these are like catching lightning in a bottle, but if you fill out the bottom of your staff with high-BPI arms, you give yourself a bigger bottle.

Mounce,Tony

LH Starter | AGE 29 Pre-Peak | TYPE | R X HIGH | I EXP con | S pt STB | K BRN | LIMA F EP: 35%

Yr	Tm	W	L	Sv	IP	K	ERA	Br/IP	R$	BF/G	OBA	vL	vR	H%	xERA	RAR	Ctl	Dom	Cmd	hr/9	G/F	S%	BPV	BPX
99	a/a	5	3	0	79	75	4.22	1.62	$2	8.0	271			34%	4.49	13.9	5.1	8.5	1.7	0.7		75%	66	154
00	aaa	1	4	1	62	43	7.11	1.87	($8)	9.3	332			38%	6.29 +	-11.2	4.2	6.2	1.5	0.7		60%	35	84
01		0	0	0	0	0	0.00	0.00																
02	a/a	5	4	0	62	37	6.24	1.76	($4)	22.3	342			37%	6.86 -	-8.1	2.6	5.4	2.1	1.5		67%	18	36
03	TEX	* 10	10	0	166	91	4.98	1.67	($2)	24.6	306	310	320	33%	5.87 -	12.2	3.8	4.9	1.3	1.2	0.73	73%	15	31
1st Half		7	5	0	91	45	3.85	1.63	$3	26.0	300			32%	5.40 -	20.5	3.8	4.4	1.2	0.9	0.67	79%	19	42
2nd Half		3	5	0	75	46	6.34	1.72	($6)	23.2	314			34%	6.44	-8.2	3.8	5.5	1.4	1.6	0.78	66%	9	19
04	Proj	2	2	0	40	23	5.63	1.73	($2)	23.2	316			33%	6.51 -	-0.5	3.8	5.2	1.4	1.6	F	71%	4	9

1-5, 7.20 ERA in 50 IP at TEX. BPIs were marginal before arm troubles, and they have been even more marginal since working his way back. Flyball hurler in TEX is no picnic either (2.0 hr/9 at home).

Moyer,Jamie

LH Starter | AGE 41 Decline | TYPE Finesse | R Moderate | I con | S pt | K AGE | LIMA F EP: 40%

Yr	Tm	W	L	Sv	IP	K	ERA	Br/IP	R$	BF/G	OBA	vL	vR	H%	xERA	RAR	Ctl	Dom	Cmd	hr/9	G/F	S%	BPV	BPX
99	SEA	14	8	0	228	137	3.87	1.24	$23	29.6	268	234	278	30%	3.92	61.2	1.9	5.4	2.9	0.9	1.07	71%	67	167
00	SEA	13	10	0	154	98	5.49	1.47	$8	26.0	285	290	278	31%	5.05	8.6	3.1	5.7	1.8	1.3	1.16	65%	33	85
01	SEA	20	6	0	209	119	3.44	1.10	$29	25.5	241	255	234	26%	3.33	57.2	1.9	5.1	2.7	1.0	0.90	73%	63	127
02	SEA	13	8	0	230	147	3.33	1.08	$25	27.0	234	276	206	25%	3.28	65.7	2.0	5.8	2.9	1.1	0.84	74%	72	147
03	SEA	21	7	0	215	129	3.27	1.23	$28	27.1	247	275	233	27%	3.54	65.1	2.8	5.4	2.0	0.8	0.79	76%	55	119
1st Half		11	5	0	107	73	3.02	1.18	$16	25.8	227			26%	3.18	35.9	3.1	6.1	2.0	0.8	0.84	78%	63	135
2nd Half		10	2	0	108	56	3.51	1.29	$12	28.4	266			29%	3.90	29.1	2.4	4.7	1.9	0.8	0.75	75%	48	103
04	Proj	13	8	0	180	100	3.95	1.29	$15	28.1	259			28%	3.98	38.3	2.8	5.0	1.8	1.0	F	72%	43	92

Ageless? Maybe, though you can see his BPIs starting to tire out a bit in the 2nd half. The percentage play is to expect this trend to carry over into 2004... but we also said that after 2000.

Mulder,Mark

LH Starter | AGE 26 Growth | TYPE | R Moderate | I con | S pt | K brn | LIMA C EP: 50%

Yr	Tm	W	L	Sv	IP	K	ERA	Br/IP	R$	BF/G	OBA	vL	vR	H%	xERA	RAR	Ctl	Dom	Cmd	hr/9	G/F	S%	BPV	BPX
99	aaa	6	7	0	128	71	4.92	1.55	$1	26.0	319			35%	5.27	10.4	2.0	5.0	2.4	0.9		69%	45	105
00	OAK	9	10	0	154	88	5.44	1.69	($0)	26.3	305	368	288	33%	5.92	9.8	4.0	5.1	1.3	1.3	1.68	70%	13	34
01	OAK	21	8	0	229	153	3.46	1.16	$29	27.5	249	242	251	29%	3.18	62.2	2.0	6.0	3.0	0.6	1.93	71%	85	171
02	OAK	19	7	0	207	159	3.48	1.14	$27	28.0	238	244	228	27%	3.31	54.9	2.4	6.9	2.9	0.9	1.58	73%	82	169
03	OAK	15	9	0	186	128	3.14	1.18	$24	29.4	255	252	260	29%	3.45	59.4	1.9	6.2	3.2	0.7	1.91	76%	87	187
1st Half		11	5	0	121	74	3.27	1.24	$15	29.6	261			29%	3.63	36.6	2.2	5.5	2.6	0.7	1.91	75%	69	149
2nd Half		4	4	0	65	54	2.91	1.08	$9	28.9	243			29%	3.12	22.8	1.5	7.5	4.9	0.8	1.91	77%	129	279
04	Proj	16	10	0	200	144	3.42	1.19	$24	28.3	254			29%	3.53	56.8	2.1	6.5	3.1	0.8	G	74%	85	181

It was shaping up to be a career year for his BPIs when a stress fracture in his hip put an early end to it. If he's healthy, he could pick up from where he left off, but "stress fracture in his hip" sure sounds mighty nasty.

Mulholland,Terry

Mulholland,Terry		Tm	W	L	Sv	IP	K	ERA	Br/IP	R$	BF/G	OBA	vL	vR	H%	xERA	RAR	Ctl	Dom	Cmd	hr/9	G/F	S%	BPV	BPX
LH Reliever	99	2NL	10	8	1	170	83	4.39	1.45	$7	17.7	295	290	299	31%	4.68	19.2	2.4	4.4	1.8	1.1	1.65	72%	28	60
AGE 41 Decline	00	ATL	9	9	1	156	78	5.13	1.53	$3	12.9	310	294	312	32%	5.73 -	10.5	2.4	4.5	1.9	1.4	1.95	70%	18	41
TYPE Finesse	01	2NL	1	1	0	65	42	4.69	1.46	($1)	7.0	298	266	308	32%	5.60 -	5.9	2.3	5.8	2.5	1.7	1.62	73%	32	60
R X HIGH	02	2TM	3	2	0	79	38	5.70	1.54	($3)	9.5	312	312	315	32%	6.07	-4.5	2.4	4.3	1.8	1.7	1.31	67%	5	10
I CON	03	CLE	3	4	0	99	42	4.91	1.56	($2)	9.8	295	246	320	30%	5.76 -	8.2	3.4	3.8	1.1	1.5	1.07	73%	-4	-8
S pt STB	1st Half		1	1	0	43	15	3.76	1.69	($1)	7.6	291			30%	5.39 -	10.2	4.8	3.1	0.7	0.8	1.09	80%	4	9
K AGE BRN	2nd Half		2	3	0	56	27	5.80	1.45	($1)	12.9	298			29%	6.04	-2.0	2.3	4.3	1.9	2.1	1.04	66%	-1	-2
LIMA F EP: 35%	04	Proj	**1**	**1**	**0**	**40**	**14**	**5.18**	**1.68**	**($2)**	**9.7**	**303**			**30%**	**6.20 -**	**1.9**	**4.1**	**3.2**	**0.8**	**1.6**	**--**	**73%**	**-18**	**-38**

His late-career resurgence finally petered out in 2003. Actually, if you look at his xERAs, there was no late career resurgence at all, and he's been a high-priced inning-eater for some time.

Munro,Peter

Munro,Peter		Tm	W	L	Sv	IP	K	ERA	Br/IP	R$	BF/G	OBA	vL	vR	H%	xERA	RAR	Ctl	Dom	Cmd	hr/9	G/F	S%	BPV	BPX
RH Reliever	99	TOR	* 6	3	0	124	97	4.72	1.64	$1	11.5	297			35%	5.30 -	19.2	4.0	7.0	1.8	0.9	1.38	72%	49	122
AGE 28 Pre-Peak	00	TOR	* 6	6	0	119	66	4.31	1.54	$5	22.1	278			31%	4.35	25.5	4.1	5.0	1.2	0.5	2.78	71%	41	108
TYPE	01	aaa	8	6	0	88	63	6.14	1.69	($2)	12.3	301			33%	6.13	-8.4	4.3	6.4	1.5	1.5		66%	19	36
R Very High	02	HOU	* 12	6	0	174	105	3.57	1.24	$15	19.1	264	328	255	30%	3.35	35.8	2.1	5.4	2.6	0.5	1.63	71%	76	144
I EXP CON	03	HOU	3	4	0	54	27	4.67	1.65	($1)	6.2	293	293	295	31%	5.53 -	4.4	4.3	4.5	1.0	1.2	1.89	74%	10	20
S PT stb	1st Half		3	3	0	39	23	5.05	1.71	($1)	5.9	285			31%	5.54 -	1.2	5.3	5.3	1.0	1.1	1.79	73%	16	31
K	2nd Half		0	1	0	15	4	3.65	1.49	($0)	7.2	313			31%	5.50 -	3.2	1.8	2.4	1.3	1.2	2.17	80%	-1	-3
LIMA D EP: 40%	04	Proj	**4**	**3**	**0**	**60**	**38**	**4.95**	**1.57**	**$0**	**10.0**	**284**			**31%**	**5.04**	**2.5**	**4.1**	**5.7**	**1.4**	**1.1**	**G**	**70%**	**31**	**59**

A season nothing like 2002, except the fact that he still can't get LHers out. Kinda makes 2002 look like the outlier now.

Mussina,Mike

Mussina,Mike		Tm	W	L	Sv	IP	K	ERA	Br/IP	R$	BF/G	OBA	vL	vR	H%	xERA	RAR	Ctl	Dom	Cmd	hr/9	G/F	S%	BPV	BPX
RH Starter	99	BAL	18	7	0	203	172	3.50	1.28	$27	27.5	266	268	268	32%	3.77	64.4	2.3	7.6	3.3	0.7	1.55	74%	96	240
AGE 35 Decline	00	BAL	11	15	0	237	210	3.79	1.19	$24	28.7	261	223	281	31%	3.77	67.3	1.7	8.0	4.6	1.1	1.49	72%	115	298
TYPE	01	NYY	17	11	0	228	214	3.16	1.07	$30	26.8	239	240	234	30%	2.96	71.2	1.7	8.4	5.1	0.8	1.02	73%	141	283
R Low	02	NYY	18	10	0	215	182	4.06	1.19	$22	26.8	255	257	248	30%	3.86	40.3	2.0	7.6	3.8	1.1	1.08	69%	95	196
I con	03	NYY	17	8	0	214	195	3.40	1.08	$28	27.7	241	229	247	29%	3.14	60.9	1.7	8.2	4.9	0.9	0.88	72%	132	285
S	1st Half		10	4	0	106	104	2.97	1.00	$19	27.7	229			28%	2.89	36.4	1.4	8.8	6.1	1.0	0.86	76%	160	346
K age	2nd Half		7	4	0	108	91	3.83	1.17	$11	27.6	253			31%	3.39	24.5	1.9	7.6	4.0	0.7	0.91	68%	111	239
LIMA C+ EP: 60%	04	Proj	**19**	**9**	**0**	**225**	**200**	**3.28**	**1.13**	**$30**	**27.6**	**248**			**30%**	**3.38**	**68.1**	**1.8**	**8.0**	**4.4**	**0.9**	**--**	**74%**	**119**	**255**

Hard to believe he's never had a 20-win season; with these BPIs, he certainly deserves it. That window will start closing as he gets older, but he's still got a shot as long as his supporting cast stays relatively intact.

Myers,Brett

Myers,Brett		Tm	W	L	Sv	IP	K	ERA	Br/IP	R$	BF/G	OBA	vL	vR	H%	xERA	RAR	Ctl	Dom	Cmd	hr/9	G/F	S%	BPV	BPX
RH Starter	99		0	0	0	0	0	0.00	0.00																
AGE 23 Growth	00		0	0	0	0	0	0.00	0.00																
TYPE	01	aa	13	4	0	156	118	4.56	1.42	$8	26.1	286			33%	4.91	18.0	2.7	6.8	2.6	1.2		71%	56	108
R High	02	PHI	* 13	11	0	200	127	4.19	1.27	$13	27.0	266	225	314	30%	3.88	24.7	2.2	5.7	2.6	0.9	1.72	69%	62	118
I EXP	03	PHI	14	9	0	193	143	4.43	1.46	$8	26.4	274	270	273	32%	4.53	21.9	3.5	6.7	1.9	0.9	1.53	71%	52	100
S pt	1st Half		7	6	0	102	70	3.62	1.23	$10	26.4	230			26%	3.41	22.7	3.4	6.2	1.8	1.0	1.38	74%	55	105
K age brn	2nd Half		7	3	0	91	73	5.34	1.71	($2)	26.4	317			37%	5.79	-0.8	3.7	7.2	2.0	0.9	1.73	69%	50	96
LIMA C+ EP: 50%	04	Proj	**14**	**9**	**0**	**200**	**143**	**4.01**	**1.37**	**$13**	**26.0**	**268**			**31%**	**4.21**	**33.7**	**3.0**	**6.4**	**2.2**	**0.9**	**G**	**73%**	**57**	**110**

ERA tanked in the 2nd half, but that was a mirage driven by 37/69% hit/strand rates. In some respects, his skills got better as the year progressed. But his overall performance was still off of history, so there's still work.

Myers,Mike

Myers,Mike		Tm	W	L	Sv	IP	K	ERA	Br/IP	R$	BF/G	OBA	vL	vR	H%	xERA	RAR	Ctl	Dom	Cmd	hr/9	G/F	S%	BPV	BPX
LH Reliever	99	MIL	2	1	0	41	35	5.27	1.44	$0	2.5	285	190	392	33%	4.86	-0.2	2.9	7.7	2.7	1.5	1.48	67%	55	119
AGE 34 Decline	00	COL	0	1	1	45	41	2.00	1.06	$6	2.3	159	120	224	20%	1.64	21.9	4.8	8.2	1.7	0.4	1.41	83%	96	212
TYPE Power	01	COL	2	3	0	40	36	3.60	1.40	$2	2.4	221	231	216	28%	3.25	9.5	5.4	8.1	1.5	0.5	1.96	74%	77	144
R Low	02	ARI	4	3	4	37	31	4.38	1.51	$4	2.4	272	241	317	34%	4.15	3.6	4.1	7.5	1.8	0.5	2.73	70%	70	131
I con	03	ARI	0	1	0	36	21	5.73	1.63	($4)	2.6	272	237	290	30%	5.03 +	-2.2	5.2	5.2	1.0	1.1	2.00	65%	23	45
S stb	1st Half		0	0	0	21	11	5.14	1.62	($2)	2.6	280			32%	4.17 +	0.4	4.7	4.7	1.0	0.0	2.92	65%	48	93
K age	2nd Half		0	1	0	15	10	6.56	1.66	($2)	2.6	260			25%	6.22	-2.6	6.0	6.0	1.0	2.4	1.25	67%	-12	-23
LIMA D EP: 50%	04	Proj	**1**	**2**	**0**	**40**	**29**	**4.95**	**1.53**	**($1)**	**2.5**	**257**			**29%**	**4.41 +**	**1.7**	**5.0**	**6.5**	**1.3**	**0.9**	**G**	**68%**	**43**	**84**

Hard to believe that he put up some of his best years in COL. Ctl has always been a problem, now Dom has been in a freefall. But heck, southpaws live forever.

Nathan,Joe

Nathan,Joe		Tm	W	L	Sv	IP	K	ERA	Br/IP	R$	BF/G	OBA	vL	vR	H%	xERA	RAR	Ctl	Dom	Cmd	hr/9	G/F	S%	BPV	BPX
RH Reliever	99	SF	* 13	9	1	173	132	4.47	1.46	$9	22.3	252	231	250	28%	4.39	17.6	4.6	6.9	1.5	1.5	1.00	74%	33	72
AGE 29 Pre-Peak	00	SF	* 5	4	0	107	68	5.12	1.61	($1)	21.1	256	295	214	28%	5.02	7.3	5.8	5.7	1.0	1.3	0.86	71%	21	46
TYPE Power	01	a/a	3	11	0	109	41	8.50	2.13	($24)	17.8	344			34%	8.37	-45.0	5.9	3.4	0.6	2.0		62%	-41	-78
R X HIGH	02	aaa	6	12	0	149	97	6.70	1.83	($16)	20.2	319			36%	6.30	-28.6	4.5	5.9	1.3	1.1	0.29	63%	21	41
I EXP CON	03	SF	12	4	0	79	83	2.96	1.06	$17	4.0	186	276	136	24%	2.28 +	24.5	3.8	9.5	2.5	0.8	0.50	75%	103	199
S PT STB	1st Half		7	3	0	43	44	4.19	1.16	$8	4.5	209			24%	3.42 +	6.3	3.8	9.2	2.4	1.5	0.45	70%	76	146
K	2nd Half		5	1	0	36	39	1.50	0.94	$10	3.6	158			23%	0.91 +	18.2	3.7	9.7	2.6	0.0	0.58	82%	137	263
LIMA C EP: 45%	04	Proj	**8**	**5**	**0**	**80**	**70**	**3.60**	**1.26**	**$10**	**4.2**	**226**			**27%**	**3.34**	**17.8**	**3.9**	**7.9**	**2.0**	**0.9**	**F**	**74%**	**72**	**139**

The ultimate vulture -- notched a giant "W" every 6.5 IP. Began with 22.1 scoreless IP, then hit a rough spot in May (with a 17.0 Cmd ratio but 45% strand rate!) before surging down the stretch. It was a fantasy season.

Neagle,Denny

Neagle,Denny		Tm	W	L	Sv	IP	K	ERA	Br/IP	R$	BF/G	OBA	vL	vR	H%	xERA	RAR	Ctl	Dom	Cmd	hr/9	G/F	S%	BPV	BPX
LH Reliever	99	CIN	* 11	5	0	128	84	4.36	1.16	$14	22.7	229	198	237	23%	3.63 +	15.0	3.0	5.9	2.0	1.8	0.59	70%	34	74
AGE 35 Decline	00	2TM	15	9	0	209	146	4.52	1.39	$15	26.5	263	295	249	29%	4.60	34.7	3.5	6.3	1.8	1.3	0.75	72%	38	90
TYPE	01	COL	9	8	0	170	139	5.39	1.48	($1)	25.0	286	300	279	32%	5.35	-0.6	3.2	7.4	2.3	1.5	0.60	67%	45	83
R High	02	COL	8	11	0	164	111	5.27	1.42	($1)	20.3	269	315	251	29%	4.77 +	-3.6	3.5	6.1	1.8	1.4	1.08	66%	32	60
I con	03	COL	* 5	4	0	59	34	6.70	1.68	($3)	24.7	332	415	283	34%	7.28 -	-11.3	2.4	5.2	2.1	2.3	0.79	65%	-4	-8
S pt stb	1st Half		5	1	0	42	27	4.70	1.52	$3	26.7	321			34%	6.14 -	3.2	1.7	5.8	3.4	1.7	0.95	75%	45	87
K age	2nd Half		0	3	0	17	7	11.65	2.06	($6)	21.2	360			33%	10.08 +	-14.5	4.2	3.7	0.9	3.7	0.65	46%	-88	-169
LIMA F EP: 45%	04	Proj	**1**	**2**	**0**	**20**	**12**	**5.40**	**1.50**	**($0)**	**9.8**	**290**			**30%**	**5.67**	**-0.4**	**3.2**	**5.4**	**1.7**	**1.8**	**F**	**69%**	**11**	**22**

Another Tommy John surgery recipient, he wants to return by the All Star Break as a reliever. More likely, he'll miss nearly all of 2004.

Nelson,Jeff

Nelson,Jeff		Tm	W	L	Sv	IP	K	ERA	Br/IP	R$	BF/G	OBA	vL	vR	H%	xERA	RAR	Ctl	Dom	Cmd	hr/9	G/F	S%	BPV	BPX
RH Reliever	99	NYY	2	1	1	30	35	4.20	1.63	$2	3.5	242	229	253	34%	4.22	6.7	6.6	10.5	1.6	0.6	1.82	74%	85	213
AGE 37 Decline	00	NYY	8	4	0	69	71	2.47	1.29	$13	4.0	184	232	157	25%	2.30	31.9	5.9	9.2	1.6	0.3	0.89	80%	99	257
TYPE Power	01	SEA	4	3	4	65	88	2.76	1.14	$11	3.8	140	167	119	22%	1.62 +	23.7	6.1	12.2	2.0	0.4	0.97	76%	129	259
R High	02	SEA	3	2	2	45	55	4.00	1.40	$4	4.7	221	224	218	31%	3.60	8.8	5.4	11.0	2.0	0.8	0.50	73%	96	196
I con	03	2AL	4	2	8	55	68	3.76	1.36	$9	3.4	247	273	233	35%	3.68	13.0	3.9	11.1	2.8	0.7	0.79	73%	112	242
S pt stb	1st Half		3	1	7	27	31	4.32	1.48	$6	3.6	261			35%	4.48	4.4	4.3	10.3	2.4	1.0	0.81	73%	85	183
K AGE	2nd Half		1	1	1	28	37	3.21	1.25	$3	3.2	233			35%	2.89	8.7	3.5	11.9	3.4	0.3	0.76	74%	141	304
LIMA B+ EP: 60%	04	Proj	**3**	**2**	**1**	**50**	**57**	**4.14**	**1.50**	**$2**	**3.9**	**254**			**34%**	**4.18**	**9.4**	**4.9**	**10.3**	**2.1**	**0.7**	**F**	**73%**	**88**	**190**

Solid season, though 35% hit rate inflated his ERA a bit. At 37, there's really only one direction it can go from here, and it's not likely the direction that Mr. Steinbrenner wants.

Neu,Mike

Neu,Mike		Tm	W	L	Sv	IP	K	ERA	Br/IP	R$	BF/G	OBA	vL	vR	H%	xERA	RAR	Ctl	Dom	Cmd	hr/9	G/F	S%	BPV	BPX
RH Reliever	99		0	0	0	0	0	0.00	0.00																
AGE 26 Growth	00		0	0	0	0	0	0.00	0.00																
TYPE Power	01		0	0	0	0	0	0.00	0.00																
R Moderate	02	a/a	3	3	23	67	69	3.49	1.36	$17	4.7	256			34%	3.64	16.0	3.5	9.3	2.7	0.5		75%	99	194
I EXP con	03	OAK	0	0	1	42	20	3.64	1.64	($1)	6.0	266	214	295	29%	4.50 -	10.6	5.6	4.3	0.8	0.4	1.74	78%	31	66
S pt	1st Half		0	0	0	24	16	2.60	1.40	$1	5.8	252			29%	3.99 -	9.5	4.1	6.0	1.5	0.7	1.52	84%	49	105
K	2nd Half		0	0	1	18	4	5.06	1.97	($2)	6.2	285			30%	5.20	1.1	7.6	2.0	0.3	0.0	2.07	71%	16	34
LIMA D EP: 40%	04	Proj	**0**	**0**	**0**	**20**	**13**	**4.50**	**1.65**	**($1)**	**5.4**	**281**			**33%**	**4.72**	**2.8**	**5.0**	**5.9**	**1.2**	**0.5**	**G**	**72%**	**45**	**97**

Rule 5 pick who took a solid BPI foundation as a minor league closer and turned it into a season devoid of skill. In the 2nd half, walked 15, K'd just 4 and escaped with a 5.06 ERA.

Nomo,Hideo

RH	Starter		
AGE	35 Decline		
TYPE	Power		
R	Moderate		
I		con	
S		STB	
K	age		
LIMA	D	EP:	40%

Yr	Tm	W	L	Sv	IP	K	ERA	Br/IP	R$	BF/G	OBA	vL	vR	H%	xERA	RAR	Ctl	Dom	Cmd	hr/9	G/F	S%	BPV	BPX
99	MIL	* 14	9	0	200	183	4.32	1.40	$12	27.0	253	280	235	30%	4.05	24.5	4.0	8.2	**2.1**	1.3	0.83	73%	59	129
00	DET	8	12	0	190	181	4.74	1.47	$6	26.1	263	241	284	31%	4.90	29.9	4.2	8.6	**2.0**	1.5	0.88	72%	53	136
01	BOS	13	10	0	198	220	4.50	1.35	$10	25.6	234	221	242	30%	3.96 +	26.1	4.4	10.0	**2.3**	1.2	1.08	70%	81	162
02	LA	16	6	0	220	193	3.40	1.32	$18	27.4	234	218	253	28%	3.68	50.4	4.1	7.9	**1.9**	1.1	0.95	78%	64	121
03	LA	16	13	0	218	177	3.09	1.25	$23	27.6	222	213	232	26%	3.37	63.8	4.0	7.3	**1.8**	1.0	0.94	80%	63	121
1st Half		9	6	0	123	103	2.41	1.08	$19	29.0	193			23%	2.49	47.2	3.7	7.5	**2.1**	0.9	0.98	83%	79	151
2nd Half		7	7	0	95	74	3.98	1.47	$5	26.1	256			29%	4.51 -	16.5	4.5	7.0	**1.5**	1.1	0.90	77%	44	85
04	**Proj**	**14**	**10**	**0**	**200**	**161**	**3.65**	**1.34**	**$15**	**26.6**	**241**			**28%**	**3.88**	**43.4**	**4.0**	**7.2**	**1.8**	**1.1**	**--**	**77%**	**56**	**109**

23/83% hit/strand rates pushed down his ERA in the 1st half. Shoulder problems affected his BPIs in the 2nd half. These naggy ills will likely become more frequent, gradually eating into his BPIs some more.

Obermueller,Wes

RH	Starter		
AGE	27 Growth		
TYPE	Finesse		
R	High		
I	EXP		
S	pt		
K		BRN	
LIMA	F	EP:	40%

Yr	Tm	W	L	Sv	IP	K	ERA	Br/IP	R$	BF/G	OBA	vL	vR	H%	xERA	RAR	Ctl	Dom	Cmd	hr/9	G/F	S%	BPV	BPX
99		0	0	0	0	0	0.00	0.00																
00		0	0	0	0	0	0.00	0.00																
01		0	0	0	0	0	0.00	0.00																
02	aa	9	5	0	105	49	4.37	1.67	$2	28.3	307			33%	5.34 -	12.6	3.8	4.2	**1.1**	0.7		74%	22	43
03	MIL	* 12	12	0	186	93	4.97	1.56	$1	26.1	295	301	301	31%	5.30	7.6	3.4	4.5	**1.3**	1.1	1.24	70%	17	33
1st Half		9	5	0	98	48	5.87	1.64	($1)	28.0	308			33%	5.69	-7.8	3.5	4.4	**1.3**	1.1		65%	13	26
2nd Half		3	7	0	88	45	3.98	1.47	$1	24.2	280			30%	4.86 -	15.4	3.4	4.6	**1.4**	1.1		76%	21	41
04	**Proj**	**3**	**5**	**0**	**60**	**29**	**4.95**	**1.60**	**($1)**	**27.1**	**299**			**32%**	**5.22**	**2.5**	**3.6**	**4.4**	**1.2**	**0.9**	**--**	**70%**	**20**	**38**

2-5, 5.12 ERA in 65 IP at MIL. Soft-tosser with poor command who gives up a lot of hits and has a name that won't fit on his uniform without making everyone turn their heads and read upside down.

Ohka,Tomokazu

RH	Starter		
AGE	28 Pre-Peak		
TYPE	Finesse		
R	Very High		
I	exp	con	
S	PT	STB	
K			
LIMA	C+	EP:	50%

Yr	Tm	W	L	Sv	IP	K	ERA	Br/IP	R$	BF/G	OBA	vL	vR	H%	xERA	RAR	Ctl	Dom	Cmd	hr/9	G/F	S%	BPV	BPX
99	a/a	16	2	0	153	109	3.12	1.33	$22	20.3	272			31%	4.07 -	49.4	2.5	6.4	**2.6**	1.0		81%	64	147
00	BOS	* 12	12	0	199	105	3.61	1.26	$22	26.1	264	277	243	28%	4.02	61.4	2.3	4.7	**2.1**	1.0	1.36	75%	44	113
01	2TM	* 5	14	0	149	95	5.92	1.59	($8)	22.4	321	329	290	36%	5.89	-9.9	2.3	5.7	**2.5**	1.2	1.48	64%	41	79
02	MON	13	8	0	192	118	3.19	1.24	$18	25.0	264	218	298	29%	3.75 -	49.3	2.1	5.5	**2.6**	0.9	1.36	78%	64	121
03	MON	10	12	0	199	118	4.16	1.40	$7	25.3	293	311	279	32%	4.83 -	29.8	2.0	5.3	**2.6**	1.1	1.13	73%	51	98
1st Half		7	7	0	92	50	4.50	1.41	$4	23.5	294			30%	5.32 -	9.7	2.1	4.9	**2.3**	1.6	1.32	74%	26	51
2nd Half		3	5	0	107	68	3.87	1.38	$3	27.1	293			33%	4.40 -	20.1	1.9	5.7	**3.0**	0.7	0.99	73%	73	140
04	**Proj**	**12**	**10**	**0**	**200**	**122**	**3.87**	**1.33**	**$13**	**24.3**	**279**			**31%**	**4.26**	**37.3**	**2.1**	**5.5**	**2.6**	**0.9**	**--**	**73%**	**58**	**113**

BPIs don't look much different from 2002, but he added a run to his ERA. Blame some slight adjustments to H%/S% and 1st half gopheritis. Made only marginal improvement to BA vs RHers, which has to improve.

Oliver,Darren

LH	Starter		
AGE	33 Past		
TYPE			
R	X HIGH		
I		CON	
S	PT	STB	
K	age	BRN	
LIMA	C	EP:	45%

Yr	Tm	W	L	Sv	IP	K	ERA	Br/IP	R$	BF/G	OBA	vL	vR	H%	xERA	RAR	Ctl	Dom	Cmd	hr/9	G/F	S%	BPV	BPX
99	STL	9	9	0	196	119	4.27	1.38	$8	28.1	263	320	254	29%	3.68 +	25.3	3.4	5.5	**1.6**	0.7	1.44	70%	47	102
00	TEX	2	9	0	108	49	7.42	1.79	($12)	24.2	331	376	326	35%	6.65 +	-21.8	3.5	4.1	**1.2**	1.3	1.01	59%	-2	-6
01	TEX	11	11	0	154	104	6.02	1.65	($4)	25.1	303	311	304	33%	5.88	-11.0	3.8	6.1	**1.6**	1.3	1.24	65%	24	48
02	BOS	* 4	7	0	74	40	5.84	1.84	($6)	18.5	304	462	272	33%	6.07	-3.8	5.5	4.9	**0.9**	1.0	1.41	69%	13	27
03	COL	13	11	0	180	88	5.05	1.45	$4	23.9	284	256	292	30%	4.80	5.6	3.0	4.4	**1.4**	1.0	1.25	67%	23	45
1st Half		5	5	0	93	45	4.84	1.48	$1	24.1	280			30%	4.75	5.5	3.5	4.4	**1.3**	1.0	1.05	69%	22	43
2nd Half		8	6	0	87	43	5.27	1.42	$3	23.6	287			30%	4.86	0.1	2.6	4.4	**1.7**	1.1	1.52	65%	26	50
04	**Proj**	**12**	**13**	**0**	**180**	**96**	**5.10**	**1.56**	**$1**	**24.4**	**289**			**31%**	**5.16**	**4.0**	**3.8**	**4.8**	**1.3**	**1.1**	**--**	**69%**	**20**	**38**

Looking for something good:
- Knocked 20 pts off his OBA
- Greatly improved BA vs LHers
- Improved Ctl, esp. in 2nd half
- xERA dipped under 5.00

And the most amazing thing of all... he did it in Colorado.

Oropesa,Eddie

LH	Reliever		
AGE	32 Peak		
TYPE	Power		
R	X HIGH		
I	EXP	CON	
S	PT	STB	
K			
LIMA	D+	EP:	60%

Yr	Tm	W	L	Sv	IP	K	ERA	Br/IP	R$	BF/G	OBA	vL	vR	H%	xERA	RAR	Ctl	Dom	Cmd	hr/9	G/F	S%	BPV	BPX
99	aaa	6	5	0	102	49	5.21	1.75	($2)	22.7	306			32%	5.96 -	4.4	4.5	4.3	**1.0**	1.3		73%	0	0
00	aa	2	4	4	76	50	4.86	2.01	($4)	6.4	325			36%	6.85 -	9.2	5.9	5.9	**1.0**	1.1		78%	15	35
01	PHI	* 2	1	0	34	24	4.50	1.68	($0)	3.6	267			31%	4.65	3.9	5.8	6.4	**1.1**	0.5	3.00	73%	47	87
02	ARI	* 3	0	0	50	38	7.56	1.90	($7)	4.0	322			36%	6.78 +	-16.4	5.0	6.8	**1.4**	1.4	1.66	61%	17	32
03	ARI	* 3	4	0	53	47	5.07	1.61	($1)	3.9	268	206	294	33%	4.43 +	1.5	5.2	7.9	**1.5**	0.5	1.78	67%	66	126
1st Half		2	2	0	37	32	2.90	1.18	$4	4.0	205			26%	2.51	11.8	4.1	7.7	**1.9**	0.5	1.63	76%	86	165
2nd Half		1	2	0	16	15	10.06	2.61	($5)	3.7	381			47%	8.86 +	-10.3	7.8	8.4	**1.1**	0.6	2.00	59%	35	67
04	**Proj**	**2**	**2**	**0**	**40**	**34**	**4.73**	**1.58**	**($0)**	**3.7**	**267**			**32%**	**4.66**	**2.9**	**5.0**	**7.7**	**1.5**	**0.9**	**G**	**71%**	**53**	**102**

3-3, 5.92 ERA in 38 IP at ARI.
3.00 ERA on Aug 12, but then....
8/16: 0.2 IP, 5 ER.
Next 5 outings, 4 IP, 2 ER
9/23: 1 IP, 4 ER
9/25: 0 IP, 3 ER
End of story.

Orosco,Jesse

LH	Reliever		
AGE	47 Decline		
TYPE	Power		
R	X HIGH		
I		CON	
S	PT	STB	
K	AGE		
LIMA	D	EP:	70%

Yr	Tm	W	L	Sv	IP	K	ERA	Br/IP	R$	BF/G	OBA	vL	vR	H%	xERA	RAR	Ctl	Dom	Cmd	hr/9	G/F	S%	BPV	BPX
99	BAL	0	2	1	32	35	5.34	1.50	($0)	2.2	237			29%	4.58 +	2.3	5.6	9.8	**1.8**	1.4	1.09	67%	61	154
00	STL	* 0	1	0	3	4	3.00	2.33	($0)	2.0	321			40%	9.37 -	1.1	9.0	12.0	**1.3**	3.0	1.00	100%	1	2
01	LA	* 1	1	0	23	30	2.74	1.30	$2	2.2	245	300	275	34%	3.95 -	8.1	3.5	11.7	**3.3**	1.2	1.23	85%	111	206
02	LA	1	2	1	27	22	3.00	1.33	$2	2.1	240	238	214	27%	4.05 -	7.6	4.0	7.3	**1.8**	1.3	0.74	84%	50	94
03	2TM	2	2	2	34	29	7.68	1.82	($3)	2.5	300	231	390	36%	5.97 +	-10.4	5.6	7.7	**1.4**	1.1	0.53	57%	38	78
1st Half		1	1	2	21	20	8.49	1.93	($3)	2.9	349			42%	7.25 +	-8.8	3.8	8.5	**2.2**	1.3	0.76	55%	45	91
2nd Half		1	1	0	13	9	6.33	1.64	($1)	1.9	200			23%	3.85 +	-1.6	8.4	6.3	**0.8**	0.7	0.27	60%	48	97
04	**Proj**	**1**	**1**	**0**	**20**	**15**	**4.50**	**1.45**	**$0**	**2.4**	**262**			**29%**	**4.75**	**2.4**	**4.1**	**6.8**	**1.7**	**1.4**	**F**	**73%**	**38**	**76**

A lot of bad luck here -- moreso than bad skill -- but you still have to wonder whether this represents the end of the line. He still did get LHers out, after all.

Ortiz,Ramon

RH	Starter		
AGE	30 Peak		
TYPE			
R	Low		
I		con	
S			
K			
LIMA	C	EP:	50%

Yr	Tm	W	L	Sv	IP	K	ERA	Br/IP	R$	BF/G	OBA	vL	vR	H%	xERA	RAR	Ctl	Dom	Cmd	hr/9	G/F	S%	BPV	BPX
99	ANA	* 16	10	0	203	175	4.57	1.43	$15	26.8	263	293	233	31%	4.58	35.5	3.9	7.8	**2.0**	1.2	1.67	71%	55	139
00	ANA	* 14	12	0	200	139	5.31	1.36	$12	25.9	243	250	219	27%	4.08 +	16.2	4.1	6.3	**1.5**	1.2	1.30	63%	41	106
01	ANA	13	11	0	208	135	4.37	1.44	$8	28.3	275	285	263	30%	4.68	31.2	3.3	5.8	**1.8**	1.1	1.31	72%	40	80
02	ANA	15	9	0	217	162	3.77	1.18	$21	27.8	235	218	243	25%	4.07	49.0	2.8	6.7	**2.4**	1.7	1.04	76%	49	100
03	ANA	16	13	0	180	94	5.20	1.51	$6	24.9	292	291	282	30%	5.44	7.8	3.2	4.7	**1.5**	1.4	0.80	69%	14	31
1st Half		9	6	0	100	53	4.68	1.50	$5	26.0	295			31%	5.33 -	11.4	2.9	4.8	**1.7**	1.3	0.74	72%	22	47
2nd Half		7	7	0	80	41	5.86	1.53	$1	23.7	288			29%	5.59	-3.6	3.5	4.6	**1.3**	1.6	0.88	65%	6	12
04	**Proj**	**16**	**12**	**0**	**200**	**129**	**4.55**	**1.39**	**$12**	**26.1**	**267**			**28%**	**4.79**	**26.6**	**3.2**	**5.8**	**1.8**	**1.4**	**F**	**72%**	**31**	**66**

Diagnosis of a disappointment :
- Sharp drop in dominance
- Unsupportive bullpen
- Hit rate reverted to mean
- 9.20 ERA in final 3 starts after death of his father.

Should bounce back some.

Ortiz,Russ

RH	Starter		
AGE	29 Peak		
TYPE	Power		
R	Low		
I		con	
S			
K		brn	
LIMA	D	EP:	45%

Yr	Tm	W	L	Sv	IP	K	ERA	Br/IP	R$	BF/G	OBA	vL	vR	H%	xERA	RAR	Ctl	Dom	Cmd	hr/9	G/F	S%	BPV	BPX
99	SF	18	9	0	207	164	3.83	1.52	$14	27.8	245	251	238	28%	4.04	39.1	5.4	7.1	**1.3**	1.0	1.23	78%	45	98
00	SF	14	12	0	195	167	5.03	1.56	$6	26.5	259	267	255	30%	4.92	15.8	5.2	7.7	**1.5**	1.3	1.27	71%	42	93
01	SF	17	9	0	218	169	3.30	1.27	$22	27.7	233	275	191	28%	3.17	60.4	3.8	7.0	**1.9**	0.5	1.21	75%	73	136
02	SF	14	10	0	214	137	3.62	1.33	$15	27.6	240	247	235	27%	3.41	42.7	4.0	5.8	**1.5**	0.6	1.24	74%	53	101
03	ATL	21	7	0	212	149	3.82	1.32	$22	26.4	228	265	187	26%	3.38	41.5	4.3	6.3	**1.5**	0.7	0.99	72%	56	108
1st Half		10	4	0	115	68	3.37	1.27	$13	26.8	221			25%	2.94	29.5	4.2	5.3	**1.3**	0.5	1.21	74%	55	106
2nd Half		11	3	0	97	81	4.36	1.37	$9	26.0	237			28%	3.89	12.0	4.4	7.5	**1.7**	1.0	0.76	70%	58	111
04	**Proj**	**15**	**10**	**0**	**200**	**145**	**3.92**	**1.36**	**$14**	**26.7**	**238**			**28%**	**3.60**	**36.1**	**4.3**	**6.5**	**1.5**	**0.8**	**--**	**72%**	**56**	**107**

From a skills perspective, not all that different from 2002, but other owners will see those 21 wins and overbid. With this skill set, another 21-win season would be a small miracle.

Osuna,Antonio

RH	Reliever		
AGE	31 Peak		
TYPE	Power		
R	High		
I		con	
S	PT	stb	
K			
LIMA	A	EP:	55%

Yr	Tm	W	L	Sv	IP	K	ERA	Br/IP	R$	BF/G	OBA	vL	vR	H%	xERA	RAR	Ctl	Dom	Cmd	hr/9	G/F	S%	BPV	BPX
99	LA	0	0	0	5	5	7.20	1.40	($0)	4.3	221			31%	2.45 +	-1.3	5.4	9.0	**1.7**	0.0	0.80	43%	100	217
00	LA	3	6	0	67	70	3.76	1.37	$4	6.3	231	229	229	30%	3.75	16.8	4.7	9.4	**2.0**	0.9	0.58	75%	79	174
01	CHW	0	0	0	4	6	21.95	2.44	($3)	5.5	409			47%	14.64 +	-9.0	4.4	13.2	**3.0**	6.6	0.38	0%	-82	-165
02	CHW	8	2	11	67	66	3.90	1.37	$14	4.9	253	250	250	34%	3.34 +	14.0	3.8	8.9	**2.4**	0.1	0.89	69%	103	211
03	NYY	2	5	0	50	47	3.76	1.55	$1	4.7	291	305	266	37%	4.69 -	11.8	3.6	8.4	**2.4**	0.5	0.60	76%	81	174
1st Half		2	2	0	27	25	2.00	1.37	$4	4.8	240			31%	3.33 -	12.7	4.3	8.3	**1.9**	0.3	0.75	86%	87	189
2nd Half		0	3	0	23	22	5.82	1.77	($3)	4.5	342			42%	6.27	-0.9	2.7	8.5	**3.1**	0.8	0.45	67%	81	174
04	**Proj**	**5**	**4**	**0**	**60**	**58**	**3.45**	**1.42**	**$5**	**4.8**	**262**			**34%**	**3.84**	**16.8**	**3.8**	**8.7**	**2.3**	**0.5**	**F**	**76%**	**90**	**193**

An underachiever, thanks to a growing history of high hit rates, but there's no question of the skill. Groin injury and mother's illness contributed to poor 2nd half. But it looks like it was not poor skill, just poor focus.

Oswalt,Roy

		Tm	W	L	Sv	IP	K	ERA	Br/IP	R$	BF/G	OBA	vL	vR	H%	xERA	RAR	Ctl	Dom	Cmd	hr/9	G/F	S%	BPV	BPX
RH Starter	99		0	0	0	0	0	0.00	0.00																
AGE 26 Growth	00	aa	11	4	0	129	117	2.79	1.23	$20	28.2	269			34%	3.48 -	51.3	1.7	8.2	4.7	0.5		78%	134	317
TYPE	01	HOU	* 16	6	0	172	173	3.30	1.13	$24	21.1	253	241	228	32%	3.42	47.7	1.6	9.1	5.8	0.9	1.46	74%	152	281
R High	02	HOU	19	9	0	233	208	3.01	1.19	$28	27.4	247	251	244	31%	3.14	65.3	2.4	8.0	3.4	0.7	1.41	77%	105	198
I EXP con	03	HOU	10	5	0	127	108	2.97	1.14	$17	24.6	245	263	234	29%	3.45	39.2	2.1	7.6	3.7	1.1	1.26	79%	98	189
S PT	1st Half		4	4	0	73	71	3.07	1.27	$7	25.6	261			33%	3.80 -	21.6	2.5	8.7	3.6	0.9	1.40	79%	104	200
K brn	2nd Half		6	1	0	54	37	2.84	0.96	$11	23.3	221			23%	2.97	17.6	1.5	6.2	4.1	1.3	1.11	80%	94	181
LIMA B EP: 55%	04	Proj	17	7	0	200	173	3.02	1.13	$27	24.5	245			29%	3.29	60.2	1.9	7.8	4.0	0.9	--	78%	109	210

Groin injury may have cut into his innings but it barely affected his BPIs. If healthy, he should be right back in track.

Padilla,Vicente

		Tm	W	L	Sv	IP	K	ERA	Br/IP	R$	BF/G	OBA	vL	vR	H%	xERA	RAR	Ctl	Dom	Cmd	hr/9	G/F	S%	BPV	BPX
RH Starter	99	aaa	7	4	0	93	49	3.87	1.40	$8	22.3	295			33%	4.22	20.7	1.9	4.7	2.5	0.6	0.50	73%	58	135
AGE 26 Growth	00	2NL	* 4	8	3	87	72	4.02	1.61	$4	5.7	295	337	252	36%	4.85 -	18.9	3.9	7.4	1.9	0.5	2.31	75%	65	143
TYPE Finesse	01	PHI	* 10	1	0	115	97	3.60	1.21	$13	12.2	260	308	258	31%	3.59	27.2	2.0	7.6	3.9	0.8	2.50	72%	107	198
R Very High	02	PHI	14	11	0	206	128	3.28	1.22	$20	26.6	254	272	236	29%	3.38	50.5	2.3	5.6	2.4	0.7	1.98	75%	67	128
I exp con	03	PHI	14	12	0	208	133	3.63	1.24	$18	27.1	250	267	239	28%	3.69	45.9	2.7	5.7	2.1	1.0	1.26	74%	56	108
S PT stb	1st Half		7	7	0	102	68	3.70	1.24	$9	26.6	252			28%	3.81	21.6	2.6	6.0	2.3	1.1	1.17	74%	56	109
K brn	2nd Half		7	5	0	106	65	3.57	1.24	$10	27.5	249			28%	3.57	24.3	2.7	5.5	2.0	0.8	1.34	74%	56	107
LIMA D+ EP: 50%	04	Proj	14	10	0	200	128	3.56	1.26	$18	26.9	257			29%	3.65	45.8	2.5	5.8	2.3	0.8	--	74%	62	119

Dom has leveled off, but most of his other BPIs are still declining. His DOM/DIS splits describe it::
2002: 44% DOM, 9% DIS
2003: 59% DOM, 16% DIS
A bit more dominant, but also more inconsistent.

Park,Chan Ho

		Tm	W	L	Sv	IP	K	ERA	Br/IP	R$	BF/G	OBA	vL	vR	H%	xERA	RAR	Ctl	Dom	Cmd	hr/9	G/F	S%	BPV	BPX
RH Starter	99	LA	13	11	0	194	174	5.24	1.59	$1	26.5	275	358	207	32%	5.01	-0.2	4.6	8.1	1.7	1.4	1.17	70%	42	91
AGE 30 Peak	00	LA	18	10	0	226	217	3.27	1.31	$26	28.1	213	229	199	27%	3.29	71.5	4.9	8.6	1.8	0.8	1.22	78%	76	167
TYPE Power	01	LA	15	11	0	234	218	3.50	1.17	$23	26.6	217	230	204	27%	3.03	58.5	3.5	8.4	2.4	0.9	1.00	73%	86	159
R Moderate	02	TEX	9	9	0	148	124	6.32	1.66	($7)	26.1	283	287	254	33%	5.52 +	-17.1	4.9	7.5	1.5	1.2	1.10	63%	39	80
I CON	03	TEX	* 3	3	0	58	29	7.72	2.21	($11)	24.9	351	367	235	37%	8.47 -	-17.1	6.2	4.5	0.7	1.7	0.97	67%	-24	-52
S pt	1st Half		3	3	0	58	29	7.72	2.21	($11)	24.9	351			37%	8.47 -	-17.1	6.2	4.5	0.7	1.7	0.97	67%	-24	-52
K	2nd Half		0	0	0	0	0	0.00	0.00																
LIMA D EP: 55%	04	Proj	5	8	0	120	99	5.48	1.64	($5)	26.1	281			32%	5.46	1.0	4.9	7.4	1.5	1.3	--	69%	37	80

That makes two lost seasons, this one due to a bad back. Quite honestly, I have no clue what he is capable of doing now, and whether or not he will be healthy. If anyone else tells you otherwise, they're lying.

Parrish,John

		Tm	W	L	Sv	IP	K	ERA	Br/IP	R$	BF/G	OBA	vL	vR	H%	xERA	RAR	Ctl	Dom	Cmd	hr/9	G/F	S%	BPV	BPX
LH Reliever	99	aa	0	2	0	55	35	4.91	1.78	($4)	21.6	262			29%	4.92	4.6	7.0	5.7	0.8	0.8		73%	30	68
AGE 26 Growth	00	BAL	* 10	11	0	156	120	5.42	1.61	$2	24.4	257	182	297	30%	4.76 +	10.3	5.7	6.9	1.2	1.0	1.18	67%	39	103
TYPE Power	01	BAL	* 8	9	0	155	133	4.76	1.47	$2	16.2	266			32%	4.58	15.0	4.1	7.7	1.9	1.0	1.21	70%	57	114
R X HIGH	02		0	0	0	0	0	0.00	0.00																
I EXP CON	03	BAL	* 3	4	6	99	82	2.81	1.42	$9	6.8	253	194	212	30%	4.18 -	36.1	4.2	7.4	1.8	0.9	1.35	84%	59	128
S pt stb	1st Half		1	1	5	50	48	2.15	1.33	$7	6.7	245			31%	3.67 -	22.7	3.8	8.6	2.3	0.7		87%	84	182
K BRN	2nd Half		2	3	1	49	34	3.48	1.51	$2	7.0	261			29%	4.70 -	13.4	4.6	6.2	1.4	1.1		81%	36	77
LIMA B EP: 30%	04	Proj	2	3	0	60	48	3.90	1.43	$2	10.0	259			30%	4.28	13.2	4.1	7.2	1.8	0.9	--	75%	57	122

0-1, 1.96 ERA in 23 IP at BAL. An 84% strand rate artificially helped his ERA, but his control is not good enough to keep up that illusion. Add another run to that ERA in 2004.

Patterson,Danny

		Tm	W	L	Sv	IP	K	ERA	Br/IP	R$	BF/G	OBA	vL	vR	H%	xERA	RAR	Ctl	Dom	Cmd	hr/9	G/F	S%	BPV	BPX
RH Reliever	99	TEX	2	0	0	60	43	5.70	1.60	($2)	5.1	313	353	280	36%	5.34	1.4	2.9	6.5	2.3	0.8	1.86	64%	56	141
AGE 33 Past	00	DET	5	1	0	56	29	4.00	1.48	$5	4.3	303	292	323	33%	4.76 -	14.4	2.2	4.6	2.1	0.6	3.05	73%	46	121
TYPE Finesse	01	DET	5	4	1	64	27	3.08	1.18	$9	4.4	261	327	231	28%	3.38	20.6	1.7	3.8	2.3	0.6	3.28	75%	56	112
R Low	02	DET	* 0	2	0	8	3	5.63	1.25	($0)	3.0	237			26%	2.75 +	-0.2	3.4	3.4	1.0	0.0	2.00	50%	49	100
I con	03	DET	* 1	0	3	28	24	3.83	1.17	$4	4.0	232	176	281	29%	2.72 +	6.4	2.9	7.7	2.7	0.3	2.10	66%	101	218
S pt	1st Half		0	0	0	4	2	2.25	1.75	($0)	4.7	307			35%	4.97 -	1.8	4.5	4.5	1.0	0.0		86%	42	90
K	2nd Half		1	0	3	24	22	4.09	1.07	$4	3.9	218			28%	2.34 +	4.6	2.6	8.2	3.1	0.4		60%	115	249
LIMA B EP: 60%	04	Proj	4	1	2	60	39	4.05	1.32	$6	4.3	271			31%	3.89	12.0	2.4	5.9	2.4	0.6	G	69%	69	148

3 Sv, 4.24 ERA in 17 IP at DET, but aside from one bad outing vs CHW (0.1 IP, 4 ER), his ERA would have been 2.08. Good signs of skill here, but at 33, you have to wonder how much opportunity he's going to get.

Patterson,John

		Tm	W	L	Sv	IP	K	ERA	Br/IP	R$	BF/G	OBA	vL	vR	H%	xERA	RAR	Ctl	Dom	Cmd	hr/9	G/F	S%	BPV	BPX
RH Starter	99	a/a	9	11	0	131	131	5.22	1.43	$5	22.8	273			34%	4.42 +	5.4	3.3	9.0	2.7	1.1		65%	79	182
AGE 26 Growth	00	aaa	0	2	0	15	9	8.40	2.13	($4)	25.3	342			38%	7.58 +	-5.3	6.0	5.4	0.9	1.2		60%	2	4
TYPE	01	a/a	3	9	0	93	51	6.00	1.73	($8)	24.0	319			35%	6.08	-7.2	3.7	4.9	1.3	1.1		66%	17	33
R X HIGH	02	ARI	* 12	5	0	142	118	4.44	1.43	$7	23.8	279	236	233	32%	4.83	12.7	3.0	7.5	2.5	1.3	0.49	73%	56	105
I EXP CON	03	ARI	* 11	9	1	164	107	4.11	1.50	$7	21.3	274	281	281	31%	4.50	25.6	3.9	5.9	1.5	0.8	0.71	74%	44	85
S PT STB	1st Half		6	5	0	78	47	4.36	1.54	$2	25.0	282			31%	5.09 -	9.6	3.9	5.4	1.4	1.1	0.86	75%	25	49
K	2nd Half		5	4	1	86	60	3.89	1.46	$4	18.8	267			32%	3.96	16.0	3.9	6.3	1.6	0.4	0.55	73%	61	117
LIMA C+ EP: 50%	04	Proj	8	7	0	120	86	4.58	1.51	$3	22.1	282			32%	4.79	11.1	3.6	6.5	1.8	1.0	F	71%	46	88

1-4, 6.05 ERA in 55 IP at ARI. Gave back the gains he made in 2002, and now it's questionable when, or if, he will take that next step up. BPIs are all over the board, as has been his health, so it's a tough call.

Pavano,Carl

		Tm	W	L	Sv	IP	K	ERA	Br/IP	R$	BF/G	OBA	vL	vR	H%	xERA	RAR	Ctl	Dom	Cmd	hr/9	G/F	S%	BPV	BPX
RH Starter	99	MON	6	8	0	104	70	5.63	1.46	$0	24.0	285	290	279	33%	4.15 +	-5.4	3.0	6.1	2.0	0.7	1.74	60%	56	121
AGE 28 Pre-Peak	00	MON	8	4	0	97	64	3.06	1.27	$13	27.1	245	312	188	28%	3.52	33.3	3.2	5.9	1.9	0.7	1.58	78%	59	130
TYPE Finesse	01	MON	* 3	7	0	69	52	5.74	1.62	($4)	26.1	319	384	295	36%	6.25 -	-3.4	2.7	6.8	2.5	1.6	1.26	68%	37	69
R High	02	2NL	* 9	10	0	156	100	5.02	1.60	($2)	17.6	315	357	276	35%	5.59 -	1.8	2.7	5.8	2.1	1.1	1.49	70%	38	73
I con	03	FLA	12	13	0	201	133	4.30	1.26	$12	25.5	265	267	263	30%	3.84	26.4	2.2	6.0	2.7	0.9	0.92	67%	69	133
S PT stb	1st Half		6	9	0	104	69	4.75	1.21	$6	23.9	272			30%	4.08 +	7.4	1.4	6.0	4.3	1.1	0.93	63%	93	179
K	2nd Half		6	4	0	97	64	3.81	1.31	$7	27.3	256			30%	3.58	19.0	3.1	6.0	1.9	0.6	0.91	71%	63	122
LIMA C+ EP: 55%	04	Proj	15	10	0	200	134	3.96	1.28	$16	25.4	267			30%	3.96	34.9	2.3	6.0	2.7	0.9	--	71%	66	127

Strand rates played games with his ERA a bit, but overall it was a good growth season. Big gains in BA vs LHers and Ctl, leaving him poised to take another step up in 2004.

Peavy,Jake

		Tm	W	L	Sv	IP	K	ERA	Br/IP	R$	BF/G	OBA	vL	vR	H%	xERA	RAR	Ctl	Dom	Cmd	hr/9	G/F	S%	BPV	BPX
RH Starter	99		0	0	0	0	0	0.00	0.00																
AGE 22 Growth	00		0	0	0	0	0	0.00	0.00																
TYPE Power	01	aa	2	1	0	28	37	3.21	1.18	$3	23.0	210			30%	3.01	8.3	3.9	11.9	3.1	1.0		77%	120	231
R Very High	02	SD	* 10	12	0	177	165	4.02	1.37	$8	24.5	264	321	225	33%	3.93	25.8	3.3	8.4	2.6	0.8	1.26	72%	84	158
I EXP con	03	SD	12	11	0	194	156	4.12	1.31	$12	25.7	240	246	230	26%	4.27	30.0	3.8	7.2	1.9	1.5	0.88	75%	44	85
S pt	1st Half		8	5	0	107	82	3.86	1.31	$9	26.6	243			27%	4.04	20.3	3.6	6.9	1.9	1.3	0.99	75%	50	96
K AGE brn	2nd Half		4	6	0	87	74	4.45	1.32	$3	24.6	237			25%	4.55	9.7	4.0	7.7	1.9	1.9	0.75	74%	38	72
LIMA D+ EP: 45%	04	Proj	10	11	0	180	145	4.65	1.42	$4	25.2	261			30%	4.52	14.8	3.9	7.3	1.9	1.3	--	71%	48	93

A young pitcher's dominance trend is the first place to look to see if he's pitched too many innings. This trend here is not encouraging, but feeding 200 IP to a 22-year-old is just asking for trouble.

Penny,Brad

		Tm	W	L	Sv	IP	K	ERA	Br/IP	R$	BF/G	OBA	vL	vR	H%	xERA	RAR	Ctl	Dom	Cmd	hr/9	G/F	S%	BPV	BPX
RH Starter	99	aa	3	7	0	122	112	4.94	1.48	($0)	23.3	298			37%	4.63	9.6	2.5	8.3	3.3	0.8		67%	90	208
AGE 25 Growth	00	FLA	* 10	7	0	134	94	4.49	1.48	$8	22.7	253	249	274	29%	4.32	20.4	4.7	6.3	1.3	0.9	1.27	71%	42	93
TYPE	01	FLA	10	10	0	205	154	3.69	1.16	$17	27.0	240	236	244	28%	3.09 +	46.1	2.4	6.8	2.9	0.7	1.50	69%	88	162
R Very High	02	FLA	8	7	0	129	93	4.67	1.53	$1	23.9	289	294	284	32%	5.18 -	7.5	3.5	6.5	1.9	1.3	1.31	73%	37	71
I exp CON	03	FLA	14	10	0	196	138	4.13	1.28	$14	25.7	261	269	258	30%	3.94	30.1	2.6	6.3	2.5	1.0	1.13	70%	64	123
S PT	1st Half		6	6	0	101	75	4.80	1.46	$2	26.1	284			33%	4.65	6.5	3.1	6.7	2.1	0.9	1.28	68%	57	109
K brn	2nd Half		8	4	0	95	63	3.41	1.09	$13	25.3	235			26%	3.18	23.7	2.0	6.0	3.0	1.0	1.00	73%	76	146
LIMA C+ EP: 50%	04	Proj	15	9	0	200	144	3.74	1.24	$19	24.4	254			29%	3.68	41.0	2.5	6.5	2.6	0.9	--	73%	70	135

BPIs bounced back, and after an excellent 2nd half, may be starting to mature as a pitcher. His big test now is being able to string two of these seasons together. I think he can.

Percival,Troy

	Yr	Tm	W	L	Sv	IP	K	ERA	Br/IP	R$	BF/G	OBA	vL	vR	H%	xERA	RAR	Ctl	Dom	Cmd	hr/9	G/F	S%	BPV	BPX
RH Reliever	99	ANA	4	6	31	57	58	3.79	1.05	$26	3.8	191	214	152	22%	2.92 +	15.9	3.5	9.2	2.6	1.4	0.55	71%	84	212
AGE 34 Decline	00	ANA	5	5	32	50	49	4.50	1.44	$23	4.0	230	237	220	28%	4.17	9.5	5.4	8.8	1.6	1.3	0.65	72%	59	152
TYPE Power	01	ANA	4	2	39	57	71	2.67	1.00	$31	3.9	195	176	202	29%	1.91 +	21.5	2.8	11.2	3.9	0.5	0.81	74%	152	304
R Low	02	ANA	4	1	40	56	68	1.93	1.13	$32	3.9	194	247	138	27%	2.59 -	26.5	4.0	10.9	2.7	0.8	0.53	88%	115	235
I CON	03	ANA	0	5	33	49	48	3.48	1.14	$23	3.8	192	165	205	22%	3.06	13.4	4.2	8.8	2.1	1.3	0.33	76%	75	161
S	1st Half		0	2	16	24	24	3.00	0.88	$12	3.6	161			19%	1.90 +	8.1	3.0	9.0	3.0	1.1	0.37	72%	106	229
K age	2nd Half		0	3	17	25	24	3.94	1.39	$10	4.0	220			25%	4.18	5.3	5.4	8.6	1.6	1.4	0.30	77%	53	115
LIMA D+ EP: 40%	04	Proj	2	4	34	50	49	3.60	1.20	$24	4.0	203			25%	3.14	13.0	4.3	8.8	2.0	1.1	F	74%	78	167

With the fall of Hoffman and Nen, now owns the longest current streak of 25-save seasons with 8. This year, the third sub-100 BPV level of that streak, perhaps due to his hip condition.

Perez,Odalis

	Yr	Tm	W	L	Sv	IP	K	ERA	Br/IP	R$	BF/G	OBA	vL	vR	H%	xERA	RAR	Ctl	Dom	Cmd	hr/9	G/F	S%	BPV	BPX
LH Starter	99	ATL	4	6	0	93	82	6.00	1.65	($5)	23.6	276			33%	4.90 +	-9.5	5.1	7.9	1.5	1.2	2.14	65%	45	98
AGE 26 Growth	00	ATL	0	0	0	0	0	0.00	0.00																
TYPE	01	ATL *	8	8	0	118	90	4.65	1.49	$3	18.0	289	342	278	34%	4.56	11.3	3.1	6.9	2.2	0.6	1.60	68%	66	123
R Moderate	02	LA	15	10	0	222	155	3.00	0.99	$30	27.1	225	223	226	25%	2.56	62.6	1.5	6.3	4.1	0.9	1.36	73%	108	204
I CON	03	LA	12	12	0	185	141	4.52	1.28	$11	25.9	268	201	284	30%	4.41	18.8	2.2	6.9	3.1	1.4	1.80	69%	66	127
S pt	1st Half		4	7	0	101	79	4.45	1.32	$3	26.8	273			31%	4.46	11.2	2.3	7.0	3.0	1.2	2.01	70%	69	133
K brn	2nd Half		8	5	0	84	62	4.61	1.24	$8	24.9	262			29%	4.35	7.6	2.1	6.6	3.1	1.5	1.58	68%	63	120
LIMA B EP: 60%	04	Proj	14	11	0	200	154	3.87	1.18	$19	23.4	251			29%	3.58	37.3	2.1	6.9	3.3	1.0	G	70%	84	162

A deceptive year, because it was just 4 bad starts out of 29:
5/29 @ COL: 3 IP, 9 ER
7/20 vs STL: 3.2 IP, 7 ER
7/31 @ PHI: 4.1 IP, 6 ER
8/26 @ HOU: 4.2 IP, 10 ER
Without them, his ERA was 3.24.

Perez,Oliver

	Yr	Tm	W	L	Sv	IP	K	ERA	Br/IP	R$	BF/G	OBA	vL	vR	H%	xERA	RAR	Ctl	Dom	Cmd	hr/9	G/F	S%	BPV	BPX
LH Starter	99		0	0	0	0	0	0.00	0.00																
AGE 22 Growth	00		0	0	0	0	0	0.00	0.00																
TYPE Power	01		0	0	0	0	0	0.00	0.00																
R High	02	SD *	5	5	0	113	123	3.11	1.30	$8	23.8	207	294	191	26%	3.33	30.3	5.1	9.8	1.9	1.1	0.80	81%	79	150
I EXP	03	2NL *	7	13	0	173	183	4.83	1.51	($1)	24.0	262	292	258	32%	4.91	10.5	4.5	9.5	2.1	1.4	0.73	72%	62	119
S pt	1st Half		5	6	0	91	84	4.53	1.54	$1	24.0	265			31%	5.03 -	9.2	4.7	8.3	1.8	1.4	0.73	75%	47	90
K AGE brn	2nd Half		2	7	0	82	99	5.16	1.46	($2)	24.0	259			34%	4.77	1.3	4.3	10.9	2.5	1.4	0.73	68%	79	152
LIMA B EP: 55%	04	Proj	10	11	0	180	196	4.20	1.39	$7	23.5	241			30%	4.20	25.6	4.5	9.8	2.2	1.3	F	74%	73	141

4-10, 5.50 ERA in 126 IP at SD and PIT. There was very little middle ground in '03. Either his starts were dominating (44%) or disasters (36%). That's good news. The skill is already there; consistency can be trained.

Pettitte,Andy

	Yr	Tm	W	L	Sv	IP	K	ERA	Br/IP	R$	BF/G	OBA	vL	vR	H%	xERA	RAR	Ctl	Dom	Cmd	hr/9	G/F	S%	BPV	BPX
LH Starter	99	NYY	14	11	0	191	121	4.71	1.60	$8	27.8	286	275	293	32%	5.11	29.7	4.2	5.7	1.4	0.9	2.08	72%	32	81
AGE 31 Peak	00	NYY	19	9	0	204	125	4.36	1.46	$18	28.0	276	256	275	31%	4.40	42.3	3.5	5.5	1.6	0.7	1.70	71%	43	112
TYPE	01	NYY	15	10	0	200	164	4.00	1.32	$15	27.4	284	251	289	34%	4.08	39.8	1.8	7.4	4.0	0.6	1.50	70%	108	215
R Low	02	NYY *	13	5	0	140	100	3.21	1.28	$17	25.6	271	255	276	32%	3.61	42.1	2.1	6.4	3.1	0.4	1.34	75%	93	192
I con	03	NYY	21	8	0	208	180	4.02	1.33	$21	26.8	279	321	254	34%	4.31	41.9	2.2	7.8	3.6	0.9	1.57	72%	94	204
S pt	1st Half		9	6	0	101	86	4.80	1.43	$5	25.9	293			35%	4.92	9.8	2.4	7.6	3.2	1.1	1.31	68%	77	167
K brn	2nd Half		12	2	0	107	94	3.28	1.23	$16	27.8	266			33%	3.74	32.1	1.9	7.9	4.1	0.8	1.88	76%	112	243
LIMA C EP: 60%	04	Proj	17	9	0	200	159	3.83	1.33	$18	26.6	277			33%	4.11	45.9	2.3	7.2	3.2	0.7	G	72%	88	188

236 LHed batters faced him in '03, and batted .321, about 65 points higher than the past 3 years. That's the only apparent kink in the armor, though it could be symptomatic of future kinks. For now, ride it out.

Phelps,Tommy

	Yr	Tm	W	L	Sv	IP	K	ERA	Br/IP	R$	BF/G	OBA	vL	vR	H%	xERA	RAR	Ctl	Dom	Cmd	hr/9	G/F	S%	BPV	BPX
LH Reliever	99	aa	3	6	0	64	29	7.31	1.84	($7)	23.5	335			34%	7.29	-15.3	3.8	4.1	1.1	2.0		63%	-24	-56
AGE 30 Peak	00	aa	6	6	0	102	46	6.53	1.64	($3)	12.2	329			34%	6.40	-10.5	2.3	4.1	1.8	1.5		62%	6	14
TYPE	01	a/a	4	3	3	92	63	4.79	1.80	($3)	9.9	347			40%	6.18 -	7.7	2.7	6.2	2.3	0.5		73%	55	106
R Very High	02	aaa	4	2	2	74	51	3.28	1.39	$6	6.3	285			33%	4.33 -	19.7	2.4	6.2	2.6	0.7		78%	67	131
I EXP con	03	FLA	3	2	0	63	43	4.00	1.48	$2	10.3	283	233	298	33%	4.24	10.8	3.3	6.1	1.9	0.4	0.82	72%	62	119
S pt STB	1st Half		3	2	0	52	39	3.97	1.48	$2	11.5	283			34%	4.17	9.1	3.3	6.7	2.1	0.3	0.87	72%	72	138
K	2nd Half		0	0	0	11	4	4.13	1.47	($0)	6.8	281			29%	4.59	1.7	3.3	3.3	1.0	0.8	0.65	73%	15	29
LIMA B EP: 50%	04	Proj	3	3	0	60	40	4.20	1.45	$2	7.1	284			32%	4.46	8.5	3.0	6.0	2.0	0.8	--	72%	54	104

First it was 7 starts -- 3 DOM and 4 DIS (5.67 ERA, 3.0 Cmd), followed by 30 IP of bullpen work (2.12 ERA, 1.3 Cmd), followed by elbow tendinitis. There's promise but problems: What role do you give to a 30-year-old?

Pineiro,Joel

	Yr	Tm	W	L	Sv	IP	K	ERA	Br/IP	R$	BF/G	OBA	vL	vR	H%	xERA	RAR	Ctl	Dom	Cmd	hr/9	G/F	S%	BPV	BPX
RH Starter	99	aa	10	15	0	166	103	6.23	1.69	($6)	27.3	325			36%	6.04	-15.7	3.0	5.6	1.8	1.2		64%	25	57
AGE 25 Growth	00	SEA *	10	2	0	132	86	4.64	1.42	$10	21.2	270	357	294	31%	4.29	22.5	3.4	5.9	1.7	0.8	1.03	68%	48	124
TYPE	01	SEA *	12	5	0	152	114	3.08	1.18	$19	17.8	226	230	150	27%	2.92	49.0	3.3	6.8	2.1	0.6	1.00	75%	76	152
R Moderate	02	SEA	14	7	0	194	136	3.25	1.25	$20	21.9	257	270	240	29%	4.03 -	57.5	2.5	6.3	2.5	1.1	1.28	79%	61	125
I exp con	03	SEA	16	11	0	211	151	3.79	1.27	$19	27.6	244	234	251	28%	3.59	49.0	3.2	6.4	2.0	0.8	1.11	72%	62	135
S pt	1st Half		8	5	0	108	76	3.67	1.24	$11	28.1	234			27%	3.18	26.9	3.4	6.3	1.9	0.6	1.29	71%	68	146
K brn	2nd Half		8	6	0	103	75	3.92	1.30	$9	27.2	254			29%	4.02	22.1	3.1	6.5	2.1	1.0	0.94	73%	57	123
LIMA D+ EP: 50%	04	Proj	15	9	0	200	143	3.65	1.26	$20	23.9	246			28%	3.67	50.7	3.0	6.4	2.1	0.9	--	74%	62	133

Control took a slight step back, but it wasn't enough to set him off course. Good, not great, skills, but enough to bank on.

Plesac,Dan

	Yr	Tm	W	L	Sv	IP	K	ERA	Br/IP	R$	BF/G	OBA	vL	vR	H%	xERA	RAR	Ctl	Dom	Cmd	hr/9	G/F	S%	BPV	BPX
LH Reliever	99	2TM	2	4	1	44	53	5.93	1.52	($0)	3.1	287	192	364	38%	5.15 +	-2.4	3.5	10.8	3.1	1.4	0.84	63%	85	197
AGE 42 Decline	00	ARI	5	1	0	40	45	3.15	1.50	$6	2.9	232	260	194	31%	4.03 -	13.3	5.9	10.1	1.7	0.9	1.05	82%	79	174
TYPE Power	01	TOR	4	5	1	45	68	3.59	1.29	$5	3.1	211	184	234	34%	3.12	11.4	4.8	13.6	2.8	0.8	0.87	74%	130	260
R High	02	2TM	3	3	1	36	41	4.25	1.25	$4	2.5	210	120	300	26%	3.67 +	4.9	4.5	10.3	2.3	1.5	0.72	72%	77	152
I CON	03	PHI	2	1	2	33	37	2.72	1.21	$5	2.4	237	224	235	32%	3.27 -	11.3	3.0	10.1	3.4	0.8	0.63	81%	114	220
S STB	1st Half		1	0	0	14	16	2.54	1.34	$2	2.4	259			33%	4.31 -	5.2	3.2	10.1	3.2	1.3	0.69	88%	93	179
K AGE	2nd Half		1	1	2	19	21	2.86	1.11	$3	2.3	220			30%	2.48	6.1	2.9	10.0	3.5	0.5	0.59	75%	130	251
LIMA A EP: 50%	04	Proj	3	3	2	35	43	3.60	1.29	$5	2.7	227			31%	3.49	7.8	4.1	11.1	2.7	1.0	F	76%	102	196

There's nothing bad you can say about a 100+ BPV at age 42. The beauty of this is, you know that he will likely go undrafted, and that makes him the perfect reserve player. If he doesn't retire, of course.

Politte,Cliff

	Yr	Tm	W	L	Sv	IP	K	ERA	Br/IP	R$	BF/G	OBA	vL	vR	H%	xERA	RAR	Ctl	Dom	Cmd	hr/9	G/F	S%	BPV	BPX
RH Reliever	99	aa	9	8	5	109	82	4.62	1.57	$8	13.2	305			35%	5.40 -	13.2	3.0	6.8	2.3	1.2	1.16	74%	45	105
AGE 30 Peak	00	PHI *	12	7	0	171	146	3.68	1.36	$16	22.2	250	224	263	30%	3.87	44.7	3.7	7.7	2.1	0.8	1.06	75%	69	152
TYPE Power	01	PHI	2	3	0	26	23	2.42	1.23	$4	4.7	247	231	257	30%	3.38 -	10.2	2.8	8.0	2.9	0.7	1.70	83%	93	173
R Very High	02	2TM	3	3	1	73	72	3.70	1.16	$6	4.4	217	272	159	28%	2.72 +	15.4	3.5	8.9	2.6	0.6	0.87	69%	100	197
I exp CON	03	TOR	1	5	12	49	40	5.68	1.41	$6	3.9	273	287	250	29%	5.46	-1.0	3.1	7.3	2.4	2.0	0.66	66%	33	72
S PT STB	1st Half		1	5	11	33	28	6.51	1.60	$4	4.2	310			32%	7.39 -	-4.4	3.0	7.6	2.5	3.0	0.54	69%	3	6
K	2nd Half		0	0	1	16	12	3.96	1.01	$2	3.5	182			23%	1.42 +	3.3	3.4	6.8	2.0	0.0	0.94	56%	101	219
LIMA B EP: 55%	04	Proj	2	3	6	60	51	3.90	1.27	$7	4.9	242			28%	3.77	13.2	3.3	7.7	2.3	1.1	F	72%	70	149

There is evidence of Talent, he was given the Opportunity, but could not nail down the closer's role? Lack of Guile? He's converted only 25% and 67% of his save opps the past two years. Ya gotta wonder.

Ponson,Sidney

	Yr	Tm	W	L	Sv	IP	K	ERA	Br/IP	R$	BF/G	OBA	vL	vR	H%	xERA	RAR	Ctl	Dom	Cmd	hr/9	G/F	S%	BPV	BPX
RH Starter	99	BAL	12	12	0	210	112	4.71	1.46	$10	28.8	277	287	277	29%	5.17	32.6	3.4	4.8	1.4	1.5	1.03	72%	13	32
AGE 27 Pre-Peak	00	BAL	9	13	0	222	152	4.82	1.38	$10	29.8	263	259	258	29%	4.44	32.3	3.4	6.2	1.8	1.2	1.13	68%	41	108
TYPE	01	BAL	5	10	0	138	84	4.95	1.43	$0	26.1	292	321	258	31%	5.20	9.8	2.4	5.5	2.3	1.4	1.28	69%	36	72
R High	02	BAL	7	9	0	176	120	4.09	1.34	$7	26.7	257	243	273	28%	4.45	32.2	3.2	6.1	1.9	1.3	1.48	74%	40	83
I con	03	2TM	17	12	0	216	134	3.75	1.26	$21	29.1	257	271	243	29%	3.59	47.5	2.5	5.6	2.2	0.7	1.59	71%	63	128
S pt	1st Half		10	5	0	109	79	3.96	1.33	$10	29.0	265			31%	3.79	20.9	2.8	6.5	2.3	0.6	1.27	70%	73	147
K BRN	2nd Half		7	7	0	107	55	3.53	1.19	$11	29.3	249			27%	3.39	26.7	2.3	4.6	2.0	0.8	1.99	72%	53	108
LIMA D EP: 50%	04	Proj	15	9	0	200	134	3.65	1.25	$19	27.8	254			29%	3.64	46.9	2.6	6.0	2.3	0.8	G	73%	65	131

Since '00, a perfect correlation: the harder he throws, the more batters he walks. But there are good signs in '03, most notably an increased G/F ratio leading to fewer HRs. Could return $20 again in 2004.

Powell,Jay

RH Reliever | AGE 32 Peak | TYPE Power | R Moderate | I con | S pt stb | K | LIMA D | EP: 70%

Yr	Tm	W	L	Sv	IP	K	ERA	Br/IP	R$	BF/G	OBA	vL	vR	H%	xERA	RAR	Ctl	Dom	Cmd	hr/9	G/F	S%	BPV	BPX
99	HOU	5	4	4	75	77	4.32	1.63	$4	5.1	279	304	265	37%	4.14	9.2	4.8	9.2	1.9	0.4	1.54	72%	84	183
00	HOU	1	1	0	27	16	5.67	1.78	($2)	4.4	276	233	297	32%	4.84 +	-0.1	6.3	5.3	0.8	0.3	1.23	66%	40	87
01	2NL	5	3	7	75	54	3.24	1.41	$10	4.4	262	296	233	30%	4.42 -	21.4	3.7	6.5	1.7	1.1	2.50	81%	46	85
02	TEX *	5	2	0	59	41	5.34	1.68	($1)	4.4	296	222	270	33%	5.77	0.9	4.4	6.3	1.4	1.2	2.07	70%	26	54
03	TEX	3	0	0	58	40	7.89	1.87	($8)	5.5	314	255	362	35%	6.38 +	-18.4	5.3	6.2	1.2	1.1	1.40	57%	22	47
1st Half		1	0	0	29	20	10.48	2.36	($9)	6.4	368			41%	8.70 +	-19.4	6.5	6.2	1.0	1.2	1.68	54%	1	3
2nd Half		2	0	0	29	20	5.28	1.38	$1	4.6	248			28%	4.05 +	1.0	4.0	6.2	1.5	0.9	1.17	62%	47	101
04	Proj	2	2	0	50	36	5.22	1.68	($2)	4.9	291			33%	5.55	2.1	4.7	6.5	1.4	1.1	--	71%	32	69

A lot of bad karma, but he didn't help himself much by walking 6.5 batters per 9 IP in the 1st half. At normal hit/strand rate levels, this is a 4.81 season, which won't win any awards but at least is back on the planet.

Prior,Mark

RH Starter | AGE 23 Growth | TYPE Power | R Moderate | I EXP | S pt | K age brn | LIMA C | EP: 50%

Yr	Tm	W	L	Sv	IP	K	ERA	Br/IP	R$	BF/G	OBA	vL	vR	H%	xERA	RAR	Ctl	Dom	Cmd	hr/9	G/F	S%	BPV	BPX
99		0	0	0	0	0	0.00	0.00																
00		0	0	0	0	0	0.00	0.00																
01		0	0	0	0	0	0.00	0.00																
02	CHC *	11	8	0	167	217	3.07	1.17	$18	24.4	229	204	242	33%	2.96	45.5	3.0	11.7	3.9	0.8	0.81	77%	138	261
03	CHC	18	6	0	211	245	2.43	1.10	$33	27.4	235	240	223	32%	2.81	80.5	2.1	10.4	4.9	0.6	0.93	81%	154	297
1st Half		8	3	0	110	127	2.62	1.11	$16	27.7	236			32%	2.85	39.3	2.1	10.4	4.9	0.7	1.16	79%	153	294
2nd Half		10	3	0	101	118	2.23	1.10	$18	27.1	234			32%	2.77 -	41.3	2.1	10.5	4.9	0.6	0.73	83%	156	300
04	Proj	21	7	0	225	274	2.96	1.13	$33	26.0	232			33%	2.88	69.4	2.5	11.0	4.4	0.7	--	76%	146	281

A slightly elevated strand rate will push his ERA up a few points, and maybe he could be better served by more of a ground ball tendency... but so what? 2004 will become his first of many 20-win seasons.

Quantrill,Paul

RH Reliever | AGE 35 Decline | TYPE Finesse | R Moderate | I con | S pt | K age | LIMA B | EP: 40%

Yr	Tm	W	L	Sv	IP	K	ERA	Br/IP	R$	BF/G	OBA	vL	vR	H%	xERA	RAR	Ctl	Dom	Cmd	hr/9	G/F	S%	BPV	BPX
99	TOR	3	2	0	48	28	3.38	1.46	$4	5.1	281	261	294	31%	4.69 -	16.1	3.2	5.3	1.6	0.9	2.15	80%	37	92
00	TOR	2	5	1	83	47	4.54	1.50	$2	5.4	299	299	296	33%	4.86	15.2	2.7	5.1	1.9	0.8	1.70	70%	42	110
01	TOR	11	2	2	83	58	3.04	1.18	$16	4.3	269	355	232	31%	3.53 -	27.2	1.3	6.3	4.8	0.7	2.06	76%	121	242
02	LA	5	4	1	76	53	2.72	1.38	$7	3.8	272	254	275	33%	3.48 -	24.3	3.0	6.3	2.1	0.1	2.25	79%	79	150
03	LA	2	5	1	77	44	1.75	0.99	$12	3.4	219	198	243	25%	1.98	36.4	1.8	5.1	2.9	0.2	1.65	82%	97	186
1st Half		1	2	0	34	20	1.58	0.94	$6	3.4	219			25%	1.89	16.9	1.3	5.3	4.0	0.3	1.73	84%	119	229
2nd Half		1	3	1	43	24	1.88	1.02	$7	3.4	219			25%	2.05	19.5	2.1	5.0	2.4	0.2	1.59	81%	85	164
04	Proj	4	4	1	75	47	3.00	1.24	$8	3.8	262			30%	3.26	22.7	2.2	5.6	2.6	0.4	G	76%	81	155

Reasons why he'll have a 3.00 ERA in 2004...
- 25% hit rate
- 82% strand rate
- Declining strikeout rate
- 35 years old
- Lightning only strikes once

Quevedo,Ruben

RH Starter | AGE 25 Growth | TYPE Power | R X HIGH | I EXP CON | S pt stb | K age brn | LIMA D | EP: 40%

Yr	Tm	W	L	Sv	IP	K	ERA	Br/IP	R$	BF/G	OBA	vL	vR	H%	xERA	RAR	Ctl	Dom	Cmd	hr/9	G/F	S%	BPV	BPX
99	aaa	9	6	0	150	147	4.92	1.27	$9	22.4	253			30%	3.99 +	12.3	2.8	8.8	3.1	1.4		65%	82	189
00	CHC *	10	12	0	162	131	6.16	1.56	($2)	21.4	270	245	289	30%	5.28 +	-11.5	4.7	7.3	1.6	1.5	0.71	63%	32	72
01	MIL *	13	10	0	197	195	3.56	1.32	$16	26.1	250	275	241	31%	3.84	47.6	3.4	8.9	2.6	0.9	0.59	76%	86	159
02	MIL	6	11	0	141	96	5.68	1.62	($7)	23.7	287	271	302	30%	5.88	-10.8	4.4	6.1	1.4	1.8	0.60	70%	10	19
03	MIL *	3	5	0	67	38	5.34	1.66	($3)	22.1	299	297	326	31%	6.19 -	-0.6	4.1	5.1	1.2	1.7	0.62	73%	-1	-1
1st Half		3	5	0	66	38	5.16	1.64	($3)	23.3	297			31%	6.02 -	1.1	4.1	5.2	1.3	1.6	0.63	73%	4	8
2nd Half		0	0	0	1	0	16.35	2.72	($1)	6.2	392			24%	16.60	-1.6	8.2	0.0	0.0	8.2	0.33	50%	************	
04	Proj	3	4	0	60	46	4.95	1.50	($0)	24.1	274			30%	5.15	2.5	3.9	6.9	1.8	1.5	F	71%	34	65

1-4, 6.86 ERA in 42 IP at MIL. After such a promising 2001 season, it all went splat. There's lots of speculation as to why, but the fact is, there are very few successful players who look like David Wells.

Radke,Brad

RH Starter | AGE 31 Peak | TYPE Finesse | R Moderate | I con | S pt | K BRN | LIMA B | EP: 60%

Yr	Tm	W	L	Sv	IP	K	ERA	Br/IP	R$	BF/G	OBA	vL	vR	H%	xERA	RAR	Ctl	Dom	Cmd	hr/9	G/F	S%	BPV	BPX
99	MIN	12	14	0	218	121	3.76	1.30	$20	27.9	280	281	278	30%	4.47 -	61.7	1.8	5.0	2.8	1.2	1.35	75%	52	131
00	MIN	12	16	0	226	141	4.46	1.38	$14	28.6	290	297	274	32%	4.71	44.1	2.0	5.6	2.8	1.1	1.34	70%	56	146
01	MIN	15	11	0	226	137	3.94	1.15	$21	27.9	269	271	271	30%	3.77	46.7	1.0	5.5	5.3	1.0	1.11	68%	116	232
02	MIN	9	5	0	118	62	4.73	1.22	$9	23.3	271	247	300	29%	3.98 +	11.5	1.5	4.7	3.1	0.9	1.05	62%	67	137
03	MIN	14	10	0	212	120	4.50	1.27	$14	26.9	288	297	278	31%	4.75	29.2	1.2	5.1	4.3	1.4	0.90	69%	77	167
1st Half		5	7	0	99	52	5.64	1.40	$0	26.8	302			31%	5.47	-1.5	1.6	4.7	2.9	1.5	0.91	63%	37	80
2nd Half		9	3	0	113	68	3.50	1.16	$14	27.1	275			30%	4.11 -	30.6	0.8	5.4	6.8	1.2	0.89	75%	139	301
04	Proj	17	10	0	225	127	3.88	1.21	$22	25.8	276			30%	4.22	50.0	1.2	5.1	4.2	1.2	--	72%	84	181

A finesse pitcher with superb control and a touch of gopheritis. But every time he bears down and gets that Dom rate up a bit, he soars. He's <this close> to a major breakout season.

Ramirez,Erasmo

LH Reliever | AGE 28 Pre-Peak | TYPE Finesse | R High | I EXP con | S pt stb | K | LIMA B | EP: 55%

Yr	Tm	W	L	Sv	IP	K	ERA	Br/IP	R$	BF/G	OBA	vL	vR	H%	xERA	RAR	Ctl	Dom	Cmd	hr/9	G/F	S%	BPV	BPX
99		0	0	0	0	0	0.00	0.00																
00	aa	0	5	1	58	36	8.69	2.09	($13)	7.4	377			42%	8.13 +	-22.8	3.4	5.6	1.6	1.2		58%	10	24
01	aa	4	1	1	50	46	3.96	1.30	$5	6.2	277			34%	4.33	9.8	2.0	8.3	4.2	1.1		73%	105	201
02	a/a	8	3	3	75	40	3.48	1.29	$11	5.4	284			33%	3.52	18.0	1.6	4.8	3.1	0.1		71%	88	173
03	TEX *	6	2	4	87	46	3.51	1.30	$10	6.2	291	250	252	32%	4.07 -	23.5	1.2	4.8	3.8	0.5	1.15	73%	90	195
1st Half		3	1	3	39	23	3.89	1.60	$3	6.3	347			39%	5.90 -	8.6	0.9	5.3	5.8	0.7	0.92	77%	117	253
2nd Half		3	1	1	48	23	3.20	1.05	$7	6.1	238			26%	2.56 +	14.9	1.5	4.3	2.9	0.4	1.21	69%	83	178
04	Proj	6	3	3	80	44	3.60	1.21	$11	5.9	271			30%	3.60	20.8	1.5	5.0	3.4	0.6	--	71%	85	181

3-1, 3.86 ERA in 49 IP at TEX. Though he's a soft- tosser, his BPIs are excellent and trending up. However, as a soft-tosser he'll also be prone to ERA swings like his monthlies in '03: 7.56, 2.35, 2.33, 5.11.

Ramirez,Horacio

LH Starter | AGE 24 Growth | TYPE | R X HIGH | I EXP con | S pt | K age BRN | LIMA D+ | EP: 45%

Yr	Tm	W	L	Sv	IP	K	ERA	Br/IP	R$	BF/G	OBA	vL	vR	H%	xERA	RAR	Ctl	Dom	Cmd	hr/9	G/F	S%	BPV	BPX
99		0	0	0	0	0	0.00	0.00																
00		0	0	0	0	0	0.00	0.00																
01	aa	1	1	0	14	15	7.07	2.00	($2)	23.0	336			42%	7.20	-3.1	5.1	9.6	1.9	1.3		65%	46	89
02	aa	9	5	0	92	54	3.52	1.37	$9	24.7	268			30%	3.82	21.5	3.0	5.3	1.7	0.5		74%	55	108
03	ATL	12	4	0	182	100	4.00	1.39	$10	27.1	261	206	278	28%	4.30	31.1	3.6	4.9	1.4	1.0	1.55	74%	31	59
1st Half		7	2	0	79	48	3.98	1.40	$6	26.3	264			29%	4.36	13.7	3.5	5.5	1.5	1.0	1.55	75%	37	71
2nd Half		5	2	0	103	52	4.02	1.38	$4	27.7	258			27%	4.25	17.4	3.6	4.5	1.3	1.0	1.55	74%	26	50
04	Proj	11	8	0	160	85	4.39	1.47	$6	27.0	275			30%	4.48	18.8	3.6	4.8	1.3	0.8	G	71%	31	60

Got by with marginal skills because of the ATL aura... or something. Don't be surprised if a 4.00 ERA is well beyond reach in 2004.

Randolph,Steve

LH Reliever | AGE 30 Peak | TYPE Power | R X HIGH | I EXP CON | S PT STB | K | LIMA C+ | EP: 40%

Yr	Tm	W	L	Sv	IP	K	ERA	Br/IP	R$	BF/G	OBA	vL	vR	H%	xERA	RAR	Ctl	Dom	Cmd	hr/9	G/F	S%	BPV	BPX
99	a/a	2	9	0	86	52	5.13	1.65	($3)	20.7	277			31%	4.82	4.6	5.1	5.4	1.1	0.8		69%	29	68
00	aaa	0	0	0	13	5	9.69	2.46	($4)	14.0	247			20%	8.46 +	-6.8	13.8	3.5	0.3	2.8		64%	-51	******
01	a/a	7	6	0	96	61	7.03	2.03	($12)	13.2	302			33%	6.79	-20.7	7.3	5.7	0.8	1.3		66%	6	12
02	aaa	15	7	0	163	100	4.14	1.58	$8	26.2	278			31%	4.86 -	24.7	4.4	5.5	1.3	0.9		76%	32	63
03	ARI *	9	1	0	69	55	4.17	1.53	$6	5.4	235	222	229	27%	4.31	10.3	6.0	7.2	1.2	1.0	0.70	76%	45	86
1st Half		4	0	0	35	28	4.08	1.56	$2	5.5	249			29%	4.53	5.7	5.6	7.1	1.3	1.0	0.75	76%	44	85
2nd Half		5	1	0	34	27	4.26	1.51	$4	5.3	221			25%	4.08	4.6	6.4	7.2	1.1	1.1	0.66	74%	46	88
04	Proj	5	5	0	70	55	4.76	1.63	$0	8.6	259			30%	4.82	4.8	5.8	7.1	1.2	1.0	F	73%	40	78

8-1, 4.05 ERA in 60 IP at ARI. Eight wins with these BPIs? In his 8 wins, he had 13 IP, 1.38 ERA and 1.1 Cmd. In his 26 other outings, he had 47 IP, 4.78 ERA and 1.2 Cmd. He may never see 8 wins again.

Redding,Tim

RH Starter | AGE 26 Growth | TYPE | R Very High | I EXP con | S PT | K brn | LIMA B | EP: 50%

Yr	Tm	W	L	Sv	IP	K	ERA	Br/IP	R$	BF/G	OBA	vL	vR	H%	xERA	RAR	Ctl	Dom	Cmd	hr/9	G/F	S%	BPV	BPX
99		0	0	0	0	0	0.00	0.00																
00	aa	2	0	0	26	20	4.50	1.65	$1	23.8	197			22%	4.15	4.4	8.7	6.9	0.8	1.0		75%	43	101
01	HOU *	17	4	0	183	188	4.28	1.27	$17	23.3	240	247	311	30%	3.80	26.7	3.4	9.2	2.7	1.1	0.98	70%	85	158
02	HOU *	6	9	0	111	106	6.00	1.50	($4)	16.9	272	258	290	32%	5.01 +	-13.3	4.0	8.6	2.2	1.5	0.99	62%	54	102
03	HOU	10	14	0	176	116	3.68	1.39	$10	23.0	265	297	229	30%	4.13	37.6	3.3	5.9	1.8	0.8	1.04	75%	51	97
1st Half		4	8	0	90	55	4.00	1.52	$1	23.5	280			32%	4.58 -	15.5	3.8	5.5	1.4	0.7	0.92	75%	41	79
2nd Half		6	6	0	86	61	3.35	1.25	$9	22.4	248			28%	3.66	22.2	2.8	6.4	2.3	0.9	1.19	77%	63	121
04	Proj	14	10	0	180	138	3.80	1.29	$16	23.0	251			29%	3.68	35.3	3.1	6.9	2.2	0.9	--	73%	67	130

Got off to a slow start, but began putting it together in the 2nd half and could be poised to take the next step up in 2004.

Redman,Mark

	Yr	Tm	W	L	Sv	IP	K	ERA	Br/IP	R$	BF/G	OBA	vL	vR	H%	xERA	RAR	Ctl	Dom	Cmd	hr/9	G/F	S%	BPV	BPX
LH Starter	99	aaa	9	9	0	133	100	5.55	1.52	$2	24.6	290			34%	4.57 +	-0.3	3.3	6.8	2.0	0.7	1.29	63%	58	135
AGE 30 Peak	00	MIN	12	9	0	151	117	4.77	1.41	$11	20.4	283	282	281	32%	4.88	23.2	2.7	7.0	2.6	1.3	0.75	70%	56	144
TYPE	01	MIN	* 2	7	0	73	43	5.18	1.55	($2)	21.7	299	333	285	32%	5.47	3.0	3.1	5.3	1.7	1.2	0.93	69%	26	52
R High	02	DET	8	15	0	203	109	4.21	1.29	$9	28.5	269	289	261	30%	3.90	33.9	2.3	4.8	2.1	0.7	1.01	68%	55	113
I exp CON	03	FLA	14	9	0	190	151	3.60	1.23	$19	27.2	243	200	248	29%	3.36	42.8	2.9	7.1	2.5	0.8	0.86	72%	79	151
S pt STB	1st Half		6	3	0	87	64	2.79	1.14	$12	27.2	234			28%	2.61	29.0	2.5	6.6	2.7	0.3	0.82	75%	95	182
K	2nd Half		8	6	0	103	87	4.28	1.30	$8	27.2	250			29%	3.99	13.8	3.2	7.6	2.4	1.1	0.90	70%	66	127
LIMA C EP: 55%	04	Proj	15	10	0	200	150	3.74	1.22	$19	25.1	249			29%	3.49	41.0	2.6	6.8	2.6	0.9	--	72%	75	145

As typical, this LHer enjoyed an early advantage over NLers. Cranked it up in the 2nd half, posting the highest Dom rate in his MLB career... but also the worst Ctl. He needs to take it back a notch and he'll be fine.

Reed,Rick

	Yr	Tm	W	L	Sv	IP	K	ERA	Br/IP	R$	BF/G	OBA	vL	vR	H%	xERA	RAR	Ctl	Dom	Cmd	hr/9	G/F	S%	BPV	BPX
RH Starter	99	NYM	11	5	0	149	104	4.59	1.41	$8	24.8	280	296	269	31%	4.59	12.9	2.8	6.3	2.2	1.4	1.39	72%	42	90
AGE 38 Decline	00	NYM	11	5	0	184	121	4.11	1.23	$16	25.4	270	273	260	29%	4.34	37.5	1.7	5.9	3.6	1.4	1.24	72%	70	155
TYPE Finesse	01	2TM	12	12	0	202	142	4.05	1.20	$16	26.0	270	276	260	30%	4.15	37.1	1.4	6.3	4.6	1.2	1.07	71%	98	188
R High	02	MIN	15	7	0	188	121	3.78	1.16	$21	23.2	266	262	257	28%	4.32 -	42.2	1.2	5.8	4.7	1.5	0.91	75%	88	181
I CON	03	MIN	6	12	0	135	71	5.07	1.36	$2	21.4	289	264	310	30%	5.04	8.3	1.9	4.7	2.4	1.4	0.77	66%	35	75
S pt stb	1st Half		3	8	0	76	38	4.85	1.37	$1	25.1	284			30%	4.65	6.9	2.2	4.5	2.0	1.1	0.87	66%	35	76
K AGE	2nd Half		3	4	0	59	33	5.35	1.36	$1	18.0	296			30%	5.54	1.4	1.5	5.0	3.3	1.8	0.65	66%	40	87
LIMA C+ EP: 50%	04	Proj	5	10	0	120	67	4.88	1.33	$3	22.1	281			29%	4.90	10.7	2.0	5.0	2.5	1.5	F	68%	36	77

Back problems took care of the length and quality of his season, and at 38, has to be considered questionable for making his way back to a draftable level.

Reed,Steve

	Yr	Tm	W	L	Sv	IP	K	ERA	Br/IP	R$	BF/G	OBA	vL	vR	H%	xERA	RAR	Ctl	Dom	Cmd	hr/9	G/F	S%	BPV	BPX
RH Reliever	99	CLE	3	2	0	61	44	4.28	1.46	$3	4.2	286	267	295	32%	5.26 -	13.0	3.0	6.5	2.2	1.5	1.33	76%	39	97
AGE 38 Decline	00	CLE	2	0	0	56	39	4.34	1.41	$3	4.3	269	271	268	30%	4.52	11.8	3.4	6.3	1.9	1.1	1.61	72%	44	115
TYPE	01	2TM	3	3	1	58	46	3.56	1.29	$5	3.5	241	514	148	28%	3.69	14.5	3.6	7.1	2.0	0.9	0.87	75%	64	122
R High	02	2NL	2	5	1	67	50	2.01	1.04	$9	4.2	229	181	259	28%	2.19	27.7	1.9	6.7	3.6	0.3	1.78	81%	117	220
I CON	03	COL	5	3	0	63	39	3.28	1.35	$6	4.0	249	374	165	26%	4.26 -	16.9	3.7	5.6	1.5	1.3	1.32	82%	32	61
S STB	1st Half		4	1	0	36	20	3.25	1.25	$5	4.1	240			26%	3.63	9.8	3.3	5.0	1.5	1.0	1.26	78%	39	76
K AGE	2nd Half		1	2	0	27	19	3.32	1.48	$1	4.0	261			28%	5.09 -	7.1	4.3	6.3	1.5	1.7	1.42	86%	22	41
LIMA C EP: 30%	04	Proj	3	3	0	60	38	3.90	1.30	$4	4.0	249			27%	3.88	11.0	3.3	5.7	1.7	1.1	--	73%	44	85

Here's an interesting split:
His lifetime ERA in the NL, which includes 6 years in COL: 3.20.
His lifetime AL ERA: 4.54
Hit/strand rates helped him overcome mediocre BPIs in '03. Can't count on that every year.

Reith,Brian

	Yr	Tm	W	L	Sv	IP	K	ERA	Br/IP	R$	BF/G	OBA	vL	vR	H%	xERA	RAR	Ctl	Dom	Cmd	hr/9	G/F	S%	BPV	BPX
RH Reliever	99		0	0	0	0	0	0.00	0.00																
AGE 26 Growth	00	aa	1	3	0	30	26	4.80	1.57	$0	26.9	299			35%	5.42 -	3.9	3.3	7.8	2.4	1.2		72%	56	132
TYPE Power	01	CIN	* 6	11	0	149	107	5.74	1.62	($7)	24.2	303	324	340	34%	5.96	-7.4	3.6	6.5	1.8	1.5	0.81	68%	26	48
R X HIGH	02	aaa	8	13	0	150	94	5.52	1.52	($3)	24.7	295			33%	5.09	-5.0	3.1	5.6	1.8	1.0		64%	38	74
I EXP CON	03	CIN	* 5	4	2	84	63	3.75	1.43	$5	6.3	240	206	287	27%	4.03	17.3	4.8	6.7	1.4	1.0	0.84	77%	48	92
S pt STB	1st Half		4	1	1	42	39	3.41	1.26	$6	5.7	217			28%	2.79 +	10.5	4.3	8.3	2.0	0.4	1.80	73%	90	172
K	2nd Half		1	3	1	42	24	4.08	1.60	($0)	7.0	262			27%	5.28 -	6.7	5.4	5.2	1.0	1.5	0.61	80%	9	16
LIMA C+ EP: 40%	04	Proj	3	4	0	60	42	4.65	1.50	$0	7.4	271			30%	4.83	4.9	4.1	6.3	1.6	1.2	--	72%	35	68

2-3, 4.13 ERA in 61 IP at CIN, with a 1.1 Cmd and an xERA about a run higher. Tried throwing harder this year, but by the 2nd half, home plate had become a foreign object. Forget seeing a 4.00 ERA in 2004.

Reitsma,Chris

	Yr	Tm	W	L	Sv	IP	K	ERA	Br/IP	R$	BF/G	OBA	vL	vR	H%	xERA	RAR	Ctl	Dom	Cmd	hr/9	G/F	S%	BPV	BPX
RH Reliever	99		0	0	0	0	0	0.00	0.00																
AGE 26 Growth	00	aa	7	2	0	90	48	3.30	1.26	$12	26.8	266			29%	3.72	29.7	2.1	4.8	2.3	0.7		75%	58	136
TYPE Finesse	01	CIN	7	15	0	182	96	5.29	1.42	($1)	21.9	289	279	296	31%	4.90	1.8	2.4	4.7	2.0	1.1	1.05	64%	33	61
R Very High	02	CIN	* 8	12	0	159	95	3.74	1.35	$8	19.4	265	265	268	29%	4.21	29.2	2.9	5.4	1.8	1.1	1.46	76%	40	76
I EXP con	03	CIN	* 10	7	12	102	62	4.50	1.39	$14	7.2	291	298	270	31%	5.00 -	10.6	2.1	5.5	2.6	1.3	1.84	72%	44	85
S pt	1st Half		8	4	0	62	34	4.92	1.46	$5	10.9	300			32%	5.29	3.0	2.3	4.9	2.1	1.3	1.71	70%	30	58
K BRN	2nd Half		2	3	12	40	28	3.84	1.28	$9	4.6	277			31%	4.54 -	7.6	1.8	6.3	3.5	1.4	2.03	76%	70	135
LIMA C EP: 50%	04	Proj	5	6	7	80	48	4.16	1.36	$8	5.6	281			31%	4.56	11.8	2.4	5.4	2.3	1.1	G	73%	46	88

9-5,. 4.29 ERA in 84 IP, with 12 saves. A legitimate closer? No:
- Closed only 67% of save opps
- Dom too low, hr/9 too high
- .298 OBA vs LHers
- .291 OBA in first 15 pitches
- .289 OBA with runners on

Remlinger,Mike

	Yr	Tm	W	L	Sv	IP	K	ERA	Br/IP	R$	BF/G	OBA	vL	vR	H%	xERA	RAR	Ctl	Dom	Cmd	hr/9	G/F	S%	BPV	BPX
LH Reliever	99	ATL	10	1	1	83	81	2.39	1.22	$16	4.7	220	205	219	27%	2.90 -	31.7	3.8	8.8	2.3	1.0	1.12	86%	83	180
AGE 38 Decline	00	ATL	5	3	12	72	72	3.49	1.27	$15	4.3	213	203	209	27%	3.10	20.7	4.6	9.0	1.9	0.7	1.60	74%	85	187
TYPE Power	01	ATL	3	3	1	75	93	2.76	1.20	$8	4.2	241	322	194	33%	3.55 -	26.2	2.8	11.2	4.0	1.1	0.91	83%	126	234
R Low	02	ATL	7	3	0	68	69	1.99	1.12	$13	3.8	200	235	184	27%	2.13	28.4	3.7	9.1	2.5	0.4	1.32	84%	110	207
I con	03	CHC	6	5	0	69	83	3.65	1.35	$6	4.0	217	263	180	28%	3.94	15.0	5.1	10.8	2.1	1.4	0.72	79%	78	150
S	1st Half		4	1	0	34	49	3.97	1.38	$4	3.8	200			27%	4.20	6.0	6.1	13.0	2.1	1.9	0.71	80%	82	158
K AGE	2nd Half		2	4	0	35	34	3.34	1.31	$3	4.2	233			29%	3.70	9.1	4.1	8.7	2.1	1.0	0.73	79%	75	144
LIMA B EP: 50%	04	Proj	6	4	0	70	73	3.60	1.31	$7	4.1	230			29%	3.74	15.6	4.2	9.4	2.2	1.2	F	77%	77	149

Was killing them in the 1st half, striking out everyone, walking everyone, giving up HRs to everyone. It was amazing he didn't bust a blood vessel. Settled down in the 2nd half, 'cause it's tiring being a maniac.

Reyes,Carlos

	Yr	Tm	W	L	Sv	IP	K	ERA	Br/IP	R$	BF/G	OBA	vL	vR	H%	xERA	RAR	Ctl	Dom	Cmd	hr/9	G/F	S%	BPV	BPX
RH Starter	99	SD	2	4	1	77	57	3.74	1.30	$4	5.0	259	289	228	29%	3.92	15.4	2.8	6.7	2.4	1.3	1.97	76%	54	118
AGE 35 Decline	00	SD	* 1	5	2	59	38	4.26	1.33	$3	6.3	255	213	259	26%	4.83 -	10.9	3.3	5.8	1.7	1.8	1.03	76%	20	45
TYPE Finesse	01	aaa	2	1	0	40	27	8.01	1.75	($5)	7.5	313			34%	6.35 +	-13.9	4.2	6.0	1.4	1.4		54%	15	29
R X HIGH	02		0	0	0	0	0	0.00	0.00																
I EXP con	03	TAM	* 10	6	0	171	77	4.20	1.26	$12	22.3	287	243	284	30%	4.45	30.3	1.1	4.0	3.7	1.1	0.96	70%	66	142
S pt stb	1st Half		7	3	0	92	45	2.64	1.02	$15	22.7	253			27%	3.28 -	35.5	0.6	4.4	7.5	1.0	1.00	80%	159	343
K age BRN	2nd Half		3	3	0	79	32	6.02	1.53	($3)	22.0	322			33%	5.82	-5.2	1.7	3.6	2.1	1.2	0.92	62%	20	43
LIMA C+ EP: 45%	04	Proj	2	2	0	40	22	5.40	1.43	$0	24.8	290			31%	5.15	0.7	2.5	5.0	2.0	1.4	--	65%	28	61

0-3, 5.31 ERA in 39 IP at TAM. Returned to the majors as a a low-speed, super-finesse guy... which worked for about 3 months. After that 2nd half, I'm going to keep my excitement under control.

Reynolds,Shane

	Yr	Tm	W	L	Sv	IP	K	ERA	Br/IP	R$	BF/G	OBA	vL	vR	H%	xERA	RAR	Ctl	Dom	Cmd	hr/9	G/F	S%	BPV	BPX
RH Starter	99	HOU	16	14	0	231	197	3.86	1.24	$21	27.5	277	282	269	33%	3.66	42.6	1.4	7.7	5.3	0.9	1.81	71%	131	284
AGE 36 Decline	00	HOU	7	8	0	131	93	5.22	1.49	$2	26.3	289	278	294	32%	5.27	7.1	3.1	6.4	2.1	1.4	1.76	68%	38	83
TYPE Finesse	01	HOU	14	11	0	182	102	4.35	1.34	$12	27.7	288	303	279	31%	4.72	24.9	1.8	5.0	2.8	1.2	1.86	71%	52	96
R X HIGH	02	HOU	3	6	0	74	47	4.86	1.43	($0)	24.8	277	257	284	29%	5.06	2.4	3.2	5.7	1.8	1.6	1.80	71%	24	46
I CON	03	ATL	11	9	0	167	94	5.44	1.50	$0	24.6	288	254	320	31%	5.00	-3.6	3.2	5.1	1.6	1.1	1.26	65%	29	55
S PT	1st Half		5	3	0	74	45	6.06	1.60	($3)	24.0	286			31%	5.25 +	-7.8	4.2	5.5	1.3	1.1	1.10	63%	25	48
K age BRN	2nd Half		6	6	0	93	49	4.94	1.41	$2	25.1	290			31%	4.80	4.2	2.3	4.7	2.0	1.1	1.40	67%	36	70
LIMA C EP: 50%	04	Proj	6	9	0	120	67	4.95	1.49	($0)	25.2	285			30%	5.02	5.0	3.3	5.0	1.5	1.2	--	69%	24	47

Aha!! Leo Mazzone can't work miracles with everybody! My faith is restored in the grand order of the world.

Rhodes,Arthur

	Yr	Tm	W	L	Sv	IP	K	ERA	Br/IP	R$	BF/G	OBA	vL	vR	H%	xERA	RAR	Ctl	Dom	Cmd	hr/9	G/F	S%	BPV	BPX
LH Reliever	99	BAL	3	4	3	53	59	5.43	1.66	$1	5.6	223	206	228	27%	4.93 +	3.1	7.6	10.0	1.3	1.5	0.95	71%	52	131
AGE 34 Decline	00	SEA	5	8	0	69	77	4.30	1.16	$9	3.9	207	220	193	28%	2.73 +	14.9	3.8	10.0	2.7	0.8	1.17	64%	106	275
TYPE Power	01	SEA	8	0	3	68	83	1.72	0.85	$19	3.6	193	200	177	27%	1.72	34.3	1.6	11.0	6.9	0.7	1.22	85%	208	416
R Low	02	SEA	10	4	2	69	81	2.35	0.84	$19	3.9	188	158	215	27%	1.54 +	28.7	1.7	10.6	6.2	0.5	1.40	74%	196	402
I CON	03	SEA	3	3	3	54	48	4.17	1.31	$5	3.4	258	269	243	32%	3.75	9.8	3.0	8.0	2.7	0.7	1.11	69%	87	189
S pt	1st Half		1	1	3	36	31	2.99	1.02	$6	3.7	191			25%	1.79 +	12.2	3.2	7.7	2.4	0.2	1.08	69%	106	229
K age	2nd Half		2	2	0	18	17	6.54	1.90	($1)	3.1	365			44%	7.71 -	-2.4	2.5	8.5	3.4	1.5	1.19	68%	59	128
LIMA A EP: 65%	04	Proj	6	4	2	65	68	2.77	0.94	$14	3.3	204			27%	2.12 +	24.1	1.9	9.4	4.9	0.7	--	73%	152	326

Sprained his ankle in late July and it dogged him the rest of the season. For those concerned about his lower 1st half Cmd:

	1st half	2nd half
2001	4.4	19.5
2002	4.0	8.8

Riedling,John

Riedling,John	Yr	Tm	W	L	Sv	IP	K	ERA	Br/IP	R$	BF/G	OBA	vL	vR	H%	xERA	RAR	Ctl	Dom	Cmd	hr/9	G/F	S%	BPV	BPX
RH Reliever	99	a/a	10	5	6	77	59	2.92	1.34	$17	5.1	233			28%	2.97	26.9	4.3	6.9	1.6	0.4		78%	73	169
AGE 28 Pre-Peak	00	CIN	* 9	4	6	90	84	2.90	1.33	$17	5.8	246	280	143	30%	3.82 -	32.9	3.7	8.4	2.3	0.9	3.67	82%	77	169
TYPE Power	01	CIN	1	1	1	33	23	2.44	1.08	$5	4.6	190	185	188	23%	1.94 +	13.0	3.8	6.2	1.6	0.3	2.25	77%	81	150
R Very High	02	CIN	* 4	5	0	63	41	4.57	1.63	($1)	6.2	277	320	163	33%	4.35	4.5	5.0	5.9	1.2	0.3	3.96	70%	51	96
I exp con	03	CIN	2	3	1	101	65	4.90	1.52	($3)	8.2	273	245	286	31%	4.41	5.1	4.2	5.8	1.4	0.6	1.52	67%	45	87
S PT	1st Half		0	3	1	53	26	6.61	1.85	($8)	12.1	309			34%	5.82 +	-9.5	5.3	4.4	0.8	0.7	1.45	63%	17	32
K BRN	2nd Half		2	0	0	48	39	3.01	1.17	$5	5.8	228			28%	2.85	14.6	3.0	7.3	2.4	0.6	1.60	75%	88	168
LIMA C EP: 60%	04	Proj	4	3	11	80	61	3.83	1.30	$11	4.8	244			30%	3.25 +	15.4	3.5	6.9	2.0	0.5	G	70%	75	145

Was given a 5 1/2 week trial in the rotation, but you have to wonder how it could have lasted that long. PQS : 0,0,3,0,4,0,0,0 He was so happy that was over that he put up career-best BPIs in the 2nd half... from the pen.

Rincon,Juan

Rincon,Juan	Yr	Tm	W	L	Sv	IP	K	ERA	Br/IP	R$	BF/G	OBA	vL	vR	H%	xERA	RAR	Ctl	Dom	Cmd	hr/9	G/F	S%	BPV	BPX
RH Reliever	99		0	0	0	0	0	0.00	0.00																
AGE 25 Growth	00	aa	3	9	0	89	67	6.37	1.76	($7)	27.8	316			36%	6.12	-7.3	4.1	6.8	1.6	1.1		64%	33	79
TYPE Power	01	aa	14	6	0	158	117	4.61	1.56	$6	21.5	284			33%	4.85	17.1	4.0	6.7	1.7	0.8	0.40	71%	49	95
R Very High	02	MIN	* 7	6	0	129	85	5.44	1.60	($3)	20.1	309	283	415	35%	5.68	0.3	3.0	5.9	2.0	1.1	1.22	67%	37	75
I EXP CON	03	MIN	5	6	0	85	63	3.70	1.31	$6	6.2	235	222	239	28%	3.33	20.9	4.0	6.7	1.7	0.5	0.92	72%	67	144
S pt	1st Half		1	3	0	41	25	3.29	1.32	$2	7.2	227			27%	2.96	12.3	4.4	5.5	1.3	0.2	1.04	74%	62	134
K age	2nd Half		4	3	0	44	38	4.07	1.31	$4	5.5	243			29%	3.68	8.6	3.7	7.7	2.1	0.8	0.81	70%	73	157
LIMA C+ EP: 50%	04	Proj	5	5	0	80	58	4.28	1.46	$3	9.7	271			31%	4.43	13.5	3.7	6.5	1.8	0.8	--	72%	53	114

Has shown small flashes of solid performance, including a nice 2nd half run, but BPIs are still borderline. It's tough to project him taking the next step up with much conviction.

Rincon,Ricardo

Rincon,Ricardo	Yr	Tm	W	L	Sv	IP	K	ERA	Br/IP	R$	BF/G	OBA	vL	vR	H%	xERA	RAR	Ctl	Dom	Cmd	hr/9	G/F	S%	BPV	BPX
LH Reliever	99	CLE	2	3	0	44	30	4.50	1.48	$2	3.3	248	233	261	27%	4.54	8.1	4.9	6.1	1.3	1.2	1.14	73%	32	79
AGE 34 Past	00	CLE	2	0	0	20	20	2.70	1.50	$3	2.5	232	216	240	31%	3.59 -	8.6	5.9	9.0	1.5	0.5	0.87	83%	81	212
TYPE Power	01	CLE	2	1	2	54	50	2.83	1.20	$6	3.3	224	213	233	29%	2.84	19.2	3.5	8.3	2.4	0.5	1.19	77%	95	191
R Moderate	02	OAK	1	4	1	56	49	4.18	1.04	$4	3.1	229	203	267	30%	2.22 +	9.6	1.8	7.9	4.5	0.2	1.07	56%	145	298
I CON	03	OAK	8	4	0	55	40	3.27	1.40	$8	3.7	225	200	250	26%	3.52	16.7	5.2	6.5	1.3	0.7	0.89	78%	56	121
S pt	1st Half		4	3	0	29	24	4.33	1.37	$3	4.0	226			27%	3.74 +	4.7	4.9	7.4	1.5	0.9	1.18	70%	58	125
K age	2nd Half		4	1	0	26	16	2.08	1.42	$5	3.4	223			26%	3.29 -	12.0	5.5	5.5	1.0	0.3	0.67	86%	54	117
LIMA B+ EP: 50%	04	Proj	5	3	0	55	43	3.11	1.20	$8	3.3	229			28%	2.92	17.9	3.3	7.0	2.2	0.5	--	75%	82	175

Outwardly solid ERA masked a sharp drop in BPIs. Hurt his hamstring during spring training and it probably affected him all year. But when he rebounds in '04, those who bid on ERA alone will just assume it's status quo.

Riske,David

Riske,David	Yr	Tm	W	L	Sv	IP	K	ERA	Br/IP	R$	BF/G	OBA	vL	vR	H%	xERA	RAR	Ctl	Dom	Cmd	hr/9	G/F	S%	BPV	BPX
RH Reliever	99	CLE	* 4	1	18	65	65	3.05	1.05	$21	4.4	186	316	341	25%	1.91 +	24.6	3.6	9.0	2.5	0.4	0.88	71%	112	280
AGE 27 Pre-Peak	00	a/a	0	0	1	7	1	2.57	1.14	$1	5.7	202			18%	3.21 -	3.0	3.9	1.3	0.3	1.3		86%	-9	-22
TYPE Power	01	CLE	* 3	2	16	80	91	2.70	1.35	$15	5.3	244	143	232	33%	3.62 -	29.8	3.9	10.2	2.6	0.7	0.93	82%	102	204
R Very High	02	CLE	* 2	3	4	66	87	5.18	1.56	$0	4.6	253	253	259	34%	5.19	2.5	5.5	11.9	2.2	1.6	0.73	71%	72	148
I EXP CON	03	CLE	2	2	8	74	82	2.30	0.97	$15	4.2	199	145	241	25%	2.52	32.0	2.4	9.9	4.1	1.1	0.83	84%	128	277
S pt stb	1st Half		1	1	1	37	41	3.15	1.10	$4	4.3	234			30%	3.38	11.9	2.2	9.9	4.6	1.2	0.58	78%	127	275
K	2nd Half		1	1	7	37	41	1.46	0.84	$11	4.2	161			20%	1.65	20.1	2.7	10.0	3.7	1.0	1.19	93%	132	285
LIMA B EP: 45%	04	Proj	2	2	30	75	86	3.12	1.11	$25	4.4	215			28%	3.04	24.3	3.0	10.3	3.4	1.1	--	77%	114	244

These are truly closer-caliber BPIs. Blew 5 of his first 6 save opps when he wasn't officially the closer, but when he was handed the job on 8/23, reeled off 7 straight. Bob Wickman, who?

Ritchie,Todd

Ritchie,Todd	Yr	Tm	W	L	Sv	IP	K	ERA	Br/IP	R$	BF/G	OBA	vL	vR	H%	xERA	RAR	Ctl	Dom	Cmd	hr/9	G/F	S%	BPV	BPX
RH Starter	99	PIT	15	9	0	172	107	3.51	1.30	$19	25.9	258	280	243	29%	3.54	39.8	2.8	5.6	2.0	0.9	1.81	76%	52	113
AGE 32 Peak	00	PIT	9	8	0	187	124	4.81	1.39	$7	26.0	283	311	258	31%	4.81	20.4	2.5	6.0	2.4	1.3	1.55	68%	48	105
TYPE Finesse	01	PIT	11	15	0	207	124	4.48	1.27	$10	26.3	265	286	236	29%	4.04	24.7	2.3	5.4	2.4	1.0	1.35	67%	54	101
R Low	02	CHW	5	15	0	133	77	6.09	1.71	($10)	23.7	319	349	282	35%	6.23	-11.2	3.5	5.2	1.5	1.2	1.14	66%	17	35
I con	03	MIL	1	2	0	28	15	5.12	1.64	($1)	25.6	312	409	261	33%	5.91 -	0.6	3.2	4.8	1.5	1.3	0.97	71%	14	28
S pt stb	1st Half		1	2	0	28	15	5.12	1.64	($1)	25.6	312			33%	5.91 -	0.6	3.2	4.8	1.5	1.3	0.97	71%	14	28
K	2nd Half		0	0	0	0	0	0.00	0.00																
LIMA D EP: 45%	04	Proj	6	9	0	120	70	4.95	1.48	$0	25.2	293			32%	5.04	5.0	2.9	5.3	1.8	1.1	--	69%	33	64

His season was ended by shoulder surgery, but his BPIs have been in a freefall for some time. No guarantees that we'll have anything draftable here once he's healthy, but you never know.

Rivera,Mariano

Rivera,Mariano	Yr	Tm	W	L	Sv	IP	K	ERA	Br/IP	R$	BF/G	OBA	vL	vR	H%	xERA	RAR	Ctl	Dom	Cmd	hr/9	G/F	S%	BPV	BPX
RH Reliever	99	NYY	4	3	45	69	52	1.83	0.88	$41	4.0	181	143	219	22%	1.32 +	37.4	2.3	6.8	2.9	0.3	2.05	80%	112	282
AGE 34 Past	00	NYY	7	4	36	75	58	2.87	1.10	$35	4.6	215	210	206	26%	2.43	30.6	3.0	6.9	2.3	0.5	1.47	75%	88	229
TYPE	01	NYY	4	6	50	80	83	2.36	0.91	$41	4.3	212	187	229	28%	2.01	33.6	1.3	9.3	6.9	0.6	2.13	76%	197	394
R Low	02	NYY	1	4	28	46	41	2.74	1.00	$22	4.0	212	181	225	27%	2.32	16.8	2.2	8.0	3.7	0.6	1.41	74%	121	249
I CON	03	NYY	5	2	40	70	63	1.67	1.01	$37	4.3	236	197	283	30%	2.42 -	36.3	1.3	8.1	6.3	0.4	1.88	85%	177	383
S pt	1st Half		2	0	15	30	29	1.79	0.93	$15	4.5	220			29%	1.94	15.0	1.2	8.7	7.3	0.3	2.41	81%	206	445
K age	2nd Half		3	2	25	40	34	1.57	1.07	$23	4.2	247			31%	2.78 -	21.2	1.3	7.6	5.7	0.4	1.61	88%	157	339
LIMA C EP: 45%	04	Proj	4	4	44	75	68	2.76	1.05	$36	4.3	235			30%	2.61	27.9	1.7	8.2	4.9	0.5	G	75%	145	310

Superb BPIs, but if I'm going to find anything to rant about, it will be his BA vs RHers. Might be a one-season aberration, but if it's not, that could be a sign of impending trouble.

Roa,Joe

Roa,Joe	Yr	Tm	W	L	Sv	IP	K	ERA	Br/IP	R$	BF/G	OBA	vL	vR	H%	xERA	RAR	Ctl	Dom	Cmd	hr/9	G/F	S%	BPV	BPX
RH Reliever	99		0	0	0	0	0	0.00	0.00																
AGE 32 Past	00	aa	6	5	0	103	38	5.59	1.83	($4)	25.8	325			34%	6.34 -	2.3	4.3	3.3	0.8	1.0		70%	-3	-6
TYPE Finesse	01	a/a	6	8	0	160	74	5.06	1.56	($3)	27.5	338			36%	6.06 -	7.7	1.1	4.2	3.9	1.2		70%	59	113
R X HIGH	02	PHI	* 18	4	0	182	100	3.02	1.15	$26	23.9	258	328	244	28%	3.29	50.9	1.5	4.9	3.2	0.7	0.95	76%	79	149
I EXP CON	03	2NL	* 3	5	0	78	54	6.32	1.65	($6)	10.2	339	434	257	37%	6.66	-10.9	1.8	6.2	3.4	1.6	1.33	64%	47	91
S pt STB	1st Half		2	3	0	36	26	6.45	1.68	($3)	16.7	345			39%	6.51	-5.7	1.7	6.4	3.7	1.2	2.42	63%	65	126
K	2nd Half		1	2	0	42	28	6.21	1.62	($4)	7.6	333			36%	6.79 -	-5.3	1.9	6.0	3.1	1.9	1.00	66%	32	62
LIMA B EP: 60%	04	Proj	2	2	0	40	23	4.05	1.28	$2	12.9	276			29%	4.48	6.5	1.8	5.2	2.9	1.4	--	73%	51	98

1-3, 6.17 ERA in 54 IP at PHI and SD, but if "they" looked at BPIs, they'd have seen his 3.4 Cmd and his ERA inflated by 37/64% hit/strand rates. He showed something in '02, but likely won't get any more chances at age 32.

Robertson,Jeriome

Robertson,Jeriome	Yr	Tm	W	L	Sv	IP	K	ERA	Br/IP	R$	BF/G	OBA	vL	vR	H%	xERA	RAR	Ctl	Dom	Cmd	hr/9	G/F	S%	BPV	BPX
LH Reliever	99	aa	15	7	0	191	111	3.72	1.35	$19	29.1	281			31%	4.30 -	46.2	2.3	5.2	2.3	1.0		76%	48	111
AGE 27 Growth	00	a/a	3	9	0	111	49	7.46	1.77	($12)	26.1	328			33%	7.23	-25.3	3.6	4.0	1.1	2.0		61%	-24	-57
TYPE	01	aa	5	1	0	73	59	5.30	1.81	($3)	6.1	346			39%	7.33 -	1.2	2.8	7.3	2.6	1.7		75%	31	60
R X HIGH	02	aaa	12	10	0	189	103	3.76	1.40	$11	21.5	283			30%	4.63 -	38.2	2.6	4.9	1.9	1.0	0.86	76%	37	72
I EXP CON	03	HOU	15	9	0	160	99	5.11	1.52	$5	22.2	285	243	300	31%	5.21	3.6	3.6	5.6	1.5	1.3	1.11	69%	25	48
S PT STB	1st Half		6	3	0	80	51	5.29	1.56	($0)	22.4	294			33%	5.18	-0.1	3.5	5.7	1.6	1.0	1.15	67%	35	67
K brn	2nd Half		9	6	0	80	48	4.94	1.48	$5	22.1	275			29%	5.24	3.7	3.7	5.4	1.5	1.6	1.07	71%	16	30
LIMA C EP: 50%	04	Proj	10	11	0	160	99	4.84	1.53	$2	15.8	295			32%	5.41 -	9.1	3.2	5.6	1.8	1.4	--	72%	26	50

Old school: "Wow! He won 15 games. He's so valuable to this team and has earned a spot in the rotation next year."
New school: "Yuck. Mediocre BPIs won't find their way onto MY team. 15 wins? FLUKE."

Robertson,Nate

Robertson,Nate	Yr	Tm	W	L	Sv	IP	K	ERA	Br/IP	R$	BF/G	OBA	vL	vR	H%	xERA	RAR	Ctl	Dom	Cmd	hr/9	G/F	S%	BPV	BPX
LH Starter	99		0	0	0	0	0	0.00	0.00																
AGE 26 Growth	00		0	0	0	0	0	0.00	0.00																
TYPE Finesse	01		0	0	0	0	0	0.00	0.00																
R Low	02	aa	10	9	0	163	86	4.20	1.50	$5	26.7	291			32%	4.67	23.5	3.1	4.7	1.5	0.7		73%	38	74
I EXP	03	DET	* 10	9	0	199	119	4.47	1.51	$4	27.6	291	300	307	32%	4.97 -	28.1	3.2	5.4	1.7	0.9	1.31	72%	38	81
S	1st Half		5	5	0	95	53	4.45	1.52	$2	28.2	300			33%	5.00 -	13.7	2.8	5.0	1.8	0.8		72%	39	85
K	2nd Half		5	4	0	104	66	4.50	1.50	$2	27.1	283			31%	4.94	14.3	3.5	5.7	1.7	1.0		72%	36	78
LIMA C+ EP: 45%	04	Proj	7	6	0	120	69	4.35	1.51	$3	26.6	291			32%	4.88 -	19.1	3.2	5.2	1.6	0.8	--	72%	38	80

1-2, 5.52 ERA in 44 IP at DET. Mediocre skill, marginal growth, and an OBA that won't make too many friends. Interesting, of his 8 starts, 4 were dominating (50%), 3 were disasters (38%), so there may be something here.

Roberts,Willis

	Yr	Tm	W	L	Sv	IP	K	ERA	Br/IP	R$	BF/G	OBA	vL	vR	H%	xERA	RAR	Ctl	Dom	Cmd	hr/9	G/F	S%	BPV	BPX
RH Reliever	99	aaa	5	8	0	92	47	7.04	1.98	($10)	14.5	323			35%	6.68	-18.6	5.7	4.6	**0.8**	1.2		65%	-0	-1
AGE 28 Pre-Peak	00	a/a	11	8	0	156	80	6.52	1.75	($6)	24.3	317			33%	6.32	-15.8	4.0	4.6	**1.2**	1.3		64%	4	9
TYPE	01	BAL	9	10	6	132	95	4.91	1.49	$6	12.7	276	264	284	31%	4.77	10.2	3.8	6.5	**1.7**	1.0	1.48	69%	44	89
R: Very High	02	BAL	5	4	1	75	51	3.36	1.48	$5	5.0	272	276	266	32%	4.34 -	21.1	3.8	6.1	**1.6**	0.6	1.61	78%	53	108
I: exp, CON	03	BAL	3	1	0	39	26	5.75	1.46	$0	6.6	271	298	258	29%	5.20 +	-1.2	3.7	6.0	**1.6**	1.6	1.73	64%	22	49
S: PT, stb	1st Half		3	1	0	39	26	5.75	1.46	$0	6.6	271			29%	5.20 +	-1.2	3.7	6.0	**1.6**	1.6	1.73	64%	22	49
K	2nd Half		0	0	0	0	0	0.00	0.00																
LIMA C+ **EP:** 50%	04	Proj	**3**	**4**	**0**	**60**	**40**	**4.80**	**1.48**	**$1**	**6.3**	**271**			**30%**	**4.88**	**5.9**	**3.9**	**6.0**	**1.5**	**1.2**	**G**	**70%**	**33**	**71**

Diagnosed with a ligament tear in July, ending his season. Up until that point, it was 2 1/2 years of eerily identical BPIs, but volatile ERAs left to the whims of his strand rate. Consistent, yes. Particularly good, no.

Rodriguez,Felix

	Yr	Tm	W	L	Sv	IP	K	ERA	Br/IP	R$	BF/G	OBA	vL	vR	H%	xERA	RAR	Ctl	Dom	Cmd	hr/9	G/F	S%	BPV	BPX
RH Reliever	99	SF	2	3	0	66	55	3.82	1.45	$2	6.1	265	223	288	32%	3.94	12.5	4.0	7.5	**1.9**	0.8	0.96	76%	62	135
AGE 31 Peak	00	SF	4	2	3	81	95	2.66	1.32	$11	4.5	221	160	267	31%	3.11	32.3	4.7	10.5	**2.3**	0.6	0.86	81%	105	231
TYPE Power	01	SF	9	1	0	80	91	1.69	1.00	$18	3.9	190	150	213	26%	1.95	39.5	3.0	10.2	**3.4**	0.6	0.65	87%	132	245
R: Low	02	SF	8	6	0	69	58	4.17	1.19	$9	4.0	214	234	196	26%	2.72 +	8.6	3.8	7.6	**2.0**	0.7	0.76	65%	80	151
I: CON	03	SF	8	2	2	61	46	3.10	1.44	$9	3.9	255	264	255	30%	4.06 -	17.8	4.3	6.8	**1.6**	0.7	0.71	81%	56	107
S	1st Half		4	0	1	36	30	3.74	1.47	$4	4.3	272			32%	4.59 -	7.4	3.7	7.5	**2.0**	1.0	0.55	78%	58	111
K	2nd Half		4	2	1	25	16	2.17	1.41	$5	3.5	230			27%	3.29 -	10.4	5.1	5.8	**1.1**	0.4	0.97	85%	57	109
LIMA B+ **EP:** 45%	04	Proj	**8**	**3**	**1**	**65**	**63**	**3.05**	**1.22**	**$11**	**3.9**	**221**			**28%**	**2.95**	**19.3**	**3.7**	**8.7**	**2.3**	**0.7**	**F**	**77%**	**91**	**176**

Pitched through an injury for the second time in two years. It's not like he can really hide the REAL results, from us anyway. Others will look at his 3.10 ERA and see nothing wrong. But next year, it might be a REAL 3.10 ERA.

Rodriguez,Francisco

	Yr	Tm	W	L	Sv	IP	K	ERA	Br/IP	R$	BF/G	OBA	vL	vR	H%	xERA	RAR	Ctl	Dom	Cmd	hr/9	G/F	S%	BPV	BPX
RH Reliever	99		0	0	0	0	0	0.00	0.00																
AGE 22 Green	00		0	0	0	0	0	0.00	0.00																
TYPE Power	01		0	0	0	0	0	0.00	0.00																
R: High	02	a/a	5	6	50	83	113	2.39	1.06	$40	22.0	212			33%	2.09	32.1	2.7	12.3	**4.5**	0.3		78%	171	336
I: EXP, con	03	ANA	8	3	2	86	95	3.03	0.99	$16	5.7	171	186	156	20%	2.40 +	28.7	3.7	9.9	**2.7**	1.3	1.11	77%	100	216
S: pt	1st Half		4	1	1	41	41	3.50	1.02	$7	5.6	177			22%	2.20 +	11.2	3.7	9.0	**2.4**	0.9	1.10	68%	98	211
K: AGE	2nd Half		4	2	1	45	54	2.61	0.96	$9	5.8	165			19%	2.59	17.5	3.6	10.8	**3.0**	1.6	1.11	86%	102	220
LIMA C+ **EP:** 45%	04	Proj	**7**	**4**	**2**	**85**	**93**	**3.60**	**1.28**	**$10**	**6.0**	**233**			**30%**	**3.59**	**22.1**	**3.8**	**9.8**	**2.6**	**1.0**	**--**	**75%**	**93**	**199**

Excellent debut season, made even moreso by his ability to improve his BPIs as AL batters got a second and third look at him. However, a 20% hit rate means his ERA is going up, so be cautious biddng.

Rodriguez,Ricardo

	Yr	Tm	W	L	Sv	IP	K	ERA	Br/IP	R$	BF/G	OBA	vL	vR	H%	xERA	RAR	Ctl	Dom	Cmd	hr/9	G/F	S%	BPV	BPX
RH Starter	99		0	0	0	0	0	0.00	0.00																
AGE 25 Growth	00		0	0	0	0	0	0.00	0.00																
TYPE Finesse	01		0	0	0	0	0	0.00	0.00																
R: Moderate	02	CLE *	11	7	0	145	78	4.16	1.40	$9	26.1	279	278	235	30%	4.44	25.3	2.8	4.8	**1.7**	0.8	1.41	72%	40	83
I: EXP, con	03	2AL	3	9	0	81	41	5.76	1.44	($2)	23.6	280	143	500	28%	5.45	-2.6	3.1	4.5	**1.5**	1.8	1.48	64%	4	8
S: pt	1st Half		3	8	0	80	39	5.40	1.38	($0)	24.5	274			27%	5.11	1.3	2.8	4.4	**1.6**	1.7	1.48	65%	9	19
K	2nd Half		0	1	0	1	2	29.98	5.83	($2)	10.5	542			68%	27.71 +	-3.9	22.5	15.0	**0.7**	7.5	2.00	50%	******	******
LIMA F **EP:** 50%	04	Proj	**4**	**6**	**0**	**80**	**41**	**4.73**	**1.39**	**$2**	**24.6**	**276**			**29%**	**4.86**	**8.7**	**2.8**	**4.6**	**1.6**	**1.4**	**--**	**70%**	**21**	**46**

Season ended by hip surgery, but he probably was suffering from it as early as late April. Track his PQS scores:
APRIL: 4,5,3,4,3,2 (3.32 ERA)
MAY: 2,0,3,1,3 (6.04 ERA)
JUNE:1,0,5,0 (9.88 ERA)

Rogers,Kenny

	Yr	Tm	W	L	Sv	IP	K	ERA	Br/IP	R$	BF/G	OBA	vL	vR	H%	xERA	RAR	Ctl	Dom	Cmd	hr/9	G/F	S%	BPV	BPX
LH Starter	99	2TM	10	4	0	195	126	4.20	1.41	$10	27.2	273	204	264	31%	4.05	34.7	3.2	5.8	**1.8**	0.7	1.86	71%	52	120
AGE 39 Decline	00	TEX	13	13	0	227	127	4.56	1.48	$12	29.4	286	314	276	32%	4.63	41.2	3.1	5.0	**1.6**	0.8	1.69	70%	38	100
TYPE Finesse	01	TEX	5	7	0	120	74	6.21	1.66	($8)	27.5	307	323	302	33%	5.96	-11.8	3.7	5.5	**1.5**	1.3	1.47	64%	18	36
R: Very High	02	TEX	13	8	0	210	107	3.86	1.34	$14	27.1	264	193	280	28%	4.17	45.1	3.0	4.6	**1.5**	0.9	2.02	74%	35	72
I: CON	03	MIN	13	8	0	195	116	4.57	1.42	$8	25.6	292	251	307	32%	4.86	25.0	2.3	5.4	**2.3**	1.0	1.00	70%	47	101
S: pt, stb	1st Half		7	3	0	95	60	4.93	1.47	$3	26.1	304			34%	4.92	7.6	2.2	5.7	**2.6**	0.8	1.00	67%	60	130
K: AGE	2nd Half		6	5	0	100	56	4.23	1.37	$5	25.2	281			30%	4.79 -	17.3	2.4	5.0	**2.1**	1.3	1.00	73%	35	75
LIMA C **EP:** 50%	04	Proj	**11**	**9**	**0**	**180**	**103**	**4.75**	**1.47**	**$5**	**26.3**	**291**			**32%**	**4.98**	**19.0**	**2.8**	**5.2**	**1.8**	**1.1**	**--**	**70%**	**35**	**75**

His ERA might have eroded by 0.71, but his BPIs were much better. The reason was his new home ballpark:

Cmd	Home	Road
2000-02	1.5	1.6
2003	2.8	1.8

Romero,J.C.

	Yr	Tm	W	L	Sv	IP	K	ERA	Br/IP	R$	BF/G	OBA	vL	vR	H%	xERA	RAR	Ctl	Dom	Cmd	hr/9	G/F	S%	BPV	BPX
LH Reliever	99	a/a	8	5	8	73	65	3.82	1.68	$10	6.6	270			33%	4.80 -	16.7	5.8	8.0	**1.4**	0.9		79%	52	121
AGE 27 Pre-Peak	00	MIN *	6	9	4	122	82	5.45	1.59	$3	19.0	287	281	322	32%	5.14	7.6	4.0	6.0	**1.5**	1.0	1.79	67%	34	89
TYPE Power	01	MIN *	4	7	0	128	86	5.34	1.53	($4)	21.9	291	286	276	33%	5.05	2.4	3.4	6.0	**1.8**	1.0	1.44	66%	41	83
R: High	02	MIN	9	2	1	81	76	1.89	1.21	$16	4.1	213	216	211	28%	2.62 -	38.7	4.0	8.4	**2.1**	0.3	1.84	85%	97	200
I: exp, CON	03	MIN	2	0	0	63	50	5.00	1.71	($3)	4.0	271	214	314	32%	5.26	4.4	6.0	7.1	**1.2**	1.0	1.55	72%	39	84
S: pt	1st Half		2	0	0	32	24	4.21	1.65	$0	4.3	249			30%	4.39	5.7	6.4	6.7	**1.0**	0.6	1.64	75%	51	109
K	2nd Half		0	0	0	31	26	5.83	1.78	($4)	3.7	292			34%	6.16	-1.2	5.5	7.6	**1.4**	1.5	1.44	70%	27	58
LIMA D+ **EP:** 50%	04	Proj	**4**	**2**	**0**	**70**	**57**	**4.24**	**1.46**	**$3**	**4.8**	**265**			**31%**	**4.42**	**12.1**	**4.0**	**7.3**	**1.8**	**0.9**	**G**	**73%**	**58**	**124**

One bizarre season...
4/15: Sore shoulder
6/9: Sore groin
7/25: Food poisoning
8/20: Struck in head by foul ball
9/15: Buttock laceration
You can't make this stuff up.

Roney,Matt

	Yr	Tm	W	L	Sv	IP	K	ERA	Br/IP	R$	BF/G	OBA	vL	vR	H%	xERA	RAR	Ctl	Dom	Cmd	hr/9	G/F	S%	BPV	BPX
RH Reliever	99		0	0	0	0	0	0.00	0.00																
AGE 24 Growth	00		0	0	0	0	0	0.00	0.00																
TYPE	01		0	0	0	0	0	0.00	0.00																
R: X HIGH	02	aa	3	6	0	70	53	8.36	1.71	($10)	25.0	308			35%	6.02 +	-28.9	4.1	6.8	**1.7**	1.3		50%	30	60
I: EXP, con	03	DET	1	9	0	100	47	5.48	1.50	($5)	9.8	265	297	232	27%	5.15	0.6	4.3	4.2	**1.0**	1.5	0.76	67%	2	4
S: pt	1st Half		0	2	0	43	21	3.97	1.35	$1	7.7	238			25%	3.95	9.0	4.2	4.4	**1.1**	1.0	0.58	74%	24	53
K: age, BRN	2nd Half		1	7	0	57	26	6.62	1.61	($5)	12.3	284			28%	6.06 +	-8.4	4.4	4.1	**0.9**	1.9	0.92	63%	-15	-31
LIMA F **EP:** 40%	04	Proj	**2**	**7**	**0**	**80**	**47**	**4.95**	**1.46**	**($1)**	**7.5**	**259**			**27%**	**4.91**	**6.3**	**4.3**	**5.3**	**1.2**	**1.5**	**F**	**70%**	**17**	**36**

Diary of a failed starter:
- PQS log: 0,0,4,2,5,1,3,0,0,2,0
- Avg PQS for 3 home starts: 3.6
- Avg PQS for 8 road starts: 0.8
- Did not last past pitch #65 in any of his final 4 starts.
- ERA in bullpen: 4.18

Rueter,Kirk

	Yr	Tm	W	L	Sv	IP	K	ERA	Br/IP	R$	BF/G	OBA	vL	vR	H%	xERA	RAR	Ctl	Dom	Cmd	hr/9	G/F	S%	BPV	BPX
LH Starter	99	SF	15	10	0	184	94	5.43	1.49	$5	24.6	297	236	312	31%	5.04	-4.8	2.7	4.6	**1.7**	1.4	0.91	66%	18	39
AGE 33 Past	00	SF	11	9	0	184	71	3.96	1.45	$11	25.1	283	244	301	29%	4.89 -	41.1	3.0	3.5	**1.1**	1.1	1.02	76%	9	21
TYPE Finesse	01	SF	14	12	0	195	83	4.43	1.43	$9	25.0	279	278	284	29%	4.80	24.5	3.0	3.8	**1.3**	1.2	1.02	72%	14	26
R: Low	02	SF	14	8	0	203	76	3.24	1.27	$18	25.8	263	244	267	27%	3.91 -	50.8	2.4	3.4	**1.4**	1.0	1.31	78%	23	43
I: CON	03	SF	10	5	0	147	41	4.53	1.48	$4	23.9	291	212	326	29%	4.80	14.7	2.9	2.5	**0.9**	0.9	1.37	70%	5	9
S: pt	1st Half		7	2	0	100	27	3.87	1.47	$5	25.8	291			30%	4.41 -	18.9	2.8	2.4	**0.9**	0.4	1.38	73%	16	31
K	2nd Half		3	3	0	47	14	5.95	1.49	($1)	20.7	290			28%	5.64	-4.2	3.1	2.7	**0.9**	1.7	1.36	64%	-20	-39
LIMA C **EP:** 40%	04	Proj	**11**	**10**	**0**	**180**	**62**	**4.25**	**1.42**	**$7**	**23.7**	**282**			**29%**	**4.52**	**24.4**	**2.8**	**3.1**	**1.1**	**0.9**	**--**	**72%**	**14**	**26**

The horror continues... Forget the 2nd half -- he had a bum shoulder. His 1st half BPIs got worse than ever and he STILL managed a 3.87 ERA. xERA says that this is a 4.80 ERA pitcher. One day he will be.

Rusch,Glendon

	Yr	Tm	W	L	Sv	IP	K	ERA	Br/IP	R$	BF/G	OBA	vL	vR	H%	xERA	RAR	Ctl	Dom	Cmd	hr/9	G/F	S%	BPV	BPX
LH Starter	99	aaa	4	7	0	114	86	5.05	1.67	($3)	26.1	331			39%	5.71 -	7.3	2.4	6.8	**2.8**	0.9	0.63	70%	62	143
AGE 29 Pre-Peak	00	NYM	11	11	0	190	157	4.02	1.26	$16	25.7	268	304	256	32%	3.89	40.9	2.1	7.4	**3.6**	0.9	1.09	70%	95	210
TYPE	01	NYM	8	12	0	179	156	4.63	1.45	$2	23.7	300	300	301	36%	5.11	17.8	2.2	7.8	**3.6**	1.2	1.11	71%	84	155
R: High	02	MIL	10	16	0	210	140	4.71	1.44	$2	26.9	277	237	292	30%	4.81	11.0	3.3	6.0	**1.8**	1.3	1.57	71%	36	67
I: exp, CON	03	MIL *	2	13	1	144	109	6.31	1.68	($14)	18.4	322	307	338	37%	5.89	-19.9	3.1	6.8	**2.2**	1.0	1.01	62%	48	93
S: pt, stb	1st Half		2	12	0	90	68	7.89	1.89	($16)	25.5	345			40%	6.90 +	-31.5	3.6	6.8	**1.9**	1.1	1.17	57%	33	64
K	2nd Half		0	1	1	54	41	3.67	1.33	$1	12.1	279			33%	4.21 -	11.7	2.2	6.8	**3.2**	0.8	0.79	75%	81	157
LIMA B **EP:** 65%	04	Proj	**5**	**6**	**0**	**120**	**91**	**4.35**	**1.40**	**$3**	**23.6**	**281**			**32%**	**4.49**	**14.7**	**2.7**	**6.8**	**2.5**	**1.0**	**--**	**71%**	**64**	**123**

1-12, 6.44 ERA in 123 IP at MIL. Hidden in this season were the facts that, prior to hitting the DL, he posted a 3.12 ERA in his last 4 starts (PQS 4/5 in the last 2). After the DL, posted a 2.35 ERA (4.0 Cmd) in 13 G in the pen.

Ryan,B.J.

LH Reliever
AGE 28 Pre-Peak
TYPE Power
R Low
I CON
S
K
LIMA A+ EP: 65%

Yr	Tm	W	L	Sv	IP	K	ERA	Br/IP	R$	BF/G	OBA	vL	vR	H%	xERA	RAR	Ctl	Dom	Cmd	hr/9	G/F	S%	BPV	BPX
99	2TM	* 4	1	7	85	93	3.28	1.26	$12	5.0	224			30%	2.79 +	25.6	4.0	9.8	**2.4**	0.5	1.50	75%	105	243
00	BAL	* 2	4	0	66	66	5.96	1.55	($2)	5.3	252	175	252	30%	5.09 +	-0.5	5.4	8.9	**1.7**	1.6	0.92	65%	44	115
01	BAL	2	4	2	53	54	4.25	1.45	$2	3.8	239	198	261	30%	4.14	8.8	5.1	9.2	**1.8**	1.0	1.16	73%	69	139
02	BAL	2	1	1	57	56	4.74	1.47	$0	3.7	241	192	283	30%	4.35	5.5	5.2	8.8	**1.7**	1.1	1.36	70%	62	128
03	BAL	4	1	0	50	63	3.41	1.38	$5	2.8	229	186	273	34%	3.04	14.2	4.9	11.3	**2.3**	0.2	1.49	74%	121	261
1st Half		3	0	0	23	33	6.21	1.64	$0	2.9	276			43%	4.51 +	-2.1	5.0	12.8	**2.5**	0.4	2.70	59%	118	255
2nd Half		1	1	0	27	30	1.00	1.15	$4	2.7	183			27%	1.77 -	16.3	4.7	10.0	**2.1**	0.0	1.00	90%	124	267
04	**Proj**	**3**	**2**	**1**	**50**	**56**	**3.78**	**1.36**	**$4**	**3.3**	**230**			**31%**	**3.35**	**11.8**	**4.7**	**10.1**	**2.2**	**0.5**	**--**	**72%**	**99**	**211**

His monthly ERAs: 0.96, 12.00, 8.59, 2.46, 0.73, 0.84... and his hit/strand rates charting the wild half-season swings. Control is still an issue, which is one of the reasons for this volatility. Gotta love a 100+ BPV, though.

Saarloos,Kirk

RH Reliever
AGE 24 Growth
TYPE
R Very High
I EXP
S pt
K age BRN
LIMA B EP: 60%

Yr	Tm	W	L	Sv	IP	K	ERA	Br/IP	R$	BF/G	OBA	vL	vR	H%	xERA	RAR	Ctl	Dom	Cmd	hr/9	G/F	S%	BPV	BPX
99		0	0	0	0	0	0.00	0.00																
00		0	0	0	0	0	0.00	0.00																
01		0	0	0	0	0	0.00	0.00																
02	HOU	* 18	8	0	184	141	3.86	1.21	$20	22.3	248	301	302	29%	3.28 +	30.6	2.5	6.9	**2.8**	0.7	2.45	69%	83	157
03	HOU	* 7	1	0	110	72	4.66	1.37	$4	9.6	282	270	287	32%	4.25	9.2	2.4	5.9	**2.5**	0.7	1.81	66%	64	123
1st Half		6	0	0	74	48	4.25	1.20	$7	12.2	254			29%	3.43 +	10.2	2.2	5.8	**2.7**	0.7	1.72	65%	73	141
2nd Half		1	1	0	36	24	5.48	1.72	($3)	7.0	334			38%	5.95	-1.0	2.7	6.0	**2.2**	0.7	1.89	68%	48	91
04	**Proj**	**6**	**2**	**0**	**80**	**56**	**3.94**	**1.28**	**$7**	**10.8**	**262**			**30%**	**3.74**	**14.2**	**2.5**	**6.3**	**2.5**	**0.8**	**G**	**71%**	**70**	**136**

2-1, 4.96 ERA in 49 IP at HOU. There is skill here, but they need to find a way to cultivate it. Failed as a starter (PQS scores of 0,0,0,0), posted a 2.97 ERA from the pen. Any questions?

Sabathia,C.C.

LH Starter
AGE 23 Growth
TYPE
R High
I exp
S pt
K age BRN
LIMA D EP: 45%

Yr	Tm	W	L	Sv	IP	K	ERA	Br/IP	R$	BF/G	OBA	vL	vR	H%	xERA	RAR	Ctl	Dom	Cmd	hr/9	G/F	S%	BPV	BPX
99		0	0	0	0	0	0.00	0.00																
00	aa	3	7	0	90	81	4.20	1.40	$4	22.9	244			30%	3.76	18.8	4.4	8.1	**1.8**	0.7		71%	72	172
01	CLE	17	5	0	180	171	4.40	1.35	$14	23.3	227	254	223	28%	3.68 +	26.2	4.7	8.5	**1.8**	0.9	0.79	69%	70	141
02	CLE	13	11	0	210	149	4.37	1.36	$10	27.2	251	240	255	29%	3.86 +	30.6	3.8	6.4	**1.7**	1.2	1.22	68%	57	117
03	CLE	13	9	0	197	141	3.61	1.30	$17	27.7	255	275	248	29%	3.87	50.7	3.0	6.4	**2.1**	0.9	1.00	75%	62	133
1st Half		7	3	0	101	67	3.48	1.32	$9	26.7	256			29%	3.71	27.7	3.1	6.0	**1.9**	0.6	0.76	75%	61	132
2nd Half		6	6	0	96	74	3.74	1.28	$8	28.9	253			29%	4.03	23.0	2.9	6.9	**2.4**	1.1	1.36	75%	62	135
04	**Proj**	**11**	**12**	**0**	**200**	**140**	**4.46**	**1.38**	**$9**	**26.9**	**258**			**29%**	**4.23**	**29.0**	**3.6**	**6.3**	**1.8**	**1.0**	**--**	**70%**	**48**	**103**

I went out on a limb last year and projected that his workload and svelte physique would lead to an implosion. It didn't happen but he's not out of the woods yet. He did take a step up, but he's also still racking up the IP.

Santana,Johan

LH Starter
AGE 25 Growth
TYPE Power
R Moderate
I exp con
S pt
K age
LIMA C+ EP: 55%

Yr	Tm	W	L	Sv	IP	K	ERA	Br/IP	R$	BF/G	OBA	vL	vR	H%	xERA	RAR	Ctl	Dom	Cmd	hr/9	G/F	S%	BPV	BPX
99		0	0	0	0	0	0.00	0.00													1.35			
00	MIN	2	3	0	86	64	6.49	1.81	($7)	13.6	296	263	317	34%	5.95 +	-6.6	5.7	6.7	**1.2**	1.2	0.88	65%	26	68
01	MIN	1	0	0	43	28	4.79	1.53	($1)	12.8	291	290	293	32%	5.30 -	4.0	3.3	5.8	**1.8**	1.3	1.18	72%	31	62
02	MIN	* 13	8	1	156	201	3.12	1.28	$18	17.2	220	195	216	32%	3.27	49.0	4.3	11.6	**2.7**	0.8	0.70	78%	113	231
03	MIN	12	3	0	158	169	3.07	1.10	$22	14.1	222	191	227	28%	3.00	51.9	2.7	9.6	**3.6**	1.0	0.52	76%	115	248
1st Half		4	1	0	59	68	2.43	1.15	$9	8.9	216			30%	2.57	24.5	3.3	10.3	**3.1**	0.5	0.42	80%	125	270
2nd Half		8	2	0	99	101	3.46	1.07	$14	21.9	225			27%	3.27	27.4	2.3	9.2	**4.0**	1.3	0.57	74%	112	241
04	**Proj**	**14**	**7**	**0**	**180**	**200**	**3.40**	**1.17**	**$22**	**23.0**	**229**			**30%**	**3.30**	**51.6**	**3.0**	**10.0**	**3.3**	**1.0**	**F**	**75%**	**109**	**234**

Finally got a chance to start, and did superbly. Apparently, there is concern about his long-term stamina, so he might not fare well crossing the 200 IP threshold. Monitor that closely, but enjoy the ride in the interim.

Santiago,Jose

RH Reliever
AGE 29 Pre-Peak
TYPE Finesse
R Very High
I exp con
S pt stb
K BRN
LIMA C+ EP: 30%

Yr	Tm	W	L	Sv	IP	K	ERA	Br/IP	R$	BF/G	OBA	vL	vR	H%	xERA	RAR	Ctl	Dom	Cmd	hr/9	G/F	S%	BPV	BPX
99	KC	* 3	5	2	58	15	3.10	1.24	$8	6.2	262	210	284	26%	4.04 -	21.5	2.2	2.3	**1.1**	1.1	2.78	80%	7	16
00	KC	* 8	7	6	86	56	3.87	1.40	$13	6.6	273	230	298	31%	4.37 -	23.5	3.0	5.9	**1.9**	0.9	2.00	75%	48	124
01	PHI	4	6	0	91	43	4.64	1.40	$1	5.4	292	352	252	32%	4.30	8.9	2.2	4.2	**2.0**	0.5	2.94	66%	48	90
02	PHI	* 4	5	7	75	48	4.80	1.49	$4	5.2	299	304	282	34%	4.83	3.1	2.6	5.8	**2.2**	0.8	2.36	69%	50	95
03	CLE	* 4	6	2	97	41	3.33	1.84	($0)	9.3	336	353	278	37%	5.93 -	28.7	3.7	3.8	**1.0**	0.3	3.16	81%	24	51
1st Half		2	1	2	49	24	2.02	1.73	$3	7.6	320			36%	5.31 -	23.0	3.7	4.4	**1.2**	0.2	4.57	88%	37	80
2nd Half		2	5	0	48	17	4.65	1.94	($3)	11.8	352			38%	6.56 -	5.7	3.7	3.2	**0.9**	0.4	2.33	75%	10	22
04	**Proj**	**4**	**6**	**1**	**80**	**40**	**4.61**	**1.58**	**$1**	**6.9**	**294**			**32%**	**4.85**	**9.9**	**3.6**	**4.5**	**1.3**	**0.6**	**G**	**70%**	**33**	**70**

1-3, 2.90 ERA in 31 IP at CLE. Improving Dom and Ctl both took a step backwards in 2003, despite outwardly better ERA. xERA shows a HUGE variance, and points to a coming ERA spike.

Sasaki,Kazuhiro

RH Reliever
AGE 36 Decline
TYPE Power
R High
I CON
S pt
K age
LIMA B+ EP: 55%

Yr	Tm	W	L	Sv	IP	K	ERA	Br/IP	R$	BF/G	OBA	vL	vR	H%	xERA	RAR	Ctl	Dom	Cmd	hr/9	G/F	S%	BPV	BPX
99	JPN	1	1	19	23	34	1.96	1.09	$15	4.0	227			37%	2.23	11.0	2.3	13.3	**5.7**	0.4		83%	197	456
00	SEA	2	5	37	62	78	3.18	1.17	$29	4.0	193	198	170	25%	3.22	22.7	4.5	11.3	**2.5**	1.4	0.88	81%	94	243
01	SEA	0	4	45	66	62	3.26	0.89	$31	3.7	205	218	168	25%	2.11 +	19.7	1.5	8.4	**5.6**	0.8	0.76	66%	159	317
02	SEA	4	5	37	60	73	2.55	1.07	$30	3.9	206	207	194	28%	2.68	23.4	3.0	11.0	**3.7**	0.9	0.97	81%	129	265
03	SEA	1	2	10	33	29	4.08	1.39	$7	4.1	249	235	242	31%	3.71	6.4	4.1	7.9	**1.9**	0.5	0.44	70%	77	166
1st Half		1	1	10	19	21	4.22	1.35	$7	3.7	260			35%	3.67 +	3.4	3.3	9.8	**3.0**	0.5	0.56	68%	111	240
2nd Half		0	1	0	14	8	3.88	1.44	($0)	4.7	234			26%	3.76	3.1	5.2	5.2	**1.0**	0.6	0.32	74%	41	88
04	**Proj**	**2**	**4**	**31**	**60**	**55**	**3.45**	**1.28**	**$22**	**3.9**	**239**			**30%**	**3.48**	**16.8**	**3.6**	**8.3**	**2.3**	**0.8**	**F**	**75%**	**82**	**177**

INJ: Broken ribs.
I think I'll start the comments like that from now on. It seems like over 50% of the players have some ailment that affects their stats. Here, advancing age may preclude a full return to form.

Sauerbeck,Scott

LH Reliever
AGE 32 Peak
TYPE Power
R Low
I con
S
K
LIMA C EP: 50%

Yr	Tm	W	L	Sv	IP	K	ERA	Br/IP	R$	BF/G	OBA	vL	vR	H%	xERA	RAR	Ctl	Dom	Cmd	hr/9	G/F	S%	BPV	BPX
99	PIT	4	1	2	67	55	2.01	1.36	$9	4.4	219	167	252	26%	3.10 -	28.9	5.1	7.4	**1.4**	0.8	2.27	89%	62	134
00	PIT	5	4	1	75	83	4.07	1.82	$1	4.8	264	222	305	36%	4.87 -	15.7	7.3	9.9	**1.4**	0.5	2.39	77%	76	168
01	PIT	2	2	2	62	79	5.64	1.62	($3)	4.0	258	272	248	37%	4.38 +	-2.3	5.8	11.4	**2.0**	0.6	1.40	64%	96	178
02	PIT	5	4	0	62	70	2.32	1.24	$8	3.3	222	147	273	30%	2.87 -	23.1	3.9	10.2	**2.6**	0.6	2.02	84%	109	205
03	2TM	3	5	0	56	50	4.80	1.60	($1)	3.2	229	192	257	27%	4.33	4.4	6.9	8.0	**1.2**	1.0	2.05	71%	53	107
1st Half		3	4	0	34	31	4.49	1.38	$2	3.3	213			24%	3.91 +	4.1	5.5	8.2	**1.5**	1.3	2.00	71%	53	107
2nd Half		0	1	0	22	19	5.29	1.95	($3)	3.1	252			32%	4.99	0.3	9.0	7.7	**0.9**	0.4	2.13	71%	57	115
04	**Proj**	**3**	**4**	**0**	**60**	**56**	**4.05**	**1.45**	**$2**	**3.3**	**239**			**30%**	**3.86**	**10.8**	**5.1**	**8.4**	**1.6**	**0.8**	**G**	**73%**	**70**	**141**

INJ: Blister in 2nd half (maybe)
Tough year, but completely bombed in BOS. Home plate became a moving target, the strike zone a foreign concept, the umpires space aliens... you get the drift.

Schilling,Curt

RH Starter
AGE 37 Decline
TYPE Power
R High
I CON
S pt stb
K AGE brn
LIMA B EP: 55%

Yr	Tm	W	L	Sv	IP	K	ERA	Br/IP	R$	BF/G	OBA	vL	vR	H%	xERA	RAR	Ctl	Dom	Cmd	hr/9	G/F	S%	BPV	BPX
99	PHI	15	6	0	180	152	3.55	1.13	$24	30.4	239	246	227	27%	3.17	40.6	2.2	7.6	**3.5**	1.3	1.21	74%	88	191
00	2NL	11	12	0	210	168	3.81	1.19	$20	29.7	256	243	268	29%	3.83	51.1	1.9	7.2	**3.7**	1.2	1.17	72%	91	200
01	ARI	22	6	0	256	293	2.99	1.08	$37	29.3	247	248	242	32%	3.54 -	81.7	1.4	10.3	**7.5**	1.3	1.10	80%	186	345
02	ARI	23	7	0	259	316	3.23	0.97	$39	28.0	230	242	208	31%	2.67 +	65.0	1.1	11.0	**9.6**	1.0	1.18	71%	246	465
03	ARI	8	9	0	168	194	2.95	1.05	$20	27.8	233	255	210	31%	2.90	52.5	1.7	10.4	**6.1**	0.9	0.99	76%	171	328
1st Half		4	3	0	71	82	3.04	0.99	$10	27.7	209			28%	2.55 +	21.3	2.2	10.4	**4.8**	1.0	0.88	74%	146	282
2nd Half		4	6	0	97	112	2.88	1.09	$11	27.8	250			34%	3.16	31.2	1.4	10.4	**7.5**	0.8	1.08	77%	199	383
04	**Proj**	**14**	**9**	**0**	**200**	**227**	**3.33**	**1.12**	**$23**	**27.9**	**247**			**32%**	**3.35**	**51.8**	**1.8**	**10.2**	**5.8**	**1.0**	**--**	**75%**	**158**	**305**

INJ: Hand, knee, groin, neck
He's at the age when the moving parts occasionally need some servicing. BPIs have remained superb throughout, so any stretches of good health will yield solid numbers.

Schmidt,Jason

RH Starter
AGE 31 Peak
TYPE Power
R Moderate
I con
S pt stb
K
LIMA C EP: 50%

Yr	Tm	W	L	Sv	IP	K	ERA	Br/IP	R$	BF/G	OBA	vL	vR	H%	xERA	RAR	Ctl	Dom	Cmd	hr/9	G/F	S%	BPV	BPX
99	PIT	13	11	0	212	148	4.20	1.43	$10	28.0	268	288	241	30%	4.14	29.3	3.6	6.3	**1.7**	1.0	1.53	73%	45	98
00	PIT	2	5	0	63	51	5.42	1.77	($4)	26.9	285	250	307	34%	5.44	1.8	5.8	7.3	**1.2**	0.9	1.53	70%	42	93
01	2NL	* 14	8	0	166	159	3.74	1.30	$16	24.1	246	282	217	31%	3.54	36.1	3.4	8.6	**2.6**	0.7	1.06	72%	90	167
02	SF	* 15	8	0	197	205	3.47	1.20	$20	26.2	225	259	180	29%	2.89 +	43.1	3.4	9.4	**2.7**	0.7	0.77	72%	103	195
03	SF	17	5	0	207	208	2.35	0.96	$37	27.7	206	197	204	27%	2.07	81.4	2.0	9.0	**4.5**	0.6	0.76	78%	145	278
1st Half		8	3	0	118	122	2.14	0.93	$21	28.4	198			26%	1.90	49.7	2.1	9.3	**4.4**	0.6	0.87	80%	144	278
2nd Half		9	2	0	89	86	2.62	0.99	$17	26.8	218			28%	2.28	31.7	1.8	8.7	**4.8**	0.6	0.63	76%	146	280
04	**Proj**	**18**	**8**	**0**	**200**	**205**	**2.75**	**1.06**	**$32**	**25.7**	**221**			**29%**	**2.54**	**67.5**	**2.3**	**9.2**	**3.9**	**0.7**	**F**	**77%**	**129**	**248**

INJ: Torm elbow tendon
Has entered the Elite and could be our next 20-game winner if he stays healthy.

Schoeneweis,Scott

LH Starter
AGE 30 Peak
TYPE
R Moderate
I CON
S PT
K
LIMA B EP: 55%

Yr	Tm	W	L	Sv	IP	K	ERA	Br/IP	R$	BF/G	OBA	vL	vR	H%	xERA	RAR	Ctl	Dom	Cmd	hr/9	G/F	S%	BPV	BPX
99	ANA *	3	5	0	74	47	8.39	2.01	($12)	9.1	367	266	313	40%	7.99	-25.0	3.4	5.7	1.7	1.5	2.03	58%	7	18
00	ANA	7	10	0	170	78	5.45	1.47	$2	27.6	276	294	271	29%	4.79 +	10.4	3.5	4.1	1.2	1.1	2.44	64%	16	41
01	ANA	10	11	0	205	104	5.09	1.48	$1	28.2	282	209	304	30%	4.75	10.8	3.4	4.6	1.4	0.9	1.84	66%	27	54
02	ANA	9	8	1	118	65	4.88	1.42	$5	9.5	263	202	290	28%	4.74	9.1	3.7	5.0	1.3	1.3	1.30	69%	21	43
03	2AL	3	2	0	64	56	4.21	1.29	$3	4.6	261	227	275	33%	3.51 +	11.3	2.7	7.9	2.9	0.4	1.53	66%	99	214
1st Half		1	0	0	27	20	4.98	1.37	$0	3.7	275			33%	3.81 +	2.0	2.7	6.6	2.5	0.3	2.00	61%	82	178
2nd Half		2	2	0	37	36	3.64	1.24	$3	5.5	251			32%	3.28	9.4	2.7	8.7	3.3	0.5	1.24	70%	111	241
04	Proj	6	6	0	120	85	4.80	1.40	$3	25.9	271			31%	4.31 +	11.9	3.2	6.4	2.0	0.8	G	66%	57	122

Became a LIMA-caliber arm in his first full season in the pen. Over the past 4 years, a 5.12 ERA and 1.3 Cmd as a starter, 4.04/2.8 in relief. So what happens? CHW is talking about moving him back to the rotation.

Sele,Aaron

RH Starter
AGE 33 Past
TYPE Finesse
R Moderate
I CON
S pt stb
K age
LIMA F EP: 45%

Yr	Tm	W	L	Sv	IP	K	ERA	Br/IP	R$	BF/G	OBA	vL	vR	H%	xERA	RAR	Ctl	Dom	Cmd	hr/9	G/F	S%	BPV	BPX
99	TEX	18	9	0	205	186	4.79	1.53	$12	27.7	297	286	299	36%	5.06	29.8	3.1	8.2	2.7	0.9	1.86	70%	73	183
00	SEA	17	10	0	211	137	4.52	1.40	$18	26.8	271	276	265	31%	4.14	39.4	3.2	5.8	1.9	0.7	1.28	68%	53	138
01	SEA	15	5	0	215	114	3.60	1.24	$20	26.3	263	231	296	28%	3.99	54.3	2.1	4.8	2.2	1.0	1.01	75%	47	93
02	ANA	8	9	0	160	82	4.89	1.49	$1	27.2	296	315	283	31%	5.29	12.1	2.8	4.6	1.7	1.2	1.17	70%	23	47
03	ANA	7	11	0	121	53	5.79	1.59	($3)	21.9	283	252	322	29%	5.40	-4.3	4.3	3.9	0.9	1.3	0.87	65%	3	7
1st Half		4	6	0	48	23	6.35	1.70	($2)	22.3	303			30%	6.53	-5.3	4.3	4.3	1.0	1.9	1.02	67%	-15	-32
2nd Half		3	5	0	73	30	5.42	1.52	($2)	21.6	270			28%	4.66 +	1.0	4.3	3.7	0.9	0.9	0.79	64%	15	33
04	Proj	7	10	0	140	66	4.89	1.50	$1	22.1	283			30%	5.07	12.2	3.5	4.2	1.2	1.2	--	70%	15	32

INJ: Bum shoulder
While this likely bothered him all year, a scan of his BPI trends say that some level of decline was likely anyway. Negative momentum can become relentless. Stay clear.

Seo,Jae

RH Starter
AGE 26 Growth
TYPE Finesse
R High
I EXP con
S pt
K brn
LIMA C EP: 50%

Yr	Tm	W	L	Sv	IP	K	ERA	Br/IP	R$	BF/G	OBA	vL	vR	H%	xERA	RAR	Ctl	Dom	Cmd	hr/9	G/F	S%	BPV	BPX
99		0	0	0	0	0	0.00	0.00																
00		0	0	0	0	0	0.00	0.00																
01	a/a	7	3	0	108	59	3.17	1.22	$12	21.3	271			30%	3.61	32.6	1.6	4.9	3.1	0.6		75%	78	150
02	a/a	6	9	0	134	76	4.90	1.49	($1)	21.1	318			35%	5.37	6.6	1.6	5.1	3.2	1.0	1.00	69%	58	115
03	NYM	9	12	0	188	110	3.83	1.27	$12	24.6	267	223	291	29%	3.91	36.5	2.2	5.3	2.4	0.9	0.74	72%	58	111
1st Half		5	3	0	93	49	3.09	1.24	$9	25.8	270			30%	3.52	27.2	1.7	4.7	2.7	0.5	0.60	75%	72	139
2nd Half		4	9	0	95	61	4.55	1.31	$3	23.6	264			29%	4.30	9.3	2.7	5.8	2.2	1.2	0.92	68%	46	88
04	Proj	9	11	0	180	104	4.15	1.34	$8	22.6	286			31%	4.37	26.9	2.0	5.2	2.7	0.9	F	71%	58	112

Not a bad rookie campaign, but clearly did not adjust well in the 2nd half. Threw harder, walked more, gave up more HRs, and negated some of the 1st half gains. 2004 will likely be an adjustment year.

Sheets,Ben

RH Starter
AGE 25 Growth
TYPE
R Moderate
I EXP con
S pt
K brn
LIMA B EP: 60%

Yr	Tm	W	L	Sv	IP	K	ERA	Br/IP	R$	BF/G	OBA	vL	vR	H%	xERA	RAR	Ctl	Dom	Cmd	hr/9	G/F	S%	BPV	BPX
99		0	0	0	0	0	0.00	0.00																
00	a/a	8	8	0	154	103	2.57	1.26	$19	23.8	248			29%	3.20 -	65.8	3.0	6.0	2.0	0.4		80%	72	170
01	MIL *	12	11	0	161	99	4.75	1.45	$6	26.0	286	324	251	31%	5.06	13.3	2.9	5.5	1.9	1.3	1.59	70%	33	62
02	MIL	11	16	0	216	170	4.17	1.42	$6	27.6	280	318	247	33%	4.40	27.2	2.9	7.1	2.4	0.9	1.47	72%	66	125
03	MIL	11	13	0	220	157	4.46	1.25	$11	27.0	272	247	286	30%	4.22	24.3	1.8	6.4	3.7	1.2	0.99	67%	80	154
1st Half		6	6	0	123	88	4.31	1.16	$8	27.9	255			27%	4.23	16.0	1.8	6.4	3.7	1.7	0.86	70%	69	133
2nd Half		5	7	0	97	69	4.64	1.36	$3	26.0	292			34%	4.21	8.3	1.8	6.4	3.6	0.6	1.18	65%	95	182
04	Proj	16	11	0	225	165	3.88	1.20	$20	25.8	260			30%	3.70	41.7	1.9	6.6	3.4	1.0	--	70%	86	166

BPIs are developing nicely, but a 5% drop in his strand rate from 2002 served to hide those gains in a higher ERA. Keep a close eye on this one. He's at the prime spot to post a break-out season. Major sleeper.

Shields,Scot

RH Starter
AGE 28 Pre-Peak
TYPE
R Very High
I EXP con
S PT stb
K brn
LIMA C+ EP: 45%

Yr	Tm	W	L	Sv	IP	K	ERA	Br/IP	R$	BF/G	OBA	vL	vR	H%	xERA	RAR	Ctl	Dom	Cmd	hr/9	G/F	S%	BPV	BPX
99	aa	4	4	0	74	69	4.01	1.35	$5	31.6	254			30%	4.30	15.0	3.5	8.4	2.4	1.5		76%	61	141
00	aaa	7	13	0	163	134	6.68	1.62	($7)	27.4	286			34%	5.23 +	-20.1	4.4	7.4	1.7	1.0		58%	46	109
01	aaa	6	11	0	148	94	5.29	1.37	$1	21.9	286	63	292	30%	5.14	2.6	2.2	5.7	2.6	1.6	0.71	66%	40	76
02	ANA *	7	5	1	96	71	2.81	1.06	$15	6.7	217	184	191	25%	2.78	34.0	2.5	6.7	2.6	0.8	1.92	77%	81	167
03	ANA	5	6	1	148	111	2.86	1.19	$14	13.8	248	229	264	29%	3.37 -	52.9	2.3	6.7	2.9	0.7	1.41	79%	85	184
1st Half		2	1	1	60	49	1.65	1.10	$9	9.7	221			27%	2.52 -	31.2	2.7	7.3	2.7	0.4	1.29	87%	99	213
2nd Half		3	5	0	88	62	3.68	1.25	$6	19.3	266			30%	3.95	21.7	2.0	6.3	3.1	0.9	1.49	73%	77	167
04	Proj	6	6	0	120	89	3.45	1.21	$11	21.5	249			28%	3.65	33.6	2.5	6.7	2.7	1.0	--	75%	73	156

Starter or reliever? You decide:

	IP	ERA	Ctl	Dom
SP	78	3.89	1.5	6.3
RP	70	1.68	3.2	7.2

This one's not so clear cut. Fared slightly better as a RP in '02, but might do well either way.

Shouse,Brian

LH Reliever
AGE 35 Decline
TYPE
R X HIGH
I EXP CON
S PT stb
K age
LIMA B+ EP: 50%

Yr	Tm	W	L	Sv	IP	K	ERA	Br/IP	R$	BF/G	OBA	vL	vR	H%	xERA	RAR	Ctl	Dom	Cmd	hr/9	G/F	S%	BPV	BPX
99	aaa	3	4	0	44	25	7.16	2.02	($5)	7.2	367			41%	7.22	-9.6	3.5	5.1	1.5	0.8		64%	19	43
00	aaa	4	5	2	61	45	4.57	1.66	$3	5.9	328			38%	5.97 -	9.7	2.5	6.6	2.6	1.0		74%	54	128
01	aaa	2	2	1	53	46	3.91	1.51	$1	4.2	297			36%	4.94 -	10.8	2.9	7.8	2.7	0.8		76%	74	142
02	KC *	1	0	0	37	29	6.32	1.59	($3)	3.6	306			35%	5.93	-4.3	3.2	7.1	2.2	1.5	2.15	62%	39	80
03	TEX	0	1	1	61	40	3.10	1.25	$4	4.1	265	195	364	32%	3.20	19.8	2.1	5.9	2.9	0.1	2.64	73%	93	201
1st Half		0	1	0	35	19	3.58	1.22	$2	4.9	266			30%	3.27	9.2	1.8	4.9	2.7	0.3	2.22	69%	80	173
2nd Half		0	0	1	26	21	2.44	1.28	$2	3.4	263			33%	3.11 -	10.7	2.4	7.3	3.0	0.0	3.58	79%	109	236
04	Proj	1	1	1	60	40	3.90	1.35	$2	3.9	274			32%	4.02	13.2	2.6	6.0	2.4	0.6	G	71%	68	145

Ageless lefty racked up some nice stats, especially impressive given his home ballpark (posted 4.24/1.67 ERA home/road splits). Platoon splits confirm where his narrow value lies, but that's till LIMA-worthy.

Shuey,Paul

RH Reliever
AGE 33 Past
TYPE Power
R Low
I con
S pt stb
K age
LIMA B EP: 40%

Yr	Tm	W	L	Sv	IP	K	ERA	Br/IP	R$	BF/G	OBA	vL	vR	H%	xERA	RAR	Ctl	Dom	Cmd	hr/9	G/F	S%	BPV	BPX
99	CLE	8	5	6	81	103	3.56	1.33	$14	4.8	229	223	223	32%	3.57	25.1	4.4	11.4	2.6	0.9	2.88	76%	105	264
00	CLE	4	2	0	63	69	3.42	1.28	$8	4.7	222	203	235	30%	3.03	21.1	4.3	9.8	2.3	0.6	1.62	74%	101	261
01	CLE	5	3	2	54	70	2.83	1.46	$7	5.0	258	280	225	39%	3.58 -	19.2	4.3	11.6	2.7	0.2	2.47	79%	125	250
02	2TM	8	2	1	70	66	3.34	1.27	$10	4.3	227	226	217	30%	2.91	18.1	4.0	8.5	2.1	0.4	2.64	73%	94	184
03	LA	6	4	0	69	60	3.00	1.20	$9	4.6	204	224	193	25%	2.84	21.1	4.3	7.8	1.8	0.8	2.34	78%	76	146
1st Half		3	1	0	31	27	1.16	0.90	$8	4.6	162			21%	1.14	17.2	3.2	7.8	2.5	0.3	1.42	89%	112	216
2nd Half		3	3	0	38	33	4.51	1.45	$2	4.6	236			27%	4.24	3.9	5.2	7.8	1.5	1.2	3.93	72%	51	98
04	Proj	6	5	0	70	61	3.86	1.36	$6	4.7	236			29%	3.58	13.2	4.4	7.8	1.8	0.8	G	73%	69	134

Excellent 1st half ERA masked all signs of 2nd half struggles, for when you start with a 1.16 ERA, it takes awhile for it to make it up to that 3.00 finishing line. Of course, his full season stats do not raise any concern.

Silva,Carlos

RH Reliever
AGE 25 Growth
TYPE Finesse
R High
I EXP con
S pt
K age
LIMA C+ EP: 50%

Yr	Tm	W	L	Sv	IP	K	ERA	Br/IP	R$	BF/G	OBA	vL	vR	H%	xERA	RAR	Ctl	Dom	Cmd	hr/9	G/F	S%	BPV	BPX
99		0	0	0	0	0	0.00	0.00																
00		0	0	0	0	0	0.00	0.00																
01	aa	15	8	0	180	91	4.60	1.39	$10	27.7	304			33%	4.94	19.8	1.5	4.6	3.1	1.0		69%	57	110
02	PHI	5	0	2	87	42	3.10	1.26	$9	5.2	264	292	276	29%	3.37	23.3	2.3	4.3	1.9	0.4	2.81	75%	56	106
03	PHI	3	1	1	87	48	4.44	1.48	$0	6.2	272	300	266	30%	4.40	9.7	3.8	5.0	1.3	0.7	1.79	70%	36	69
1st Half		3	1	1	47	26	4.21	1.49	$2	6.3	266			28%	4.72 -	6.7	4.2	5.0	1.2	1.1	1.57	75%	22	42
2nd Half		0	0	0	40	22	4.71	1.47	($2)	6.1	280			32%	4.01 +	3.0	3.4	4.9	1.5	0.2	2.10	66%	53	101
04	Proj	4	1	0	85	44	4.02	1.39	$3	6.5	275			30%	4.09	14.1	2.9	4.7	1.6	0.6	G	71%	43	83

There is debate about him returning to a starting role, as he was in the minors. His two years in the bullpen have shown nothing special, but as a soft-tosser his ceiling will be low no matter where he ends up.

Simontacchi,Jason

RH Reliever
AGE 30 Peak
TYPE Finesse
R High
I EXP con
S pt
K
LIMA D EP: 50%

Yr	Tm	W	L	Sv	IP	K	ERA	Br/IP	R$	BF/G	OBA	vL	vR	H%	xERA	RAR	Ctl	Dom	Cmd	hr/9	G/F	S%	BPV	BPX
99		0	0	0	0	0	0.00	0.00																
00		0	0	0	0	0	0.00	0.00																
01	aaa	7	13	0	143	67	6.67	1.76	($12)	20.9	361			38%	7.25 -	-23.9	1.5	4.2	2.8	1.4		64%	23	45
02	STL *	16	6	0	185	95	3.79	1.34	$15	26.3	266	248	257	28%	4.11	32.5	2.9	4.6	1.6	1.0	1.15	75%	34	65
03	STL	9	5	1	126	74	5.57	1.54	($0)	12.2	301	307	294	32%	5.68	-4.9	2.9	5.3	1.8	1.5	1.15	67%	19	37
1st Half		5	4	0	75	40	6.59	1.60	($4)	22.6	303			30%	6.49	-13.2	3.4	4.8	1.4	2.2	1.04	64%	-12	-22
2nd Half		4	1	1	51	34	4.06	1.45	$3	7.2	298			35%	4.50	8.3	2.3	6.0	2.6	0.5	1.35	72%	70	136
04	Proj	5	4	0	80	45	4.39	1.45	$3	7.8	292			32%	4.73	9.4	2.6	5.1	2.0	0.9	--	71%	41	79

Starter/reliever? Here we go...

	IP	ERA	Ctl	Dom
SP	85	6.33	3.2	5.5
RP	41	3.95	2.4	4.8

Slight edge to the pen, but given he's posted a 5.43 ERA since July 2002, take the edge.

Smith,Dan		Tm	W	L	Sv	IP	K	ERA	Br/IP	R$	BF/G	OBA	vL	vR	H%	xERA	RAR	Ctl	Dom	Cmd	hr/9	G/F	S%	BPV	BPX
RH Reliever	99	aaa	5	4	0	71	46	4.94	1.48	$3	28.4	275			31%	4.52	5.6	3.7	5.8	1.6	1.0	0.95	68%	38	88
AGE 28 Pre-Peak	00	aaa	7	10	0	124	57	6.39	1.64	($4)	23.5	315			33%	5.86 +	-10.4	3.0	4.1	1.4	1.2	0.43	61%	10	25
TYPE	01	aaa	6	4	0	106	56	6.03	1.70	($6)	23.3	311			32%	6.63 -	-8.6	3.8	4.8	1.2	1.9		69%	-9	-17
R X HIGH	02	MON *	6	5	2	129	83	4.12	1.26	$8	11.5	251	151	239	27%	4.02	17.1	2.8	5.8	2.1	1.3	0.90	72%	43	82
I EXP CON	03	MON	2	2	0	37	35	5.32	1.61	($1)	5.3	286	273	284	31%	6.71 -	-0.2	4.4	8.5	1.9	2.7	1.39	78%	10	19
S PT	1st Half		2	2	0	37	35	5.32	1.61	($1)	5.3	286			31%	6.71 -	-0.2	4.4	8.5	1.9	2.7	1.39	78%	10	19
K brn	2nd Half		0	0	0	0	0	0.00	0.00																
LIMA F EP: 30%	04	Proj	2	4	0	50	31	4.86	1.46	($0)	7.1	273			29%	5.16	2.7	3.6	5.6	1.6	1.6	--	72%	18	34

INJ: Rotator cuff inflammation Allowed a HR about every 3 innings, with a G/F ratio of 1.39, which is a sign that something is very wrong. This is what happens when players play through injuries.

Smoltz,John		Tm	W	L	Sv	IP	K	ERA	Br/IP	R$	BF/G	OBA	vL	vR	H%	xERA	RAR	Ctl	Dom	Cmd	hr/9	G/F	S%	BPV	BPX
RH Reliever	99	ATL	11	8	0	186	156	3.19	1.12	$22	25.9	243	264	229	29%	2.67 +	50.9	1.9	7.5	3.9	0.7	1.37	73%	113	246
AGE 36 Decline	00	ATL	0	0	0	0	0	0.00	0.00																
TYPE Power	01	ATL	3	3	10	59	57	3.36	1.07	$13	6.5	242	263	211	30%	3.25	15.9	1.5	8.7	5.7	1.1	1.21	73%	147	272
R Moderate	02	ATL	3	2	55	80	85	3.26	1.04	$38	4.2	207	213	199	28%	2.05 +	19.8	2.7	9.6	3.5	0.5	1.28	68%	132	249
I con	03	ATL	0	2	45	64	73	1.12	0.87	$35	3.9	210	189	218	30%	1.58	35.7	1.1	10.2	9.1	0.3	1.13	89%	258	496
S pt	1st Half		0	1	29	42	48	0.86	0.86	$24	4.1	196			29%	1.11	24.9	1.5	10.3	6.9	0.0	1.11	89%	221	426
K AGE	2nd Half		0	1	16	22	25	1.64	0.91	$12	3.7	234			31%	2.48 -	10.7	0.4	10.2	25.0	0.8	1.16	89%	570	1096
LIMA C EP: 45%	04	Proj	2	3	44	80	80	3.38	1.16	$31	4.9	247			32%	3.02	20.2	2.1	9.0	4.2	0.6	--	72%	131	253

INJ: Elbow tendinitis... ... and was en route to a record-setting saves season when it hit. Amazing BPIs, but a 258 BPV is still short of the record... 347 by Dennis Eckersley in 1990. Oh, and be worried about the elbow.

Snyder,Kyle		Tm	W	L	Sv	IP	K	ERA	Br/IP	R$	BF/G	OBA	vL	vR	H%	xERA	RAR	Ctl	Dom	Cmd	hr/9	G/F	S%	BPV	BPX
RH Starter	99		0	0	0	0	0	0.00	0.00																
AGE 26 Growth	00		0	0	0	0	0	0.00	0.00																
TYPE Finesse	01		0	0	0	0	0	0.00	0.00																
R Very High	02	aa	2	2	0	25	14	6.48	1.44	($0)	18.2	284			28%	5.81 +	-4.0	2.9	5.0	1.8	2.2		60%	0	1
I EXP con	03	KC *	4	6	0	119	52	4.69	1.36	$2	24.3	285	273	297	30%	4.73	13.4	2.1	3.9	1.9	1.1	1.07	68%	27	57
S pt	1st Half		4	4	0	93	46	4.25	1.36	$4	24.9	288			30%	4.70	15.8	2.0	4.4	2.2	1.1	1.09	72%	38	83
K BRN	2nd Half		0	2	0	26	6	6.23	1.35	($1)	22.2	276			26%	4.82 +	-2.5	2.4	2.1	0.9	1.4	1.00	55%	-11	-25
LIMA C EP: 45%	04	Proj	3	8	0	120	45	4.73	1.35	$2	23.3	281			28%	4.77	13.1	2.3	3.4	1.5	1.3	--	68%	12	27

1-6, 5.19 ERA in 85 IP at KC. INJ: Shoulder surgery, which follows elbow surgery two years ago. Good Ctl, but most other BPIs are marginal, or worse. Just say no.

Soriano,Rafael		Tm	W	L	Sv	IP	K	ERA	Br/IP	R$	BF/G	OBA	vL	vR	H%	xERA	RAR	Ctl	Dom	Cmd	hr/9	G/F	S%	BPV	BPX
RH Reliever	99		0	0	0	0	0	0.00	0.00																
AGE 24 Growth	00		0	0	0	0	0	0.00	0.00																
TYPE Power	01	aa	2	2	0	48	48	3.94	1.13	$4	24.3	224			28%	3.04 +	9.5	2.8	9.0	3.2	0.9		67%	103	198
R X HIGH	02	SEA *	2	6	1	93	76	3.87	1.25	$5	19.4	243	297	179	27%	4.14	19.8	3.1	7.4	2.4	1.5	0.54	75%	57	117
I EXP con	03	SEA *	7	3	1	115	125	2.82	0.90	$19	8.6	198	191	132	28%	1.61 +	41.7	1.9	9.8	5.2	0.3	0.61	68%	174	376
S pt	1st Half		4	3	0	69	67	3.77	1.04	$8	16.1	226			30%	2.25 +	16.2	2.0	8.7	4.5	0.3	0.30	61%	148	320
K age BRN	2nd Half		3	0	1	46	58	1.38	0.70	$12	4.9	151			23%	0.63 +	25.4	1.8	11.4	6.4	0.4	0.67	83%	217	468
LIMA B+ EP: 70%	04	Proj	5	2	3	80	81	2.70	0.96	$15	10.4	210			27%	2.24	30.4	1.9	9.1	4.8	0.7	F	75%	147	316

3-0, 1.53 ERA in 53 IP at SEA. We've been waiting for his arrival, but these BPI levels are far beyond what we would have expected, at least not this soon. The best part is he'll never get drafted at full value.

Sosa,Jorge		Tm	W	L	Sv	IP	K	ERA	Br/IP	R$	BF/G	OBA	vL	vR	H%	xERA	RAR	Ctl	Dom	Cmd	hr/9	G/F	S%	BPV	BPX
RH Starter	99		0	0	0	0	0	0.00	0.00																
AGE 27 Growth	00		0	0	0	0	0	0.00	0.00																
TYPE	01		0	0	0	0	0	0.00	0.00																
R Low	02	TAM	2	7	0	106	51	5.18	1.41	($2)	13.9	239	289	183	24%	4.52 +	4.0	4.7	4.3	0.9	1.4	0.69	67%	9	19
I EXP con	03	TAM *	6	13	0	152	87	5.08	1.61	($4)	20.9	291	315	241	32%	5.29	9.1	4.1	5.1	1.3	1.0	0.76	70%	24	52
S pt	1st Half		2	7	0	72	36	5.86	1.75	($6)	18.7	316			34%	6.03	-3.2	4.0	4.5	1.1	1.0	0.71	67%	12	27
K	2nd Half		4	6	0	80	51	4.38	1.48	$2	23.5	266			29%	4.63	12.3	4.2	5.7	1.4	1.0	0.80	73%	35	75
LIMA F EP: 45%	04	Proj	4	9	0	120	70	5.10	1.61	($4)	23.6	285			31%	5.40	7.1	4.4	5.3	1.2	1.2	F	71%	19	40

5-12, 4.64 ERA in 128 IP at TAM. Soft skills with little visible upside, and one trend that I'll bet nobody picked up on... The three times he clocked 110 pitches or more, he struggled mightily in his next start.

Sparks,Steve		Tm	W	L	Sv	IP	K	ERA	Br/IP	R$	BF/G	OBA	vL	vR	H%	xERA	RAR	Ctl	Dom	Cmd	hr/9	G/F	S%	BPV	BPX
RH Reliever	99	ANA	5	11	0	148	73	5.41	1.67	($4)	24.3	283	293	270	29%	5.58	9.1	5.0	4.4	0.9	1.3	1.17	70%	5	13
AGE 38 Decline	00	DET *	12	12	1	194	90	4.17	1.38	$16	23.2	270	269	255	29%	4.04	45.3	3.0	4.2	1.4	0.6	1.40	70%	36	92
TYPE Finesse	01	DET	14	9	0	232	116	3.65	1.33	$17	28.2	272	280	263	29%	4.15 -	57.1	2.5	4.5	1.8	0.9	1.53	75%	40	80
R X HIGH	02	DET *	8	16	0	205	106	6.37	1.72	($15)	22.1	314	299	312	34%	6.04	-24.9	3.9	4.7	1.2	1.1	1.42	63%	13	26
I CON	03	2AL	0	6	2	107	54	4.88	1.42	($2)	9.1	276	286	270	29%	4.70	9.3	3.1	4.5	1.5	1.1	1.24	68%	25	54
S pt stb	1st Half		0	4	2	58	34	3.88	1.33	$2	9.1	248			27%	4.07	12.8	3.6	5.3	1.5	1.1	1.14	74%	35	77
K AGE BRN	2nd Half		0	2	0	49	20	6.06	1.53	($4)	9.1	306			32%	5.45 +	-3.5	2.6	3.7	1.4	1.1	1.36	61%	13	27
LIMA F EP: 45%	04	Proj	2	5	0	80	39	5.18	1.51	($2)	9.6	290			31%	5.05	3.9	3.3	4.4	1.3	1.0	--	67%	21	46

I suppose, a 38-year-old knuckleballer is just beginning his career, but he has to be at least marginally effective. 2002 was completely horrible, and from May 28 on in 2003, he posted a 5.64 ERA. Forget it.

Speier,Justin		Tm	W	L	Sv	IP	K	ERA	Br/IP	R$	BF/G	OBA	vL	vR	H%	xERA	RAR	Ctl	Dom	Cmd	hr/9	G/F	S%	BPV	BPX
RH Reliever	99	ATL *	2	4	3	69	56	5.61	1.64	($2)	6.8	291	275	226	33%	5.37	-3.4	4.3	7.3	1.7	1.4	1.00	69%	33	72
AGE 30 Peak	00	CLE *	5	2	9	81	79	3.66	1.27	$14	5.7	239	171	274	30%	3.63	24.4	3.4	8.8	2.5	1.0	0.59	74%	83	216
TYPE Power	01	COL *	7	3	2	88	75	4.30	1.26	$8	5.7	253	221	234	29%	4.14	12.6	2.8	7.7	2.8	1.3	0.65	70%	69	128
R Low	02	COL *	7	1	3	76	58	4.50	1.28	$8	4.3	259	240	197	29%	4.26	6.2	2.6	6.9	2.6	1.4	0.63	69%	57	108
I exp con	03	COL	3	1	9	73	66	4.06	1.31	$8	4.3	262	273	245	31%	4.38	11.9	2.8	8.1	2.9	1.4	0.63	74%	71	137
S stb	1st Half		2	1	1	42	35	3.42	1.33	$3	4.6	261			31%	3.96 -	10.5	3.0	7.5	2.5	0.9	0.59	77%	74	143
K	2nd Half		1	0	8	31	31	4.94	1.29	$5	4.0	262			30%	4.96	1.4	2.6	9.0	3.4	2.0	0.69	70%	68	131
LIMA B EP: 55%	04	Proj	2	3	12	70	64	4.37	1.29	$9	4.5	259			30%	4.30	8.4	2.7	8.2	3.0	1.4	F	71%	74	143

A legitimate option at closer? BPIs show promise, however... The period of time when he posted the most saves is also when he was allowing 2.0 hr/9. If that's not a receipe for disaster in COL, I don't know what is.

Spooneybarger,Tim		Tm	W	L	Sv	IP	K	ERA	Br/IP	R$	BF/G	OBA	vL	vR	H%	xERA	RAR	Ctl	Dom	Cmd	hr/9	G/F	S%	BPV	BPX
RH Reliever	99		0	0	0	0	0	0.00	0.00																
AGE 24 Growth	00		0	0	0	0	0	0.00	0.00																
TYPE	01	a/a	4	2	5	76	79	2.49	1.21	$12	5.1	233			32%	2.71	29.9	3.2	9.4	2.9	0.2	1.75	79%	119	228
R Very High	02	ATL *	2	0	12	71	52	2.15	1.21	$14	4.3	206	150	234	24%	2.68 -	28.1	4.3	6.6	1.5	0.6	1.80	85%	66	126
I EXP con	03	FLA	1	2	0	42	32	4.07	0.90	$4	4.9	186	152	224	23%	1.35 +	6.8	2.4	6.9	2.9	0.2	2.72	51%	114	219
S pt stb	1st Half		1	2	0	42	32	4.07	0.90	$4	4.9	186			23%	1.35 +	6.8	2.4	6.9	2.9	0.2	2.72	51%	114	219
K age	2nd Half		0	0	0	0	0	0.00	0.00																
LIMA A EP: 65%	04	Proj	0	0	0	10	7	2.70	1.30	$0	5.3	242			30%	2.80	3.4	3.6	6.3	1.8	0.0	G	77%	81	157

INJ: Tommy John surgery BPIs were just fine, 51% strand rate is horrible luck. Might not be back until 2005.

Spurling,Chris		Tm	W	L	Sv	IP	K	ERA	Br/IP	R$	BF/G	OBA	vL	vR	H%	xERA	RAR	Ctl	Dom	Cmd	hr/9	G/F	S%	BPV	BPX
RH Reliever	99		0	0	0	0	0	0.00	0.00																
AGE 26 Growth	00		0	0	0	0	0	0.00	0.00																
TYPE Finesse	01	aa	5	7	1	121	51	4.39	1.65	($1)	16.3	329			35%	5.89 -	16.7	2.5	3.8	1.5	0.9		75%	18	34
R High	02	aa	4	3	20	70	46	2.96	1.16	$19	5.6	259			28%	3.79 -	21.7	1.5	5.9	3.8	1.2		81%	84	166
I EXP con	03	DET	1	3	3	77	38	4.68	1.30	$3	4.9	264	352	200	28%	4.19	8.8	2.6	4.4	1.7	1.1	1.01	66%	34	72
S pt	1st Half		0	1	3	36	20	4.74	1.25	$2	4.4	272			28%	4.58	3.8	1.7	5.0	2.9	1.5	0.83	67%	46	99
K	2nd Half		1	2	0	41	18	4.62	1.34	$1	5.5	257			28%	3.85 +	5.0	3.3	4.0	1.2	0.7	1.19	65%	33	71
LIMA C+ EP: 45%	04	Proj	2	3	2	60	30	4.80	1.37	$2	6.0	271			29%	4.46	5.9	2.9	4.5	1.6	1.1	--	67%	29	63

Low dominance and high hr/9 limit him in any closing role. Problem is, he set the bar much higher after '02's performance, so we now expect more. 2nd half letdown shows he's not really ready for the bigs just yet.

Standridge,Jason	Yr	Tm	W	L	Sv	IP	K	ERA	Br/IP	R$	BF/G	OBA	vL	vR	H%	xERA	RAR	Ctl	Dom	Cmd	hr/9	G/F	S%	BPV	BPX
RH Starter	99		0	0	0	0	0	0.00	0.00																
AGE 25 Growth	00	aa	6	8	0	97	48	4.36	1.43	$6	24.8	262			29%	3.89	18.2	3.9	4.5	**1.1**	0.5		69%	39	93
TYPE	01	a/a	5	12	0	131	57	6.73	1.98	($17)	20.7	340			35%	7.43 -	-23.0	4.8	3.9	**0.8**	1.4	1.08	68%	-16	-30
R X HIGH	02	aaa	10	9	0	176	95	3.99	1.55	$4	26.2	289			32%	4.79 -	30.2	3.6	4.9	**1.4**	0.7	1.00	75%	33	65
I EXP CON	03	TAM *	2	9	1	95	52	5.96	1.64	($6)	21.7	293	250	297	31%	5.63	-5.6	4.3	4.9	**1.2**	1.2	1.15	65%	13	29
S PT STB	1st Half		2	6	1	69	40	5.32	1.54	($2)	23.8	290			32%	5.17	1.9	3.5	5.2	**1.5**	1.0	1.12	67%	28	61
K age	2nd Half		0	3	0	26	12	7.67	1.90	($5)	17.8	299			30%	6.86 +	-7.4	6.3	4.2	**0.7**	1.7	1.23	61%	-18	-39
LIMA F EP: 45%	04	Proj	**1**	**3**	**0**	**40**	**20**	**5.85**	**1.70**	**($3)**	**23.1**	**299**			**32%**	**5.76**	**-1.7**	**4.5**	**4.5**	**1.0**	**1.1**	**--**	**67%**	**10**	**20**

0-5, 6.43 ERA in 35 IP at TAM. Here's how the PQS system can describe pitching performance in a way that no other system can. The scores of his 7 starts: 4-4-2-2-1-0-0

Stanford,Jason	Yr	Tm	W	L	Sv	IP	K	ERA	Br/IP	R$	BF/G	OBA	vL	vR	H%	xERA	RAR	Ctl	Dom	Cmd	hr/9	G/F	S%	BPV	BPX
LH Starter	99		0	0	0	0	0	0.00	0.00																
AGE 27 Growth	00		0	0	0	0	0	0.00	0.00																
TYPE	01	a/a	7	11	0	151	98	5.25	1.48	($1)	26.6	310			35%	5.08	3.6	2.0	5.8	**3.0**	0.8		65%	65	126
R High	02	a/a	10	7	0	138	89	4.50	1.64	$1	26.2	314			36%	5.41 -	14.2	3.2	5.8	**1.8**	0.7		73%	44	86
I EXP con	03	CLE *	11	7	0	176	119	4.40	1.39	$8	23.0	288	260	241	32%	4.77	26.6	2.3	6.1	**2.7**	1.1	0.55	71%	58	126
S pt	1st Half		8	2	0	97	67	4.27	1.40	$6	27.9	296			34%	4.78 -	16.3	1.9	6.2	**3.2**	0.9		71%	72	156
K	2nd Half		3	5	0	79	52	4.56	1.38	$2	18.9	279			31%	4.77	10.2	2.6	5.9	**2.3**	1.3		70%	45	97
LIMA C+ EP: 50%	04	Proj	**7**	**6**	**0**	**120**	**80**	**4.35**	**1.38**	**$6**	**23.4**	**278**			**31%**	**4.48**	**19.1**	**2.6**	**6.0**	**2.3**	**1.0**	**F**	**70%**	**54**	**116**

1-3, 3.60 ERA in 50 IP at CLE. PQS can do similarly here, even though we already know this is a better skill set: 2,3,0,0,4,4,4,3 That late surge could open up more opportunities.

Stanton,Mike	Yr	Tm	W	L	Sv	IP	K	ERA	Br/IP	R$	BF/G	OBA	vL	vR	H%	xERA	RAR	Ctl	Dom	Cmd	hr/9	G/F	S%	BPV	BPX
LH Reliever	99	NYY	2	2	0	62	59	4.35	1.44	$2	3.7	289	256	308	36%	4.51	12.6	2.6	8.6	**3.3**	0.7	1.07	70%	96	240
AGE 36 Decline	00	NYY	2	3	0	68	75	4.10	1.35	$4	4.2	262	339	199	35%	3.81	16.5	3.2	9.9	**3.1**	0.7	1.06	70%	108	280
TYPE	01	NYY	9	4	0	80	78	2.58	1.36	$12	4.5	262	283	251	34%	3.67 -	31.1	3.3	8.8	**2.7**	0.4	0.96	82%	98	197
R Low	02	NYY	7	1	6	78	44	3.00	1.29	$13	4.2	249	268	247	28%	3.44	25.7	3.2	5.1	**1.6**	0.5	0.96	77%	55	112
I con	03	NYM	2	7	5	45	34	4.59	1.24	$5	3.8	225	206	226	25%	3.59 +	4.2	3.8	6.8	**1.8**	1.2	0.65	66%	52	101
S pt	1st Half		2	3	0	21	13	4.71	1.33	$1	3.6	243			27%	3.74 +	1.6	3.9	5.6	**1.4**	0.9	0.72	65%	44	86
K AGE	2nd Half		0	4	5	24	21	4.48	1.16	$3	3.9	209			23%	3.47 +	2.6	3.7	7.8	**2.1**	1.5	0.58	67%	59	114
LIMA B EP: 50%	04	Proj	**4**	**6**	**2**	**60**	**42**	**3.90**	**1.37**	**$5**	**4.1**	**259**			**29%**	**4.04**	**11.0**	**3.5**	**6.3**	**1.8**	**0.9**	**F**	**74%**	**52**	**101**

Skills have been off the past two years, and while he pitched better than a 4.59 ERA in 2003, his BPIs look like he's going to be a 4.00 ERA pitcher more often than a 3.00 pitcher from now on.

Stark,Dennis	Yr	Tm	W	L	Sv	IP	K	ERA	Br/IP	R$	BF/G	OBA	vL	vR	H%	xERA	RAR	Ctl	Dom	Cmd	hr/9	G/F	S%	BPV	BPX
RH Starter	99	aa	9	11	0	147	86	6.24	1.80	($8)	26.7	317			34%	6.09	-14.1	4.4	5.3	**1.2**	1.2		66%	13	31
AGE 29 Peak	00	aa	4	3	0	49	33	3.31	1.33	$6	26.0	237			29%	3.02	16.1	4.0	6.1	**1.5**	0.2		73%	70	166
TYPE	01	a/a	16	3	0	172	124	3.51	1.35	$17	25.4	268	320	342	31%	4.24 -	44.1	2.9	6.5	**2.3**	0.9	0.59	77%	59	114
R Very High	02	COL *	12	6	0	165	95	4.20	1.38	$9	18.2	243	228	224	24%	4.55	20.0	4.3	5.2	**1.2**	1.7	1.01	77%	12	24
I EXP CON	03	COL	3	3	0	78	30	5.87	1.68	($5)	21.1	308	346	268	31%	6.04	-6.2	3.8	3.5	**0.9**	1.4	0.81	67%	-8	-16
S PT stb	1st Half		0	0	0	0	0	0.00	0.00																
K	2nd Half		3	3	0	78	30	5.87	1.68	($5)	21.1	308			31%	6.04	-6.2	3.8	3.5	**0.9**	1.4		67%	-8	-16
LIMA F EP: 50%	04	Proj	**8**	**7**	**0**	**140**	**80**	**4.63**	**1.49**	**$2**	**22.1**	**277**			**30%**	**4.86**	**11.9**	**3.7**	**5.1**	**1.4**	**1.2**	**--**	**72%**	**25**	**48**

INJ: Torn right lat muscle in the 1st half, and struggled upon his return. Of course, it would have been nice if he had a more friendly home ballpark:
7 starts at home: PQS Avg = 1
6 starts on the road: Avg = 3

Stephenson,Garrett	Yr	Tm	W	L	Sv	IP	K	ERA	Br/IP	R$	BF/G	OBA	vL	vR	H%	xERA	RAR	Ctl	Dom	Cmd	hr/9	G/F	S%	BPV	BPX
RH Starter	99	STL *	7	4	0	116	77	4.03	1.38	$7	21.7	273	320	236	30%	4.14	18.7	2.9	6.0	**2.1**	1.1	0.82	74%	47	103
AGE 32 Peak	00	STL	16	9	0	200	123	4.50	1.36	$16	26.8	270	310	231	29%	4.70	30.3	2.8	5.5	**2.0**	1.4	0.98	71%	33	73
TYPE Finesse	01	aaa	0	0	0	2	2	0.00	1.00	$0	7.8	262			35%	2.34 -	1.5	0.0	9.0		0.0		100%	57	109
R X HIGH	02	STL *	2	6	0	57	44	5.37	1.60	($3)	17.2	285	355	223	34%	4.68 +	-2.0	4.3	6.9	**1.6**	0.6	0.73	66%	55	104
I exp CON	03	STL	7	13	0	174	91	4.60	1.30	$5	22.9	253	280	238	25%	4.44	15.8	3.1	4.7	**1.5**	1.6	0.68	70%	18	35
S PT stb	1st Half		4	7	0	100	53	4.32	1.33	$3	26.6	246			25%	4.33	12.8	3.7	4.8	**1.3**	1.4	0.64	73%	18	35
K BRN	2nd Half		3	6	0	74	38	4.98	1.26	$2	19.3	262			26%	4.60	3.0	2.3	4.6	**2.0**	1.7	0.74	66%	21	41
LIMA D+ EP: 40%	04	Proj	**8**	**12**	**0**	**160**	**88**	**4.78**	**1.38**	**$3**	**20.9**	**267**			**28%**	**4.57**	**10.3**	**3.2**	**5.0**	**1.5**	**1.3**	**F**	**69%**	**25**	**48**

He may be back, in body anyway, but his skills are not. Only two positive signs: A .238 OBA vs RH and some 2nd half improvement, but I need to see much more before I project better days.

Stewart,Scott	Yr	Tm	W	L	Sv	IP	K	ERA	Br/IP	R$	BF/G	OBA	vL	vR	H%	xERA	RAR	Ctl	Dom	Cmd	hr/9	G/F	S%	BPV	BPX
LH Reliever	99	a/a	7	4	0	105	78	4.80	1.54	$3	13.0	299			35%	4.79	9.1	3.1	6.7	**2.2**	0.8		69%	58	134
AGE 28 Pre-Peak	00	aaa	3	5	5	72	48	4.00	1.49	$6	6.0	305			36%	4.55 -	17.0	2.3	6.0	**2.7**	0.4		72%	75	177
TYPE	01	MON	3	1	3	47	39	3.83	1.19	$6	3.1	245	286	215	29%	3.51	9.7	2.5	7.5	**3.0**	1.0	1.07	71%	85	158
R Very High	02	MON	4	2	17	64	67	3.09	1.11	$17	3.8	214	159	235	28%	2.42 +	17.3	3.1	9.4	**3.0**	0.6	2.06	73%	116	219
I exp CON	03	MON	3	1	0	43	29	3.98	1.51	$2	3.7	300	283	318	34%	5.17 -	7.5	2.7	6.1	**2.2**	1.0	0.88	77%	47	90
S PT stb	1st Half		3	1	0	34	23	2.63	1.37	$4	3.7	272			30%	4.42 -	12.1	2.9	6.1	**2.1**	1.1	0.75	86%	49	95
K	2nd Half		0	0	0	9	6	9.20	2.05	($2)	4.0	392			44%	8.11 +	-4.6	2.0	6.1	**3.0**	1.0	1.71	53%	46	88
LIMA B+ EP: 45%	04	Proj	**4**	**2**	**5**	**60**	**45**	**3.45**	**1.30**	**$8**	**4.1**	**262**			**31%**	**3.77**	**14.6**	**2.7**	**6.8**	**2.5**	**0.8**	**--**	**75%**	**73**	**141**

INJ: Appendectomy
It was thought that he might be the favorite for saves, but he got only one save opp all year. Serves him right for being a lefty. BPIs are still good, not great, but good enough for LIMA.

Stone,Ricky	Yr	Tm	W	L	Sv	IP	K	ERA	Br/IP	R$	BF/G	OBA	vL	vR	H%	xERA	RAR	Ctl	Dom	Cmd	hr/9	G/F	S%	BPV	BPX
RH Reliever	99	aaa	6	10	0	167	109	5.50	1.65	($5)	28.3	311			35%	5.61	0.8	3.4	5.9	**1.7**	1.1		68%	30	70
AGE 29 Pre-Peak	00	aaa	9	5	5	120	63	5.03	1.61	$6	11.3	311			34%	5.19	11.8	3.0	4.7	**1.6**	0.6		68%	36	86
TYPE	01	aaa	6	3	2	102	69	4.68	1.57	$2	8.0	308			35%	5.39 -	10.2	2.8	6.1	**2.2**	1.0	2.83	72%	46	88
R High	02	HOU	3	3	1	77	63	3.62	1.45	$3	4.3	264	288	258	31%	4.42 -	15.3	4.0	7.4	**1.9**	1.1	2.10	79%	54	101
I EXP con	03	HOU	6	4	1	83	47	3.69	1.29	$8	5.4	245	290	217	26%	3.98	17.7	3.4	5.1	**1.5**	1.2	2.09	76%	33	63
S pt	1st Half		4	2	0	44	22	3.87	1.36	$4	5.7	261			26%	4.78 -	8.3	3.3	4.5	**1.4**	1.6	1.75	79%	10	19
K brn	2nd Half		2	2	1	39	25	3.48	1.21	$4	5.0	226			26%	3.07	9.3	3.5	5.8	**1.7**	0.7	2.67	73%	59	113
LIMA C EP: 40%	04	Proj	**4**	**4**	**1**	**80**	**53**	**4.28**	**1.41**	**$3**	**5.7**	**267**			**30%**	**4.37**	**10.6**	**3.5**	**6.0**	**1.7**	**1.0**	**G**	**72%**	**43**	**83**

BPIs took a step back in most critical areas, but his ERA held on thanks to a 26% hit rate. When that regresses to the 30% mean, unless his BPI trend reverses, he'll be looking down at a 4.00 ERA.

Strickland,Scott	Yr	Tm	W	L	Sv	IP	K	ERA	Br/IP	R$	BF/G	OBA	vL	vR	H%	xERA	RAR	Ctl	Dom	Cmd	hr/9	G/F	S%	BPV	BPX
RH Reliever	99	MON *	4	2	8	75	84	3.00	1.35	$11	6.4	246	400	156	34%	2.96	22.5	3.8	10.1	**2.6**	0.4	1.36	78%	111	240
AGE 28 Pre-Peak	00	MON	4	3	9	48	48	3.00	1.13	$13	4.0	219	290	174	29%	2.62	16.9	3.0	9.0	**3.0**	0.6	1.22	75%	111	245
TYPE Power	01	MON	2	6	9	81	85	3.22	1.33	$9	4.5	227	274	189	29%	3.65	23.3	4.5	9.4	**2.1**	1.0	0.97	80%	80	148
R Moderate	02	2NL	6	9	2	68	69	3.57	1.38	$7	4.2	241	313	188	31%	3.80	14.0	4.4	9.1	**2.1**	0.9	0.89	77%	78	147
I con	03	NYM	0	2	0	20	16	2.25	1.30	$1	4.4	221	222	217	27%	2.98 -	8.1	4.5	7.2	**1.6**	0.5	1.00	84%	74	143
S PT stb	1st Half		0	2	0	20	16	2.25	1.30	$1	4.4	221			27%	2.98 -	8.1	4.5	7.2	**1.6**	0.5	1.00	84%	74	143
K	2nd Half		0	0	0	0	0	0.00	0.00																
LIMA B+ EP: 40%	04	Proj	**1**	**2**	**1**	**20**	**19**	**3.15**	**1.30**	**$2**	**4.4**	**232**			**29%**	**3.49**	**5.7**	**4.1**	**8.6**	**2.1**	**0.9**	**--**	**79%**	**77**	**149**

INJ: Ligament tear in elbow, and that means only one thing -- yet ANOTHER pitcher having Tommy John surgery. His was in June, so he might be back late in 2004.

Sturtze,Tanyon	Yr	Tm	W	L	Sv	IP	K	ERA	Br/IP	R$	BF/G	OBA	vL	vR	H%	xERA	RAR	Ctl	Dom	Cmd	hr/9	G/F	S%	BPV	BPX
RH Reliever	99	aaa	9	4	3	104	82	4.67	1.34	$10	13.4	250			30%	3.43 +	11.9	3.5	7.1	**2.0**	0.6	0.56	64%	71	165
AGE 33 Past	00	2AL	5	2	0	68	44	4.76	1.48	$4	10.3	273	269	275	30%	4.70	10.5	3.8	5.8	**1.5**	1.1	1.51	70%	35	92
TYPE	01	TAM	11	12	1	195	110	4.43	1.43	$7	21.8	267	283	261	29%	4.53	27.6	3.6	5.1	**1.4**	1.1	0.95	71%	30	59
R Very High	02	TAM	4	18	0	224	137	5.18	1.61	($10)	30.7	300	323	282	32%	5.76 -	8.3	3.6	5.5	**1.5**	1.3	0.89	71%	21	42
I CON	03	TOR	7	6	0	89	54	5.96	1.68	($3)	10.3	299	271	321	32%	5.99	-5.2	4.3	5.5	**1.3**	1.4	1.09	67%	12	26
S PT STB	1st Half		6	4	0	65	37	5.38	1.56	$1	11.2	292			31%	5.70	1.2	3.6	5.1	**1.4**	1.5	0.95	69%	11	25
K age	2nd Half		1	2	0	24	17	7.53	2.01	($4)	8.4	315			36%	6.79 +	-6.4	6.4	6.4	**1.0**	1.1	1.65	62%	18	38
LIMA F EP: 45%	04	Proj	**4**	**6**	**0**	**80**	**48**	**5.74**	**1.73**	**($4)**	**12.8**	**301**			**32%**	**6.06**	**-2.1**	**4.6**	**5.4**	**1.2**	**1.4**	**--**	**69%**	**11**	**24**

I won't bore you with his starter/ reliever splits, because they were both terrible. All you really need to know you learned in kindergarten: "What's the next value in this series?"
BPX: 165, 92, 59, 42, 26, ??

Sullivan,Scott

RH Reliever
AGE 33 Past
TYPE Power
R: Low
I: CON
S:
K:
LIMA C+ | EP: 45%

Yr	Tm	W	L	Sv	IP	K	ERA	Br/IP	R$	BF/G	OBA	vL	vR	H%	xERA	RAR	Ctl	Dom	Cmd	hr/9	G/F	S%	BPV	BPX
99	CIN	5	4	3	113	78	3.03	1.19	$13	5.9	216	242	202	24%	2.65	33.4	3.7	6.2	1.7	0.8	0.89	78%	60	130
00	CIN	3	6	3	106	96	3.48	1.18	$11	5.5	225	214	235	26%	3.43	30.6	3.2	8.1	2.5	1.2	0.77	76%	76	168
01	CIN	7	1	0	103	82	3.32	1.26	$10	5.5	244	252	237	29%	3.60	28.3	3.1	7.2	2.3	0.9	1.01	77%	71	131
02	CIN	6	5	1	78	78	6.12	1.59	($2)	5.0	297	357	253	35%	5.86	-10.5	3.6	9.0	2.5	1.7	0.80	65%	50	95
03	2TM	6	0	0	64	56	3.66	1.25	$7	4.1	210	238	187	25%	3.11 +	14.9	4.5	7.9	1.8	0.8	0.50	73%	72	145
1st Half		6	0	0	39	38	4.38	1.44	$5	4.5	236			29%	3.97	5.3	5.1	8.8	1.7	0.9	0.39	71%	69	140
2nd Half		0	0	0	25	18	2.52	0.96	$3	3.6	166			19%	1.77 +	9.6	3.6	6.5	1.8	0.7	0.70	77%	77	156
04	Proj	4	2	0	70	55	4.37	1.36	$3	4.6	248			29%	4.02	9.6	3.9	7.1	1.8	1.0	F	70%	56	112

The burnout symptoms we were expecting in 2002 -- but didn't get, despite his ERA spike -- seem to have appeared in 2003 -- despite the ERA rebound, thanks to a 25% hit rate. Got all that? Trust this projection.

Suppan,Jeff

RH Starter
AGE 29 Pre-Peak
TYPE Finesse
R: Moderate
I: CON
S:
K: brn
LIMA D+ | EP: 45%

Yr	Tm	W	L	Sv	IP	K	ERA	Br/IP	R$	BF/G	OBA	vL	vR	H%	xERA	RAR	Ctl	Dom	Cmd	hr/9	G/F	S%	BPV	BPX
99	KC	10	12	0	208	103	4.54	1.37	$12	27.9	275	259	289	29%	4.62	37.0	2.7	4.5	1.7	1.2	1.57	70%	25	64
00	KC	10	9	0	217	128	4.94	1.49	$6	27.4	282	284	283	30%	5.27	28.4	3.5	5.3	1.5	1.5	1.39	71%	18	46
01	KC	10	14	0	218	120	4.37	1.38	$7	27.6	270	235	306	29%	4.46	32.4	3.1	5.0	1.6	1.1	1.36	71%	33	65
02	KC	9	16	0	208	109	5.32	1.43	($0)	27.4	281	276	281	29%	5.08	3.8	2.9	4.7	1.6	1.4	1.30	66%	19	40
03	2TM	13	11	0	204	110	4.19	1.31	$13	27.0	274	310	239	29%	4.30	32.8	2.3	4.9	2.2	1.0	1.30	71%	44	90
1st Half		6	7	0	102	57	3.79	1.28	$8	26.8	267			30%	3.83	21.9	2.3	5.0	2.2	0.7	1.66	72%	57	115
2nd Half		7	4	0	102	53	4.59	1.34	$5	27.2	280			29%	4.76	10.9	2.2	4.7	2.1	1.3	1.03	70%	32	64
04	Proj	12	11	0	200	109	4.14	1.29	$13	27.2	267			28%	4.22	33.6	2.4	4.9	2.1	1.1	--	71%	41	82

Had a nice little run in PIT (3.57 ERA, 2.5 Cmd) but reverted to his old American League BPIs when he was traded to BOS. There is a serviceable arm here with some upside, but he just might need to be in the NL.

Tam,Jeff

RH Reliever
AGE 33 Past
TYPE Finesse
R: Moderate
I: exp con
S: pt stb
K: age
LIMA D | EP: 45%

Yr	Tm	W	L	Sv	IP	K	ERA	Br/IP	R$	BF/G	OBA	vL	vR	H%	xERA	RAR	Ctl	Dom	Cmd	hr/9	G/F	S%	BPV	BPX
99	2TM	* 2	3	3	58	26	3.88	1.47	$4	6.1	297	200	185	32%	4.60 -	12.8	2.5	4.0	1.6	0.8	2.11	75%	31	71
00	OAK	3	3	3	85	46	2.64	1.28	$12	5.0	264	360	209	30%	3.37 -	37.3	2.4	4.9	2.0	0.3	2.49	79%	64	166
01	OAK	2	4	3	74	44	3.03	1.31	$7	4.5	245	247	251	28%	3.28	24.4	3.5	5.3	1.5	0.4	2.08	77%	59	118
02	OAK	* 2	5	2	69	35	5.48	1.57	($2)	5.2	316	300	352	35%	5.16	-0.2	2.3	4.6	1.9	0.5	2.54	63%	44	91
03	TOR	* 1	4	5	61	36	4.69	1.73	($0)	4.7	311	303	319	34%	5.78 -	6.9	4.1	5.3	1.3	0.9	1.84	74%	25	54
1st Half		0	2	1	39	25	6.00	1.95	($5)	4.9	321			36%	6.76 -	-2.5	5.5	5.8	1.0	1.2	1.79	70%	13	27
2nd Half		1	2	4	22	11	2.41	1.34	$5	4.3	292			32%	4.08 -	9.3	1.6	4.4	2.8	0.4	2.20	83%	69	149
04	Proj	1	3	0	40	22	4.50	1.58	($1)	4.9	307			34%	5.15 -	5.6	2.9	5.0	1.7	0.7	G	72%	39	83

0-4, 5.73 ERA in 44 IP at TOR. Two straight years of .300+ OBA have been boosted by high hit rates, but could be for real. With falling BPIs, there little support for these struggles to be just random chance.

Tavarez,Julian

RH Reliever
AGE 30 Peak
TYPE Finesse
R: Very High
I: CON
S: PT STB
K:
LIMA D+ | EP: 55%

Yr	Tm	W	L	Sv	IP	K	ERA	Br/IP	R$	BF/G	OBA	vL	vR	H%	xERA	RAR	Ctl	Dom	Cmd	hr/9	G/F	S%	BPV	BPX
99	SF	2	0	0	54	33	6.00	1.67	($4)	5.3	299	345	265	33%	5.33 +	-5.5	4.2	5.5	1.3	1.2	2.20	65%	21	45
00	COL	11	5	1	120	62	4.43	1.48	$9	10.3	268	260	273	29%	4.44	19.3	4.0	4.7	1.2	0.8	2.86	71%	29	64
01	CHC	10	9	0	161	107	4.53	1.50	$4	20.9	275	320	249	31%	4.48	18.2	3.9	6.0	1.6	0.7	2.86	70%	47	87
02	FLA	10	12	0	153	67	5.41	1.71	($6)	24.4	303	332	285	33%	5.19	-6.3	4.4	3.9	0.9	0.5	1.94	67%	21	40
03	PIT	3	3	11	83	39	3.68	1.23	$11	5.4	242	292	215	27%	2.77 +	17.8	2.9	4.2	1.4	0.1	3.10	67%	59	113
1st Half		0	2	0	34	14	3.95	1.32	$0	4.8	266			30%	3.23 +	6.1	2.6	3.7	1.4	0.0	2.71	67%	53	102
2nd Half		3	1	11	49	25	3.49	1.16	$11	5.9	224			26%	2.46 +	11.7	3.1	4.6	1.5	0.2	3.44	68%	63	121
04	Proj	4	4	2	80	40	4.39	1.45	$3	6.7	274			30%	4.05	9.4	3.5	4.5	1.3	0.5	G	69%	41	79

Another test to see if we can resist. Opportunity has provided him the chance to save games, but BPIs hardly support future success. Do you bid on the save opps to continue or on the lack of skill to kick in?

Tejera,Michael

LH Reliever
AGE 27 Pre-Peak
TYPE Power
R: Moderate
I: EXP con
S: pt
K:
LIMA B | EP: 55%

Yr	Tm	W	L	Sv	IP	K	ERA	Br/IP	R$	BF/G	OBA	vL	vR	H%	xERA	RAR	Ctl	Dom	Cmd	hr/9	G/F	S%	BPV	BPX
99		0	0	0	0	0	0.00	0.00																
00		0	0	0	0	0	0.00	0.00																
01	aa	9	8	0	141	108	5.04	1.62	($1)	25.6	313			36%	5.87 -	7.2	3.0	6.9	2.3	1.3		72%	44	84
02	FLA	8	8	1	139	95	4.47	1.47	$3	13.0	269	228	280	30%	4.57	11.9	3.9	6.2	1.6	1.1	1.07	72%	38	73
03	FLA	3	4	2	81	58	4.67	1.46	$1	7.1	264	392	224	31%	4.15 +	6.6	4.0	6.4	1.6	0.7	1.18	68%	55	105
1st Half		1	3	1	54	41	5.49	1.63	($3)	9.8	292			34%	5.13	-1.5	4.2	6.8	1.6	0.8	1.16	66%	47	90
2nd Half		2	1	1	27	17	3.01	1.12	$4	4.3	200			23%	2.17 +	8.2	3.7	5.7	1.5	0.3	1.21	72%	71	138
04	Proj	7	6	0	120	88	4.20	1.38	$5	16.1	254			29%	3.92	17.1	3.8	6.6	1.8	0.8	--	71%	56	108

Starter? Reliever? Whatever.

	IP	ERA	Ctl	Dom
SP	30	5.40	3.9	7.5
RP	51	4.24	4.1	5.8

Fared better as a starter. Last year he fared better as a RP. Overall, didn't improve much.

Telemaco,Amaury

RH Starter
AGE 30 Peak
TYPE Finesse
R: X HIGH
I: EXP con
S: PT STB
K: BRN
LIMA C+ | EP: 55%

Yr	Tm	W	L	Sv	IP	K	ERA	Br/IP	R$	BF/G	OBA	vL	vR	H%	xERA	RAR	Ctl	Dom	Cmd	hr/9	G/F	S%	BPV	BPX
99	2NL	* 4	3	0	71	58	5.70	1.52	($1)	5.1	270	304	235	30%	4.85 +	-4.5	4.3	7.4	1.7	1.5	1.03	66%	35	77
00	PHI	* 9	6	0	147	100	5.08	1.49	$4	19.1	277	233	313	30%	5.02	10.8	3.7	6.1	1.7	1.3	0.77	69%	33	72
01	PHI	* 6	7	0	113	81	5.65	1.52	($2)	17.9	294	289	257	32%	5.65	-4.4	3.1	6.5	2.1	1.6	1.28	66%	31	57
02	a/a	1	0	0	6	4	3.00	1.00	$1	11.8	262			24%	5.16 -	1.8	0.0	6.0		3.0		100%	-51	******
03	PHI	* 11	13	0	200	122	4.36	1.18	$13	24.9	262	288	202	28%	3.82 +	24.6	1.7	5.5	3.3	1.1	1.21	66%	72	139
1st Half		5	7	0	107	60	4.37	1.05	$9	25.0	245			26%	3.36 +	13.0	1.2	5.0	4.3	1.2		61%	91	175
2nd Half		6	6	0	93	62	4.35	1.34	$5	24.8	280			31%	4.36	11.6	2.2	6.0	2.7	1.0		70%	63	121
04	Proj	7	7	0	120	76	4.13	1.24	$8	22.7	260			28%	3.96	18.3	2.3	5.7	2.5	1.1	--	70%	57	109

1-4, 4.00 ERA in 45 IP at PHI, but solid BPIs during that stretch as well as a dominant stint in AAA. The prospect tag is long gone, but it's always good to grab a peaking player and hope that peak occurs in the bigs.

Thomson,John

RH Starter
AGE 30 Peak
TYPE Finesse
R: Moderate
I: con
S: pt stb
K:
LIMA C+ | EP: 60%

Yr	Tm	W	L	Sv	IP	K	ERA	Br/IP	R$	BF/G	OBA	vL	vR	H%	xERA	RAR	Ctl	Dom	Cmd	hr/9	G/F	S%	BPV	BPX
99	COL	* 1	12	0	83	49	8.78	2.04	($19)	21.7	344	278	361	37%	7.43 +	-39.4	5.0	5.3	1.1	1.6	1.44	57%	-8	-18
00	COL	0	0	0	0	0	0.00	0.00																
01	COL	* 9	8	0	161	111	4.25	1.35	$8	26.4	282	177	294	31%	4.84 -	24.1	2.2	6.2	2.8	1.4	1.16	73%	54	100
02	2NL	9	14	0	181	107	4.72	1.35	$4	25.8	283	285	264	32%	3.79 +	9.3	2.2	5.3	2.4	0.3	0.87	63%	71	134
03	TEX	13	14	0	217	136	4.85	1.30	$10	26.2	277	281	270	30%	4.43	19.5	2.0	5.6	2.8	1.1	1.32	65%	58	126
1st Half		5	9	0	103	64	5.93	1.39	($1)	24.7	295			31%	5.34 +	-5.6	1.8	5.6	3.0	1.6	1.16	60%	46	100
2nd Half		8	5	0	114	72	3.88	1.23	$11	27.8	259			29%	3.61	25.1	2.2	5.7	2.6	0.7	1.50	69%	70	151
04	Proj	13	12	0	200	127	3.96	1.23	$17	24.4	262			29%	3.91	42.3	2.1	5.7	2.8	1.0	--	71%	65	140

There is nothing wrong with these BPIs that a little bit of extra bullpen support and a few less HRs can't cure. Take a good look at his 2nd half and know that those levels represent a very attainable upside.

Timlin,Mike

RH Reliever
AGE 38 Decline
TYPE Finesse
R: Very High
I: CON
S: pt STB
K: AGE
LIMA B+ | EP: 55%

Yr	Tm	W	L	Sv	IP	K	ERA	Br/IP	R$	BF/G	OBA	vL	vR	H%	xERA	RAR	Ctl	Dom	Cmd	hr/9	G/F	S%	BPV	BPX
99	BAL	3	9	27	63	50	3.57	1.17	$23	4.2	223	198	240	25%	3.50	19.4	3.3	7.1	2.2	1.3	2.30	75%	60	151
00	2TM	5	4	12	64	52	4.21	1.59	$11	4.7	270	311	241	31%	4.99 -	13.4	4.9	7.3	1.5	1.1	1.44	77%	42	100
01	STL	4	5	3	72	47	4.11	1.34	$5	4.6	277	319	257	31%	4.15	12.1	2.4	5.9	2.5	0.7	2.84	70%	64	119
02	2NL	4	6	0	96	50	3.00	0.93	$12	5.1	217	208	214	24%	2.04 +	27.1	1.3	4.7	3.6	0.6	1.83	69%	98	185
03	BOS	6	4	2	83	65	3.57	1.03	$12	4.6	247	287	198	28%	3.40	21.8	1.0	7.0	7.2	1.2	1.52	71%	164	354
1st Half		3	2	2	46	34	3.51	1.02	$7	5.2	249			27%	3.55	12.4	0.8	6.6	8.5	1.4	1.50	73%	183	394
2nd Half		3	2	0	37	31	3.64	1.05	$5	4.0	245			29%	3.20	9.4	1.2	7.5	6.2	1.0	1.55	69%	152	329
04	Proj	5	5	1	80	56	3.60	1.13	$10	4.6	252			28%	3.53	20.8	1.6	6.3	4.0	1.0	G	72%	96	206

From a BPI perspective, a career year. His trends saw it coming, but at this age, you'd always bet against. He's now 38; you can't reasonably expect it to get better... but we would have said the same thing last year.

Tomko,Brett

RH Starter
AGE 31 Peak
TYPE Finesse
R: Very High
I: CON
S: PT STB
K:
LIMA C+ | EP: 50%

Yr	Tm	W	L	Sv	IP	K	ERA	Br/IP	R$	BF/G	OBA	vL	vR	H%	xERA	RAR	Ctl	Dom	Cmd	hr/9	G/F	S%	BPV	BPX
99	CIN	* 7	7	0	184	140	4.94	1.37	$3	22.6	269	250	275	30%	4.50	7.3	3.0	6.8	2.3	1.6	1.00	69%	44	95
00	SEA	7	5	1	92	59	4.69	1.43	$7	12.5	262	270	260	28%	4.53	15.1	3.9	5.8	1.5	1.2	1.09	70%	33	86
01	SEA	* 13	7	0	161	121	5.03	1.44	$6	23.4	294	365	229	33%	5.10	9.8	2.4	6.8	2.8	1.2	0.80	68%	59	118
02	SD	10	10	0	204	126	4.50	1.33	$6	27.1	269	270	264	29%	4.50	16.6	2.6	5.6	2.1	1.4	1.50	71%	38	71
03	STL	13	9	0	202	114	5.30	1.53	$0	27.3	306	325	292	32%	5.80 -	-0.5	2.5	5.1	2.0	1.6	1.24	69%	19	37
1st Half		4	5	0	106	55	5.69	1.62	($6)	28.3	316			33%	6.17	-5.8	2.9	4.7	1.6	1.5	1.34	68%	8	15
2nd Half		9	4	0	96	59	4.86	1.42	$5	26.1	296			31%	5.40 -	5.3	2.2	5.5	2.6	1.6	1.14	71%	35	68
04	Proj	10	12	0	200	125	4.95	1.45	$2	24.9	291			31%	5.20	8.4	2.6	5.6	2.2	1.4	--	70%	33	63

Allowed 35 HRs, most in the NL, which is a huge problem for him. There is some talent here, though declining Dom and increasing hr/9 are slowly whittling that talent away.

Torres,Salomon

Torres,Salomon	Yr	Tm	W	L	Sv	IP	K	ERA	Br/IP	R$	BF/G	OBA	vL	vR	H%	xERA	RAR	Ctl	Dom	Cmd	hr/9	G/F	S%	BPV	BPX
RH Reliever	99		0	0	0	0	0	0.00	0.00																
AGE 32 Peak	00		0	0	0	0	0	0.00	0.00																
TYPE	01	KOR	0	2	2	5	5	19.80	5.00	($4)		515			52%	26.19 -				0.5	9.0		70%		0
R Low	02	PIT	*10	6	0	192	116	4.78	1.55	($1)	27.7	311	241	273	35%	5.04	8.4	2.5	5.4	2.1	0.7	1.73	69%	50	94
I EXP	03	PIT	7	5	2	121	84	4.76	1.40	$4	12.8	273	307	252	30%	4.84	8.4	3.1	6.2	2.0	1.4	1.78	70%	38	72
S pt	1st Half		5	2	1	63	42	4.71	1.35	$4	10.0	271			28%	5.10	4.8	2.7	6.0	2.2	1.9	1.32	72%	28	53
K	2nd Half		2	3	1	58	42	4.81	1.47	($0)	18.2	275			32%	4.57	3.6	3.6	6.5	1.8	0.9	2.56	68%	50	95
LIMA B EP: 50%	04	Proj	6	5	0	120	84	4.35	1.38	$4	16.7	273			31%	4.35	14.7	2.9	6.3	2.2	1.0	G	71%	54	105

Struggled with the longball in the 1st half, but got it under control down the stretch, thanks in part to being able to keep the ball down more (higher G/F). All things considered, there might be a bit more BPI upside here.

Towers,Josh

Towers,Josh	Yr	Tm	W	L	Sv	IP	K	ERA	Br/IP	R$	BF/G	OBA	vL	vR	H%	xERA	RAR	Ctl	Dom	Cmd	hr/9	G/F	S%	BPV	BPX
RH Starter	99	aa	12	7	0	189	86	4.62	1.38	$11	28.0	305			31%	5.08	23.1	1.3	4.1	3.2	1.4		71%	44	102
AGE 27 Growth	00	aaa	8	6	0	148	91	4.32	1.37	$10	26.5	304			33%	5.04 -	28.6	1.3	5.5	4.3	1.2		72%	82	194
TYPE Finesse	01	BAL	*11	11	0	181	82	4.52	1.30	$10	25.5	293	307	288	31%	4.69	23.3	1.2	4.1	3.4	1.1	0.79	68%	58	117
R X HIGH	02	BAL	*0	12	0	96	49	8.72	1.93	($21)	23.3	380			38%	9.18	-41.9	1.8	4.6	2.6	2.6	0.77	59%	-18	-37
I EXP CON	03	TOR	*13	8	1	196	106	4.49	1.31	$12	23.7	293	281	250	31%	4.80	27.1	1.3	4.9	3.8	1.2	0.91	69%	68	147
S pt STB	1st Half		4	6	0	87	46	4.95	1.49	$0	22.6	313			34%	5.37	6.7	1.9	4.7	2.6	1.0	0.43	68%	44	94
K BRN	2nd Half		9	2	1	109	60	4.13	1.17	$12	24.7	276			29%	4.34	20.4	0.8	5.0	6.0	1.4	0.96	70%	113	245
LIMA B EP: 55%	04	Proj	8	8	0	140	78	4.31	1.28	$9	23.5	286			30%	4.66	23.1	1.4	5.0	3.7	1.3	--	70%	67	144

8-1, 4.50 ERA in 64 IP at TOR. The next Brian Anderson? Stingy with the walks, stingy with the strikeouts, but boy do those HRs fly. There is some potential here but not a high ceiling.

Traber,Billy

Traber,Billy	Yr	Tm	W	L	Sv	IP	K	ERA	Br/IP	R$	BF/G	OBA	vL	vR	H%	xERA	RAR	Ctl	Dom	Cmd	hr/9	G/F	S%	BPV	BPX
LH Starter	99		0	0	0	0	0	0.00	0.00																
AGE 24 Growth	00		0	0	0	0	0	0.00	0.00																
TYPE	01	a/a	4	4	0	50	38	4.68	1.52	$1	24.7	305			36%	4.99	5.0	2.5	6.8	2.7	0.7		69%	70	135
R Very High	02	a/a	17	5	0	162	99	3.89	1.37	$15	25.7	292			33%	4.43 -	30.0	1.9	5.5	2.9	0.8		73%	68	133
I EXP con	03	CLE	6	9	0	111	88	5.26	1.55	($1)	15.1	296	219	318	34%	5.40	3.9	3.2	7.1	2.2	1.2	1.46	68%	48	104
S pt	1st Half		3	4	0	54	46	3.99	1.50	$2	11.4	265			32%	4.31	11.1	4.3	7.7	1.8	0.7	1.76	74%	65	141
K age	2nd Half		3	5	0	57	42	6.46	1.59	($3)	21.5	323			36%	6.45	-7.2	2.2	6.6	3.0	1.7	1.25	63%	41	89
LIMA D+ EP: 60%	04	Proj	9	8	0	120	91	4.58	1.40	$6	22.5	284			33%	4.69	15.5	2.6	6.8	2.7	1.1	--	69%	64	137

Starter or reliever? Yet again:

	IP	ERA	Ctl	Dom
SP	89	5.68	2.5	6.7
RP	23	3.52	5.9	8.6

Overthrowing the ball from the pen; the better results are as a SP, despite 33/50 DOM/DIS.

Trachsel,Steve

Trachsel,Steve	Yr	Tm	W	L	Sv	IP	K	ERA	Br/IP	R$	BF/G	OBA	vL	vR	H%	xERA	RAR	Ctl	Dom	Cmd	hr/9	G/F	S%	BPV	BPX
RH Starter	99	CHC	8	18	0	205	149	5.58	1.41	($1)	26.1	281	285	276	31%	4.64 +	-9.3	2.8	6.5	2.3	1.4	1.27	63%	45	97
AGE 33 Past	00	2AL	8	15	0	200	110	4.81	1.53	$4	26.2	291	298	290	31%	5.20	29.5	3.3	4.9	1.5	1.2	1.13	71%	23	59
TYPE Finesse	01	NYM	*13	13	0	192	153	4.45	1.24	$13	25.8	255	232	273	29%	4.11	23.5	2.5	7.2	2.8	1.3	1.31	68%	67	125
R Low	02	NYM	12	11	0	178	108	3.29	1.39	$13	24.8	257	233	281	29%	3.96 -	43.4	3.7	5.5	1.5	0.8	1.39	79%	43	81
I CON	03	NYM	16	10	0	204	111	3.79	1.32	$17	26.2	262	199	312	28%	4.23	40.7	2.9	4.9	1.7	1.1	0.85	75%	34	64
S stb	1st Half		7	5	0	103	53	4.36	1.43	$4	26.4	271			28%	4.81	12.7	3.5	4.6	1.3	1.3	0.93	74%	17	33
K age	2nd Half		9	5	0	101	58	3.21	1.20	$13	26.0	252			27%	3.64	28.0	2.2	5.2	2.3	1.0	0.77	77%	55	106
LIMA D EP: 40%	04	Proj	13	13	0	200	117	4.05	1.34	$12	25.8	263			28%	4.19	32.5	3.0	5.3	1.8	1.1	--	73%	39	75

Overall, Dom has declined over the past 2 years, although he did show a bit more oomph in the 2nd half. BA vs RHers, Declining G/F, more reasons that his 3.79 was not as good as it looked.

Tucker,T.J.

Tucker,T.J.	Yr	Tm	W	L	Sv	IP	K	ERA	Br/IP	R$	BF/G	OBA	vL	vR	H%	xERA	RAR	Ctl	Dom	Cmd	hr/9	G/F	S%	BPV	BPX
RH Reliever	99	aa	8	5	0	116	74	4.81	1.37	$7	26.2	273			30%	4.15 +	11.2	2.8	5.7	2.1	0.9		66%	50	116
AGE 25 Growth	00	aa	2	2	0	52	22	5.37	1.33	$1	22.1	250			22%	5.16	2.8	3.5	3.8	1.1	2.3	0.71	68%	-17	-39
TYPE	01	a/a	8	10	0	166	100	4.34	1.46	$4	27.0	266			28%	4.94 -	24.1	4.0	5.4	1.4	1.4		75%	21	40
R X HIGH	02	MON	6	3	4	61	42	4.13	1.64	$4	4.9	286	269	300	33%	4.92 -	8.0	4.6	6.2	1.4	0.7	1.77	76%	41	78
I EXP CON	03	MON	*3	3	0	96	52	4.40	1.39	$1	8.6	283	254	294	31%	4.53	11.3	2.5	4.9	1.9	0.9	1.52	70%	40	77
S PT stb	1st Half		0	1	0	41	27	5.24	1.41	($2)	6.1	270			29%	4.93	0.2	3.3	5.9	1.8	1.5	1.29	67%	28	54
K BRN	2nd Half		3	2	0	55	25	3.77	1.38	$3	12.4	292			32%	4.23	11.1	2.0	4.1	2.1	0.5	1.82	73%	50	96
LIMA C+ EP: 45%	04	Proj	4	3	0	80	47	4.39	1.46	$1	6.7	281			31%	4.70	9.4	3.3	5.3	1.6	1.0	G	72%	34	66

2-3, 4.73 ERA in 80 IP at MON. His Seven Bizarre Starts:
- 4.05 ERA, 16.0 Cmd
- WIthout last start: 2.42 ERA
- Walked just 1 batter in 27 IP
- PQS scores: 0,0,0,4,0,4,0
- Lasted past 5th inn. only twice

Urbina,Ugueth

Urbina,Ugueth	Yr	Tm	W	L	Sv	IP	K	ERA	Br/IP	R$	BF/G	OBA	vL	vR	H%	xERA	RAR	Ctl	Dom	Cmd	hr/9	G/F	S%	BPV	BPX
RH Reliever	99	MON	6	6	41	75	100	3.72	1.27	$31	4.4	218	198	215	32%	2.73 +	15.2	4.3	12.0	2.8	0.7	0.89	72%	120	261
AGE 30 Peak	00	MON	0	1	8	13	22	4.12	1.22	$5	4.2	229	269	174	40%	3.05 +	2.6	3.4	15.1	4.4	0.7	1.00	67%	172	378
TYPE Power	01	2TM	2	2	24	66	89	3.67	1.24	$18	4.3	237	278	196	33%	3.73	15.5	3.3	12.1	3.7	1.2	0.83	75%	121	233
R High	02	BOS	1	6	40	60	71	3.00	1.07	$29	3.9	206	257	143	27%	2.96	19.8	3.0	10.7	3.6	1.2	0.51	79%	116	238
I con	03	2TM	3	4	32	77	78	2.81	1.13	$27	4.3	205	182	229	26%	2.82	26.7	3.6	9.1	2.5	0.9	0.41	80%	93	189
S PT STB	1st Half		0	3	22	34	33	4.24	1.29	$13	4.2	226			26%	4.11	5.3	4.2	8.7	2.1	1.6	0.33	74%	58	117
K	2nd Half		3	1	10	43	45	1.67	1.00	$14	4.4	188			25%	1.80	21.4	3.1	9.4	3.0	0.4	0.49	85%	124	252
LIMA C+ EP: 50%	04	Proj	3	4	38	70	80	3.09	1.14	$29	4.2	212			28%	2.99	21.6	3.5	10.3	3.0	1.0	F	78%	106	214

There has been a gradual decline in his BPIs over the past few years, but they are still very closer-caliber. If he finds a front-line closing job, he should do very well. Except in a flyball ballpark.

Valdes,Ismael

Valdes,Ismael	Yr	Tm	W	L	Sv	IP	K	ERA	Br/IP	R$	BF/G	OBA	vL	vR	H%	xERA	RAR	Ctl	Dom	Cmd	hr/9	G/F	S%	BPV	BPX
RH Starter	99	LA	9	14	0	203	143	3.99	1.33	$11	27.0	271	271	269	30%	4.31	33.9	2.6	6.3	2.5	1.4	0.93	76%	48	104
AGE 30 Peak	00	2NL	2	7	0	107	74	5.64	1.53	($4)	22.7	291	330	261	31%	5.87	-0.1	3.4	6.2	1.9	1.9	0.79	68%	17	38
TYPE Finesse	01	ANA	9	13	0	163	100	4.47	1.39	$6	26.1	278	294	261	30%	4.63	22.2	2.8	5.5	2.0	1.1	1.08	71%	41	83
R Very High	02	2AL	8	12	0	196	102	4.18	1.23	$11	26.2	260	255	259	27%	4.11	33.6	2.2	4.7	2.2	1.2	0.93	70%	41	84
I CON	03	TEX	*9	10	0	128	51	5.90	1.56	($2)	23.0	317	283	350	32%	6.18	-6.5	2.2	3.6	1.6	1.6	1.18	66%	-2	-4
S PT STB	1st Half		6	5	0	73	35	5.90	1.50	$0	23.1	317			33%	6.01	-3.7	1.7	4.3	2.5	1.6	1.31	64%	22	47
K	2nd Half		3	5	0	55	16	5.90	1.64	($2)	22.8	317			31%	6.41 -	-2.8	3.0	2.6	0.9	1.6	1.02	68%	-23	-50
LIMA C EP: 45%	04	Proj	7	9	0	120	57	5.18	1.45	$2	23.8	294			30%	5.35	5.8	2.5	4.3	1.7	1.4	--	68%	15	33

Diary of a Workload Abuse Case

Age	IP	BPV	Age	IP	BPV
22	198	88	27	107	17
23	225	88	28	163	41
24	197	87	29	196	41
25	174	54	30	128	-2
26	203	48			

Valverde,Jose

Valverde,Jose	Yr	Tm	W	L	Sv	IP	K	ERA	Br/IP	R$	BF/G	OBA	vL	vR	H%	xERA	RAR	Ctl	Dom	Cmd	hr/9	G/F	S%	BPV	BPX
RH Reliever	99		0	0	0	0	0	0.00	0.00																
AGE 24 Growth	00		0	0	0	0	0	0.00	0.00																
TYPE Power	01	aa	2	2	13	41	62	4.39	1.56	$8	4.7	252			41%	3.79 +	5.7	5.5	13.6	2.5	0.2		70%	132	253
R Very High	02	aaa	2	4	5	47	54	6.51	1.49	$0	4.2	270			34%	5.08 +	-7.8	4.0	10.3	2.6	1.5		58%	71	140
I EXP con	03	ARI	*3	2	15	79	94	2.73	1.16	$16	4.2	192	169	112	27%	2.37	27.0	4.4	10.7	2.4	0.6	0.57	78%	114	220
S pt stb	1st Half		2	1	14	43	41	2.93	1.30	$11	5.0	234			30%	3.30	13.5	4.0	8.6	2.2	0.6	0.85	79%	86	166
K age	2nd Half		1	1	1	36	53	2.49	1.00	$5	3.5	136			22%	1.26 +	13.5	5.0	13.2	2.7	0.5	0.47	76%	148	284
LIMA A EP: 55%	04	Proj	3	4	3	80	101	3.71	1.29	$6	4.2	224			31%	3.33	16.6	4.3	11.4	2.7	0.9	F	74%	107	207

10 Sv, 2.16 ERA in 50 IP at ARI. Kept the hot seat warm for Kim's return, and then Mantei, and got only 2 save opps after June 29. He deserves another shot. Hard-thrower still trying to learn control, but improving.

Van Poppel,Todd

Van Poppel,Todd	Yr	Tm	W	L	Sv	IP	K	ERA	Br/IP	R$	BF/G	OBA	vL	vR	H%	xERA	RAR	Ctl	Dom	Cmd	hr/9	G/F	S%	BPV	BPX
RH Reliever	99	aaa	10	6	0	163	127	5.96	1.63	($3)	27.5	305			35%	5.74	-9.4	3.5	7.0	2.0	1.4		66%	35	80
AGE 32 Peak	00	CHC	*7	9	2	126	122	3.63	1.41	$10	9.0	252	234	261	32%	4.04	33.7	4.1	8.7	2.1	0.9	0.97	77%	75	166
TYPE Power	01	CHC	4	1	0	75	90	2.52	1.35	$7	5.4	230	281	194	31%	3.79 -	28.6	4.6	10.8	2.4	1.1	0.88	87%	91	169
R Very High	02	TEX	3	2	1	72	85	5.50	1.51	($1)	6.4	283	291	262	36%	5.61	-0.4	3.6	10.6	2.9	1.8	0.76	68%	71	146
I exp con	03	2TM	*7	4	1	111	74	4.94	1.40	$4	12.6	288	225	289	32%	4.84	6.7	2.3	6.0	2.6	1.1	0.71	67%	53	107
S PT STB	1st Half		4	0	1	36	25	4.96	1.65	$2	11.1	315			37%	5.26	2.1	3.2	6.2	1.9	0.5	0.71	69%	55	111
K	2nd Half		3	4	0	75	49	4.93	1.28	$2	13.7	275			30%	4.63	4.6	1.9	5.9	3.1	1.4	0.71	65%	56	114
LIMA B EP: 55%	04	Proj	7	4	0	120	98	4.58	1.40	$4	8.6	274			32%	4.72	13.2	3.0	7.4	2.5	1.3	F	71%	57	116

3-1, 5.63 ER in 48 IP at TEX & CIN. Entered the rotation in Sept. for his first regular starting gig in 5 years, and posted PQS scores of 4,5,3,5,4... For CIN, a team that used 14 other SPs in '03, it might open doors.

Vargas,Claudio

Info	Yr	Tm	W	L	Sv	IP	K	ERA	Br/IP	R$	BF/G	OBA	vL	vR	H%	xERA	RAR	Ctl	Dom	Cmd	hr/9	G/F	S%	BPV	BPX
RH Starter	99		0	0	0	0	0	0.00	0.00																
AGE 25 Growth	00		0	0	0	0	0	0.00	0.00																
TYPE	01		0	0	0	0	0	0.00	0.00																
R Low	02	a/a	6	13	0	109	84	6.28	1.60	($6)	19.7	300			34%	5.71 +	-14.7	3.5	6.9	2.0	1.4		62%	36	72
I EXP	03	MON *	7	8	0	135	82	3.93	1.29	$8	21.1	248	270	242	27%	3.98	24.5	3.3	5.5	1.7	1.1	0.61	73%	39	76
S	1st Half		6	3	0	96	64	2.52	1.17	$12	23.2	227			25%	3.20 -	35.6	3.1	6.0	1.9	0.9	0.60	83%	58	112
K	2nd Half		1	5	0	39	18	7.42	1.60	($5)	17.5	296			30%	5.89 +	-11.1	3.7	4.2	1.1	1.6	0.64	55%	-4	-8
LIMA C EP: 40%	04	Proj	11	12	0	160	107	4.33	1.36	$9	22.8	264			29%	4.53	20.0	3.2	6.0	1.9	1.4	F	73%	38	73

INJ: Sore shoulder, which kept him out most of the 2nd half. The 1st half was pretty good, but not 2.52 ERA good. There are signs of upside here, but don't be taken in by that 1st half. Goal: a sub-4.00 ERA.

Vazquez,Javier

Info	Yr	Tm	W	L	Sv	IP	K	ERA	Br/IP	R$	BF/G	OBA	vL	vR	H%	xERA	RAR	Ctl	Dom	Cmd	hr/9	G/F	S%	BPV	BPX
RH Starter	99	MON *	13	10	0	196	155	5.28	1.40	$6	25.6	272	234	272	31%	4.34 +	-1.2	3.1	7.1	2.3	1.3	1.20	65%	53	115
AGE 27 Pre-Peak	00	MON	11	9	0	217	196	4.06	1.42	$12	28.6	287	279	291	35%	4.70 -	45.6	2.5	8.1	3.2	1.0	1.51	74%	84	185
TYPE Power	01	MON	16	11	0	223	208	3.43	1.08	$27	27.9	238	220	246	29%	3.14	58.0	1.8	8.4	4.7	1.0	1.28	72%	128	237
R Low	02	MON	10	13	0	230	179	3.91	1.27	$11	28.3	273	282	262	31%	4.12	36.8	1.9	7.0	3.7	1.1	0.94	73%	86	163
I CON	03	MON	13	12	0	230	241	3.25	1.11	$25	27.3	234	233	225	29%	3.24	62.7	2.2	9.4	4.2	1.1	0.73	76%	121	232
S	1st Half		6	6	0	113	127	4.06	1.19	$8	25.8	248			31%	4.10	18.5	2.4	10.1	4.2	1.6	0.68	73%	107	206
K brn	2nd Half		7	6	0	117	114	2.46	1.02	$17	28.9	220			28%	2.41	44.2	2.1	8.8	4.2	0.6	0.78	79%	134	258
LIMA C+ EP: 55%	04	Proj	16	9	0	225	221	3.12	1.12	$27	27.5	239			29%	3.26	64.6	2.1	8.8	4.2	1.0	F	77%	117	225

Got off to a slow start, thanks to a bit of gopheritis, but made his way back, big time, in the 2nd half. The longball may become his Achilles Heel, as his G/F trend is not encouraging. Still, a breakout is waiting to happen.

Veres,Dave

Info	Yr	Tm	W	L	Sv	IP	K	ERA	Br/IP	R$	BF/G	OBA	vL	vR	H%	xERA	RAR	Ctl	Dom	Cmd	hr/9	G/F	S%	BPV	BPX
RH Reliever	99	COL	4	8	31	77	71	5.14	1.62	$16	4.8	288	328	263	34%	5.47	1.0	4.3	8.3	1.9	1.6	1.63	73%	38	83
AGE 37 Decline	00	STL	3	5	29	75	67	2.87	1.20	$26	4.4	235	210	261	29%	3.15	27.8	3.0	8.0	2.7	0.7	1.66	79%	91	200
TYPE	01	STL	3	2	15	65	61	3.73	1.30	$13	3.9	237	237	229	27%	4.33 -	14.3	3.9	8.4	2.2	1.7	1.32	79%	54	101
R High	02	STL	5	8	4	82	68	3.51	1.29	$8	4.9	225	190	246	25%	3.74	17.5	4.3	7.5	1.7	1.3	1.13	79%	52	98
I CON	03	CHC *	2	2	1	48	36	4.29	1.24	$3	4.8	284	174	359	32%	4.33	6.4	1.1	6.7	6.0	1.1	1.00	69%	131	252
S pt stb	1st Half		0	2	0	19	14	5.16	1.25	($0)	5.3	298			33%	4.82	0.3	0.5	6.6	14.0	1.4	1.17	62%	287	551
K AGE	2nd Half		2	0	1	29	22	3.72	1.24	$3	4.5	275			32%	4.00	6.0	1.6	6.8	4.4	0.9	0.97	73%	105	203
LIMA B EP: 60%	04	Proj	3	4	4	60	49	3.75	1.28	$6	4.6	262			30%	4.14	12.2	2.6	7.4	2.9	1.2	--	75%	71	138

2-1, 4.78 ERA in 32 IP at CHC. INJ: Shoulder tendinitis In his brief season, he posted career-high command, but it's a small sample. Continues to be a lefty-killer, but a .359 OBA vs RHers could be a concern.

Villafuerte,Brandon

Info	Yr	Tm	W	L	Sv	IP	K	ERA	Br/IP	R$	BF/G	OBA	vL	vR	H%	xERA	RAR	Ctl	Dom	Cmd	hr/9	G/F	S%	BPV	BPX
RH Reliever	99	aa	6	10	5	124	94	3.77	1.46	$10	14.7	269			32%	4.18	29.2	3.8	6.8	1.8	0.8		76%	56	130
AGE 28 Pre-Peak	00	aa	4	9	4	87	68	8.17	2.05	($11)	9.4	350			42%	6.93 +	-28.1	4.8	7.0	1.5	0.6	3.00	58%	40	94
TYPE Power	01	aaa	5	5	10	68	61	4.50	1.71	$6	7.1	312			38%	5.87 -	8.4	3.8	8.1	2.1	1.1	1.09	76%	53	103
R X HIGH	02	SD *	9	6	2	90	70	2.00	1.26	$15	4.8	235	286	213	29%	2.92 -	37.4	3.5	7.0	2.0	0.4	2.30	85%	80	151
I EXP CON	03	SD *	3	3	14	83	65	3.03	1.50	$11	5.5	268	200	284	31%	4.50 -	25.1	4.2	7.0	1.7	0.9	1.37	83%	53	101
S pt stb	1st Half		1	2	2	43	38	4.18	1.67	($0)	6.2	283			33%	5.69 -	6.4	5.0	7.9	1.6	1.5	1.57	80%	35	68
K	2nd Half		2	1	12	40	27	1.80	1.32	$11	4.9	252			30%	3.23 -	18.7	3.4	6.1	1.8	0.2	1.00	87%	72	139
LIMA C+ EP: 30%	04	Proj	4	3	4	60	47	3.45	1.48	$6	5.7	271			32%	4.36 -	14.6	3.9	7.1	1.8	0.8	--	79%	58	113

2 L, 2 Sv, 3 blown Sv, 4.38 ERA in 39 IP at SD, which was the full extent of his opportunity to be the closer. Excelled as their AAA closer, but BPIs were still off from 2002. Don't over-value.

Villarreal,Oscar

Info	Yr	Tm	W	L	Sv	IP	K	ERA	Br/IP	R$	BF/G	OBA	vL	vR	H%	xERA	RAR	Ctl	Dom	Cmd	hr/9	G/F	S%	BPV	BPX
RH Reliever	99		0	0	0	0	0	0.00	0.00																
AGE 22 Green	00		0	0	0	0	0	0.00	0.00																
TYPE Power	01	aa	6	9	0	140	102	4.37	1.47	$2	22.8	278			33%	4.26	19.7	3.5	6.6	1.9	0.5		70%	63	121
R X HIGH	02	a/a	9	6	0	148	116	4.07	1.22	$11	25.5	253			30%	3.28 +	23.7	2.4	7.1	2.9	0.5		66%	91	179
I EXP con	03	ARI	10	7	0	98	80	2.57	1.29	$14	4.8	224	252	204	27%	3.08 -	35.5	4.2	7.3	1.7	0.6	1.14	82%	74	143
S pt stb	1st Half		5	4	0	48	36	3.19	1.56	$4	5.2	254			30%	4.17 -	13.4	5.4	6.8	1.2	0.6	1.65	81%	54	104
K AGE BRN	2nd Half		5	3	0	50	44	1.98	1.02	$10	4.4	194			24%	2.03	22.1	3.1	7.9	2.6	0.5	0.80	83%	102	196
LIMA C+ EP: 40%	04	Proj	6	5	0	80	65	3.26	1.26	$8	5.0	239			29%	3.19	21.4	3.4	7.3	2.2	0.6	--	75%	80	154

BPIs were borderline in the 1st half, but took a big step up after the Break. Hit/strand rates served to depress his ERA a bit, but he's got the momentum to post LIMA-caliber stats in 2004.

Villone,Ron

Info	Yr	Tm	W	L	Sv	IP	K	ERA	Br/IP	R$	BF/G	OBA	vL	vR	H%	xERA	RAR	Ctl	Dom	Cmd	hr/9	G/F	S%	BPV	BPX
LH Starter	99	CIN *	11	7	3	161	118	3.91	1.30	$15	14.4	215	253	212	25%	2.61 +	28.5	4.8	6.6	1.4	0.5	1.30	70%	66	143
AGE 34 Past	00	CIN	10	10	0	141	77	5.43	1.65	$0	18.4	279	252	296	29%	5.57	3.8	5.0	4.9	1.0	1.4	1.02	70%	7	16
TYPE Power	01	2NL	6	10	0	114	113	5.91	1.63	($5)	9.8	292	250	300	35%	5.69	-8.3	4.2	8.9	2.1	1.4	1.45	66%	52	97
R High	02	PIT	4	6	0	93	55	5.81	1.39	($2)	8.9	266	233	289	30%	4.03 +	-8.7	3.3	5.3	1.6	0.8	1.22	57%	44	84
I con	03	HOU *	10	8	1	160	123	3.76	1.34	$11	17.5	241	267	221	28%	3.87	32.6	4.0	6.9	1.7	1.0	0.80	75%	54	104
S pt STB	1st Half		4	2	1	72	48	2.86	1.31	$7	13.3	247			28%	3.53 -	23.4	3.5	6.0	1.7	0.6	1.31	80%	59	113
K age brn	2nd Half		6	6	0	88	75	4.49	1.36	$4	23.6	237			27%	4.15	9.2	4.4	7.7	1.7	1.3	0.73	71%	50	97
LIMA C+ EP: 40%	04	Proj	5	5	0	80	57	4.50	1.45	$2	20.6	257			29%	4.33	8.2	4.3	6.4	1.5	1.0	--	71%	43	83

6-6, 4.16 ERA in 106 IP at HOU. Got everyone all excited by posting early PQS scores of 5,4,4,4,3,5, but only had 3 more DOM starts in his next 13. BPIs were as mediocre as ever, so keep your excitement in check.

Vizcaino,Luis

Info	Yr	Tm	W	L	Sv	IP	K	ERA	Br/IP	R$	BF/G	OBA	vL	vR	H%	xERA	RAR	Ctl	Dom	Cmd	hr/9	G/F	S%	BPV	BPX
RH Reliever	99	a/a	8	8	0	118	84	5.34	1.53	$2	16.4	289			32%	5.04	3.0	3.5	6.4	1.8	1.2	2.33	67%	37	87
AGE 29 Peak	00	OAK *	6	3	5	67	53	6.72	1.70	$2	6.9	300	270	333	35%	5.53 +	-7.2	4.4	7.1	1.6	0.9	0.89	60%	43	112
TYPE Power	01	OAK *	4	3	8	78	79	3.46	1.24	$11	5.2	257	241	282	31%	4.30 -	21.1	2.4	9.1	3.8	1.5	1.09	80%	92	185
R Moderate	02	MIL	5	3	5	81	79	3.00	1.05	$13	4.2	194	225	170	25%	2.14 +	22.9	3.3	8.8	2.6	0.7	0.65	73%	104	197
I exp con	03	MIL	4	3	0	62	61	6.39	1.44	($1)	3.6	268	253	269	30%	5.68 +	-9.2	3.6	8.9	2.4	2.3	0.65	62%	36	69
S pt stb	1st Half		2	3	0	30	30	9.27	1.89	($6)	3.9	336			37%	8.80	-16.1	4.2	9.0	2.1	3.3	0.61	57%	-12	-23
K	2nd Half		2	0	0	32	31	3.67	1.00	$4	3.3	189			21%	2.74 +	6.9	3.1	8.7	2.8	1.4	0.70	70%	86	166
LIMA C+ EP: 65%	04	Proj	4	3	2	70	66	3.73	1.17	$7	4.1	230			27%	3.51	14.4	3.0	8.5	2.9	1.3	F	74%	82	157

Missed a week of spring training with a sore quad muscle, a fact that disappeared during his struggles. This was really only a horrible half season, but that 9.27 1st half ERA hid his solid 2nd half return to form.

Voyles,Brad

Info	Yr	Tm	W	L	Sv	IP	K	ERA	Br/IP	R$	BF/G	OBA	vL	vR	H%	xERA	RAR	Ctl	Dom	Cmd	hr/9	G/F	S%	BPV	BPX
RH Reliever	99		0	0	0	0	0	0.00	0.00																
AGE 27 Growth	00		0	0	0	0	0	0.00	0.00																
TYPE Power	01	aa	1	0	10	41	41	1.32	1.32	$10	5.3	189			26%	2.44 -	22.5	5.9	9.0	1.5	0.2	0.67	91%	96	185
R High	02	KC *	3	6	6	59	54	5.80	1.75	($0)	5.7	278			34%	5.51	-2.7	5.9	8.2	1.4	1.1	0.71	68%	46	94
I EXP con	03	KC *	2	4	2	112	79	4.89	1.52	($2)	12.4	288	357	333	33%	4.97	9.5	3.4	6.3	1.9	1.0	0.52	69%	46	99
S pt	1st Half		1	2	2	56	36	3.52	1.51	$2	9.2	287			34%	4.35 -	15.1	3.4	5.8	1.7	0.3	0.47	76%	58	126
K brn	2nd Half		1	2	0	56	43	6.28	1.52	($4)	19.1	289			32%	5.60 +	-5.6	3.4	6.9	2.0	1.6	0.55	61%	33	72
LIMA D+ EP: 55%	04	Proj	2	3	1	50	41	4.86	1.56	($0)	6.6	269			32%	4.75	4.5	4.7	7.4	1.6	0.9	F	70%	52	110

0-2, 7.55 ERA in 31 IP at KC. He's showing some small signs of improvement, but the going is slow. At this rate, he'll break out at about age 45, and teams don't tend to exhibit THAT much patience.

Wagner,Billy

Info	Yr	Tm	W	L	Sv	IP	K	ERA	Br/IP	R$	BF/G	OBA	vL	vR	H%	xERA	RAR	Ctl	Dom	Cmd	hr/9	G/F	S%	BPV	BPX
LH Reliever	99	HOU	4	1	39	74	124	1.58	0.78	$38	4.2	144	152	131	26%	0.54 +	36.2	2.8	15.1	5.4	0.6	1.08	85%	212	460
AGE 32 Past	00	HOU	2	4	6	27	28	6.29	1.69	$3	4.5	267	321	232	31%	6.02	-2.4	6.0	9.3	1.6	2.0	0.73	68%	30	67
TYPE Power	01	HOU	2	5	39	62	79	2.75	1.03	$31	3.8	201	261	182	29%	2.29	21.8	2.9	11.4	4.0	0.7	1.19	76%	145	268
R Low	02	HOU	4	2	35	75	88	2.52	0.97	$30	4.2	194	180	201	26%	2.09	26.0	2.6	10.6	4.0	0.8	1.10	79%	138	262
I con	03	HOU	1	4	44	86	105	1.78	0.87	$37	4.2	177	216	154	24%	1.71	40.3	2.4	11.0	4.6	0.8	0.95	87%	156	301
S pt	1st Half		1	3	22	45	60	2.20	0.93	$19	4.2	196			29%	2.03	18.6	2.2	12.0	5.5	0.8	1.00	82%	178	343
K	2nd Half		0	1	22	41	45	1.32	0.81	$19	4.1	154			19%	1.35	21.7	2.6	9.9	3.8	0.9	0.90	93%	136	262
LIMA C EP: 40%	04	Proj	2	3	42	80	95	2.48	0.96	$34	4.2	193			26%	2.05	29.9	2.6	10.7	4.1	0.8	--	79%	144	277

Cruising. Won't likely see a sub-2.00 ERA again, but who cares? Having spent the last few seasons in a hitter-friendly park, we shouldn't have to worry TOO much should he leave HOU.

Wakefield,Tim

	Yr	Tm	W	L	Sv	IP	K	ERA	Br/IP	R$	BF/G	OBA	vL	vR	H%	xERA	RAR	Ctl	Dom	Cmd	hr/9	G/F	S%	BPV	BPX
RH Starter	99	BOS	6	11	15	140	104	5.08	1.56	$10	12.8	270	280	256	30%	5.03	14.9	4.6	6.7	1.4	1.2	0.92	70%	35	87
AGE 37 Decline	00	BOS	6	10	0	159	102	5.49	1.48	$1	13.7	275	250	289	29%	5.37	9.0	3.7	5.8	1.6	1.8	1.00	68%	15	39
TYPE Power	01	BOS	9	12	3	168	148	3.91	1.36	$11	16.0	247	230	261	30%	3.73	35.6	3.9	7.9	2.0	0.7	1.24	72%	75	150
R Low	02	BOS	11	5	3	163	134	2.82	1.06	$25	14.4	208	195	213	25%	2.64	57.7	2.8	7.4	2.6	0.8	0.98	77%	88	181
I con	03	BOS	11	7	1	202	169	4.10	1.31	$13	24.4	253	266	228	30%	4.00	38.6	3.2	7.5	2.4	1.0	0.92	71%	69	149
S pt	1st Half		6	3	1	95	84	4.73	1.46	$3	23.1	264			32%	4.55	10.1	4.1	7.9	2.0	1.0	0.76	70%	60	129
K AGE	2nd Half		5	4	0	107	85	3.53	1.17	$10	25.7	243			28%	3.51	28.5	2.4	7.1	3.0	1.0	1.08	73%	83	179
LIMA C+ EP: 55%	04	Proj	10	8	0	180	148	3.80	1.27	$14	24.3	243			29%	3.70	41.9	3.3	7.4	2.3	1.0	--	73%	70	150

As knuckleballers go, he's got BPIs levels that you rarely see. Eventually, the innings will catch up with him, but probably not for a few more years.

Walker,Jamie

	Yr	Tm	W	L	Sv	IP	K	ERA	Br/IP	R$	BF/G	OBA	vL	vR	H%	xERA	RAR	Ctl	Dom	Cmd	hr/9	G/F	S%	BPV	BPX
LH Reliever	99	aaa	0	1	0	17	10	5.29	1.65	($1)	19.4	324			37%	5.25	0.5	2.6	5.3	2.0	0.5		67%	48	111
AGE 32 Past	00	aaa	3	10	0	101	39	6.86	1.94	($12)	20.5	375			36%	9.18 -	-14.9	2.2	3.5	1.6	2.8		72%	-49	-117
TYPE	01	aaa	7	2	2	93	40	5.61	1.80	($3)	11.5	343			35%	7.20 -	-2.4	2.9	3.9	1.3	1.6		73%	-12	-23
R Very High	02	DET *	1	2	2	56	48	3.54	0.93	$7	3.2	202	202	194	21%	3.13	14.4	1.9	7.7	4.0	1.8	0.73	73%	92	188
I EXP CON	03	DET	4	3	3	65	45	3.32	1.20	$9	3.4	250	212	276	27%	3.91 -	19.2	2.4	6.2	2.6	1.2	0.67	78%	61	131
S PT	1st Half		2	2	0	27	19	3.67	1.26	$3	3.1	247			27%	4.11	6.7	3.0	6.3	2.1	1.3	0.80	77%	48	103
K	2nd Half		2	1	3	38	26	3.08	1.16	$6	3.7	251			28%	3.77 -	12.4	1.9	6.2	3.3	1.2	0.58	79%	74	161
LIMA C+ EP: 40%	04	Proj	3	3	2	65	46	3.74	1.22	$6	4.2	253			27%	4.11	15.7	2.4	6.4	2.7	1.4	F	75%	58	124

You gotta love guys that fly under the radar, with solid BPIs on poor teams. They will almost always be reserve picks. And they almost always return a profit. From last year: "Take a cheap flyer." $1 buys $9.

Walker,Pete

	Yr	Tm	W	L	Sv	IP	K	ERA	Br/IP	R$	BF/G	OBA	vL	vR	H%	xERA	RAR	Ctl	Dom	Cmd	hr/9	G/F	S%	BPV	BPX
RH Reliever	99	aaa	8	4	5	62	44	6.24	1.77	$3	6.1	319			34%	6.89 -	-5.9	4.1	6.4	1.6	2.0		70%	2	3
AGE 35 Decline	00	aaa	7	3	5	73	51	4.32	1.55	$8	5.6	282			33%	4.60	14.1	3.9	6.3	1.6	0.6	1.83	72%	51	121
TYPE Finesse	01	aaa	13	4	0	174	90	3.98	1.36	$12	26.6	273			30%	4.12	33.5	2.7	4.7	1.7	0.7	2.00	72%	43	83
R X HIGH	02	2TM *	10	5	1	149	85	4.35	1.40	$7	16.1	271	288	254	29%	4.55	18.4	3.1	5.1	1.6	1.1	1.17	72%	32	62
I EXP CON	03	TOR *	2	4	0	70	36	6.03	1.55	($4)	10.5	293	278	276	30%	5.82	-4.7	3.5	4.6	1.3	1.7	1.03	65%	2	5
S PT stb	1st Half		1	2	0	34	18	6.07	1.76	($3)	9.4	314			31%	7.33 -	-2.5	4.2	4.8	1.1	2.4	1.08	73%	-27	-58
K age	2nd Half		1	2	0	36	18	5.98	1.36	($1)	11.9	272			29%	4.39 +	-2.2	2.7	4.5	1.6	1.0	0.97	56%	32	69
LIMA C EP: 45%	04	Proj	4	4	0	80	44	4.95	1.48	$1	11.7	283			30%	5.17	6.3	3.3	5.0	1.5	1.4	--	70%	19	42

INJ: Strained left knee
Marginal skills set treaded ever closer to that margin in 2003, injury or not. You can't squeeze blood out of a turnip, but sometimes you think that's what teams try to do with these BPIs.

Washburn,Jarrod

	Yr	Tm	W	L	Sv	IP	K	ERA	Br/IP	R$	BF/G	OBA	vL	vR	H%	xERA	RAR	Ctl	Dom	Cmd	hr/9	G/F	S%	BPV	BPX
LH Starter	99	ANA *	5	10	0	120	87	6.23	1.43	($0)	19.3	270	216	273	31%	4.53 +	-5.7	3.5	6.5	1.9	1.1	0.90	56%	48	121
AGE 29 Peak	00	ANA *	10	2	0	114	66	3.94	1.35	$13	25.7	244	215	215	25%	4.31	30.2	3.9	5.2	1.3	1.4	0.62	76%	23	59
TYPE Finesse	01	ANA	11	10	0	193	126	3.78	1.29	$14	27.1	265	287	257	29%	4.25	44.2	2.5	5.9	2.3	1.2	0.65	75%	51	103
R Moderate	02	ANA	18	6	0	206	139	3.15	1.17	$27	26.4	240	199	246	27%	3.34	63.8	2.6	6.1	2.4	0.8	0.60	76%	68	140
I CON	03	ANA	10	15	0	207	118	4.43	1.25	$11	27.0	260	230	264	27%	4.40	30.3	2.3	5.1	2.2	1.5	0.58	70%	35	76
S pt	1st Half		6	9	0	107	55	4.20	1.22	$8	27.7	258			26%	4.43	19.0	2.2	4.6	2.1	1.6	0.58	72%	28	60
K	2nd Half		4	6	0	100	63	4.68	1.28	$4	26.3	262			28%	4.38	11.3	2.5	5.7	2.3	1.3	0.57	67%	43	94
LIMA D+ EP: 50%	04	Proj	12	11	0	200	125	3.96	1.23	$16	26.8	251			27%	3.98	42.3	2.6	5.6	2.2	1.2	F	72%	48	103

BPIs took a step back in 2003. Of most concern is his Dom, which is borderline to begin with. As a flyball pitcher, and prone to the longball as has happened in '03, he has little margin for error. Success depends on k/9.

Weathers,Dave

	Yr	Tm	W	L	Sv	IP	K	ERA	Br/IP	R$	BF/G	OBA	vL	vR	H%	xERA	RAR	Ctl	Dom	Cmd	hr/9	G/F	S%	BPV	BPX
RH Reliever	99	MIL	7	4	2	93	74	4.65	1.51	$5	6.5	280	290	273	32%	4.80	7.4	3.7	7.2	1.9	1.4	1.49	73%	42	92
AGE 34 Decline	00	MIL	3	5	1	76	50	3.07	1.38	$7	4.7	254	223	278	29%	3.99 -	26.0	3.8	5.9	1.6	0.8	1.34	81%	48	105
TYPE Power	01	2NL	4	5	4	86	66	2.41	1.15	$13	4.4	211	213	218	25%	2.68	34.1	3.6	6.9	1.9	0.6	1.11	82%	76	141
R Low	02	NYM	6	3	0	77	61	2.92	1.36	$7	4.6	241	267	232	29%	3.56 -	22.5	4.2	7.1	1.7	0.7	1.49	81%	64	121
I con	03	NYM	1	6	7	87	75	3.10	1.46	$6	5.0	261	239	276	32%	4.05 -	25.5	4.1	7.7	1.9	0.6	1.38	80%	70	135
S stb	1st Half		1	4	0	45	38	3.40	1.38	$2	4.5	257			32%	3.79	11.3	3.6	7.6	2.1	0.6	1.63	76%	75	145
K age	2nd Half		0	2	7	42	37	2.77	1.54	$4	5.5	265			33%	4.34 -	14.2	4.7	7.9	1.7	0.6	1.17	84%	65	126
LIMA B EP: 40%	04	Proj	3	4	2	80	65	3.49	1.39	$5	4.9	250			30%	3.74	19.0	4.1	7.3	1.8	0.7	--	76%	67	129

Stopgap closer, he converted 78% of his save opps despite a decline in his control. Continues to succeed by keeping the ball in the park and keeping runners from scoring. It's life on the edge but always worth a few bucks.

Weaver,Jeff

	Yr	Tm	W	L	Sv	IP	K	ERA	Br/IP	R$	BF/G	OBA	vL	vR	H%	xERA	RAR	Ctl	Dom	Cmd	hr/9	G/F	S%	BPV	BPX
RH Starter	99	DET	9	12	0	163	114	5.58	1.42	$4	23.6	277	310	236	30%	5.05 +	6.4	3.1	6.3	2.0	1.5	1.20	64%	35	89
AGE 27 Pre-Peak	00	DET	11	15	0	200	136	4.32	1.29	$17	27.1	267	267	266	29%	4.22	42.6	2.3	6.1	2.6	1.2	1.51	70%	58	151
TYPE	01	DET	13	16	0	229	152	4.09	1.32	$14	29.5	267	278	253	30%	3.96	42.9	2.7	6.0	2.2	0.7	1.21	70%	62	124
R Moderate	02	2AL	11	11	2	199	132	3.53	1.21	$18	25.7	256	233	268	30%	3.38	51.5	2.2	6.0	2.8	0.5	1.27	71%	81	166
I CON	03	NYY	7	9	0	159	93	6.00	1.62	($7)	22.6	320	342	290	35%	5.69	-10.0	2.7	5.3	2.0	0.9	0.97	63%	37	80
S stb	1st Half		4	6	0	95	51	5.59	1.60	($3)	25.3	316			35%	5.45	-0.8	2.7	4.8	1.8	0.8	1.05	65%	36	78
K brn	2nd Half		3	3	0	64	42	6.60	1.65	($5)	19.5	325			36%	6.05 +	-9.2	2.7	5.9	2.2	1.1	0.85	60%	38	82
LIMA D+ EP: 60%	04	Proj	8	9	0	160	104	4.33	1.33	$8	22.6	270			30%	4.18	25.9	2.5	5.9	2.3	0.9	--	69%	58	123

The only real skills deficiencies in this debacle were his drop in Dom and increasing flyball tendency, which affected his HR rate in the 2nd half. At normal hit and strand rates, his ERA would have been 4.30.

Webb,Brandon

	Yr	Tm	W	L	Sv	IP	K	ERA	Br/IP	R$	BF/G	OBA	vL	vR	H%	xERA	RAR	Ctl	Dom	Cmd	hr/9	G/F	S%	BPV	BPX
RH Starter	99		0	0	0	0	0	0.00	0.00																
AGE 24 Growth	00		0	0	0	0	0	0.00	0.00																
TYPE Power	01		0	0	0	0	0	0.00	0.00																
R High	02	a/a	10	7	0	159	106	3.57	1.38	$10	25.3	264			31%	3.54	36.3	3.3	6.0	1.8	0.2		73%	70	137
I EXP con	03	ARI *	11	10	0	198	187	3.22	1.20	$19	25.5	223	257	167	28%	2.81	54.5	3.5	8.5	2.4	0.5	2.95	74%	96	185
S	1st Half		5	3	0	95	73	3.03	1.11	$11	25.5	216			26%	2.46 +	28.6	2.9	6.9	2.4	0.5	3.25	73%	88	170
K age	2nd Half		6	7	0	103	114	3.40	1.28	$9	25.5	228			31%	3.14	25.9	4.0	9.9	2.5	0.6	2.71	74%	103	198
LIMA C+ EP: 55%	04	Proj	13	9	0	200	169	3.38	1.28	$18	25.4	240			30%	3.08	50.6	3.5	7.6	2.2	0.4	G	73%	87	167

10-9, 2.85 ERA in 180 IP at ARI. The most positive signs here:
- Incredible .167 OBA vs RHers
- Outstanding G/F ratio
- Improved his BPI as the season progressed.

A keeper, especially under $15.

Weber,Ben

	Yr	Tm	W	L	Sv	IP	K	ERA	Br/IP	R$	BF/G	OBA	vL	vR	H%	xERA	RAR	Ctl	Dom	Cmd	hr/9	G/F	S%	BPV	BPX
RH Reliever	99	aaa	2	4	8	86	53	3.66	1.36	$9	7.2	266			30%	3.64	21.5	3.0	5.5	1.8	0.5		73%	58	134
AGE 34 Past	00	2TM *	5	10	7	101	73	4.08	1.40	$10	7.4	287	250	188	33%	4.46	22.8	2.4	6.5	2.7	0.8	2.14	72%	69	164
TYPE Finesse	01	ANA	6	2	0	68	40	3.44	1.42	$6	5.3	256	210	278	29%	3.87	18.7	4.1	5.3	1.3	0.5	2.65	76%	47	94
R Moderate	02	ANA	7	2	7	78	43	2.54	1.18	$16	5.1	241	243	253	27%	3.05 -	30.5	2.5	5.0	2.0	0.5	3.66	80%	64	131
I exp con	03	ANA	5	1	0	80	46	2.70	1.32	$8	5.5	271	268	282	30%	4.09 -	30.3	2.5	5.2	2.1	0.8	1.97	83%	52	113
S pt stb	1st Half		2	0	0	42	23	3.00	1.29	$4	5.0	266			29%	4.00 -	14.2	2.4	4.9	2.1	0.9	1.41	80%	49	107
K age	2nd Half		3	1	0	38	23	2.36	1.36	$5	6.0	276			31%	4.19 -	16.1	2.6	5.4	2.1	0.7	3.05	86%	55	119
LIMA C+ EP: 30%	04	Proj	6	2	2	80	47	3.04	1.31	$10	5.6	262			29%	3.83 -	26.8	2.8	5.3	1.9	0.7	G	79%	54	115

Solid, consistent, unspectacular. His BPIs dropped a bit, due to his hit rate reverting to normal and him allowing 3 more HRs in 2003. Strand rate could drop in 2004, which would hurt his ERA, but he's a decent end-gamer.

Wellemeyer,Todd

	Yr	Tm	W	L	Sv	IP	K	ERA	Br/IP	R$	BF/G	OBA	vL	vR	H%	xERA	RAR	Ctl	Dom	Cmd	hr/9	G/F	S%	BPV	BPX
RH Reliever	99		0	0	0	0	0	0.00	0.00																
AGE 25 Growth	00		0	0	0	0	0	0.00	0.00																
TYPE Power	01		0	0	0	0	0	0.00	0.00																
R High	02	aa	3	3	0	46	31	6.26	1.30	$0	24.3	236			28%	3.13 +	-6.1	3.9	6.1	1.6	0.4		48%	65	128
I EXP con	03	CHC *	7	7	1	114	105	6.69	1.71	($8)	16.5	286	219	257	35%	5.48 +	-21.7	5.2	8.3	1.6	1.1	1.04	61%	48	92
S pt	1st Half		3	3	1	53	59	5.76	1.49	($1)	13.8	254			33%	4.38 +	-3.5	4.7	10.0	2.1	1.0	0.95	62%	78	150
K brn	2nd Half		4	4	0	61	46	7.50	1.90	($8)	19.6	311			36%	6.43 +	-18.2	5.6	6.8	1.2	1.2	1.33	60%	23	45
LIMA D EP: 65%	04	Proj	2	4	0	40	32	5.18	1.55	($1)	9.4	267			31%	4.60 +	0.5	4.7	7.2	1.5	0.9	--	67%	50	96

1-1, 6.67 ERA in 27 IP at CHC. Hard thrower, poor movement, poor location, poor composure with men on base. And very unlucky. Had a 1.29 ERA in his 1st 13 IP, then gave up 10 runs in his next 2 outings. Game over.

Wells,David

		Tm	W	L	Sv	IP	K	ERA	Br/IP	R$	BF/G	OBA	vL	vR	H%	xERA	RAR	Ctl	Dom	Cmd	hr/9	G/F	S%	BPV	BPX
LH Starter	99	TOR	17	10	0	231	169	4.83	1.33	$17	28.9	274	295	266	31%	4.55	32.2	2.4	6.6	**2.7**	1.2	1.27	67%	60	149
AGE 40 Decline	00	TOR	20	8	0	229	166	4.12	1.30	$26	27.6	292	288	289	34%	4.35	54.9	1.2	6.5	**5.4**	0.9	1.19	70%	121	315
TYPE Finesse	01	CHW	5	7	0	100	59	4.49	1.41	$3	27.1	298	206	328	33%	4.95	13.3	1.9	5.3	**2.8**	1.1	1.12	71%	54	108
R Very High	02	NYY	19	7	0	206	137	3.76	1.24	$22	27.6	266	213	274	30%	3.93	46.9	2.0	6.0	**3.0**	0.9	1.08	72%	74	152
I CON	03	NYY	15	7	0	213	101	4.14	1.23	$18	28.5	287	274	290	30%	4.31	39.5	0.8	4.3	**5.1**	1.0	1.09	69%	99	213
S pt stb	1st Half		10	2	0	113	58	3.42	1.11	$16	28.5	277			30%	3.73	31.9	0.3	4.6	**14.5**	0.9	0.94	72%	306	660
K AGE	2nd Half		5	5	0	100	43	4.96	1.36	$3	28.5	299			31%	4.97	7.5	1.4	3.9	**2.7**	1.2	1.27	66%	40	86
LIMA D EP: 50%	**04**	**Proj**	**11**	**9**	**0**	**160**	**79**	**4.73**	**1.41**	**$7**	**28.9**	**296**			**31%**	**5.11**	**17.4**	**2.0**	**4.4**	**2.2**	**1.2**	**--**	**70%**	**31**	**67**

Reasons why the end is near:
1. Sharp drop in Dom, which got worse in the 2nd half. Ctl is impressive but easier to achieve. Dom requires strength.
2. He's over 40 and not exactly a physical specimen.

Wells,Kip

		Tm	W	L	Sv	IP	K	ERA	Br/IP	R$	BF/G	OBA	vL	vR	H%	xERA	RAR	Ctl	Dom	Cmd	hr/9	G/F	S%	BPV	BPX
RH Starter	99	CHW	* 12	3	0	105	67	3.60	1.25	$17	24.3	227	267	209	26%	3.11 +	31.9	3.8	5.7	**1.5**	0.6	1.32	72%	58	146
AGE 27 Growth	00	CHW	* 12	12	0	167	110	6.41	1.85	($7)	22.2	314	290	339	34%	6.63	-11.1	5.1	5.9	**1.2**	1.5	1.19	67%	9	22
TYPE Power	01	CHW	* 12	12	0	158	120	4.84	1.56	$3	16.1	284	267	294	33%	5.01	13.6	4.0	6.8	**1.7**	1.0	1.52	70%	46	92
R Moderate	02	PIT	12	14	0	198	134	3.59	1.35	$12	25.6	261	274	249	29%	4.04	40.2	3.2	6.1	**1.9**	1.0	1.98	77%	50	95
I exp con	03	PIT	10	9	0	197	147	3.29	1.25	$16	26.5	235	252	219	26%	3.65	52.5	3.5	6.7	**1.9**	1.1	1.54	78%	56	108
S pt	1st Half		2	3	0	85	66	3.60	1.26	$4	25.4	226			25%	3.71	19.2	3.9	7.0	**1.8**	1.3	1.76	77%	51	98
K	2nd Half		8	6	0	112	81	3.05	1.25	$12	27.5	242			27%	3.62 -	33.4	3.1	6.5	**2.1**	1.0	1.39	80%	60	116
LIMA D+ EP: 45%	**04**	**Proj**	**12**	**11**	**0**	**200**	**154**	**3.78**	**1.28**	**$14**	**23.3**	**244**			**28%**	**3.74**	**39.7**	**3.3**	**6.9**	**2.1**	**1.0**	**G**	**74%**	**60**	**117**

While his ERA has made huge gains over the past 3 years, his BPIs are developing at a much slower pace. The good news is that the long-term looks optimistic. The bad news is that there may be short term bumps.

Wendell,Turk

		Tm	W	L	Sv	IP	K	ERA	Br/IP	R$	BF/G	OBA	vL	vR	H%	xERA	RAR	Ctl	Dom	Cmd	hr/9	G/F	S%	BPV	BPX
RH Reliever	99	NYM	5	4	3	85	77	3.07	1.38	$9	4.6	250	260	235	30%	3.67 -	24.6	3.9	8.2	**2.1**	1.0	0.62	81%	69	150
AGE 36 Decline	00	NYM	8	6	1	82	73	3.61	1.23	$12	4.4	206	225	196	24%	3.13	22.2	4.5	8.0	**1.8**	1.0	0.94	74%	70	153
TYPE	01	2NL	4	5	1	67	56	4.43	1.45	$3	4.2	250	295	222	28%	4.84	8.4	4.6	7.5	**1.6**	1.6	0.76	75%	36	67
R High	02	PHI	0	0	0	0	0	0.00	0.00																
I con	03	PHI	3	3	1	64	27	3.38	1.28	$5	4.8	230	302	194	24%	3.45	16.3	3.9	3.8	**1.0**	0.8	0.88	76%	27	51
S pt stb	1st Half		1	1	0	27	12	0.67	0.93	$6	4.3	165			19%	1.00	16.7	3.3	4.0	**1.2**	0.0	0.94	92%	71	137
K AGE brn	2nd Half		2	2	1	37	15	5.35	1.54	($0)	5.2	272			27%	5.25	-0.4	4.4	3.6	**0.8**	1.5	0.84	69%	-4	-7
LIMA D+ EP: 30%	**04**	**Proj**	**2**	**5**	**0**	**60**	**29**	**4.50**	**1.50**	**($0)**	**4.7**	**268**			**28%**	**4.66**	**6.1**	**4.2**	**4.4**	**1.0**	**1.1**	**--**	**72%**	**18**	**34**

An amazing 1st half, highlighted by media accolades, despite no semblance of skill whatsoever. What was really amazing was witnessing the outer limits of random chance... a 19% hit rate and a 92% strand rate.

Westbrook,Jake

		Tm	W	L	Sv	IP	K	ERA	Br/IP	R$	BF/G	OBA	vL	vR	H%	xERA	RAR	Ctl	Dom	Cmd	hr/9	G/F	S%	BPV	BPX
RH Starter	99	aa	11	5	0	174	77	4.71	1.53	$6	28.7	294			31%	4.66	19.2	3.2	4.0	**1.2**	0.7		69%	25	57
AGE 26 Growth	00	aaa	5	7	0	89	53	5.36	1.57	$1	25.0	293			34%	4.53 +	4.8	3.6	5.4	**1.5**	0.3	1.09	64%	50	119
TYPE Finesse	01	CLE	* 12	5	0	128	87	5.06	1.52	$4	16.3	294	298	313	34%	4.74	7.2	3.2	6.1	**1.9**	0.6	1.98	66%	55	109
R X HIGH	02	CLE	* 2	4	0	62	29	6.39	1.44	($3)	18.0	303	292	300	32%	5.09 +	-7.7	1.9	4.2	**2.2**	1.0	1.83	55%	36	74
I EXP con	03	CLE	7	10	0	133	58	4.33	1.49	$3	17.2	275	276	287	30%	4.40	21.3	3.8	3.9	**1.0**	0.6	2.67	71%	27	59
S PT stb	1st Half		3	4	0	61	24	4.57	1.47	$1	12.8	283			30%	4.47	7.8	3.2	3.5	**1.1**	0.6	2.69	69%	25	54
K BRN	2nd Half		4	6	0	72	34	4.13	1.50	$2	24.5	267			29%	4.35	13.4	4.3	4.3	**1.0**	0.6	2.65	73%	29	63
LIMA C+ EP: 45%	**04**	**Proj**	**7**	**8**	**0**	**120**	**59**	**4.28**	**1.41**	**$5**	**23.6**	**271**			**30%**	**4.14**	**20.3**	**3.2**	**4.4**	**1.4**	**0.6**	**G**	**70%**	**38**	**82**

The good news...
- Extreme GB pitcher won't have to worry about gopheritis
- Late adjustment led to PQS scores of 4,4,3 in last 3 starts.

The bad news...
- Pretty much everything else.

Wheeler,Dan

		Tm	W	L	Sv	IP	K	ERA	Br/IP	R$	BF/G	OBA	vL	vR	H%	xERA	RAR	Ctl	Dom	Cmd	hr/9	G/F	S%	BPV	BPX
RH Reliever	99	a/a	10	5	0	140	102	4.24	1.33	$11	25.9	286			32%	4.67	24.1	1.8	6.6	**3.6**	1.4	0.82	73%	71	165
AGE 26 Growth	00	aaa	5	11	0	150	83	5.46	1.46	$0	25.3	302			31%	5.91	6.0	2.2	5.0	**2.3**	1.9	0.76	68%	15	36
TYPE	01	a/a	* 4	7	0	98	56	6.78	1.60	($7)	13.1	326			34%	6.49	-17.9	2.1	5.1	**2.4**	1.7	0.79	60%	19	37
R X HIGH	02	aaa	9	6	0	155	92	5.69	1.48	($2)	25.2	301			32%	5.48	-8.7	2.4	5.3	**2.2**	1.5		64%	30	60
I EXP CON	03	NYM	* 5	5	6	96	72	4.30	1.44	$6	7.4	279	208	279	32%	4.58	12.6	3.2	6.7	**2.1**	0.9	0.93	72%	56	108
S PT STB	1st Half		4	2	5	54	42	4.48	1.49	$5	8.6	288			34%	4.73	5.8	3.1	7.0	**2.2**	0.8	0.82	71%	61	117
K BRN	2nd Half		1	3	1	42	30	4.08	1.38	$1	6.2	267			30%	4.39	6.7	3.2	6.4	**2.0**	1.1	0.96	74%	50	96
LIMA B EP: 50%	**04**	**Proj**	**3**	**3**	**2**	**60**	**43**	**3.90**	**1.38**	**$4**	**7.8**	**278**			**32%**	**4.34**	**11.0**	**2.7**	**6.5**	**2.4**	**0.9**	**--**	**74%**	**61**	**118**

1-3, 3.71 ERA in 51 IP at NYM. Skills development continues, slowly but surely. Has a good shot at getting his ERA under 4.00 in 2004.

White,Gabe

		Tm	W	L	Sv	IP	K	ERA	Br/IP	R$	BF/G	OBA	vL	vR	H%	xERA	RAR	Ctl	Dom	Cmd	hr/9	G/F	S%	BPV	BPX
LH Reliever	99	CIN	1	2	0	61	61	4.43	1.34	$1	5.2	283	355	247	33%	4.95 -	6.6	2.1	9.0	**4.4**	1.9	0.51	75%	86	188
AGE 32 Peak	00	2NL	11	2	5	84	84	2.36	0.94	$24	4.8	213	200	217	28%	2.16	36.8	1.6	9.0	**5.6**	0.6	0.62	78%	165	363
TYPE Finesse	01	COL	1	7	0	67	47	6.29	1.43	($4)	4.2	270	269	271	27%	5.82	-8.4	3.5	6.3	**1.8**	2.4	0.62	63%	4	8
R High	02	CIN	6	1	0	54	41	3.00	1.09	$9	3.5	243	202	267	29%	2.72	15.2	1.7	6.8	**4.1**	0.5	0.64	73%	118	224
I CON	03	2TM	5	1	0	46	29	4.09	1.13	$6	4.1	252	247	255	27%	3.85	8.1	1.6	5.6	**3.6**	1.4	0.54	69%	74	149
S pt STB	1st Half		3	0	0	34	23	3.96	1.23	$4	4.2	272			30%	4.34	6.6	1.6	6.1	**3.8**	1.3	0.56	73%	78	158
K	2nd Half		2	1	0	12	6	4.46	0.83	$3	3.8	190			18%	2.45 +	1.5	1.5	4.5	**3.0**	1.5	0.48	50%	62	126
LIMA C+ EP: 50%	**04**	**Proj**	**4**	**2**	**0**	**50**	**35**	**3.96**	**1.20**	**$5**	**4.2**	**258**			**28%**	**4.15**	**9.6**	**2.0**	**6.3**	**3.2**	**1.4**	**F**	**73%**	**65**	**131**

Didn't much like it at home in 2003, posting a 5.03 ERA at Great American, and then a 6.14 ERA in Yankee Stadium... and a 2.29 ERA on the road. BPIs are fairly stable -- same strengths, same weaknesses.

White,Rick

		Tm	W	L	Sv	IP	K	ERA	Br/IP	R$	BF/G	OBA	vL	vR	H%	xERA	RAR	Ctl	Dom	Cmd	hr/9	G/F	S%	BPV	BPX
RH Reliever	99	TAM	5	3	0	108	81	4.08	1.57	$4	7.7	302	309	301	36%	5.03 -	25.9	3.2	6.8	**2.1**	0.7	1.56	75%	60	150
AGE 35 Decline	00	2TM	5	9	3	99	67	3.54	1.22	$12	6.2	229	268	193	26%	3.24	29.5	3.4	6.1	**1.8**	0.8	1.22	73%	58	138
TYPE	01	NYM	4	5	2	69	51	3.90	1.27	$6	5.3	267	271	249	31%	3.97	13.6	2.2	6.6	**3.0**	0.9	1.60	72%	77	143
R Moderate	02	2NL	* 5	8	0	67	46	4.57	1.40	$3	4.4	270	295	245	32%	3.91 +	4.8	3.2	6.2	**1.9**	0.5	1.50	67%	62	117
I con	03	2TM	1	2	1	67	54	5.78	1.42	($2)	5.9	281	223	322	31%	5.33	-3.4	2.8	7.3	**2.6**	1.7	1.18	63%	44	89
S pt STB	1st Half		0	1	0	32	24	6.15	1.49	($3)	5.7	290			31%	5.83	-3.3	3.1	6.7	**2.2**	2.0	1.09	63%	24	50
K age	2nd Half		1	1	1	35	30	5.43	1.35	$0	6.2	274			31%	4.86 +	-0.2	2.6	7.8	**3.0**	1.6	1.28	63%	63	128
LIMA D+ EP: 55%	**04**	**Proj**	**3**	**4**	**1**	**65**	**49**	**4.29**	**1.38**	**$3**	**5.5**	**273**			**31%**	**4.65**	**9.6**	**2.9**	**6.8**	**2.3**	**1.2**	**--**	**73%**	**53**	**107**

Massive acute gopheritis hit him in CHW, as he posted a 2.1 hr/9. The cure was to trade him to HOU, where the malady resolved itself quickly (0.9). Low strand rate hurt his ERA; that should improve in '04.

Williamson,Scott

		Tm	W	L	Sv	IP	K	ERA	Br/IP	R$	BF/G	OBA	vL	vR	H%	xERA	RAR	Ctl	Dom	Cmd	hr/9	G/F	S%	BPV	BPX
RH Reliever	99	CIN	12	7	19	93	107	2.42	1.04	$31	5.9	171	171	172	23%	1.68 +	35.1	4.2	10.4	**2.5**	0.8	0.90	81%	112	243
AGE 28 Pre-Peak	00	CIN	5	8	6	112	136	3.29	1.49	$10	10.3	226	251	204	32%	3.61	35.0	6.0	10.9	**1.8**	0.6	1.15	79%	97	213
TYPE Power	01	CIN	0	0	0	0	0	0.00	0.00		1.8						0.1	90.0	0.0	**0.0**	0.0	1.00	100%	55	
R Low	02	CIN	3	4	8	74	84	2.92	1.11	$12	4.7	181	198	170	25%	2.06 +	21.7	4.4	10.2	**2.3**	0.6	0.86	75%	111	210
I con	03	2TM	5	4	21	62	74	4.20	1.41	$16	4.1	235	200	245	32%	3.97	10.0	4.9	10.7	**2.2**	1.0	0.92	73%	87	177
S pt	1st Half		4	3	18	32	38	3.66	1.44	$14	4.4	224			29%	4.25 -	7.4	5.6	10.7	**1.9**	1.4	0.69	80%	72	146
K	2nd Half		1	1	3	30	36	4.77	1.39	$2	3.8	247			35%	3.67 +	2.5	4.2	10.7	**2.6**	0.6	1.24	65%	106	215
LIMA B EP: 60%	**04**	**Proj**	**5**	**4**	**24**	**70**	**82**	**3.60**	**1.30**	**$20**	**4.8**	**215**			**29%**	**3.18**	**16.8**	**4.8**	**10.5**	**2.2**	**0.8**	**--**	**74%**	**99**	**200**

Hard thrower, but control continues to be a problem. Has yet to hit the magic 80% for successful saves conversion rate. His last 4 years: 73%, 75%, 67%, 75%... though he was 3 for 3 in the ALCS.

Williams,Jerome

		Tm	W	L	Sv	IP	K	ERA	Br/IP	R$	BF/G	OBA	vL	vR	H%	xERA	RAR	Ctl	Dom	Cmd	hr/9	G/F	S%	BPV	BPX
RH Starter	99		0	0	0	0	0	0.00	0.00																
AGE 22 Green	00		0	0	0	0	0	0.00	0.00																
TYPE	01	aa	9	7	0	130	77	4.15	1.12	$13	22.9	242			26%	3.27 +	22.1	2.0	5.3	**2.7**	0.9		65%	67	129
R Very High	02	aaa	6	11	0	160	128	3.60	1.11	$13	23.0	232			28%	2.85 +	35.8	2.4	7.2	**3.0**	0.7		69%	96	188
I EXP con	03	SF	* 11	7	0	188	125	3.06	1.22	$19	25.1	238	215	266	28%	3.12	55.8	3.0	6.0	**2.0**	0.6	1.18	76%	68	130
S stb	1st Half		6	3	0	94	57	2.97	1.22	$10	24.3	236			28%	2.75	29.1	3.2	5.5	**1.7**	0.2	0.96	74%	71	137
K AGE brn	2nd Half		5	4	0	94	68	3.16	1.21	$9	25.9	241			27%	3.49	26.7	2.9	6.5	**2.3**	1.0	1.28	78%	65	125
LIMA C EP: 50%	**04**	**Proj**	**11**	**7**	**0**	**180**	**127**	**3.40**	**1.17**	**$18**	**23.7**	**237**			**27%**	**3.06**	**44.9**	**2.6**	**6.4**	**2.4**	**0.7**	**--**	**72%**	**76**	**147**

7-5, 3.30 ERA in 131 IP at SF. Solid debut season, and the best part is his improvement in command in the 2nd half. Seeds are here for further growth.

Williams,Mike

		Tm	W	L	Sv	IP	K	ERA	Br/IP	R$	BF/G	OBA	vL	vR	H%	xERA	RAR	Ctl	Dom	Cmd	hr/9	G/F	S%	BPV	BPX
RH Reliever	99	PIT	3	4	23	58	76	5.12	1.72	$11	4.6	278	253	289	38%	5.31	0.9	5.7	11.8	**2.1**	1.4	1.44	74%	71	155
AGE 34 Decline	00	PIT	3	4	24	72	71	3.50	1.33	$20	4.3	216	233	208	27%	3.53	20.5	5.0	8.9	**1.8**	1.0	1.68	77%	72	159
TYPE Power	01	2NL	6	4	22	64	59	3.80	1.48	$18	4.3	250	259	231	30%	4.59 -	13.5	4.9	8.3	**1.7**	1.3	1.40	79%	52	97
R Low	02	PIT	2	6	46	61	43	2.95	1.23	$30	4.3	239	281	180	27%	3.37	17.6	3.1	6.3	**2.0**	0.9	1.40	80%	62	117
I con	03	2NL	1	7	28	63	39	6.14	1.70	$9	4.3	271	277	261	31%	4.91 +	-7.3	5.9	5.6	**1.0**	0.7	1.59	63%	33	63
S STB	1st Half		0	2	21	30	13	5.66	1.62	$9	4.2	260			27%	4.76 +	-1.6	5.7	3.9	**0.7**	0.9	1.47	65%	14	26
K age	2nd Half		1	5	7	33	26	6.59	1.77	$0	4.4	280			34%	5.04 +	-5.7	6.0	7.1	**1.2**	0.5	1.73	61%	50	96
LIMA C EP: 60%	**04**	**Proj**	**2**	**6**	**11**	**65**	**49**	**4.85**	**1.58**	**$4**	**4.4**	**268**			**31%**	**4.64**	**3.6**	**5.0**	**6.8**	**1.4**	**0.8**	**G**	**70%**	**46**	**88**

Talent, Opportunity, Guile... TALENT: Very little, it seems. Poor BPIs, .305 OBA when runners are on base. OPPTY: He's had it. But again? GUILE: Converted 87% of saves opps in 2000-02; 80% in 2003.

Williams,Woody

		Tm	W	L	Sv	IP	K	ERA	Br/IP	R$	BF/G	OBA	vL	vR	H%	xERA	RAR	Ctl	Dom	Cmd	hr/9	G/F	S%	BPV	BPX
RH Starter	99	SD	12	12	0	208	137	4.41	1.38	$10	27.1	266	260	275	29%	4.36	22.9	3.2	5.9	**1.9**	1.4	0.86	73%	34	74
AGE 37 Decline	00	SD	10	8	0	168	111	3.75	1.23	$17	30.3	243	232	245	26%	3.84	42.3	2.9	5.9	**2.1**	1.2	1.02	74%	48	106
TYPE	01	2NL	15	9	0	220	154	4.05	1.27	$16	27.1	265	251	281	29%	4.45	38.8	2.3	6.3	**2.8**	1.4	1.00	74%	55	101
R X HIGH	02	STL	10	4	0	108	82	2.50	1.03	$19	23.7	218	182	256	25%	2.55	37.7	2.2	6.8	**3.2**	0.8	1.07	80%	94	177
I con	03	STL	18	9	0	220	153	3.88	1.25	$21	27.0	262	268	246	30%	3.74	41.2	2.2	6.3	**2.8**	0.8	0.82	71%	74	143
S PT stb	1st Half		10	2	0	112	77	2.97	1.12	$17	28.3	242			28%	2.90	34.6	1.9	6.2	**3.2**	0.6	0.85	75%	94	181
K AGE BRN	2nd Half		8	7	0	108	76	4.82	1.39	$4	25.9	281			32%	4.60	6.6	2.6	6.3	**2.5**	1.1	0.78	67%	56	107
LIMA D+ EP: 50%	**04**	**Proj**	**14**	**11**	**0**	**200**	**137**	**4.14**	**1.27**	**$15**	**26.2**	**263**			**30%**	**3.92**	**30.1**	**2.3**	**6.2**	**2.6**	**1.0**	**--**	**70%**	**65**	**126**

Healthy in alternating years, so 2004 does not look good. At 37, and with his 2nd half decline, stamina may become an issue, making 2004 all that more risky. But there's no question about his solid, stable skill set.

Willis,Dontrelle

		Tm	W	L	Sv	IP	K	ERA	Br/IP	R$	BF/G	OBA	vL	vR	H%	xERA	RAR	Ctl	Dom	Cmd	hr/9	G/F	S%	BPV	BPX
LH Starter	99		0	0	0	0	0	0.00	0.00																
AGE 22 Green	00		0	0	0	0	0	0.00	0.00																
TYPE Power	01		0	0	0	0	0	0.00	0.00																
R Moderate	02		0	0	0	0	0	0.00	0.00																
I EXP	03	FLA	* 18	6	0	196	171	3.03	1.23	$25	24.7	240	216	250	29%	3.27	59.2	3.1	7.8	**2.6**	0.7	0.96	78%	87	167
S	1st Half		12	1	0	99	91	2.08	1.13	$20	25.1	229			29%	2.63 -	42.5	2.6	8.2	**3.1**	0.5	1.02	83%	111	214
K AGE brn	2nd Half		6	5	0	97	80	3.99	1.34	$6	24.3	252			30%	3.92	16.7	3.5	7.4	**2.1**	0.9	0.93	73%	66	126
LIMA C+ EP: 45%	**04**	**Proj**	**15**	**10**	**0**	**200**	**164**	**3.87**	**1.35**	**$15**	**25.1**	**253**			**30%**	**3.90**	**37.3**	**3.5**	**7.4**	**2.1**	**0.9**	**--**	**73%**	**66**	**127**

14-6, 3.32 ERA in 160 IP at FLA. The exhorbitant number of IP at his age, combined with a 6.82 Aug ERA, make the immediate future less rosy than it looked back in early summer. Still a keeper, but not a $20 keeper.

Wilson,Kris

		Tm	W	L	Sv	IP	K	ERA	Br/IP	R$	BF/G	OBA	vL	vR	H%	xERA	RAR	Ctl	Dom	Cmd	hr/9	G/F	S%	BPV	BPX
RH Reliever	99	a/a	5	8	0	80	42	6.53	1.54	($2)	14.9	328			34%	6.23	-10.7	1.5	4.7	**3.2**	1.8		61%	32	73
AGE 27 Pre-Peak	00	KC	* 7	4	0	136	74	4.36	1.35	$10	14.2	285	306	267	30%	4.61	28.4	2.0	4.9	**2.4**	1.1	1.41	71%	44	114
TYPE Finesse	01	KC	* 8	7	1	138	82	4.83	1.49	$3	17.4	300	346	251	31%	5.88 -	12.2	2.5	5.3	**2.2**	1.8	1.23	74%	18	35
R Very High	02	KC	* 7	3	1	92	47	4.30	1.64	$2	12.7	350			37%	6.63 -	14.2	1.1	4.6	**4.3**	1.3	0.86	78%	64	131
I EXP CON	03	KC	* 6	5	0	84	49	6.19	1.61	($3)	11.2	330	355	253	35%	6.49	-7.5	2.0	5.2	**2.6**	1.6	0.94	64%	27	57
S pt	1st Half		3	0	0	42	24	5.79	1.52	($0)	11.0	313			34%	5.70	-1.5	2.1	5.1	**2.4**	1.3	1.13	64%	35	76
K	2nd Half		3	5	0	42	25	6.60	1.70	($3)	11.5	346			36%	7.28 -	-6.1	1.9	5.3	**2.8**	1.9	0.73	65%	19	40
LIMA D EP: 55%	**04**	**Proj**	**4**	**7**	**0**	**90**	**51**	**5.30**	**1.56**	**($2)**	**12.6**	**321**			**34%**	**6.19 -**	**2.9**	**2.0**	**5.1**	**2.6**	**1.6**	**--**	**70%**	**27**	**58**

6-3, 5.38 ERA in 72 IP at KC. Soft-tosser with good control, but little movement on his pitches. Once a batter makes contact, it falls for a hit or clears the fence at a rate far beyond the norm. It's chronic. Pass.

Wilson,Paul

		Tm	W	L	Sv	IP	K	ERA	Br/IP	R$	BF/G	OBA	vL	vR	H%	xERA	RAR	Ctl	Dom	Cmd	hr/9	G/F	S%	BPV	BPX
RH Starter	99		0	0	0	0	0	0.00	0.00																
AGE 31 Peak	00	TAM	* 6	9	0	134	89	3.96	1.24	$12	21.4	252	228	189	29%	3.30 +	35.0	2.6	6.0	**2.3**	0.5	1.31	68%	72	188
TYPE Finesse	01	TAM	8	9	0	151	119	4.88	1.44	$3	17.8	279	286	270	32%	4.88	12.2	3.1	7.1	**2.3**	1.3	1.13	69%	52	105
R Low	02	TAM	6	12	0	193	111	4.85	1.48	($2)	28.3	287	309	267	30%	5.27	15.8	3.1	5.2	**1.7**	1.4	1.22	71%	23	47
I exp con	03	CIN	8	10	0	166	93	4.66	1.44	$2	25.9	288	290	282	31%	5.08	13.8	2.7	5.0	**1.9**	1.3	1.10	71%	28	53
S pt	1st Half		5	5	0	91	50	4.64	1.45	$2	26.5	300			31%	5.43 -	7.7	2.2	4.9	**2.3**	1.5	1.15	73%	28	54
K	2nd Half		3	5	0	75	43	4.67	1.44	$0	25.2	274			30%	4.64	6.1	3.4	5.2	**1.5**	1.1	1.05	70%	31	60
LIMA C+ EP: 45%	**04**	**Proj**	**7**	**10**	**0**	**160**	**93**	**4.67**	**1.43**	**$2**	**24.0**	**282**			**30%**	**4.80**	**12.8**	**2.9**	**5.2**	**1.8**	**1.2**	**--**	**70%**	**32**	**62**

INJ: Shoulder tendinitis. Has settled into a zone, a performance range that's not very good and is showing no signs of growth. The promise he had in 1994-95 is gone for good. Thanks, Mets.

Witasick,Jay

		Tm	W	L	Sv	IP	K	ERA	Br/IP	R$	BF/G	OBA	vL	vR	H%	xERA	RAR	Ctl	Dom	Cmd	hr/9	G/F	S%	BPV	BPX
RH Reliever	99	KC	9	12	0	158	102	5.58	1.73	($3)	23.0	300	322	286	33%	6.01	6.1	4.7	5.8	**1.2**	1.3	1.11	70%	16	41
AGE 31 Peak	00	SD	6	10	0	150	121	5.82	1.67	($6)	20.9	296	287	281	34%	5.90	-3.8	4.4	7.3	**1.7**	1.4	1.58	68%	31	68
TYPE Power	01	2TM	8	2	1	79	106	3.30	1.41	$9	5.4	259	305	271	37%	4.15 -	22.4	3.8	12.1	**3.2**	0.9	1.42	80%	116	222
R High	02	SF	1	0	0	70	56	2.44	1.16	$6	6.2	230	228	238	28%	2.60	25.0	2.8	7.2	**2.5**	0.4	1.59	79%	94	178
I CON	03	SD	3	7	2	45	42	4.58	1.48	$2	4.3	248	292	215	30%	4.47	4.2	5.0	8.4	**1.7**	1.2	1.71	72%	55	106
S pt STB	1st Half		1	1	2	7	6	5.07	1.13	$2	2.9	231			22%	4.62	0.2	2.5	7.6	**3.0**	2.5	1.29	67%	41	80
K	2nd Half		2	6	0	38	36	4.49	1.55	$0	4.7	251			31%	4.44	4.0	5.4	8.5	**1.6**	0.9	1.81	73%	60	116
LIMA B+ EP: 55%	**04**	**Proj**	**4**	**5**	**0**	**70**	**63**	**3.86**	**1.31**	**$4**	**6.3**	**245**			**30%**	**3.70**	**13.2**	**3.6**	**8.1**	**2.3**	**0.9**	**G**	**73%**	**75**	**145**

From Rotowire: Supposedly, he hurt his arm when tossing away a trash bag with a watermelon inside. Witasick: "That's not how it happened. I threw two IP the day before I took out the trash. My elbow was already sore."

Wolf,Randy

		Tm	W	L	Sv	IP	K	ERA	Br/IP	R$	BF/G	OBA	vL	vR	H%	xERA	RAR	Ctl	Dom	Cmd	hr/9	G/F	S%	BPV	BPX
LH Starter	99	PHI	* 10	14	0	198	178	4.91	1.51	$2	25.8	268	209	278	32%	4.55	8.7	4.3	8.1	**1.9**	1.3	0.71	70%	51	111
AGE 27 Pre-Peak	00	PHI	11	9	0	206	160	4.37	1.42	$10	28.0	265	227	276	31%	4.49	34.8	3.6	7.0	**1.9**	1.1	0.82	72%	52	114
TYPE Power	01	PHI	10	11	0	163	152	3.70	1.23	$14	24.2	246	171	268	30%	3.50	36.4	2.8	8.4	**3.0**	0.8	0.79	72%	94	174
R Low	02	PHI	11	9	0	210	172	3.21	1.12	$21	27.4	225	258	216	26%	3.00	53.2	2.7	7.4	**2.7**	1.0	0.99	75%	82	155
I con	03	PHI	16	10	0	200	177	4.23	1.27	$16	25.4	238	232	234	28%	3.83	28.1	3.5	8.0	**2.3**	1.2	0.92	70%	66	128
S pt	1st Half		9	3	0	102	93	3.17	1.10	$15	25.7	202			24%	2.88	28.9	3.4	8.2	**2.4**	1.1	1.06	77%	79	153
K brn	2nd Half		7	7	0	98	84	5.34	1.45	$1	25.2	272			32%	4.82 +	-0.8	3.6	7.7	**2.2**	1.3	0.80	66%	54	103
LIMA D+ EP: 50%	**04**	**Proj**	**13**	**11**	**0**	**200**	**169**	**4.41**	**1.39**	**$9**	**26.9**	**263**			**31%**	**4.35**	**22.9**	**3.5**	**7.6**	**2.2**	**1.1**	**--**	**71%**	**60**	**117**

BPIs are on an overall decline, and all the innings may finally be catching up to him. He clocked 9 games with 110+ pitch counts... his performance crashed in 7 of the subsequent starts. Be afraid. Be very afraid.

Wood,Kerry

		Tm	W	L	Sv	IP	K	ERA	Br/IP	R$	BF/G	OBA	vL	vR	H%	xERA	RAR	Ctl	Dom	Cmd	hr/9	G/F	S%	BPV	BPX
RH Starter	99		0	0	0	0	0	0.00	0.00																
AGE 26 Growth	00	CHC	8	7	0	137	132	4.80	1.45	$5	26.0	225	223	229	27%	4.04 +	15.3	5.7	8.7	**1.5**	1.1	0.98	69%	60	133
TYPE Power	01	CHC	12	6	0	174	217	3.36	1.26	$17	26.0	206	201	203	29%	3.03	46.8	4.8	11.2	**2.4**	0.8	0.86	76%	106	196
R Low	02	CHC	12	11	0	213	217	3.68	1.25	$15	26.9	220	223	219	28%	3.19	40.8	4.1	9.2	**2.2**	0.9	0.83	73%	85	161
I con	03	CHC	14	11	0	211	266	3.20	1.19	$22	27.1	203	198	206	28%	3.00	58.8	4.3	11.3	**2.7**	1.0	1.01	78%	108	207
S pt	1st Half		8	5	0	115	143	2.90	1.14	$15	27.5	202			28%	2.84	36.7	3.8	11.2	**2.9**	1.0	0.98	80%	113	217
K brn	2nd Half		6	6	0	96	123	3.56	1.26	$8	26.8	205			29%	3.20	22.1	4.8	11.5	**2.4**	1.0	1.04	75%	103	198
LIMA C+ EP: 55%	**04**	**Proj**	**19**	**8**	**0**	**225**	**268**	**3.36**	**1.24**	**$25**	**26.8**	**210**			**28%**	**3.16**	**57.4**	**4.4**	**10.7**	**2.4**	**1.0**	**--**	**77%**	**98**	**189**

BPIs keep edging upward, but don't cast a blind eye to some warning signs:
- Below optimal control
- Excessive workload. Wracked up 100+ pitch counts in 75% of his starts; 120+ in 38% of starts.

Worrell,Tim

		Tm	W	L	Sv	IP	K	ERA	Br/IP	R$	BF/G	OBA	vL	vR	H%	xERA	RAR	Ctl	Dom	Cmd	hr/9	G/F	S%	BPV	BPX
RH Reliever	99	OAK	2	2	0	69	62	4.17	1.49	$2	5.7	262	285	229	32%	4.33	15.7	4.4	8.1	**1.8**	0.8	0.98	73%	66	165
AGE 36 Decline	00	2TM	* 7	6	3	79	63	3.29	1.46	$11	5.3	268	221	276	30%	4.98 -	26.2	3.9	7.2	**1.9**	1.5	0.96	84%	39	92
TYPE Power	01	SF	2	5	0	78	63	3.46	1.33	$3	4.5	244	248	234	30%	3.38	20.0	3.8	7.3	**1.9**	0.5	0.94	74%	76	141
R Moderate	02	SF	8	2	0	72	55	2.25	1.18	$13	3.7	213	204	218	26%	2.44	27.5	3.8	6.9	**1.8**	0.4	0.72	82%	81	153
I con	03	SF	4	4	38	78	65	2.88	1.31	$28	4.3	251	241	250	31%	3.50 -	25.1	3.2	7.5	**2.3**	0.6	1.33	79%	81	156
S stb	1st Half		2	3	17	42	30	1.71	1.19	$15	4.7	233			27%	3.05 -	20.0	3.0	6.4	**2.1**	0.6	1.22	89%	73	140
K AGE	2nd Half		2	1	21	36	35	4.24	1.44	$13	4.0	272			35%	4.04	5.0	3.5	8.7	**2.5**	0.5	1.52	70%	91	174
LIMA D+ EP: 50%	**04**	**Proj**	**4**	**3**	**34**	**75**	**62**	**3.24**	**1.29**	**$25**	**4.2**	**246**			**30%**	**3.39**	**20.3**	**3.4**	**7.4**	**2.2**	**0.6**	**--**	**76%**	**79**	**152**

Legitimate closer? Check TOG: TALENT: Okay, but you'd like to see a more dominant arm. OPPTY: Had it in 2003. GUILE: Converted 84% of save opps. That will draw second looks... as will his age.

Wright,Danny

RH Reliever
AGE 26 Growth
TYPE

RISK		
R	High	
I	EXP	con
S	pt	
K		

LIMA F EP: 50%

Yr	Tm	W	L	Sv	IP	K	ERA	Br/IP	R$	BF/G	OBA	vL	vR	H%	xERA	RAR	Ctl	Dom	Cmd	hr/9	G/F	S%	BPV	BPX
99		0	0	0	0	0	0.00	0.00																
00	aa	2	4	0	43	27	3.56	1.42	$3	26.7	224			25%	3.70	12.7	5.4	5.7	**1.0**	0.8		77%	41	97
01	CHW	* 12	10	0	200	146	4.37	1.48	$7	26.6	274	264	342	32%	4.58	30.0	3.7	6.6	**1.8**	0.9	1.62	72%	50	100
02	CHW	14	12	0	196	136	5.19	1.38	$7	25.6	266	257	270	29%	4.82	7.1	3.3	6.2	**1.9**	1.5	1.13	66%	35	73
03	CHW	* 2	10	1	119	70	6.12	1.49	($6)	18.7	265	280	271	27%	5.31 +	-9.5	4.2	5.3	**1.3**	1.7	1.02	62%	8	17
1st Half		0	5	0	66	46	4.89	1.37	($1)	21.9	246			26%	4.53	5.7	4.1	6.2	**1.5**	1.5	1.02	69%	31	66
2nd Half		2	5	1	53	24	7.67	1.63	($5)	16.0	287			28%	6.29 +	-15.2	4.4	4.1	**0.9**	2.0	1.02	55%	-20	-43
04	**Proj**	**3**	**6**	**0**	**80**	**50**	**5.06**	**1.51**	**($1)**	**16.1**	**274**			**29%**	**5.23**	**5.1**	**4.1**	**5.6**	**1.4**	**1.5**	**--**	**70%**	**19**	**41**

1-7, 6.17 ERA in 86 IP at CHW. Managed a 3.24 ERA out of the bullpen (in 16.2 IP) , but that came along with a 2.7 strikeout rate, 1.0 command ratio and a 21% hit rate. DO NOT roster him until he shows signs of life.

Wright,Jamey

RH Starter
AGE 29 Pre-Peak
TYPE Power

RISK		
R	High	
I	exp	CON
S	pt	STB
K		

LIMA D EP: 50%

Yr	Tm	W	L	Sv	IP	K	ERA	Br/IP	R$	BF/G	OBA	vL	vR	H%	xERA	RAR	Ctl	Dom	Cmd	hr/9	G/F	S%	BPV	BPX
99	COL	* 9	10	0	194	112	6.31	1.79	($14)	27.7	322	331	291	35%	6.14	-27.9	4.1	5.2	**1.3**	1.3	1.66	66%	10	21
00	MIL	7	9	0	164	96	4.11	1.49	$6	27.9	253	266	257	28%	4.11	33.4	4.8	5.3	**1.1**	0.7	2.15	73%	39	86
01	MIL	11	12	0	194	129	4.91	1.54	$1	26.2	268	260	282	29%	4.95	11.8	4.5	6.0	**1.3**	1.2	1.90	71%	29	53
02	2NL	* 8	14	0	144	87	5.31	1.60	($4)	25.0	270	271	267	29%	4.89	-4.0	5.0	5.4	**1.1**	1.1	1.70	68%	25	47
03	KC	* 7	11	0	163	113	6.13	1.79	($12)	24.8	310	296	175	34%	6.40	-13.1	4.7	6.2	**1.3**	1.4	1.50	68%	17	36
1st Half		3	5	0	69	40	7.96	2.07	($12)	21.5	350			38%	7.97	-22.5	5.0	5.2	**1.1**	1.6		63%	-9	-19
2nd Half		4	6	0	94	73	4.78	1.58	($1)	28.3	278			32%	5.25	9.4	4.5	7.0	**1.6**	1.2		73%	37	79
04	**Proj**	**5**	**10**	**0**	**120**	**79**	**5.18**	**1.61**	**($3)**	**24.7**	**278**			**31%**	**5.28**	**5.8**	**4.7**	**5.9**	**1.3**	**1.2**	**--**	**70%**	**25**	**54**

1-2, 4.32 ERA in 25 IP at KC, and PQS scores of 4,4,5,0. For the past 7 years, he's posted Cmd ratios between 0.8 and 1.3. There's nothing he could do at this point to lead us to believe it's going to get any better.

Wright,Jaret

RH Reliever
AGE 28 Pre-Peak
TYPE Power

RISK		
R	Moderate	
I	exp	CON
S	pt	
K		

LIMA B EP: 60%

Yr	Tm	W	L	Sv	IP	K	ERA	Br/IP	R$	BF/G	OBA	vL	vR	H%	xERA	RAR	Ctl	Dom	Cmd	hr/9	G/F	S%	BPV	BPX
99	CLE	8	10	0	133	91	6.09	1.66	($3)	23.4	277	294	261	31%	5.40 +	-3.9	5.2	6.2	**1.2**	1.2	1.08	65%	25	62
00	CLE	3	4	0	52	36	4.67	1.38	$3	24.9	231	295	182	26%	3.87 +	8.6	4.8	6.2	**1.3**	1.0	1.10	68%	42	109
01	CLE	* 5	3	0	65	44	5.95	1.63	($2)	19.7	276	281	353	31%	5.08 +	-4.1	5.0	6.1	**1.2**	1.0	1.03	64%	33	66
02	CLE	* 7	6	0	73	48	8.01	2.15	($11)	20.6	350			39%	7.86	-25.0	5.7	5.9	**1.0**	1.2	0.60	63%	5	11
03	2NL	* 4	6	2	75	66	5.87	1.76	($4)	5.7	307	365	313	37%	5.92	-6.0	4.6	7.9	**1.7**	1.1	1.34	67%	45	87
1st Half		3	6	2	44	39	6.73	2.02	($4)	6.6	333			39%	7.31 -	-8.6	5.5	8.0	**1.4**	1.4	1.21	68%	24	46
2nd Half		1	0	0	31	27	4.65	1.39	$0	4.6	268			33%	3.93 +	2.6	3.2	7.8	**2.5**	0.6	1.52	66%	83	159
04	**Proj**	**4**	**4**	**0**	**60**	**51**	**4.65**	**1.52**	**$1**	**8.1**	**274**			**33%**	**4.62**	**4.9**	**4.1**	**7.7**	**1.9**	**0.9**	**--**	**71%**	**59**	**113**

2-5, 7.39 ERA in 56 IP at ATL. Another arm with little in the BPI department, likely done in by overuse in his early years. But then... comes to ATL, pitches in 11 games -- 9-7-2-0-3-9.... Mazzone lives! Arrrgh!

Wunsch,Kelly

LH Reliever
AGE 31 Peak
TYPE Power

RISK		
R	High	
I	exp	CON
S	PT	
K		

LIMA B EP: 40%

Yr	Tm	W	L	Sv	IP	K	ERA	Br/IP	R$	BF/G	OBA	vL	vR	H%	xERA	RAR	Ctl	Dom	Cmd	hr/9	G/F	S%	BPV	BPX
99	a/a	6	2	1	92	46	3.91	1.55	$5	10.8	292			32%	4.48 -	19.9	3.5	4.5	**1.3**	0.5		75%	36	83
00	CHW	6	3	1	61	51	2.95	1.29	$11	3.1	225	160	275	27%	3.13	24.3	4.3	7.5	**1.8**	0.6	3.42	79%	74	193
01	CHW	2	1	0	22	16	7.74	1.36	($1)	2.9	252			27%	4.67 +	-6.7	3.7	6.5	**1.8**	1.6	2.05	42%	32	64
02	CHW	* 3	1	0	43	29	3.35	1.60	$2	3.2	266	208	268	31%	4.60 -	12.2	5.2	6.1	**1.2**	0.6	2.55	80%	44	90
03	CHW	0	0	0	36	33	2.75	1.19	$3	3.4	151	127	153	20%	1.78 +	13.4	6.3	8.3	**1.3**	0.3	1.27	76%	95	204
1st Half		0	0	0	15	12	1.18	0.92	$3	2.7	104			14%	0.41 +	8.8	5.3	7.1	**1.3**	0.0	1.69	86%	105	226
2nd Half		0	0	0	21	21	3.89	1.39	$0	4.3	181			24%	2.77 +	4.5	6.9	9.1	**1.3**	0.4	1.00	71%	88	190
04	**Proj**	**2**	**1**	**0**	**40**	**32**	**4.28**	**1.55**	**$1**	**3.8**	**252**			**31%**	**4.06**	**6.8**	**5.4**	**7.2**	**1.3**	**0.5**	**--**	**72%**	**62**	**133**

It's tough to pull a 95 BPV with a 1.3 command ratio. You have to give up virtually no hits... which is what he did, thanks to a 20% hit rate. That won't last. Nor will a sub-3.00 ERA. And likely, nor will his draft-worthiness.

Yan,Esteban

RH Reliever
AGE 28 Pre-Peak
TYPE Power

RISK		
R	Moderate	
I		CON
S	pt	
K		

LIMA D EP: 60%

Yr	Tm	W	L	Sv	IP	K	ERA	Br/IP	R$	BF/G	OBA	vL	vR	H%	xERA	RAR	Ctl	Dom	Cmd	hr/9	G/F	S%	BPV	BPX
99	TAM	3	4	0	61	46	5.90	1.79	($3)	5.7	309	310	342	35%	6.15	-0.2	4.7	6.8	**1.4**	1.2	1.19	68%	29	72
00	TAM	7	8	0	137	111	6.23	1.46	$0	14.0	290	316	258	32%	5.48 +	-5.9	2.8	7.3	**2.6**	1.7	1.07	60%	45	117
01	TAM	4	6	22	62	64	3.91	1.21	$18	4.7	268	272	252	34%	3.90	13.1	1.6	9.3	**5.8**	1.0	1.42	71%	149	298
02	TAM	7	8	19	69	53	4.30	1.43	$16	5.5	265	273	246	30%	4.77	10.7	3.8	6.9	**1.8**	1.3	1.06	74%	43	88
03	2TM	2	1	1	66	53	6.39	1.62	($5)	5.6	310	309	307	35%	6.29	-8.8	3.1	7.2	**2.3**	1.8	1.13	64%	32	64
1st Half		2	1	0	40	33	7.18	1.65	($4)	5.7	315			36%	6.25 +	-9.6	3.1	7.4	**2.4**	1.6	1.23	58%	39	79
2nd Half		0	0	1	26	20	5.17	1.57	($1)	5.3	303			33%	6.34 -	0.8	3.1	6.9	**2.2**	2.1	1.00	74%	20	41
04	**Proj**	**1**	**3**	**0**	**40**	**33**	**4.95**	**1.43**	**($0)**	**5.4**	**276**			**31%**	**5.09**	**2.4**	**3.2**	**7.4**	**2.4**	**1.6**	**--**	**70%**	**47**	**94**

It's been all downhill since 2001. Ctl/Dom/Cmd have not been terrible, but has been unable to keep the ball in the park, is killed by LHers, and, well, also by RHers. H% and S% have not been kind either. It's just bad.

Zambrano,Carlos

RH Starter
AGE 22 Growth
TYPE Power

RISK		
R	X HIGH	
I	EXP	con
S	PT	stb
K	AGE	BRN

LIMA C EP: 50%

Yr	Tm	W	L	Sv	IP	K	ERA	Br/IP	R$	BF/G	OBA	vL	vR	H%	xERA	RAR	Ctl	Dom	Cmd	hr/9	G/F	S%	BPV	BPX
99		0	0	0	0	0	0.00	0.00																
00	a/a	5	6	6	117	87	2.62	1.22	$18	11.3	214			26%	2.58	49.3	4.1	6.7	**1.6**	0.3		78%	78	184
01	aaa	11	7	0	157	157	4.30	1.23	$12	20.4	224			29%	2.91 +	23.6	3.7	9.0	**2.4**	0.5	1.22	64%	99	191
02	CHC	4	8	0	117	104	3.38	1.40	$4	14.4	225	209	253	28%	3.43	27.0	5.2	8.0	**1.5**	0.7	2.10	77%	69	131
03	CHC	13	11	0	214	168	3.11	1.32	$18	28.3	238	245	235	29%	3.17	62.1	4.0	7.1	**1.8**	0.4	2.00	76%	76	146
1st Half		6	6	0	103	83	3.14	1.34	$8	27.5	234			29%	3.14	29.6	4.3	7.2	**1.7**	0.3	1.56	76%	77	148
2nd Half		7	5	0	111	85	3.09	1.30	$10	29.2	241			29%	3.19	32.5	3.7	6.9	**1.9**	0.4	2.56	76%	76	146
04	**Proj**	**12**	**10**	**0**	**200**	**164**	**3.29**	**1.27**	**$17**	**27.0**	**231**			**28%**	**3.02**	**53.0**	**3.8**	**7.4**	**2.0**	**0.5**	**G**	**74%**	**79**	**153**

First, the bad news... 32 starts, 23 of them over 100 pitches, 14 over 110 pitches, and 214 IP at age 21. Oh, and his control can still use work. Now the good news... It'll be a fun ride until the breakdown.

Zambrano,Victor

RH Starter
AGE 29 Peak
TYPE Power

RISK		
R	X HIGH	
I	EXP	CON
S	PT	stb
K		brn

LIMA C EP: 45%

Yr	Tm	W	L	Sv	IP	K	ERA	Br/IP	R$	BF/G	OBA	vL	vR	H%	xERA	RAR	Ctl	Dom	Cmd	hr/9	G/F	S%	BPV	BPX
99	aa	7	2	1	82	65	5.93	1.84	($2)	9.8	324			39%	5.84	-4.4	4.4	7.1	**1.6**	0.7		67%	47	110
00	aaa	0	6	8	62	47	5.37	1.69	$1	5.4	308			35%	6.00 -	3.2	3.9	6.8	**1.7**	1.3		71%	32	75
01	TAM	* 7	4	14	81	82	3.00	1.26	$18	5.2	237	205	198	30%	3.50 -	27.0	3.4	9.1	**2.6**	0.9	1.12	80%	91	182
02	TAM	* 8	9	2	128	85	5.20	1.59	$0	11.1	266	292	266	29%	5.08	4.4	5.1	6.0	**1.2**	1.2	1.07	69%	27	54
03	TAM	12	10	0	188	132	4.21	1.44	$9	24.1	237	263	206	27%	4.13	33.1	5.1	6.3	**1.2**	1.0	1.23	73%	41	90
1st Half		5	4	0	84	52	4.06	1.39	$5	20.2	218			24%	3.62	16.5	5.5	5.6	**1.0**	0.9	1.35	72%	41	88
2nd Half		7	6	0	104	80	4.33	1.48	$4	28.6	253			29%	4.54	16.6	4.8	6.9	**1.5**	1.1	1.12	74%	43	93
04	**Proj**	**11**	**14**	**0**	**200**	**150**	**4.64**	**1.51**	**$4**	**26.0**	**254**			**29%**	**4.53**	**24.2**	**4.9**	**6.8**	**1.4**	**1.0**	**--**	**71%**	**43**	**91**

Unexciting skill set with a few anomalies that artificially depressed his ERA, such as a .206 OBA vs RHers. Won't happen again, which means his ERA goes up, which is not good when it's already in the mid-4's.

Zerbe,Chad

LH Reliever
AGE 32 Peak
TYPE Finesse

RISK		
R	High	
I	EXP	con
S	pt	stb
K		

LIMA C+ EP: 45%

Yr	Tm	W	L	Sv	IP	K	ERA	Br/IP	R$	BF/G	OBA	vL	vR	H%	xERA	RAR	Ctl	Dom	Cmd	hr/9	G/F	S%	BPV	BPX
99	aa	1	3	0	41	13	2.85	1.32	$3	24.8	266			28%	3.48 -	14.7	2.6	2.9	**1.1**	0.4		79%	28	66
00	a/a	9	4	0	120	53	4.80	1.63	$4	21.0	332			36%	5.52 -	15.4	2.1	4.0	**1.9**	0.5	6.00	70%	36	87
01	SF	* 6	4	5	64	35	3.94	1.44	$8	6.3	288	396	215	32%	4.52 -	12.2	2.7	4.9	**1.8**	0.7	1.71	74%	45	83
02	SF	* 2	0	0	66	30	2.59	1.30	$5	5.3	250	247	248	27%	3.27 -	22.2	3.3	4.1	**1.3**	0.4	2.00	81%	44	82
03	SF	* 2	2	2	59	23	4.40	1.48	$1	6.5	304	365	277	32%	4.92 -	7.0	2.3	3.5	**1.5**	0.8	1.57	71%	25	47
1st Half		1	1	1	31	11	4.33	1.41	$1	6.1	296			31%	4.71	4.0	2.0	3.2	**1.6**	0.9	1.80	71%	22	42
2nd Half		1	1	1	28	12	4.48	1.57	$0	7.0	312			34%	5.14 -	3.0	2.6	3.8	**1.5**	0.6	1.35	71%	28	54
04	**Proj**	**2**	**1**	**0**	**40**	**17**	**4.28**	**1.43**	**$1**	**6.7**	**290**			**31%**	**4.44**	**5.3**	**2.5**	**3.8**	**1.5**	**0.7**	**G**	**70%**	**32**	**62**

1-1, 4.78 ERA in 49 IP at SF. Soft-tosser, getting more and more soft, and doing less and less real tossing. If there's nobody going to draft him anyway, do I have to write anything more?

Zito,Barry

LH Starter
AGE 25 Growth
TYPE

RISK		
R	Moderate	
I	exp	con
S	pt	
K		BRN

LIMA D EP: 40%

Yr	Tm	W	L	Sv	IP	K	ERA	Br/IP	R$	BF/G	OBA	vL	vR	H%	xERA	RAR	Ctl	Dom	Cmd	hr/9	G/F	S%	BPV	BPX
99	a/a	3	1	0	28	30	4.82	1.57	$2	25.2	269			36%	4.28 +	2.7	4.8	9.6	**2.0**	0.6		69%	82	190
00	OAK	* 15	9	0	193	156	3.44	1.33	$23	25.7	234	194	195	29%	3.28	63.9	4.2	7.3	**1.7**	0.5	0.82	74%	72	188
01	OAK	17	8	0	214	205	3.49	1.23	$23	25.4	234	234	229	29%	3.27	57.2	3.4	8.6	**2.6**	0.8	0.85	74%	91	182
02	OAK	23	5	0	229	182	2.75	1.14	$36	26.5	220	275	203	25%	3.09	83.0	3.1	7.2	**2.3**	0.9	0.74	81%	75	153
03	OAK	14	12	0	231	146	3.31	1.19	$24	27.1	222	223	218	25%	3.05	68.6	3.4	5.7	**1.7**	0.7	0.82	74%	57	124
1st Half		7	5	0	113	69	3.18	1.17	$13	27.2	212			23%	3.16	35.5	3.7	5.5	**1.5**	1.0	0.82	77%	46	99
2nd Half		7	7	0	118	77	3.43	1.20	$12	27.0	231			27%	2.94 +	33.1	3.2	5.9	**1.8**	0.5	0.81	71%	69	149
04	**Proj**	**15**	**12**	**0**	**225**	**147**	**3.84**	**1.26**	**$19**	**26.9**	**235**			**27%**	**3.41**	**51.2**	**3.5**	**5.9**	**1.7**	**0.8**	**--**	**71%**	**56**	**119**

A troubling season. Dom is on a 3-year skid, and only a 25% hit rate has kept his ERA in check. With all the innings on his arm and a hit rate looking to revert to the mean, his ERA could spike. In 2004? It's possible.

Pure Quality Starts

PQS is the next step in following pitching lines. The old Quality Start method — minimum 6 IP, maximum 3 earned runs — is overly simplistic and does not measure any real skill. Bill James' "game score" methodology is better, but is not feasible for quick calculation.

In PQS, we give a starting pitcher credit for exhibiting certain skills in each of his starts. Then by tracking his "PQS Score" over time, we can follow his progress. Here are the criteria...

1. The pitcher must have gone a minimum of 6 innings. This measures stamina. For a 6 IP performance, the pitcher gets 1 point. If he goes less than 5 innings, he automatically gets a total PQS score of zero, no matter what other stats he produces.

2. He must have allowed no more than an equal number of hits to the number of innings pitched. This measures hit prevention and earns him 1 point.

3. His number of strikeouts must be no fewer than two less than his innings pitched (IP minus K must be 2 or less). This measures dominance and earns him 1 point.

4. He must have struck out at least twice as many batters as he walked. This measures command and earns him 1 point.

5. He must have allowed no more than one home run. This measures his ability to keep the ball in the park and earns him 1 point.

At first it may seem like a bit of work, but guaranteed, after a week or so, you'll be able to glance at a pitcher's stat line and immediately determine his PQS score. A perfect PQS score would be 5. Any pitcher who averages 3 or more over the course of the season is probably performing admirably. The nice thing about PQS is it allows you to approach each start as more than an all-or-nothing event.

Note the absence of earned runs. Just as BPV serves as a leading indicator to ERA — without the use of earned runs — so does PQS. No matter how many runs a pitcher allows, if he scores high on the PQS scale, he has hurled a good game in terms of his base skills. The number of runs allowed — a function of not only the pitcher's ability but that of his bullpen and defense — will even out over time.

PQS Pitching Logs

We've always approached performance measures on an aggregate basis. Each individual event that our statistics chronicle gets dumped into a huge pool of data. We then use our formulas to try to sort and slice and manipulate the data into more usable information.

Pure Quality Starts (PQS) take a different approach. It says that the smallest unit of measure should not be the "event" but instead be the "game." Within that game, we can accumulate all the strikeouts, hits and walks, and evaluate that outing as a whole. After all, when a pitcher takes the mound, he is either "on" or "off" his game; he is either dominant or struggling, or somewhere in between.

PQS captures the array of events and slaps an evaluative label on that outing, on a scale of 0 to 5. It doesn't matter if a few extra balls got through the infield, or the pitcher was given the hook in the 4th or 6th inning, or the bullpen was able to strand their inherited baserunners. When we look at performance in the aggregate, *those events do matter,* and will affect a pitcher's BPIs and ERA. But with PQS, the minutia is less relevant than the overall performance.

In the end, a dominating performance is a dominating performance, whether Mark Prior is hurling a 2-hit shutout or giving up 4 runs while striking out 11 in 7 IP. And a disaster is still a disaster, whether Nate Cornejo gets a 1st inning hook after giving up 7 hits, or "takes one for the team" getting shelled for 5 IP.

With the addition of Gene McCaffrey's Domination and Disaster percentages, we can sort out the PQS scores even more.

Domination Per Cent (DOM%) measures the portion of a pitcher's starts that scored a 4 or 5 on the PQS scale.

Disaster Per Cent (DIS%) measures the portion of a pitcher's starts that scored a 0 or 1 on the PQS scale.

DOM/DIS percentages open up a new perspective, providing us with two separate scales of performance. In tandem, they measure something completely different — *consistency.* For instance, a pitcher with a 66/33% DOM/DIS split was dominating in two thirds of his starts but was rocked once every three outings. Compare him to a pitcher with a 66/10% split — also dominating two thirds of the time but saw an early shower only once every 10 times out.

This is important because a pitcher might possess incredible skill but be unable to sustain it on a start-by-start basis. For instance, a pitcher who posts PQS scores of 5,0,5,0,5 might have a seasonal stat line that is identical to another pitcher who posts scores of 3,3,3,3,3 — less skill, but more consistent. ERAs, WHIPs, and even BPIs don't capture that subtle difference. DOM/DIS *does* capture that difference, and in doing so, helps us identify pitchers who might be better or worse than their stats — and sabermetrics — indicate.

The final step is to convert a pitcher's DOM/DIS split back to an expected ERA. By creating a grid of individual DOM and DIS levels, we can determine the average ERA at each cross point. The result is an ERA based purely on PQS, and so we can call it the PQS ERA, or *qERA* for short. When we look at this in tandem with a pitcher's true ERA and his xERA, it gives us a broad picture of where he is versus where he could, or should, be.

The following pitching logs include:

- Up to three years of data for all pitchers who had at least five starts in 2003.
- Number of starts in that year. (No.)
- Start-by-start listing of PQS scores, separated by half season. These are not time-phased, so any gaps between half seasons do not necessarily represent gaps of time.
- Average pitch counts for all starts (PC)
- Domination and Disaster percentages (DOM, DIS)
- Earned Run Average (ERA)
- Expected Earned Run Average (xERA)
- PQS Earned Run Average (qERA)

PQS PITCHING LOGS

Pitcher	Year	No.	FIRST HALF	SECOND HALF	PC	DOM	DIS	ERA	xERA	qERA
Abbott,Paul	2001	27	0 3 4 5 0 3 2 3 5 2 3 3 4	2 5 3 5 4 3 4 0 2 2 3 3 1 3	100	30%	15%	4.25	4.23	4.60
	2002	5	0 2 3 0 0		91	0%	60%	12.12	8.60	9.02
	2003	8		0 3 4 0 4 2 2 0	91	25%	38%	5.36	5.26	5.27
Acevedo,Jose	2001	18	0 0 5 3	4 0 1 3 0 5 4 0 5 5 0 5 4 4	85	50%	39%	5.07	4.60	4.87
Adams,Terry	2001	22	0 5 2 2 3 5 4	3 5 1 5 0 4 5 3 0 4 5 4 4 3 3	100	50%	18%	4.33	3.81	4.37
	2002	19	3 2 1 3 5 0 5 2 4 3 0 3 5 3 3 3 0	0 1	90	21%	32%	4.37	3.90	5.21
Affeldt,Jeremy	2002	7	0 0 3 3 0 5 0		86	14%	57%	4.45	4.47	7.77
	2003	18	4 4 2 0 0 4 3 3 4 3 0 3 3 0 4 3	3 4	88	33%	22%	3.93	3.98	4.71
Ainsworth,Kurt	2003	11	4 4 2 0 3 0 4 2 3 4 4		96	45%	18%	4.10	4.72	4.40
Alvarez,Wilson	2002	10	0 4 0 5 0 3 1 4 0	0	81	30%	60%	4.88	5.05	7.45
	2003	13	2 0 3	5 5 5 0 2 3 5 4 5 0	88	46%	23%	2.37	2.56	4.53
Anderson,Brian	2001	22	0 0 3 2 3 5 2 3 4 4 5	4 3 3 0 0 3 2 0 0 3 0	81	23%	32%	5.21	5.44	5.21
	2002	24	0 0 4 2 5 3 2 4 1 3 0 4 3	3 2 5 4 4 1 4 3 3 0 0	87	33%	29%	4.79	4.80	4.90
	2003	31	4 2 2 1 1 2 0 3 1 3 0 4 5 4 2 3 3	2 3 5 0 5 5 5 4 2 3 0 3 3 3	95	29%	23%	3.79	4.55	4.73
Anderson,Jimmy	2001	34	3 0 4 5 3 2 3 2 4 1 5 2 3 5 1 3 0 2	4 2 3 0 0 2 3 3 2 0 4 2 3 3 3	93	21%	21%	5.11	4.67	4.75
	2002	25	2 3 4 1 0 2 3 1 3 1 0 3 1 3 1 3 0 1	0 3 2 2 2 3 2 0	86	4%	44%	5.46	5.80	5.90
	2003	7	0 2 2 1 2 4 0		84	14%	43%	9.00	8.07	5.70
Appier,Kevin	2001	33	5 2 2 4 2 3 0 3 4 5 5 5 5 5 0 5 5 5	5 5 0 3 5 3 2 5 0 4 3 3 4 5 5	100	58%	12%	3.58	3.40	3.97
	2002	32	2 5 5 0 4 4 4 5 4 2 3 0 0 0 5 3 4	5 2 3 4 4 2 3 4 3 5 5 3 0 1 4	99	50%	19%	3.93	4.24	4.37
	2003	23	0 5 2 0 2 5 0 5 4 4 1 2 3 4 0 3	0 3 0 3 4 2 0	87	30%	35%	5.43	5.44	5.19
Armas Jr.,Tony	2001	34	4 2 5 3 3 5 3 4 5 5 3 3 4 4 4 3 0 5 4	5 5 0 4 0 5 4 5 3 5 5 5 0 1 3 0	99	56%	18%	4.04	3.86	4.10
	2002	29	2 5 3 4 5 5 5 4 4 1 4 3 3 2 3 0 5 5 2	2 0 4 0 0 0 4 5 4 3 4	94	48%	21%	4.45	4.27	4.53
	2003	5	4 1 5 3 3		96	40%	20%	2.61	3.07	4.56
Asencio,Miguel	2002	21	3 3 3 3 1 0 2	3 0 2 0 3 3 1 2 4 3 2 4 2 3	91	10%	24%	5.12	5.31	4.79
	2003	8	2 1 3 4 3 4 2 3		98	25%	13%	5.25	4.89	4.50
Ashby,Andy	2001	2	3 3		85	0%	0%	4.02	5.40	4.50
	2002	30	5 3 2 4 5 2 4 3 5 3 4 2 3 4 0 2 3	1 3 1 3 4 5 3 3 2 0 2 0 0	91	30%	20%	3.93	4.21	4.71
	2003	12	0 0 2 3 4 0 3	1 3 0 4 3	79	17%	42%	5.18	5.06	5.60
Astacio,Pedro	2001	26	5 4 4 5 4 0 2 0 4 5 3 5 0 3 2 3 2 5	3 5 0 4 3 4 4 5	99	54%	15%	5.11	4.61	4.37
	2002	31	4 4 5 2 4 4 4 5 4 2 3 5 4 5 3 2 0	2 4 5 4 5 2 0 1 4 4 0 0 5 2	97	58%	16%	4.81	4.69	4.10
	2003	7	5 0 4 2 0 3 0		90	29%	43%	7.50	7.07	5.40
Austin,Jeff	2003	7	4 4 2 4 0 0 0		78	43%	43%	8.68	6.93	5.21
Baldwin,James	2001	28	3 0 2 4 3 2 0 4 0 2 3 3 1 0	4 4 4 5 5 5 3 3 4 0 4 2 2 3	98	36%	21%	4.42	4.98	4.64
	2002	23	5 4 0 3 0 2 3 3 2 5 5 0 4 3 3 2 3	4 4 1 5 0 0	88	35%	26%	5.28	5.56	4.82
Bale,John	2003	9		0 5 3 0 4 3 3 0 0	81	22%	44%	4.50	4.72	5.50
Batista,Miguel	2001	18	1 0 0 0 5 4 1 2	2 2 4 3 4 4 0 5 5 2	87	39%	33%	3.36	3.27	5.00
	2002	29	3 2 3 4 5 3 0 4 2 5 3 2 0 4	3 2 5 4 3 3 5 2 4 0 3 3 3 1 3	92	31%	14%	4.30	3.60	4.49
	2003	29	3 0 2 5 4 5 2 2 4 5 5 4 4 4 5 0	4 4 5 3 3 4 3 3 5 0 4 0 4 1	93	55%	17%	3.54	3.79	4.10
Beckett,Josh	2001	4		4 5 4 5	87	100%	0%	1.50	2.40	2.00
	2002	21	4 4 4 5 3 2 5 5 0 0	3 5 4 4 3 0 3 0 0 0 3	83	43%	29%	4.12	3.77	4.74
	2003	22	0 5 3 5 5 5 4 0 5 3	5 4 5 1 3 5 5 4 4 5 4 5	97	73%	14%	3.04	3.46	3.51
Bell,Rob	2001	27	3 4 4 0 0 2 5 0 2 0 2 0 4	3 4 1 0 2 3 5 3 0 4 4 1 0 1	89	30%	41%	6.34	6.21	5.29
	2002	15	4 4 1 0 5 5 3 4 1	4 1 2 2 3 0	97	40%	33%	6.22	5.68	4.92
	2003	18	0 4 0 1 3	4 0 0 3 3 3 4 3 3 2 0 4 0	84	22%	39%	5.52	4.78	5.36
Benoit,Joaquin	2002	14	3 2	3 4 0 5 3 0 4 0 0 2 4 0	97	29%	36%	5.36	5.04	5.27
	2003	18	3 4 0 5 0 1 4 3 0 4	1 0 5 0 0 0 3 0 0	90	28%	56%	5.49	5.19	7.14
Benson,Kris	2002	25	0 5 0 0 2 2 0 0 3 3 5	1 1 0 3 2 3 2 4 4 4 1 4 1 1	83	24%	44%	4.32	4.98	5.50
	2003	18	3 5 5 3 4 4 0 4 5 3 3 2 0 2 2 5 2	0	96	39%	17%	4.97	5.41	4.52
Bere,Jason	2001	32	3 5 5 5 5 0 4 0 3 4 2 3 3 4 5	5 3 5 3 5 5 0 4 0 5 4 0 5 0 2 3	93	50%	22%	4.31	3.99	4.50
	2002	16	5 4 0 0 3 3 2 4 1 3 4 5 5 5 0	0	86	44%	31%	5.72	5.33	4.92
Bernero,Adam	2002	11	4 3 0 3 5 4 3 0 0	2 0	92	27%	36%	6.24	5.84	5.27
	2003	17	3 2 1 4 3 0 5 0 5 5 5 4 5 0 5 3 0		93	47%	29%	5.89	4.73	4.69
Biddle,Rocky	2001	21	3 4 3 2 3 2 3 0 3 5 0 4 4 3 5	3 4 0 1 3 5	91	33%	19%	5.41	4.81	4.60
	2002	7	0 0 0 3 3 3 1		72	0%	57%	4.09	4.62	8.24
Bierbrodt,Nick	2003	6	0 0 0 0 3 0		74	0%	83%	9.21	8.30	12.14
Bonderman,Jeremy	2003	28	0 0 3 4 3 5 3 3 2 5 0 3 3 4 3 4 5 4	0 3 0 3 3 0 4 0 0 0	86	29%	32%	5.56	5.52	5.13
Brazelton,Dewon	2003	10	2 3 2 2 4 3 0 1 0 0		82	10%	40%	6.94	6.20	5.70
Brower,Jim	2003	5	4 0	5 4 1	76	60%	40%	3.96	3.48	4.67
Brown,Kevin	2001	19	5 3 5 5 5 5 5 0 3 2 3 5 2	4 2 1 3 5 2	93	47%	11%	2.66	2.81	4.28
	2002	10	0 5 0 4 4 5 4 2 0	3	75	50%	30%	4.86	4.94	4.71
	2003	32	5 4 2 2 5 5 4 5 5 5 5 5 5 4 3 3 3	5 5 3 4 4 5 4 4 4 5 5 5 2 3	97	75%	0%	2.39	2.76	2.84
Buehrle,Mark	2001	32	4 0 2 3 5 3 2 4 3 4 4 3 3 3 4	4 5 5 3 4 3 2 3 3 4 4 0 3 3 2 5	103	44%	6%	3.30	3.07	4.11
	2002	34	5 4 3 4 4 0 5 3 4 3 4 4 5 3 4 2 4 2 2 4	5 3 3 4 2 3 4 5 3 4 1 3 4 2 4	103	53%	6%	3.58	3.74	3.85
	2003	35	3 4 3 4 0 4 3 3 1 0 3 3 4 5 0 4 2 5 4 4	2 4 5 3 2 4 2 4 4 2 3 2 4 4 4	100	49%	11%	4.15	4.37	4.28
Burba,Dave	2001	27	5 0 4 3 3 3 4 0 5 2 2 0 5 0 4 2 0	5 4 4 0 0 4 3 0 0 4	88	41%	33%	6.23	5.47	4.92
	2002	22	3 2 2 5 0 5 4 4 3 2 2 2 0 4 3 2 0	3 2 2 4 2	95	27%	14%	5.21	3.79	4.50
Burkett,John	2001	34	2 0 4 5 5 5 5 5 2 5 5 5 1 5 5 5 5 2	3 5 4 5 5 1 4 5 4 2 0 2 3 2 3	97	62%	12%	3.04	3.05	3.71
	2002	29	2 5 5 4 4 4 3 3 1 2 3 3 5 2 2	3 4 2 5 0 4 0 3 2 0 3 4 0 5 5	93	38%	17%	4.53	4.99	4.52
	2003	31	2 3 4 0 3 1 3 2 4 3 0 2 4 5 5 5 1 4	3 2 2 3 2 5 4 2 5 2 4 4 0	91	39%	16%	5.17	4.62	4.52
Burnett,A.J.	2001	27	4 4 2 0 3 4 4 5 1 4 0 3	4 2 3 3 3 0 3 4 1 4 4 5 3 5 5	103	48%	19%	4.06	3.70	4.40
	2002	29	3 5 5 4 4 3 3 5 2 3 5 4 4 4 5 3 4 5 5	5 0 5 5 5 3 5 5 4 4	110	72%	3%	3.31	2.71	2.99
Bynum,Mike	2003	5	5 0	0 3 0	77	20%	60%	8.75	7.80	7.98
Byrd,Paul	2001	16	3 2 2 2 3 0	3 1 4 4 2 5 3 0 3 2	90	19%	19%	4.45	4.86	4.65
	2002	33	3 4 4 4 3 4 3 5 4 4 3 0 2 0 2 4 1 1	3 3 5 4 4 2 4 4 4 2 0 1 5 4 2	97	48%	18%	3.91	3.94	4.40
Callaway,Mickey	2002	6		4 5 4 0 0 5	90	67%	33%	4.24	3.62	4.29
	2003	7	5 1 0 0	5 0 0	87	29%	71%	6.60	6.40	8.88
Capuano,Chris	2003	5	0 5	0 4 0	84	40%	60%	4.64	3.00	7.05

PQS PITCHING LOGS

Pitcher	Year	No.	FIRST HALF	SECOND HALF	PC	DOM	DIS	ERA	xERA	qERA
Carpenter,Chris	2001	34	5 5 3 2 5 3 3 0 4 4 5 3 3 2 0 4 4 3	5 3 0 3 0 0 2 1 5 1 5 2 5 0 3 5	97	38%	24%	4.10	4.72	4.64
	2002	13	0 0 1 3 3 2	5 3 4 3 0 3 3	90	15%	31%	5.30	5.61	5.29
Chacon,Shawn	2001	27	2 0 4 3 5 4 1 5 5 3 3 3 2	5 5 2 2 2 0 4 3 4 5 3 3 3	101	37%	11%	4.79	4.89	4.41
	2002	21	0 5 3 2 3 4 4 3 3 3 4 0 3	3 3 0 4 0 0 3 2	96	24%	24%	5.75	5.61	4.75
	2003	22	5 2 3 5 5 2 4 0 3 3 5 4 0 3 4 5 0	0 5 3 1 4	98	45%	18%	4.60	3.65	4.53
Clemens,Roger	2001	33	4 4 4 3 4 4 3 5 5 4 3 3 5 5 5 5 4 5	4 1 3 4 5 5 5 3 4 5 3 3 4 4 3	108	70%	3%	3.52	3.55	2.99
	2002	29	0 5 3 5 5 4 4 5 3 5 5 0 4 5 5 2 0 2 2	4 5 2 4 5 2 5 5 2 4 4	104	62%	10%	4.35	3.73	3.71
	2003	33	5 5 5 5 5 3 5 5 3 4 3 4 5 5 5 4 5 0 5 4	0 4 4 4 3 4 0 3 0 4 4 4 3	104	70%	12%	3.92	3.76	3.51
Clement,Matt	2001	31	2 5 2 5 2 0 0 3 5 2 3 0 5 3 1 3 0 0	5 3 0 4 5 3 4 3 4 3 0 5 0	90	32%	29%	5.06	4.46	4.90
	2002	32	3 5 5 3 4 0 3 3 5 5 5 3 3 4 2 5 3	5 5 3 3 5 4 2 4 3 5 5 0 3 5 0	101	50%	9%	3.60	3.09	3.85
	2003	32	0 3 5 5 4 2 4 4 4 1 5 5 4 0 2 4 4 5	5 3 5 5 1 4 0 5 4 1 3 5 0 5	99	63%	22%	4.12	3.41	3.95
Colon,Bartolo	2001	34	4 3 4 5 4 5 3 2 5 3 3 2 5 5 0 5 0 3	5 4 2 4 5 4 3 4 4 4 1 2 5 5 5 0	108	59%	12%	4.09	4.32	3.97
	2002	33	4 4 0 2 2 5 5 3 3 4 4 4 0 3 4 2 5 3	3 3 2 5 3 4 4 4 3 5 3 5 3 1 3	108	45%	9%	2.94	3.60	3.98
	2003	34	3 5 5 3 1 4 1 3 4 4 4 4 4 3 4 1 4 4	0 4 5 5 5 3 0 4 4 3 3 3 1 2 3	104	53%	18%	3.87	3.76	4.37
Condrey,Clay	2003	6	2 0 3 4 0 2		92	17%	33%	8.47	7.00	5.29
Contreras,Jose	2003	9	5 5	5 0 5 0 5 4 5	98	78%	22%	3.30	2.55	3.65
Cook,Aaron	2003	16	0 1 3 3 0 0 3 2 3 4 2 3 0 2 0 2		89	6%	38%	6.02	5.57	5.63
Cornejo,Nate	2003	32	0 2 3 3 3 3 2 0 4 3 2 1 1 0 0 2 0 3	3 3 0 0 3 3 3 2 3 3 1 3 2 2	93	3%	31%	4.64	5.12	5.53
Correia,Kevin	2003	7		4 3 5 3 0 0 2	82	29%	29%	3.69	5.06	4.93
Cruz,Juan	2001	8		5 4 3 4 0 4 2 4	85	63%	13%	3.26	3.59	3.71
	2002	9	0 5 0 3 4 1 0 0 5		89	33%	56%	3.99	4.20	6.91
	2003	6		4 5 3 5 3 0	96	50%	17%	6.05	4.85	4.37
Cruz,Nelson	2002	5	0 5	0 4 0	70	40%	60%	4.50	5.45	7.05
	2003	7	2 4 2 1 0 2 0		83	14%	43%	7.30	6.50	5.70
D'Amico,Jeff	2001	10	3 5 5 0	0 0 0 3 0 2	80	20%	50%	6.11	6.61	6.74
	2002	22	5 5 4 4 2 5 0 5 5 5 0 5 0 3 3 0 2	2 2 3 0 1	94	41%	27%	4.97	4.48	4.74
	2003	29	0 2 2 3 4 4 2 5 4 4 2 0 4 2 1 4 3	3 2 3 2 4 4 3 0 0 5 5 2	91	38%	17%	4.78	4.92	4.52
Daal,Omar	2001	32	3 2 5 5 2 5 2 1 5 3 3 0 3 0 4 0 2 3	4 2 2 3 4 1 1 2 2 0 0 5 5 4	89	31%	25%	4.47	4.71	4.90
	2002	23	5 5 4 2 0 4 3 2 0	2 3 4 5 4 3 3 3 0 0 0 2 5	85	35%	22%	3.91	3.71	4.64
	2003	17	4 3 0 4 2 2 0 4 3 4 4 0 2 3 0	0 0	86	29%	35%	6.39	6.53	5.27
Davis,Doug	2001	30	0 2 2 0 0 2 0 0 4 4 5 3 3 3	4 4 3 4 3 3 4 3 4 3 5 4 0 2 3	102	37%	20%	4.39	4.72	4.64
	2002	10	5 4 4 3 0 1 2 1 2 0		95	30%	40%	5.03	4.93	5.29
	2003	20	0 2 3 0 0 2 3 0 4 3 0 0	4 1 4 4 0 1 3 4	94	25%	45%	4.05	5.43	5.98
Davis,Jason	2003	27	0 0 2 2 2 0 0 5 1 4 4 4 0 4 1 5 0 3	5 0 3 1 4 5 3 2 1	91	33%	41%	4.69	4.66	5.29
Day,Zach	2003	23	3 0 4 5 3 4 3 2 0 2 1	0 3 3 4 4 4 0 1 2 3 4 0	90	30%	30%	4.19	4.04	5.08
Dempster,Ryan	2001	34	3 4 3 4 4 0 2 4 5 5 2 4 5 2 4 5 2 3 5	4 5 3 5 4 3 0 2 4 4 4 0 3 0 0	105	50%	18%	4.95	4.70	4.37
	2002	33	5 5 2 4 3 4 5 5 1 3 3 0 3 5 5 4 3	0 3 0 3 0 4 3 2 3 4 0 2 5 2 3	101	36%	18%	5.38	4.66	4.52
	2003	19	2 3 0 2 4 0 3 2 3 2 4 5 1 3 0 0 4	3 2	95	21%	26%	6.57	5.75	4.98
Dessens,Elmer	2001	34	4 0 4 1 1 2 2 4 3 5 5 4 2 3 2 3 3 3	3 4 4 4 3 0 3 2 2 2 4 0 3 0 5 2	94	32%	18%	4.48	4.78	4.60
	2002	30	0 4 4 4 3 4 4 3 3 3 0 3 2 3 1 4 3 0	3 4 4 3 0 1 4 3 4 2 3 4	90	37%	20%	3.03	4.13	4.64
	2003	30	2 3 3 1 3 5 2 4 3 0 3 3 4 2 0 3 4 2 5 0	3 5 2 0 3 4 0 2 2 3	92	23%	20%	5.09	5.32	4.75
Dickey,R.A.	2003	13	1	4 2 5 5 2 5 2 0 0 0 5 5	96	46%	31%	5.12	5.25	4.82
Dreifort,Darren	2001	16	0 3 5 4 5 4 3 5 2 4 5 0 3 3 3 2		95	44%	13%	5.12	4.24	4.32
	2003	10	5 3 5 3 5 3 4 5 5 0		99	60%	10%	4.05	4.02	3.71
Drese,Ryan	2001	4		1 2 4 4	98	50%	25%	3.48	3.29	4.61
	2002	26	1 2 0 0 4 2 4 5 3 4 0 4 3 3 0 3 5	0 2 0 1 2 4 0 1 2	94	27%	38%	6.57	5.93	5.27
	2003	8	0 3 0 3 0	3 0 4	84	13%	50%	6.85	6.91	7.08
Driskill,Travis	2002	19	5 4 5 2 5 1 1 3	1 0 3 0 5 4 3 1 1 0 3	97	32%	42%	4.98	5.24	5.29
Dubose,Eric	2003	10	5	3 2 0 3 5 3 3 3 2	97	20%	10%	3.82	3.07	4.51
Duckworth,Brandon	2001	11		4 5 3 5 3 2 3 4 3 3 0	102	36%	9%	3.63	3.69	4.29
	2002	29	5 4 5 0 3 3 5 0 2 3 0 4 5 5 0 4 1	4 4 5 0 4 0 0 5 3 0 5 3	98	48%	31%	5.41	4.94	4.82
	2003	18	0 2 3 0 3 5 0 5 2 0 5 0 4	0 2 4 3 0	85	28%	39%	4.94	4.89	5.27
Durbin,Chad	2001	29	0 3 4 3 3 0 5 2 4 0 3 2 0 0	3 5 2 4 0 2 1 4 2 3 3 0 0 5 1	100	24%	34%	4.81	4.90	5.21
Eaton,Adam	2001	17	2 3 2 4 5 3 3 5 4 3 4 2 5 5 4 4 4		108	59%	0%	4.34	4.35	3.38
	2002	6		0 0 3 5 4 5	90	50%	33%	5.45	4.21	4.71
	2003	31	2 4 5 4 5 0 4 3 1 3 5 3 5 5 2 0 4 4 0	5 3 1 5 3 0 4 4 3 5 3 3 4	98	48%	19%	4.08	3.90	4.40
Elarton,Scott	2001	23	4 0 4 5 4 1 2 2 3 2 3 2 0 3 5 3 1 0	0 2 4 4 0	95	30%	30%	7.08	6.21	5.08
	2003	10	2 2 2 1 1 1	0 4 0	91	10%	50%	6.35	7.74	7.08
Erickson,Scott	2002	28	3 4 3 0 2 3 3 0 2 5 0 3 2 1 4 2 4 3	3 5 1 0 0 3 0 0 0 0	94	18%	39%	5.57	5.45	5.45
Escobar,Kelvim	2003	26	0 3 0 4 5 4 5 2 4 2 2 0	4 4 3 3 5 4 4 3 4 3 0 3 5 4	102	50%	15%	4.30	4.46	4.37
Estes,Shawn	2001	27	0 5 4 3 4 2 5 4 3 3 4 4 1 3 0 0	3 4 4 3 0 0 3 0 5 5 0	93	41%	30%	4.02	3.91	4.92
	2002	29	5 5 1 1 5 3 2 4 4 1 2 2 5 2 4 0 2	2 3 5 3 5 0 2 2 4 1 0 0	94	34%	28%	5.12	4.14	4.90
	2003	28	0 4 4 0 0 2 4 4 3 3 0 2 5 2 0 4 4 2 1	0 4 4 3 0 0 0 2 4	93	36%	36%	5.74	5.84	5.13
Etherton,Seth	2003	7		0 5 3 3 0 0 0	78	14%	57%	6.90	6.28	7.77
Fassero,Jeff	2003	6		0 3 5 0 3 1	79	17%	50%	5.73	6.39	6.90
Fernandez,Jared	2002	8	3	5 2 4 3 0 0 3	93	25%	25%	4.50	5.41	4.93
	2003	6		4 0 0 2 4 2	81	33%	33%	4.03	3.45	5.08
Fogg,Josh	2002	33	5 5 3 3 3 4 5 5 3 0 4 2 2 2 1 4 4	3 0 0 4 2 2 2 3 1 4 0 4 2 4 2 4	89	39%	18%	4.36	4.68	4.52
	2003	26	3 5 3 0 4 3 0 3 5 2 2 5 0	0 0 0 3 0 4 2 4 3 4 4 0 3	82	31%	31%	5.26	5.25	5.08
Foppert,Jesse	2003	21	0 4 3 2 4 4 0 5 2 5 0 0 0 2 0	4 5 0 3 2 0	94	33%	38%	5.03	4.73	5.19
Fossum,Casey	2001	7		0 1 3 0 3 4 0	87	14%	57%	4.90	4.28	7.77
	2002	13		5 3 5 3 3 4 0 3 5 0 5 2 3	98	38%	15%	3.48	4.23	4.52
	2003	14	3 0 4 3 5 0 3 4 5 3 2 0	2 1	85	29%	29%	5.47	4.66	4.93
Franklin,Ryan	2002	12	3 3	0 1 1 3 5 2 0 5 4 2	86	25%	33%	4.04	3.71	5.13
	2003	32	4 2 2 4 2 3 3 0 2 2 4 4 4 4 5 1 1 3	3 3 2 3 0 0 3 2 2 4 4 3 4 4	99	34%	16%	3.57	4.21	4.60
Franklin,Wayne	2003	34	2 4 0 3 2 3 0 0 4 4 5 3 2 0 2 3 4 3 4 5	1 4 4 1 0 3 1 5 1 2 0 3 0 0	94	29%	35%	5.52	5.32	5.27

Pitcher	Year	No.	FIRST HALF	SECOND HALF	PC	DOM	DIS	ERA	xERA	qERA
Garcia,Freddy	2001	34	0 2 5 5 2 4 3 0 4 2 3 3 4 5 5 3 3 4	3 0 3 3 4 4 5 4 3 4 5 5 5 3 3 4	104	50%	9%	3.06	2.82	3.85
	2002	34	2 3 3 0 2 5 5 5 5 3 4 4 4 5 5 5 0 4 5	1 0 4 5 3 2 2 2 3 3 3 4 3 2 3	106	44%	12%	4.40	4.19	4.32
	2003	33	0 3 3 3 2 4 4 0 4 2 3 4 5 4 3 3 4 4 3	2 0 1 0 4 3 5 1 4 3 5 3 0 4	102	39%	21%	4.52	4.49	4.64
Garland,Jon	2001	16	0 2 0 4 3	3 2 2 3 4 3 2 0 2 3 4	89	19%	19%	3.66	4.76	4.65
	2002	33	1 0 5 1 2 4 1 1 0 4 4 4 3 0 3 3 2 3	3 0 0 4 5 4 0 1 5 4 2 3 2 2 4	94	33%	33%	4.59	4.27	5.08
	2003	32	0 3 5 0 3 1 2 4 3 5 0 5 3 3 1 4 3 0	4 3 3 1 3 2 2 5 5 5 3 5 0 0 3	95	28%	28%	4.52	4.57	4.93
George,Chris	2001	13		1 0 0 4 3 2 3 2 2 3 2 0 3	89	8%	31%	4.62	4.60	5.45
	2002	6	2 3 1 1 0 0		81	0%	67%	5.67	5.67	9.80
	2003	18	4 1 0 3 1 2 3 3 3 0 2 0 2 1 1 0 0 1		91	6%	56%	7.16	7.14	7.99
Glavine,Tom	2001	35	3 2 4 4 1 5 2 2 2 5 3 1 2 0 2 2 3 0 3	3 3 4 3 4 4 3 0 2 5 4 3 3 3 3 4	98	29%	14%	3.57	4.28	4.50
	2002	36	5 3 4 4 5 3 5 2 2 3 4 5 3 5 4 2 5 2 0 0	0 3 1 2 3 3 4 3 3 4 2 4 2 4 1 0	100	39%	17%	2.97	3.78	4.52
	2003	32	0 4 3 4 2 2 2 2 3 3 4 0 1 0 3 3 0 5 1 2	0 2 4 3 3 4 4 4 3 4 1 1 2	91	28%	28%	4.52	4.86	4.93
Glover,Gary	2001	11		0 0 2 2 5 3 1 4 3 5 0	86	27%	36%	4.30	3.75	5.27
	2002	22	0 0 2 0 1 5 0 0 3 3	2 3 4 4 1 4 0 3 2 0 0 3	88	18%	45%	5.22	4.44	6.25
Gobble,Jimmy	2003	9		4 3 0 0 3 5 5 5 3	92	44%	22%	4.67	4.86	4.56
Gonzalez,Jeremi	2003	25	5 4 3 4 4 3 4 4 1 2 4	5 3 1 3 3 3 2 3 0 3 2 4 4 3 0	108	40%	16%	3.92	3.69	4.44
Good,Andrew	2003	10	0 3 1 5 4 3 3 3 2 5		88	30%	20%	5.32	5.50	4.71
Graves,Danny	2003	26	2 1 1 2 3 5 3 3 2 2 2 0 1 1 3 3 3 0 0	2 3 4 3 3 1 2	92	8%	31%	5.33	5.55	5.45
Greisinger,Seth	2002	8	3 0 3 0 3 4 0 0		80	13%	50%	6.32	5.63	7.08
Griffiths,Jeremy	2003	7	1 0	4 4 0 0 0	90	29%	71%	7.02	6.56	8.88
Halama,John	2001	17	0 4 5 4 0 4 2 2 0 0 2 0 5 3 0 1	0	77	29%	47%	4.12	4.70	5.98
	2002	10	5 2 4 0 3 1 2 0 0 0		83	20%	50%	3.56	4.40	6.74
	2003	13	2 2 0 3 0 3 4 2 0 3	0 3 0	83	8%	38%	4.25	5.12	5.63
Halladay,Roy	2001	16	4	2 0 5 4 4 3 5 5 4 5 0 5 5 2 5	93	69%	13%	3.12	2.91	3.61
	2002	34	5 5 4 5 0 4 4 5 3 4 4 4 4 4 5 4 4 4	4 3 5 4 4 5 4 3 1 3 2 3 4 4 4 4	103	76%	6%	2.94	2.92	3.13
	2003	36	0 3 5 4 4 3 4 4 5 5 4 5 4 5 5 5 5 2 3 4	5 4 2 4 4 4 0 4 3 5 4 3 5 4 *	101	75%	6%	3.25	3.29	3.13
Hall,Josh	2003	5		2 0 5 3 0	85	20%	40%	6.75	7.25	5.50
Hampton,Mike	2001	32	3 2 3 4 3 4 3 2 3 3 5 1 1 4 0 2 2 2	0 1 4 0 3 1 0 5 5 5 3 2 4 3	104	28%	25%	5.41	5.56	4.93
	2002	30	0 2 2 3 0 3 2 4 4 3 0 2 1 1 3 4 2 2	2 1 2 2 1 3 4 3 4 1 3 2	100	17%	27%	6.17	6.33	5.03
	2003	31	1 3 4 3 2 4 0 5 2 0 3 3 3 0 4 1	3 3 1 5 4 4 4 2 3 3 3 2 3 3 0	96	26%	23%	3.84	3.89	4.73
Harang,Aaron	2002	15	5 4 3 0 5 5 3 0	2 0 3 3 2 0 4	94	27%	33%	4.85	4.83	5.13
	2003	15	0 0 3 0 4 0	4 3 5 2 2 0 3 4 1	82	27%	40%	5.33	5.08	5.40
Harden,Rich	2003	13		4 4 5 5 3 0 0 3 5 0 1 3 3	97	38%	31%	4.50	4.20	5.00
Haren,Danny	2003	14	3 0 5	3 3 4 4 1 3 4 2 1 0 0	83	29%	36%	5.13	5.03	5.27
Haynes,Jimmy	2001	29	0 2 0 3 2 3 4 3 5 4 5 2 2 2 5 4 0 2 5	0 4 3 4 3 4 5 3 0 0	93	38%	21%	4.86	4.79	4.64
	2002	34	0 5 4 3 1 3 1 2 2 4 3 2 4 3 4 4 2 4	5 4 3 2 1 2 2 0 2 5 4 2 3 5 4 3	95	38%	15%	4.13	4.74	4.52
	2003	18	0 0 1 0 3 3 2 4 1 3 3 2 2 4	0 4 0 0	94	17%	44%	6.32	6.46	5.60
Heilman,Aaron	2003	13	3 3 0 0	2 3 2 0 3 3 0 0 3	91	0%	38%	6.78	6.72	5.72
Helling,Rick	2001	34	4 0 0 2 5 4 1 1 1 2 3 5 4 5 2 4 3 3 3	5 3 3 4 0 2 3 3 4 4 4 3 4 1 2	106	38%	21%	5.19	5.58	4.64
	2002	30	3 4 3 2 4 0 5 2 4 2 3 1 4 4 5 4 4 0	0 4 5 5 4 4 0 1 4 3 3 3	93	50%	20%	4.53	4.76	4.50
	2003	24	3 3 3 4 0 0 2 4 3 0 3 0 3 1 1 3 4 4	4 4 4 3 3 0	100	29%	29%	5.17	5.16	4.93
Hendrickson,Mark	2003	30	0 2 4 2 3 0 4 3 2 2 0 0 4 3 0 3 2	3 2 0 5 3 1 4 0 0 0 3 1	85	17%	37%	5.53	5.97	5.45
Hentgen,Pat	2001	9	4 4 5 1 3 2 2 3 3		106	33%	11%	3.48	3.19	4.49
	2002	4		0 0 4 2	94	25%	50%	6.43	7.33	6.56
	2003	22	0 1 3 3 0 2 4 1 4	5 5 5 3 3 4 3 0 5 3 2 4 4	102	41%	23%	4.11	4.34	4.56
Hermanson,Dustin	2001	33	2 2 0 3 4 3 4 4 3 0 2 0 0 4 0 5 5 4	3 4 5 5 4 3 2 2 1 2 2 3 4 5 0	96	39%	21%	4.45	4.90	4.64
	2002	1		3	83	0%	0%	7.77	7.16	4.50
	2003	6		5 4 4 1 3 4	91	67%	17%	4.10	4.50	3.73
Hernandez,Carlos	2001	3		5 5 0	92	67%	33%	1.05	1.99	4.29
	2002	21	1 2 5 5 5 3 5 3 4 4 2 0 2 0 0	0 5 0 4 3 1	90	38%	33%	4.35	4.42	5.00
Hernandez,Livan	2001	34	5 0 2 2 0 4 4 1 4 2 5 2 4 1 4 2 3 2 4	4 3 2 3 2 5 3 4 0 3 3 3 3 0 3	109	32%	18%	5.25	5.13	4.60
	2002	33	3 4 2 3 4 3 3 3 0 1 5 4 5 2 0 4 0 0	5 4 2 2 3 3 3 5 3 2 4 5 2 0 4	105	36%	18%	4.38	4.41	4.52
	2003	33	2 4 2 2 3 4 3 4 4 2 4 3 0 3 1 4 5 4	4 5 5 4 5 5 5 5 3 4 0 4 4	108	64%	9%	3.21	3.75	3.50
Hernandez,Orlando	2001	16	0 4 0 3 2 3 3 5 0	0 5 3 5 4 4 0	99	38%	31%	4.87	4.96	5.00
	2002	22	5 4 5 5 3 4 4 0 5	2 4 5 3 0 2 3 4 4 5 4 4 5	101	68%	9%	3.64	3.33	3.38
Hernandez,Runelvys	2002	12		3 5 2 3 4 3 3 4 4 3 1 3	96	33%	8%	4.72	4.65	4.48
	2003	16	5 4 4 3 3 4 4 3 2 0	2 2 0 1 5 0	89	38%	25%	4.65	4.07	4.82
Hitchcock,Sterling	2001	12	5	4 2 3 2 0 2 4 4 1 0 5	91	42%	25%	5.48	5.28	4.74
	2002	2	0 0		91	0%	100%	5.54	6.48	15.00
	2003	7		3 5 5 0 3 2 4	88	43%	14%	4.76	4.85	4.32
Howard,Ben	2003	6		2 4 2 2 2 5	87	33%	0%	3.71	5.47	4.46
Hudson,Tim	2001	35	3 5 0 5 0 3 4 5 4 4 4 5 5 5 4 5 1 5 4	5 5 3 2 4 4 4 0 3 3 4 5 0 3 3 4	103	63%	14%	3.37	3.43	3.71
	2002	34	5 4 4 3 4 4 2 4 1 2 2 4 4 5 5 4 2 3 4	3 1 4 3 5 4 4 5 4 4 4 3 4 3	102	65%	6%	2.99	3.58	3.38
	2003	34	4 1 2 5 4 4 4 4 4 4 0 2 3 5 3 5 4 4 5	3 5 4 4 4 5 5 3 5 0 3 4 4 5	103	71%	9%	2.70	2.67	3.25
Ishii,Kazuhisa	2002	28	4 4 4 2 5 4 3 3 2 3 3 4 0 5 4 0 4	3 4 4 0 2 3 4 3 0 4 0	96	46%	18%	4.27	4.66	4.40
	2003	27	0 4 4 4 3 3 4 4 3 5 4 3 3 1 4 3	3 3 5 3 0 5 3 0 0	98	37%	19%	3.86	4.33	4.52
Jarvis,Kevin	2001	32	3 0 3 3 5 3 4 4 5 3 5 0 2 2 2 3 5 5	1 4 5 1 2 3 5 3 3 2 4 3 0 2	90	34%	16%	4.80	4.51	4.60
	2002	7	4 3 4 4 4 0 0		79	57%	29%	4.37	4.50	4.39
	2003	16	1 3 4 2 3 2	3 4 2 0 2 3 3 0 0 0	91	13%	31%	5.87	5.78	5.37
Jennings,Jason	2001	7		5 4 3 2 0 0 4	90	43%	29%	4.60	4.41	4.74
	2002	32	4 0 2 3 3 0 4 5 0 3 5 3 4 0 1 2 3	1 5 3 3 4 4 3 4 4 0 4 1 2 2 3	94	34%	25%	4.52	5.01	4.90
	2003	32	0 3 3 0 4 5 4 2 0 2 0 4 4 4 3 4 1 3 0 4	0 3 3 3 0 3 1 1 5 2 3 2	95	28%	31%	5.12	5.38	5.13
Jensen,Ryan	2001	7	2	0 1 4 0 4 0	87	29%	57%	3.71	4.05	7.14
	2002	31	4 5 0 3 0 5 3 4 4 1 0 3 3 3 3 2 5	1 5 5 1 4 2 0 3 3 0 0 0 2 4	88	32%	32%	4.53	4.80	5.08
Jimenez,Jose	2003	7		3 3 3 2 1 3 4	86	14%	14%	5.26	5.58	4.53
Johnson,Jason	2001	32	4 0 3 3 0 4 4 0 4 4 4 5 3 0 0 3 3 4	4 5 3 3 5 0 5 2 0 3 2 5 2 2	102	38%	22%	4.09	4.53	4.64
	2002	22	5 1 0 5 3 5 0 5 4 1	4 1 2 4 5 3 3 3 0 3 4 4	96	45%	27%	4.60	4.67	4.67
	2003	31	3 5 4 3 3 5 4 0 5 3 0 0 0 2 3 2 1 5	4 3 0 1 3 4 2 5 4 3 2 2 2	101	32%	23%	4.19	5.22	4.71

135

PQS PITCHING LOGS

Pitcher	Year	No.	FIRST HALF	SECOND HALF	PC	DOM	DIS	ERA	xERA	qERA
Johnson,Randy	2001	34	5 2 5 5 5 4 5 5 5 3 4 5 4 5 5 4 5 4 5 5 5	5 5 5 5 5 5 4 5 5 5 4 4 5 4 5	117	94%	0%	2.49	2.24	2.39
	2002	35	5 5 5 4 5 5 5 5 3 5 5 2 4 5 4 5 5 5 5 4 5	4 4 2 5 5 5 5 5 5 5 5 3 5 4 5 5 5	113	89%	0%	2.32	2.65	2.54
	2003	18	4 4 0 4	5 5 5 3 3 2 5 3 4 2 5 5 4 4	100	67%	6%	4.26	4.58	3.38
Kennedy,Joe	2001	20	3 5 0 4 4 2 4	3 4 2 5 0 3 5 4 4 2 3 2 3	94	45%	10%	3.27	3.63	4.28
	2002	30	2 2 2 3 3 4 4 3 5 1 2 3 4 2 2 4 4	2 0 0 4 3 2 3 3 0 1 2 3 4	103	27%	17%	4.55	4.19	4.62
	2003	22	3 2 2 1 4 2 4 0 3 0 0 0 1	0 5 0 0 2 3 0 3 0	92	14%	50%	6.16	5.85	7.08
Kile,Darryl	2001	34	1 2 3 4 5 4 3 4 4 5 4 5 2 2 4 4 3 5	3 4 4 2 5 4 3 5 3 2 3 4 5 5 4 3	99	59%	3%	3.09	3.92	3.38
	2002	14	4 4 4 4 2 2 2 3 4 4 3 0 0 4		97	50%	14%	3.75	4.05	4.23
Kim,Byung-Hyun	2003	12	4 4 5 3 5 2 5 4 2 4 3 3		94	58%	0%	3.32	3.16	3.38
Kinney,Matt	2002	12	3 0 5 4 0 3 4 3 2 0 2 1		90	25%	33%	4.64	6.13	5.13
	2003	31	3 3 5 4 4 5 4 5 3 3 2 4 0 2 4 2 4 2	3 0 3 5 3 4 4 5 1 3 4 0 1	100	45%	16%	5.21	4.89	4.40
Knotts,Gary	2003	18	4 5 0 0 3 1 4 0 5 0 0 3 0	3 0 0 0 0	87	22%	61%	6.06	5.80	7.98
Lackey,John	2002	18	5 3 3	4 0 4 3 5 5 4 3 2 3 5 0 3 0 2	98	39%	17%	3.67	4.06	4.52
	2003	33	0 3 2 2 0 3 5 2 4 4 4 5 3 0 4 5 5 4	2 4 5 0 5 5 5 0 2 3 3 1 4 4	99	48%	18%	4.63	5.00	4.40
Lawrence,Brian	2001	15	5 5	4 3 0 5 3 3 4 4 3 5 4 5 0	93	60%	13%	3.68	3.66	3.71
	2002	31	2 4 4 5 4 3 4 0 3 4 5 5 5 5 4 2 0 5	4 5 3 4 5 3 4 2 3 4 3 3 3	97	58%	6%	3.69	4.18	3.68
	2003	33	3 4 5 5 5 0 3 0 2 2 4 5 4 2 2 0 5 4 3 2	3 2 2 4 5 3 4 4 4 2 0 3 3	94	42%	12%	4.20	4.02	4.32
Ledezma,Wil	2003	8	4 4	0 3 0 0 0 0	83	25%	63%	5.79	5.62	7.72
Lee,Cliff	2003	9	4	4 5 4 0 3 5 5 0	89	67%	22%	3.63	3.58	3.85
Leiter,Al	2001	29	5 3 5 0 5 5 3 5 3 5 4 5 3 2	5 5 4 4 0 3 4 5 5 5 3 3 5 5 0	104	62%	10%	3.32	3.54	3.71
	2002	33	5 5 0 5 5 4 0 4 4 3 3 0 3 3 5 5 4 2	4 4 0 5 3 3 4 5 5 0 3 5 5 2 0	103	55%	18%	3.49	3.96	4.10
	2003	30	3 3 3 4 3 4 4 3 0 4 4 0 1 2 1	3 5 4 4 4 4 5 3 5 1 3 4	108	50%	17%	4.00	4.23	4.37
Lewis,Colby	2003	26	4 0 2 3 3 0 0 0 3 0 4 2 0 0	2 4 0 3 5 0 0 3 0 2 5 2	88	19%	42%	7.30	6.81	5.60
Lidle,Cory	2001	29	0 4 5 4 2 4 3 2 3 5 5 5 0 2 4	3 1 3 5 4 4 4 3 0 3 4 4 4 5	94	55%	14%	3.59	3.55	3.97
	2002	30	2 4 0 3 5 3 2 3 0 2 0 3 3 3 3	0 4 1 3 5 3 4 5 3 5 4 1 3 3 3	95	27%	20%	3.89	3.51	4.73
	2003	31	3 5 4 1 4 4 4 3 2 3 4 5 2 2 3 3 0 2 0 0	0 2 3 1 0 4 5 0 4 4 5	95	39%	26%	5.77	4.92	4.82
Lieber,Jon	2001	34	5 5 5 4 5 5 4 1 4 4 4 5 4 4 4 4 3 3	2 3 4 5 4 4 4 4 3 0 4 1 2 5 3	96	68%	9%	3.80	3.59	3.38
	2002	21	2 5 3 4 4 2 4 3 3 4 1 3 4 5 4 2 4	4 3 2 5	93	52%	5%	3.70	3.98	3.85
Lilly,Ted	2001	21	3 4 0 0 0 4 0 2 5 3 5 0 4	0 0 3 4 3 0 0 4	90	33%	43%	5.09	4.72	5.29
	2002	16	5 5 1 2 5 3 3 0 2 5 0	5 2 0 0 3	87	31%	31%	3.69	2.42	5.08
	2003	31	3 4 3 3 3 0 4 0 4 3 5 0 5 3 3 0 1	1 5 5 0 5 0 4 5 5 4 4 5 0	94	45%	29%	4.35	4.67	4.67
Lima,Jose	2001	27	0 4 3 0 0 1 5 0 0 2 1 2	0 4 2 3 4 2 3 0 2 0 3 4 3 2 2	87	19%	37%	5.56	5.76	5.45
	2002	12	0 0 5 0	0 5 2 0 2 0 4 0	70	25%	58%	7.81	5.92	7.14
	2003	14	3 2 3 4 4 4	4 4 0 0 0 2 0 1	87	36%	36%	4.93	4.65	5.13
Linebrink,Scott	2003	6	3 2 3 0 2 1		86	0%	33%	3.33	4.20	5.53
Loaiza,Esteban	2001	30	4 4 3 4 3 4 2 0 4 3 2 5 4 1 0 4 2 0	3 4 3 3 2 2 2 4 0 5 2	96	37%	17%	5.02	5.45	4.52
	2002	25	2 5 3 3 0 0 2 3 0 2 0	5 3 3 3 4 3 0 4 2 1 3 2 0 4	94	20%	28%	5.72	5.32	4.98
	2003	34	4 4 5 5 5 0 3 5 2 4 4 5 4 3 5 5 2 3 5	5 3 4 4 5 3 4 5 5 3 5 0 4 4 5	102	71%	6%	2.91	2.98	3.25
Loewer,Carlton	2003	5	2 3 0 3 0		73	0%	40%	6.86	7.97	5.90
Lohse,Kyle	2001	16	4 5 1 5	2 0 0 2 3 4 1 4 3 0 0 0	88	31%	44%	4.78	4.98	5.29
	2002	31	0 0 5 5 3 0 5 2 4 3 2 2 0 0 5 3 0 4	5 3 3 3 2 3 5 2 4 3 5 3	96	32%	19%	4.25	4.49	4.60
	2003	33	4 4 5 0 0 3 4 4 3 5 4 4 5 2 2 3 2 0 0	3 0 4 3 4 3 3 2 2 5 4 4 0	92	42%	18%	4.61	4.43	4.44
Lopez,Rodrigo	2002	28	1 2 3 5 3 5 2 4 4 3 4 1 4 4	3 4 5 5 1 3 3 4 3 3 3 3 0 5	99	43%	14%	3.58	3.42	4.32
	2003	26	4 0 4 0 2 0 4 2 0 4 5 4	4 0 0 5 4 4 0 5 0 3 1 0 3 4	96	46%	38%	5.82	5.98	4.98
Lowe,Derek	2001	3		4 4 5	73	100%	0%	3.55	4.47	2.00
	2002	32	3 3 5 3 4 5 3 4 4 5 5 3 4 2 5 4 5 2	4 4 5 3 4 5 2 3 3 2 4 4 5 3 4	96	59%	0%	2.59	2.04	3.38
	2003	33	3 2 4 2 0 3 0 0 3 3 2 3 5 1 2 4 5 2 2	0 3 2 2 3 3 4 3 3 2 5 5 2 3	95	21%	15%	4.48	4.37	4.63
Maddux,Greg	2001	34	4 5 5 5 2 5 4 5 3 4 4 4 4 4 5 5 4	3 5 4 4 4 3 4 4 3 5 4 3 3 4 4 4	88	76%	0%	3.05	3.09	2.84
	2002	34	4 0 3 0 2 4 5 4 3 3 3 5 3 3 4 3 4	4 4 4 4 3 4 4 2 3 3 5 1 0 4 5 4	79	50%	12%	2.62	3.47	4.23
	2003	36	4 0 2 4 2 4 5 2 3 2 0 4 2 3 4 5 4 3 0 3	5 4 4 2 4 5 2 4 5 5 2 3 0 4 3 *	81	47%	11%	3.96	3.82	4.28
Maroth,Mike	2002	21	3 4 2 0 3 0	5 0 4 0 4 4 2 3 3 2 1 4 4 4 4	95	43%	24%	4.50	3.78	4.56
	2003	33	4 0 4 2 4 0 4 3 3 0 3 0 4 2 2 4 3 1 2	2 0 2 1 4 1 4 2 1 0 5 3 1 3	94	27%	33%	5.74	5.61	5.13
Martinez,Pedro	2001	18	5 5 5 4 5 5 5 5 5 5 5 5 4 0	0 5 0	99	83%	17%	2.40	1.78	3.43
	2002	30	0 5 4 5 5 3 0 5 5 5 5 4 3 4 5 4 5 4	5 5 5 5 5 4 5 5 4 4 4	103	87%	7%	2.26	1.85	2.88
	2003	29	5 5 0 3 4 4 5 3 5 0 3 5 4 5 5 5	5 4 5 4 4 5 5 0 5 5 4 5 0	98	76%	14%	2.23	2.26	3.41
Mays,Joe	2001	34	4 4 2 3 3 5 2 5 3 4 3 3 2 2 2 4 4 3	0 3 3 5 4 2 0 5 5 5 4 4 4 5 3 3	100	47%	6%	3.16	3.36	3.98
	2002	17	0 0 0	3 2 3 2 4 4 0 2 1 3 3 4 0 5	89	24%	35%	5.40	5.18	5.36
	2003	22	4 1 3 3 4 3 0 3 3 2 2 2 2 0 3 0 0 0	3 3 3 0	82	9%	32%	6.30	5.73	5.45
May,Darrell	2002	22	0 0 0 5 2 2 1 3 4 0 5	4 3 0 0 2 2 3 3 5 3 3	92	23%	32%	5.02	5.27	5.21
	2003	32	0 4 0 4 4 1 3 3 3 3 2 3 4 3 3 3 3	3 2 2 5 5 2 3 4 4 4 3 0 3 4 3	99	31%	13%	3.77	4.00	4.49
McClung,Seth	2003	5	3 0 5 3 0		78	20%	40%	5.45	4.74	5.50
Meadows,Brian	2001	10	0 4 3 0 2 0 3 3 0 0		79	10%	50%	7.32	7.54	7.08
	2002	11		3 4 0 4 3 3 4 0 3 4 1	83	36%	27%	3.92	3.96	4.82
	2003	7	0	4 0 2 1 0 0	67	14%	71%	4.74	4.63	9.84
Meche,Gil	2003	32	2 2 5 5 4 4 4 4 5 3 3 3 5 4 2 3 0 2	4 3 2 4 5 0 2 0 5 4 3 0 0 1	96	44%	19%	4.60	4.67	4.44
Mendoza,Ramiro	2003	5	1 4	2 0 0	77	20%	60%	6.82	6.99	7.98
Miller,Wade	2001	32	5 5 4 4 3 4 3 3 4 4 2 1 3 0 4 3 5 1	3 2 5 5 0 4 5 3 5 5 4 4 5 5	104	59%	13%	3.40	3.78	3.97
	2002	26	0 4 1 0 1 5 5 3 3 3 1 5	3 3 4 2 4 3 4 5 5 5 4 4 5 4 3	99	54%	19%	3.29	3.67	4.37
	2003	33	0 5 3 3 0 1 4 0 2 5 2 5 5 4 2 5 5 4 2 5	4 5 0 5 5 4 5 5 3 0 4 4 0	94	58%	21%	4.14	3.60	4.23
Millwood,Kevin	2001	21	4 3 4 2 4 2 0	3 4 4 0 4 3 5 2 5 0 5 4 3 3	88	48%	14%	4.31	4.59	4.28
	2002	35	4 5 4 0 0 3 5 3 4 0 3 5 0 4 4 5 5 4	4 5 5 3 4 5 5 3 4 5 3 2 3 5	95	63%	11%	3.24	3.05	3.71
	2003	35	5 0 4 0 4 5 3 5 5 4 3 5 3 5 0 2 2 3 5 3	4 0 0 5 2 4 3 3 4 5 2 2 5 3 0	99	46%	17%	4.01	3.54	4.40
Milton,Eric	2001	34	2 3 5 4 3 2 5 3 0 3 3 5 0 4 1 2 3 5	5 4 0 1 3 4 3 4 4 4 2 4 4 0	103	44%	18%	4.33	4.46	4.44
	2002	29	4 0 4 4 0 4 3 0 2 4 5 0 3 4 5 0 0 5 3	5 4 5 5 5 0 0 4 4	93	55%	31%	4.84	3.95	4.55
Morris,Matt	2001	34	0 5 4 5 4 5 4 5 5 5 2 5 2 4 3 2 3 4 0	5 5 4 0 4 4 5 4 2 4 5 0 5 0 5 5	98	68%	15%	3.17	3.53	3.73
	2002	32	5 5 4 3 4 5 5 5 3 0 2 3 5 5 4 5 3 1	5 5 5 0 4 5 3 5 2 3 0 4 4	100	56%	13%	3.43	3.82	3.97
	2003	27	2 5 3 4 3 5 4 3 5 5 3 5 3 3 0 3 3 0 1	0 2 4 4 5 5 5 2 4	93	44%	15%	3.77	3.65	4.44

Pitcher	Year	No.	FIRST HALF	SECOND HALF	PC	DOM	DIS	ERA	xERA	qERA
Moss, Damian	2002	29	5 4 4 3 4 2 3 3 4 4 3 0 5 4 2	1 5 3 4 4 1 3 1 2 3 4 0 4 0 5	98	45%	21%	3.42	3.50	4.53
	2003	29	3 1 3 4 3 4 4 4 3 3 0 3 2 0 2 2 0 0	3 3 4 3 3 2 2 3 0 0 0 1	93	14%	31%	5.18	5.67	5.37
Mounce, Tony	2003	11	0 2 3 4 2 0 0	0 2 4 0	84	18%	45%	7.20	6.77	6.25
Moyer, Jamie	2001	33	2 2 5 2 3 4 0 2 4 2 3 5 2 4 4 1 3	3 3 4 4 5 3 0 4 5 5 4 4 4 3 4 4	94	52%	9%	3.44	3.34	3.85
	2002	34	5 3 3 1 4 4 1 4 0 4 4 1 4 4 0 5 3 4 3	4 3 5 5 4 4 2 4 5 5 3 0 5 0 4	101	59%	21%	3.33	3.13	4.23
	2003	33	0 5 4 4 5 4 3 3 4 3 3 5 4 3 4 1 3 3 4	2 2 2 5 1 1 2 5 4 2 4 4 4 2	104	48%	12%	3.27	3.57	4.28
Mulder, Mark	2001	34	2 5 5 3 4 5 3 4 4 4 2 0 4 3 2 1 5 5	5 3 1 5 5 4 5 0 0 3 5 5 3 4 2 4	97	56%	15%	3.46	3.19	4.10
	2002	30	5 3 0 0 1 0 4 3 5 3 3 5 3 5	4 5 4 2 5 3 3 4 3 5 3 5 2 5 4 5	100	50%	13%	3.48	3.16	4.23
	2003	26	2 2 3 4 4 4 4 5 4 4 3 0 3 4 3 4 3 4 4	4 5 4 5 3 4 0	100	62%	8%	3.15	3.48	3.50
Mulholland, Terry	2003	5		0 0 1 5 2	88	20%	60%	4.91	5.78	7.98
Mussina, Mike	2001	34	4 4 4 0 4 5 3 3 2 5 5 3 3 4 4 2 4 5	0 2 4 5 0 3 4 4 5 5 5 5 4 5 4 0	102	65%	12%	3.16	2.96	3.61
	2002	33	4 4 5 3 2 3 5 4 3 5 3 5 4 1 2 4 2 4	5 4 4 0 3 4 4 3 5 3 5 4 5 5 3	101	61%	6%	4.06	3.71	3.50
	2003	31	4 5 5 5 5 5 5 0 5 4 4 2 4 4 3 0 5 4	4 3 5 2 3 5 3 3 5 5 3 4 3	104	65%	6%	3.41	3.17	3.38
Myers, Brett	2002	12		4 0 2 2 3 1 2 2 1 4 0 2	89	17%	33%	4.25	4.09	5.29
	2003	32	5 1 3 5 4 3 5 5 3 5 4 0 0 2 3 2 4 4 4	5 0 5 2 0 4 1 1 0 4 4 0 2	94	47%	28%	4.43	4.52	4.67
Neagle, Denny	2001	30	2 5 3 4 4 4 5 4 3 4 1 2 3 4 0	1 1 2 0 4 2 4 4 3 5 5 5 0 3	99	50%	20%	5.39	5.34	4.50
	2002	28	5 0 3 2 5 5 3 4 5 0 3 2 2 3 3 0 0	5 5 3 1 4 5 3 1 0 0 0	89	32%	32%	5.27	4.92	5.08
	2003	7	1 5 5 0 2 0	0	86	29%	57%	7.97	7.88	7.14
Nomo, Hideo	2001	33	5 4 4 0 4 5 2 0 3 5 4 4 5 5 2 5 3 4 4	2 3 5 4 0 3 3 4 5 2 3 5 0 4 5	98	58%	12%	4.50	3.96	3.97
	2002	34	0 3 4 4 4 4 2 0 1 5 4 2 3 4 3 4 5 5	4 4 3 3 3 4 3 5 5 5 5 4 4 4 3 5 5	102	62%	9%	3.40	3.83	3.50
	2003	33	5 5 2 2 4 3 3 3 4 4 5 4 4 4 5 5 5 4 5 3	4 3 3 0 2 2 3 5 2 3 3 1 4	99	52%	6%	3.10	3.37	3.85
Obermueller, Wes	2003	11		3 5 0 0 2 3 4 4 0 2 3	81	27%	27%	5.12	5.89	4.93
Ohka, Tomo	2001	21	0 4 4 3 2 0 2 0 1	4 0 4 0 1 1 2 2 3 5 2 5	81	29%	38%	5.47	5.55	5.27
	2002	31	2 5 0 5 5 2 4 2 4 5 4 5 3 3 2 3 5	4 0 3 0 3 1 5 3 3 5 3 0 3 5	91	42%	16%	3.19	3.91	4.44
	2003	34	0 4 2 3 0 0 3 0 4 4 3 0 2 0 3 5 4 1 4	3 4 3 4 0 5 2 3 5 4 0 4 3 5 4	87	41%	26%	4.16	4.82	4.74
Oliver, Darren	2001	27	3 3 2 4 0 0 0 4 2 3 0 3 1 0	3 4 2 4 0 3 2 3 0 1 4 1 4	90	22%	37%	6.02	5.88	5.36
	2002	9	3 3 0 4 3 0 2 0 0		84	11%	44%	4.66	5.54	5.70
	2003	32	3 0 4 0 4 2 4 2 4 3 2 3 3 3 4 1 3 3	1 5 3 1 1 2 0 5 4 0 4 2 2 0	84	28%	28%	5.05	4.80	4.93
Ortiz, Ramon	2001	32	5 5 2 2 4 2 4 5 2 2 4 5 1 2 2 4 4	4 3 5 3 5 0 3 4 2 2 5 3 0 3 2	99	44%	9%	4.37	4.68	4.11
	2002	32	2 3 2 5 4 4 5 3 2 4 4 5 4 3 4 1 2 3 4 5	0 5 1 3 0 1 5 2 4 5 3 5 5 2	101	50%	13%	3.77	3.92	4.23
	2003	32	2 0 5 3 3 3 3 0 1 2 4 0 3 3 4 5 2 0 3 4	3 5 0 3 0 0 3 3 4 2 0 3 2	94	22%	28%	5.20	5.47	4.98
Ortiz, Russ	2001	33	1 5 5 5 4 2 5 4 5 2 2 2 0 3 4 2 5 4	4 4 2 4 4 4 4 3 3 4 0 4 5 5 4	106	64%	9%	3.30	3.17	3.50
	2002	33	4 2 4 3 3 3 3 4 5 2 1 4 5 0 4 3 2 3	5 3 2 0 5 4 3 3 3 5 3 5 3 3 5	109	39%	9%	3.62	3.57	4.29
	2003	33	3 3 0 2 5 3 2 3 5 1 3 2 2 3 3 4 4 3 4	4 4 2 4 4 4 3 3 4 4 0 4 2 5 0 2	104	33%	9%	3.82	3.37	4.48
Oswalt, Roy	2001	20	5 1 4 5 5 5	5 0 4 4 5 1 5 5 5 5 5 5 0 0	93	75%	25%	3.30	3.42	3.87
	2002	34	5 3 4 5 5 2 5 3 5 4 3 4 1 4 4 5 5 3	5 4 3 5 4 3 4 3 5 5 3 5 4 5 5 0	100	68%	6%	3.01	3.29	3.38
	2003	21	3 5 3 3 3 5 4 4 4 5 4 0 4 4	3 3 0 4 5 5 5	92	62%	10%	2.98	3.44	3.71
Padilla, Vicente	2002	32	5 3 5 5 4 4 3 5 3 4 3 3 4 3 4 5 2 0 5	3 3 2 3 4 2 5 5 4 3 1 3 2 0	95	44%	9%	3.28	3.53	4.11
	2003	32	4 4 4 4 5 3 0 0 5 3 3 2 4 4 5 0 3	3 1 4 4 1 3 4 5 4 5 2 5 4 4	99	59%	16%	3.63	3.68	4.10
Park, Chan Ho	2001	35	5 3 5 3 3 5 5 5 5 4 5 4 4 4 5 5 5 4 5	0 5 5 3 3 2 4 2 5 1 4 0 5 3 4 0	105	66%	11%	3.50	3.02	3.61
	2002	25	2 4 3 0 3 0 4 3 4 3 4	4 2 3 3 2 0 4 5 4 3 3 3 0 5	102	36%	16%	5.77	5.09	4.52
	2003	7	0 0 3 4 2 0 0		80	14%	57%	7.76	6.96	7.77
Parque, Jim	2001	5	1 0 3 3 0		88	0%	60%	8.04	6.88	9.02
	2002	4		2 0 4 0	74	25%	50%	10.08	9.48	6.56
	2003	5	1 0 3 0 0		72	0%	80%	12.18	8.84	12.14
Parris, Steve	2001	19	0 0 1 3 2 0 2 4 3 2 0 3 4 3 3 4	5 3 3	94	21%	26%	4.66	5.62	4.98
	2002	14	1 0 4 2 4	4 2 0 3 4 0 0 1 0	93	29%	50%	6.00	6.36	6.56
	2003	7	3 3 2 2 0 2 0		89	0%	29%	6.28	7.61	5.18
Patterson, John	2002	5		5 5 0 5 3	92	0%	0%	3.28	4.30	4.50
	2003	8	0 2 2 0 5 1 3 0		93	13%	50%	6.05	5.34	7.08
Pavano, Carl	2001	8		0 0 0 3 5 5 4 3	89	38%	38%	5.74	6.25	5.13
	2002	22	3 4 2 4 2 2 3 0 4 0 3 4 0 0	0 0 4 3 4 5 3 0	84	32%	32%	5.16	5.01	5.08
	2003	32	2 4 2 5 5 0 4 4 4 4 4 0 5 3 3 5 0 4 4	4 0 2 5 4 2 4 5 4 4 1 0 5	94	63%	19%	4.30	3.83	3.83
Peavy, Jake	2002	17	5 0 4	5 4 0 3 4 5 0 5 5 5 0 2 5 3	96	59%	24%	4.55	4.63	4.23
	2003	32	4 3 4 2 5 5 3 3 3 2 4 2 3 0 3 3 4 0 1	3 4 4 4 3 5 0 5 4 0 4 4 5	101	47%	16%	4.13	4.27	4.40
Penny, Brad	2001	31	4 5 2 5 0 4 5 4 5 5 0 3 4 5 5 5 5 3	4 3 3 5 3 5 4 4 3 4 5 5 3	94	65%	6%	3.69	3.08	3.38
	2002	24	3 0 2 2 3 0 4 0 0 0	0 5 0 3 5 5 3 1 5 4 0 5 1 1	87	29%	46%	4.67	5.34	5.98
	2003	32	2 3 5 3 2 2 3 2 5 5 3 5 0 4 0 3 0 5 4	5 2 4 4 3 5 2 0 4 4 0 4 3	95	44%	16%	4.13	3.93	4.44
Perez, Odalis	2001	16	0 3 0 0 3 5 4 4 5 4 3 4 4 3	0 0	92	44%	31%	4.92	4.72	4.92
	2002	32	4 4 4 4 4 3 5 3 0 4 4 5 5 4 4 4 3	3 3 2 5 3 2 5 3 4 5 2 3 5 5	94	63%	3%	3.00	2.72	3.29
	2003	29	5 3 4 4 5 2 5 5 2 0 5 3 5 3 3 3 4 1	0 0 5 4 2 4 0 4 4 5 0	95	52%	21%	4.52	4.40	4.50
Perez, Oliver	2002	15	3 3 4 3 5	5 5 3 4 4 4 3 0 0 5	100	53%	13%	3.50	3.92	4.23
	2003	25	0 3 0 0 5 0 5 3 3 4 5 0	0 5 5 3 5 4 0 4 0 5 5 2 0	96	44%	36%	5.50	5.43	5.07
Pettitte, Andy	2001	31	5 3 2 5 3 5 5 4 5 3 3 3 4 0 5 4	3 0 4 4 5 3 4 3 4 3 0 5 5 0 2	101	52%	13%	4.00	4.08	4.23
	2002	22	5 0 0 0 0 2 5 0	4 3 3 5 4 3 5 4 3 4 4 5 5 4	97	55%	23%	3.29	3.63	4.23
	2003	33	5 2 0 5 1 5 0 1 4 0 5 5 0 5 5 4 2 5 2	5 5 4 5 4 1 4 4 5 0 5 2 4 3	102	61%	24%	4.02	4.34	3.95
Phelps, Tommy	2003	7	0 4 4 1 0 5 1		80	43%	57%	4.00	4.23	6.59
Pineiro, Joel	2001	11		0 5 5 5 4 0 3 2 4 4 0	85	55%	27%	3.08	2.92	4.39
	2002	28	0 5 2 5 2 0 1 3 4 3 4 3 3	4 2 4 3 2 2 3 5 4 3 5 5 4 2 3	100	39%	11%	3.25	3.88	4.41
	2003	32	3 3 3 4 3 2 4 2 5 2 5 4 3 4 5 4 5 3 5	3 5 4 0 3 3 0 2 4 5 3 4 5	109	50%	6%	3.80	3.62	3.85
Ponson, Sidney	2001	23	4 0 2 0 3 3 4 4 2 2 4 2 4 0	2 0 2 2 4 0 2 3 0	93	26%	26%	4.95	5.20	4.93
	2002	28	3 0 4 4 5 3 4 4 4 5 0 4 3 4 0 2 0 3	2 3 4 4 4 3 4 4 3 5	99	54%	14%	4.09	4.30	4.23
	2003	31	0 4 4 4 4 5 5 4 2 5 5 5 5 2 3 4 3 4	2 3 3 3 2 4 4 4 4 2 3 3 3	99	55%	3%	3.75	3.56	3.38
Prior, Mark	2002	19	5 5 0 5 5 2 5 3 5	4 5 4 3 5 5 5 0 5 3	106	68%	11%	3.34	3.39	3.61
	2003	30	5 5 5 4 5 5 5 3 5 4 4 4 3 3 4 5 4 5 0	5 5 4 5 5 5 4 3 5 5 4	113	83%	3%	2.43	2.80	2.69
Quevedo, Ruben	2001	10		0 5 5 5 4 5 3 5 2 0	101	60%	20%	3.56	3.84	3.95
	2002	25	0 0 2 4 1 2 0 3 5 5 5 5 1 0 0 4 1 0	3 1 1 4 0 0 2	95	28%	52%	5.76	6.11	6.56
	2003	8	3 2 3 4 0 2 1 0		86	13%	38%	6.86	7.51	5.54

Pitcher	Year	No.	FIRST HALF	SECOND HALF	PC	DOM	DIS	ERA	xERA	qERA
Radke,Brad	2001	33	4 3 5 4 3 4 4 0 4 0 3 3 4 5 4 2 4 3 4	3 1 4 3 0 3 5 4 3 4 3 0 3 3	96	45%	15%	3.94	3.77	4.40
	2002	21	0 4 3 1 0 1 5 3 0 0	5 4 4 2 2 3 4 4 3 0 5	82	38%	33%	4.73	3.83	5.00
	2003	33	4 0 1 2 4 2 5 2 3 1 3 4 4 1 5 4 2 4 4	3 4 4 3 3 3 3 4 0 4 3 3 5 3	95	42%	15%	4.50	4.78	4.44
Ramirez,Horacio	2003	29	5 3 1 5 3 2 3 3 4 1 0 5 4 3 5 0	0 3 1 2 2 0 3 3 4 4 4 0 4	98	34%	28%	4.01	4.29	4.90
Redding,Tim	2001	9	2 5 0	3 2 3 0 2 0	93	11%	33%	4.28	3.79	5.37
	2002	14	0 0 5 4 3 5 4 0 0 0 4 3 2	0	86	36%	43%	5.42	5.13	5.25
	2003	32	4 3 0 5 5 1 2 2 4 3 1 0 5 0 5 2 0 4 5	0 4 5 2 2 4 4 0 4 3 3 3 4	91	44%	25%	3.68	4.12	4.74
Redman,Mark	2001	11	0 4 3 0 2 1 4 2 4	2 0	94	27%	36%	5.18	5.47	5.27
	2002	30	0 3 5 2 5 4 2 4 2 4 5 3 3 3 3 4 2	3 4 5 4 5 4 0 5 3 4 2 0 0	105	47%	13%	4.21	3.74	4.28
	2003	29	4 3 2 3 5 5 5 5 0 3 3 5 2 4 3 0	5 3 4 5 5 3 1 4 5 4 4 3 4 5	109	55%	10%	3.60	3.35	3.97
Reed,Rick	2001	31	4 4 5 4 5 5 3 5 4 4 3 3 5 4 4 0 5	5 0 3 3 2 4 0 4 0 4 3 3 2 0	93	55%	16%	4.05	4.15	4.10
	2002	32	2 3 0 3 4 4 4 0 0 4 0 4 1 2 5 0 3 4	4 3 1 5 3 4 5 5 5 4 4 3 0 1	88	47%	28%	3.78	4.17	4.67
	2003	21	3 0 5 0 5 0 4 2 4 2 0 5 3 5 0	2 3 4 4 5 0	90	43%	29%	5.07	5.06	4.74
Reitsma,Chris	2001	29	5 5 3 4 0 2 4 3 2 3 2 4 1 0 3 2 2 2	1 3 0 4 1 0 4 4 4 0 0	92	31%	31%	5.29	4.89	5.08
	2002	21	3 0 3 0 3 3 4 3 5 1 0 3 5 1 4 2 0	3 0 3 0	86	19%	38%	3.65	4.52	5.45
Reyes,Carlos	2003	5	3 0 4	0 4	80	40%	40%	5.31	5.08	5.21
Reynolds,Shane	2001	28	3 0 0 5 4 4 4 3 4 4 4 3 5 4 3	0 1 4 4 4 2 3 5 5 1 3 4 3	91	54%	18%	4.35	4.72	4.37
	2002	13	2 0 2 2 5 4 4 3 4 2 3 0 0		91	31%	23%	4.86	5.22	4.71
	2003	29	4 3 0 3 4 3 5 4 3 0 3 0 0 0 3 3 4	0 4 4 3 1 4 3 3 5 0 3 3	91	31%	28%	5.44	4.99	4.90
Riedling,John	2003	8	0 0 3 0 4 0 0 0		81	13%	75%	4.90	4.40	10.53
Ritchie,Todd	2001	33	4 2 2 1 3 2 4 1 2 3 4 1 2 3 5 4 4 3	4 3 0 5 3 3 0 3 0 5 4 3 0 4	91	39%	18%	4.48	4.04	4.52
	2002	23	5 2 3 5 5 1 1 1 2 0 0 3 4 3 0 3 3 3 4 0	3 3 0 2	97	22%	35%	6.09	6.08	5.36
	2003	5	3 5 0 2 2		91	20%	20%	5.14	5.93	4.75
Roa,Joe	2002	11		0 3 3 4 3 4 4 3 4 3 0	88	36%	18%	4.06	4.72	4.52
Robertson,Jeriome	2003	31	0 5 0 3 0 0 4 4 4 4 0 1 2 2 3 3 5	2 3 0 0 0 3 0 0 3 0 4 4 3 0 0	82	26%	42%	5.12	5.21	5.40
Robertson,Nate	2003	8		5 4 1 2 4 0 1 4	95	50%	38%	5.52	6.18	4.87
Rodriguez,Ricardo	2002	7		2 4 0 3 3 0 4	95	29%	29%	5.69	4.43	4.93
	2003	15	4 5 3 4 3 2 2 0 3 1 3 1 0 5 0		88	27%	33%	5.78	5.49	5.13
Rogers,Kenny	2001	20	4 2 3 3 4 2 2 2 1 4 5 4 5 3 2 0 0 4	4 0	98	40%	20%	6.21	5.96	4.56
	2002	33	3 5 2 4 5 3 0 4 2 3 4 3 1 0 0 4 3 0	3 3 4 0 2 4 3 4 1 2 4 4 2 5 4	101	39%	21%	3.86	4.01	4.64
	2003	31	0 4 5 2 3 2 3 4 2 5 0 4 3 2 1 5 3 2	2 4 3 3 4 5 2 1 4 2 2 4 4	99	39%	13%	4.57	4.88	4.41
Roney,Matt	2003	11	0 0 4 2 5	1 3 0 0 2 0	79	18%	55%	5.49	5.19	7.55
Rueter,Kirk	2001	34	0 4 4 0 1 2 0 3 3 2 3 1 3 4 4 1 4 2	3 3 0 3 3 5 2 2 2 3 3 2 1 3 4 3	94	21%	24%	4.43	4.80	4.75
	2002	33	2 2 3 4 2 1 2 2 4 2 0 3 3 2 2	3 2 4 4 1 1 1 4 3 4 4 0 2 3 2	99	27%	18%	3.24	4.06	4.62
	2003	27	2 3 3 0 2 2 5 4 3 2 0 4 2 2 1 2 0 0 0	3 1 0 0 4 2 3 3	89	15%	33%	4.53	4.79	5.29
Rusch,Glendon	2001	33	0 5 5 0 0 5 2 0 2 0 5 0 0 5 4 3 4 4	5 2 3 4 5 0 0 2 0 4 5 0 3 3 5	93	42%	33%	4.63	5.11	4.92
	2002	34	3 4 4 5 5 5 0 3 4 0 1 4 3 3 4 4 4 0	0 3 4 4 2 3 3 2 2 5 4 3 4 3 0 3	106	44%	18%	4.71	4.96	4.44
	2003	19	3 5 2 0 4 0 0 2 0 0 2 3 3 0 0 3	0 5 4	95	21%	37%	6.44	6.03	5.36
Sabathia,C.C.	2001	33	2 2 3 2 3 4 2 0 0 3 5 5 5 0 5 0	5 3 4 4 0 4 4 5 0 5 5 0 1 5 4 4	95	48%	27%	4.40	3.68	4.67
	2002	33	4 3 5 0 0 1 4 2 4 5 0 4 2 4 3 3 2	3 2 2 2 5 4 3 4 4 4 4 3 4 3 4	102	45%	12%	4.37	3.71	4.28
	2003	30	3 2 3 3 3 5 3 3 4 5 3 0 3 5 3 5 4 4	4 2 2 3 3 5 3 3 5 4 5 4	104	43%	3%	3.61	3.90	3.89
Santana,Johan	2001	4	0 2 3 1		78	0%	50%	4.79	5.30	7.46
	2002	14	4 0 5 0 5 5	0 0 5 5 4 4 5 4	99	71%	29%	3.00	2.75	3.97
	2003	18	4 5 5 5	5 2 2 5 3 5 5 5 5 0 5 3 4 4	95	72%	6%	3.08	3.03	3.25
Schilling,Curt	2001	35	5 5 3 4 3 3 4 3 5 4 5 4 5 4 3 4 4 4 5	3 0 5 2 5 5 5 5 3 5 5 5 2 5 5 4	106	71%	3%	2.99	3.54	2.99
	2002	35	5 5 4 4 5 4 4 5 5 4 5 5 5 4 4 4 3 5	5 4 5 5 5 5 5 5 4 4 4 5 5 5 3 4	106	94%	0%	3.23	2.82	2.39
	2003	24	4 3 5 5 1 5 5 4 4 4 4	4 4 5 5 5 4 4 5 5 4 4 1	102	88%	8%	2.95	2.89	2.88
Schmidt,Jason	2001	25	4 4 2 2 5 0 4 0 5 5 3	4 5 5 5 0 3 5 3 4 5 4 4 3	100	64%	12%	3.74	3.54	3.71
	2002	29	2 0 0 0 5 0 4 5 5 5 5 3 5 1	4 4 4 5 5 5 4 5 5 4 5 5 3 5 5	104	72%	17%	3.45	3.03	3.63
	2003	29	5 3 4 5 5 5 0 4 5 4 5 5 2 5 4 4 5 5	4 5 4 0 5 5 4 5 5 5 4	106	86%	7%	2.35	2.06	2.88
Sele,Aaron	2001	33	2 4 0 4 2 5 3 2 3 3 3 4 0 0 3 3 2 4	3 5 3 2 1 5 3 4 3 4 0 4 4 5 1	98	36%	18%	3.60	3.99	4.52
	2002	26	1 1 4 2 1 3 3 3 2 3 2 4 2 1 0 4 3	2 4 4 2 5 3 3 2 0	100	23%	23%	4.89	5.13	4.75
	2003	25	3 0 5 0 1 4 0 3 0 2 2 2	2 3 3 1 0 0 3 4 0 2 0 0 4	83	16%	44%	5.80	5.44	5.60
Seo,Jae Weong	2003	31	0 3 4 4 5 2 2 5 4 3 2 4 4 2 0 3 4	0 3 4 0 3 2 4 4 5 3 2 5 5 4	92	48%	13%	3.83	3.91	4.28
Sheets,Ben	2001	25	4 4 4 3 4 3 0 0 4 3 4 2 4 3 4 2	5 0 4 4 1 3 0 2 3	95	44%	20%	4.75	5.05	4.56
	2002	34	4 4 4 0 0 2 5 3 5 5 2 3 2 0 5 3 1 5	5 5 3 1 3 1 5 5 1 5 4 4 4 4 5 5	103	56%	21%	4.17	4.56	4.23
	2003	34	2 3 3 5 4 4 2 3 3 4 5 1 3 5 4 4 3 5 5 4 5	3 5 4 3 5 5 2 0 1 3 4 4 3 3	99	50%	9%	4.46	4.22	3.85
Shields,Scot	2003	13	4 1	3 5 4 4 0 1 1 0 5 5 4	94	54%	38%	2.86	3.40	4.87
Simontacchi,Jason	2002	24	4 1 4 2 3 2 4 0 3 3	3 3 1 0 0 3 3 5 3 2 4 2 5 3	91	25%	21%	4.03	4.53	4.73
	2003	17	0 0 3 3 3 4 0 3 0 4 2 3 4 0 4 3	4	87	29%	29%	5.57	5.68	4.93
Snyder,Kyle	2003	15	2 3 4 1 4 1 5 3 0 4 0	3 2 2 0	84	27%	33%	5.19	4.71	5.13
Sosa,Jorge	2002	14	0 3 3	3 4 3 1 0 0 4 3 1 1 3	90	14%	43%	5.18	4.36	5.70
	2003	20	2 2 1 3 0 3 2 2	3 0 2 5 0 4 5 4 3 2 1 1	89	20%	30%	4.64	4.90	5.21
Sparks,Steve	2001	33	0 4 1 3 3 3 0 1 4 2 4 5 2 3 3 4 4	4 3 1 5 0 0 5 5 2 4 3 5 4 3 4 3	107	42%	21%	3.65	4.16	4.56
	2002	30	3 4 1 3 1 3 2 0 3 0 2 0 0 3 2 3	0 2 4 5 4 5 3 2 4 0 2 0 3 2	98	20%	27%	5.52	5.54	4.98
Standridge,Jason	2003	7	4 4 2 2 1 0 0		77	29%	43%	6.43	5.72	5.40
Stanford,Jason	2003	8	2 3	0 0 4 4 4 3	85	38%	25%	3.60	3.88	4.82
Stark,Denny	2002	20	3 5 2 2 4	4 3 0 3 3 3 3 1 1 0 3 4 2 3 0	89	20%	25%	4.01	4.50	4.98
	2003	13	0 3 2	4 0 0 0 2 4 3 2 0 5	92	23%	38%	5.88	6.06	5.36
Stephenson,Garrett	2002	10	0 5 0 0 3 3 0	0 0 2	78	10%	60%	5.40	4.91	8.46
	2003	27	3 5 0 0 3 3 0 3 4 1 1 1 4 4 4 3 3 3 1	0 4 3 3 4 0 0 5	97	30%	37%	4.60	4.44	5.19
Stephens,John	2002	10		0 5 5 5 3 1 4 4 4 1	95	60%	30%	6.09	5.19	4.39
Stewart,Josh	2003	5	2 0 3 2 0		96	0%	40%	6.12	6.03	5.90
Sturtze,Tanyon	2001	27	3 5 0 3 3 4 1 3 4 3 3 4	5 2 1 1 4 3 5 4 2 3 1 3 2 4	106	33%	19%	4.43	4.53	4.60
	2002	33	1 2 2 4 4 2 2 4 2 2 2 2 3 5 3 4 1 4	4 2 0 1 2 3 3 4 2 3 3 2 0 5 3	108	27%	21%	5.18	5.63	4.62
	2003	8	3 5 0 0 4 0 0 3		98	25%	50%	5.97	6.03	6.56
Suppan,Jeff	2001	34	0 3 4 3 3 4 2 4 0 3 4 2 3 3 4 2 3 2	4 4 4 3 3 3 3 2 1 4 2 0 2 2 3	105	29%	12%	4.37	4.46	4.50
	2002	33	2 4 3 4 4 4 0 4 4 5 3 0 2 3 3 4 2 4	2 2 3 4 3 1 2 1 0 3 2 3 4	104	33%	15%	5.32	4.93	4.60
	2003	31	4 5 3 4 3 3 3 2 4 0 1 2 5 3 4 2 4 2 4	2 3 4 2 4 2 4 2 3 2 2 4 3	101	39%	6%	4.19	4.35	4.29

Pitcher	Year	No.	FIRST HALF	SECOND HALF	PC	DOM	DIS	ERA	xERA	qERA
Tejera,Michael	2002	18	0 3 5 3 5 4	4 3 2 3 5 1 4 4 0 0 1 0	99	39%	33%	4.47	4.73	5.00
	2003	6	4 4 0 2 0 5		82	50%	33%	4.67	4.14	4.71
Telemaco,Amaury	2003	8		5 1 4 3 4 1 5 0	84	50%	38%	4.00	3.43	4.87
Thomson,John	2001	14	1 4 2	5 4 3 5 2 4 4 3 3 5 5	99	57%	7%	4.25	4.83	3.68
	2002	30	4 4 4 0 5 5 2 4 3 4 2 0 3 1 2 2 3 4	1 2 3 2 0 4 3 5 1 0 2 5	98	37%	23%	4.72	3.94	4.64
	2003	35	0 4 4 0 4 1 4 0 3 4 3 3 1 5 0 5 0 3 5 3	5 0 4 4 2 0 4 2 4 3 5 4 3 3 3	95	43%	26%	4.85	4.46	4.74
Tomko,Brett	2001	4	0 4 0	4	87	50%	50%	5.03	5.10	5.81
	2002	32	3 2 4 5 4 2 4 3 2 0 5 3 4 1 4 2 2 3	4 3 2 0 4 0 4 4 0 4 4 3 0 0	96	41%	22%	4.50	4.66	4.56
	2003	33	3 3 3 4 4 3 3 2 0 4 5 2 0 0 2 2 3 3 2	3 3 3 3 4 3 0 3 3 0 5 3 5 1	99	21%	18%	5.30	5.80	4.63
Torres,Salomon	2002	5		4 0 3 1 2	83	20%	40%	2.70	2.93	5.50
	2003	16	3 3 2 2 2 4 0	3 5 2 2 4 4 0 3 3	81	25%	13%	4.76	4.84	4.50
Towers,Josh	2001	20	2 4 4 3 3 2 3 3	3 3 2 2 2 3 2 3 3 4 2 3	92	15%	0%	4.52	4.69	4.48
	2002	3	1 2 1		96	0%	67%	8.00	9.07	9.80
	2003	8		3 1 4 5 3 5 0 4	92	50%	25%	4.50	4.93	4.61
Traber,Billy	2003	18	0 0 0 2 5 5 0 4 4	5 0 5 0 2 0 3 0 0	80	33%	50%	5.27	5.44	6.37
Trachsel,Steve	2001	28	1 5 0 3 5 3 4 0 4 4 5 3 4 0	4 4 5 5 0 3 5 4 3 4 3 4 5	97	61%	18%	4.45	4.11	3.83
	2002	30	2 1 3 0 0 3 1 3 3 5 3 4 4 3 5 4 0	4 4 1 4 0 3 4 4 3 0 5 3 3	95	37%	27%	3.38	4.13	4.82
	2003	33	1 4 4 1 4 2 4 2 4 1 4 0 0 3 3 3 3 4 0	2 1 2 4 1 3 4 4 5 4 5 3 5 5	100	45%	24%	3.79	4.23	4.53
Tsao,Chin-Hui	2003	8		3 0 4 3 0 0 0 5	88	25%	50%	6.07	6.27	6.56
Tucker,T.J.	2003	7	0	0 0 4 0 4 0	60	29%	71%	4.73	4.47	8.88
Valdes,Ismael	2001	27	4 3 2 5 3 3 1 3 5 4 0 4	4 5 1 5 3 3 3 0 0 3 3 2 0 0 3	96	30%	26%	4.47	4.63	4.90
	2002	31	4 0 3 2 5 4 4 2 1 3 4 3 0 3 5 1	3 2 4 4 3 5 3 4 2 2 4 2 5 0 1	95	39%	19%	4.18	3.13	4.52
	2003	22	1 5 0 5 0 2 3 2 4 4 4 0 0 0 4 0	4 0 3 0 1 1	83	32%	50%	6.10	6.26	6.37
Van Hekken,Andy	2002	5		3 3 0 3 3	89	0%	20%	3.00	4.92	4.83
Van Poppel,Todd	2003	6	0	4 5 3 5 4	89	67%	17%	5.63	4.85	3.73
Vargas,Claudio	2003	20	4 4 2 3 4 0 4 2 3 4 4 4 3 1 0	5 2 0 0 0	90	40%	30%	4.34	4.30	4.92
Vazquez,Javier	2001	32	2 5 0 5 0 0 3 5 5 3 3 5 4 5 3 3 5 2 4	5 5 5 2 5 4 5 5 3 5 5 5 3	106	59%	9%	3.43	3.14	3.68
	2002	34	4 4 3 5 4 5 4 4 5 4 2 3 5 2 2 4 0 2 3	4 5 4 4 0 4 5 0 1 2 3 5 5 3 4	104	59%	12%	3.91	4.27	3.97
	2003	34	3 5 5 4 5 4 5 4 0 4 5 2 4 4 3 3 4 3 4 4	5 5 2 5 3 4 5 5 5 3 5 5 5 4	109	74%	3%	3.25	3.24	2.99
Villone,Ron	2001	12	2 0 0 0 3 3	4 3 0 3 4 0	90	17%	42%	5.91	5.69	5.60
	2002	7	3 3 0 3 0 4 3		90	14%	29%	5.81	4.19	5.08
	2003	19	5 4 4 4 3	5 3 3 0 4 3 3 5 5 5 0 3 0 3 3	94	42%	16%	4.16	4.00	4.44
Vogelsong,Ryan	2003	5	2	0 2 5 0	82	20%	40%	6.55	5.63	5.50
Waechter,Doug	2003	5		5 3 3 3 4	99	40%	0%	3.34	3.57	3.89
Wakefield,Tim	2001	17	5 5 5 4 4 5 5 4 4	4 2 0 4 4 1 4 3	101	76%	12%	3.91	3.73	3.41
	2002	16	4 5 3 5	4 4 2 5 4 4 5 5 5 4 3 3	95	75%	0%	2.82	2.48	2.84
	2003	33	4 3 5 2 3 2 4 5 5 3 0 0 5 4 5 2 5 5 4	5 4 5 4 4 5 3 0 4 3 5 4 4 0	94	64%	12%	4.10	4.03	3.71
Walker,Pete	2002	20	0 4 4 0 2	0 4 1 0 4 3 4 3 4 0 3 1 4 2 3	93	35%	35%	4.37	4.46	5.13
	2003	7	3 2 1 0	0 4 3	80	14%	43%	4.91	5.61	5.70
Washburn,Jarrod	2001	30	2 1 0 2 5 5 2 2 4 3 3 3 5 5 4	3 4 3 4 0 5 5 4 4 2 5 3 2 0	102	43%	13%	3.78	4.25	4.32
	2002	32	3 3 0 3 3 3 4 2 5 5 5 2 5 2 4 5 5	3 3 3 3 4 3 4 2 2 4 3 3 4 4 2	105	41%	3%	3.15	3.19	3.89
	2003	32	3 3 4 1 3 3 4 5 4 4 3 5 2 2 1 3 2 2 5	4 0 5 3 5 3 3 3 4 2 5 2 0	101	38%	13%	4.43	4.43	4.41
Weaver,Jeff	2001	33	3 3 2 4 2 4 5 2 4 4 5 4 4 3 2 3 1 4	3 3 3 3 4 3 4 0 0 4 0 5 4	110	45%	6%	4.09	3.96	3.98
	2002	26	2 2 2 1 4 4 4 3 5 5 2 0 5 5 4 4 4	4 2 4 3 3 4 4 4	109	58%	8%	3.53	3.23	3.68
	2003	24	4 4 5 2 0 3 3 2 1 3 3 3 0 1 3 3 5	0 3 4 0 4 1 2	102	25%	29%	6.00	5.72	4.93
Webb,Brandon	2003	28	5 3 4 3 4 4 5 5 5 3 4 4 5 4	5 4 3 4 5 3 5 0 5 4 4 3 0 0	100	68%	11%	2.85	2.68	3.61
Wells,David	2001	16	2 3 1 4 3 3 3 2 3 0 0 5 4 3 0		90	19%	25%	4.49	4.95	5.03
	2002	31	3 4 3 1 3 4 0 0 5 5 3 4 5 5 1	3 4 4 4 0 3 1 3 5 4 4 4 4 4	101	58%	16%	3.76	3.78	4.10
	2003	31	4 4 3 4 3 4 3 3 3 3 3 4 4 4 3 2 3	3 1 4 3 0 3 2 3 4 3 3 3 4	97	32%	6%	4.14	4.34	4.48
Wells,Kip	2001	20	3 5 4 4 3 2 5 3 3 4	3 4 0 0 0 0 0 3 0 0	89	30%	35%	4.84	5.02	5.19
	2002	33	2 0 1 5 4 4 3 5 4 3 4 2 4 0 5 3 3 0	4 3 2 5 4 2 2 2 5 1 5 2 5 5	94	45%	15%	3.59	4.20	4.40
	2003	31	3 0 4 5 4 4 3 5 5 1 2 3 3 4 5 1 3	4 4 3 3 3 4 2 5 3 4 5 4 3 4	103	52%	10%	3.29	3.65	4.23
Westbrook,Jake	2003	22	4 2 1 1 1 3 0 2 0 2	3 4 0 1 3 2 3 1 4 0 4 3	86	18%	41%	4.33	4.43	5.60
Williams,David	2001	18	1 3 3	3 4 5 1 0 0 2 3 2 5 0 2 3 4 0	87	22%	33%	3.59	3.90	5.21
	2002	9	5 4 2 5 0 0 0 0 4		85	44%	44%	5.02	4.99	5.21
Williams,Jerome	2003	21	0 5 3 3 3 4 5 4 5	3 5 4 1 0 3 5 3 3 5 3 4	97	48%	14%	3.30	3.33	4.28
Williams,Woody	2001	34	2 2 4 3 0 5 3 4 5 4 3 2 4 5 2 0 2 5	1 5 1 4 0 0 2 4 4 3 5 5 4	103	50%	18%	4.05	4.44	4.37
	2002	17	0 5 5 4 2 3 4 4 5 5 4	0 5 4 4 0	92	71%	18%	2.53	2.90	3.63
	2003	33	5 3 5 3 5 4 5 4 5 5 3 4 2 1 5 4 3 5 3	2 2 4 5 2 2 4 5 0 4 0 5 5 2	110	58%	9%	3.89	3.73	3.68
Willis,Dontrelle	2003	27	4 3 0 5 5 3 4 5 4 4 5 4 3	0 4 5 5 0 4 1 2 5 5 2 3 3 4	99	59%	15%	3.32	3.53	4.10
Wilson,Paul	2001	24	3 4 0 0 3 2 3 3 5 0 0	4 4 2 5 1 2 5 3 5 5 4 5	94	42%	21%	4.88	4.88	4.56
	2002	30	3 3 2 2 4 3 3 2 4 2 0 4 3 2 4	5 3 4 4 3 4 3 3 2 0 0 3 0 0	104	27%	17%	4.85	5.12	4.62
	2003	28	2 4 0 5 2 0 3 3 4 4 5 5 3 4 1 3 4 0	4 2 3 4 2 4 5 4 2 2	92	46%	14%	4.66	5.07	4.28
Wolf,Randy	2001	25	0 2 0 3 3 4 5 5 5 4 0 4 2 0 3	5 4 4 5 3 4 0 5 4 5	100	56%	20%	3.70	3.50	4.23
	2002	31	4 4 3 2 0 4 3 4 2 4 4 2 4 4 3 4	5 5 5 3 4 5 4 5 1 4 5 5 5 3	103	68%	6%	3.21	3.16	3.38
	2003	33	3 3 5 2 5 4 3 4 4 4 4 4 5 2 4 4 3 5	4 3 3 3 5 0 0 5 5 3 4 5 0	99	61%	9%	4.23	3.82	3.50
Wood,Kerry	2001	28	4 0 5 4 5 3 5 0 4 5 5 4 3 5 3 3 4 3	4 5 3 5 5 5 3 4 5	108	64%	7%	3.36	3.02	3.50
	2002	33	4 5 3 0 2 3 5 4 4 4 2 4 4 0 3 2 4	4 5 4 4 5 5 2 4 5 3 4 4 4 3 5 5	103	67%	6%	3.68	3.35	3.38
	2003	32	3 5 5 3 5 4 3 5 5 0 0 5 5 5 3 5 4 4 0 5	4 2 5 5 5 0 0 5 5 5 5 5	110	72%	13%	3.20	2.99	3.51
Wright,Danny	2001	12		2 3 4 2 0 0 1 1 3 2 3 0	93	8%	42%	4.37	4.58	5.80
	2002	33	3 4 0 1 4 3 0 0 4 4 0 3 5 2 3 0 4	3 4 4 4 0 3 2 5 3 4 2 5 4 5	95	45%	21%	5.19	4.66	4.53
	2003	16	0 4 0 4 0 4 2 4 3 0 0	3 4 3 0 0	80	31%	44%	6.17	5.66	5.29
Zambrano,Carlos	2002	16	0 3	3 5 4 0 4 5 0 4 3 4 0 5 4 3	99	50%	25%	3.67	3.91	4.61
	2003	32	4 4 5 3 4 4 3 3 0 4 3 2 2 3 2	4 5 2 4 5 4 4 4 4 4 5 0 2	106	59%	6%	3.11	3.16	3.68
Zambrano,Victor	2002	11		5 2 5 4 2 2 2 3 3 3 4	94	36%	0%	5.53	5.16	4.18
	2003	28	0 0 3 3 1 3 5 4 3 4 4 3 3 4	2 2 2 4 1 4 0 2 5 5 0 3 2 5	106	36%	21%	4.21	4.15	4.64
Zito,Barry	2001	35	4 3 3 5 5 5 0 0 5 5 5 2 2 3 4 5 3 3 5	4 0 0 5 5 3 2 5 5 3 5 5 4 4 4 3	101	57%	11%	3.49	3.27	3.97
	2002	35	5 5 4 0 5 0 5 4 5 3 4 5 2 4 5 5 0 3 5	3 4 4 3 2 4 4 3 3 5 3 5 5 2 2 5	105	60%	6%	2.75	2.94	3.50
	2003	35	3 4 0 4 3 3 3 3 5 3 4 3 3 2 4 3 2 3 1 3	5 4 4 0 4 3 5 1 3 5 1 5 4 4 3	107	40%	14%	3.31	3.08	4.32

Bullpen Indicators

2003 Volatility Report

Closer volatility in 2003 reached record levels. Nearly 60% of those pitchers anointed with the "Closer Role" on Opening Day ended up in other places, from the DL to mop-up duty. For Rotisserie leaguers, saves investments returned just 41 cents on every dollar spent.

This 41% percentage play, which represented our success rate for 2003, indicates a decision point not worth taking. It says, *don't invest in closers at all.* But can we afford to blow off an entire category? Well... this has become a successful strategy in 5x5 leagues, but it's still very risky..

Over the past five years, the play has been closer to 67%, which is borderline, but still worthwhile. Going back to the mid-1990s, saves used to be a stable commodity that almost always paid off, with top closers garnering bids in the high $30's. But, as the turnover has increased, the risk of investing even $30 in a closer has skyrocketed.

As for 2004, who knows? We've watched as the average closer price has dropped from a high of $32 in 1998 to $22 the past two years. After this season's debacle, might it fall even further? You'll have to lay off the early bidding on saves to see where market forces are going to land.

Of course, the flipside to this horror story had names like Rocky Biddle, Joe Borowski, Tim Worrell and Rod Beck. These were surprise saves sources whose owners reaped the benefit of being lucky. But in a game like Rotisserie, where the saves category constitutes 20%-25% of a team's score, this type of turnover — *through no fault or skill of any roto owner* — can have a dramatic impact on the final standings.

The Closer Volatility Chart summarizes all this.

A bit of explanation... CLOSERS DRAFTED refers to the number of top saves sources purchased in both AL and NL Rotisserie Leagues each year. For the most part, these only include relievers drafted for at least $15 or so. AVG $ refers to the average 4x4 purchase price of these pitchers. FAILED is the number (and percentage) of CLOSERS DRAFTED that did not return at least 50% of their value that year. The Failures include those that lost their value due to ineffectiveness, injury or managerial decision. NEW SOURCES are arms that had no previous saves value coming into the season but finished with enough saves to rank among the top closers for that year. The body of the chart lists the pitchers who make up the study.

So what is an intelligent fantasy leaguer to do?

1. We can discount closers at the draft table... but that only softens the blow of overspending; it does not address the risk of losing your investment completely for every other closer you buy.

2. We can pay top dollar for the cream of the crop in hopes of better assuring a return on investment... but Jose Mesa, Billy Koch and Kaz Sasaki were all once considered in that "cream" class.

3. We can play it close to the vest and spend prudently, buying only bargains and loading our reserves with contingency plans... but that might yield an even lower return than buying arms at the 59% failure rate.

4. We can punt saves completely and focus on skills, speculative saves and firming up the other categories... but that can put us at a competitive disadvantage.

5. Or we can just assume the risk and pray a lot.

The percentage plays are underwhelming, which leaves us being more *reactive than proactive when it comes to* managing our bullpens. It's a heckuva way to run a fantasy team, yet that's what we've been doing.

Tools for Speculation

A little bit of structured analysis might help in the speculating process. We use the Rule of TOG here, which captures the elements that lead to saves as well as anything else. Talent, Opportunity and Guile are the three qualities that are required for saves. A complete description appears in the Forecaster's Toolbox.

We've been playing with TOG for seven years now, and while it is the most logical approach to saves prospecting, it still falls short. Talent is measurable, Opportunity comes and goes, and as for the quest for the Holy Guile, well, we're all still out there clapping coconut shells.

Still, I think we need to be grounded in at least a little bit of science. To aid in this process, the following Bullpen Indicator Charts (which are compiled by HQ analyst Matt Dodge) help focus on many of the statistical and situational factors that might go into a manager's decision to grant any individual pitcher a save opportunity. It's not all-encompassing, but it's a good start. In the following pages, we provide a three-year scan of indicators for all pitchers who posted at least 1 save and/or 3 holds in 2003.

Some of the tidbits worthy of analysis...

Saves Percentage... which could be the single most important number on the chart, especially for identifying closers who might be in danger of losing their job. What it says is simple... "Who is getting it done?" and that is probably the biggest determining factor for a manager. Bottom line is that, skills or no skills, a pitcher will not keep getting the call if he is not consistently converting his save opportunities at about an 80% rate.

Base Performance Value... The components of BPV are evaluated in many ways. Big league managers tend to look for a pitcher who can strike out eight or nine batters per 9 IP, sometimes even if he's also walking that many. In using BPV, we set a benchmark of 75 as the minimum necessary for success. BPV's over 100 are much better, however.

Situational Performance... is the last piece of the puzzle. Our chart includes the opposition batting averages for each pitcher versus RH and LH hitters, with runners on base, in his first 15 pitches, etc. which are all good indicators. We'll set a benchmark of a .250 BA; anything over and the risk level increases.

The tools are here. Whether or not a major league manager will make a decision reflective of this information remains to be seen. But I do think the data can help us increase our odds of uncovering those elusive saves and minimizing at least some of the risk.

Closer Volatility Analysis

FAILURES

1998	1999	2000	2001	2002	2003
Bottalico	Acevedo	Howry	Jones,T	Alfonseca	Alfonseca
Brantley	Beck	Jackson	Kohlmeier	Anderson,M	Anderson,M
Eckersely	Gordon	Mantei	Leskanic	Foulke	Benitez
Hernandez,R	Ligtenberg	Rocker	Lowe	Fox	Dejean
Jones,D	Taylor,B	Shuey	Mantei	Gordon	Embree
Jones,T		Timlin	Rocker	Strickland	Escobar
Loiselle		Trombley	Veres	Wickman	Hoffman
Mesa		Urbina		Zimmerman	Isringhausen
Myers,R		Wagner			Jimenez
Slocumb		Williamson			Koch
Wohlers					Mesa
					Nen
					Sasaki
					Stewart
					Urbina
					Williams,M
					Williamson

NEW SOURCES

1998	1999	2000	2001	2002	2003
Acevedo	Foulke	Dotel	Fassero	Acevedo	Beck
Benitez	Graves	Isringhausen	Gordon	Baez	Biddle
Howry	Koch	Jimenez	Kim	Cordero	Borowski
Jackson,M	Lowe	Kohlmeir	Mesa	DeJean	Carter,L
Ligtenberg	Rocker	Leskanic	Prinz	Gagne	Cordero,F
Mantei	Williamson	Sasaki	Yan	Irabu	Gordon,T
Olsen,G	Zimmerman	Strickland	Zimmerman	Julio	Hasegawa,S
Taylor,B		Wells,B		Looper	Kolb,D
Wickman		Williams,M		Marte	Lopez,Aq
				Nunez,V	MacDougal,M
				Osuna	Marte
				Williamson	Politte
					Tavarez
					Worrell

SUMMARY

NUMBER OF CLOSERS

YEAR	Drafted	*Avg R$	Failed	Failure %	New Sources
1996	24	$30	3	13%	2
1997	26	$30	5	19%	8
1998	25	$32	11	44%	9
1999	23	$25	5	22%	7
2000	27	$25	10	37%	9
2001	25	$26	7	28%	7
2002	28	$22	8	29%	12
2003	29	$22	17	59%	14

* 4x4 prices from LABR experts league

Bullpen Indicators

Pitcher	Th	Yr	Tm	BPIs			Results		Runners		Pitch Ct		Platoon	
				IP/g	bpv	S%	Sv%	Eff%	Emp	On	0-15	16-30	vLH	vRH
Acevedo,Juan	R	01	FLA	1.0	28	77%	0%	38%	269	296	303	302	319	264
		02	DET	1.1	66	79%	80%	71%	293	199	263	197	264	228
		03	FA	1.0	7	66%	75%	61%	325	314	294	386	292	341
Adams,Terry	R	01	LA	3.9	91	67%	0%	64%	255	282	250	241	232	295
		02	PHI	3.0	59	69%	0%	66%	235	281	268	179	246	263
		03	PHI	1.0	67	79%		81%	293	244	301	205	264	271
Affeldt,Jeremy	L	02	KC	2.3	56	66%	0%	44%	298	254	257	225	283	271
		03	KC	3.5	78	72%	100%	70%	274	243	234	184	223	272
Alfonseca,Antoni	R	01	FLA	1.1	70	81%	82%	76%	313	241	281	278	302	259
		02	CHC	1.1	64	73%	68%	60%	270	245	247	287	304	220
		03	CHC	1.1	52	63%	0%	71%	240	338	314	250	340	259
Almanza,Armand	L	01	FLA	0.8	45	73%	0%	78%	244	212	282	139	210	244
		02	FLA	0.9	80	73%	50%	81%	222	225	198	293	255	208
		03	FLA	1.0	36	68%	0%	59%	402	214	317	290	277	306
Almonte,Hector	R	03	MON	1.0	30	61%	0%	57%	234	362	241	288	326	280
Alvarez,Juan	L	02	TEX	0.8	26	71%	0%	59%	194	288	229	313	233	250
Anderson,Matt	R	01	DET	0.9	108	61%	92%	92%	242	268	255	271	291	222
		03	DET	1.0	4	69%	75%	78%	304	239	294	208	286	263
Ayala,Luis	R	03	MON	1.1	93	79%	63%	85%	242	248	253	232	337	188
Baez,Danys	R	01	CLE	1.2	99	82%	0%	83%	176	214	159	273	188	193
		02	CLE	4.2	55	71%	75%	55%	237	282	168	258	278	233
		03	CLE	1.0	87	71%	71%	63%	257	197	255	157	285	165
Bauer,Rick	R	02	BAL	1.5	19	77%	20%	63%	266	269	239	258	288	253
		03	BAL	1.7	60	66%	0%	75%	216	293	237	256	247	261
Beck,Rod	R	01	BOS	1.2	43	78%	55%	75%	266	233	281	195	213	285
		03	SD	1.0	97	91%	100%	92%	230	151	219	129	159	341
Beimel,Joe	L	02	PIT	1.6	29	72%	0%	54%	265	268	260	272	262	269
		03	PIT	0.9	30	71%	0%	62%	266	340	288	328	311	288
Benitez,Armando	R	01	NYM	1.0	80	77%	93%	88%	225	198	221	179	212	215
		02	NYM	1.1	114	86%	89%	89%	216	149	202	183	160	220
		03	SEA	1.1	77	81%	72%	71%	236	197	217	227	214	221
Betancourt,Rafae	R	03	CLE	1.2	90	89%	33%	64%	231	150	232	125	270	133
Biddle,Rocky	R	02	CHW	1.8	37	78%	33%	57%	220	278	282	182	287	205
		03	MON	1.0	31	73%	83%	74%	290	220	264	206	242	264
Bland,Nate	L	03	HOU	0.9	35	68%	0%	57%	261	323	271	261	273	303
Boehringer,Brian	R	01	SF	1.4	67	76%	100%	56%	196	305	245	305	333	202
		02	PIT	1.1	78	73%	17%	79%	220	241	205	291	250	218
		03	PIT	1.0	27	67%	0%	74%	274	259	238	348	193	309
Bong,Jung	L	03	ATL	1.3	39	70%	33%	69%	236	298	260	296	264	268
Borowski,Joe	R	02	CHC	1.3	108	82%	33%	69%	252	220	247	262	209	260
		03	CHC	1.0	121	78%	89%	86%	197	220	211	219	212	204
Boyd,Jason	R	02	SD	1.2	-3	55%	0%	63%	254	353	308	268	235	356
		03	CLE	1.2	46	65%	0%	85%	153	250	195	185	232	176
Bradford,Chad	R	01	OAK	1.0	132	88%	25%	64%	293	268	289	237	300	274
		02	OAK	1.0	129	72%	40%	86%	241	269	268	186	267	247
		03	OAK	1.1	71	79%	40%	82%	217	260	237	263	326	190
Brower,Jim	R	01	CIN	2.8	41	75%	50%	48%	258	232	234	226	272	228
		02	MON	1.5	64	67%	0%	75%	225	287	252	303	254	251
		03	SF	2.0	56	70%	67%	67%	235	270	216	276	291	220
Bump,Nate	R	03	FLA	1.1	24	68%		100%	200	316	250	263	229	258
Calero,Kiko	R	03	STL	1.5	98	84%	25%	43%	175	263	262	159	222	205
Carrara,Giovanni	R	01	LA	1.8	80	79%	0%	79%	237	207	221	309	259	267
		02	LA	1.4	37	81%	17%	72%	229	267	273	247	248	240
		03	SEA	1.3	-21	67%		100%	293	371	426	297	387	276
Carrasco,D.J.	R	03	KC	1.6	42	69%	40%	64%	247	297	288	245	290	255
Carrasco,Hector	R	01	BAL	1.3		70%	50%	60%	254	297	296	281	318	251
		03	BAL	1.0	30	71%	33%	58%	295	233	252	324	288	256
Carter,Lance	R	02	TAM	2.5	112	66%	100%	100%	255	111	167	160	212	195
		03	TAM	1.3	55	67%	79%	74%	214	292	270	208	222	271
Christiansen,Jaso	L	01	2TM	0.7	77	79%	75%	89%	224	226	233	154	254	200
		03	SF	0.7	61	64%	0%	88%	220	293	277	118	208	288
Colome,Jesus	R	01	TAM	1.6	24	81%		73%	208	208	270	136	188	220
		02	TAM	1.3	9	61%	0%	29%	328	351	420	213	414	287
		03	TAM	1.4	49	74%	25%	55%	283	213	227	301	218	269
Cordero,Chad	R	03	MON	0.9	152	83%	100%	100%	115	100	65	400	111	111
Cordero,Francisc	R	02	TEX	1.2	121	84%	83%	87%	181	246	188	226	189	216
		03	TEX	1.1	103	78%	60%	68%	211	250	213	221	236	223
Corey,Mark	R	02	2TM	0.9	93	69%		25%	375	298	364	300	342	333
		03	PIT	1.4	88	58%		67%	224	281	273	256	316	221
Cormier,Rheal	L	01	PHI	0.9	66	69%	17%	62%	221	282	247	250	294	223
		02	PHI	1.1	49	67%	0%	61%	242	295	275	217	291	253
		03	PHI	1.3	106	83%	25%	88%	171	198	181	186	119	207
Cressend,Jack	R	01	MIN	1.3	53	74%	0%	67%	281	186	238	213	294	198
		02	MIN	1.4	4	72%		0%	338	273	397	143	355	261
		03	CLE	1.3	107	77%	0%	78%	242	266	276	185	253	250
Crudale,Mike	R	02	STL	1.1	118	85%	0%	90%	242	214	248	220	247	216
		03	MIL	0.9	38	83%	0%	67%	128	212	173	111	105	189
Cunnane,Will	R	01	MIL	1.7	48	70%		25%	340	301	326	254	295	336
		02	CHC	1.7	87	69%	0%	50%	235	306	300	154	395	194
		03	ATL	1.0	115	78%	100%	83%	163	240	135	318	200	182
De los Santos,Va	L	02	MIL	1.1	59	75%		75%	218	200	215	183	219	207
	L	03	PHI	1.0	38	71%	25%	73%	250	229	242	218	267	228

Bullpen Indicators

Pitcher	Th	Yr	Tm	BPIs			Results		Runners		Pitch Ct		Platoon	
				IP/g	bpv	S%	Sv%	Eff%	Emp	On	0-15	16-30	vLH	vRH
DeJean,Mike	R	01	MIL	1.1	73	80%	50%	78%	258	214	252	198	227	242
		02	MIL	1.1	61	81%	90%	78%	242	230	228	254	259	213
		03	STL	1.1	43	73%	70%	68%	287	248	283	229	329	216
Donnelly,Brendar	R	02	ANA	1.1	125	80%	33%	83%	156	218	189	143	242	148
		03	ANA	1.2	135	86%	60%	89%	230	176	180	247	199	202
Dotel,Octavio	R	01	HOU	1.7	137	79%	50%	77%	182	236	200	148	238	178
		02	HOU	1.2	161	83%	60%	84%	190	144	179	167	190	159
		03	HOU	1.1	117	80%	67%	88%	162	186	178	167	152	186
Eischen,Joey	L	02	MON	0.9	119	88%	67%	90%	212	239	244	151	173	261
		03	MON	0.8	76	83%	25%	78%	257	312	248	372	255	308
Eldred,Cal	R	03	STL	1.1	68	77%	57%	72%	250	245	281	192	295	227
Embree,Alan	L	01	CHW	0.9	62	56%	0%	59%	295	299	320	266	220	352
		02	BOS	0.9	144	87%	29%	69%	188	226	241	96	156	244
		03	BOS	0.9	90	65%	50%	90%	184	315	249	206	263	221
Estrella,Leo	R	03	MIL	1.1	7	74%	38%	70%	306	272	312	232	290	289
Eyre,Scott	L	01	TOR	0.9	90	76%	67%	67%	276	250	238	444	192	323
		02	SF	1.1	61	71%	0%	80%	268	282	266	258	233	317
		03	SF	0.8	43	79%	33%	88%	250	284	271	250	219	305
Farnsworth,Kyle	R	01	CHC	1.1	134	80%	67%	81%	222	202	204	242	223	207
		02	CHC	1.0	38	57%	14%	48%	240	353	261	349	392	216
		03	CHC	1.0	109	73%	0%	81%	194	198	192	232	189	199
Fassero,Jeff	L	01	CHC	0.9	118	73%	71%	82%	215	258	241	210	247	228
		02	STL	1.0	71	64%	0%	70%	257	333	271	364	318	275
		03	STL	1.2	10	71%	50%	60%	291	304	307	308	337	278
Foster,John	L	03	MIL	0.9	11	82%	0%	71%	514	216	361	318	391	323
Foulke,Keith	R	01	CHW	1.1	131	76%	93%	79%	182	221	213	145	212	183
		02	CHW	1.2	127	75%	79%	75%	211	253	219	198	266	185
		03	OAK	1.2	138	85%	90%	90%	215	138	196	178	158	210
Fox,Chad	R	01	MIL	1.0	98	89%	50%	87%	185	176	193	151	158	197
		03	FLA	1.1	70	81%	60%	72%	279	189	274	159	205	241
Franco,John	L	01	NYM	0.9	67	76%	29%	78%	241	293	273	233	236	275
		03	NYM	0.9	15	88%	67%	60%	311	207	277	233	267	264
Fuentes,Brian	L	01	SEA	1.2	103	67%	0%	50%	133	200	111	214	111	235
		02	COL	0.9	92	71%		100%	241	261	333	94	381	155
		03	COL	1.0	92	82%	67%	84%	255	205	224	250	238	227
Fultz,Aaron	L	01	SF	1.1	92	67%	50%	89%	259	259	241	291	237	276
		02	SF	1.0	47	71%	0%	67%	235	360	300	302	302	284
		03	TEX	1.1	48	68%		87%	267	313	315	238	218	345
Gagne,Eric	R	02	LA	1.1	228	82%	93%	92%	212	157	204	131	213	163
		03	LA	1.1	258	84%	100%	95%	139	121	147	86	130	135
Gallo,Mike	L	03	HOU	0.9	44	80%	0%	88%	348	203	267	286	227	295
Garcia,Rosman	R	03	TEX	1.0	20	67%	0%	67%	350	289	331	279	333	312
German,Franklyn	R	02	DET	1.0	139	66%	100%	100%	231	0	167	0	100	200
		03	DET	1.0	24	71%	71%	65%	247	293	270	250	238	304
Gonzalez,Mike	L	03	PIT	0.5	-76	67%		75%	250	214	250	0	222	238
Gordon,Tom	R	01	CHC	1.0	160	70%	87%	82%	200	171	177	237	188	188
		02	HOU	1.2	117	75%		70%	266	254	253	291	269	255
		03	CHW	1.1	125	74%	71%	70%	177	256	204	202	231	196
Graves,Danny	R	01	CIN	1.2	75	68%	82%	76%	238	301	249	322	301	243
		02	CIN	1.4	70	76%	82%	80%	236	295	281	280	272	259
		03	CIN	5.6	5	67%	100%	29%	297	300	292	270	297	299
Grimsley,Jason	R	01	KC	1.1	69	79%	0%	69%	239	245	236	256	261	218
		02	KC	1.0	67	72%	33%	67%	214	257	223	269	248	225
		03	KC	1.0	51	69%	0%	70%	250	342	337	203	316	282
Groom,Buddy	L	01	BAL	0.9	168	68%	85%	82%	281	222	263	222	194	291
		02	BAL	0.9	130	87%	50%	86%	192	202	201	151	181	208
		03	BAL	0.8	48	69%	33%	78%	297	322	302	314	270	343
Gryboski,Kevin	R	02	ATL	0.9	17	83%	0%	81%	283	233	293	154	169	306
		03	ATL	0.7	51	75%	0%	69%	246	290	254	355	227	288
Guardado,Eddie	L	01	MIN	1.0	111	68%	86%	92%	202	194	172	270	167	216
		02	MIN	1.0	118	79%	88%	84%	204	235	225	182	263	200
		03	MIN	1.0	129	75%	91%	83%	201	218	193	246	175	291
Guthrie,Mark	L	01	OAK	1.0	79	69%	33%	83%	277	219	220	263	239	241
		02	NYM	0.7	95	80%	50%	85%	232	176	224	115	187	223
		03	CHC	0.7	17	88%	0%	75%	301	222	258	273	280	241
Hackman,Luther	R	01	STL	1.0	49	71%	33%	64%	264	150	208	233	308	172
		02	STL	1.9	31	75%	0%	55%	309	265	351	266	298	279
		03	SD	1.2	39	65%	0%	76%	245	277	234	318	238	277
Hammond,Chris	L	02	ATL	1.2	98	92%	0%	86%	212	175	213	160	174	206
		03	NYY	1.0	114	79%	25%	81%	280	260	265	288	292	257
Harper,Travis	R	02	TAM	2.3	41	67%	50%	47%	306	272	336	271	301	280
		03	TAM	1.5	63	72%	17%	61%	235	276	209	316	287	223
Harville,Chad	R	03	OAK	1.0	18	72%	100%	100%	318	268	288	333	303	288
Hasegawa,Shige	R	01	ANA	1.2	66	70%	0%	59%	246	250	234	276	221	270
		02	SEA	1.3	50	76%	20%	71%	233	244	219	222	284	199
		03	SEA	1.2	57	91%	94%	86%	317	134	250	188	246	221
Hawkins,LaTroy	R	01	MIN	0.8	31	67%	76%	67%	235	331	321	196	276	305
		02	MIN	1.2	133	81%	0%	86%	209	228	258	155	225	211
		03	MIN	1.0	158	85%	25%	81%	229	250	257	171	205	263
Heredia,Felix	L	01	CHC	0.7	28	67%	0%	67%	339	296	287	355	292	333
		02	TOR	1.0	33	78%	0%	67%	216	299	282	189	224	281
		03	NYY	1.3	35	84%	20%	67%	232	223	220	232	233	225

Bullpen Indicators

Pitcher			Tm	IP/g	bpv	S%	Sv%	Eff%	Emp	On	0-15	16-30	vLH	vRH
				BPIs			Results		Runners		Pitch Ct		Platoon	
Herges,Matt	R	01	LA	1.3	57	78%	13%	63%	252	268	280	218	280	243
		02	MON	1.0	37	80%	43%	57%	346	267	321	286	315	300
		03	SF	1.2	95	79%	50%	75%	252	214	246	187	209	249
Hermanson,Dusti	R	02	BOS	1.8	30	59%	0%	60%	362	346	282	405	325	373
		03	SF	2.1	34	74%	17%	38%	280	259	356	179	282	264
Hernandez,Rob	R	01	KC	1.1	50	73%	82%	73%	270	262	249	322	299	230
		02	KC	1.0	78	72%	79%	73%	311	287	302	295	282	317
		03	ATL	0.9	12	80%	0%	77%	248	279	278	179	248	276
Hodges,Trey	R	02	ATL	2.9	54	69%		100%	318	375	400	333	273	371
		03	ATL	1.3	54	74%	0%	58%	245	297	287	278	269	268
Hoffman,Trevor	R	01	SD	1.0	87	78%	93%	87%	216	216	216	226	214	218
		02	SD	1.0	146	76%	93%	83%	250	214	229	267	186	275
		03	SD	1.0	127	89%			333	67	250	0	182	273
Holmes,Darren	R	02	ATL	1.0	133	84%	50%	77%	268	133	222	162	230	198
		03	ATL	0.9	120	72%	0%	80%	242	333	254	357	355	236
Isringhausen,Jas	R	01	OAK	1.1	120	78%	79%	76%	196	212	220	165	240	152
		02	STL	1.1	154	72%	86%	83%	199	200	213	161	247	164
		03	STL	1.1	100	81%	88%	85%	282	131	223	128	254	159
Jimenez,Jose	R	01	COL	1.0	46	74%	77%	79%	278	250	278	240	255	271
		02	COL	1.0	110	73%	87%	73%	218	336	261	232	266	264
		03	FA	1.6	31	68%	87%	65%	312	332	356	306	382	266
Jones,Todd	R	01	MIN	1.0	41	79%	62%	68%	321	303	302	311	325	301
		02	COL	1.0	75	68%	33%	84%	240	303	280	261	233	301
		03	BOS	1.2	39	61%	0%	41%	304	340	343	286	323	323
Julio,Jorge	R	01	BAL	1.2	80	78%	0%	67%	333	259	321	269	290	286
		02	BAL	1.0	77	87%	81%	72%	230	195	217	206	213	214
		03	BAL	1.0	34	76%	82%	72%	291	215	262	242	273	239
Karsay,Steve	R	01	ATL	1.2	119	81%	67%	72%	231	224	204	290	257	203
		02	NYY	1.1	70	77%	75%	80%	299	218	267	202	243	269
Kershner,Jason	L	02	TOR	1.0	37	68%	50%	50%	200	250	148	308	256	192
		03	TOR	1.4	67	74%	0%	71%	227	203	177	316	178	250
Kim,Byung-Hyun	R	01	ARI	1.3	105	76%	83%	78%	151	208	166	207	199	151
		02	ARI	1.2	133	84%	86%	83%	219	196	208	222	220	198
		03	BOS	2.2	97	74%	84%	67%	210	245	204	245	221	227
King,Ray	R	01	MIL	0.7	71	75%	25%	73%	247	236	244	241	210	276
		02	MIL	0.9	72	79%	0%	86%	272	237	257	255	219	280
		03	ATL	0.7	69	71%	0%	81%	131	319	218	194	200	223
Kline,Steve	L	01	STL	0.8	82	85%	90%	88%	197	210	194	250	149	237
		02	STL	0.9	73	74%	75%	91%	281	218	275	156	230	266
		03	STL	0.8	32	73%	43%	74%	250	221	237	262	243	233
Koch,Billy	R	01	TOR	1.0	52	68%	82%	75%	254	278	268	276	289	245
		02	OAK	1.1	84	76%	88%	85%	206	225	207	208	237	196
		03	CHW	1.0	20	69%	73%	65%	280	282	267	302	294	267
Kolb,Danny	R	01	TEX	0.9	46	74%		100%	182	360	238	313	261	257
		02	TEX	0.9	45	71%	25%	40%	222	231	197	250	291	172
		03	MIL	1.1	89	86%	91%	87%	235	203	240	182	209	230
Koplove,Mike	R	02	ARI	1.1	86	69%		94%	217	207	224	131	174	230
		03	ARI	1.2	88	84%	0%	89%	226	222	193	277	224	225
Leskanic,Curtis	R	01	MIL	1.0	56	80%	71%	62%	242	241	245	193	275	220
		03	KC	1.0	86	83%	67%	95%	202	206	205	180	176	228
Levine,Al	R	01	ANA	1.2	40	86%	33%	66%	217	306	261	153	288	229
		02	ANA	1.2	26	75%	71%	76%	265	238	280	200	240	263
		03	KC	1.3	16	85%	25%	61%	245	259	278	221	218	284
Lidge,Brad	R	02	HOU	1.4	63	71%		100%	429	273	462	167	500	227
		03	HOU	1.1	102	71%	17%	81%	180	232	201	202	230	279
Ligtenberg,Kerry	R	01	ATL	1.1	78	79%	50%	50%	246	204	213	243	241	216
		02	ATL	1.3	57	81%		63%	229	185	177	227	200	216
		03	BAL	0.9	81	80%	25%	79%	246	284	246	308	356	206
Lincoln,Mike	R	01	PIT	1.3	71	79%	0%	75%	238	209	247	186	196	240
		02	PIT	1.3	52	82%	0%	65%	285	296	255	333	276	296
		03	PIT	1.0	53	65%	63%	65%	306	246	283	265	333	250
Linebrink,Scott	R	01	HOU	1.2	87	75%			188	167	105	308	67	263
		02	HOU	1.1		60%		100%	321	271	350	200	265	327
		03	SD	1.8	57	79%		82%	311	219	262	237	275	265
Lloyd,Graeme	L	01	MON	0.8	60	69%	33%	75%	281	262	281	235	252	284
		02	FLA	0.9	72	62%	63%	71%	277	319	320	167	326	281
		03	KC	0.9	49	68%	0%	62%	312	355	369	246	338	333
Looper,Braden	R	01	FLA	1.0	53	76%	50%	79%	240	245	269	194	250	236
		02	FLA	1.1	62	76%	81%	79%	238	221	204	276	278	191
		03	FLA	1.1	69	73%	82%	77%	250	277	278	247	280	250
Lopez,Aquilino	R	03	TOR	1.0	77	74%	88%	86%	267	162	236	163	250	186
Lopez,Javier	L	03	COL	0.8	94	71%	50%	91%	246	273	242	370	250	266
Lowe,Sean	R	01	CHW	2.8	61	73%	100%	79%	259	253	236	257	281	233
		02	COL	1.6	66	65%	0%	75%	351	280	315	287	348	294
		03	FA	1.6	14	65%	0%	80%	292	310	308	257	267	333
Lyon,Brandon	R	03	BOS	1.2	73	76%	75%	63%	299	292	314	234	317	276
Macdougal,Mike	R	02	KC	1.5	12	66%		0%	133	188	125	231	176	143
		03	KC	0.9	70	73%	77%	70%	256	277	251	328	230	314
Mahay,Ron	L	03	TEX	1.3	79	74%	0%	67%	200	189	209	138	208	190
Malaska,Mark	L	03	TAM	0.7	86	80%	0%	69%	263	216	243	235	219	250
Manon,Julio	R	03	MON	1.2	19	75%	100%	80%	190	350	211	314	195	290

Bullpen Indicators

Pitcher			Tm	IP/g	bpv	S%	Sv%	Eff%	Emp	On	0-15	16-30	vLH	vRH
				BPIs			Results		Runners		Pitch Ct		Platoon	
Mantei,Matt	R	01	ARI	0.9	82	100%	100%	100%	267	167	263	125	455	62
		02	ARI	0.8	80	71%	0%	57%	222	250	275	67	200	250
		03	ARI	1.1	135	80%	91%	83%	222	132	203	170	155	218
Marte,Damaso	L	02	CHW	0.9	143	75%	83%	89%	157	270	227	135	149	252
		03	CHW	1.1	119	86%	61%	76%	175	195	202	148	168	199
Martin,Tom	L	01	NYM	1.2		48%		100%	238	433	314	545	250	375
		03	LA	0.6	78	74%	0%	91%	174	233	203	152	189	211
Mateo,Julio	R	02	SEA	1.8	75	66%		100%	222	267	342	100	333	167
		03	SEA	1.7	135	76%	100%	100%	237	192	222	211	220	219
Matthews,Mike	L	01	STL	1.8	67	78%	33%	54%	194	283	189	205	133	268
		02	MIL	1.0	64	72%	0%	67%	299	210	306	224	208	292
		03	SD	0.8	54	69%	0%	76%	248	291	288	236	294	254
Mears,Chris	R	03	DET	1.4	36	64%	100%	70%	300	313	281	275	405	221
Mecir,Jim	R	01	OAK	1.2	93	74%	38%	63%	234	226	255	202	195	267
		02	OAK	1.1	64	71%	17%	75%	294	226	267	211	204	297
		03	OAK	0.9	41	63%	50%	79%	321	226	286	257	311	256
Mendoza,Ramiro	R	01	NYY	1.8	91	68%	75%	82%	214	277	241	202	248	236
		02	NYY	1.5	100	75%	50%	75%	277	273	282	289	261	286
		03	BOS	1.8	19	63%	0%	50%	311	391	353	341	320	372
Mercado,Hector	L	01	CIN	1.0	69	77%	0%	67%	255	279	254	318	287	252
		02	PHI	1.3	77	67%		71%	179	263	183	342	125	252
		03	PHI	1.4	-7	72%	50%	50%	316	182	258	333	158	288
Mercker,Kent	L	02	COL	0.8	1	72%	0%	75%	319	278	309	279	209	350
		03	ATL	0.8	53	92%	20%	67%	297	157	252	189	222	230
Mesa,Jose	R	01	PHI	1.0	102	83%	91%	87%	303	180	264	182	236	255
		02	PHI	1.0	67	80%	83%	77%	233	230	248	194	225	237
		03	PHI	1.0	34	63%	86%	74%	270	322	297	286	213	349
Miceli,Dan	R	01	2TM	0.9	80	70%	25%	58%	238	295	241	359	361	196
		03	HOU	1.2	54	83%	50%	62%	242	198	218	212	194	244
Miller,Trever	L	03	TOR	0.7	46	70%	80%	88%	283	187	241	195	226	237
Mota,Guillermo	R	01	MON	0.9	25	67%	0%	68%	252	294	310	128	310	248
		02	LA	1.4	75	65%	0%	56%	223	183	193	205	188	213
		03	LA	1.4	131	84%	33%	80%	189	238	232	176	181	220
Munro,Peter	R	03	HOU	1.4	11	74%	0%	55%	274	315	288	265	293	295
Myers,Mike	L	01	COL	0.6	71	74%	0%	71%	235	216	244	105	231	216
		02	ARI	0.5	70	70%	44%	76%	281	269	269	333	241	317
		03	ARI	0.6	20	65%	0%	60%	258	266	261	250	237	290
Nakamura,Mike	R	03	MIN	1.0	112	61%	100%	100%	407	281	361	250	385	303
Nathan,Joe	R	03	SF	1.0	101	75%	0%	82%	179	195	164	233	276	136
Nelson,Jeff	R	01	SEA	0.9	116	76%	80%	89%	122	153	125	158	167	119
		02	SEA	1.1	89	73%	50%	81%	210	232	258	169	224	218
		03	NYY	0.8	112	73%	57%	76%	191	313	248	170	273	233
Nen,Robb	R	01	SF	1.0	149	73%	87%	80%	182	238	220	138	240	162
		02	SF	1.1	150	80%	84%	83%	232	232	214	294	224	242
Neu,Mike	R	03	OAK	1.3	26	78%	100%	100%	274	250	247	351	214	295
Norton,Phil	L	03	CIN	0.9	55	67%		100%	156	154	195	63	214	100
Oropesa,Eddie	L	01	PHI	0.6	41	72%	0%	88%	296	190	245	200	156	297
		02	ARI	0.8	-16	52%	0%	90%	283	423	325	320	340	356
		03	ARI	0.8	60	65%		81%	200	308	264	229	206	294
Orosco,Jesse	L	01	LA	0.5	84	81%	0%	77%	261	289	281	250	275	300
		02	LA	0.5	49	84%	100%	90%	302	177	245	91	238	214
		03	MIN	0.5	35	57%	50%	79%	322	282	308	263	231	390
Osuna,Antonio	R	02	CHW	1.1	104	69%	79%	85%	223	278	294	224	250	250
		03	NYY	1.0	83	76%	0%	65%	294	268	309	254	305	266
Painter,Lance	L	01	2TM	1.3	-22	71%		50%	300	333	277	364	360	286
		03	STL	0.8	27	62%	0%	71%	270	219	245	267	290	211
Patterson,Danny	R	01	DET	1.1	64	75%	20%	73%	315	238	244	356	327	231
		03	DET	0.9	158	61%	100%	100%	108	379	192	357	176	281
Percival,Troy	R	01	ANA	1.0	154	74%	93%	90%	195	174	182	203	176	202
		02	ANA	1.0	112	88%	91%	90%	202	170	231	91	247	138
		03	ANA	0.9	71	76%	89%	79%	192	175	200	167	165	205
Plesac,Dan	L	01	TOR	0.7	125	74%	50%	78%	210	205	220	152	184	234
		02	PHI	0.6	73	72%	25%	79%	200	200	216	105	120	300
		03	PHI	0.6	117	81%	50%	82%	192	292	261	0	227	235
Politte,Cliff	R	02	TOR	1.1	101	69%	25%	83%	178	257	211	183	272	159
		03	TOR	0.9	37	66%	67%	66%	284	253	279	241	287	250
Quantrill,Paul	L	01	TOR	1.0	131	76%	22%	79%	310	233	287	257	355	232
		02	LA	0.9	83	79%	33%	87%	292	237	283	233	254	275
		03	LA	0.9	104	82%	20%	78%	244	204	211	283	198	243
Raggio,Brady	R	03	ARI	0.8	39	64%	100%	100%	273	300	316	293	333	273
Reed,Steve	R	01	ATL	0.8	65	75%	50%	79%	279	179	267	143	181	259
		02	NYM	1.1	132	79%	25%	71%	279	179	267	143	181	259
		03	COL	0.9	32	82%	0%	79%	298	219	269	207	374	165
Reith,Brian	R	03	CIN	1.5	20	78%	100%	70%	246	284	297	247	206	287
Reitsma,Chris	R	03	CIN	1.5	54	73%	67%	69%	277	289	291	238	298	270
Remlinger,Mike	L	01	ATL	1.0	130	83%	20%	83%	256	203	246	211	322	194
		02	ATL	0.9	108	84%	0%	82%	210	186	211	175	235	184
		03	CHC	1.0	72	79%		82%	207	215	242	147	263	180
Rhodes,Arthur	R	01	SEA	1.0	215	85%	43%	91%	174	208	151	321	198	179
		02	SEA	1.1	203	74%	29%	81%	163	220	182	211	158	215
		03	SEA	0.8	91	69%	50%	80%	230	280	261	250	269	243

Bullpen Indicators

				BPIs			Results		Runners		Pitch Ct		Platoon	
Pitcher			Tm	IP/g	bpv	S%	Sv%	Eff%	Emp	On	0-15	16-30	vLH	vRH
Riedling,John	R	01	CIN	1.1	79	77%	33%	70%	230	140	192	184	185	188
		02	CIN	1.4	52	81%		71%	250	213	226	259	320	163
		03	CIN	1.8	45	67%	25%	60%	221	328	247	184	245	286
Rincon,Juan	R	01	MIN	1.4	53	66%			364	273	333	250	500	250
		02	MIN	2.9	42	66%	0%	0%	397	306	346	292	283	415
		03	MIN	1.5	66	72%	0%	59%	222	242	223	214	222	239
Rincon,Ricardo	R	01	CLE	0.8	96	77%	50%	84%	269	172	224	222	213	233
		02	OAK	0.8	153	56%	20%	78%	219	242	199	349	203	267
		03	OAK	0.9	50	78%	0%	75%	245	213	254	163	200	250
Riske,David	R	01	CLE	1.0	66	91%	100%	100%	244	179	273	125	143	232
		02	CLE	1.0	62	71%	100%	80%	228	283	268	226	253	259
		03	CLE	1.1	132	84%	62%	79%	208	282	195	213	145	241
Rivera,Mariano	L	01	NYY	1.1	206	76%	88%	81%	191	235	200	238	187	229
		02	NYY	1.0	127	74%	88%	79%	185	225	226	156	181	225
		03	NYY	1.1	187	85%	87%	85%	258	212	268	138	197	283
Roberts,Grant	R	01	NYM	1.6	76	70%	0%	67%	222	261	239	219	303	209
		02	NYM	1.3	67	86%		75%	277	224	269	196	261	248
		03	NYM	1.1	111	64%	100%	63%	204	360	232	353	231	271
Rodney,Fernando	R	02	DET	0.9	110	66%	0%	13%	400	304	347	333	241	383
		03	DET	1.1	77	64%	50%	54%	180	377	292	300	345	246
Rodriguez,Felix	R	01	SF	1.0	133	87%	0%	91%	199	172	189	188	150	213
		02	SF	1.0	79	65%	0%	73%	168	271	231	175	234	196
		03	SF	0.9	55	81%	67%	91%	278	239	250	278	264	255
Rodriguez,Franci	R	02	ANA	1.1	172	100%			333	0	83	250	286	91
		03	ANA	1.5	97	77%	33%	71%	165	183	174	182	186	156
Rodriguez,Rich	R	01	CLE	0.7	69	71%	0%	71%	250	289	256	370	189	346
		02	TEX	0.5	46	63%	33%	67%	320	176	255	0	214	294
Romero,J.C.	L	02	MIN	1.0	95	85%	20%	88%	228	199	263	82	216	211
		03	MIN	0.9	33	72%	0%	86%	232	305	306	175	214	314
Roney,Matt	R	03	DET	2.2	1	67%	0%	39%	273	249	258	238	297	232
Ryan,B.J.	L	01	BAL	0.9	65	73%	50%	75%	194	273	203	222	198	261
		02	BAL	0.9	58	70%	50%	88%	227	252	253	182	192	283
		03	BAL	0.7	116	74%	0%	88%	218	234	239	222	186	273
Saarloos,Kirk	R	03	HOU	1.4	81	66%		86%	274	308	283	288	275	299
Sadler,Carl	L	02	CLE	0.8	86	67%	0%	67%	200	222	232	154	205	219
		03	CLE	0.5	95	88%		100%	325	286	286	375	333	278
Santiago,Jose	R	01	PHI	1.3	56	66%	0%	62%	279	306	299	252	352	252
		02	PHI	1.1	37	56%	0%	71%	296	284	287	294	304	282
		03	CLE	1.2	28	84%	0%	50%	290	306	303	298	353	278
Sasaki,Kazuhiro	R	01	SEA	1.0	167	66%	87%	80%	187	208	195	213	218	168
		02	SEA	1.0	131	81%	82%	76%	215	179	207	190	207	194
		03	SEA	0.9	76	70%	71%	65%	281	206	300	91	239	250
Sauerbeck,Scott	L	01	PIT	0.9	90	64%	50%	85%	208	308	241	328	272	248
		02	PIT	0.8	107	84%		89%	241	200	220	226	147	273
		03	BOS	0.7	42	71%	0%	68%	159	302	219	239	192	257
Schoenewels,S	L	02	ANA	2.2	22	69%	25%	66%	238	297	244	188	202	290
		03	CHW	1.1	104	66%	0%	64%	223	288	286	188	227	275
Service,Scott	R	03	FA	1.0	121	67%	50%	57%	274	290	280	275	327	250
Shields,Scot	R	02	ANA	1.7	57	83%		73%	198	172	198	160	184	191
		03	ANA	3.4	91	79%	100%	60%	243	252	223	215	229	264
Shiell,Jason	R	02	SD	0.4	74	60%			500	833	571	1000	600	800
		03	BOS	1.4	30	78%	50%	75%	256	250	250	212	195	300
Shouse,Brian	L	02	KC	0.6	74	66%		100%	250	265	280	125	276	241
		03	TEX	1.0	100	73%	100%	92%	246	289	259	298	195	364
Shuey,Paul	R	01	CLE	1.2	124	79%	40%	73%	293	218	298	187	280	225
		02	LA	1.0	89	74%	20%	82%	214	228	247	160	226	217
		03	LA	1.1	72	78%	0%	76%	199	222	223	197	224	193
Silva,Carlos	R	02	PHI	1.2	60	75%	20%	78%	304	255	330	242	292	276
		03	PHI	1.4	37	70%	33%	73%	276	283	272	276	300	266
Smoltz,John	R	01	ATL	1.6	155	73%	91%	82%	238	238	196	229	263	211
		02	ATL	1.1	135	68%	93%	91%	167	261	183	264	213	199
		03	ATL	1.0	268	89%	92%	88%	226	169	238	83	189	218
Soriano,Rafael	R	02	SEA	4.7	40	70%	100%	25%	234	262	281	286	297	179
		03	SEA	1.3	204	83%	50%	90%	156	169	135	206	185	135
Sparks,Steve	R	03	OAK	2.1	29	68%	50%	20%	251	302	226	252	286	270
Speier,Justin	R	01	COL	1.4	74	67%	0%	71%	242	254	283	202	247	247
		02	COL	1.0	67	66%	25%	86%	209	225	216	227	240	197
		03	COL	1.0	75	74%	75%	86%	276	234	250	291	273	245
Spooneybarger,T	R	02	ATL	1.0	49	82%	100%	100%	207	205	228	152	150	234
		03	FLA	1.3	117	51%	0%	70%	133	318	180	234	152	224
Springer,Russ	R	03	STL	1.0	-52	53%	0%	75%	174	458	260	316	240	289
Spurling,Chris	R	03	DET	1.2	39	66%	50%	60%	286	247	247	280	352	200
Stanton,Mike	L	01	NYY	1.1	101	82%	0%	86%	260	267	239	329	283	251
		02	NYY	1.0	57	77%	67%	88%	283	229	260	274	268	247
		03	NYM	0.9	52	66%	71%	65%	194	254	208	244	206	226
Stechschulte,G	R	01	STL	1.0	39	78%	75%	74%	286	260	272	296	284	268
		02	STL	1.1	33	68%	0%	73%	169	320	173	346	263	221
Stewart,Scott	L	01	MON	0.8	90	71%	75%	88%	236	250	215	344	286	215
		02	MON	1.0	118	73%	89%	90%	180	245	205	196	159	235
		03	MON	0.8	53	77%	0%	89%	349	264	302	333	283	318

Bullpen Indicators

				BPIs			Results		Runners		Pitch Ct		Platoon	
Pitcher			Tm	IP/g	bpv	S%	Sv%	Eff%	Emp	On	0-15	16-30	vLH	vRH
Stone,Ricky	R	02	HOU	1.0	54	79%	50%	80%	252	281	250	305	288	258
		03	HOU	1.3	34	76%	100%	78%	259	238	239	267	290	221
Strickland,Scott	R	01	MON	1.1	77	80%	75%	72%	230	213	256	181	274	189
		02	NYM	1.0	76	77%	33%	64%	256	212	244	217	313	188
		03	NYM	1.1	71	84%	0%	57%	216	222	283	115	222	217
Sullivan,Scott	R	01	CIN	1.3	73	77%	0%	87%	237	250	232	273	252	237
		02	CIN	1.1	54	65%	33%	79%	279	311	293	255	357	253
		03	CHW	1.0	68	73%	0%	95%	183	228	217	190	238	187
Tam,Jeff	R	01	OAK	1.1	60	77%	50%	81%	257	242	253	186	247	251
		02	OAK	1.0	23	69%	0%	40%	273	385	360	277	300	352
		03	FA	1.0	14	71%	50%	58%	350	286	311	327	303	319
Tavarez,Julian	R	03	PIT	1.3	62	67%	79%	79%	188	304	254	263	292	215
Tejera,Michael	L	02	FLA	3.0	39	72%	33%	63%	270	267	190	297	228	280
		03	FLA	1.6	55	68%	100%	71%	233	306	193	304	392	224
Timlin,Mike	R	01	STL	1.1	71	70%	43%	68%	247	317	248	382	319	257
		02	PHI	1.3	107	69%	0%	71%	218	198	213	189	208	214
		03	BOS	1.2	175	71%	33%	76%	217	268	214	313	287	198
Torres,Salomon	R	03	PIT	3.0	41	70%	67%	71%	264	293	252	226	307	252
Tucker,T.J.	R	02	MON	1.1	41	76%	57%	82%	354	232	314	232	269	300
		03	MON	1.8	59	67%	0%	50%	254	311	274	274	254	294
Urbina,Ugueth	R	01	BOS	1.0	123	75%	86%	83%	212	257	242	217	278	196
		02	BOS	1.0	118	79%	87%	77%	211	184	199	178	257	143
		03	FLA	1.1	93	80%	84%	82%	212	195	228	147	182	229
Valverde,Jose	R	03	ARI	0.9	130	83%	91%	91%	77	202	123	176	169	112
Veres,Dave	R	01	STL	0.9	54	79%	79%	81%	241	219	240	228	237	229
		02	STL	1.2	50	79%	50%	68%	234	210	255	163	190	246
		03	CHC	1.0	127	65%	50%	78%	283	297	303	273	174	359
Villafuerte,Brand	R	02	SD	1.0	77	92%	100%	83%	275	227	238	290	286	213
		03	SD	1.3	24	79%	40%	44%	221	282	319	120	200	284
Villarreal,Oscar	R	03	ARI	1.1	72	82%	0%	65%	195	251	248	181	252	204
Vizcaino,Luis	R	01	OAK	1.0	46	74%	100%	86%	264	268	230	341	241	282
		02	MIL	1.1	104	73%	83%	88%	197	185	209	149	225	170
		03	MIL	0.8	38	62%	0%	59%	262	264	261	278	253	269
Wagner,Billy	L	01	HOU	1.0	147	76%	95%	85%	182	224	207	182	261	182
		02	HOU	1.1	141	79%	85%	83%	187	213	207	167	180	201
		03	HOU	1.1	160	87%	94%	87%	170	167	202	86	216	154
Wagner,Ryan	R	03	CIN	1.2	93	91%	0%	89%	200	143	209	80	240	140
Walker,Jamie	L	02	DET	0.8	107	72%	25%	64%	205	193	203	184	202	194
		03	DET	0.8	66	78%	43%	73%	264	229	247	263	212	276
Weathers,David	R	01	CHC	1.1	76	82%	40%	69%	291	144	222	183	213	218
		02	NYM	1.1	63	81%	0%	75%	283	208	299	122	267	232
		03	NYM	1.1	70	80%	78%	81%	292	237	319	197	239	276
Weber,Ben	R	01	ANA	1.2	46	76%	0%	80%	254	248	249	234	210	278
		02	ANA	1.2	68	80%	64%	84%	253	244	251	268	243	253
		03	ANA	1.3	58	83%	0%	89%	284	266	289	247	268	282
Wellemeyer,Todd	R	03	CHC	1.8	41	62%	100%	67%	164	366	282	233	219	257
Wendell,Turk	R	01	2TM	1.0	36	75%	33%	65%	222	280	270	179	295	222
		03	PHI	1.1	26	76%	20%	63%	226	243	241	227	294	199
Wheeler,Dan	R	01	TAM	1.4	21	56%		100%	378	372	476	300	364	389
		03	NYM	1.5	56	75%	67%	43%	245	271	258	243	217	274
White,Gabe	L	01	COL	1.0	7	63%	0%	50%	249	317	262	293	269	271
		02	CIN	0.9	127	73%	0%	93%	214	269	233	256	202	267
		03	NYY	1.0	82	69%	0%	85%	282	222	238	306	247	255
White,Rick	R	01	NYM	1.3	84	72%	50%	70%	235	285	235	333	271	249
		02	STL	1.0	83	64%	0%	72%	311	200	267	266	295	245
		03	HOU	1.4	49	63%	100%	75%	291	274	257	287	227	324
Wickman,Bob	R	01	CLE	1.0	150	80%	91%	93%	265	206	252	191	279	205
		02	CLE	1.0	109	71%	91%	81%	299	268	311	185	275	294
Williamson,Scott	R	02	CIN	1.2	106	75%	67%	70%	174	190	207	141	198	170
		03	BOS	0.9	83	73%	75%	74%	208	248	263	123	339	313
Williams,Mike	R	01	HOU	1.0	49	79%	88%	82%	283	206	269	169	256	233
		02	PIT	1.0	64	80%	92%	83%	254	206	241	213	281	180
		03	PHI	0.9	27	63%	80%	69%	232	305	273	263	275	267
Witasick,Jay	R	01	NYY	1.3	117	80%	25%	79%	229	274	276	260	288	234
		02	SF	1.6	97	80%		100%	264	192	237	191	228	238
		03	SD	1.0	51	72%	29%	59%	211	271	269	174	292	215
Worrell,Tim	R	01	SF	1.1	76	74%	0%	65%	255	223	264	179	248	234
		02	SF	0.9	80	82%	0%	91%	227	198	209	220	204	218
		03	SF	1.0	84	79%	84%	80%	245	247	257	220	241	250
Wright,Jaret	R	02	CLE	2.3	23	48%		40%	414	444	529	519	458	109
		03	ATL	1.1	29	62%	40%	50%	323	333	350	297	361	310
Wunsch,Kelly	L	01	CHW	0.7	33	42%	0%	63%	190	302	274	83	262	233
		02	CHW	0.6	39	79%	0%	85%	204	250	253	71	208	268
		03	CHW	0.8	81	76%		100%	135	143	159	103	127	153
Yan,Esteban	R	01	TAM	1.2	158	71%	71%	63%	285	230	282	219	272	252
		02	TAM	1.3	44	74%	70%	62%	265	252	280	224	273	246
		03	FA	1.2	36	64%	100%	88%	273	340	346	338	309	307
Zambrano,Victor	R	01	TAM	1.4	112	76%	33%	68%	225	167	252	101	205	198
		02	TAM	2.7	18	68%	33%	60%	289	268	235	303	292	266
Zimmerman,Jeff	R	01	TEX	1.1	133	83%	90%	84%	193	190	215	138	220	163

Off-Season Injury Report

Jose Acevedo (RHP, CIN, fractured right foot) has the green light and will be ready by Opening Day, though rusty.

Terry Adams (RHP, PHI, elbow bone spurs) had surgery in late October and will likely begin the year on the DL.

Kurt Ainsworth (RHP, BAL, stress fracture in his right shoulder blade): Look for a tentative spring.

Armando Almanza (LHP, FLA, elbow surgery): A slow start is anticipated and he should be left behind in Florida for a couple of weeks when camp breaks.

Kevin Appier's (RHP, KC, torn flexor tendon) surgery was successful. He'll be rusty early on but will improve as the season moves along.

Tony Armas Jr. (RHP, MON, labrum and rotator cuff surgery) was throwing by the end of the season but wasn't strong enough for activation. He'll be 10 months post surgery in spring training and very close to 100%.

Miguel Asencio (RHP, KC, elbow bone chips) will be rusty in the spring, but has a good chance to record at least a half of a productive season, if not more.

Pedro Astacio's (RHP, NYM, torn labrum). Surgery in June should allow him enough time to recover completely when pitchers report to camp.

David Bell (3B, PHI, back) is attempting a rehab program to rebuild the strength in his back. His medical situation makes him a big risk entering 2004.

Kris Benson (RHP, PIT, elbow irritation) was shut down in August for about six weeks, then a rehab program was started. The Pirates believe he'll be ready for spring training, but he's an injury risk this season.

Jason Bere (RHP, CLE, frayed labrum and rotator cuff): June surgery corrected the problem but a long rehab is needed. Could begin the year on the DL.

Milton Bradley's (OF, CLE, herniated disc) problem has cleared up with a rehab program. He'll be tentative early on but at full strength (and confidence) by May.

Ellis Burks (DH, FA, damaged ulnar nerve) responded nicely to surgery and all of the feeling (and strength) has returned to his lower right arm.

Marlon Byrd's (OF, PHI, labrum tear) surgery was a success. He's expected to be watched closely early in spring training but will be ready for the start of the season.

Chris Carpenter (RHP, STL, shoulder) underwent arthroscopic surgery to remove scar tissue. Risky for 2004.

Shawn Chacon (RHP, COL, elbow tendinitis) didn't need surgery and is expected to be ready for April, but his control might not be.

Greg Colbrunn (OF, SEA, wrist tendon) had two surgeries and will likely start in extended spring training.

Ryan Dempster (RHP, CIN): Tommy John surgery will keep him out till 2004.

Brendan Donnelly (RHP, ANA, torn cartilage in knee, bone chips in pitching elbow) had surgery in September. Look for a slow start.

Darren Dreifort (RHP, LA, medial collateral ligament, damaged hip cartilage) has had two surgeries in the last few months.. He's a huge injury risk — avoid!

Darin Erstad (OF, ANA, hamstring): No surgery is planned, rather an extensive rehab. This injury may become chronic, making him a higher injury risk in 2004.

Bobby Estalella (C, COL, elbow bone chips) is a good candidate to stay behind in extended spring training and start the year on the DL.

Cliff Floyd (OF, NYM, Achilles tendon) had surgery in August and should be ready for the start of the season.

Brad Fullmer's (DH, ANA, ruptured patellar tendon): His early 2004 season is cloudy due to the injury.

Jason Giambi (1B, NYY, sore knee) was scheduled to have surgery this fall after the playoffs. This is an impact injury that may curtail some of his production.

Jeremy Giambi (DH, BOS, torn shoulder ligament) could get off to a slow start this spring as he recovers.

Troy Glaus' (3B, ANA, frayed labrum) will rely on an extensive rehab program to recover. He's at risk to struggle early on or begin the year on the disabled list.

Juan Gonzalez' (OF, TEX, torn right calf muscle) is expected to heal by spring training and without surgery. That's his agent's line; his history hints at more problems.

Shawn Green (OF, LA, shoulder surgery) will be back for spring training and most of his shoulder strength should return by May-June.

Ben Grieve (OF, TAM, rib surgery) had a blot clot that ended his season. He's got the green light and there isn't any reason to believe he won't be 100% in spring training.

Ken Griffey Jr. (OF, CIN, torn ankle ligament, torn labrum and rotator cuff): At best, he'll play in April and be rusty. More likely May. But when will he get hurt again?

Jose Guillen's (OF, OAK, fractured hamate bone) power numbers will drop some in 2004 due to the surgery.

Ricky Gutierrez' (SS, CLE, spinal cord compression) 2004 season and career is in doubt. Kudos for coming back this far, but he might not improve enough to play again .

Jerry Hairston (2B, BALT, fractured right foot) is expected to be 100% in spring training.

Carlos Hernandez (LHP, HOU, torn labrum and rotator cuff): By the end of the 2003 season, he was throwing breaking balls and reporting no discomfort. He'll be 100% for spring training.

Orlando Hernandez (RHP, MON, rotator cuff tear): Barring any setbacks, the Expos believe he'll be game ready by Opening Day.

Runelvys Hernandez (RHP, KC) had Tommy John surgery in September and is gone for the year.

Bobby Hill (2B, PIT, back): Pittsburgh did not want to risk serious injury by playing him late in the season. If Hill doesn't have any disc involvement, then he shouldn't have any problems securing a job in 2004.

Eric Hinske (3B, TOR, fractured right hand) is healed and in the middle of a full rehab program. The hand will be 100% at the start of spring training.

Kevin Jarvis (RHP, SD, flexor tendon) had surgery in 2002 but has battled setbacks and several cases of tendinitis. No signs his elbow is 100%. Avoid on draft day.

Geoff Jenkins (OF, MIL, fractured thumb): MIL expects him to be ready for the start of spring training though he could struggle gripping a bat early on.

Derek Jeter (SS, NYY, shoulder) won't need more surgery, just a strong rehab program. The shoulder is expected to be 100% by the start of spring training.

Brian Jordan's (OF, LA, left patellar tendon) rehab is right on schedule and he'll be ready for spring training. How well the knee holds up is a lingering question.

Steve Karsay (RHP, NYY, rotator cuff): Because he had surgery back in May, it will be long enough recovery that his only problem is rust this spring.

Austin Kearns (OF, CIN, rotator cuff): CIN believes he'll be game ready for the start of the season.

Ryan Klesko (OF, SD, shoulder surgery) started lifting weights in November and is expected to be close to 100% in spring training.

Corey Koskie (3B, MIN, wrist): A slow start is almost a given due to a late surgery date.

Brandon Larson (3B, CIN, torn labrum): Look for a slow start in spring training.

Matt Lawton (OF, CLE, torn knee cartilage, hand tendon) is healing slightly ahead of schedule and should avoid starting the year on the disabled list.

Cory Lidle (RHP, TOR, strained right groin): Groin injuries tend to re-occur so he isn't out of the woods in '04.

Kevin Mench (OF, TEX, fractured left wrist): TEX is not happy he isn't planning on playing winter ball. A slow start is almost assured.

Doug Mientkiewicz (1B, MIN, wrist): Look for a slow start as he regains strength in the wrist and hand.

Bengie Molina (C, ANA, fractured forearm) had surgery in Sept. and is expected to be ready for spring training.

Melvin Mora (OF, BAL, torn knee ligament): Look for a slow start early in the season.

Mark Mulder (LHP, OAK, thigh bone fracture): This is a very rare injury in athletes and a prognosis is difficult. It might curtail his career or we may never hear about it again. A tough call.

Eric Munson (3B, DET, fractured left thumb) will be ready for the start of spring training.

Robb Nen (RHP, SF, rotator cuff surgery) has had three surgeries in six months. Avoid him no matter how desperate you are for a closer in 2004.

Nick Neugebauer (RHP, MIL, shoulder) needed his second operation in less than two years. No value for 2004 as he recovers from more surgery.

Rey Ordonez (SS, TAM, torn knee ligament) is expected to be close to 100% by spring training.

Roy Oswalt (RHP, HOU, groin muscle injury): The hope is he'll avoid a nagging injury that has plagued him off and on since 2001.

Dean Palmer (3B, DET, neck, back): Career over?

Danny Patterson (RHP, DET, elbow) had surgery in 2002 and finished the 2003 campaign with more elbow pain. A high injury risk candidate this season.

Troy Percival (RHP, ANA, degenerative hip condition) has talked about retiring soon but will give it a go this year.

Rick Reed (RHP, MIN, herniated disc) avoided surgery this off-season but the back ailment will return in 2004 if his personal history is any indication.

Pokey Reese (2B, PIT, torn thumb tendon): Extra rehab time should allow him to completely recover in time for spring training and the opening of the season.

Desi Relaford (UT, KC, torn wrist ligament): KC expects him to be 100% by the end of spring training.

Jose Reyes' (SS, NYM, sprained ankle) injury will cause him to miss winter ball. Five months should be enough time for it to heal unless there is more damage than is being reported. His status is in question until spring training starts.

Chris Richard (OF, COL, torn labrum): COL expects him to be 100% recovered at the start of spring training.

Todd Ritchie (RHP, MIL, rotator cuff) will get off to a slow start this season due to a long rehab.

Ricardo Rodriguez (RHP, TEX, right hip, torn labrum): Look for a slow start to his 2004 season, maybe even landing in extended spring training.

Johan Santana (LHP, MIN, elbow bone spur). MIN plans to watch him closely this spring but expects him to be at full strength by the end of April.

Kaz Sasaki (RHP, SEA, elbow bone spurs): Will his velocity return? It should, but it's not a given that it will. There might be too many miles on that elbow.

Jason Schmidt (RHP, SF, elbow surgery) is expected to be ready for spring training, but one has to wonder since the surgery took place so late in the year. Caution needed here.

John Smoltz (RHP, ATL, elbow surgery) ATL indicates he'll be ready for the start of spring training. Smoltz stated if he needs one more surgery on his right arm, he'll retire.

Kyle Snyder (RHP, KC, rotator cuff). Cross him off for the first quarter, maybe half of the 2004 season.

Tim Spooneybarger (RHP, FLA) had Tommy John surgery and is out until 2005.

A.J. Burnett (RHP, FLA) had Tommy John surgery in April. While he'll return this season, pitchers coming off TJ surgery are not good investments in their first season back.

Gene Stechschulte (RHP, STL, frayed labrum) suffered a couple of setbacks during his rehab but is on course now.

Mike Sweeney (1B, KC, disc) is an injury risk on draft day. While the ailment has cleared up, he could very well suffer a relapse. Bid accordingly.

Fernando Tatis (3B, MON, chest injury): His status is currently up in the air.

Reggie Taylor (OF, CIN, torn labrum) should be close to 100% by the end of April.

Omar Vizquel (SS, CLE, knee surgery) will begin the year slowly. Forget about him for stolen bases.

Larry Walker (OF, COL, damaged labrum) had his left knee scoped and cartilage removed. As usual, he will start slow due to the rehab work. A DL stint is possible.

Bob Wickman (RHP, CLE) had Tommy John surgery in 2002 and was throwing with good velocity late in the year. Should begin slow but a second half surge is possible .

Jeff Zimmerman (RHP, TEX) had Tommy John surgery in 2002 and developed nerve damage during his comeback. He's a huge injury risk in 2004.

IV.
MINOR
LEAGUES

Top Prospects for 2004

For many minor leaguers that have potential to make an impact in the majors in 2004, a narrow focus on statistics is often inadequate to describe their skills and upside.

Sometimes a player's stats will be distorted by the fact that, in a given year, their organization has them focus on a particular element of their game to the exclusion of others. For instance, a pitcher that has already proven the capabilities of his fastball will spend a year working on an off-speed pitch.

And sometimes a player's body type lends itself to future development in an area that the statistics don't reveal early on. For instance, a batter might be viewed as a long-term power threat "once he fills out" but you'd never think he could even reach the warning track by a scan of his yearly home run totals.

For these reasons, it's comforting to know that there are many astute baseball people who can identify a player's true skills and put some perspective on what the statistics seem to say. Some of these people become baseball scouts (but as it turns out, only some baseball scouts actually have this ability), and those that are not allowed into this exclusive network become writers and analysts.

We are fortunate that these analysts exist. They are often far more objective than people who are actually paid to scout for major league clubs. They don't have to follow the often archaic rules that organizations rely on. The growing crop of intelligent minor league analysts would actually consider a right-handed pitcher under 6 feet tall as a player worth pursuing, a possibility that 80% of the major clubs would never even entertain.

And I am personally fortunate that one of these analysts writes for Baseball HQ and has been contributing to this book for the past eight years. Deric McKamey is an amazing repository of information. But more than that, he knows talent.

Over the next six pages, Deric will introduce you to 54 of the names you need to tuck away for 2004. It is important to note that these are players expected to hit the majors this coming year, and does not necessarily represent the prospects with the best long-term upside overall. There are still players in the lower minors that could become bigger names, but will not likely see the majors until 2005 at the earliest. You'll be able to find information on those players at Baseball HQ over the winter. In fact, Deric's annual organizational reports are online at this very moment.

The following section is a minor league extension of the player boxes that appear in the main part of the book. As such, the player boxes themselves will be familiar to you. They contain much of the same information as those for the major league players. Some statistical gauges have been omitted as they are not relevant to an evaluation of prospects, such as Rotisserie values. Other data, like RH/LH splits, were just not available. The number to the left of each player box is his relative rank among the batters and the pitchers.

We have listed a preliminary projection for each player. These are all highly speculative and represent a most likely scenario if three conditions occur in 2004:

1. They make their respective teams.
2. They get the playing time we expect.
3. They overcome the mental hurdle of jumping to the majors and perform at the level they are probably capable of as a first year player.

These unknowns can turn the hottest of prospects into a non-entity. Just ask Brandon Phillips. As such, you'll note that there is no Forecast Risk listed for any of these players. It is safe to assume that all of them — all essentially unproven — are high risks.

The snapshot section of each player box contains some new information that helps put each player's potential into better perspective. The following abbreviations pertain to each player's ability, as of the moment, and are subjective assessments.

BATTERS

PWR: The ability to hit for power
SPD: Speed and baserunning ability
BAVG: The ability to hit for batting average and judge the strike zone.
DEF: Overall defense, which includes range, hands, throwing arm and agility. While Rotisserie types might not have direct interest in defense, simulation players certainly do, and Deric often notes that defense is what gets a player to the majors (and offense is what keeps him there). This alone can explain why apparently solid minor league hitters, like Jack Cust, might never get a legitimate chance that many casual observers think they rightfully deserve.

PITCHERS

VEL: Velocity of a pitcher's fastball, with movement factored in slightly
BRE: Quality of breaking pitch(es)
CHG: Ability to change speeds, along with the quality of change-up
PIT: Pitchability. This is the mental aspect of the game, a pitcher's ability to work hitters, set up pitches, establish command, and a pitcher's level of poise.

15 Amezaga,Alfredo

Pos SS
Bats B
Age 26 Pre-Peak
PWR +
SPD + + + + +
BAVG +
DEF + + + +

Year	Lev	Tm	AB	R	H	HR	RBI	SB	Avg	OB	Slg	OPS	bb%	ct%	Eye	PX	SX	RC/G	BPV
2001	aa	ANA	263	48	81	3	17	23	308	361	414	776	8	80	0.42	62	183	5.06	38
2002	aaa	ANA	518	77	130	6	51	23	251	311	361	672	8	81	0.45	69	149	3.82	23
2002	MLB	ANA	13	3	7	0	2	1	538	538	692	1231	0	92	0.00	133		21.79	137
2003	aaa	ANA	317	55	110	3	45	14	347	386	470	856	6	88	0.51	83	147	6.93	62
2003	MLB	ANA	105	15	22	2	7	2	210	272	333	605	8	78	0.39	71	153	2.93	8
2002	MLE		518	58	113	5	39	17	218	266	305	571	6	86	0.46	58	108	2.50	7
2003	MLE		317	44	98	2	36	11	309	342	404	746	5	91	0.53	67	109	4.80	43
2004	Projection		350	52	92	3	37	15	263	308	364	672	6	86	0.48	68	134	3.72	27

Strong indications are that he cannot hit MLB pitching, but has enough secondary skills to be a useful utilityman. His defense is solid. Speed is disruptive and could steal plenty of bases, even in limited AB.

20 Atkins,Garrett

Pos 3B
Bats R
Age 24 Growth
PWR + +
SPD +
BAVG + + + +
DEF +

Year	Lev	Tm	AB	R	H	HR	RBI	SB	Avg	OB	Slg	OPS	bb%	ct%	Eye	PX	SX	RC/G	BPV
2000	a	COL	251	34	76	7	47	2	303	409	434	843	15	81	0.94	84	40	7.25	55
2001	a	COL	465	70	151	5	67	6	325	417	471	888	14	79	0.76	104	94	7.94	69
2002	aa	COL	510	71	138	12	61	6	271	346	406	752	10	85	0.77	86	78	5.11	43
2003	aaa	COL	439	80	140	13	67	2	319	382	481	863	9	88	0.87	113	59	7.04	70
2003	MLB	COL	69	6	11	0	4	0	159	194	188	383	4	80	0.21	26	45	1.18	-32
2002	MLE		510	51	132	11	44	3	259	313	380	693	7	89	0.71	81	61	4.31	35
2003	MLE		439	60	134	12	50	1	305	355	458	813	7	92	0.94	104	41	5.96	64
2004	Projection		350	50	93	9	43	2	266	332	410	742	9	88	0.83	98	60	4.89	46

COL gave him a brief look at 3B, but was overmatched by MLB pitching. Not a power hitter, but should hit for BA and doubles. His defense is well-below average, and that will be the deciding factor as to whether he gets PT.

2 Bay,Jason

Pos CF
Bats R
Age 25 Pre-Peak
PWR + + + +
SPD + +
BAVG + +
DEF + + +

Year	Lev	Tm	AB	R	H	HR	RBI	SB	Avg	OB	Slg	OPS	bb%	ct%	Eye	PX	SX	RC/G	BPV
2001	a	MON	441	79	139	14	71	25	315	404	488	892	13	80	0.75	106	135	8.03	64
2002	a	NYM	261	48	71	9	54	22	272	356	437	793	12	79	0.63	97	144	6.23	46
2002	aa	2TM	188	33	56	8	31	17	298	389	516	905	13	76	0.62	124	188	7.70	66
2003	aaa	SD	307	64	93	20	59	23	303	409	541	950	15	77	0.77	141	118	8.95	74
2003	MLB	2TM	85	15	25	4	14	3	294	412	541	953	17	67	0.61	156	125	9.10	76
2002	MLE		188	29	48	7	27	14	255	340	441	781	11	76	0.53	109	165	5.25	42
2003	MLE		307	52	80	15	49	19	261	353	443	796	13	80	0.72	104	109	5.86	46
2004	Projection		500	89	140	24	84	21	280	374	482	856	13	78	0.68	116	127	6.69	56

He drove the ball well in his Sept trial and is a lock for an outfield spot in '03. Improved plate discipline and physical maturity drove his power spike and could get 25 HR if given 500 AB. His defense works better in the corners.

14 Cash,Kevin

Pos CA
Bats R
Age 26 Pre-Peak
PWR + +
SPD +
BAVG + +
DEF + + + +

Year	Lev	Tm	AB	R	H	HR	RBI	SB	Avg	OB	Slg	OPS	bb%	ct%	Eye	PX	SX	RC/G	BPV
2002	aa	TOR	213	38	59	8	44	5	277	382	469	851	14	79	0.82	120	89	6.84	60
2002	aaa	TOR	236	27	52	10	26	0	220	295	424	719	10	69	0.35	126	22	4.35	37
2002	MLB	TOR	14	1	2	0	0	0	143	200	143	343	7	71	0.25		30	0.96	-47
2003	aaa	TOR	326	37	88	8	37	1	270	330	442	771	8	75	0.36	117	65	5.37	48
2003	MLB	TOR	103	9	14	1	8	0	136	168	194	362	4	79	0.18	40	48	1.01	-34
2002	MLE		449	51	100	14	55	4	223	298	392	690	10	80	0.53	112	56	3.99	33
2003	MLE		326	32	83	7	32	1	255	310	414	724	7	78	0.37	113	48	4.62	41
2004	Projection		350	40	87	5	42	2	249	317	378	695	9	77	0.43	94	59	4.33	32

TOR was so impressed with his defense that he got most of the reps behind the plate in Sept. His lack of offense was not a surprise, as he lacks good bat speed and strike zone judgment. Needs to find a platoon partner.

4 Crosby,Bobby

Pos SS
Bats R
Age 24 Growth
PWR + +
SPD + + +
BAVG + + +
DEF + + +

Year	Lev	Tm	AB	R	H	HR	RBI	SB	Avg	OB	Slg	OPS	bb%	ct%	Eye	PX	SX	RC/G	BPV
2001	a	OAK	38	7	15	1	3	0	395	439	605	1044	7	79	0.38	152	34	11.57	104
2002	a	OAK	280	47	86	2	38	5	307	380	404	784	11	85	0.77	67	105	6.21	48
2002	aa	OAK	228	31	64	7	31	9	281	336	443	779	8	82	0.46	107		5.57	49
2003	aaa	OAK	465	86	143	22	90	24	308	390	544	934	12	76	0.57	143	155	8.43	76
2003	MLB	OAK	10	0	0	0	0	0	0	91	0	91	9	50	0.20	0	-9	0.06	-96
2002	MLE		228	27	57	6	27	8	250	299	390	690	7	85	0.46	94	80	4.17	33
2003	MLE		465	69	125	18	72	19	269	340	462	802	10	80	0.55	119	123	5.80	52
2004	Projection		500	76	135	12	66	15	270	339	418	757	9	81	0.55	97	109	5.27	43

Takes over as the OAK SS, and though his stats were PCL-enhanced, has enough power and speed to be useful on offense. Lacks the range of a typical SS, but makes the plays and has a strong arm. Could take time to adjust.

10 DeJesus,David

Pos CF
Bats L
Age 24 Growth
PWR +
SPD + + + +
BAVG + + +
DEF + + +

Year	Lev	Tm	AB	R	H	HR	RBI	SB	Avg	OB	Slg	OPS	bb%	ct%	Eye	PX	SX	RC/G	BPV
2002	a	KC	334	69	99	4	41	15	296	385	434	819	13	87	1.14	89	163	6.46	60
2002	aa	KC	79	7	20	2	15	3	253	322	443	765	9	87	0.80	111	152	5.10	50
2003	aa	KC	71	14	24	2	10	1	338	413	479	891	11	89	1.13	91	56	7.05	75
2003	aaa	KC	215	49	64	5	23	8	298	394	470	863	14	86	1.13	112	145	7.08	70
2003	MLB	KC	71	14	24	2	10	1	338	413	479	891	11	89	1.13	92	58	7.05	75
0	MLE		0	0	0	0	0	0	0					0		0			
2003	MLE		286	52	84	6	27	7	294	369	437	806	11	90	1.13	96	96	5.74	62
2004	Projection		350	71	99	6	38	13	283	370	434	804	12	88	1.14	99	141	5.92	60

Has the ability of a leadoff hitter (OBP/speed), though his durability is in question. Can flag down flyballs in all directions in CF. Will take over for Carlos Beltran should he leave for free agency, but spends career as 4th OF.

5 Greene,Khalil

Pos SS
Bats R
Age 24 Growth
PWR + + +
SPD + + +
BAVG + + +
DEF + +

Year	Lev	Tm	AB	R	H	HR	RBI	SB	Avg	OB	Slg	OPS	bb%	ct%	Eye	PX	SX	RC/G	BPV
2001	r	SD	37	5	10	0	6	1	270	357	297	654	12	84	0.83	24	55	4.32	17
2002	a	SD	183	33	58	9	32	0	317	359	525	884	6	82	0.36	120	60	7.26	66
2003	aa	SD	229	20	63	3	20	2	275	322	406	729	7	76	0.29	91	76	4.60	37
2003	aaa	SD	319	42	92	10	47	5	288	330	442	772	6	84	0.38	106	61	5.23	47
2003	MLB	SD	62	8	14	2	6	0	226	273	419	692	6	71	0.22	123	130	3.62	31
0	MLE		0	0	0	0	0	0	0					0		0			
2003	MLE		548	54	137	10	58	6	250	289	365	654	5	83	0.32	81	57	3.53	24
2004	Projection		450	51	124	8	53	4	276	319	398	716	6	80	0.32	86	68	4.47	34

Does not overwhelm with the bat, but adjusts to level of play. BA/OBP may be low initially, but he can drive the ball. Defense is average, but has solid instincts. Must be judged by his total contributions.

19 Hairston,Scott

Pos 2B
Bats R
Age 23 Growth
PWR + + + +
SPD + +
BAVG + + +
DEF +

Year	Lev	Tm	AB	R	H	HR	RBI	SB	Avg	OB	Slg	OPS	bb%	ct%	Eye	PX	SX	RC/G	BPV
			0	0	0	0	0	0	0					0					
2001	r	ARI	291	81	101	14	65	2	347	422	588	1010	12	83	0.76	136	151	10.06	91
2002	a	ARI	394	79	131	16	72	9	332	418	563	982	13	81	0.78	146	120	9.54	90
2002	a	ARI	79	20	32	6	26	1	405	447	797	1245	7	80	0.38	263	125	15.79	149
2003	aa	ARI	337	53	93	10	47	6	276	335	469	804	8	76	0.38	121	168	5.77	50
2003	MLE		0	0	0	0	0	0	0					0		0			
2003	MLE		337	40	85	8	36	5	252	300	415	715	6	83	0.40	104	138	4.39	35
2004	Projection		150	30	42	6	26	2	280	353	500	853	10	82	0.64	136	157	6.53	63

His bat may be ready for the Majors right now, with his ability to make contact and hit for power. Defensively, he is well-below average and will need more time in minors. He may surface in the 2nd half if ARI struggles.

18 Hardy,JJ

Pos SS
Bats R
Age 21 Growth
PWR + +
SPD + + + +
BAVG + + +
DEF + + + +

Year	Lev	Tm	AB	R	H	HR	RBI	SB	Avg	OB	Slg	OPS	bb%	ct%	Eye	PX	SX	RC/G	BPV
2001	r	MIL	20	6	5	0	1	0	250	286	450	736	5	90	0.50	131	273	4.50	48
2001	r	MIL	125	20	31	2	15	1	248	329	336	665	11	90	1.25	58	56	3.88	33
2002	a	MIL	335	53	98	6	48	9	293	331	409	739	5	89	0.50	78	102	5.02	42
2002	aa	MIL	145	14	33	1	13	1	228	273	297	569	6	87	0.47	56	49	2.66	8
2003	aa	MIL	416	67	116	12	62	6	279	367	428	795	12	87	1.07	101	63	5.90	57
2002	MLE		145	13	33	1	12	1	228	268	290	558	5	90	0.53	48	47	2.54	7
2003	MLE		416	61	109	11	57	5	262	343	401	744	11	88	1.04	95	60	5.01	48
2004	Projection		250	31	62	4	28	3	248	306	346	652	8	88	0.73	70	59	3.68	27

Will start in AAA, but should assume the SS role when MIL realizes that Bill Hall cannot hit. Improved strength and approach to the plate led to outstanding season with the bat. One of the better fielding SS's in the minors.

BATTERS

21 Hill,Koyie

	Year	Lev	Tm	AB	R	H	HR	RBI	SB	Avg	OB	Slg	OPS	bb%	ct%	Eye	PX	SX	RC/G	BPV
Pos CA	2001	a	LA	498	65	150	8	79	21	301	364	398	761	9	84	0.60	63	87	5.37	39
Bats B	2002	aa	LA	468	67	127	11	64	5	271	373	400	773	14	81	0.86	82	59	5.71	44
Age 25 Pre-Peak	2003	aa	LA	101	9	23	0	7	2	228	271	297	568	6	81	0.32	59	64	2.75	8
	2003	aaa	LA	312	48	98	3	36	5	314	346	401	746	5	88	0.38	69	84	5.41	40
PWR +	2003	MLB	LA	3	0	1	0	0	0	333	333	667	1000	0	33	0.00	298		8.50	136
SPD ++	2002	MLE		468	62	114	10	59	5	244	343	359	702	13	81	0.81	77	64	4.56	30
BAVG +++	2003	MLE		413	48	104	3	36	6	252	283	322	605	4	87	0.33	55	79	3.25	14
DEF ++	2004	Projection		**200**	**25**	**50**	**2**	**21**	**3**	**250**	**304**	**338**	**641**	**7**	**85**	**0.50**	**66**	**70**	**3.70**	**21**

Ability to switch-hit and play defense could land him a P/T role. Has doubles power, makes contact, and runs well for a CA, giving him some value offensively. Defense won't hold up as a regular, but can also play 1B and 3B.

17 Hummell,Tim

	Year	Lev	Tm	AB	R	H	HR	RBI	SB	Avg	OB	Slg	OPS	bb%	ct%	Eye	PX	SX	RC/G	BPV
Pos 3B	2000	a	CHW	242	37	79	2	30	9	326	409	426	835	12	87	1.06	72	88	7.03	61
Bats R	2001	aa	CHW	295	40	79	3	33	6	268	331	373	704	9	87	0.72	66	123	4.58	33
Age 25 Pre-Peak	2002	aaa	CHW	523	55	136	4	41	6	260	326	346	672	9	82	0.54	66	49	4.07	26
	2003	aaa	CHW	476	72	135	15	80	9	284	347	443	790	9	83	0.55	99	99	5.75	48
PWR +	2003	MLB	CIN	80	9	18	2	10	0	225	295	363	658	9	85	0.67	95	27	3.78	28
SPD +	2002	MLE		523	49	126	4	36	5	241	305	321	626	8	84	0.56	63	46	3.41	18
BAVG ++	2003	MLE		476	63	126	15	70	8	265	324	416	740	8	85	0.58	96	86	4.90	40
DEF ++	2004	Projection		**150**	**19**	**40**	**3**	**19**	**2**	**267**	**331**	**396**	**727**	**9**	**84**	**0.59**	**86**	**85**	**4.77**	**37**

Can play all four infield spots and has some pop in his bat, making him a solid utility infielder. His bat isn't strong enough to play full-time and can be stretched defensively in the middle for an extended time.

22 Kelton,Dave

	Year	Lev	Tm	AB	R	H	HR	RBI	SB	Avg	OB	Slg	OPS	bb%	ct%	Eye	PX	SX	RC/G	BPV
Pos 1B	2000	a	CHC	523	75	140	18	84	7	268	317	455	772	7	77	0.32	114	113	4.97	43
Bats R	2001	aa	CHC	224	33	70	12	45	1	313	379	549	928	10	75	0.44	129	109	7.73	70
Age 24 Growth	2002	aaa	CHC	498	68	130	20	79	12	261	331	462	793	9	74	0.40	119	127	5.45	47
	2003	aaa	CHC	442	62	119	16	67	8	269	338	446	784	9	74	0.40	115	103	5.59	44
PWR +++	2003	MLB	CHC	11	1	2	0	1	0	182	182	273	455	0	64	0.00	81	54	1.55	-5
SPD +	2002	MLE		498	60	119	18	69	11	239	305	416	720	9	77	0.41	110	103	4.34	34
BAVG +	2003	MLE		442	52	106	14	57	7	240	303	391	694	8	77	0.40	96	87	4.22	28
DEF +	2004	Projection		**150**	**19**	**37**	**5**	**22**	**1**	**247**	**313**	**422**	**735**	**9**	**76**	**0.40**	**110**	**73**	**4.59**	**36**

CHC loves his power, but he does not make good contact, and now that he isn't playing 3B, his value is on the wane. Poor plate discipline and not using the whole field limits usefulness of his power. Could land role as utilityman.

27 Krynzel,Dave

	Year	Lev	Tm	AB	R	H	HR	RBI	SB	Avg	OB	Slg	OPS	bb%	ct%	Eye	PX	SX	RC/G	BPV
Pos CF	2001	a	MIL	141	22	43	1	19	11	305	347	348	694	6	80	0.32	23	122	4.43	18
Bats L	2001	a	MIL	383	65	106	5	33	34	277	324	392	716	7	68	0.22	73	175	4.29	29
Age 22 Growth	2002	a	MIL	365	76	98	11	45	29	268	378	460	838	15	73	0.64	104	256	6.06	48
	2002	aa	MIL	129	13	31	2	13	13	240	263	349	612	3	77	0.13	61	211	2.95	7
PWR +	2003	aa	MIL	457	72	122	2	34	43	267	352	357	709	12	74	0.50	54	213	4.48	22
SPD ++++	2002	MLE		129	12	30	2	12	12	233	250	326	576	2	81	0.13	52	170	2.44	2
BAVG ++	2003	MLE		457	66	114	2	31	39	249	327	324	651	10	76	0.49	46	179	3.58	12
DEF +++	2004	Projection		**150**	**20**	**38**	**2**	**14**	**10**	**253**	**309**	**355**	**664**	**7**	**77**	**0.34**	**57**	**181**	**3.54**	**15**

The emergence of Scott Podsednik limits his urgency, as he is the same type of player. Improving his leadoff skills, but his aggressiveness can get him in trouble. Could be the first outfielder called if injury hits MIL outfield.

6 LaForest,Pete

	Year	Lev	Tm	AB	R	H	HR	RBI	SB	Avg	OB	Slg	OPS	bb%	ct%	Eye	PX	SX	RC/G	BPV
Pos CA	2002	aa	TAM	359	57	97	20	64	9	270	375	493	868	14	74	0.64	128	74	6.76	58
Bats L	2002	aaa	TAM	66	7	17	3	15	0	258	290	439	729	4	58	0.11	105	33	4.18	35
Age 26 Pre-Peak	2003	aa	TAM	72	9	18	3	15	0	250	386	486	872	18	76	0.94	159		7.14	71
	2003	aaa	TAM	201	40	54	14	38	2	269	380	567	947	15	72	0.64	175	104	8.05	78
PWR ++++	2003	MLB	TAM	48	0	8	0	6	0	167	184	208	392	2	71	0.07	36	-9	1.20	-27
SPD +	2002	MLE		425	53	103	19	66	8	242	324	428	752	11	74	0.46	111	63	4.73	38
BAVG ++	2003	MLE		273	43	65	14	46	2	238	346	484	829	14	74	0.63	152	81	6.05	57
DEF +	2004	Projection		**200**	**33**	**51**	**9**	**35**	**1**	**255**	**358**	**471**	**830**	**14**	**73**	**0.60**	**132**	**62**	**6.10**	**54**

Unique hitter, in that he hits for power and will draw walks, but doesn't hit for a high BA. Slow actions behind the plate preclude him from playing regularly, despite good arm strength, but could help TAM in a C/1B/DH role.

8 Lane,Jason

	Year	Lev	Tm	AB	R	H	HR	RBI	SB	Avg	OB	Slg	OPS	bb%	ct%	Eye	PX	SX	RC/G	BPV
Pos RF	2001	aa	HOU	313	65	108	28	86	10	345	413	690	1103	10	85	0.75	201	95	11.83	114
Bats R	2002	aaa	HOU	426	65	116	15	83	13	272	322	472	793	7	79	0.34	128	109	5.54	54
Age 27 Peak	2002	MLB	HOU	69	12	20	4	10	1	290	380	536	916	13	83	0.83	137	112	7.51	73
	2003	aaa	HOU	248	37	74	7	39	2	298	374	452	826	11	90	1.15	109	51	6.52	67
PWR +++	2003	MLB	HOU	23	4	6	3	8	0	261	261	696	957	0	96	0.00	243	33	6.26	89
SPD +	2002	MLE		426	56	111	15	72	11	261	305	460	765	6	81	0.33	135	106	4.99	50
BAVG +++	2003	MLE		248	32	70	7	34	2	282	350	431	782	9	90	1.04	102	48	5.67	58
DEF +	2004	Projection		**350**	**51**	**100**	**13**	**60**	**6**	**286**	**349**	**476**	**825**	**9**	**86**	**0.68**	**126**	**81**	**6.23**	**62**

He is an aggressive hitter with moderate power and the ability to get on base, and has hit MLB pitching in his brief tenure. If he stays in an outfield corner, his defense will be respectable.

24 Linden,Todd

	Year	Lev	Tm	AB	R	H	HR	RBI	SB	Avg	OB	Slg	OPS	bb%	ct%	Eye	PX	SX	RC/G	BPV
Pos RF				0	0	0	0	0	0	0					0					
Bats B	2002	aa	SF	392	64	123	12	52	9	314	406	482	888	13	74	0.60	106	84	7.71	64
Age 23 Growth	2002	aaa	SF	100	18	25	3	10	2	250	375	380	755	17	65	0.57	71	116	5.64	26
	2003	aaa	SF	471	75	131	11	56	14	278	335	412	747	8	78	0.38	91	120	5.13	37
PWR +++	2003	MLB	SF	36	2	8	1	6	0	222	243	333	577	3	83	0.17	68	6	2.72	6
SPD +	2002	MLE		492	72	134	11	54	10	272	363	407	769	12	76	0.60	90	93	5.51	40
BAVG ++	2003	MLE		471	61	114	7	45	11	242	290	346	636	6	82	0.38	71	110	3.50	18
DEF ++	2004	Projection		**350**	**53**	**88**	**8**	**38**	**8**	**251**	**329**	**378**	**707**	**10**	**76**	**0.49**	**83**	**105**	**4.55**	**29**

2003 was disappointing from an offensive standpoint, showing decreased power and OBP. He could make the team in a RF platoon if SF doesn't acquire an OF. Good pitching can get him out and needs to make adjustments.

13 Mauer,Joe

	Year	Lev	Tm	AB	R	H	HR	RBI	SB	Avg	OB	Slg	OPS	bb%	ct%	Eye	PX	SX	RC/G	BPV
Pos CA				0	0	0	0	0	0	0					0					
Bats L	2001	r	MIN	110	14	44	0	14	4	400	488	491	979	15	91	1.90	61	120	11.51	99
Age 21 Growth	2002	a	MIN	411	58	124	4	62	0	302	392	392	784	13	90	1.45	65	34	6.16	58
	2003	a	MIN	233	25	78	1	44	3	335	397	412	809	9	90	1.00	59	65	6.78	57
PWR ++	2003	aa	MIN	276	48	94	4	41	0	341	395	453	848	8	91	1.00	79	50	7.28	67
SPD +	0	MLE		0	0	0	0	0	0	0					0		0			
BAVG ++++	2003	MLE		276	43	92	3	37	0	333	383	438	821	7	92	1.05	77	47	6.72	65
DEF ++++	2004	Projection		**150**	**21**	**44**	**1**	**22**	**1**	**293**	**370**	**389**	**760**	**11**	**91**	**1.32**	**69**	**71**	**5.68**	**54**

Top prospect in baseball. Has a mature approach to the plate, hitting for BA and judging the strike zone, but power has yet to surface, as he likes using the middle of the field. Defense is ready and could debut by mid-'04.

1 Morneau,Justin

	Year	Lev	Tm	AB	R	H	HR	RBI	SB	Avg	OB	Slg	OPS	bb%	ct%	Eye	PX	SX	RC/G	BPV
Pos 1B	2001	a	MIN	433	75	142	16	93	0	328	398	524	922	10	82	0.63	118	78	8.36	73
Bats L	2001	aa	MIN	38	3	6	0	4	0	158	220	184	404	7	79	0.38	22	32	1.36	-30
Age 22 Growth	2002	aa	MIN	494	72	147	16	80	7	298	353	474	826	8	82	0.48	110	101	6.44	57
	2003	aaa	MIN	265	39	71	16	42	0	268	338	498	836	10	79	0.50	131	44	6.00	56
PWR ++++	2003	MLB	MIN	103	13	23	4	16	0	223	286	369	655	8	71	0.30	85	30	3.67	17
SPD +	2002	MLE		494	60	137	13	66	6	277	325	431	756	7	85	0.47	100	90	5.23	45
BAVG ++++	2003	MLE		344	47	90	18	48	0	262	321	471	792	8	82	0.48	120	50	5.34	49
DEF +	2004	Projection		**500**	**71**	**139**	**22**	**77**	**2**	**278**	**338**	**474**	**812**	**8**	**82**	**0.50**	**116**	**67**	**5.88**	**53**

Power is developing and stays back on the ball really well, making 30+ HR very achievable with regular playing time. His defense is average at best and is a liability on the bases. An All-Star in four years.

9 Nivar,Ramon

Pos 2B CF
Bats B
Age 24 Growth

PWR +
SPD +++++
BAVG +++
DEF +++

Year	Lev	Tm	AB	R	H	HR	RBI	SB	Avg	OB	Slg	OPS	bb%	ct%	Eye	PX	SX	RC/G	BPV
2001	a	TEX	515	69	124	2	32	28	241	280	295	575	5	87	0.43	41	111	2.67	6
2002	a	TEX	472	98	144	3	41	39	305	349	403	752	6	91	0.73	61	187	5.19	43
2003	aa	TEX	317	53	110	4	37	9	347	386	464	849	6	93	0.87	76	110	6.65	66
2003	aaa	TEX	89	11	30	2	12	6	337	372	472	844	5	94	1.00	73	157	7.14	64
2003	MLB	TEX	90	9	19	0	7	4	211	245	267	511	4	89	0.40	29	164	2.12	-9
	MLE		0	0	0	0	0	0	0					0		0			
2003	MLE		406	56	134	6	43	13	330	364	446	810	5	94	0.92	74	111	5.91	60
2004	**Projection**		**350**	**59**	**99**	**3**	**33**	**8**	**283**	**324**	**381**	**705**	**6**	**92**	**0.73**	**64**	**119**	**4.12**	**37**

Athletic player with speed and contact ability. Will have to maintain a high BA, as he rarely walks and doesn't hit for power. Shows plenty of range in CF. TEX would like for him to take the CF/leadoff role, but needs a good spring.

3 Reed,Jeremy

Pos CF
Bats L
Age 22 Growth

PWR ++
SPD ++++
BAVG ++++
DEF +++

Year	Lev	Tm	AB	R	H	HR	RBI	SB	Avg	OB	Slg	OPS	bb%	ct%	Eye	PX	SX	RC/G	BPV
			0	0	0	0	0	0	0					0					
			0	0	0	0	0	0	0					0					
2002	a	CHW	210	37	67	4	32	17	319	353	448	801	5	89	0.46	91	109	6.02	55
2003	a	CHW	222	37	74	4	52	27	333	437	477	915	16	92	2.41	102	118	8.97	103
2003	aa	CHW	242	51	99	7	43	18	409	472	591	1063	11	92	1.53	116	128	11.09	117
	MLE		0	0	0	0	0	0	0					0		0			
2003	MLE		242	48	96	8	41	17	397	461	579	1040	11	93	1.61	115	109	10.21	114
2004	**Projection**		**200**	**36**	**55**	**5**	**36**	**12**	**275**	**346**	**426**	**772**	**10**	**91**	**1.20**	**101**	**117**	**5.11**	**59**

Led minors with a .373 BA / .453 OBP. Sprays line-drives to all fields, has excellent strike zone judgment, and runs the bases intelligently. Only deficiencies are a lack of power and range that may not be suitable for CF.

25 Ross,Cody

Pos RF
Bats R
Age 23 Growth

PWR +++
SPD +
BAVG +
DEF ++

Year	Lev	Tm	AB	R	H	HR	RBI	SB	Avg	OB	Slg	OPS	bb%	ct%	Eye	PX	SX	RC/G	BPV
2000	a	DET	434	71	116	7	68	11	267	350	396	746	11	81	0.66	75	166	5.24	35
2001	a	DET	482	84	133	15	80	28	276	337	461	797	8	80	0.46	113	157	5.84	52
2002	aa	DET	400	73	112	19	72	16	280	351	508	859	10	79	0.51	139	126	6.79	64
2003	aaa	DET	470	74	135	20	61	15	287	333	515	848	6	82	0.37	140	141	6.19	64
2003	MLB	DET	19	1	4	1	5	0	211	250	421	671	5	84	0.33	126	-9	3.51	31
2002	MLE		400	60	97	13	59	13	243	308	415	723	9	84	0.58	108	123	4.64	39
2003	MLE		470	75	132	17	61	15	281	328	494	822	7	84	0.45	131	155	5.82	59
2004	**Projection**		**150**	**24**	**41**	**6**	**22**	**3**	**273**	**330**	**479**	**809**	**8**	**82**	**0.48**	**126**	**124**	**5.69**	**55**

Torn ACL kept him from a Sept. audition, but is the only upper-level bat capable of contributing for DET. Surprising power for his size, but doesn't hit for BA or draw walks. He can play solid defense in either corner.

11 Ryan,Michael

Pos RF
Bats L
Age 26 Pre-Peak

PWR +++
SPD ++
BAVG +
DEF +++

Year	Lev	Tm	AB	R	H	HR	RBI	SB	Avg	OB	Slg	OPS	bb%	ct%	Eye	PX	SX	RC/G	BPV
2001	aaa	MIN	527	89	152	18	73	1	288	352	486	838	9	77	0.43	121	104	6.42	56
2002	aaa	MIN	540	92	141	31	101	4	261	329	522	852	9	77	0.44	149	105	6.05	63
2002	MLB	MIN	11	3	1	0	0	0	91	91	91	182	0	82	0.00			0.23	-70
2003	aaa	MIN	408	56	92	15	60	6	225	291	404	696	9	78	0.43	107	117	4.14	30
2003	MLB	MIN	61	13	24	5	13	2	393	448	754	1202	9	80	0.50	225	65	14.12	138
2002	MLE		540	66	122	21	72	3	226	278	420	698	7	83	0.42	121	74	3.84	36
2003	MLE		408	49	84	12	52	5	206	264	360	624	7	79	0.38	94	111	3.24	17
2004	**Projection**		**200**	**27**	**46**	**8**	**29**	**2**	**230**	**291**	**418**	**710**	**8**	**79**	**0.41**	**114**	**100**	**4.20**	**34**

Was the regular RF for MIN during Sept and should go into '04 in a platoon. Free swinger, with moderate power, but will likely be a streaky hitter and has plenty of competition for playing time. Plays all three OF spots.

7 Sanchez,Freddy

Pos SS 3B
Bats R
Age 26 Pre-Peak

PWR +
SPD +++
BAVG +++
DEF ++

Year	Lev	Tm	AB	R	H	HR	RBI	SB	Avg	OB	Slg	OPS	bb%	ct%	Eye	PX	SX	RC/G	BPV
2001	aa	BOS	311	60	102	3	38	19	328	399	437	837	11	86	0.82	80	119	7.31	60
2002	aaa	BOS	183	25	55	4	28	5	301	344	432	775	6	89	0.57	82	87	5.16	48
2002	MLB	BOS	16	3	3	0	2	0	188	278	188	465	11	81	0.67			1.92	-24
2003	aaa	2TM	216	47	74	5	25	8	343	425	495	920	13	83	0.84	111	96	9.10	77
2003	MLB	BOS	34	6	8	0	2	0	235	235	294	529	0	76	0.00	51	82	2.31	0
2002	MLE		494	67	141	5	52	19	285	336	387	723	7	89	0.68	74	101	4.83	40
2003	MLE		216	40	68	4	21	7	315	388	449	838	11	87	0.90	97	89	7.19	65
2004	**Projection**		**450**	**80**	**122**	**8**	**51**	**7**	**271**	**343**	**402**	**745**	**10**	**86**	**0.79**	**92**	**85**	**5.09**	**46**

Will start at either 3B or 2B. Makes the plays with little flash. Offensively, he's a singles hitter who draws walks, but can turn on a mistake. A starter for a few years, but falls back into a utility role.

16 Sledge,Termel

Pos RF
Bats L
Age 27 Peak

PWR +++
SPD ++
BAVG +++
DEF ++

Year	Lev	Tm	AB	R	H	HR	RBI	SB	Avg	OB	Slg	OPS	bb%	ct%	Eye	PX	SX	RC/G	BPV
2000	a	SEA	407	95	135	11	78	36	332	436	516	952	16	87	1.44	110	191	9.23	86
2001	aa	MON	273	41	68	5	26	17	249	314	374	688	9	83	0.57	77	145	4.32	28
2002	aa	MON	396	74	119	8	43	11	301	386	437	823	12	82	0.79	82	138	6.36	52
2002	aaa	MON	80	12	21	1	11	1	263	352	413	764	12	81	0.73	101	158	5.27	43
2003	aaa	MON	497	95	161	22	92	13	324	398	545	943	11	81	0.66	132	157	8.54	77
2002	MLE		476	68	123	8	43	10	258	330	376	706	10	84	0.69	77	109	4.32	32
2003	MLE		497	70	139	16	68	10	280	338	445	783	8	86	0.61	103	109	5.45	48
2004	**Projection**		**350**	**57**	**98**	**8**	**42**	**9**	**280**	**355**	**422**	**776**	**10**	**84**	**0.74**	**90**	**121**	**5.45**	**46**

Financial restraints prevented him from playing in Sept, but MON needs to find out if he can be a starter or is a 4th OF. Power spiked in '03, and has always been able to get on base. Speed is declining and defense is marginal.

23 Snelling,Chris

Pos LF
Bats L
Age 22 Growth

PWR ++
SPD ++++
BAVG +++
DEF +++

Year	Lev	Tm	AB	R	H	HR	RBI	SB	Avg	OB	Slg	OPS	bb%	ct%	Eye	PX	SX	RC/G	BPV
2001	a	SEA	450	90	151	7	73	12	336	396	491	887	9	86	0.71	97	170	7.73	68
2002	aa	SEA	89	10	29	1	12	5	326	406	506	912	12	88	1.09	120	150	8.40	84
2002	MLB	SEA	27	2	4	1	3	0	148	207	259	466	7	85	0.50	56		1.72	-16
2003	aa	SEA	186	24	62	3	25	1	333	361	468	829	4	84	0.27	90	82	5.66	55
2003	aaa	SEA	67	11	18	3	10	1	269	319	433	752	7	82	0.42	94	63	5.12	38
	MLE		0	0	0	0	0	0	0					0		0			
2003	MLE		253	35	78	5	35	2	308	345	431	775	5	85	0.37	82	60	4.98	45
2004	**Projection**		**200**	**32**	**57**	**3**	**29**	**3**	**285**	**332**	**427**	**758**	**7**	**85**	**0.47**	**91**	**122**	**4.81**	**44**

LF could be an open spot, but he must prove he can remain healthy, something his reckless abandon play barely allows. He has surprising power for his size and does little things to help a team win. A sleeper if he plays.

26 Tracy,Chad

Pos 3B
Bats L
Age 23 Growth

PWR +
SPD +
BAVG ++++
DEF ++

Year	Lev	Tm	AB	R	H	HR	RBI	SB	Avg	OB	Slg	OPS	bb%	ct%	Eye	PX	SX	RC/G	BPV
			0	0	0	0	0	0	0					0					
2001	a	ARI	36	2	10	0	5	1	278	333	306	639	8	86	0.60	24	36	4.02	15
2001	a	ARI	215	43	73	4	36	3	340	393	447	840	8	91	1.00	72	78	7.24	65
2002	aa	ARI	514	80	177	8	74	2	344	389	486	876	7	90	0.76	104	81	7.52	72
2003	aaa	ARI	522	91	169	10	80	0	324	373	456	829	7	90	0.79	90	68	6.60	61
2002	MLE		514	63	163	6	58	2	317	354	438	791	5	93	0.76	88	66	5.81	58
2003	MLE		522	71	156	8	62	0	299	339	412	751	6	93	0.82	79	54	5.20	49
2004	**Projection**		**150**	**22**	**44**	**2**	**20**	**1**	**293**	**339**	**419**	**758**	**6**	**92**	**0.81**	**89**	**76**	**5.26**	**52**

Hits for BA and has plate discipline, which gets people excited, but doesn't hit for power and his defense is average. ARI neglected to give him playing time in Sept, which means he isn't highly thought of.

12 Weeks,Rickie

Pos 2B
Bats R
Age 21 Growth

PWR +++
SPD ++++
BAVG +++
DEF ++

Year	Lev	Tm	AB	R	H	HR	RBI	SB	Avg	OB	Slg	OPS	bb%	ct%	Eye	PX	SX	RC/G	BPV
			0	0	0	0	0	0	0					0					
			0	0	0	0	0	0	0					0					
2003	r	MIL	4	2	2	0	4	1	500	600	500	1100	20	50	0.50		124	21.27	77
2003	a	MIL	63	13	22	1	16	2	349	474	556	1030	19	86	1.67	158	125	11.78	114
2003	MLB	MIL	8	0	1	0	0	0	125	222	125	347	11	50	0.25	0	-10	1.02	-53
	MLE		0	0	0	0	0	0	0					0		0			
	MLE		0	0	0	0	0	0	0					0					
2004	**Projection**		**200**	**17**	**53**	**4**	**20**	**3**	**265**	**329**	**389**	**718**	**9**	**94**	**1.67**	**82**	**61**	**4.80**	**56**

Will need very little time in the minors, as he is an athletic player who can hit for BA & power, runs the bases, and judges the strike zone. His defense needs work, but should provide enough offense to offset it.

9　Balfour, Grant

	Year	Lev	Tm	W	L	Sv	IP	ERA	Br/IP	BF/G	OBA	OOB	H%	xERA		Ctl	Dom	Cmd	hr/9	S%	BPV
Th R	2001	aa	MIN	2	1	13	50	1.08	0.96	5.5	156	254	27%	1.09		4.0	13.0	3.3	0.2	89%	165
Role Reliever	2001	aaa	MIN	2	2	0	16	5.63	1.75	6.8	285	383	36%	5.58		5.6	9.6	1.7	1.1	69%	57
Age 26 Growth	2002	aaa	MIN	2	4	8	71	4.18	1.27	5.1	230	310	34%	2.94	+	3.8	11.1	2.9	0.4	66%	126
Type Power	2003	aaa	MIN	5	2	5	71	2.41	0.90	12.9	193	242	27%	1.98		2.0	11.0	5.4	0.8	78%	174
VEL ++++	2003	MLB	MIN	1	0	0	25	4.32	1.40	6.8	230	332	29%	4.30		5.0	10.1	2.0	1.4	74%	68
BRE +++	2002	MLE		2	4	8	71	4.44	1.32	5.2	245	319	33%	3.31	+	3.7	9.5	2.6	1.0	65%	106
CHG +	2003	MLE		5	2	5	71	3.17	1.06	13.4	225	273	29%	2.86		2.2	9.3	4.3	0.9	74%	129
PIT ++	2004	Projection		4	3	1	80	3.71	1.28	6.6	242	311	31%	3.74		3.4	9.3	2.8	1.0	74%	90

It is apparent that he pitches better out of the bullpen than the rotation, but MIN wanted to give it a shot. His power sinker and slider can be plus pitches. With the MIN bullpen losing a couple of members, a bullpen spot could be his.

25　Burnett, Sean

	Year	Lev	Tm	W	L	Sv	IP	ERA	Br/IP	BF/G	OBA	OOB	H%	xERA		Ctl	Dom	Cmd	hr/9	S%	BPV
Th L	2000	r	PIT	2	1	0	31	4.06	1.10	15.6	262	280	33%	2.24	+	0.9	7.0	8.0	0.0	59%	212
Role Starter	2001	a	PIT	11	8	0	161	2.63	1.22	25.7	265	303	32%	3.54	-	1.8	7.5	4.1	0.6	81%	114
Age 21 Green	2002	a	PIT	13	4	0	155	1.80	0.97	23.2	213	257	25%	1.89		1.9	5.6	2.9	0.2	82%	100
Type Finesse	2003	aa	PIT	14	6	0	159	3.22	1.17	24.1	260	294	30%	2.81		1.6	4.9	3.0	0.1	70%	91
VEL ++	2003	MLB	PIT	0	2	0	23	4.70	1.57	25.8	217	357	27%	3.91	+	7.0	8.2	1.2	0.8	71%	62
BRE ++++		MLE		0	0	0	0	0.00	0.00												
CHG ++++	2003	MLE		14	6	0	159	4.47	1.39	25.4	301	331	34%	4.03		1.6	4.2	2.6	0.1	65%	70
PIT ++++	2004	Projection		6	6	0	100	4.14	1.34	23.7	282	322	31%	4.06		2.1	5.0	2.4	0.6	69%	60

His ability to change speeds and command his curveball is impressive, and has been able to win, despite a below average fastball and poor dominance. He has won at every level, posting similar base skills.

21　Capuano, Chris

	Year	Lev	Tm	W	L	Sv	IP	ERA	Br/IP	BF/G	OBA	OOB	H%	xERA		Ctl	Dom	Cmd	hr/9	S%	BPV
Th L	2000	a	ARI	10	4	0	101	2.22	1.12	22.7	192	284	27%	1.56	+	4.0	9.3	2.3	0.2	79%	116
Role Starter	2001	aa	ARI	10	11	0	159	5.32	1.63	25.8	291	366	38%	5.02		4.2	9.4	2.2	0.7	67%	78
Age 25 Growth	2002	a	ARI	4	1	0	36	2.74	1.14	24.4	228	287	28%	2.48		2.7	7.2	2.6	0.2	75%	101
Type Finesse	2003	aaa	ARI	9	5	0	142	3.35	1.24	25.7	249	305	30%	3.22		2.7	6.8	2.5	0.6	74%	82
VEL ++	2003	MLB	ARI	2	4	0	33	4.64	1.15	14.9	225	290	26%	3.01	+	3.0	6.3	2.1	0.8	60%	67
BRE ++++	2002	MLE		4	1	0	36	3.00	1.19	24.7	245	298	29%	2.85		2.5	6.0	2.4	0.3	74%	85
CHG ++++	2003	MLE		9	5	0	142	4.05	1.36	26.4	275	325	32%	4.02		2.6	5.9	2.3	0.6	70%	65
PIT ++++	2004	Projection		5	5	0	80	4.05	1.34	26.2	262	322	30%	3.90		3.0	6.2	2.0	0.8	71%	59

Fully recovered from TJS in '01, he likes to pitch to the outside part of the plate, mixing a plus slider and a quality change-up. His command is outstanding, but will be a pitcher with low DOM and a high oppBA.

1　Claussen, Brandon

	Year	Lev	Tm	W	L	Sv	IP	ERA	Br/IP	BF/G	OBA	OOB	H%	xERA		Ctl	Dom	Cmd	hr/9	S%	BPV
Th L	2001	a/a	NYY	14	4	0	187	2.31	1.16	26.3	219	291	31%	2.52		3.3	10.6	3.2	0.4	81%	131
Role Starter	2002	aaa	NYY	2	8	0	93	3.29	1.41	26.9	245	333	30%	3.48		4.4	7.1	1.6	0.4	76%	70
Age 25 Growth	2003	a	NYY	2	0	0	22	1.64	0.86	20.8	205	234	31%	1.26		1.2	10.6	8.7	0.0	79%	260
Type Power	2003	2TM		2	2	0	84	3.64	1.12	24.3	228	284	26%	2.90	+	2.6	5.9	2.3	0.7	69%	70
VEL +++	2003	MLB	NYY	1	0	0	6	1.48	1.48	26.8	317	343	36%	5.80	-	1.5	7.4	5.0	1.5	100%	97
BRE +++	2002	MLE		2	8	0	93	3.68	1.47	27.2	262	343	31%	3.95		4.3	6.3	1.5	0.4	74%	60
CHG +++	2003	MLE		2	2	0	84	4.71	1.26	25.1	257	309	28%	3.91	+	2.6	5.0	2.0	1.0	64%	46
PIT +++	2004	Projection		7	11	0	140	4.31	1.42	26.4	259	335	30%	4.26		3.9	6.7	1.7	0.9	71%	52

He might be the best pitcher CIN has and will get a rotation spot. He sinks and cuts his fastball, mixing a slurvy slider, all with a hint of deception. His strikeout rate is low, which could mean his elbow wasn't fully recovered.

5　Cordero, Chad

	Year	Lev	Tm	W	L	Sv	IP	ERA	Br/IP	BF/G	OBA	OOB	H%	xERA		Ctl	Dom	Cmd	hr/9	S%	BPV
Th R				0	0	0	0	0.00	0.00												
Role Reliever				0	0	0	0	0.00	0.00												
Age 22 Green				0	0	0	0	0.00	0.00												
Type Power	2003	a	MON	1	1	6	26	2.07	1.03	5.4	188	268	22%	1.75		3.4	5.9	1.7	0.3	81%	78
VEL +++	2003	MLB	MON	1	0	1	11	1.64	0.64	3.3	114	184	14%	0.47	+	2.5	9.8	4.0	0.8	83%	151
BRE ++++		MLE		0	0	0	0	0.00	0.00												
CHG		MLE		0	0	0	0	0.00	0.00												
PIT +++	2004	Projection		2	2	13	50	3.96	1.34	4.3	246	322	27%	3.81		3.8	5.6	1.5	0.9	73%	43

Ended the season as the MON closer and will go into spring training as the favorite. He isn't a strike thrower and his strikeout rate isn't what a closer should have, but has a power sinker and gets hitters to chase his quality slider.

14　Correia, Kevin

	Year	Lev	Tm	W	L	Sv	IP	ERA	Br/IP	BF/G	OBA	OOB	H%	xERA		Ctl	Dom	Cmd	hr/9	S%	BPV
Th R				0	0	0	0	0.00	0.00												
Role Starter				0	0	0	0	0.00	0.00												
Age 23 Growth	2002	r	SF	2	2	0	38	4.50	1.34	16.2	257	322	31%	3.82	+	3.3	7.3	2.2	0.7	67%	73
Type Power	2003	aa	SF	6	6	0	86	3.66	1.28	22.6	248	312	31%	3.06	+	3.1	7.6	2.4	0.3	70%	93
VEL +++	2003	MLB	SF	2	1	0	33	3.52	1.42	16.0	255	334	27%	4.82	-	4.1	6.5	1.6	1.6	83%	28
BRE +++		MLE		0	0	0	0	0.00	0.00												
CHG +	2003	MLE		6	7	0	105	3.68	1.26	23.1	256	308	31%	3.30		2.6	6.9	2.7	0.4	70%	89
PIT +++	2004	Projection		6	8	0	120	4.43	1.40	23.6	259	332	29%	4.47		3.8	6.5	1.7	1.3	72%	41

Unheralded prospect, but rose through the minors with impressive command of a sinker and slider. He doesn't change speeds well and will need to pitch with confidence in the Majors, something he failed to show in '03.

16　Cotts, Neal

	Year	Lev	Tm	W	L	Sv	IP	ERA	Br/IP	BF/G	OBA	OOB	H%	xERA		Ctl	Dom	Cmd	hr/9	S%	BPV
Th L	2001	a	OAK	1	0	0	35	3.09	1.17	15.9	221	293	32%	2.70		3.3	11.3	3.4	0.5	74%	134
Role Starter	2001	a	OAK	3	2	0	31	2.32	1.35	18.9	236	325	34%	2.85	-	4.4	9.9	2.3	0.0	81%	115
Age 24 Growth	2002	a	OAK	12	6	0	138	4.11	1.52	21.9	240	350	36%	3.65		5.7	11.6	2.0	0.3	72%	110
Type Finesse	2003	aa	CHW	9	7	0	108	2.16	1.14	20.9	180	287	27%	1.86		4.7	11.1	2.4	0.1	80%	130
VEL ++	2003	MLB	CHW	1	1	4	13	8.24	2.44		289	464	34%	7.06	+			0.6	0.7	65%	
BRE ++++		MLE		0	0	0	0	0.00	0.00												
CHG +++	2003	MLE		9	7	0	108	3.16	1.37	22.1	220	327	31%	2.98		5.2	9.7	1.9	0.2	76%	102
PIT ++	2004	Projection		5	5	0	80	4.39	1.51	25.3	247	349	33%	4.09		5.3	9.8	1.9	0.7	71%	83

Has posted outstanding K rates without much velocity, owing his Dom to deception, a solid change-up and sinker. He walks too many batters as a result of not repeating his delivery. Needs some fine-tuning.

7　Crain, Jesse

	Year	Lev	Tm	W	L	Sv	IP	ERA	Br/IP	BF/G	OBA	OOB	H%	xERA		Ctl	Dom	Cmd	hr/9	S%	BPV
Th R	2002	r	MIN	2	1	2	16	0.56	0.69	6.4	81	196	13%	-0.45	+	3.9	10.1	2.6	0.0	91%	153
Role Reliever	2002	a	MIN	1	1	1	12	1.50	0.83	5.0	151	228	21%	0.56	+	3.0	8.3	2.8	0.0	80%	132
Age 22 Growth	2003	a	MIN	2	1	0	19	2.84	0.79	7.0	157	219	26%	0.53	+	2.4	11.8	5.0	0.0	60%	200
Type Power	2003	aa	MIN	1	1	9	39	0.69	0.59	6.2	106	173	19%	-0.45	+	2.3	12.9	5.6	0.0	87%	229
VEL ++++	2003	aaa	MIN	3	1	10	26	3.12	1.31	4.8	247	317	37%	2.92		3.5	11.4	3.3	0.0	74%	144
BRE +++		MLE		0	0	0	0	0.00	0.00												
CHG +	2003	MLE		4	2	19	65	2.08	1.00	5.7	194	262	29%	1.50	+	2.9	10.4	3.6	0.0	77%	154
PIT +++	2004	Projection		2	1	3	40	3.38	1.25	4.9	237	307	33%	3.07		3.4	10.4	3.1	0.5	73%	121

Easily the most dominant reliever in the minors, putting up obscene BPIs at 3 levels, with a fastball that reaches 97 MPH and three other pitches that can be thrown for strikes. Aggressive approach could make him a future closer.

26　DePaula, Julio

	Year	Lev	Tm	W	L	Sv	IP	ERA	Br/IP	BF/G	OBA	OOB	H%	xERA		Ctl	Dom	Cmd	hr/9	S%	BPV
Th R	2001	a	2TM	7	2	0	73	2.96	1.05	26.4	208	272	30%	2.15	+	2.8	11.5	4.0	0.6	74%	149
Role Starter	2001	a	NYY	9	5	0	83	3.58	1.42	22.5	217	335	28%	3.10		5.7	8.3	1.5	0.3	74%	82
Age 24 Growth	2002	aa	NYY	14	6	0	175	3.45	1.10	26.1	222	281	28%	2.63	+	2.7	7.8	2.9	0.6	69%	102
Type Power	2003	aaa	NYY	10	11	0	167	4.36	1.35	26.4	263	323	30%	4.41		3.1	6.7	2.2	1.2	71%	53
VEL ++++	2003	MLB	NYY	0	0	0	11	0.81	0.36	9.1	87	113	8%	-0.38	+	0.8	5.7	7.0	0.8	100%	194
BRE +	2002	MLE		14	6	0	175	5.35	1.54	28.9	292	354	33%	4.99		3.4	5.6	1.6	0.8	65%	40
CHG ++	2003	MLE		10	11	0	167	5.28	1.49	27.3	289	346	31%	5.34		3.1	5.8	1.9	1.4	68%	30
PIT ++	2004	Projection		4	3	0	60	4.35	1.47	8.8	284	342	32%	4.87	-	3.2	6.0	1.9	1.1	73%	43

NYY top pitching prospect, who pitched well in his brief MLB stint. Ball comes out very clean and can touch 95 MPH. Worked hard to improve change and has three quality pitches to work with.

15 Dominguez,Juan

Th R | Role Starter | Age 23 Growth | Type Power | VEL +++ | BRE + | CHG ++++ | PIT +++

Year	Lev	Tm	W	L	Sv	IP	ERA	Br/IP	BF/G	OBA	OOB	H%	xERA	Ctl	Dom	Cmd	hr/9	S%	BPV
2002	r	TEX	0	0	0	1	0.00	1.00	3.9	262	262	26%	2.43 -	0.0	0.0		0.0	100%	3
2002	a	TEX	1	3	1	67	2.15	1.06	16.7	209	273	28%	2.28	2.8	9.4	3.3	0.5	82%	123
2003	a	TEX	4	0	1	63	2.85	1.13	16.0	236	285	33%	2.71	2.3	10.3	4.5	0.4	75%	151
2003	aa	TEX	5	0	0	55	2.61	1.02	24.1	184	265	25%	1.77 +	3.4	8.8	2.6	0.3	74%	115
2003	MLB	TEX	0	2	0	16	7.27	1.74	12.5	261	381	25%	6.86	6.7	7.3	1.1	2.8	65%	-15
	MLE		0	0	0	0	0.00	0.00											
2003	MLE		6	0	0	73	3.69	1.09	24.5	217	280	27%	2.50 +	2.8	7.6	2.7	0.5	66%	99
2004	**Projection**		**2**	**1**	**0**	**40**	**4.50**	**1.28**	**24.0**	**242**	**311**	**28%**	**3.86 +**	**3.4**	**7.9**	**2.3**	**1.1**	**67%**	**69**

His deceptive delivery and plus circle-change was enough to destroy hitters at two levels. He runs his fastball into the mid-90's, but struggles to spin the ball. He needs more time in the minors to set up hitters better.

13 Duchscherer,Justin

Th R | Role Starter | Age 26 Growth | Type Finesse | VEL ++ | BRE +++ | CHG ++++ | PIT ++++

Year	Lev	Tm	W	L	Sv	IP	ERA	Br/IP	BF/G	OBA	OOB	H%	xERA	Ctl	Dom	Cmd	hr/9	S%	BPV
			0	0	0	0	0.00	0.00											
2001	aa	2TM	8	3	0	87	2.27	0.85	23.5	194	232	25%	1.67 +	1.5	8.6	5.5	0.6	76%	165
2002	aaa	OAK	2	4	0	63	5.57	1.43	19.6	291	336	34%	4.80 +	2.4	7.4	3.1	1.0	61%	76
2003	aaa	OAK	14	2	0	155	3.25	1.09	25.9	257	279	30%	3.23	1.0	6.8	6.5	0.7	72%	160
2003	MLB	OAK	1	1	0	16	3.35	1.24	16.8	272	306	34%	3.66	1.7	8.4	5.0	0.6	74%	139
2002	MLE		2	4	0	63	5.43	1.43	19.6	297	336	34%	4.79 +	2.1	6.3	2.9	0.9	62%	69
2003	MLE		14	2	0	155	3.60	1.18	26.5	274	295	31%	3.68	1.0	5.7	5.5	0.7	71%	129
2004	**Projection**		**6**	**3**	**0**	**80**	**4.28**	**1.35**	**24.4**	**281**	**324**	**32%**	**4.39**	**2.3**	**6.1**	**2.7**	**0.9**	**70%**	**65**

Finesse pitchers live and die with their ability to change speeds and command the plate, and he happened to have everything going in '03. He dominated the PCL, though he found life tough with OAK.

2 Greinke,Zach

Th R | Role Starter | Age 20 Green | Type Finesse | VEL +++ | BRE ++++ | CHG ++++ | PIT ++++

Year	Lev	Tm	W	L	Sv	IP	ERA	Br/IP	BF/G	OBA	OOB	H%	xERA	Ctl	Dom	Cmd	hr/9	S%	BPV
2002	r	KC	0	0	0	5	1.80	1.20	6.9	175	299	23%	1.80	5.4	7.2	1.3	0.0	83%	91
2002	a	KC	0	0	0	5	7.20	1.80	11.8	390	390	50%	6.44 +	0.0	9.0		0.0	56%	31
2002	a	KC	0	0	0	2	0.00	0.50	6.8	151	151	15%	-0.15	0.0	0.0		0.0	100%	25
2003	a	KC	11	1	0	87	1.14	0.79	23.1	186	220	23%	1.42	1.3	8.1	6.0	0.5	91%	177
2003	aa	KC	4	3	0	53	3.23	1.19	24.2	280	297	31%	3.93 -	0.8	5.8	6.8	0.8	76%	151
	MLE		0	0	0	0	0.00	0.00											
2003	MLE		4	3	0	53	4.08	1.30	24.9	300	316	33%	4.68 -	0.8	5.3	6.2	1.0	71%	126
2004	**Projection**		**3**	**5**	**0**	**60**	**4.20**	**1.35**	**25.6**	**290**	**324**	**32%**	**4.39**	**1.8**	**5.3**	**2.9**	**0.8**	**70%**	**67**

Uncharacteristic polish for his age, he has enough pitchability and stuff to hold his own in the Majors right now. Doesn't walk anyone and can get strikeouts by changing speeds and pitching to the corners.

12 Griffiths,Jeremy

Th R | Role Starter | Age 26 Growth | Type Power | VEL +++ | BRE +++ | CHG + | PIT ++

Year	Lev	Tm	W	L	Sv	IP	ERA	Br/IP	BF/G	OBA	OOB	H%	xERA	Ctl	Dom	Cmd	hr/9	S%	BPV
2001	a	NYM	7	8	0	132	3.75	1.22	23.8	253	302	30%	3.01 +	2.4	6.5	2.7	0.6	70%	82
2001	aa	NYM	2	0	0	13	0.69	0.92	25.0	179	247	24%	1.13	2.8	8.3	3.0	0.0	92%	132
2002	aa	NYM	8	6	0	152	3.90	1.39	24.3	268	330	32%	4.08	3.2	7.5	2.3	0.7	73%	74
2003	aaa	NYM	7	6	1	115	2.74	1.04	21.7	225	270	26%	2.33	2.0	6.1	3.0	0.5	75%	96
2003	MLB	NYM	1	3	0	37	6.81	1.81	21.9	324	391	36%	6.24 +	4.1	5.6	1.4	1.0	62%	23
2002	MLE		8	6	0	152	4.50	1.55	25.2	296	355	34%	4.89	3.3	6.0	1.8	0.7	71%	49
2003	MLE		7	6	1	115	3.37	1.19	22.5	253	297	28%	3.24	2.1	5.0	2.4	0.5	72%	68
2004	**Projection**		**7**	**10**	**0**	**120**	**4.65**	**1.47**	**23.9**	**281**	**342**	**31%**	**4.67**	**3.3**	**5.6**	**1.7**	**1.0**	**70%**	**39**

A workhorse, who will mix four pitches, showing above average command. None of his pitches are considered "out" pitches, but they work well together and he doesn't cave in to any hitter.

23 Guzman,Angel

Th R | Role Starter | Age 22 Green | Type Power | VEL ++++ | BRE +++ | CHG ++ | PIT ++

Year	Lev	Tm	W	L	Sv	IP	ERA	Br/IP	BF/G	OBA	OOB	H%	xERA	Ctl	Dom	Cmd	hr/9	S%	BPV
2000	r	CHC	1	1	0	33	1.91	0.88	17.9	205	238	26%	0.97 +	1.4	6.8	5.0	0.0	76%	160
2001	a	CHC	9	1	0	77	2.22	1.13	22.3	238	286	30%	2.59	2.2	7.4	3.3	0.2	80%	114
2002	a	CHC	5	2	0	62	1.89	0.94	26.6	194	249	24%	1.75	2.3	7.1	3.1	0.4	82%	110
2002	a	CHC	6	2	0	94	2.39	1.40	25.4	272	332	34%	3.60 -	3.2	7.1	2.2	0.2	82%	84
2003	aa	CHC	3	3	0	89	2.83	1.22	24.6	248	302	31%	3.45 -	2.6	8.8	3.3	0.8	80%	104
	MLE		0	0	0	0	0.00	0.00											
2003	MLE		3	3	0	89	3.63	1.41	25.8	280	334	34%	4.48 -	2.8	7.8	2.8	0.9	77%	76
2004	**Projection**		**4**	**2**	**0**	**60**	**4.05**	**1.40**	**25.9**	**274**	**332**	**32%**	**4.33**	**3.0**	**7.1**	**2.4**	**0.9**	**73%**	**65**

Minor shoulder surgery has been the only thing holding him back. Has a dynamic fastball with impressive arm action, and has gradually improved his comp pitches. CHC has a loaded rotation, but could sneak in by mid-'04.

22 Hanrahan,Joel

Th R | Role Starter | Age 22 Growth | Type Power | VEL +++ | BRE ++ | CHG +++ | PIT +++

Year	Lev	Tm	W	L	Sv	IP	ERA	Br/IP	BF/G	OBA	OOB	H%	xERA	Ctl	Dom	Cmd	hr/9	S%	BPV
2001	a	LA	9	11	0	144	3.38	1.33	22.6	251	320	30%	3.43	3.4	7.3	2.1	0.8	77%	68
2002	a	LA	10	6	0	144	4.19	1.25	24.0	241	307	31%	3.34 +	3.2	8.7	2.7	0.7	67%	96
2002	aa	LA	1	1	0	11	10.64	2.00	18.0	326	415	38%	7.37 +	5.7	8.2	1.4	1.6	45%	20
2003	aa	LA	10	4	0	133	2.43	1.28	24.3	238	312	31%	2.93 -	3.6	8.8	2.5	0.3	81%	102
2003	aaa	LA	1	2	0	25	10.08	2.24	25.8	338	443	37%	7.33 +	7.2	4.7	0.7	0.7	52%	8
	MLE		0	0	0	0	0.00	0.00											
2003	MLE		11	6	0	158	4.04	1.51	25.0	273	349	33%	4.15	4.1	7.2	1.8	0.4	72%	69
2004	**Projection**		**4**	**3**	**0**	**60**	**4.35**	**1.55**	**24.4**	**284**	**355**	**33%**	**4.84 -**	**3.9**	**7.2**	**1.8**	**0.9**	**74%**	**53**

Overlooked, but is LA's most developed pitching prospect and led the SL in ERA. He has a plus slider and can move his fastball in all directions. Needs to improve command within strike zone.

10 Jackson,Edwin

Th R | Role Starter | Age 20 Green | Type Power | VEL +++++ | BRE +++ | CHG +++ | PIT +++

Year	Lev	Tm	W	L	Sv	IP	ERA	Br/IP	BF/G	OBA	OOB	H%	xERA	Ctl	Dom	Cmd	hr/9	S%	BPV
			0	0	0	0	0.00	0.00											
2001	r	LA	2	1	0	22	2.45	1.50	8.1	184	347	25%	3.01 -	7.8	9.4	1.2	0.4	84%	88
2002	a	LA	5	2	0	105	1.97	1.07	22.0	211	274	27%	2.03	2.8	7.3	2.6	0.2	81%	106
2003	aa	LA	7	7	0	148	2.19	1.17	22.5	225	294	30%	2.70 -	3.2	9.5	3.0	0.5	84%	113
2003	MLB	LA	2	1	0	22	2.45	1.27	23.1	215	311	26%	3.18 -	4.5	7.8	1.7	0.8	85%	70
	MLE		0	0	0	0	0.00	0.00											
2003	MLE		7	7	0	148	4.38	1.25	22.9	242	307	31%	3.24 +	3.2	8.9	2.8	0.6	65%	101
2004	**Projection**		**6**	**5**	**0**	**120**	**3.98**	**1.38**	**24.6**	**245**	**329**	**30%**	**3.82**	**4.2**	**7.7**	**1.8**	**0.8**	**73%**	**65**

Fluid arm action and plus command of three pitches allowed him to post terrific BPIs in AA. Was impressive in three late-season starts for LA, but may need additional time in the minors. Potential #1 starter.

17 Martinez,Luis

Th L | Role Starter | Age 24 Growth | Type Power | VEL +++ | BRE ++ | CHG ++ | PIT +++

Year	Lev	Tm	W	L	Sv	IP	ERA	Br/IP	BF/G	OBA	OOB	H%	xERA	Ctl	Dom	Cmd	hr/9	S%	BPV
2001	a/a	MIL	8	9	0	122	5.31	1.62	19.1	267	365	36%	4.22 +	5.4	9.9	1.8	0.7	67%	80
2002	aa	MIL	8	8	1	109	5.20	1.64	17.1	271	368	35%	4.54 +	5.4	8.8	1.6	0.5	67%	73
2003	aa	MIL	8	5	0	115	2.58	1.28	24.1	223	312	30%	2.83	4.2	9.1	2.1	0.3	80%	101
2003	aaa	MIL	4	0	0	45	1.00	1.24	26.9	225	305	31%	2.36 -	3.8	9.2	2.4	0.0	91%	116
2003	MLB	MIL	0	2	0	12	8.93	2.81	23.1	358	499	41%	8.43 +	11.2	5.2	0.5	0.0	65%	25
2002	MLE		8	8	1	109	6.61	1.83	17.8	304	393	37%	5.56 +	5.4	7.5	1.4	0.6	62%	51
2003	MLE		12	5	0	160	2.75	1.42	25.8	253	335	32%	3.54 -	4.2	7.6	1.8	0.3	80%	80
2004	**Projection**		**5**	**9**	**0**	**120**	**4.58**	**1.63**	**23.7**	**278**	**366**	**35%**	**4.65**	**4.9**	**8.0**	**1.6**	**0.6**	**72%**	**64**

Was overwhelmed by Major League hitters, as he failed to attack and didn't trust his stuff. Struck out over a batter per IP at two levels, mixing three above average pitches. If he learns from his mistakes, he could bounce back strong.

18 Nageotte,Clint

Th R | Role Starter | Age 23 Growth | Type Power | VEL ++++ | BRE +++++ | CHG + | PIT ++

Year	Lev	Tm	W	L	Sv	IP	ERA	Br/IP	BF/G	OBA	OOB	H%	xERA	Ctl	Dom	Cmd	hr/9	S%	BPV
			0	0	0	0	0.00	0.00											
2000	R	SEA	4	1	1	50	2.16	1.14	16.9	171	288	26%	1.52 +	5.0	10.6	2.1	0.0	79%	129
2001	a	SEA	11	8	0	152	3.14	1.26	22.7	248	308	35%	3.33	3.0	11.1	3.7	0.6	76%	133
2002	a	SEA	9	6	0	165	4.53	1.34	24.2	247	322	36%	3.54 +	3.7	11.7	3.1	0.5	65%	125
2003	aa	SEA	11	7	0	154	3.10	1.26	23.8	226	309	30%	2.89	3.9	9.2	2.3	0.4	75%	103
	MLE		0	0	0	0	0.00	0.00											
2003	MLE		11	7	0	154	3.80	1.40	24.6	252	331	32%	3.57	4.0	8.2	2.0	0.4	72%	87
2004	**Projection**		**4**	**3**	**0**	**60**	**3.90**	**1.42**	**12.4**	**255**	**334**	**34%**	**3.75**	**4.1**	**9.5**	**2.3**	**0.5**	**72%**	**96**

Possesses one of the best sliders in the minors, and is slowly improving his fastball command. Pitched well enough as a starter to lead the TL in strikeouts, but arm action and lack of a change may mean a move to the pen.

11 Riley,Matt

		Year	Lev	Tm	W	L	Sv	IP	ERA	Br/IP	BF/G	OBA	OOB	H%	xERA	Ctl	Dom	Cmd	hr/9	S%	BPV
Th	L	2001	DNP	INJ	0	0	0	0	0.00	0.00											
Role	Starter	2002	aa	BAL	4	10	0	109	6.35	1.69	22.8	307	374	38%	5.66 +	4.0	8.7	2.2	1.0	62%	62
Age	24 Growth	2003	aa	BAL	5	2	0	72	3.12	1.10	20.7	216	280	29%	2.46 +	2.9	9.1	3.2	0.5	72%	118
Type	Power	2003	aaa	BAL	4	2	0	70	3.59	1.40	23.3	262	331	35%	3.78	3.6	9.9	2.8	0.5	74%	104
VEL	+++	2003	MLB	BAL	1	0	0	10	1.80	1.20	20.6	199	299	23%	2.92 -	4.5	7.2	1.6	0.9	91%	65
BRE	+++	2002	MLE		4	10	0	109	7.60	1.89	23.8	338	401	40%	6.71 +	4.0	7.1	1.8	1.0	59%	37
CHG	+	2003	MLE		9	4	0	142	4.49	1.46	23.1	277	342	34%	4.34	3.4	8.0	2.4	0.6	69%	78
PIT	+	2004	Projection		7	8	0	120	4.43	1.49	23.0	273	346	33%	4.58	3.9	8.2	2.1	0.9	72%	66

Once-prized prospect has returned with a vengeance from TJS, matching his pre-surgery velocity and having good snap to his curveball. Command is much better and the time off has left him more mature.

20 Ring,Royce

		Year	Lev	Tm	W	L	Sv	IP	ERA	Br/IP	BF/G	OBA	OOB	H%	xERA	Ctl	Dom	Cmd	hr/9	S%	BPV
Th	L				0	0	0	0	0.00	0.00											
Role	Reliever				0	0	0	0	0.00	0.00											
Age	23 Growth	2002	r	CHW	0	0	0	5	0.00	0.40	5.5	124	124	28%	-0.84 +	0.0	16.2		0.0	100%	127
Type	Power	2002	a	CHW	2	0	5	23	3.91	1.35	4.7	236	323	30%	3.57	4.3	8.6	2.0	0.8	72%	78
VEL	++	2003	aa	2TM	4	4	26	57	2.21	1.24	4.4	222	306	30%	2.88 -	3.9	9.8	2.5	0.5	84%	107
BRE	++++		MLE		0	0	0	0	0.00	0.00											
CHG	++	2003	MLE		4	4	26	57	2.68	1.38	4.6	248	329	31%	3.72 -	4.1	8.2	2.0	0.6	83%	78
PIT	++++	2004	Projection		4	4	7	60	3.90	1.37	4.6	242	326	30%	3.70	4.2	8.4	2.0	0.8	73%	77

Power LHer with a plus slider and a fastball hard enough to overmatch hitters. Shows good command and attacks hitters aggressively. He'll settle into a setup role, getting some save opps along the way.

3 Rodney,Fernando

		Year	Lev	Tm	W	L	Sv	IP	ERA	Br/IP	BF/G	OBA	OOB	H%	xERA	Ctl	Dom	Cmd	hr/9	S%	BPV
Th	R	2002	aa	DET	1	0	11	20	1.34	0.95	3.7	198	251	27%	1.32	2.2	8.1	3.6	0.0	84%	139
Role	Reliever	2002	aaa	DET	1	1	4	22	0.81	1.00	4.3	173	261	24%	1.61 -	3.7	10.2	2.8	0.4	95%	128
Age	27 Growth	2002	MLB	DET	1	3	0	18	6.00	1.94	4.4	330	408	36%	6.73 -	5.0	5.0	1.0	1.0	70%	10
Type	Power	2003	aaa	DET	1	1	23	40	1.34	0.87	4.0	163	236	28%	0.74 +	2.9	13.0	4.5	0.0	83%	194
VEL	++++	2003	MLB	DET	1	3	3	29	6.16	1.78	5.1	298	387	40%	5.41 +	5.2	10.2	1.9	0.6	64%	79
BRE	+++	2002	MLE		2	1	15	42	1.29	1.10	4.1	213	280	28%	2.16 -	3.0	7.9	2.6	0.2	89%	109
CHG	++	2003	MLE		1	1	23	40	1.79	1.00	4.1	192	261	30%	1.44	2.9	11.0	3.8	0.0	80%	162
PIT	+	2004	Projection		1	2	16	60	4.65	1.57	4.7	274	357	37%	4.49	4.5	9.9	2.2	0.6	70%	88

Finished '03 as the DET closer, though he was the lesser of the evils rather than the standout. Live fastball, can get the strikeout, and pitched well in the 2nd half, but tends to overthrow, flattening-out his pitches.

19 Rosario,Rodrigo

		Year	Lev	Tm	W	L	Sv	IP	ERA	Br/IP	BF/G	OBA	OOB	H%	xERA	Ctl	Dom	Cmd	hr/9	S%	BPV
Th	R	2000	a	HOU	5	6	0	76	3.43	1.30	22.9	238	316	30%	3.10	3.8	7.9	2.1	0.4	73%	88
Role	Starter	2001	a	HOU	13	4	2	147	2.14	0.96	19.0	202	254	25%	1.95	2.2	8.0	3.6	0.5	80%	124
Age	26 Growth	2002	aa	HOU	11	6	0	130	3.11	1.27	21.0	224	310	27%	2.82	4.1	6.5	1.6	0.3	75%	72
Type	Power	2003	aaa	HOU	5	7	0	87	4.03	1.18	23.8	224	296	27%	3.01 +	3.3	7.0	2.1	0.7	67%	75
VEL	+++	2003	MLB	HOU	1	0	0	8	1.13	1.00	15.7	181	262	23%	1.37	3.4	6.8	2.0	0.0	88%	101
BRE	+++	2002	MLE		11	6	0	130	3.81	1.39	21.6	248	331	29%	3.57	4.2	5.6	1.4	0.4	72%	55
CHG	+++	2003	MLE		5	7	0	87	5.79	1.41	25.1	264	334	29%	4.42 +	3.6	5.9	1.6	1.0	59%	41
PIT	++	2004	Projection		7	7	0	100	4.14	1.35	23.7	250	324	28%	3.84	3.7	6.1	1.7	0.8	71%	52

Would have spent '03 as HOU 5th starter, but had minor surgery on his shoulder. His whip-like delivery gives him excellent movement to two breaking pitches, and is tough on RH batters. Should be ready by spring training.

8 Tsao,Chin-hui

		Year	Lev	Tm	W	L	Sv	IP	ERA	Br/IP	BF/G	OBA	OOB	H%	xERA	Ctl	Dom	Cmd	hr/9	S%	BPV
Th	R	2001	a	COL	0	4	0	17	4.76	1.65	19.4	324	369	42%	5.37 -	2.6	9.5	3.6	0.5	70%	107
Role	Starter	2002	a	COL	0	0	0	11	0.00	0.73	13.4	162	205	29%	0.41	1.6	13.1	8.0	0.0	100%	269
Age	22 Growth	2002	a	COL	4	2	0	47	2.11	0.98	20.4	204	258	26%	2.04	2.3	8.6	3.8	0.6	81%	127
Type	Power	2003	aa	COL	11	4	0	113	2.47	1.01	24.7	216	263	29%	2.28	2.1	9.9	4.8	0.6	78%	156
VEL	++++	2003	MLB	COL	3	3	0	43	6.06	1.58	21.5	283	359	29%	6.29	4.2	6.1	1.5	2.3	68%	-4
BRE	+++	2003	MLE		0	0	0	0	0.00	0.00											
CHG	++	2003	MLE		11	4	0	113	3.58	1.20	25.9	256	299	32%	3.68	2.1	8.7	4.2	1.0	73%	115
PIT	+++	2004	Projection		7	9	0	120	4.95	1.44	26.2	276	338	32%	5.13	3.3	7.9	2.4	1.6	70%	50

A shame that he'll be pitching half his games in Coors, as his skills are as solid as any minor leaguer. His electric fastball/slider combo from a deceptive delivery helped him lead the TL in ERA, though he struggled in COL

24 VanBenschoten,John

			Lev	Tm	W	L	Sv	IP	ERA	Br/IP	BF/G	OBA	OOB	H%	xERA	Ctl	Dom	Cmd	hr/9	S%	BPV
Th	R				0	0	0	0	0.00	0.00											
Role	Starter	2001	a	PIT	0	2	0	26	3.46	1.27	12.1	239	310	30%	2.74 +	3.5	6.6	1.9	0.0	70%	87
Age	24 Growth	2002	a	PIT	11	4	0	148	2.80	1.22	22.7	222	302	29%	2.67	3.8	8.8	2.3	0.4	77%	102
Type	Power	2003	a	PIT	6	0	0	48	2.24	1.06	21.3	195	273	27%	1.82	3.4	9.1	2.7	0.2	78%	122
VEL	++++	2003	aa	PIT	7	6	0	90	3.70	1.43	23.1	272	337	34%	4.05	3.4	7.8	2.3	0.5	74%	81
BRE	+++		MLE		0	0	0	0	0.00	0.00											
CHG	++	2003	MLE		7	6	0	90	5.29	1.72	24.6	321	379	38%	5.62	3.5	6.5	1.9	0.6	68%	51
PIT	+++	2004	Projection		5	5	0	80	4.28	1.44	23.2	269	338	33%	3.97	3.6	7.5	2.1	0.5	69%	77

His base skills held up well with a promotion to AA, and his development has progressed as scheduled. With fluid arm action, he throws four pitches for strikes and is learning how to use his arsenal. Potential #2 starter.

27 Vogelsong,Ryan

		Year	Lev	Tm	W	L	Sv	IP	ERA	Br/IP	BF/G	OBA	OOB	H%	xERA	Ctl	Dom	Cmd	hr/9	S%	BPV
Th	R	2001	MLB	SF	0	5	0	34	6.84	1.73	10.6	288	380	31%	6.02 +	5.3	6.3	1.2	1.6	62%	13
Role	Reliever	2002	a	PIT	1	1	0	16	7.88	1.63	18.2	296	366	43%	4.39 +	3.9	11.3	2.9	0.0	46%	123
Age	26 Growth	2002	aa	PIT	1	5	0	43	5.63	1.32	22.9	278	319	33%	4.32 +	2.1	7.3	3.5	1.0	58%	85
Type	Power	2003	aaa	PIT	12	8	0	149	4.29	1.32	24.3	253	318	32%	3.69 +	3.3	8.8	2.7	0.7	68%	92
VEL	+++	2003	MLB	PIT	2	2	0	22	6.55	1.77	17.2	326	386	38%	5.67 +	3.7	6.1	1.7	0.4	61%	49
BRE	++	2002	MLE		1	5	0	43	7.74	1.63	24.4	331	366	36%	6.19 +	2.1	5.7	2.7	1.3	52%	42
CHG	+++	2003	MLE		12	8	0	149	5.80	1.53	25.5	292	352	35%	4.86 +	3.3	7.3	2.2	0.8	61%	63
PIT	+++	2004	Projection		6	10	0	120	4.58	1.48	24.0	288	345	34%	4.64	3.1	7.3	2.4	0.8	70%	68

BPIs describe an under-achiever, though he will need to stop nibbling at the Major League level. Fares better when he only has to use two pitches and can "air-out" his fastball, so relief work could be in his future.

6 Waechter,Doug

		Year	Lev	Tm	W	L	Sv	IP	ERA	Br/IP	BF/G	OBA	OOB	H%	xERA	Ctl	Dom	Cmd	hr/9	S%	BPV
Th	R	2002	a	TAM	9	6	0	144	2.88	1.38	25.8	274	328	35%	4.02 -	2.8	8.6	3.0	0.7	81%	95
Role	Starter	2002	aa	TAM	1	3	0	18	9.00	2.22	23.1	347	441	41%	8.63	6.5	9.0	1.4	2.0	61%	9
Age	23 Growth	2003	aa	TAM	5	3	0	76	4.14	1.22	24.2	256	302	29%	3.53 +	2.2	5.3	2.4	0.7	67%	64
Type	Power	2003	aaa	TAM	3	3	0	51	3.35	1.23	21.2	261	304	28%	4.40 -	2.1	6.2	2.9	1.6	81%	53
VEL	+++	2003	MLB	TAM	3	2	0	35	3.33	1.25	24.4	227	308	26%	3.50	3.8	7.4	1.9	1.0	78%	64
BRE	+++		MLE		0	0	0	0	0.00	0.00											
CHG	+++	2003	MLE		8	6	0	127	5.02	1.43	24.1	293	337	31%	5.06	2.3	4.8	2.1	1.2	67%	32
PIT	++++	2004	Projection		8	6	0	120	4.05	1.31	24.2	263	317	30%	4.14	2.7	6.2	2.3	1.1	72%	57

Though his W/L didn't show it, he pitched very well for TAM. He won't overpower anyone, but throws four pitches for strikes and repeats his delivery. Upside is limited, but will be a solid starter.

4 Wagner,Ryan

		Year	Lev	Tm	W	L	Sv	IP	ERA	Br/IP	BF/G	OBA	OOB	H%	xERA	Ctl	Dom	Cmd	hr/9	S%	BPV
Th	R				0	0	0	0	0.00	0.00											
Role	Reliever				0	0	0	0	0.00	0.00											
Age	21 Green	2003	aa	CIN	1	0	0	5	0.00	0.80	3.7	124	221	20%	0.17	3.6	10.8	3.0	0.0	100%	158
Type	Power	2003	aaa	CIN	0	1	0	4	4.50	1.25	4.2	307	307	41%	3.63 +	0.0	9.0		0.0	60%	48
VEL	++++	2003	MLB	CIN	2	0	0	21	1.70	1.18	5.1	179	295	24%	2.55 -	5.1	10.6	2.1	0.8	91%	101
BRE	++++		MLE		0	0	0	0	0.00	0.00											
CHG		2003	MLE		1	1	0	9	3.00	1.11	4.0	240	283	33%	2.32 +	2.0	9.0	4.5	0.0	70%	156
PIT	++	2004	Projection		3	6	0	80	3.83	1.45	11.7	244	340	32%	4.07	4.8	9.7	2.0	0.9	76%	79

The first 2003 draftee to debut in the Majors, he held his own despite only 9 IP in the minors. Slider is a lethal pitch and has enough fastball to blow hitters away. Would work great in a setup role, but CIN may try him as a starter.

Major League Equivalents

In his 1985 *Baseball Abstract*, Bill James introduced the concept of major league equivalencies. His assertion was that, with the proper adjustments, a minor leaguer's statistics could be converted to an equivalent major league level performance with a great deal of accuracy.

Because of wide variations in the level of play among different minor leagues, it is difficult to get a true reading on a player's potential. For instance, a .300 AVG achieved in the high-offense Pacific Coast League is not nearly as much of an accomplishment as a similar level in the Eastern League. MLEs normalize these type of variances, for all statistical categories.

The actual MLEs are not projections. They represent how a player's previous performance might look at the major league level. However, that MLE stat line can be used in forecasting future performance in just the same way as a major league stat line would.

The model we use contains a few minor variations to James' version and updates all of the minor league and ballpark factors. In addition, we have designed a module to project pitching statistics, which is something James did not do.

Another of the enhancements we made is to include an adjustment for each player's age and relative level reached at that age. This serves to truly separate the prospects from the suspects. In other words, it might seem that Phil Hiatt's 25 HR, .272 season may look worthy of another shot in the majors, but a 34-year-old facing young Triple-A pitching is bound to put up good numbers. His MLE of 19 HRs, .218 shows the appropriate — albeit radical — adjustment facing potential big league pitchers, and diffuses any thought of him being able to help a major league club.

Do MLEs really work?

Used correctly, MLEs are excellent indicators of potential. But, just like we cannot take traditional major league statistics at face value, the same goes for MLEs. The underlying measures of base skill — batting eye ratios, pitching command ratios, etc. — are far more accurate in evaluating future talent than raw home runs, batting averages or ERAs.

The charts we present here also provide the unique perspective of looking at two year's worth of data. These are only short-term trends, for sure. But even here we can find small indications of players improving their skills, or struggling, as they rise through more difficult levels of competition. Since players — especially those with any modicum of talent — are promoted rapidly through major league systems, a two-year scan is often all we get to spot any trends.

Here are some things to look for as you scan these charts:

Target players who...
- spent a full season in Double-A and then a full season at Triple-A
- had consistent playing time from one year to the next
- maintained or improved their base skills levels as they were promoted.

Raise the warning flag for players who...
- were stuck at the same level both years, or regressed
- displayed marked changes in playing time from one year to the next.
- showed large drops in BPIs from one year to the next.

Also be sure to keep an eye on each player's age. While minor leaguers over 26 have officially lost their "prospect" status, there are still some who will make it to the majors. Don't discount them completely or you might end up missing out on a player like Scott Podsednik.

Players are listed on the charts if they spent at least part of 2002 or 2003 in Triple-A or Double-A and had at least 100 at bats or 30 innings pitched within those two levels. Each is listed with the organization they finished the season with.

Only statistics accumulated in Triple-A and Double-A ball are included (and players who split a season are indicated as a/a); major league and Single-A stats are excluded.

Each player's actual AB and IP totals are used as the base for the conversion. However, it is more useful to compare performances using common levels, so rely on the ratios and sabermetric gauges. Complete explanations of these formulas appear in the glossary.

BATTER	Yr	Age	Pos	Lev	Org	ab	r	h	d	t	hr	rbi	bb	k	sb	cs	ba	ob	slg	ops	bb%	ct%	eye	px	sx	rc/g	bpv
Abad,Andy	02	30	8	aaa	FLA	352	32	80	22	2	6	46	38	37	0	4	227	303	352	655	10%	89%	1.03	87	39	3.62	32
	03	31	38	aaa	BOS	504	61	131	32	2	9	74	42	67	0	3	259	316	382	698	8%	87%	0.63	86	42	4.30	35
Abbott,Jeff	02	30	8	aaa	BOS	367	36	87	24	1	7	32	19	42	3	2	237	275	365	640	5%	89%	0.45	90	63	3.42	25
Abercrombie,Reggie	03	22	8	aa	LA	448	56	107	22	5	14	51	16	161	27	10	239	265	404	669	3%	64%	0.10	102	169	3.52	24
Abernathy,Brent	03	26	4	aaa	KC	373	51	104	21	0	7	35	28	32	11	8	278	329	390	719	7%	91%	0.88	79	76	4.51	43
Abreu,Dennis	02	24	4	aa	CHC	402	38	101	15	3	6	43	21	97	15	15	251	288	348	637	5%	76%	0.22	63	102	3.13	14
Acevas,Jon	02	25	2	a/a	CHW	165	23	35	7	1	3	14	20	32	0	1	212	297	321	619	11%	81%	0.63	71	68	3.31	13
Acevedo,Anthony	03	25	8	aa	HOU	459	45	108	19	2	8	41	40	90	7	5	235	296	337	633	8%	80%	0.44	67	73	3.48	15
Aceves,Jon	03	26	2	a/a	CHW	151	17	34	8	0	3	17	14	38	0	2	226	293	333	627	9%	75%	0.38	74	36	3.27	13
Ackerman,Scott	03	24	2	aa	MON	292	23	55	10	2	6	32	12	36	0	2	189	222	296	518	4%	88%	0.35	68	54	2.06	-2
Acuna,Ron	03	24	8	aa	NYM	474	55	120	23	2	2	39	26	78	19	13	253	291	321	612	5%	84%	0.33	52	102	3.09	12
Adams,Russ	03	23	6	aa	TOR	271	34	67	10	3	3	20	24	31	7	1	247	309	336	645	8%	89%	0.78	58	119	3.84	22
Agbayani,Benny	02	31	8	aaa	BOS	164	23	36	8	1	8	26	23	37	1	0	220	316	427	742	12%	77%	0.62	124	72	4.81	37
	03	32	8	aaa	KC	299	35	59	7	0	13	32	37	51	0	2	199	287	349	636	11%	83%	0.72	87	26	3.39	16
Aguila,Chris	02	24	8	aa	FLA	429	49	109	24	3	5	37	39	89	11	9	254	316	359	675	8%	79%	0.44	74	95	3.91	24
	03	25	8	aa	FLA	337	48	95	19	3	9	46	31	65	5	2	282	343	431	774	9%	81%	0.48	97	99	5.51	43
Ahumada,Alex	02	24	6	aa	BOS	185	23	39	4	2	1	15	12	34	8	4	211	259	270	529	6%	82%	0.35	37	139	2.32	-7
Airoso,Kurt	02	28	0	aa	DET	386	51	80	12	0	11	43	41	100	4	3	207	283	324	607	10%	74%	0.41	72	62	3.14	7
	03	29	8	aa	BAL	354	37	61	10	2	13	40	35	109	3	2	172	247	316	563	9%	69%	0.32	84	74	2.55	-2
Alcantara,Israel	02	29	8	aaa	MIL	410	50	96	18	1	24	54	42	86	7	3	234	305	459	764	9%	79%	0.49	132	68	4.87	42
Aldridge,Cory	03	24	8	aa	ATL	448	48	95	18	1	14	43	31	126	10	3	212	264	352	616	7%	72%	0.25	87	86	3.15	11
Alexander,Chad	02	28	8	aaa	DET	313	31	73	20	4	5	29	18	54	2	4	233	275	371	646	5%	83%	0.33	93	95	3.34	23
Alexander,Manny	03	33	6	aaa	TEX	450	41	99	14	5	4	38	23	70	22	10	220	259	296	555	5%	84%	0.33	50	128	2.53	0
Alfaro,Jason	02	25	5	aa	HOU	455	53	125	32	2	13	55	37	63	9	10	275	329	440	769	8%	86%	0.59	110	73	4.97	49
	03	26	56	a/a	HOU	442	41	106	21	3	8	47	28	65	2	4	241	285	352	638	6%	85%	0.42	74	60	3.41	19
Alfonzo,Eliezer	02	24	2	aa	MIL	244	19	57	14	1	6	32	8	48	2	3	234	258	373	631	3%	80%	0.17	92	57	3.11	19
Allegra,Matt	03	22	8	aa	OAK	452	44	94	19	1	12	56	26	130	4	2	208	251	334	585	5%	71%	0.20	80	67	2.79	6
Allensworth,Jermair	02	31	8	aa	ATL	270	27	48	11	1	1	21	27	56	5	1	178	253	237	490	9%	79%	0.48	45	90	2.10	-13
Allen,Chad	02	28	8	aaa	CLE	311	40	84	20	1	10	55	13	39	0	1	270	299	437	737	4%	87%	0.33	110	49	4.62	42
	03	29	8	aaa	FLA	337	32	88	25	2	6	37	13	41	7	12	262	290	397	687	4%	88%	0.32	96	79	3.52	34
Allen,Luke	02	24	8	aaa	LA	501	60	137	23	1	8	55	40	56	3	8	273	327	371	698	7%	89%	0.71	67	46	4.24	33
	03	25	8	aaa	COL	438	48	113	20	2	6	34	38	55	7	14	258	316	353	669	8%	88%	0.69	65	65	3.63	26
Almonte,Erick	02	25	6	a/a	NYY	408	45	87	15	1	15	52	39	102	10	3	213	282	365	647	9%	75%	0.38	92	83	3.56	17
	03	26	6	aaa	NYY	179	22	39	10	1	4	22	14	39	3	3	216	272	348	620	7%	78%	0.35	88	91	3.08	15
Alvarez,Gabe	03	30	3	aa	CHW	410	43	92	24	0	9	56	43	108	2	4	225	298	349	648	9%	74%	0.40	86	34	3.57	18
Alvarez,Jimmy	02	23	4	aa	TOR	497	62	120	30	2	6	51	59	96	15	13	241	322	346	668	11%	81%	0.61	76	87	3.81	24
	03	24	64	aaa	TOR	342	40	83	13	5	4	22	40	80	10	5	243	322	345	667	10%	77%	0.50	65	132	3.99	18
Alvarez,Nick	03	27	38	aa	LA	292	32	64	12	1	4	38	18	53	16	10	218	264	310	573	6%	82%	0.35	63	107	2.58	5
Alvarez,Tony	02	23	8	aa	PIT	507	63	144	35	1	11	48	21	57	23	20	284	313	422	735	4%	89%	0.37	96	92	4.23	42
	03	24	8	aaa	PIT	349	43	97	26	2	7	46	24	56	19	10	278	324	424	748	6%	84%	0.43	102	111	4.75	43
Alviso,Jerome	02	27	6	aaa	COL	304	20	82	12	0	1	16	8	18	3	1	270	288	319	608	3%	94%	0.44	40	45	3.28	15
	03	28	4	a/a	BAL	248	18	48	4	0	0	9	9	26	5	3	192	221	209	430	4%	90%	0.36	15	69	1.51	-23
Ambres,Chip	03	24	8	aa	FLA	380	63	88	21	8	8	47	63	76	8	7	232	342	391	732	14%	80%	0.83	99	153	4.70	35
Amezaga,Alfredo	02	25	6	aaa	ANA	518	58	113	22	4	5	39	34	74	17	17	218	266	305	571	6%	86%	0.46	59	110	2.50	6
	03	26	6	aaa	ANA	317	44	98	18	3	2	36	16	30	11	10	309	342	403	745	5%	90%	0.52	68	111	4.78	41
Amezcua,Adan	02	29	2	a/a	SD	229	19	57	9	1	4	26	11	33	0	0	249	283	349	633	5%	86%	0.33	66	36	3.48	17
Amrhein,Mike	02	27	2	a/a	CHC	317	29	79	15	1	4	30	20	31	3	4	249	294	341	634	6%	90%	0.65	64	56	3.41	22
Anderson,Bryan	03	25	6	aa	CIN	101	9	18	7	0	1	10	9	26	0	1	178	245	276	522	8%	75%	0.35	77	40	2.18	-2
Andrews,Shane	02	31	5	aaa	BOS	390	47	83	17	1	15	48	39	117	1	1	213	284	377	661	9%	70%	0.33	100	52	3.68	19
	03	32	5	aaa	MIN	445	41	98	29	2	8	48	34	129	2	2	220	276	348	624	7%	71%	0.27	89	58	3.28	16
Ansman,Craig	03	26	2	aa	ARI	213	31	57	14	1	11	32	22	47	4	4	266	334	494	828	9%	78%	0.46	142	75	5.73	57
Ardoin,Danny	02	28	2	a/a	TEX	183	15	34	7	0	4	16	16	47	1	0	186	251	290	541	8%	74%	0.34	68	39	2.48	-3
	03	29	2	aaa	TEX	239	27	50	10	2	6	27	16	54	0	2	209	260	346	607	6%	77%	0.30	85	71	2.94	11
Arias,Alex	02	35	6	aaa	NYY	263	24	50	14	0	1	18	15	23	2	2	190	234	255	489	5%	91%	0.65	53	58	1.93	-2
Arteaga,Joshua	03	24	64	a/a	CHC	230	30	53	12	0	1	15	8	35	1	1	230	256	296	552	3%	85%	0.23	53	67	2.55	3
Asche,Kirk	02	25	8	aa	OAK	376	39	73	11	6	9	43	31	126	7	6	194	256	327	583	8%	66%	0.25	77	144	2.68	1
Ashby,Chris	03	29	83	a/a	FLA	308	20	65	12	1	3	29	9	44	5	2	210	233	287	520	3%	86%	0.21	54	71	2.21	-4
Athas,Jamie	03	24	6	aa	SF	444	49	105	13	2	2	34	38	70	10	12	236	296	286	582	8%	84%	0.54	36	79	2.80	4
Atkins,Garrett	02	23	5	aa	COL	510	51	132	25	2	11	44	43	52	4	7	259	316	380	697	8%	90%	0.83	80	51	4.17	36
	03	24	5	aaa	COL	439	60	134	29	1	12	50	34	36	1	5	305	355	458	813	7%	92%	0.94	103	40	5.96	63
Aven,Bruce	02	31	0	aaa	PHI	324	32	69	14	0	10	44	40	56	3	1	213	299	349	648	11%	83%	0.71	86	45	3.69	21
	03	32	8	aaa	TOR	192	16	35	5	0	3	14	21	42	1	1	183	262	248	511	10%	78%	0.49	43	37	2.23	-12
Bacani,David	03	24	4	aa	NYM	103	10	21	3	0	0	6	16	17	4	4	203	311	231	542	14%	84%	0.96	24	63	2.48	-3
Badeaux,Brooks	02	26	4	aaa	TAM	340	39	78	14	2	2	25	24	39	7	2	229	280	300	580	7%	89%	0.62	51	101	2.97	10
	03	27	45	a/a	TAM	287	28	58	13	2	2	14	21	53	2	3	201	254	276	530	7%	81%	0.39	54	75	2.31	-3
Bailey,Jeff	02	24	3	aa	MON	309	35	77	16	1	11	41	49	63	2	4	249	352	414	766	14%	80%	0.78	104	43	5.22	41
	03	25	328	a/a	MON	379	45	83	19	2	11	48	27	63	2	1	220	272	366	638	7%	83%	0.43	93	73	3.41	21
Bair,Rod	02	28	8	aaa	COL	258	20	59	15	1	3	23	11	31	9	7	229	260	329	590	4%	88%	0.35	73	85	2.68	13
Baker,John	03	23	2	aa	OAK	150	13	31	3	0	1	17	11	38	0	0	207	261	247	508	7%	75%	0.29	28	27	2.23	-14
Baldelli,Rocco	02	21	8	a/a	TAM	166	22	56	10	2	4	19	4	27	4	9	337	353	494	847	2%	84%	0.15	101	108	5.47	57
Balfe,Ryan	03	28	32	a/a	MON	261	29	60	14	0	5	29	19	51	0	0	230	283	343	626	7%	81%	0.38	78	30	3.39	16
Banks,Brian	02	32	3	aaa	FLA	439	59	104	30	2	12	59	49	66	6	5	237	314	396	710	10%	85%	0.74	107	79	4.32	38
Barbier,Blair	03	26	5	aa	CHC	137	7	26	2	0	1	14	14	21	0	3	191	263	223	486	9%	85%	0.64	22	18	1.88	-15
Barden,Brian	03	23	5	aa	ARI	383	37	100	22	4	2	42	22	56	7	5	261	301	355	656	5%	85%	0.39	68	101	3.72	23
Bard,Josh	02	25	2	aaa	CLE	344	33	98	25	1	6	49	18	42	0	0	285	320	416	736	5%	88%	0.43	94	32	4.91	42
	03	26	2	aaa	CLE	115	13	36	7	0	5	19	13	16	1	2	310	379	499	879	10%	86%	0.80	120	31	6.99	69
Barker,Kevin	02	27	3	aaa	SD	390	45	82	11	1	10	40	37	66	1	1	210	279	321	599	9%	83%	0.56	67	52	3.08	9
Barkett,Andy	02	28	3	aa	SEA	421	43	79	18	1	6	47	43	93	7	7	188	263	278	541	9%	78%	0.46	62	72	2.39	-3
	03	29	3	aaa	SEA	401	34	80	17	1	10	51	34	85	4	3	200	262	322	584	8%	79%	0.40	79	54	2.81	7
Barmes,Clint	02	24	6	aa	COL	438	44	111	20	2	14	42	21	49	11	13	253	288	404	692	5%	89%	0.43	94	77	3.66	32
	03	25	6	aaa	COL	493	47	129	33	1	7	40	17	44	9	8	262	286	375	662	3%	91%	0.39	83	69	3.60	29

Major League Equivalent Statistics

BATTER	Yr	Age	Pos	Lev	Org	ab	r	h	d	t	hr	rbi	bb	k	sb	cs	ba	ob	slg	ops	bb%	ct%	eye	px	sx	rc/g	bpv
Barnes,John	02	26	8	aaa	COL	269	28	68	17	1	5	18	12	10	3	5	253	285	379	664	4%	96%	1.20	88	65	3.52	45
	03	27	8	aaa	PIT	402	50	116	29	1	10	57	23	35	12	8	288	327	444	771	5%	91%	0.66	107	84	5.12	53
Barnes,Larry	02	28	3	aaa	ANA	452	50	116	24	6	16	68	20	72	6	1	257	288	442	731	4%	84%	0.28	114	119	4.51	38
	03	29	3	aaa	LA	302	31	64	15	2	10	41	17	55	3	1	211	254	371	624	5%	82%	0.31	99	81	3.15	18
Barns,B.J.	03	26	8	aa	PIT	202	18	39	8	0	0	18	23	49	0	3	194	278	233	510	10%	76%	0.48	34	31	2.18	-12
Barnwell,Chris	03	25	46	aa	MIL	313	34	68	7	0	3	22	23	45	5	6	219	272	267	539	7%	86%	0.50	33	62	2.39	-4
Baron,Brian	02	24	8	aa	MIN	390	36	102	21	0	1	27	15	42	2	1	262	289	323	612	4%	89%	0.36	52	48	3.31	16
	03	25	8	aa	MIN	276	26	59	10	2	0	26	15	17	1	4	212	253	261	514	5%	94%	0.92	38	67	2.12	4
Bartee,Kimera	02	30	8	aaa	CHC	419	37	79	20	1	6	41	26	88	15	15	189	236	284	520	6%	79%	0.30	67	89	1.94	-4
Barthol,Blake	02	30	2	aaa	SEA	178	23	35	14	2	2	14	19	43	0	2	197	274	331	606	10%	76%	0.44	97	95	2.97	14
	03	31	2	aaa	PIT	102	12	19	5	0	2	9	7	20	1	1	185	239	282	521	7%	80%	0.36	66	64	2.18	-4
Bartlett,Jason	03	24	6	aa	MIN	548	80	147	30	7	6	40	47	61	34	26	269	326	381	707	8%	89%	0.77	76	141	4.02	36
Basak,Chris	02	24	64	a/a	NYM	437	51	97	17	3	3	34	34	95	20	16	222	278	295	573	7%	78%	0.36	51	117	2.59	2
	03	25	6	a/a	NYM	475	57	110	27	1	6	42	34	114	17	15	231	282	329	611	7%	76%	0.30	71	94	2.96	12
Bass,Jayson	02	28	8	aaa	CHC	419	51	94	11	2	14	52	34	70	8	8	224	283	360	643	8%	83%	0.49	79	83	3.33	17
Bates,Fletcher	02	29	8	a/a	NYM	268	29	60	13	3	6	33	17	46	4	5	224	270	362	632	6%	83%	0.37	87	104	3.13	18
	03	30	8	a/a	BAL	149	16	25	8	1	1	13	9	33	1	0	171	218	253	471	6%	78%	0.27	62	90	1.82	-12
Battersby,Eric	02	27	3	a/a	CHW	385	32	84	16	1	6	31	31	63	4	4	218	276	312	588	7%	84%	0.49	63	55	2.90	9
Battle,Howard	02	31	5	aaa	MON	193	15	39	10	0	4	14	8	27	0	1	202	234	316	550	4%	86%	0.30	78	29	2.37	5
Baughman,Justin	02	28	8	aaa	CHW	420	47	83	10	0	6	31	27	72	25	9	198	246	264	510	6%	83%	0.38	43	108	2.18	-9
Bautista,Rayner	02	24	6	aa	DET	302	27	67	16	2	3	26	18	58	4	2	222	266	318	584	6%	81%	0.31	68	86	2.87	8
	03	25	6	aa	DET	398	36	95	14	5	7	39	14	91	4	3	237	264	351	615	3%	77%	0.16	70	99	3.11	11
Bay,Jason	02	24	8	aa	SD	188	29	48	8	3	7	27	24	45	14	6	255	340	441	781	11%	76%	0.53	109	165	5.25	41
	03	25	8	aaa	SD	307	52	80	9	1	15	49	44	61	19	5	261	353	442	795	12%	80%	0.72	103	110	5.84	44
Beattie,Andrew	03	26	4	a/a	CIN	453	44	102	29	1	6	33	37	74	4	10	224	283	329	612	8%	84%	0.50	77	50	3.00	17
Beattie,Andy	02	25	8	aa	CIN	166	18	36	9	1	5	14	13	24	2	2	217	274	373	647	7%	86%	0.54	100	77	3.37	24
Beinbrink,Andrew	03	27	5	aa	TEX	451	48	95	19	1	8	46	44	92	19	10	210	280	311	591	9%	80%	0.48	68	91	2.92	7
Beinbrink,Andy	02	26	5	a/a	TAM	426	48	110	23	1	3	49	46	75	17	11	258	331	338	669	10%	82%	0.61	61	84	3.95	23
Bellinger,Clay	02	34	8	aaa	ANA	324	31	66	14	3	10	28	9	71	3	2	204	225	358	583	3%	78%	0.13	94	100	2.58	9
	03	35	58	aaa	SF	377	40	78	14	3	9	40	18	64	2	2	208	244	332	576	5%	83%	0.28	77	81	2.65	7
Bell,Mike	02	28	5	aaa	COL	240	20	58	16	1	3	21	10	26	3	5	242	272	354	626	4%	89%	0.38	82	64	3.06	22
	03	29	4	aaa	ARI	416	43	93	22	2	8	50	19	47	1	4	224	257	347	603	4%	89%	0.39	83	56	2.90	16
Bell,Rick	02	24	5	aaa	LA	448	42	98	21	2	9	54	11	54	0	1	219	237	335	572	2%	88%	0.20	77	51	2.61	9
	03	25	53	aaa	LA	343	39	85	21	4	4	39	13	36	2	2	248	275	367	643	4%	90%	0.36	83	98	3.45	24
Benick,Jon	03	24	3	aa	SD	123	10	21	6	0	1	8	7	32	0	1	170	212	239	452	5%	74%	0.21	53	41	1.58	-17
Benjamin,Al	02	25	8	a/a	SD	221	19	41	11	1	3	15	5	46	1	2	186	204	285	489	2%	79%	0.11	69	74	1.77	-7
Bergeron,Peter	02	25	8	aaa	MON	340	45	93	9	3	1	25	33	56	6	8	274	338	326	664	9%	84%	0.59	36	93	3.88	18
	03	26	8	aaa	MON	388	47	102	18	4	1	24	27	48	9	4	263	310	337	647	6%	88%	0.55	54	113	3.76	21
Berger,Brandon	02	28	8	aaa	KC	261	27	67	14	1	10	36	19	36	9	2	257	307	433	740	7%	86%	0.53	110	87	4.79	42
	03	29	8	aaa	KC	226	32	53	14	2	9	39	22	47	5	1	235	303	436	740	9%	79%	0.47	126	109	4.69	39
Berroa,Angel	02	25	6	aaa	KC	297	30	59	10	3	7	28	12	65	5	5	199	230	323	553	4%	78%	0.18	75	113	2.28	1
Betemit,Wilson	02	22	6	aaa	ATL	343	40	82	17	1	7	32	30	68	7	6	239	300	356	656	8%	80%	0.44	78	76	3.62	21
	03	22	5	aaa	ATL	478	57	132	24	11	9	68	39	96	9	6	276	330	428	758	7%	80%	0.40	94	157	5.08	39
Betts,Todd	02	29	3	aaa	BOS	416	46	102	15	2	10	35	47	55	3	5	245	322	363	685	10%	87%	0.85	73	56	4.10	29
Bierek,Kurt	02	30	8	aaa	TEX	220	14	37	8	1	2	14	13	36	1	1	168	215	241	456	6%	84%	0.36	50	57	1.66	-16
Bigbie,Larry	02	25	8	aaa	BAL	348	37	95	20	1	2	31	30	71	6	3	273	331	353	684	8%	80%	0.42	62	72	4.31	25
	03	26	8	aaa	BAL	117	22	37	12	2	3	20	13	29	0	0	313	381	525	906	10%	75%	0.44	144	114	7.83	73
Bikowski,Scott	02	26	8	aa	CHW	395	38	86	14	1	4	29	50	69	14	11	218	306	289	594	11%	83%	0.72	49	76	3.01	7
	03	27	8	aa	CHW	394	44	103	19	2	3	40	44	70	3	6	261	334	338	672	10%	82%	0.62	57	55	4.00	23
Blakely,Darren	02	26	8	a/a	SD	439	57	82	19	3	8	52	60	125	9	4	187	285	298	583	12%	72%	0.48	73	108	2.96	2
Blake,Casey	02	29	5	aaa	MIN	482	58	119	22	2	12	38	35	65	16	10	247	298	376	673	7%	87%	0.54	83	95	3.78	27
Blalock,Hank	02	22	5	aaa	TEX	387	53	117	32	1	7	52	29	41	2	1	302	351	444	795	7%	89%	0.71	103	60	5.92	58
Bledsoe,Hunter	02	27	3	aa	LA	348	32	78	15	1	3	31	45	47	3	3	224	313	299	612	11%	86%	0.96	54	52	3.34	16
	03	28	3	aa	KC	110	12	22	2	0	2	7	4	17	1	1	204	233	272	504	4%	85%	0.25	43	61	2.04	-9
Bloomquist,Willie	02	25	8	aaa	SEA	337	42	82	13	2	5	42	26	39	18	11	243	298	338	636	7%	88%	0.67	62	113	3.33	20
Bocachica,Hiram	03	28	84	aaa	DET	322	44	68	16	4	10	33	22	54	10	6	212	262	375	637	6%	83%	0.41	101	138	3.17	20
Bolivar,Papo	02	24	8	aa	MIN	547	63	138	34	2	10	70	38	87	15	6	252	301	377	677	6%	84%	0.44	87	94	3.99	29
	03	25	8	aa	STL	474	49	119	22	2	4	46	43	73	27	11	251	313	329	641	8%	85%	0.59	57	102	3.65	19
Bonifay,Josh	03	25	8	aa	PIT	386	41	95	27	0	8	46	32	101	1	4	245	302	378	680	8%	74%	0.31	94	33	3.91	27
Borchard,Joe	02	24	8	aaa	CHW	438	55	112	32	1	20	52	46	124	2	4	256	326	470	797	10%	72%	0.37	137	45	5.38	49
	03	25	8	aaa	CHW	435	54	103	18	1	13	46	25	88	2	4	237	278	372	651	5%	80%	0.28	85	58	3.47	20
Borders,Pat	02	39	2	aaa	SEA	317	33	68	14	1	9	22	9	46	3	2	215	236	350	586	3%	85%	0.20	86	75	2.69	11
	03	40	2	aaa	SEA	293	31	76	23	1	9	43	17	58	1	2	258	299	433	732	6%	80%	0.30	118	48	4.49	41
Boscan,Jean	03	24	2	a/a	ATL	142	12	26	7	0	2	15	14	35	0	1	183	256	275	531	9%	75%	0.40	65	31	2.32	-4
Bost,Tom	03	28	8	aa	FLA	126	10	20	2	2	2	8	12	35	2	1	159	232	248	480	9%	72%	0.34	48	138	1.90	-21
Botts,Jason	03	23	8	aa	TEX	194	22	47	11	1	4	22	17	39	5	1	240	303	365	668	8%	80%	0.45	84	92	3.99	24
Bourgeois,Jason	03	22	4	aa	TEX	202	24	48	5	3	4	18	14	38	3	1	238	287	351	639	6%	81%	0.37	66	124	3.54	14
Bowen,Rob	03	23	2	a/a	MIN	239	27	64	20	1	6	29	21	44	0	0	268	327	435	762	8%	82%	0.48	117	40	5.21	47
Bowers,Jason	02	25	6	aa	STL	343	34	83	15	2	2	28	21	40	2	2	242	286	315	601	6%	88%	0.53	53	68	3.12	13
	03	26	6	aaa	STL	415	39	95	14	5	7	32	24	66	6	6	229	271	336	607	5%	84%	0.36	66	101	3.00	11
Boyd,Patrick	03	25	8	aa	TEX	160	16	26	5	2	3	7	13	37	7	3	163	224	264	489	7%	77%	0.34	61	143	1.92	-14
Bozied,Tagg	02	23	3	aa	SD	234	30	43	12	0	8	28	14	41	1	0	184	230	338	567	6%	82%	0.34	98	65	2.55	9
	03	24	3	aaa	SD	450	48	106	21	1	11	48	30	67	1	0	236	283	360	643	6%	85%	0.45	81	50	3.58	21
Branson,Jeff	02	36	5	aaa	LA	233	19	41	11	0	2	16	13	42	0	1	176	220	249	468	5%	82%	0.31	55	37	1.75	-12
Bravo,Danny	02	25	5	aa	CHW	138	14	28	6	0	1	13	13	20	5	5	203	272	268	540	9%	86%	0.65	50	74	2.27	1
	03	26	635	aa	SD	365	33	66	12	0	3	30	37	56	0	1	181	256	236	492	9%	85%	0.65	41	31	2.06	-10
Brazell,Craig	02	22	3	aa	NYM	130	12	35	7	0	5	16	1	24	0	2	269	275	438	713	1%	82%	0.04	107	30	3.91	35
	03	23	3	a/a	NYM	478	54	123	23	1	14	66	20	93	3	1	257	287	397	685	4%	81%	0.22	90	63	4.02	27
Brewer,Jace	02	23	6	aa	TAM	153	11	30	5	0	1	14	3	24	2	0	196	212	248	460	2%	84%	0.13	39	62	1.75	-16
	03	24	6	aa	TAM	281	22	57	16	1	4	17	10	60	1	1	203	231	308	539	4%	79%	0.17	75	55	2.32	2
Bridges,Kary	02	31	4	aaa	NYY	502	52	104	6	2	6	29	34	23	5	7	207	257	263	520	6%	95%	1.48	33	69	2.21	12

Major League Equivalent Statistics

BATTER	Yr	Age	Pos	Lev	Org	ab	r	h	d	t	hr	rbi	bb	k	sb	cs	ba	ob	slg	ops	bb%	ct%	eye	px	sx	rc/g	bpv
Brinkley,Darryl	02	34	8	aaa	BAL	509	46	119	24	2	6	58	20	67	15	5	234	263	324	587	4%	87%	0.30	63	97	2.91	10
Brisson,Dustin	03	26	3	aa	BOS	211	18	40	14	0	3	25	11	41	3	1	188	227	290	517	5%	81%	0.26	76	65	2.16	-1
Brito,Juan	02	23	2	a/a	KC	311	37	78	12	0	6	35	19	36	1	1	251	294	347	641	6%	88%	0.53	64	46	3.60	21
	03	24	2	aaa	KC	122	11	27	2	0	2	10	2	19	0	2	221	234	287	521	2%	84%	0.11	40	43	2.03	-8
Brock,Tarrik	02	29	8	aa	LA	325	45	64	12	1	7	36	55	113	6	7	197	313	305	618	14%	65%	0.49	69	76	3.26	4
	03	30	38	a/a	LA	337	39	62	16	3	7	40	45	115	2	7	185	281	319	600	12%	66%	0.39	86	92	2.88	5
Broussard,Ben	02	26	83	aaa	CLE	340	54	82	20	1	16	46	49	76	4	1	241	337	447	784	13%	78%	0.64	128	76	5.49	46
	03	27	3	aaa	CLE	120	14	27	2	1	3	13	8	28	3	0	222	268	325	593	6%	76%	0.27	58	108	3.10	3
Brown,Adrian	02	29	8	aaa	PIT	184	28	53	7	1	2	12	18	15	17	7	288	351	370	721	9%	92%	1.20	55	123	4.77	43
	03	30	8	aaa	BOS	482	65	117	15	2	4	25	37	79	27	11	244	298	304	602	7%	84%	0.47	42	117	3.20	8
Brown,Dee	02	25	8	aaa	KC	458	54	116	21	1	14	61	34	87	8	5	253	305	395	700	7%	81%	0.39	90	72	4.20	29
Brown,Emil	02	28	8	aaa	TAM	422	48	106	23	3	10	48	28	75	9	2	251	298	391	689	6%	82%	0.37	91	104	4.16	29
	03	29	8	aaa	CIN	369	44	96	20	2	10	47	20	65	14	3	260	298	406	704	5%	83%	0.32	94	110	4.37	32
Brown,Jason	02	28	2	aa	MON	106	6	16	6	0	2	8	6	41	0	0	151	196	264	461	5%	61%	0.15	79	15	1.65	-14
Brown,Jeremy	03	24	2	aa	OAK	233	29	54	9	1	4	29	32	33	2	0	233	326	329	655	12%	86%	0.97	63	68	4.00	23
Brown,Kevin	02	38	2	aaa	BOS	246	25	49	12	1	5	19	15	62	0	0	199	245	317	562	6%	75%	0.24	78	50	2.60	4
Brown,Tonayne	02	25	8	aa	BOS	472	49	101	19	5	8	41	24	76	8	17	214	252	326	578	5%	84%	0.32	71	103	2.35	7
	03	26	8	aa	DET	464	49	95	18	7	3	45	22	86	3	3	204	240	291	531	4%	81%	0.25	57	119	2.28	-3
Brumbaugh,Cliff	02	28	8	aaa	COL	505	50	125	30	1	12	48	34	69	4	3	248	295	382	677	6%	86%	0.49	91	55	3.93	30
	03	29	8	aaa	CHW	223	26	59	11	1	8	24	19	45	1	3	265	323	433	756	8%	80%	0.42	104	51	4.87	40
Bruntlett,Eric	02	25	6	a/a	HOU	532	75	127	23	2	2	41	54	60	30	15	239	309	301	610	9%	89%	0.90	47	114	3.26	17
	03	26	64	aaa	HOU	324	43	80	10	0	2	24	31	46	8	4	248	313	296	609	9%	86%	0.66	37	77	3.35	11
Bubela,Jaime	03	25	8	aa	SEA	473	50	108	24	5	3	51	27	113	22	11	228	270	316	586	5%	76%	0.24	63	134	2.83	7
Buck,John	02	22	2	aa	HOU	448	38	108	27	3	10	70	24	74	2	4	241	280	382	661	5%	83%	0.32	94	59	3.58	26
	03	23	2	aaa	HOU	274	29	68	18	2	2	35	12	48	1	0	248	280	350	630	4%	82%	0.25	76	78	3.45	19
Budde,Ryan	03	24	2	aa	ANA	342	37	64	8	1	9	33	29	67	1	1	186	249	289	538	8%	80%	0.42	61	57	2.40	-4
Budzinski,Mark	02	29	8	a/a	CHC	459	53	108	16	4	3	28	39	79	15	8	235	295	307	602	8%	83%	0.49	49	115	3.15	8
	03	30	8	aaa	CIN	418	65	100	22	2	2	22	42	91	14	5	239	309	312	621	9%	78%	0.46	56	113	3.48	12
Buford,Damon	02	32	8	aaa	CHW	169	20	32	7	0	3	10	14	27	5	1	189	251	284	535	8%	84%	0.52	64	88	2.46	-0
Burford,Kevin	02	25	3	aa	COL	266	30	67	21	1	3	23	33	36	1	7	252	334	372	707	11%	86%	0.92	91	46	4.16	40
	03	26	3	aa	COL	271	28	62	14	1	6	25	32	39	4	1	229	311	355	667	11%	86%	0.83	83	66	4.00	27
Burke,Chris	02	23	4	aa	HOU	481	52	116	18	7	3	29	30	49	13	18	241	286	326	612	6%	90%	0.61	56	120	2.86	16
	03	24	46	aa	HOU	549	69	147	21	6	3	32	44	47	26	12	269	322	345	667	7%	91%	0.92	52	128	4.00	29
Burke,Jamie	02	31	2	aaa	ANA	316	32	77	10	2	6	31	14	31	1	4	244	276	345	621	4%	90%	0.45	63	60	3.13	16
	03	32	2	aaa	CHW	323	37	87	11	0	5	40	16	38	1	1	270	305	354	659	5%	88%	0.43	55	42	3.88	22
Burkhart,Lance	02	28	2	a/a	MIL	154	16	28	10	0	4	14	27	51	2	3	182	304	325	629	15%	67%	0.53	98	44	3.30	11
	03	29	2	a/a	TEX	116	9	19	5	1	3	9	14	46	0	1	161	254	308	562	11%	60%	0.31	91	64	2.54	-3
Burkhart,Morgan	03	32	3	aaa	KC	382	39	81	15	0	14	41	34	56	2	0	212	277	358	635	8%	85%	0.62	90	43	3.44	20
Burnham,Gary	02	28	3	aaa	TOR	537	53	130	32	1	12	67	40	57	1	2	242	295	372	667	7%	89%	0.70	89	38	3.83	31
	03	29	3	aaa	TOR	349	36	84	24	1	7	42	20	51	0	1	240	282	378	660	6%	86%	0.40	97	41	3.68	28
Burns,Kevan	02	26	8	aa	ARI	187	25	51	7	4	2	18	15	21	2	5	273	327	385	712	7%	89%	0.71	69	130	4.20	33
	03	27	8	aa	STL	312	29	68	12	3	3	24	20	67	5	3	218	265	304	569	6%	79%	0.30	57	108	2.69	2
Burns,Kevin	02	27	3	aa	ANA	169	14	22	8	1	3	15	23	48	1	0	130	234	243	477	12%	72%	0.48	75	69	1.93	-16
Burroughs,Sean	02	22	4	aaa	SD	179	26	50	15	1	2	21	19	14	1	0	279	348	408	756	10%	92%	1.36	96	71	5.40	60
Butler,Brent	02	25	6	aaa	COL	105	13	32	8	1	2	11	4	7	0	0	305	330	457	787	4%	93%	0.57	105	63	5.66	56
	03	26	4	aaa	COL	205	28	64	18	1	6	20	14	14	0	1	314	357	497	855	6%	93%	0.98	126	49	6.71	76
Bynum,Freddie	03	24	4	aa	OAK	510	66	113	16	6	4	46	44	116	17	9	223	284	299	582	8%	77%	0.37	49	138	2.91	2
Byrd,Marlon	02	25	8	aaa	PHI	538	85	147	38	5	12	52	41	89	13	1	273	325	429	754	7%	83%	0.46	105	134	5.22	44
Byrnes,Eric	02	27	8	aaa	OAK	119	12	25	6	0	3	12	5	11	4	1	210	242	336	578	4%	91%	0.45	84	82	2.72	14
Cabrera,Jolbert	02	30	8	aaa	LA	193	25	46	10	0	1	12	15	22	4	6	238	293	306	599	7%	89%	0.68	54	71	2.86	15
Cabrera,Miguel	03	20	5	aa	FLA	266	43	95	29	3	8	55	29	43	8	5	355	419	584	1004	10%	84%	0.69	157	115	9.70	97
Cabrera,Ray	02	24	8	aa	BAL	243	21	58	17	0	3	24	6	27	5	6	239	257	346	603	2%	89%	0.22	81	65	2.74	17
Caceres,Wilmy	02	29	6	aaa	TAM	347	33	76	5	5	0	15	18	45	13	8	219	258	262	520	5%	87%	0.40	25	136	2.21	-8
	03	30	68	a/a	CIN	364	37	74	10	1	3	18	17	39	14	8	202	237	259	497	4%	89%	0.43	39	101	1.96	-8
Cadiente,Brett	02	25	8	a/a	TEX	319	34	68	15	4	2	20	31	61	11	6	213	283	304	587	9%	81%	0.51	62	129	2.92	7
Calabrese,Tony	03	25	4	aa	NYM	110	7	23	5	0	2	12	6	24	1	0	207	246	302	549	5%	78%	0.24	65	34	2.54	1
Calloway,Ron	02	26	8	aaa	MON	447	61	108	21	3	12	50	37	78	14	13	242	300	383	682	8%	83%	0.47	89	105	3.71	27
Calzado,Napolean	02	26	5	aa	BAL	482	55	108	15	2	3	32	26	49	32	12	224	264	282	546	5%	90%	0.53	41	125	2.53	2
Calzado,Napoleon	03	27	58	a/a	BAL	362	40	88	10	3	1	23	16	46	17	5	244	276	293	569	4%	87%	0.36	35	125	2.85	3
Cameron,Troy	02	24	54	aa	COL	325	26	67	13	2	8	28	20	66	0	1	206	252	332	584	6%	80%	0.30	79	47	2.78	7
Camilli,Jason	02	27	4	aa	ANA	338	29	61	10	1	3	21	27	61	4	5	180	241	243	484	7%	82%	0.44	43	66	1.87	-13
Camilo,Juan	02	26	8	aa	DET	156	12	24	5	3	3	15	11	43	3	0	154	210	282	492	7%	72%	0.26	75	153	1.96	-13
Campo,Mike	03	27	8	aa	OAK	304	32	61	8	1	3	27	23	68	5	4	200	258	266	524	7%	78%	0.35	43	79	2.26	-9
Cancel,Robinson	02	26	2	aa	OAK	402	42	88	17	1	9	48	23	69	8	7	219	261	333	595	5%	83%	0.33	74	78	2.80	10
Candelaria,Ben	02	28	8	a/a	FLA	128	9	29	10	0	1	14	6	19	2	2	227	261	328	589	4%	85%	0.32	81	52	2.77	15
Canizaro,Jay	02	29	4	aaa	MIN	247	28	56	9	1	9	25	20	38	4	4	227	285	381	665	7%	85%	0.53	92	72	3.57	24
	03	30	4	aaa	TAM	92	11	19	6	0	3	11	7	19	2	0	205	263	362	625	7%	79%	0.38	106	68	3.31	20
Cannizaro,Andy	03	25	64	aa	NYY	369	39	86	20	1	1	30	20	21	7	5	234	274	301	575	5%	94%	0.95	54	80	2.78	19
Cano,Robinson	03	21	4	aa	NYY	164	18	43	8	1	1	12	7	12	0	0	263	294	346	640	4%	92%	0.59	61	55	3.63	24
Cantu,Jorge	02	21	6	aa	TAM	512	45	122	32	1	3	39	20	61	2	7	238	267	322	589	4%	88%	0.33	66	44	2.79	13
	03	22	56	a/a	TAM	358	39	93	27	1	6	45	16	43	2	4	261	292	396	688	4%	88%	0.37	97	57	3.92	35
Capista,Aaron	02	23	4	aa	BOS	174	16	38	9	1	1	8	11	21	4	2	218	265	299	564	6%	88%	0.52	60	89	2.67	8
Carroll,Jamey	02	29	45	a/a	MON	430	46	105	18	1	7	39	31	34	5	10	244	295	340	635	7%	92%	0.91	64	56	3.26	26
Carter,Charley	02	27	3	aa	DET	492	44	104	23	1	12	65	38	80	1	0	211	268	335	603	7%	84%	0.48	81	43	3.09	13
Caruso,Joe	02	32	58	a/a	KC	354	32	77	14	4	4	36	17	47	3	4	218	253	314	567	5%	87%	0.36	62	93	2.58	6
	03	33	54	aa	PIT	224	18	29	4	0	1	18	18	53	2	1	131	194	169	363	7%	76%	0.33	26	62	1.09	-39
Caruso,Mike	02	25	46	a/a	KC	233	27	67	3	2	3	23	11	11	9	3	288	320	356	676	5%	95%	1.00	39	109	4.20	32
Carvajal,Jhonny	02	29	5	aa	SF	419	37	80	20	3	3	22	23	75	7	4	191	233	274	507	5%	82%	0.31	60	100	2.08	-6
	03	30	45	a/a	ARI	254	16	43	11	1	4	18	12	41	2	5	170	208	268	475	5%	84%	0.29	66	52	1.61	-10
Casanova,Raul	03	31	2	aaa	BAL	284	27	66	18	0	5	37	18	32	0	0	231	277	352	629	6%	89%	0.56	86	25	3.39	24
Cash,Kevin	02	25	2	a/a	TOR	449	51	100	32	1	14	55	48	90	4	4	223	298	392	690	10%	80%	0.53	113	58	3.99	32
	03	26	2	aaa	TOR	326	32	83	29	1	7	32	26	71	1	0	255	310	413	723	7%	78%	0.36	114	49	4.61	39

Major League Equivalent Statistics

BATTERS

BATTER	Yr	Age	Pos	Lev	Org	ab	r	h	d	t	hr	rbi	bb	k	sb	cs	ba	ob	slg	ops	bb%	ct%	eye	px	sx	rc/g	bpv
Casillas,Uriel	02	27	54	a/a	PHI	252	31	62	10	2	2	26	25	35	3	1	246	314	325	639	9%	86%	0.71	54	90	3.73	19
	03	28	54	a/a	PHI	241	19	48	9	0	2	20	20	27	4	1	201	261	261	522	8%	89%	0.72	45	61	2.39	0
Castellano,John	02	25	8	aa	SEA	194	14	44	9	0	1	18	9	32	3	3	227	261	289	550	4%	84%	0.28	49	52	2.46	1
Castillo,Carlos	02	23	6	aa	DET	112	6	21	4	2	0	5	3	26	1	1	188	209	259	468	3%	77%	0.12	47	120	1.68	-16
Castillo,Jose	03	23	46	aa	PIT	498	62	137	24	4	4	60	36	69	17	11	275	324	363	687	7%	86%	0.52	62	109	4.14	28
Castillo,Ruben	02	24	6	aa	SEA	394	38	77	11	3	3	34	15	88	10	7	195	225	261	486	4%	78%	0.17	43	116	1.83	-14
	03	25	6	aaa	SEA	337	31	64	13	0	0	14	21	68	16	11	191	238	229	467	6%	80%	0.31	34	92	1.70	-16
Castro,Bernabel	02	23	4	aa	SD	419	53	95	12	2	0	28	45	65	47	21	227	302	265	567	10%	84%	0.69	30	132	2.79	2
	03	24	4	aaa	SD	424	47	114	14	3	2	20	20	36	40	16	269	302	330	632	5%	92%	0.56	43	132	3.45	18
Castro,Nelson	02	26	68	a/a	SF	394	36	74	15	5	6	28	12	70	18	11	188	212	297	509	3%	82%	0.17	68	152	1.84	-6
Castro,Ramon	02	23	64	a/a	ATL	331	62	92	23	2	9	33	46	53	17	13	278	366	441	807	12%	84%	0.87	109	115	5.60	55
	03	24	56	a/a	ATL	288	41	69	11	1	5	26	34	55	4	5	240	320	337	657	11%	81%	0.62	64	74	3.74	19
Cepicky,Matt	02	25	8	aa	MON	419	41	101	24	1	12	58	25	78	6	1	241	284	389	673	6%	81%	0.32	97	73	3.88	27
	03	26	8	aaa	MON	442	46	116	22	2	5	48	23	62	5	2	262	298	354	652	5%	86%	0.37	65	77	3.77	22
Cervenak,Mike	02	26	3	aa	NYY	492	57	110	28	1	17	70	24	82	3	2	224	260	388	648	5%	83%	0.29	106	65	3.38	24
	03	27	53	aa	SF	511	52	100	20	1	11	64	25	81	2	1	195	232	300	533	5%	84%	0.31	69	60	2.30	-1
Cesar,Dionys	02	26	4	aaa	MIL	479	46	113	20	2	6	33	26	69	7	8	236	275	324	599	5%	86%	0.38	60	72	2.93	11
	03	27	4	a/a	CIN	102	10	30	9	0	0	13	5	11	1	1	290	325	375	700	5%	89%	0.45	75	48	4.41	37
Chamblee,Jim	02	27	53	a/a	STL	444	61	103	27	2	13	57	40	82	7	2	232	295	390	685	8%	82%	0.49	103	95	4.05	30
	03	28	53	a/a	CIN	365	32	88	18	2	7	35	26	79	3	1	240	290	354	643	7%	78%	0.32	76	69	3.62	18
Chapman,Travis	02	24	5	aa	PHI	478	50	126	33	1	11	60	46	73	3	1	264	328	406	734	9%	85%	0.63	99	53	4.89	41
	03	25	5	aaa	PHI	478	54	120	36	0	10	72	40	94	2	2	251	308	387	695	8%	80%	0.42	98	44	4.23	32
Charles,Frank	02	34	3	aaa	HOU	332	23	76	9	2	5	39	14	83	1	3	229	260	313	573	4%	75%	0.17	53	53	2.68	1
Chavez,Endy	02	25	8	aaa	MON	405	59	132	29	3	4	36	28	32	18	14	326	370	442	811	6%	92%	0.88	85	107	5.86	61
Chavez,Raul	02	30	2	aaa	HOU	373	19	74	9	0	3	29	16	49	3	4	198	231	247	478	4%	87%	0.33	34	35	1.82	-13
	03	30	25	aaa	HOU	355	38	86	25	1	5	38	11	43	0	2	241	264	364	628	3%	88%	0.25	90	48	3.21	22
Chen,Chin-Feng	02	25	3	aaa	LA	511	63	119	21	2	18	59	41	115	1	0	233	290	387	677	7%	77%	0.36	94	60	3.94	24
	03	26	8	aaa	LA	474	65	111	25	3	20	67	48	87	5	5	234	304	424	728	9%	82%	0.55	116	82	4.40	37
Chevalier,Virgil	02	29	2	a/a	NYM	397	50	97	21	0	6	42	41	44	4	3	244	315	343	658	9%	89%	0.93	70	57	3.86	29
	03	30	28	a/a	NYM	281	21	43	10	0	3	21	25	45	2	2	152	222	222	444	8%	84%	0.56	49	51	1.62	-18
Chiaffredo,Paul	02	26	2	aa	TOR	258	25	38	6	1	7	25	9	70	3	0	147	176	260	436	3%	73%	0.13	66	103	1.45	-21
	03	27	2	a/a	TOR	217	22	48	9	1	5	22	18	60	1	1	221	281	341	622	8%	72%	0.31	76	57	3.29	11
Choi,Hee Seop	02	24	3	aaa	CHC	478	66	115	20	2	18	68	68	85	2	3	241	335	404	739	12%	82%	0.80	99	56	4.86	37
Christensen,McKay	02	27	8	aaa	NYM	377	44	92	20	4	4	26	22	69	17	14	244	286	350	636	6%	82%	0.32	73	130	3.13	18
	03	28	8	aaa	PHI	181	21	37	9	1	3	11	12	49	6	2	206	255	313	569	6%	73%	0.24	74	112	2.70	4
Christensen,Mike	02	26	5	aa	ANA	413	24	73	15	1	4	25	11	93	1	2	177	198	247	445	3%	77%	0.12	49	44	1.52	-18
Christenson,Ryan	02	29	8	aaa	MIL	260	32	58	15	1	5	25	15	27	9	5	223	265	346	612	5%	90%	0.56	84	105	3.00	20
	03	30	8	aaa	TEX	195	24	53	14	1	5	19	23	42	9	1	271	347	420	767	10%	79%	0.54	102	102	5.65	43
Christianson,Ryan	02	21	2	aa	SEA	190	20	46	11	0	5	17	16	35	0	2	242	301	379	680	8%	82%	0.46	92	29	3.87	28
Church,Ryan	02	24	8	aa	CLE	291	34	80	16	3	12	45	11	54	1	0	275	301	474	776	4%	81%	0.20	122	83	5.15	46
	03	25	8	aa	CLE	371	41	87	16	2	11	45	28	62	4	3	236	288	382	670	7%	83%	0.44	91	73	3.77	25
Cintron,Alex	02	24	6	aaa	ARI	351	40	103	20	2	3	20	8	24	7	6	293	309	387	697	2%	93%	0.33	69	87	4.16	33
	03	25	6	aaa	ARI	107	16	39	10	2	2	16	6	5	1	0	364	398	551	950	5%	95%	1.20	128	114	9.12	98
Clapinski,Chris	02	31	6	aaa	LA	342	37	75	18	1	7	36	25	41	1	0	219	272	339	612	7%	88%	0.61	81	57	3.20	19
	03	32	6	aaa	CIN	307	35	82	16	3	9	43	19	43	5	2	267	309	425	734	6%	86%	0.44	100	94	4.70	39
Clapp,Stubby	02	30	4	aaa	STL	359	37	72	15	1	2	15	37	65	2	7	201	275	265	540	9%	82%	0.57	48	53	2.36	-2
	03	31	46	aaa	ATL	286	37	53	10	6	3	20	39	68	5	2	186	283	293	575	12%	76%	0.57	65	168	2.91	0
Clark,Brady	02	29	8	aaa	CIN	109	12	27	6	0	1	12	2	8	0	2	248	261	330	592	2%	93%	0.25	63	51	2.70	14
Clark,Daryl	03	24	8	aa	MIL	202	24	42	10	1	2	14	33	60	5	1	207	319	292	611	14%	70%	0.55	60	89	3.49	5
Clark,Doug	02	27	8	a/a	SF	350	31	81	15	2	5	27	28	76	7	11	231	288	329	617	7%	78%	0.37	65	74	2.97	11
	03	28	8	a/a	SF	417	37	96	18	3	3	35	33	66	6	6	229	286	309	595	7%	84%	0.50	56	84	2.98	10
Clark,Howie	02	29	8	aaa	BAL	418	47	110	18	3	6	35	33	27	3	5	263	317	364	681	7%	94%	1.22	67	68	4.04	40
	03	30	4	aaa	TOR	252	23	56	13	1	4	24	17	19	1	0	224	274	325	599	6%	93%	0.93	70	52	3.10	22
Clark,Jermaine	02	26	4	aaa	TEX	425	44	100	14	4	5	29	51	53	26	18	235	317	322	640	11%	88%	0.96	56	114	3.40	21
	03	27	8	aaa	TEX	331	42	71	8	5	10	29	31	44	21	4	215	283	353	636	9%	87%	0.71	77	159	3.58	18
Clemente,Edgard	02	27	8	aaa	MIL	373	33	82	17	1	8	35	20	92	5	1	220	260	335	595	5%	75%	0.22	76	74	2.98	9
Closser,J.D.	02	23	2	aa	COL	315	31	85	25	1	12	45	32	46	6	4	270	337	470	807	9%	85%	0.70	132	61	5.66	58
	03	24	2	aa	COL	410	48	111	26	4	13	42	37	60	2	2	270	330	445	775	8%	85%	0.62	113	75	5.32	49
Coffie,Ivanon	02	25	5	aaa	CHC	373	38	72	26	3	5	36	29	46	1	6	193	251	319	570	7%	88%	0.63	90	71	2.49	14
	03	26	5	aaa	BAL	353	44	73	16	0	15	41	40	73	1	4	207	287	382	669	10%	79%	0.54	108	35	3.63	24
Colangelo,Mike	02	26	8	aaa	OAK	217	16	38	7	0	0	16	24	26	2	4	175	257	207	465	10%	88%	0.92	29	42	1.75	-11
	03	27	8	aaa	TOR	310	36	81	20	2	4	39	32	66	4	2	260	329	375	704	9%	79%	0.49	83	82	4.52	31
Coleman,Michael	02	27	8	aaa	BOS	204	22	42	7	1	7	18	23	51	0	0	206	286	353	639	10%	75%	0.45	88	44	3.51	14
Cole,Eric	02	27	8	a/a	TEX	397	30	83	19	2	5	32	21	78	2	3	209	249	305	554	5%	80%	0.27	66	59	2.48	2
	03	28	38	a/a	HOU	408	35	85	15	1	5	29	15	63	13	8	209	237	288	525	3%	85%	0.23	54	89	2.16	-3
Colina,Javier	02	24	4	a/a	COL	458	39	107	26	3	4	32	20	47	3	6	234	266	330	595	4%	90%	0.43	70	66	2.85	15
	03	25	45	aa	COL	388	46	102	24	2	16	46	10	45	6	0	262	280	458	737	2%	88%	0.21	123	93	4.56	42
Collier,Lou	02	29	8	aaa	MON	307	38	84	25	4	5	41	29	65	4	2	274	336	430	766	9%	79%	0.45	109	112	5.30	45
	03	30	86	aaa	BOS	392	46	98	17	3	10	55	25	93	6	7	250	296	383	679	6%	76%	0.27	84	89	3.77	23
Collins,Mike	02	26	4	aa	LA	384	34	101	12	1	0	39	38	39	6	1	263	329	299	629	9%	90%	0.97	30	68	3.76	20
	03	27	64	aa	LA	279	16	53	3	0	0	20	14	31	1	3	190	229	203	431	5%	89%	0.45	11	30	1.46	-23
Connacher,Kevin	02	28	4	aa	MIN	356	33	67	21	2	8	32	28	88	17	9	188	247	326	573	7%	75%	0.32	92	114	2.53	7
	03	29	45	a/a	MIN	163	12	30	5	2	2	11	12	56	3	3	183	238	266	504	7%	65%	0.21	53	103	1.95	-13
Connors,Greg	02	28	38	a/a	SEA	366	33	71	24	0	8	47	25	80	3	3	194	246	325	571	6%	78%	0.31	92	51	2.59	9
	03	29	5	aaa	SEA	113	12	23	4	0	3	11	5	29	0	1	201	232	306	538	4%	75%	0.16	66	47	2.25	-3
Conti,Jason	03	29	8	aaa	MIL	456	48	99	15	2	8	33	20	117	11	8	216	248	312	560	4%	74%	0.17	61	97	2.46	1
Coolbaugh,Mike	02	30	5	aaa	STL	411	47	82	16	1	23	57	41	117	7	3	200	272	411	683	9%	72%	0.35	123	73	3.74	24
	03	31	5	aa	HOU	147	13	25	4	0	4	16	12	49	1	0	167	229	281	510	7%	67%	0.25	70	42	2.13	-11
Coquillette,Trace	02	28	58	a/a	PIT	254	26	41	10	1	4	24	20	68	2	4	161	223	256	479	7%	73%	0.29	63	77	1.74	-14
	03	29	4	a/a	BOS	391	42	85	23	1	8	36	27	121	6	7	218	269	344	613	6%	69%	0.22	86	70	2.95	13
Corr,Frank	03	25	8	aa	NYM	170	18	37	10	0	3	13	9	30	1	6	217	256	323	579	5%	82%	0.30	76	52	2.34	10
Cortez,Fernando	03	22	4	aa	TAM	114	14	35	3	1	1	6	3	21	1	2	307	325	377	702	3%	82%	0.14	45	87	4.29	24

Major League Equivalent Statistics

BATTER	Yr	Age	Pos	Lev	Org	ab	r	h	d	t	hr	rbi	bb	k	sb	cs	ba	ob	slg	ops	bb%	ct%	eye	px	sx	rc/g	bpv
Cosme,Caonabo	03	25	4	aa	STL	495	56	121	31	2	6	40	30	112	8	6	244	287	349	637	6%	77%	0.27	77	83	3.43	19
Coste,Chris	02	30	3	aaa	CLE	478	49	134	28	1	7	56	28	55	0	0	280	320	387	707	6%	88%	0.51	76	32	4.56	35
Cota,Humberto	02	24	2	aaa	PIT	404	42	99	26	1	7	45	25	82	4	9	245	289	366	655	6%	80%	0.30	86	57	3.41	23
	03	25	2	aaa	PIT	200	20	38	9	0	6	23	17	48	2	0	190	253	325	578	8%	76%	0.35	86	55	2.81	6
Cota,Jesus	03	22	8	aa	ARI	364	38	89	15	2	1	27	20	41	1	6	245	284	305	589	5%	89%	0.49	46	58	2.84	10
Crawford,Carl	02	21	8	aaa	TAM	353	56	109	19	9	7	50	19	55	25	10	309	344	473	817	5%	84%	0.35	101	205	5.89	51
Crede,Joe	02	24	5	aaa	CHW	359	50	107	19	0	24	57	25	43	0	1	298	344	552	895	7%	88%	0.58	150	23	7.03	73
Crespo,Cesar	02	23	4	aaa	SD	322	37	73	15	1	7	32	43	70	18	8	227	318	345	663	12%	78%	0.61	78	96	3.86	20
	03	24	84	aaa	BOS	465	60	118	31	2	7	51	34	83	11	9	254	305	374	679	7%	82%	0.41	86	92	3.87	28
Crespo,Felipe	03	31	3	aaa	CIN	360	32	75	19	0	5	35	32	47	6	5	208	271	298	569	8%	87%	0.68	66	57	2.68	10
Cresse,Brad	02	24	2	a/a	ARI	366	36	78	22	0	4	28	15	85	1	0	213	244	306	550	4%	77%	0.18	70	51	2.52	3
	03	25	2	aaa	ARI	306	31	63	20	1	8	36	14	67	0	0	207	241	356	597	4%	78%	0.21	100	45	2.85	15
Crisp,Coco	03	24	8	aaa	CLE	225	39	77	19	4	1	22	24	22	18	9	342	406	476	881	10%	90%	1.09	97	161	7.36	76
Cromer,Tripp	02	35	3	aaa	HOU	265	24	59	12	2	6	21	7	42	0	0	223	243	351	594	3%	84%	0.17	82	57	2.85	11
	03	36	4	aaa	HOU	242	23	53	14	3	4	29	14	41	0	0	219	261	342	603	5%	83%	0.33	82	72	3.04	14
Crosby,Bobby	02	23	6	aa	OAK	228	27	57	14	0	6	27	16	35	8	2	250	299	390	690	7%	85%	0.46	95	82	4.17	32
	03	24	6	aaa	OAK	465	69	125	28	4	18	72	50	91	19	5	269	340	462	802	10%	80%	0.55	121	125	5.80	50
Crosby,Bubba	02	26	8	a/a	LA	429	29	87	14	2	8	41	22	63	7	5	203	242	301	542	5%	85%	0.35	62	70	2.34	0
	03	27	8	aaa	NYY	340	52	102	23	5	11	51	25	52	9	0	299	346	495	841	7%	85%	0.48	124	142	6.64	60
Crozier,Eric	02	24	3	aa	CLE	142	16	38	8	1	1	11	18	47	1	0	268	350	359	709	11%	67%	0.38	67	75	4.82	24
	03	25	3	aa	CLE	347	42	73	9	2	16	42	41	94	5	3	210	294	386	681	11%	73%	0.44	100	78	3.90	20
Cruz,Edgar	03	25	2	aa	PHI	213	13	37	9	0	3	16	8	36	0	0	173	204	254	457	4%	83%	0.23	57	20	1.65	-14
Cruz,Ivan	02	34	3	aaa	STL	461	63	106	22	0	28	77	40	90	0	0	230	291	460	751	8%	80%	0.44	136	27	4.66	42
Cruz,Jacob	03	31	8	aaa	CIN	132	18	40	7	0	5	22	10	19	2	0	300	349	477	826	7%	86%	0.52	112	54	6.40	57
Cuddyer,Michael	02	24	8	aaa	MIN	330	51	90	15	6	14	39	26	59	9	9	273	326	482	808	7%	82%	0.44	122	147	5.25	50
	03	25	8	aaa	MIN	186	22	55	17	0	2	31	22	45	4	4	296	370	419	790	11%	76%	0.49	98	54	5.69	49
Cummings,Midre	03	32	8	aaa	CHC	385	41	78	17	1	14	41	31	84	1	3	203	262	365	627	7%	78%	0.36	99	44	3.13	16
Cunningham,Marco	02	25	8	aa	KC	215	32	34	6	0	4	23	28	37	11	8	158	255	242	497	12%	83%	0.76	54	105	1.95	-10
	03	26	8	aa	KC	319	44	74	10	2	5	26	21	46	10	9	232	279	325	604	6%	86%	0.45	59	107	2.90	11
Curry,Chris	03	26	2	aa	SF	219	17	45	9	0	3	14	10	47	0	0	205	240	284	523	4%	79%	0.21	55	25	2.27	-4
Curry,Mike	02	26	8	a/a	CIN	263	30	58	8	1	1	11	31	47	10	7	221	303	270	573	11%	82%	0.66	36	91	2.83	2
	03	27	8	aa	SEA	518	72	114	24	6	2	42	57	126	47	10	220	297	301	597	10%	76%	0.45	57	172	3.34	6
Cust,Jack	02	24	8	aaa	COL	359	47	87	21	0	19	35	53	71	4	4	242	340	460	799	13%	80%	0.75	134	43	5.52	51
	03	25	8	aaa	BAL	333	51	88	15	1	9	54	75	85	5	2	264	400	396	796	18%	74%	0.88	84	68	6.28	41
Daigle,Leo	03	24	3	aa	DET	412	50	84	21	1	10	47	35	74	3	1	203	266	327	593	8%	82%	0.48	83	72	2.97	11
Dalesandro,Mark	02	34	2	aaa	CHW	160	10	30	6	0	2	8	5	13	0	0	188	212	263	475	3%	92%	0.38	53	21	1.80	-8
Dallimore,Brian	02	29	5	aaa	ARI	419	44	103	22	2	5	35	20	56	9	5	246	280	344	624	5%	87%	0.36	69	91	3.29	18
	03	30	45	aaa	SF	330	39	93	14	2	3	35	27	33	5	5	281	336	358	695	8%	90%	0.83	54	74	4.36	33
Darula,Bobby	02	28	8	a/a	CIN	372	37	93	16	2	3	29	34	26	7	3	250	313	328	641	8%	93%	1.31	55	81	3.71	32
DaVanon,Jeff	02	29	8	aaa	ANA	100	15	27	8	1	4	13	12	19	4	4	270	348	490	838	11%	81%	0.63	142	114	5.61	61
Davidson,Cleatus	02	26	40	aa	NYY	118	15	24	2	2	1	15	9	26	5	6	203	260	280	540	7%	78%	0.35	43	160	2.06	-7
Davis,Glenn	02	27	3	aa	MON	114	12	24	3	1	5	12	11	31	1	1	211	280	386	666	9%	73%	0.35	99	81	3.61	18
	03	28	3	aa	MON	333	22	52	15	1	6	31	20	88	1	2	157	205	259	464	6%	74%	0.23	69	46	1.66	-15
Davis,John-Paul	03	25	3	aa	TAM	110	19	25	9	0	1	15	13	28	0	0	225	308	328	636	11%	74%	0.47	82	51	3.64	18
Davis,J.J.	02	24	8	aa	PIT	348	41	88	16	2	15	49	26	80	6	5	253	305	440	744	7%	77%	0.33	113	81	4.57	37
	03	25	8	aaa	PIT	426	59	112	28	3	21	58	30	69	20	7	263	311	491	802	7%	84%	0.43	141	121	5.34	54
Davis,Tommy	02	29	20	aaa	CLE	289	22	66	14	1	9	42	5	71	0	1	228	241	377	619	2%	75%	0.07	94	37	2.99	16
Dawkins,Gookie	02	23	6	a/a	CIN	322	28	76	15	2	1	16	28	47	6	9	236	297	304	601	8%	85%	0.60	52	74	2.94	12
	03	24	6	a/a	KC	340	30	74	16	1	6	43	21	53	7	6	217	263	322	585	6%	85%	0.41	72	72	2.75	10
De la rosa,Tomas	02	25	65	aaa	MON	351	33	73	17	1	3	29	22	44	9	6	208	255	288	542	6%	87%	0.50	59	85	2.39	4
	03	26	64	aaa	PIT	263	28	60	12	1	3	26	21	31	5	2	230	286	316	602	7%	88%	0.66	61	81	3.17	15
De Los Santos,Luis	02	25	3	aaa	BAL	187	18	45	7	1	5	14	12	39	0	0	241	286	369	655	6%	79%	0.31	79	43	3.71	19
De Renne,Keoni	02	23	4	aa	ATL	320	42	77	22	2	2	38	32	33	2	5	241	310	341	650	9%	90%	0.97	76	73	3.60	31
	03	24	46	aa	NYY	137	8	27	4	0	1	7	11	25	0	1	194	256	243	499	8%	82%	0.45	35	20	2.07	-12
Deardorff,Jeff	02	24	8	aa	MIL	425	57	96	20	1	16	50	48	117	10	7	226	304	391	695	10%	72%	0.41	102	81	4.04	26
	03	25	35	a/a	MIN	479	63	134	33	4	14	67	36	123	15	7	280	330	454	784	7%	74%	0.29	115	115	5.40	46
DeHaan,Kory	02	26	8	aaa	SD	442	54	108	26	10	2	33	26	90	19	10	244	286	362	648	6%	80%	0.29	79	186	3.47	20
	03	27	8	aaa	SD	183	20	29	6	1	1	9	12	29	6	1	161	214	218	432	6%	84%	0.42	40	120	1.59	-21
DeJesus,David	03	24	8	a/a	KC	286	52	84	19	2	6	27	34	30	7	8	294	369	437	806	11%	90%	1.13	97	98	5.74	61
Del Chiaro,Brent	03	24	2	aa	ANA	154	14	22	10	1	1	9	8	49	0	0	142	182	234	417	5%	68%	0.15	70	77	1.34	-21
Delgado,Alex	03	33	2	aaa	MIL	155	10	41	6	0	2	13	7	18	2	0	267	300	343	642	4%	89%	0.41	54	39	3.76	19
Delgado,Wilson	02	30	6	aaa	STL	365	23	77	15	1	5	27	18	50	2	5	211	248	299	547	5%	86%	0.36	60	40	2.35	2
Dellaero,Jason	02	26	65	a/a	CHW	264	26	52	11	1	9	26	10	76	5	4	197	226	348	575	4%	71%	0.13	93	89	2.43	7
DeMent,Dan	03	25	45	aa	TAM	349	34	77	20	1	3	29	32	66	2	2	222	288	307	595	8%	81%	0.49	64	54	3.08	10
Depastino,Joe	02	29	2	aaa	NYM	248	19	61	13	2	4	22	10	47	4	0	246	275	363	638	4%	81%	0.21	78	91	3.55	19
	03	30	2	aaa	NYM	277	22	61	14	0	2	18	16	53	2	1	221	264	289	553	6%	81%	0.30	53	45	2.62	2
Derosso,Tony	02	27	5	aa	PIT	182	16	27	4	2	5	23	19	43	2	0	148	229	275	504	9%	76%	0.44	72	100	2.11	-12
Deschaine,Jim	02	25	5	aa	TOR	405	41	72	12	0	11	46	35	72	2	4	178	243	289	532	8%	82%	0.49	68	44	2.25	-3
	03	26	35	aa	PHI	258	25	57	9	0	9	31	17	29	0	3	223	269	357	627	6%	89%	0.58	82	26	3.10	20
Devore,Doug	02	25	8	aaa	ARI	436	44	103	18	5	11	44	20	74	7	7	236	270	376	646	4%	83%	0.27	86	105	3.30	20
	03	26	8	aaa	ARI	462	56	124	27	6	11	57	35	72	4	8	268	319	422	741	7%	84%	0.48	99	95	4.60	40
Dewey,Jason	02	25	2	a/a	COL	358	31	76	22	0	10	41	18	67	3	5	212	250	358	608	5%	81%	0.27	98	44	2.82	16
	03	26	2	aa	TEX	225	19	37	7	1	5	15	15	78	0	2	162	214	271	485	6%	65%	0.19	67	54	1.80	-15
Diaz,Alejandro	02	24	8	aa	CIN	150	10	29	7	2	1	14	9	26	5	2	193	239	287	526	6%	83%	0.35	63	122	2.25	-2
	03	25	8	aa	CIN	360	32	82	16	2	4	23	14	48	12	11	228	255	313	568	4%	87%	0.28	60	93	2.44	6
Diaz,Felix	03	26	5	aa	MON	185	12	28	3	2	5	13	10	71	1	1	150	192	273	465	5%	61%	0.13	69	87	1.62	-19
Diaz,Juan	02	29	3	aaa	BOS	389	37	86	13	0	15	42	19	97	0	0	221	257	370	628	5%	75%	0.20	89	21	3.23	14
	03	30	3	aa	BAL	248	21	48	14	0	11	40	19	80	1	0	194	250	387	637	7%	68%	0.23	121	27	3.23	19
Diaz,Maikell	02	24	6	a/a	BAL	153	11	21	3	2	0	9	5	28	2	1	137	165	183	348	3%	82%	0.18	29	127	0.92	-39
Diaz,Matt	02	25	8	aa	TAM	449	58	109	26	1	9	41	28	66	26	10	243	287	365	652	6%	85%	0.42	84	114	3.58	24
	03	26	8	a/a	TAM	480	58	155	37	3	10	75	30	67	13	8	323	363	477	840	6%	86%	0.45	107	90	6.50	61

Major League Equivalent Statistics

BATTER	Yr	Age	Pos	Lev	Org	ab	r	h	d	t	hr	rbi	bb	k	sb	cs	ba	ob	slg	ops	bb%	ct%	eye	px	sx	rc/g	bpv
Diaz,Victor	02	21	3	aa	LA	152	22	32	6	0	4	24	7	39	7	5	211	245	329	574	4%	74%	0.18	76	110	2.42	5
	03	22	4	aa	NYM	491	67	144	29	1	15	73	32	90	14	16	293	337	448	785	6%	82%	0.36	101	76	5.06	47
Dillon,Joe	02	27	50	a/a	MIN	362	35	73	17	2	6	37	37	59	3	1	202	276	309	585	9%	84%	0.63	72	73	2.96	10
Dina,Allen	02	29	8	aa	FLA	182	21	31	11	1	4	12	5	36	3	3	170	193	308	500	3%	80%	0.14	92	121	1.72	-2
DiSarcina,Gary	02	35	4	aaa	BOS	144	17	30	10	2	1	7	6	14	0	1	208	240	326	566	4%	90%	0.43	84	105	2.51	13
Dodson,Jeremy	03	26	8	aa	STL	112	11	21	5	0	3	8	11	32	5	2	186	261	303	564	9%	71%	0.35	77	81	2.68	1
Dominique,Andy	02	27	3	aa	BOS	361	27	77	17	1	5	35	23	54	2	1	213	260	307	568	6%	85%	0.43	66	51	2.72	7
	03	28	23	a/a	BOS	386	46	101	22	0	11	59	29	62	2	1	261	313	406	718	7%	84%	0.46	95	45	4.57	36
Donnels,Chris	03	37	3	aaa	FLA	263	33	61	11	0	9	32	43	40	1	1	233	341	376	717	14%	85%	1.08	89	34	4.71	36
Donovan,Todd	02	24	8	aa	SD	114	14	21	4	1	2	8	12	31	5	3	184	262	289	551	10%	73%	0.39	66	127	2.45	-4
	03	25	8	aa	SD	420	50	68	8	5	6	26	37	83	25	11	163	230	249	479	8%	80%	0.44	50	157	1.85	-16
Doster,Dave	03	33	45	aaa	PIT	456	53	106	28	3	9	44	15	50	3	5	233	258	365	623	3%	89%	0.31	90	78	3.04	21
Doster,David	02	32	4	aaa	PHI	579	69	142	26	7	7	69	32	87	7	3	245	285	351	635	5%	85%	0.37	69	117	3.49	18
Dransfeldt,Kelly	02	27	6	aaa	TEX	507	43	98	18	5	10	48	31	102	7	4	193	240	308	547	6%	80%	0.30	71	101	2.41	-0
	03	28	6	aaa	BOS	354	35	65	19	2	6	36	20	82	0	2	184	227	294	521	5%	77%	0.24	76	63	2.12	-3
Dubois,Jason	03	25	0	aa	CHC	443	51	105	27	3	13	66	52	122	2	4	238	318	401	719	11%	72%	0.43	105	64	4.46	31
Duffy,Chris	03	23	8	aa	PIT	494	74	125	22	4	1	37	39	69	30	13	253	308	320	628	7%	86%	0.56	50	138	3.49	16
Duncan,Carlos	02	25	4	aa	ANA	215	23	50	9	1	5	17	8	40	12	5	233	260	353	614	4%	81%	0.20	77	116	3.01	13
	03	26	8	aa	ANA	303	25	59	16	2	3	21	9	92	19	3	195	218	293	511	3%	70%	0.09	69	140	2.15	-5
Duncan,Jeff	03	25	8	a/a	NYM	293	43	73	11	3	5	22	30	61	21	11	248	318	354	672	9%	79%	0.49	67	142	3.86	20
Dunwoody,Todd	02	28	8	aaa	CLE	363	49	88	29	3	7	26	10	61	7	3	242	263	397	659	3%	83%	0.16	108	125	3.51	29
	03	28	8	aaa	STL	334	33	65	23	1	8	33	17	78	11	4	195	233	345	579	5%	76%	0.21	103	106	2.61	12
Durham,Chad	02	24	8	aa	CHW	366	53	90	10	1	0	30	33	69	33	19	246	308	279	587	8%	81%	0.48	27	122	2.88	3
	03	25	8	aa	CHW	408	50	95	11	1	1	32	35	84	13	15	232	292	269	562	8%	79%	0.42	29	84	2.51	-3
Durrington,Trent	02	27	28	a/a	ANA	450	45	84	17	3	9	39	29	77	19	16	187	236	298	534	6%	83%	0.38	70	115	2.05	-1
	03	28	45	aaa	ANA	447	60	113	23	3	6	40	45	62	26	9	252	320	354	673	9%	86%	0.72	71	121	4.09	27
Dzurilla,Mike	03	25	84	a/a	CHC	359	46	81	21	2	10	42	22	65	4	3	225	269	381	650	6%	82%	0.33	101	88	3.43	23
Eberwein,Kevin	02	26	5	aaa	SD	320	28	57	15	0	10	31	27	92	0	1	178	242	319	561	8%	71%	0.29	90	25	2.52	2
Echevarria,Angel	02	31	8	aaa	CHC	217	25	49	9	2	8	29	11	39	0	0	226	263	396	659	5%	82%	0.28	102	68	3.55	23
Edwards,Mike	02	26	8	a/a	CIN	481	48	133	23	2	10	51	34	53	7	12	277	324	395	719	7%	89%	0.64	78	58	4.32	37
	03	27	8	aaa	OAK	436	60	110	19	3	12	74	47	66	4	2	251	324	389	713	10%	85%	0.71	87	84	4.56	34
Ellison,Jason	02	25	8	aaa	SF	196	28	56	8	1	2	7	19	24	14	3	286	349	367	716	9%	88%	0.79	56	118	5.03	34
	03	26	8	aaa	SF	461	59	118	20	4	4	32	31	42	17	16	256	302	341	643	6%	91%	0.72	59	112	3.34	24
Encarnacion,Edwin	03	21	5	aa	CIN	254	34	68	14	1	5	30	18	32	6	3	269	317	393	709	7%	87%	0.55	83	90	4.43	35
Encarnacion,Mario	02	27	8	aaa	CHC	200	16	45	7	0	5	19	11	46	0	3	225	265	335	600	5%	77%	0.24	70	23	2.83	9
Ensberg,Morgan	02	27	5	aaa	HOU	292	42	77	11	3	7	31	42	53	8	5	264	356	394	750	13%	82%	0.79	80	108	5.15	37
Erickson,Corey	02	26	5	aa	CLE	345	40	68	18	2	17	51	27	101	3	3	197	255	409	664	7%	71%	0.27	128	81	3.37	24
	03	27	5	aa	STL	359	36	58	20	0	11	40	36	92	3	1	162	238	313	551	9%	74%	0.39	98	60	2.46	2
Erickson,Matt	02	27	4	aaa	FLA	379	44	87	25	2	1	19	22	51	10	5	230	272	314	586	5%	87%	0.43	67	106	2.89	13
	03	28	54	aaa	FLA	298	31	83	19	3	1	25	32	35	10	10	278	347	368	715	10%	88%	0.89	68	95	4.41	39
Escalona,Felix	03	25	46	a/a	BAL	123	15	26	8	0	1	12	6	19	2	0	213	248	300	548	5%	85%	0.31	68	78	2.58	5
Escobar,Alex	03	25	8	aaa	CLE	439	56	104	21	1	23	70	22	124	7	3	237	273	444	717	5%	72%	0.18	124	83	4.11	34
Espada,Joe	02	27	4	aaa	KC	223	14	44	10	0	0	18	14	21	10	5	197	245	242	487	6%	91%	0.67	40	77	1.95	-5
Espy,Nate	02	24	3	aa	PHI	517	66	120	27	2	11	60	61	78	14	1	232	313	356	669	11%	85%	0.78	83	103	4.13	27
	03	25	3	aa	PHI	347	35	67	12	0	6	35	40	74	7	6	192	275	280	555	10%	79%	0.53	58	61	2.56	-1
Estrada,Johnny	02	26	2	aaa	PHI	434	40	108	26	0	9	54	22	49	1	0	249	285	371	656	5%	89%	0.45	85	37	3.73	27
	03	27	2	aaa	ATL	354	36	106	27	0	10	60	27	29	0	0	301	349	456	806	7%	92%	0.90	108	17	6.06	63
Evans,Lee	02	25	52	a/a	CHW	308	34	68	18	2	8	25	19	88	4	1	221	266	370	636	6%	71%	0.22	98	97	3.37	18
	03	26	2	a/a	ATL	236	22	48	8	1	3	16	22	57	3	0	202	269	278	547	8%	76%	0.38	51	73	2.65	-4
Evans,Tom	03	29	5	aaa	COL	137	15	20	5	1	3	5	12	34	4	0	146	214	252	466	8%	75%	0.35	66	121	1.84	-17
Everett,Adam	02	26	6	aaa	HOU	345	45	91	16	7	2	22	21	54	11	3	264	306	368	674	6%	84%	0.39	68	167	4.08	24
	03	27	6	aaa	HOU	100	20	23	6	1	1	8	6	14	3	1	233	275	340	614	5%	86%	0.40	75	154	3.23	17
Fabregas,Jorge	03	34	2	aaa	TAM	140	11	36	6	0	2	14	8	10	1	0	257	298	341	638	5%	93%	0.81	60	35	3.67	27
Fagan,Shawn	02	25	3	aa	TOR	421	52	96	22	0	9	50	75	71	5	4	228	345	344	689	15%	83%	1.06	79	49	4.36	30
	03	26	35	a/a	TOR	479	68	128	16	2	4	45	52	93	4	2	268	340	333	673	10%	81%	0.56	46	76	4.26	19
Faison,Vince	02	22	8	aa	SD	359	36	82	20	4	6	40	35	97	5	8	228	297	357	654	9%	73%	0.36	85	98	3.46	18
	03	23	8	aa	SD	392	38	81	13	0	3	26	41	108	12	2	207	282	263	545	9%	72%	0.38	41	82	2.71	-7
Fasano,Sal	02	31	2	aaa	ANA	173	13	32	9	0	5	14	6	39	1	0	185	212	324	536	3%	77%	0.15	91	42	2.23	2
Feliciano,Jesus	02	23	8	aa	LA	245	29	52	5	1	0	12	12	28	9	11	212	249	241	490	5%	89%	0.43	22	105	1.72	-12
	03	24	8	aa	TAM	332	35	76	10	0	2	24	24	43	9	4	229	280	278	558	7%	87%	0.55	37	77	2.72	2
Fernandez,Alex	02	21	8	a/a	SD	489	46	134	21	0	8	68	12	71	25	13	274	291	366	657	2%	85%	0.17	63	85	3.59	21
	03	22	8	a/a	SD	454	49	122	24	2	9	54	14	61	16	10	269	291	390	680	3%	87%	0.23	81	97	3.79	28
Figgins,Chone	02	25	4	aaa	ANA	511	77	136	22	9	6	47	40	62	30	10	266	319	380	699	7%	88%	0.65	72	172	4.39	31
	03	26	46	aaa	ANA	285	44	78	13	9	3	24	23	28	13	7	274	328	413	741	7%	90%	0.81	84	205	4.76	42
Figueroa,Franky	02	26	3	a/a	BAL	229	26	53	8	1	3	27	9	47	0	0	231	261	314	575	4%	79%	0.19	55	57	2.81	4
Figueroa,Luis	02	26	5	aa	SEA	180	23	52	12	0	1	23	22	16	2	1	289	366	372	739	11%	91%	1.38	68	51	5.27	52
	03	27	5	aaa	SEA	423	36	107	16	0	2	45	42	34	1	5	252	319	305	624	9%	92%	1.23	42	23	3.44	26
Figueroa,Luis	02	29	6	a/a	MON	336	37	63	15	3	2	27	20	29	4	9	188	233	268	501	6%	91%	0.69	57	100	1.83	-0
	03	30	46	aaa	MON	480	46	123	26	1	2	30	24	25	5	8	256	291	326	617	5%	95%	0.94	56	53	3.16	27
Fiore,Curtis	02	25	8	aa	ATL	319	31	72	17	1	6	31	29	43	3	0	226	290	342	632	8%	87%	0.67	79	66	3.54	21
Firlit,Dan	03	25	6	aa	ARI	147	7	26	2	1	1	9	3	35	2	1	174	190	220	410	2%	76%	0.08	27	74	1.30	-29
Fischer,Mark	02	26	8	aa	BOS	131	11	15	4	0	2	6	8	39	2	1	115	165	191	356	6%	70%	0.21	51	81	0.97	-37
Fitzgerald,Jason	02	27	8	a/a	CLE	405	36	88	21	0	10	46	32	91	17	7	217	275	343	618	7%	78%	0.35	84	79	3.18	14
	03	28	83	a/a	ATL	429	37	88	12	2	5	36	32	87	16	7	206	262	277	539	7%	80%	0.37	46	96	2.46	-5
Flaherty,Tim	02	26	2	aa	SF	247	17	42	9	2	3	25	21	77	0	1	170	235	259	494	8%	69%	0.27	58	62	1.99	-14
Fleming,Ryan	02	27	8	a/a	TOR	298	30	64	14	0	3	28	21	24	3	5	215	266	292	558	7%	92%	0.88	57	53	2.52	13
	03	28	8	aa	TEX	423	43	90	18	3	0	17	31	51	10	11	212	265	271	536	7%	88%	0.61	45	100	2.28	1
Flores,Jose	02	29	6	aaa	OAK	363	44	86	15	1	1	25	38	44	11	5	237	309	292	601	9%	88%	0.86	43	90	3.26	14
	03	30	84	aaa	OAK	370	51	78	10	1	2	27	44	43	12	2	212	296	258	553	11%	88%	1.02	33	104	2.86	5
Fontenot,Mike	03	23	4	aa	BAL	449	59	134	20	3	13	62	48	87	15	5	298	365	441	806	10%	81%	0.55	89	101	6.17	47
Forbes,P.J.	02	35	8	aaa	PHI	355	34	80	16	1	1	32	18	47	3	1	225	263	285	547	5%	87%	0.38	47	71	2.58	2

Major League Equivalent Statistics

BATTER	Yr	Age	Pos	Lev	Org	ab	r	h	d	t	hr	rbi	bb	k	sb	cs	ba	ob	slg	ops	bb%	ct%	eye	px	sx	rc/g	bpv
Ford,Lew	02	26	8	a/a	MIN	566	85	147	33	3	14	52	43	61	20	6	260	312	403	715	7%	89%	0.70	95	117	4.52	40
	03	27	8	aaa	MIN	211	29	58	17	2	2	27	9	27	4	5	275	303	401	704	4%	87%	0.31	94	106	4.03	36
Foster,Quincy	02	28	8	aa	MON	264	27	56	7	2	2	22	12	41	17	12	212	246	277	523	4%	84%	0.29	42	130	2.00	-6
	03	29	8	aa	MON	216	22	46	6	1	2	11	7	26	14	6	211	237	267	503	3%	88%	0.27	38	122	2.05	-9
Fox,Jason	02	26	8	aa	MIL	147	9	23	5	2	0	13	5	33	3	1	156	184	218	402	3%	78%	0.15	42	128	1.26	-27
Francia,Dave	02	27	8	aaa	PHI	117	10	22	7	1	1	8	4	18	3	2	188	215	291	505	3%	85%	0.22	74	113	1.91	-2
Franco,Matt	02	33	3	aaa	ATL	173	19	41	9	0	5	23	11	18	1	0	237	283	376	658	6%	90%	0.61	91	46	3.73	29
Franklin,Micah	02	30	8	aaa	ARI	311	43	72	15	0	12	41	32	59	4	4	232	303	395	699	9%	81%	0.54	102	59	4.08	30
Frank,Mike	02	28	8	a/a	STL	324	26	71	10	2	6	34	19	24	7	3	219	262	318	580	6%	93%	0.79	61	84	2.82	14
Freel,Ryan	02	27	4	aaa	TAM	448	54	107	25	4	7	41	31	46	31	11	239	288	359	647	6%	90%	0.67	81	139	3.56	27
	03	28	4	aaa	CIN	215	29	53	10	1	3	10	16	26	19	7	247	300	345	645	7%	88%	0.61	67	130	3.62	23
Freeman,Choo	02	23	8	aa	COL	430	58	120	17	5	11	46	46	68	11	16	279	349	419	767	10%	84%	0.68	85	103	4.87	42
	03	24	8	aaa	COL	327	33	79	9	3	7	27	17	49	1	9	242	279	352	631	5%	85%	0.35	66	68	3.01	15
Freire,Alejandro	02	28	3	a/a	SF	322	26	68	14	1	8	29	25	67	0	2	211	268	335	603	7%	79%	0.37	80	32	2.99	11
	03	29	3	aa	SF	498	45	103	22	1	9	51	30	97	1	0	206	251	307	559	6%	80%	0.31	68	44	2.61	3
French,Anton	03	28	8	aaa	BOS	314	42	81	8	7	2	18	24	59	33	12	258	311	349	660	7%	81%	0.41	54	208	3.80	16
Frese,Nate	02	25	6	aa	CHC	230	19	43	8	1	2	14	19	59	4	3	187	249	257	506	8%	74%	0.32	48	78	2.10	-11
	03	26	6	aaa	CHC	309	30	64	12	1	5	26	32	58	0	0	207	282	298	580	9%	81%	0.55	60	37	2.95	5
Frias,Hanley	02	29	64	aaa	ARI	427	44	91	16	6	4	26	22	47	5	2	213	252	307	558	5%	89%	0.47	60	121	2.60	5
Frye,Jeff	02	36	45	aaa	HOU	397	36	98	13	0	1	19	26	37	4	4	247	293	287	580	6%	91%	0.70	33	49	2.93	10
Fuentes,Omar	03	24	2	aa	NYY	250	23	51	14	0	4	21	21	33	0	0	206	268	307	575	8%	87%	0.65	72	26	2.83	11
Furmaniak,J.J.	03	24	6	aa	SD	103	9	23	3	1	3	10	7	26	0	0	221	269	350	619	6%	74%	0.25	75	57	3.23	10
Gall,John	02	25	3	aa	STL	526	62	141	38	2	16	62	30	62	3	1	268	308	439	747	5%	88%	0.48	114	66	4.85	46
	03	26	83	a/a	STL	513	60	145	23	1	17	75	39	60	5	3	283	334	431	765	7%	88%	0.65	93	56	5.29	46
Gandolfo,Rob	02	25	4	a/a	SEA	201	16	35	4	1	1	14	14	25	1	3	174	228	219	447	7%	88%	0.56	30	63	1.55	-18
	03	26	4	a/a	SEA	195	21	44	6	1	0	14	9	34	9	5	226	260	268	528	4%	82%	0.26	33	111	2.32	-6
Garabito,Eddy	02	26	6	aaa	BAL	434	46	100	18	3	3	28	21	43	10	9	230	266	306	572	5%	90%	0.49	54	99	2.63	9
	03	27	6	aaa	BAL	459	54	114	23	3	3	50	28	66	13	9	249	293	332	625	6%	86%	0.43	60	105	3.30	17
Garbe,B.J.	03	23	8	aa	MIN	225	23	37	9	1	2	18	13	52	4	3	164	210	240	450	5%	77%	0.25	53	101	1.57	-18
Garcia,Danny	03	23	4	a/a	NYM	505	58	126	31	3	6	66	27	71	11	3	250	288	358	646	5%	86%	0.38	78	105	3.65	23
Garcia,Douglas	02	23	8	a/a	TEX	153	8	40	8	0	1	15	2	28	0	0	261	271	333	604	1%	82%	0.07	56	12	3.15	12
Garcia,Jesse	02	29	4	aaa	ATL	230	24	58	10	1	5	14	13	31	7	5	252	292	370	662	5%	87%	0.42	76	86	3.60	24
	03	30	6	aaa	ATL	425	39	113	15	2	2	26	10	51	25	8	267	284	324	608	2%	88%	0.19	42	111	3.24	10
Garcia,Karim	02	27	8	aaa	CLE	379	53	107	21	4	15	63	26	60	1	6	282	328	478	806	6%	84%	0.43	120	77	5.42	52
Garcia,Luis	02	24	8	aa	CLE	474	57	120	23	1	16	50	39	80	4	2	253	310	407	717	8%	83%	0.49	97	61	4.50	34
	03	25	38	aaa	CLE	432	37	88	26	1	7	46	20	89	2	4	204	239	317	556	4%	79%	0.22	80	53	2.42	6
Garrett,Shawn	02	24	8	aa	PIT	489	57	125	22	5	8	58	26	70	16	7	256	293	370	663	5%	86%	0.37	74	123	3.77	23
	03	25	8	aa	PIT	468	59	123	28	4	10	58	31	86	17	8	262	308	404	712	6%	82%	0.36	94	119	4.36	33
Gautreau,Jake	03	24	4	aa	SD	438	43	92	20	0	12	49	43	127	1	4	210	280	337	617	9%	71%	0.34	82	28	3.16	11
Gemoll,Brandon	03	23	3	aa	MIL	456	47	113	30	2	10	57	43	99	6	10	249	313	387	700	9%	78%	0.43	95	62	4.05	31
Gemoll,Justin	03	26	5	aa	KC	382	40	91	16	0	1	26	34	52	12	5	238	301	287	588	8%	86%	0.65	41	76	3.09	9
German,Amado	02	25	8	aa	TAM	344	45	82	10	4	2	28	31	87	12	16	238	301	308	609	8%	75%	0.36	45	126	2.85	5
	03	26	8	aa	TAM	395	33	93	23	3	4	41	28	88	5	5	235	285	333	618	7%	78%	0.32	71	76	3.22	14
German,Esteban	02	25	4	aaa	OAK	458	54	105	14	2	1	32	57	49	19	18	229	315	275	590	11%	89%	1.16	34	90	2.90	14
	03	26	4	aaa	OAK	467	68	124	18	5	2	41	44	54	26	10	265	328	337	665	9%	89%	0.81	50	138	4.05	25
German,Ramon	03	24	5	aa	HOU	115	4	22	1	0	1	6	9	22	0	1	194	251	228	479	7%	81%	0.40	21	10	1.88	-19
Gerut,Jody	02	25	8	a/a	CLE	439	65	120	20	3	10	51	49	48	17	13	273	346	401	747	10%	89%	1.02	82	103	4.85	45
Gettis,Byron	03	24	8	aa	KC	510	66	144	29	3	15	85	44	91	13	12	281	338	436	774	8%	82%	0.48	100	87	5.13	45
Gibbs,Kevin	02	29	8	aa	NYY	217	26	47	6	2	2	13	15	36	14	7	217	267	290	558	6%	83%	0.42	47	139	2.53	-0
Gibralter,Dave	02	27	8	aa	CHC	166	16	30	6	0	2	13	9	30	1	1	181	223	253	476	5%	82%	0.30	51	57	1.81	-13
Gilbert,Shawn	02	35	5	aaa	PIT	143	14	32	2	1	1	11	17	27	2	5	224	306	273	579	11%	81%	0.63	29	72	2.69	-1
Giles,Marcus	02	24	4	aaa	ATL	115	22	34	6	0	3	14	11	13	3	0	296	357	426	783	9%	89%	0.85	87	85	6.01	51
Gil,Geronimo	03	28	2	aaa	BAL	134	13	41	8	0	1	15	7	28	0	3	305	338	389	726	5%	79%	0.23	66	30	4.54	34
Ginter,Keith	02	26	4	aaa	HOU	435	60	108	27	1	12	47	48	90	3	4	248	323	398	721	10%	79%	0.53	100	59	4.53	35
Gipson,Charles	03	31	8	aaa	NYY	120	13	27	5	1	0	4	7	17	4	6	225	269	285	554	6%	86%	0.43	46	102	2.14	3
Glavine,Mike	03	31	3	aaa	NYM	169	13	37	9	0	4	14	20	38	0	0	218	300	336	636	10%	78%	0.52	80	12	3.59	16
Gload,Ross	02	27	3	aaa	COL	442	43	123	24	4	13	44	12	36	6	5	278	297	439	736	3%	92%	0.33	102	84	4.51	41
	03	28	38	aaa	CHW	508	60	143	35	4	17	58	26	55	5	3	281	315	466	781	5%	89%	0.47	120	82	5.27	52
Godwin,Tyrell	03	24	8	aa	TOR	123	16	33	6	2	1	10	3	23	5	1	270	287	371	658	2%	81%	0.12	67	155	3.83	20
Goelz,Jim	03	28	68	a/a	BOS	222	20	41	7	0	0	9	6	34	1	2	184	206	216	422	3%	84%	0.18	28	59	1.38	-24
Gomes,Jonny	03	23	8	a/a	TAM	461	64	110	30	4	15	52	50	142	21	2	239	313	419	732	10%	69%	0.35	116	143	4.85	34
Gomez,Alexis	02	22	8	aa	KC	461	64	131	20	7	13	67	38	72	32	26	284	339	443	781	8%	84%	0.53	95	148	4.73	45
	03	23	8	aaa	KC	456	39	115	22	6	7	46	20	69	3	6	252	284	373	656	4%	85%	0.29	78	87	3.52	22
Gomez,Rich	02	26	8	aaa	SD	334	36	67	13	1	9	45	20	69	11	6	201	246	326	572	6%	79%	0.29	79	98	2.56	5
	03	27	8	a/a	SD	320	37	70	9	1	10	44	20	59	22	1	220	266	351	617	6%	82%	0.34	77	123	3.46	12
Gonzalez,Adrian	02	20	3	aa	FLA	508	60	125	33	1	14	83	47	90	5	4	246	310	398	708	8%	82%	0.52	102	61	4.32	34
	03	21	3	a/a	TEX	449	42	119	20	3	5	45	35	60	2	1	264	317	358	675	7%	87%	0.58	64	66	4.14	26
Gonzalez,Jimmy	02	30	2	aa	NYM	299	20	47	7	1	4	23	27	57	2	3	157	227	227	454	8%	81%	0.47	44	51	1.66	-20
Gonzalez,Luis	02	23	4	a/a	CLE	282	38	69	10	2	6	23	12	37	4	0	245	276	358	634	4%	87%	0.32	71	109	3.50	17
	03	24	34	aa	CLE	431	63	124	21	3	7	54	40	40	1	0	287	347	395	742	8%	91%	1.00	73	71	5.21	45
Gonzalez,Raul	02	29	8	aaa	CIN	432	66	122	24	1	10	50	43	47	7	9	282	347	412	759	9%	89%	0.91	87	70	5.06	48
	03	30	8	aaa	NYM	120	15	36	3	1	3	15	13	24	5	2	303	370	410	780	10%	80%	0.53	62	96	5.83	37
Gonzalez,Wiki	03	29	2	aaa	SD	149	13	33	6	1	3	15	15	11	1	0	220	293	330	623	9%	93%	1.41	72	56	3.45	31
Gordon,Brian	02	24	8	aa	ARI	477	54	120	29	8	8	49	26	87	2	7	252	290	396	686	5%	82%	0.30	95	107	3.81	29
	03	25	8	aaa	ARI	449	45	109	19	6	11	53	26	70	1	4	243	284	384	667	5%	84%	0.37	86	81	3.66	24
Gorneault,Nick	03	24	8	aa	ANA	110	16	33	6	3	2	16	7	22	2	0	302	342	458	800	6%	80%	0.30	96	171	6.03	46
Grabowski,Jason	02	26	8	aaa	OAK	265	36	64	18	2	9	38	28	43	4	5	242	314	426	740	10%	84%	0.65	119	88	4.50	43
	03	27	8	aaa	OAK	250	33	61	10	1	7	30	24	40	6	2	243	309	372	681	9%	84%	0.59	82	89	4.12	27
Gredvig,Doug	02	23	3	aa	BAL	465	40	112	18	1	12	67	38	86	2	3	241	298	361	660	8%	82%	0.44	76	38	3.75	21
	03	24	3	aa	BAL	100	5	19	5	0	1	11	5	20	1	0	190	227	266	493	5%	80%	0.24	57	34	2.02	-9
Greene,Charlie	02	32	2	aaa	FLA	320	23	60	19	0	5	27	7	44	0	0	188	205	294	499	2%	86%	0.16	77	27	1.93	-3
Greene,Khalil	03	24	6	a/a	SD	548	54	137	31	1	10	58	30	95	6	8	250	289	365	654	5%	83%	0.32	80	56	3.53	23

Major League Equivalent Statistics

BATTER	Yr	Age	Pos	Lev	Org	ab	r	h	d	t	hr	rbi	bb	k	sb	cs	ba	ob	slg	ops	bb%	ct%	eye	px	sx	rc/g	bpv
Greene,Todd	02	31	2	aaa	TEX	277	33	73	17	0	12	49	8	40	2	0	264	284	455	739	3%	86%	0.20	121	55	4.59	42
Green,Andy	03	26	46	aa	ARI	490	45	117	30	2	2	33	25	43	11	10	238	275	318	593	5%	91%	0.59	64	81	2.87	17
Green,Chad	02	27	8	a/a	MIN	296	30	57	12	2	6	30	12	66	10	3	193	224	307	531	4%	78%	0.18	73	125	2.24	-2
	03	28	8	aaa	MIN	397	42	88	23	3	7	24	18	85	10	7	223	256	344	600	4%	79%	0.21	83	109	2.81	13
Green,Nick	02	24	4	aa	ATL	355	39	72	13	1	11	40	28	79	2	6	203	261	338	599	7%	78%	0.35	83	55	2.78	9
	03	25	4	aaa	ATL	399	38	94	25	1	10	48	24	74	7	5	236	279	377	656	6%	82%	0.32	96	69	3.52	24
Gregorio,Tom	02	25	2	a/a	ANA	239	19	51	12	1	3	13	9	39	2	1	213	242	310	552	4%	84%	0.23	68	67	2.48	4
	03	26	8	aaa	ANA	181	19	34	9	0	4	18	11	35	0	0	188	233	300	533	6%	81%	0.30	76	38	2.30	-0
Griffin,John-Ford	03	24	8	aa	TOR	373	38	93	22	2	11	60	40	71	2	0	250	322	406	728	10%	81%	0.56	102	61	4.77	36
Grindell,Nate	02	26	8	aa	CLE	435	59	105	21	5	10	49	27	61	4	3	241	286	382	667	6%	86%	0.44	88	110	3.74	26
	03	27	8	a/a	CLE	272	31	53	19	1	5	30	26	48	2	4	195	266	321	587	9%	82%	0.55	90	65	2.76	13
Gripp,Ryan	02	24	5	aa	CHC	380	43	76	21	1	9	41	39	80	4	2	200	274	332	606	9%	79%	0.49	88	71	3.11	13
	03	25	3	aa	MIL	144	18	35	5	0	5	18	18	37	1	0	244	328	369	697	11%	75%	0.49	76	42	4.47	22
Gross,Gabe	02	23	8	aa	TOR	403	44	85	17	3	7	42	41	54	6	2	211	284	320	604	9%	87%	0.76	71	94	3.18	15
	03	24	8	a/a	TOR	492	63	139	40	3	10	63	71	92	3	3	283	373	437	810	13%	81%	0.77	109	65	6.19	54
Grove,Jason	03	25	8	aa	NYY	244	21	57	10	0	4	21	17	44	0	2	232	283	317	600	7%	82%	0.38	59	24	3.04	9
Grummitt,Dan	02	26	3	aa	TAM	363	41	74	18	1	6	35	26	94	3	3	204	257	309	566	7%	74%	0.28	72	72	2.62	3
	03	27	3	a/a	TAM	349	29	71	18	1	9	44	25	118	1	2	204	258	337	595	7%	66%	0.21	87	42	2.88	8
Gubanich,Creighton	03	32	2	aa	CIN	119	7	18	5	0	1	8	4	29	0	0	147	176	224	400	3%	76%	0.15	55	25	1.23	-25
Guerrero,Cristian	02	22	8	aa	MIL	394	41	82	15	1	7	42	22	86	18	10	208	250	305	555	5%	78%	0.26	63	104	2.42	1
	03	23	8	aa	MIL	123	7	21	6	0	0	6	4	27	3	1	173	199	221	420	3%	78%	0.14	42	67	1.41	-22
Guerrero,Wilton	03	29	84	aaa	CIN	476	52	115	20	1	1	22	20	48	23	9	242	272	293	565	4%	90%	0.40	41	107	2.74	6
Guevara,Giomar	02	30	6	aa	OAK	363	32	61	11	2	1	12	24	103	5	5	168	220	218	437	6%	72%	0.23	36	92	1.51	-24
Guiel,Aaron	02	30	8	aaa	KC	215	32	64	9	1	7	37	21	30	6	1	298	360	447	807	9%	86%	0.70	92	92	6.24	51
	03	31	8	aaa	KC	190	27	45	7	2	6	22	23	36	2	0	237	318	393	711	11%	81%	0.63	93	96	4.55	30
Guiel,Jeff	02	29	8	a/a	ANA	330	36	64	17	2	9	33	31	68	5	3	194	263	339	603	9%	79%	0.46	93	89	2.96	12
	03	30	35	aaa	ANA	325	35	63	13	1	9	35	34	67	2	1	193	269	322	591	9%	79%	0.50	81	59	2.95	8
Gulan,Mike	03	33	5	aaa	PIT	417	41	103	25	2	7	46	20	94	5	4	246	280	367	647	5%	77%	0.21	84	74	3.50	21
Gutierrez,Jesse	03	25	3	aa	CIN	107	9	20	7	1	4	14	6	13	0	0	185	230	370	600	6%	88%	0.47	119	52	2.78	20
Gutierrez,Vic	03	26	5	aa	MON	262	23	51	8	1	1	14	11	37	5	2	196	228	244	472	4%	86%	0.29	36	92	1.84	-14
Guzman,Edwards	02	26	2	aaa	SF	390	39	103	21	0	4	48	14	24	1	3	264	290	349	638	3%	94%	0.58	64	37	3.48	26
	03	27	2	aaa	MON	213	19	64	11	1	2	20	6	15	4	1	299	317	388	705	3%	93%	0.39	65	73	4.57	34
Guzman,Elpidio	02	26	8	aa	ANA	454	43	92	13	5	4	32	31	84	16	11	203	254	280	533	6%	81%	0.37	49	124	2.26	-5
	03	27	8	aa	SEA	475	49	104	10	4	3	43	17	71	23	10	220	247	277	524	4%	85%	0.24	36	135	2.26	-7
Guzman,Freddy	03	23	8	a/a	SD	187	27	45	4	1	1	10	22	31	36	8	241	321	289	609	11%	83%	0.71	32	154	3.76	8
Haad,Yamid	02	25	2	a/a	TAM	231	20	41	4	0	3	27	10	40	3	1	177	212	234	445	4%	83%	0.25	35	68	1.61	-21
	03	26	23	a/a	SD	287	21	53	12	1	8	31	14	58	3	2	185	222	317	538	4%	80%	0.23	83	59	2.24	0
Haas,Chris	02	26	305	a/a	TEX	289	28	53	15	1	10	28	33	85	0	0	183	267	346	613	10%	71%	0.39	103	36	3.13	11
Hafner,Travis	02	25	3	aaa	TEX	401	60	122	20	1	17	58	60	58	2	1	304	395	486	881	13%	86%	1.03	112	50	7.57	68
	03	26	3	aaa	CLE	100	14	25	4	0	2	9	21	25	2	1	252	384	349	733	18%	75%	0.86	64	49	5.25	28
Hairston,Scott	03	23	4	a/a	ARI	337	40	85	19	6	8	36	23	58	5	2	252	300	415	715	6%	83%	0.40	102	136	4.39	34
Hallmark,Pat	02	29	8	aa	KC	362	39	70	10	1	2	23	24	68	30	10	193	244	243	487	6%	81%	0.35	35	129	2.02	-14
	03	30	8	aa	SF	485	35	75	15	2	3	37	25	97	20	11	155	196	210	406	5%	80%	0.25	40	105	1.26	-27
Hall,Bill	02	23	6	aaa	MIL	465	34	105	20	1	4	29	23	89	16	12	226	262	299	561	5%	81%	0.26	53	78	2.50	2
	03	24	46	aaa	MIL	354	52	94	24	1	5	29	24	72	9	12	266	312	381	694	6%	80%	0.33	84	89	3.84	30
Hall,Billy	03	34	85	aa	FLA	367	36	58	6	2	1	20	22	61	27	3	158	205	198	404	6%	83%	0.35	26	152	1.50	-29
Hall,Noah	03	26	8	aa	MON	449	66	109	20	2	7	49	61	61	23	10	242	333	341	674	12%	86%	1.00	67	108	4.15	28
Hall,Victor	02	22	8	aa	ARI	161	14	43	4	4	0	9	5	17	5	5	267	289	342	631	3%	89%	0.29	44	154	3.16	13
	03	23	8	aa	ARI	490	54	130	12	10	0	32	38	65	16	22	265	318	329	647	7%	87%	0.58	39	139	3.30	16
Haltiwanger,Garrick	02	28	0	aa	TOR	133	13	22	7	1	2	12	12	36	5	2	165	234	278	513	8%	73%	0.33	77	119	2.13	-7
Hamilton,Jon	02	25	8	aa	CHC	386	49	86	17	5	9	46	29	76	8	4	223	277	363	640	7%	80%	0.38	87	131	3.40	18
	03	26	8	aa	CHW	411	45	87	17	1	7	40	41	84	20	9	212	283	311	594	9%	79%	0.48	66	97	3.00	8
Hammock,Rob	02	25	2	aa	ARI	441	48	105	23	3	8	51	30	57	4	5	238	287	358	645	6%	87%	0.53	80	77	3.47	23
	03	26	2	aaa	ARI	116	11	28	6	2	2	13	9	19	1	0	243	296	376	672	7%	84%	0.47	85	106	3.98	25
Hammond,Joey	02	25	45	a/a	BAL	285	32	63	10	1	1	17	36	42	3	2	221	308	274	582	11%	85%	0.86	40	67	3.06	7
	03	26	485	a/a	BAL	405	45	101	11	4	0	34	50	63	5	2	249	332	296	627	11%	84%	0.80	33	92	3.69	13
Hankins,Ryan	02	26	3	aa	CHW	422	40	97	23	1	6	57	38	78	6	6	230	293	332	625	8%	82%	0.49	72	61	3.31	16
	03	27	53	a/a	CHW	482	50	112	30	1	11	54	38	79	5	7	233	289	368	658	7%	84%	0.48	92	56	3.55	25
Hannahan,Buzz	02	26	4	aa	PHI	269	34	49	6	2	2	17	32	49	10	4	182	269	242	511	11%	82%	0.65	38	120	2.29	-11
	03	27	84	aa	PHI	380	41	73	12	1	2	17	38	77	17	4	192	266	240	506	9%	80%	0.50	36	104	2.31	-11
Hannahan,Jack	02	23	5	aa	DET	226	14	47	10	1	2	16	18	38	2	1	208	266	288	554	7%	83%	0.47	57	55	2.63	2
	03	24	5	aa	DET	471	56	107	16	0	7	40	43	68	2	0	227	291	303	594	8%	86%	0.63	51	55	3.15	9
Hansen,Jed	02	30	5	aaa	KC	339	46	74	14	3	11	36	37	73	13	5	218	295	375	670	10%	78%	0.51	95	125	3.82	22
	03	31	58	aaa	KC	364	47	81	23	2	10	39	47	89	8	7	223	311	376	687	11%	76%	0.53	101	86	3.95	26
Hardy,J.J.	02	20	6	aa	MIL	145	13	33	6	0	1	12	8	15	1	2	228	268	290	558	5%	90%	0.53	47	46	2.54	6
	03	21	6	aa	MIL	416	61	109	25	0	11	57	51	49	5	4	262	343	401	744	11%	88%	1.04	94	59	5.01	47
Harper,Brandon	03	27	2	aa	FLA	195	13	36	9	0	2	14	18	37	2	0	183	253	255	508	9%	81%	0.49	55	43	2.24	-7
Harrison,Adonis	03	27	46	a/a	ANA	317	30	75	14	3	2	23	30	36	3	7	236	303	318	621	9%	89%	0.85	57	78	3.19	19
Harris,Brendan	03	23	8	aa	CHC	435	51	110	30	5	5	48	48	73	6	7	252	326	377	703	10%	83%	0.65	88	97	4.29	33
Harris,Brian	02	27	4	aa	KC	490	61	109	18	6	2	35	37	78	7	4	222	277	296	573	7%	84%	0.47	50	122	2.82	4
	03	28	46	a/a	KC	388	37	81	14	4	3	25	31	60	5	6	208	267	291	559	7%	85%	0.52	54	97	2.55	2
Harris,Willie	02	24	4	aaa	CHW	360	48	95	15	3	5	29	31	55	28	15	264	322	364	686	8%	85%	0.56	66	131	3.97	26
	03	25	4	aaa	CHW	100	19	36	6	1	6	11	16	17	8	3	356	444	614	1058	14%	83%	0.92	153	122	11.04	100
Hart,Bo	02	26	4	aa	STL	405	42	77	13	3	3	27	31	74	10	7	190	248	259	507	7%	82%	0.42	46	108	2.09	-9
	03	27	4	aaa	STL	266	27	71	12	1	7	28	14	55	4	2	268	305	396	702	5%	79%	0.26	83	68	4.30	29
Hart,Corey	02	21	506	a/a	KC	376	46	91	17	2	3	47	48	51	8	9	242	328	322	650	11%	86%	0.94	57	79	3.66	23
	03	22	63	aa	KC	334	34	88	9	0	4	40	40	55	10	4	263	342	326	669	11%	84%	0.73	42	65	4.21	20
Hart,Corey	03	28	5	aa	MIL	493	51	112	30	1	10	69	20	116	18	7	227	257	351	608	4%	76%	0.17	86	100	3.00	15
Hart,Jason	02	25	8	aaa	TEX	514	58	119	28	1	20	62	51	91	1	0	232	301	407	707	9%	82%	0.56	110	43	4.33	34
	03	26	3	aaa	TEX	512	55	119	20	0	19	69	46	93	2	1	233	296	386	682	8%	82%	0.49	94	39	4.01	26
Harvey,Ken	02	25	3	aaa	KC	488	61	124	27	1	17	61	33	68	7	3	254	301	418	719	6%	86%	0.49	105	75	4.44	38
Haselman,Bill	03	37	2	aaa	BOS	280	29	53	5	0	5	19	7	46	1	1	190	210	257	467	3%	84%	0.16	42	60	1.72	-16

Major League Equivalent Statistics

BATTER	Yr	Age	Pos	Lev	Org	ab	r	h	d	t	hr	rbi	bb	k	sb	cs	ba	ob	slg	ops	bb%	ct%	eye	px	sx	rc/g	bpv
Haverbusch,Kevin	02	26	8	a/a	PIT	224	19	53	11	1	5	20	5	33	5	3	237	253	362	615	2%	85%	0.15	82	82	2.99	16
	03	27	8	aa	BOS	203	13	37	10	1	3	22	12	47	0	3	184	231	290	521	6%	77%	0.26	72	42	2.02	-4
Hawpe,Brad	03	24	8	aa	COL	346	39	90	25	0	16	51	24	65	1	3	261	308	472	781	6%	81%	0.36	135	29	5.04	50
Haynes,Dee	02	25	8	aa	STL	504	57	133	24	3	16	74	20	56	2	2	264	292	419	711	4%	89%	0.36	97	66	4.28	35
	03	26	8	aaa	STL	441	49	104	23	2	17	64	15	47	3	1	236	261	411	671	3%	89%	0.31	109	73	3.64	30
Haynes,Nathan	02	23	8	aaa	ANA	283	28	70	12	3	2	9	9	40	8	12	247	271	332	603	3%	86%	0.23	58	110	2.61	11
	03	24	8	a/a	ANA	492	60	119	17	8	5	40	34	78	26	10	243	291	339	631	6%	84%	0.43	61	160	3.45	15
Headley,Justin	02	27	8	aa	BOS	377	39	76	18	1	7	37	27	58	2	7	202	255	310	565	7%	85%	0.47	73	55	2.46	7
	03	28	38	a/a	BOS	495	54	102	20	2	7	48	29	78	4	3	206	250	295	545	6%	84%	0.37	61	79	2.46	1
Heintz,Chris	02	28	2	aa	STL	373	26	83	20	1	5	29	13	60	1	0	223	249	322	570	3%	84%	0.22	71	45	2.71	8
	03	29	2	aa	PIT	271	19	50	9	2	2	18	13	28	0	0	185	222	252	474	4%	90%	0.46	45	55	1.84	-10
Henson,Drew	02	23	5	aaa	NYY	471	58	104	28	2	16	55	33	117	2	1	221	272	391	662	7%	75%	0.28	109	72	3.62	24
	03	24	5	aaa	NYY	483	50	102	36	1	12	66	27	104	7	5	211	253	364	617	5%	78%	0.26	106	77	3.00	19
Hermansen,Chad	03	26	8	aaa	LA	235	33	69	13	1	7	24	16	32	3	1	293	337	442	779	6%	86%	0.49	96	77	5.56	47
Hernandez,Alex	02	25	8	a/a	CIN	307	29	67	18	1	4	26	27	67	5	0	218	281	322	604	8%	78%	0.40	75	81	3.25	12
Hernandez,Carlos	02	22	64	aaa	NYM	332	39	103	16	2	0	27	14	49	14	7	310	338	370	709	4%	85%	0.29	48	105	4.60	29
	03	28	4	a/a	HOU	318	23	56	5	0	2	17	14	54	5	1	175	210	208	418	4%	83%	0.26	23	71	1.45	-27
Hernandez,Michel	02	24	2	a/a	NYY	182	18	47	10	1	2	19	11	16	1	5	258	301	357	658	6%	91%	0.69	70	59	3.42	29
	03	25	2	aaa	NYY	282	33	71	13	0	4	25	31	30	0	2	253	326	341	667	10%	89%	1.01	62	28	3.99	30
Hessman,Mike	02	25	5	aaa	ATL	484	59	117	26	1	22	68	29	93	1	6	242	285	436	721	6%	81%	0.31	120	41	4.09	36
	03	26	38	aaa	ATL	359	45	85	15	2	15	49	22	81	3	1	237	281	414	694	6%	77%	0.27	106	82	4.02	28
Hiatt,Phil	02	33	8	aaa	LA	355	44	80	10	1	14	52	27	70	1	3	225	280	377	658	7%	80%	0.39	88	51	3.53	19
	03	34	38	aaa	CHC	478	55	104	28	1	19	68	35	108	7	2	218	272	399	671	7%	77%	0.33	115	79	3.71	27
Hill,Bobby	02	25	4	aaa	CHC	354	56	83	19	2	6	27	35	47	20	7	234	303	350	654	9%	87%	0.74	79	131	3.76	26
	03	26	4	aaa	PIT	427	49	105	24	3	6	37	37	58	8	10	246	305	357	662	8%	87%	0.64	77	85	3.62	26
Hill,Jason	02	26	2	aa	ANA	431	32	97	17	1	5	41	11	58	2	5	225	244	304	548	2%	87%	0.19	55	45	2.36	1
	03	27	23	a/a	CIN	299	18	58	10	1	5	23	7	28	4	1	193	212	277	489	2%	91%	0.26	55	65	1.90	-8
Hill,Koyie	02	24	2	aa	LA	468	62	114	22	1	10	59	71	88	5	3	244	343	359	702	13%	81%	0.81	77	63	4.56	29
	03	25	2	a/a	LA	413	48	104	20	0	3	36	18	54	6	1	251	283	322	605	4%	87%	0.34	55	77	3.25	13
Hill,Mike	02	26	8	aa	HOU	527	51	119	24	4	10	42	26	97	10	8	226	262	343	606	5%	82%	0.27	76	97	2.93	12
	03	27	8	aa	HOU	159	11	30	3	2	2	14	5	35	2	1	188	213	277	489	3%	78%	0.14	52	93	1.88	-13
Hinch,A.J.	03	29	2	aaa	DET	185	17	40	12	1	3	20	12	37	0	1	216	264	334	598	6%	80%	0.32	84	53	2.94	13
Hitchcox,Brian	02	24	4	aa	PHI	297	34	69	17	2	5	21	13	28	3	6	232	265	354	618	4%	91%	0.46	83	84	2.94	21
	03	25	4	a/a	PHI	349	30	74	13	3	5	23	33	54	7	7	212	281	308	588	9%	85%	0.62	62	85	2.85	9
Hochgesang,Josh	02	25	5	aa	OAK	354	32	67	17	0	10	48	22	89	3	5	189	237	322	559	6%	75%	0.25	86	48	2.37	4
Hodges,Scott	02	24	5	aa	MON	526	61	127	34	1	7	53	48	82	2	2	241	305	350	655	8%	84%	0.59	79	53	3.79	25
	03	25	5	aaa	MON	482	51	123	20	2	9	50	21	70	4	2	255	286	361	647	4%	85%	0.30	69	72	3.62	20
Hoffpauir,Josh	02	25	4	aa	BAL	302	24	66	9	2	1	20	16	28	8	6	219	258	272	529	5%	91%	0.57	37	90	2.27	-0
	03	26	84	aa	BAL	356	32	84	16	1	2	28	22	26	11	6	235	279	298	577	6%	93%	0.82	49	83	2.83	15
Holbert,Aaron	02	30	6	aaa	SEA	399	50	103	20	2	5	35	15	48	14	14	258	285	356	641	4%	88%	0.31	68	104	3.17	20
	03	31	6	aaa	PIT	397	44	90	18	4	2	29	14	70	23	14	227	254	304	558	4%	82%	0.21	55	141	2.39	2
Holliday,Matt	02	23	8	aa	COL	463	57	122	18	2	9	46	49	68	12	2	263	334	369	703	10%	85%	0.72	68	95	4.66	30
	03	24	8	aa	COL	522	49	126	26	4	12	55	33	56	12	10	242	287	374	660	6%	89%	0.59	86	88	3.55	28
Hollins,Damon	02	28	8	aaa	ATL	498	54	120	29	1	9	48	28	72	8	2	241	281	357	639	5%	86%	0.39	81	82	3.53	22
	03	29	8	aaa	ATL	307	34	74	20	3	10	39	18	63	6	2	240	283	421	704	6%	80%	0.29	116	108	4.12	34
Holt,Daylan	02	24	8	aa	OAK	201	15	48	9	0	3	21	12	45	1	5	239	282	328	610	6%	78%	0.27	63	30	2.90	11
Hood,Donnie	03	25	54	aa	CHC	154	14	37	14	1	1	10	6	42	3	0	241	268	364	632	4%	73%	0.14	97	97	3.44	23
Hooper,Clay	02	26	6	aa	NYY	236	26	45	5	1	2	13	17	34	0	6	191	245	246	491	7%	86%	0.50	36	60	1.79	-12
Hooper,Kevin	02	26	6	aaa	FLA	452	50	109	18	2	1	28	25	39	12	13	241	281	296	577	5%	91%	0.64	43	89	2.67	11
	03	27	46	aaa	FLA	493	56	110	8	3	1	39	26	51	18	11	222	262	256	517	5%	90%	0.52	22	113	2.22	-6
Hoover,Paul	02	26	2	aaa	TAM	227	22	46	12	3	4	16	15	60	3	3	203	252	335	587	6%	74%	0.25	86	118	2.71	8
	03	27	2	aaa	FLA	256	25	56	18	2	3	29	13	52	7	4	219	258	338	595	5%	80%	0.26	86	107	2.84	14
Hopper,Norris	03	25	8	aa	KC	424	46	116	13	2	0	32	21	49	20	10	273	307	314	621	5%	88%	0.42	32	102	3.38	13
Hopper,Shane	02	27	58	a/a	SD	173	13	36	6	2	3	19	9	48	3	1	208	247	318	565	5%	72%	0.19	68	108	2.63	1
Horner,Jim	02	29	2	a/a	SEA	229	27	54	16	1	3	25	15	56	1	1	236	283	354	636	6%	76%	0.27	86	70	3.45	19
	03	30	2	a/a	SEA	260	28	61	8	1	3	33	11	44	3	1	233	266	309	575	4%	83%	0.26	50	79	2.85	4
Howe,Matt	02	26	5	aa	OAK	187	15	37	11	1	3	14	18	49	3	3	198	268	316	584	9%	74%	0.37	82	73	2.76	7
Hubbard,Mike	02	32	2	aaa	BAL	211	21	49	9	0	4	23	14	24	1	2	232	280	332	612	6%	89%	0.58	67	41	3.13	17
	03	33	2	aaa	ATL	206	19	41	11	0	2	13	11	29	0	0	201	241	280	520	5%	86%	0.37	60	33	2.25	-1
Hubbard,Trenidad	03	37	8	aaa	CHC	348	50	90	13	1	4	21	37	29	18	7	259	330	331	661	10%	92%	1.28	50	102	4.01	33
Huber,Justin	03	21	2	aa	NYM	193	13	44	11	0	5	29	15	45	0	2	228	284	363	646	7%	77%	0.33	91	15	3.42	20
Huckaby,Ken	03	33	23	aaa	TOR	267	19	67	13	0	3	20	12	29	1	1	249	281	327	608	4%	89%	0.41	57	31	3.19	15
Hudson,Orlando	02	25	4	aaa	TOR	417	50	115	27	2	8	30	28	43	6	6	276	321	408	729	6%	90%	0.65	91	75	4.60	43
Huffman,Royce	02	26	3	aa	HOU	522	56	139	31	3	10	65	29	62	9	6	266	305	395	700	5%	88%	0.47	87	84	4.21	34
	03	27	3	aaa	HOU	460	43	124	19	2	2	52	37	63	6	3	270	324	333	657	7%	86%	0.59	48	69	3.97	21
Huff,Aubrey	02	26	3	aaa	TAM	126	16	38	9	0	3	17	10	11	0	0	302	353	444	797	7%	91%	0.91	100	26	5.99	60
Huisman,Jason	02	26	8	aa	ANA	263	30	51	12	1	4	26	10	31	8	6	194	223	293	516	4%	88%	0.32	67	111	1.97	-1
Hummel,Tim	02	24	6	aaa	CHW	523	49	126	30	0	4	36	48	85	5	6	241	305	321	626	8%	84%	0.56	63	45	3.41	17
	03	25	56	aaa	CHW	476	63	126	23	2	15	70	42	72	8	3	265	324	416	740	8%	85%	0.58	95	85	4.90	39
Hunter,Brian	02	35	3	aaa	TAM	101	6	17	5	1	3	14	7	21	0	0	168	222	327	549	6%	79%	0.33	99	49	2.35	3
Hunter,Scott	02	27	8	aa	BAL	386	37	68	18	0	5	32	17	74	8	5	176	211	262	473	4%	81%	0.23	61	85	1.72	-11
Hyzdu,Adam	02	31	8	aaa	PIT	243	24	49	14	0	7	37	22	51	1	2	202	268	346	614	8%	79%	0.43	96	38	3.06	15
	03	32	8	aaa	PIT	135	17	32	9	1	5	14	14	26	2	2	233	303	413	716	9%	81%	0.53	117	83	4.24	36
Iapoce,Anthony	02	29	8	aa	FLA	280	26	53	11	2	2	19	17	52	12	3	189	236	264	500	6%	81%	0.33	52	125	2.12	-9
	03	30	8	aaa	FLA	128	11	23	5	1	0	8	11	18	4	2	176	240	232	472	8%	86%	0.61	44	99	1.85	-11
Infante,Omar	02	21	6	aaa	DET	436	51	127	16	10	3	53	31	37	20	18	291	338	394	733	7%	92%	0.84	63	155	4.45	40
	03	22	6	aaa	DET	224	30	51	10	0	2	19	23	26	23	4	226	298	300	598	9%	88%	0.88	54	119	3.42	15
Inge,Brandon	03	26	2	aaa	DET	142	14	35	8	0	4	14	11	22	3	1	246	299	383	681	7%	85%	0.49	91	55	4.04	29
Inglett,Joe	03	25	4	aa	CLE	276	33	67	14	1	4	21	30	37	1	2	241	315	339	654	10%	87%	0.81	69	53	3.80	25
Inglin,Jeff	02	27	8	aaa	CHW	152	15	38	4	0	6	18	8	21	2	2	250	288	395	682	5%	86%	0.38	84	45	3.82	26
	03	28	8	aa	PHI	539	55	109	21	1	15	66	30	63	5	3	202	243	328	571	5%	88%	0.47	79	66	2.62	9

BATTER	Yr	Age	Pos	Lev	Org	ab	r	h	d	t	hr	rbi	bb	k	sb	cs	ba	ob	slg	ops	bb%	ct%	eye	px	sx	rc/g	bpv
Ingram,Darron	02	26	0	a/a	CHW	434	44	85	18	1	18	56	46	161	7	7	196	273	366	639	10%	63%	0.29	103	64	3.23	13
	03	27	8	aa	CHW	227	21	38	2	1	8	22	19	88	2	1	168	233	296	529	8%	61%	0.22	70	65	2.25	-11
Isenia,Chairon	03	25	2	aa	TAM	142	11	29	5	0	0	10	7	11	0	0	201	236	234	471	4%	93%	0.63	30	31	1.86	-8
Izturis,Maicer	02	22	4	aa	CLE	253	30	66	12	5	0	29	15	25	7	4	261	302	348	650	6%	90%	0.60	59	147	3.66	23
	03	23	64	a/a	CLE	519	67	132	27	6	3	45	43	47	26	13	254	311	347	658	8%	91%	0.91	65	135	3.76	30
Jackson,Nic	02	23	8	aa	CHC	131	16	34	8	1	3	17	5	22	7	2	260	287	405	691	4%	83%	0.23	96	126	4.06	31
	03	24	8	aaa	CHC	458	47	103	17	2	9	37	30	90	14	10	225	273	330	602	6%	80%	0.33	67	92	2.92	9
Jackson,Ryan	02	31	8	aaa	DET	420	33	94	28	1	5	41	11	80	5	3	224	244	331	575	3%	81%	0.14	80	69	2.65	10
	03	32	38	aaa	TAM	519	62	134	41	4	10	57	23	86	2	4	258	290	408	698	4%	84%	0.27	105	73	4.07	35
Jackson,Steve	03	26	23	aa	OAK	274	26	58	10	1	7	35	20	68	1	1	210	263	332	595	7%	75%	0.29	76	52	2.95	7
Jacobsen,Bucky	02	27	3	aa	STL	300	29	59	14	1	10	39	22	63	2	2	197	252	350	602	7%	79%	0.35	96	59	2.88	12
	03	28	3	aa	STL	447	62	101	18	1	23	62	44	108	2	1	226	295	426	721	9%	76%	0.41	118	61	4.38	32
Jacobson,Russ	02	25	2	aa	PHI	282	15	48	14	0	2	27	15	73	1	0	170	212	241	453	5%	74%	0.21	55	35	1.67	-17
	03	26	2	aa	PHI	109	6	24	4	0	1	4	5	16	1	1	223	260	281	540	5%	86%	0.35	42	34	2.44	-1
Jacobs,Greg	03	27	8	aa	SEA	126	9	31	5	0	1	11	7	15	1	3	249	288	311	599	5%	88%	0.47	47	34	2.91	12
Jacobs,Mike	03	23	2	aa	NYM	407	46	118	32	1	14	67	22	74	0	4	290	326	477	803	5%	82%	0.30	125	31	5.51	54
James,Kenny	02	26	8	aa	TOR	414	37	85	15	1	2	23	18	57	28	14	205	238	261	499	4%	86%	0.32	42	113	1.95	-8
	03	27	8	aa	ANA	447	45	103	19	1	3	35	25	62	10	7	230	271	294	565	5%	86%	0.41	49	79	2.66	5
Jeffcoat,Bryon	03	24	3	aa	ATL	100	13	24	5	0	0	10	14	22	1	0	238	333	285	618	12%	78%	0.64	42	53	3.64	9
Jennings,Doug	03	39	3	aaa	MIL	169	14	37	11	1	5	19	14	49	1	1	218	276	373	649	7%	71%	0.28	102	57	3.48	21
Jennings,Robin	02	31	8	aaa	CIN	351	20	63	18	0	3	33	18	46	3	5	179	220	256	476	5%	87%	0.39	59	41	1.73	-8
	03	31	38	a/a	CIN	249	18	42	12	1	2	11	14	49	2	2	170	213	244	457	5%	80%	0.28	55	64	1.65	-15
Jensen,Marcus	02	30	2	aaa	MIL	183	20	36	6	0	4	21	27	38	0	0	197	300	295	595	13%	79%	0.71	63	24	3.18	6
	03	31	2	aaa	NYY	196	15	36	6	0	3	12	27	50	0	0	184	283	257	540	12%	74%	0.54	50	16	2.59	-7
Jester,Joe	02	24	4	aa	SF	359	43	86	18	2	8	32	24	58	11	6	240	287	368	655	6%	84%	0.41	84	103	3.57	23
	03	25	4	aa	SF	121	14	22	5	0	1	8	14	24	5	2	179	261	245	506	10%	80%	0.55	51	87	2.22	-8
Jimenez,D'Angelo	02	25	6	aaa	CHW	157	21	41	10	1	6	16	23	13	5	2	261	356	452	808	13%	92%	1.77	121	87	5.92	72
Joffrion,Jack	03	28	6	aa	COL	124	10	24	4	0	2	8	2	33	2	0	194	209	284	493	2%	74%	0.07	59	63	1.95	-10
Johnson,Ben	02	21	8	aa	SD	456	52	98	20	3	8	50	57	119	10	10	215	302	325	627	11%	74%	0.48	72	90	3.29	11
	03	22	8	aa	SD	127	7	21	4	0	1	6	9	33	0	1	165	221	220	441	7%	74%	0.27	40	25	1.54	-23
Johnson,Brian	02	25	2	aa	KC	109	12	23	5	0	1	11	5	16	3	0	211	246	284	530	4%	85%	0.31	55	85	2.47	-1
Johnson,Dan	03	24	3	a/a	OAK	542	71	134	23	3	21	89	52	70	6	5	247	313	419	732	9%	87%	0.75	104	75	4.59	40
Johnson,Gary	02	27	8	a/a	ANA	532	56	112	20	3	8	58	46	110	10	10	211	273	305	578	8%	79%	0.42	62	87	2.72	4
	03	28	8	aaa	ANA	447	48	96	20	4	10	55	45	91	3	2	215	286	340	626	9%	80%	0.49	80	84	3.36	14
Johnson,Jason	02	25	8	aa	PHI	411	30	96	14	0	0	34	13	76	14	11	234	257	268	525	3%	82%	0.17	30	72	2.18	-6
Johnson,Kade	03	25	2	aa	MIL	213	22	34	7	1	4	25	17	66	5	3	161	223	254	476	7%	69%	0.26	60	97	1.80	-17
Johnson,Keith	02	31	5	aaa	ANA	367	38	82	17	2	11	38	7	53	5	4	223	238	371	609	2%	86%	0.13	92	89	2.82	15
	03	32	5	aaa	ANA	451	36	104	27	1	8	45	14	60	5	6	229	252	347	599	3%	87%	0.23	83	55	2.79	15
Johnson,Kelly	03	22	6	aa	ATL	334	43	88	21	4	6	42	32	73	9	3	263	328	404	732	9%	78%	0.44	94	126	4.85	35
Johnson,Mark	02	27	3	aaa	NYM	270	38	60	14	1	11	31	27	52	1	0	222	293	404	697	9%	81%	0.52	112	66	4.15	31
	03	28	2	aaa	OAK	162	20	30	9	1	2	22	25	20	0	1	184	293	287	580	13%	87%	1.23	74	61	2.93	16
Johnson,Reed	02	26	8	aaa	TOR	159	21	33	8	2	2	8	10	18	1	5	208	254	321	575	6%	89%	0.56	75	113	2.37	11
	03	27	8	aaa	TOR	101	12	30	4	1	2	14	3	11	3	1	298	317	413	730	3%	89%	0.26	72	103	4.80	34
Johnson,Rontrez	02	26	8	aaa	KC	403	57	111	25	3	8	43	39	40	25	13	275	339	412	751	9%	90%	0.98	92	121	4.90	49
	03	27	8	aaa	ATL	322	35	60	10	2	4	20	21	28	14	8	187	237	265	502	6%	91%	0.77	51	118	1.99	-2
Johnson,Russ	03	31	5	aaa	NYM	349	31	82	14	0	3	32	35	47	5	5	235	305	297	601	9%	87%	0.75	46	46	3.16	12
Jones,Chris	02	37	8	aaa	MIL	273	28	66	11	3	3	24	21	50	5	5	242	296	337	633	7%	82%	0.42	62	101	3.36	15
Jones,Damien	02	23	8	aa	ATL	211	16	40	7	1	1	10	18	46	7	6	190	253	246	500	8%	78%	0.39	41	86	1.97	-12
Jones,Jason	02	26	3	aa	TEX	471	66	120	28	2	11	60	70	93	10	7	255	351	393	744	13%	80%	0.75	93	81	5.02	38
	03	27	8	aaa	TEX	375	44	100	27	0	9	47	43	70	6	2	266	341	409	750	10%	81%	0.61	100	59	5.19	42
Jones,Jeremy	02	25	2	aa	TEX	132	14	25	4	0	2	6	13	20	1	1	189	262	265	527	9%	85%	0.65	50	51	2.34	-3
Jones,Mitch	02	25	5	aa	NYY	216	27	41	14	0	9	23	15	56	1	4	190	242	380	622	6%	74%	0.27	122	57	2.77	19
	03	26	8	aa	NYY	463	56	91	14	0	18	68	43	120	4	5	196	265	344	609	9%	74%	0.36	88	52	2.99	9
Jones,Ryan	02	28	3	aa	SD	266	29	42	7	1	9	40	22	63	2	1	158	222	293	515	8%	76%	0.35	79	77	2.10	-8
Jordan,Kevin	02	33	45	aaa	CIN	270	19	50	7	1	2	15	12	28	1	0	185	220	241	461	4%	90%	0.43	38	56	1.75	-14
	03	34	4	aaa	DET	160	9	30	5	0	2	14	7	17	1	1	186	221	253	474	4%	90%	0.43	47	35	1.79	-10
Jorgensen,Ryan	02	23	2	aa	FLA	144	12	27	4	0	1	11	10	29	2	1	188	240	236	476	6%	80%	0.34	35	58	1.90	-16
	03	24	2	aa	FLA	211	23	44	14	0	5	29	26	52	1	0	207	293	342	635	11%	76%	0.50	95	42	3.54	18
Jurries,James	03	24	53	aa	ATL	465	65	120	32	3	8	48	42	102	4	2	257	319	388	707	8%	78%	0.41	92	88	4.47	32
Kata,Matt	02	25	4	aa	ARI	578	70	150	29	8	9	43	27	63	9	8	260	293	384	677	4%	89%	0.43	81	118	3.82	28
	03	26	4	aaa	ARI	201	24	53	12	4	2	19	7	22	2	4	266	290	394	684	3%	89%	0.31	85	129	3.75	30
Kaup,Nathan	02	25	5	aa	TAM	272	19	58	12	0	2	22	21	42	1	4	213	270	279	549	7%	85%	0.50	50	28	2.45	2
Keene,Kurt	03	26	56	a/a	TOR	293	29	64	12	1	3	28	18	38	2	2	218	263	292	555	6%	87%	0.48	52	62	2.59	4
Keith,Rusty	02	25	8	aa	OAK	358	41	77	13	0	1	17	20	42	5	5	215	257	260	516	5%	88%	0.48	36	71	2.19	-4
Kellner,Ryan	03	26	2	aaa	LA	153	7	27	9	0	0	11	6	39	1	0	175	206	233	438	4%	74%	0.15	52	39	1.56	-17
Kelly,Heath	02	27	5	aa	FLA	180	17	27	6	1	4	17	11	71	2	0	150	199	261	460	6%	61%	0.15	69	100	1.69	-19
Kelly,Kenny	02	24	8	aaa	SEA	391	45	87	12	6	9	47	23	82	10	3	223	266	353	619	6%	79%	0.28	76	148	3.20	11
	03	25	8	aaa	NYM	433	50	97	19	5	14	40	30	95	22	8	224	274	388	662	6%	78%	0.32	99	145	3.57	22
Kelly,Mike	03	33	8	aaa	KC	368	46	92	24	1	11	47	35	67	5	1	249	315	408	723	9%	82%	0.53	106	73	4.65	37
Kelton,Dave	02	23	3	aa	CHC	498	60	119	26	4	18	69	47	116	11	7	239	305	416	720	9%	77%	0.41	109	101	4.34	33
	03	24	85	aaa	CHC	442	52	106	21	2	14	57	40	101	7	2	240	303	391	694	8%	77%	0.40	95	86	4.22	27
Kieschnick,Brooks	02	30	0	aaa	CHW	189	25	44	9	0	12	32	12	46	0	0	233	279	471	750	6%	76%	0.26	140	27	4.51	41
Kinchen,Jason	02	27	0	aa	NYY	123	10	22	4	1	5	14	12	29	1	1	179	252	350	601	9%	76%	0.41	99	69	2.85	9
Kingsale,Eugene	02	26	8	aaa	SEA	188	21	43	14	2	5	22	13	27	9	3	229	279	404	683	6%	86%	0.48	116	132	3.82	34
	03	27	8	aaa	DET	160	17	36	5	6	0	10	10	22	8	5	226	269	327	596	6%	86%	0.43	58	221	2.80	8
King,Brad	02	28	25	a/a	TEX	198	27	40	4	0	3	14	31	31	1	1	202	310	268	578	14%	84%	1.00	41	49	3.02	4
	03	29	2	aaa	PIT	197	21	36	7	0	2	17	33	39	0	3	184	303	250	553	15%	80%	0.86	48	29	2.63	-2
King,Brennan	02	22	5	aa	LA	435	59	110	18	1	7	60	56	47	1	1	253	338	347	685	11%	89%	1.19	64	50	4.37	34
	03	23	5	aa	LA	434	45	96	13	1	8	41	43	90	0	3	221	291	311	602	9%	79%	0.48	57	34	3.12	7
Kinkade,Mike	02	29	8	aaa	LA	287	41	74	16	3	7	33	19	40	4	3	258	304	408	712	6%	86%	0.48	96	109	4.31	35
Klassen,Danny	02	27	6	a/a	ARI	426	35	81	19	3	3	32	18	109	4	1	190	223	270	493	4%	74%	0.17	57	96	1.98	-10
	03	28	64	aaa	DET	407	56	87	16	5	8	43	25	105	10	5	215	260	338	599	6%	74%	0.24	76	145	2.94	8

Major League Equivalent Statistics

BATTER	Yr	Age	Pos	Lev	Org	ab	r	h	d	t	hr	rbi	bb	k	sb	cs	ba	ob	slg	ops	bb%	ct%	eye	px	sx	rc/g	bpv
Klimek,Josh	02	29	5	aaa	TOR	424	37	94	26	1	6	44	30	58	1	2	222	273	330	603	7%	86%	0.52	78	42	3.06	17
Knorr,Randy	02	34	2	aaa	MON	338	24	74	23	1	6	30	24	50	0	0	219	271	346	617	7%	85%	0.48	90	26	3.22	20
	03	35	2	aaa	MON	316	25	77	16	1	5	32	19	48	1	0	242	285	342	627	6%	85%	0.40	70	44	3.44	17
Knott,Jon	03	25	83	a/a	SD	458	72	98	27	0	21	72	68	112	4	3	214	316	409	724	13%	76%	0.61	122	58	4.51	34
Knox,Ryan	02	25	8	aa	MIL	217	20	39	6	1	0	7	19	41	14	7	180	246	217	462	8%	81%	0.46	29	115	1.76	-19
	03	26	8	a/a	MIL	471	62	98	23	3	2	22	24	97	38	12	208	247	279	526	5%	79%	0.25	53	156	2.33	-4
Knupfer,Jason	02	28	64	a/a	PHI	299	37	61	11	2	2	23	31	75	10	3	204	279	274	553	9%	75%	0.41	49	119	2.72	-4
	03	29	6	aaa	PHI	398	40	72	18	0	2	17	38	93	11	1	181	252	240	492	9%	77%	0.41	48	91	2.17	-12
Koonce,Graham	02	27	3	aa	OAK	470	61	95	21	0	17	69	95	122	2	0	202	336	355	692	17%	74%	0.78	96	43	4.41	22
	03	28	3	aaa	OAK	480	60	108	19	1	26	85	72	104	0	0	225	325	430	756	13%	78%	0.69	120	27	5.02	38
Kopitzke,Casey	02	24	2	aa	CHC	244	13	48	5	0	0	16	11	32	2	3	197	231	217	449	4%	87%	0.34	18	38	1.60	-20
	03	25	0	aa	CHC	318	23	70	8	1	0	22	25	49	3	5	221	278	252	530	7%	85%	0.52	25	48	2.36	-6
Krause,Scott	02	29	8	a/a	SEA	140	8	24	6	0	2	10	7	30	2	1	171	211	257	468	5%	79%	0.23	60	49	1.73	-13
	03	30	8	a/a	STL	211	26	48	13	1	4	17	15	43	4	2	227	279	353	632	7%	80%	0.36	86	87	3.33	19
Kremblas,Mike	02	27	2	aa	OAK	141	11	21	2	0	0	5	12	36	1	2	149	216	163	379	8%	74%	0.33	13	51	1.13	-39
	03	28	2	aa	MIL	198	17	29	6	0	3	14	18	60	4	2	145	218	222	440	9%	70%	0.31	50	68	1.56	-25
Kroeger,Josh	03	21	8	aa	ARI	208	19	52	8	2	2	16	8	39	2	6	250	278	337	614	4%	81%	0.21	57	84	2.88	11
Krynzel,Dave	02	21	8	aa	MIL	129	12	30	2	2	2	12	3	24	12	6	233	250	326	576	2%	81%	0.13	51	167	2.44	1
	03	22	8	aa	MIL	457	66	114	12	8	2	31	53	109	39	23	249	327	324	651	10%	76%	0.49	46	176	3.58	12
Kuzmic,Craig	02	25	5	a/a	SEA	454	50	85	21	4	9	45	60	144	9	2	187	282	311	593	12%	68%	0.42	79	116	3.08	4
	03	26	45	aaa	SF	303	35	65	11	4	6	34	34	85	5	4	214	294	333	627	10%	72%	0.40	72	117	3.34	9
Labandeira,John	03	25	6	aa	MON	238	19	49	16	1	2	20	14	32	0	2	208	252	307	560	6%	87%	0.45	76	45	2.52	10
LaForest,Pete	02	25	2	a/a	TAM	425	53	103	20	1	19	66	51	110	8	8	242	324	428	752	11%	74%	0.46	113	64	4.73	37
	03	26	2	a/a	TAM	273	43	65	21	2	14	46	45	72	2	1	237	344	484	828	14%	74%	0.62	155	81	6.01	55
Laird,Gerald	02	23	2	aa	TEX	442	62	116	20	3	10	60	40	82	7	7	262	324	389	713	8%	81%	0.49	81	91	4.40	31
	03	24	2	aaa	TEX	338	44	84	19	4	9	37	33	52	8	3	249	315	408	724	9%	85%	0.63	101	120	4.60	37
Laker,Tim	02	33	2	aaa	CLE	216	19	42	9	0	4	23	17	53	2	0	194	253	292	545	7%	75%	0.32	66	52	2.54	-2
Lamb,David	02	27	6	aaa	MIN	440	50	114	23	2	7	50	31	45	1	8	259	308	368	676	7%	90%	0.69	75	48	3.79	31
	03	28	6	aaa	MIN	405	37	93	14	2	2	26	40	60	2	6	230	299	287	586	9%	85%	0.66	42	50	2.93	7
Lamb,Mike	03	28	5	aaa	TEX	274	36	71	17	3	8	37	34	41	1	1	258	341	431	772	11%	85%	0.84	110	78	5.38	48
Landry,Jacques	02	29	8	a/a	OAK	290	32	54	11	1	9	40	34	96	7	5	186	272	324	596	10%	67%	0.35	85	84	2.89	4
	03	30	38	a/a	HOU	412	40	78	20	2	12	38	23	131	8	3	188	232	336	568	5%	68%	0.18	93	105	2.52	5
Lane,Jason	02	26	8	aaa	HOU	426	56	111	36	2	15	72	27	82	11	3	261	305	460	765	6%	81%	0.33	133	104	4.99	48
	03	27	8	aaa	HOU	248	32	70	16	0	7	34	26	25	2	1	282	350	430	780	10%	90%	1.06	101	47	5.65	57
Lane,Rich	03	24	3	aa	MON	207	15	38	3	1	3	18	5	33	1	0	183	201	248	450	2%	84%	0.15	38	63	1.61	-20
Langaigne,Selwyn	02	27	8	a/a	TOR	277	18	53	11	1	4	16	12	57	1	5	191	225	282	507	4%	79%	0.21	61	46	1.89	-7
Langerhans,Ryan	02	23	8	aa	ATL	391	48	88	21	1	7	52	55	68	8	6	225	321	338	658	12%	83%	0.81	78	72	3.81	23
	03	24	8	a/a	ATL	468	52	117	32	3	9	46	52	104	11	12	250	325	389	714	10%	78%	0.50	96	85	4.27	33
LaRocca,Greg	02	30	5	aaa	CLE	382	58	98	25	1	6	35	40	49	15	4	257	327	374	701	9%	87%	0.82	85	106	4.53	37
	03	31	5	aaa	CLE	500	51	124	29	1	9	56	32	54	5	3	248	294	364	658	6%	89%	0.60	80	60	3.75	28
LaRoche,Adam	02	23	3	aa	ATL	173	14	45	8	0	3	16	15	31	1	1	260	319	358	678	8%	82%	0.48	68	30	4.12	24
	03	24	3	a/a	ATL	483	70	134	32	1	19	67	56	101	2	4	277	353	466	818	10%	79%	0.55	121	47	6.00	54
Larson,Brandon	02	26	5	aaa	CIN	297	36	89	18	1	20	52	17	54	1	1	300	338	569	907	5%	82%	0.31	161	42	7.10	73
	03	27	5	aaa	CIN	282	40	83	19	1	17	57	22	58	2	0	293	344	549	893	7%	79%	0.38	156	61	7.11	70
Latham,Chris	02	29	8	aaa	NYM	405	48	76	18	4	5	35	49	103	21	9	188	275	289	564	11%	75%	0.48	67	139	2.71	-0
Lawrence,Joe	02	26	4	aaa	TOR	108	10	16	4	1	2	9	11	18	2	0	148	227	259	486	9%	83%	0.61	70	101	2.01	-10
	03	27	2	aaa	MIL	137	16	25	7	0	2	7	19	31	2	2	184	285	276	561	12%	77%	0.63	66	59	2.69	1
Leach,Jalal	02	34	8	aaa	NYY	287	25	57	11	3	5	21	14	44	5	5	199	236	310	546	5%	85%	0.32	70	103	2.27	1
	03	35	8	aaa	SEA	250	21	60	6	1	5	23	19	53	5	5	241	295	328	622	7%	79%	0.35	53	62	3.25	9
LeBron,Juan	02	25	8	aa	SEA	311	40	63	16	1	5	30	22	79	5	4	203	255	309	564	7%	75%	0.28	73	93	2.57	3
LeCroy,Matthew	02	27	0	aaa	MIN	174	26	52	7	1	8	36	12	27	1	0	299	344	489	833	6%	84%	0.44	112	70	6.37	55
Lemonis,Chris	03	30	3	a/a	BAL	222	24	38	8	0	2	27	13	58	1	2	169	215	227	442	5%	74%	0.22	43	63	1.54	-21
Lennon,Pat	03	35	3	aaa	DET	203	23	41	8	1	6	28	20	56	2	1	204	275	346	620	9%	73%	0.36	87	71	3.24	11
Leone,Justin	03	27	5	aa	SEA	455	84	104	30	4	15	75	77	114	17	6	228	340	411	751	15%	75%	0.68	118	136	5.05	38
Leon,Carlos	02	23	4	aa	BOS	265	33	65	10	1	1	16	20	25	12	11	245	298	302	600	7%	91%	0.80	43	98	2.87	15
	03	24	4	aa	BOS	259	37	70	10	3	2	19	17	32	9	7	271	317	352	669	6%	88%	0.54	54	123	3.82	23
Leon,Donny	02	26	5	a/a	CIN	476	50	110	30	1	16	57	33	89	10	8	231	281	399	680	6%	81%	0.37	110	72	3.69	30
	03	27	5	a/a	CHC	431	41	99	26	1	11	46	13	71	2	1	230	253	373	626	3%	83%	0.18	96	55	3.18	20
Leon,Jose	02	26	5	aaa	BAL	312	34	78	14	1	7	35	16	49	0	0	250	287	369	655	5%	84%	0.33	77	41	3.72	22
	03	27	5	aaa	BAL	309	30	73	16	1	4	35	14	44	1	1	235	268	330	597	4%	86%	0.31	67	55	3.01	12
Lesher,Brian	02	32	8	aaa	TOR	248	24	53	12	1	5	20	14	48	5	1	214	256	331	586	5%	81%	0.29	78	88	2.89	9
Levis,Jesse	02	34	2	aaa	CIN	254	17	59	10	1	2	17	21	16	1	1	232	291	303	594	8%	94%	1.31	51	42	3.10	25
	03	35	2	aaa	PHI	265	21	62	14	0	0	24	14	19	1	0	234	274	289	562	5%	93%	0.76	48	39	2.78	13
Lewis,Richard	03	23	4	aa	ATL	460	52	102	21	2	6	42	39	93	17	10	221	282	314	596	8%	80%	0.42	64	103	2.98	9
Liefer,Jeff	03	29	8	aaa	TAM	157	16	35	9	3	5	19	11	48	0	0	226	276	423	700	7%	69%	0.23	121	106	4.02	30
Linden,Todd	02	22	8	a/a	SF	492	72	134	27	3	11	54	70	117	10	6	272	363	407	769	12%	76%	0.60	89	92	5.51	39
	03	23	8	aaa	SF	471	61	114	22	3	7	45	32	84	11	5	242	290	346	636	6%	82%	0.38	70	108	3.50	17
Lindsey,John	03	27	3	aa	SEA	307	32	72	17	1	6	35	18	89	7	1	235	278	357	635	6%	71%	0.21	83	91	3.52	17
Lindsey,Rodney	02	27	8	a/a	DET	402	36	87	12	6	1	17	24	88	24	10	216	261	284	544	6%	78%	0.27	43	156	2.47	-4
Liniak,Cole	03	27	5	a/a	TEX	266	25	53	12	2	5	28	14	40	3	4	200	239	317	557	5%	85%	0.35	77	80	2.35	5
Littleton,Brandon	03	24	8	a/a	BAL	254	33	54	13	1	0	24	16	43	8	5	214	262	271	533	6%	83%	0.38	47	109	2.35	-2
Little,Mark	03	31	8	aaa	CLE	241	27	60	9	3	6	24	6	66	5	3	250	269	388	658	3%	73%	0.10	83	125	3.52	20
Lockwood,Mike	02	26	8	aa	OAK	501	52	96	20	5	3	38	46	63	4	6	192	260	269	529	8%	87%	0.73	53	90	2.30	1
	03	27	8	a/a	OAK	356	41	81	15	2	6	29	24	41	1	4	228	277	334	611	6%	88%	0.59	70	60	3.07	17
Loeb,Bryan	03	26	2	a/a	ARI	197	22	49	10	2	3	19	6	31	2	1	251	272	366	638	3%	85%	0.19	78	98	3.42	19
Lofton,James	02	29	6	a/a	BOS	426	32	82	12	1	3	26	17	79	7	5	192	223	246	470	4%	81%	0.22	38	74	1.75	-16
Logan,Kyle	02	27	8	aaa	HOU	335	46	92	19	3	11	38	20	45	18	9	275	315	448	763	6%	87%	0.44	109	128	4.83	45
	03	28	8	aaa	HOU	460	36	106	23	2	5	37	18	85	12	8	230	259	319	578	4%	82%	0.21	64	85	2.68	7
Logan,Matt	02	23	3	aa	TOR	345	34	73	24	0	2	37	26	49	6	1	212	267	299	565	7%	86%	0.53	71	75	2.79	10
	03	24	3	aa	TOR	299	35	70	13	1	3	29	30	32	2	2	235	306	315	620	9%	89%	0.96	57	61	3.41	21
Logan,Nook	03	24	8	aa	DET	514	62	116	14	8	3	33	45	90	32	14	226	288	300	588	8%	83%	0.50	46	160	2.99	4

Major League Equivalent Statistics

BATTER	Yr	Age	Pos	Lev	Org	ab	r	h	d	t	hr	rbi	bb	k	sb	cs	ba	ob	slg	ops	bb%	ct%	eye	px	sx	rc/g	bpv
Lomasney,Steve	02	25	2	a/a	BOS	368	33	63	16	2	6	44	43	126	4	6	171	258	274	532	10%	66%	0.34	69	74	2.28	-8
	03	26	2	aaa	BAL	253	25	54	9	1	0	17	25	87	2	1	215	286	257	543	9%	66%	0.29	34	70	2.62	-9
Lombard,George	03	28	8	aaa	TAM	438	47	102	23	4	13	53	37	139	19	7	234	294	393	686	8%	68%	0.27	101	125	3.99	25
Lopez,Felipe	02	22	6	aaa	TOR	173	29	53	12	1	2	14	24	28	11	0	306	391	422	813	12%	84%	0.86	84	122	7.06	54
	03	23	6	aaa	CIN	143	18	38	11	0	2	15	10	30	2	6	266	314	385	698	7%	79%	0.33	90	58	3.70	32
Lopez,Jose	03	20	64	aa	SEA	538	84	140	35	1	12	70	29	48	19	10	260	297	397	694	5%	91%	0.59	95	108	4.03	37
Lopez,Luis	02	29	5	aaa	OAK	516	45	111	22	0	6	49	43	52	1	4	215	275	293	568	8%	90%	0.83	56	28	2.72	11
	03	30	4	aaa	BAL	326	27	61	12	0	6	36	11	47	1	2	188	214	282	495	3%	86%	0.23	62	43	1.90	-7
Lopez,Luis	03	33	5	aaa	OAK	498	48	95	22	0	14	51	28	61	0	1	192	234	316	551	5%	88%	0.46	80	32	2.42	6
Lopez,Mendy	02	28	6	aaa	PIT	385	47	85	24	0	8	56	27	81	3	1	221	272	345	617	7%	79%	0.33	87	65	3.23	16
Lopez,Mickey	02	29	64	a/a	CHC	400	39	78	20	1	3	31	30	51	9	7	195	251	273	524	7%	87%	0.59	58	83	2.21	1
	03	30	46	aaa	SEA	455	57	105	19	3	5	35	41	52	17	12	230	294	320	614	8%	89%	0.79	61	107	3.14	18
Lopez,Pee Wee	02	26	2	a/a	ATL	127	12	25	3	0	3	13	10	20	1	1	197	255	291	547	7%	84%	0.50	57	46	2.47	-1
Lorenzana,Luis	02	24	6	aa	SD	288	28	61	7	1	2	17	35	40	0	1	212	297	264	561	11%	86%	0.88	35	40	2.80	3
Lorenzo,Juan	02	24	6	aa	MIN	215	26	52	6	1	2	16	7	20	1	2	242	266	307	573	3%	91%	0.35	43	74	2.71	5
Loyd,Brian	02	29	2	a/a	SD	257	22	47	8	0	3	23	10	44	0	1	183	213	249	463	4%	83%	0.23	46	40	1.69	-16
	03	30	2	aa	BOS	100	6	20	5	0	1	8	5	13	1	0	203	237	270	507	4%	87%	0.34	51	37	2.16	-5
Luderer,Brian	02	24	2	aa	CLE	155	25	34	10	1	3	14	10	31	0	0	219	267	355	622	6%	80%	0.32	93	83	3.24	18
	03	25	2	aa	CLE	245	23	50	11	1	4	28	20	34	0	1	206	265	301	566	7%	86%	0.57	65	45	2.69	7
Ludwick,Ryan	02	24	8	aaa	TEX	305	47	78	24	3	12	40	29	56	2	2	256	320	472	792	9%	82%	0.52	139	96	5.34	53
	03	25	8	aaa	TEX	317	44	91	23	2	16	54	29	61	1	1	287	347	522	868	8%	81%	0.47	146	62	6.69	66
Luke,Matt	02	32	3	aaa	TAM	106	11	21	5	0	1	9	11	27	0	0	198	274	274	547	9%	75%	0.41	56	31	2.61	-3
Lunar,Fernando	02	25	2	aaa	BAL	145	6	25	1	0	2	7	3	24	1	0	172	189	221	410	2%	83%	0.13	27	31	1.34	-29
	03	26	2	aaa	KC	251	21	48	8	0	5	18	8	26	0	0	189	214	278	492	3%	90%	0.30	57	31	1.92	-7
Luna,Hector	03	24	6	aa	CLE	462	78	126	18	1	2	34	42	62	16	5	273	333	330	663	8%	87%	0.67	44	106	4.14	22
Lunsford,Trey	02	23	2	a/a	SF	267	25	62	13	0	2	25	30	49	4	2	232	310	303	613	10%	82%	0.61	55	53	3.39	12
	03	24	2	aaa	SF	206	16	51	9	1	1	16	13	26	0	1	248	292	316	608	6%	87%	0.50	50	42	3.22	13
Luther,Ryan	02	26	2	a/a	SF	116	10	28	6	0	1	14	11	25	4	0	241	307	319	626	9%	78%	0.44	59	66	3.73	14
Luuloa,Keith	02	28	5	a/a	MIL	340	45	68	10	3	7	32	45	53	3	3	200	294	309	602	12%	84%	0.85	66	90	3.13	11
	03	29	354	aaa	MIL	359	42	81	23	2	9	46	29	44	3	3	225	283	378	661	7%	88%	0.65	102	72	3.62	30
Machado,Albenis	02	24	4	a/a	MON	281	33	62	11	2	3	28	45	38	6	6	221	328	306	634	14%	86%	1.18	57	83	3.54	21
	03	25	65	aa	MON	339	35	62	12	0	0	19	38	43	2	4	182	265	219	483	10%	87%	0.88	32	48	1.96	-8
Machado,Alejandro	03	21	4	aa	MIL	444	60	106	16	4	1	36	39	57	25	12	239	300	300	600	8%	87%	0.68	43	134	3.13	11
Machado,Andy	02	22	6	aa	PHI	450	59	103	24	2	10	64	63	105	33	13	229	324	358	681	12%	77%	0.60	86	116	4.11	24
	03	23	6	aa	PHI	423	63	73	18	3	4	16	87	102	39	18	173	314	258	571	17%	76%	0.85	59	136	2.93	-1
Machado,Robert	03	30	2	aaa	BAL	221	25	62	14	0	7	32	14	37	0	0	281	325	440	765	6%	83%	0.39	105	23	5.26	45
Mackowiak,Rob	03	27	3	aaa	PIT	217	17	45	10	1	2	19	14	43	6	3	206	255	289	544	6%	80%	0.33	60	85	2.45	-0
Maddox,Garry	03	29	8	a/a	PHI	236	23	49	9	1	9	33	14	59	3	7	209	255	364	618	6%	75%	0.25	94	62	2.72	13
Magee,Wendell	03	31	8	aaa	DET	419	29	91	19	3	4	37	16	71	2	9	217	246	301	547	4%	83%	0.23	59	55	2.24	1
Magness,Pat	03	26	3	aa	FLA	132	8	24	6	0	2	14	20	37	0	1	184	291	273	563	13%	72%	0.54	63	15	2.75	-2
Magruder,Chris	02	25	8	aaa	CLE	191	26	49	10	1	5	15	24	32	3	2	257	340	398	737	11%	83%	0.75	91	78	4.90	38
	03	26	8	a/a	CLE	150	16	43	6	1	3	14	14	30	5	1	288	347	396	743	8%	80%	0.45	70	87	5.27	34
Mahoney,Mike	02	30	2	aaa	CHC	223	21	43	9	1	1	12	11	34	1	1	193	231	256	486	5%	85%	0.32	47	71	1.93	-10
	03	31	2	aaa	CHC	190	14	39	9	1	2	14	8	31	0	1	204	236	289	525	4%	84%	0.26	61	50	2.21	-2
Maldonado,Carlos	02	24	2	a/a	HOU	152	12	34	8	0	4	18	19	25	0	0	224	310	355	665	11%	84%	0.76	87	11	3.95	26
	03	25	2	aa	CHW	408	45	98	22	1	6	56	41	49	1	1	240	309	340	649	9%	88%	0.83	71	46	3.77	26
Malloy,Marty	02	30	4	aaa	CIN	180	17	36	6	1	3	11	14	20	5	5	200	258	294	552	7%	89%	0.70	60	87	2.35	6
	03	31	4	aaa	STL	264	22	52	11	1	2	14	16	34	5	2	198	244	266	510	6%	87%	0.47	50	78	2.18	-4
Marsters,Brandon	02	28	2	a/a	MIN	260	26	54	14	0	4	24	13	51	0	0	208	245	308	553	5%	80%	0.25	71	34	2.53	4
	03	29	2	aaa	MIN	359	33	77	23	0	7	37	14	99	0	2	215	244	342	586	4%	72%	0.14	89	31	2.72	11
Martinez,Felix	02	28	6	a/a	LA	386	39	70	11	2	3	30	20	67	4	4	181	222	244	465	5%	83%	0.30	42	89	1.71	-16
Martinez,Gabby	03	30	8	a/a	TAM	152	16	41	6	0	2	7	4	17	6	2	270	289	356	645	3%	89%	0.24	58	79	3.67	19
Martinez,Greg	02	31	8	aa	TAM	101	5	14	1	1	0	6	4	19	4	1	139	171	168	340	4%	81%	0.21	18	119	0.94	-42
Martinez,Sandy	02	32	2	aaa	MON	133	9	25	3	1	3	14	8	39	2	0	188	234	293	527	6%	71%	0.21	62	82	2.33	-8
Martinez,Victor	02	24	2	aa	CLE	443	73	139	38	0	20	74	50	58	3	3	314	383	535	918	10%	87%	0.86	146	48	7.88	82
	03	25	2	a/a	CLE	286	38	87	20	0	7	42	22	32	3	5	305	356	448	803	7%	89%	0.70	100	47	5.76	57
Martin,Billy	02	26	8	aa	ARI	264	23	45	13	0	5	26	21	79	0	0	170	232	277	508	7%	70%	0.27	73	27	2.12	-8
	03	27	3	a/a	ARI	339	39	94	26	2	10	44	27	70	1	0	277	330	457	787	7%	79%	0.38	120	58	5.58	50
Martin,Tyler	03	26	5	aa	TEX	121	10	19	2	1	3	8	12	29	2	1	158	235	252	487	9%	76%	0.42	52	80	1.96	-17
Massiatte,Danny	03	25	2	aa	TAM	169	15	31	6	0	2	12	14	39	0	1	181	242	250	492	7%	77%	0.35	49	37	1.99	-12
Mateo,Henry	02	26	4	aaa	MON	285	31	67	10	4	4	22	15	45	13	7	235	273	340	614	5%	84%	0.33	65	143	3.05	12
Mateo,Ruben	02	25	8	aaa	CIN	209	29	57	14	0	7	18	8	29	5	2	273	300	440	740	4%	86%	0.28	111	81	4.65	42
	03	26	8	aaa	CIN	217	29	67	15	1	8	41	21	27	2	1	310	371	497	868	9%	87%	0.76	121	62	7.09	69
Mathis,Jared	02	27	5	aa	MIL	203	17	37	4	2	2	13	7	27	3	5	182	210	251	461	3%	87%	0.26	41	102	1.51	-17
Matos,Julius	02	28	6	aaa	SD	186	17	49	14	0	3	22	8	19	1	2	263	294	387	681	4%	90%	0.42	92	39	3.88	34
	03	29	6	aaa	KC	371	33	93	17	0	6	36	9	26	7	6	251	269	341	610	2%	93%	0.36	63	63	3.04	17
Matos,Luis	02	24	8	aa	BAL	218	28	52	12	1	8	34	26	41	12	5	239	320	413	733	11%	81%	0.63	110	103	4.60	37
	03	25	8	aaa	BAL	175	26	48	14	2	1	23	12	31	6	1	274	321	394	715	6%	82%	0.39	90	137	4.73	36
Matranga,Dave	02	26	4	aaa	HOU	300	41	78	15	3	7	35	24	72	6	2	260	315	400	715	7%	76%	0.33	89	118	4.55	30
	03	27	46	aaa	HOU	315	30	72	16	4	3	22	18	66	3	3	228	271	329	600	6%	79%	0.28	69	103	2.99	10
Matthews,Lamont	02	24	8	aa	LA	317	37	53	15	1	8	29	61	99	3	3	167	302	297	598	16%	69%	0.62	84	61	3.12	3
Mauer,Joe	03	20	2	aa	MIN	276	43	92	18	1	3	37	22	21	0	0	335	384	441	825	7%	92%	1.05	78	48	6.80	65
Maule,Jason	02	25	5	aa	HOU	171	23	37	3	0	2	11	14	24	9	5	216	276	269	545	8%	86%	0.58	34	98	2.48	-2
	03	26	8	aa	NYY	117	15	25	3	0	0	10	16	16	3	1	216	308	238	546	12%	86%	0.97	20	74	2.80	-1
Maxwell,Jason	02	31	6	aaa	CIN	269	31	66	18	2	2	22	24	37	4	5	245	307	349	657	8%	86%	0.65	77	86	3.64	27
	03	32	46	aaa	CIN	361	38	80	15	1	6	33	21	50	2	1	222	264	322	586	5%	86%	0.41	67	61	2.90	10
Maynard,Scott	03	26	2	aa	SEA	237	23	39	4	1	1	15	17	68	0	2	165	220	202	422	7%	71%	0.24	25	61	1.42	-30
McCarthy,Bill	03	24	8	aa	ATL	276	31	64	17	1	6	42	36	55	5	1	232	320	366	686	12%	80%	0.66	92	76	4.28	28
McCarty,Dave	02	33	3	aaa	TAM	114	20	32	6	1	6	17	11	32	0	1	281	344	509	853	9%	72%	0.34	136	86	6.28	56
McCarty,David	03	34	3	aaa	OAK	352	50	75	18	1	11	51	32	64	3	1	212	277	361	637	8%	82%	0.49	95	78	3.44	20
McDonald,Darnell	02	24	8	a/a	BAL	476	56	125	26	5	9	44	46	94	17	7	263	328	395	723	9%	80%	0.49	87	121	4.67	33
	03	25	8	aaa	BAL	152	18	42	6	1	0	19	17	25	5	8	276	349	329	678	10%	84%	0.68	41	86	3.72	23

Major League Equivalent Statistics

BATTER	Yr	Age	Pos	Lev	Org	ab	r	h	d	t	hr	rbi	bb	k	sb	cs	ba	ob	slg	ops	bb%	ct%	eye	px	sx	rc/g	bpv
McDonald,Donzell	02	28	8	aaa	KC	452	48	105	13	12	6	27	42	83	23	7	232	298	354	652	9%	82%	0.51	69	195	3.73	16
	03	29	8	aaa	ATL	464	54	105	16	7	2	17	54	112	27	9	226	307	301	608	10%	76%	0.48	49	153	3.35	5
McDonald,Keith	02	30	2	aaa	STL	267	25	60	16	0	10	28	12	51	1	2	225	258	397	655	4%	81%	0.24	111	36	3.36	25
	03	31	2	aaa	CHC	280	23	54	12	0	11	34	23	43	0	0	193	255	350	605	8%	85%	0.54	97	14	3.00	15
McDougall,Marshall	02	24	5	aa	OAK	341	55	92	21	4	8	50	37	53	6	5	270	341	425	766	10%	84%	0.70	101	115	5.19	46
	03	25	6	a/a	TEX	529	61	127	18	4	14	66	48	77	16	4	240	303	367	670	8%	85%	0.61	77	111	4.00	24
McDowell,Arturo	02	23	8	aa	SF	221	15	35	3	1	0	9	13	39	8	6	158	205	181	386	6%	82%	0.33	16	96	1.13	-34
McGowan,Sean	02	25	3	a/a	SF	217	11	45	15	2	1	15	5	40	1	1	207	225	309	534	2%	82%	0.13	76	71	2.24	3
	03	26	3	aa	BOS	299	31	77	18	0	4	30	15	39	3	0	256	291	361	652	5%	87%	0.38	77	59	3.77	25
McGuire,Ryan	02	31	3	aaa	BAL	315	35	74	12	1	9	37	23	69	0	1	235	287	365	652	7%	78%	0.33	81	43	3.62	18
	03	32	38	aaa	MIN	267	21	56	12	1	2	21	23	57	0	1	209	273	280	553	8%	79%	0.41	52	38	2.62	-1
McKay,Cody	02	29	2	aaa	OAK	378	38	86	13	1	8	40	15	47	1	1	228	257	331	588	4%	88%	0.32	66	53	2.87	9
	03	30	2	aaa	MIL	371	26	73	13	1	5	35	21	49	2	2	196	239	280	519	5%	87%	0.42	55	47	2.20	-3
McKeel,Walt	02	31	2	aaa	COL	130	5	26	5	0	2	6	9	18	0	0	200	252	285	536	6%	86%	0.50	58	2	2.43	1
McKinley,Dan	02	26	8	a/a	MON	294	24	54	12	3	3	24	10	51	4	5	184	211	276	486	3%	83%	0.20	61	105	1.73	-10
McKinley,Josh	02	23	4	aa	MON	325	31	67	16	0	6	25	32	65	2	5	206	277	311	588	9%	80%	0.49	72	38	2.82	8
	03	24	4	aa	MON	458	63	114	30	1	11	57	44	72	13	6	249	314	394	708	9%	84%	0.61	99	91	4.39	36
McKnight,Lukas	03	24	6	aa	CHC	112	7	20	1	0	0	10	10	26	2	0	182	247	191	438	8%	77%	0.38	8	49	1.71	-29
McMillon,Billy	02	31	8	aaa	NYY	442	53	106	26	2	6	33	44	64	2	5	240	309	348	657	9%	86%	0.69	77	58	3.71	25
	03	32	8	aaa	OAK	153	23	41	8	0	6	25	13	28	1	1	265	321	441	762	8%	82%	0.45	111	50	5.05	43
McNally,Sean	02	30	5	aa	TEX	243	15	39	5	1	5	27	19	83	3	2	160	221	251	472	7%	66%	0.23	54	65	1.79	-20
McNamara,Rusty	02	28	5	aa	ATL	448	37	91	14	1	4	37	23	47	5	1	203	242	266	508	5%	90%	0.49	43	72	2.18	-5
McNeal,Aaron	02	24	3	a/a	NYM	434	49	104	15	0	16	64	42	107	1	2	240	307	385	692	9%	75%	0.39	88	31	4.15	24
	03	25	3	aa	PHI	421	29	86	17	1	9	51	18	98	0	1	203	236	312	548	4%	77%	0.18	71	28	2.41	1
McPherson,Dallas	03	23	5	aa	ANA	102	18	29	9	1	4	23	16	22	3	0	285	380	504	884	13%	79%	0.72	143	113	7.56	68
Meadows,Randy	02	26	6	aa	PIT	111	11	11	2	0	1	5	4	25	2	1	99	130	144	275	3%	77%	0.16	30	123	0.56	-51
Meadows,Tydus	02	25	8	aa	KC	119	19	36	10	3	4	16	11	22	4	2	303	362	538	899	8%	82%	0.50	149	178	7.16	72
	03	26	8	aa	KC	421	44	103	23	3	14	59	30	69	10	8	244	293	409	703	7%	84%	0.43	104	89	4.00	33
Medrano,Anthony	03	29	6	aaa	MON	425	44	85	16	2	2	33	33	39	4	5	199	258	258	516	7%	91%	0.86	44	72	2.20	2
Medrano,Jesus	02	24	4	aa	FLA	414	60	105	23	5	2	25	63	74	30	20	254	352	348	700	13%	82%	0.85	67	138	4.23	29
	03	25	4	a/a	FLA	365	45	75	15	3	2	30	44	65	19	9	206	291	278	569	11%	82%	0.67	52	125	2.83	3
Medrano,Tony	02	28	6	aaa	MON	438	40	93	17	2	2	35	30	42	10	1	212	263	274	537	6%	90%	0.71	45	98	2.56	4
Meier,Dan	02	25	8	aa	PIT	237	20	48	9	1	5	24	17	57	2	3	203	256	312	568	7%	76%	0.30	70	61	2.58	2
Melhuse,Adam	02	31	2	aaa	COL	341	33	87	23	1	10	34	25	47	3	5	255	306	416	722	7%	86%	0.53	108	50	4.32	40
	03	32	2	aaa	OAK	147	19	33	7	0	2	13	19	29	0	1	227	315	312	627	11%	80%	0.65	62	38	3.50	14
Meliah,Dave	02	26	8	a/a	TEX	328	35	71	16	2	8	35	16	40	2	5	216	253	351	604	5%	88%	0.40	86	72	2.79	16
	03	27	5	aaa	TEX	185	18	43	7	0	5	16	9	36	0	0	231	265	346	611	5%	80%	0.24	73	27	3.15	12
Melian,Jackson	02	23	8	aa	CHC	418	52	104	21	1	9	44	47	112	18	10	249	325	368	693	10%	73%	0.42	80	90	4.19	24
	03	24	8	a/a	CHC	381	31	80	11	2	9	33	25	68	11	8	210	259	320	579	6%	82%	0.37	67	85	2.65	5
Melo,Juan	02	26	4	aaa	SF	479	59	119	27	2	12	55	29	82	5	8	248	291	388	680	6%	83%	0.35	92	72	3.75	28
Mench,Kevin	02	25	8	aaa	TEX	98	13	18	7	0	5	11	13	24	0	0	184	279	408	687	12%	76%	0.54	142	29	3.86	31
	03	26	8	a/a	TEX	116	14	27	8	0	4	17	17	15	2	0	229	328	393	721	13%	87%	1.16	109	53	4.78	44
Mendez,Carlos	02	28	2	aaa	OAK	404	41	103	20	1	8	52	8	42	2	1	255	269	369	638	2%	90%	0.19	77	60	3.43	20
	03	29	3	aaa	BAL	248	27	73	15	2	4	35	9	29	1	2	294	319	411	730	4%	88%	0.32	81	67	4.70	38
Mendez,Donaldo	02	24	6	a/a	SD	441	58	82	21	1	8	31	27	109	22	10	186	233	293	525	6%	75%	0.25	72	129	2.16	-3
	03	25	654	aaa	SD	358	40	68	14	0	4	29	20	70	8	8	191	233	263	496	5%	81%	0.28	51	82	1.88	-10
Mendoza,Carlos	02	23	6	aa	SF	377	37	83	19	2	1	24	57	35	10	10	220	323	289	612	13%	91%	1.63	53	76	3.24	28
	03	24	4	a/a	SF	204	21	41	11	0	3	16	10	26	1	1	201	238	299	537	5%	87%	0.38	70	55	2.33	4
Menechino,Frank	02	32	6	aaa	OAK	314	33	59	9	0	4	33	31	48	6	4	188	261	255	516	9%	85%	0.65	45	68	2.24	-6
Mensik,Todd	02	28	0	aa	OAK	251	27	44	9	0	4	22	28	66	2	1	175	258	259	517	10%	74%	0.42	56	56	2.29	-10
	03	29	8	aa	TEX	197	14	31	7	0	2	10	17	49	2	2	158	225	231	456	8%	75%	0.34	51	44	1.68	-19
Meran,Jorge	02	28	2	aa	DET	184	12	33	3	2	2	11	11	53	1	0	179	226	250	476	6%	71%	0.21	41	87	1.88	-19
Merrill,Ronnie	03	25	6	aa	COL	199	24	33	8	3	2	15	14	31	2	2	167	223	263	485	7%	85%	0.47	61	130	1.85	-10
Metcalfe,Mike	02	30	4	aaa	KC	149	20	31	5	0	1	11	8	10	7	2	208	248	262	510	5%	93%	0.80	40	110	2.24	2
Meyers,Chad	02	27	8	aaa	STL	412	54	93	16	1	8	29	53	57	34	10	226	314	328	642	11%	86%	0.93	67	114	3.77	21
	03	28	8	aaa	SEA	377	44	97	17	2	3	30	27	47	32	12	257	306	333	639	7%	87%	0.57	55	123	3.59	20
Michaelis,Derek	03	25	3	aa	LA	378	50	87	24	1	11	46	48	127	9	0	231	317	390	707	11%	66%	0.37	105	95	4.56	28
Miles,Aaron	02	26	4	aa	CHW	531	55	145	33	1	8	56	35	46	21	15	273	318	384	702	6%	91%	0.76	80	81	4.15	39
	03	27	4	aaa	CHW	546	68	150	30	3	11	43	36	46	7	10	275	320	400	720	6%	92%	0.77	84	73	4.41	42
Miller,Corky	02	27	2	aaa	CIN	134	11	27	5	0	5	16	12	15	1	2	201	267	351	618	8%	89%	0.80	91	33	3.00	21
	03	28	2	aaa	CIN	354	38	80	28	0	10	33	27	47	0	0	225	280	384	663	7%	87%	0.56	110	27	3.71	32
Minges,Tyler	03	24	8	aa	CLE	422	44	86	17	3	9	39	23	62	5	4	205	246	322	568	5%	85%	0.38	75	90	2.57	7
Minor,Damon	03	30	3	aaa	PHI	469	45	87	16	1	17	62	25	84	1	2	186	227	336	562	5%	82%	0.29	90	45	2.44	5
Minor,Ryan	02	29	5	aaa	SEA	157	12	30	6	1	1	7	9	27	0	0	191	235	261	496	5%	83%	0.33	49	51	2.04	-9
Mitchell,Derek	02	28	46	a/a	CIN	184	17	29	5	0	2	17	21	46	3	3	158	244	217	461	10%	75%	0.46	41	59	1.74	-21
Mitchell,Keith	03	34	8	a/a	CIN	107	10	19	5	1	2	8	15	24	1	0	179	282	284	566	12%	78%	0.64	69	73	2.84	1
Moeller,Chad	02	28	2	aaa	ARI	211	27	58	7	2	8	34	20	36	1	0	275	338	441	778	9%	83%	0.56	96	78	5.56	43
Molina,Izzy	02	31	2	a/a	BAL	342	23	54	8	0	5	23	19	64	2	1	158	202	225	427	5%	81%	0.30	43	47	1.46	-24
Molina,Jose	02	27	2	aaa	ANA	290	22	75	11	1	3	31	9	47	0	4	259	281	334	615	3%	84%	0.19	53	34	3.09	12
Molina,Yadier	03	21	2	aa	STL	364	30	94	12	1	2	47	25	43	0	1	258	306	313	619	6%	88%	0.58	40	32	3.44	14
Monahan,Shane	02	28	8	aa	KC	391	39	92	20	2	7	42	12	56	8	9	235	258	350	608	3%	86%	0.21	78	88	2.82	15
Monroe,Craig	02	26	8	aaa	DET	358	55	105	27	5	7	45	34	49	6	3	293	355	455	810	9%	86%	0.69	109	122	6.05	57
Moon,Brian	02	25	2	a/a	MIL	221	18	42	8	0	1	15	23	49	4	1	190	266	240	506	9%	78%	0.47	39	60	2.27	-11
Moore,Frank	02	24	4	aa	TAM	331	33	83	16	0	2	28	24	57	8	8	251	301	317	619	7%	83%	0.42	52	63	3.21	14
	03	25	438	a/a	TAM	392	33	92	15	6	4	31	23	87	8	1	235	277	332	609	5%	78%	0.26	62	130	3.26	9
Moore,Jason	02	25	6	aa	TEX	417	46	91	19	3	11	58	41	85	3	4	218	288	357	646	9%	80%	0.48	88	75	3.48	18
Morales,Steve	02	24	2	aa	FLA	164	12	36	9	0	4	19	4	20	0	1	220	238	348	586	2%	88%	0.20	86	27	2.66	13
	03	25	2	a/a	CHW	123	9	26	2	1	3	12	6	19	0	0	209	244	309	553	4%	85%	0.30	56	45	2.52	-1
Morales,Willie	02	30	2	aaa	ARI	315	30	79	20	0	5	36	10	47	3	5	251	274	362	636	3%	85%	0.21	81	50	3.23	21
	03	31	2	a/a	COL	263	20	53	11	2	7	25	7	49	1	1	201	222	338	560	3%	81%	0.15	85	60	2.41	5
Moreta,Ramon	02	27	8	aa	SF	273	24	53	9	2	2	27	14	52	12	15	194	233	264	497	5%	81%	0.27	47	113	1.61	-11

Major League Equivalent Statistics

BATTER	Yr	Age	Pos	Lev	Org	ab	r	h	d	t	hr	rbi	bb	k	sb	cs	ba	ob	slg	ops	bb%	ct%	eye	px	sx	rc/g	bpv
Morgan,Scott	02	29	8	aaa	SD	384	33	79	14	0	7	35	15	99	3	1	206	236	297	532	4%	74%	0.15	60	56	2.32	-3
	03	30	8	aaa	CHW	359	37	79	18	1	8	38	30	96	4	4	221	280	343	624	8%	73%	0.31	82	62	3.24	13
Moriarty,Mike	02	29	6	aaa	BAL	311	39	73	15	1	4	21	30	48	4	1	235	302	328	630	9%	85%	0.63	65	80	3.57	18
	03	30	56	aaa	HOU	348	34	71	13	1	6	24	27	55	5	2	204	262	301	563	7%	84%	0.50	63	76	2.69	4
Morneau,Justin	02	21	3	aa	MIN	494	60	137	31	3	13	66	35	75	6	0	277	325	431	756	7%	85%	0.47	102	92	5.23	44
	03	22	3	a/a	MIN	344	47	90	14	2	18	48	30	63	0	2	262	321	471	792	8%	82%	0.48	122	51	5.34	47
Morrissey,Adam	02	21	4	aa	OAK	302	33	63	13	1	2	19	32	61	3	2	209	284	278	563	10%	80%	0.52	51	70	2.77	1
	03	22	54	aa	OAK	469	54	109	24	1	4	53	40	83	7	1	232	293	313	606	8%	82%	0.48	60	84	3.31	12
Morris,Warren	02	29	4	aaa	BOS	356	41	86	20	4	5	35	17	46	3	3	242	276	362	638	5%	87%	0.37	81	101	3.38	21
	03	30	4	aaa	DET	206	23	49	10	5	2	16	14	25	4	1	239	286	358	644	6%	88%	0.54	76	150	3.60	22
Mosquera,Julio	02	31	82	a/a	TEX	278	27	59	10	0	5	21	10	51	9	1	212	240	302	542	3%	82%	0.20	60	92	2.50	-1
	03	32	2	aaa	SEA	291	30	68	14	1	3	18	10	44	5	4	235	260	315	576	3%	85%	0.22	58	84	2.72	7
Mota,Tony	02	25	8	aaa	STL	136	18	27	6	0	3	11	13	23	3	2	199	268	309	577	9%	83%	0.57	73	77	2.75	8
Mottola,Chad	02	31	8	aaa	TOR	476	55	102	32	1	9	48	36	76	9	2	214	270	342	612	7%	84%	0.47	91	91	3.19	18
	03	32	8	aaa	BOS	285	28	67	9	2	6	37	20	47	5	4	234	283	344	628	6%	84%	0.42	68	80	3.29	14
Mouton,James	02	34	8	aaa	ARI	333	41	77	20	2	5	29	23	78	7	6	231	281	348	629	6%	77%	0.29	82	100	3.23	17
Mouton,Lyle	03	34	8	aaa	CLE	352	41	86	20	1	13	50	32	100	7	2	245	307	414	722	8%	72%	0.32	107	79	4.55	32
Moylan,Dan	03	24	2	aa	STL	182	19	45	3	1	2	20	28	28	1	0	245	345	303	647	13%	84%	0.97	35	56	4.01	15
Munoz,Billy	02	27	3	aa	CLE	248	27	49	17	1	4	32	31	51	0	1	198	287	323	609	11%	79%	0.61	89	48	3.18	15
	03	28	3	a/a	DET	384	39	83	11	3	11	48	37	86	3	0	217	286	350	636	9%	78%	0.44	78	92	3.54	13
Munson,Eric	02	25	3	aaa	DET	477	69	112	27	5	18	76	73	99	1	3	235	336	426	762	13%	79%	0.74	118	78	5.10	42
Murphy,Nate	02	27	8	aaa	ARI	245	29	59	11	4	8	23	25	45	6	5	241	311	416	727	9%	82%	0.56	105	127	4.36	35
	03	28	8	a/a	CHW	415	50	88	20	1	13	43	30	91	7	6	211	264	356	620	7%	78%	0.33	93	78	3.05	15
Murray,Calvin	02	31	8	aaa	TEX	139	15	30	5	1	2	10	7	17	3	0	216	253	309	563	5%	88%	0.41	60	103	2.75	5
	03	32	8	aaa	LA	312	32	61	14	3	2	29	20	46	9	5	196	244	274	518	6%	85%	0.43	55	118	2.20	-3
Myers,Adrian	02	27	8	aa	SEA	449	51	96	22	5	3	41	25	89	13	7	214	255	305	560	5%	80%	0.28	64	135	2.56	3
	03	28	8	aaa	SEA	428	49	98	21	2	4	41	31	76	20	11	228	280	313	593	7%	82%	0.40	62	109	2.90	9
Myers,Corey	03	23	3	aa	ARI	428	46	109	24	2	7	43	31	58	2	4	254	304	367	671	7%	87%	0.54	79	56	3.88	28
Myrow,Brian	02	26	5	aa	NYY	188	29	46	13	0	3	23	33	44	3	0	245	357	362	719	15%	77%	0.75	86	66	5.02	32
	03	27	54	aa	NYY	461	68	105	23	4	13	54	74	114	4	3	229	335	383	719	14%	75%	0.65	97	94	4.63	29
Nady,Xavier	02	24	8	aaa	SD	315	40	79	11	1	8	37	17	54	0	1	251	289	368	657	5%	83%	0.31	73	51	3.71	20
	03	25	8	aaa	SD	136	16	31	6	0	5	19	9	23	0	0	228	276	382	658	6%	83%	0.39	96	30	3.64	23
Navarrete,Ray	03	25	45	aa	PIT	285	26	63	18	1	4	29	12	38	1	5	221	252	328	580	4%	87%	0.31	78	53	2.59	12
Navarro,Dioner	03	20	2	aa	NYY	208	25	70	15	0	4	34	17	20	2	4	338	387	476	863	7%	90%	0.83	98	40	6.89	70
Neal,Steve	02	26	3	aa	ARI	407	41	95	24	0	12	53	43	89	2	1	233	307	381	688	10%	78%	0.48	98	39	4.15	28
	03	27	3	aaa	ARI	285	24	62	16	2	6	27	17	60	0	1	218	263	347	610	6%	79%	0.29	86	53	3.06	14
Nelson,Brad	03	21	8	aa	MIL	143	15	29	12	0	1	14	11	30	2	2	206	260	308	568	7%	79%	0.36	83	65	2.60	10
Nelson,Bryant	02	29	8	aaa	BOS	223	20	57	7	2	6	19	11	17	1	6	256	291	386	676	5%	92%	0.65	77	62	3.51	30
Nelson,John	03	25	6	aa	STL	506	53	107	20	1	5	37	41	117	9	5	212	271	283	555	7%	77%	0.35	51	78	2.63	-1
Nettles,Jeff	02	24	6	a/a	NYY	168	12	39	9	1	3	18	16	36	1	2	232	299	351	650	9%	79%	0.44	80	52	3.57	19
Neuberger,Scott	02	25	8	aa	TAM	348	32	83	11	2	4	26	29	57	3	4	239	297	316	613	8%	84%	0.51	51	64	3.23	11
	03	26	8	aaa	TAM	205	25	50	12	0	4	17	16	39	0	4	246	302	360	662	7%	81%	0.42	80	37	3.57	23
Nevers,Tom	02	31	3	aa	CIN	444	33	90	18	1	8	44	20	84	5	5	203	237	302	539	4%	81%	0.24	66	59	2.28	-1
Newhan,David	03	30	4	aaa	COL	244	29	73	14	2	3	19	11	28	4	5	299	328	406	734	4%	89%	0.39	76	83	4.68	39
Nicholson,Derek	02	26	80	a/a	DET	326	42	76	22	5	5	50	46	73	1	1	233	328	377	705	12%	78%	0.63	97	105	4.48	30
	03	27	8	a/a	DET	346	36	72	14	1	3	32	42	74	3	2	209	294	284	578	11%	79%	0.57	53	64	2.97	3
Nicholson,Kevin	02	27	6	a/a	STL	392	39	84	20	3	4	41	31	57	4	10	214	272	311	583	7%	85%	0.54	68	77	2.63	10
	03	28	5	aa	PIT	405	47	95	26	2	5	34	31	46	6	7	234	288	346	634	7%	89%	0.67	81	84	3.28	25
Nicholson,Tommy	03	24	54	a/a	CHW	168	14	37	8	1	1	11	20	28	2	2	219	304	294	598	11%	83%	0.73	55	63	3.14	10
Niekro,Lance	02	24	3	aa	SF	297	27	81	18	1	3	28	6	28	0	2	273	287	370	657	2%	91%	0.21	72	41	3.66	25
	03	25	5	aaa	SF	381	35	101	14	2	3	33	15	31	2	4	265	293	336	629	4%	92%	0.48	49	57	3.38	18
Nieves,Jose	03	28	6	aaa	NYY	217	21	41	4	4	2	16	10	30	4	1	189	225	266	491	5%	86%	0.34	44	141	1.98	-12
Nieves,Raul	03	25	6	aa	BOS	253	26	57	9	1	0	17	19	26	4	7	225	279	267	546	7%	90%	0.72	33	70	2.39	3
Nieves,Wil	02	25	2	aaa	SD	237	21	64	18	1	6	25	4	36	0	0	270	282	430	713	2%	85%	0.11	110	37	4.29	38
	03	26	2	aaa	ANA	361	37	88	15	1	3	29	19	42	1	2	245	283	314	597	5%	88%	0.46	51	51	3.07	12
Niles,Drew	02	26	5	aa	FLA	259	20	47	8	6	0	12	11	64	2	2	181	215	259	474	4%	75%	0.17	48	154	1.75	-16
	03	27	54	aa	FLA	390	49	82	14	3	2	28	30	83	1	3	210	265	272	538	7%	79%	0.36	44	79	2.43	-5
Nivar,Ramon	03	24	48	a/a	TEX	406	56	134	19	5	6	43	22	24	13	11	330	364	446	810	5%	94%	0.92	75	114	5.91	59
Nix,Laynce	03	23	8	aa	TEX	335	45	91	22	0	14	55	30	57	8	2	272	332	463	794	8%	83%	0.53	123	73	5.64	52
Nunez,Abraham	02	26	8	aaa	FLA	428	49	88	21	4	14	43	38	85	22	8	206	270	371	642	8%	80%	0.45	102	134	3.35	20
	03	27	8	aaa	FLA	212	25	55	12	2	8	28	24	45	7	5	261	337	444	780	10%	79%	0.53	113	101	5.19	44
Nunez,Jorge	02	28	4	aaa	MON	282	35	73	9	3	0	17	10	39	23	8	259	284	312	596	3%	86%	0.26	38	154	3.10	7
	03	29	6	aaa	CHW	350	28	70	7	1	1	21	10	74	12	8	199	222	231	453	3%	79%	0.14	23	94	1.58	-21
Nunnally,Jon	02	31	8	aaa	STL	360	42	71	15	1	14	44	33	93	11	5	197	265	361	626	8%	74%	0.35	100	93	3.15	14
	03	32	8	aaa	STL	428	68	98	17	4	21	44	86	132	16	11	229	359	431	790	17%	69%	0.65	118	112	5.44	38
Nye,Rodney	02	26	5	aa	NYM	394	38	73	14	0	9	39	40	92	3	2	185	260	289	550	9%	77%	0.43	67	49	2.54	-2
	03	27	5	a/a	NYM	481	61	119	33	3	7	55	45	76	3	5	247	311	372	684	9%	84%	0.60	89	68	4.02	31
O'Keefe,Mike	02	24	3	aa	ANA	468	58	115	29	4	18	63	49	64	8	3	246	317	440	757	9%	86%	0.77	122	98	4.97	48
	03	25	3	aa	ANA	444	41	97	22	1	8	56	48	67	5	9	219	295	326	621	10%	85%	0.72	73	46	3.16	17
Ojeda,Augie	02	28	6	aaa	CHC	291	36	52	15	2	1	18	21	22	3	4	179	234	254	488	7%	92%	0.95	57	100	1.88	2
	03	29	64	aaa	CHC	283	33	59	8	2	2	18	27	24	3	0	207	276	269	545	9%	92%	1.14	42	89	2.66	9
Olivares,Teuris	02	24	4	aa	NYY	142	19	33	6	1	2	13	12	28	4	3	232	292	331	623	8%	80%	0.43	65	106	3.24	13
	03	25	6	a/a	NYY	220	21	46	7	0	5	27	16	31	2	5	207	263	304	567	7%	86%	0.53	61	46	2.49	5
Oliver,Brian	02	26	4	aa	TEX	356	46	82	15	1	3	21	26	52	3	4	230	283	303	586	7%	85%	0.50	53	72	2.90	9
Olivo,Miguel	02	24	2	aa	CHW	359	44	98	22	7	6	43	37	64	25	13	273	341	423	764	9%	82%	0.58	97	166	5.01	43
Olmedo,Rainer	03	22	6	a/a	CIN	185	22	50	12	0	3	15	13	27	2	3	270	318	384	702	7%	85%	0.48	83	52	4.22	34
Olmedo,Ranier	02	21	6	aa	CIN	478	50	108	21	1	3	24	42	66	12	19	226	288	293	581	8%	86%	0.64	50	70	2.60	9
Olson,Tim	02	24	6	aa	ARI	433	46	103	21	2	8	48	19	72	7	12	238	270	351	621	4%	83%	0.26	76	78	2.91	16
	03	25	6	a/a	ARI	453	46	99	21	0	6	34	27	74	8	5	218	261	302	563	6%	84%	0.36	60	69	2.64	5
Ordaz,Luis	02	27	6	aaa	KC	330	36	84	18	3	2	26	13	31	7	3	255	283	345	628	4%	91%	0.42	66	109	3.40	20
	03	28	65	aaa	KC	178	11	37	11	0	0	16	7	15	2	0	209	241	272	512	4%	92%	0.49	55	50	2.23	2
Orie,Kevin	02	30	5	aaa	CHC	294	32	67	12	2	13	40	16	32	0	1	228	268	415	683	5%	89%	0.50	111	54	3.73	32

Major League Equivalent Statistics

BATTER	Yr	Age	Pos	Lev	Org	ab	r	h	d	t	hr	rbi	bb	k	sb	cs	ba	ob	slg	ops	bb%	ct%	eye	px	sx	rc/g	bpv
Orr,Pete	02	23	6	aa	ATL	305	29	67	9	1	2	29	16	39	18	5	220	259	275	534	5%	87%	0.41	39	112	2.49	-2
	03	24	6	aa	ATL	257	19	52	10	1	2	28	22	45	12	5	203	266	270	536	8%	82%	0.48	47	93	2.47	-3
Ortega,Bill	02	27	8	aaa	STL	293	37	64	14	1	6	29	30	38	1	5	218	291	334	625	9%	87%	0.79	77	55	3.19	20
Ortiz,Hector	02	33	2	aaa	KC	181	10	35	5	0	1	9	15	27	1	1	193	255	238	493	8%	85%	0.56	33	30	2.06	-11
	03	34	2	aaa	TAM	221	21	46	13	0	0	20	16	23	0	1	208	262	265	527	7%	89%	0.69	50	37	2.34	4
Ortiz,Jose	02	25	6	aaa	COL	111	15	34	8	1	5	12	3	8	1	1	306	325	532	856	3%	93%	0.38	141	84	6.23	68
Ortiz,Luis	02	32	3	aaa	MON	382	37	95	35	0	4	50	17	33	1	0	249	281	372	652	4%	91%	0.52	97	44	3.66	33
	03	33	3	aaa	MON	190	21	47	11	0	7	26	9	21	1	0	246	280	417	697	5%	89%	0.43	109	43	4.09	36
Ortiz,Nick	03	30	6	aa	KC	274	22	52	10	0	3	16	15	80	1	2	189	232	255	488	5%	71%	0.19	47	39	1.90	-14
Ottavinia,Paul	02	29	8	aa	TEX	522	51	97	23	2	5	40	35	67	10	6	186	237	266	503	6%	87%	0.52	57	91	2.05	-4
	03	30	8	a/a	TEX	433	30	86	11	3	2	34	27	63	12	6	200	247	257	504	6%	86%	0.44	38	97	2.12	-9
Overbay,Lyle	02	26	3	aaa	ARI	525	62	161	37	0	15	82	31	64	0	0	307	345	463	808	6%	88%	0.48	107	24	6.07	56
	03	27	3	aaa	ARI	119	18	30	10	0	3	12	21	14	0	0	253	366	408	774	15%	88%	1.48	110	30	5.68	59
Owens,Jeremy	03	27	8	aa	BOS	471	48	101	22	5	15	51	30	163	11	7	214	262	377	639	6%	65%	0.19	99	128	3.21	16
Owens,Ryan	02	25	45	a/a	COL	337	27	79	19	1	9	36	30	70	5	5	234	297	377	674	8%	79%	0.43	94	54	3.78	25
	03	26	48	aa	MIN	351	41	72	17	2	6	32	32	89	1	5	205	272	318	590	8%	75%	0.36	75	64	2.79	7
Ozuna,Pablo	02	28	4	aaa	FLA	261	25	67	13	1	5	22	12	30	11	4	257	289	372	661	4%	89%	0.40	77	94	3.74	25
	03	29	48	a/a	COL	278	21	58	12	5	1	13	7	24	10	7	209	230	298	528	3%	91%	0.30	59	144	2.06	0
Pachot,John	02	28	2	aa	PIT	321	21	64	23	0	2	30	4	29	1	0	199	209	290	499	1%	91%	0.14	73	44	1.96	-1
	03	29	2	aa	SF	320	21	60	21	0	2	24	6	44	2	1	188	201	275	476	2%	86%	0.13	69	50	1.76	-6
Padgett,Matt	02	25	8	aa	FLA	406	38	75	21	1	11	46	32	123	5	5	185	244	323	567	7%	70%	0.26	90	67	2.51	4
	03	26	8	aa	FLA	462	50	102	23	1	12	58	34	110	2	3	220	274	354	628	7%	76%	0.31	87	50	3.27	16
Padilla,Jorge	02	23	8	aa	PHI	484	57	111	29	2	6	52	34	70	26	13	229	280	335	615	7%	86%	0.49	76	115	3.10	17
	03	24	8	aa	PHI	173	16	44	11	1	2	18	14	26	9	10	253	309	362	672	8%	85%	0.54	80	92	3.37	28
Parrish,Dave	02	23	2	aa	NYY	341	33	72	16	1	4	36	35	59	12	7	211	285	299	584	9%	83%	0.59	62	85	2.88	8
	03	24	2	aa	NYY	103	12	19	4	1	1	11	8	16	2	0	184	241	267	508	7%	85%	0.48	55	114	2.23	-6
Pascucci,Val	02	24	8	aa	MON	459	56	95	14	1	21	64	71	93	2	0	207	313	379	692	13%	80%	0.76	100	51	4.25	25
	03	25	83	aaa	MON	459	60	114	28	1	12	64	73	98	2	2	248	352	392	744	14%	79%	0.74	96	48	5.11	37
Patterson,Jarrod	02	29	5	aaa	DET	447	55	111	27	6	9	58	40	67	3	1	248	310	396	706	8%	85%	0.60	97	107	4.40	35
	03	30	53	aaa	KC	478	53	104	28	2	14	66	35	77	3	1	217	270	373	643	7%	84%	0.46	102	69	3.44	23
Paulino,Ronny	03	22	2	aa	PIT	159	17	34	6	1	5	17	11	30	0	2	214	265	358	623	6%	81%	0.37	88	61	3.04	15
Paul,Josh	02	27	2	aaa	CHW	231	15	55	13	1	0	14	15	42	9	4	238	285	303	588	6%	82%	0.36	54	85	2.99	9
	03	28	2	aaa	CHC	210	14	40	3	1	3	16	10	41	1	3	190	228	252	480	5%	81%	0.25	36	52	1.78	-17
Paz,Rich	02	25	5	aa	KC	479	67	117	23	0	5	59	62	76	4	6	244	331	324	654	11%	84%	0.82	59	52	3.84	22
	03	26	4	a/a	MIL	359	42	86	19	0	1	23	59	54	5	5	241	347	301	648	14%	85%	1.07	50	53	3.90	23
Pecci,Jay	02	26	4	aa	SEA	271	26	62	9	1	1	22	22	37	8	8	229	287	280	567	8%	86%	0.59	38	80	2.62	4
	03	27	4	a/a	SF	223	16	42	5	0	0	10	14	26	3	3	187	235	211	446	6%	88%	0.53	21	57	1.63	-19
Peeples,Mike	02	26	8	a/a	FLA	314	30	59	15	2	5	31	15	54	6	6	188	225	296	521	5%	83%	0.28	73	99	2.02	-2
	03	27	3	aaa	DET	163	10	29	6	0	0	13	8	28	1	2	181	217	216	433	4%	83%	0.27	31	44	1.46	-22
Pelaez,Alex	02	27	5	aaa	SD	411	40	110	26	1	9	54	16	37	0	1	268	295	401	697	4%	91%	0.43	92	34	4.18	36
	03	28	5	aaa	SD	292	29	69	12	0	5	38	9	27	0	0	238	259	329	588	3%	91%	0.31	63	31	2.91	11
Pellow,Kit	02	29	5	aaa	KC	402	48	97	21	2	21	56	15	70	3	2	241	269	460	729	4%	83%	0.21	132	74	4.17	39
	03	30	32	aaa	COL	320	32	81	13	1	16	38	17	58	1	1	253	291	450	741	5%	82%	0.30	116	40	4.56	38
Pena,Angel	02	28	2	aaa	SF	248	23	56	10	2	6	29	12	51	2	2	226	262	355	616	5%	79%	0.24	80	80	3.08	13
Pena,Carlos	02	24	3	aaa	OAK	175	22	35	8	1	7	24	18	36	2	0	200	275	377	652	9%	79%	0.50	107	84	3.59	21
Pena,Elvis	02	28	4	a/a	MIL	397	44	86	11	3	2	23	36	79	24	12	217	282	275	556	8%	80%	0.46	39	125	2.62	-3
Pena,Wily Mo	02	21	8	aa	CIN	388	40	96	24	1	9	40	29	92	6	0	247	300	384	684	7%	76%	0.32	93	79	4.18	27
Peralta,Jhonny	03	21	6	aaa	CLE	237	25	64	13	1	1	21	14	38	1	3	269	311	348	659	6%	84%	0.37	61	59	3.73	22
Peralta,John	02	20	6	aa	CLE	470	58	132	28	3	15	58	42	84	4	2	281	340	449	789	8%	82%	0.50	108	76	5.64	48
Perez,Antonio	02	23	4	aa	SEA	240	30	59	8	1	2	24	11	63	15	9	246	279	313	591	4%	74%	0.17	46	120	2.79	4
	03	24	4	a/a	TAM	215	39	57	17	3	7	27	25	52	5	2	265	342	470	811	10%	76%	0.48	133	144	5.85	53
Perez,Jerson	02	27	6	aaa	TOR	203	21	43	7	1	3	12	11	40	2	2	212	252	300	553	5%	80%	0.28	58	78	2.48	-0
Perez,Jhonny	03	27	48	a/a	DET	283	25	55	11	2	2	24	13	44	15	4	194	228	264	492	4%	84%	0.28	49	129	2.04	-9
Perez,Johnny	02	26	4	aa	DET	343	33	84	11	2	2	34	23	43	6	6	245	292	306	598	6%	87%	0.53	43	79	3.03	10
Perez,Josue	02	25	8	aa	PHI	196	11	34	7	0	1	13	10	40	5	5	173	214	224	438	5%	80%	0.25	40	61	1.42	-21
	03	26	8	a/a	PHI	306	24	68	11	0	2	23	16	56	9	9	221	260	274	533	5%	82%	0.29	40	66	2.21	-4
Perez,Robert	02	33	8	aaa	NYY	460	40	93	23	2	11	45	11	51	6	7	202	221	333	553	2%	89%	0.22	85	78	2.23	7
Perez,Santiago	03	28	86	a/a	CIN	285	38	70	13	3	4	24	30	77	17	10	244	315	354	669	9%	73%	0.38	72	131	3.73	19
Pernalete,Marco	02	24	53	a/a	SF	314	30	73	8	1	4	26	12	56	3	1	232	261	303	563	4%	82%	0.21	45	71	2.71	0
	03	25	5	a/a	SF	175	17	30	5	1	3	23	16	33	0	0	172	239	261	500	8%	81%	0.47	55	55	2.09	-11
Perry,Chan	02	30	3	aa	KC	399	37	85	13	1	9	46	18	54	4	4	213	247	318	565	4%	86%	0.33	66	63	2.55	5
	03	31	3	a/a	PIT	415	34	89	20	1	5	46	21	44	3	2	214	251	301	552	5%	89%	0.48	62	58	2.54	7
Petersen,Chris	02	32	4	aaa	ATL	223	23	42	5	1	0	12	14	38	0	2	188	236	220	456	6%	83%	0.37	24	63	1.67	-20
Peterson,Brian	03	25	2	aa	CIN	100	11	22	7	0	0	3	8	18	2	1	219	274	285	559	7%	82%	0.42	59	71	2.69	6
Petrick,Ben	02	26	8	aaa	COL	265	33	77	16	3	13	35	26	46	6	8	291	354	521	875	9%	83%	0.57	139	95	6.28	66
	03	27	832	aaa	COL	228	27	55	15	2	10	29	18	38	3	5	243	299	451	750	7%	83%	0.48	130	84	4.38	44
Phelps,Josh	02	24	2	aaa	TOR	257	40	68	20	1	19	51	26	66	0	0	265	332	572	904	9%	74%	0.39	187	44	6.89	73
Phillips,Andy	02	26	4	a/a	NYY	477	73	118	30	2	24	70	36	93	3	5	247	300	470	770	7%	81%	0.39	137	72	4.78	47
Phillips,Brandon	02	21	6	a/a	CLE	503	67	153	32	1	18	64	30	68	14	5	304	343	479	822	6%	86%	0.44	113	85	6.14	57
	03	22	4	aaa	CLE	154	14	27	7	0	3	13	12	19	6	3	177	235	286	521	7%	88%	0.61	74	82	2.13	2
Phillips,Dan	02	24	8	aa	COL	287	18	57	9	4	2	16	9	49	6	8	199	223	279	502	3%	83%	0.18	51	112	1.79	-9
Phillips,Jason	02	26	2	aaa	NYM	323	30	80	19	1	11	56	20	28	1	0	248	292	415	706	6%	91%	0.71	108	44	4.27	41
Phillips,J.R.	03	33	3	aaa	SEA	310	30	76	16	0	11	45	14	78	4	3	244	277	401	678	4%	75%	0.19	100	50	3.76	26
Piatt,Adam	02	27	8	aaa	OAK	234	33	56	13	0	6	32	25	23	3	4	239	313	372	685	10%	90%	1.09	89	59	3.96	38
Pickler,Jeff	02	27	4	a/a	TEX	418	48	101	16	0	0	23	41	41	14	8	242	309	280	589	9%	90%	1.00	34	78	3.09	15
	03	28	4	aaa	TEX	486	56	97	18	4	2	29	53	65	27	5	199	278	264	542	10%	87%	0.82	46	134	2.72	2
Piedra,Jorge	03	24	8	aa	COL	357	42	92	15	6	17	40	24	39	4	2	258	304	476	781	6%	89%	0.61	126	111	5.10	50
Piniella,Juan	02	25	8	aa	CHW	153	19	42	8	0	1	10	16	33	10	8	275	343	346	690	9%	78%	0.48	56	82	3.95	24
	03	26	8	aa	CHW	346	39	87	21	1	4	23	25	86	10	5	252	303	349	652	7%	75%	0.29	71	88	3.73	19
Podsednik,Scott	02	27	8	aaa	SEA	438	54	107	22	4	7	52	37	64	30	15	244	303	361	664	8%	85%	0.58	77	133	3.67	25
Pogue,Jamie	02	25	2	aa	STL	208	14	32	9	0	2	18	24	32	1	1	154	241	226	467	10%	85%	0.75	53	35	1.84	-12
Polanco,Enohel	03	28	6	aa	COL	135	10	26	8	1	1	10	4	26	1	1	196	219	284	503	3%	81%	0.15	67	75	1.98	-4

Major League Equivalent Statistics

BATTER	Yr	Age	Pos	Lev	Org	ab	r	h	d	t	hr	rbi	bb	k	sb	cs	ba	ob	slg	ops	bb%	ct%	eye	px	sx	rc/g	bpv
Pond,Simon	03	27	5	a/a	TOR	476	59	130	35	1	9	65	42	70	2	2	272	332	407	738	8%	85%	0.60	96	51	4.94	43
Porter,Bo	02	30	8	a/a	ATL	447	42	94	22	2	6	46	37	136	14	10	210	271	309	579	8%	70%	0.27	68	94	2.72	4
	03	31	8	aaa	ATL	267	29	55	12	4	5	26	22	80	12	4	206	265	327	592	7%	70%	0.27	77	154	2.96	6
Porter,Colin	02	27	8	aaa	HOU	461	50	114	29	5	6	32	39	118	24	8	247	306	371	677	8%	74%	0.33	85	139	4.03	24
	03	28	8	aaa	HOU	356	45	105	22	5	10	43	18	76	19	6	296	330	472	803	5%	79%	0.24	112	148	5.73	50
Pose,Scott	02	36	8	aaa	TEX	158	11	25	4	1	0	10	16	10	4	5	158	236	196	432	9%	94%	1.60	28	82	1.42	-4
Post,Dave	02	29	4	aaa	PIT	345	45	88	15	1	5	29	28	48	8	5	255	311	348	659	8%	86%	0.58	63	85	3.81	23
	03	30	84	aaa	COL	275	27	54	11	2	4	21	23	30	3	3	196	259	288	547	8%	89%	0.78	61	78	2.47	6
Powers,John	02	28	4	aa	CHC	198	23	43	6	1	4	16	22	34	6	2	217	295	318	614	10%	83%	0.65	63	93	3.34	11
	03	29	5	a/a	TEX	140	11	22	3	1	0	7	19	26	2	2	158	258	193	451	12%	82%	0.74	26	78	1.76	-22
Pratt,Scott	02	26	8	a/a	CLE	466	71	113	16	3	15	49	54	86	16	5	242	321	386	707	10%	82%	0.63	86	115	4.49	29
	03	27	84	aaa	CLE	357	38	81	11	3	4	27	13	67	16	10	226	252	304	556	3%	81%	0.19	50	126	2.41	-0
Pressley,Josh	02	23	3	a/a	TAM	389	42	104	20	0	3	43	42	46	4	8	267	339	342	681	10%	88%	0.91	57	41	4.07	31
	03	24	3	a/a	NYM	159	15	31	7	0	1	12	13	26	0	1	195	256	258	514	8%	84%	0.50	49	38	2.19	-5
Pride,Curtis	02	34	8	aaa	PIT	385	53	95	19	1	7	34	24	64	16	8	247	291	356	647	6%	83%	0.38	74	107	3.52	20
	03	35	8	aaa	NYY	225	33	53	9	2	5	26	15	46	5	7	236	285	364	649	6%	80%	0.34	80	113	3.22	18
Prieto,Alex	02	26	4	aaa	MIN	276	27	62	13	1	5	20	14	36	3	5	225	262	333	595	5%	87%	0.39	73	66	2.77	13
	03	27	6	aaa	MIN	234	23	56	9	1	4	18	10	47	5	3	240	272	333	605	4%	80%	0.22	61	82	3.05	9
Prieto,Chris	03	31	8	aaa	OAK	390	50	86	10	4	3	39	34	37	4	4	219	282	284	566	8%	91%	0.93	41	96	2.75	9
Pritchett,Chris	02	33	3	aaa	PIT	397	40	95	14	1	6	45	34	82	2	0	239	299	325	624	8%	79%	0.41	57	57	3.51	12
	03	34	3	aaa	CHC	102	6	13	3	0	3	11	10	20	0	0	124	201	229	430	9%	80%	0.50	64	13	1.49	-22
Punto,Nick	02	25	6	aaa	PHI	443	62	110	12	4	1	24	68	76	35	9	248	348	300	649	13%	83%	0.89	35	137	4.16	15
	03	26	6	aaa	PHI	111	17	33	7	1	0	8	6	12	6	1	294	330	375	705	5%	89%	0.49	63	131	4.78	34
Quatraro,Matt	02	29	3	aaa	TAM	101	9	18	4	1	0	6	4	25	0	0	178	210	238	447	4%	75%	0.16	44	83	1.61	-19
Quinlan,Robb	02	26	8	aaa	ANA	528	72	154	28	7	17	85	31	71	6	2	292	331	468	799	6%	87%	0.44	109	116	5.73	51
	03	27	8	aaa	ANA	393	43	106	16	2	7	52	19	47	8	4	269	303	370	674	5%	88%	0.41	66	85	3.98	25
Quinn,Mark	03	29	8	aaa	TAM	240	27	49	14	1	6	25	21	51	0	0	205	269	349	617	8%	79%	0.41	95	47	3.20	16
Quintero,Humberto	02	23	2	a/a	CHW	178	13	42	8	0	1	20	8	19	1	3	236	269	298	567	4%	89%	0.42	48	37	2.58	7
	03	24	2	aa	SD	386	32	99	22	0	3	46	16	41	0	0	256	286	335	621	4%	89%	0.39	62	23	3.39	19
Quiroz,Guillermo	03	22	2	aa	TOR	369	52	97	27	0	17	65	37	67	0	0	263	330	474	804	9%	82%	0.55	136	28	5.71	55
Rabe,Josh	02	24	8	aa	MIN	183	16	39	10	0	1	15	8	27	3	1	213	246	284	530	4%	85%	0.30	57	67	2.36	0
	03	25	8	a/a	MIN	497	66	129	20	2	13	71	34	79	17	4	260	307	384	691	6%	84%	0.43	79	108	4.29	28
Rachels,Wes	02	27	4	aa	BAL	199	14	31	4	1	0	14	16	33	3	0	156	219	186	405	7%	83%	0.48	22	83	1.42	-29
Radmanovich,Ryan	02	31	8	aaa	PIT	271	26	50	14	0	5	20	22	50	2	5	185	246	292	537	8%	82%	0.44	74	48	2.21	1
Raines Jr,Tim	03	24	8	a/a	BAL	461	75	126	22	6	7	46	37	74	47	16	274	327	391	719	7%	84%	0.50	77	171	4.62	33
Raines,Tim	02	23	8	aa	BAL	491	55	112	15	3	4	21	28	92	27	16	228	270	295	565	5%	81%	0.30	45	121	2.57	1
Ramirez,Dan	02	29	8	aaa	ARI	236	22	60	5	3	1	14	11	39	5	10	254	287	314	601	4%	83%	0.28	37	104	2.69	5
	03	30	8	a/a	ARI	254	16	48	4	0	2	15	4	44	9	5	187	200	223	423	2%	83%	0.09	24	81	1.36	-26
Ramirez,Julio	02	25	8	aaa	ANA	139	13	33	3	3	2	8	3	23	6	4	237	254	345	599	2%	83%	0.13	60	166	2.71	7
	03	26	8	aaa	ANA	402	38	96	15	3	8	37	9	68	13	7	239	255	347	603	2%	83%	0.13	68	109	2.89	10
Ransom,Cody	02	27	6	aaa	SF	449	46	81	16	4	9	40	40	134	5	4	180	247	294	541	8%	70%	0.30	70	102	2.38	-5
	03	28	6	aaa	SF	396	43	82	13	4	8	38	33	76	10	5	206	268	317	584	8%	81%	0.44	68	116	2.86	6
Redman,Prentice	02	23	8	aa	NYM	491	63	117	30	1	8	50	46	98	34	11	238	304	352	656	9%	80%	0.47	81	114	3.80	22
	03	24	8	aaa	NYM	433	55	100	26	1	10	44	35	90	22	9	231	288	365	653	7%	79%	0.39	91	108	3.58	22
Redman,Tike	02	26	8	aaa	PIT	311	33	76	9	2	2	17	17	19	13	8	244	284	305	589	5%	94%	0.89	41	105	2.89	16
	03	27	8	aaa	PIT	360	50	96	12	4	3	24	30	27	35	10	267	323	345	668	8%	93%	1.12	51	152	4.17	32
Reed,Jeremy	03	22	8	aa	CHW	242	48	96	16	2	8	41	29	18	17	14	397	461	579	1040	11%	93%	1.61	117	112	10.21	113
Reed,Keith	02	24	8	aa	BAL	488	47	103	16	1	12	52	32	99	3	10	211	260	322	581	6%	80%	0.32	69	46	2.59	5
	03	25	8	aa	BAL	419	54	92	9	1	9	33	27	98	14	8	219	266	309	576	6%	77%	0.28	54	99	2.71	1
Reese,Kevin	02	25	8	aa	NYY	514	68	130	21	4	4	38	67	83	19	14	253	339	333	672	12%	84%	0.81	55	105	4.00	23
	03	26	8	a/a	NYY	364	42	82	12	1	4	19	25	59	22	6	224	274	295	569	6%	84%	0.42	48	115	2.87	3
Renick,Josh	03	25	4	aa	MIN	328	46	69	8	3	0	30	23	46	10	6	211	263	252	515	6%	86%	0.49	28	131	2.23	-8
Repko,Jason	03	23	8	aa	LA	416	59	91	12	3	9	22	41	87	20	9	219	289	327	616	9%	79%	0.47	65	129	3.23	9
Requena,Alex	03	23	8	aa	CLE	150	16	24	2	1	1	5	9	37	5	3	162	208	207	415	5%	75%	0.24	27	121	1.35	-30
Restovich,Michael	02	24	8	aaa	MIN	518	69	130	30	5	20	71	38	113	8	9	251	302	444	746	7%	78%	0.34	120	103	4.48	40
	03	25	8	aaa	MIN	454	67	119	35	2	13	65	41	108	9	3	262	323	434	757	8%	76%	0.38	116	99	5.08	43
Reyes,Guillermo	03	22	6	aa	CHW	376	38	76	9	1	4	32	32	66	14	8	202	265	263	528	8%	82%	0.48	40	92	2.33	-6
Reyes,Jose	02	19	6	aa	NYM	275	44	79	16	6	2	23	15	31	25	15	287	324	411	735	5%	89%	0.48	82	196	4.28	39
	03	20	6	aaa	NYM	160	30	45	6	3	0	14	15	20	28	6	280	342	359	701	9%	88%	0.75	51	221	4.94	29
Reyes,Rene	02	25	8	aa	COL	455	44	121	29	3	12	37	20	48	7	12	266	297	422	719	4%	89%	0.42	103	72	4.02	39
	03	26	8	aaa	COL	370	45	120	22	2	6	37	17	39	9	10	324	353	441	795	4%	89%	0.43	82	80	5.54	50
Richardson,Corey	02	26	8	aa	DET	377	39	76	10	1	1	16	46	68	22	5	202	288	241	530	11%	82%	0.68	30	106	2.64	-7
	03	27	8	aa	DET	128	11	17	3	1	1	9	7	28	2	2	136	180	197	378	5%	78%	0.25	41	106	1.06	-33
Richardson,Juan	03	25	5	aa	PHI	248	29	56	9	0	11	26	13	62	2	1	226	265	398	664	5%	75%	0.21	102	51	3.57	22
Rich,Dominic	02	23	4	aa	TOR	132	11	31	4	1	1	11	14	19	2	5	235	308	303	611	10%	86%	0.74	45	70	2.94	12
	03	24	4	aa	TOR	390	38	88	21	1	3	36	24	41	1	5	227	271	307	578	6%	89%	0.58	61	46	2.73	12
Rifkin,Aaron	02	24	3	aa	NYY	235	35	52	12	1	4	29	25	60	4	3	221	296	332	628	10%	74%	0.42	75	93	3.38	13
	03	25	3	aa	NYY	510	55	117	25	1	16	70	38	92	4	7	229	283	376	659	7%	82%	0.41	94	51	3.51	23
Riggs,Adam	02	30	8	aaa	STL	122	20	23	7	0	2	8	18	26	4	1	189	293	295	588	13%	79%	0.69	76	92	3.12	8
	03	31	83	aaa	ANA	394	42	94	29	0	10	59	26	58	5	2	238	285	386	671	6%	85%	0.45	104	65	3.83	31
Riggs,Eric	02	26	6	aa	LA	455	57	91	29	1	6	57	52	83	3	3	200	282	308	590	10%	82%	0.63	79	66	2.98	12
	03	27	56	aaa	LA	410	52	92	25	3	6	44	38	63	2	1	225	291	341	631	8%	85%	0.60	81	82	3.47	20
Rigsby,Randy	02	26	8	aa	FLA	156	7	30	8	0	3	15	7	46	3	2	192	227	301	528	4%	71%	0.15	75	44	2.16	-2
Rios,Alexis	03	23	8	aa	TOR	514	71	168	32	7	9	68	33	70	9	3	327	367	469	836	6%	86%	0.47	94	121	6.72	57
Rios,Armando	03	32	8	aaa	CHW	155	18	42	7	1	5	23	12	29	4	6	273	324	435	759	7%	81%	0.41	100	78	4.44	40
Rios,Brian	02	28	5	aaa	DET	262	23	60	10	4	2	23	16	41	0	2	229	273	321	594	6%	84%	0.39	59	86	2.93	9
Risinger,Ben	02	25	5	aa	SD	466	37	115	22	0	3	38	34	61	1	2	247	298	313	611	7%	87%	0.56	52	28	3.30	15
	03	26	52	aaa	SD	278	26	59	15	0	4	29	18	25	2	2	214	261	310	571	6%	91%	0.71	69	49	2.70	14
Rivera,Carlos	02	24	3	aa	PIT	494	52	129	26	1	16	66	21	61	1	1	261	291	415	706	4%	88%	0.34	99	43	4.25	35
	03	25	3	aaa	PIT	262	24	63	18	0	7	27	11	31	3	1	242	272	389	661	4%	88%	0.35	101	53	3.65	29
Rivera,Juan	02	24	8	aaa	NYY	265	33	77	19	1	7	38	11	32	4	1	291	319	449	768	4%	88%	0.34	108	80	5.27	48
	03	25	8	aaa	NYY	308	40	90	19	0	6	32	22	32	1	3	293	339	411	751	7%	90%	0.67	84	39	5.07	46

Major League Equivalent Statistics

BATTER	Yr	Age	Pos	Lev	Org	ab	r	h	d	t	hr	rbi	bb	k	sb	cs	ba	ob	slg	ops	bb%	ct%	eye	px	sx	rc/g	bpv
Rivera,Mike	02	26	2	aaa	DET	265	38	56	10	1	15	48	33	57	0	1	211	299	426	725	11%	78%	0.58	124	49	4.36	33
	03	27	2	aaa	CHW	295	30	74	10	0	11	44	14	62	0	2	251	286	403	688	5%	79%	0.23	91	24	3.92	26
Rivera,Ruben	02	29	8	a/a	TEX	303	40	71	14	5	12	46	26	65	4	3	234	295	432	727	8%	79%	0.40	117	131	4.34	34
	03	30	8	a/a	BAL	176	22	34	6	2	7	21	12	52	2	1	196	248	359	607	7%	70%	0.23	95	108	2.93	9
Roberge,J.P.	02	30	83	a/a	PHI	431	39	94	23	1	6	37	24	74	5	1	218	259	318	577	5%	83%	0.32	71	73	2.83	8
	03	31	3	aaa	PHI	338	32	76	20	2	3	28	19	58	3	0	224	265	317	582	5%	83%	0.33	69	81	2.92	10
Roberts,Brian	02	25	4	aaa	BAL	313	43	77	8	5	3	26	34	41	19	4	246	320	332	652	10%	87%	0.83	52	160	4.02	20
	03	26	4	aaa	BAL	178	34	50	11	1	0	14	25	11	18	7	284	371	356	727	12%	94%	2.23	59	132	5.05	63
Robinson,Bo	02	27	3	aa	SEA	420	32	81	16	0	2	34	37	60	1	2	193	258	245	503	8%	86%	0.62	41	32	2.15	-6
	03	28	5	a/a	NYY	235	20	43	13	0	2	14	16	42	2	1	181	234	257	490	6%	82%	0.38	59	55	1.99	-8
Rodriguez,Guillermo	02	24	2	a/a	SF	156	11	33	6	2	2	12	9	29	1	3	212	255	314	569	5%	81%	0.31	65	87	2.48	4
	03	25	2	aaa	SF	238	25	57	7	4	3	29	11	20	1	0	241	274	341	616	4%	92%	0.54	60	106	3.28	16
Rodriguez,John	02	25	8	aa	NYY	354	43	67	16	2	13	53	30	88	11	3	189	253	356	609	8%	75%	0.34	102	116	3.00	12
	03	26	8	aaa	NYY	232	30	54	8	1	9	28	20	43	5	0	235	295	393	687	8%	81%	0.46	93	92	4.18	26
Rodriguez,Luis	02	29	6	aa	MIN	455	40	86	14	2	5	26	40	48	2	2	189	255	262	516	8%	89%	0.83	48	59	2.25	-0
	03	30	4	aaa	MIN	518	53	134	33	2	1	36	37	47	5	8	258	308	334	642	7%	91%	0.79	62	58	3.53	27
Rodriguez,Luis	02	28	2	aaa	BOS	259	19	51	11	4	5	24	9	57	0	3	197	224	328	552	3%	78%	0.16	81	92	2.24	2
	03	29	2	aaa	STL	199	18	40	6	1	2	8	17	43	2	0	201	264	271	535	8%	78%	0.40	47	74	2.52	-6
Rodriguez,Victor	02	26	4	aa	PIT	188	22	45	5	0	2	14	6	17	2	0	239	263	298	561	3%	91%	0.35	40	69	2.75	3
	03	27	64	aa	LA	338	32	75	14	0	3	31	15	32	3	2	221	254	286	540	4%	90%	0.46	48	57	2.44	3
Rogers,Ed	02	24	6	aa	BAL	422	48	94	22	1	9	47	13	65	11	5	223	246	344	590	3%	85%	0.20	81	100	2.77	12
	03	25	6	aa	BAL	340	41	60	10	1	5	31	11	67	23	7	177	203	259	462	3%	80%	0.16	53	150	1.67	-16
Rolison,Nate	02	26	3	aaa	SEA	411	49	95	19	1	14	47	32	124	1	0	231	287	384	671	7%	70%	0.26	96	55	3.86	22
	03	27	3	aaa	NYY	385	44	83	16	1	14	45	39	99	0	3	217	288	368	656	9%	74%	0.39	93	36	3.58	18
Rolls,Damian	02	25	8	a/a	TAM	251	34	61	6	4	5	29	18	40	12	1	243	294	359	652	7%	84%	0.45	66	164	3.91	17
Romano,Jason	02	23	8	aaa	COL	325	31	84	13	2	3	24	16	40	12	8	258	293	338	632	5%	88%	0.40	55	97	3.33	17
	03	24	8	aaa	LA	216	36	56	15	2	3	18	9	26	8	7	259	289	389	678	4%	88%	0.35	91	139	3.56	31
Romero,Armando	02	35	2	aaa	PIT	283	30	69	22	0	12	38	18	41	1	1	244	289	449	738	6%	86%	0.44	134	36	4.48	46
Romero,Mandy	03	36	2	aaa	COL	250	20	64	9	1	4	21	13	29	0	0	256	291	342	633	5%	88%	0.44	57	31	3.54	18
Roneberg,Brett	02	24	8	a/a	FLA	219	29	56	13	2	3	28	23	31	2	2	256	326	374	701	10%	86%	0.74	82	88	4.38	34
	03	25	38	aa	PIT	442	52	112	28	3	9	53	34	51	10	6	254	307	387	694	7%	89%	0.68	91	96	4.16	36
Rosamond,Mike	02	24	8	aa	HOU	422	35	85	20	4	10	36	21	100	5	10	201	239	339	578	5%	76%	0.21	87	89	2.41	7
	03	25	8	aa	HOU	455	40	103	20	2	8	31	22	110	5	8	225	261	330	591	5%	76%	0.20	70	66	2.73	8
Rose,Mike	02	26	2	a/a	KC	265	28	57	15	3	4	23	30	52	2	4	215	295	340	635	10%	80%	0.58	83	89	3.34	18
	03	27	2	aaa	OAK	221	33	48	9	1	7	23	33	43	2	1	215	318	352	670	13%	80%	0.77	85	74	4.02	22
Ross,Cody	02	22	8	aa	DET	400	60	97	24	3	13	59	38	66	13	2	243	308	415	723	9%	84%	0.58	110	126	4.64	38
	03	23	8	aaa	DET	470	75	132	33	8	17	61	33	73	15	6	281	328	494	822	6%	84%	0.44	132	160	5.80	57
Ross,Dave	02	26	2	aaa	LA	293	34	70	13	1	11	48	25	63	1	1	239	299	403	701	8%	78%	0.40	100	53	4.21	29
Rouse,Michael	02	22	6	aa	TOR	231	27	53	11	0	7	33	22	36	5	7	229	296	368	664	9%	84%	0.61	89	59	3.46	25
	03	23	6	a/a	OAK	464	62	122	29	2	3	44	51	69	6	2	263	336	353	689	10%	85%	0.74	69	84	4.44	31
Rowand,Aaron	03	26	8	aaa	CHW	120	13	26	8	0	3	11	10	10	0	0	218	277	356	632	7%	91%	0.94	95	27	3.40	31
Ruan,Wilkin	02	24	8	a/a	LA	477	49	111	19	5	2	49	16	42	27	4	233	258	306	564	3%	91%	0.38	51	149	2.82	6
	03	25	8	aaa	LA	403	46	105	5	2	0	32	8	31	33	9	260	275	283	557	2%	92%	0.25	15	133	2.79	-2
Ruiz,Carlos	03	25	2	aa	PHI	169	17	38	6	0	2	12	10	14	1	1	225	266	292	558	5%	92%	0.69	47	49	2.64	8
Rumfield,Toby	02	30	2	aaa	STL	198	16	45	6	0	3	21	14	29	0	2	227	278	303	581	7%	85%	0.48	50	24	2.81	6
Rushford,Jim	02	29	8	a/a	MIL	424	43	105	27	2	6	53	36	47	1	2	248	307	363	670	8%	89%	0.77	82	51	3.93	32
	03	30	38	aaa	MIL	457	39	109	14	1	7	46	28	41	5	3	239	283	321	604	6%	91%	0.69	53	56	3.15	15
Ryan,Mike	02	25	8	aa	MIN	540	66	122	34	4	21	72	39	93	3	6	226	278	420	698	7%	83%	0.42	122	76	3.84	34
	03	26	8	aaa	MIN	408	49	84	19	4	12	52	32	85	5	1	207	265	359	624	7%	79%	0.38	95	111	3.24	16
Ryan,Rob	02	29	8	aaa	OAK	442	53	86	23	2	11	39	40	65	3	1	195	261	330	592	8%	85%	0.62	89	80	2.93	14
	03	30	8	aaa	SF	289	34	57	18	2	5	26	25	43	3	3	196	261	318	578	8%	85%	0.58	85	87	2.73	12
Sadler,Ray	03	23	8	aa	PIT	465	58	126	35	3	6	45	32	88	16	7	271	318	396	714	6%	81%	0.37	91	110	4.51	35
Salas,Juan	03	25	5	aa	TAM	279	27	69	8	2	3	36	9	43	1	2	249	271	320	591	3%	85%	0.20	46	68	2.93	6
Salazar,Jeremy	02	27	2	aaa	PHI	129	8	24	6	0	0	8	10	31	1	0	186	245	233	477	7%	76%	0.32	41	40	1.97	-15
	03	28	2	aaa	PHI	231	13	37	7	0	3	21	13	51	0	0	160	206	226	432	5%	78%	0.26	45	18	1.51	-23
Salazar,Oscar	02	24	46	a/a	DET	285	18	50	16	1	5	26	19	46	2	3	175	227	291	518	6%	84%	0.41	80	51	2.07	-0
	03	25	465	a/a	KC	456	48	122	21	4	10	53	34	58	5	6	267	318	398	716	7%	87%	0.59	83	75	4.43	35
Salazar,Ruben	02	25	40	a/a	MIN	397	39	95	22	2	3	31	20	62	5	0	239	276	327	603	5%	84%	0.32	65	90	3.21	13
Salzano,Jerry	02	28	8	a/a	BOS	445	50	89	23	0	8	47	37	72	13	5	200	261	306	567	8%	84%	0.51	74	87	2.70	7
Sanchez,Freddy	02	25	6	a/a	BOS	494	67	141	31	2	5	52	38	56	19	7	285	336	387	723	7%	89%	0.68	75	104	4.83	40
	03	26	64	aaa	PIT	216	40	68	17	0	4	21	26	29	7	0	316	389	449	838	11%	86%	0.88	97	90	7.21	63
Sanchez,Tino	02	24	8	aa	COL	272	22	71	15	1	3	18	30	20	8	5	261	334	357	691	10%	93%	1.50	69	68	4.29	46
	03	25	28	aa	COL	313	25	67	11	2	2	27	20	24	3	1	215	263	282	545	6%	92%	0.82	47	72	2.55	8
Sandberg,Jared	02	25	5	aaa	TAM	114	17	30	9	0	3	18	12	37	1	0	263	333	421	754	10%	68%	0.32	111	55	5.23	40
	03	26	5	aaa	TAM	272	35	58	17	1	10	33	26	87	1	0	215	283	393	676	9%	68%	0.30	114	66	3.85	25
Sanders,Anthony	02	29	8	aaa	CIN	335	23	67	13	2	9	34	12	75	5	4	200	228	331	559	3%	78%	0.16	81	76	2.37	3
	03	30	8	a/a	TOR	352	39	68	16	2	10	40	21	96	3	2	193	239	331	570	6%	73%	0.22	87	86	2.60	5
Sandoval,Danny	02	24	6	aa	CHW	504	76	121	27	1	5	40	43	53	34	25	240	300	327	627	8%	89%	0.81	65	114	3.08	23
	03	25	46	aa	CHW	478	56	124	28	1	3	44	41	66	19	11	260	319	340	658	8%	86%	0.62	62	89	3.79	25
Sandusky,Scott	02	27	2	aa	MON	354	26	57	14	1	2	24	21	59	0	2	161	208	223	431	6%	83%	0.36	46	44	1.46	-20
	03	28	2	a/a	MON	192	11	39	9	1	1	13	10	36	2	1	204	245	272	517	5%	81%	0.29	51	60	2.23	-5
Santana,Pedro	02	28	4	aa	CIN	350	27	75	14	2	4	20	17	73	8	8	214	251	300	551	5%	79%	0.23	58	85	2.34	0
Santangelo,F.P.	02	35	68	aaa	OAK	101	7	12	3	0	1	4	12	19	2	4	119	212	178	391	11%	81%	0.63	42	58	1.08	-31
Santiago,Ramon	02	23	6	a/a	DET	103	15	30	1	2	2	11	5	13	5	2	291	324	398	722	5%	87%	0.38	56	159	4.66	28
Santora,Jack	02	26	64	a/a	ARI	190	18	31	3	2	1	5	14	29	2	5	163	221	216	436	7%	85%	0.48	31	101	1.39	-23
Santos,Angel	02	23	4	aaa	BOS	350	34	84	15	2	8	42	32	60	10	9	240	304	363	667	8%	83%	0.53	78	82	3.65	23
	03	24	46	aaa	CLE	260	31	58	10	0	6	25	32	52	12	4	223	308	331	639	11%	80%	0.62	70	83	3.67	15
Santos,Chad	03	22	3	aa	KC	396	41	103	20	2	10	42	29	93	3	0	260	311	396	707	7%	77%	0.31	88	73	4.49	29
Santos,Deivis	02	23	83	a/a	SF	495	54	139	35	5	4	61	17	48	7	5	281	305	396	701	3%	90%	0.35	84	100	4.25	35
Santos,Francisco	03	30	83	aaa	SF	301	16	57	12	4	4	31	7	33	1	0	190	210	290	500	2%	89%	0.22	64	76	1.97	-6
Santos,Jose	02	29	5	aa	FLA	214	15	31	6	1	2	22	15	60	2	2	145	201	210	411	7%	72%	0.25	43	74	1.32	-29
Santos,Sergio	03	20	6	aa	ARI	137	11	34	6	1	2	13	6	17	0	0	245	278	353	631	4%	87%	0.37	71	46	3.43	18

BATTER	Yr	Age	Pos	Lev	Org	ab	r	h	d	t	hr	rbi	bb	k	sb	cs	ba	ob	slg	ops	bb%	ct%	eye	px	sx	rc/g	bpv
Sapp,Damian	02	26	2	aa	CIN	137	13	26	9	0	3	9	17	39	0	1	190	279	321	600	11%	72%	0.44	92	29	3.01	10
Sardinha,Dane	02	24	2	aa	CIN	394	26	72	19	0	3	31	11	90	0	2	183	205	254	459	3%	77%	0.12	54	30	1.62	-14
	03	25	2	aa	CIN	246	16	56	14	0	3	25	16	49	4	3	228	275	321	596	6%	80%	0.33	69	46	2.97	11
Sasser,Rob	02	28	5	aaa	MIL	185	16	38	8	0	3	15	16	28	6	0	205	269	297	566	8%	85%	0.57	63	75	2.90	6
	03	29	3	a/a	BAL	276	25	43	13	1	3	20	11	49	6	1	157	190	237	427	4%	82%	0.22	58	108	1.45	-19
Saunders,Chris	02	32	53	a/a	CHW	352	23	58	14	0	4	30	18	90	0	1	165	205	239	444	5%	74%	0.20	53	27	1.55	-19
Saylor,Jamie	02	28	6	aaa	HOU	237	19	47	7	3	3	10	17	58	4	1	198	252	291	543	7%	76%	0.29	57	114	2.50	-5
Scales,Bobby	02	25	4	aa	SD	250	32	56	11	2	3	22	22	59	5	3	224	287	320	607	8%	76%	0.37	65	108	3.15	9
	03	26	5	a/a	SD	344	39	80	23	2	2	31	32	68	9	2	233	299	324	623	9%	80%	0.48	71	102	3.52	16
Scanlon,Matt	02	24	8	aa	MIN	197	19	33	6	2	2	20	12	35	3	1	168	215	249	464	6%	82%	0.34	52	115	1.75	-16
	03	25	8	aa	MIN	358	34	75	20	3	5	32	31	69	7	8	209	271	317	588	8%	81%	0.44	75	91	2.74	9
Scarborough,Steve	02	25	64	a/a	MIL	438	50	106	32	1	8	45	49	87	9	10	242	318	374	693	10%	80%	0.56	95	68	4.03	31
	03	26	64	aaa	MIL	428	42	95	24	5	7	39	25	105	4	7	222	265	349	614	5%	75%	0.24	84	99	2.95	14
Scheschuk,John	02	26	3	aa	SD	153	14	33	8	1	1	22	26	20	1	2	216	330	301	630	15%	87%	1.30	62	57	3.55	24
Schrager,Tony	02	25	4	aa	CHC	350	45	66	19	3	8	38	63	92	7	3	189	312	329	641	15%	74%	0.68	91	105	3.66	14
	03	26	654	aa	BOS	461	41	89	23	2	7	47	49	107	3	5	192	270	294	564	10%	77%	0.46	70	57	2.63	2
Schramek,Mark	03	23	5	aa	CIN	141	11	22	9	0	0	8	6	43	2	1	158	192	220	412	4%	69%	0.13	55	72	1.32	-22
Schumaker,Skip	03	24	8	aa	STL	342	39	79	18	2	2	19	35	53	6	6	230	301	312	613	9%	85%	0.66	61	83	3.21	15
Scott,Bill	02	24	3	aa	MIL	249	14	53	8	0	3	22	13	55	3	2	213	252	281	533	5%	78%	0.24	47	41	2.36	-5
Scott,Luke	03	25	8	aa	CLE	183	17	43	12	1	6	31	9	38	0	1	236	272	413	685	5%	79%	0.24	114	47	3.77	31
Scutaro,Marco	02	27	4	aaa	NYM	354	42	100	19	4	6	24	25	58	6	9	282	330	410	739	7%	84%	0.43	84	98	4.59	37
Scutaro,Marcos	03	28	54	aaa	NYM	244	36	67	15	2	8	28	28	34	10	7	273	346	444	790	10%	86%	0.82	110	106	5.37	53
Seabol,Scott	02	27	3	aaa	NYY	428	43	93	25	1	12	52	23	77	2	4	217	257	364	622	5%	82%	0.30	97	52	3.05	18
	03	28	5	aaa	MIL	388	40	98	20	2	14	58	30	82	2	1	252	305	422	727	7%	79%	0.36	107	58	4.57	35
Seale,Marvin	03	24	8	aa	NYM	345	28	64	10	1	4	23	21	89	10	10	184	231	251	482	6%	74%	0.23	44	83	1.72	-16
Sears,Todd	02	27	3	aaa	MIN	484	62	129	33	3	14	71	42	110	1	1	267	325	434	759	8%	77%	0.38	111	65	5.13	42
	03	28	3	aaa	MIN	283	29	65	11	1	6	35	31	87	5	1	228	305	336	641	10%	69%	0.36	70	76	3.71	12
Secrist,Reed	02	32	5	aaa	PIT	358	44	76	21	2	8	41	38	74	5	5	212	288	349	637	10%	79%	0.51	91	84	3.36	19
	03	33	8	a/a	CLE	123	14	22	7	0	4	11	7	30	1	2	182	227	338	566	6%	76%	0.24	102	65	2.35	8
Seestedt,Mike	03	26	2	a/a	BAL	131	8	28	3	0	0	6	13	17	0	1	210	283	232	515	9%	87%	0.79	19	20	2.29	-6
Sefcik,Kevin	02	32	4	aa	PIT	467	40	93	22	1	1	29	25	47	7	6	199	240	257	497	5%	90%	0.53	47	73	1.99	-4
	03	33	8	aaa	PHI	492	60	116	29	3	8	53	32	50	8	4	236	283	355	638	6%	90%	0.65	82	96	3.48	26
Seguignol,Fernandc	03	29	3	aaa	NYY	402	61	117	24	1	23	69	27	75	0	0	291	336	530	866	6%	81%	0.36	145	39	6.62	64
Selby,Bill	02	32	8	aaa	CLE	184	23	48	13	1	5	18	16	34	4	1	261	320	424	744	8%	82%	0.47	109	89	4.94	41
	03	33	84	aaa	STL	279	28	62	10	4	7	34	22	33	5	1	223	278	361	640	7%	88%	0.65	83	110	3.51	21
Sellier,Brian	03	26	8	a/a	OAK	361	50	84	17	3	5	42	43	60	7	5	232	313	334	647	11%	83%	0.71	69	101	3.68	20
Senjem,Guye	03	28	8	aa	CIN	351	48	70	17	1	10	39	35	78	6	2	201	273	342	615	9%	78%	0.45	90	87	3.18	13
Sequea,Jorge	02	22	4	aa	DET	397	45	93	20	3	3	32	35	60	11	2	234	296	322	619	8%	85%	0.58	63	113	3.47	16
	03	23	46	a/a	TOR	382	51	100	22	3	4	37	35	55	6	10	262	324	366	690	8%	86%	0.64	74	88	3.98	31
Sergio,Tom	02	27	80	a/a	BOS	486	55	104	23	2	9	54	32	77	4	6	214	263	325	588	6%	84%	0.42	74	72	2.78	10
Servais,Scott	02	35	2	aaa	SF	136	18	32	11	0	1	21	5	21	0	0	235	262	338	601	4%	85%	0.24	83	49	3.04	17
Sexton,Chris	02	31	5	aaa	CIN	414	56	107	25	3	5	34	29	33	2	2	258	307	370	677	7%	92%	0.88	79	81	4.03	36
Shabala,Adam	02	25	8	aa	SF	148	11	28	8	0	1	13	5	31	3	1	189	216	264	479	3%	79%	0.16	58	70	1.85	-10
	03	26	8	aa	SF	513	54	110	18	5	5	41	34	91	7	7	214	263	302	565	6%	82%	0.38	57	105	2.60	2
Shackelford,Brian	02	26	0	aa	KC	244	23	44	8	0	4	24	17	41	3	3	180	234	262	496	7%	83%	0.41	54	60	1.95	-9
Shaffer,Josh	02	22	5	aa	CHW	210	23	45	7	1	0	15	32	54	1	5	214	318	257	575	13%	74%	0.59	34	57	2.80	-3
	03	23	56	aa	CHW	304	16	57	7	1	0	19	16	67	1	2	188	230	217	447	5%	78%	0.25	23	42	1.62	-23
Sheets,Andy	02	31	5	aaa	TAM	374	43	94	23	5	11	54	22	70	5	2	251	293	428	721	6%	81%	0.31	112	118	4.38	36
Shelton,Chris	03	23	3	aa	PIT	122	15	32	10	1	0	13	7	21	0	1	262	301	358	659	5%	83%	0.33	77	75	3.74	26
Sherrod,Justin	02	25	8	aa	BOS	243	28	52	17	1	6	35	21	67	6	5	214	277	366	643	8%	72%	0.31	104	91	3.27	20
	03	26	8	aa	BOS	448	54	98	25	2	11	58	36	140	5	5	219	277	356	633	7%	69%	0.26	91	78	3.26	16
Shinjo,Tsuyoshi	03	32	8	aaa	NYM	111	10	30	5	1	3	7	7	18	0	1	268	312	397	709	6%	84%	0.41	81	55	4.34	31
Shipp,Brian	02	24	4	aa	NYM	375	39	69	22	2	6	38	17	84	6	9	184	219	301	521	4%	78%	0.20	81	99	1.92	-1
	03	25	4	a/a	NYM	183	18	30	5	1	6	20	10	64	4	0	166	211	296	507	5%	65%	0.16	76	106	2.08	-10
Shoppach,Kelly	03	23	2	aa	BOS	340	38	88	29	2	10	50	29	75	0	0	260	318	442	760	8%	78%	0.39	125	47	5.09	46
Short,Rick	02	30	0	aaa	ANA	410	50	118	24	1	5	47	15	35	2	2	288	313	388	701	4%	91%	0.43	73	59	4.38	35
Simmons,Brian	02	29	8	aaa	SF	319	36	77	16	4	7	33	27	73	5	4	241	301	382	683	8%	77%	0.37	89	112	3.94	25
	03	30	8	aaa	PHI	198	19	41	8	1	4	12	6	47	2	2	205	229	309	538	3%	76%	0.14	68	79	2.25	-1
Singleton,Justin	03	24	8	aa	TOR	244	32	54	10	3	3	24	17	62	3	0	222	273	323	596	7%	75%	0.28	66	127	3.11	7
Sing,Brandon	03	23	3	aa	CHC	139	14	27	6	0	5	22	10	38	2	1	194	248	345	594	7%	73%	0.26	94	57	2.82	9
Sitzman,Jay	02	25	8	aa	PHI	385	47	85	20	5	7	45	24	77	14	10	221	267	353	620	6%	80%	0.31	86	143	2.98	15
	03	26	8	aa	PHI	249	16	55	11	0	1	6	11	53	6	1	220	253	275	528	4%	79%	0.20	44	69	2.43	-4
Sizemore,Grady	03	21	8	aa	CLE	496	88	143	26	7	12	71	42	68	9	10	288	344	442	785	8%	86%	0.62	96	127	5.36	48
Skrehot,Shaun	02	27	6	aa	PIT	312	29	59	12	2	2	17	17	53	6	4	189	231	260	491	5%	83%	0.32	50	100	1.92	-10
	03	28	6	aa	PIT	304	31	66	12	2	1	25	20	49	9	7	218	266	278	545	6%	84%	0.40	45	98	2.43	-0
Sledge,Terrmel	02	26	8	a/a	MON	476	68	123	22	5	8	43	51	74	10	10	258	330	376	706	10%	84%	0.69	76	108	4.32	31
	03	27	8	aaa	MON	497	70	139	24	5	16	68	44	72	10	6	279	337	447	784	8%	85%	0.60	103	105	5.45	48
Smitherman,Stephe	03	25	8	a/a	CIN	428	47	108	21	1	16	60	44	93	9	3	253	322	420	742	9%	78%	0.47	104	70	4.88	37
Smith,Bobby	02	28	5	aaa	MIL	293	22	61	19	0	7	26	20	55	9	2	208	259	345	603	6%	81%	0.36	94	71	3.05	16
	03	30	68	aaa	NYY	458	53	106	30	3	6	54	31	69	3	5	232	281	352	633	6%	85%	0.45	85	74	3.32	21
Smith,Casey	03	25	4	aa	ANA	324	38	81	9	1	4	27	15	39	4	8	249	283	317	600	4%	88%	0.39	44	68	2.87	9
Smith,Corey	03	21	5	aa	CLE	473	46	121	27	2	9	58	45	92	6	2	256	320	378	699	9%	81%	0.49	84	72	4.42	30
Smith,Jason	02	25	6	aaa	TAM	206	25	52	11	2	3	24	8	39	4	1	252	280	369	649	4%	81%	0.21	78	116	3.64	21
	03	26	64	aaa	TAM	515	65	135	19	13	13	61	10	120	12	10	262	275	422	697	2%	77%	0.08	93	185	3.80	27
Smith,Jeff	02	28	2	a/a	MIN	324	26	69	14	0	7	33	15	52	1	2	213	248	321	569	4%	84%	0.29	72	34	2.60	6
	03	29	2	aa	TEX	137	6	26	3	1	2	10	5	24	1	0	186	212	252	464	3%	82%	0.19	41	49	1.75	-17
Smith,Mark	02	32	8	aaa	FLA	389	40	86	23	0	7	36	27	67	4	3	221	272	334	606	6%	83%	0.40	80	57	3.07	15
	03	33	8	aaa	MIL	388	38	96	22	1	13	50	17	59	3	2	248	280	406	686	4%	85%	0.29	102	54	3.91	30
Smith,Will	03	22	8	aa	TEX	253	31	60	11	2	5	25	15	45	1	0	237	280	356	636	6%	82%	0.33	76	84	3.49	17
Smothers,Stewart	02	26	8	a/a	ATL	105	7	14	1	0	2	7	13	33	0	3	133	229	200	429	11%	69%	0.39	38	28	1.35	-32
Snead,Esix	02	26	8	aa	NYM	401	44	77	7	3	2	30	31	69	47	18	192	250	239	489	7%	83%	0.45	30	154	2.00	-15
	03	27	8	aaa	NYM	472	55	89	12	4	3	27	34	81	52	8	189	244	250	494	7%	83%	0.42	40	169	2.30	-12

Major League Equivalent Statistics

BATTER	Yr	Age	Pos	Lev	Org	ab	r	h	d	t	hr	rbi	bb	k	sb	cs	ba	ob	slg	ops	bb%	ct%	eye	px	sx	rc/g	bpv
Snelling,Chris	02	21	8	aa	SEA	89	11	29	9	1	1	13	13	10	5	1	326	412	483	895	13%	89%	1.30	117	111	8.23	83
	03	22	8	a/a	SEA	253	35	78	14	1	5	35	14	38	2	8	307	343	432	774	5%	85%	0.36	84	62	4.92	44
Snyder,Chris	03	23	2	aa	ARI	188	15	34	13	0	3	19	14	21	0	0	181	238	298	535	7%	89%	0.67	86	24	2.35	9
Snyder,Earl	02	26	5	aaa	CLE	400	61	98	27	1	18	59	38	92	0	2	245	311	453	763	9%	77%	0.41	132	48	4.90	44
	03	27	5	aaa	BOS	467	50	106	24	1	17	59	20	106	0	0	228	259	393	652	4%	77%	0.19	104	37	3.46	22
Socarras,Tony	03	25	2	aa	LA	182	20	31	7	1	5	28	17	52	1	0	172	243	298	541	9%	72%	0.33	77	76	2.43	-4
Solano,Danny	02	27	6	aa	TOR	249	26	45	10	2	3	24	30	45	4	3	181	269	273	542	11%	82%	0.67	61	93	2.48	-1
	03	28	65	aa	TOR	396	37	80	25	2	2	29	34	64	2	2	201	264	289	554	8%	84%	0.53	68	69	2.60	6
Soler,Ramon	02	25	4	a/a	NYM	185	23	37	6	0	1	10	20	33	13	8	200	278	249	527	10%	82%	0.61	37	100	2.26	-6
	03	26	4	aa	SF	184	20	37	3	1	0	9	11	31	7	2	199	245	227	472	6%	83%	0.36	21	113	1.95	-18
Sorensen,Zach	02	26	4	aaa	CLE	455	50	114	12	9	7	50	22	68	12	6	251	285	363	648	5%	85%	0.32	65	152	3.54	17
	03	27	4	aaa	CLE	238	34	52	12	2	3	25	19	40	11	5	220	279	322	601	8%	83%	0.48	69	133	3.04	12
Sosa,Juan	03	28	68	aaa	PHI	298	25	64	10	1	3	21	10	40	8	2	215	241	284	525	3%	87%	0.26	48	93	2.33	-3
Soules,Ryan	03	28	3	aa	TEX	229	24	48	11	1	6	24	21	61	0	1	210	276	341	617	8%	73%	0.34	84	47	3.19	12
Specht,Brian	02	22	6	aa	ANA	476	54	109	22	2	12	51	41	107	15	5	229	290	359	649	8%	78%	0.38	84	100	3.64	19
	03	23	6	aa	ANA	458	54	107	17	3	12	55	39	95	10	9	234	294	362	656	8%	79%	0.41	79	93	3.54	19
Sprague,Ed	02	35	0	aaa	TEX	400	35	86	21	1	7	44	28	76	0	1	215	266	325	591	7%	81%	0.37	76	35	2.93	10
Stanley,Henri	02	25	8	aa	HOU	456	67	126	32	9	13	53	53	72	10	10	276	352	471	823	10%	84%	0.74	124	141	5.83	58
	03	26	8	aaa	HOU	506	76	143	28	7	11	43	52	85	14	8	282	349	428	778	9%	83%	0.62	94	130	5.47	45
Stanley,Steve	03	24	8	aa	OAK	479	54	121	9	2	0	31	44	57	11	8	253	316	279	595	8%	88%	0.77	20	81	3.16	8
Stefanski,Mike	02	33	2	aaa	CIN	203	16	46	7	1	5	16	9	21	0	0	227	259	345	604	4%	90%	0.43	73	36	3.05	14
	03	34	2	aaa	CIN	202	14	37	6	1	3	14	9	26	1	1	183	218	263	480	4%	87%	0.35	52	58	1.83	-11
Stenson,Dernell	02	24	8	aaa	BOS	368	37	85	20	1	7	30	31	82	3	3	231	291	348	639	8%	78%	0.38	80	58	3.48	18
	03	25	38	a/a	CIN	415	46	111	30	0	16	68	33	68	3	6	268	322	458	780	7%	84%	0.49	125	35	5.10	51
Stotts,J.T.	03	24	4	aa	OAK	176	19	46	7	0	0	11	15	36	3	2	259	316	298	613	8%	79%	0.40	34	59	3.39	8
Stratton,Rob	02	25	8	aaa	NYM	336	50	71	9	1	22	52	21	116	5	4	211	258	440	698	6%	65%	0.18	128	91	3.65	27
	03	26	8	aaa	FLA	372	46	64	10	2	21	59	27	141	4	5	172	228	381	609	7%	62%	0.19	117	91	2.66	9
Strong,Jamal	02	24	8	aa	SEA	503	60	126	15	3	1	29	58	89	44	16	250	328	298	626	10%	82%	0.65	35	124	3.65	11
	03	25	8	aaa	SEA	210	35	58	6	1	2	18	24	36	24	12	278	352	344	696	10%	83%	0.65	44	129	4.26	24
St. Pierre,Maxim	02	22	2	a/a	DET	209	21	49	8	0	2	25	15	25	0	1	234	286	301	587	7%	88%	0.60	49	33	2.98	10
	03	23	2	aa	DET	399	44	82	14	0	8	48	29	58	2	0	207	261	299	560	7%	86%	0.50	60	56	2.68	4
Sullivan,Cory	03	24	8	aa	COL	557	61	155	31	7	5	46	29	64	13	14	278	314	384	698	5%	88%	0.46	74	108	4.05	32
Sullivan,Kevin	03	26	3	a/a	COL	154	7	31	5	0	0	10	5	31	2	0	199	221	234	455	3%	80%	0.14	31	45	1.74	-18
Sutton,Larry	02	32	3	aaa	OAK	431	56	95	31	1	8	55	62	90	1	0	220	318	353	671	13%	79%	0.69	94	54	4.08	26
Swann,Pedro	02	32	8	aaa	TOR	368	37	83	15	2	10	44	27	68	1	4	226	278	359	637	7%	82%	0.40	83	54	3.30	17
	03	33	8	aaa	BAL	418	51	97	16	1	9	44	30	73	4	6	233	283	340	624	7%	82%	0.41	70	62	3.19	14
Sweeney,Mark	03	34	8	aaa	COL	165	16	42	8	1	5	23	23	24	1	5	256	349	398	747	12%	85%	0.96	90	46	4.71	42
Swisher,Nick	03	23	8	aa	OAK	287	29	57	21	1	4	35	30	63	0	1	199	274	321	595	9%	78%	0.48	89	46	2.99	13
Taguchi,So	02	33	8	a/a	STL	411	38	78	19	0	4	34	15	60	6	4	190	218	265	484	4%	85%	0.25	56	75	1.83	-9
	03	34	8	aaa	STL	258	26	56	7	1	2	20	20	38	12	5	216	272	272	544	7%	85%	0.52	39	100	2.57	-2
Tamargo,John	02	27	4	aaa	NYM	101	10	17	3	0	2	8	10	9	2	0	168	243	257	501	9%	91%	1.11	57	65	2.19	2
	03	28	54	aa	HOU	288	16	47	3	1	2	18	22	38	3	2	164	222	197	419	7%	87%	0.58	21	57	1.46	-25
Tarasco,Tony	02	32	8	aaa	NYM	153	17	35	5	1	1	14	7	16	4	3	229	263	294	557	4%	90%	0.44	45	101	2.51	3
Taveras,Luis	02	27	2	aa	ATL	156	7	30	7	1	3	17	12	24	1	1	192	250	308	558	7%	85%	0.50	75	47	2.53	5
	03	28	2	a/a	DET	185	17	33	5	1	3	18	16	28	1	0	179	245	257	502	8%	85%	0.57	50	63	2.15	-8
Taylor,Seth	02	25	4	aa	COL	161	13	36	12	0	3	17	9	24	1	1	224	265	354	619	5%	85%	0.38	95	40	3.14	21
	03	26	456	aa	COL	322	35	72	14	3	9	35	16	46	7	2	224	260	365	625	5%	86%	0.34	87	109	3.24	18
Teixeira,Mark	02	22	5	aa	TEX	171	28	52	10	3	9	25	23	31	3	2	304	387	556	942	12%	82%	0.74	149	127	8.13	78
Terrero,Luis	02	22	8	aa	ARI	360	38	95	18	5	6	42	17	67	14	26	264	297	392	689	5%	81%	0.25	82	125	3.05	27
	03	23	8	aaa	ARI	467	64	125	19	12	2	35	24	77	18	23	268	303	373	676	5%	84%	0.31	65	183	3.40	22
Terveen,Bryce	02	25	2	aa	ATL	172	18	31	7	0	2	10	22	36	0	2	180	273	256	529	11%	79%	0.61	54	35	2.33	-5
	03	26	2	aa	ATL	178	14	30	6	0	0	14	24	49	1	0	167	267	202	469	12%	73%	0.50	31	40	1.96	-22
Thames,Marcus	02	26	8	aaa	NYY	386	41	69	19	2	11	36	35	58	4	5	179	247	324	571	8%	85%	0.60	92	77	2.54	10
	03	27	8	aaa	NYY	260	30	63	17	1	4	30	21	56	4	4	243	300	362	662	8%	79%	0.38	86	75	3.69	24
Theodorou,Nick	02	27	46	a/a	LA	198	15	35	7	0	0	17	28	28	3	0	177	279	212	491	12%	86%	1.00	31	54	2.22	-8
	03	28	6	a/a	LA	151	18	31	6	0	0	8	21	32	1	2	203	301	242	543	12%	79%	0.67	35	48	2.59	-5
Theriot,Ryan	03	24	6	aa	CHC	178	18	38	3	0	1	8	27	22	8	8	213	317	245	562	13%	88%	1.25	23	65	2.63	5
Thomas,Charles	03	25	8	aa	ATL	176	26	51	13	3	0	20	15	24	5	4	291	348	399	747	8%	86%	0.63	81	134	4.99	43
Thomas,Chuck	02	24	8	aa	ATL	229	32	47	7	0	2	15	22	36	4	3	205	275	262	537	9%	84%	0.61	41	78	2.46	-3
Thomas,Juan	02	30	0	aaa	SEA	429	38	92	28	1	13	46	34	100	3	1	214	272	375	647	7%	77%	0.34	107	55	3.49	22
Thompson,Andy	02	27	80	a/a	TAM	282	23	53	10	2	5	33	12	55	1	1	188	221	291	512	4%	80%	0.22	65	72	2.07	-6
Thompson,Kevin	03	24	8	aa	NYY	328	37	63	13	1	4	15	29	49	37	9	191	256	272	528	8%	85%	0.58	56	138	2.50	-2
Thompson,Rich	02	23	8	aa	TOR	554	82	134	13	2	2	33	38	68	34	16	242	291	283	574	6%	88%	0.56	30	125	2.84	4
	03	24	8	a/a	PIT	403	54	105	10	2	0	21	22	43	38	8	260	299	294	592	5%	89%	0.52	26	140	3.36	7
Thompson,Ryan	02	35	8	aaa	MIL	273	30	68	10	2	11	32	9	46	0	4	249	273	421	694	3%	83%	0.20	101	59	3.71	29
Thrower,Jake	02	27	4	aaa	SD	362	38	83	26	1	3	28	19	49	1	0	229	268	331	599	5%	86%	0.39	79	60	3.07	17
	03	28	456	a/a	MON	279	25	57	14	1	3	24	15	31	3	2	203	243	287	530	5%	89%	0.48	61	69	2.30	2
Thurston,Joe	02	23	4	aaa	LA	587	76	162	32	6	9	39	18	44	16	12	276	298	397	694	3%	93%	0.41	81	119	3.99	34
	03	24	4	aaa	LA	538	61	132	22	3	5	54	25	39	1	15	245	279	325	604	4%	93%	0.64	56	55	2.78	18
Tiffee,Terry	03	24	5	aa	MIN	530	63	148	29	3	10	75	25	45	3	1	280	312	405	717	4%	91%	0.55	84	73	4.60	39
Timmons,Ozzie	02	32	8	aaa	ATL	496	43	106	19	1	12	60	30	87	5	1	214	259	329	587	6%	82%	0.34	73	65	2.90	8
	03	33	8	aa	ARI	216	16	42	11	1	4	21	12	31	0	3	194	237	301	538	5%	85%	0.38	74	41	2.21	3
Toca,Jorge	02	28	3	aaa	NYM	195	18	42	8	0	2	12	8	29	2	1	215	246	287	533	4%	85%	0.28	52	59	2.36	-1
	03	29	3	aaa	PIT	458	37	112	30	0	7	52	16	72	6	2	244	269	357	626	3%	84%	0.22	83	58	3.31	20
Tonis,Mike	03	25	2	aa	KC	307	28	67	16	0	2	19	18	44	3	1	217	260	288	548	6%	86%	0.41	56	58	2.57	4
Topolski,Jon	02	26	8	aa	HOU	300	29	59	5	2	7	24	33	78	2	6	197	276	297	573	10%	74%	0.42	57	65	2.63	-3
	03	27	3	a/a	HOU	218	24	43	5	4	5	24	22	51	7	6	198	270	318	588	9%	77%	0.42	68	144	2.70	3
Torcato,Tony	02	23	8	aaa	SF	490	60	135	24	3	11	60	27	54	4	7	276	313	404	717	5%	89%	0.50	84	70	4.37	36
	03	24	38	aaa	SF	423	29	109	16	2	2	39	5	26	3	0	258	266	319	586	1%	94%	0.19	45	66	2.98	8
Torrealba,Steve	02	25	2	aaa	ATL	191	17	41	10	0	3	16	16	27	0	0	215	275	314	589	8%	86%	0.59	71	23	3.00	13
	03	26	2	aaa	STL	117	15	30	9	1	2	17	16	19	1	1	254	343	398	741	12%	84%	0.83	101	78	4.96	43

Major League Equivalent Statistics

BATTERS

BATTER	Yr	Age	Pos	Lev	Org	ab	r	h	d	t	hr	rbi	bb	k	sb	cs	ba	ob	slg	ops	bb%	ct%	eye	px	sx	rc/g	bpv
Torres,Andres	02	25	8	aaa	DET	462	72	115	15	9	3	38	50	99	38	13	249	322	340	662	10%	79%	0.51	56	193	3.99	16
	03	26	8	aaa	DET	271	34	64	11	4	2	15	17	55	26	12	237	282	329	611	6%	80%	0.31	60	174	3.00	10
Torres,Gabby	02	25	2	aa	MIN	191	16	47	12	1	2	19	22	23	0	2	246	324	351	675	10%	88%	0.96	76	40	4.00	33
	03	26	2	a/a	MIN	210	25	54	14	3	1	16	11	29	1	0	258	296	366	662	5%	86%	0.39	79	103	3.90	26
Tousa,Scott	03	24	4	aa	DET	437	48	95	14	9	4	44	60	72	9	3	217	312	315	627	12%	84%	0.84	60	142	3.57	14
Tracy,Andy	02	29	5	aaa	NYM	432	50	72	13	1	15	50	45	120	4	1	167	245	306	551	9%	72%	0.38	82	76	2.50	-3
	03	30	53	aa	COL	384	44	86	17	1	19	37	25	113	2	2	223	270	418	688	6%	70%	0.22	117	50	3.76	27
Tracy,Chad	02	22	5	aa	ARI	514	63	163	36	4	6	58	29	38	2	4	317	354	438	791	5%	93%	0.76	87	65	5.81	57
	03	23	5	aaa	ARI	522	71	156	29	3	8	62	32	39	0	2	299	339	412	751	6%	93%	0.82	78	53	5.20	48
Treanor,Matt	02	27	2	a/a	FLA	251	23	51	10	1	6	32	28	41	3	1	203	283	323	606	10%	84%	0.68	76	65	3.19	13
	03	28	2	aaa	FLA	315	32	70	15	1	8	29	29	37	7	5	223	288	350	637	8%	88%	0.77	83	73	3.39	24
Tremie,Chris	02	33	2	aa	HOU	134	9	20	2	0	1	11	7	20	0	1	149	191	187	378	5%	85%	0.35	25	38	1.10	-33
	03	34	2	aa	HOU	301	18	47	7	1	6	20	14	57	0	1	156	193	240	433	4%	81%	0.25	51	33	1.45	-22
Truby,Chris	03	30	53	aaa	TAM	430	46	96	25	0	12	39	35	77	4	6	224	283	364	647	8%	82%	0.46	93	46	3.39	22
Tyler,Brad	02	34	8	aaa	LA	148	22	26	6	1	1	8	26	29	0	3	176	299	250	549	15%	80%	0.90	52	74	2.51	-2
Tyner,Jason	02	25	8	aaa	TAM	351	50	95	12	4	0	23	29	24	17	8	271	326	328	654	8%	93%	1.21	40	133	3.87	31
	03	26	8	aaa	TAM	275	29	82	11	5	0	20	18	24	9	8	300	344	374	718	6%	91%	0.78	50	125	4.53	36
Ugueto,Luis	03	25	46	a/a	SEA	376	55	88	14	1	2	40	30	77	24	11	235	291	292	583	7%	79%	0.39	42	122	2.95	3
Ullery,Dave	02	28	2	aa	BAL	106	8	15	3	0	1	4	11	34	0	0	142	222	198	420	9%	68%	0.32	40	25	1.49	-30
	03	29	2	a/a	KC	124	9	20	3	0	0	9	5	28	0	0	165	198	192	389	4%	77%	0.18	24	36	1.22	-32
Umbria,Jose	02	25	2	a/a	TOR	116	8	23	3	0	0	7	6	23	1	1	198	238	224	462	5%	80%	0.26	23	46	1.75	-19
Unroe,Tim	02	32	3	aaa	ATL	264	26	53	11	1	8	32	22	82	1	2	201	262	341	603	8%	69%	0.27	87	56	2.94	8
Upton,B.J.	03	19	6	aa	TAM	105	14	31	9	0	1	17	17	22	2	4	293	389	409	798	14%	79%	0.76	90	51	5.54	50
Urquhart,Derick	02	27	8	a/a	ANA	287	23	48	10	2	3	16	22	37	5	6	167	227	247	474	7%	87%	0.59	53	87	1.71	-10
Ust,Brant	02	24	5	aa	DET	209	22	33	9	1	6	15	16	44	0	1	158	218	297	514	7%	79%	0.36	87	64	2.03	-4
	03	25	56	a/a	DET	457	44	105	30	5	8	49	19	80	3	3	231	261	368	629	4%	82%	0.24	94	91	3.21	20
Utley,Chase	02	23	5	aaa	PHI	464	64	119	41	1	15	61	43	76	7	3	256	320	446	766	8%	84%	0.57	130	78	5.10	50
	03	25	4	aaa	PHI	431	72	130	26	2	16	69	38	72	9	4	302	358	483	841	8%	83%	0.53	115	95	6.51	59
Valderrama,Carlos	02	25	0	aa	SF	135	10	28	3	1	3	12	8	20	3	0	207	252	311	563	6%	85%	0.40	61	85	2.74	2
	03	26	8	a/a	SF	442	45	109	17	3	3	22	29	54	16	16	247	293	318	611	6%	88%	0.53	50	96	2.95	14
Valdez,Mario	02	28	3	aaa	OAK	304	30	63	14	1	2	18	41	44	1	0	207	301	280	581	12%	86%	0.93	54	52	3.07	10
	03	29	83	aaa	SD	226	18	48	12	0	4	19	25	38	0	0	214	293	317	609	10%	83%	0.67	73	15	3.28	15
Valdez,Wilson	02	24	6	aa	FLA	375	40	83	16	4	1	23	11	42	14	7	221	244	293	537	3%	89%	0.26	51	137	2.31	0
	03	25	64	a/a	FLA	482	56	121	15	5	0	25	28	48	38	16	250	291	302	592	5%	90%	0.57	37	142	3.02	10
Valencia,Vic	03	26	2	a/a	CLE	242	23	54	12	1	8	28	16	64	2	1	223	272	379	651	6%	73%	0.25	98	59	3.51	20
Valentin,Javier	02	27	2	aaa	MIN	455	48	108	29	1	14	55	29	76	0	1	237	283	398	681	6%	83%	0.38	106	36	3.88	30
Valent,Eric	02	26	8	aaa	PHI	546	57	125	34	2	7	69	43	85	0	2	229	285	337	622	7%	84%	0.51	78	42	3.32	19
	03	27	8	aaa	PHI	450	53	88	26	2	10	44	52	100	0	0	196	280	328	608	10%	78%	0.52	89	50	3.18	12
Valenzuela,Mario	03	27	8	aaa	CHW	114	12	26	5	0	3	9	3	22	1	0	230	249	349	598	2%	81%	0.13	77	54	2.97	11
Valera,Yohanny	02	26	2	a/a	DET	146	12	28	7	1	1	5	5	37	0	0	192	219	274	493	3%	75%	0.14	59	62	1.95	-9
	03	27	2	aaa	DET	188	18	32	10	0	2	16	10	59	1	1	172	212	258	469	5%	69%	0.16	65	61	1.73	-13
Van Iten,Bobby	02	25	2	aa	PHI	313	31	59	11	2	3	24	16	77	4	2	188	228	265	493	5%	75%	0.21	52	100	1.97	-12
Varner,Noochie	03	23	8	aa	MIL	468	47	121	17	3	8	66	23	70	6	3	259	293	359	652	5%	85%	0.33	64	84	3.71	19
Vaughn,Greg	03	38	8	aaa	COL	116	17	31	6	1	10	23	11	21	1	0	264	326	590	916	9%	82%	0.51	187	72	6.99	75
Velandia,Jorge	02	28	6	aaa	NYM	407	36	69	17	1	5	31	25	76	4	2	170	218	253	471	6%	81%	0.33	58	75	1.78	-13
	03	29	6	aaa	NYM	374	38	74	19	1	9	41	31	90	2	5	199	260	328	588	8%	76%	0.34	85	53	2.74	8
Velazquez,Gil	02	23	4	a/a	NYM	105	7	19	3	0	0	5	9	21	0	3	181	246	210	455	8%	80%	0.43	25	33	1.53	-21
	03	24	6	a/a	NYM	157	15	32	5	0	2	18	12	31	1	5	204	260	274	534	7%	80%	0.39	48	46	2.11	-5
Velazquez,Jose	03	28	3	aa	CHC	138	8	25	2	0	1	17	16	28	1	1	180	265	214	479	10%	80%	0.58	24	29	1.99	-18
Vento,Mike	02	24	8	aa	NYY	227	25	47	14	1	4	22	22	46	3	3	207	277	330	608	9%	80%	0.48	86	76	3.04	14
	03	25	8	a/a	NYY	498	59	130	29	2	11	69	29	79	4	7	261	301	395	696	5%	84%	0.36	89	63	4.05	31
Veras,Wilton	02	25	5	a/a	BOS	471	42	127	30	2	5	66	26	34	0	2	270	308	374	682	5%	93%	0.76	77	36	4.09	37
	03	26	5	aaa	MIL	402	32	82	13	1	2	21	20	33	2	4	204	242	256	498	5%	92%	0.59	38	50	2.00	-4
Victorino,Shane	02	22	8	aa	LA	481	58	116	14	1	4	32	45	48	43	17	241	306	299	605	9%	90%	0.94	40	113	3.25	16
	03	23	8	a/a	LA	307	37	80	9	4	3	21	20	41	14	9	261	306	345	651	6%	87%	0.49	53	133	3.56	18
Vitiello,Joe	02	33	3	aaa	MON	431	45	122	32	0	13	65	30	56	1	0	283	330	448	778	7%	87%	0.54	112	33	5.48	51
	03	34	3	aaa	MON	171	14	34	11	0	2	12	13	22	0	0	200	255	295	550	7%	87%	0.57	72	25	2.55	8
Wakeland,Chris	02	28	8	aaa	DET	297	33	60	9	1	7	27	21	98	5	3	202	255	310	564	7%	67%	0.21	66	86	2.61	-1
	03	29	8	aaa	CLE	264	25	58	11	1	6	25	14	69	2	2	221	259	341	600	5%	74%	0.20	77	61	2.93	9
Waldron,Jeff	02	26	2	a/a	ARI	214	16	53	9	0	1	19	20	33	0	2	248	312	304	616	9%	85%	0.61	44	20	3.33	13
	03	27	2	a/a	ARI	176	11	33	5	0	2	14	17	37	0	1	188	261	247	508	9%	79%	0.47	42	20	2.18	-11
Walker,Matt	03	26	8	aa	DET	291	35	63	14	0	6	36	17	57	2	2	216	260	331	591	6%	81%	0.30	77	59	2.87	10
Walter,Scott	03	25	2	aa	KC	167	17	41	12	1	5	17	6	31	1	1	245	270	415	685	3%	82%	0.19	115	70	3.78	33
Ward,Daryle	03	28	3	a/a	LA	144	12	30	7	0	3	19	8	26	0	0	207	247	307	554	5%	82%	0.30	69	24	2.54	3
Ware,Jeremy	02	27	8	a/a	CLE	230	25	56	14	1	6	29	11	41	2	1	243	278	391	669	5%	82%	0.27	98	72	3.75	27
	03	28	8	a/a	MON	274	24	60	9	1	9	36	11	40	1	0	219	250	352	602	4%	85%	0.28	80	49	2.98	12
Warner,Michael	02	31	8	aaa	OAK	103	6	14	2	1	2	8	10	22	4	4	136	212	233	445	9%	79%	0.45	56	103	1.39	-23
Warren,Chris	02	26	4	aa	COL	205	20	38	5	1	6	14	15	44	1	2	185	241	307	548	7%	79%	0.34	71	64	2.36	-2
Warriax,Brandon	02	23	6	aa	ANA	316	26	52	8	2	5	16	25	77	3	2	165	226	250	476	7%	76%	0.32	53	81	1.84	-17
Washington,Rico	02	24	5	aa	PIT	359	41	68	10	2	6	27	47	54	2	5	189	283	279	562	12%	85%	0.87	55	63	2.64	3
	03	25	5	a/a	SD	460	58	92	17	2	13	58	43	81	2	3	200	268	333	601	9%	82%	0.53	81	67	2.98	11
Waszgis,B.J.	03	33	2	aa	LA	116	5	13	2	0	1	6	18	49	1	1	115	235	151	386	14%	58%	0.37	25	24	1.28	-44
Wathan,Derek	02	26	6	aaa	FLA	329	31	77	15	5	3	30	17	33	5	14	234	272	337	609	5%	90%	0.52	68	107	2.62	16
	03	27	38	aaa	FLA	409	40	102	20	6	3	40	26	45	16	10	249	294	349	643	6%	89%	0.58	68	128	3.45	22
Wathan,Dusty	02	29	2	a/a	KC	185	16	39	8	1	1	20	12	40	1	1	211	259	281	540	6%	78%	0.30	51	67	2.45	-3
	03	30	2	a/a	CLE	221	18	46	7	0	2	14	13	40	2	0	210	253	264	517	5%	82%	0.32	40	55	2.33	-7
Watson,Brandon	03	22	8	aa	MON	565	70	163	17	4	1	32	30	48	15	20	288	324	338	662	5%	92%	0.63	36	92	3.63	23
Watson,Matt	02	24	8	aa	NYM	441	44	102	22	1	8	52	29	46	10	9	231	279	340	619	6%	90%	0.63	74	73	3.10	20
	03	25	8	a/a	NYM	282	38	73	18	1	10	46	20	23	3	3	259	308	431	740	7%	92%	0.86	112	69	4.62	50
Weber,Jake	02	26	8	a/a	SEA	255	23	59	6	0	2	22	17	31	5	4	231	279	278	558	6%	88%	0.55	33	59	2.63	2
	03	27	8	aa	ANA	539	48	125	24	2	3	47	34	46	8	5	233	278	302	580	6%	92%	0.74	52	73	2.89	14

Major League Equivalent Statistics

BATTER	Yr	Age	Pos	Lev	Org	ab	r	h	d	t	hr	rbi	bb	k	sb	cs	ba	ob	slg	ops	bb%	ct%	eye	px	sx	rc/g	bpv
Weekly,Chris	02	26	5	a/a	CHC	139	14	28	9	0	0	7	15	34	0	4	201	279	266	545	10%	76%	0.44	57	40	2.30	-0
	03	27	584	aa	STL	279	22	58	10	0	3	25	33	57	4	1	209	293	274	567	11%	79%	0.58	48	53	2.92	1
Werth,Jayson	02	23	8	aaa	TOR	443	52	103	25	1	14	65	53	98	19	8	233	315	388	703	11%	78%	0.54	101	90	4.28	30
	03	24	8	aaa	TOR	236	32	54	19	1	8	30	13	59	10	1	229	269	419	689	5%	75%	0.22	127	127	3.97	33
Wesson,Barry	02	26	8	aaa	HOU	413	38	116	25	5	11	53	14	91	4	8	281	304	446	750	3%	78%	0.15	106	89	4.53	40
	03	27	8	aaa	ANA	475	48	114	24	3	7	41	29	69	13	4	241	285	347	632	6%	85%	0.42	73	102	3.47	19
Weston,Aron	03	23	8	aa	CHC	194	25	36	5	1	3	13	12	53	11	4	186	233	268	501	6%	73%	0.23	51	139	2.05	-12
West,Kevin	03	24	8	aa	MIN	494	45	125	40	1	11	65	21	99	3	6	253	284	403	687	4%	80%	0.22	106	46	3.82	33
West,Todd	02	24	4	aa	MIL	120	11	23	5	0	0	7	7	21	5	3	192	236	233	470	6%	83%	0.33	37	87	1.76	-14
Whiteman,Tommy	03	24	65	aa	HOU	532	49	122	16	2	10	53	26	86	2	9	229	264	325	589	5%	84%	0.30	60	46	2.73	7
Whiteside,Eli	03	24	2	aa	BAL	265	19	49	11	1	1	21	5	42	0	1	183	198	242	439	2%	84%	0.11	45	48	1.52	-18
Widger,Chris	02	31	2	aaa	NYY	217	19	42	11	1	7	28	13	28	0	4	194	239	350	589	6%	87%	0.46	99	47	2.51	15
Wigginton,Ty	02	25	5	aaa	NYM	383	44	104	24	2	5	43	38	46	4	3	272	337	384	721	9%	88%	0.83	80	70	4.75	40
Wilken,Kris	03	24	35	aa	BAL	426	36	100	16	1	2	39	24	58	5	1	234	275	290	565	5%	86%	0.41	42	68	2.81	4
Williams,Gerald	02	36	8	aaa	STL	278	31	53	11	2	3	12	11	41	6	5	191	221	277	498	4%	85%	0.27	58	116	1.88	-7
	03	37	8	aaa	FLA	327	40	77	17	4	9	34	17	40	10	13	237	275	394	668	5%	88%	0.43	99	119	3.20	28
Williams,Glenn	02	25	5	aaa	TOR	339	39	83	18	2	12	37	16	64	2	0	245	279	416	695	5%	81%	0.25	107	78	4.06	31
	03	26	5	aaa	TOR	210	23	45	10	2	3	20	11	51	2	1	212	251	319	569	5%	76%	0.21	71	104	2.67	4
Wilson,Craig	02	32	4	aaa	DET	415	40	91	17	2	1	38	39	37	2	2	219	286	277	563	9%	91%	1.05	44	61	2.78	12
	03	33	4		NYY	403	40	87	14	0	5	31	29	51	1	2	217	269	293	561	7%	87%	0.56	52	38	2.68	5
Wilson,John	03	25	2	a/a	NYM	208	20	46	7	0	1	14	17	32	2	1	219	279	265	543	8%	85%	0.54	35	52	2.59	-2
Wilson,Josh	03	23	6	aa	FLA	434	46	102	28	6	2	50	24	64	5	6	235	275	341	616	5%	85%	0.38	76	112	3.10	17
Wilson,Travis	02	25	8	aaa	ATL	494	51	119	21	3	11	62	11	93	9	3	241	257	362	620	2%	81%	0.12	77	102	3.16	15
	03	26	83	aaa	ATL	409	35	98	24	3	6	36	8	104	5	2	240	254	356	609	2%	75%	0.07	81	93	3.04	15
Wise,Dewayne	02	25	8	aa	TOR	340	44	86	20	2	8	36	22	40	11	10	253	298	394	692	6%	88%	0.55	94	101	3.80	34
	03	26	8	aaa	TOR	285	32	58	11	3	9	32	15	63	10	3	205	244	358	602	5%	78%	0.24	91	136	2.89	11
Witt,Kevin	02	27	3	aaa	CIN	509	57	118	30	1	19	81	24	106	0	1	232	266	407	673	5%	79%	0.23	112	39	3.67	28
	03	28	3	aaa	DET	133	20	36	9	0	7	26	15	35	0	0	271	346	486	832	10%	74%	0.44	134	28	6.24	55
Woods,Ken	02	32	8	a/a	PHI	241	26	50	10	2	3	19	8	33	5	4	207	233	300	536	3%	86%	0.24	63	113	2.20	7
Wood,Jason	02	33	5	aaa	FLA	457	51	110	29	2	9	46	25	78	2	0	241	280	372	652	5%	83%	0.32	91	72	3.65	24
	03	34	53	aaa	FLA	473	54	109	21	3	10	57	32	84	4	1	230	278	348	626	6%	82%	0.37	76	84	3.38	16
Wright,Gavin	03	24	8	aaa	HOU	372	29	80	13	1	2	22	16	65	6	9	215	247	271	518	4%	82%	0.25	42	64	2.06	-6
Wright,Ron	02	27	0	aaa	SEA	359	45	86	18	1	12	49	33	80	0	1	240	304	390	699	8%	78%	0.41	99	43	4.22	29
	03	28	3	a/a	DET	193	20	38	7	0	6	33	24	45	0	1	198	288	329	617	11%	77%	0.54	81	26	3.25	10
Youkilis,Kevin	02	24	5	aa	BOS	160	26	49	10	0	4	19	23	14	4	5	306	393	444	837	13%	91%	1.64	94	60	6.36	74
	03	25	5	aaa	BOS	421	70	111	25	1	6	44	86	56	6	1	263	388	369	757	17%	87%	1.55	76	76	5.71	50
Young,Ernie	02	33	8	aaa	ARI	160	20	42	7	1	10	33	16	27	0	4	263	330	506	836	9%	83%	0.59	141	49	5.46	58
	03	34	8	aaa	DET	454	49	99	18	0	15	72	43	119	9	5	218	286	359	645	9%	74%	0.36	87	62	3.48	16
Zamora,Junior	03	27	53	aa	ANA	430	44	93	19	2	7	39	22	99	2	1	216	254	318	572	5%	77%	0.22	68	82	2.73	5
Zapp,A.J.	02	24	3	a/a	ATL	392	38	78	16	0	15	44	33	94	1	0	199	261	355	616	8%	76%	0.35	95	35	3.14	13
	03	25	3	aa	SEA	528	70	121	29	1	20	77	41	188	6	8	228	283	399	682	7%	64%	0.22	108	70	3.71	25
Zinter,Alan	02	34	3	aaa	HOU	225	23	45	13	0	10	31	17	63	2	0	200	256	391	647	7%	72%	0.27	120	50	3.39	22
	03	35	32	aaa	HOU	342	39	76	15	0	14	46	29	77	1	0	221	282	392	674	8%	78%	0.38	105	38	3.83	24
Zoccolillo,Peter	02	26	8	aaa	MIL	227	33	57	10	1	10	35	31	48	5	7	251	341	436	777	12%	79%	0.65	111	75	4.96	42
	03	27	8	aaa	MIL	443	50	113	33	1	11	64	44	66	3	5	254	321	405	726	9%	85%	0.66	105	49	4.55	41
Zuber,Jon	02	33	3	aaa	MIL	385	44	78	11	2	2	21	55	49	5	2	203	302	257	559	13%	87%	1.12	38	81	2.85	6
Zuleta,Julio	02	28	8	aaa	CHC	444	53	104	16	0	21	69	29	80	0	1	234	281	412	693	6%	82%	0.36	105	28	3.98	29
	03	29	3	aaa	BOS	204	23	49	10	0	9	40	10	45	0	0	242	278	429	706	5%	78%	0.23	115	25	4.13	33
Zuniga,Tony	02	28	5	aaa	SF	304	18	63	15	1	4	28	15	35	0	4	207	245	303	547	5%	88%	0.43	67	29	2.32	5
	03	29	5	aaa	TOR	261	27	69	20	1	10	33	22	44	0	2	264	322	456	778	8%	83%	0.51	127	20	5.17	50
Zywica,Mike	02	28	38	a/a	CHW	189	17	33	5	0	5	18	13	49	3	0	175	228	280	508	6%	74%	0.27	64	65	2.16	-10

					Actual				Major League Equivalents																
PITCHER	Yr	Age	Lev	Org	w	l	g	sv	ip	h	er	hr	bb	k	era	br/ip	bf/g	oob	ctl	dom	cmd	hr/9	h%	s%	bpv
Abbott,Jim	03	24	aa	MIN	4	2	10	0	45	53	16	4	15	29	3.30	1.51	19.9	349	3.1	5.8	1.9	0.8	33%	81%	48
Abbott,Paul	03	36	aaa	ARI	3	4	11	0	54	75	29	3	12	42	4.89	1.59	22.2	361	1.9	6.9	3.6	0.5	39%	68%	93
Abreu,Winston	02	26	aa	KC	4	0	34	2	55	51	40	4	46	54	6.52	1.76	7.6	384	7.5	8.8	1.2	0.7	32%	61%	65
Acevedo,Jose	02	25	aaa	CIN	12	7	23	0	154	158	60	17	31	107	3.50	1.23	27.8	303	1.8	6.2	3.5	1.0	30%	75%	83
	03	26	aaa	CIN	6	2	29	0	60	68	30	7	20	49	4.54	1.46	9.1	341	3.0	7.3	2.4	1.1	33%	71%	62
Achilles,Matt	02	26	aa	CHC	8	7	41	1	115	166	71	8	45	54	5.55	1.83	13.3	394	3.5	4.2	1.2	0.6	37%	69%	21
Adams,Brian	02	25	aa	BOS	1	0	16	1	31	36	12	1	20	13	3.48	1.81	9.2	390	5.8	3.8	0.7	0.3	32%	80%	26
	03	26	aa	MIL	3	2	39	3	72	84	34	1	57	29	4.30	1.96	9.0	410	7.2	3.6	0.5	0.1	32%	76%	26
Adams,Mike	03	25	aa	MIL	3	7	45	14	74	76	38	8	38	63	4.59	1.53	7.3	352	4.6	7.7	1.7	0.9	32%	72%	56
Adkins,Jon	02	25	aaa	OAK	11	8	28	0	143	193	83	11	41	90	5.22	1.64	23.3	367	2.6	5.7	2.2	0.7	37%	68%	51
	03	26	aaa	CHW	7	8	26	1	122	145	72	15	36	52	5.31	1.48	20.7	345	2.7	3.9	1.5	1.1	31%	66%	17
Adkins,Tim	02	28	a/a	DET	2	3	34	0	74	101	56	6	41	46	6.80	1.92	10.5	405	5.0	5.6	1.1	0.7	37%	63%	27
	03	29	a/a	NYY	3	5	49	0	68	85	48	5	49	39	6.29	1.97	6.8	412	6.5	5.1	0.8	0.6	34%	67%	23
Agamennone,Brando	02	27	a/a	MON	7	1	35	2	67	89	36	10	24	38	4.82	1.68	8.8	374	3.2	5.1	1.6	1.3	34%	75%	16
	03	28	a/a	BAL	3	4	34	1	68	102	51	14	22	35	6.69	1.83	9.5	393	2.9	4.6	1.6	1.8	36%	67%	-7
Agosto,Stevenson	02	27	aa	TAM	3	1	7	0	38	60	17	5	16	20	4.02	1.99	26.8	414	3.8	4.7	1.3	1.2	39%	83%	4
Aguilar,Ray	03	24	a/a	ATL	4	4	36	1	98	101	40	10	23	81	3.67	1.27	11.4	310	2.1	7.4	3.5	0.9	32%	74%	94
Ahearne,Pat	02	33	aaa	DET	5	4	12	0	82	95	38	3	13	42	4.16	1.31	29.0	318	1.4	4.6	3.2	0.3	33%	67%	84
	03	34	a/a	DET	8	6	27	0	184	204	79	13	49	86	3.86	1.38	29.3	328	2.4	4.2	1.8	0.7	31%	73%	43
Ainsworth,Kurt	02	24	aaa	SF	8	6	20	0	116	113	51	6	41	102	3.96	1.33	24.6	320	3.2	7.9	2.5	0.5	32%	70%	91
Aldred,Scott	02	34	aaa	LA	2	2	42	2	44	52	21	2	18	40	4.28	1.58	4.7	360	3.7	8.1	2.2	0.4	37%	72%	81
	03	35	a/a	BOS	2	1	29	8	33	30	11	1	16	23	3.03	1.38	4.9	329	4.2	6.1	1.4	0.3	29%	78%	66
Almanzar,Carlos	03	30	aaa	CIN	2	2	42	23	46	62	26	3	3	42	5.15	1.41	4.7	333	0.6	8.2	12.7	0.6	40%	63%	289
Almonte,Ed	02	26	aaa	CHW	2	3	50	26	60	63	20	8	13	51	3.00	1.26	5.0	310	1.9	7.6	3.9	1.2	32%	82%	94
Almonte,Edwin	03	27	aaa	NYM	3	7	46	20	51	69	36	7	21	31	6.34	1.75	5.2	383	3.6	5.5	1.5	1.3	35%	65%	18
Altman,Gene	02	24	aa	MIL	0	3	24	1	33	38	42	4	44	19	11.42	2.48	7.4	468	12.0	5.2	0.4	1.1	31%	51%	6
Alvarado,Carlo	03	26	aa	DET	3	2	37	0	66	71	31	4	29	43	4.24	1.52	7.9	350	3.9	5.9	1.5	0.6	32%	72%	50
Alvarez,Juan	03	30	aaa	FLA	3	2	51	0	52	80	39	9	26	35	6.73	2.03	5.0	419	4.4	6.1	1.4	1.5	39%	69%	5
Alvarez,Oscar	03	23	aa	CLE	2	2	13	0	33	41	21	3	14	16	5.62	1.69	11.7	374	3.9	4.5	1.1	0.8	33%	67%	21
Alvarez,Victor	02	26	aaa	LA	10	7	34	3	122	131	58	9	34	91	4.27	1.35	15.3	324	2.5	6.7	2.7	0.7	32%	69%	78
	03	27	aaa	LA	4	4	22	1	63	57	20	2	14	41	2.79	1.13	11.6	286	2.1	5.8	2.8	0.3	28%	75%	93
Alvarez,Wilson	03	34	aaa	LA	5	1	8	0	47	39	7	1	6	28	1.41	0.96	22.8	255	1.2	5.3	4.4	0.2	27%	86%	128
Anderson,Craig	02	22	aa	SEA	7	7	27	0	152	173	73	14	67	80	4.32	1.58	25.3	359	4.0	4.7	1.2	0.8	31%	74%	28
	03	23	aaa	SEA	13	11	28	0	177	206	83	26	45	63	4.21	1.42	27.4	334	2.3	3.2	1.4	1.3	29%	75%	8
Anderson,Jason	02	23	a/a	NYY	6	2	42	9	53	45	16	4	16	44	2.71	1.15	5.2	289	2.7	7.4	2.8	0.7	28%	79%	92
	03	24	aaa	NYM	1	3	16	7	31	23	8	3	9	18	2.32	1.03	7.7	268	2.6	5.2	2.0	0.9	22%	83%	62
Anderson,Jimmy	03	28	aaa	SF	7	5	17	0	104	142	59	5	28	38	5.10	1.64	27.9	368	2.5	3.3	1.3	0.5	35%	68%	25
Anderson,Luke	02	25	aa	SF	2	4	26	11	32	36	12	1	13	38	3.38	1.53	5.5	352	3.7	10.7	2.9	0.3	40%	77%	116
Anderson,Matt	03	27	aaa	DET	1	3	23	3	38	62	22	4	8	26	5.24	1.86	7.9	397	2.0	6.1	3.0	1.0	42%	73%	54
Anderson,Travis	03	26	aaa	COL	3	8	31	0	86	131	81	19	44	56	8.48	2.04	13.8	420	4.6	5.8	1.3	2.0	38%	60%	-11
Andrade,Stephen	03	26	aa	ANA	5	1	36	7	51	33	21	2	21	57	3.73	1.07	5.6	275	3.7	10.0	2.7	0.4	26%	64%	123
Ankiel,Rick	03	24	aa	STL	2	6	20	0	54	57	54	6	55	56	8.93	2.06	13.5	422	9.1	9.3	1.0	1.1	34%	55%	48
An,Byeong	03	23	aa	CHW	5	3	16	0	80	97	52	6	38	40	5.80	1.69	23.0	374	4.3	4.5	1.0	0.7	33%	65%	24
Aquino,Greg	03	25	aa	ARI	7	3	20	0	106	134	48	5	38	76	4.10	1.62	24.1	364	3.2	6.4	2.0	0.4	36%	74%	62
Arias,Pablo	02	26	aa	DET	5	8	29	0	106	167	98	22	60	43	8.31	2.14	18.5	431	5.1	3.6	0.7	1.9	36%	63%	-34
Arnold,Jamie	02	29	aaa	FLA	3	8	16	0	67	89	57	9	29	20	7.66	1.76	19.6	384	3.9	2.7	0.7	1.2	32%	56%	-13
Arnold,Jason	02	23	aa	NYY	6	3	13	0	75	70	30	4	31	61	3.60	1.34	23.0	323	3.7	7.3	2.0	0.5	30%	73%	77
	03	24	a/a	TOR	7	9	27	0	156	166	82	22	59	97	4.76	1.44	25.2	338	3.4	5.6	1.7	1.2	30%	70%	32
Arroyo,Bronson	02	26	aaa	PIT	8	6	22	0	143	145	58	10	26	98	3.65	1.20	26.8	298	1.6	6.2	3.8	0.6	31%	70%	101
	03	27	aaa	BOS	12	6	24	0	149	178	74	10	25	127	4.48	1.36	26.6	326	1.5	7.7	5.1	0.6	36%	67%	132
Arteaga,J.D.	02	28	aaa	HOU	9	10	42	3	119	177	85	27	47	61	6.42	1.88	13.6	400	3.5	4.6	1.3	2.0	35%	71%	-19
Atchison,Scott	02	27	aaa	SEA	5	10	27	2	124	143	78	13	31	93	5.66	1.40	19.9	332	2.2	6.7	3.0	0.9	34%	60%	74
	03	28	aaa	SEA	6	9	39	1	108	139	67	8	40	71	5.60	1.65	12.7	370	3.3	5.9	1.8	0.7	36%	65%	46
Austin,Jeff	02	26	aaa	KC	4	0	39	2	52	63	23	2	14	36	3.97	1.48	5.9	344	2.4	6.2	2.6	0.3	35%	72%	77
	03	27	aaa	CIN	4	2	9	0	45	57	30	7	20	31	5.95	1.69	23.1	374	3.9	6.2	1.6	1.4	34%	67%	22
Autrey,Scott	03	23	aa	TAM	5	4	12	0	78	96	35	11	16	32	4.03	1.43	28.3	337	1.8	3.7	2.0	1.3	31%	76%	22
Averette,Robert	02	26	aa	COL	1	6	11	0	61	124	76	11	25	25	11.18	2.43	29.8	463	3.7	3.7	1.0	1.6	43%	53%	-32
Avery,Steve	03	33	aaa	DET	1	4	22	0	34	46	16	6	11	11	4.17	1.67	7.1	372	2.8	3.0	1.1	1.7	32%	81%	-18
Axelson,Josh	03	25	aa	STL	4	2	27	0	75	85	33	9	21	50	3.92	1.42	12.0	335	2.5	6.0	2.4	1.1	32%	76%	51
Aybar,Manny	02	30	aaa	SF	1	4	45	24	50	57	27	6	19	41	4.85	1.52	4.9	350	3.4	7.4	2.2	1.1	34%	70%	56
	03	31	aaa	SF	2	4	52	17	57	61	28	5	22	36	4.48	1.46	4.8	341	3.5	5.7	1.6	0.8	31%	70%	45
Backe,Brandon	02	25	aa	TAM	4	6	20	2	92	111	63	11	40	36	6.16	1.64	21.0	368	3.9	3.5	0.9	1.1	31%	63%	4
	03	26	aaa	TAM	2	1	16	0	33	39	22	1	14	23	6.06	1.62	9.4	365	3.9	6.2	1.6	0.3	35%	60%	60
Bacsik,Mike	02	25	aaa	NYM	5	5	25	0	108	153	54	13	26	63	4.50	1.66	19.8	370	2.2	5.2	2.4	1.1	37%	75%	40
	03	26	aaa	NYM	2	9	22	0	117	151	81	14	35	51	6.21	1.59	24.0	360	2.7	4.0	1.5	1.1	33%	61%	16
Baek,Cha Seung	03	23	aa	SEA	3	3	9	0	56	58	21	2	19	40	3.31	1.36	26.6	326	3.0	6.4	2.1	0.3	32%	75%	76
Baerlocher,Ryan	02	25	a/a	KC	8	4	24	0	110	129	67	16	47	61	5.47	1.60	20.7	362	3.8	5.0	1.3	1.3	31%	68%	16
	03	26	a/a	KC	6	8	31	0	154	204	118	26	61	81	6.87	1.72	23.1	379	3.6	4.7	1.3	1.5	34%	62%	4
Baisley,Brad	02	23	aa	PHI	7	9	21	0	116	130	67	13	56	57	5.19	1.60	25.0	362	4.3	4.4	1.0	1.0	30%	69%	17
Bajenaru,Jeff	03	26	aa	CHW	4	2	50	14	64	73	37	3	33	50	5.14	1.66	5.9	371	4.7	7.1	1.5	0.5	35%	68%	59
Baker,Brad	02	22	aa	SD	4	4	12	0	64	53	38	5	46	48	5.34	1.54	23.8	354	6.5	6.7	1.0	0.7	27%	65%	52
	03	23	aa	SD	1	6	17	0	50	57	38	3	37	44	6.81	1.87	14.2	399	6.6	7.9	1.2	0.5	36%	62%	55
Baker,Chris	02	25	aaa	TOR	4	7	18	0	89	106	51	13	28	36	5.15	1.50	21.9	348	2.8	3.6	1.3	1.3	30%	69%	7
	03	26	a/a	TOR	9	7	27	0	154	218	100	14	46	77	5.84	1.71	26.4	377	2.7	4.5	1.7	0.8	36%	66%	27
Baker,Ryan	03	26	aa	FLA	5	2	44	4	64	69	28	1	44	45	3.91	1.77	6.8	386	6.3	6.3	1.0	0.2	33%	76%	56
Baldwin,James	03	32	aaa	MIN	3	4	13	0	76	86	36	6	17	34	4.24	1.36	25.0	325	2.0	4.1	2.0	0.7	31%	70%	43
Bale,John	03	29	aaa	CIN	4	2	34	4	57	65	34	1	19	46	5.37	1.46	7.4	342	2.9	7.2	2.4	0.2	36%	60%	88
	02	28	aaa	NYM	2	2	12	0	28	27	14	2	8	21	4.50	1.25	9.7	307	2.6	6.8	2.6	0.6	30%	64%	82
Balfour,Grant	02	25	aaa	MIN	2	4	58	8	71	65	35	3	29	75	4.43	1.32	5.2	319	3.7	9.5	2.6	0.4	33%	65%	107
	03	26	aaa	MIN	5	2	21	5	71	58	25	7	17	73	3.20	1.05	13.4	272	2.2	9.3	4.3	0.9	28%	73%	130
Banks,Willie	03	35	aaa	CHC	4	3	56	20	70	75	27	6	27	46	3.51	1.46	5.5	341	3.5	5.9	1.7	0.8	31%	78%	47
Barry,Kevin	03	25	aa	ATL	4	4	51	5	56	72	47	1	37	52	7.49	1.94	5.3	408	5.9	8.4	1.4	0.2	40%	58%	69

Major League Equivalent Statistics

					Actual				Major League Equivalents																
PITCHER	Yr	Age	Lev	Org	w	l	g	sv	ip	h	er	hr	bb	k	era	br/ip	bf/g	oob	ctl	dom	cmd	hr/9	h%	s%	bpv
Bartosh,Cliff	02	23	aa	SD	2	4	62	25	70	63	31	4	34	57	3.97	1.38	4.9	329	4.4	7.3	1.7	0.5	30%	71%	72
	03	24	aaa	SD	2	5	64	10	71	71	36	4	21	42	4.56	1.29	4.7	315	2.7	5.3	2.0	0.5	30%	64%	63
Basham,Bobby	03	24	aa	CIN	5	10	17	0	94	162	72	22	25	47	6.91	1.99	27.1	413	2.4	4.5	1.9	2.1	39%	69%	-15
Bauer,Greg	02	25	aa	LA	2	4	38	1	70	76	29	6	33	31	3.73	1.56	8.2	356	4.2	4.0	0.9	0.8	30%	78%	21
	03	26	aa	LA	6	6	46	2	86	118	39	2	48	49	4.07	1.93	9.1	406	5.0	5.1	1.0	0.2	37%	78%	36
Bauer,Peter	02	24	aa	TOR	6	13	28	0	177	237	101	14	53	78	5.14	1.64	28.8	367	2.7	4.0	1.5	0.7	35%	68%	25
	03	25	aa	TOR	5	6	29	0	103	139	72	7	46	49	6.25	1.80	16.8	389	4.0	4.3	1.1	0.6	35%	64%	21
Bauer,Rick	03	27	aaa	BAL	3	1	7	0	36	37	13	1	13	17	3.33	1.40	22.3	331	3.3	4.3	1.3	0.3	30%	75%	49
Baugh,Kenny	03	25	aa	DET	7	9	19	0	109	134	72	16	32	48	5.90	1.51	25.5	349	2.6	4.0	1.5	1.3	31%	63%	13
Bausher,Andy	02	26	a/a	SD	5	1	42	0	74	98	33	8	21	37	4.01	1.61	8.0	363	2.6	4.5	1.8	1.0	34%	77%	27
Bautista,Denny	03	21	aa	FLA	4	5	11	0	53	49	26	5	35	58	4.36	1.58	21.7	359	6.0	9.8	1.6	0.8	32%	73%	76
Bazzell,Shane	02	24	aa	OAK	5	7	39	3	97	116	60	3	47	73	5.56	1.68	11.5	373	4.4	6.8	1.6	0.3	36%	64%	62
	03	25	aa	OAK	3	6	34	1	56	65	34	4	26	34	5.39	1.63	7.5	366	4.2	5.5	1.3	0.7	33%	66%	38
Beal,Andy	02	24	a/a	NYY	6	9	18	0	107	119	62	10	43	82	5.21	1.51	26.4	349	3.6	6.9	1.9	0.8	33%	66%	56
	03	25	a/a	NYY	7	6	25	0	113	148	75	14	32	75	5.99	1.60	20.4	361	2.5	5.9	2.3	1.1	35%	63%	43
Bean,Colter	03	27	a/a	NYY	4	2	53	4	73	69	29	7	32	61	3.55	1.38	5.9	329	4.0	7.5	1.9	0.8	30%	76%	67
Beasley,Ray	02	26	aaa	ATL	6	5	64	4	55	64	20	3	16	38	3.26	1.45	3.8	339	2.6	6.2	2.4	0.5	34%	78%	71
	03	27	a/a	TEX	5	5	46	7	55	81	40	6	22	27	6.55	1.88	5.7	400	3.6	4.4	1.2	0.9	37%	65%	13
Bechler,Steve	02	23	a/a	BAL	8	12	28	0	173	204	90	18	58	76	4.68	1.51	27.4	349	3.0	4.0	1.3	0.9	31%	70%	21
Beck,Rod	03	35	aaa	CHC	1	1	21	4	30	29	2	2	7	22	0.63	1.22	6.0	302	2.2	6.5	3.0	0.6	30%	100%	87
Bedard,Erik	02	24	aa	BAL	6	3	13	0	68	49	18	0	31	54	2.38	1.17	21.5	294	4.1	7.1	1.7	0.0	26%	78%	95
Beech,Matt	02	31	a/a	NYY	6	8	23	0	120	179	81	10	71	74	6.07	2.08	26.1	425	5.3	5.5	1.0	0.7	39%	70%	20
Beirne,Kevin	02	29	aaa	LA	10	3	22	0	125	137	56	11	39	72	4.03	1.41	24.6	333	2.8	5.2	1.8	0.8	31%	73%	47
Belflower,Jay	02	23	aa	ARI	5	3	36	2	55	75	29	5	13	44	4.73	1.59	6.9	361	2.1	7.2	3.4	0.8	39%	71%	81
	03	24	aa	ARI	4	2	53	2	70	120	46	7	23	30	5.96	2.03	6.5	419	2.9	3.9	1.3	0.9	40%	71%	4
Belisle,Matt	02	22	aa	ATL	5	9	26	0	159	181	89	19	37	103	5.03	1.37	26.3	327	2.1	5.8	2.8	1.1	32%	65%	60
	03	23	a/a	CIN	8	12	28	0	171	226	99	11	51	102	5.21	1.62	27.7	365	2.7	5.4	2.0	0.6	36%	67%	50
Belitz,Todd	02	27	aaa	COL	1	3	22	2	44	62	30	8	19	24	6.14	1.84	9.5	395	3.9	4.9	1.3	1.6	35%	70%	-3
	03	28	aaa	TAM	3	1	40	0	50	65	33	3	14	29	5.85	1.57	5.6	358	2.5	5.3	2.2	0.6	36%	61%	53
Bell,Heath	02	25	a/a	NYM	4	4	46	11	69	71	24	2	16	62	3.12	1.26	6.3	308	2.1	8.1	3.9	0.3	34%	74%	125
	03	26	aaa	NYM	2	3	40	3	49	64	33	4	8	44	6.03	1.47	5.4	342	1.5	8.0	5.3	0.8	39%	58%	130
Bell,Rob	02	26	a/a	TEX	6	0	13	0	83	89	44	12	25	49	4.77	1.37	27.4	327	2.7	5.3	2.0	1.3	29%	69%	35
	03	27	aaa	TAM	6	4	12	0	71	88	42	11	16	40	5.34	1.46	26.0	341	2.1	5.0	2.4	1.4	32%	67%	33
Beltran,Francis	03	24	aaa	CHC	6	2	31	4	48	51	18	2	19	29	3.36	1.45	6.8	340	3.5	5.4	1.5	0.4	31%	76%	55
Beltran,Francis	02	22	aa	CHC	2	2	39	23	41	32	15	2	20	38	3.28	1.26	4.4	309	4.4	8.3	1.9	0.4	28%	74%	90
Beltran,Rigo	03	34	aaa	BAL	5	4	31	1	103	95	42	4	43	57	3.68	1.34	14.2	322	3.8	5.0	1.3	0.4	28%	72%	54
Benedetti,John	03	25	aa	TAM	5	5	42	3	65	93	41	8	30	40	5.68	1.89	7.5	402	4.1	5.5	1.3	1.1	37%	71%	17
Benes,Alan	02	31	aaa	CHC	10	9	28	0	113	147	76	17	53	68	6.05	1.77	18.9	386	4.2	5.4	1.3	1.4	34%	68%	12
	03	32	aaa	CHC	7	7	19	0	114	151	82	15	46	67	6.48	1.73	27.9	380	3.7	5.3	1.5	1.2	35%	63%	20
Bennett,Jeff	03	23	a/a	PIT	5	7	42	1	83	85	47	7	35	67	5.10	1.45	8.6	339	3.8	7.3	1.9	0.8	32%	65%	64
Bennett,Steve	03	27	aa	NYM	1	3	28	0	45	89	46	8	40	29	9.12	2.85	9.3	503	7.9	5.8	0.7	1.7	45%	69%	-26
Benoit,Joaquin	02	25	aaa	TEX	8	4	16	0	98	82	44	8	35	89	4.03	1.19	25.2	297	3.2	8.2	2.5	0.7	28%	67%	91
	03	26	aaa	TEX	2	1	6	0	33	35	20	4	11	26	5.34	1.41	23.8	333	3.1	7.1	2.3	1.1	32%	63%	59
Bentz,Chad	03	23	aa	MON	1	4	52	16	84	84	29	4	39	45	3.09	1.46	7.1	341	4.2	4.8	1.1	0.4	29%	79%	44
Bergman,Dusty	02	25	a/a	ANA	6	1	56	4	85	95	43	11	16	53	4.55	1.30	6.4	316	1.7	5.6	3.3	1.2	31%	68%	68
	03	26	a/a	ANA	6	6	51	0	110	144	61	8	35	67	4.99	1.62	9.8	365	2.8	5.4	1.9	0.7	36%	69%	45
Bergman,Sean	03	34	aaa	FLA	8	11	28	0	170	213	96	17	44	86	5.07	1.51	26.9	349	2.3	4.6	2.0	0.9	33%	67%	37
Bernero,Adam	02	26	aaa	DET	2	2	9	0	57	54	12	2	12	44	1.89	1.16	25.8	291	1.9	6.9	3.7	0.3	31%	84%	115
Betancourt,Rafael	03	28	a/a	CLE	0	0	35	17	52	55	15	1	19	59	2.65	1.43	6.5	336	3.3	10.2	3.1	0.2	38%	81%	122
Bevel,Bobby	02	29	a/a	SEA	6	2	51	1	55	84	46	10	26	36	7.50	1.99	5.3	414	4.2	5.9	1.4	1.6	38%	64%	2
	03	30	a/a	CIN	3	3	44	1	58	79	29	5	26	34	4.53	1.80	6.2	390	4.0	5.2	1.3	0.8	36%	76%	28
Beverlin,Jason	02	29	aaa	DET	13	8	27	0	137	154	73	11	46	100	4.79	1.46	22.2	341	3.0	6.6	2.2	0.7	33%	67%	63
Bevis,P.J.	02	22	aa	ARI	5	5	53	11	70	61	24	3	30	64	3.08	1.30	5.6	315	3.8	8.2	2.1	0.4	30%	76%	92
	03	23	a/a	NYM	5	7	50	6	79	64	38	4	32	90	4.32	1.21	6.5	301	3.6	10.2	2.8	0.5	31%	63%	118
Billingsley,Brent	02	27	a/a	MON	4	9	34	1	108	149	92	15	47	69	7.66	1.81	15.0	391	3.9	5.7	1.5	1.2	36%	57%	19
Blackley,Travis	03	21	aa	SEA	17	3	27	0	162	137	55	10	61	135	3.07	1.22	24.9	302	3.4	7.5	2.2	0.6	28%	76%	84
Blank,Matt	02	27	aaa	MON	11	7	31	0	147	164	71	15	58	76	4.35	1.51	21.0	349	3.6	4.7	1.3	0.9	31%	73%	28
	03	28	aaa	SF	2	3	15	0	70	84	33	5	20	42	4.19	1.49	20.6	345	2.6	5.4	2.1	0.7	34%	72%	53
Blanton,Joe	03	23	aa	OAK	3	1	7	1	35	23	6	1	7	26	1.53	0.85	19.0	232	1.8	6.6	3.7	0.3	23%	83%	129
Blevins,Jeremy	02	25	a/a	NYY	5	3	36	1	50	60	24	4	29	34	4.32	1.78	6.5	387	5.2	6.1	1.2	0.7	34%	76%	36
Bochtler,Doug	02	32	aaa	MIN	7	4	34	0	88	80	41	6	45	65	4.19	1.42	11.2	335	4.6	6.6	1.4	0.6	29%	71%	59
	03	33	aaa	FLA	5	3	23	1	53	67	35	8	18	34	5.88	1.60	10.5	362	3.0	5.8	1.9	1.4	34%	66%	27
Bohanon,Brian	02	34	aaa	CIN	3	0	14	0	44	59	27	7	19	19	5.51	1.77	14.8	385	3.9	3.9	1.0	1.4	33%	72%	-6
Bones,Ricky	02	34	aaa	LA	0	2	30	9	30	35	13	2	12	12	3.89	1.56	4.5	356	3.6	3.6	1.0	0.6	31%	76%	23
Bong,Jung	02	22	aa	ATL	7	8	27	2	122	152	51	6	43	90	3.76	1.60	20.4	362	3.2	6.6	2.1	0.4	36%	76%	66
Bonilla,Henry	03	25	aa	MIN	9	7	26	0	142	184	73	9	43	59	4.65	1.60	24.7	363	2.7	3.7	1.4	0.6	34%	71%	27
Bonser,Boof	03	22	a/a	SF	8	12	28	0	158	141	69	10	66	117	3.91	1.31	23.9	317	3.7	6.6	1.8	0.6	28%	70%	67
Bootcheck,Chris	02	24	a/a	ANA	12	10	28	0	174	217	101	18	49	109	5.22	1.53	27.6	352	2.5	5.6	2.2	0.9	34%	67%	48
	03	25	aaa	ANA	8	9	28	0	171	214	91	20	41	70	4.79	1.49	27.0	346	2.2	3.7	1.7	1.1	32%	70%	21
Borkowski,Dave	03	27	aa	BAL	6	8	30	0	128	180	67	13	28	53	4.68	1.62	19.4	365	1.9	3.7	1.9	0.9	35%	72%	26
Borland,Toby	02	33	aaa	FLA	5	2	56	14	70	59	23	2	29	63	2.96	1.26	5.2	308	3.7	8.1	2.2	0.3	30%	76%	97
Borrell,Danny	02	24	aa	NYY	9	4	21	0	128	138	42	6	41	79	2.95	1.40	26.3	331	2.9	5.6	1.9	0.4	32%	79%	62
	03	25	aaa	NYY	4	2	10	0	55	63	22	5	22	26	3.59	1.54	24.6	354	3.6	4.2	1.2	0.8	31%	79%	25
Bost,Heath	02	28	aaa	OAK	1	5	52	12	78	73	29	7	18	56	3.35	1.17	6.1	293	2.1	6.5	3.1	0.8	29%	74%	86
Bottalico,Ricky	03	34	aaa	ARI	2	2	31	0	39	46	20	5	16	24	4.60	1.59	5.7	360	3.6	5.5	1.5	1.2	32%	74%	25
Bouknight,Kip	03	25	aa	COL	10	7	26	0	158	201	108	28	61	84	6.17	1.66	27.8	370	3.5	4.8	1.4	1.6	32%	66%	3
Bowers,Cedrick	02	25	aaa	TAM	4	3	47	0	69	87	30	10	44	67	3.91	1.90	7.1	402	5.7	8.7	1.5	1.3	38%	83%	40
	03	26	aaa	TAM	4	3	32	2	83	89	54	7	41	67	5.79	1.57	11.7	357	4.5	7.3	1.6	0.8	33%	62%	56
Bowe,Brandon	02	27	aa	FLA	6	4	45	4	75	111	39	7	26	41	4.68	1.83	7.9	393	3.1	4.9	1.6	0.8	38%	75%	25
Bowie,Micah	02	28	aaa	OAK	3	2	46	4	54	43	20	2	23	52	3.32	1.22	4.9	302	3.8	8.6	2.3	0.3	29%	72%	102
Bowles,Brian	02	26	aaa	TOR	4	7	59	14	59	54	27	4	32	45	4.12	1.46	4.4	341	4.9	6.9	1.4	0.6	29%	72%	60
	03	27	aaa	TOR	2	3	41	14	47	59	19	1	23	27	3.62	1.74	5.4	382	4.4	5.1	1.1	0.2	35%	78%	44

					Actual				Major League Equivalents																
PITCHER	Yr	Age	Lev	Org	w	l	g	sv	ip	h	er	hr	bb	k	era	br/ip	bf/g	oob	ctl	dom	cmd	hr/9	h%	s%	bpv
Boyd,Jason	02	30	aaa	SD	1	1	28	5	42	38	12	5	18	28	2.57	1.33	6.4	321	3.9	6.0	1.6	1.1	27%	86%	44
Braswell,Bryan	02	27	aa	NYM	3	1	24	1	34	63	31	1	13	13	8.18	2.23	7.3	441	3.4	3.4	1.0	0.3	43%	60%	11
Brazelton,Dewon	02	22	a/a	TAM	6	9	27	0	151	155	67	8	70	97	3.99	1.49	24.7	346	4.2	5.8	1.4	0.5	31%	73%	52
	03	23	a/a	TAM	4	2	7	0	36	37	20	1	20	20	4.99	1.58	23.2	359	5.0	5.0	1.0	0.2	31%	66%	46
Brea,Lesli	02	24	aaa	BAL	3	7	60	3	86	91	37	4	37	63	3.86	1.48	6.3	345	3.9	6.6	1.7	0.4	33%	73%	65
Brewington,Jamie	02	31	aaa	BOS	5	6	18	0	91	105	59	19	38	49	5.83	1.57	22.7	358	3.8	4.8	1.3	1.9	29%	68%	-2
Bridges,Donnie	02	24	aa	FLA	4	8	20	0	78	103	75	7	62	47	8.63	2.11	19.7	428	7.1	5.4	0.8	0.8	36%	57%	17
	03	25	aa	FLA	10	2	31	0	134	102	54	6	78	93	3.60	1.34	18.4	322	5.2	6.2	1.2	0.4	25%	73%	64
Brink,Jim	02	26	aa	TEX	7	5	42	0	85	141	72	17	24	31	7.61	1.94	9.9	407	2.5	3.3	1.3	1.8	37%	63%	-24
Brittan,Corey	02	28	aaa	COL	3	6	35	0	97	144	76	21	44	58	7.04	1.94	13.5	407	4.1	5.4	1.3	1.9	36%	67%	-11
	03	29	aaa	DET	5	5	44	1	62	94	37	3	24	20	5.29	1.88	6.8	401	3.4	2.8	0.8	0.5	37%	71%	7
Brohawn,Troy	02	30	aaa	SF	3	3	56	1	69	87	35	7	22	43	4.57	1.58	5.5	359	2.9	5.6	2.0	0.9	35%	73%	42
Brooks,Frank	03	25	a/a	PIT	5	4	51	9	89	80	34	9	24	79	3.40	1.17	7.1	293	2.4	8.0	3.3	1.0	29%	74%	95
Brown,Derek	02	26	aa	BAL	3	6	41	0	87	148	64	11	29	39	6.62	2.03	10.5	419	3.0	4.0	1.3	1.1	40%	68%	-0
Brown,Elliot	02	27	aa	SF	8	4	25	0	111	173	72	6	39	27	5.83	1.91	21.5	403	3.2	2.2	0.7	0.5	37%	68%	-1
	03	28	a/a	SF	4	5	16	0	60	82	46	6	21	14	6.86	1.72	17.5	379	3.2	2.0	0.6	0.9	33%	59%	-10
Brown,Eric	03	25	a/a	CHC	6	1	47	1	54	73	26	2	16	40	4.28	1.65	5.3	370	2.7	6.6	2.4	0.3	39%	73%	72
Brown,Jamie	02	26	aa	CLE	9	5	18	0	103	129	47	7	20	56	4.10	1.44	25.0	339	1.7	4.9	2.8	0.6	34%	72%	65
	03	27	aaa	BOS	8	5	31	1	113	102	48	5	24	53	3.86	1.11	14.7	283	1.9	4.2	2.2	0.4	27%	64%	68
Bruback,Matt	02	24	aa	CHC	9	7	28	0	174	187	77	10	51	135	3.98	1.37	26.6	327	2.6	7.0	2.6	0.5	33%	71%	83
	03	25	aaa	SD	10	10	26	0	157	163	76	14	47	93	4.35	1.34	25.7	322	2.7	5.3	2.0	0.8	30%	68%	52
Brueggemann,Dean	02	27	aa	COL	0	3	34	0	51	84	62	7	37	27	10.90	2.36	8.0	456	6.5	4.7	0.7	1.2	40%	52%	-10
Brunette,Justin	02	27	a/a	NYM	3	2	48	2	81	102	46	5	24	33	5.11	1.56	7.6	356	2.7	3.7	1.4	0.6	33%	66%	29
Brunet,Mike	03	27	aa	ANA	6	8	32	0	126	178	95	22	49	64	6.80	1.80	18.6	390	3.5	4.6	1.3	1.6	35%	64%	-2
Bruney,Brian	03	22	a/a	ARI	3	3	60	26	63	56	21	1	28	56	2.99	1.33	4.5	320	3.9	7.9	2.0	0.1	31%	76%	94
Bruso,Greg	03	23	aa	MIL	6	5	13	0	86	98	40	6	18	41	4.20	1.34	28.2	322	1.8	4.3	2.3	0.6	31%	69%	54
Buchholz,Taylor	03	22	aa	PHI	9	11	25	0	144	148	63	14	34	100	3.93	1.26	24.1	309	2.1	6.2	2.9	0.9	30%	71%	76
Bucktrot,Keith	03	23	aa	PHI	3	1	7	0	45	37	14	3	15	26	2.79	1.15	26.3	290	3.0	5.2	1.7	0.6	25%	78%	61
Buddie,Mike	02	32	aaa	MON	4	4	29	2	42	42	26	2	24	14	5.57	1.57	6.5	358	5.1	3.0	0.6	0.4	28%	63%	21
	03	33	aaa	MIL	0	4	18	0	36	40	20	6	13	14	5.00	1.46	8.8	341	3.2	3.6	1.1	1.6	28%	70%	-2
Buglovsky,Chris	03	24	aa	COL	10	10	28	0	158	263	127	18	63	63	7.22	2.06	28.1	422	3.6	3.6	1.0	1.0	39%	65%	-5
Bukvich,Ryan	02	24	a/a	KC	2	1	35	16	48	26	6	0	23	51	1.13	1.02	5.4	266	4.3	9.6	2.2	0.0	24%	88%	128
	03	25	aaa	KC	1	2	34	5	36	45	25	2	24	36	6.28	1.93	5.2	406	6.0	8.9	1.5	0.5	40%	66%	64
Bullard,Jim	03	24	aa	CHW	5	3	53	3	90	132	55	9	46	53	5.46	1.98	8.3	412	4.6	5.3	1.1	0.9	38%	73%	17
Bullinger,Kirk	02	33	aaa	HOU	4	1	55	4	75	78	34	8	13	38	4.07	1.21	5.6	301	1.6	4.6	2.9	1.0	29%	69%	62
	03	34	aaa	HOU	3	3	55	20	65	73	21	4	16	37	2.91	1.36	5.1	325	2.2	5.1	2.3	0.6	32%	80%	62
Bumatay,Mike	03	24	aa	COL	4	1	40	1	55	55	24	7	31	58	3.87	1.55	6.2	355	5.1	9.5	1.9	1.2	33%	79%	65
Bump,Nate	02	26	aa	FLA	7	6	20	0	127	138	61	6	33	62	4.32	1.34	27.1	323	2.3	4.4	1.9	0.4	31%	67%	54
	03	27	aaa	FLA	6	5	15	0	85	98	45	3	24	45	4.79	1.43	24.7	337	2.6	4.7	1.8	0.3	33%	65%	56
Bumstead,Mike	03	26	aa	SD	1	2	37	0	68	85	30	1	32	31	3.94	1.72	8.6	379	4.2	4.1	1.0	0.2	34%	75%	36
Burba,Dave	03	37	aaa	MIL	6	7	14	0	72	100	45	7	22	35	5.64	1.69	23.8	375	2.8	4.4	1.6	0.9	35%	67%	23
Burke,Erick	03	26	aa	TEX	4	4	64	3	59	70	26	5	31	38	4.03	1.71	4.3	378	4.7	5.8	1.2	0.7	34%	77%	37
Burnett,Sean	03	21	aa	PIT	14	6	27	0	159	193	79	2	29	74	4.47	1.39	25.4	331	1.6	4.2	2.6	0.1	34%	65%	72
Burnside,Adrian	02	26	aa	PIT	6	9	32	0	130	152	89	20	70	94	6.15	1.71	18.8	377	4.8	6.5	1.3	1.4	33%	66%	24
	03	27	aa	DET	2	4	15	2	67	107	66	9	29	35	8.79	2.02	22.1	418	3.9	4.7	1.2	1.2	39%	55%	1
Burns,Mike	03	25	aa	HOU	2	13	38	0	105	164	98	20	33	68	8.37	1.88	13.3	400	2.9	5.8	2.0	1.7	39%	56%	11
Bush,David	03	24	aa	TOR	7	3	14	0	81	86	31	4	20	62	3.44	1.30	24.4	315	2.2	6.9	3.2	0.5	33%	73%	96
Bynum,Mike	02	25	a/a	SD	7	2	13	0	74	61	23	6	14	52	2.80	1.01	22.4	264	1.7	6.3	3.7	0.7	26%	75%	105
	03	26	aaa	SD	7	12	24	0	125	139	71	10	58	87	5.09	1.57	23.4	358	4.1	6.3	1.5	0.7	33%	68%	47
Cabrera,Fernando	03	22	aa	CLE	9	4	36	5	109	115	48	10	43	98	3.96	1.45	13.2	340	3.6	8.1	2.3	0.8	33%	74%	74
Cabrera,Jose	03	35	aaa	PHI	3	4	25	1	45	55	18	2	12	28	3.56	1.47	7.9	342	2.3	5.5	2.4	0.4	35%	75%	67
Calero,Kiko	02	28	a/a	KC	8	7	25	0	141	164	76	17	45	90	4.84	1.48	24.9	344	2.9	5.7	2.0	1.1	32%	69%	42
Callaway,Mickey	02	27	aaa	ANA	9	2	17	0	91	91	20	8	21	61	1.98	1.23	22.2	304	2.1	6.0	2.9	0.8	30%	88%	77
	03	28	aaa	TEX	3	0	11	0	38	46	13	1	12	16	3.05	1.52	15.4	351	2.8	3.7	1.3	0.3	33%	79%	39
Cameron,Ryan	02	25	a/a	COL	5	8	38	0	119	107	67	14	58	116	5.06	1.39	13.5	329	4.4	8.8	2.0	1.1	30%	65%	71
	03	26	a/a	BOS	3	7	37	1	108	136	67	8	59	63	5.56	1.80	13.8	390	4.9	5.3	1.1	0.6	35%	68%	29
Cammack,Eric	02	27	a/a	NYM	3	4	47	5	64	72	52	6	63	51	7.30	2.11	6.9	428	8.8	7.2	0.8	0.8	34%	64%	34
	03	28	a/a	HOU	1	2	45	6	61	69	25	6	25	39	3.65	1.54	6.0	354	3.6	5.8	1.6	0.9	32%	79%	41
Campos,Francisco	03	31	aaa	MIL	2	4	8	0	39	65	34	9	13	22	7.75	1.99	24.0	414	2.9	5.0	1.7	2.2	39%	65%	-17
Camp,Shawn	02	27	aaa	PIT	4	1	39	2	58	59	27	5	14	49	4.18	1.26	6.2	308	2.2	7.6	3.5	0.8	32%	68%	99
	03	28	a/a	PIT	0	3	51	0	72	106	59	6	30	53	7.32	1.88	6.8	400	3.7	6.6	1.8	0.7	40%	59%	44
Candelario,Eddie	03	26	aa	NYY	8	5	28	1	93	118	61	11	52	54	5.90	1.82	15.8	393	5.0	5.2	1.0	1.1	34%	69%	15
Cannon,Jon	02	28	a/a	SF	2	5	41	4	67	76	39	6	49	43	5.24	1.87	7.8	398	6.6	5.8	0.9	0.8	32%	72%	28
Capuano,Chris	02	24	aaa	ARI	4	1	6	0	36	33	12	1	10	24	2.99	1.19	24.7	297	2.5	6.0	2.4	0.2	29%	74%	86
	03	25	aaa	ARI	9	5	23	0	142	152	64	10	41	94	4.03	1.36	26.4	325	2.6	6.0	2.3	0.6	32%	71%	66
Caraccioli,Lance	02	25	a/a	CLE	12	5	28	1	164	193	87	10	78	101	4.77	1.65	26.8	369	4.3	5.5	1.3	0.5	34%	70%	42
	03	26	aaa	CLE	4	8	34	2	100	148	77	14	37	70	6.90	1.85	14.1	397	3.4	6.3	1.9	1.3	39%	64%	27
Carlyle,Buddy	03	26	a/a	KC	3	3	17	3	32	29	13	3	8	35	3.54	1.18	7.7	295	2.4	9.9	4.2	0.9	32%	73%	127
Carnes,Matt	02	27	a/a	MIN	11	6	42	1	124	176	97	9	49	63	7.03	1.81	14.0	391	3.6	4.6	1.3	0.7	37%	59%	24
	03	28	a/a	MIN	3	10	31	0	149	240	127	20	46	69	7.66	1.92	23.3	405	2.8	4.2	1.5	1.2	38%	60%	4
Carrasco,Hector	03	34	aaa	BAL	4	2	33	4	44	40	15	3	21	39	3.00	1.38	5.8	329	4.3	7.9	1.9	0.6	30%	80%	75
Carter,Lance	02	28	aaa	TAM	12	2	33	1	132	136	54	18	13	72	3.68	1.13	16.2	286	0.9	4.9	5.5	1.2	28%	73%	112
Carter,Ryan	03	24	aa	PHI	2	7	17	0	75	121	58	7	35	39	6.95	2.08	22.0	424	4.2	4.7	1.1	0.9	40%	66%	9
Casadiego,Gerardo	02	22	aa	MON	1	3	9	0	35	52	32	8	15	21	8.21	1.91	18.8	404	3.8	5.4	1.4	2.1	36%	59%	-12
	03	23	aa	MON	1	4	22	1	61	80	52	11	40	26	7.67	1.97	13.6	411	5.9	3.8	0.7	1.6	32%	62%	-19
Casey,Joe	02	24	a/a	TOR	1	1	29	1	35	47	28	5	27	10	7.18	2.11	6.1	428	6.9	2.6	0.4	1.3	32%	67%	-23
Cash,David	02	23	aa	SF	5	8	34	5	109	106	42	7	38	73	3.46	1.32	13.6	319	3.1	6.0	1.9	0.6	30%	74%	64
	03	24	aa	CHC	2	5	50	11	59	80	45	9	31	67	6.88	1.87	5.7	398	4.6	10.1	2.2	1.4	41%	65%	55
Cassidy,Scott	03	28	aaa	TOR	3	4	57	4	80	96	41	4	51	60	4.59	1.82	6.7	393	5.7	6.8	1.2	0.5	36%	74%	48
Castellanos,Hugo	02	22	a/a	TOR	3	5	52	18	57	55	39	6	29	31	6.15	1.47	4.8	343	4.6	4.9	1.1	0.9	27%	58%	29
	03	23	aa	TOR	3	7	21	0	33	48	24	3	13	23	6.45	1.87	7.5	399	3.6	6.3	1.7	0.8	39%	65%	37
Castillo,Carlos	03	28	a/a	CHW	3	2	11	0	40	67	45	11	16	21	10.01	2.08	18.3	424	3.7	4.8	1.3	2.4	38%	53%	-33

Major League Equivalent Statistics

					Actual				Major League Equivalents																
PITCHER	Yr	Age	Lev	Org	w	l	g	sv	ip	h	er	hr	bb	k	era	br/ip	bf/g	oob	ctl	dom	cmd	hr/9	h%	s%	bpv
Castillo,Frank	03	35	aaa	OAK	5	5	23	0	114	165	69	18	44	59	5.48	1.84	23.6	395	3.5	4.7	1.3	1.4	36%	73%	2
Cercy,Rick	02	26	aa	COL	3	4	47	1	65	93	56	9	51	59	7.75	2.22	7.1	440	7.1	8.2	1.2	1.2	40%	65%	25
Cerda,Jaime	02	24	a/a	NYM	5	1	26	1	52	34	10	0	17	42	1.72	0.98	7.8	257	2.9	7.2	2.5	0.0	24%	80%	114
	03	25	aaa	NYM	3	0	22	0	32	33	7	3	10	29	1.96	1.34	6.2	322	2.8	8.1	2.9	0.8	33%	90%	87
Cerros,Juan	02	26	a/a	NYM	1	3	28	2	40	49	18	2	12	20	4.03	1.52	6.4	350	2.7	4.5	1.7	0.4	33%	73%	45
Cervantes,Chris	02	24	aa	ARI	6	4	33	0	121	151	54	7	23	72	4.01	1.44	16.0	337	1.7	5.3	3.1	0.5	35%	72%	77
	03	25	aaa	ARI	3	4	11	1	42	46	22	3	23	24	4.70	1.64	17.4	368	4.9	5.1	1.0	0.6	31%	71%	34
Chacin,Gustavo	02	22	aa	TOR	6	5	35	1	119	145	70	12	56	59	5.29	1.69	15.7	374	4.2	4.5	1.1	0.9	32%	69%	18
	03	23	aa	TOR	3	4	46	2	69	89	41	1	29	48	5.34	1.71	7.0	377	3.8	6.3	1.7	0.1	37%	66%	62
Chantres,Carlos	02	27	a/a	TAM	9	10	28	0	147	208	101	21	80	60	6.18	1.96	25.6	410	4.9	3.7	0.8	1.3	34%	70%	-11
Chapman,Jake	03	30	aaa	BOS	6	1	35	0	57	100	37	7	29	31	5.88	2.27	8.5	445	4.6	4.8	1.0	1.1	42%	75%	-0
Chavez,Wilton	02	24	aa	CHC	8	5	18	0	103	118	56	8	42	72	4.89	1.55	25.6	355	3.7	6.3	1.7	0.7	33%	68%	51
	03	25	a/a	CHC	11	7	28	0	148	179	86	20	58	107	5.25	1.60	23.9	362	3.5	6.5	1.9	1.2	34%	69%	38
Chen,Bruce	03	26	aaa	BOS	5	5	16	1	85	97	53	13	16	60	5.57	1.33	22.6	321	1.7	6.4	3.6	1.4	32%	61%	71
Chiasson,Scott	02	25	a/a	CHC	1	4	30	7	31	44	29	9	14	26	8.39	1.86	5.0	398	4.1	7.5	1.9	2.6	36%	59%	-4
Chiavacci,Ron	02	25	aa	MON	6	9	35	0	111	132	70	8	70	75	5.67	1.82	15.0	392	5.7	6.1	1.1	0.6	34%	68%	37
	03	26	a/a	MON	5	10	31	0	137	187	108	18	63	89	7.07	1.82	21.0	393	4.2	5.8	1.4	1.2	36%	61%	21
Childers,Jason	02	28	a/a	MIL	3	4	40	0	79	108	49	10	49	38	5.58	1.98	9.7	413	5.6	4.3	0.8	1.1	35%	73%	-1
	03	29	aaa	MIL	5	4	46	10	63	63	23	8	23	36	3.23	1.37	5.9	326	3.2	5.2	1.6	1.1	28%	81%	36
Childers,Matt	02	24	a/a	MIL	2	5	37	12	86	123	54	8	30	52	5.65	1.78	10.9	387	3.1	5.4	1.7	0.8	38%	68%	33
	03	25	a/a	MIL	4	0	47	8	92	100	33	5	32	51	3.22	1.43	8.5	337	3.1	5.0	1.6	0.5	31%	78%	50
Childress,Daylan	03	25	aa	CIN	2	4	9	0	48	70	51	6	29	27	9.58	2.06	26.6	422	5.4	5.1	0.9	1.0	37%	51%	7
Choate,Randy	02	27	aaa	NYY	3	2	31	1	36	28	8	0	16	27	1.99	1.22	4.8	301	4.0	6.7	1.7	0.0	27%	82%	89
	03	28	aaa	NYY	3	5	54	1	71	92	40	5	26	45	5.04	1.66	6.0	371	3.3	5.7	1.7	0.7	36%	70%	43
Cho,Jin Ho	02	27	aaa	BOS	3	6	20	2	54	91	44	11	13	16	7.32	1.92	13.1	405	2.2	2.7	1.2	1.8	37%	65%	-31
Christensen,Ben	02	25	aa	CHC	2	6	12	0	64	88	59	7	38	30	8.30	1.97	26.1	411	5.3	4.2	0.8	1.0	35%	56%	3
Chrysler,Clint	02	27	aa	PIT	3	2	51	3	56	72	34	8	23	19	5.44	1.69	5.1	375	3.7	3.0	0.8	1.3	31%	70%	-9
Chulk,Vinny	02	24	a/a	TOR	13	6	27	1	156	155	61	12	57	95	3.51	1.36	24.7	325	3.3	5.5	1.7	0.7	29%	76%	51
	03	25	aaa	TOR	8	10	23	0	119	140	73	17	47	79	5.52	1.57	23.3	358	3.6	6.0	1.7	1.3	32%	67%	30
Clark,Jeff	02	22	aa	SF	2	2	6	0	35	49	22	4	2	17	5.63	1.45	25.6	339	0.5	4.3	8.5	1.0	35%	62%	164
	03	23	aa	SF	2	4	7	0	37	51	22	3	5	26	5.25	1.50	23.4	347	1.3	6.4	5.1	0.8	38%	65%	114
Claussen,Brandon	02	23	aaa	NYY	2	8	15	0	93	93	38	4	44	65	3.67	1.47	27.3	343	4.3	6.3	1.5	0.4	31%	74%	61
	03	24	aaa	CIN	2	2	14	0	84	82	44	9	24	47	4.71	1.26	25.1	309	2.6	5.0	2.0	1.0	28%	64%	47
Clontz,Brad	03	32	aaa	COL	3	2	57	30	55	68	29	6	27	52	4.81	1.74	4.5	381	4.5	8.5	1.9	1.0	38%	74%	56
Cloude,Ken	02	28	aaa	SEA	9	4	15	0	92	87	31	9	21	42	3.03	1.17	25.1	293	2.0	4.1	2.0	0.9	26%	78%	46
	03	29	aaa	SEA	4	4	21	0	75	110	67	16	41	33	7.98	2.00	17.6	415	4.9	3.9	0.8	1.9	34%	62%	-29
Coco,Pasqual	02	25	aaa	TOR	4	9	30	0	141	165	92	18	56	84	5.87	1.57	21.1	357	3.6	5.4	1.5	1.1	32%	64%	27
	03	26	aaa	MIL	10	9	27	0	146	204	103	21	48	81	6.35	1.73	25.2	380	3.0	5.0	1.7	1.3	36%	64%	18
Cogan,Tony	02	26	aa	KC	4	6	17	0	90	123	52	6	29	46	5.19	1.69	24.4	374	2.9	4.6	1.6	0.6	36%	68%	34
Cole,Joey	02	25	a/a	NYM	2	4	11	0	48	69	35	6	24	24	6.55	1.93	21.2	407	4.5	4.5	1.0	1.1	36%	67%	3
	03	26	aa	NYM	8	7	25	0	113	152	77	10	67	57	6.12	1.93	22.0	406	5.3	4.5	0.8	0.8	35%	68%	12
Collazo,William	02	23	aa	ATL	4	2	51	4	72	78	32	7	26	62	3.99	1.44	6.2	338	3.2	7.7	2.4	0.9	33%	74%	71
	03	24	aa	ATL	6	2	39	0	46	52	27	4	23	28	5.22	1.61	5.4	363	4.4	5.5	1.2	0.8	32%	68%	35
Collins,Pat	02	25	aa	MON	3	0	29	7	50	51	13	3	19	41	2.33	1.39	7.5	331	3.4	7.4	2.2	0.5	32%	85%	77
	03	26	aa	STL	3	5	30	0	65	88	61	3	53	36	8.44	2.16	11.0	434	7.4	5.0	0.7	0.5	36%	58%	22
Colon,Jose	02	28	aa	CLE	5	4	46	5	76	102	31	10	10	31	3.67	1.47	7.3	343	1.2	3.7	3.1	1.2	33%	79%	44
Colon,Roman	03	24	aa	ATL	11	3	39	2	107	133	57	12	36	47	4.78	1.57	12.3	358	3.0	3.9	1.3	1.0	32%	71%	17
Colyer,Steve	02	24	aa	LA	5	4	59	21	62	60	31	7	43	57	4.49	1.66	4.8	370	6.2	8.2	1.3	1.0	31%	75%	52
	03	25	aaa	LA	2	3	44	23	47	46	17	1	21	44	3.24	1.42	4.7	335	4.0	8.4	2.1	0.2	34%	76%	94
Condrey,Clay	02	27	aaa	SD	10	4	25	0	133	145	61	11	41	60	4.12	1.40	23.0	331	2.8	4.1	1.5	0.7	30%	71%	33
	03	28	aaa	SD	3	3	11	0	63	72	32	6	12	36	4.51	1.32	24.3	319	1.7	5.2	3.1	0.9	32%	67%	68
Connelly,Steve	03	29	aaa	SF	3	4	38	0	59	112	56	8	24	23	8.53	2.31	8.1	450	3.7	3.5	0.9	1.2	42%	62%	-18
Connolly,Mike	03	21	aa	PIT	7	8	25	0	127	150	67	12	38	77	4.74	1.48	22.4	344	2.7	5.5	2.0	0.8	33%	69%	47
Cook,Aaron	02	24	a/a	COL	11	6	24	0	159	163	53	15	35	79	3.00	1.24	27.6	306	2.0	4.5	2.3	0.8	29%	79%	52
Cook,Andy	02	26	aa	NYM	6	3	30	0	55	78	38	7	24	30	6.22	1.85	8.8	397	3.9	4.9	1.3	1.1	36%	67%	11
Cook,B.R.	02	25	aa	STL	7	13	28	0	163	209	99	16	65	96	5.46	1.68	26.8	373	3.6	5.3	1.5	0.9	35%	68%	30
	03	26	a/a	STL	1	1	42	1	52	69	41	6	36	26	7.08	2.02	6.1	417	6.2	4.4	0.7	1.1	34%	65%	1
Cooper,Brian	02	28	aaa	TOR	9	9	27	0	155	212	111	22	48	57	6.44	1.68	26.4	373	2.8	3.3	1.2	1.3	33%	63%	-2
	03	29	aaa	CHW	15	9	28	0	174	254	110	26	40	87	5.68	1.69	28.6	374	2.0	4.5	2.2	1.4	36%	69%	21
Corcoran,Tim	02	24	aa	BAL	0	5	35	1	49	72	24	5	31	39	4.41	2.10	7.0	427	5.7	7.2	1.3	0.9	40%	81%	30
	03	25	aa	BAL	4	1	26	3	44	49	30	1	22	26	6.14	1.62	7.7	364	4.5	5.3	1.2	0.2	33%	59%	50
Cordova,Jorge	02	25	a/a	CIN	5	2	37	13	40	44	21	4	13	26	4.71	1.42	4.7	335	2.9	5.8	2.0	0.9	31%	68%	50
	03	26	aa	DET	1	1	30	0	47	60	32	7	17	24	6.14	1.62	7.1	365	3.2	4.6	1.5	1.3	33%	63%	15
Corey,Bryan	02	29	aaa	LA	5	4	37	1	53	84	25	4	17	27	4.23	1.90	6.9	402	2.9	4.6	1.6	0.7	39%	78%	25
	03	30	aaa	LA	4	5	60	3	91	108	33	8	30	37	3.26	1.51	6.7	349	2.9	3.7	1.3	0.8	31%	81%	23
Corey,Mark	03	29	aaa	PIT	1	3	46	30	45	47	31	6	19	50	6.21	1.47	4.3	343	3.9	10.0	2.6	1.3	35%	59%	78
Cormier,Lance	03	23	a/a	ARI	3	4	14	0	69	95	42	4	26	33	5.48	1.75	23.0	383	3.4	4.3	1.3	0.5	36%	68%	28
Cornejo,Nate	02	23	aaa	DET	9	8	21	0	132	188	80	10	29	78	5.45	1.64	28.7	368	2.0	5.3	2.7	0.7	38%	66%	57
Correa,Cristobal	02	23	aa	STL	6	9	26	0	137	158	78	9	56	69	5.12	1.56	23.6	356	3.7	4.5	1.2	0.6	32%	66%	34
Correia,Kevin	03	23	a/a	SF	6	7	19	0	105	102	43	5	30	81	3.68	1.26	23.1	308	2.6	6.9	2.7	0.4	31%	70%	91
Cotts,Neal	03	24	aa	CHW	9	7	21	0	108	86	38	3	62	117	3.18	1.36	22.1	326	5.1	9.8	1.9	0.3	31%	76%	103
Coughenour,Jory	02	24	aa	HOU	3	2	32	3	61	86	31	2	28	38	4.57	1.87	9.1	398	4.1	5.6	1.4	0.3	38%	74%	43
	03	25	aa	HOU	2	5	34	3	53	91	58	4	33	26	9.79	2.34	8.2	454	5.6	4.4	0.8	0.8	41%	56%	1
Coward,Chad	02	24	aa	TAM	9	4	37	0	87	100	38	7	36	48	3.92	1.56	10.6	356	3.7	5.0	1.3	0.7	32%	76%	35
Cox,Ryan	02	26	aa	SF	7	9	27	0	145	201	87	13	33	56	5.39	1.61	24.4	364	2.0	3.5	1.7	0.8	35%	67%	23
	03	27	aa	SF	1	3	26	0	60	110	62	6	30	27	9.29	2.33	12.1	453	4.5	4.0	0.9	0.9	42%	58%	-5
Cozier,Vance	02	25	aa	SF	3	7	21	0	67	104	56	8	40	19	7.50	2.14	16.2	432	5.4	2.5	0.5	1.1	36%	65%	-21
	03	26	aa	SF	6	7	26	0	100	145	57	5	39	26	5.17	1.84	18.3	395	3.5	2.3	0.7	0.4	35%	71%	4
Crabtree,Robbie	02	30	aaa	TOR	4	8	56	2	84	100	74	8	38	49	7.92	1.64	6.8	368	4.1	5.2	1.3	0.9	33%	49%	30
Crain,Jesse	03	22	a/a	MIN	4	2	45	19	65	44	15	0	21	75	2.08	1.00	5.7	262	2.9	10.4	3.6	0.0	29%	77%	155
Crawford,Paxton	02	25	a/a	BOS	3	3	10	0	53	76	36	9	21	23	6.11	1.83	25.2	394	3.6	3.9	1.1	1.5	35%	69%	-10
Cressend,Jack	03	28	a/a	CLE	3	0	16	1	30	31	4	0	11	16	1.05	1.36	8.1	326	3.2	4.8	1.5	0.0	31%	91%	64

					Actual				Major League Equivalents																
PITCHER	Yr	Age	Lev	Org	w	l	g	sv	ip	h	er	hr	bb	k	era	br/ip	bf/g	oob	ctl	dom	cmd	hr/9	h%	s%	bpv
Cromer,Jason	03	23	aa	TAM	1	5	6	0	34	47	30	4	15	14	7.89	1.81	27.0	391	3.9	3.7	0.9	1.1	34%	55%	1
Croushore,Rick	02	32	aaa	TAM	5	4	36	7	64	67	32	6	28	49	4.50	1.48	7.8	345	3.9	6.9	1.8	0.8	32%	71%	55
Crouthers,Dave	03	24	aa	BAL	4	2	9	0	45	45	26	5	20	24	5.15	1.44	21.8	339	3.9	4.9	1.2	1.0	28%	66%	28
Crowell,Jim	03	29	aaa	PHI	0	8	54	9	54	80	34	7	27	34	5.66	1.99	4.9	413	4.6	5.6	1.2	1.1	38%	73%	14
Cruceta,Francisco	03	22	aa	CLE	13	9	27	0	163	169	75	9	71	115	4.14	1.47	26.5	343	3.9	6.3	1.6	0.5	32%	71%	60
Crudale,Mike	03	27	aaa	MON	5	5	34	6	31	44	26	9	12	19	7.43	1.82	4.3	392	3.6	5.6	1.6	2.7	34%	65%	-24
Crumpton,Chuck	02	26	a/a	MON	2	5	40	3	84	116	52	5	29	34	5.56	1.72	9.8	379	3.1	3.6	1.2	0.5	35%	66%	21
	03	27	a/a	MON	6	7	45	7	110	139	62	9	48	37	5.09	1.70	11.3	376	3.9	3.0	0.8	0.7	32%	70%	7
Cruz,Juan	03	25	aaa	CHC	4	0	9	0	50	41	13	1	11	41	2.33	1.04	22.1	269	2.0	7.4	3.7	0.2	28%	76%	128
Cubillan,Darwin	02	30	aaa	MON	1	1	29	6	36	36	20	5	23	27	5.00	1.64	5.7	368	5.8	6.8	1.2	1.3	29%	72%	32
	03	29	aaa	BAL	5	6	65	20	73	72	35	9	37	62	4.37	1.49	5.0	345	4.5	7.7	1.7	1.1	31%	73%	55
Cueto,Jose	02	26	aa	FLA	1	4	9	0	43	43	24	6	24	36	5.00	1.55	21.5	355	5.0	7.5	1.5	1.3	30%	70%	43
	03	27	aa	FLA	5	3	35	1	58	67	30	2	45	32	4.66	1.93	8.1	406	6.9	5.0	0.7	0.4	33%	75%	32
Cullen,Ryan	03	24	aa	OAK	2	1	30	2	45	61	20	1	13	20	3.91	1.65	6.9	369	2.7	4.1	1.5	0.2	36%	75%	42
Cumberland,Chris	02	30	a/a	TOR	0	5	37	1	45	70	29	1	27	18	5.77	2.15	6.2	432	5.4	3.6	0.7	0.2	39%	71%	15
Cummings,Jeremy	02	26	aa	STL	4	3	14	0	78	83	40	7	24	42	4.62	1.37	23.9	327	2.8	4.8	1.8	0.8	30%	67%	43
	03	27	a/a	STL	15	9	28	0	162	189	107	30	50	83	5.93	1.47	25.4	343	2.8	4.6	1.7	1.7	30%	63%	10
Cummings,Ryan	02	26	a/a	ANA	7	5	43	1	62	82	32	8	30	26	4.64	1.80	6.8	390	4.3	3.8	0.9	1.2	33%	77%	-1
	03	27	a/a	ANA	2	8	49	0	79	140	70	8	33	21	7.99	2.20	8.2	438	3.8	2.4	0.6	0.9	40%	63%	-21
Cunnane,Will	02	28	aaa	CHC	4	1	43	2	73	73	18	3	23	57	2.21	1.31	7.2	317	2.8	7.0	2.5	0.4	32%	84%	87
	03	29	aaa	ATL	1	1	27	2	37	35	5	0	11	27	1.33	1.24	5.7	306	2.7	6.6	2.5	0.0	31%	88%	98
Currier,Rik	03	25	aaa	NYY	1	0	7	0	34	28	13	1	17	26	3.51	1.30	20.6	315	4.4	6.9	1.6	0.3	27%	72%	77
Curtis,Daniel	02	23	aa	ATL	4	2	10	0	54	68	34	7	17	24	5.66	1.57	24.3	358	2.8	4.0	1.4	1.2	32%	65%	13
	03	24	aa	ATL	6	4	17	0	78	90	35	5	15	39	4.04	1.35	19.6	323	1.8	4.5	2.5	0.6	32%	70%	60
Cyr,Eric	02	24	a/a	SD	4	6	23	0	86	85	36	6	45	64	3.76	1.51	16.6	348	4.7	6.7	1.4	0.6	31%	76%	56
	03	25	aa	ANA	6	6	21	0	105	118	78	12	54	64	6.67	1.63	22.8	367	4.6	5.5	1.2	1.0	31%	59%	27
D'Amico,Jeff	02	28	aaa	CIN	6	10	27	1	118	148	75	19	37	58	5.72	1.57	19.6	357	2.8	4.4	1.6	1.4	32%	66%	11
Daigle,Casey	02	22	aa	ARI	3	2	7	0	44	51	18	5	8	24	3.67	1.34	26.8	322	1.6	4.9	3.0	1.0	31%	76%	60
	03	23	aa	ARI	11	11	29	0	176	241	101	10	48	101	5.16	1.64	27.7	368	2.5	5.2	2.1	0.5	37%	67%	51
Darensbourg,Vic	03	33	aaa	MON	3	3	31	0	36	41	14	1	12	21	3.41	1.46	5.1	341	2.9	5.2	1.8	0.3	33%	76%	60
Darnell,Paul	02	26	a/a	CIN	3	4	39	0	68	73	32	11	32	46	4.23	1.54	7.8	353	4.2	6.1	1.4	1.5	30%	78%	24
Davey,Tom	02	29	aaa	SD	2	1	22	4	32	20	8	1	13	17	2.25	1.03	5.7	268	3.7	4.8	1.3	0.3	21%	78%	67
Davis,Doug	02	27	aaa	TEX	4	3	9	0	61	81	40	7	11	40	5.89	1.51	30.0	348	1.6	5.9	3.6	1.0	36%	61%	73
	03	28	a/a	MIL	5	2	10	0	68	88	39	7	16	31	5.13	1.54	30.4	353	2.2	4.0	1.9	0.9	33%	67%	29
Davis,Jason	02	22	aa	CLE	6	2	10	0	59	75	30	3	17	39	4.58	1.56	26.4	356	2.6	5.9	2.3	0.5	36%	70%	64
Davis,Kane	03	28	aaa	CHC	2	1	22	2	30	25	10	3	13	20	2.88	1.25	5.7	306	3.8	5.8	1.5	1.0	25%	81%	49
Davis,Lance	02	26	a/a	CIN	4	10	23	0	127	183	71	17	34	59	5.03	1.71	25.6	377	2.4	4.2	1.7	1.2	36%	73%	14
	03	27	aaa	CIN	8	9	26	0	138	208	97	20	44	50	6.31	1.83	25.2	393	2.9	3.3	1.1	1.3	36%	67%	-9
Dawley,Joey	02	31	aaa	ATL	9	7	24	0	140	137	53	12	38	108	3.40	1.25	24.3	307	2.4	6.9	2.8	0.8	30%	75%	83
	03	32	aaa	ATL	3	5	46	23	56	61	31	5	25	59	4.89	1.54	5.4	353	4.0	9.4	2.3	0.8	36%	69%	81
Dawson,Layne	03	24	aa	PHI	1	9	14	0	74	117	71	13	29	38	8.58	1.98	25.9	412	3.6	4.6	1.3	1.5	38%	57%	-6
Day,Zach	02	24	aaa	MON	5	6	17	0	90	91	46	6	33	58	4.60	1.38	22.8	328	3.3	5.8	1.8	0.6	30%	66%	57
De La Rosa,Jorge	02	22	aa	BOS	3	7	35	6	51	62	35	1	23	25	6.18	1.67	6.7	371	4.1	4.4	1.1	0.2	34%	60%	40
	03	23	a/a	BOS	7	5	27	1	123	133	52	6	50	101	3.80	1.49	20.1	345	3.7	7.4	2.0	0.4	34%	74%	75
De Los Santos,Luis	02	25	aaa	TAM	9	2	24	0	115	122	39	9	22	58	3.05	1.25	20.0	307	1.7	4.5	2.6	0.7	30%	78%	63
De Paula,Jorge	03	25	aaa	NYY	10	11	27	0	167	192	98	26	57	108	5.28	1.49	27.3	346	3.1	5.8	1.9	1.4	31%	68%	31
Deago,Roger	03	26	aa	SD	8	7	26	0	118	166	72	10	60	78	5.52	1.91	21.9	404	4.6	6.0	1.3	0.8	38%	71%	30
DeHart,Blair	02	24	aa	SD	2	3	7	0	32	53	20	2	9	24	5.61	1.93	22.2	406	2.5	6.7	2.7	0.6	43%	70%	62
Dehart,Casey	03	26	aa	CIN	3	2	41	2	74	102	46	3	48	39	5.53	2.02	8.9	418	5.8	4.7	0.8	0.4	37%	71%	24
	02	25	aa	CIN	1	3	21	1	30	38	26	4	15	19	7.77	1.76	6.7	384	4.5	5.7	1.3	1.2	34%	55%	19
DeHart,Rick	02	33	aaa	KC	1	0	49	1	57	66	32	5	21	36	5.03	1.52	5.2	350	3.3	5.7	1.7	0.8	33%	67%	45
Denney,Kyle	02	25	aa	CLE	3	1	6	0	34	30	9	3	6	25	2.37	1.05	22.6	272	1.6	6.6	4.2	0.8	27%	82%	112
	03	26	a/a	CLE	9	4	24	0	134	176	68	16	40	87	4.55	1.61	25.3	363	2.7	5.9	2.2	1.0	35%	74%	43
DePaula,Julio	02	23	aa	NYY	14	6	27	0	175	204	104	16	66	108	5.35	1.54	28.9	354	3.4	5.6	1.6	0.8	33%	65%	41
DePaula,Sean	02	29	aaa	CLE	2	3	34	9	57	71	37	9	20	43	5.84	1.60	7.6	361	3.2	6.8	2.2	1.4	34%	66%	38
Dequin,Benji	03	23	aa	MON	2	4	22	0	40	55	25	7	20	35	5.55	1.85	8.7	396	4.4	7.8	1.8	1.6	38%	74%	27
Devey,Phil	02	25	a/a	LA	5	5	34	0	122	178	65	9	41	45	4.79	1.79	16.9	389	3.0	3.3	1.1	0.7	36%	73%	11
Diaz,Felix	02	22	aa	SF	7	5	19	0	91	86	33	4	29	67	3.26	1.26	20.0	309	2.9	6.6	2.3	0.4	30%	74%	83
	03	23	aaa	CHW	5	7	27	0	115	145	66	16	34	75	5.16	1.55	19.1	355	2.7	5.9	2.2	1.3	34%	69%	39
Dickey,R.A.	02	28	aaa	TEX	8	7	37	0	154	203	82	8	46	90	4.79	1.62	18.9	364	2.7	5.3	2.0	0.5	36%	69%	51
Dickson,Jason	02	30	aaa	TAM	3	4	9	0	47	69	41	11	26	25	7.83	2.02	25.8	417	5.0	4.8	1.0	2.1	35%	64%	-26
DiFelice,Mark	03	27	aa	COL	7	6	21	0	113	182	82	33	29	54	6.51	1.86	25.8	398	2.3	4.3	1.9	2.6	36%	72%	-29
Diggins,Ben	02	23	aa	MIL	2	1	7	0	37	31	10	0	15	28	2.42	1.24	22.1	305	3.6	6.8	1.9	0.0	29%	78%	90
	03	24	aa	MIL	3	2	8	0	45	51	17	2	18	26	3.35	1.51	25.1	349	3.6	5.1	1.4	0.4	32%	78%	48
Dillinger,John	02	29	a/a	NYY	5	2	22	0	97	172	94	18	40	55	8.70	2.18	22.5	436	3.7	5.1	1.4	1.7	41%	61%	-11
Dinardo,Lenny	03	24	aa	NYM	1	3	7	0	40	40	18	3	14	29	4.03	1.34	24.4	322	3.1	6.4	2.1	0.7	30%	71%	65
Dittfurth,Ryan	02	23	aa	TEX	1	3	9	0	41	51	35	1	24	28	7.66	1.82	21.7	393	5.3	6.1	1.2	0.2	36%	54%	50
Dohmann,Scott	03	26	aa	COL	9	4	50	4	93	131	69	20	33	80	6.65	1.76	8.7	385	3.2	7.7	2.4	1.9	38%	66%	29
Dominguez,Juan	03	21	a/a	TEX	6	0	12	0	73	57	30	4	23	62	3.63	1.09	24.5	280	2.8	7.6	2.7	0.5	27%	66%	101
Donaldson,Bo	02	28	a/a	NYY	5	5	46	0	106	128	62	11	38	71	5.26	1.57	10.3	357	3.2	6.0	1.9	0.9	34%	67%	44
Donnelly,Brendan	02	31	aaa	ANA	4	0	25	6	33	31	15	5	11	34	4.07	1.27	5.6	310	3.0	9.2	3.1	1.4	30%	73%	86
Dotel,Melido	03	26	aa	COL	4	6	49	1	66	102	55	11	44	44	7.50	2.21	6.9	439	5.9	6.0	1.0	1.6	39%	68%	-4
Dougherty,Jim	02	35	a/a	PIT	3	4	40	4	55	68	39	7	26	32	6.37	1.71	6.4	377	4.2	5.2	1.2	1.1	33%	63%	18
Douglass,Ryan	03	25	aa	KC	0	3	28	1	66	120	49	12	17	30	6.75	2.07	11.8	424	2.3	4.1	1.8	1.6	41%	70%	-6
Douglass,Sean	02	23	aaa	BAL	4	6	14	0	66	74	41	4	35	60	5.57	1.65	21.6	369	4.8	8.2	1.7	0.5	36%	65%	68
	03	24	aaa	BAL	10	8	27	0	143	167	69	8	58	103	4.34	1.57	23.8	358	3.7	6.5	1.8	0.5	35%	72%	59
Downs,Scott	03	28	aaa	MON	8	9	21	0	121	136	66	14	39	43	4.92	1.44	25.2	338	2.9	3.2	1.1	1.0	29%	67%	11
Drese,Ryan	03	28	a/a	TEX	9	7	22	0	131	211	103	14	46	57	7.11	1.97	29.1	411	3.2	3.9	1.2	0.9	39%	63%	5
Drew,Tim	02	24	aaa	MON	14	7	28	0	181	206	81	13	48	61	4.03	1.40	27.9	332	2.4	3.0	1.3	0.6	30%	72%	24
	03	25	aaa	MON	5	9	27	2	93	139	82	10	33	45	7.91	1.86	16.5	397	3.2	4.3	1.3	1.0	37%	56%	12
Driskill,Travis	03	32	aaa	BAL	4	0	9	0	50	57	21	11	6	29	3.77	1.26	23.3	309	1.1	5.3	4.7	1.9	29%	80%	72

Major League Equivalent Statistics

					Actual				Major League Equivalents																
PITCHER	Yr	Age	Lev	Org	w	l	g	sv	ip	h	er	hr	bb	k	era	br/ip	bf/g	oob	ctl	dom	cmd	hr/9	h%	s%	bpv
Drumright,Mike	02	28	aaa	BAL	6	8	30	0	150	189	85	12	54	86	5.10	1.62	22.7	365	3.2	5.2	1.6	0.7	34%	68%	38
	03	29	a/a	BAL	6	6	29	0	126	187	105	16	63	78	7.49	1.98	21.3	413	4.5	5.6	1.2	1.1	38%	62%	13
Dubose,Eric	02	26	a/a	BAL	5	3	42	3	65	59	24	2	26	50	3.32	1.31	6.5	317	3.6	6.9	1.9	0.3	30%	73%	81
	03	27	aaa	BAL	9	5	19	0	114	138	58	9	36	88	4.57	1.52	26.7	351	2.8	7.0	2.5	0.7	36%	71%	68
Duchscherer,Justin	02	25	aaa	OAK	2	4	14	0	63	75	38	6	15	44	5.43	1.43	19.6	336	2.1	6.3	2.9	0.9	34%	62%	71
	03	26	aaa	OAK	14	2	24	0	155	165	62	12	18	99	3.58	1.18	26.5	295	1.1	5.7	5.4	0.7	31%	71%	129
Duff,Matt	02	28	a/a	STL	11	1	51	5	69	53	15	5	28	72	1.95	1.17	5.6	293	3.6	9.4	2.6	0.7	28%	87%	104
	03	29	aaa	STL	4	2	32	3	34	37	14	5	16	27	3.77	1.58	4.8	359	4.4	7.2	1.7	1.5	32%	82%	35
Duncan,Courtney	02	28	aaa	CHC	3	5	55	6	68	77	35	5	32	53	4.62	1.60	5.6	362	4.2	7.0	1.7	0.7	34%	71%	56
	03	29	aaa	ANA	2	6	56	18	63	86	42	4	42	42	5.95	2.02	5.6	417	5.9	6.0	1.0	0.6	37%	70%	30
Dunn,Scott	02	24	aa	CIN	5	7	37	1	110	116	58	12	53	91	4.74	1.53	13.3	352	4.3	7.4	1.7	1.0	32%	71%	53
	03	25	a/a	CHW	7	3	48	9	63	62	39	5	34	74	5.55	1.52	5.8	350	4.8	10.6	2.2	0.7	35%	63%	92
Durbin,Chad	03	26	a/a	CLE	5	6	13	0	70	73	45	14	19	61	5.80	1.30	22.8	316	2.4	7.8	3.2	1.8	30%	59%	64
Durbin,J.D.	03	22	aa	MIN	6	3	14	0	94	118	41	10	30	59	3.92	1.57	30.2	358	2.9	5.6	2.0	1.0	34%	78%	41
Duvall,Mike	03	29	aaa	MIN	1	4	24	0	44	76	39	9	17	23	7.90	2.12	9.3	429	3.5	4.7	1.4	1.8	40%	65%	-15
Eason,Clay	02	27	a/a	CHW	5	2	40	4	88	93	38	9	41	61	3.89	1.52	9.8	351	4.2	6.2	1.5	0.9	31%	77%	43
	03	28	a/a	CHW	1	3	25	1	54	107	61	20	30	41	10.15	2.53	11.8	473	5.0	6.8	1.4	3.3	44%	65%	-54
Ebert,Derrin	02	26	aaa	MIL	6	4	50	4	74	81	40	14	27	38	4.85	1.46	6.5	340	3.3	4.6	1.4	1.7	28%	72%	7
	03	27	aaa	ARI	1	3	25	0	30	48	18	2	13	14	5.33	2.02	6.0	418	3.8	4.2	1.1	0.6	40%	73%	14
Echols,Justin	03	23	aa	TEX	1	3	8	0	44	39	33	7	27	28	6.75	1.50	24.3	347	5.5	5.8	1.0	1.5	25%	56%	21
Eckenstahler,Eric	02	26	aaa	DET	2	4	52	0	67	67	41	7	33	62	5.51	1.49	5.7	346	4.4	8.3	1.9	0.9	32%	63%	65
	03	27	aaa	DET	3	6	39	0	42	39	20	2	25	34	4.18	1.51	4.8	349	5.3	7.2	1.4	0.4	30%	72%	66
Edmondson,Brian	02	30	aa	DET	5	2	43	6	52	79	29	5	16	29	5.02	1.83	5.7	393	2.8	5.0	1.8	0.9	39%	73%	29
Elarton,Scott	03	28	aaa	COL	6	8	20	0	118	185	100	24	40	76	7.61	1.91	28.5	403	3.0	5.8	1.9	1.8	38%	62%	4
Elder,Dave	02	27	a/a	CLE	5	2	45	14	70	70	28	3	39	64	3.60	1.56	7.0	356	5.0	8.2	1.6	0.4	33%	76%	76
Ellison,Jason	02	25	aa	SEA	1	6	36	2	73	102	47	1	37	37	5.79	1.90	9.8	403	4.6	4.6	1.0	0.1	37%	67%	35
Ellis,Robert	02	32	aaa	LA	9	7	29	0	172	201	75	15	34	91	3.92	1.36	25.4	326	1.8	4.8	2.7	0.8	32%	73%	59
	03	33	aaa	TEX	3	10	27	3	118	162	92	17	38	41	6.98	1.69	20.2	375	2.9	3.1	1.1	1.3	33%	59%	-6
Elmore,Chris	02	25	a/a	BOS	8	5	21	0	114	141	54	4	36	70	4.26	1.55	24.3	355	2.8	5.5	1.9	0.3	35%	71%	60
	03	26	a/a	BOS	3	3	11	0	46	62	34	3	32	20	6.71	2.04	20.8	420	6.3	3.9	0.6	0.6	35%	66%	8
Emanuel,Brandon	02	27	a/a	ANA	7	6	21	0	119	168	71	23	31	57	5.37	1.67	26.0	372	2.3	4.3	1.8	1.7	34%	73%	2
	03	28	aaa	ANA	6	10	29	2	147	216	100	27	37	58	6.12	1.72	23.5	379	2.3	3.5	1.6	1.7	35%	68%	-8
Emiliano,Jamie	02	28	aa	ATL	3	3	42	3	54	48	15	5	29	26	2.50	1.42	5.6	335	4.8	4.3	0.9	0.8	25%	86%	28
	03	29	aaa	ATL	0	7	53	1	73	108	51	7	34	31	6.23	1.94	6.7	408	4.2	3.8	0.9	0.8	37%	67%	5
Ennis,John	02	23	aa	ATL	9	9	26	0	148	146	80	7	59	86	4.86	1.38	24.5	329	3.6	5.2	1.5	0.4	30%	63%	54
	03	24	a/a	DET	3	11	32	0	119	177	97	15	44	77	7.32	1.85	17.8	397	3.3	5.8	1.8	1.1	38%	60%	25
Enochs,Chris	02	27	a/a	OAK	7	13	29	0	164	220	110	19	77	87	6.04	1.81	26.8	391	4.2	4.8	1.1	1.0	35%	67%	13
	03	28	aaa	OAK	6	3	37	0	62	86	41	2	31	40	5.96	1.88	8.1	401	4.4	5.8	1.3	0.3	38%	66%	43
Erdos,Todd	02	29	aaa	BOS	4	4	52	10	78	109	38	4	23	38	4.38	1.69	6.9	375	2.7	4.4	1.7	0.5	37%	73%	37
	03	30	aaa	MIN	2	2	29	11	33	55	25	3	5	13	6.85	1.82	5.4	392	1.5	3.5	2.3	0.9	39%	62%	25
Espina,Rendy	02	24	aaa	BAL	2	2	45	0	53	73	47	13	31	32	7.97	1.96	5.8	410	5.3	5.4	1.0	2.2	34%	63%	-21
Esslinger,Cam	02	26	a/a	COL	0	2	35	2	39	44	32	3	20	24	7.38	1.64	5.1	368	4.6	5.5	1.2	0.7	32%	52%	37
Estrada,Horacio	02	27	aaa	ARI	8	7	29	1	163	188	81	23	38	87	4.47	1.38	24.2	329	2.1	4.8	2.3	1.3	31%	71%	37
Estrella,Leo	02	28	a/a	CHC	4	4	32	1	74	98	46	5	39	38	5.58	1.85	11.1	396	4.7	4.6	1.0	0.6	35%	69%	23
Estrella,Luis	02	28	aaa	SF	7	13	38	7	144	201	88	15	66	78	5.50	1.85	18.1	397	4.1	4.9	1.2	0.9	36%	71%	16
	03	29	aaa	SF	2	9	51	5	89	121	63	4	41	40	6.33	1.82	8.3	392	4.1	4.0	1.0	0.4	36%	63%	23
Etherton,Seth	03	27	aaa	CIN	7	7	21	0	123	177	80	15	27	57	5.88	1.66	26.8	370	2.0	4.2	2.1	1.1	36%	66%	25
Evans,Keith	03	28	aaa	CHC	2	2	22	1	41	55	24	5	13	13	5.30	1.64	8.5	368	2.8	2.9	1.1	1.2	33%	69%	-3
Evans,Kyle	03	25	aa	CLE	9	5	28	1	133	177	75	4	42	56	5.06	1.65	21.7	369	2.8	3.8	1.3	0.3	35%	67%	35
Evert,Brett	02	22	aa	ATL	5	8	16	0	93	105	59	15	34	70	5.70	1.49	25.7	346	3.3	6.8	2.1	1.4	32%	65%	40
	03	23	aa	ATL	4	9	33	1	116	152	70	15	45	87	5.43	1.70	16.2	376	3.5	6.7	1.9	1.2	36%	70%	39
Eyre,Willie	02	24	aa	MIN	6	4	28	2	50	48	24	1	23	35	4.32	1.42	7.8	335	4.1	6.3	1.5	0.2	31%	67%	70
	03	25	a/a	MIN	6	7	35	0	120	153	72	9	60	71	5.36	1.77	16.1	386	4.5	5.3	1.2	0.7	35%	69%	30
Falkenborg,Brian	02	25	aaa	SEA	4	4	9	0	49	58	18	3	13	36	3.30	1.45	23.8	339	2.4	6.6	2.8	0.5	35%	78%	79
	03	26	aaa	SEA	4	2	17	0	79	77	32	7	27	55	3.67	1.31	19.7	318	3.1	6.3	2.0	0.8	29%	74%	62
Farmer,Tom	02	23	a/a	LA	9	9	25	0	145	175	82	14	41	70	5.08	1.49	25.6	345	2.5	4.3	1.7	0.9	32%	66%	32
	03	24	a/a	LA	7	10	25	0	145	165	61	10	35	72	3.77	1.38	25.0	328	2.2	4.4	2.0	0.6	31%	73%	50
Farnsworth,Jeff	03	28	aa	DET	3	3	8	0	53	85	29	8	11	25	4.87	1.81	31.4	391	1.9	4.2	2.2	1.3	38%	76%	18
Feliciano,Pedro	02	26	a/a	CIN	3	2	53	6	74	100	33	6	17	42	4.01	1.58	6.3	359	2.1	5.1	2.5	0.7	36%	76%	52
Ferguson,Ian	02	23	aa	KC	6	2	11	0	76	74	31	9	18	49	3.67	1.21	28.5	300	2.1	5.8	2.7	1.1	28%	73%	65
	03	24	a/a	KC	2	3	16	0	39	62	41	4	30	16	9.52	2.35	12.9	455	6.9	3.8	0.6	1.0	38%	58%	-10
Fernandez,Jared	02	31	aaa	CIN	12	5	26	1	128	182	68	17	31	60	4.78	1.66	22.6	371	2.2	4.2	1.9	1.2	35%	74%	20
	03	32	aaa	HOU	7	10	26	0	156	213	98	23	42	41	5.65	1.63	27.3	367	2.4	2.4	1.0	1.3	32%	68%	-14
Fernandez,Osvaldo	02	34	aaa	MON	7	6	28	0	103	138	72	9	34	52	6.28	1.67	16.9	371	3.0	4.5	1.5	0.8	35%	61%	28
Ferrari,Anthony	02	24	aa	MON	7	4	44	6	75	95	42	2	35	43	5.03	1.73	7.9	380	4.2	5.2	1.2	0.2	36%	69%	44
	03	25	a/a	MON	7	2	42	5	65	88	33	3	24	21	4.50	1.73	7.2	380	3.3	2.9	0.9	0.4	34%	73%	14
Fesh,Sean	02	30	aaa	FLA	1	1	24	5	42	51	29	1	29	32	6.18	1.90	8.5	402	6.2	6.8	1.1	0.2	36%	65%	54
	03	31	a/a	FLA	10	1	55	7	83	96	34	1	33	54	3.65	1.55	6.8	354	3.5	5.8	1.6	0.1	34%	75%	64
Field,Nate	03	28	a/a	KC	3	2	34	7	42	48	24	9	14	27	5.15	1.47	5.4	343	2.9	5.8	2.0	2.0	30%	72%	15
Field,Nathan	02	27	aaa	NYY	2	2	39	7	55	76	40	6	29	33	6.55	1.91	6.8	404	4.7	5.4	1.1	1.0	36%	66%	18
Figueroa,Juan	02	23	aa	BAL	1	6	24	1	89	114	60	15	27	56	6.07	1.58	16.7	360	2.7	5.7	2.1	1.5	34%	64%	26
	03	28	aa	STL	5	2	34	2	37	45	20	8	20	32	4.86	1.76	5.1	384	4.9	7.8	1.6	1.8	34%	78%	22
Figueroa,Nelson	02	28	aaa	MIL	5	0	6	0	39	51	23	3	14	20	5.28	1.66	29.9	370	3.2	4.6	1.4	0.7	35%	68%	30
	03	29	aaa	PIT	12	5	23	0	151	188	71	13	40	94	4.25	1.51	29.1	348	2.4	5.6	2.4	0.8	34%	73%	55
Fikac,Jeremy	03	29	aaa	OAK	3	3	42	4	56	46	16	4	14	40	2.59	1.08	5.3	276	2.2	6.4	2.9	0.7	26%	79%	89
File,Bob	02	26	aaa	TOR	0	0	33	2	36	44	28	2	15	20	6.98	1.63	5.0	367	3.7	5.0	1.3	0.5	34%	54%	39
Fiore,Tony	03	32	aaa	MIN	5	6	16	1	84	101	52	6	24	39	5.52	1.49	23.2	346	2.6	4.2	1.6	0.7	32%	62%	35
Fischer,Rich	02	22	aa	ANA	1	3	7	0	44	46	26	10	10	31	5.29	1.27	26.4	310	2.0	6.3	3.1	2.0	28%	65%	44
	03	23	aa	ANA	5	11	26	0	154	185	99	16	43	105	5.78	1.48	26.1	344	2.5	6.1	2.4	0.9	34%	61%	57
Fisher,Pete	03	26	aa	MIN	4	1	8	0	45	75	33	2	13	17	6.67	1.94	27.3	408	2.5	3.3	1.3	0.5	40%	64%	16
Fitzgerald,Brian	02	28	aaa	COL	3	4	36	2	57	77	42	7	25	34	6.62	1.79	7.5	388	3.9	5.4	1.4	1.1	36%	63%	19
Flannery,Mike	03	24	aa	FLA	7	3	56	23	58	51	19	1	28	43	2.94	1.36	4.4	325	4.4	6.6	1.5	0.2	29%	77%	76

					Actual				Major League Equivalents																
PITCHER	Yr	Age	Lev	Org	w	l	g	sv	ip	h	er	hr	bb	k	era	br/ip	bf/g	oob	ctl	dom	cmd	hr/9	h%	s%	bpv
Flohr,Adam	02	26	aa	MIN	4	5	43	0	82	107	31	4	22	36	3.40	1.57	8.6	358	2.4	3.9	1.6	0.4	35%	78%	38
	03	27	a/a	MIN	2	1	45	0	70	96	60	8	46	36	7.70	2.01	7.7	417	5.8	4.6	0.8	1.0	35%	61%	6
Flores,Randy	02	27	aaa	COL	3	3	22	1	56	68	32	3	22	36	5.14	1.61	11.5	363	3.5	5.8	1.6	0.5	35%	67%	51
	03	28	aaa	COL	10	8	28	0	142	202	115	27	71	94	7.28	1.92	24.6	405	4.5	5.9	1.3	1.7	36%	64%	2
Flores,Ron	03	24	a/a	OAK	5	2	51	6	73	67	33	6	19	63	4.07	1.17	5.9	294	2.3	7.8	3.4	0.8	30%	66%	102
Florie,Bryce	02	32	aaa	OAK	4	6	18	0	83	98	48	11	36	56	5.20	1.61	20.9	364	3.9	6.1	1.6	1.2	33%	70%	31
Flury,Pat	03	31	a/a	KC	2	0	31	0	44	66	34	6	34	27	6.90	2.27	7.4	446	6.9	5.6	0.8	1.3	38%	71%	-1
Foppert,Jesse	02	22	a/a	SF	6	9	25	0	140	127	61	13	53	156	3.92	1.28	23.6	313	3.4	10.0	2.9	0.8	32%	71%	105
Fordham,Tom	03	30	a/a	PIT	7	4	26	0	107	179	87	17	48	56	7.27	2.12	20.8	429	4.0	4.7	1.2	1.4	40%	67%	-8
Ford,Ben	02	27	aaa	CHC	6	11	32	0	142	167	78	12	69	70	4.94	1.66	20.3	371	4.4	4.4	1.0	0.8	32%	71%	23
	03	28	aaa	MIL	5	4	26	1	84	101	39	10	20	56	4.15	1.45	14.1	339	2.2	6.0	2.7	1.0	34%	74%	59
Fortunato,Bartolome	02	28	a/a	TAM	4	0	12	0	30	31	12	4	15	25	3.60	1.53	11.1	352	4.5	7.5	1.7	1.2	31%	81%	47
	03	29	a/a	TAM	5	4	40	1	74	91	41	10	40	58	5.03	1.78	8.7	386	4.9	7.1	1.4	1.2	35%	74%	33
Forystek,Brian	03	25	aa	BAL	9	9	29	0	124	146	66	12	45	86	4.81	1.54	19.1	354	3.3	6.2	1.9	0.8	34%	70%	49
Foster,John	02	24	aaa	ATL	8	4	55	8	62	77	36	5	28	40	5.23	1.69	5.2	375	4.1	5.8	1.4	0.7	35%	69%	38
	03	25	aaa	MIL	2	2	27	0	41	53	22	5	13	31	4.87	1.60	6.9	362	2.9	6.7	2.3	1.1	36%	72%	50
Francisco,Frank	03	24	aa	TEX	2	3	7	0	35	55	46	7	19	18	11.88	2.10	25.2	427	4.9	4.6	1.0	1.9	37%	41%	-24
Franco,Martire	02	25	aa	PHI	4	8	16	0	89	131	72	15	28	44	7.28	1.79	26.2	388	2.8	4.4	1.6	1.5	36%	60%	2
	03	26	aa	PHI	4	7	28	4	86	141	68	10	29	37	7.08	1.97	15.1	412	3.0	3.9	1.3	1.0	39%	64%	2
Franklin,Wayne	02	29	aaa	HOU	13	9	29	0	179	201	92	22	69	113	4.63	1.51	27.3	348	3.5	5.7	1.6	1.1	31%	72%	35
Frasor,Jason	03	26	aa	LA	1	0	35	17	36	44	17	2	17	38	4.29	1.68	4.8	374	4.3	9.5	2.2	0.6	39%	75%	83
Frederick,Kevin	02	26	aaa	MIN	3	6	46	22	55	69	30	7	20	40	4.91	1.62	5.4	365	3.3	6.5	2.0	1.1	35%	72%	42
	03	27	a/a	TOR	3	5	49	9	55	92	47	10	29	37	7.64	2.20	5.7	438	4.7	6.0	1.3	1.6	41%	67%	-4
Freed,Mark	02	24	aa	CHC	9	11	29	0	132	193	99	17	63	88	6.74	1.94	22.1	407	4.3	6.0	1.4	1.2	38%	66%	19
	03	25	aa	ARI	4	3	67	1	63	92	42	4	39	34	6.01	2.07	4.7	424	5.5	4.9	0.9	0.6	38%	70%	17
Frendling,Neal	02	23	aa	TAM	5	6	22	0	112	128	72	16	69	56	5.79	1.76	23.8	384	5.5	4.5	0.8	1.3	30%	69%	4
Frick,Mike	03	24	aa	OAK	1	2	28	0	35	53	23	5	9	17	5.80	1.76	5.9	384	2.4	4.5	1.9	1.3	37%	69%	14
Fuentes,Brian	02	27	aaa	COL	3	3	41	1	49	52	24	0	31	51	4.40	1.69	5.5	375	5.7	9.3	1.6	0.0	37%	71%	92
Fussell,Chris	02	26	aaa	KC	12	6	28	0	164	195	101	26	70	82	5.54	1.61	26.6	364	3.8	4.5	1.2	1.4	31%	69%	6
	03	27	aaa	ATL	7	11	29	0	152	183	100	16	81	105	5.92	1.74	24.4	381	4.8	6.2	1.3	0.9	34%	66%	33
Fyhrie,Mike	02	33	aaa	OAK	7	2	13	0	77	66	21	3	22	55	2.45	1.14	24.1	288	2.6	6.4	2.5	0.4	28%	79%	90
	03	34	aaa	FLA	9	9	28	0	154	186	87	16	55	88	5.11	1.57	24.7	357	3.2	5.2	1.6	0.9	33%	68%	34
Gaal,Bryan	02	26	aa	SD	4	1	32	3	36	50	16	1	12	24	3.98	1.71	5.2	378	3.0	6.0	2.0	0.2	39%	75%	61
	03	27	a/a	SD	3	6	64	3	74	80	32	8	31	59	3.91	1.50	5.1	347	3.8	7.1	1.9	0.9	32%	76%	55
Gallo,Mike	03	26	a/a	HOU	4	1	33	2	37	38	9	1	9	27	2.30	1.28	4.7	312	2.3	6.5	2.8	0.3	32%	82%	93
Galva,Claudio	02	26	aa	OAK	3	3	62	4	65	80	34	9	36	41	4.71	1.78	4.9	388	5.0	5.7	1.1	1.2	33%	77%	16
Garcia,Gerardo	02	23	a/a	TAM	4	8	25	0	102	119	72	10	43	66	6.35	1.59	18.4	360	3.8	5.8	1.5	0.9	33%	59%	39
	03	24	a/a	TAM	2	2	10	0	40	49	22	5	14	20	4.94	1.57	18.0	358	3.1	4.5	1.4	1.1	32%	71%	19
Garcia,Jose	02	24	a/a	MIL	5	11	28	0	144	175	93	11	71	66	5.81	1.71	23.8	377	4.4	4.1	0.9	0.7	33%	65%	20
	03	25	aa	ANA	2	2	6	0	33	50	23	6	17	19	6.33	2.01	27.3	416	4.5	5.1	1.1	1.5	37%	71%	-4
Garcia,Mike	03	35	aaa	BAL	2	2	34	13	35	37	14	3	14	36	3.51	1.44	4.5	338	3.5	9.3	2.6	0.8	35%	78%	89
Garcia,Reynaldo	02	28	a/a	TEX	7	3	43	4	100	116	54	18	51	65	4.86	1.67	10.7	372	4.6	5.9	1.3	1.6	31%	76%	11
	03	29	aaa	TEX	4	3	39	9	61	85	37	4	21	51	5.51	1.73	7.3	380	3.1	7.5	2.4	0.6	40%	67%	68
Garcia,Rosman	02	24	aa	TEX	8	5	53	6	74	93	35	1	34	32	4.25	1.71	6.5	378	4.1	3.9	0.9	0.1	34%	73%	34
Garcia,Sonny	02	26	aa	OAK	4	3	21	1	59	87	34	6	22	28	5.18	1.84	13.4	395	3.4	4.3	1.3	0.9	37%	73%	13
	03	27	aa	OAK	3	5	10	0	50	100	51	6	24	18	9.09	2.48	27.0	468	4.3	3.3	0.8	1.1	43%	62%	-23
Gardner,Hayden	03	23	aa	TEX	4	1	33	0	52	78	36	9	26	24	6.25	2.00	7.8	415	4.5	4.2	0.9	1.6	36%	72%	-16
Gardner,Lee	02	28	aaa	TAM	2	1	45	25	49	61	17	1	16	42	3.11	1.57	4.9	357	2.9	7.7	2.6	0.2	38%	79%	91
	03	29	aaa	TAM	3	7	57	30	62	86	35	11	16	45	5.13	1.64	5.0	368	2.3	6.5	2.8	1.6	37%	73%	41
Garza,Alberto	02	25	aa	CLE	2	0	20	1	36	20	10	3	33	35	2.49	1.46	7.9	342	8.2	8.7	1.1	0.7	20%	86%	75
Gassner,Dave	02	24	a/a	TOR	1	3	5	0	30	32	11	1	9	13	3.29	1.36	25.8	326	2.7	3.9	1.4	0.3	30%	75%	46
	03	25	a/a	TOR	11	4	36	1	150	172	59	12	30	81	3.52	1.35	17.8	323	1.8	4.9	2.7	0.7	32%	76%	63
Geary,Geoff	02	26	aaa	PHI	4	2	38	1	101	128	42	10	35	73	3.74	1.61	12.1	364	3.1	6.5	2.1	0.9	36%	79%	51
	03	27	aaa	PHI	9	4	46	5	87	89	27	3	15	67	2.82	1.20	7.8	298	1.5	6.9	4.5	0.3	32%	76%	129
George,Chris	02	23	aaa	KC	6	12	22	0	127	166	101	17	63	78	7.15	1.80	27.3	390	4.5	5.5	1.2	1.2	35%	60%	16
	03	24	aaa	KC	3	5	10	0	54	83	55	10	21	23	9.15	1.92	26.2	405	3.5	3.8	1.1	1.7	36%	52%	-18
Germano,Justin	03	21	aa	SD	2	5	9	0	58	68	33	6	13	36	5.12	1.40	27.8	331	2.0	5.6	2.8	0.9	33%	64%	61
German,Franklyn	02	23	a/a	DET	2	2	60	29	64	48	21	0	31	82	2.95	1.23	4.4	304	4.4	11.5	2.6	0.0	33%	73%	139
	03	24	aaa	DET	1	4	24	4	29	25	10	2	9	28	3.09	1.17	5.0	293	2.8	8.7	3.1	0.6	30%	75%	108
Giese,Dan	02	25	aa	BOS	5	7	55	3	102	133	48	10	23	68	4.24	1.53	8.3	352	2.0	6.0	3.0	0.9	36%	74%	65
	03	26	a/a	PHI	6	1	48	1	70	73	39	13	17	59	4.99	1.28	6.1	313	2.1	7.6	3.6	1.7	30%	67%	72
Gilfillan,Jason	02	26	a/a	KC	4	4	54	4	76	88	38	9	44	44	4.49	1.73	6.6	381	5.2	5.2	1.0	1.1	32%	76%	19
	03	27	aaa	KC	6	0	35	7	52	57	16	5	13	26	2.72	1.33	6.3	321	2.2	4.4	2.0	0.9	30%	84%	43
Gil,Dave	02	24	a/a	CIN	12	7	27	0	132	148	76	27	44	98	5.18	1.45	21.4	340	3.0	6.7	2.2	1.8	31%	70%	31
	03	25	a/a	CIN	1	3	46	11	80	98	40	9	24	48	4.49	1.52	7.7	351	2.7	5.3	2.0	1.1	33%	73%	37
Ginter,Matt	03	26	aaa	CHW	3	5	49	14	68	79	30	3	23	47	4.00	1.50	6.1	347	3.1	6.1	2.0	0.4	34%	72%	65
Giron,Rob	03	28	aaa	MIL	1	5	52	15	59	80	42	4	31	45	6.42	1.87	5.4	399	4.7	6.8	1.5	0.6	38%	64%	44
Giron,Roberto	02	27	a/a	MIL	2	4	51	11	70	76	39	6	48	60	5.01	1.77	6.4	386	6.2	7.7	1.3	0.8	34%	72%	50
Gissell,Chris	02	25	aaa	CHC	8	12	28	0	154	180	100	16	55	117	5.84	1.52	24.5	351	3.2	6.8	2.1	0.9	34%	62%	55
	03	26	aaa	COL	8	4	38	1	109	117	59	12	34	71	4.84	1.39	12.4	330	2.8	5.9	2.1	1.0	31%	67%	50
Glaser,Eric	02	25	aa	BOS	2	9	33	1	113	168	85	15	33	65	6.76	1.78	16.1	386	2.6	5.2	2.0	1.2	38%	62%	24
	03	26	a/a	BOS	5	3	33	0	84	91	52	16	33	48	5.53	1.47	11.2	342	3.5	5.1	1.5	1.7	28%	67%	11
Glen,Will	03	26	aa	PHI	3	6	31	0	103	121	54	14	60	63	4.75	1.76	15.6	384	5.2	5.5	1.1	1.3	32%	76%	15
Glick,David	03	28	aa	NYY	4	0	45	0	40	78	34	4	29	22	7.55	2.67	5.0	486	6.5	5.0	0.8	0.8	45%	71%	-3
Glynn,Ryan	02	28	aaa	FLA	8	11	26	0	141	189	89	12	52	70	5.67	1.71	25.1	377	3.3	4.5	1.3	0.8	35%	66%	24
	03	29	aaa	ATL	6	5	16	0	92	111	45	5	34	59	4.41	1.57	25.9	358	3.4	5.7	1.7	0.5	34%	72%	51
Gobble,Jimmy	02	21	aa	KC	5	7	13	0	69	86	35	4	19	43	4.56	1.52	23.6	350	2.5	5.6	2.3	0.5	35%	69%	61
	03	22	aa	KC	12	8	22	0	132	155	64	15	40	83	4.36	1.48	26.4	343	2.7	5.7	2.1	1.0	33%	73%	45
Gomes,Wayne	02	30	aaa	BOS	5	4	48	4	81	104	51	10	45	47	5.67	1.84	8.0	395	5.0	5.2	1.0	1.1	34%	71%	14
	03	31	aaa	PHI	4	2	46	14	48	40	19	1	29	34	3.53	1.43	4.6	336	5.4	6.4	1.2	0.2	28%	74%	68
Gonzalez,Alfredo	02	23	a/a	LA	2	4	27	4	41	38	10	1	10	36	2.18	1.17	6.2	292	2.2	7.9	3.6	0.2	32%	81%	123
	03	24	a/a	LA	5	4	12	0	57	80	35	6	21	36	5.52	1.77	22.3	386	3.2	5.7	1.7	1.0	37%	70%	31

Major League Equivalent Statistics

					Actual				Major League Equivalents																
PITCHER	Yr	Age	Lev	Org	w	l	g	sv	ip	h	er	hr	bb	k	era	br/ip	bf/g	oob	ctl	dom	cmd	hr/9	h%	s%	bpv
Gonzalez,Dicky	02	24	aaa	MON	8	5	23	0	124	170	68	13	36	67	4.93	1.66	24.7	370	2.6	4.9	1.9	0.9	36%	72%	31
	03	25	aaa	BOS	8	8	27	0	151	210	86	14	30	88	5.12	1.59	25.2	360	1.8	5.2	2.9	0.8	37%	68%	59
Gonzalez,Edgar	03	21	a/a	ARI	10	9	26	0	165	168	71	5	34	96	3.86	1.22	26.3	302	1.8	5.2	2.8	0.3	31%	67%	85
Gonzalez,Jeremi	02	28	aaa	TEX	6	5	46	14	92	99	40	8	38	77	3.91	1.49	8.8	346	3.7	7.5	2.0	0.8	33%	75%	65
	03	29	aaa	TAM	1	0	7	0	32	30	13	2	6	26	3.63	1.14	18.6	288	1.8	7.3	4.0	0.6	30%	69%	117
Gonzalez,Mike	02	24	aa	PIT	8	4	16	0	85	93	46	4	46	67	4.86	1.63	24.2	367	4.9	7.1	1.5	0.4	34%	69%	61
Gooch,Arnie	02	26	aa	CIN	3	3	7	0	37	56	33	2	17	21	7.98	1.96	25.9	410	4.1	5.1	1.2	0.5	39%	56%	29
Good,Andrew	02	23	aa	ARI	13	6	28	0	178	195	82	23	25	103	4.15	1.24	26.4	305	1.3	5.2	4.1	1.2	30%	70%	83
	03	24	aaa	ARI	4	4	11	0	63	88	41	14	12	40	5.86	1.59	25.8	360	1.7	5.7	3.3	2.0	35%	69%	35
Gosling,Mike	02	22	aa	ARI	14	5	27	0	166	166	67	7	58	96	3.63	1.35	26.3	323	3.1	5.2	1.7	0.4	30%	72%	59
	03	23	aaa	ARI	9	12	26	0	136	214	100	15	54	78	6.61	1.97	25.6	411	3.6	5.2	1.4	1.0	39%	66%	17
Grabow,John	02	24	aa	PIT	8	13	28	0	146	213	111	10	45	81	6.84	1.77	24.5	385	2.8	5.0	1.8	0.6	38%	59%	38
	03	25	a/a	PIT	6	3	41	1	107	146	61	10	27	82	5.11	1.62	11.9	364	2.3	6.9	3.1	0.9	38%	69%	71
Gracesqui,Frank	02	23	aa	TOR	4	2	41	1	42	45	26	3	34	40	5.55	1.87	4.9	399	7.3	8.5	1.2	0.6	35%	70%	58
	03	24	aa	FLA	3	3	44	5	58	53	20	0	47	64	3.10	1.72	6.1	379	7.4	9.9	1.3	0.0	35%	80%	95
Grace,Bryan	03	28	aa	NYY	1	2	7	0	31	73	40	4	12	10	11.51	2.75	25.2	494	3.5	2.9	0.8	1.0	47%	56%	-31
Graham,Tom	02	25	a/a	TEX	1	2	26	0	44	56	27	3	13	43	5.50	1.56	7.6	356	2.6	8.8	3.3	0.6	39%	64%	98
	03	26	a/a	TEX	5	2	38	3	63	78	51	8	21	41	7.21	1.57	7.5	357	3.0	5.8	1.9	1.2	34%	53%	35
Graman,Alex	02	25	a/a	NYY	11	11	28	0	174	216	97	14	52	112	5.02	1.54	27.7	353	2.7	5.8	2.2	0.7	35%	67%	54
	03	26	aaa	NYY	9	10	26	0	142	156	87	16	65	94	5.50	1.55	24.4	354	4.1	6.0	1.5	1.0	31%	65%	36
Gray,Brett	02	26	aa	CIN	6	6	48	0	94	113	38	6	22	44	3.64	1.44	8.5	337	2.1	4.2	2.0	0.6	33%	75%	47
	03	27	aa	CIN	5	3	43	1	64	108	43	13	17	41	6.10	1.96	7.3	410	2.4	5.7	2.4	1.9	41%	73%	11
Gray,Mike	02	26	a/a	ARI	1	2	25	0	36	67	24	2	15	22	5.97	2.27	7.5	445	3.7	5.5	1.5	0.5	45%	73%	26
Green,Steve	03	26	aaa	ANA	9	5	21	0	110	133	65	6	44	59	5.29	1.62	23.8	364	3.6	4.9	1.3	0.5	34%	66%	39
Gregg,Kevin	02	24	a/a	OAK	5	8	27	0	96	125	73	9	39	75	6.84	1.71	16.5	377	3.7	7.0	1.9	0.8	37%	59%	51
	03	25	a/a	ANA	11	7	30	0	158	179	84	14	38	109	4.80	1.37	22.6	327	2.2	6.2	2.9	0.8	33%	65%	74
Greinke,Zack	03	20	aa	KC	4	3	9	0	53	64	24	6	5	31	4.01	1.29	24.8	313	0.8	5.2	6.8	1.1	33%	72%	138
Greisinger,Seth	02	27	a/a	DET	3	1	7	0	36	34	14	1	17	25	3.49	1.41	22.3	334	4.2	6.2	1.5	0.2	30%	74%	67
	03	28	aaa	DET	6	9	25	0	136	196	83	17	24	65	5.48	1.61	24.7	364	1.6	4.3	2.8	1.1	36%	68%	38
Grezlovski,Ben	02	26	aa	ANA	0	2	38	1	59	90	47	4	38	23	7.15	2.16	7.9	434	5.8	3.5	0.6	0.6	37%	65%	2
Griffiths,Jeremy	02	25	aa	NYM	8	6	27	0	152	180	76	12	56	102	4.49	1.55	25.2	355	3.3	6.0	1.8	0.7	34%	71%	50
	03	26	aaa	NYM	7	6	21	1	115	110	43	7	27	64	3.40	1.19	22.5	298	2.1	5.0	2.4	0.6	28%	72%	69
Grilli,Jason	03	27	aaa	FLA	6	2	12	0	66	69	26	3	30	33	3.50	1.50	24.4	346	4.1	4.5	1.1	0.4	30%	76%	40
Guerra,Mark	02	31	aaa	HOU	6	11	28	0	173	248	118	24	42	68	6.14	1.68	28.4	373	2.2	3.5	1.6	1.2	35%	65%	7
Guerrier,Matt	02	24	aaa	PIT	7	12	27	0	157	176	97	20	44	111	5.56	1.40	25.1	332	2.5	6.4	2.5	1.1	32%	62%	56
	03	25	aaa	PIT	4	6	20	0	105	129	70	17	18	66	5.97	1.40	22.7	332	1.6	5.7	3.6	1.5	33%	60%	62
Guillory,Dan	02	26	aa	CLE	3	3	19	2	32	28	6	1	24	26	1.68	1.62	7.7	365	6.7	7.3	1.1	0.3	30%	90%	67
	03	27	aa	TAM	2	2	23	0	41	57	29	0	23	22	6.33	1.93	8.7	407	5.0	4.7	0.9	0.0	38%	64%	39
Gulin,Lindsay	02	26	a/a	LA	10	4	33	3	130	149	62	14	43	114	4.29	1.48	17.3	344	3.0	7.9	2.7	1.0	35%	73%	73
	03	27	aaa	LA	10	10	28	0	154	164	86	14	61	110	5.00	1.46	24.1	341	3.6	6.4	1.8	0.8	32%	66%	53
Guthrie,Jeremy	03	25	a/a	CLE	10	11	28	0	159	213	109	20	48	81	6.18	1.65	25.9	369	2.7	4.6	1.7	1.1	34%	63%	21
Guy,Brad	02	27	aa	PIT	3	2	26	1	76	114	38	8	17	30	4.49	1.72	13.6	379	2.0	3.5	1.8	0.9	36%	76%	17
	03	28	aa	PHI	3	8	39	3	83	129	72	12	27	31	7.84	1.87	10.2	399	2.9	3.3	1.2	1.3	36%	58%	-9
Guzman,Angel	03	22	aa	CHC	3	3	15	0	89	98	36	9	28	77	3.63	1.41	25.8	334	2.8	7.8	2.8	0.9	34%	77%	77
Haines,Talley	02	26	aaa	TAM	4	7	48	0	75	98	47	10	25	51	5.63	1.64	7.1	367	3.0	6.1	2.0	1.2	35%	67%	37
	03	27	aaa	TAM	5	3	50	2	67	69	25	6	12	53	3.31	1.21	5.6	301	1.7	7.1	4.3	0.8	32%	75%	112
Hall,Josh	02	22	aa	CIN	7	8	22	0	132	156	63	8	46	97	4.30	1.53	26.7	352	3.1	6.6	2.1	0.5	35%	72%	65
	03	23	aa	CIN	8	10	26	0	153	179	76	12	53	97	4.47	1.52	26.1	350	3.1	5.7	1.8	0.7	33%	71%	49
Halsey,Brad	03	23	aa	NYY	7	5	15	0	91	138	59	5	22	67	5.83	1.76	28.4	384	2.2	6.6	3.0	0.5	41%	65%	76
Hamann,Rob	02	26	a/a	TOR	0	0	19	1	35	48	17	3	12	10	4.37	1.71	8.5	378	3.1	2.6	0.8	0.8	34%	75%	1
Hamilton,Jimmy	02	27	aa	PHI	3	2	46	4	71	76	31	7	49	42	3.93	1.76	7.2	384	6.2	5.3	0.9	0.9	30%	80%	25
Hamilton,Joey	03	33	aaa	CIN	8	3	33	1	86	129	43	7	19	36	4.51	1.72	12.1	379	2.0	3.8	1.9	0.8	37%	75%	27
Hampton,Matt	02	25	aa	SD	6	5	57	0	94	116	49	11	32	75	4.69	1.57	7.4	358	3.1	7.2	2.3	1.1	36%	72%	56
	03	26	aaa	SD	1	3	33	0	46	56	32	6	22	29	6.24	1.68	6.4	373	4.2	5.7	1.3	1.2	33%	64%	23
Hamulack,Tim	02	26	aa	FLA	8	4	38	6	78	89	31	7	32	42	3.58	1.55	9.2	355	3.7	4.8	1.3	0.8	32%	79%	31
	03	27	a/a	SEA	1	1	50	1	61	61	23	1	27	53	3.44	1.44	5.3	338	3.9	7.8	2.0	0.2	33%	74%	88
Hancock,Josh	02	24	a/a	BOS	7	6	23	1	129	141	62	11	45	81	4.33	1.44	24.5	338	3.1	5.7	1.8	0.8	31%	71%	49
	03	25	aaa	PHI	10	9	28	0	165	172	89	16	51	106	4.84	1.35	25.2	323	2.8	5.8	2.1	0.9	30%	65%	55
Hanrahan,Joel	03	22	a/a	LA	11	6	28	0	158	167	71	7	72	127	4.04	1.51	25.0	349	4.1	7.2	1.8	0.4	33%	72%	70
Hansell,Greg	03	33	a/a	NYY	0	2	26	1	34	56	20	1	8	26	5.26	1.85	6.3	396	2.0	6.9	3.4	0.3	44%	70%	86
Harang,Aaron	02	24	a/a	OAK	5	3	11	0	55	59	18	1	15	49	2.94	1.34	21.4	323	2.5	8.0	3.3	0.2	35%	77%	113
	03	25	aaa	CIN	8	3	13	0	72	77	31	7	18	54	3.90	1.32	23.5	318	2.3	6.8	3.0	0.9	32%	72%	79
Harden,Rich	02	21	aa	OAK	8	3	16	0	85	71	31	2	49	91	3.28	1.41	23.0	333	5.2	9.6	1.9	0.2	32%	75%	101
	03	22	a/a	OAK	11	4	18	0	101	74	32	6	32	97	2.88	1.05	22.3	272	2.9	8.6	3.0	0.5	27%	74%	114
Haren,Dan	03	23	a/a	STL	8	1	16	0	100	103	40	10	15	77	3.59	1.18	25.7	295	1.3	6.9	5.1	0.9	31%	72%	125
Harikkala,Tim	02	31	aaa	MIL	8	10	31	1	162	218	88	11	25	73	4.89	1.50	23.1	347	1.4	4.1	2.9	0.6	35%	67%	59
	03	32	aaa	BAL	5	0	20	2	44	34	5	0	7	24	1.07	0.93	8.5	248	1.5	4.8	3.2	0.0	25%	87%	110
Harnisch,Pete	03	37	aaa	CIN	0	4	8	0	34	74	53	8	12	14	13.93	2.51	23.1	471	3.1	3.8	1.2	2.2	44%	42%	-49
Harvey,Ian	02	26	aa	SD	6	1	12	0	57	68	16	2	17	33	2.53	1.49	21.0	346	2.7	5.2	1.9	0.3	34%	83%	60
	03	27	aa	PHI	6	1	17	1	33	47	22	6	15	24	5.92	1.87	9.4	399	4.1	6.6	1.6	1.6	37%	71%	17
Harville,Chad	02	26	aaa	OAK	1	2	24	5	30	34	19	4	12	21	5.70	1.53	5.6	352	3.6	6.3	1.8	1.2	32%	64%	38
	03	27	aaa	OAK	3	5	48	18	57	47	15	5	21	47	2.33	1.20	4.9	299	3.3	7.4	2.2	0.8	27%	85%	76
Hasselhoff,Derek	02	29	aaa	BOS	0	4	39	11	44	59	34	5	9	23	6.92	1.54	5.1	353	1.8	4.7	2.6	1.0	35%	54%	43
Hazlett,Andy	02	27	a/a	SD	1	1	27	0	54	63	37	10	18	31	6.14	1.49	8.9	346	3.0	5.1	1.7	1.7	30%	62%	15
Heams,Shane	02	27	a/a	COL	2	3	34	0	40	54	53	11	55	24	11.90	2.72	6.6	491	12.3	5.4	0.4	2.5	33%	57%	-41
Heaverlo,Jeff	03	26	aaa	SEA	5	12	24	0	123	175	92	8	39	66	6.71	1.74	23.9	381	2.9	4.8	1.7	0.6	37%	59%	36
Hebson,Bryan	02	27	a/a	MON	11	1	43	7	103	88	32	7	30	66	2.79	1.14	9.8	288	2.6	5.8	2.2	0.6	26%	77%	72
	03	28	aaa	BOS	8	1	48	6	69	71	35	7	29	53	4.52	1.45	6.3	339	3.8	6.9	1.8	1.0	31%	70%	54
Hee,Aaron	03	25	aa	NYM	2	2	22	0	40	31	29	2	44	30	6.63	1.87	8.7	399	9.9	6.8	0.7	0.5	26%	62%	55
Heilman,Aaron	02	24	a/a	NYM	6	7	27	0	146	141	68	10	44	112	4.19	1.27	22.6	310	2.7	6.9	2.5	0.6	30%	67%	82
	03	25	aaa	NYM	6	4	16	0	94	114	42	5	33	59	4.02	1.56	26.4	356	3.2	5.6	1.8	0.5	35%	74%	53
Heiserman,Rick	02	30	aaa	STL	1	1	22	1	38	53	29	15	11	13	6.85	1.68	8.0	373	2.6	3.1	1.2	3.5	29%	71%	-73

					Actual				Major League Equivalents																
PITCHER	Yr	Age	Lev	Org	w	l	g	sv	ip	h	er	hr	bb	k	era	br/ip	bf/g	oob	ctl	dom	cmd	hr/9	h%	s%	bpv
Hendrickson,Ben	02	22	aa	MIL	4	2	13	0	69	67	29	2	35	43	3.77	1.47	23.4	343	4.6	5.6	1.2	0.3	30%	73%	57
	03	23	aa	MIL	7	6	17	0	78	97	39	7	29	47	4.49	1.61	20.8	364	3.3	5.4	1.6	0.8	34%	73%	38
Hendrickson,Mark	02	28	aaa	TOR	7	5	19	0	92	109	45	13	23	55	4.40	1.43	21.1	337	2.3	5.4	2.4	1.3	32%	73%	42
Henkel,Rob	02	24	aa	FLA	5	4	13	0	70	62	35	6	28	57	4.50	1.29	22.6	313	3.6	7.3	2.0	0.8	29%	65%	72
	03	25	aa	DET	9	3	16	0	82	86	42	8	28	55	4.62	1.38	22.1	328	3.0	6.0	2.0	0.9	31%	67%	54
Henrie,Matt	03	24	a/a	ARI	5	7	15	0	95	134	50	3	18	40	4.73	1.60	28.6	362	1.7	3.8	2.2	0.3	36%	68%	51
Henriquez,Oscar	02	29	aaa	DET	2	1	33	17	32	38	16	4	14	33	4.47	1.61	4.4	364	3.9	9.2	2.4	1.1	37%	75%	69
Hensley,Matt	02	24	aaa	ANA	7	5	19	0	117	143	71	17	36	91	5.45	1.53	27.4	351	2.8	7.0	2.5	1.3	34%	67%	52
	03	25	aaa	ANA	8	12	27	0	158	216	98	17	46	72	5.58	1.66	26.8	371	2.6	4.1	1.6	1.0	35%	67%	19
Hernandez,Adrian	02	28	aaa	NYY	6	7	20	0	109	132	75	9	46	92	6.18	1.63	24.8	366	3.8	7.6	2.0	0.7	36%	61%	62
	03	29	a/a	NYY	8	5	33	1	105	129	53	8	60	81	4.53	1.80	15.0	390	5.1	6.9	1.3	0.7	36%	75%	44
Hernandez,Buddy	02	24	aa	ATL	4	0	40	1	59	41	9	0	23	66	1.37	1.08	5.9	278	3.5	10.1	2.9	0.0	29%	86%	137
	03	25	aaa	ATL	4	3	53	4	71	80	38	3	32	69	4.82	1.58	6.0	359	4.1	8.7	2.2	0.4	37%	68%	86
Hernandez,Runelvys	02	22	aa	KC	8	3	16	0	106	116	43	4	24	71	3.65	1.32	28.1	319	2.0	6.0	3.0	0.3	33%	71%	89
Hernandez,Yoel	03	21	a/a	PHI	6	3	45	2	77	112	41	4	31	45	4.79	1.87	8.2	398	3.7	5.3	1.4	0.4	39%	73%	37
Herndon,Junior	02	24	aaa	SD	7	13	28	0	159	190	105	27	52	50	5.94	1.52	25.2	351	2.9	2.8	1.0	1.5	29%	64%	-12
	03	25	aa	BOS	9	8	25	0	133	199	100	20	36	52	6.76	1.76	24.9	384	2.4	3.5	1.5	1.4	36%	63%	-1
Herrera,Alex	02	26	a/a	CLE	0	3	35	5	68	72	45	11	42	57	5.95	1.67	8.9	372	5.6	7.5	1.4	1.5	31%	67%	32
	03	27	aaa	CLE	4	6	34	1	56	63	45	11	49	38	7.29	2.01	8.1	416	8.0	6.1	0.8	1.8	30%	66%	-3
High,Andy	02	28	aa	MIL	1	1	16	1	31	51	16	3	14	20	4.62	2.08	9.8	425	4.0	5.8	1.4	0.9	41%	79%	22
Hiles,Cary	02	27	a/a	PHI	5	8	47	8	83	119	51	3	39	41	5.52	1.90	8.5	402	4.2	4.4	1.1	0.3	37%	69%	28
Hiljus,Erik	02	30	aaa	OAK	1	3	9	0	37	62	34	3	15	24	8.23	2.07	20.6	423	3.6	5.8	1.6	0.7	42%	58%	29
	03	31	aaa	OAK	11	10	29	0	174	209	110	31	57	99	5.68	1.52	26.7	351	2.9	5.1	1.7	1.6	31%	66%	16
Hill,Jeremy	02	25	aa	KC	4	7	56	19	76	81	30	6	36	59	3.55	1.54	6.1	353	4.3	7.0	1.6	0.7	33%	78%	57
	03	26	a/a	NYM	1	5	39	1	55	67	60	9	64	41	9.80	2.38	7.5	458	10.5	6.6	0.6	1.5	33%	58%	6
Hill,Terry	02	27	aa	BOS	6	5	45	3	83	137	71	10	40	64	7.70	2.13	9.3	431	4.3	6.9	1.6	1.1	43%	63%	25
Hoard,Brent	02	26	aa	MIN	11	8	31	0	161	198	92	13	60	97	5.14	1.60	23.5	362	3.4	5.4	1.6	0.7	34%	68%	40
	03	27	a/a	MIN	3	5	16	0	70	119	56	12	21	27	7.12	1.99	21.6	414	2.7	3.5	1.3	1.6	38%	66%	-18
Hodges,Trey	02	24	aaa	ATL	15	9	28	0	172	182	75	10	55	97	3.92	1.38	26.4	328	2.9	5.1	1.8	0.5	31%	71%	54
Hodge,Kevin	02	26	aa	MIN	3	2	24	6	30	29	14	3	9	22	4.19	1.26	5.2	309	2.7	6.6	2.4	0.9	29%	69%	69
	03	27	aa	MIN	6	8	56	9	93	116	57	10	33	49	5.56	1.60	7.5	363	3.2	4.7	1.5	1.0	33%	66%	24
Hoerman,Jared	03	26	aa	SEA	3	6	56	36	58	82	36	5	28	44	5.51	1.88	5.0	400	4.3	6.7	1.6	0.7	39%	70%	42
Holsten,Ryan	03	24	aa	ARI	2	8	38	0	101	161	93	11	54	34	8.25	2.12	13.4	430	4.8	3.0	0.6	0.9	37%	60%	-12
Holtz,Mike	03	31	aaa	PIT	3	2	45	0	44	59	34	9	21	38	7.05	1.82	4.6	392	4.3	7.7	1.8	1.8	37%	64%	22
Holt,Chris	02	31	aaa	COL	6	3	12	1	70	80	36	14	16	44	4.62	1.37	25.1	327	2.1	5.6	2.8	1.8	30%	73%	37
Holzemer,Mark	02	33	aaa	ARI	2	3	51	2	34	41	23	4	19	27	6.09	1.76	3.1	385	5.0	7.1	1.4	1.1	35%	66%	38
Hooten,Dave	02	27	aa	CHC	5	1	65	9	76	69	17	5	24	48	2.01	1.22	4.8	303	2.8	5.7	2.0	0.6	28%	86%	66
	03	28	aa	OAK	7	8	39	0	111	168	76	11	40	52	6.17	1.87	13.6	398	3.2	4.2	1.3	0.9	37%	67%	12
Horgan,Joe	02	25	a/a	SF	6	5	37	0	113	156	77	12	41	59	6.12	1.74	14.3	382	3.3	4.7	1.4	1.0	36%	65%	21
	03	26	aaa	SF	7	7	55	3	74	87	49	7	28	53	6.00	1.54	6.0	354	3.4	6.5	1.9	0.9	34%	61%	51
Houlton,D.J.	03	24	a/a	HOU	8	8	29	0	170	200	107	30	51	122	5.67	1.47	25.8	343	2.7	6.5	2.4	1.6	32%	65%	40
House,Craig	03	26	a/a	FLA	2	1	34	2	43	52	39	0	47	30	8.10	2.29	6.6	448	9.7	6.2	0.6	0.0	36%	61%	47
Housman,Jeff	03	22	aa	MIL	3	2	8	0	46	58	22	5	18	22	4.30	1.65	26.3	369	3.5	4.3	1.2	1.0	33%	76%	17
Howard,Ben	02	24	a/a	SD	3	5	17	0	78	82	45	12	32	47	5.19	1.46	20.1	341	3.7	5.4	1.5	1.4	29%	68%	24
	03	25	aaa	SD	7	9	22	0	130	125	69	15	46	56	4.77	1.31	25.1	318	3.2	3.9	1.2	1.0	26%	65%	23
Howington,Ty	02	22	aa	CIN	1	5	15	0	65	72	42	5	31	43	5.82	1.58	19.5	360	4.3	6.0	1.4	0.7	32%	62%	44
Hudson,Luke	02	25	aaa	CIN	5	9	30	3	117	112	65	6	52	107	4.99	1.40	16.9	332	4.0	8.2	2.1	0.5	32%	63%	84
Hughes,Travis	02	24	aa	TEX	9	7	26	0	143	176	79	15	88	114	4.97	1.84	26.2	395	5.5	7.2	1.3	0.9	36%	74%	38
	03	25	a/a	TEX	5	11	35	0	131	202	107	14	57	78	7.37	1.97	18.3	412	3.9	5.3	1.4	0.9	39%	62%	19
Huisman,Justin	03	24	aa	COL	7	2	57	26	61	73	18	2	7	38	2.63	1.31	4.5	317	1.1	5.6	5.2	0.3	34%	80%	130
Hundley,Jeff	02	26	a/a	ANA	1	5	42	1	69	81	40	9	26	37	5.21	1.55	7.4	354	3.4	4.8	1.4	1.2	31%	68%	21
Hunter,Johnny	02	27	a/a	SD	5	5	33	1	113	152	72	11	51	44	5.73	1.79	16.2	389	4.1	3.5	0.9	0.9	34%	68%	5
Hurtado,Edwin	02	33	aaa	KC	4	4	11	0	60	83	38	6	19	36	5.70	1.70	25.2	376	2.9	5.4	1.9	0.9	37%	67%	36
Hutchinson,Trevor	03	24	aa	FLA	3	3	8	0	35	39	19	1	15	15	4.87	1.53	19.5	352	3.8	3.9	1.0	0.3	31%	66%	37
Hutchison,Ryan	03	25	aa	PHI	3	2	34	5	52	66	27	7	19	14	4.60	1.62	7.0	365	3.3	2.3	0.7	1.1	31%	74%	-11
Hutchison,Wesley	02	23	a/a	SF	3	13	39	3	101	136	79	10	42	53	7.04	1.76	12.1	385	3.7	4.7	1.3	0.9	35%	59%	20
Ireland,Eric	03	27	aa	HOU	1	5	32	0	67	113	55	8	34	41	7.40	2.19	10.7	437	4.6	5.5	1.2	1.1	41%	66%	7
Izquierdo,Hansel	02	26	a/a	FLA	4	6	14	0	78	105	46	9	24	33	5.31	1.65	25.5	370	2.8	3.8	1.4	1.0	34%	69%	12
	03	27	aaa	MON	2	3	21	3	64	111	74	6	26	33	10.42	2.14	15.4	431	3.6	4.6	1.3	0.9	42%	48%	9
Jackson,Dan	03	25	aa	TOR	5	1	33	2	47	58	28	2	27	30	5.32	1.80	6.7	389	5.1	5.7	1.1	0.4	35%	69%	40
Jackson,Edwin	03	20	aa	LA	7	7	27	0	148	133	72	10	52	147	4.40	1.25	22.9	308	3.2	8.9	2.8	0.6	31%	64%	103
Jacobsen,Landon	03	24	aa	PIT	9	11	27	0	162	201	78	14	42	65	4.32	1.50	26.5	347	2.3	3.6	1.5	0.8	32%	72%	26
Jacome,Jason	02	32	aaa	STL	8	6	28	1	105	138	62	17	24	60	5.30	1.54	16.8	353	2.1	5.1	2.5	1.5	34%	69%	33
Jacquez,Tom	02	27	aaa	CHW	0	7	14	0	61	97	63	10	23	41	9.28	1.96	21.3	411	3.4	6.0	1.8	1.5	40%	52%	14
James,Delvin	02	25	a/a	TAM	3	3	10	0	47	63	26	7	6	32	4.98	1.47	20.6	342	1.1	6.1	5.3	1.3	36%	69%	101
	03	26	aaa	TAM	5	10	34	0	137	204	104	23	38	55	6.82	1.77	18.9	385	2.5	3.6	1.4	1.5	35%	63%	-6
James,Mike	02	35	aaa	COL	1	1	24	1	31	45	35	7	16	21	10.16	1.97	6.3	411	4.6	6.1	1.3	2.0	36%	48%	-8
Jamison,Ryan	02	25	aa	HOU	3	6	42	1	94	125	54	6	42	73	5.16	1.77	10.5	386	4.0	7.0	1.7	0.6	38%	70%	54
Janke,Cheyenne	02	26	aa	STL	12	8	28	0	150	174	73	16	43	92	4.38	1.45	23.4	339	2.6	5.5	2.1	1.0	32%	72%	47
	03	27	aa	HOU	2	5	37	1	73	111	60	9	37	46	7.36	2.03	9.8	418	4.5	5.7	1.3	1.1	39%	64%	13
Jarvis,Matt	02	31	aaa	SF	5	4	43	3	56	71	27	3	21	38	4.32	1.64	6.0	367	3.4	6.1	1.8	0.5	36%	73%	55
	03	32	aaa	SF	1	2	23	0	31	46	16	0	11	13	4.58	1.83	6.4	394	3.1	3.9	1.3	0.0	38%	72%	37
Jean,Domingo	02	34	a/a	NYY	0	6	55	19	70	83	44	11	28	46	5.65	1.58	5.7	360	3.6	5.9	1.6	1.4	32%	67%	25
Jenks,Bobby	02	22	aa	ANA	3	6	10	0	58	57	37	2	44	50	5.74	1.74	27.0	382	6.8	7.8	1.1	0.3	33%	65%	66
	03	23	aa	ANA	7	2	16	0	83	65	25	2	51	88	2.71	1.40	22.4	331	5.5	9.5	1.7	0.2	30%	80%	100
Jensen,Ryan	03	28	aaa	SF	1	10	27	0	103	129	68	11	35	39	5.91	1.59	17.3	361	3.1	3.4	1.1	0.9	32%	63%	10
Jimenez,Jason	02	27	aaa	TAM	2	2	44	3	51	57	20	3	16	46	3.52	1.43	5.1	336	2.8	8.1	2.9	0.5	36%	76%	93
	03	28	aaa	DET	1	2	47	2	49	53	29	2	29	29	5.41	1.68	4.8	373	5.4	5.4	1.0	0.4	32%	66%	43
Johnson,Adam	02	23	aaa	MIN	13	8	27	0	151	196	99	23	53	96	5.90	1.65	25.6	369	3.2	5.7	1.8	1.4	34%	66%	25
	03	24	aaa	MIN	6	11	28	0	114	153	90	8	52	66	7.10	1.80	19.2	389	4.1	5.2	1.3	0.6	36%	58%	31
Johnson,James	03	27	a/a	BOS	3	5	41	5	58	54	33	8	24	50	5.16	1.35	6.0	323	3.7	7.8	2.1	1.2	29%	64%	60

Major League Equivalent Statistics

					Actual				Major League Equivalents																
PITCHER	Yr	Age	Lev	Org	w	l	g	sv	ip	h	er	hr	bb	k	era	br/ip	bf/g	oob	ctl	dom	cmd	hr/9	h%	s%	bpv
Johnson,Jeremy	02	20	aa	DET	6	1	8	0	48	52	22	6	12	25	4.11	1.33	25.6	320	2.2	4.7	2.1	1.1	29%	72%	39
	03	21	aa	DET	5	3	10	0	60	60	23	5	14	27	3.44	1.23	25.0	304	2.1	4.0	1.9	0.7	28%	74%	46
Johnson,Jonathan	02	28	a/a	SD	0	4	29	1	66	100	68	11	22	38	9.26	1.85	10.9	396	3.0	5.2	1.7	1.5	37%	49%	9
	03	29	aaa	HOU	5	4	13	0	78	100	53	5	32	47	6.09	1.69	27.7	375	3.7	5.5	1.5	0.6	35%	63%	39
Johnson,Mark	02	27	a/a	DET	4	2	17	0	52	77	36	3	20	24	6.21	1.86	14.7	397	3.4	4.1	1.2	0.5	38%	65%	22
	03	28	aa	DET	8	3	48	4	87	125	54	8	23	38	5.55	1.69	8.4	375	2.3	3.9	1.7	0.8	36%	67%	24
Johnson,Mike	02	27	aaa	LA	2	1	8	0	44	56	19	5	17	29	3.89	1.66	25.2	370	3.5	5.9	1.7	1.0	35%	79%	35
	03	28	aaa	SF	4	3	30	1	65	66	30	4	26	44	4.16	1.40	9.4	332	3.6	6.0	1.7	0.6	30%	70%	58
Johnson,Rett	02	23	aa	SEA	10	4	21	0	117	133	65	6	57	86	5.00	1.62	25.3	365	4.4	6.6	1.5	0.5	34%	68%	56
	03	24	a/a	SEA	11	4	25	0	154	163	58	9	41	98	3.37	1.33	26.2	320	2.4	5.7	2.4	0.5	31%	75%	70
Johnston,Mike	03	25	aa	PIT	6	2	46	7	72	63	25	5	28	53	3.15	1.27	6.6	311	3.5	6.6	1.9	0.7	28%	77%	68
Jones,Bobby M.	02	31	aaa	NYM	1	4	13	0	40	53	24	4	17	27	5.39	1.75	14.4	382	3.8	6.1	1.6	0.9	36%	70%	35
	03	31	aaa	ATL	2	5	57	6	71	65	32	8	37	53	3.99	1.43	5.4	337	4.7	6.7	1.4	1.1	28%	75%	46
Jones,Chris	02	37	aa	SF	1	7	36	0	84	124	78	14	44	42	8.35	2.00	11.5	415	4.7	4.5	1.0	1.5	36%	58%	-10
Jones,Greg	02	26	aaa	ANA	7	4	39	2	62	75	33	5	20	47	4.77	1.53	7.1	351	2.9	6.8	2.4	0.7	35%	69%	65
	03	27	aaa	ANA	2	3	33	4	47	41	27	4	9	47	5.13	1.07	5.7	276	1.8	8.9	5.0	0.8	30%	51%	144
Jones,Marcus	02	28	aa	OAK	1	4	7	0	31	49	27	4	20	17	7.79	2.21	22.9	440	5.8	4.9	0.9	1.2	39%	65%	-2
Jones,Mike	03	20	aa	MIL	7	2	17	0	97	98	32	5	47	56	3.00	1.49	25.2	346	4.3	5.2	1.2	0.4	30%	80%	46
Jongejan,Ferenc	02	24	aa	CHC	3	4	62	2	67	70	32	4	30	44	4.29	1.49	4.8	346	4.0	5.9	1.5	0.5	31%	71%	52
Joseph,Jake	02	25	a/a	NYM	6	5	15	0	90	100	39	4	28	35	3.90	1.42	26.1	335	2.8	3.5	1.3	0.4	30%	72%	35
	03	26	a/a	NYM	7	10	30	0	124	195	98	12	38	57	7.09	1.87	19.8	399	2.7	4.1	1.5	0.8	38%	61%	16
Joseph,Kevin	02	26	aaa	STL	1	1	31	2	35	44	9	2	11	13	2.30	1.56	5.1	357	2.8	3.3	1.2	0.5	33%	87%	24
	03	27	aaa	MON	2	7	29	1	75	123	65	14	31	30	7.83	2.05	12.9	421	3.7	3.6	1.0	1.6	38%	63%	-23
Journell,Jimmy	02	25	a/a	STL	5	7	17	0	103	102	42	7	36	86	3.67	1.34	25.8	322	3.1	7.5	2.4	0.6	32%	73%	81
	03	26	aaa	STL	6	6	40	5	78	97	45	4	34	63	5.24	1.68	9.0	374	4.0	7.3	1.8	0.5	37%	67%	64
Judd,Mike	02	27	aaa	FLA	8	6	23	0	125	146	74	9	49	84	5.32	1.56	24.4	356	3.5	6.0	1.7	0.6	34%	65%	51
	03	28	aaa	FLA	4	9	30	4	58	66	43	6	31	46	6.67	1.67	8.9	372	4.8	7.1	1.5	1.0	33%	60%	42
Junge,Eric	02	26	aaa	PHI	12	6	29	0	180	196	87	17	73	114	4.35	1.49	27.4	346	3.6	5.7	1.6	0.8	31%	72%	42
	03	27	aaa	PHI	1	0	10	0	47	45	21	2	18	36	3.95	1.34	20.0	322	3.4	6.9	2.0	0.4	31%	69%	78
Kalita,Tim	02	24	aaa	DET	1	9	15	0	87	107	59	9	21	43	6.09	1.47	25.5	342	2.2	4.4	2.0	0.9	33%	58%	38
	03	25	aa	DET	0	5	15	0	50	91	52	7	23	24	9.27	2.27	17.3	446	4.2	4.3	1.0	1.3	41%	58%	-14
Karnuth,Jason	02	26	a/a	STL	3	4	59	4	71	93	37	9	24	38	4.69	1.65	5.5	369	3.0	4.8	1.6	1.1	34%	74%	21
	03	27	a/a	CHC	3	6	58	14	67	100	39	9	28	33	5.24	1.90	5.6	403	3.7	4.4	1.2	1.2	37%	75%	2
Karp,Josh	02	23	aa	MON	7	5	16	0	86	97	45	7	34	56	4.70	1.52	23.9	350	3.5	5.8	1.6	0.7	32%	69%	47
	03	24	aa	MON	4	10	23	0	122	148	83	14	51	61	6.12	1.63	24.2	366	3.7	4.5	1.2	1.0	32%	63%	18
Kaye,Justin	02	26	aaa	SEA	3	7	47	6	62	63	34	2	42	54	4.93	1.69	6.1	375	6.1	7.8	1.3	0.3	33%	69%	69
	03	27	aaa	CHC	3	6	51	4	73	82	43	5	39	38	5.31	1.66	6.6	370	4.8	4.7	1.0	0.6	31%	67%	29
Keisler,Randy	03	28	aaa	HOU	7	6	22	0	102	129	61	12	40	48	5.38	1.66	21.3	371	3.5	4.3	1.2	1.0	33%	69%	15
Keller,Kris	02	25	aaa	ATL	3	0	46	2	61	53	25	5	30	34	3.69	1.36	5.7	325	4.4	5.0	1.1	0.7	26%	74%	41
	03	26	a/a	CIN	3	3	55	12	63	88	38	6	31	31	5.40	1.89	5.5	401	4.4	4.5	1.0	0.9	36%	72%	12
Kelley,Rich	02	32	aaa	ANA	6	5	40	0	119	146	62	17	39	59	4.69	1.55	13.3	355	2.9	4.5	1.5	1.3	32%	73%	16
Kelly,Steve	03	24	aa	CIN	4	2	6	0	38	42	13	0	13	25	2.98	1.43	27.7	337	3.0	5.8	2.0	0.0	34%	77%	76
Kemp,Beau	03	23	aa	MIN	5	6	36	11	52	73	29	1	24	32	5.02	1.87	6.9	398	4.2	5.5	1.3	0.2	39%	71%	46
Kent,Steve	03	25	aa	FLA	4	5	37	0	58	73	47	3	42	24	7.22	1.99	7.7	413	6.5	3.8	0.6	0.5	33%	61%	14
Keppel,Bob	03	21	aa	NYM	7	4	18	0	94	100	35	6	26	39	3.34	1.34	22.3	322	2.5	3.7	1.5	0.6	29%	76%	38
Kershner,Jason	02	26	aaa	SD	7	2	31	0	86	73	33	8	26	69	3.45	1.15	11.3	290	2.7	7.2	2.7	0.8	27%	73%	84
	03	27	aaa	TOR	6	1	24	0	45	52	16	1	9	25	3.28	1.35	8.0	323	1.8	5.0	2.7	0.2	33%	74%	80
Kester,Tim	03	32	aa	BOS	10	10	27	0	164	264	101	22	26	92	5.55	1.76	28.5	385	1.4	5.0	3.5	1.2	39%	70%	52
Kibler,Ryan	02	22	aa	COL	7	8	25	0	143	190	105	10	63	51	6.61	1.77	26.8	386	4.0	3.2	0.8	0.6	34%	61%	10
Kida,Masao	03	35	aaa	LA	2	4	21	1	84	97	49	8	23	48	5.29	1.43	17.4	336	2.5	5.2	2.1	0.9	32%	63%	46
Kieschnick,Brooks	02	30	aaa	CHW	0	1	25	0	31	40	13	1	12	25	3.76	1.67	5.7	372	3.5	7.2	2.1	0.3	38%	76%	72
Kim,Sun-woo	03	26	aaa	MON	10	8	22	0	132	164	82	19	52	67	5.62	1.63	27.3	366	3.5	4.6	1.3	1.3	32%	68%	12
	02	25	aaa	MON	7	2	15	0	89	76	29	7	33	54	2.93	1.22	24.6	303	3.3	5.5	1.6	0.7	26%	78%	56
Kingrey,Jarrod	02	26	aaa	TOR	4	1	26	1	41	37	27	6	20	23	5.91	1.39	6.8	330	4.4	5.0	1.2	1.3	25%	59%	23
Kinney,Josh	03	25	aaa	STL	2	1	29	2	39	24	4	2	14	42	0.97	0.97	5.3	255	3.1	9.6	3.1	0.5	24%	94%	127
Kinney,Matt	02	26	a/a	MIN	2	1	6	0	31	54	37	11	5	20	10.71	1.90	25.0	402	1.4	5.8	4.0	3.2	39%	46%	4
Klepacki,Ed	02	24	aa	FLA	2	1	19	2	33	26	15	2	24	17	4.08	1.51	7.7	349	6.5	4.6	0.7	0.5	24%	73%	39
Knight,Brandon	02	27	aaa	NYY	2	7	36	12	80	77	41	6	38	68	4.60	1.43	9.7	337	4.3	7.6	1.8	0.7	31%	68%	69
Knotts,Gary	02	26	aaa	FLA	5	3	42	3	53	55	24	3	30	39	4.08	1.60	5.7	363	5.1	6.6	1.3	0.5	32%	74%	54
	03	27	aaa	DET	4	6	13	0	79	120	60	15	28	53	6.81	1.87	29.1	398	3.2	6.1	1.9	1.8	38%	66%	11
Knott,Eric	02	28	aaa	ARI	8	10	31	1	150	220	97	13	23	74	5.82	1.62	22.0	365	1.4	4.4	3.2	0.8	37%	63%	59
	03	29	aaa	MON	6	5	24	0	77	121	44	7	13	29	5.14	1.74	15.0	382	1.5	3.4	2.2	0.8	38%	71%	29
Kohlmeier,Ryan	02	25	aaa	CHW	2	1	38	0	65	79	48	17	21	53	6.64	1.54	7.6	353	2.9	7.3	2.5	2.4	32%	63%	23
	03	26	aaa	CHW	7	4	33	0	116	158	81	25	22	64	6.31	1.54	15.7	354	1.7	5.0	3.0	1.9	34%	63%	26
Kolb,Brandon	02	29	aaa	CHC	3	3	53	1	64	76	35	3	37	43	4.91	1.76	5.7	385	5.2	6.0	1.2	0.4	35%	71%	45
Kolb,Dan	03	29	aaa	MIL	0	1	26	4	39	33	9	1	14	36	1.98	1.21	6.2	300	3.2	8.3	2.6	0.2	30%	84%	107
Komine,Shane	03	23	aa	OAK	4	6	19	0	103	118	48	6	30	64	4.19	1.44	23.6	337	2.6	5.6	2.1	0.5	33%	70%	61
Komiyama,Satoru	02	37	aaa	NYM	3	1	17	0	44	33	8	4	9	34	1.63	0.95	10.0	252	1.8	6.9	3.8	0.8	24%	89%	111
Koplove,Mike	02	26	aaa	ARI	1	2	23	3	30	24	4	1	4	25	1.19	0.93	5.1	247	1.2	7.5	6.3	0.3	28%	89%	179
Koronka,John	02	22	aa	CIN	2	8	16	0	95	121	61	11	48	58	5.77	1.78	27.9	386	4.5	5.5	1.2	1.0	34%	68%	21
	03	23	aa	CHC	7	13	26	0	162	202	86	9	62	101	4.75	1.63	28.4	366	3.4	5.6	1.6	0.5	35%	70%	48
Kozlowski,Ben	02	22	aa	TEX	4	2	8	0	52	34	15	4	22	36	2.60	1.08	26.0	276	3.8	6.2	1.6	0.7	21%	79%	69
	03	23	aa	TEX	3	2	11	0	54	88	45	5	28	24	7.53	2.13	24.9	430	4.6	4.0	0.9	0.9	39%	64%	1
Krawczyk,Jack	02	27	a/a	MIL	5	3	46	5	69	78	33	6	21	54	4.30	1.43	6.5	337	2.7	7.0	2.6	0.8	34%	71%	72
	03	28	aa	ARI	1	3	21	0	41	79	45	4	13	19	9.88	2.23	10.0	441	2.7	4.2	1.5	0.8	44%	53%	8
Krawiec,Aaron	03	25	aa	CHC	3	4	8	0	44	62	22	7	11	20	4.51	1.65	25.2	369	2.1	4.1	1.9	1.5	34%	77%	9
Kroon,Marc	03	31	aaa	ANA	5	4	46	6	59	54	31	4	41	48	4.77	1.61	5.8	363	6.3	7.3	1.2	0.6	30%	70%	59
Kubes,Greg	02	26	aa	PHI	13	7	28	0	174	223	89	19	53	87	4.60	1.59	28.0	360	2.7	4.5	1.6	1.0	34%	73%	26
	03	27	aaa	PHI	6	3	37	3	95	140	58	8	18	53	5.47	1.66	11.8	371	1.7	5.1	3.0	0.8	38%	67%	59
Kusiewicz,Mike	02	26	a/a	BOS	7	8	23	0	114	131	63	9	35	69	4.97	1.45	21.7	340	2.8	5.4	2.0	0.7	33%	66%	51
	03	27	a/a	OAK	3	2	45	1	51	56	29	2	20	32	5.09	1.48	5.0	344	3.5	5.5	1.6	0.4	32%	64%	55
Lackey,John	02	24	aaa	ANA	8	2	16	0	101	97	32	5	26	70	2.85	1.22	26.2	301	2.3	6.2	2.7	0.4	30%	77%	86

Major League Equivalent Statistics

					Actual				Major League Equivalents																
PITCHER	Yr	Age	Lev	Org	w	l	g	sv	ip	h	er	hr	bb	k	era	br/ip	bf/g	oob	ctl	dom	cmd	hr/9	h%	s%	bpv
Lail,Denny	02	28	aaa	STL	1	3	10	0	41	52	28	3	28	20	6.13	1.95	20.0	408	6.1	4.4	0.7	0.7	34%	68%	16
Lambert,Jeremy	03	25	a/a	STL	1	2	45	2	53	52	21	7	22	58	3.50	1.38	5.1	329	3.7	9.9	2.7	1.2	33%	80%	84
Lamber,Justin	02	26	aa	SEA	1	2	34	0	33	48	18	1	18	18	4.89	1.99	4.8	414	4.9	4.9	1.0	0.3	38%	74%	31
	03	27	aa	SEA	3	2	39	0	58	90	33	2	18	27	5.04	1.87	7.1	398	2.8	4.1	1.5	0.4	39%	72%	30
Langen,Brian	02	25	aa	STL	2	0	46	0	53	56	28	3	32	29	4.75	1.66	5.3	371	5.4	4.9	0.9	0.5	31%	71%	35
Langone,Steve	02	25	aa	LA	2	2	14	1	32	26	6	0	14	14	1.68	1.24	9.6	306	3.9	3.9	1.0	0.0	25%	85%	56
	03	26	a/a	LA	3	0	28	1	58	60	22	2	13	50	3.42	1.25	8.7	307	2.0	7.8	4.0	0.3	34%	72%	123
Lankford,Frank	02	32	aaa	OAK	6	6	46	0	80	99	42	8	21	46	4.72	1.50	7.7	347	2.4	5.2	2.2	0.9	34%	70%	46
Lantigua,Delvis	02	23	a/a	CHW	7	7	31	0	137	136	90	22	68	99	5.90	1.49	19.5	345	4.5	6.5	1.5	1.4	28%	63%	31
Larrison,Preston	03	23	a/a	DET	4	13	25	0	132	191	101	11	58	49	6.89	1.89	25.4	401	4.0	3.3	0.8	0.8	36%	62%	4
Larson,Ryan	02	23	a/a	CLE	2	3	33	8	37	48	12	5	7	27	2.92	1.49	4.9	345	1.7	6.6	3.9	1.2	36%	86%	77
	03	24	aa	CLE	2	6	40	2	63	99	38	11	20	24	5.40	1.89	7.6	401	2.9	3.4	1.2	1.5	36%	75%	-15
Lavigne,Tim	02	24	aa	NYM	2	3	23	9	34	34	13	1	16	20	3.42	1.46	6.5	341	4.2	5.3	1.3	0.3	30%	76%	54
	03	25	a/a	NYM	3	5	47	11	72	101	43	6	43	40	5.39	2.00	7.5	415	5.4	5.0	0.9	0.8	37%	73%	16
Laxton,Brett	02	29	aaa	KC	9	13	29	0	156	229	115	16	52	78	6.63	1.80	25.4	389	3.0	4.5	1.5	0.9	37%	63%	19
Layfield,Scotty	02	26	aa	STL	6	4	58	24	65	69	22	6	26	50	3.05	1.46	4.9	341	3.6	6.9	1.9	0.8	32%	82%	59
Leek,Randy	02	25	aa	LA	7	5	15	0	95	122	32	7	12	44	3.03	1.41	27.5	333	1.1	4.2	3.7	0.7	34%	80%	76
Lee,Cliff	02	24	a/a	CLE	5	3	11	0	59	58	38	10	35	40	5.78	1.57	24.2	358	5.3	6.1	1.1	1.5	27%	66%	20
	03	25	a/a	CLE	7	1	13	0	75	87	35	6	39	60	4.16	1.68	26.6	374	4.7	7.2	1.5	0.8	35%	76%	51
Lee,Corey	02	28	aaa	CHW	7	6	38	0	111	163	67	18	41	81	5.43	1.84	13.9	395	3.3	6.6	2.0	1.5	38%	74%	25
Lee,Dave	02	30	aaa	MIN	9	1	51	5	64	95	38	5	33	55	5.33	1.99	6.2	414	4.6	7.7	1.7	0.7	42%	73%	48
	03	31	aaa	LA	3	2	56	9	60	54	23	4	38	49	3.49	1.53	4.8	352	5.7	7.3	1.3	0.7	29%	78%	58
Lee,Derek	02	28	aa	MIL	5	10	34	0	127	203	69	9	56	71	4.89	2.04	18.5	419	4.0	5.0	1.3	0.6	40%	76%	22
	03	29	a/a	MIL	13	7	34	0	147	201	89	10	59	79	5.45	1.77	20.3	385	3.6	4.8	1.3	0.6	36%	68%	30
Lee,Garrett	02	26	a/a	KC	8	2	37	2	92	120	42	9	21	35	4.11	1.53	11.1	352	2.1	3.4	1.7	0.9	33%	75%	22
	03	27	aa	KC	5	9	30	1	118	212	107	28	40	51	8.17	2.13	19.9	431	3.0	3.9	1.3	2.1	39%	65%	-35
Lee,Seung	03	24	a/a	PHI	11	8	28	0	152	184	114	25	51	97	6.77	1.54	24.2	353	3.0	5.7	1.9	1.5	32%	57%	27
Lehr,Justin	02	25	aa	OAK	8	3	58	4	80	110	47	8	33	45	5.29	1.79	6.5	388	3.7	5.1	1.4	0.9	36%	71%	23
	03	26	aaa	OAK	3	2	53	4	75	82	35	3	27	53	4.21	1.46	6.2	341	3.2	6.4	2.0	0.4	33%	70%	69
Leicester,Jon	03	25	a/a	CHC	6	7	46	6	111	112	63	8	59	94	5.09	1.54	10.8	353	4.8	7.6	1.6	0.7	32%	66%	63
Levrault,Allen	02	25	aaa	OAK	7	8	24	0	111	151	79	13	41	68	6.40	1.73	21.5	380	3.3	5.5	1.7	1.1	36%	63%	28
Lewis,Colby	02	23	aaa	TEX	5	6	20	0	106	110	48	4	26	86	4.07	1.28	22.3	312	2.2	7.3	3.3	0.3	33%	67%	106
	03	24	aaa	TEX	5	1	7	0	47	43	21	8	19	38	4.00	1.31	28.5	318	3.6	7.2	2.0	1.5	27%	76%	47
Lewis,Derrick	02	26	a/a	ATL	4	5	19	0	83	101	51	11	40	41	5.53	1.70	20.2	376	4.3	4.4	1.0	1.2	32%	69%	9
	03	27	a/a	ATL	2	5	39	0	70	133	89	11	39	38	11.38	2.46	9.7	466	5.0	4.9	1.0	1.5	43%	52%	-18
Lidge,Brad	02	26	a/a	HOU	6	6	29	0	122	115	61	13	56	105	4.49	1.40	18.2	332	4.1	7.7	1.9	1.0	30%	70%	63
Lidle,Kevin	02	31	aa	DET	2	11	23	0	91	187	91	13	37	29	9.00	2.46	21.3	466	3.7	2.9	0.8	1.3	43%	63%	-33
Linton,Doug	02	38	aaa	ATL	9	11	28	0	174	202	63	16	27	127	3.26	1.32	26.3	318	1.4	6.6	4.7	0.8	34%	78%	111
	03	38	aaa	TOR	2	10	32	0	109	165	87	17	20	66	7.21	1.70	15.7	376	1.7	5.4	3.3	1.4	38%	58%	46
Lira,Felipe	02	30	aaa	CIN	4	6	32	1	99	130	66	8	30	43	6.00	1.62	14.0	364	2.7	3.9	1.4	0.7	34%	62%	25
Lira,James	02	25	aa	HOU	3	4	28	3	43	44	21	7	19	23	4.40	1.47	6.7	342	4.0	4.8	1.2	1.5	27%	75%	13
	03	26	aa	SF	1	6	24	1	63	107	53	7	31	37	7.55	2.19	13.4	437	4.4	5.2	1.2	1.0	41%	65%	8
Liriano,Pedro	03	23	aa	MIL	9	13	27	0	142	163	78	14	64	97	4.94	1.60	23.8	361	4.1	6.1	1.5	0.9	33%	70%	41
Lockwood,Luke	03	22	aa	MON	8	11	26	0	144	196	97	17	40	53	6.05	1.64	25.3	367	2.5	3.3	1.3	1.1	34%	63%	7
Loewer,Carlton	03	30	aaa	SD	7	8	23	0	125	190	88	9	30	42	6.32	1.76	25.4	384	2.2	3.0	1.4	0.6	37%	63%	15
Looney,Brian	02	33	a/a	BAL	1	2	19	0	35	40	23	7	17	17	5.88	1.62	8.4	365	4.3	4.3	1.0	1.8	29%	68%	-8
Looper,Aaron	02	26	aa	SEA	6	1	57	0	90	106	36	6	36	54	3.59	1.57	7.1	358	3.6	5.4	1.5	0.6	33%	78%	43
	03	27	aaa	SEA	5	2	46	5	75	87	34	11	28	57	4.04	1.54	7.3	353	3.4	6.8	2.0	1.3	33%	78%	43
Lopez,Aquilino	02	27	aaa	SEA	4	4	34	5	109	106	37	6	28	84	3.05	1.23	13.3	303	2.3	6.9	3.0	0.5	31%	76%	95
Lopez,Javier	02	25	aa	ARI	2	2	61	6	46	42	18	3	17	35	3.51	1.28	3.2	312	3.3	6.8	2.1	0.6	29%	73%	74
Lorraine,Andrew	02	30	aaa	MIL	7	11	25	0	165	210	83	20	48	67	4.53	1.56	29.6	357	2.6	3.7	1.4	1.1	32%	74%	13
	03	31	aaa	LA	8	9	30	0	158	231	77	16	39	65	4.38	1.71	24.4	377	2.2	3.7	1.7	0.9	36%	76%	18
Loux,Shane	02	23	aaa	DET	11	10	26	0	158	227	103	10	36	79	5.86	1.66	27.9	371	2.0	4.5	2.2	0.6	37%	63%	45
	03	24	aaa	DET	11	6	21	0	128	152	55	5	29	51	3.87	1.41	26.4	334	2.0	3.6	1.8	0.4	32%	72%	45
Lovingier,Kevin	02	31	a/a	NYY	0	4	40	1	48	78	32	1	39	25	6.00	2.44	6.4	464	7.3	4.7	0.6	0.2	41%	73%	19
Lowe,Sean	03	33	aaa	KC	4	0	14	0	52	66	25	4	19	21	4.36	1.63	17.0	367	3.3	3.6	1.1	0.7	33%	74%	17
Lowry,Noah	03	23	a/a	SF	10	6	27	0	137	152	71	5	49	93	4.66	1.47	22.3	342	3.2	6.1	1.9	0.3	33%	66%	67
Luebbers,Larry	02	33	aaa	OAK	11	11	28	0	168	218	95	16	53	65	5.08	1.61	27.2	364	2.8	3.5	1.2	0.9	33%	69%	14
Lugo,Ruddy	02	22	aa	LA	3	1	11	1	33	40	19	3	14	20	5.17	1.63	13.7	366	3.8	5.4	1.4	0.8	34%	69%	35
	03	23	aa	HOU	4	15	41	1	118	158	100	14	55	92	7.62	1.80	13.6	389	4.2	7.0	1.7	1.1	37%	57%	37
Lukasiewicz,Mark	02	30	aaa	ANA	3	2	35	0	43	55	23	7	18	37	4.81	1.70	5.7	376	3.8	7.7	2.1	1.5	36%	76%	40
	03	31	aaa	ANA	2	2	40	1	62	91	52	9	19	40	7.57	1.77	7.3	386	2.7	5.7	2.1	1.3	38%	57%	28
Lundberg,Spike	02	25	a/a	TEX	11	9	29	0	164	227	100	18	42	78	5.49	1.64	25.8	368	2.3	4.3	1.9	1.0	35%	67%	26
	03	26	a/a	TEX	4	5	59	31	69	91	28	6	19	46	3.61	1.59	5.3	360	2.5	6.0	2.4	0.7	36%	79%	58
Lundquist,Dave	02	29	aaa	SD	1	4	30	21	32	34	25	7	16	24	7.03	1.56	4.8	357	4.5	6.8	1.5	2.0	29%	58%	15
Lyons,Mike	03	28	aa	STL	3	4	57	31	53	75	34	3	31	46	5.72	2.00	4.6	415	5.3	7.9	1.5	0.4	41%	70%	55
Lyon,Brandon	02	23	aaa	TOR	4	9	14	0	75	111	50	4	18	30	5.98	1.72	24.9	378	2.2	3.6	1.7	0.5	37%	63%	30
Mabeus,Chris	03	25	aa	OAK	1	3	32	13	38	43	18	1	9	32	4.23	1.38	5.1	329	2.2	7.6	3.4	0.2	36%	67%	109
MacDougal,Mike	02	26	a/a	KC	4	6	16	0	70	78	53	6	82	34	6.79	2.28	22.8	447	10.5	4.4	0.4	0.8	31%	69%	12
MacRae,Scott	02	28	aaa	CIN	4	2	49	2	72	86	31	5	27	42	3.86	1.57	6.6	357	3.4	5.2	1.6	0.6	33%	76%	42
Madritsch,Bobby	03	28	aa	SEA	13	7	27	0	158	184	95	13	83	115	5.41	1.69	27.0	375	4.7	6.5	1.4	0.8	34%	68%	43
Madson,Ryan	02	22	aa	PHI	16	4	26	0	171	171	73	12	57	121	3.84	1.33	28.0	321	3.0	6.4	2.1	0.6	31%	72%	68
	03	23	aaa	PHI	12	8	26	0	157	182	76	10	46	122	4.36	1.45	26.4	340	2.6	7.0	2.7	0.6	35%	70%	79
Magrane,Jim	02	24	a/a	TAM	7	11	29	0	156	204	115	23	73	64	6.63	1.77	25.3	386	4.2	3.7	0.9	1.3	32%	64%	-6
	03	25	a/a	TAM	10	7	27	0	155	203	86	18	62	74	5.01	1.71	26.6	377	3.6	4.3	1.2	1.0	34%	72%	13
Mahay,Ron	02	31	aaa	CHC	0	1	39	2	46	34	11	3	15	42	2.14	1.06	4.7	273	2.9	8.2	2.8	0.6	26%	83%	105
	03	32	aaa	TEX	4	2	26	3	42	45	28	7	11	42	6.06	1.32	6.9	319	2.2	8.9	4.0	1.6	33%	57%	91
Mahomes,Pat	02	32	aaa	CHC	4	5	44	14	72	61	28	11	19	59	3.50	1.11	6.6	282	2.4	7.4	3.1	1.4	26%	75%	78
	03	33	aaa	PIT	8	4	38	2	64	68	26	4	21	23	3.70	1.40	7.3	331	3.0	3.2	1.1	0.6	29%	74%	26
Mairena,Ozwaldo	03	29	aaa	FLA	6	4	61	1	86	126	63	11	30	45	6.56	1.81	6.7	392	3.1	4.7	1.5	1.2	37%	64%	13
Majewski,Gary	02	23	aa	CHW	5	3	57	3	74	74	30	4	36	69	3.64	1.48	5.7	345	4.4	8.4	1.9	0.5	33%	75%	80
	03	24	aaa	CHW	6	4	42	4	72	73	42	4	30	65	5.24	1.43	7.5	336	3.7	8.1	2.2	0.5	33%	62%	83

Major League Equivalent Statistics

PITCHER	Yr	Age	Lev	Org	Actual				Major League Equivalents																
					w	l	g	sv	ip	h	er	hr	bb	k	era	br/ip	bf/g	oob	ctl	dom	cmd	hr/9	h%	s%	bpv
Malaska,Mark	02	25	aa	TAM	4	5	12	1	70	100	38	4	31	39	4.87	1.87	28.0	398	4.0	5.0	1.3	0.5	38%	73%	30
	03	26	a/a	TAM	2	2	34	1	48	57	23	3	14	36	4.34	1.47	6.2	343	2.6	6.8	2.6	0.6	35%	70%	76
Mallette,Brian	02	28	aaa	MIL	3	2	45	25	45	49	20	5	19	41	3.99	1.51	4.4	348	3.8	8.2	2.2	1.0	34%	76%	65
Malone,Corwin	02	22	aa	CHW	10	7	22	0	124	140	88	8	95	82	6.38	1.89	27.2	402	6.9	5.9	0.9	0.6	33%	65%	36
	03	23	aa	CHW	4	2	8	0	40	64	35	3	31	24	7.89	2.37	26.5	457	7.0	5.5	0.8	0.7	41%	65%	13
Maness,Nick	02	24	a/a	NYM	7	9	28	1	149	151	84	15	80	102	5.07	1.55	23.8	355	4.8	6.2	1.3	0.9	30%	68%	40
Mangrum,Micah	02	25	aa	KC	1	2	23	1	38	61	22	2	10	14	5.21	1.87	7.9	399	2.4	3.3	1.4	0.5	39%	71%	19
Mangum,Mark	02	24	aa	MON	7	5	18	2	80	101	46	14	25	32	5.18	1.58	20.0	358	2.8	3.6	1.3	1.6	31%	71%	-4
Manning,Charlie	02	24	aa	NYY	4	2	11	0	63	66	32	1	28	52	4.57	1.49	25.3	346	4.0	7.4	1.9	0.1	34%	67%	81
	03	25	aa	NYY	0	2	23	0	46	63	40	1	37	28	7.83	2.17	10.2	435	7.2	5.4	0.7	0.2	38%	61%	33
Manning,David	02	30	aa	MIN	3	3	11	0	62	114	57	4	40	22	8.26	2.48	30.5	468	5.8	3.2	0.6	0.6	42%	65%	-9
	03	31	aaa	MIL	6	8	23	0	99	127	73	8	65	61	6.60	1.95	20.9	408	5.9	5.5	0.9	0.8	35%	65%	24
Mann,Jim	02	28	a/a	HOU	0	3	34	22	36	46	25	10	9	23	6.22	1.52	4.7	350	2.2	5.7	2.6	2.5	31%	67%	8
	03	29	aaa	PIT	3	2	51	5	61	48	29	10	22	38	4.27	1.14	4.9	288	3.2	5.6	1.8	1.4	22%	68%	41
Manon,Julio	02	29	a/a	MON	13	7	34	2	144	170	82	16	60	92	5.12	1.60	19.1	361	3.7	5.7	1.5	1.0	33%	69%	34
	03	30	aaa	MON	3	1	35	14	42	40	12	4	20	36	2.62	1.43	5.2	336	4.3	7.7	1.8	1.0	30%	86%	61
Markwell,Diego	03	23	aa	TOR	5	7	28	0	110	172	107	23	55	58	8.77	2.06	19.6	422	4.5	4.8	1.1	1.9	37%	59%	-20
Markwell,Diegomar	02	22	aa	TOR	13	9	28	1	168	192	93	23	57	87	4.98	1.48	26.4	344	3.1	4.7	1.5	1.2	30%	69%	22
Maroth,Mike	02	25	aaa	DET	8	1	11	0	73	62	28	6	21	46	3.45	1.14	27.0	287	2.6	5.7	2.2	0.7	26%	71%	68
Marquez,Rob	02	29	aaa	MIL	4	7	47	8	68	80	43	14	27	34	5.68	1.57	6.5	358	3.6	4.5	1.3	1.9	29%	69%	-4
	03	30	aaa	MIL	0	2	30	0	56	72	36	8	29	33	5.70	1.80	8.8	390	4.6	5.3	1.2	1.2	34%	70%	13
Marquis,Jason	03	25	aaa	ATL	8	4	15	0	94	115	49	6	35	62	4.74	1.60	28.3	362	3.4	6.0	1.8	0.6	35%	70%	51
Marrero,Darwin	02	22	aa	MON	6	5	19	0	105	135	56	18	20	46	4.80	1.47	24.3	343	1.7	3.9	2.3	1.5	32%	72%	20
Marshall,Lee	02	26	aaa	BAL	4	6	59	4	78	118	52	6	33	29	6.00	1.94	6.4	407	3.8	3.3	0.9	0.7	37%	68%	5
	03	27	a/a	ARI	5	6	55	1	71	133	63	7	28	37	8.01	2.27	6.7	446	3.5	4.7	1.4	0.9	44%	63%	7
Marsonek,Sam	02	24	aa	NYY	5	8	19	0	100	136	74	7	37	64	6.65	1.73	24.5	380	3.3	5.7	1.7	0.6	37%	60%	43
	03	25	aaa	NYY	4	4	54	18	83	97	55	10	31	49	5.90	1.54	6.9	353	3.4	5.2	1.5	1.1	32%	62%	29
Martines,Jason	02	27	aa	ARI	2	1	27	2	40	57	28	3	14	18	6.28	1.77	7.0	386	3.1	4.0	1.3	0.7	36%	63%	21
Martinez,Anastacio	02	22	aa	BOS	5	12	27	0	139	168	93	11	73	107	6.02	1.73	24.0	381	4.7	6.9	1.5	0.7	36%	64%	47
	03	25	a/a	PIT	5	2	45	14	58	59	19	6	28	36	2.88	1.49	5.7	346	4.3	5.6	1.3	1.0	29%	85%	35
Martinez,Gustavo	02	27	a/a	SEA	3	6	22	0	102	126	53	8	52	61	4.67	1.74	21.6	382	4.6	5.4	1.2	0.7	34%	74%	31
	03	28	aa	SEA	7	6	35	0	92	106	47	10	61	55	4.60	1.82	12.5	392	6.0	5.4	0.9	0.9	32%	76%	21
Martinez,Luis	02	23	aa	MIL	8	8	29	1	109	134	80	7	65	91	6.61	1.83	17.8	393	5.4	7.5	1.4	0.6	37%	62%	53
	03	24	a/a	MIL	12	5	27	0	160	153	49	5	75	136	2.75	1.42	25.8	335	4.2	7.6	1.8	0.3	32%	80%	81
Martin,Chandler	02	29	a/a	COL	8	8	27	0	141	202	92	15	61	71	5.87	1.86	25.0	398	3.9	4.5	1.2	1.0	36%	69%	12
Mata,Gustavo	03	20	aa	MON	6	8	22	0	107	150	66	10	36	37	5.52	1.74	22.7	382	3.0	3.1	1.0	0.8	35%	68%	6
Mateo,Julio	02	25	a/a	SEA	5	2	32	6	48	57	20	4	11	33	3.74	1.41	6.5	334	2.1	6.2	3.0	0.7	34%	75%	75
Matos,Josue	02	25	a/a	SEA	5	7	28	0	150	218	127	30	43	90	7.62	1.74	25.0	382	2.6	5.4	2.1	1.8	36%	58%	11
	03	26	aa	SEA	7	2	48	4	88	74	30	9	42	84	3.06	1.32	7.8	320	4.3	8.6	2.0	0.9	28%	80%	76
Mattioni,Nick	03	25	aa	NYM	0	3	42	4	75	85	35	1	41	54	4.16	1.68	8.2	374	4.9	6.5	1.3	0.1	35%	73%	62
Mattox,David	03	23	aa	NYM	8	7	21	0	113	115	49	7	40	70	3.94	1.38	23.1	328	3.2	5.6	1.7	0.6	30%	72%	56
Maurer,Dave	02	28	aaa	CLE	5	1	36	5	68	63	32	8	27	60	4.23	1.32	8.0	319	3.6	7.9	2.2	1.1	29%	71%	69
Maust,David	03	25	aa	MON	3	6	17	1	66	68	24	5	21	26	3.29	1.35	16.6	324	2.9	3.5	1.2	0.7	28%	78%	28
Mayo,Blake	02	30	a/a	ARI	1	5	19	0	55	93	55	5	34	28	8.98	2.30	15.2	450	5.6	4.6	0.8	0.8	41%	59%	2
McAdoo,Duncan	03	25	aa	SD	6	8	30	0	130	161	80	10	34	82	5.53	1.50	19.2	348	2.4	5.7	2.4	0.7	35%	62%	59
McAvoy,Jeff	02	26	a/a	MON	3	3	17	3	39	55	33	5	13	18	7.58	1.73	10.7	381	3.0	4.1	1.4	1.1	35%	56%	10
McClaskey,Tim	03	28	aa	HOU	5	4	15	1	65	95	51	8	18	39	6.98	1.74	20.2	381	2.5	5.4	2.2	1.2	37%	60%	31
McClung,Seth	02	22	aa	TAM	5	7	20	0	114	160	85	13	54	54	6.71	1.88	27.3	400	4.3	4.3	1.0	1.0	35%	64%	6
McConnell,Sam	02	27	a/a	PHI	2	7	36	3	104	151	57	16	41	54	4.92	1.84	13.8	395	3.5	4.7	1.3	1.4	36%	77%	3
	03	28	a/a	ATL	9	4	38	0	108	156	55	7	25	53	4.59	1.68	13.1	373	2.1	4.4	2.1	0.6	37%	72%	42
McCrotty,Will	02	23	aa	LA	1	4	43	6	52	44	19	3	32	49	3.28	1.46	5.3	340	5.5	8.4	1.5	0.5	29%	78%	78
	03	24	aa	LA	3	5	32	1	93	107	55	7	45	57	5.30	1.64	13.3	368	4.4	5.5	1.3	0.7	33%	67%	36
McDade,Neal	02	26	aa	PIT	8	3	49	3	78	111	47	13	17	38	5.42	1.64	7.3	368	2.0	4.4	2.2	1.5	35%	70%	18
	03	27	aa	PIT	1	6	38	4	72	111	37	7	22	34	4.66	1.84	9.0	394	2.7	4.2	1.6	0.9	38%	76%	17
McDonald,Jon	02	25	aa	MIN	3	8	21	0	72	94	64	4	52	23	7.99	2.02	17.0	418	6.5	2.9	0.4	0.5	33%	58%	5
McGowan,Dustin	03	22	aa	TOR	7	0	14	0	76	89	32	1	19	63	3.78	1.42	23.6	334	2.2	7.4	3.3	0.1	37%	71%	109
McKnight,Tony	02	25	aaa	PIT	11	14	30	0	175	229	125	22	42	102	6.42	1.55	26.1	354	2.2	5.2	2.4	1.1	35%	59%	42
McLeary,Marty	02	28	a/a	BOS	1	3	29	0	52	83	52	7	36	22	8.98	2.28	9.3	447	6.2	3.8	0.6	1.2	38%	60%	-16
	03	29	a/a	FLA	2	2	31	0	63	80	28	5	39	30	4.03	1.88	9.8	400	5.5	4.2	0.8	0.7	34%	79%	16
McWhirter,Kris	03	24	aa	CHW	3	8	25	0	60	78	57	3	49	36	8.50	2.12	12.1	429	7.4	5.4	0.7	0.5	36%	57%	27
Meadows,Brian	02	27	aaa	PIT	9	8	23	0	126	156	75	15	26	81	5.35	1.44	23.9	339	1.9	5.8	3.1	1.1	34%	64%	63
	03	28	aaa	PIT	7	0	9	0	51	40	11	2	0	32	1.86	0.78	21.0	218	0.0	5.7		0.4	25%	78%	36
Mears,Chris	02	25	aa	SEA	6	9	30	0	143	176	71	19	42	84	4.47	1.52	21.2	351	2.6	5.3	2.0	1.2	33%	74%	34
	03	26	aaa	DET	5	1	25	2	58	64	23	5	18	24	3.60	1.41	10.1	333	2.8	3.7	1.3	0.8	29%	76%	26
Meaux,Ryan	03	25	aa	CHW	1	2	26	2	38	53	14	0	3	23	3.42	1.49	6.4	346	0.8	5.5	7.0	0.0	39%	75%	171
Meche,Gil	02	24	aa	SEA	4	6	25	0	65	86	66	9	35	46	9.14	1.86	12.4	398	4.8	6.4	1.3	1.2	36%	49%	21
Medders,Brandon	03	24	aa	ARI	5	3	56	7	69	74	39	3	25	61	5.10	1.43	5.4	337	3.2	8.0	2.5	0.4	35%	62%	89
Mendoza,Geronimo	02	23	aaa	CHW	1	9	11	0	53	77	61	13	25	35	10.36	1.92	23.3	406	4.2	5.9	1.4	2.2	36%	46%	-13
Mendoza,Hatuey	02	25	aa	ANA	3	10	29	0	90	138	73	14	38	36	7.29	1.95	15.1	409	3.8	3.6	0.9	1.4	36%	64%	-14
Mendoza,Marcos	02	22	aa	CLE	2	5	21	0	37	36	13	3	25	23	3.15	1.64	8.1	368	6.1	5.6	0.9	0.7	29%	83%	36
Mendoza,Mario	02	24	a/a	ANA	0	5	13	1	54	76	32	5	19	32	5.32	1.76	19.5	384	3.2	5.3	1.7	0.8	37%	70%	32
Mercado,Hector	02	28	a/a	PHI	3	1	26	3	33	27	8	2	14	36	2.18	1.24	5.3	305	3.8	9.8	2.6	0.5	30%	85%	108
	03	29	a/a	PHI	0	3	15	0	34	46	7	2	16	15	1.94	1.83	10.8	393	4.2	3.9	0.9	0.6	35%	92%	15
Messenger,Randall	03	22	aa	FLA	5	7	29	0	113	157	84	7	54	70	6.68	1.86	18.7	398	4.3	5.6	1.3	0.6	38%	62%	35
Meyers,Mike	03	26	aaa	CHC	5	2	30	0	74	86	43	9	36	40	5.28	1.65	11.3	369	4.4	4.8	1.1	1.1	31%	70%	17
Meyer,Jake	02	28	a/a	SEA	2	1	29	0	50	54	29	6	29	31	5.21	1.66	7.9	370	5.2	5.6	1.1	1.1	30%	70%	25
	03	29	a/a	ARI	2	4	40	1	54	72	33	4	25	28	5.48	1.78	6.4	387	4.1	4.7	1.1	0.6	35%	68%	27
Miadich,Bart	02	27	aaa	ANA	4	3	59	14	80	67	37	5	62	77	4.15	1.61	6.2	363	7.0	8.6	1.2	0.6	29%	74%	72
	03	28	aaa	ANA	5	5	46	16	51	45	25	4	41	53	4.45	1.69	5.1	375	7.2	9.4	1.3	0.7	31%	74%	70
Michalak,Chris	02	32	aaa	BOS	5	9	18	0	94	153	79	17	34	43	7.55	1.99	25.7	413	3.2	4.1	1.3	1.6	38%	64%	-14
	03	33	aaa	CIN	9	10	33	1	146	208	95	37	49	73	5.83	1.76	20.8	385	3.0	4.5	1.5	2.3	34%	74%	-21

					Actual				Major League Equivalents																
PITCHER	Yr	Age	Lev	Org	w	l	g	sv	ip	h	er	hr	bb	k	era	br/ip	bf/g	oob	ctl	dom	cmd	hr/9	h%	s%	bpv
Middlebrook,Jason	02	27	aaa	NYM	4	6	15	0	60	66	38	7	15	44	5.69	1.35	17.1	323	2.2	6.6	2.9	1.0	32%	58%	70
	03	28	aaa	NYM	7	10	23	0	118	151	78	25	37	71	5.98	1.58	23.1	360	2.8	5.4	1.9	1.9	32%	67%	11
Miller,Greg	02	23	aa	HOU	3	6	14	0	68	91	47	7	21	43	6.21	1.64	22.2	368	2.8	5.7	2.0	0.9	36%	62%	42
	03	24	a/a	HOU	4	8	40	0	144	188	110	21	71	98	6.88	1.79	17.0	389	4.4	6.1	1.4	1.3	35%	62%	20
Miller,Josh	03	25	aa	PHI	0	3	43	1	84	113	58	9	20	33	6.20	1.58	8.8	359	2.1	3.6	1.7	1.0	34%	61%	18
Miller,Justin	02	25	aaa	TOR	3	2	8	0	44	38	9	0	16	25	1.83	1.22	22.9	302	3.3	5.1	1.6	0.0	28%	83%	73
Miller,Matt	02	31	aaa	OAK	3	7	54	6	71	92	37	4	28	49	4.69	1.69	6.1	375	3.5	6.2	1.8	0.5	37%	72%	52
	03	32	aaa	COL	5	0	61	3	63	59	21	0	24	68	3.00	1.32	4.4	318	3.5	9.8	2.8	0.0	35%	75%	124
Miller,Ryan	03	26	aa	MIL	1	8	50	4	86	104	53	4	53	62	5.57	1.83	8.2	394	5.6	6.5	1.2	0.5	36%	68%	46
Miller,Travis	02	30	aaa	CLE	1	3	40	1	55	84	37	5	21	29	6.03	1.90	6.7	403	3.4	4.7	1.4	0.8	38%	68%	19
	03	31	a/a	MIL	6	3	21	0	55	113	48	8	13	26	7.76	2.27	13.6	446	2.0	4.2	2.0	1.2	45%	66%	4
Miller,Trever	02	29	aaa	CIN	9	5	65	0	82	90	35	7	23	61	3.84	1.38	5.4	328	2.5	6.7	2.7	0.8	33%	74%	73
Mills,Ryan	02	25	aa	MIN	3	11	26	0	105	151	88	12	79	52	7.53	2.19	20.7	437	6.8	4.4	0.7	1.0	36%	65%	-1
	03	26	aaa	MIN	5	1	32	0	61	76	38	4	34	42	5.62	1.81	9.0	390	5.0	6.1	1.2	0.6	36%	68%	39
Milo,Tony	02	24	aa	ANA	2	4	15	0	44	69	51	7	25	29	10.41	2.13	14.9	430	5.1	5.9	1.2	1.4	39%	49%	2
Minix,Travis	02	25	aa	TAM	5	7	38	0	68	90	32	3	33	37	4.24	1.81	8.5	391	4.4	4.9	1.1	0.4	36%	76%	34
	03	26	aa	TAM	5	3	44	0	79	120	53	9	17	52	6.02	1.73	8.4	380	2.0	5.9	3.0	1.0	39%	66%	55
Mitre,Sergio	03	23	aa	CHC	7	9	25	0	145	191	70	7	44	113	4.34	1.62	26.4	365	2.7	7.0	2.6	0.4	38%	72%	76
Mohler,Mike	02	34	aaa	BAL	1	2	34	1	49	61	19	2	16	35	3.49	1.57	6.5	358	2.9	6.4	2.2	0.4	36%	77%	69
	03	35	aaa	BAL	6	5	50	1	72	85	42	5	44	42	5.26	1.80	6.8	389	5.5	5.2	0.9	0.7	33%	70%	29
Molina,Gabe	02	27	aaa	STL	5	4	56	12	71	73	22	8	25	47	2.78	1.38	5.5	328	3.2	5.9	1.9	1.0	30%	84%	48
	03	28	aaa	STL	2	9	57	9	63	94	52	12	35	40	7.35	2.04	5.5	420	5.1	5.7	1.1	1.7	37%	66%	-5
Montero,Agustin	02	25	aa	LA	1	3	31	0	41	49	26	7	33	20	5.71	2.00	6.5	415	7.2	4.4	0.6	1.5	31%	75%	-10
	03	26	a/a	LA	4	3	51	1	77	98	46	6	48	41	5.32	1.89	7.3	401	5.6	4.8	0.9	0.6	34%	71%	22
Montes,Albert	03	24	aa	SF	3	1	36	5	63	82	35	2	18	24	5.01	1.59	7.9	360	2.5	3.5	1.4	0.3	34%	66%	34
Montgomery,Matt	02	26	aa	PIT	3	0	44	3	66	82	43	3	28	37	5.85	1.66	6.9	371	3.8	5.0	1.3	0.4	35%	63%	41
	03	27	a/a	SF	6	5	52	14	76	92	38	6	29	55	4.49	1.59	6.6	360	3.4	6.5	1.9	0.7	35%	72%	55
Moore,Darin	03	27	aa	TEX	0	3	22	1	36	51	37	1	28	20	9.17	2.17	8.3	434	6.9	5.0	0.7	0.3	38%	54%	27
Moreno,Edwin	03	23	aa	TEX	6	5	29	0	112	130	57	9	35	63	4.56	1.47	17.0	343	2.8	5.1	1.8	0.7	32%	70%	44
Moreno,Orber	03	26	a/a	NYM	7	1	42	13	57	50	16	2	20	49	2.45	1.23	5.6	303	3.2	7.7	2.4	0.4	30%	80%	95
Moreno,Victor	03	24	aa	MIN	1	1	24	0	33	45	34	5	24	22	9.13	2.09	6.9	426	6.6	5.9	0.9	1.4	36%	56%	3
Moseley,Dustin	02	21	aa	CIN	5	6	13	0	80	96	40	5	32	46	4.49	1.60	27.9	361	3.6	5.2	1.4	0.6	34%	72%	41
	03	22	a/a	CIN	7	9	26	0	162	183	78	19	40	90	4.33	1.37	26.8	328	2.2	5.0	2.3	1.1	31%	71%	45
Moser,Todd	03	27	aa	FLA	6	4	18	0	97	140	52	9	34	61	4.79	1.80	25.5	389	3.2	5.6	1.8	0.9	38%	74%	34
Mota,Guillermo	02	29	aaa	LA	1	3	20	1	36	36	12	1	8	30	2.98	1.22	7.5	301	2.0	7.5	3.8	0.2	33%	74%	120
Mottl,Ryan	03	26	aa	CIN	6	7	26	0	130	169	82	20	58	92	5.68	1.75	23.4	383	4.0	6.4	1.6	1.4	35%	70%	23
Mounce,Tony	02	28	a/a	TEX	5	4	13	0	62	91	43	10	18	37	6.22	1.75	22.4	383	2.6	5.4	2.1	1.4	37%	67%	20
	03	29	a/a	TEX	9	5	20	0	116	142	52	13	46	61	4.01	1.62	26.4	365	3.6	4.7	1.3	1.0	33%	78%	22
Mullen,Scott	02	28	aaa	KC	1	2	19	0	31	39	12	0	9	16	3.48	1.55	7.3	354	2.6	4.6	1.8	0.0	35%	75%	60
	03	29	aaa	LA	9	5	27	1	110	140	52	8	37	60	4.22	1.60	18.4	362	3.0	4.9	1.7	0.6	35%	74%	40
Munoz,Arnaldo	02	20	aa	CHW	6	0	51	6	72	71	28	8	30	76	3.50	1.40	6.1	332	3.7	9.5	2.5	1.0	33%	78%	85
	03	21	aaa	CHW	4	3	49	6	55	56	35	8	25	63	5.65	1.49	4.9	345	4.2	10.3	2.5	1.3	34%	64%	76
Munoz,Bobby	02	35	aaa	NYM	1	4	18	0	47	94	63	7	32	36	12.06	2.68	14.6	487	6.1	6.9	1.1	1.3	47%	53%	-2
Munro,Pete	02	27	aaa	HOU	7	1	19	0	94	87	37	4	17	60	3.54	1.11	19.9	282	1.6	5.7	3.5	0.4	29%	67%	104
Murphy,Bill	03	22	aa	OAK	3	3	11	0	55	48	28	4	26	29	4.58	1.35	21.3	323	4.3	4.7	1.1	0.7	26%	66%	41
Murray,A.J.	03	22	aa	TEX	10	4	27	0	144	161	77	17	64	79	4.81	1.56	23.9	357	4.0	4.9	1.2	1.1	31%	71%	23
Murray,Dan	02	29	aaa	TEX	5	7	39	2	109	156	91	16	52	43	7.50	1.90	13.5	403	4.3	3.5	0.8	1.3	35%	61%	-12
	03	30	aaa	TEX	5	9	41	2	81	143	78	13	40	39	8.66	2.25	10.2	444	4.4	4.3	1.0	1.5	41%	62%	-17
Musser,Neal	03	23	aa	NYM	5	9	20	0	100	121	58	9	39	62	5.19	1.60	22.6	361	3.5	5.6	1.6	0.8	34%	68%	38
Myers,Brett	02	22	aaa	PHI	9	6	19	0	128	131	59	10	20	93	4.15	1.18	27.6	295	1.4	6.5	4.7	0.7	31%	65%	119
Myers,Rodney	02	33	aaa	SD	5	2	42	4	48	56	24	2	14	29	4.48	1.45	5.0	340	2.6	5.4	2.1	0.4	34%	68%	63
	03	34	aaa	LA	9	1	46	1	71	73	27	4	22	41	3.47	1.33	6.6	321	2.8	5.2	1.8	0.5	30%	74%	57
Myette,Aaron	02	25	aaa	TEX	7	4	16	0	106	95	41	5	41	91	3.48	1.28	27.8	313	3.5	7.7	2.2	0.4	30%	73%	88
	03	26	a/a	PHI	5	4	37	1	97	106	60	10	53	68	5.56	1.64	12.0	367	4.9	6.3	1.3	0.9	32%	66%	38
Nageotte,Clint	03	23	aa	SEA	11	7	27	0	154	146	65	6	69	141	3.80	1.40	24.6	331	4.0	8.2	2.0	0.4	32%	72%	88
Nagy,Charles	02	35	aaa	CLE	1	2	5	0	36	48	19	8	4	15	4.72	1.44	31.5	337	1.0	3.7	3.8	2.0	31%	75%	34
Nakamura,Micheal	02	26	aaa	MIN	4	3	46	2	87	94	51	7	22	66	5.27	1.33	8.1	321	2.3	6.8	3.0	0.7	33%	60%	83
	03	27	aaa	MIN	6	6	43	2	78	89	37	4	32	76	4.25	1.55	8.1	355	3.6	8.8	2.4	0.5	37%	72%	87
Nance,Shane	02	25	aaa	MIL	14	3	46	1	75	85	36	6	33	53	4.32	1.57	7.3	358	4.0	6.4	1.6	0.7	33%	73%	49
	03	26	aaa	MIL	2	4	35	3	52	41	10	5	13	43	1.78	1.05	5.9	271	2.3	7.4	3.2	0.9	26%	90%	97
Nannini,Mike	02	22	aa	HOU	7	10	29	0	141	173	110	17	65	103	7.02	1.69	22.4	374	4.1	6.6	1.6	1.1	35%	58%	36
	03	23	aa	CHC	10	9	31	0	154	189	82	14	53	135	4.82	1.57	22.3	357	3.1	7.9	2.6	0.8	37%	70%	72
Narveson,Chris	03	22	aa	STL	4	3	10	0	57	67	25	7	28	31	3.95	1.67	26.1	371	4.4	4.9	1.1	1.1	32%	80%	17
Natale,Mike	02	23	aa	KC	4	3	24	0	48	48	39	7	46	42	7.30	1.95	9.8	409	8.6	7.9	0.9	1.3	30%	63%	31
	03	24	aa	KC	1	2	20	4	38	41	17	3	20	22	3.97	1.60	8.6	362	4.7	5.1	1.1	0.7	31%	76%	33
Nathan,Joe	02	28	aaa	SF	6	12	31	0	146	196	111	18	75	95	6.84	1.85	22.5	397	4.6	5.9	1.3	1.1	36%	63%	20
Neal,Blaine	02	25	aaa	FLA	3	1	29	11	31	27	10	2	14	23	2.90	1.32	4.5	319	4.1	6.7	1.6	0.6	28%	79%	66
	03	26	aaa	FLA	3	2	40	21	46	59	12	1	15	29	2.37	1.60	5.2	362	3.0	5.6	1.9	0.2	36%	85%	62
Nelson,Bubba	03	22	a/a	ATL	8	11	34	0	133	141	62	10	52	71	4.19	1.45	17.1	340	3.5	4.8	1.4	0.7	30%	72%	39
Neu,Mike	02	25	a/a	CIN	3	3	61	23	67	65	26	4	26	69	3.49	1.36	4.7	325	3.5	9.3	2.7	0.5	34%	75%	100
Nichting,Chris	02	36	aaa	COL	1	4	22	1	32	63	45	11	21	18	12.66	2.63	8.1	482	5.9	5.1	0.9	3.1	42%	53%	-70
Nickle,Doug	02	28	aaa	STL	6	6	48	10	76	88	37	9	25	40	4.38	1.48	7.0	345	3.0	4.7	1.6	1.1	31%	73%	28
	03	29	aaa	CHW	3	3	45	6	64	70	16	2	22	32	2.31	1.44	6.2	338	3.1	4.5	1.4	0.3	31%	84%	48
Nickoli,Michael	02	23	aa	ANA	3	10	17	0	82	134	69	11	45	27	7.56	2.18	24.6	436	4.9	3.0	0.6	1.2	38%	65%	-23
Nicolas,Mike	03	22	aa	BOS	4	3	25	1	39	32	39	3	44	41	8.98	1.94	7.6	408	10.1	9.4	0.9	0.7	30%	51%	67
Nina,Elvin	02	27	aaa	ANA	5	9	26	0	108	129	63	16	48	56	5.24	1.64	19.0	367	4.0	4.7	1.2	1.3	31%	71%	10
Nitkowski,C.J.	02	30	aaa	TEX	3	5	49	2	47	64	31	4	21	35	5.92	1.80	4.5	390	4.0	6.7	1.7	0.8	38%	67%	44
	03	31	aaa	TEX	5	4	33	2	81	118	56	9	36	41	6.17	1.89	11.8	401	3.9	4.6	1.2	1.0	37%	68%	11
Nolasco,Dave	03	25	aa	MIL	2	2	8	0	31	41	18	1	14	12	5.16	1.75	18.2	384	3.9	3.6	0.9	0.3	35%	69%	24
Nomura,Takahito	02	34	aaa	MIL	1	2	31	0	33	48	29	5	12	19	7.91	1.82	5.0	392	3.3	5.2	1.6	1.4	37%	56%	12
Norton,Phil	03	28	aaa	CHC	4	2	48	1	47	52	24	4	25	36	4.62	1.63	4.5	366	4.8	6.9	1.4	0.8	33%	72%	48
Noyce,Dave	02	26	aa	CHC	3	2	53	0	76	82	31	9	41	43	3.67	1.62	6.5	365	4.9	5.1	1.0	1.1	30%	81%	22

					Actual				Major League Equivalents																
PITCHER	Yr	Age	Lev	Org	w	l	g	sv	ip	h	er	hr	bb	k	era	br/ip	bf/g	oob	ctl	dom	cmd	hr/9	h%	s%	bpv
Nunez,Vladimir	03	29	aaa	FLA	4	1	46	5	68	75	40	12	20	46	5.27	1.41	6.4	333	2.7	6.0	2.2	1.6	30%	67%	36
O'Brien,Matt	02	26	aa	OAK	1	3	54	2	63	59	27	8	22	38	3.85	1.28	4.9	313	3.1	5.4	1.7	1.1	27%	74%	41
	03	27	a/a	OAK	7	1	46	0	62	80	41	4	31	44	5.96	1.79	6.4	388	4.5	6.4	1.4	0.6	37%	66%	43
O'Connor,Brian	02	26	a/a	PIT	5	8	28	0	90	112	65	6	56	47	6.49	1.86	15.4	398	5.6	4.7	0.8	0.6	34%	64%	23
Obermueller,Wes	02	26	aa	KC	9	5	17	0	105	131	51	8	44	49	4.36	1.66	28.4	371	3.8	4.2	1.1	0.7	33%	74%	23
	03	27	aaa	MIL	10	7	20	0	121	139	66	13	46	59	4.90	1.53	27.0	352	3.4	4.4	1.3	1.0	31%	69%	22
Ogiltree,John	03	25	aa	TOR	4	4	45	2	61	70	31	1	34	30	4.58	1.71	6.3	377	5.1	4.4	0.9	0.2	33%	71%	38
Ohme,Kevin	02	31	aaa	STL	4	3	56	2	87	124	57	13	22	48	5.88	1.67	7.2	373	2.3	5.0	2.2	1.3	36%	67%	25
	03	32	aaa	STL	5	5	49	1	66	97	44	11	23	28	6.01	1.81	6.4	391	3.1	3.7	1.2	1.4	35%	69%	-7
Olore,Kevin	03	25	aa	SEA	0	2	13	0	39	67	34	4	20	32	7.91	2.21	15.5	439	4.6	7.2	1.6	1.0	44%	64%	27
Olsen,Kevin	02	26	aaa	FLA	2	5	8	0	49	47	21	5	13	21	3.86	1.22	25.4	303	2.4	3.9	1.6	0.9	26%	71%	35
	03	27	aaa	FLA	2	1	7	0	38	40	9	1	7	24	2.24	1.24	22.7	306	1.7	5.6	3.2	0.2	32%	82%	96
Oquendo,Ian	03	22	aa	PIT	4	0	6	0	36	44	11	2	10	20	2.73	1.49	26.6	346	2.5	5.0	2.0	0.5	34%	83%	53
Orloski,Joe	02	23	aa	TOR	6	5	54	4	60	79	41	4	29	38	6.15	1.80	5.2	390	4.4	5.7	1.3	0.6	36%	64%	37
Ormond,Rodney	03	26	aa	BAL	7	2	46	1	85	97	41	8	37	55	4.38	1.57	8.3	357	3.9	5.8	1.5	0.9	32%	73%	40
Ortiz,Javier	03	24	aa	NYY	6	11	28	0	150	210	116	12	73	77	6.99	1.89	25.8	401	4.4	4.6	1.0	0.7	36%	62%	17
Ortiz,Omar	02	25	aa	FLA	4	8	33	3	103	130	76	18	77	59	6.63	2.01	15.4	416	6.7	5.1	0.8	1.6	33%	69%	-5
Osting,Jimmy	02	26	aaa	MIL	5	7	22	0	126	139	67	9	39	95	4.78	1.41	24.8	333	2.8	6.8	2.4	0.6	33%	66%	73
	03	27	aaa	KC	1	4	9	0	49	58	40	12	23	21	7.37	1.64	24.9	367	4.2	3.9	0.9	2.3	28%	59%	-27
Outlaw,Mark	02	26	aa	PHI	6	2	41	2	50	57	33	3	40	24	5.92	1.93	5.9	407	7.2	4.3	0.6	0.5	31%	68%	21
Oxspring,Chris	03	26	aa	SD	10	6	40	0	135	138	61	7	72	93	4.06	1.56	15.1	356	4.8	6.2	1.3	0.5	31%	73%	54
Ozias,Todd	02	26	aa	PHI	3	1	46	3	59	74	28	3	25	48	4.26	1.68	5.9	373	3.8	7.3	1.9	0.5	37%	74%	65
	03	27	aa	PIT	2	2	51	21	61	69	18	2	20	37	2.67	1.46	5.2	341	3.0	5.4	1.8	0.4	33%	82%	58
Ozuna,Francisco	02	21	aa	TOR	2	2	44	0	70	81	41	12	18	30	5.27	1.41	6.9	334	2.3	3.9	1.7	1.5	29%	67%	10
Pacheco,Enemencio	03	25	aa	CHW	12	2	30	0	151	180	68	8	61	95	4.04	1.60	22.7	361	3.6	5.6	1.5	0.5	34%	74%	49
Padilla,Juan	02	26	aa	MIN	3	5	54	29	65	89	33	2	21	40	4.56	1.69	5.6	375	2.9	5.5	1.9	0.3	38%	71%	56
	03	27	aaa	MIN	7	4	57	6	91	116	46	8	19	56	4.59	1.48	7.0	345	1.8	5.6	3.0	0.8	35%	70%	67
Palki,Jeromy	02	26	a/a	MIN	6	6	56	3	91	119	48	11	37	77	4.74	1.71	7.5	378	3.7	7.6	2.1	1.1	37%	74%	50
	03	27	aaa	MIN	7	6	47	1	101	133	64	7	35	73	5.72	1.66	9.8	370	3.1	6.5	2.1	0.7	37%	64%	57
Palma,Rick	02	23	a/a	CHC	2	3	55	0	71	72	16	3	20	60	2.03	1.30	5.4	315	2.5	7.6	3.0	0.4	33%	85%	101
	03	24	aa	PIT	6	5	35	0	68	91	41	4	25	49	5.42	1.70	9.0	376	3.3	6.5	2.0	0.6	38%	67%	56
Paradis,Mike	02	24	aa	BAL	8	13	27	0	151	204	116	13	69	76	6.90	1.81	26.5	390	4.1	4.5	1.1	0.8	35%	60%	19
	03	25	aa	BAL	5	10	25	0	124	172	108	19	92	65	7.81	2.13	25.1	430	6.7	4.7	0.7	1.4	35%	64%	-8
Parker,Christian	03	28	a/a	NYY	8	8	24	0	137	202	95	7	65	37	6.26	1.95	27.8	409	4.3	2.4	0.6	0.5	36%	66%	0
Parker,Matt	02	24	aa	MIL	4	4	40	2	77	89	43	6	35	66	5.02	1.61	8.7	363	4.1	7.7	1.9	0.7	35%	69%	63
	03	25	aa	MIL	8	6	42	6	95	119	45	12	39	57	4.28	1.66	10.4	370	3.7	5.4	1.5	1.1	34%	77%	25
Paronto,Chad	03	28	aaa	CLE	3	5	49	18	56	83	39	3	26	38	6.22	1.94	5.6	407	4.1	6.1	1.5	0.5	40%	66%	40
Parque,Jim	02	27	aaa	CHW	7	9	20	0	105	162	104	30	41	56	8.90	1.93	25.5	406	3.5	4.8	1.4	2.6	35%	57%	-34
	03	29	aaa	TAM	5	7	21	0	121	167	75	15	53	39	5.59	1.81	27.3	391	3.9	2.9	0.7	1.1	33%	71%	-10
Parrish,John	03	26	aa	BAL	3	3	49	6	76	78	26	8	38	67	3.02	1.52	6.9	350	4.5	7.9	1.8	0.9	32%	84%	60
Parrish,Wade	02	25	a/a	CHW	9	9	28	0	160	224	101	20	63	64	5.67	1.79	27.0	388	3.5	3.6	1.0	1.1	34%	70%	-1
	03	26	aa	COL	4	6	24	0	73	127	72	9	42	26	8.89	2.31	15.9	450	5.2	3.2	0.6	1.1	40%	60%	-20
Parrott,Rhett	02	23	aa	STL	4	1	9	0	66	59	24	3	12	34	3.27	1.08	29.3	276	1.6	4.6	2.8	0.4	27%	69%	83
	03	24	a/a	STL	10	12	28	0	164	193	81	16	63	125	4.44	1.56	26.3	356	3.5	6.9	2.0	0.9	34%	73%	54
Patterson,John	02	25	aaa	ARI	10	5	19	0	112	128	59	14	41	87	4.73	1.51	26.1	348	3.3	7.0	2.1	1.1	33%	71%	52
	03	26	aaa	ARI	10	5	18	0	109	114	38	7	41	64	3.17	1.43	26.3	336	3.4	5.3	1.6	0.6	31%	79%	49
Pautz,Brad	02	26	aa	PHI	4	6	43	3	79	89	36	9	31	49	4.10	1.52	8.2	350	3.5	5.6	1.6	1.0	31%	76%	35
	03	27	aa	PHI	4	5	29	1	48	75	52	7	23	26	9.70	2.04	8.2	419	4.3	4.9	1.1	1.3	38%	51%	-0
Payne,Jerrod	02	25	a/a	TOR	2	0	27	0	35	34	18	3	15	15	4.60	1.39	5.6	330	3.8	3.8	1.0	0.8	27%	67%	26
Pearce,Josh	03	26	aaa	STL	5	4	15	0	79	113	53	14	13	39	6.07	1.60	23.8	362	1.5	4.4	2.9	1.6	35%	65%	27
Pearsall,J.J.	02	29	a/a	FLA	3	3	45	1	63	76	35	6	34	47	4.99	1.74	6.5	382	4.8	6.7	1.4	0.9	35%	72%	40
Pearson,Jason	02	27	aaa	SF	3	0	57	0	66	69	24	7	25	38	3.27	1.42	5.0	336	3.4	5.2	1.5	1.0	30%	80%	37
	03	28	a/a	STL	4	4	53	3	63	66	28	5	14	37	3.93	1.26	5.0	308	2.0	5.3	2.7	0.7	30%	69%	72
Pearson,Terry	02	31	a/a	DET	3	8	55	6	61	108	45	3	23	30	6.62	2.14	5.6	432	3.4	4.4	1.3	0.4	42%	67%	20
	03	32	a/a	DET	6	3	54	2	60	94	39	1	21	30	5.82	1.92	5.4	405	3.2	4.4	1.4	0.2	40%	67%	36
Peavy,Jake	02	21	aa	SD	4	5	14	0	80	73	30	4	31	75	3.37	1.30	24.1	315	3.5	8.4	2.4	0.4	31%	74%	95
Peguero,Darwin	02	24	aa	HOU	3	2	54	1	60	77	37	7	30	34	5.54	1.78	5.2	387	4.5	5.1	1.1	1.0	34%	70%	17
Pember,David	02	24	aa	MIL	10	6	27	0	156	194	74	17	56	90	4.27	1.60	26.1	362	3.2	5.2	1.6	1.0	34%	76%	31
Pena,Jesus	02	28	a/a	TEX	3	9	46	2	79	128	76	11	56	55	8.66	2.33	9.0	452	6.4	6.3	1.0	1.3	41%	62%	4
Pena,Juan	02	25	aaa	BOS	4	11	17	0	82	97	61	21	37	50	6.68	1.63	22.0	366	4.1	5.5	1.4	2.3	29%	65%	-10
	03	26	aa	STL	6	5	29	0	95	134	54	10	52	57	5.15	1.96	16.0	410	4.9	5.4	1.1	0.9	37%	75%	16
Penney,Mike	02	26	aa	MIL	7	4	37	3	57	69	21	6	24	29	3.30	1.63	7.0	366	3.8	4.6	1.2	0.9	32%	83%	21
Peralta,Joel	03	28	a/a	ANA	5	4	48	20	52	51	17	3	15	36	2.98	1.26	4.5	308	2.6	6.2	2.4	0.6	30%	78%	74
Perez,Beltran	02	21	aa	ARI	3	8	20	0	97	121	65	10	30	68	6.03	1.56	21.7	356	2.8	6.3	2.3	0.9	35%	61%	53
	03	22	aa	ARI	2	11	29	0	147	198	98	14	51	78	5.99	1.69	23.4	375	3.1	4.8	1.5	0.9	35%	64%	27
Perez,Frank	02	27	aa	DET	0	4	20	1	33	46	23	4	17	25	6.27	1.91	8.0	404	4.6	6.8	1.5	1.1	38%	68%	29
	02	24	aa	PHI	2	0	28	5	45	53	21	6	13	26	4.18	1.46	7.1	341	2.6	5.2	2.0	1.2	32%	75%	35
Perez,Juan	03	25	aa	BOS	3	3	18	0	30	48	18	4	12	18	5.30	1.99	8.2	413	3.6	5.4	1.5	1.3	39%	76%	8
Perez,Oliver	03	22	aaa	SD	3	3	8	0	47	45	16	5	10	42	3.09	1.17	24.1	293	2.0	8.0	4.0	0.9	31%	77%	111
Perez,Yorkis	02	35	aaa	BAL	1	1	28	0	40	49	21	4	21	35	4.71	1.75	6.7	382	4.7	7.9	1.7	0.9	37%	74%	51
Perisho,Matt	02	27	aaa	DET	4	4	51	1	66	76	23	4	19	38	3.14	1.44	5.6	338	2.6	5.2	2.0	0.5	33%	79%	55
	03	28	aaa	COL	8	5	46	1	66	99	67	10	31	47	9.09	1.97	7.0	411	4.3	6.5	1.5	1.3	39%	53%	18
Peterson,Matt	03	22	aa	NYM	1	2	6	0	31	31	13	2	20	19	3.76	1.64	23.6	368	5.8	5.5	1.0	0.6	30%	78%	40
Peters,Chris	02	31	aa	DET	3	3	43	0	59	109	49	4	31	36	7.47	2.37	7.3	457	4.7	5.5	1.2	0.6	45%	67%	17
Pettyjohn,Adam	03	26	aa	DET	1	4	19	0	81	115	51	9	20	37	5.62	1.66	19.5	371	2.2	4.2	1.9	1.0	36%	67%	24
Phelps,Tommy	02	29	aaa	FLA	4	2	51	2	74	83	27	6	20	51	3.28	1.39	6.3	330	2.4	6.2	2.6	0.7	33%	78%	68
Phelps,Travis	02	25	aaa	TAM	3	2	27	8	31	34	19	2	14	29	5.52	1.55	5.1	354	4.1	8.4	2.1	0.6	35%	63%	77
	03	26	aaa	ATL	9	5	47	4	93	97	52	14	41	75	4.98	1.48	8.7	345	4.0	7.2	1.8	1.4	31%	70%	42
Phillips,Jason	02	26	aaa	CLE	7	4	16	0	98	109	52	11	19	59	4.77	1.30	25.9	316	1.7	5.4	3.1	1.0	31%	65%	67
	03	30	aaa	CLE	10	1	13	0	85	89	30	5	22	44	3.14	1.31	27.6	316	2.3	4.6	2.0	0.6	30%	77%	54
Pickford,Kevin	02	28	aaa	SD	4	7	20	1	69	92	55	5	33	32	7.15	1.81	16.4	390	4.3	4.2	1.0	0.7	35%	58%	18
	03	29	aaa	SF	9	8	25	0	145	191	91	12	55	50	5.67	1.70	26.8	376	3.4	3.1	0.9	0.7	33%	66%	9

Major League Equivalent Statistics

					Actual				Major League Equivalents																
PITCHER	Yr	Age	Lev	Org	w	l	g	sv	ip	h	er	hr	bb	k	era	br/ip	bf/g	oob	ctl	dom	cmd	hr/9	h%	s%	bpv
Pilkington,Brian	03	21	aa	LA	3	0	5	0	32	36	15	3	2	21	4.21	1.18	26.3	296	0.6	5.9	10.5	0.8	32%	66%	230
Pina,Rafael	02	31	aaa	BAL	6	5	50	10	111	139	54	11	33	60	4.38	1.55	9.9	355	2.7	4.9	1.8	0.9	34%	73%	36
	03	32	a/a	BAL	2	6	13	1	52	71	42	7	27	22	7.31	1.88	19.2	400	4.6	3.7	0.8	1.2	34%	61%	-4
Pineda,Isauro	02	24	aa	BOS	9	13	28	0	156	196	114	20	68	99	6.58	1.69	25.7	375	3.9	5.7	1.5	1.2	34%	61%	25
Pine,Chris	02	26	a/a	ANA	2	9	36	1	79	117	67	12	40	29	7.61	1.98	10.8	413	4.5	3.3	0.7	1.4	35%	62%	-18
Porzio,Mike	02	30	aaa	CHW	6	5	14	0	75	110	56	13	34	50	6.70	1.91	26.0	404	4.1	6.0	1.5	1.6	37%	67%	8
	03	31	aaa	CHW	8	6	26	0	133	155	86	27	51	99	5.83	1.54	22.9	353	3.4	6.7	2.0	1.8	32%	67%	24
Pote,Lou	02	31	aaa	ANA	2	1	7	0	39	48	29	3	9	35	6.69	1.46	24.4	341	2.1	8.1	3.9	0.7	38%	52%	105
Powell,Brian	02	29	aaa	DET	10	3	20	0	119	162	70	8	27	67	5.29	1.59	26.8	360	2.0	5.1	2.5	0.6	36%	66%	56
	03	30	aaa	PHI	9	12	31	0	153	210	89	10	49	76	5.23	1.69	22.8	375	2.9	4.5	1.5	0.6	36%	68%	33
Powell,Greg	03	25	aa	HOU	7	9	36	0	141	198	83	9	43	61	5.32	1.71	18.1	377	2.8	3.9	1.4	0.6	36%	68%	26
Pratt,Andy	02	23	a/a	ATL	8	11	26	0	133	144	69	7	52	86	4.66	1.47	22.5	343	3.5	5.8	1.7	0.5	32%	67%	56
	03	24	a/a	ATL	7	10	28	0	156	179	82	13	80	136	4.73	1.66	25.5	371	4.6	7.8	1.7	0.8	35%	72%	59
Pridie,Jon	02	23	aa	MIN	5	3	16	0	94	110	66	7	48	60	6.32	1.68	27.0	373	4.6	5.7	1.3	0.7	33%	61%	38
	03	24	aa	MIN	6	9	27	0	111	163	82	7	38	53	6.69	1.81	19.5	391	3.1	4.3	1.4	0.6	37%	61%	26
Prinz,Bret	02	25	aaa	ARI	1	0	37	18	39	46	14	4	8	28	3.22	1.38	4.5	329	1.8	6.4	3.5	0.9	34%	80%	82
	03	26	a/a	NYY	0	2	22	0	26	52	26	3	6	17	8.81	2.21	6.1	440	1.9	5.9	3.1	1.1	46%	59%	39
Prior,Mark	02	22	a/a	CHC	5	2	9	0	51	42	14	1	17	70	2.47	1.16	23.1	291	3.0	12.4	4.1	0.2	36%	78%	166
Proctor,Scott	02	26	aa	LA	7	9	26	0	133	144	73	12	99	103	4.94	1.83	24.3	393	6.7	7.0	1.0	0.8	33%	74%	40
	03	27	a/a	NYY	7	4	51	1	85	89	31	6	27	66	3.29	1.36	7.1	325	2.8	6.9	2.5	0.6	32%	77%	78
Puello,Ignacio	03	23	aa	MON	1	0	18	0	35	45	34	7	27	17	8.69	2.05	9.7	420	6.9	4.3	0.6	1.8	32%	58%	-20
Puffer,Brandon	03	28	aaa	HOU	7	3	44	5	52	67	26	1	18	33	4.45	1.63	5.4	366	3.2	5.6	1.8	0.2	36%	71%	60
Pulido,Carlos	03	32	aaa	MIN	12	5	25	0	149	183	82	15	45	70	4.96	1.53	26.6	352	2.7	4.2	1.6	0.9	32%	68%	27
Pulsipher,Bill	03	30	aaa	BAL	4	5	51	3	54	77	48	4	32	34	7.95	2.01	5.2	416	5.4	5.7	1.1	0.7	38%	59%	24
Pumphrey,Ken	02	26	a/a	PHI	13	9	28	0	171	219	108	13	54	80	5.68	1.59	27.6	361	2.8	4.2	1.5	0.7	34%	63%	30
	03	27	aaa	PHI	5	7	17	0	81	132	87	11	37	39	9.70	2.08	23.8	424	4.1	4.3	1.1	1.2	39%	51%	-3
Putz,J.J.	02	26	a/a	SEA	5	14	24	0	138	166	76	13	53	81	4.96	1.59	25.9	360	3.5	5.3	1.5	0.8	33%	69%	35
	03	27	aaa	SEA	0	3	41	11	86	82	31	4	36	52	3.24	1.38	9.0	328	3.8	5.5	1.5	0.4	29%	77%	56
Qualls,Chad	02	24	aa	HOU	6	13	29	0	163	209	101	12	72	116	5.58	1.72	26.1	379	4.0	6.4	1.6	0.7	36%	67%	46
	03	25	aa	HOU	8	11	28	0	175	222	102	16	68	101	5.25	1.66	28.6	370	3.5	5.2	1.5	0.8	34%	68%	33
Raggio,Brady	03	31	aaa	ARI	4	4	18	0	56	72	27	5	8	27	4.38	1.42	13.6	335	1.3	4.3	3.2	0.8	33%	70%	61
Rakers,Aaron	02	26	aa	BAL	5	1	36	10	48	48	14	3	13	34	2.63	1.27	5.6	311	2.4	6.4	2.6	0.6	31%	81%	80
	03	27	a/a	BAL	7	4	52	9	65	61	39	11	34	53	5.37	1.47	5.5	342	4.8	7.3	1.5	1.5	28%	67%	37
Ramirez,Emmanuel	03	24	aa	COL	3	1	26	0	37	38	12	0	27	35	3.00	1.75	6.7	383	6.5	8.5	1.3	0.0	35%	81%	81
Ramirez,Erasmo	02	26	a/a	TEX	8	3	59	3	75	84	29	1	13	40	3.48	1.29	5.4	314	1.6	4.8	3.1	0.1	33%	71%	89
	03	27	a/a	TEX	3	1	25	4	38	55	13	1	3	18	2.99	1.54	6.8	353	0.8	4.3	5.3	0.3	38%	80%	118
Ramirez,Horacio	02	23	aa	ATL	9	5	16	0	92	95	36	5	31	54	3.52	1.37	24.7	327	3.0	5.3	1.7	0.5	30%	74%	56
Ramirez,Jose	02	27	aa	DET	0	3	28	0	45	71	40	7	30	28	8.00	2.24	8.3	443	6.0	5.6	0.9	1.4	39%	65%	-4
Ramirez,Santiago	02	24	a/a	HOU	7	2	51	5	84	75	35	7	40	74	3.74	1.37	7.1	326	4.3	7.9	1.9	0.7	29%	74%	72
Ramos,Mario	02	25	aaa	TEX	3	8	34	0	121	178	112	21	49	65	8.32	1.87	17.1	399	3.6	4.8	1.3	1.6	36%	56%	-2
	03	26	a/a	TEX	8	10	24	0	153	214	105	14	43	104	6.18	1.68	29.3	373	2.5	6.1	2.4	0.8	38%	62%	53
Randall,Scott	02	27	a/a	MIN	14	0	24	0	136	168	64	10	31	56	4.23	1.46	24.9	341	2.0	3.7	1.8	0.7	33%	71%	36
	03	28	aaa	CIN	10	4	30	3	136	214	97	13	41	70	6.41	1.87	21.7	399	2.7	4.7	1.7	0.8	39%	65%	24
Randolph,Steve	02	28	aaa	ARI	15	7	28	0	163	177	75	16	80	100	4.14	1.58	26.2	358	4.4	5.5	1.3	0.9	31%	76%	34
Ratliff,Jon	02	31	aaa	TOR	2	4	28	1	37	60	29	3	24	14	7.04	2.26	6.9	445	5.8	3.4	0.6	0.7	39%	68%	-5
Rauch,Jon	02	24	aaa	CHW	7	8	19	0	109	109	69	19	44	90	5.69	1.40	24.8	332	3.6	7.4	2.0	1.6	29%	63%	44
	03	25	aaa	CHW	7	1	24	0	124	144	75	22	36	84	5.42	1.46	22.6	340	2.6	6.1	2.3	1.6	31%	67%	35
Rayborn,Kenny	03	29	a/a	CLE	5	1	6	0	32	48	13	1	7	16	3.63	1.72	24.8	379	2.0	4.5	2.3	0.3	39%	78%	52
Ray,Ken	03	29	a/a	MIL	2	1	31	4	61	96	34	9	33	33	4.97	2.11	9.9	428	4.8	4.8	1.0	1.3	39%	79%	-4
Reames,Britt	02	29	aaa	MON	3	2	7	0	42	41	19	4	15	20	4.07	1.33	25.5	321	3.2	4.3	1.3	0.9	27%	71%	33
	03	30	aaa	MON	5	13	25	0	118	176	86	9	48	64	6.53	1.89	22.7	402	3.6	4.9	1.3	0.7	38%	64%	24
Redding,Tim	02	25	aaa	HOU	3	3	11	0	38	39	30	8	14	43	7.11	1.39	14.9	331	3.3	10.2	3.1	1.9	33%	51%	72
Regilio,Nick	02	24	a/a	TEX	7	8	20	0	109	126	58	10	53	53	4.78	1.64	24.9	368	4.4	4.4	1.0	0.8	31%	72%	21
Reichert,Dan	03	27	aaa	TOR	4	3	41	0	58	68	32	2	38	49	4.90	1.83	6.7	394	5.9	7.7	1.3	0.3	37%	72%	61
Reid,Justin	02	25	aa	PIT	11	8	25	0	153	191	99	23	29	83	5.82	1.44	26.7	337	1.7	4.9	2.9	1.4	32%	61%	44
	03	26	aaa	PIT	3	7	34	1	82	110	59	10	23	43	6.44	1.62	11.0	365	2.5	4.7	1.9	1.1	35%	61%	26
Reimers,Cameron	02	24	a/a	TOR	5	9	25	0	116	192	81	18	30	41	6.28	1.91	22.4	404	2.3	3.2	1.4	1.4	38%	69%	-11
	03	25	aa	TOR	10	5	28	0	163	214	74	12	41	76	4.11	1.57	26.1	357	2.3	4.2	1.8	0.7	34%	74%	36
Reith,Brian	02	25	aaa	CIN	8	13	27	0	150	177	92	17	51	94	5.51	1.52	24.7	350	3.1	5.6	1.8	1.0	33%	64%	39
Rekar,Bryan	02	30	aaa	COL	7	10	25	0	147	253	121	28	41	85	7.41	2.00	28.9	415	2.5	5.2	2.1	1.7	41%	65%	4
Reyes,Al	02	32	aaa	PIT	7	3	43	1	66	48	25	5	22	73	3.40	1.06	6.1	273	3.0	9.9	3.3	0.7	27%	69%	124
Reyes,Carlos	03	34	aaa	TAM	10	3	22	0	132	154	57	11	16	64	3.87	1.28	25.2	313	1.1	4.3	4.0	0.7	32%	71%	87
Reyes,Dennys	03	26	aaa	ARI	2	1	33	2	31	28	12	0	22	25	3.57	1.59	4.3	360	6.2	7.3	1.2	0.0	31%	75%	76
Reynoso,Edison	03	28	aa	NYY	8	8	22	0	77	148	83	10	27	31	9.70	2.27	18.2	446	3.1	3.6	1.2	1.1	43%	55%	-12
Rheinecker,John	02	23	aa	OAK	7	7	20	0	128	158	58	7	25	83	4.08	1.43	27.8	336	1.8	5.8	3.3	0.5	35%	71%	86
	03	24	a/a	OAK	11	6	29	0	180	262	103	14	44	95	5.15	1.70	28.7	376	2.2	4.8	2.1	0.7	37%	70%	40
Rigdon,Paul	03	28	aaa	CLE	3	0	6	0	30	39	18	4	6	12	5.39	1.48	22.1	344	1.8	3.5	1.9	1.1	32%	65%	23
Riggan,Jerrod	02	28	aaa	CLE	4	1	27	3	45	52	17	4	13	30	3.39	1.44	7.3	338	2.6	6.0	2.3	0.8	33%	79%	59
Rijo,Fernando	02	25	aa	LA	8	8	27	0	142	160	79	16	79	87	5.01	1.68	24.2	374	5.0	5.5	1.1	1.0	31%	72%	25
	03	26	a/a	BAL	5	10	22	0	112	147	87	26	54	69	7.01	1.79	24.0	389	4.3	5.6	1.3	2.1	33%	65%	-10
Riley,Matt	02	23	aa	BAL	4	10	22	0	109	157	92	12	49	86	7.59	1.89	23.8	401	4.0	7.1	1.8	1.0	40%	59%	39
	03	24	a/a	BAL	9	4	27	0	142	154	71	10	54	127	4.50	1.46	23.1	341	3.4	8.0	2.4	0.7	34%	69%	79
Rincon,Juan	02	24	aaa	MIN	7	4	19	0	101	119	58	11	34	64	5.16	1.51	23.6	349	3.0	5.7	1.9	1.0	33%	67%	42
Ring,Royce	03	23	aa	NYM	4	4	54	26	57	53	17	4	26	52	2.68	1.38	4.6	329	4.1	8.2	2.0	0.6	31%	83%	79
Rivard,Reggie	03	26	a/a	TEX	0	2	35	1	60	106	47	7	31	39	7.11	2.28	8.9	447	4.6	5.8	1.3	1.1	43%	69%	8
Rivera,Homero	02	25	a/a	DET	6	4	52	8	82	87	34	5	23	39	3.73	1.34	6.7	322	2.5	4.3	1.7	0.5	30%	72%	47
	03	26	aa	DET	13	4	54	1	72	100	33	8	24	27	4.16	1.72	6.2	379	3.0	3.4	1.1	1.0	34%	78%	4
Rivera,Saul	02	25	aa	MON	2	5	45	16	57	55	25	2	33	38	3.93	1.54	5.7	353	5.2	6.0	1.2	0.3	30%	73%	56
Rizzo,Todd	03	32	a/a	BAL	2	4	54	0	67	94	48	7	43	33	6.41	2.05	6.2	421	5.8	4.5	0.8	0.9	36%	69%	6
Roach,Jason	02	26	a/a	NYM	9	10	27	0	150	194	66	13	48	67	3.95	1.61	25.2	364	2.9	4.0	1.4	0.8	34%	77%	24
	03	27	aaa	NYM	5	11	31	0	120	171	88	14	39	78	6.62	1.74	18.1	382	2.9	5.8	2.0	1.0	38%	62%	36
Roa,Joe	02	31	aaa	PHI	14	0	17	0	111	100	29	4	18	65	2.35	1.06	26.0	274	1.5	5.3	3.6	0.3	28%	78%	106

					Actual				Major League Equivalents																
PITCHER	Yr	Age	Lev	Org	w	l	g	sv	ip	h	er	hr	bb	k	era	br/ip	bf/g	oob	ctl	dom	cmd	hr/9	h%	s%	bpv
Robbins,Jake	02	26	aaa	ATL	2	6	58	3	68	91	59	7	57	43	7.79	2.17	6.0	435	7.5	5.7	0.8	0.9	36%	63%	14
	03	27	aa	CLE	6	3	34	8	58	64	23	1	31	27	3.55	1.64	7.8	367	4.9	4.1	0.8	0.2	31%	77%	37
Robertson,Jeriome	02	26	aaa	HOU	12	8	27	0	180	197	72	18	49	97	3.60	1.37	28.6	326	2.5	4.9	2.0	0.9	30%	76%	44
Robertson,Nate	03	26	aaa	DET	9	7	24	0	155	176	72	14	47	86	4.19	1.44	28.2	339	2.8	5.0	1.8	0.8	32%	72%	42
Robertson,Nathan	02	25	aa	FLA	10	9	27	0	163	189	76	12	56	86	4.20	1.50	26.7	348	3.1	4.7	1.5	0.7	32%	73%	39
Roberts,Nick	02	26	aa	HOU	12	7	28	0	172	248	112	20	48	76	5.86	1.72	28.5	379	2.5	4.0	1.6	1.0	36%	67%	15
	03	27	aa	HOU	2	8	13	0	72	102	56	9	30	37	7.02	1.83	26.4	394	3.7	4.7	1.3	1.1	36%	62%	10
Roberts,Rick	02	23	aa	LA	8	2	51	2	87	79	40	6	45	72	4.13	1.42	7.4	335	4.6	7.4	1.6	0.6	30%	71%	67
Rodgers,Bobby	02	28	a/a	FLA	5	5	28	2	104	138	73	18	65	61	6.31	1.95	18.1	409	5.6	5.3	0.9	1.6	34%	70%	-3
Rodney,Fernando	02	26	a/a	DET	2	1	41	15	42	32	6	1	14	37	1.28	1.09	4.1	279	3.0	7.9	2.6	0.2	27%	89%	110
	03	27	aaa	DET	1	1	38	23	40	27	8	0	13	49	1.85	1.00	4.1	262	3.0	11.1	3.7	0.0	30%	79%	162
Rodriguez,Eddy	03	22	aa	BAL	3	4	56	13	73	59	25	4	36	58	3.08	1.30	5.5	316	4.4	7.2	1.6	0.5	27%	77%	74
Rodriguez,Francisco	02	21	a/a	ANA	5	6	50	15	83	63	22	3	25	113	2.38	1.06	6.6	273	2.7	12.2	4.5	0.3	33%	78%	172
Rodriguez,Jose	03	29	aaa	MON	0	1	19	1	31	44	26	4	17	16	7.47	1.97	8.0	411	5.0	4.6	0.9	1.2	36%	62%	-1
Rodriguez,Nerio	02	32	aaa	ATL	7	3	21	0	126	118	40	15	23	69	2.86	1.12	24.2	284	1.6	4.9	3.0	1.1	26%	80%	67
	03	33	aaa	STL	5	1	11	0	76	72	22	4	14	47	2.61	1.12	28.0	284	1.6	5.5	3.4	0.5	29%	78%	96
Rodriguez,Ricardo	02	24	a/a	CLE	9	5	17	0	104	118	41	8	27	54	3.54	1.39	26.4	330	2.3	4.7	2.0	0.7	31%	76%	48
Rodriguez,Rich	03	41	aaa	ANA	3	2	34	1	43	55	15	3	12	14	3.07	1.54	5.7	352	2.4	3.0	1.2	0.7	32%	82%	18
Rogers,Brian	02	25	a/a	NYY	13	8	27	0	139	173	79	14	44	85	5.11	1.56	23.1	356	2.8	5.5	1.9	0.9	34%	68%	42
	03	27	a/a	ANA	3	4	40	1	76	104	51	7	39	37	6.04	1.88	9.1	400	4.6	4.4	0.9	0.8	35%	67%	14
Rojas,Chris	02	26	aa	SD	6	8	25	0	126	157	96	11	84	61	6.85	1.91	24.4	404	6.0	4.4	0.7	0.8	33%	63%	13
	03	27	aa	SD	5	10	32	0	109	123	71	7	62	66	5.87	1.69	15.7	375	5.1	5.4	1.1	0.6	32%	64%	37
Rojas,Jose	02	21	aa	LA	3	4	10	0	54	62	35	9	30	37	5.83	1.70	25.0	377	5.0	6.2	1.2	1.5	31%	69%	16
Roller,Adam	03	25	aa	NYY	4	3	36	10	40	61	17	2	17	28	3.74	1.94	5.4	408	3.7	6.3	1.7	0.5	41%	81%	44
Romero,Josmir	03	23	aa	MIN	2	5	27	0	63	93	47	4	26	42	6.69	1.88	11.2	400	3.7	6.0	1.6	0.6	40%	63%	41
Roney,Matt	02	23	aa	COL	3	6	13	0	70	88	65	10	32	53	8.33	1.71	25.0	377	4.1	6.8	1.7	1.3	35%	50%	32
Rosario,Juan	02	27	a/a	BAL	4	10	27	0	130	184	96	13	61	68	6.65	1.88	23.1	401	4.2	4.7	1.1	0.9	36%	64%	14
Rosario,Rodrigo	02	23	aa	HOU	11	6	26	0	130	121	55	6	60	81	3.80	1.39	21.6	330	4.2	5.6	1.4	0.4	29%	72%	56
	03	26	aaa	HOU	5	7	15	0	87	88	56	10	35	57	5.75	1.42	25.2	334	3.7	5.9	1.6	1.0	29%	60%	42
Rose,Teddy	02	29	a/a	CLE	4	3	11	0	57	80	39	10	22	22	6.16	1.79	24.4	388	3.5	3.5	1.0	1.6	34%	68%	-15
Rudrude,Brett	03	25	aa	BOS	1	2	6	0	31	47	20	1	11	13	5.77	1.86	24.8	397	3.0	3.8	1.3	0.3	38%	67%	27
Ruhl,Nathan	02	26	aa	CIN	1	5	44	19	48	60	34	5	36	30	6.38	2.00	5.4	415	6.8	5.6	0.8	0.9	34%	68%	18
Runser,Greg	02	24	aa	TEX	1	4	61	25	61	92	36	4	31	22	5.31	2.02	4.9	417	4.6	3.2	0.7	0.6	37%	73%	4
Rupe,Ryan	03	29	aaa	BOS	8	4	20	0	102	117	51	13	22	60	4.46	1.36	21.8	325	1.9	5.3	2.8	1.1	31%	70%	55
Rust,Evan	03	25	a/a	TAM	3	5	56	12	70	76	32	1	28	49	4.06	1.49	5.5	346	3.7	6.4	1.7	0.1	34%	70%	71
Ryan,Jason	03	28	aaa	STL	8	6	29	0	189	245	80	23	51	96	3.81	1.56	29.3	357	2.4	4.6	1.9	1.1	34%	79%	28
Ryu,Jae-kuk	03	20	aa	CHC	2	5	11	0	58	70	43	4	26	42	6.65	1.66	24.1	370	4.0	6.5	1.6	0.6	35%	58%	52
Saarloos,Kirk	02	23	a/a	HOU	12	1	17	0	99	71	22	3	24	87	2.00	0.96	22.6	254	2.2	7.9	3.6	0.3	26%	79%	131
	03	24	aaa	HOU	5	0	13	0	61	67	30	5	12	29	4.42	1.29	19.8	314	1.8	4.3	2.4	0.7	30%	66%	55
Sabel,Erik	02	28	aaa	DET	5	5	39	1	77	100	53	6	23	46	6.18	1.59	8.9	361	2.7	5.4	2.0	0.7	35%	60%	47
	03	29	aaa	ARI	2	3	42	1	62	96	43	8	18	28	6.24	1.84	7.0	395	2.7	4.1	1.5	1.1	38%	67%	9
Sadler,Carl	02	26	a/a	CLE	5	2	33	3	65	73	22	1	22	41	3.05	1.46	8.6	341	3.0	5.7	1.9	0.1	34%	78%	68
	03	27	aaa	CLE	2	1	31	3	53	76	51	5	34	26	8.58	2.08	8.6	425	5.8	4.4	0.8	0.9	37%	57%	6
Saenz,Jason	02	26	a/a	NYM	6	3	41	2	78	93	58	6	68	40	6.68	2.06	9.5	422	7.8	4.6	0.6	0.7	33%	66%	16
	03	27	aa	NYM	4	3	32	2	58	72	36	2	45	26	5.51	2.01	9.0	417	6.9	4.0	0.6	0.4	34%	71%	21
Saipe,Mike	02	29	aaa	ATL	4	6	42	1	94	135	54	5	29	48	5.17	1.74	10.4	382	2.8	4.6	1.7	0.5	37%	69%	37
	03	30	aaa	LA	6	5	21	0	101	142	62	12	37	50	5.54	1.77	22.6	386	3.3	4.5	1.4	1.1	36%	70%	13
Saladin,Miguel	02	27	a/a	HOU	4	5	55	24	58	53	21	6	31	36	3.25	1.44	4.6	339	4.8	5.6	1.2	0.9	27%	81%	37
	03	28	aaa	HOU	5	6	55	3	84	99	42	4	39	47	4.49	1.64	7.0	367	4.1	5.1	1.2	0.5	33%	72%	40
Sampson,Benj	02	27	a/a	MIN	6	8	29	0	149	206	102	20	31	46	6.16	1.59	23.2	361	1.9	2.8	1.5	1.2	33%	62%	2
	03	28	aa	COL	5	6	18	0	107	183	80	21	31	42	6.72	1.99	29.3	414	2.6	3.6	1.4	1.8	38%	69%	-22
Sanches,Brian	02	24	aa	KC	10	6	33	0	116	141	81	11	46	80	6.27	1.61	15.9	363	3.6	6.2	1.7	0.9	34%	60%	44
	03	25	aa	KC	1	5	38	2	85	113	46	12	19	55	4.82	1.55	10.0	355	2.0	5.8	2.9	1.3	35%	72%	49
Sanchez,Duaner	02	23	a/a	PIT	5	7	55	20	63	69	34	4	24	56	4.84	1.47	5.0	343	3.4	8.0	2.3	0.6	35%	66%	80
	03	24	aaa	PIT	4	4	41	1	61	75	33	3	26	29	4.87	1.66	6.8	370	3.8	4.3	1.1	0.4	33%	69%	32
Sanchez,Felix	03	22	aa	CHC	2	2	30	0	64	67	30	4	33	48	4.22	1.56	9.6	357	4.6	6.8	1.5	0.6	32%	73%	56
Sanchez,Jesus	02	28	aaa	CHC	8	9	26	0	125	154	82	24	62	79	5.90	1.73	22.3	380	4.5	5.7	1.3	1.7	32%	70%	5
	03	29	aaa	COL	2	0	46	2	63	80	41	6	28	42	5.83	1.70	6.3	377	4.0	6.0	1.5	0.9	33%	66%	34
Sanders,Dave	02	23	aa	CHW	3	1	47	0	63	70	19	4	31	54	2.71	1.60	6.1	362	4.4	7.7	1.7	0.6	35%	85%	66
Sanders,Scott	03	35	aaa	FLA	7	5	19	0	117	137	55	11	33	94	4.21	1.45	26.9	339	2.5	7.2	2.9	0.8	35%	72%	77
Sansom,Trevor	02	26	aa	STL	4	4	47	0	79	99	47	14	32	40	5.34	1.65	7.7	370	3.6	4.5	1.3	1.6	32%	72%	1
Santana,Johan	02	24	aaa	MIN	5	2	11	0	48	40	18	7	26	64	3.36	1.37	18.8	327	4.9	12.0	2.5	1.3	31%	81%	95
Santiago,Jose	03	29	aaa	CLE	3	3	25	2	66	102	26	1	26	26	3.51	1.93	12.9	407	3.5	3.5	1.0	0.1	39%	81%	24
Santos,Alex	02	25	aa	TAM	1	4	7	0	31	63	40	4	10	11	11.54	2.34	23.4	453	2.9	3.2	1.1	1.2	43%	48%	-19
	03	26	aa	TAM	3	2	25	0	40	72	43	5	18	17	9.55	2.26	8.3	445	4.1	3.9	0.9	1.0	41%	56%	-9
Santos,Victor	02	26	aaa	COL	4	9	21	0	118	170	91	25	40	113	6.94	1.78	26.4	387	3.1	8.6	2.8	1.9	40%	64%	43
	03	27	aaa	TEX	5	4	20	1	108	142	58	8	38	54	4.82	1.67	24.8	371	3.2	4.5	1.4	0.7	35%	71%	29
Scanlan,Bob	02	36	aaa	NYY	2	3	51	3	70	115	42	3	23	27	5.39	1.97	6.7	411	3.0	3.5	1.2	0.4	40%	71%	17
	03	37	a/a	HOU	1	9	36	0	101	128	60	11	40	41	5.34	1.66	12.9	370	3.6	3.6	1.0	1.0	32%	69%	8
Scheffer,Aaron	02	27	aaa	OAK	4	1	35	1	52	58	28	1	23	29	4.84	1.55	6.7	355	4.0	5.0	1.3	0.2	33%	66%	51
Schmack,Brian	02	29	a/a	TEX	1	7	41	1	92	149	78	9	28	48	7.63	1.92	10.9	406	2.7	4.7	1.7	0.9	40%	59%	21
	03	30	aa	DET	3	3	53	29	57	81	21	3	12	31	3.37	1.64	4.9	367	1.9	4.9	2.6	0.4	38%	79%	60
Schmitt,Eric	03	25	a/a	NYY	6	2	34	1	111	145	56	11	33	76	4.52	1.60	14.8	362	2.6	6.2	2.3	0.9	36%	73%	53
Schneider,Scott	03	25	aa	ANA	8	4	33	0	71	81	44	9	28	40	5.63	1.53	9.6	352	3.5	5.0	1.4	1.1	31%	64%	25
Schoening,Brent	02	25	aa	MIN	3	1	21	0	62	74	47	14	25	47	6.80	1.59	13.4	361	3.6	6.8	1.9	2.0	32%	61%	17
	03	26	aa	MIN	12	6	26	0	147	181	90	18	50	80	5.51	1.57	25.4	358	3.1	4.9	1.6	1.1	33%	66%	26
Schrenk,Steve	02	34	aaa	CHW	2	7	38	0	77	93	48	12	27	39	5.60	1.55	9.1	355	3.1	4.5	1.4	1.4	31%	67%	12
Schroder,Chris	03	25	aa	MON	9	2	49	4	82	84	33	6	51	60	3.65	1.65	7.7	369	5.6	6.6	1.2	0.6	32%	79%	49
Schurman,Ryan	02	26	aa	STL	0	3	18	0	51	85	52	11	22	31	9.18	2.10	14.2	427	3.9	5.5	1.4	1.9	40%	57%	-13
Scobie,Jason	03	25	a/a	NYM	3	7	17	0	77	102	54	5	24	31	6.26	1.64	20.7	367	2.8	3.7	1.3	0.6	34%	60%	23
Seale,Dustin	02	25	a/a	MON	1	2	30	0	68	80	35	13	16	43	4.62	1.41	9.8	333	2.1	5.7	2.7	1.7	31%	73%	37
	03	26	aa	MON	1	2	26	1	46	59	32	12	24	17	6.28	1.80	8.4	390	4.8	3.3	0.7	2.4	29%	72%	-43

					Actual				Major League Equivalents																
PITCHER	Yr	Age	Lev	Org	w	l	g	sv	ip	h	er	hr	bb	k	era	br/ip	bf/g	oob	ctl	dom	cmd	hr/9	h%	s%	bpv
Seanez,Rudy	03	35	aaa	CHC	3	5	35	5	38	41	24	6	25	37	5.73	1.75	5.1	382	6.0	8.8	1.5	1.5	33%	70%	40
Seay,Bobby	02	24	a/a	TAM	2	0	25	0	50	55	30	3	18	31	5.38	1.45	8.8	340	3.2	5.6	1.7	0.5	32%	61%	54
	03	25	aaa	TAM	3	0	25	0	30	27	9	1	16	25	2.73	1.45	5.2	339	4.8	7.4	1.5	0.3	30%	81%	75
Secoda,Jason	02	28	aaa	FLA	6	3	35	0	116	117	60	11	41	52	4.65	1.36	14.2	325	3.2	4.0	1.3	0.9	28%	67%	29
Sedlacek,Shawn	02	25	a/a	KC	8	6	14	0	98	100	48	7	20	65	4.40	1.22	29.1	302	1.8	6.0	3.3	0.6	30%	64%	88
	03	27	a/a	KC	5	13	32	0	123	230	129	21	36	49	9.40	2.16	19.5	433	2.6	3.6	1.4	1.5	41%	56%	-18
Seibel,Phil	02	24	aa	NYM	10	8	28	0	149	165	74	16	49	93	4.46	1.43	23.2	337	3.0	5.6	1.9	1.0	31%	71%	45
	03	25	a/a	NYM	7	8	28	0	117	135	67	11	51	78	5.15	1.59	18.8	360	3.9	6.0	1.5	0.9	33%	68%	40
Seifert,Ryan	02	27	aaa	COL	1	5	21	0	62	95	60	21	27	29	8.68	1.96	14.5	410	3.9	4.2	1.1	3.0	34%	61%	-57
Seo,Jae Weong	02	25	a/a	NYM	6	9	27	0	133	176	73	15	24	75	4.93	1.50	21.8	347	1.6	5.1	3.1	1.0	35%	69%	58
Sequea,Jacobo	02	21	a/a	BAL	2	10	20	0	100	102	67	18	44	47	6.02	1.46	21.9	341	4.0	4.2	1.1	1.6	26%	62%	3
	03	22	aa	BAL	1	3	12	0	40	52	32	7	29	21	7.20	2.03	16.5	418	6.5	4.7	0.7	1.6	33%	66%	-10
Sergent,Joe	02	24	aa	FLA	3	6	20	0	70	98	58	13	23	34	7.46	1.73	16.3	380	3.0	4.4	1.5	1.7	34%	58%	-3
Serrano,Elio	02	24	aaa	PHI	1	3	43	5	71	73	28	7	18	41	3.55	1.28	6.9	312	2.3	5.2	2.3	0.9	29%	75%	55
	03	25	aaa	ANA	5	4	46	2	68	93	41	7	21	39	5.41	1.67	6.8	372	2.8	5.1	1.9	0.9	36%	68%	33
Serrano,Jim	02	26	aaa	NYM	8	6	53	3	74	103	41	3	33	62	4.99	1.84	6.6	395	4.0	7.5	1.9	0.4	41%	71%	64
	03	27	aaa	KC	4	4	46	3	77	84	36	5	33	59	4.18	1.52	7.4	350	3.8	6.9	1.8	0.6	33%	73%	61
Serrano,Wascar	02	25	aaa	SEA	1	3	41	5	71	97	61	6	29	48	7.72	1.77	8.1	386	3.7	6.1	1.7	0.8	37%	54%	40
Serrano,Willy	02	26	aa	BAL	4	4	27	0	48	93	52	11	33	22	9.71	2.61	9.9	481	6.2	4.1	0.7	2.1	42%	64%	-48
Service,Scott	02	36	aaa	PIT	4	4	47	6	61	57	29	8	24	57	4.26	1.32	5.5	319	3.5	8.4	2.4	1.2	30%	71%	72
Sessions,Doug	02	26	a/a	HOU	2	2	41	0	58	82	53	14	29	33	8.20	1.91	6.9	403	4.5	5.1	1.1	2.2	34%	60%	-21
	03	27	aaa	HOU	9	5	31	1	157	194	76	23	48	74	4.34	1.54	22.6	353	2.8	4.2	1.5	1.3	32%	76%	13
Severino,Ronni	02	27	aa	TAM	0	4	25	0	35	48	26	1	25	35	6.67	2.08	7.0	424	6.4	9.0	1.4	0.3	42%	65%	67
Shackelford,Brian	03	27	a/a	CIN	4	2	25	1	35	56	26	5	24	22	6.76	2.29	7.3	448	6.2	5.6	0.9	1.2	40%	71%	1
Shaffar,Ben	02	25	a/a	PIT	9	7	19	0	116	141	53	7	42	82	4.11	1.58	27.5	359	3.3	6.4	2.0	0.5	35%	74%	59
	03	26	a/a	PIT	1	3	17	0	76	106	52	6	29	48	6.18	1.77	21.0	385	3.4	5.6	1.7	0.7	38%	64%	39
Shearn,Tom	02	25	aaa	HOU	4	6	57	8	83	95	37	10	45	68	4.01	1.68	6.7	374	4.9	7.4	1.5	1.1	34%	79%	42
Shelley,Jason	03	27	aa	MIL	3	2	9	0	54	52	24	7	25	38	4.01	1.42	26.1	335	4.2	6.4	1.5	1.1	28%	75%	41
Shepard,David	02	29	a/a	NYY	8	8	43	1	92	124	65	11	31	51	6.35	1.68	9.9	374	3.0	5.0	1.6	1.1	35%	63%	24
	03	30	a/a	NYY	8	8	61	12	82	102	45	13	26	56	4.94	1.56	6.0	356	2.8	6.1	2.2	1.5	34%	72%	33
Sheredy,Kevin	02	28	aaa	STL	1	2	35	2	41	51	28	3	23	30	6.12	1.80	5.6	389	5.0	6.6	1.3	0.7	36%	65%	43
Shibilo,Andy	02	26	a/a	BOS	5	4	56	6	82	107	51	3	28	65	5.60	1.65	6.7	369	3.1	7.1	2.3	0.3	38%	64%	75
	03	27	a/a	BOS	3	3	51	2	65	80	39	5	34	50	5.39	1.76	6.0	385	4.8	7.0	1.5	0.6	36%	69%	49
Shields,Scot	02	27	aaa	ANA	2	2	28	1	47	44	18	5	6	41	3.45	1.06	6.7	274	1.1	7.9	6.8	1.0	30%	71%	168
Shiell,Jason	02	26	aaa	SD	4	3	56	6	74	70	26	6	29	62	3.16	1.34	5.6	321	3.5	7.5	2.1	0.7	30%	78%	74
Silva,Jesus	03	21	aa	ARI	5	4	55	3	66	89	40	8	18	51	5.45	1.61	5.4	364	2.5	7.0	2.8	1.0	37%	67%	63
Silva,Jose	02	29	aaa	CIN	1	2	20	1	35	47	11	1	4	21	2.81	1.45	7.7	339	1.0	5.4	5.3	0.3	37%	80%	127
	03	30	aaa	CHC	1	7	27	0	55	82	37	4	27	27	6.09	1.99	10.0	414	4.5	4.5	1.0	0.7	38%	69%	13
Simas,Bill	02	31	aaa	CHW	1	3	28	2	40	61	23	7	9	18	5.18	1.75	6.7	383	2.0	4.1	2.0	1.6	36%	75%	5
	03	32	aaa	LA	4	0	26	0	46	51	11	3	8	21	2.06	1.28	7.4	312	1.6	4.1	2.5	0.6	30%	87%	58
Simontacchi,Jason	02	29	aaa	STL	5	1	6	0	42	55	14	2	5	23	2.99	1.43	30.5	336	1.1	4.9	4.6	0.4	36%	79%	106
Simon,Ben	02	28	a/a	LA	7	0	38	1	116	140	60	14	51	59	4.66	1.65	13.9	369	4.0	4.6	1.2	1.1	32%	74%	16
Simpson,Allan	02	25	aa	SEA	10	5	56	7	82	71	42	6	58	77	4.60	1.57	6.6	358	6.4	8.4	1.3	0.7	30%	71%	68
	03	26	aaa	SEA	2	5	43	1	62	71	37	7	44	60	5.37	1.86	6.9	397	6.4	8.7	1.4	1.0	36%	72%	48
Sims,Ken	02	27	aa	BAL	5	11	28	0	107	176	93	7	48	37	7.82	2.09	19.2	426	4.0	3.1	0.8	0.6	39%	60%	0
Sinclair,Steve	02	31	aaa	CHC	6	2	52	1	73	76	33	4	32	49	4.06	1.48	6.2	343	3.9	6.0	1.5	0.5	31%	72%	56
Skrmetta,Matt	02	30	aaa	LA	9	1	47	1	68	67	24	5	35	51	3.17	1.50	6.4	347	4.6	6.7	1.5	0.7	31%	80%	56
Sloan,Brandon	02	25	a/a	FLA	2	8	45	8	73	89	38	7	33	40	4.67	1.67	7.5	371	4.1	4.9	1.2	0.9	33%	73%	25
Small,Aaron	02	31	aaa	ATL	0	3	14	0	31	61	30	2	16	14	8.71	2.48	12.0	468	4.6	4.1	0.9	0.6	45%	63%	-0
	03	32	a/a	FLA	9	8	22	0	130	172	83	18	36	65	5.76	1.60	26.7	362	2.5	4.5	1.8	1.2	34%	65%	21
Smith,Brian	02	30	aaa	PIT	3	3	33	7	37	47	21	2	11	19	5.08	1.56	5.0	356	2.7	4.6	1.7	0.5	34%	66%	44
Smith,Bud	02	23	aaa	PHI	3	1	9	0	55	59	20	1	19	43	3.27	1.42	26.5	334	3.1	7.0	2.3	0.2	34%	75%	86
	03	24	aa	PHI	1	1	8	0	37	45	25	6	15	20	6.02	1.64	21.1	368	3.8	5.0	1.3	1.5	32%	66%	8
Smith,Chuck	03	34	a/a	ATL	2	2	6	0	36	37	17	3	16	19	4.14	1.44	26.3	338	3.9	4.7	1.2	0.8	29%	73%	32
Smith,Clint	02	26	aa	DET	5	13	38	0	120	210	105	17	61	60	7.86	2.25	16.4	444	4.6	4.5	1.0	1.3	41%	65%	-10
Smith,Dan	02	27	aaa	MON	5	4	14	0	83	88	41	13	19	49	4.44	1.29	25.0	313	2.1	5.3	2.6	1.4	29%	70%	46
Smith,Hans	02	24	aa	TAM	2	4	46	0	54	66	33	2	31	36	5.49	1.79	5.5	389	5.2	6.0	1.2	0.3	35%	67%	46
Smith,Matt	02	23	aa	NYY	3	8	17	0	89	134	69	9	39	60	6.97	1.94	25.5	408	3.9	6.1	1.5	0.9	40%	63%	28
	03	24	aa	NYY	2	3	9	0	50	67	29	7	25	29	5.28	1.85	26.6	396	4.5	5.3	1.2	1.3	35%	74%	9
Smith, Matt	03	25	aa	CHW	4	1	52	2	69	102	48	11	37	36	6.22	2.01	6.6	416	4.8	4.7	1.0	1.4	36%	71%	-7
Smith,Mike	02	25	aaa	TOR	8	4	20	0	121	120	56	10	42	65	4.16	1.34	25.8	322	3.1	4.8	1.5	0.7	28%	70%	44
	03	26	aaa	TOR	8	9	26	0	131	171	98	16	61	76	6.72	1.77	23.6	386	4.2	5.2	1.2	1.1	34%	62%	17
Smith,Roy	02	26	aaa	CLE	5	4	36	1	70	80	42	3	32	54	5.39	1.60	8.8	362	4.1	6.9	1.7	0.4	35%	64%	64
	03	27	aaa	OAK	7	4	52	3	72	87	48	3	49	38	6.04	1.90	6.7	402	6.2	4.7	0.8	0.4	34%	66%	29
Smith,Travis	02	30	aaa	STL	4	7	16	0	85	96	30	9	15	51	3.17	1.30	22.5	316	1.6	5.4	3.4	1.0	31%	79%	75
Smyth,Steve	02	24	a/a	CHC	7	6	17	0	104	108	55	11	28	84	4.76	1.31	25.9	317	2.4	7.3	3.0	1.0	32%	65%	81
	03	25	aaa	CHC	6	11	25	0	130	161	88	17	74	85	6.07	1.80	24.6	390	5.1	5.9	1.2	1.2	34%	67%	20
Snare,Ryan	02	24	aa	FLA	4	2	16	0	61	58	26	6	23	48	3.84	1.33	16.2	320	3.4	7.1	2.1	0.9	30%	73%	66
	03	25	a/a	TEX	9	9	27	0	157	190	82	12	52	89	4.72	1.53	25.9	352	3.0	5.1	1.7	0.7	33%	69%	42
Sneed,John	02	26	a/a	MIN	3	7	40	1	92	119	66	13	50	62	6.46	1.84	10.9	394	4.9	6.1	1.2	1.3	35%	66%	18
Snow,Bert	03	27	a/a	OAK	2	5	44	13	52	63	41	6	33	35	7.10	1.86	5.7	397	5.8	6.1	1.1	1.0	34%	61%	26
Snyder,John	02	28	aaa	SD	7	12	26	0	144	185	81	12	54	73	5.06	1.66	25.4	370	3.4	4.6	1.4	0.7	34%	70%	27
	03	29	aaa	ANA	3	2	10	0	55	73	37	5	20	25	6.10	1.68	25.3	373	3.2	4.0	1.2	0.9	34%	63%	16
Snyder,Kyle	03	26	a/a	KC	3	0	6	0	34	40	13	4	7	13	3.53	1.37	24.3	327	1.8	3.3	1.9	1.2	30%	79%	22
Sobkowiak,Scott	02	25	a/a	ATL	3	2	17	0	39	35	22	3	31	35	5.06	1.69	10.6	374	7.1	8.1	1.1	0.7	30%	70%	59
Sodowsky,Clint	03	31	a/a	FLA	1	3	8	0	41	64	32	6	6	28	7.06	1.70	23.8	377	1.2	6.1	5.0	1.2	40%	59%	91
Sollecito,Gabe	02	31	a/a	ARI	3	3	50	6	51	61	26	6	15	27	4.58	1.49	4.5	345	2.6	4.8	1.8	1.1	32%	71%	32
Song,Seung	02	22	aa	MON	7	7	22	0	113	126	63	12	36	102	5.01	1.43	22.4	337	2.9	8.1	2.8	1.0	34%	66%	79
	03	23	a/a	MON	12	4	26	0	146	136	56	12	54	70	3.45	1.30	23.7	316	3.3	4.3	1.3	0.7	27%	75%	38
Soriano,Rafael	02	23	aa	SEA	2	3	10	0	46	39	16	7	16	44	3.12	1.19	19.0	297	3.1	8.6	2.8	1.4	27%	81%	78
	03	24	aaa	SEA	4	3	11	0	62	50	27	2	12	57	3.92	1.00	22.1	262	1.7	8.3	4.8	0.3	29%	58%	152
Spencer,Corey	02	26	a/a	BOS	2	4	47	7	74	112	62	8	44	55	7.52	2.10	7.9	427	5.3	6.7	1.3	1.0	40%	64%	24

					Actual				Major League Equivalents																
PITCHER	Yr	Age	Lev	Org	w	l	g	sv	ip	h	er	hr	bb	k	era	br/ip	bf/g	oob	ctl	dom	cmd	hr/9	h%	s%	bpv
Spiegel,Mike	02	27	a/a	CLE	7	3	26	0	95	96	53	11	64	68	5.01	1.68	16.8	373	6.1	6.4	1.1	1.0	30%	72%	33
	03	28	aa	DET	0	5	24	0	44	59	22	4	23	20	4.44	1.86	8.8	398	4.7	4.1	0.9	0.7	35%	77%	13
Spiehs,R.D.	03	24	aa	SD	2	7	54	7	79	82	37	4	36	54	4.23	1.50	6.5	347	4.1	6.2	1.5	0.5	32%	71%	57
Spille,Ryan	02	26	aa	TOR	7	12	27	0	159	231	116	24	57	76	6.56	1.81	27.9	391	3.2	4.3	1.3	1.4	36%	65%	2
Sprague,Kevin	03	27	aa	STL	3	4	53	2	63	92	56	6	47	49	8.03	2.20	6.1	439	6.7	6.9	1.0	0.8	40%	62%	27
Springer,Dennis	02	38	aaa	LA	7	8	26	1	143	209	87	18	34	31	5.48	1.70	25.4	376	2.1	2.0	0.9	1.1	34%	69%	-15
Spurgeon,Jay	02	26	aaa	BAL	4	14	29	0	154	214	111	18	43	69	6.49	1.67	24.4	372	2.5	4.0	1.6	1.1	35%	61%	17
Spurling,Chris	02	25	aa	PIT	4	3	51	20	70	69	23	9	12	46	2.96	1.16	5.6	291	1.5	5.9	3.8	1.2	28%	81%	86
Stamler,Keith	02	23	aa	TEX	6	7	30	0	134	196	91	6	29	50	6.11	1.68	20.6	373	1.9	3.4	1.7	0.4	37%	61%	33
	03	24	a/a	TEX	4	7	51	1	79	92	45	5	21	35	5.11	1.43	6.8	336	2.4	4.0	1.7	0.6	32%	63%	40
Standridge,Jason	02	24	aaa	TAM	10	9	29	0	173	195	75	13	66	94	3.90	1.51	26.4	349	3.4	4.9	1.4	0.7	32%	75%	38
	03	25	aaa	TAM	2	4	12	1	60	73	38	6	29	32	5.70	1.70	23.1	376	4.4	4.8	1.1	0.9	33%	67%	21
Stanford,Jason	02	26	a/a	CLE	10	7	24	0	138	178	69	11	49	89	4.50	1.64	26.2	368	3.2	5.8	1.8	0.7	36%	73%	45
	03	27	aaa	CLE	10	4	20	0	126	153	66	16	28	89	4.71	1.43	27.4	337	2.0	6.4	3.2	1.2	34%	70%	67
Stanifer,Rob	03	32	aaa	HOU	4	2	44	4	63	78	38	5	19	34	5.40	1.53	6.4	352	2.7	4.9	1.8	0.7	34%	64%	40
Stark,Dennis	02	28	aaa	COL	1	2	7	0	37	41	20	6	14	31	4.84	1.48	23.4	344	3.4	7.5	2.2	1.5	32%	71%	48
Steenstra,Kennie	02	32	aaa	ARI	2	3	18	0	53	97	57	5	18	25	9.66	2.17	15.0	434	3.1	4.2	1.4	0.8	42%	53%	7
Steffek,Brian	03	26	aa	LA	1	5	24	1	30	52	37	3	27	25	10.93	2.61	7.0	481	7.9	7.5	0.9	1.0	45%	56%	16
Stein,Blake	03	30	a/a	MON	3	5	21	2	74	131	83	10	43	32	10.03	2.35	18.6	454	5.2	3.9	0.8	1.2	41%	56%	-18
Stemle,Steve	02	25	a/a	STL	12	6	28	0	137	168	73	13	39	69	4.80	1.51	21.7	349	2.6	4.5	1.8	0.9	33%	69%	35
	03	26	aaa	STL	6	11	26	0	156	191	82	15	39	79	4.76	1.47	26.4	343	2.3	4.5	2.0	0.9	33%	69%	39
Stephens,Jason	02	27	a/a	ANA	1	8	10	0	57	95	49	13	16	23	7.74	1.95	27.7	408	2.5	3.6	1.4	2.1	37%	63%	-27
Stephens,John	02	23	aaa	BAL	11	5	21	0	142	135	54	10	22	105	3.42	1.10	27.2	281	1.4	6.6	4.8	0.6	30%	70%	127
	03	24	aaa	BAL	6	7	27	0	158	182	89	19	39	115	5.06	1.40	25.3	331	2.2	6.5	2.9	1.1	33%	65%	67
Stevens,Josh	02	23	aa	NYY	1	1	24	0	40	60	22	2	8	28	4.95	1.70	7.7	376	1.8	6.3	3.5	0.5	41%	70%	85
	03	24	aa	BOS	10	9	25	0	154	199	87	12	21	77	5.10	1.43	26.8	336	1.2	4.5	3.7	0.7	34%	64%	77
Stewart,Cory	03	24	aa	SD	12	7	24	0	125	122	64	10	53	107	4.59	1.39	22.5	330	3.8	7.7	2.0	0.7	31%	67%	71
Stewart,Josh	02	24	aa	CHW	11	7	26	0	150	180	82	16	62	82	4.92	1.61	26.2	364	3.7	4.9	1.3	1.0	32%	71%	25
Stewart,Paul	02	24	aa	MIL	12	9	27	0	161	177	77	15	43	103	4.30	1.36	25.6	326	2.4	5.8	2.4	0.8	32%	70%	60
	03	25	aaa	BOS	6	8	27	0	121	155	73	17	44	64	5.43	1.64	20.5	368	3.3	4.8	1.5	1.3	33%	69%	15
Stockman,Phil	03	24	a/a	ARI	12	8	28	0	156	162	76	10	64	133	4.38	1.45	24.4	339	3.7	7.7	2.1	0.6	33%	69%	75
Stocks,Nick	03	25	aa	STL	10	8	27	0	151	213	118	23	69	90	7.02	1.87	26.8	399	4.1	5.4	1.3	1.4	36%	64%	8
Stokes,Brian	03	24	aa	TAM	2	5	10	0	50	71	25	2	15	27	4.53	1.70	23.2	376	2.6	4.8	1.8	0.4	37%	72%	45
Stokley,Billy	02	25	aa	ANA	4	14	38	1	131	200	87	14	38	32	5.98	1.82	16.3	392	2.6	2.2	0.8	1.0	36%	67%	-12
	03	26	a/a	ANA	2	14	35	1	158	219	103	18	39	57	5.88	1.63	20.6	366	2.2	3.2	1.5	1.0	34%	64%	10
Strange,Pat	02	22	aaa	NYM	10	10	29	0	165	179	80	11	58	97	4.36	1.44	24.8	337	3.2	5.3	1.7	0.6	31%	69%	50
	03	23	aaa	NYM	5	4	31	1	89	128	70	9	46	54	7.07	1.95	14.0	409	4.6	5.5	1.2	0.9	38%	63%	19
Stull,Everett	02	31	aaa	MIL	11	11	24	0	151	188	92	18	54	97	5.48	1.60	28.5	362	3.2	5.8	1.8	1.1	34%	67%	35
	03	32	aaa	MIN	4	6	11	0	57	85	54	8	23	29	8.46	1.90	25.0	402	3.7	4.5	1.2	1.3	37%	55%	0
Stults,Eric	03	24	aa	LA	3	4	9	1	38	55	27	5	14	12	6.35	1.82	20.0	392	3.4	2.8	0.8	1.2	34%	66%	-14
Sturdy,Tim	02	24	aa	MIN	1	0	35	0	53	77	51	5	32	17	8.63	2.05	7.6	421	5.4	2.9	0.5	0.8	35%	56%	-8
Surkont,Keith	02	26	aa	OAK	2	3	27	1	65	87	37	6	38	28	5.12	1.92	11.7	405	5.3	3.9	0.7	0.8	34%	74%	6
Suzuki,Mac	02	27	a/a	KC	0	4	30	0	58	85	39	8	26	36	6.03	1.91	9.4	403	4.0	5.6	1.4	1.2	38%	70%	14
Sweeney,Brian	02	28	aaa	SEA	9	5	30	2	142	191	76	17	29	90	4.82	1.55	21.2	355	1.8	5.7	3.1	1.1	36%	71%	59
	03	29	aaa	SEA	11	10	29	0	141	210	91	19	36	94	5.82	1.75	22.7	382	2.3	6.0	2.6	1.2	39%	68%	42
Switzer,Jon	03	24	a/a	TAM	9	8	23	0	131	152	67	12	35	85	4.60	1.42	24.7	336	2.4	5.9	2.4	0.8	33%	69%	59
Sylvester,Billy	02	26	a/a	ATL	2	3	58	26	58	51	30	8	40	40	4.64	1.56	4.5	357	6.2	6.2	1.0	1.2	26%	73%	30
	03	27	a/a	ATL	1	2	53	18	60	46	24	1	52	60	3.61	1.63	5.2	366	7.7	9.0	1.2	0.2	29%	76%	87
Szuminski,Jason	03	25	a/a	CHC	7	4	32	2	72	73	25	1	22	43	3.09	1.32	9.5	318	2.7	5.3	2.0	0.1	31%	75%	73
Tadano,Kazuhito	03	23	a/a	CLE	4	1	33	3	79	81	17	5	20	72	1.93	1.28	10.1	311	2.3	8.2	3.6	0.6	33%	88%	111
Taglienti,Jeff	02	27	aa	CIN	2	0	24	0	30	47	16	1	7	13	4.77	1.79	5.9	388	2.1	3.9	1.9	0.3	39%	72%	39
Takeoka,Kazuhiro	02	28	a/a	ATL	2	3	44	4	65	84	41	1	34	30	5.68	1.82	7.0	392	4.7	4.2	0.9	0.1	35%	66%	33
	03	29	a/a	ATL	2	1	29	1	38	60	34	7	14	12	8.04	1.94	6.4	408	3.3	2.8	0.8	1.7	36%	60%	-30
Tallet,Brian	02	25	a/a	CLE	12	4	26	0	146	177	69	14	54	81	4.25	1.58	25.3	359	3.3	5.0	1.5	0.9	33%	75%	32
	03	26	aaa	CLE	4	4	15	0	84	109	66	13	37	55	7.07	1.74	26.1	382	4.0	5.9	1.5	1.4	35%	60%	17
Tamayo,Danny	03	24	aa	KC	11	14	27	0	154	202	112	22	59	75	6.52	1.70	26.3	375	3.4	4.4	1.3	1.3	33%	63%	7
Tankersley,Dennis	02	24	a/a	SD	6	7	19	0	101	101	45	7	52	91	4.00	1.51	23.6	349	4.6	8.1	1.8	0.6	33%	74%	71
	03	25	aaa	SD	8	11	27	0	151	158	82	13	64	123	4.89	1.47	24.6	343	3.8	7.3	1.9	0.8	32%	67%	63
Taschner,Jack	03	25	aa	SF	0	6	34	0	75	93	58	6	47	35	6.91	1.86	10.6	398	5.6	4.2	0.8	0.7	33%	61%	16
Taylor,Aaron	02	25	aa	SEA	4	3	61	24	77	69	30	7	40	72	3.51	1.42	5.5	334	4.7	8.4	1.8	0.8	30%	77%	72
	03	26	aaa	SEA	1	3	33	16	40	36	14	3	13	30	3.24	1.23	5.0	304	3.0	6.7	2.2	0.7	28%	76%	75
Tekavec,Nate	02	23	aa	DET	6	9	27	0	141	220	125	27	48	49	7.98	1.90	25.2	403	3.1	3.1	1.0	1.7	36%	59%	-26
Telemaco,Amaury	03	30	aaa	PHI	10	9	25	0	155	159	77	19	26	93	4.46	1.20	25.5	298	1.5	5.4	3.5	1.1	29%	65%	77
Telford,Anthony	02	37	aaa	TEX	8	2	35	5	50	55	22	3	21	29	3.95	1.52	6.4	350	3.8	5.2	1.4	0.5	32%	74%	44
Tessmer,Jay	02	31	aaa	NYY	5	4	63	4	78	132	47	7	16	43	5.42	1.90	6.0	402	1.8	5.0	2.7	0.8	41%	72%	44
Teut,Nate	02	27	aaa	FLA	5	6	27	0	116	138	67	15	49	70	5.20	1.61	19.5	364	3.8	5.4	1.4	1.2	32%	70%	25
	03	28	aaa	CHC	3	9	23	0	101	147	79	20	33	50	7.02	1.78	20.7	387	2.9	4.5	1.5	1.8	35%	63%	-6
Thames,Charlie	02	23	aa	ANA	1	3	38	4	53	54	38	5	36	35	6.43	1.69	6.5	375	6.1	5.9	1.0	0.8	30%	61%	34
Thomas,Brad	02	25	aaa	MIN	6	12	28	0	152	188	104	19	52	83	6.16	1.58	24.4	359	3.1	4.9	1.6	1.1	33%	62%	25
	03	26	aaa	MIN	0	3	15	0	58	82	31	3	11	42	4.84	1.60	17.5	362	1.7	6.4	3.7	0.5	39%	69%	93
Thomas,Evan	02	28	aaa	PHI	10	2	22	0	113	130	63	8	43	64	5.02	1.53	22.9	352	3.4	5.1	1.5	0.6	32%	67%	41
	03	29	aaa	TOR	4	8	20	0	94	141	77	14	33	50	7.36	1.85	22.4	396	3.2	4.8	1.5	1.4	37%	61%	7
Thompson,Doug	02	26	aa	COL	6	2	50	6	70	86	49	9	29	51	6.29	1.64	6.4	368	3.7	6.5	1.8	1.2	34%	62%	37
	03	27	a/a	COL	1	4	39	1	77	114	68	16	37	44	7.93	1.96	9.6	409	4.3	5.2	1.2	1.9	36%	62%	-12
Thompson,Eric	02	25	a/a	OAK	6	5	35	3	114	142	60	11	36	65	4.74	1.56	14.6	356	2.8	5.1	1.8	0.9	34%	71%	38
	03	26	a/a	KC	11	3	28	1	112	122	52	11	47	50	4.19	1.51	17.7	348	3.7	4.0	1.1	0.9	29%	74%	21
Thompson,Mark	02	32	a/a	COL	1	4	20	0	58	104	50	17	16	32	7.75	2.07	14.5	423	2.5	5.0	2.0	2.6	40%	68%	-28
Thompson,Travis	02	25	a/a	CIN	1	7	23	0	81	122	58	5	21	52	6.44	1.76	16.5	385	2.3	5.8	2.5	0.6	40%	62%	57
Thornton,Matt	02	26	aa	SEA	1	5	12	0	62	72	39	3	34	33	5.66	1.71	23.9	377	4.9	4.8	1.0	0.4	33%	65%	34
	03	27	a/a	SEA	3	2	6	0	34	29	13	2	14	18	3.34	1.25	23.7	307	3.6	4.8	1.3	0.6	25%	74%	49
Thurman,Corey	03	25	aaa	TOR	6	4	17	0	86	106	53	10	27	63	5.54	1.54	22.6	354	2.8	6.6	2.3	1.0	35%	65%	53

Major League Equivalent Statistics

					Actual				Major League Equivalents																
PITCHER	Yr	Age	Lev	Org	w	l	g	sv	ip	h	er	hr	bb	k	era	br/ip	bf/g	oob	ctl	dom	cmd	hr/9	h%	s%	bpv
Thurman,Mike	02	29	aaa	NYY	7	3	12	0	76	100	36	9	15	41	4.25	1.51	28.1	349	1.8	4.8	2.7	1.1	34%	75%	48
	03	30	aaa	NYY	7	7	26	1	94	146	67	14	26	58	6.38	1.82	17.1	392	2.4	5.5	2.3	1.4	39%	67%	25
Tolar,Kevin	02	32	aaa	PIT	6	1	44	1	78	80	28	5	26	67	3.23	1.36	7.6	325	3.0	7.7	2.6	0.6	33%	77%	86
	03	33	aaa	BOS	5	1	47	4	31	23	11	3	19	28	3.04	1.35	2.8	324	5.5	7.9	1.5	0.9	25%	81%	65
Tollberg,Brian	03	31	aaa	SD	5	3	20	0	82	105	53	12	13	35	5.77	1.44	17.9	337	1.4	3.9	2.8	1.3	32%	61%	37
Torres,Salomon	02	31	aaa	PIT	8	5	26	0	162	216	93	13	41	104	5.16	1.59	28.1	360	2.3	5.8	2.5	0.7	37%	67%	59
Totten,Heath	02	24	aa	LA	3	3	9	0	49	56	21	2	16	25	3.86	1.47	23.9	343	2.9	4.6	1.6	0.4	32%	73%	48
	03	25	aa	LA	11	12	28	0	181	252	94	18	20	91	4.69	1.50	28.6	348	1.0	4.5	4.5	0.9	36%	70%	86
Towers,Josh	02	26	aaa	BAL	0	9	15	0	69	124	69	17	14	36	9.00	2.00	22.6	415	1.8	4.7	2.6	2.2	40%	57%	-6
	03	27	aaa	TOR	5	7	21	0	132	162	66	12	21	64	4.49	1.38	27.1	329	1.4	4.4	3.1	0.8	33%	68%	62
Traber,Billy	02	23	a/a	CLE	17	5	27	0	162	188	70	14	34	99	3.89	1.37	25.8	327	1.9	5.5	2.9	0.8	33%	73%	69
Tremblay,Max	03	27	aa	HOU	2	3	41	0	32	52	31	2	17	25	8.81	2.15	4.0	432	4.7	7.0	1.5	0.7	43%	56%	36
Trujillo,J.J.	02	27	a/a	SD	5	0	49	20	68	70	22	3	23	57	2.91	1.37	6.0	327	3.0	7.5	2.5	0.4	33%	79%	88
	03	28	a/a	SD	2	3	55	6	73	87	48	8	26	39	5.94	1.55	5.9	354	3.2	4.8	1.5	1.0	32%	62%	27
Tsao,Chin-hui	03	22	aa	COL	11	4	18	0	113	110	45	12	26	109	3.58	1.20	25.9	299	2.1	8.7	4.2	1.0	32%	73%	116
Tucker,Rusty	03	23	aa	SD	2	6	51	28	53	58	27	4	32	50	4.55	1.69	4.8	375	5.4	8.6	1.6	0.7	35%	73%	64
Turman,Jason	03	28	aaa	KC	2	5	31	4	74	83	42	11	36	35	5.11	1.61	10.8	363	4.3	4.3	1.0	1.3	29%	71%	7
Turnbow,Derrick	03	26	aaa	ANA	2	2	42	5	69	86	44	6	29	67	5.77	1.68	7.6	373	3.8	8.7	2.3	0.8	38%	65%	70
Ulacia,Dennis	02	22	aa	CHW	6	14	28	1	145	209	106	21	55	81	6.57	1.82	24.6	392	3.4	5.0	1.5	1.3	36%	65%	11
	03	23	aa	CHW	1	5	11	0	49	73	36	6	23	28	6.59	1.95	21.8	409	4.2	5.1	1.2	1.1	38%	67%	11
Ulloa,Enmanuel	02	24	aaa	SEA	4	7	38	2	77	103	61	13	28	35	7.13	1.70	9.4	376	3.3	4.1	1.3	1.5	33%	59%	-3
	03	25	a/a	MON	0	3	17	1	30	57	46	5	23	21	13.87	2.64	9.8	483	6.8	6.4	0.9	1.5	45%	44%	-12
Ungs,Nic	03	24	aa	FLA	3	4	10	0	58	74	29	4	8	31	4.56	1.41	25.2	333	1.3	4.8	3.7	0.7	34%	68%	82
Urban,Jeff	02	26	aaa	SF	5	7	35	0	103	128	45	8	34	61	3.93	1.57	13.2	358	3.0	5.3	1.8	0.7	34%	76%	44
	03	27	aaa	SF	3	10	29	0	127	180	78	8	44	72	5.55	1.77	20.5	386	3.1	5.1	1.6	0.6	38%	68%	37
Urdaneta,Lino	03	24	aa	LA	0	8	44	6	65	81	39	4	26	36	5.42	1.65	6.8	369	3.6	5.0	1.4	0.6	34%	66%	37
Valentine,Joe	02	23	aa	CHW	4	1	55	36	59	44	18	1	32	58	2.74	1.29	4.5	313	4.9	8.8	1.8	0.2	28%	77%	101
	03	24	aaa	CIN	2	3	49	5	63	55	34	6	38	52	4.84	1.47	5.7	343	5.4	7.4	1.4	0.9	28%	68%	57
Valverde,Jose	02	23	aaa	ARI	2	4	49	5	47	49	34	8	21	54	6.48	1.48	4.2	345	4.0	10.3	2.6	1.5	34%	58%	73
	03	24	aaa	ARI	1	1	22	5	29	29	12	1	13	23	3.72	1.45	5.8	339	4.0	7.1	1.8	0.3	32%	73%	75
Van Dusen,Derrick	02	21	aa	TEX	2	3	8	0	37	54	31	5	15	19	7.54	1.86	22.1	398	3.6	4.6	1.3	1.2	36%	59%	6
	03	22	aa	CLE	10	8	28	0	139	219	101	14	55	66	6.54	1.97	24.3	411	3.6	4.3	1.2	0.9	39%	67%	9
Van Hekken,Andy	02	23	aaa	DET	9	7	28	0	183	202	76	12	41	102	3.74	1.33	27.8	320	2.0	5.0	2.5	0.6	31%	72%	65
	03	24	a/a	DET	9	12	26	0	152	219	107	24	35	49	6.34	1.67	26.8	371	2.1	2.9	1.4	1.4	34%	64%	-7
Van Poppel,Todd	03	32	a/a	CIN	4	3	22	1	63	76	31	6	14	40	4.44	1.43	12.5	336	2.1	5.7	2.7	0.8	34%	70%	64
VanBenschoten,Johr	03	23	aa	PIT	7	6	17	0	90	120	53	6	35	65	5.25	1.72	24.6	378	3.5	6.5	1.9	0.6	37%	69%	52
Vance,Cory	02	23	aa	COL	10	8	25	0	150	176	88	13	77	96	5.28	1.69	27.7	374	4.6	5.8	1.2	0.8	33%	69%	35
	03	24	aaa	COL	9	11	24	0	157	216	109	28	49	84	6.24	1.69	30.2	374	2.8	4.8	1.7	1.6	34%	66%	8
Vargas,Claudio	02	23	a/a	FLA	6	13	25	0	109	132	76	17	42	84	6.27	1.59	19.7	361	3.5	6.9	2.0	1.4	34%	62%	38
Vargas,Jose	02	26	aa	CLE	4	1	18	2	39	56	28	1	19	26	6.43	1.91	10.5	404	4.4	6.0	1.4	0.2	39%	64%	47
	03	27	a/a	CLE	3	2	38	8	53	77	21	6	34	41	3.58	2.09	7.0	426	5.8	7.0	1.2	0.9	40%	85%	28
Vargas,Martin	02	26	aaa	CLE	3	2	22	8	35	43	12	3	12	16	3.09	1.57	7.1	358	3.1	4.1	1.3	0.8	33%	83%	25
Vasquez,Jorge	03	25	aa	KC	3	1	36	22	51	52	17	4	20	39	2.93	1.41	6.2	333	3.5	6.8	1.9	0.8	31%	82%	61
Vega,Rene	02	26	aa	NYM	1	6	26	2	45	76	45	7	21	25	8.98	2.15	8.8	433	4.2	5.0	1.2	1.4	40%	58%	-5
Vent,Kevin	02	25	aa	SF	9	4	45	3	81	101	38	6	30	24	4.22	1.62	8.2	364	3.3	2.7	0.8	0.7	32%	74%	8
	03	26	a/a	SF	6	5	43	1	84	109	53	6	37	41	5.71	1.73	9.1	380	3.9	4.4	1.1	0.6	35%	66%	26
Veras,Jose	03	23	a/a	TAM	6	9	30	0	135	140	73	15	58	103	4.86	1.46	19.8	342	3.9	6.9	1.8	1.0	31%	68%	51
Veronie,Shanin	02	26	aa	ATL	2	2	29	0	52	69	31	6	24	23	5.34	1.78	8.5	387	4.1	4.0	1.0	1.0	34%	71%	6
Verplancke,Jeff	02	25	aaa	SF	3	5	51	3	64	67	31	5	24	44	4.35	1.42	5.5	335	3.4	6.2	1.8	0.7	31%	70%	57
Viera,Rolando	02	29	a/a	BOS	5	1	48	10	84	128	63	20	46	34	6.75	2.07	8.7	423	4.9	3.6	0.7	2.1	35%	72%	-40
Villafuerte,Brandon	02	27	aaa	SD	8	4	47	1	58	49	15	2	23	45	2.33	1.24	5.1	306	3.6	7.0	2.0	0.3	28%	81%	84
	03	28	aaa	SD	3	1	37	12	44	47	9	1	14	31	1.94	1.39	5.1	330	2.8	6.4	2.3	0.2	33%	86%	81
Villalon,Julio	03	25	aa	STL	4	7	12	0	66	96	50	11	28	40	6.81	1.87	26.4	398	3.8	5.4	1.4	1.5	37%	65%	6
Villarreal,Oscar	02	21	a/a	ARI	9	6	24	0	148	141	67	9	40	116	4.07	1.22	25.6	302	2.4	7.0	2.9	0.5	30%	66%	93
Villegas,Felix	03	25	aa	BOS	1	8	23	0	53	79	53	4	32	26	9.02	2.09	11.6	425	5.5	4.4	0.8	0.8	38%	54%	9
Villone,Ron	03	34	aaa	HOU	4	2	20	1	54	53	18	2	23	32	2.97	1.40	11.7	331	3.8	5.4	1.4	0.3	30%	79%	56
Vining,Ken	02	28	aaa	CHW	2	5	44	1	47	46	21	6	27	30	4.02	1.55	4.8	355	5.2	5.7	1.1	1.1	28%	78%	28
	03	29	aaa	HOU	3	5	41	1	64	99	56	12	26	23	7.86	1.95	7.6	409	3.6	3.3	0.9	1.7	36%	61%	-26
Vogelsong,Ryan	02	25	aa	PIT	1	5	8	0	43	60	37	6	10	27	7.71	1.62	24.5	365	2.1	5.6	2.7	1.3	36%	52%	43
	03	26	aaa	PIT	12	8	26	0	149	173	96	13	55	121	5.79	1.53	25.5	352	3.3	7.3	2.2	0.8	35%	62%	64
Voyles,Brad	02	26	aaa	KC	3	4	26	5	32	33	18	2	21	28	5.05	1.68	5.7	374	5.9	7.9	1.3	0.6	33%	69%	61
	03	27	aaa	KC	2	2	29	2	81	81	35	6	24	55	3.89	1.30	11.8	315	2.6	6.1	2.3	0.7	30%	71%	69
Wade,Travis	02	27	a/a	HOU	3	8	48	1	68	102	57	14	38	35	7.54	2.06	7.1	422	5.0	4.6	0.9	1.9	36%	66%	-21
	03	28	aa	SF	2	4	47	5	54	99	46	4	29	20	7.71	2.36	6.1	456	4.8	3.3	0.7	0.6	42%	66%	-6
Waechter,Doug	03	23	a/a	TAM	8	6	23	0	127	149	71	17	33	68	5.02	1.43	24.1	337	2.3	4.8	2.1	1.2	31%	67%	34
Wainwright,Adam	03	22	aa	ATL	10	8	27	0	149	161	76	11	38	108	4.58	1.33	23.5	321	2.3	6.5	2.8	0.7	32%	65%	80
Walker,Kevin	03	27	aaa	SD	3	1	34	0	46	59	23	4	9	34	4.52	1.48	6.0	345	1.8	6.7	3.6	0.8	36%	70%	85
Walker,Tyler	02	26	aaa	NYM	10	5	28	1	142	178	78	13	40	89	4.94	1.54	22.6	352	2.5	5.6	2.2	0.8	35%	68%	51
	03	27	aaa	DET	2	9	26	0	131	173	88	14	48	97	6.07	1.69	23.2	374	3.3	6.7	2.0	0.9	37%	64%	47
Walk,Mitch	02	25	aa	SF	6	5	33	1	124	152	46	5	49	55	3.33	1.62	17.1	365	3.6	4.0	1.1	0.4	33%	79%	33
	03	26	aa	SF	6	13	36	7	137	177	76	8	58	58	4.96	1.71	17.6	377	3.8	3.8	1.0	0.5	34%	70%	22
Walling,Dave	02	24	aaa	NYY	2	7	11	0	67	80	38	8	11	41	5.10	1.36	26.1	325	1.5	5.5	3.7	1.1	33%	64%	76
Walrond,Les	02	26	a/a	STL	10	8	32	0	145	173	92	25	75	123	5.71	1.71	21.0	377	4.7	7.6	1.6	1.6	34%	70%	31
	03	27	a/a	KC	5	1	34	2	60	60	26	7	26	37	3.82	1.42	7.7	335	3.8	5.5	1.4	1.0	29%	76%	38
Wang,Chien-Ming	03	24	aa	NYY	7	6	21	0	122	166	76	8	33	71	5.63	1.63	26.4	366	2.4	5.2	2.1	0.6	37%	64%	50
Ward,Bryan	02	31	aaa	COL	1	2	6	0	38	47	28	7	16	21	6.63	1.66	29.0	370	3.8	5.0	1.3	1.7	32%	63%	3
Ward,Jeremy	02	25	aaa	ARI	4	6	54	1	62	74	33	5	13	34	4.77	1.40	5.0	332	1.9	4.9	2.6	0.7	33%	66%	60
Wasdin,John	03	31	aaa	TOR	10	5	28	0	133	163	71	6	27	114	4.77	1.43	20.7	337	1.9	7.7	4.2	0.4	38%	65%	117
Waters,Chris	03	23	aa	ATL	3	8	17	0	85	130	59	14	28	45	6.21	1.85	23.9	396	2.9	4.7	1.6	1.5	37%	69%	3
Watkins,Steve	02	24	aa	SD	4	8	37	0	116	147	61	8	53	70	4.72	1.72	14.6	379	4.1	5.4	1.3	0.6	35%	72%	36
	03	25	a/a	SD	6	4	32	0	127	139	66	8	47	77	4.69	1.46	17.4	342	3.4	5.4	1.6	0.6	32%	67%	49

Major League Equivalent Statistics

PITCHERS

PITCHER	Yr	Age	Lev	Org	Actual w	l	g	sv	Major League Equivalents ip	h	er	hr	bb	k	era	br/ip	bf/g	oob	ctl	dom	cmd	hr/9	h%	s%	bpv
Watson,Mark	02	29	aaa	COL	6	0	44	3	60	81	48	9	32	35	7.18	1.88	6.6	400	4.8	5.2	1.1	1.3	35%	63%	6
	03	30	aaa	CIN	4	4	44	4	53	69	37	1	15	35	6.32	1.59	5.5	361	2.6	6.0	2.3	0.2	37%	57%	72
Wayne,Justin	02	23	a/a	FLA	8	6	26	0	152	131	58	11	49	77	3.43	1.18	24.0	295	2.9	4.6	1.6	0.7	25%	72%	50
	03	24	aaa	FLA	4	12	23	0	136	145	65	9	39	74	4.30	1.35	25.3	324	2.6	4.9	1.9	0.6	31%	68%	53
Weatherby,Charlie	03	25	aa	BOS	2	2	30	1	51	83	45	3	22	20	7.96	2.06	8.5	422	3.9	3.5	0.9	0.6	39%	59%	7
Weaver,Eric	02	29	aa	PHI	5	4	37	7	45	57	33	11	37	32	6.60	2.09	6.1	426	7.4	6.4	0.9	2.2	33%	73%	-15
Webb,Alan	03	24	a/a	SD	1	3	59	2	86	66	36	7	48	64	3.77	1.33	6.2	320	5.1	6.7	1.3	0.8	25%	73%	59
Webb,Brandon	02	23	a/a	ARI	10	7	27	0	159	161	63	4	58	106	3.57	1.38	25.3	328	3.3	6.0	1.8	0.2	31%	73%	71
Webb,John	02	23	aa	CHC	4	5	11	0	61	62	39	6	24	39	5.74	1.41	24.1	333	3.5	5.7	1.6	0.9	30%	59%	46
	03	24	aa	CHC	5	8	30	1	132	167	89	14	59	71	6.10	1.71	20.4	378	4.0	4.9	1.2	0.9	34%	64%	21
Wedel,Jeremy	02	26	aaa	PHI	7	1	43	1	60	70	22	1	21	31	3.29	1.51	6.2	349	3.1	4.6	1.5	0.1	33%	77%	52
Weibl,Clint	02	28	aaa	STL	5	8	24	0	110	147	56	19	25	54	4.57	1.56	20.6	356	2.0	4.4	2.2	1.6	33%	76%	18
	03	29	aaa	STL	3	6	20	1	95	131	69	17	38	50	6.51	1.78	22.3	386	3.6	4.8	1.3	1.6	34%	66%	-1
Wellemeyer,Todd	02	24	aa	CHC	3	3	8	0	46	40	32	2	20	31	6.26	1.30	24.3	316	3.9	6.1	1.6	0.4	28%	48%	66
	03	25	a/a	CHC	6	6	17	0	87	104	65	9	47	75	6.74	1.74	23.9	382	4.9	7.8	1.6	1.0	36%	61%	47
Wengert,Don	02	33	aaa	BOS	8	12	29	0	169	265	112	20	36	60	5.96	1.78	27.4	387	1.9	3.2	1.7	1.1	37%	67%	7
West,Brian	02	22	aa	CHW	9	11	27	0	149	156	98	13	76	84	5.92	1.56	24.7	356	4.6	5.1	1.1	0.8	30%	61%	32
	03	23	a/a	CHW	4	5	13	0	59	90	52	9	31	35	7.92	2.05	22.6	421	4.7	5.3	1.1	1.4	38%	62%	1
Wheeler,Dan	02	25	aaa	ATL	9	6	27	0	155	188	98	25	41	92	5.69	1.48	25.2	344	2.4	5.3	2.2	1.5	32%	64%	32
	03	26	aaa	NYM	4	2	22	4	45	56	25	4	17	37	5.03	1.61	9.3	363	3.4	7.3	2.1	0.8	36%	69%	60
White,Bill	03	25	aa	ARI	1	3	15	0	39	48	32	4	22	21	7.29	1.81	12.3	391	5.1	4.8	0.9	1.0	33%	59%	15
White,Matt	02	24	aa	TAM	1	2	7	0	34	44	32	9	23	15	8.53	1.99	23.9	309	6.2	4.1	0.7	2.4	31%	60%	-39
	03	25	aa	TAM	0	4	7	0	31	53	39	10	28	14	11.29	2.62	24.5	371	8.1	3.9	0.5	2.9	37%	59%	-73
White,Matt	02	25	a/a	CLE	6	2	34	1	106	160	71	14	53	58	6.04	2.01	15.4	341	4.5	4.9	1.1	1.2	38%	72%	2
	03	26	a/a	CLE	2	3	23	0	49	51	14	4	21	32	2.65	1.47	9.4	263	3.9	6.0	1.5	0.8	31%	85%	46
Wiggins,Scott	02	27	a/a	TOR	5	2	52	1	61	47	17	1	22	46	2.51	1.13	4.8	286	3.2	6.8	2.1	0.1	27%	76%	93
	03	28	a/a	TOR	2	3	52	1	53	89	48	7	28	27	8.18	2.19	5.2	437	4.7	4.6	1.0	1.2	40%	62%	-5
Wilkerson,Wes	03	27	aa	KC	6	6	32	1	105	170	92	13	55	24	7.85	2.15	16.6	432	4.8	2.1	0.4	1.1	37%	63%	-29
Wilkins,Marc	02	32	aaa	CHC	2	0	31	1	41	45	22	1	12	24	4.81	1.38	5.7	329	2.6	5.2	2.0	0.2	32%	63%	67
	03	33	aaa	FLA	1	1	20	1	36	51	29	5	17	23	7.37	1.87	8.6	399	4.2	5.7	1.4	1.3	37%	61%	13
Williams,Dave	03	25	aaa	PIT	7	4	16	0	77	93	47	8	29	48	5.49	1.58	21.7	359	3.4	5.6	1.7	0.9	33%	66%	37
Williams,Jeff	02	30	aaa	LA	6	4	56	28	79	88	23	2	21	59	2.61	1.38	6.1	328	2.4	6.7	2.8	0.2	34%	80%	92
Williams,Jerome	02	21	aaa	SF	6	11	28	0	160	136	64	12	42	128	3.60	1.11	23.1	283	2.4	7.2	3.0	0.7	28%	69%	97
	03	22	aaa	SF	4	2	10	0	57	50	16	2	14	37	2.58	1.12	23.0	284	2.2	5.9	2.7	0.3	28%	76%	93
Williams,Randy	03	28	a/a	SEA	6	3	47	3	67	79	33	6	22	43	4.42	1.51	6.3	348	3.0	5.8	1.9	0.8	33%	72%	50
Williams,Todd	02	32	aaa	MON	3	5	46	24	48	71	27	5	13	17	5.06	1.75	4.9	383	2.4	3.2	1.3	0.9	36%	72%	6
	03	33	aaa	TAM	3	2	56	4	69	68	16	2	16	29	2.05	1.22	5.1	301	2.1	3.8	1.9	0.3	29%	83%	58
Willis,Dontrelle	03	22	aa	FLA	4	0	6	0	36	27	7	2	9	29	1.75	1.00	23.6	261	2.2	7.2	3.2	0.5	26%	85%	110
Wilson,C.J.	02	22	aa	TEX	1	0	5	0	30	28	8	0	12	15	2.40	1.33	25.5	321	3.6	4.5	1.3	0.0	29%	80%	60
	03	23	aa	TEX	6	9	22	0	123	162	92	15	39	78	6.73	1.63	25.5	367	2.9	5.7	2.0	1.1	35%	59%	36
Wilson,Jeff	02	26	aa	BAL	4	4	50	10	91	92	29	6	36	58	2.87	1.41	7.9	333	3.6	5.7	1.6	0.6	30%	81%	54
	03	27	aa	BAL	5	7	28	0	81	122	54	6	30	37	6.02	1.87	13.9	399	3.3	4.1	1.2	0.7	38%	67%	17
Wilson,Kris	02	26	a/a	KC	5	3	21	1	74	111	27	6	6	37	3.28	1.58	15.9	359	0.7	4.5	6.2	0.7	38%	81%	122
Wilson,Mike	03	23	aa	SF	3	2	11	0	40	49	22	6	20	18	4.86	1.72	16.9	379	4.4	4.1	0.9	1.4	31%	75%	-1
Wilson,Phil	02	22	aa	ANA	2	4	7	0	42	66	42	12	14	13	8.96	1.90	29.0	402	3.0	2.8	0.9	2.6	34%	56%	-55
Wimberly,Larry	02	27	aa	PIT	1	2	26	1	53	67	35	5	20	26	5.93	1.64	9.3	367	3.4	4.4	1.3	0.8	33%	63%	23
Winchester,Scott	02	29	aaa	TOR	2	4	44	2	63	91	54	11	21	32	7.69	1.77	6.7	386	3.0	4.6	1.5	1.6	35%	57%	1
	03	30	aaa	LA	2	9	19	0	87	154	64	10	19	31	6.65	1.99	22.5	413	1.9	3.2	1.6	1.0	40%	67%	1
Wise,Matt	02	27	aaa	ANA	3	4	16	0	78	114	53	13	14	63	6.12	1.64	22.2	368	1.6	7.3	4.5	1.5	39%	65%	81
Withers,Darvin	03	23	aa	OAK	7	4	23	0	119	180	82	6	35	57	6.24	1.81	24.5	391	2.7	4.3	1.6	0.5	38%	64%	33
Wolfe,Brian	03	23	aa	MIN	5	7	30	3	82	129	73	10	25	36	7.99	1.87	13.1	399	2.7	3.9	1.4	1.1	38%	56%	6
Woodards,Orlando	02	25	a/a	FLA	5	9	29	1	103	118	42	6	35	52	3.67	1.48	15.7	345	3.1	4.5	1.5	0.5	32%	76%	41
Woodard,Steve	02	27	aaa	PHI	5	4	22	5	65	84	43	9	11	48	5.95	1.46	12.9	341	1.5	6.6	4.4	1.2	36%	60%	88
	03	28	aaa	BOS	6	7	31	2	94	129	67	11	14	46	6.38	1.52	13.5	350	1.3	4.4	3.3	1.0	35%	58%	55
Wood,Mike	02	22	aa	OAK	11	3	17	0	105	115	43	8	28	54	3.68	1.36	26.5	325	2.4	4.6	1.9	0.7	31%	74%	48
	03	23	aaa	OAK	9	3	16	0	91	94	34	5	22	50	3.36	1.27	23.9	311	2.2	4.9	2.3	0.5	30%	74%	65
Wrightsman,Dusty	03	24	aa	KC	4	4	20	1	75	122	71	20	18	41	8.51	1.85	17.9	396	2.1	4.9	2.3	2.3	37%	57%	-9
Wright,Chris	02	25	aa	SEA	6	4	37	0	70	102	40	7	32	32	5.13	1.91	9.2	404	4.1	4.1	1.0	0.9	36%	74%	7
	03	26	a/a	SEA	7	12	29	0	142	211	100	18	74	91	6.33	2.01	24.2	416	4.7	5.8	1.2	1.1	38%	69%	14
Wright,Danny	03	26	aaa	CHW	1	3	8	0	33	30	22	7	10	23	6.06	1.22	17.1	303	2.8	6.2	2.3	1.9	25%	55%	34
Wright,Jamey	03	29	aaa	KC	6	9	27	0	138	184	99	24	74	94	6.45	1.87	24.5	399	4.8	6.1	1.3	1.5	35%	68%	9
Wright,Jaret	02	27	aaa	CLE	5	3	10	0	55	71	33	7	27	36	5.38	1.78	25.9	386	4.4	5.9	1.3	1.1	35%	71%	23
Wrigley,Jase	02	27	a/a	COL	2	3	53	10	71	92	32	3	37	31	4.04	1.81	6.4	391	4.7	3.9	0.8	0.4	34%	77%	23
Wuertz,Mike	02	24	aaa	CHC	9	5	28	0	154	188	91	21	63	115	5.32	1.63	25.0	366	3.7	6.7	1.8	1.2	34%	70%	38
	03	25	aaa	CHC	3	9	43	1	124	155	72	17	35	81	5.23	1.53	12.8	352	2.5	5.9	2.3	1.2	34%	68%	42
Wylie,Mitch	02	26	aaa	CHW	2	3	6	0	34	52	24	8	5	21	6.35	1.68	26.0	373	1.3	5.6	4.2	2.1	37%	67%	44
	03	27	aa	CHW	3	5	14	0	57	76	46	3	21	33	7.25	1.69	18.8	375	3.3	5.2	1.6	0.5	36%	54%	41
Yarnall,Ed	03	28	aaa	OAK	3	3	18	0	64	82	31	6	31	37	4.28	1.75	16.7	384	4.3	5.2	1.2	0.9	34%	77%	24
Yates,Tyler	02	25	aaa	NYM	2	2	24	6	34	33	6	1	13	29	1.59	1.35	6.1	324	3.4	7.7	2.2	0.3	32%	89%	90
	03	26	a/a	NYM	2	4	12	0	59	69	36	6	29	39	5.41	1.65	22.5	370	4.4	5.9	1.3	0.8	33%	67%	36
Yennaco,Jay	03	28	aaa	STL	0	3	8	0	34	52	35	4	20	13	9.20	2.11	21.4	427	5.3	3.5	0.7	1.1	36%	55%	-12
Yofu,Tetsu	03	30	a/a	CHW	9	9	32	2	140	194	95	20	54	92	6.10	1.77	20.5	385	3.5	5.9	1.7	1.3	36%	67%	24
Young,Chris	03	24	aa	MON	4	4	15	0	83	98	45	11	22	50	4.91	1.45	24.2	339	2.4	5.5	2.3	1.1	32%	68%	44
Young,Colin	03	26	aa	COL	2	2	40	2	45	52	20	2	22	33	3.91	1.63	5.1	367	4.4	6.6	1.5	0.5	34%	76%	56
Young,Jason	02	23	a/a	COL	13	9	27	0	168	184	88	16	64	131	4.71	1.48	27.4	343	3.4	7.0	2.0	0.9	33%	69%	60
	03	24	aaa	COL	6	7	23	0	116	154	69	15	36	86	5.35	1.64	23.0	367	2.8	6.7	2.4	1.2	37%	69%	48
Young,Tim	02	29	aaa	BOS	5	3	57	4	72	70	39	5	41	49	4.86	1.54	5.6	353	5.1	6.1	1.2	0.6	30%	68%	48
	03	30	aaa	COL	4	3	48	1	52	62	45	8	37	41	7.80	1.90	5.2	403	6.5	7.1	1.1	1.3	34%	59%	23
Zamora,Pete	02	27	aaa	PHI	5	2	55	15	62	76	31	2	33	28	4.50	1.76	5.3	384	4.8	4.1	0.8	0.3	34%	73%	29
	03	28	aaa	NYM	5	3	55	1	90	117	46	4	35	41	4.62	1.69	7.6	375	3.5	4.1	1.2	0.4	35%	72%	29
Ziegler,Mike	03	24	aa	OAK	12	9	27	0	165	214	86	6	31	86	4.71	1.48	26.9	344	1.7	4.7	2.8	0.3	35%	66%	70
Zink,Charlie	03	24	aa	BOS	3	2	6	0	39	25	20	1	16	14	4.60	1.05	25.9	271	3.6	3.3	0.9	0.2	20%	53%	50

V.
RATINGS
and
RANKINGS

Draft Guide History

The draft guide history (DGH) provides a capsule summary of each player's last few seasons along with their projection for 2004 using several different measures of performance. The players are then ranked by primary position. The true value of this exercise is not so much the projections themselves (which will change over the next few months, as uniforms and playing time expectations change), but the historical ratings. They keep every player's performance in perspective.

The DGH summarizes the tons of information in the forecast boxes. So, you can look at potential draft picks here, and if you're undecided about any player, you can refer back to their forecast box for more detailed information.

UNIVERSAL DISCLAIMER... This section is intended solely as a preliminary look based on current factors. Do not treat this guide as the Draft Day gospel. Use the ratings and rankings as a rough guide to get a general sense of where a player falls. For Draft Day, you will need to make your own adjustments based upon about seven thousand different criteria that can impact the world between now and then. Updates will appear next spring online at BaseballHQ.com. And don't forget the free projections update at BaseballForecaster.com.

Standard Rotisserie

The standard Rotisserie listings are provided for leagues that use the 4x4 statistical categories (HR, RBI, SB, BA for batters; W, Sv, ERA, WHIP for pitchers) but can also be used as rough guides by leagues with other formats.

Runs Created per Game

This category can be used for many any other fantasy formats, from point systems to simulation leagues to table/computer games. RC/G gives you a sense of overall value, but it does not take playing time into account. As such, a platoon or bench player projected to post a 5.00 RC/G will be ranked right up there with a 600 AB regular.

The value of this? It allows you to do some cherry-picking. Players with high value, but low-playing time, are your best late-round roster fillers. When a Doug Mirabelli or a Henry Mateo finish in the Top 10 of *anything,* you might scratch your head. But when it's two in the morning and you have the catcher and middle infielder slots open and $2 left to spend, you'll thank this list.

Power and Speed

These are rankings using our league-normalized power and speed indices (PX and SX). They are very insightful, but they, too, do not account for playing time. They just tell you where each player falls on the skills scale.

There are plenty of no-brainer rankings on these lists, but there are plenty of surprises as well. The value is in picking out the high-ranked lesser names. These are players who may be prime fodder for further analysis, or again, could be excellent late-round cherry-picking targets.

For example, if you have one last catcher slot open and have drafted a team short on speed, you can use the SX ranking to pick out that one backstop whose one extra potential stolen base might put you over the top come October. Who woulda thunk that Gerald Laird could be your man?

Base Performance Value

For pitchers, BPV gets you beyond the erratic trends and noise inherent in ERA. Just pure skills. No playing time is taken into account here either. The relievers list will go a long way to helping you fill out a LIMA Plan pitching staff.

Within each of the above five categories, players are rated as part of the entire population, not within each position. So those who qualify at multiple positions may be moved around freely without affecting their ratings. Of course, their ranking within a new position will likely change.

Runs Above Replacement (RAR)

The most important use for RAR is that it allows us to integrate batters and pitchers in the ranking process. To those who play Scoresheet Baseball, or some other simulation game, RAR is probably the single best gauge for your draft — if you've got a firm handle on projected playing time. Which we don't. Not yet, anyway. In addition, we're still playing around with the entire concept of replacement levels, and were forced to apply some adjustments to these numbers in order to generate a more "real world" ranking list. What's important right now is each player's relative rank, not the RAR values (which will not tie out to the levels in the player boxes), so don't obsess over them.

As such, consider these lists preliminary, but probably the best you'll find for your early stage drafts. Over the winter, there will be monthly updates. Come March, RAR will provide no better evaluator.

Catchers

Std Rotisserie	'99	'00	'01	'02	'03	'04Prj
Rodriguez,Ivan	39	25	23	19	22	**22**
Lopez,Javy	11	18	12	6	34	**20**
Kendall,Jason	19	25	12	13	20	**18**
Piazza,Mike	30	32	26	24	8	**17**
Posada,Jorge	6	18	18	17	21	**17**
Lieberthal,Mike	23	12	0	12	19	**17**
Molina,Ben	7	11	5	3	13	**15**
LeCroy,Matt	4	5	4	13	13	**15**
Varitek,Jason	12	5	6	10	18	**14**
Pierzynski,A.J.	-0	10	10	11	17	**14**
LoDuca,Paul	3	10	25	13	8	**12**
Hernandez,Ramon	8	5	9	2	15	**11**
Hall,Toby	2	13	23	8	6	**11**
Barrett,Michael	9	2	3	11	2	**10**
Martinez,Victor				21	13	**10**
Santiago,Benito	3	6	7	16	10	**9**
Johnson,Charles	7	22	12	2	9	**8**
Schneider,Brian	5	0	2	6	3	**8**
Bard,Josh			4	9	9	**8**
Estrada,Johnny		4	5	6	13	**7**
Laird,Gerald				11	8	**7**
Moeller,Chad	-1	0	2	10	5	**6**
Ross,David			5	7	5	**6**
Myers,Greg	3	-0	4	2	13	**6**
LaRue,Jason	2	5	5	8	7	**6**
Ojeda,Miguel		14	13	21	2	**6**
Miller,Damian	7	8	9	7	3	**5**
Olivo,Miguel			7	16	3	**5**
Torrealba,Yorvit	-0	4	1	3	4	**5**
Alomar Jr.,Sandy	8	7	2	7	4	**5**
Estalella,Bobby	2	7	2	6	2	**5**
Castro,Ramon	-0	8	13	3	3	**5**
Hammock,Robby		-1	-3	5	9	**5**
Greene,Todd	7	4	1	14	3	**5**
Wilson,Dan	6	1	8	9	2	**4**
Melhuse,Adam	4	5	0	6	3	**4**
Bennett,Gary	2	8	2	4	3	**4**
Hundley,Todd	6	15	0	5	1	**4**
Zaun,Gregg	1	7	6	1	2	**4**
Ausmus,Brad	11	8	1	6	2	**4**
Mayne,Brent	7	11	6	2	2	**4**
Davis,Ben	7	4	6	6	3	**3**
Wilson,Vance	1	4	1	3	5	**3**
Mirabelli,Doug	8	2	4	3	3	**3**
Miller,Corky	-1	-0	13	3	2	**3**
Matheny,Mike	-1	4	0	3	5	**3**
Diaz,Einar	8	4	8	-4	4	**3**
Machado,Robert	-2	6	2	3	6	**3**
Fordyce,Brook	10	11	-2	-0	6	**3**
Inge,Brandon		3	-2	1	3	**3**
Redmond,Mike	5	-0	5	7	-0	**2**
Gil,Geronimo	4	6	3	5	4	**2**
Gonzalez,Wiki	10	1	6	-0	0	**2**
Wilson,Tom	2	5	1	5	4	**2**
Pratt,Todd	4	5	-2	5	3	**2**
Perez,Eddie	2	-0	2	-2	9	**2**
Barajas,Rod	10	-1	4	3	0	**1**
Flaherty,John	11	4	2	4	2	**1**
Hinch,A.J.	4	2	6	5	0	**1**
Rivera,Mike	0	-4	11	5	5	**1**
Laker,Tim	-2	1	5	-1	2	**1**
Stinnett,Kelly	5	1	5	-1	1	**1**
Molina,Jose	-1	-4	4	4	-3	**1**
Valentin,Javier	2	7	6	6	0	**1**
Widger,Chris	9	4		1	0	**1**
DiFelice,Mike	6	1	-2	1	3	**0**
Osik,Keith	-3	5	-0	-2	1	**-0**
Bako,Paul	-0	-1	-0	1	-1	**-0**
Blanco,Henry	3	2	0	-0	-2	**-1**
Walbeck,Matt	0	-1	1	-2	-3	**-1**

RC/Gm	'99	'00	'01	'02	'03	'04Prj
Piazza,Mike	7.58	9.10	7.86	6.71	6.54	**6.76**
Lopez,Javy	6.98	5.81	4.61	3.50	9.66	**6.73**
Posada,Jorge	4.60	7.69	5.76	6.01	7.04	**6.46**
Rodriguez,Ivan	7.28	9.45	6.77	6.91	6.14	**6.41**
Lieberthal,Mike	7.14	5.76	3.46	5.17	6.06	**5.85**
Pratt,Todd	5.13	5.90	3.03	8.29	6.19	**5.63**
LeCroy,Matt	4.86	4.32	13.18	5.28	5.80	**5.61**
Varitek,Jason	5.52	4.41	6.51	4.35	6.16	**5.54**
Pierzynski,A.J.	2.89	5.01	4.63	5.03	5.92	**5.49**
Melhuse,Adam	4.09	4.14	3.00	4.13	4.52	**5.48**
Moeller,Chad	2.84	3.22	3.35	5.58	4.89	**5.22**
Kendall,Jason	8.38	6.83	3.66	4.24	5.76	**5.21**
Molina,Ben	4.28	4.71	3.54	2.95	4.72	**5.21**
Barrett,Michael	5.28	3.52	3.57	4.77	3.53	**5.11**
Martinez,Victor				7.48	4.96	**5.10**
LoDuca,Paul	4.15	4.79	7.37	4.57	4.23	**5.01**
Ojeda,Miguel		7.59	5.59	7.75	3.79	**4.99**
Schneider,Brian	3.59	3.01	7.00	5.34	3.90	**4.97**
Johnson,Charles	4.74	8.15	4.91	3.67	4.73	**4.83**
Ross,David			4.16	4.07	4.56	**4.80**
Castro,Ramon	2.86	4.91	5.37	5.03	7.16	**4.78**
Myers,Greg	4.49	3.06	4.60	4.27	6.72	**4.78**
Hundley,Todd	4.12	7.69	2.88	4.06	3.75	**4.74**
Hernandez,Ramc	4.31	3.96	4.30	3.42	5.13	**4.64**
Mirabelli,Doug	4.85	4.12	4.81	4.10	4.69	**4.63**
Zaun,Gregg	3.57	5.53	7.23	2.84	3.50	**4.60**
Santiago,Benito	3.95	4.32	3.69	4.99	4.87	**4.52**
Hall,Toby	2.96	4.92	6.30	4.05	3.70	**4.49**
Bard,Josh			4.03	4.39	4.36	**4.48**
Miller,Corky	2.96	2.57	5.43	3.50	3.63	**4.48**
Estalella,Bobby	3.43	5.63	3.25	4.93	3.84	**4.37**
Machado,Robert	1.94	3.98	3.15	4.13	4.88	**4.36**
Miller,Damian	4.90	5.30	4.88	4.95	3.82	**4.36**
Laird,Gerald				4.16	4.44	**4.33**
Estrada,Johnny		3.70	3.56	3.47	5.61	**4.30**
Hammock,Robby		2.29	0.93	3.31	4.90	**4.30**
Redmond,Mike	4.74	3.03	5.84	4.91	2.93	**4.26**
Alomar Jr.,Sandy	6.03	4.56	3.21	4.37	4.01	**4.20**
Torrealba,Yorvit	2.71	3.95	2.90	4.87	4.17	**4.03**
LaRue,Jason	3.08	3.61	3.80	4.08	3.97	**3.88**
Flaherty,John	4.42	3.85	3.27	3.74	4.67	**3.76**
Wilson,Tom	3.73	4.45	3.38	4.33	4.44	**3.76**
Wilson,Dan	4.23	3.19	4.17	4.73	3.13	**3.74**
Olivo,Miguel			4.19	4.75	3.26	**3.72**
Fordyce,Brook	5.69	6.26	2.64	2.97	3.92	**3.65**
Bennett,Gary	3.76	5.50	3.85	3.54	3.05	**3.64**
Greene,Todd	3.79	4.81	2.44	4.85	3.40	**3.63**
Mayne,Brent	5.78	5.74	4.06	3.10	3.45	**3.62**
Davis,Ben	4.15	3.85	3.94	4.29	3.67	**3.61**
Gonzalez,Wiki	4.94	3.42	5.31	3.22	2.93	**3.61**
Gil,Geronimo	4.07	3.72	3.08	3.18	3.58	**3.49**
Wilson,Vance	3.12	2.82	2.76	3.34	3.45	**3.48**
Perez,Eddie	3.64	1.29	6.04	2.32	4.52	**3.43**
Rivera,Mike	3.54	1.77	4.15	3.58	3.38	**3.40**
Valentin,Javier	4.09	7.50	4.13	3.73	2.91	**3.39**
Matheny,Mike	2.68	3.93	2.66	3.25	3.85	**3.38**
Ausmus,Brad	4.85	4.43	3.22	3.75	2.87	**3.37**
Stinnett,Kelly	4.11	3.03	4.86	2.59	3.44	**3.36**
Bako,Paul	3.58	3.15	3.50	3.12	3.30	**3.33**
Widger,Chris	4.60	4.32		2.77	3.04	**3.29**
Inge,Brandon		3.00	2.29	3.08	3.02	**3.24**
Hinch,A.J.	3.34	3.28	3.85	4.05	2.88	**3.21**
Diaz,Einar	4.10	4.10	4.07	2.21	3.25	**3.12**
Barajas,Rod	4.25	2.10	3.53	3.82	2.83	**3.06**
DiFelice,Mike	5.82	3.81	2.09	3.58	3.93	**3.04**
Molina,Jose	2.97	1.85	3.92	3.04	1.31	**3.02**
Laker,Tim	2.47	3.11	3.41	2.38	3.30	**2.98**
Osik,Keith	1.86	6.17	2.73	1.58	3.62	**2.88**
Blanco,Henry	4.16	4.06	3.19	2.77	2.15	**2.64**
Walbeck,Matt	3.00	2.57	3.05	1.97	1.35	**1.89**

Power	'99	'00	'01	'02	'03	'04Prj
Lopez,Javy	136	113	92	91	210	**152**
Ross,David			100	106	147	**146**
Johnson,Charles	96	155	121	112	138	**144**
Piazza,Mike	155	163	157	160	123	**135**
Estalella,Bobby	100	141	108	182	123	**135**
Posada,Jorge	95	141	121	129	139	**132**
Hundley,Todd	130	165	104	127	122	**127**
Mirabelli,Doug	101	83	133	111	126	**126**
Castro,Ramon	90	105	128	133	181	**124**
Varitek,Jason	134	92	121	85	146	**121**
LeCroy,Matt	125	117	222	113	123	**120**
Pratt,Todd	58	106	74	142	129	**119**
LaRue,Jason	99	111	104	102	123	**119**
Melhuse,Adam	96	71	72	109	102	**118**
Greene,Todd	128	115	78	135	121	**118**
Barrett,Michael	99	62	83	103	113	**118**
Schneider,Brian	86	70	99	133	114	**118**
Rodriguez,Ivan	130	180	137	143	117	**116**
Moeller,Chad	60	73	81	112	113	**114**
Hammock,Robby		47	47	81	108	**113**
Ojeda,Miguel		146	78	114	82	**106**
Pierzynski,A.J.	41	94	107	94	102	**106**
Miller,Corky	118	75	128	108	106	**104**
Molina,Ben	85	82	57	54	103	**103**
Hernandez,Ramc	89	87	98	69	111	**102**
Lieberthal,Mike	151	123	82	111	95	**102**
Miller,Damian	113	109	94	127	91	**101**
Hall,Toby	105	92	129	78	83	**100**
Valentin,Javier	85	148	99	107	86	**96**
Widger,Chris	113	121		90	96	**95**
Santiago,Benito	83	88	71	110	94	**94**
Bard,Josh			85	93	91	**93**
Estrada,Johnny		82	88	85	102	**92**
Laird,Gerald				82	99	**92**
Myers,Greg	64	75	120	93	120	**92**
Martinez,Victor				148	74	**92**
Rivera,Mike	169	71	115	105	81	**90**
Stinnett,Kelly	115	74	123	79	88	**90**
Alomar Jr.,Sandy	129	71	63	86	93	**90**
Hinch,A.J.	67	64	118	89	93	**89**
Machado,Robert	77	79	87	89	94	**88**
Perez,Eddie	83	39	112	67	100	**87**
LoDuca,Paul	77	86	134	90	76	**87**
Zaun,Gregg	44	83	135	66	81	**86**
Inge,Brandon		83	77	92	87	**86**
Davis,Ben	94	89	75	89	101	**85**
Barajas,Rod	92	79	104	98	82	**85**
Torrealba,Yorvit	67	59	73	92	85	**83**
Wilson,Tom	114	108	78	79	94	**83**
Laker,Tim	83	101	104	66	87	**82**
Flaherty,John	83	69	87	83	124	**81**
Wilson,Vance	90	88	72	89	80	**79**
Gonzalez,Wiki	109	74	107	61	72	**78**
Olivo,Miguel			119	99	84	**77**
Bako,Paul	81	56	91	63	76	**74**
DiFelice,Mike	103	100	49	95	103	**74**
Blanco,Henry	90	109	86	86	58	**74**
Wilson,Dan	77	65	88	66	66	**72**
Fordyce,Brook	108	120	79	65	61	**70**
Gil,Geronimo	104	81	68	82	55	**68**
Bennett,Gary	57	109	82	60	54	**67**
Kendall,Jason	115	93	59	56	65	**66**
Diaz,Einar	59	77	83	61	57	**63**
Redmond,Mike	39	36	67	67	57	**62**
Matheny,Mike	59	68	55	53	69	**61**
Mayne,Brent	96	80	41	45	67	**59**
Ausmus,Brad	87	64	73	67	42	**58**
Osik,Keith	39	97	54	60	58	**57**
Molina,Jose	66	33	84	49	31	**49**
Walbeck,Matt	42	89	66	37	43	**42**

Speed	'99	'00	'01	'02	'03	'04Prj
Laird,Gerald				91	124	**113**
Olivo,Miguel			67	168	83	**107**
Hammock,Robby		83	57	78	115	**105**
Ojeda,Miguel		113	103	95	32	**101**
Rodriguez,Ivan	105	103	92	83	101	**96**
Kendall,Jason	146	120	83	89	77	**89**
Inge,Brandon		98	58	129	83	**84**
Ausmus,Brad	117	93	100	74	70	**84**
Barrett,Michael	49	52	59	65	76	**80**
Bako,Paul	54	36	87	47	100	**77**
Hinch,A.J.	93	72	42	75	61	**74**
Pierzynski,A.J.	30	84	58	93	75	**70**
DiFelice,Mike	23	49	72	21	87	**69**
Greene,Todd	41	43	61	51	58	**65**
Torrealba,Yorvit	49	52	68	28	85	**64**
Diaz,Einar	85	94	51	43	63	**64**
LaRue,Jason	71	63	73	52	70	**64**
Moeller,Chad	56	80	52	71	57	**64**
Estalella,Bobby	63	100	58	29	53	**63**
Santiago,Benito	57	47	80	94	53	**62**
Wilson,Vance	87	75	26	42	54	**57**
Bennett,Gary		33	46	58	54	**56**
Wilson,Dan	85	43	60	47	53	**53**
Laker,Tim	65	95	43	52	55	**50**
Varitek,Jason	55	44	35	61	53	**50**
Alomar Jr.,Sandy	77	69	44	37	31	**49**
Fordyce,Brook	54	39	42	30	51	**48**
LoDuca,Paul	51	72	37	64	39	**47**
Redmond,Mike		38	26		61	**47**
Mayne,Brent	38	22	37	73	36	**45**
Martinez,Victor				49	42	**45**
Schneider,Brian	45	50		72	35	**44**
Matheny,Mike	27	33	33	44	49	**44**
Flaherty,John	28		50	45	43	**41**
Lopez,Javy	39	28	41		63	**39**
Lieberthal,Mike	36	49	54	32	35	**38**
Posada,Jorge	62	48	32	49	24	**37**
Zaun,Gregg	90	66	30	69	34	**37**
Widger,Chris	37	58		37	45	**37**
Davis,Ben	68	69	46	54	24	**36**
Molina,Jose	36	31	57	28	57	**36**
Walbeck,Matt	51	45	34		75	**36**
Melhuse,Adam	42	80	46	50	34	**35**
Stinnett,Kelly	47	22	55	51	16	**35**
Pratt,Todd	50	43	36	45	58	**35**
LeCroy,Matt	73	40		58	18	**35**
Wilson,Tom		40	46	26	34	**34**
Hernandez,Ramc	53	42	36	33	40	**34**
Barajas,Rod	66	49	47	35	25	**34**
Bard,Josh			28	30	28	**33**
Miller,Damian	23	42	24	27	46	**33**
Gonzalez,Wiki	38	40	41	44	47	**33**
Miller,Corky	51	43	48	27	27	**32**
Gil,Geronimo	53	44	33	33	31	**32**
Rivera,Mike	21	38	59	53	20	**32**
Hall,Toby	37	36	48	40	28	**31**
Blanco,Henry	64	20	96	38	23	**31**
Ross,David			57	53	27	**30**
Valentin,Javier	38	72	27	36	59	**29**
Mirabelli,Doug	73	67			35	**29**
Osik,Keith	42	73	35		22	**29**
Johnson,Charles	36	50	21		32	**28**
Hundley,Todd	50	21			7	**28**
Piazza,Mike	45	51		35	27	**28**
Machado,Robert	34	32	24	39	26	**27**
Myers,Greg			24		26	**26**
Estrada,Johnny		36	22	36	17	**25**
Castro,Ramon		24	41		-1	**24**
Molina,Ben	34	58	24	22	27	**18**
Perez,Eddie	22				21	**16**

1Bmen

Std Rotisserie

Std Rotisserie	'99	'00	'01	'02	'03	'04Prj
Helton,Todd	32	46	45	34	38	39
Thome,Jim	20	20	31	34	29	32
Bagwell,Jeff	40	37	33	28	29	32
Sexson,Richie	18	18	28	23	29	31
Ortiz,David	15	9	8	15	22	29
Delgado,Carlos	26	36	36	33	33	28
Giambi,Jason	28	35	36	34	22	28
Klesko,Ryan	19	26	32	28	14	27
Nevin,Phil	15	25	33	14	10	26
Lee,Derrek	5	17	18	26	28	26
Thomas,Frank	16	35	1	17	24	24
Spiezio,Scott	10	7	11	16	14	23
Palmeiro,Rafael	37	25	22	26	22	23
Konerko,Paul	18	18	9	8	12	22
Johnson,Nick	13	7	21	16	19	21
Millar,Kevin		18	28	19	17	21
Sweeney,Mike	25	34	28	30	17	21
Teixeira,Mark				9	15	20
Lee,Travis	9	6	14	13	16	18
Durazo,Erubiel	30	5	8	12	13	18
Conine,Jeff	12	10	24	14	20	17
Olerud,John	20	14	22	6	11	17
Casey,Sean	27	21	20	7	18	16
Martinez,Tino	17	11	24	15	13	16
Mientkiewicz,Doug	-1	16	18	9	15	16
Hillenbrand,Shea	2	9	9	9	17	16
Phillips,Jason L.	0		8	20	17	14
Hafner,Travis				11	11	14
Pena,Carlos		22	16	11	9	14
Cordero,Wil	7	11	2	6	14	13
Simon,Randall	7	8	15	11	13	13
Broussard,Ben		0	6	13	13	13
Fick,Robert	2	0	12	12	12	12
Karros,Eric	29	17	11	14	10	11
Harvey,Ken					11	10
Hatteberg,Scott	0	5	1	13	7	9
Witt,Kevin	5	6	14	4	10	9
Wooten,Shawn	5	14	9	4	3	9
McGriff,Fred	25	18	26	23	6	8
Choi,Hee Seop		6		18	7	8
Quinlan,Robb				6	20	7
Snow,J.T.	17	17	7	5	8	7
Galarraga,Andres	24	11	7	11		7
Overbay,Lyle		9	16	11	6	7
Colbrunn,Greg	6	14	16	9		6
Perry,Herbert	7	13	5	2		6
Ventura,Robin	26	11	9	16	7	5
Baerga,Carlos	-2	8	8	10		4
Franco,Julio	21	16	43	6	6	4
Clark,Tony	20	7	14	7	7	4
Ward,Daryle	18	10	9	-1	4	3
Daubach,Brian	16	9	13	13	2	3
Hansen,Dave	5	6	1	4	1	2
Riggs,Adam	6	5	-0		9	2
Rivera,Carlos			11	4		2
Lopez,Mendy	6	3	7	4	3	2
Coomer,Ron	10	11	7	2	4	2
Vaughn,Mo	21	21	2	15	0	1
Franco,Matt	1	-2	-1	12	1	

RC/Gm

RC/Gm	'99	'00	'01	'02	'03	'04Prj
Helton,Todd	8.38	13.11	11.09	9.47	11.27	11.41
Thome,Jim	8.11	7.38	9.23	10.92	7.52	8.76
Giambi,Jason	8.62	11.78	12.14	9.39	7.09	8.51
Delgado,Carlos	7.31	11.84	7.59	7.73	8.96	8.37
Ortiz,David	5.95	5.85	5.14	5.86	7.83	8.13
Sexson,Richie	5.23	6.04	6.30	6.37	7.07	7.50
Bagwell,Jeff	9.61	9.26	8.05	7.36	6.79	7.48
Thomas,Frank	6.98	10.20	4.63	5.84	7.45	7.32
Klesko,Ryan	7.26	7.24	7.56	7.54	5.33	7.22
Colbrunn,Greg	7.32	7.53	6.19	8.90	5.09	6.96
Johnson,Nick	7.95		4.16	4.82	6.89	6.96
Franco,Julio	12.42	6.02	12.90	4.91	5.92	6.95
Sweeney,Mike	7.46	8.00	7.44	8.64	6.55	6.93
Palmeiro,Rafael	9.84	7.93	7.44	7.83	6.27	6.84
Mientkiewicz,Dou	3.46	5.58	6.27	4.84	6.44	6.63
Nevin,Phil	6.55	7.41	8.16	5.16	6.41	6.55
Spiezio,Scott	6.17	5.08	4.90	5.55	5.05	6.50
Lee,Derrek	3.30	6.41	5.69	6.35	6.55	6.47
Teixeira,Mark				7.66	5.15	6.33
Durazo,Erubiel	9.85	5.80	6.92	7.53	5.53	6.33
Konerko,Paul	6.50	6.22	6.18	6.45	4.01	6.24
Millar,Kevin	5.20	5.98	7.63	6.45	5.74	6.23
Olerud,John	7.14	6.10	6.92	7.24	4.96	6.11
Lee,Travis	4.27	4.25	4.99	4.49	5.67	5.99
Hafner,Travis				5.87	6.54	5.64
Phillips,Jason L.	2.95	6.48	4.57	4.30	5.99	5.57
Conine,Jeff	5.30	5.23	6.14	4.99	5.60	5.54
Karros,Eric	7.17	4.97	3.89	4.43	5.38	5.54
Martinez,Tino	5.29	4.66	5.75	5.07	5.17	5.42
Galarraga,Andres		6.47	4.72	4.39	5.94	5.42
Casey,Sean	7.99	7.35	4.72	5.18	5.18	5.34
Cordero,Wil	6.42	5.15	6.10	4.29	5.53	5.18
Daubach,Brian	7.08	4.69	3.58	5.18	4.53	5.15
Pena,Carlos		4.69	6.14	5.48	4.71	5.09
Snow,J.T.	5.69	5.80	6.65	4.22	5.42	5.04
Hillenbrand,Shea	2.73	3.94	3.70	5.27	5.17	4.88
Hatteberg,Scott	4.09	5.49	3.75	5.64	4.34	4.87
Simon,Randall	5.24	3.63	5.50	5.64	4.63	4.85
Broussard,Ben	2.86	4.60	5.50	5.29	4.21	4.84
McGriff,Fred	8.31	6.05	5.75	4.72	4.65	4.76
Overbay,Lyle		6.03	5.62	6.15	5.15	4.72
Fick,Robert	4.40	3.29	5.62	6.88	4.93	4.66
Ward,Daryle	6.55	5.50	5.44	4.89	1.94	4.61
Baerga,Carlos	2.32		5.15	4.73	7.03	4.56
Hansen,Dave	5.46	8.25	5.57	4.43	4.04	4.52
Perry,Herbert	4.73	5.81	4.29	5.22	1.88	4.50
Riggs,Adam	2.60	3.58	2.61	2.78	3.94	4.46
Clark,Tony	6.39	6.49	6.45	2.47	4.69	4.46
Lopez,Mendy	4.65	4.40	4.87	3.07	4.95	4.45
Quinlan,Robb				5.56	4.04	4.45
Choi,Hee Seop		7.90		4.30	5.56	3.93	4.44
Ventura,Robin	7.28	4.77	4.87	5.73	4.58	4.44
Harvey,Ken					5.20	4.75	4.36
Witt,Kevin	5.03	4.00	4.45	4.27	4.26	4.11
Wooten,Shawn	3.40	5.90	5.72	4.18	4.76	4.06
Rivera,Carlos			2.71	3.35		3.85
Coomer,Ron	4.50	4.60	4.27	4.14	3.50	3.78
Vaughn,Mo	6.26	6.22	3.76		3.23	3.66
Franco,Matt	4.47	2.49	2.68	5.58	3.56	3.46

Power

Power	'99	'00	'01	'02	'03	'04Prj
Thome,Jim	150	148	186	203	178	192
Helton,Todd	159	197	207	159	171	191
Ortiz,David	128	110	141	143	185	189
Sexson,Richie	139	131	152	145	160	171
Giambi,Jason	141	173	192	165	158	166
Delgado,Carlos	173	191	151	161	172	163
Thomas,Frank	109	171	127	131	173	156
Bagwell,Jeff	169	174	165	144	145	153
Klesko,Ryan	144	139	148	155	123	148
Teixeira,Mark				151	131	145
Colbrunn,Greg	108	127	133	198	109	142
Lee,Derrek	93	125	119	142	145	138
Millar,Kevin	98	136	151	145	120	135
Palmeiro,Rafael	171	148	166	174	139	134
Nevin,Phil	156	141	161	84	122	133
Durazo,Erubiel	138	109	157	181	107	130
Konerko,Paul	128	110	135	118	99	127
Spiezio,Scott	133	120	106	101	119	126
Choi,Hee Seop		164		120	146	125
Pena,Carlos		134	115	113		121
Hafner,Travis				151	108	120
Clark,Tony		148	145	58	144	119
Daubach,Brian	159	120	121	119	102	118
Lee,Travis	79	86	110	87	118	117
Sweeney,Mike	125	109	150	138	104	117
Lopez,Mendy	95	100	131	88	117	116
Hillenbrand,Shea	75	72	80	107	122	116
Riggs,Adam	69	85	87	77	109	114
Galarraga,Andres	129	89	127	88	118	114
Broussard,Ben	117	89		104	118	113
Phillips,Jason L.	95	26	93	107	105	110
Johnson,Nick	113		108	92	117	109
Conine,Jeff	105	91	82	108	113	108
Martinez,Tino	113	101	126	113	100	106
Cordero,Wil	128	116	61	109	113	105
Ward,Daryle	152	152	124	106	47	104
Mientkiewicz,Dou	67	76	121	106	101	103
Fick,Robert	118	115	125	113	103	102
Witt,Kevin	92		98	108	101	102
Overbay,Lyle		95	88	101		102
Karros,Eric	150	121	95	88	101	102
Simon,Randall	93	96	94	92	98	99
Franco,Julio	121	85	138	67	99	98
Olerud,John	72	97	106	122	104	97
Perry,Herbert	105	103	106	104	85	96
Rivera,Carlos			97	122	56	96
Harvey,Ken					100	95
McGriff,Fred	140	96	136	144	111	94
Ventura,Robin	140	120	107	120	98	97
Hatteberg,Scott	66	105	76	92	89	91
Snow,J.T.	106	108	81	84	95	91
Vaughn,Mo	127	128		120	82	86
Quinlan,Robb				93	65	83
Wooten,Shawn	80	123	90	110	73	78
Casey,Sean	130	124	101	79	77	77
Franco,Matt	79	39	67	115	75	76
Coomer,Ron	99	89	84	72	79	75
Hansen,Dave	102	155	83	73	56	74
Baerga,Carlos	47		98	69	86	68

Speed

Speed	'99	'00	'01	'02	'03	'04Prj
Lee,Derrek	63	46	89	134	99	107
Quinlan,Robb				63	117	95
Broussard,Ben	76	128	68	68	105	94
Teixeira,Mark				128	70	93
Lopez,Mendy	51	60	86	65	118	92
Colbrunn,Greg	125	34	21	73	110	91
Pena,Carlos		100	80	85	97	89
Bagwell,Jeff	86	80	110	72	87	87
Conine,Jeff	32	69	72	101	90	86
Spiezio,Scott	42	68	88	71	110	86
Baerga,Carlos	54		166	75	44	80
Franco,Julio	146	32	113	83	74	77
Helton,Todd	91	69	76	90	62	74
Hafner,Travis				42	53	70
Lee,Travis	108	79	56	62	80	68
Hansen,Dave	53	93	63	44	63	64
Sweeney,Mike	84	63	70	65	55	63
Casey,Sean	47	51	50	55	77	62
Perry,Herbert	51	85	64	65	21	61
Riggs,Adam	99	99	68	93	77	61
Snow,J.T.	37	49	44	43	72	61
Klesko,Ryan	66	98	143	68	23	58
Harvey,Ken					74	75	57
Choi,Hee Seop		61		62	54	60	56
Johnson,Nick	88		64	39	59	56
Martinez,Tino	60	81	48	39	50	55	54
Durazo,Erubiel	75	48	34	90	39	54
Fick,Robert	56	86	48	39	50	53
Sexson,Richie	117	61	48	39	47	53
Nevin,Phil	30	54	46	42	61	52
Millar,Kevin	84	66	68	61	56	52
Hillenbrand,Shea	69	64	61	89	45	51
Cordero,Wil	69	75	41	56	35	47
Giambi,Jason	46	49	55	51	37	46
Delgado,Carlos	43	30	55	63	37	45
Mientkiewicz,Dou	71	74	36	39	58	44
Witt,Kevin	45	61	60	40	30	44
Thome,Jim	48	49	29	46	51	41
Palmeiro,Rafael	31	62	27	44	59	41
Karros,Eric	46	48	43	54	42	40
Overbay,Lyle		60	57	24	33	38
Ortiz,David	50	51	54	40	46	38
Simon,Randall	41	71	29	27	25	37
Vaughn,Mo		44		24	24	37
Thomas,Frank	40	85	66	57	24	36
Franco,Matt	21	45	48	43	55	35
Hatteberg,Scott	27	66	40	36	35	30
Olerud,John	52	23	51	48	35	30
Ventura,Robin	30	41	34	42	21	30
Coomer,Ron	51	54	20	23	26	27
Clark,Tony	37	25	56	41	15	26
McGriff,Fred	35	41	36	41	16	24
Konerko,Paul	67	54	41	26	20	24
Phillips,Jason L.	34		45	20		22
Ward,Daryle	41	54	25	22	23	18

2Bmen

Std Rotisserie	'99	'00	'01	'02	'03	'04Prj
Soriano,Alfonso	16	10	27	44	37	36
Boone,Bret	12	12	38	24	32	28
Kent,Jeff	23	37	25	35	23	28
Vidro,Jose	13	28	19	26	19	27
Giles,Marcus		14	19	8	27	25
Polanco,Placido	3	11	15	13	19	21
Castillo,Luis	22	32	15	28	21	19
Kennedy,Adam	17	14	9	19	16	18
Jimenez,D'Angelo	23	-0	8	11	14	18
Loretta,Mark	11	7	6	8	21	18
Walker,Todd	12	17	18	19	15	18
Young,Mike		9	12	10	22	17
Hairston Jr.,Jerry	17	8	11	12	7	17
Durham,Ray	24	21	20	24	10	15
Young,Eric	22	28	18	17	16	15
Hudson,Orlando		-0	17	12	10	15
Rivas,Luis	11	10	16	7	11	14
Roberts,Brian			15	11	21	14
Utley,Chase				12	22	12
Anderson,Marlon	7	14	16	8	15	12
Alomar,Roberto	39	33	37	15	7	11
Spivey,Junior	4	3	6	23	10	11
Grudzielanek,Mark	15	11	11	10	13	10
Belliard,Ron	13	8	8	-1	11	10
Relaford,Desi	2	3	14	10	12	9
Vina,Fernando	3	11	20	12	3	8
Phillips,Brandon			11	23	-0	8
Hall,Bill			3	4	11	8
Ellis,Mark		1	7	8	6	8
Ginter,Keith		27	10	8	8	8
Butler,Brent	4	7	10	10	6	7
Cabrera,Jolbert	4	6	6	-1	9	6
Jackson,Damian	12	12	9	6	6	6
Morris,Warren	14	5	5	3	8	6
Cora,Alex	4	6	-3	9	3	6
DeRosa,Mark	2	6	9	7	4	6
Reese,Pokey	22	15	10	10	2	6
Martinez,Ramon	5	7	3	5	6	5
Perez,Antonio			-1	7	8	5
Perez,Neifi	15	13	13	2	3	4
Scutaro,Marcos	9	3	9	8	10	4
Nunez,Abraham	0	4	4	0	6	4
Cairo,Miguel	14	11	6	2	4	4
Febles,Carlos	12	7	8	7	2	3
Fox,Andy	4	3	2	14	-2	3
Mateo,Henry		15	17	5	3	3
Kata,Matt			1	9	8	2
Santos,Angel		6	15	7	6	2
Garcia,Danny					10	2
Menechino,Frank	7	5	6	-1	-1	2
Berg,Dave	5	2	1	5	2	2
Clark,Howie	3	3	14	7	3	2
McEwing,Joe	9	3	9	0	0	2
Castro,Juan	-3	3	-1	0	5	2
Gomez,Chris	0	-1	10	8	1	2
Gil,Benji	3	4	9	6	-0	2
Hart,Bo				-2	12	2
Hocking,Denny	8	10	3	2	1	1
Lockhart,Keith	2	4	-0	0	1	1
Reboulet,Jeff	-5	0	3	-0	1	0
McDonald,John	6	1	1	1	-1	-1

RC/Gm	'99	'00	'01	'02	'03	'04Prj
Vidro,Jose	5.76	7.67	6.55	6.85	6.77	7.38
Giles,Marcus		4.98	5.25	4.58	7.48	6.74
Kent,Jeff	6.58	9.30	6.57	7.68	6.39	6.71
Boone,Bret	4.18	4.57	7.97	5.42	7.09	6.37
Polanco,Placido	3.50	5.23	4.77	4.58	5.62	5.93
Walker,Todd	4.67	5.65	5.59	5.43	5.10	5.86
Loretta,Mark	4.88	4.87	4.18	5.58	6.09	5.79
Soriano,Alfonso	3.91	3.78	4.47	6.27	6.19	5.79
Jimenez,D'Angel	5.62	2.52	4.05	4.29	4.97	5.60
Durham,Ray	5.83	5.52	5.33	6.03	5.47	5.43
Castillo,Luis	5.22	6.22	3.96	4.89	5.19	5.00
Kennedy,Adam	5.01	4.13	3.90	5.68	4.60	4.98
Butler,Brent	3.38	4.92	4.69	4.07	5.06	4.97
Utley,Chase				4.85	5.58	4.95
Hudson,Orlando		2.75	5.44	4.54	4.35	4.94
Belliard,Ron	5.04	4.70	5.12	2.30	5.05	4.90
Spivey,Junior	4.01	5.07	3.47	6.41	4.60	4.80
Hairston Jr.,Jerry	4.14	4.32	3.30	4.25	4.41	4.76
Young,Mike		3.68	4.23	3.95	5.67	4.75
Grudzielanek,Ma	5.84	4.54	4.13	3.82	5.47	4.67
Alomar,Roberto	8.77	6.90	8.77	4.37	4.08	4.67
Scutaro,Marcos	4.01	3.32	4.04	4.17	4.86	4.63
Young,Eric	4.51	5.62	4.38	4.33	4.30	4.60
Anderson,Marlon	3.65	4.07	5.03	4.09	4.42	4.55
Rivas,Luis	3.56	4.12	3.95	3.94	3.91	4.49
Martinez,Ramon	4.47	6.12	3.78	4.75	4.45	4.47
Ginter,Keith		7.76	4.60	4.32	4.75	4.46
Relaford,Desi	3.24	3.46	6.09	4.38	4.06	4.28
DeRosa,Mark	2.77	3.86	4.46	4.40	4.07	4.18
Roberts,Brian			3.87	3.58	4.45	4.06
Ellis,Mark		4.63	3.42	4.65	3.87	4.04
Morris,Warren	5.27	3.81	3.00	3.13	3.88	4.02
Menechino,Frank	4.12	5.24	4.33	2.37	2.87	3.91
Clark,Howie	3.96	4.17	5.79	3.94	3.50	3.89
Perez,Antonio			0.61	2.72	5.04	3.75
Cabrera,Jolbert	2.98	3.96	3.58	2.09	4.84	3.73
Berg,Dave	4.61	3.97	3.44	4.14	3.81	3.72
Cora,Alex	3.20	3.78	2.66	5.57	3.12	3.68
Cairo,Miguel	4.39	3.69	4.37	3.54	3.58	3.65
Gomez,Chris	3.36	2.27	4.08	4.11	3.35	3.65
Santos,Angel		3.46	4.29	3.44	3.37	3.64
Lockhart,Keith	3.66	4.14	2.70	2.99	4.41	3.63
Vina,Fernando	3.76	4.85	5.08	3.63	3.48	3.61
Perez,Neifi	4.36	4.70	4.23	2.52	3.37	3.61
Phillips,Brandon			4.63	5.97	2.16	3.57
Hocking,Denny	3.87	5.55	3.66	3.33	3.50	3.57
Jackson,Damian	3.79	4.56	3.65	3.97	3.03	3.50
Nunez,Abraham	2.68	2.82	3.83	3.12	3.70	3.49
Kata,Matt			7.21	3.71	4.13	3.42
Reese,Pokey	5.00	4.38	3.33	4.14	2.62	3.40
Hall,Bill			3.10	2.41	3.88	3.35
Fox,Andy	4.39	3.18	4.15	3.87	1.85	3.31
Febles,Carlos	4.68	3.59	4.08	3.66	2.79	3.31
Castro,Juan	2.29	3.92	2.60	2.66	3.74	3.28
Garcia,Danny					3.45	3.27
Reboulet,Jeff	1.81	3.11	4.94	2.85	3.03	3.23
Gil,Benji	2.75	3.51	5.44	5.18	1.81	3.07
McEwing,Joe	4.53	3.13	4.94	1.94	3.03	3.06
Hart,Bo				1.95	4.20	3.04
Mateo,Henry		3.56	3.44	2.90	2.96	2.99
McDonald,John	3.45	2.99	2.25	3.13	2.21	2.30

Power	'99	'00	'01	'02	'03	'04Prj
Kent,Jeff	141	153	132	161	139	145
Soriano,Alfonso	100	97	103	151	137	140
Giles,Marcus		93	96	102	142	131
Boone,Bret	106	98	146	113	142	129
Vidro,Jose	120	133	108	121	109	114
Durham,Ray	85	100	123	102	107	110
Spivey,Junior	87	126	74	117	114	107
Utley,Chase				132	112	106
Walker,Todd	83	82	104	97	96	105
Ginter,Keith		138	115	107	104	103
Polanco,Placido	48	63	54	84	105	101
Belliard,Ron	82	79	123	58	94	101
Kennedy,Adam	94	84	70	92	79	98
Butler,Brent	69	93	88	103	107	96
Jimenez,D'Angel	92	43	72	77	87	95
Scutaro,Marcos	68	56	78	83	108	93
Gil,Benji	91	71	110	134	66	91
Phillips,Brandon			96	115	69	89
Menechino,Frank	85	119	83	55	37	89
Hudson,Orlando		60	99	93	79	88
Kata,Matt			108	82	96	87
Loretta,Mark	71	83	44	82	85	85
Young,Mike		82	93	75	87	85
Cabrera,Jolbert	43	66	63	44	115	84
Santos,Angel		66	89	79	77	82
Hall,Bill			77	54	96	82
Alomar,Roberto	129	103	122	74	66	81
Castro,Juan	61	91	54	61	86	81
Grudzielanek,Ma	72	73	74	67	82	80
Ellis,Mark		38	84	80	82	80
Relaford,Desi	61	53	117	67	80	80
DeRosa,Mark	45	58	80	79	82	79
Rivas,Luis	80	86	60	93	72	78
Gomez,Chris	40		93	97	68	78
Berg,Dave	70	68	80	81	76	77
Garcia,Danny					80	77
Anderson,Marlon	75	73	84	86	73	77
Cairo,Miguel	46	49	76	73	88	76
Martinez,Ramon	80	115	65	97	68	76
Hairston Jr.,Jerry	83	76	72	75	70	76
Perez,Antonio				47	110	75
Young,Eric	56	74	82	69	89	74
Lockhart,Keith	31	57	54	77	106	72
Morris,Warren	84	62	83	81	69	72
Hocking,Denny	71	78	62	55	80	71
Cora,Alex	52	74	59	96	64	71
Clark,Howie	77	70	100	67	68	68
Hart,Bo				47	80	66
Fox,Andy	78	58	77	55	50	66
Perez,Neifi	75	88	73	46	67	65
Vina,Fernando	50	65	73	53	86	64
Jackson,Damian	85	79	66	81	47	63
Reese,Pokey	89	77	76	70	31	62
McEwing,Joe	81	93	103	65	41	61
Nunez,Abraham	22	33	48	67	63	56
Reboulet,Jeff	22	32	89	48	53	56
Roberts,Brian			54	51	64	56
Febles,Carlos	91	41	81	68	34	54
Castillo,Luis	48	37	47	40	53	48
Mateo,Henry		63	55	64	23	45
McDonald,John	46	55	41	52	48	44

Speed	'99	'00	'01	'02	'03	'04Prj
Mateo,Henry		163	178	155	164	172
Rivas,Luis	136	138	130	141	163	149
Jackson,Damian	126	149	172	111	144	139
Soriano,Alfonso	103	127	126	134	136	130
Roberts,Brian			136	148	130	129
Kata,Matt			60	119	133	129
Durham,Ray	152	155	152	147	112	128
Fox,Andy	85	112	111	152	109	125
Hairston Jr.,Jerry	122	94	125	122	117	124
Young,Mike		128	87	115	139	124
Nunez,Abraham	80	88	122	68	168	124
Relaford,Desi	107	113	86	114	135	123
Castillo,Luis	130	126	166	135	114	121
Vina,Fernando	66	116	133	106	132	119
Perez,Antonio				121	134	119
Polanco,Placido	93	93	117	79	123	116
Hart,Bo				109	117	113
Alomar,Roberto	135	126	167	107	102	113
Young,Eric	118	126	132	117	112	113
Gil,Benji	103	77	109	97	124	113
Ellis,Mark		58	81	121	106	112
Febles,Carlos	182	116	115	138	105	112
Kennedy,Adam	110	166	86	142	101	111
Anderson,Marlon	114	120	80	107	112	111
Hudson,Orlando		105	144	92	99	107
Boone,Bret	91	78	75	93	119	107
Spivey,Junior	174	150	113	127	93	105
Cairo,Miguel	132	128	91	109	120	105
Jimenez,D'Angel	95	67	61	124	108	103
Cabrera,Jolbert	140	126	139	71	93	102
Belliard,Ron	83	115	119	55	97	97
Cora,Alex	124	127	56	137	76	95
Reese,Pokey	138	152	127	83	83	95
Garcia,Danny					103	95
Utley,Chase				79	99	94
Giles,Marcus		89	101	80	102	94
Hall,Bill			92	78	101	93
Gomez,Chris	44		78	60	106	92
Scutaro,Marcos	93	94	74	102	103	91
Grudzielanek,Ma	92	124	88	58	83	91
Perez,Neifi	139	107	130	97	92	90
McDonald,John	72	69	90	124	79	89
Menechino,Frank	93	92	64	68	20	88
McEwing,Joe	88	117	125	104	64	86
Kent,Jeff	89	109	91	76	76	85
Morris,Warren	53	65	56	101	110	83
Phillips,Brandon			82	85	79	83
Ginter,Keith		113	97	53	68	80
DeRosa,Mark	76	101	83	87	60	80
Reboulet,Jeff	61	74	79	51	78	80
Lockhart,Keith	79	96	40	76	100	76
Butler,Brent	35	42	87	101	73	75
Martinez,Ramon	63	101	69	108	39	74
Santos,Angel		109	85	83	92	72
Hocking,Denny	95	103	87	30	78	70
Walker,Todd	102	114	52	80	71	65
Clark,Howie	70	59	132	62	59	65
Berg,Dave	61	75	59	50	77	63
Loretta,Mark	93	39	53	35	72	61
Vidro,Jose	41	66	77	72	47	60
Castro,Juan	57	60	38		47	53

3Bmen

Std Rotisserie

	'99	'00	'01	'02	'03	'04Prj
Lowell,Mike	7	16	18	21	24	32
Rolen,Scott	19	23	28	25	27	32
Boone,Aaron	19	11	16	25	25	29
Chavez,Eric	6	16	27	26	24	27
Ramirez,Aramis	14	10	30	9	21	27
Hinske,Eric	0	10	15	22	10	24
Blalock,Hank			14	12	24	22
Mueller,Bill	7	8	6	7	23	20
Randa,Joe	21	20	14	15	15	19
Glaus,Troy	12	30	24	21	10	19
Ensberg,Morgan			15	11	20	18
Alfonzo,Edgardo	27	26	8	20	13	17
Beltre,Adrian	17	21	14	16	12	17
Koskie,Corey	13	13	28	15	18	16
Crede,Joe		1	19	12	12	14
Batista,Tony	21	22	13	16	13	14
Burroughs,Sean		4	6	6	13	14
Munson,Eric		3	7	9	9	13
Helms,Wes	3	10	4	3	13	12
Larson,Brandon			7		9	12
Castilla,Vinny	21	0	16	6	17	11
Bell,David	6	11	4	19	12	11
Blake,Casey	14	4	10	10	14	10
Wiginton,Ty		5	8	10	12	10
Blum,Geoff	8	9	6	11	7	9
Stynes,Chris	2	16	8	3	10	8
Branyan,Russ	6	14	8	11	3	8
Cirillo,Jeff	24	24	25	7	-2	8
Hernandez,Jose	14	6	14	20	4	7
Bellhorn,Mark			1	17	5	6
Feliz,Pedro		0	2	1	9	6
Houston,Tyler	6	12	2	9	2	6
Sandberg,Jared		2	4	6	4	6
Norton,Greg	8	8	6	11	5	6
Rolls,Damian		-1	8	4	5	5
Zeile,Todd	19	14	9	17	10	5
Counsell,Craig	-2	5	8	10	4	5
Perez,Tomas	-0	7	4	7	4	4
Tatis,Fernando	32	10	1	1	-1	3
Bloomquist,Willie					2	3
Halter,Shane	-3	4	13	3	2	2
Merloni,Lou	5	2	3	6	1	2
Leon,Jose		5	5	13	1	2
Matos,Julius		-6		4	1	2
Carroll,Jamey	8	5	-2	7	2	2
Klassen,Danny	2	3	0	-4	4	1
Guzman,Edwards	2	0	3	6	6	1
Easley,Damion	14	11	9	9	0	0
Harris,Lenny	5	7	-0	6	-2	0
Delgado,Wilson	2	1	1	-1	-1	-0
Sadler,Donnie	4	-1	-3	-1	2	-0

RC/Gm

	'99	'00	'01	'02	'03	'04Prj
Rolen,Scott	6.83	7.37	6.64	5.98	7.15	7.92
Lowell,Mike	4.27	5.68	5.27	5.69	6.54	7.30
Mueller,Bill	5.01	4.43	6.42	4.89	7.85	7.28
Chavez,Eric	4.78	6.17	6.52	6.24	6.36	7.03
Blalock,Hank			7.70	4.90	6.54	6.53
Hinske,Eric	6.52	4.63	4.39	6.33	4.94	6.46
Ensberg,Morgan			6.72	4.66	7.03	6.06
Ramirez,Aramis	5.82	4.74	6.58	3.55	5.14	6.03
Randa,Joe	6.30	5.45	3.96	5.10	5.61	6.01
Koskie,Corey	6.41	6.27	6.14	5.29	6.32	5.80
Alfonzo,Edgardo	7.14	8.61	4.39	6.63	4.48	5.79
Glaus,Troy	4.94	8.28	6.59	5.40	5.39	5.60
Norton,Greg	5.06	4.62	5.83	3.65	4.94	5.38
Boone,Aaron	4.93	5.76	5.91	4.53	5.16	5.31
Burroughs,Sean		3.83	6.32	4.29	4.93	5.23
Crede,Joe	2.85	6.15	4.87	6.32	4.50	5.15
Bellhorn,Mark	3.93	5.50	3.09	6.30	4.22	4.86
Munson,Eric		3.42	3.91	4.37	4.73	4.82
Larson,Brandon	4.06	4.09	2.89	6.92	4.76	4.81
Bell,David	4.95	3.92	4.29	4.78	2.63	4.76
Branyan,Russ	3.54	5.46	5.02	4.73	4.56	4.73
Houston,Tyler	3.72	4.86	5.76	4.81	3.94	4.65
Beltre,Adrian	5.20	6.07	4.35	4.30	4.03	4.54
Helms,Wes	4.78	3.99	4.09	3.76	4.94	4.54
Blum,Geoff	4.82	5.08	3.48	5.78	3.86	4.48
Stynes,Chris	3.15	7.31	4.40	3.90	4.64	4.42
Perez,Tomas	2.70	3.90	5.24	4.26	4.12	4.26
Zeile,Todd	6.16	5.67	4.60	5.29	3.91	4.22
Sandberg,Jared		4.17	3.71	4.54	3.79	4.21
Cirillo,Jeff	6.91	6.97	6.47	3.25	2.35	4.05
Feliz,Pedro	3.22	4.54	3.18	3.24	4.69	3.93
Castilla,Vinny	6.03	5.32	4.03	4.55	3.45	3.91
Batista,Tony	5.49	2.48	4.76	3.03	4.97	3.90
Blake,Casey	3.40	4.40	4.20	3.55	4.06	3.90
Wiginton,Ty		3.76	3.27	4.92	4.26	3.89
Hernandez,Jose	4.95	3.65	3.71	5.83	3.29	3.88
Merloni,Lou	4.33	4.09	4.38	3.80	4.12	3.83
Counsell,Craig	2.36	5.91	4.04	4.26	3.33	3.77
Tatis,Fernando	7.67	5.95	5.52	3.87	2.24	3.54
Halter,Shane	1.96	3.78	2.26	2.02	2.93	3.54
Bloomquist,Willie					3.50	3.42
Carroll,Jamey	3.46	3.38	3.49	3.49	3.56	3.31
Leon,Jose		2.22	4.43	3.57	2.89	3.31
Matos,Julius	3.47	1.85	2.77	3.16	3.09	3.27
Guzman,Edward	2.84	2.62	3.44	3.66	3.42	3.20
Klassen,Danny	2.46	2.64	3.93	3.39	3.69	2.91
Rolls,Damian	3.33	4.43	3.83	1.91	2.84	2.86
Easley,Damion	4.96	4.83	3.92	2.94	1.66	2.79
Harris,Lenny	4.81	4.49	2.32	5.32	2.06	2.69
Delgado,Wilson	3.30	3.21	2.47	2.25	2.46	2.47
Sadler,Donnie	4.26	2.55	1.49	1.62	3.18	2.35

Power

	'99	'00	'01	'02	'03	'04Prj
Rolen,Scott	155	147	130	145	158	167
Lowell,Mike	89	128	107	133	153	154
Chavez,Eric	110	121	155	139	140	154
Branyan,Russ	120	157	146	133	141	144
Ramirez,Aramis	115	90	142	102	120	144
Hinske,Eric	158	104	117	126	134	142
Blalock,Hank			128	95	133	140
Larson,Brandon	138	109	85	167	127	136
Glaus,Troy	124	179	165	118	128	134
Norton,Greg	106	80	144	109	127	129
Ensberg,Morgan			147	88	139	120
Beltre,Adrian	95	112	88	107	116	120
Crede,Joe	65	113	112	143	108	119
Koskie,Corey	100	91	130	117	103	117
Boone,Aaron	100	114	118	130	115	116
Helms,Wes	126	91	121	116	115	114
Sandberg,Jared		96	98	125	122	114
Mueller,Bill	58	77	96	92	138	111
Feliz,Pedro	84	123	87	54	152	110
Randa,Joe	98	81	88	95	104	110
Bellhorn,Mark	57	116	96	156	81	109
Batista,Tony	142	143	115	129	92	109
Bell,David	100	83	100	110	63	107
Munson,Eric		91	104	108	113	103
Alfonzo,Edgardo	124	134	97	102	87	100
Castilla,Vinny	117	52	126	78	115	99
Houston,Tyler	88	139	102	102	86	99
Hernandez,Jose	95	81	114	120	75	93
Wiginton,Ty		101	73	99	96	92
Blake,Casey	98	102	84	82	101	92
Stynes,Chris	35	103	84	89	108	88
Burroughs,Sean		70	94	68	78	85
Zeile,Todd	122	121	70	99	92	84
Blum,Geoff	113	102	77	104	78	83
Perez,Tomas	62	85	84	95	80	82
Halter,Shane	46	68	115	96	68	82
Tatis,Fernando	150	141	74	110	49	80
Cirillo,Jeff	90	106	97	55	49	76
Merloni,Lou	85	71	80	91	57	71
Leon,Jose		94	91	75	60	69
Klassen,Danny	85	75	84	57	74	69
Rolls,Damian		66	57	66	72	66
Matos,Julius		66	53	64	65	61
Guzman,Edward	48	58	70	64	55	55
Sadler,Donnie	70	48	36	38	69	54
Carroll,Jamey	65	46	32	76	50	52
Harris,Lenny	69	69	38	71	29	50
Counsell,Craig	35	34	60	56	42	48
Bloomquist,Willie		24	35	63	48	45
Delgado,Wilson	48	55	61	35	45
Easley,Damion	103	96	79	79	47	42

Speed

	'99	'00	'01	'02	'03	'04Prj
Sadler,Donnie	127	132	105	161	173	146
Boone,Aaron	119	73	87	117	124	116
Rolls,Damian		41	115	154	97	115
Bloomquist,Willie		102	113	114	118	112
Bellhorn,Mark	40	183	111	114	78	108
Hinske,Eric	353	143	84	104	120	104
Klassen,Danny	110	87	64	97	140	103
Counsell,Craig	62	78	87	76	118	99
Rolen,Scott	88	129	92	120	89	96
Harris,Lenny	44	161	91	99	47	96
Wiginton,Ty		69	52	72	129	95
Easley,Damion	88	104	111	42	66	93
Carroll,Jamey	100	103	89	85	95	93
Burroughs,Sean		66	84	80	110	91
Chavez,Eric	59	82	72	83	99	88
Ensberg,Morgan			59	115	82	87
Feliz,Pedro	95	48	74	55	110	82
Koskie,Corey	42	90	110	85	85	79
Halter,Shane	87	102	102	85	56	79
Merloni,Lou	64	74	71	84	93	79
Blake,Casey	73	80	119	94	63	75
Beltre,Adrian	116	81	117	93	44	74
Stynes,Chris	85	79	78	66	93	74
Cirillo,Jeff	62	64	105	66	40	71
Hernandez,Jose	94	48	72	58	76	70
Mueller,Bill	53	94	64	68	67	67
Batista,Tony	68	74	98	66	61	67
Alfonzo,Edgardo	80	63	70	71	65	65
Glaus,Troy	63	76	78	83	100	64
Blalock,Hank			87	54	63	64
Zeile,Todd	38	53	45	29	72	62
Branyan,Russ	67	84	76	61	20	61
Sandberg,Jared		62	31	74	66	60
Blum,Geoff	93	51	73	88	34	58
Larson,Brandon		81	62	49	65	58
Castilla,Vinny	39	38	39	76	56	58
Tatis,Fernando	95	60	35	53	49	58
Randa,Joe	101	87	53	75	56	53
Perez,Tomas	54	89	48	59	51	53
Crede,Joe	60	42	63	21	54	52
Matos,Julius	98	58	63	44	63	50
Munson,Eric		92	35	70	34	50
Bell,David	79	60	50	56	28	50
Delgado,Wilson	92	75	74	41	51	49
Guzman,Edward	59	44	34	38	70	47
Houston,Tyler	47	89	88	79	47	47
Leon,Jose	41	89	88	51	53	46
Norton,Greg	46	60	83	68	46	43
Ramirez,Aramis	59	65	49	45	52	42
Helms,Wes	37	59	109	40	20	40
Lowell,Mike	103	59	31	52	58	39

Shortstops — Std Rotisserie

Std Rotisserie	'99	'00	'01	'02	'03	'04Prj
Rodriguez,Alex	32	36	45	42	38	42
Tejada,Miguel	13	21	24	42	24	35
Renteria,Edgar	21	20	13	26	37	34
Garciaparra,Nomar	35	31	4	29	31	33
Cabrera,Orlando	4	6	22	16	27	30
Furcal,Rafael		21	12	18	24	24
Berroa,Angel			1	1	21	21
Jeter,Derek	36	29	11	29	19	21
Reyes,Jose				13	24	18
Rollins,Jimmy	15	14	27	17	14	17
Lugo,Julio	13	22	10	9	15	16
Aurilia,Rich	16	14	32	10	12	15
Guzman,Cristian		-1	21	14	11	14
Cintron,Alex			7	7	22	13
Valentin,Jose	4	22	17	14	14	13
Eckstein,David	14	4	17	20	7	12
Gonzalez,Alex S.	4	8	15	11	7	10
Uribe,Juan			24	7	10	10
Izturis,Cesar			18	1	4	9
Woodward,Chris	1	4	6	6		9
Ordonez,Rey	5	-3	3	3	5	9
Guillen,Carlos		7	6	9	9	8
Vizquel,Omar	31	17	7	19	3	8
Gonzalez,Alex	11	-0	5	2	12	8
Wilson,Jack		5	1	5	7	8
Vazquez,Ramon	1	5	7	6	6	7
Womack,Tony	29	22	13	18	3	7
Graffanino,Tony	18	4	5	6		7
Lopez,Felipe			3	12	4	7
Clayton,Royce	13	7	21	8	1	6
Santiago,Ramon				11	8	6
Everett,Adam	9	2	7	7	1	4
Gutierrez,Ricky		20	16	6	1	4
Cruz,Deivi	2	12	14	6	10	4
Larkin,Barry	10	14	7	7	8	3
Punto,Nick			24	17	3	3
McLemore,Mark	10	10	22	13	6	3
Sanchez,Rey	11	5	9	6	1	3
Almonte,Erick				12	10	3
Peralta,Jhonny					14	2
Bruntlett,Eric				11	4	2
Vizcaino,Jose	1	7	11	4		2
Wilson,Enrique	3	6	-2	-1		2
Olmedo,Ranier				8	1	1
Morban,Jose					0	0
Mendez,Donaldo	2	4	-3	-1		0
Mordecai,Mike	5	6	1	1		0
Velandia,Jorge	-1	3	1	-1		-0
Cruz,Enrique					-4	-2

RC/Gm

RC/Gm	'99	'00	'01	'02	'03	'04Prj
Rodriguez,Alex	7.33	9.50	9.14	8.65	8.47	8.94
Garciaparra,Nom	9.92	10.59	6.69	6.83	6.49	7.37
Tejada,Miguel	4.46	5.90	5.13	6.46	5.67	7.16
Renteria,Edgar	4.85	5.01	4.07	5.83	7.41	7.07
Cabrera,Orlando	3.89	3.56	4.82	4.26	6.05	6.27
Jeter,Derek	9.19	7.67	6.75	5.87	6.35	5.60
Furcal,Rafael		5.45	4.30	4.18	5.79	5.34
Graffanino,Tony	5.72	4.35	5.61	4.80	4.99	5.07
Aurilia,Rich	5.15	5.23	7.86	4.25	4.65	5.07
Lugo,Julio	4.64	5.07	3.94	4.28	4.72	4.95
Berroa,Angel				2.46	3.93	5.29	4.94
Cintron,Alex		3.52	3.60	3.27	6.83	4.92
Uribe,Juan			5.88	3.27	4.24	4.76
Guillen,Carlos		4.48	4.13	4.29	4.89	4.76
Valentin,Jose	4.74	6.01	5.65	4.96	4.77	4.56
Woodward,Chris	4.19	4.56	5.09	5.52	4.22	4.54
Larkin,Barry	6.01	6.88	4.58	3.79	4.70	4.53
Rollins,Jimmy	4.29	4.52	4.94	3.81	4.14	4.50
Vizquel,Omar	6.87	4.99	3.59	4.82	3.66	4.48
Reyes,Jose				4.17	5.17	4.43
Ordonez,Rey	3.48	1.98	3.38	3.19	5.51	4.32
Guzman,Cristian	2.31	3.88	5.68	3.67	3.75	4.11
Gonzalez,Cristian	5.28	4.16	3.83	3.40	3.84	4.06
Eckstein,David	4.72	3.34	4.46	4.58	3.44	4.05
Gutierrez,Ricky	3.83	5.25	4.83	3.76	3.21	4.04
Vazquez,Ramon	3.32	4.12	4.18	4.40	4.06	4.01
Gonzalez,Alex	4.33	2.34	3.69	3.02	4.39	3.84
Almonte,Erick			4.26	4.88	3.35	3.29	3.75
Everett,Adam	3.75	3.58	3.24	3.56	3.84	3.71
Wilson,Jack		4.24	2.95	3.41	3.59	3.70
Clayton,Royce	5.30	3.75	4.12	3.68	3.29	3.61
Lopez,Felipe			2.85	5.06	4.53	3.18	3.55
Vizcaino,Jose	3.07	2.95	3.79	4.76	3.37	3.55
Peralta,Jhonny					5.37	3.24	3.47
Punto,Nick		3.05	3.32	3.70	3.55	3.45
Womack,Tony	4.67	4.16	3.67	3.63	2.45	3.42
Izturis,Cesar		2.30	4.07	2.44	3.00	3.41
McLemore,Mark	4.65	3.75	5.99	5.08	3.18	3.32
Bruntlett,Eric					3.19	3.04	3.29
Wilson,Enrique	3.71		1.94	2.13	3.21	3.27
Sanchez,Rey	4.29	5.14	3.67	3.85	2.74	3.22
Cruz,Deivi	4.41	5.06	3.72	3.63	3.38	3.10
Santiago,Ramon				3.68	2.61	3.02
Infante,Omar			4.66	4.28	2.80	2.99
Mordecai,Mike	3.29	5.12	4.54	2.97	3.11	2.88
Olmedo,Ranier		3.73		2.42	3.17	2.84
Velandia,Jorge	1.42		2.87	1.68	2.58	2.44
Mendez,Donaldo			1.09	2.06	2.06	2.30
Morban,Jose					1.50	1.96
Cruz,Enrique					0.37	0.91

Power

Power	'99	'00	'01	'02	'03	'04Prj
Rodriguez,Alex	168	163	173	179	170	181
Garciaparra,Nom	150	143	120	141	131	141
Valentin,Jose	107	128	144	135	133	127
Tejada,Miguel	106	118	123	117	122	124
Renteria,Edgar	85	92	69	97	108	119
Cabrera,Orlando	96	98	98	92	113	117
Uribe,Juan			129	92	112	114
Gonzalez,Alex S.	91	94	81	114	120	111
Woodward,Chris	73	116	142	111	91	105
Berroa,Angel				80	100	102
Aurilia,Rich	98	102	83	109	88	101
Graffanino,Tony	108	52	75	100	105	95
Gonzalez,Alex	94	74	88	70	119	94
Cintron,Alex		60	59	72	113	94
Rollins,Jimmy	77	94	86	90	88	89
Lugo,Julio	83	89	68	86	82	89
Ordonez,Rey	47	32	62	58	121	86
Almonte,Erick			86	93	80	86
Larkin,Barry	82	108	85	93	76	86
Lopez,Felipe		61	113	93	71	85
Mordecai,Mike	80	116	82	49	75	84
Jeter,Derek	120	86	105	77	82	82
Furcal,Rafael		58	69	77	96	81
Peralta,Jhonny					61	79
Guillen,Carlos		84	64	84	77	79
Cruz,Deivi	95	98	86	76	80	78
Reyes,Jose				83	70	77
Wilson,Enrique	68	87	47	62	92	74
Velandia,Jorge	18	85	86	59	82	72
Everett,Adam	64	67	67	63	80	71
Clayton,Royce	93	82	81	72	67	71
Guzman,Cristian	34	78	104	73	56	69
Vizcaino,Jose	73	58	53	90	64	68
Wilson,Jack		81	56	58	65	64
Vazquez,Ramon	69	78	69	64	51	59
Mendez,Donaldo					52	56
Santiago,Ramon					58	56
Eckstein,David	60	57	52	60	54	53
Gutierrez,Ricky	45	76	71	49	45	52
Olmedo,Ranier					80	52
Izturis,Cesar			45	58	57	52
Womack,Tony	64	65	52	58	46	50
McLemore,Mark	57	51	71	57	55	48
Infante,Omar				64	44	48
Punto,Nick		48	53	35	52	48
Bruntlett,Eric					50	48
Sanchez,Rey	49	36	41	26	43	34
Morban,Jose					13	28
Cruz,Enrique					13	0

Speed

Speed	'99	'00	'01	'02	'03	'04Prj
Reyes,Jose				105	197	191	184
Guzman,Cristian	224	205	109	188	180
Furcal,Rafael	137	100	147	174	145
Womack,Tony	186	199	151	135	152	139
Rollins,Jimmy	120	150	189	159	123	137
Graffanino,Tony	147	115	70	128	155	137
Uribe,Juan			177	135	127	135
Everett,Adam	93	100	152	159	127	134
Berroa,Angel			130	122	149	132
Garciaparra,Nom	112	83	36	93	169	129
Punto,Nick			117	137	121	122
Santiago,Ramon				181	78	118
Infante,Omar			105	156	113	115
Renteria,Edgar	118	89	106	102	107	113
Morban,Jose					213	112
Vizquel,Omar	137	102	115	111	119	112
Rodriguez,Alex	102	104	93	79	129	111
Jeter,Derek	141	125	118	113	104	109
Vazquez,Ramon	92	62	70	114	116	109
Izturis,Cesar			135	117	86	106	106
Cabrera,Orlando	97	60	109	99	115	105
Eckstein,David	120	85	111	127	98	105
Valentin,Jose	134	150	87	87	90	99
Lugo,Julio	131	150	112	96	106	96
Cintron,Alex		86	83	84	103	94
Guillen,Carlos		103	98	109	85	93
Lopez,Felipe		77	148	128	101	92
Wilson,Enrique	75	57	46	166	82	92
Almonte,Erick			101	71	84	86	91
McLemore,Mark	131	100	192	105	80	89
Clayton,Royce	110	115	106	107	63	86
Mendez,Donaldo			113	130	81	85
Woodward,Chris	85	105	93	120	69	84
Vizcaino,Jose	47	93	114	67	81	83
Wilson,Jack		112	73	105	77	82
Gutierrez,Ricky	105	87	79	30	84	80
Larkin,Barry	116	125	72	107	91	80
Gonzalez,Alex	111	119	55	91	64	79
Gonzalez,Alex S.	69	69	105	97	54	78
Sanchez,Rey	125	89	118	83	71	75
Bruntlett,Eric				107	115	74
Tejada,Miguel	94	83	98	70	83	74
Olmedo,Ranier				71	61	72
Mordecai,Mike	81	49	79	64	81	62
Peralta,Jhonny					77	52	59
Cruz,Enrique					66	56
Aurilia,Rich	39	46	70	62	54	55
Cruz,Deivi	39	65	62	54	54	54
Velandia,Jorge	82	85	72	76	61	54
Ordonez,Rey	68	19	67	69	38	47

Outfielders

Std Rotisserie	'99	'00	'01	'02	'03	'04Prj
Beltran,Carlos	29	7	34	33	38	44
Pujols,Albert			36	34	45	42
Guerrero,Vladimir	38	41	42	52	27	41
Wilson,Preston	19	32	22	18	34	35
Sheffield,Gary	28	33	32	28	44	35
Ordonez,Magglio	29	33	35	37	30	35
Ramirez,Manny	38	32	31	31	32	33
Pierre,Juan		31	33	24	34	33
Abreu,Bobby	34	32	37	34	30	33
Wells,Vernon	12	13	17	22	32	32
Jones,Chipper	41	33	36	32	26	32
Sosa,Sammy	39	40	47	33	26	32
Crawford,Carl			19	26	27	32
Bonds,Barry	23	34	51	44	36	31
Jones,Andruw	24	34	22	25	27	30
Lee,Carlos	20	24	21	16	31	30
Berkman,Lance	10	18	37	36	23	30
Huff,Aubrey	13	12	6	24	29	30
Green,Shawn	37	24	41	33	19	29
Giles,Brian	32	32	33	34	21	29
Anderson,Garret	19	25	29	30	31	28
Gonzalez,Luis	32	28	43	27	27	28
Hidalgo,Richard	7	37	16	8	28	28
Floyd,Cliff	12	27	35	26	16	27
Nixon,Trot	10	11	21	17	24	27
Mondesi,Raul	28	20	24	17	23	26
Suzuki,Ichiro	19	26	43	28	29	25
Edmonds,Jim	4	31	28	26	24	24
Damon,Johnny	29	37	14	25	21	23
Patterson,Corey		17	9	14	19	23
Sanders,Reggie	28	10	24	21	27	23
Payton,Jay	7	15	6	19	26	23
Sanchez,Alex	7	15	12	19	24	23
Gonzalez,Juan	33	14	34	8	17	23
Ibanez,Raul	8	0	10	23	21	22
Hunter,Torii	7	22	19	30	17	22
Winn,Randy	14	12	11	26	23	22
Finley,Steve	21	25	16	27	22	22
Gibbons,Jay		11	6	13	18	22
Lofton,Kenny	17	21	15	18	23	21
Encarnacion,Juan	21	18	8	25	23	21
Stewart,Shannon	27	26	26	18	18	21
Alou,Moises		33	31	15	19	21
Jones,Jacque	14	16	14	25	21	21
Jenkins,Geoff	21	28	14	5	23	21
Podsednik,Scott	-3	4	5	15	31	21
Cameron,Mike	22	19	29	22	16	20
Guillen,Jose	10	12	7	7	25	20
Kearns,Austin			5	21	13	19
Kotsay,Mark	8	19	16	20	7	19
Everett,Carl	34	27	11	12	23	19
Baldelli,Rocco				8	24	19
Matsui,Hideki	17	22	23	28	19	19
Young,Dmitri	13	19	22	7	23	19
Monroe,Craig		15	15	11	15	18
Wilkerson,Brad	-1	15	10	15	19	18
Grissom,Marquis	20	11	9	15	24	18
Gerut,Jody		11		15	21	18
Matos,Luis	4	8	4	8	22	17
Bradley,Milton	14	8	12	8	20	17
Williams,Bernie	32	29	27	30	12	17
White,Rondell	22	16	15	7	19	16
Wilson,Craig	9	12	11	12	11	16
Redman,Tike	9	4	10	5	25	16
Roberts,Dave	12	16	6	22	14	16
Drew,J.D.	14	19	27	13	12	16
Byrd,Marlon			23	15	16	15
Mora,Melvin	6	12	8	13	16	15
Salmon,Tim	12	21	7	20	15	15
Burrell,Pat	18	15	16	28	4	15
Burnitz,Jeromy	22	14	18	8	16	15
Cabrera,Miguel					28	15
Higginson,Bobby	5	27	20	15	7	15

RC/Gm	'99	'00	'01	'02	'03	'04Prj
Bonds,Barry	8.41	11.15	16.68	18.70	15.33	14.86
Pujols,Albert			9.09	7.91	11.52	10.49
Ramirez,Manny	10.82	12.44	8.85	10.17	9.38	9.56
Guerrero,Vladimi	8.15	9.93	7.36	8.90	9.20	8.87
Jones,Chipper	10.72	8.38	9.41	8.89	7.61	8.85
Giles,Brian	9.58	9.62	8.62	9.99	7.80	8.64
Sheffield,Gary	7.71	10.30	8.91	7.53	9.61	8.60
Berkman,Lance	4.99	7.98	9.57	8.30	7.42	8.50
Sosa,Sammy	8.02	9.58	12.15	8.51	6.90	8.18
Ordonez,Magglio	6.40	7.71	7.39	8.24	7.52	8.12
Beltran,Carlos	5.53	4.07	7.12	6.17	7.91	8.10
Gonzalez,Luis	8.29	7.64	10.88	7.14	7.74	7.96
Edmonds,Jim	4.71	8.65	8.33	8.52	8.11	7.69
Floyd,Cliff	6.66	7.43	8.35	7.19	7.08	7.48
Nixon,Trot	5.93	6.09	6.58	5.39	8.33	7.42
Huff,Aubrey	5.71	5.38	3.78	6.74	7.37	7.41
Wells,Vernon	5.57	4.51	4.74	4.85	7.33	7.29
Abreu,Bobby	9.32	8.60	7.55	7.81	6.93	7.27
Green,Shawn	8.06	6.06	8.07	7.51	5.72	7.15
Gonzalez,Juan	8.54	5.97	8.34	5.22	6.59	7.15
Hidalgo,Richard	4.40	8.70	5.34	4.29	7.73	6.93
Jenkins,Geoff	7.61	7.50	5.30	4.44	7.22	6.91
Wilson,Preston	6.04	5.31	5.49	4.45	6.34	6.87
Jones,Andruw	5.88	7.12	4.88	6.35	6.00	6.81
Drew,J.D.	4.93	6.61	9.53	5.02	6.64	6.80
Lee,Carlos	5.25	6.06	5.04	5.89	5.95	6.72
Michaels,Jason		3.91	4.50	4.72	8.91	6.58
Alou,Moises		10.18	8.43	5.11	5.75	6.50
Stairs,Matt	6.38	4.57	5.34	5.42	7.64	6.47
Stewart,Shannon	5.44	6.98	6.14	5.97	5.96	6.39
Anderson,Garret	5.71	5.60	5.32	6.55	6.91	6.39
Griffey Jr.,Ken	7.74	7.32	6.94	5.08	6.80	6.35
Payton,Jay	6.71	4.90	3.60	6.05	6.40	6.29
Ibanez,Raul	5.03	3.17	5.60	6.62	5.63	6.26
Walker,Larry	12.96	7.12	11.35	9.40	6.79	6.24
Mondesi,Raul	5.49	5.92	5.11	4.31	5.57	6.16
Finley,Steve	6.03	6.74	4.96	6.60	6.21	6.12
Young,Dmitri	6.46	6.07	5.96	5.34	7.05	6.08
Salmon,Tim	6.44	7.68	4.54	6.71	5.98	6.04
Sanders,Reggie	6.76	4.11	5.93	4.81	6.78	6.01
Bradley,Milton	5.40	3.85	3.88	4.17	7.76	5.99
Williams,Bernie	8.69	8.00	7.50	7.72	5.26	5.99
Wilson,Craig	4.89	5.43	7.09	4.81	5.87	5.94
Matsui,Hideki	6.68	7.66	7.94	8.47	5.44	5.89
Catalanotto,Franl	4.79	5.99	7.09	4.75	5.86	5.84
Gibbons,Jay		5.61	4.54	4.94	5.26	5.83
Wilkerson,Brad	3.27	6.33	4.99	5.74	5.86	5.81
Kotsay,Mark	4.22	5.49	5.75	5.60	4.53	5.76
White,Rondell	6.38	6.62	6.99	3.48	5.61	5.64
Bautista,Danny	4.61	5.62	5.36	6.81	4.43	5.58
Everett,Carl	8.42	7.76	4.57	4.85	6.33	5.57
Burrell,Pat	7.39	5.91	5.52	7.28	3.97	5.53
Hollandsworth,Tc	5.44	5.11	11.35	5.38	4.41	5.53
Hunter,Torii	3.81	5.77	4.75	6.09	4.55	5.53
Hammonds,Jeffre	5.90	7.76	4.20	4.40	4.68	5.52
Jones,Jacque	4.70	5.12	4.63	6.12	5.71	5.49
Suzuki,Ichiro	6.80	7.98	6.81	5.99	5.67	5.43
Guillen,Jose	4.70	5.57	4.42	3.56	7.07	5.40
Mench,Kevin			4.07	4.55	5.39	5.40
Bigbie,Larry		2.30	4.39	4.06	6.61	5.39
Winn,Randy	4.60	4.70	4.39	5.97	5.30	5.39
Kearns,Austin			3.83	7.59	5.58	5.39
McMillon,Billy	4.29	7.00	3.24	3.46	5.21	5.38
Lofton,Kenny	6.48	5.63	4.33	4.93	5.70	5.38
Dunn,Adam			9.16	5.98	5.20	5.33
Pierre,Juan		5.02	5.70	4.08	4.96	5.28
Byrd,Marlon			5.51	5.00	5.62	5.27
Monroe,Craig		5.02	4.91	5.19	4.71	5.26
Gerut,Jody		5.20		4.55	5.69	5.24
Damon,Johnny	6.84	7.42	3.92	5.71	5.02	5.23
Vitiello,Joe	3.80	5.54	4.25	5.27	3.76	5.22
Rivera,Juan			5.87	4.82	4.92	5.21
Kielty,Bobby		4.50	4.87	7.07	4.74	5.20

Power	'99	'00	'01	'02	'03	'04Prj
Bonds,Barry	200	209	292	260	233	239
Pujols,Albert			168	159	193	188
Berkman,Lance	98	159	178	176	141	176
Sosa,Sammy	190	178	225	177	159	176
Edmonds,Jim	116	160	157	159	205	173
Wilson,Preston	128	130	132	116	159	163
Gonzalez,Juan	160	128	157	113	160	163
Nixon,Trot	119	110	133	132	156	160
Guerrero,Vladimi	165	173	155	161	152	159
Ramirez,Manny	186	195	175	170	156	159
Giles,Brian	175	160	162	202	136	159
Green,Shawn	165	126	167	167	123	157
Hidalgo,Richard	121	186	109	112	167	157
Ordonez,Magglio	122	132	139	168	143	156
Jones,Chipper	186	150	157	137	133	156
Sanders,Reggie	140	108	159	127	168	154
Jones,Andruw	126	136	119	157	140	153
Stairs,Matt	154	110	128	147	164	152
Jenkins,Geoff	162	165	123	135	149	150
Wells,Vernon	91	113	105	112	144	147
Griffey Jr.,Ken	159	156	143	103	193	146
Gonzalez,Luis	134	142	201	125	148	146
Wilson,Craig	130	152	133	113	143	145
Sheffield,Gary	126	174	155	131	167	143
Floyd,Cliff	137	139	158	159	143	142
Mondesi,Raul	133	142	117	123	130	140
Hollandsworth,Tc	100	106	194	117	123	139
Cabrera,Miguel					140	138
Monroe,Craig		126	123	110	125	137
Lee,Carlos	104	107	121	130	126	137
Michaels,Jason		89	106	125	162	137
Burrell,Pat	142	126	125	167	123	135
Beltran,Carlos	93	70	121	139	116	135
Burnitz,Jeromy	173	129	146	93	147	134
Dunn,Adam			185	130	141	134
Anderson,Garret	103	135	116	149	142	134
Wilkerson,Brad	67	147	102	127	126	133
Huff,Aubrey	129	119	93	119	150	130
Kieschnick,Brook	125	123	107	142	148	129
Ledee,Ricky	108	84	91	127	139	128
Drew,J.D.	104	106	161	112	132	127
Hunter,Torii	77	109	129	142	121	125
Guillen,Jose	88	125	101	98	153	125
Finley,Steve	150	147	96	131	126	124
Piatt,Adam	167	92	67	94	155	124
Salmon,Tim	135	144	94	137	119	123
Werth,Jayson	48	70	121	98	127	123
Hammonds,Jeffre	142	114	111	96	129	123
Gibbons,Jay		113	139	140	113	122
Young,Dmitri	132	116	108	113	142	122
Ludwick,Ryan			105	125	135	122
Mench,Kevin			133	120	110	121
Perez,Eduardo	89	116	72	159	118	121
Walker,Larry	189	119	180	173	115	120
Richard,Chris	133	124	108	122	124	120
Alou,Moises		155	133	96	118	120
McMillon,Billy	101	101	101	78	114	119
Bradley,Milton	102	74	81	91	124	119
Payton,Jay	134	94	74	114	128	118
Abreu,Bobby	130	142	155	147	110	117
Petrick,Ben	152	113	114	140	120	116
Patterson,Corey		113	73	93	127	116
Cruz,Jose	105	127	152	116	103	115
Catalanotto,Franl	114	96	103	108	112	115
White,Rondell	114	116	132	87	119	115
Grissom,Marquis	91	64	105	147	108	114
Restovich,Mike			132	121	111	113
Stewart,Shannon	69	122	97	93	105	113
Ibanez,Raul	103	72	122	148	100	113
Cameron,Mike	128	100	126	119	110	113
Hyzdu,Adam	133	116	102	119	115	111
Vitiello,Joe	105	118	93	114	93	111
Kearns,Austin			87	134	114	111

Speed	'99	'00	'01	'02	'03	'04Prj
Crawford,Carl			111	191	169	173
Beltran,Carlos	143	139	181	156	185	173
Figgins,Chone			133	173	180	164
Lofton,Kenny	161	142	117	170	164	161
Torres,Andres		63	127	186	171	155
Roberts,Dave	174	122	129	179	161	155
Kingsale,Gene	107	132	138	140	163	154
Robinson,Kerry	186	135	130	181	156	153
Sanchez,Alex	114	125	151	178	154	151
Podsednik,Scott	105	134	156	131	171	151
Patterson,Corey		136	134	137	193	150
Taylor,Reggie	143	149	171	159	144	149
Goodwin,Tom	173	188	203	174	124	147
Pierre,Juan		111	173	152	151	146
Suzuki,Ichiro	112	100	151	134	146	144
Damon,Johnny	161	173	118	177	140	144
Redman,Tike	146	133	135	106	163	143
Byrnes,Eric	74	103	117	155	168	138
Crisp,Coco				118	148	136
Hunter,Brian L.	171	136	109	153	88	135
Tucker,Michael	162	153	164	143	120	135
Finley,Steve	131	111	99	115	157	133
Freel,Ryan	159	156	121	140	135	131
Winn,Randy	129	108	118	150	130	131
Harris,Willie			129	120	139	130
Cameron,Mike	171	128	147	143	116	130
Catalanotto,Franl	59	108	118	211	101	130
Chavez,Endy			80	137	138	130
Byrd,Marlon			156	136	128	129
Tyner,Jason	126	97	139	131	112	129
Duncan,Jeff					144	127
Cedeno,Roger	155	179	188	118	117	127
Baldelli,Rocco				109	144	126
Encarnacion,Juai	159	131	138	118	126	126
Sanders,Reggie	160	112	121	145	127	124
DaVanon,Jeff	176		122	109	112	118
Erstad,Darin	114	123	91	135	106	118
McCracken,Quint	110	84	88	164	106	118
Kapler,Gabe	125	70	97	134	126	116
Taguchi,So	97	116	148	80	112	114
Matos,Luis	111	160	88	101	123	112
Walker,Larry	111	145	103	94	127	112
Wilkerson,Brad	59	89	98	140	103	112
Johnson,Reed			124	114	107	110
Dellucci,David	110	92	86	88	162	110
Bautista,Danny	93	147	87	114	91	110
Ford,Lew			111	119	115	109
Hollandsworth,Tc	96	99	121	65	116	109
Drew,J.D.	166	97	145	81	106	108
Mackowiak,Rob	69	112	92	80	133	107
Grissom,Marquis	100	90	86	130	102	107
Singleton,Chris	139	147	120	164	91	107
Matthews Jr.,Gar	97	128	93	126	102	106
Escobar,Alex		144	129		80	106
Werth,Jayson	113	91	71	97	123	106
Macias,Jose	107	124	131	86	100	104
Giles,Brian	81	110	123	106	97	104
Mondesi,Raul	132	140	115	96	118	103
Benard,Marvin	126	140	115	156	110	102
Buchanan,Brian	88	73	39	71	120	102
Hunter,Torii	100	142	106	126	83	101
Kotsay,Mark	118	120	95	110	95	100
Nixon,Trot	114	150	92	80	111	100
Abreu,Bobby	165	154	128	133	86	99
Berkman,Lance	73	85	88	74	108	99
Biggio,Craig	90	138	95	128	91	99
Cabrera,Miguel					101	98
Floyd,Cliff	66	100	136	77	78	97
Bradley,Milton	115	76	135	107	97	97
Conti,Jason	134	133	78	103	92	97
Henderson,Ricke	96	122	134	124	60	97
Bragg,Darren	69	92	90	114	94	96
Sheffield,Gary	62	62	81	77	104	95

Outfielders

Std Rotisserie	'99	'00	'01	'02	'03	'04Prj
Dunn,Adam			40	20	11	**15**
Bigbie,Larry		-1	11	6	15	**15**
Mench,Kevin			11	11	6	**14**
Griffey Jr.,Ken	38	26	16	5	6	**14**
Stairs,Matt	19	8	10	9	15	**14**
Crisp,Coco				23	21	**14**
Dye,Jermaine	23	28	24	14	-3	**13**
Harris,Willie			22	17	10	**13**
Walker,Larry	40	13	42	32	17	**13**
Erstad,Darin	9	41	14	21	4	**13**
Tucker,Michael	9	12	13	15	11	**13**
Catalanotto,Frank	8	10	22	6	14	**13**
Nix,Laynce					18	**13**
Chavez,Endy			6	22	10	**13**
Cedeno,Roger	31	13	28	14	10	**13**
Escobar,Alex		15	13		16	**13**
Lawton,Matt	14	24	21	9	11	**13**
Rivera,Juan			25	10	12	**12**
Cruz,Jose	11	15	31	12	12	**12**
Biggio,Craig	24	9	20	14	13	**12**
Hollandsworth,Todd	8	16	9	17	2	**12**
Kielty,Bobby		5	7	12	9	**12**
Nady,Xavier				5	11	**12**
Bautista,Danny	10	12	7	9	6	**11**
Jordan,Brian	24	14	23	18	7	**10**
Johnson,Reed			22	-1	16	**9**
Ludwick,Ryan			12	9	17	**9**
Garcia,Karim	5	11	18	25	7	**9**
Clark,Brady	11	10	6	0	11	**9**
Byrnes,Eric	-2	18	15	4	11	**9**
Michaels,Jason		7	12	3	6	**9**
Kapler,Gabe	12	16	20	11	6	**9**
Long,Terrence	12	19	17	8	8	**8**
Matthews Jr.,Gary	4	-0	6	12	7	**8**
Hammonds,Jeffrey	11	29	5	7	2	**8**
Perez,Timo	-1	14	15	15	7	**8**
Buchanan,Brian	6	13	7	7	7	**7**
Figgins,Chone			3	17	16	**7**
Goodwin,Tom	15	24	8	7	9	**7**
Spencer,Shane	4	7	7	3	7	**6**
Brown,Dee	14	16	6	12	2	**6**
Pena,Wily Mo				7	6	**6**
Piatt,Adam	24	10	-1	7	2	**6**
Guiel,Aaron	1	5	6	13	14	**6**
Surhoff,B.J.	26	16	12	2	8	**6**
Tyner,Jason	17	12	18	9	8	**6**
Palmeiro,Orlando	4	5	3	8	5	**6**
Mateo,Ruben	17	7	1	7	11	**6**
Ledee,Ricky	9	9	2	3	7	**6**
Owens,Eric	18	19	5	15	6	**6**
Sierra,Ruben	13	11	18	12	8	**5**
Rowand,Aaron		16	19	4	5	**5**
Marrero,Eli	0	3	6	18	1	**5**
Freel,Ryan	5	13	9	13	13	**5**
Werth,Jayson	3	0	14	14	7	**5**
DaVanon,Jeff	22		8	4	17	**5**
Robinson,Kerry	15	11	7	4	5	**5**
Borchard,Joe			18	12	5	**5**
Mackowiak,Rob	1	12	6	11	7	**5**
Cuddyer,Michael		4	24	15	8	**4**
Benard,Marvin	22	14	12	4	-1	**4**
Perez,Eduardo	4	14	-0	3	10	**4**
Mohr,Dustan	-2		0	10	6	**4**
Restovich,Mike			21	14	13	**4**
Reyes,Rene				10	17	**4**
McMillon,Billy	7	15	0	2	9	**4**
Calloway,Ron			25	10	8	**4**
Smitherman,Steve					12	**4**
Singleton,Chris	22	13	14	14	4	**4**
Mabry,John	4	3	1	9	1	**4**
Petrick,Ben	23	14	7	13	6	**3**
Vander Wal,John	6	23	14	4	8	**3**

RC/Gm	'99	'00	'01	'02	'03	'04Prj
Lawton,Matt	4.52	6.80	5.53	3.97	4.75	**5.19**
Cabrera,Miguel					6.80	**5.19**
Dye,Jermaine	6.66	8.18	5.78	4.93	2.36	**5.12**
Cruz,Jose	4.93	5.02	6.20	4.76	4.99	**5.10**
Cameron,Mike	5.62	5.50	6.03	5.01	4.93	**5.08**
Cuddyer,Michael		3.87	7.33	4.95	5.06	**5.03**
Restovich,Mike			5.68	4.31	4.95	**4.99**
Higginson,Bobby	4.27	7.43	5.60	5.01	3.76	**4.95**
Buchanan,Brian	3.69	4.92	5.70	4.97	5.36	**4.94**
Grissom,Marquis	4.69	3.35	3.16	5.79	5.50	**4.94**
Mora,Melvin	3.34	4.59	3.87	4.13	7.45	**4.84**
Ledee,Ricky	5.07	4.03	3.35	4.55	5.39	**4.79**
Biggio,Craig	6.08	5.18	5.84	4.41	4.61	**4.79**
Ludwick,Ryan			3.61	4.69	5.73	**4.78**
Surhoff,B.J.	6.34	5.49	4.58	4.18	5.08	**4.77**
Rowand,Aaron		3.99	5.94	3.82	4.22	**4.76**
Werth,Jayson	4.25	3.35	5.85	4.02	3.80	**4.75**
Piatt,Adam	7.91	5.22	2.94	3.77	3.96	**4.72**
Patterson,Corey		3.93	3.06	3.77	6.00	**4.72**
Perez,Eduardo	3.09	5.46	2.74	4.07	5.91	**4.71**
Nix,Laynce					5.05	**4.66**
Garcia,Karim	4.24	4.54	5.22	5.56	3.93	**4.65**
Jordan,Brian	5.48	4.66	5.90	5.49	5.50	**4.63**
Kapler,Gabe	5.04	6.16	5.36	4.50	4.25	**4.57**
Encarnacion,Juai	4.07	5.07	3.80	4.96	4.76	**4.53**
Guiel,Aaron	3.27	4.62	3.44	4.21	4.96	**4.52**
Matthews Jr.,Gar	3.17	2.68	3.99	5.32	3.65	**4.51**
Kieschnick,Brook	3.95	4.03	4.21	4.36	5.98	**4.49**
Benard,Marvin	5.55	4.63	4.70	4.60	1.91	**4.48**
Reyes,Rene				3.92	5.01	**4.48**
Sweeney,Mark	3.97	7.25	3.75	1.75	4.32	**4.47**
Mateo,Ruben	5.87	5.39	3.01	4.44	4.78	**4.46**
Burnitz,Jeromy	7.56	5.18	5.74	3.45	4.65	**4.46**
Richard,Chris	4.92	5.12	4.70	3.81	3.71	**4.45**
Escobar,Alex		4.92	4.04		4.21	**4.43**
McCarty,Dave	2.97	5.60	4.55	3.90	3.66	**4.40**
Sierra,Ruben	5.61	4.81	5.87	4.73	4.81	**4.40**
Palmeiro,Orlandc	4.02	5.79	3.22	4.85	4.01	**4.40**
Pena,Wily Mo				3.99	4.54	**4.39**
Matos,Luis	2.61	2.79	4.49	3.72	5.30	**4.39**
Petrick,Ben	7.77	6.42	4.54	5.29	3.85	**4.39**
Crawford,Carl			3.76	4.70	4.18	**4.38**
Smitherman,Stev					4.26	**4.38**
Nady,Xavier				3.57	4.02	**4.36**
Spencer,Shane	4.27	5.29	3.76	3.88	4.40	**4.36**
Tucker,Michael	4.85	6.36	4.45	4.45	4.61	**4.35**
Perez,Timo	1.19	5.49	4.64	5.05	3.68	**4.35**
Crisp,Coco				4.95	4.63	**4.33**
Harris,Willie			3.91	3.51	4.91	**4.30**
Vander Wal,John	5.37	8.48	5.49	4.83	5.48	**4.30**
Mabry,John	4.00	3.67	3.24	5.60	3.58	**4.27**
Byrnes,Eric	1.91	4.83	4.30	3.25	5.31	**4.24**
Cedeno,Roger	6.20	5.25	4.89	3.94	4.04	**4.19**
Mohr,Dustan	1.39		2.65	4.83	4.26	**4.17**
Podsednik,Scott	0.85	3.71	3.18	3.51	6.25	**4.16**
Borchard,Joe			5.57	4.93	3.17	**4.16**
Clark,Brady	4.31	4.64	3.94	2.28	4.38	**4.15**
Redman,Tike	3.23	2.42	3.32	2.78	4.84	**4.11**
Figgins,Chone			2.36	4.20	4.51	**4.10**
Chavez,Endy			3.04	5.42	3.53	**4.08**
Banks,Brian	3.87	2.99	3.56	4.13	4.37	**4.07**
Henderson,Ricke	7.22	3.90	4.16	4.27	3.31	**4.06**
Jones,Jason			1.96	4.59	4.55	**4.06**
Marrero,Eli	2.27	4.26	4.69	5.24	3.04	**4.05**
O'Leary,Troy	5.93	4.46	4.14	4.90	3.30	**4.04**
Baldelli,Rocco				5.41	4.76	**4.03**
Roberts,Dave	3.17	4.03	3.21	4.77	3.45	**4.02**
Goodwin,Tom	3.94	4.57	3.17	3.47	4.40	**4.01**
Long,Terrence	3.87	5.74	4.94	3.75	3.78	**3.99**
Ford,Lew			2.44	4.33	5.01	**3.96**
Smith,Mark	4.15	3.94	3.35	2.91	3.87	**3.93**
DaVanon,Jeff	6.25		4.40	4.58	5.61	**3.92**

Power	'99	'00	'01	'02	'03	'04Prj
Everett,Carl	150	161	111	102	131	**111**
Gerut,Jody		89		83	140	**110**
Buchanan,Brian	78	112	130	119	117	**110**
Rivera,Juan			128	97	101	**110**
Nix,Laynce					118	**110**
Liefer,Jeff	112	139	144	86	104	**109**
Escobar,Alex		98	90		118	**109**
Encarnacion,Juai	116	85	98	109	113	**108**
Guiel,Aaron	124	103	100	81	121	**108**
Dye,Jermaine	139	140	112	124	60	**108**
Garcia,Karim	111	114	137	130	90	**107**
Pena,Wily Mo				94	107	**107**
Vander Wal,John	101	157	107	113	138	**107**
Rowand,Aaron		100	130	87	100	**107**
Marrero,Eli	67	106	104	120	79	**105**
Jones,Jacque	99	103	90	130	103	**105**
McCarty,Dave	105	115	96	106	97	**104**
Kotsay,Mark	81	92	100	102	82	**104**
DaVanon,Jeff	115		118	143	104	**104**
Borchard,Joe			117	135	80	**103**
Cuddyer,Michael		77	153	117	95	**103**
Kielty,Bobby		95	103	114	102	**102**
Williams,Bernie	112	149	134	102	91	**101**
Bigbie,Larry		38	82	63	110	**101**
Winn,Randy	83	73	84	104	88	**101**
O'Leary,Troy	127	93	114	76	91	**100**
Jones,Jason			77	94	99	**99**
Bautista,Danny	98	112	84	105	82	**99**
Biggio,Craig	115	72	102	104	103	**99**
Byrnes,Eric	67	105	105	92	120	**99**
Benard,Marvin	107	82	103	96	65	**98**
Mabry,John	97	101	98	139	94	**98**
Sweeney,Mark	87	110	82	67	103	**97**
Lawton,Matt	64	102	92	96	105	**97**
Mateo,Ruben	131	94	70	112	93	**97**
Mohr,Dustan	41		34	104	99	**97**
Tucker,Michael	95	136	94	99	107	**96**
Reyes,Rene				104	85	**96**
Lofton,Kenny	85	84	83	98	100	**95**
Smith,Mark	103	79	102	81	109	**95**
Ford,Lew			74	96	110	**94**
Matos,Luis	73	51	119	101	94	**94**
Nady,Xavier				74	86	**94**
Byrd,Marlon			110	107	80	**92**
Jordan,Brian	110	97	121	121	78	**91**
Calloway,Ron			112	90	89	**91**
Mora,Melvin	62	82	80	105	112	**91**
Smitherman,Stev					102	**90**
Mackowiak,Rob	99	84	89	120	75	**90**
Higginson,Bobby	88	141	102	87	77	**90**
Taylor,Reggie	77	75	79	112	78	**89**
Matsui,Hideki	130	138	117	145	99	**89**
Spencer,Shane	92	100	91	83	90	**88**
Sierra,Ruben	111	89	141	95	96	**88**
Long,Terrence	76	105	85	95	87	**88**
Kapler,Gabe	127	108	107	74	84	**88**
Matthews Jr.,Gar	70	65	88	105	80	**87**
Baldelli,Rocco				103	81	**86**
Damon,Johnny	106	102	72	97	84	**85**
Banks,Brian	67	56	121	107	90	**85**
Rios,Armando	99	137	120	52	78	**84**
Brown,Dee	119	111	72	89	78	**84**
Perez,Timo		86	79	98	75	**84**
Singleton,Chris	115	76	84	96	76	**83**
Merced,Orlando	122	36	110	97	102	**83**
Clark,Brady	92	107	67	58	91	**82**
Kinkade,Mike	85	89	65	109	87	**82**
Christenson,Ryar	66	71	84	89	83	**82**
Thames,Marcus	58	97	154	97	75	**81**
Freel,Ryan	83	90	78	83	77	**81**
Dellucci,David	78	67	117	99	83	**80**
Johnson,Reed			78	76	83	**78**

Speed	'99	'00	'01	'02	'03	'04Prj
Bigbie,Larry		67	82	73	104	**94**
Calloway,Ron			120	106	92	**93**
Ibanez,Raul	64	69	92	102	98	**93**
Hidalgo,Richard	78	104	66	114	100	**93**
Owens,Eric	122	132	82	142	84	**92**
Monroe,Craig		101	92	117	78	**92**
Payton,Jay	83	50	73	130	93	**91**
Mora,Melvin	98	121	69	110	79	**91**
Dunn,Adam			78	88	90	**91**
Stewart,Shannon	113	133	127	133	62	**91**
Restovich,Mike			107	104	110	**90**
Gerut,Jody		82		104	76	**89**
Marrero,Eli	102	155	156	106	108	**89**
Wilson,Craig	58	57	104	55	106	**89**
Wells,Vernon	97	141	96	101	91	**89**
Higginson,Bobby	43	110	110	92	88	**88**
Gonzalez,Raul	87	79	53	75	110	**87**
Perez,Timo	28	118	112	118	51	**87**
Lee,Carlos	78	107	97	49	97	**87**
Wilson,Preston	104	120	111	107	83	**86**
Clark,Brady	90	88	90	57	100	**86**
Hammonds,Jeffre	47	102	94	86	62	**86**
Everett,Carl	120	107	124	38	92	**85**
Guerrero,Vladimi	96	123	127	97	92	**85**
Jones,Jacque	106	99	60	76	97	**84**
Green,Shawn	97	114	120	69	74	**84**
Lawton,Matt	100	93	101	86	78	**84**
Ledee,Ricky	145	116	80	69	61	**83**
Petrick,Ben	104	87	108	94	76	**82**
Reyes,Rene				73	87	**82**
Kielty,Bobby		67	73	100	82	**82**
Mohr,Dustan	116		58	91	69	**82**
Cuddyer,Michael		100	74	127	94	**82**
Cruz,Jose	131	116	131	117	55	**82**
Glanville,Doug	138	136	121	130	67	**81**
Griffey Jr.,Ken	111	79	72		86	**81**
Michaels,Jason		93	107	155	32	**81**
Gonzalez,Luis	86	49	84	90	76	**80**
Ordonez,Magglio	93	105	88	74	79	**80**
Kearns,Austin			80	99	59	**80**
Jones,Andruw	112	126	98	64	73	**79**
Ludwick,Ryan			82	95	73	**79**
Long,Terrence	104	93	93	69	80	**78**
Merced,Orlando	60	87	108	117	94	**78**
O'Leary,Troy	59	61	116	47	63	**78**
Guiel,Aaron	83	86	77	72	77	**77**
Pena,Wily Mo				80	92	**76**
Banks,Brian	99	62	98	77	98	**75**
Brown,Dee	121	121	54	78	59	**75**
Christenson,Ryar	107	146	65	100	95	**73**
Anderson,Garret	59	79	77	78	75	**73**
Palmeiro,Orlandc	71	93	78	85	60	**73**
Williams,Bernie	94	126	69	73	78	**72**
Burnitz,Jeromy	77	68	67	70	55	**72**
Shinjo,Tsuyoshi	162	94	60	104	45	**72**
Mateo,Ruben	93	90	100	76	50	**71**
Jordan,Brian	102	80	75	72	37	**71**
Salmon,Tim	83	43	66	71	78	**70**
Pujols,Albert			64	60	77	**70**
Nix,Laynce					78	**70**
Rios,Armando	81	142	85	43	55	**70**
Young,Dmitri	82	61	79	54	91	**69**
Jones,Chipper	89	78	89	67	58	**69**
Edmonds,Jim	115	79	60	74	59	**68**
Perez,Eduardo	47	85	67	30	79	**67**
Nady,Xavier				51	78	**66**
Bonds,Barry	122	112	84	80	79	**66**
White,Rondell	108	62	48	47	61	**64**
Matsui,Hideki	60	85	89	67	45	**62**
Burrell,Pat	68	51	56	54	54	**62**
Rivera,Juan			78	75	35	**62**
Liefer,Jeff	86	41	50	35	83	**62**

Outfielders

Std Rotisserie

Name	'99	'00	'01	'02	'03	'04Prj
Ford,Lew			0	16	9	3
O'Leary,Troy	19	7	6	10	3	3
Hunter,Brian L.	12	8	7	5	0	3
Taylor,Reggie	14	10	15	10	3	3
Torres,Andres		-2	7	15	8	3
Rios,Armando	11	8	10	2	5	3
Richard,Chris	15	20	13	4	0	3
Macias,Jose	-4	0	14	7	2	3
Vitiello,Joe	7	8	10	13	2	3
Kieschnick,Brooks	6	7	7	5	3	3
Dellucci,David	6	0	8	4	4	3
Liefer,Jeff	7	12	13	2	1	3
Kinkade,Mike	7	13	4	10	1	3
Banks,Brian	3	1	6	9	3	2
Glanville,Doug	30	18	18	9	2	2
Gonzalez,Raul	15	1	9	17	6	2
Jones,Jason			-2	11	10	2
Henderson,Rickey	25	11	11	4	1	2
McCarty,Dave	3	8	3	2	6	2
Sweeney,Mark	1	4	5	1	5	2
Smith,Mark	8	3	2	2	9	2
Duncan,Jeff					9	2
Kingsale,Gene	9	2	5	12	0	2
McCracken,Quinton	5	-3	6	11	1	2
Merced,Orlando	9	11	12	4	3	1
Conti,Jason	9	15	10	5	-0	1
Shinjo,Tsuyoshi	12	5	4	8	2	1
Hyzdu,Adam		6	6	-2	5	1
Taguchi,So			6	6	-0	1
Bragg,Darren	4	2	7	6	3	1
Christenson,Ryan	5	2	1	2	5	1
Thames,Marcus	-1	3	25	-1	2	0

RC/Gm

Name	'99	'00	'01	'02	'03	'04Prj
Tyner,Jason	3.94	2.81	3.75	3.08	4.32	3.91
Erstad,Darin	3.86	8.76	3.98	4.46	3.55	3.89
Gonzalez,Raul	5.13	2.60	4.16	4.57	4.19	3.86
Rios,Armando	5.63	6.03	5.28	5.04	3.93	3.86
Freel,Ryan	4.00	4.50	3.60	3.42	3.86	3.78
Sanchez,Alex	1.77	2.72	3.58	4.31	2.90	3.77
Kinkade,Mike	3.88	4.79	4.43	4.85	2.90	3.77
Singleton,Chris	5.90	3.94	4.79	4.31	3.52	3.77
Johnson,Reed			4.49	2.26	4.91	3.77
Dellucci,David	9.75	3.20	5.75	3.92	3.80	3.76
Mackowiak,Rob	3.28	3.74	3.90	4.56	3.48	3.75
Brown,Dee	7.21	4.83	3.43	3.99	3.24	3.68
Liefer,Jeff	4.99	4.98	5.42	3.65	2.95	3.65
Hyzdu,Adam	4.61	3.82	3.34	3.69	3.98	3.64
Calloway,Ron			5.19	3.53	3.55	3.62
Robinson,Kerry	3.14	3.25	3.95	3.58	3.40	3.61
Owens,Eric	4.55	4.58	3.34	4.14	2.96	3.60
Merced,Orlando	5.69	2.10	5.25	5.60	3.40	3.54
Hunter,Brian L.	3.01	3.99	4.64	4.91	2.94	3.50
McCracken,Quint	3.50	2.04	3.52	6.05	2.57	3.45
Shinjo,Tsuyoshi	3.41	4.00	4.20	3.47	2.85	3.34
Bragg,Darren	4.79	3.42	4.56	4.62	2.72	3.34
Taylor,Reggie	2.87	3.37	3.60	3.89	3.16	3.22
Duncan,Jeff					3.16	3.19
Christenson,Ryar	3.85	4.31	3.10	2.68	3.52	3.17
Macias,Jose	2.18	3.13	4.30	3.48	3.08	3.15
Thames,Marcus	2.58	3.33	7.27	2.42	3.21	3.14
Glanville,Doug	6.77	4.10	3.74	3.56	2.72	3.10
Conti,Jason	3.86	4.12	4.60	4.05	2.47	3.03
Kingsale,Gene	2.98	3.40	2.54	4.27	2.49	3.03
Taguchi,So	3.09	3.97	3.96	1.92	2.89	3.01
Torres,Andres		0.80	3.76	3.46	2.67	2.90

Power

Name	'99	'00	'01	'02	'03	'04Prj
Macias,Jose	48	46	78	91	79	77
Shinjo,Tsuyoshi	85	89	89	84	64	76
Conti,Jason	67	79	88	87	65	76
Surhoff,B.J.	112	98	91	62	79	76
Chavez,Endy			39	94	72	75
Suzuki,Ichiro	109	77	70	66	77	73
Harris,Willie			63	57	79	71
Gonzalez,Raul	95	60	84	87	71	71
Henderson,Ricke	102	46	76	76	56	71
Podsednik,Scott	30	62	64	78	85	71
Crisp,Coco				75	70	70
Cedeno,Roger	66	58	59	60	76	68
Figgins,Chone			56	73	67	67
Taguchi,So	52	64	73	55	59	66
Hunter,Brian L.	41	27	56	111	64	66
Bragg,Darren	75	76	91	93	33	64
Erstad,Darin	73	110	71	69	51	63
Kingsale,Gene	50	59	55	91	52	63
Crawford,Carl				86	49	63
Redman,Tike		60	55	42	70	61
McCracken,Quint	56	47	72	106	31	60
Glanville,Doug	88	63	70	65	41	59
Goodwin,Tom	49	49	60	54	61	58
Palmeiro,Orlandc	40	76	55	43	54	53
Robinson,Kerry	46	39	37	65	46	52
Torres,Andres			68	51	54	51
Duncan,Jeff					55	50
Pierre,Juan		29	56	42	49	47
Sanchez,Alex	30	40	48	44	52	45
Roberts,Dave	48	63	52	57	33	45
Owens,Eric	81	53	55	65	28	43
Tyner,Jason	34	19	25	32	55	39

Speed

Name	'99	'00	'01	'02	'03	'04Prj
Vander Wal,John	35	75	94	66	55	61
Richard,Chris	70	93	94	28	205	60
Rowand,Aaron		122	80	71	31	60
Dye,Jermaine	96	44	78	63	51	59
Kinkade,Mike	94	100	47	104	51	59
Gonzalez,Juan	63	58	51	73	67	58
Thames,Marcus	60	46	51	77	53	57
Sierra,Ruben	88	67	80	57	71	56
Smitherman,Stev					52	55
Hyzdu,Adam	74	51	46	35	74	55
Guillen,Jose	49	116	45	51	90	53
Mench,Kevin			56	61	54	53
Alou,Moises		58	63	73	51	52
Jenkins,Geoff	88	130	73	68	59	52
Sosa,Sammy	60	56	75	72	48	51
Jones,Jason			20	82	36	51
Garcia,Karim	98	67	70	57	57	50
Stairs,Matt	58	61	38	52	39	49
Ramirez,Manny	73	55	39	23	59	49
McCarty,Dave	64	55	24	64	73	48
Huff,Aubrey	55	43	43	54	51	48
Spencer,Shane	38	88	88	54	37	47
Surhoff,B.J.	70	85	87	33	35	45
Smith,Mark	75	74	74	58	56	44
Borchard,Joe			55	46	53	42
Platt,Adam	79	99	69	62	33	42
Sweeney,Mark	59	30	71	28	44	40
Kieschnick,Brook	51	43	83	60	20	39
Mabry,John	55	51	36	86	23	35
McMillon,Billy	103	59	86	44	34	34
Gibbons,Jay		52	22	42	38	33
Vitiello,Joe	29	48	27	33	26	31

DH

Std Rotisserie

Name	'99	'00	'01	'02	'03	'04Prj
Fullmer,Brad	15	23	16	18	10	19
Phelps,Josh			1	25	13	16
Martinez,Edgar	26	33	25	12	21	15
Segui,David	12	24	11	2	4	12
Grieve,Ben	12	19	12	13	4	10
Burks,Ellis	22	27	19	25	1	10
Cordova,Marty	16	2	17	11	1	10
Cust,Jack				8	11	8
Giambi,Jeremy	11	6	11	11	11	6
Palmer,Dean	20	16	6	-1	-3	3
Shumpert,Terry	22	8	10	3	-0	3
Martin,Al	20	13	7	9	3	2
Trammell,Bubba	12	8	17	9	-1	1

RC/Gm

Name	'99	'00	'01	'02	'03	'04Prj
Martinez,Edgar	9.46	9.29	8.41	6.79	7.08	6.43
Segui,David	5.96	7.59	6.87	4.33	4.55	6.18
Fullmer,Brad	5.49	6.76	5.02	6.42	6.72	6.12
Burks,Ellis	7.66	10.03	7.11	6.88	5.02	5.49
Cust,Jack		5.68	5.95	4.56	5.66	5.47
Phelps,Josh		3.10	5.83	6.98	5.36	5.36
Giambi,Jeremy	6.17	4.85	5.98	7.01	3.81	5.12
Shumpert,Terry	9.91	5.04	5.29	3.72	3.27	4.90
Grieve,Ben	5.90	6.20	4.96	5.09	4.07	4.89
Cordova,Marty	5.90	3.46	6.05	4.55	5.05	4.24
Trammell,Bubba	5.78	5.55	5.21	4.50	2.58	4.18
Palmer,Dean	5.82	5.44	4.33	0.00	1.07	4.07
Martin,Al	6.13	5.12	4.21		3.59	3.77

Power

Name	'99	'00	'01	'02	'03	'04Prj
Fullmer,Brad	137	149	107	150	113	127
Phelps,Josh		102	141	169	119	125
Shumpert,Terry	162	109	92	93	109	111
Giambi,Jeremy	88	95	104	149	105	111
Cust,Jack		114	118	123	98	110
Martinez,Edgar	133	144	150	130	117	109
Burks,Ellis	164	147	156	141	99	104
Trammell,Bubba	123	112	117	107	79	100
Segui,David	106	111	108	69	77	97
Cordova,Marty	111	59	121	111	80	97
Palmer,Dean	143	119	121		20	95
Martin,Al	139	90	89		70	89
Grieve,Ben	123	124	82	114	74	89

Speed

Name	'99	'00	'01	'02	'03	'04Prj
Shumpert,Terry	141	192	190	88	169	158
Martin,Al	160	156	104	104	71	116
Fullmer,Brad	62	63	72	141	95	89
Burks,Ellis	54	106	73	47	61	71
Cordova,Marty	108	56	48	44	52	70
Grieve,Ben	62	62	76	62	35	67
Cust,Jack		95	56	42	61	59
Segui,David	58	38	50		56	49
Giambi,Jeremy	54	69	29	26	38	46
Phelps,Josh		66	62	45	47	44
Palmer,Dean	66	66	68		8	39
Trammell,Bubba	27	87	65	42	19	34
Martinez,Edgar	65	49	57	25	18	33

Starting Pitchers

Std Rotisserie	'99	'00	'01	'02	'03	'04Prj
Hudson,Tim	30	27	25	24	33	**34**
Prior,Mark				18	33	**33**
Schmidt,Jason	10	-4	16	20	37	**32**
Mussina,Mike	27	24	30	22	28	**30**
Halladay,Roy	7	-15	17	30	37	**30**
Martinez,Pedro	50	54	20	40	31	**29**
Loaiza,Esteban	9	11	3	1	34	**28**
Oswalt,Roy		20	24	28	17	**27**
Vazquez,Javier	6	12	27	11	25	**27**
Wood,Kerry		5	17	15	22	**25**
Hernandez,Livan	1	21	-1	6	23	**24**
Mulder,Mark	1	-0	29	27	24	**24**
Schilling,Curt	24	20	37	39	20	**23**
Millwood,Kevin	38	11	6	26	16	**22**
Radke,Brad	20	14	21	9	14	**22**
Contreras,Jose		54	41	44	14	**22**
Santana,Johan		-7	-1	18	22	**22**
Morris,Matt		7	28	19	16	**22**
Colon,Bartolo	24	19	12	28	21	**22**
Beckett,Josh			19	6	13	**22**
Johnson,Randy	40	39	41	44	5	**21**
Sheets,Ben		19	6	6	11	**20**
Maddux,Greg	22	38	31	25	20	**20**
Brown,Kevin	35	36	17	2	28	**20**
Pineiro,Joel	-6	10	19	20	19	**20**
Ponson,Sidney	10	10	0	7	21	**19**
Redman,Mark	2	11	-2	9	19	**19**
Zito,Barry	2	23	23	36	24	**19**
Buehrle,Mark		21	28	24	13	**19**
Penny,Brad	-0	8	17	1	14	**19**
Perez,Odalis	-5		3	30	11	**19**
Pettitte,Andy	8	18	15	17	21	**18**
Padilla,Vicente	8	4	13	20	18	**18**
Williams,Jerome			13	13	19	**18**
Webb,Brandon				10	19	**18**
Zambrano,Carlos		18	12	4	18	**17**
Thomson,John	-19		8	4	10	**17**
Miller,Wade	6	5	22	17	14	**17**
Milton,Eric	13	17	15	13	3	**17**
Pavano,Carl	0	13	-4	-2	12	**16**
Kim,Byung-Hyun	13	14	24	35	25	**16**
Washburn,Jarrod	-0	13	14	27	11	**16**
Redding,Tim		1	17	-4	10	**16**
Nomo,Hideo	12	6	10	18	23	**15**
Moyer,Jamie	23	8	29	25	28	**15**
Willis,Dontrelle					25	**15**
Williams,Woody	10	17	16	19	21	**15**
Leiter,Al	11	27	18	16	10	**15**
Alvarez,Wilson	9		2	-1	25	**15**
Lowe,Derek	27	37	18	39	12	**15**
Wells,Kip	17	-7	3	12	16	**14**
Ortiz,Russ	14	6	22	15	22	**14**
Harden,Rich				8	20	**14**
Clement,Matt	4	4	-0	17	16	**14**
Wakefield,Tim	10	1	11	25	13	**14**
Franklin,Ryan	-4	8	7	10	18	**14**
Lackey,John		5	8	22	5	**13**
Garcia,Freddy	17	11	31	15	10	**13**
Lilly,Ted	4	3	0	10	11	**13**
Lawrence,Brian		27	9	12	11	**13**
Armas Jr.,Tony	15	8	8	8	5	**13**
Suppan,Jeff	12	6	7	-0	13	**13**
May,Darrell	12	27	11	-1	17	**13**
Lopez,Rodrigo	4	1	3	21	-4	**13**
Myers,Brett			8	13	8	**13**
Ohka,Tomokazu	22	22	-8	18	7	**13**
Acevedo,Jose			3	15	9	**12**
Trachsel,Steve	-1	4	13	13	17	**12**

Base Perf Value	'99	'00	'01	'02	'03	'04Prj
Schilling,Curt	88	91	186	246	171	**158**
Martinez,Pedro	259	256	215	187	153	**153**
Prior,Mark				138	154	**146**
Schmidt,Jason	45	42	90	103	145	**129**
Halladay,Roy	18	-8	127	89	153	**128**
Johnson,Randy	164	157	184	154	118	**125**
Mussina,Mike	96	115	141	95	132	**119**
Vazquez,Javier	53	84	128	86	121	**117**
Contreras,Jose		161	207	188	107	**111**
Santana,Johan		26	31	113	115	**109**
Oswalt,Roy		134	152	105	98	**109**
Loaiza,Esteban	53	46	44	50	115	**103**
Beckett,Josh			116	86	103	**101**
Hudson,Tim	96	66	78	67	85	**98**
Wood,Kerry		60	106	85	108	**98**
Brown,Kevin	115	134	98	68	110	**95**
Harden,Rich				100	91	**90**
Pettitte,Andy	32	43	108	93	94	**88**
Webb,Brandon				70	96	**87**
Sheets,Ben		72	33	66	80	**86**
Mulder,Mark	45	13	85	82	87	**85**
Radke,Brad	52	56	116	67	77	**84**
Perez,Odalis	45		66	108	66	**84**
Kim,Byung-Hyun	110	115	109	130	92	**83**
Hernandez,Livan	45	60	35	49	80	**82**
Morris,Matt		64	104	82	75	**82**
Zambrano,Carlos		78	99	69	76	**79**
Alvarez,Wilson	43		98	31	119	**78**
Williams,Jerome			67	96	68	**76**
Foppert,Jesse				103	46	**76**
Redman,Mark	58	56	26	55	79	**75**
Harang,Aaron			64	71	55	**74**
Millwood,Kevin	107	69	40	90	75	**74**
Milton,Eric	66	74	52	87	145	**74**
Perez,Oliver				79	62	**73**
Shields,Scot	61	46	40	81	85	**73**
Clement,Matt	47	49	54	97	71	**72**
Fossum,Casey			85	94	54	**71**
Miller,Wade	50	54	66	81	73	**71**
Maddux,Greg	87	122	156	72	80	**70**
Wakefield,Tim	35	15	75	88	69	**70**
Penny,Brad	90	42	88	37	64	**70**
Affeldt,Jeremy			70	56	73	**68**
Lilly,Ted	73	55	60	64	64	**68**
Redding,Tim		43	85	54	51	**67**
Towers,Josh	44	82	58	-18	68	**67**
Ainsworth,Kurt		52	77	82	50	**67**
Acevedo,Jose			56	59	75	**67**
Dreifort,Darren	54	48	66		94	**66**
Willis,Dontrelle					87	**66**
Pavano,Carl	56	59	37	38	69	**66**
Leiter,Al	57	91	84	72	54	**66**
Thomson,John	-8		54	71	58	**65**
Williams,Woody	34	48	55	94	74	**65**
Colon,Bartolo	62	84	67	61	65	**65**
Ponson,Sidney	13	41	36	40	63	**65**
Lackey,John		77	68	68	46	**64**
Traber,Billy			70	68	48	**64**
Rusch,Glendon	62	95	84	36	48	**64**
Pineiro,Joel	25	48	76	61	62	**62**
Padilla,Vicente	58	65	107	67	56	**62**
Wells,Kip	58	9	46	50	56	**60**
Wolf,Randy	51	52	94	82	66	**60**
Ishii,Kazuhisa	103	114	82	50	59	**60**
Armas Jr.,Tony	58	34	70	48	76	**60**
Ohka,Tomokazu	64	44	41	64	51	**58**
Seo,Jae			78	58	58	**58**
Batista,Miguel	52	-23	51	54	73	**58**

Relief Pitchers

Std Rotisserie	'99	'00	'01	'02	'03	'04Prj
Gagne,Eric	28	4	11	43	48	**42**
Foulke,Keith	24	33	36	15	45	**37**
Rivera,Mariano	41	35	41	22	37	**36**
Wagner,Billy	38	3	31	30	37	**34**
Guardado,Eddie	4	14	17	32	34	**31**
Smoltz,John	22		13	38	35	**31**
Urbina,Ugueth	31	5	18	29	27	**29**
Borowski,Joe	-2	11	11	10	26	**29**
Cordero,Francisco	27	-4	-0	12	17	**28**
Isringhausen,Jason	11	27	28	27	16	**27**
Hoffman,Trevor	33	37	31	26	1	**27**
Mantei,Matt	22	10	1	2	26	**25**
Worrell,Tim	2	11	3	13	28	**25**
Riske,David	21	1	15	0	15	**25**
Carter,Lance	21	0		22	24	**24**
Percival,Troy	26	23	31	32	23	**24**
Sasaki,Kazuhiro	15	29	31	30	7	**22**
Escobar,Kelvim	3	6	12	24	11	**21**
Julio,Jorge			13	25	20	**21**
Looper,Braden	2	4	6	13	21	**21**
Williamson,Scott	31	10		12	16	**20**
Lopez,Aquilino			6	11	12	**20**
Kolb,Danny	-0	6	3	1	16	**19**
Hawkins,LaTroy	-7	15	9	15	18	**18**
Beck,Rod	5	7	10		25	**16**
Gordon,Tom	5		20	1	18	**16**
Soriano,Rafael			4	5	19	**15**
Hasegawa,Shige	4	17	5	10	20	**15**
Dotel,Octavio	10	7	14	22	17	**14**
Rhodes,Arthur	1	9	19	19	5	**14**
Marte,Damaso	-8	0	3	12	20	**14**
Gonzalez,Jeremi	-1			12	11	**13**
Ayala,Luis	7	1	1	-1	17	**12**
Baez,Danys		3	9	9	20	**12**
German,Franklyn				21	3	**12**
Rodriguez,Felix	2	11	18	9	9	**11**
Fuentes,Brian	-7	-10	9	0	8	**11**
Bradford,Chad	20	15	10	9	11	**11**
Donnelly,Brendan	8	-9	15	14	13	**11**
Riedling,John	17	17	5	-1	-3	**11**
Cruz,Juan			12	1	5	**11**
Ramirez,Erasmo		-13	5	11	10	**11**
Graves,Danny	28	32	25	27	-4	**11**
Benitez,Armando	26	36	32	25	18	**10**
Rodriguez,Francisco				40	16	**10**
Weber,Ben	9	10	6	16	8	**10**
Mateo,Julio				7	12	**10**
Timlin,Mike	23	11	5	12	12	**10**
Nathan,Joe	9	-1	-24	-16	17	**10**
Cormier,Rheal	5	4	5	0	19	**9**
Mota,Guillermo	9	11	-1	5	18	**9**
Jimenez,Jose	-4	22	15	27	4	**9**
Betancourt,Rafael	13	6	-2		19	**9**
Kershner,Jason	-2	8	-8	10	13	**9**
Speier,Justin	-2	14	8	8	8	**9**
Villarreal,Oscar			2	11	14	**8**
Reitsma,Chris		12	-1	8	14	**8**
Stewart,Scott	3	6	6	17	2	**8**
Quantrill,Paul	4	2	16	7	12	**8**
Rincon,Ricardo	2	3	6	4	8	**8**
Lyon,Brandon			14	-9	7	**8**
Koplove,Mike		7	14	15	6	**8**
Vizcaino,Luis	2	2	11	13	-1	**7**
Meadows,Brian	-0	6	-15	4	15	**7**
Lidge,Brad			4	2	9	**7**
Gallo,Mike					9	**7**
Herges,Matt	7	17	9	2	9	**7**
Politte,Cliff	8	16	4	6	6	**7**

Base Perf Value	'99	'00	'01	'02	'03	'04Prj
Gagne,Eric	94	35	77	222	255	**190**
Rhodes,Arthur	52	106	208	196	87	**152**
Soriano,Rafael			103	57	174	**147**
Rivera,Mariano	112	88	197	121	177	**145**
Wagner,Billy	212	30	145	138	156	**144**
Smoltz,John	113		147	132	258	**131**
Foulke,Keith	174	128	127	119	133	**125**
Gordon,Tom	89		159	103	126	**120**
Hawkins,LaTroy	13	57	38	125	150	**119**
Dotel,Octavio	71	56	139	158	117	**114**
Riske,David	112	-9	102	72	128	**114**
Mantei,Matt	125	87	87	70	133	**112**
Mota,Guillermo	45	39	22	87	126	**110**
Hoffman,Trevor	155	209	86	142	125	**108**
Valverde,Jose			132	71	114	**107**
Urbina,Ugueth	120	172	121	116	93	**106**
Guardado,Eddie	77	34	110	113	123	**105**
Marte,Damaso	-4	-1	84	140	121	**103**
Borowski,Joe	32	84	95	104	117	**102**
Plesac,Dan	85	79	130	77	114	**102**
Isringhausen,Jason	54	62	117	151	101	**100**
Cordero,Francisco	85	15	24	104	104	**99**
Betancourt,Rafael	112	83	159		108	**99**
Williamson,Scott	112	97	55	111	87	**99**
Ryan,B.J.	105	44	69	62	121	**99**
Donnelly,Brendan	63	-5	59	109	133	**98**
Lidge,Brad			165	63	106	**98**
Timlin,Mike	60	42	64	98	164	**96**
Rodriguez,Francisco				171	100	**93**
Fox,Chad	100		106	59	80	**92**
Farnsworth,Kyle	12	36	133	37	113	**92**
Rodriguez,Felix	62	105	132	80	56	**91**
Osuna,Antonio	100	79	-82	103	81	**90**
Bradford,Chad	106	99	167	121	70	**89**
Fuentes,Brian	44	55	92	94	93	**89**
Nelson,Jeff	85	99	129	96	112	**88**
Benitez,Armando	165	123	84	114	82	**87**
German,Franklyn				138	55	**85**
Ramirez,Erasmo		10	105	88	90	**85**
Sasaki,Kazuhiro	197	94	159	129	77	**82**
Koplove,Mike		79	69	100	83	**82**
Mateo,Julio				56	126	**82**
Embree,Alan	78	69	57	142	86	**82**
Rincon,Ricardo	32	81	95	145	56	**82**
Baez,Danys		55	100	57	83	**82**
Vizcaino,Luis	37	43	92	104	36	**82**
Spooneybarger,Tim			119	66	114	**81**
Quantrill,Paul	37	42	121	79	97	**81**
Christiansen,Jason	85	92	78	-37	61	**81**
Lopez,Aquilino			110	93	79	**80**
Villarreal,Oscar			63	91	74	**80**
Cunnane,Will	78	77	49	79	101	**79**
Worrell,Tim	66	39	76	81	81	**79**
Adams,Terry	58	51	87	59	86	**79**
Holmes,Darren	53	19		127	113	**79**
Percival,Troy	84	59	152	115	75	**78**
Cruz,Juan			88	51	93	**78**
Cormier,Rheal	66	59	63	51	104	**77**
Strickland,Scott	111	111	80	78	74	**77**
Remlinger,Mike	83	85	126	110	78	**77**
King,Ray	66	71	72	69	71	**76**
Meadows,Brian	-3	-1	7	56	144	**75**
Linebrink,Scott	18	61	86	48	55	**75**
Riedling,John	73	77	81	51	45	**75**
Witasick,Jay	16	31	116	94	55	**75**
Groom,Buddy	70	61	158	123	42	**74**
Speier,Justin	33	83	69	57	71	**74**
Stewart,Scott	58	75	85	116	47	**73**

Starting Pitchers

Std Rotisserie	'99	'00	'01	'02	'03	'04Prj
Ortiz,Ramon	15	12	8	21	6	**12**
Lohse,Kyle	-7	-22	6	10	13	**12**
Lidle,Cory	-0	12	20	13	1	**11**
Harang,Aaron			4	7	10	**11**
Shields,Scot	5	-7	1	15	14	**11**
Eaton,Adam	13	15	8	1	9	**11**
Anderson,Brian	8	17	-1	2	17	**10**
Hampton,Mike	31	23	-1	-16	13	**9**
Wolf,Randy	2	10	14	21	16	**9**
Towers,Josh	11	10	10	-21	12	**9**
Vargas,Claudio				-6	8	**9**
Sabathia,C.C.		4	14	10	17	**9**
Batista,Miguel	2	-9	15	6	12	**8**
Ainsworth,Kurt		11	8	10	4	**8**
Telemaco,Amaury	-1	4	-2	1	13	**8**
Garland,Jon	1	13	5	7	9	**8**
Day,Zach		4	5	8	6	**8**
Seo,Jae			12	-1	12	**8**
Burkett,John	1	4	22	8	6	**8**
Weaver,Jeff	4	17	14	18	-7	**8**
Glavine,Tom	11	33	16	24	2	**8**
Lee,Cliff				-1	8	**8**
Perez,Oliver				8	-1	**7**
Rueter,Kirk	5	11	9	18	4	**7**
Affeldt,Jeremy			5	-1	11	**7**
Wells,David	17	26	3	22	18	**7**
Fossum,Casey			6	5	2	**7**
Maroth,Mike		4	-5	15	-2	**6**
Traber,Billy			1	15	-1	**6**
Ramirez,Horacio			-2	9	10	**6**
Stanford,Jason			-1	1	8	**6**
Westbrook,Jake	6	1	4	-3	3	**5**
Benson,Kris	11	14		4	-1	**5**
Rogers,Kenny	10	12	-8	14	8	**5**
Johnson,Jason	6	1	9	4	4	**5**
Haren,Danny					11	**5**
Figueroa,Nelson	12	18	7	-2	10	**5**
DuBose,Eric	0	3		8	6	**5**
Peavy,Jake			3	8	12	**4**
Gobble,Jimmy				2	11	**4**
Hitchcock,Sterling	12	-1	1	-9	3	**4**
Dreifort,Darren	8	14	-1		3	**4**
Appier,Kevin	9	11	18	14	2	**4**
D'Amico,Jeff	-4	27	-3	2	3	**4**
Zambrano,Victor	-2	1	18	0	9	**4**
Good,Andrew			-7	14	-0	**4**
Davis,Jason				2	6	**4**
Benoit,Joaquin		2	1	6	3	**4**
Stephenson,Garrett	7	16	0	-3	5	**3**
Ishii,Kazuhisa	9	23	17	6	4	**3**
Robertson,Nate				5	4	**3**
Dessens,Elmer	-1	12	7	13	-2	**3**
Reed,Rick	8	16	16	21	2	**3**
Cornejo,Nate		1	22	-4	-1	**3**
Schoeneweis,Scott	-12	2	1	5	3	**3**
Hermanson,Dustin	9	8	10	-3	1	**3**
Patterson,John	5	-4	-8	7	7	**3**
Rusch,Glendon	-3	16	2	2	-14	**3**
Daal,Omar	22	-11	9	13	-8	**3**
Duckworth,Brandon		15	19	-2	-1	**2**
Villone,Ron	15	0	-5	-2	11	**2**
Rodriguez,Ricardo				9	-2	**2**
Stark,Dennis	-8	6	17	9	-5	**2**
Burnett,A.J.	-5	0	11	19	-1	**2**
Wilson,Paul		12	3	-2	2	**2**
Tomko,Brett	3	7	6	6	0	**2**
Valdes,Ismael	11	-4	6	11	-2	**2**
Snyder,Kyle				-0	2	**2**

Base Perf Value	'99	'00	'01	'02	'03	'04Prj
Weaver,Jeff	35	58	62	81	37	**58**
Haren,Danny					75	**57**
Myers,Brett			56	62	52	**57**
Schoeneweis,Scott	7	16	27	21	99	**57**
Telemaco,Amaury	35	33	31	-51	72	**57**
Lawrence,Brian		103	71	77	41	**57**
Nomo,Hideo	59	53	81	64	63	**56**
DuBose,Eric	42	41		80	57	**56**
Ortiz,Russ	45	42	73	53	56	**56**
Burkett,John	40	58	90	49	48	**56**
Zito,Barry	82	72	91	75	57	**56**
Garcia,Freddy	63	32	78	70	43	**56**
Lidle,Cory	37	63	60	68	35	**55**
Eaton,Adam	73	56	67	28	63	**54**
Stanford,Jason			65	44	58	**54**
Lopez,Rodrigo	51	48	40	59	37	**53**
Lohse,Kyle	10	15	57	38	59	**52**
Hitchcock,Sterling	70	51	48	24	44	**51**
Buehrle,Mark		60	65	51	42	**51**
Benoit,Joaquin		61	61	61	33	**51**
Burnett,A.J.	47	42	50	98	62	**49**
Peavy,Jake			120	84	44	**48**
Sabathia,C.C.		72	70	57	62	**48**
Washburn,Jarrod	48	23	51	68	35	**48**
Benson,Kris	56	66		36	34	**48**
Gobble,Jimmy				59	41	**48**
Lee,Cliff				18	54	**48**
Good,Andrew			58	82	29	**47**
Lowe,Derek	102	108	85	85	39	**47**
Duckworth,Brandon		77	77	65	30	**46**
Patterson,John	79	2	17	56	44	**46**
Day,Zach		81	44	58	33	**45**
Lewis,Colby			66	74	17	**44**
Villone,Ron	66	7	52	44	54	**43**
Moyer,Jamie	67	33	63	72	55	**43**
Heilman,Aaron				80	33	**43**
Dessens,Elmer	4	51	39	35	38	**43**
D'Amico,Jeff	-13	58	8	58	42	**43**
Zambrano,Victor	47	32	91	27	41	**43**
Figueroa,Nelson	54	53	59	14	47	**41**
Marquis,Jason	22	29	54	33	43	**41**
Suppan,Jeff	25	18	33	19	44	**41**
May,Darrell	92	123	97	29	40	**40**
Davis,Jason				63	26	**40**
Trachsel,Steve	45	23	67	43	34	**39**
Westbrook,Jake	25	50	55	36	27	**38**
Vargas,Claudio				36	39	**38**
Robertson,Nate				38	38	**38**
Estes,Shawn	46	51	53	63	23	**38**
Park,Chan Ho	42	76	86	39	-24	**37**
Kinney,Matt	14	49	27	-5	45	**37**
Reed,Rick	42	70	98	88	35	**36**
Dempster,Ryan	41	65	50	53	28	**36**
Franklin,Ryan	26	48	53	63	21	**36**
Hernandez,Runelvys				70	33	**36**
Hermanson,Dustin	56	14	24	30	40	**35**
Daal,Omar	58	11	33	50	23	**35**
Rogers,Kenny	52	38	18	35	47	**35**
Johnson,Jason	29	42	27	51	31	**34**
Bonderman,Jeremy					32	**34**
Quevedo,Ruben	82	32	86	10	-1	**34**
Jarvis,Kevin	13	13	46	62	11	**34**
Hampton,Mike	71	64	18	-4	44	**33**
Ritchie,Todd	52	48	54	17	14	**33**
Tomko,Brett	44	33	59	38	19	**33**
Astacio,Pedro	62	60	67	51	-15	**32**
Wilson,Paul		72	52	23	28	**32**
Wells,David	60	121	54	74	99	**31**

Relief Pitchers

Std Rotisserie	'99	'00	'01	'02	'03	'04Prj
Remlinger,Mike	16	15	8	13	6	**7**
Saarloos,Kirk				20	4	**7**
Adams,Terry	14	9	10	4	4	**7**
Kline,Steve	8	11	16	7	7	**7**
Ligtenberg,Kerry		11	5	5	7	**7**
Walker,Jamie	-1	-12	-3	7	9	**6**
Boyd,Jason	8	-3	10	1	8	**6**
MacDougal,Mike		-2	-4	-13	18	**6**
Veres,Dave	16	26	13	8	3	**6**
Eischen,Joey	-14	-5	6	18	4	**6**
Valverde,Jose			8	0	16	**6**
Fox,Chad	-2		15	-0	4	**6**
Shuey,Paul	14	8	7	10	9	**6**
Villafuerte,Brandon	10	-11	6	15	11	**6**
Patterson,Danny	-2	5	9	-0	4	**6**
Corey,Mark	-12	-5	26	4	14	**6**
Miceli,Dan	3	7	1	-2	6	**6**
Tejera,Michael			-1	3	1	**5**
Embree,Alan	6	3	-6	11	6	**5**
Osuna,Antonio	-0	4	-3	14	1	**5**
Helling,Rick	11	16	2	9	2	**5**
Farnsworth,Kyle	3	-2	11	-3	7	**5**
Kennedy,Joe			20	6	-8	**5**
White,Gabe	1	24	-4	9	6	**5**
Cressend,Jack	-6	6	7	-4	11	**5**
Brower,Jim	8	7	7	1	10	**5**
Harper,Travis	0	18	7	-4	7	**5**
Stanton,Mike	2	4	12	13	5	**5**
Christiansen,Jason	4	2	6	-0	-1	**5**
Meche,Gil	11	7		-11	12	**5**
Plesac,Dan	-0	6	5	4	5	**5**
Eldred,Cal	-13	9	-3		11	**5**
Weathers,Dave	5	7	13	7	6	**5**
DeJean,Mike	-11	1	8	17	11	**5**
Anderson,Matt	-5	3	14	-2	-1	**5**
Halama,John	13	8	12	3	2	**5**
Witasick,Jay	-3	-6	9	6	2	**4**
Cerda,Jaime			3	12	3	**4**
Biddle,Rocky		4	-0	4	20	**4**
Feliciano,Pedro			18	3	2	**4**
Cunnane,Will	13	8	-6	7	11	**4**
Van Poppel,Todd	-3	10	7	-1	4	**4**
Lopez,Javier			-9	6	6	**4**
de los Santos,Valeri	-2	-0	-0	4	4	**4**
Groom,Buddy	2	8	11	13	-2	**4**
Williams,Mike	11	20	18	30	9	**4**
Ryan,B.J.	12	-2	2	0	5	**4**
King,Ray	6	8	1	5	5	**4**
Mecir,Jim	1	19	6	5	0	**4**
Hodges,Trey				13	-0	**4**
Torres,Salomon			-4	-1	4	**4**
Anderson,Jason				14	7	**4**
Wheeler,Dan	11	0	-7	-2	6	**4**
Koch,Billy	21	35	19	38	6	**4**
Mears,Chris				-0	8	**4**
Leskanic,Curtis	0	19	13	0	9	**4**
Linebrink,Scott	-6	3	12	-8	4	**4**
Mendoza,Ramiro	12	8	15	12	-7	**4**
Reed,Steve	3	3	5	9	6	**4**
Rincon,Juan		-7	6	-3	6	**3**
Sullivan,Scott	13	11	10	-2	7	**3**
Silva,Carlos			10	9	0	**3**
Heredia,Felix	1	7	-3	1	10	**3**
Lincoln,Mike	-10	-1	9	4	6	**3**
Stone,Ricky	-5	6	2	3	8	**3**
Mahay,Ron	-5	-6	17	5	9	**3**
White,Rick	4	12	6	3	-2	**3**
Tavarez,Julian	-4	9	4	-6	11	**3**

Base Perf Value	'99	'00	'01	'02	'03	'04Prj
Nathan,Joe	33	21	-41	21	103	**72**
Kolb,Danny	21	57	70	43	91	**72**
Jones,Todd	66	88	39	72	37	**72**
Eischen,Joey	-15	-14	48	120	69	**72**
Veres,Dave	38	91	54	52	131	**71**
Hodges,Trey				52	54	**71**
Corey,Mark	18	11	91	59	83	**71**
Herges,Matt	41	65	58	34	94	**71**
Saarloos,Kirk				83	64	**70**
Sauerbeck,Scott	62	76	96	109	53	**70**
Politte,Cliff	45	69	93	100	33	**70**
Beck,Rod	27	104	43		92	**69**
Shuey,Paul	105	101	125	94	76	**69**
Patterson,Danny	56	46	56	49	101	**69**
Ayala,Luis	71	19	98	59	85	**68**
Shouse,Brian	19	54	74	39	93	**68**
Escobar,Kelvim	40	40	97	69	69	**67**
Leskanic,Curtis	61	72	57	88	92	**67**
Mahay,Ron	7	15	69	73	80	**67**
Kieschnick,Brooks				71	39	**67**
Bale,John	106	54	95	80	77	**67**
Weathers,Dave	42	48	76	64	70	**67**
Martin,Tom	78	36	2	92	82	**65**
Helling,Rick	15	35	38	48	26	**65**
White,Gabe	86	165	4	118	74	**65**
Ligtenberg,Kerry		71	81	61	74	**63**
Lyon,Brandon			73	12	68	**63**
Cressend,Jack	47	63	53	4	79	**63**
Wunsch,Kelly	36	74	32	44	95	**62**
Almanza,Armando	78	69	52	83	36	**62**
Looper,Braden	40	29	53	59	67	**62**
Miceli,Dan	57	74	80	17	52	**62**
Lopez,Javier			-16	73	87	**62**
Wheeler,Dan	71	15	19	30	56	**61**
de los Santos,Valeri	1	44	78	61	40	**61**
Gallo,Mike					69	**61**
Mecir,Jim	76	82	93	63	40	**61**
MacDougal,Mike		48	29	21	71	**59**
Kershner,Jason	31	46	14	70	69	**59**
Wright,Jaret	25	42	33	5	45	**59**
Villafuerte,Brandon	56	40	53	80	53	**58**
Julio,Jorge			85	77	37	**58**
Walker,Jamie	48	-49	-12	92	61	**58**
Eldred,Cal	13	58	23		69	**58**
Romero,J.C.	52	34	41	97	39	**58**
Van Poppel,Todd	35	75	91	71	53	**57**
Parrish,John	30	39	57		59	**57**
Jimenez,Jose	47	58	44	100	25	**56**
Carter,Lance	93	23		98	49	**56**
Bong,Jung				64	51	**56**
Kline,Steve	77	65	82	71	34	**56**
Tejera,Michael			44	38	55	**56**
Cerda,Jaime			102	101	47	**56**
Feliciano,Pedro			82	51	57	**56**
Sullivan,Scott	60	76	71	50	72	**56**
Torres,Salomon				50	38	**54**
Matthews,Mike	-5	68	66	70	54	**54**
Alfonseca,Antonio	53	47	63	65	50	**54**
Phelps,Tommy	-24	6	55	67	62	**54**
Weber,Ben	58	69	47	64	52	**54**
Gonzalez,Jeremi	58			64	49	**54**
Rincon,Juan		33	49	37	67	**53**
Oropesa,Eddie	0	15	47	17	66	**53**
Carrasco,Hector	66	49	72		55	**53**
Kennedy,Joe			83	41	21	**53**
Brower,Jim	5	26	44	63	55	**53**
White,Rick	60	58	77	62	44	**53**
Stanton,Mike	96	108	98	55	52	**52**

Starting Pitchers

Std Rotisserie	'99	'00	'01	'02	'03	'04Prj
Howard,Ben			4	-5	6	**1**
Astacio,Pedro	9	4	2	7	-4	**1**
Davis,Doug	13	9	6	-1	3	**1**
Jarvis,Kevin	5	6	11	2	-4	**1**
Sele,Aaron	12	18	20	1	-3	**1**
Foppert,Jesse				7	1	**1**
Lima,Jose	29	-11	-2	-6	5	**1**
Fogg,Josh	-5	11	-6	8	2	**1**
Oliver,Darren	8	-12	-4	-6	4	**1**
Marquis,Jason	1	-2	7	0	-0	**0**
Hernandez,Runelvy				12	5	**0**
Hentgen,Pat	8	10	5	-4	9	**0**
Reyes,Carlos	4	3	-5		12	**0**
Ritchie,Todd	19	7	10	-10	-1	**0**
Reynolds,Shane	21	2	12	-0	0	**-0**
Quevedo,Ruben	9	-2	16	-7	-3	**-0**
Bonderman,Jeremy					-5	**-0**
Haynes,Jimmy	-5	-1	-0	9	-12	**-1**
Bell,Rob	4	8	-10	-1	3	**-1**
Jennings,Jason		-1	-6	8	-2	**-1**
Obermueller,Wes				2	1	**-1**
Chacon,Shawn		-2	0	-5	9	**-1**
Brazelton,Dewan				2	-3	**-2**
Loux,Shane		13	-11	-5	7	**-2**
Fernandez,Jared	5	11	-10	0	-3	**-2**
Mounce,Tony	2	-8		-4	-2	**-2**
Heilman,Aaron				7	-5	**-2**
Lewis,Colby			-1	1	-5	**-2**
Dempster,Ryan	-1	19	3	-5	-13	**-3**
Abbott,Paul	10	13	13	-11	-2	**-3**
Kinney,Matt	-10	11	-11	-9	-0	**-3**
Wright,Jamey	-14	6	1	-4	-12	**-3**
Drese,Ryan			7	-5	-18	**-3**
Standridge,Jason		6	-17	4	-6	**-3**
Knotts,Gary	4	-2	0	7	-14	**-3**
Asencio,Miguel				-5	-1	**-3**
Moss,Damian	-9	7	4	15	-3	**-3**
Sosa,Jorge				-2	-4	**-4**
Park,Chan Ho	1	26	23	-7	-11	**-5**
Anderson,Jimmy	8	-1	-2	-5	-9	**-5**
George,Chris		6	12	-16	-14	**-5**
Estes,Shawn	0	10	7	-7	-9	**-5**
Elarton,Scott	14	12	-11		-18	**-6**

Base Perf Value	'99	'00	'01	'02	'03	'04Prj
Jennings,Jason		30	49	37	30	**31**
Ramirez,Horacio			46	55	31	**31**
Abbott,Paul	70	28	40	-10	46	**31**
Ortiz,Ramon	55	41	40	49	14	**31**
Glavine,Tom	45	62	28	45	17	**31**
Loux,Shane		67	-2	43	30	**31**
Davis,Doug	66	23	48	37	18	**30**
Hentgen,Pat	24	28	45	-26	33	**30**
Anderson,Brian	49	35	6	40	29	**30**
Reyes,Carlos	54	20	15		66	**28**
Knotts,Gary	33	31	64	43	7	**28**
Brazelton,Dewan				51	16	**28**
Garland,Jon	33	41	27	31	25	**28**
Drese,Ryan			56	43	1	**26**
Asencio,Miguel				6	33	**26**
Maroth,Mike		25	17	52	9	**25**
Wright,Jamey	10	39	29	25	17	**25**
Stephenson,Garrett	47	33	57	55	18	**25**
Stark,Dennis	13	70	59	12	-8	**25**
Chacon,Shawn		46	41	-1	53	**25**
Cornejo,Nate		41	74	41	-1	**24**
Reynolds,Shane	131	38	52	24	29	**24**
Bell,Rob	90	31	12	33	16	**23**
Appier,Kevin	31	32	80	50	2	**22**
Rodriguez,Ricardo				40	4	**21**
Howard,Ben			63	12	17	**21**
Haynes,Jimmy	18	11	34	38	-1	**20**
Fogg,Josh	17	61	30	29	19	**20**
Oliver,Darren	47	-2	24	13	23	**20**
Obermueller,Wes				22	17	**20**
Sosa,Jorge				9	24	**19**
Lima,Jose	98	-1	12	5	23	**17**
Valdes,Ismael	48	17	41	41	-2	**15**
Sele,Aaron	73	53	47	23	3	**15**
Fernandez,Jared	3	21	5	23	-2	**14**
Rueter,Kirk	18	9	14	23	5	**14**
Snyder,Kyle				0	27	**12**
Standridge,Jason		39	-16	33	13	**10**
Moss,Damian	-19	38	54	41	3	**9**
Anderson,Jimmy	51	30	24	-9	8	**9**
Elarton,Scott	101	30	-4		-10	**7**
Mounce,Tony	66	35		18	15	**4**
George,Chris		30	26	17	-27	**-4**

Relief Pitchers

Std Rotisserie	'99	'00	'01	'02	'03	'04Prj
Tam,Jeff	4	12	7	-2	-0	**-1**
Acevedo,Juan	-1	5	-2	22	-1	**-1**
Wellemeyer,Todd				0	-8	**-1**
Levrault,Allen	8	8	-2	-8	5	**-1**
Fultz,Aaron	4	5	3	1	-3	**-1**
Roney,Matt				-10	-5	**-1**
Ford,Matt					-2	**-1**
Wright,Danny		3	7	7	-6	**-1**
Fassero,Jeff	-16	5	14	2	-5	**-1**
McClung,Seth				-13	1	**-1**
Condrey,Clayton		3	2	11	-4	**-1**
Neu,Mike				17	-1	**-1**
Hackman,Luther	-1	1	3	1	-2	**-1**
Mercker,Kent	1	-4		-5	3	**-1**
Myers,Mike	0	6	2	4	-4	**-1**
Almonte,Hector	14	-5	-6	3	5	**-1**
Wilson,Kris	-2	10	3	2	-3	**-2**
Sparks,Steve	-4	16	17	-15	-2	**-2**
Powell,Jay	4	-2	10	-1	-8	**-2**
Mulholland,Terry	7	3	-1	-3	-2	**-2**
Bierbrodt,Nick	-1	-4	7		-11	**-2**

Base Perf Value	'99	'00	'01	'02	'03	'04Prj
Mears,Chris				32	27	**30**
Backe,Brandon			51	-0	50	**30**
Acevedo,Juan	3	37	41	62	20	**30**
Halama,John	41	24	42	58	10	**30**
Spurling,Chris			18	84	34	**29**
Wilson,Kris	32	44	18	64	27	**27**
Robertson,Jeriome	48	-24	31	37	25	**26**
Biddle,Rocky		35	36	48	34	**25**
Driskill,Travis	8	14	42	30	64	**24**
Fassero,Jeff	-1	44	115	68	8	**23**
Sparks,Steve	5	36	40	13	25	**21**
Franklin,Wayne	69	42	23	36	9	**21**
Cook,Aaron				41	12	**20**
Hendrickson,Mark	30	26	-19	49	16	**20**
Walker,Pete	2	51	43	32	2	**19**
Wright,Danny		41	50	35	8	**19**
Franco,John	97	80	67		13	**19**
Smith,Dan	38	10	-9	43	10	**18**
Wendell,Turk	69	70	36		27	**18**
Beimel,Joe		-9	21	31	31	**17**
Roney,Matt				30	2	**17**

Relief Pitchers

Std Rotisserie	'99	'00	'01	'02	'03	'04Prj
Boehringer,Brian	8	-2	2	7	0	**3**
Carrasco,Hector	3	3	2		8	**3**
Romero,J.C.	10	3	-4	16	-3	**3**
Bong,Jung				3	2	**3**
Franco,John	12	10	6		2	**3**
Bale,John	4	3	3	2	3	**3**
Simontacchi,Jason			-12	15	-0	**3**
Bauer,Rick		-8	6	4	3	**2**
Nelson,Jeff	2	13	11	4	9	**2**
Roa,Joe		-4	-3	26	-6	**2**
Shouse,Brian	-5	3	1	-3	4	**2**
Hammond,Chris			7	16	7	**2**
Gryboski,Kevin	4	1	11	2	5	**2**
Strickland,Scott	11	13	9	7	1	**2**
Levine,Al	7	5	13	5	6	**2**
Spurling,Chris			-1	19	3	**2**
Sauerbeck,Scott	9	1	-3	8	-1	**2**
Martin,Tom	1	2	-7	-0	3	**2**
Calero,Kiko	-0	-10	8	1	3	**2**
Franklin,Wayne	20	-0	-4	7	-3	**2**
Driskill,Travis	-5	-5	-0	6	5	**2**
Matthews,Mike	-9	5	8	-0	4	**2**
Miller,Trever	-1	-2	-15	8	3	**2**
Parrish,John	-4	2	2		9	**2**
Almanza,Armando	-1	0	0	3	-2	**2**
Dickey,R.A.	5	-3	4	-2	5	**2**
Phelps,Tommy	-7	-3	-3	6	2	**2**
Robertson,Jeriome	19	-12	-3	11	5	**2**
Tucker,T.J.	7	1	4	4	1	**1**
Holmes,Darren	3	-4		9	0	**1**
Garcia,Rosman			2	6	4	**1**
Eyre,Scott	1	10	4	-2	2	**1**
Callaway,Mickey	5	1	-0	17	-4	**1**
Fiore,Tony	5	14	6	13	-0	**1**
Zerbe,Chad	3	4	8	5	1	**1**
Wright,Jaret	-3	3	-2	-11	-4	**1**
Glover,Gary	11	-3	10	3	-1	**1**
Gaudin,Chad					9	**1**
Santiago,Jose	8	13	1	4	-0	**1**
Cruz,Nelson	9	9	6	-2	-7	**1**
Walker,Pete	3	8	12	7	-4	**1**
Roberts,Willis	-10	-6	6	5	0	**1**
Wunsch,Kelly	5	11	-1	2	3	**1**
Spooneybarger,Tim			12	14	4	**0**
Guthrie,Mark	-0	2	6	9	3	**0**
Orosco,Jesse	-0	-0	2	2	-3	**0**
Burba,Dave	17	13	-5	-1	-0	**0**
Bynum,Mike		5	-8	11	-6	**0**
Grimsley,Jason	9	2	5	4	-4	**0**
Colome,Jesus		14	1	-4	1	**0**
Reith,Brian		0	-7	-3	5	**0**
Randolph,Steve	-3	-4	-12	8	6	**0**
Cook,Aaron				17	-8	**0**
Munro,Peter	1	5	-2	15	-1	**0**
Voyles,Brad			10	-0	-2	**-0**
Jones,Todd	21	29	8	-1	-8	**-0**
Mesa,Jose	16	0	32	30	10	**-0**
Smith,Dan	3	-4	-6	8	-1	**-0**
Estrella,Leo		9	-8	-5	9	**-0**
Neagle,Denny	14	15	-1	-1	-3	**-0**
Alfonseca,Antonio	17	30	22	11	-3	**-0**
Wendell,Turk	9	12	3		5	**-0**
Yan,Esteban	-3	0	18	16	-5	**-0**
Oropesa,Eddie	-2	-4	-0	-7	-1	**-0**
Kieschnick,Brooks				-1	-7	**-0**
Bump,Nate	-2	-4	-4	5	5	**-1**
Hendrickson,Mark	-7	3	-6	11	-2	**-1**
Lloyd,Graeme	10		8	3	-4	**-1**

Base Perf Value	'99	'00	'01	'02	'03	'04Prj
Grimsley,Jason	43	29	67	68	50	**52**
Lincoln,Mike	-4	33	54	60	52	**52**
Boehringer,Brian	48	-20	67	79	27	**52**
Koch,Billy	60	93	53	88	22	**52**
Almonte,Hector	47	17	-3	85	58	**52**
Voyles,Brad			96	46	46	**52**
Roa,Joe		-3	59	79	47	**51**
Anderson,Jason				91	27	**50**
Wellemeyer,Todd				65	48	**50**
Miller,Trever	36	23	20	72	50	**50**
Harper,Travis	45	34	25	29	60	**49**
Bierbrodt,Nick	49	45	69		23	**49**
Fultz,Aaron	43	68	87	51	46	**47**
Boyd,Jason	53	60	74	24	60	**47**
DeJean,Mike	-20	15	74	64	43	**47**
Mendoza,Ramiro	66	21	84	91	13	**47**
Yan,Esteban	29	45	149	43	32	**47**
Colome,Jesus		60	43	43	54	**46**
Williams,Mike	71	72	52	62	33	**46**
Reitsma,Chris		58	33	40	44	**46**
Neu,Mike				99	31	**45**
Hammond,Chris			74	99	104	**45**
Hasegawa,Shige	10	36	64	50	51	**45**
Eyre,Scott	43	62	74	61	43	**45**
Anderson,Matt	0	66	104	20	31	**45**
Gryboski,Kevin	15	43	39	29	53	**45**
Dickey,R.A.	13	15	48	50	51	**44**
Cruz,Nelson	41	55	86	36	17	**44**
Reed,Steve	39	44	64	117	32	**44**
Calero,Kiko	19	-8	25	41	103	**44**
Myers,Mike	55	96	77	70	23	**43**
Silva,Carlos			57	56	36	**43**
Stone,Ricky	30	36	46	54	33	**43**
Mesa,Jose	6	61	97	71	34	**43**
Meche,Gil	41	57		20	40	**43**
Lloyd,Graeme	42		55	67	42	**42**
Gaudin,Chad					82	**42**
Simontacchi,Jason			23	34	19	**41**
Graves,Danny	49	41	68	64	-3	**41**
Tavarez,Julian	21	29	47	21	59	**41**
Randolph,Steve	29	-51	6	32	45	**40**
Bynum,Mike		55	8	68	33	**40**
Callaway,Mickey	48	14	-45	69	34	**39**
Bauer,Rick		16	42	12	54	**39**
Carrasco,D.J.			45		43	**39**
Tam,Jeff	31	64	59	44	25	**39**
Burba,Dave	48	67	53	41	35	**38**
Garcia,Rosman			100	33	40	**38**
Orosco,Jesse	61	1	111	50	38	**38**
Levrault,Allen	59	55	22	26	49	**37**
Bernero,Adam		61	31	58	27	**36**
Heredia,Felix	57	65	26	35	34	**36**
Reith,Brian		56	26	38	48	**35**
Fiore,Tony	41	28	50	35	31	**35**
Ford,Matt					27	**35**
Hackman,Luther	38	27	49	31	39	**35**
Bump,Nate	33	20	18	52	44	**34**
Tucker,T.J.	50	-17	21	41	40	**34**
Roberts,Willis	-0	4	44	53	22	**33**
Mercker,Kent	24	-16		-21	58	**33**
Santiago,Jose	7	48	48	50	24	**33**
Guthrie,Mark	38	56	77	95	20	**32**
Powell,Jay	84	40	46	26	22	**32**
Zerbe,Chad	28	36	45	44	25	**32**
Glover,Gary	66	23	53	18	35	**32**
Hernandez,Roberto	97	69	48	63	19	**32**
Condrey,Clayton		26	32	39	32	**31**
Munro,Peter	49	41	19	76	10	**31**

RAR	Pos	'04Prj
Bonds,Barry	LF	98.5
Helton,Todd	1B	97.0
Pujols,Albert	RF	93.1
Rodriguez,Alex	SS	92.5
Hudson,Tim	SP	84.0
Ramirez,Manny	LF	80.3
Halladay,Roy	SP	70.9
Guerrero,Vladimir	RF	70.2
Beltran,Carlos	CF	69.8
Prior,Mark	SP	69.4
Rolen,Scott	3B	68.8
Martinez,Pedro	SP	68.4
Mussina,Mike	SP	68.1
Schmidt,Jason	SP	67.5
Loaiza,Esteban	SP	66.9
Garciaparra,Nomar	SS	66.5
Vazquez,Javier	SP	64.6
Ordonez,Magglio	RF	64.4
Thome,Jim	1B	63.8
Vidro,Jose	2B	63.7
Lowell,Mike	3B	63.2
Renteria,Edgar	SS	62.6
Tejada,Miguel	SS	62.4
Sheffield,Gary	RF	61.3
Jones,Chipper	LF	61.1
Oswalt,Roy	SP	60.2
Wells,Vernon	CF	59.5
Giambi,Jason	1B	59.0
Giles,Brian	LF	58.9
Hernandez,Livan	SP	58.7
Edmonds,Jim	CF	57.4
Wood,Kerry	SP	57.4
Colon,Bartolo	SP	57.2
Berkman,Lance	LF	57.1
Mulder,Mark	SP	56.8
Sosa,Sammy	RF	56.7
Mueller,Bill	3B	56.6
Chavez,Eric	3B	56.3
Delgado,Carlos	1B	56.3
Cabrera,Orlando	SS	55.9
Kent,Jeff	2B	54.9
Boone,Bret	2B	54.8
Brown,Kevin	SP	54.6
Huff,Aubrey	RF	54.1
Zambrano,Carlos	SP	53.0
Ortiz,David	1B	52.7
Contreras,Jose	SP	52.4
Beckett,Josh	SP	52.2
Giles,Marcus	2B	52.0
Schilling,Curt	SP	51.8
Santana,Johan	SP	51.6
Wilson,Preston	CF	51.5
Nixon,Trot	RF	51.4
Millwood,Kevin	SP	51.3
Zito,Barry	SP	51.2
Pineiro,Joel	SP	50.7
Webb,Brandon	SP	50.6
Jones,Andruw	CF	50.4
Radke,Brad	SP	50.0
Gonzalez,Luis	LF	48.4
Soriano,Alfonso	2B	47.7
Posada,Jorge	CA	47.6
Buehrle,Mark	SP	47.6
Ponson,Sidney	SP	46.9
Sexson,Richie	1B	46.8
Rodriguez,Ivan	CA	46.8
Blalock,Hank	3B	46.7
Bagwell,Jeff	1B	46.5
Hinske,Eric	3B	46.3
Pettitte,Andy	SP	45.9
Padilla,Vicente	SP	45.8
Maddux,Greg	SP	45.8
Morris,Matt	SP	45.8
Williams,Jerome	SP	44.9
Piazza,Mike	CA	44.9
Lopez,Javy	CA	44.2
Abreu,Bobby	RF	44.0
Nomo,Hideo	SP	43.4
Green,Shawn	RF	43.3
Ramirez,Aramis	3B	42.7
Leiter,Al	SP	42.5
Lee,Carlos	LF	42.5
Thomson,John	SP	42.3
Washburn,Jarrod	SP	42.3
Johnson,Randy	SP	42.2
Wakefield,Tim	SP	41.9
Walker,Todd	2B	41.8
Sheets,Ben	SP	41.7
Alvarez,Wilson	SP	41.7
Furcal,Rafael	SS	41.2
Lawrence,Brian	SP	41.0
Redman,Mark	SP	41.0
Penny,Brad	SP	41.0
Thomas,Frank	1B	40.9
Klesko,Ryan	1B	39.8
Wells,Kip	SP	39.7
Lieberthal,Mike	CA	39.0
Floyd,Cliff	LF	38.7
Lowe,Derek	SP	38.7
May,Darrell	SP	38.7
Randa,Joe	3B	38.4
Moyer,Jamie	SP	38.3
Gonzalez,Juan	RF	37.7
Hidalgo,Richard	RF	37.6
Franklin,Ryan	SP	37.5
Lopez,Rodrigo	SP	37.5
Anderson,Garret	LF	37.4
Perez,Odalis	SP	37.3
Willis,Dontrelle	SP	37.3
Ohka,Tomokazu	SP	37.3
Miller,Wade	SP	37.3
Polanco,Placido	2B	37.2
Loretta,Mark	2B	37.2
Jimenez,D'Angelo	2B	36.9
Harden,Rich	SP	36.7
Stewart,Shannon	LF	36.6
Ensberg,Morgan	3B	36.4
Ortiz,Russ	SP	36.1
Clement,Matt	SP	36.1
Milton,Eric	SP	35.9
Lilly,Ted	SP	35.9
Varitek,Jason	CA	35.6
Redding,Tim	SP	35.3
Lackey,John	SP	35.1
Finley,Steve	CF	35.0
Johnson,Nick	1B	34.9
Pavano,Carl	SP	34.9
Kim,Byung-Hyun	SP	34.8
Gagne,Eric	RP	34.7
Alfonzo,Edgardo	3B	34.6
Armas Jr.,Tony	SP	34.4
Jeter,Derek	SS	34.3
Koskie,Corey	3B	34.3
Pierzynski,A.J.	CA	34.2
LeCroy,Matt	CA	33.9
Garcia,Freddy	SP	33.9
Myers,Brett	SP	33.7
Suppan,Jeff	SP	33.6
Shields,Scot	SP	33.6
Palmeiro,Rafael	1B	33.3
Martinez,Edgar	DH	33.3
Ibanez,Raul	LF	33.1
Aurilia,Rich	SS	33.0
Bradley,Milton	CF	32.7
Durham,Ray	2B	32.6
Trachsel,Steve	SP	32.5
Williams,Bernie	CF	32.4
Kendall,Jason	CA	32.0
Glaus,Troy	3B	31.9
Hawkins,LaTroy	RP	31.6
Griffey Jr.,Ken	CF	31.6
Johnson,Jason	SP	31.4
Lidle,Cory	SP	31.4
Kotsay,Mark	CF	31.2
Molina,Ben	CA	30.8
Affeldt,Jeremy	SP	30.7
Sweeney,Mike	1B	30.6
Young,Dmitri	LF	30.5
Soriano,Rafael	RP	30.4
Boone,Aaron	3B	30.2
Hampton,Mike	SP	30.1
Williams,Woody	SP	30.1
Wagner,Billy	RP	29.9
Gonzalez,Jeremi	RP	29.5
Jenkins,Geoff	LF	29.4
Fullmer,Brad	DH	29.3
Batista,Miguel	SP	29.3
Matsui,Hideki	LF	29.3
Nevin,Phil	1B	29.2
Cintron,Alex	SS	29.1
Mondesi,Raul	RF	29.1
Sabathia,C.C.	SP	29.0
Salmon,Tim	RF	28.9
Gibbons,Jay	RF	28.4
Lee,Derrek	1B	28.3
Hudson,Orlando	2B	28.3
Mientkiewicz,Doug	1B	28.2
Glavine,Tom	SP	28.1
Drew,J.D.	RF	28.0
Foulke,Keith	RP	28.0
Marte,Damaso	RP	28.0
Betancourt,Rafael	RP	28.0
Rivera,Mariano	RP	27.9
Spiezio,Scott	1B	27.9
Garland,Jon	SP	27.8
Eaton,Adam	SP	27.7
Kennedy,Adam	2B	27.6
Dotel,Octavio	RP	27.5
Acevedo,Jose	SP	27.2
Hunter,Torii	CF	27.1
Young,Mike	2B	27.0
Seo,Jae	SP	26.9
Weber,Ben	RP	26.8
Bradford,Chad	RP	26.7
Cordero,Francisco	RP	26.7
Barrett,Michael	CA	26.6
Ortiz,Ramon	SP	26.6
Burroughs,Sean	3B	26.6
Everett,Carl	CF	26.5
Martinez,Victor	CA	26.5
Castillo,Luis	2B	26.5
Segui,David	DH	26.4
LoDuca,Paul	CA	26.4
Lohse,Kyle	SP	26.2
Anderson,Brian	SP	26.2
Rollins,Jimmy	SS	26.1
Lugo,Julio	SS	26.1
Weaver,Jeff	SP	25.7
Crede,Joe	3B	25.7
Perez,Oliver	SP	25.6
Durazo,Erubiel	1B	25.5
Donnelly,Brendan	RP	25.5
Teixeira,Mark	1B	25.5
Lofton,Kenny	CF	25.4
Alou,Moises	LF	25.3
Pierre,Juan	CF	25.2
Ainsworth,Kurt	SP	25.2
Cruz,Juan	RP	25.2
Stairs,Matt	RF	25.1
Mota,Guillermo	RP	25.1
Hairston Jr.,Jerry	2B	24.6
Rueter,Kirk	SP	24.4
Riske,David	RP	24.3
Cornejo,Nate	SP	24.2
Zambrano,Victor	SP	24.2
Hernandez,Ramon	CA	24.1
Rhodes,Arthur	RP	24.1
Benitez,Armando	RP	24.1
Konerko,Paul	1B	23.9
Escobar,Kelvim	RP	23.8
Schneider,Brian	CA	23.8
Damon,Johnny	CF	23.8
Millar,Kevin	1B	23.7
Catalanotto,Frank	LF	23.6
Ishii,Kazuhisa	SP	23.6
Uribe,Juan	SS	23.6
Reyes,Jose	SS	23.2
Towers,Josh	SP	23.1
Lee,Cliff	SP	23.1
Hasegawa,Shige	RP	23.1
Payton,Jay	LF	23.1
Moeller,Chad	CA	23.0
Berroa,Angel	SS	22.9
Wolf,Randy	SP	22.9
Byrd,Marlon	CF	22.8
Johnson,Charles	CA	22.8
Quantrill,Paul	RP	22.7
Walker,Larry	RF	22.7
Utley,Chase	2B	22.3
Sanders,Reggie	RF	22.1
Rodriguez,Francisco	RP	22.1
Hall,Toby	CA	22.1
Mateo,Julio	RP	22.0
Gordon,Tom	RP	21.9
Lopez,Aquilino	RP	21.8
Olerud,John	1B	21.8
Belliard,Ron	2B	21.8
Alomar,Roberto	2B	21.7
Melhuse,Adam	CA	21.6
Urbina,Ugueth	RP	21.6
Isringhausen,Jason	RP	21.6
Harang,Aaron	SP	21.6
Suzuki,Ichiro	RF	21.6
Villarreal,Oscar	RP	21.4
Herges,Matt	RP	21.4
Jones,Jacque	LF	21.4
Spivey,Junior	2B	21.3
Myers,Greg	CA	21.1
Ramirez,Erasmo	RP	20.8
Timlin,Mike	RP	20.8
Kershner,Jason	RP	20.8
Anderson,Marlon	2B	20.8
Michaels,Jason	LF	20.7
Rivas,Luis	2B	20.6
Butler,Brent	2B	20.5
Guardado,Eddie	RP	20.5
Bard,Josh	CA	20.5
Wilson,Craig	RF	20.4
Borowski,Joe	RP	20.4
Colbrunn,Greg	1B	20.4
Winn,Randy	LF	20.4
Figueroa,Nelson	SP	20.4
Phelps,Josh	DH	20.3
Worrell,Tim	RP	20.3
Westbrook,Jake	SP	20.3
Munson,Eric	3B	20.3
Ross,David	CA	20.3
Adams,Terry	RP	20.2

RAR	Pos	'04Prj	RAR	Pos	'04Prj	RAR	Pos	'04Prj	RAR	Pos	'04Prj
Smoltz,John	RP	20.2	Machado,Robert	CA	16.8	Benard,Marvin	CF	14.0	Ludwick,Ryan	RF	11.9
Lidge,Brad	RP	20.2	Fox,Chad	RP	16.8	Conine,Jeff	1B	14.0	Stark,Dennis	SP	11.9
Davis,Jason	SP	20.2	Houston,Tyler	3B	16.8	Ellis,Mark	2B	13.9	Davis,Doug	SP	11.9
Cameron,Mike	CF	20.2	Relaford,Desi	2B	16.8	Gonzalez,Alex	SS	13.9	Haren,Danny	SP	11.9
Ojeda,Miguel	CA	20.2	Williamson,Scott	RP	16.8	DeRosa,Mark	2B	13.8	Lockhart,Keith	2B	11.9
Lee,Travis	1B	20.1	Ayala,Luis	RP	16.8	Galarraga,Andres	1B	13.8	Corey,Mark	RP	11.9
Rivera,Juan	CF	20.1	Osuna,Antonio	RP	16.8	Kearns,Austin	RF	13.8	Almonte,Erick	SS	11.9
Vargas,Claudio	SP	20.0	Sasaki,Kazuhiro	RP	16.8	Trammell,Bubba	DH	13.8	Gobble,Jimmy	SP	11.9
Benson,Kris	SP	20.0	Hitchcock,Sterling	SP	16.8	Martinez,Tino	1B	13.7	Schoeneweis,Scott	SP	11.9
Santiago,Benito	CA	19.9	Ginter,Keith	2B	16.7	Wilson,Tom	CA	13.6	Goodwin,Tom	CF	11.9
Bell,David	3B	19.8	Miller,Corky	CA	16.7	Santos,Angel	2B	13.6	Gil,Benji	2B	11.8
Mench,Kevin	LF	19.7	Valverde,Jose	RP	16.6	Werth,Jayson	RF	13.6	Brower,Jim	RP	11.8
Grudzielanek,Mark	2B	19.5	Meadows,Brian	RP	16.6	Rincon,Juan	RP	13.5	Reitsma,Chris	RP	11.8
Graffanino,Tony	SS	19.5	Linebrink,Scott	RP	16.6	Harper,Travis	RP	13.5	Mordecai,Mike	SS	11.8
Bigbie,Larry	LF	19.5	Scutaro,Marcos	2B	16.4	Grieve,Ben	DH	13.5	Ryan,B.J.	RP	11.8
Pratt,Todd	CA	19.4	Lawton,Matt	LF	16.4	Everett,Adam	SS	13.5	Mayne,Brent	CA	11.7
Burks,Ellis	DH	19.3	Giambi,Jeremy	DH	16.3	Vitiello,Joe	LF	13.5	Hyzdu,Adam	CF	11.7
Rodriguez,Felix	RP	19.3	Kennedy,Joe	RP	16.3	Ordonez,Rey	SS	13.4	Stinnett,Kelly	CA	11.6
Larson,Brandon	3B	19.3	Biggio,Craig	CF	16.3	German,Franklyn	RP	13.4	Hinch,A.J.	CA	11.6
Norton,Greg	3B	19.3	McMillon,Billy	LF	16.3	Valentin,Javier	CA	13.3	Perez,Eduardo	RF	11.6
Cust,Jack	DH	19.3	Woodward,Chris	SS	16.3	Hammonds,Jeffrey	LF	13.3	Wilson,Jack	SS	11.6
Bellhorn,Mark	3B	19.2	Hammock,Robby	CA	16.2	Levine,Al	RP	13.3	Feliz,Pedro	3B	11.6
Farnsworth,Kyle	RP	19.2	Vazquez,Ramon	SS	16.2	Wilson,Dan	CA	13.3	Matos,Julius	3B	11.5
Stanford,Jason	SP	19.1	Martinez,Ramon	2B	16.1	Higginson,Bobby	RF	13.2	Riggs,Adam	1B	11.4
Robertson,Nate	SP	19.1	Blum,Geoff	3B	15.9	Heredia,Felix	RP	13.2	Lopez,Mendy	1B	11.4
Fossum,Casey	SP	19.1	Bautista,Danny	RF	15.9	Miceli,Dan	RP	13.2	Ford,Lew	CF	11.4
DuBose,Eric	SP	19.1	Meche,Gil	RP	15.9	Shuey,Paul	RP	13.2	Burrell,Pat	LF	11.4
Laird,Gerald	CA	19.1	Dye,Jermaine	RF	15.8	Witasick,Jay	RP	13.2	Garcia,Karim	RF	11.4
Jimenez,Jose	RP	19.0	Wilkerson,Brad	LF	15.7	Feliciano,Pedro	RP	13.2	Jackson,Damian	2B	11.3
Weathers,Dave	RP	19.0	Redmond,Mike	CA	15.7	Parrish,John	RP	13.2	Wilson,Vance	CA	11.3
Castro,Ramon	CA	19.0	Walker,Jamie	RP	15.7	Hammond,Chris	RP	13.2	Mora,Melvin	LF	11.2
Rogers,Kenny	SP	19.0	Remlinger,Mike	RP	15.6	Politte,Cliff	RP	13.2	Lopez,Felipe	SS	11.2
Young,Eric	2B	18.8	Ledee,Ricky	CF	15.6	Shouse,Brian	RP	13.2	Bauer,Rick	RP	11.1
Dessens,Elmer	SP	18.8	Ligtenberg,Kerry	RP	15.6	Embree,Alan	RP	13.2	Buchanan,Brian	RF	11.1
Ramirez,Horacio	SP	18.8	Fuentes,Brian	RP	15.5	Van Poppel,Todd	RP	13.2	Morban,Jose	SS	11.1
Day,Zach	SP	18.8	Traber,Billy	SP	15.5	Rivera,Mike	CA	13.1	Richard,Chris	LF	11.1
Burkett,John	SP	18.6	Vizquel,Omar	SS	15.5	Snyder,Kyle	SP	13.1	Patterson,John	SP	11.1
Larkin,Barry	SS	18.6	Riedling,John	RP	15.4	McCarty,Dave	LF	13.0	Good,Andrew	SP	11.1
Franco,Julio	1B	18.3	Looper,Braden	RP	15.4	Helling,Rick	RP	13.0	Cairo,Miguel	2B	11.1
Telemaco,Amaury	SP	18.3	Stynes,Chris	3B	15.3	Percival,Troy	RP	13.0	Appier,Kevin	SP	11.0
Guillen,Carlos	SS	18.2	Phillips,Jason L.	1B	15.2	Gomez,Chris	2B	13.0	Daal,Omar	SP	11.0
Grissom,Marquis	CF	18.2	D'Amico,Jeff	SP	15.2	Punto,Nick	SS	12.9	Grimsley,Jason	RP	11.0
Koplove,Mike	RP	18.2	Patterson,Corey	CF	15.0	Fordyce,Brook	CA	12.9	Reed,Steve	RP	11.0
Beck,Rod	RP	18.2	Rowand,Aaron	CF	15.0	Zeile,Todd	3B	12.8	de los Santos,Valerio	RP	11.0
Mantei,Matt	RP	18.2	Cuddyer,Michael	RF	14.8	Surhoff,B.J.	LF	12.8	Wheeler,Dan	RP	11.0
Maroth,Mike	SP	18.2	Peavy,Jake	SP	14.8	Wilson,Paul	SP	12.8	Stanton,Mike	RP	11.0
Cressend,Jack	RP	18.2	Hafner,Travis	1B	14.8	Berg,Dave	2B	12.7	Rios,Armando	CF	10.9
Branyan,Russ	3B	18.1	Shumpert,Terry	DH	14.8	Daubach,Brian	1B	12.7	Molina,Jose	CA	10.9
Julio,Jorge	RP	18.1	Carter,Lance	RP	14.7	Greene,Todd	CA	12.7	Guiel,Aaron	RF	10.9
Mirabelli,Doug	CA	18.1	Torres,Salomon	RP	14.7	Hollandsworth,Todd	LF	12.7	Bennett,Gary	CA	10.9
Gallo,Mike	RP	18.0	Burnett,A.J.	SP	14.7	LaRue,Jason	CA	12.7	Clayton,Royce	SS	10.9
Cormier,Rheal	RP	18.0	Rusch,Glendon	SP	14.7	Matthews Jr.,Gary	CF	12.7	Palmer,Dean	DH	10.9
Hundley,Todd	CA	17.9	Restovich,Mike	RF	14.6	Olivo,Miguel	CA	12.7	Sauerbeck,Scott	RP	10.8
Rincon,Ricardo	RP	17.9	King,Ray	RP	14.6	Gutierrez,Ricky	SS	12.6	Duckworth,Brandon	SP	10.7
Nathan,Joe	RP	17.8	Kline,Steve	RP	14.6	Hocking,Denny	2B	12.6	Freel,Ryan	CF	10.7
White,Rondell	LF	17.8	Eischen,Joey	RP	14.6	Pena,Wily Mo	CF	12.6	Reyes,Rene	RF	10.7
Miller,Damian	CA	17.6	Cunnane,Will	RP	14.6	Davis,Ben	CA	12.6	DeJean,Mike	RP	10.7
Monroe,Craig	LF	17.6	Stewart,Scott	RP	14.6	Widger,Chris	CA	12.5	Reed,Rick	SP	10.7
Gerut,Jody	RF	17.5	Villafuerte,Brandon	RP	14.6	Piatt,Adam	LF	12.4	Ward,Daryle	1B	10.6
Gonzalez,Alex S.	SS	17.5	Baez,Danys	RP	14.6	Vizcaino,Jose	SS	12.4	Stone,Ricky	RP	10.6
Wells,David	SP	17.4	Flaherty,John	CA	14.5	Gil,Geronimo	CA	12.3	Bale,John	RP	10.6
Beltre,Adrian	3B	17.3	Leskanic,Curtis	RP	14.4	Merloni,Lou	3B	12.3	Casey,Sean	1B	10.6
Zaun,Gregg	CA	17.2	Lyon,Brandon	RP	14.4	Perez,Antonio	2B	12.3	Groom,Buddy	RP	10.6
Halama,John	RP	17.2	Vizcaino,Luis	RP	14.4	Sandberg,Jared	3B	12.3	Laker,Tim	CA	10.6
Tejera,Michael	RP	17.1	Roberts,Brian	2B	14.4	DiFelice,Mike	CA	12.3	Borchard,Joe	CF	10.5
Hermanson,Dustin	SP	17.1	Torrealba,Yorvit	CA	14.3	Sele,Aaron	SP	12.2	Baerga,Carlos	1B	10.5
Estalella,Bobby	CA	17.1	Dreifort,Darren	SP	14.2	Bruntlett,Eric	SS	12.2	Jones,Jason	LF	10.4
Estrada,Johnny	CA	17.1	Hodges,Trey	RP	14.2	Veres,Dave	RP	12.2	Petrick,Ben	LF	10.3
Helms,Wes	3B	17.0	Saarloos,Kirk	RP	14.2	Romero,J.C.	RP	12.1	Stephenson,Garrett	SP	10.3
Kolb,Danny	RP	17.0	Morris,Warren	2B	14.2	Boyd,Jason	RP	12.1	Velandia,Jorge	SS	10.3
Hoffman,Trevor	RP	17.0	Karros,Eric	1B	14.2	Koch,Billy	RP	12.1	Bako,Paul	CA	10.3
Alomar Jr.,Sandy	CA	16.9	Silva,Carlos	RP	14.1	Kieschnick,Brooks	RF	12.1	Bloomquist,Willie	3B	10.3
Kielty,Bobby	RF	16.9	Menechino,Frank	2B	14.1	Sweeney,Mark	RF	12.0	Garcia,Danny	2B	10.3
Guillen,Jose	RF	16.8	Clark,Howie	2B	14.1	Gonzalez,Wiki	CA	12.0	Mabry,John	RF	10.3
Valentin,Jose	SS	16.8	Perez,Tomas	3B	14.0	Patterson,Danny	RP	12.0	Duncan,Jeff	CF	10.2

Runs Above Replacement

RAR	Pos	'04Prj	RAR	Pos	'04Prj	RAR	Pos	'04Prj	RAR	Pos	'04Prj
Harris,Willie	CF	10.2	Kata,Matt	2B	8.2	Vaughn,Mo	1B	6.0	Almanza,Armando	RP	2.7
Carroll,Jamey	3B	10.2	Graves,Danny	RP	8.2	Ventura,Robin	1B	6.0	Bierbrodt,Nick	RP	2.7
Hansen,Dave	1B	10.1	Villone,Ron	SP	8.2	Acevedo,Juan	RP	5.9	Loux,Shane	SP	2.7
Guzman,Cristian	SS	10.1	Sadler,Donnie	3B	8.2	Roberts,Willis	RP	5.9	Klassen,Danny	3B	2.6
Figgins,Chone	CF	10.1	Bonderman,Jeremy	SP	8.2	Spurling,Chris	RP	5.9	Quevedo,Ruben	SP	2.5
Cirillo,Jeff	3B	10.1	Dellucci,David	RF	8.2	Delgado,Wilson	3B	5.9	Obermueller,Wes	SP	2.5
Sierra,Ruben	LF	10.1	Blanco,Henry	CA	8.2	Hackman,Luther	RP	5.9	Mesa,Jose	RP	2.5
Reboulet,Jeff	2B	10.1	Clark,Tony	1B	8.0	Valdes,Ismael	SP	5.8	Munro,Peter	RP	2.5
Christenson,Ryan	CF	10.1	Taylor,Reggie	CF	8.0	Wright,Jamey	SP	5.8	Crawford,Carl	LF	2.4
Cruz,Enrique	SS	10.1	Hernandez,Jose	3B	8.0	Overbay,Lyle	1B	5.8	Orosco,Jesse	RP	2.4
Perez,Eddie	CA	10.0	DaVanon,Jeff	RF	8.0	Howard,Ben	SP	5.8	Yan,Esteban	RP	2.4
Crisp,Coco	CF	9.9	Plesac,Dan	RP	7.8	Fiore,Tony	RP	5.8	Hatteberg,Scott	1B	2.4
Santiago,Jose	RP	9.9	Mateo,Ruben	RF	7.7	Chavez,Endy	CF	5.7	Anderson,Matt	RP	2.3
Glover,Gary	RP	9.9	Peralta,Jhonny	SS	7.6	Pena,Carlos	1B	5.7	Bynum,Mike	RP	2.2
Callaway,Mickey	RP	9.9	Singleton,Chris	CF	7.6	Strickland,Scott	RP	5.7	Estrella,Leo	RP	2.2
Mears,Chris	RP	9.9	Nunez,Abraham	2B	7.6	Tam,Jeff	RP	5.6	Powell,Jay	RP	2.1
Mendez,Donaldo	SS	9.9	Spencer,Shane	LF	7.6	Cook,Aaron	RP	5.5	Calloway,Ron	LF	2.1
Easley,Damion	3B	9.9	Martin,Tom	RP	7.5	McEwing,Joe	2B	5.5	Bragg,Darren	RF	2.1
Womack,Tony	SS	9.8	Gryboski,Kevin	RP	7.5	Reese,Pokey	2B	5.4	Mackowiak,Rob	RF	2.0
Leon,Jose	3B	9.8	Dickey,R.A.	RP	7.5	Hendrickson,Mark	RP	5.4	Mulholland,Terry	RP	1.9
Taguchi,So	CF	9.8	Matheny,Mike	CA	7.5	Zerbe,Chad	RP	5.3	Bell,Rob	SP	1.9
Eyre,Scott	RP	9.8	Inge,Brandon	CA	7.4	Franco,Matt	1B	5.2	Hall,Bill	2B	1.8
Harris,Lenny	3B	9.7	Escobar,Alex	RF	7.4	Podsednik,Scott	CF	5.2	Myers,Mike	RP	1.7
Wilson,Enrique	SS	9.7	Garcia,Rosman	RP	7.4	Ford,Matt	RP	5.1	Rolls,Damian	3B	1.7
Nix,Laynce	RF	9.7	Banks,Brian	LF	7.4	Wright,Danny	RP	5.1	Hernandez,Roberto	RP	1.5
White,Gabe	RP	9.6	Lopez,Javier	RP	7.3	Lima,Jose	SP	5.1	Carrasco,D.J.	RP	1.5
White,Rick	RP	9.6	Calero,Kiko	RP	7.3	Heilman,Aaron	SP	5.0	Clark,Brady	RF	1.4
Sullivan,Scott	RP	9.6	Matthews,Mike	RP	7.3	Ritchie,Todd	SP	5.0	Baldelli,Rocco	CF	1.4
Smith,Mark	LF	9.6	Palmeiro,Orlando	RF	7.3	Reynolds,Shane	SP	5.0	Fernandez,Jared	SP	1.3
Gaudin,Chad	RP	9.6	Fox,Andy	2B	7.3	Colome,Jesus	RP	5.0	Brazelton,Dewan	SP	1.1
Mecir,Jim	RP	9.6	O'Leary,Troy	LF	7.3	Wright,Jaret	RP	4.9	Park,Chan Ho	SP	1.0
Moss,Damian	SP	9.5	Hart,Bo	2B	7.2	Reith,Brian	RP	4.9	Foppert,Jesse	SP	1.0
Cruz,Jose	RF	9.5	Henderson,Rickey	LF	7.2	Almonte,Hector	RP	4.9	McDonald,John	2B	1.0
Martin,Al	DH	9.5	Castro,Juan	2B	7.2	Cordova,Marty	DH	4.9	Fick,Robert	1B	0.9
Benoit,Joaquin	SP	9.5	Anderson,Jason	RP	7.2	Franklin,Wayne	RP	4.8	Reyes,Carlos	SP	0.7
Counsell,Craig	3B	9.4	Jones,Todd	RP	7.2	Randolph,Steve	RP	4.8	Long,Terrence	LF	0.6
Simontacchi,Jason	RP	9.4	MacDougal,Mike	RP	7.1	Bong,Jung	RP	4.7	Wellemeyer,Todd	RP	0.5
Tucker,T.J.	RP	9.4	Rivera,Carlos	1B	7.1	Biddle,Rocky	RP	4.7	Choi,Hee Seop	1B	0.5
Tavarez,Julian	RP	9.4	Barajas,Rod	CA	7.1	Knotts,Gary	SP	4.6	Nady,Xavier	RF	0.5
Osik,Keith	CA	9.4	Sosa,Jorge	SP	7.1	Hentgen,Pat	SP	4.6	Brown,Dee	LF	0.4
Nelson,Jeff	RP	9.4	Castilla,Vinny	3B	7.0	Haynes,Jimmy	SP	4.6	Jennings,Jason	SP	0.3
Halter,Shane	3B	9.4	Kingsale,Gene	CF	6.9	Marquis,Jason	SP	4.6	Hernandez,Runelvys	SP	0.2
Eckstein,David	SS	9.3	Coomer,Ron	1B	6.9	Miller,Trever	RP	4.5	Bernero,Adam	RP	-0.1
Cordero,Wil	1B	9.2	Izturis,Cesar	SS	6.9	Voyles,Brad	RP	4.5	Chacon,Shawn	SP	-0.1
Mahay,Ron	RP	9.2	Olmedo,Ranier	SS	6.8	Batista,Tony	3B	4.5	Estes,Shawn	SP	-0.1
Robertson,Jeriome	RP	9.1	Wunsch,Kelly	RP	6.8	Quinlan,Robb	1B	4.5	Fogg,Josh	SP	-0.1
Thames,Marcus	RF	9.0	Wigginton,Ty	3B	6.7	Marrero,Eli	RF	4.4	Lewis,Colby	SP	-0.2
Snow,J.T.	1B	9.0	Cabrera,Miguel	LF	6.7	Franco,John	RP	4.3	Erstad,Darin	CF	-0.2
Febles,Carlos	2B	9.0	Roberts,Dave	CF	6.7	Astacio,Pedro	SP	4.2	Condrey,Clayton	RP	-0.3
Matos,Luis	CF	9.0	Sanchez,Rey	SS	6.7	Mercker,Kent	RP	4.1	Neagle,Denny	RP	-0.4
Holmes,Darren	RP	8.9	Burba,Dave	RP	6.6	Guthrie,Mark	RP	4.1	Mounce,Tony	SP	-0.5
Smitherman,Steve	LF	8.9	Perry,Herbert	1B	6.6	Robinson,Kerry	RF	4.1	Fassero,Jeff	RP	-0.7
Cabrera,Jolbert	2B	8.9	Cora,Alex	2B	6.6	Tucker,Michael	RF	4.1	Sanchez,Alex	CF	-0.8
Mateo,Henry	2B	8.9	Gonzalez,Raul	LF	6.6	Oliver,Darren	SP	4.0	Cruz,Deivi	SS	-1.1
Kapler,Gabe	RF	8.9	Owens,Eric	CF	6.6	Sparks,Steve	RP	3.9	Abbott,Paul	SP	-1.3
Perez,Neifi	2B	8.8	Diaz,Einar	CA	6.5	Conti,Jason	RF	3.8	Encarnacion,Juan	RF	-1.5
Shinjo,Tsuyoshi	CF	8.8	Roa,Joe	RP	6.5	Infante,Omar	SS	3.8	McClung,Seth	RP	-1.7
Byrnes,Eric	CF	8.8	McLemore,Mark	SS	6.5	Jordan,Brian	LF	3.7	Standridge,Jason	SP	-1.7
Christiansen,Jason	RP	8.7	Blake,Casey	3B	6.5	Vina,Fernando	2B	3.7	Ledezma,Wil	RP	-1.7
Rodriguez,Ricardo	SP	8.7	Lincoln,Mike	RP	6.3	Alfonseca,Antonio	RP	3.6	Harvey,Ken	1B	-1.9
Phillips,Brandon	2B	8.6	Merced,Orlando	RF	6.3	Williams,Mike	RP	3.6	Sturtze,Tanyon	RP	-2.1
Tatis,Fernando	3B	8.6	Walker,Pete	RP	6.3	Lloyd,Graeme	RP	3.6	Beimel,Joe	RP	-2.4
Kieschnick,Brooks	RP	8.5	Roney,Matt	RP	6.3	Driskill,Travis	RP	3.5	Dempster,Ryan	SP	-3.1
Phelps,Tommy	RP	8.5	Ausmus,Brad	CA	6.3	Cruz,Nelson	RP	3.5	Backe,Brandon	RP	-3.3
Walbeck,Matt	CA	8.5	Torres,Andres	CF	6.2	Spooneybarger,Tim	RP	3.4	Cedeno,Roger	RF	-3.7
Dunn,Adam	LF	8.5	Asencio,Miguel	SP	6.2	Bump,Nate	RP	3.4	Wooten,Shawn	1B	-3.7
Boehringer,Brian	RP	8.5	Vander Wal,John	RF	6.2	Jarvis,Kevin	SP	3.4	Johnson,Reed	RF	-4.3
Cerda,Jaime	RP	8.5	Redman,Tike	CF	6.2	Hillenbrand,Shea	1B	3.1	Kinney,Matt	SP	-4.5
Carrasco,Hector	RP	8.4	McGriff,Fred	1B	6.2	Oropesa,Eddie	RP	2.9	Drese,Ryan	SP	-4.5
Tomko,Brett	SP	8.4	Simon,Randall	1B	6.2	Levrault,Allen	RP	2.9	Burnitz,Jeromy	LF	-4.7
Liefer,Jeff	CF	8.4	Wendell,Turk	RP	6.1	Wilson,Kris	RP	2.9	Macias,Jose	LF	-4.8
Speier,Justin	RP	8.4	Eldred,Cal	RP	6.1	Broussard,Ben	1B	2.8	Anderson,Jimmy	SP	-5.4
Guzman,Edwards	3B	8.4	Kinkade,Mike	LF	6.1	Perez,Timo	LF	2.8	Witt,Kevin	1B	-5.7
Mendoza,Ramiro	RP	8.3	Hunter,Brian L.	RF	6.1	Glanville,Doug	CF	2.8	George,Chris	SP	-6.2
Mohr,Dustan	RF	8.3	Fultz,Aaron	RP	6.0	Neu,Mike	RP	2.8	Santiago,Ramon	SS	-6.7
Tyner,Jason	RF	8.3	McCracken,Quinton	RF	6.0	Smith,Dan	RP	2.7	Elarton,Scott	SP	-11.8

VI. 2003 Greatest Hits
Beyond the Numbers: Logic, Cynicism and Faith

Beyond this book, I also write a weekly column for about 10 months of the year that appears on BaseballHQ.com. Each week, I get to conduct new research, rehash old research and occasionally get up on my well-worn soapbox. A few times last year, I became downright curmudgeonly.

The problem is, at Baseball HQ, these essays have a life of about three weeks and then drop off the menu, disappearing forever into the far reaches of cyberspace. For the real good stuff, this is unfortunate, because I hate to expend all that effort for a shelf life of three weeks. For the not so good stuff, three weeks is often about 22 days too long.

But here we have this nice little book with a shelf life of more than three weeks. In fact, some people keep these books for many years.

Anyway, some of the best columns from 2003 appear here. For those of you who have never experienced the joys and wonders of a subscription to Baseball HQ, these essays should provide you with some exposure to what you've been missing. For those of you who already subscribe to Baseball HQ, don't think of this as rehashed content. All of these essays have been updated based on subsequent events; at minimum, all are worth re-reading.

Enjoy.

Addressing Deficiencies

At our 2001 fantasy baseball symposium at the Arizona Fall League, I offered up a little exercise as fodder for discussion... For the following player, what is the most reasonable projection for Year #5?

Batting Average

Year #	vs LHP	vs RHP
======	=====	======
1	.337	.293
2	.282	.306
3	.245	.314
4	.233	.296
5	???	???

Options:

A	.228	.290
B	.266	.290
C	.228	.265

The point of the exercise was to project out this player's batting average splits, given a consistent decline in his ability to hit left-handers. In option A, the trend of declining performance versus left-handed pitchers continues. Option B says that the trend is reversed. The final option is that the snowballing effect of the trend exacerbates and impacts his BA versus right-handed pitchers as well. Which is the most likely course of events?

As it turns out, this is less of an exercise in statistics than it is a study of logic. There is no real right or wrong answer because any of the options could happen. However, what are the odds that a batter, who has seen a three-year freefall in his ability to hit southpaws, can find a way to suddenly turn it around?

My initial thought was that, given no other changes (coaching, conditioning, etc.), the odds of a rebound are low. Why? Because if there was to be a change in fortunes, why did it not occur earlier? He must have realized that there was a problem back in year #2, and certainly by year #3. Why would he still not have addressed it in year #4? As such, there has to be a basic flaw that he cannot correct, and so, my choice for Year #5 would be either A or C.

This case of simple logic led to the following conclusion...

The odds of a player correcting a deficiency decrease with each year that he allows that deficiency to exist.

It is a statement that makes perfect sense to me. Unfortunately, this type of hypothesis is tough to prove because there are so many variables that go into every player's annual trends. If we could isolate all the players that performed well in Year #1, then tanked in years #2, #3 and #4, how many different explanations could we find? How many were the result of injury? The result of team environment? Or simply age? Isolating pure skill from all external influences, so that we can take a scientific look under a microscope, is nearly impossible. There are few players whose individual circumstances are similar enough that we can use their experiences to draw conclusions.

A bunch of years back, in our pre-internet days, we ran a study that looked to dispel the notion that some players demonstrate consistent first-half to second-half trends. Over a two year period, there were dozens of consistent 1H to 2H performances, but over three years, that number dropped sharply. After four years, there were only three batters in the entirety of baseball that demonstrated a consistent first half to second half trend. As such, attempting to cull a test group from a 5-plus year sample is just not going to happen.

So we have to rely on a little logic instead. But does the logic hold up?

Well, it doesn't in our test case above. Year #5 was 2002, and Rusty Greer batted .293 versus LHers (and .298 versus RHers), though in only 199 total

ABs. Why did he defy the logic? In this case, the turnaround could be attributed to health, at least for those 199 ABs.

Here is another interesting case...

Year	PX	Age
====	===	===
1996	85	24
1997	109	25
1998	123	26
1999	64	27
2000	102	28
2001	92	29

This batter's power skills showed nice growth from 1996 to 1998, peaking at 123 when he turned 26. We projected the upward trend to continue in 1999, but the bottom fell out. No injury. No change of environment. The power just stopped. While 2000 showed a slight rebound, 2001 fell off again, leading us to speculate that 1998 might have been more of an aberration than a point along a growth curve.

In my 2002 projections, I gave up on the expectation of a power surge. After three years of dormant skills, it appeared that the deficiency would not be addressed. However, there were still two minor variables that could support a power spike in 2002... his age (prime power peak), and the fact that "once you display a skill, you own it."

I suppose, sometimes that might just be enough, but in this case it wasn't. Matt Lawton posted a 108 PX in 2002 and 105 in 2003, though he got off to a 133 PX and 30 HR pace in '02 after six weeks. If not for his litany of injuries, perhaps he might be able to sustain that type of power stroke again. Given his history, you can't ever dismiss the possibility that it might.

One of the problems with "the odds of a player correcting a deficiency decrease with each year that he allows that deficiency to exist" is that, for many players, the decline is rapid and they never get the chance to see Year #5. Major league teams have various levels of patience, and there are a myriad of other factors that enter into the picture.

Should the Reds have been more patient with Brandon Larson this past season? Larson's fantasy owners probably thought that they were too patient. In the mid-1990s, I'm sure Phil Nevin's owners felt the same way about the Astros' and Tigers' approach to this underachieving #1 draft pick. Could Larson finally address the deficiencies like Nevin has done? It might take a move to another organization. But how much patience would you have?

Or, maybe we should all live and die by "once you display a skill, you own it," and be prepared for any eventuality that may come as a result.

It's a basic conflict in philosophies. "Addressing deficiencies" tells us to take a pessimistic approach to player potential. "Displaying a skill" appeals to our optimism and suggests that anything is possible. "Addressing deficiencies" is the risk-prudent approach. "Displaying a skill" helps us keep our eyes open so that the surprises aren't all that surprising.

In reality, our analyses have to be on a case-by-case basis. We have to assimilate as much hard data as we can while allowing the logic behind these concepts to help shape the analysis.

The Pitching Matrix

One of the themes in last year's *Baseball Forecaster* was the embracing of imprecision in our analyses. This seems counter-intuitive, especially with the growing complexity in our body of analytical knowledge. However, as shown with PQS ratings and the resulting qERA gauge, sometimes less is better.

Why?

Because it is impossible to create an absolute definition for any player's performance. A true .290 hitter can bat .254 one year and .326 the next and still be within a statistically valid range for .290. When it comes to pitching, a hurler allowing 5 runs in 2 innings will see a different ERA impact than one allowing 8 runs in 5 innings, even though, for all intents and purposes, both got rocked.

Generalizing performance is not a bad thing. For one, it simplifies our analyses. We don't get caught up in the minutia of whether a 27-HR hitter is better than a 24-HR hitter. We can group players into "pockets of talent," which can help us at the draft table. And it can help us see the forest from the trees.

In the case of projections, this is even more important. It's one thing to try to get a read on a player's actual performance level, but quite another when you add in the element of future uncertainty. I can project a player to hit 25 HRs, but how far can I be off and still consider the projection a success? 22? 29? Everyone has a different tolerance for forecasting error.

When it comes to pitching wins, we enter into a huge black hole. As I've often written, it takes five events to occur in order for a hurler to notch a single "W" — effective pitching, offensive support, defensive support, bullpen support and managerial decision to keep him in for at least 5 innings — and only one is within the control of the pitcher. So how can we accurately forecast wins for any individual?

In Rotisserie circles, this poses an even greater challenge. Wins drive a full 33% of a starting pitcher's Rotisserie dollar value in the 4x4 game (25% in 5x5). With so much uncertainty driving such a large chunk of a pitcher's value, how can we ever know what the optimal bids should be?

Take two pitchers of comparable skill and usage in 2002...

PITCHER	ERA	WHIP	IP	R$
========	=====	====	===	===
Pitcher A	3.92	1.36	188	$11
Pitcher B	3.92	1.36	181	$ 7

By all rights, both of these 2002 pitchers should have posted about the same Rotisserie value. However, one had the good fortune to win 14 games on a team that scored 851 runs, while the other eked out 9 victories on a club that scored 713 runs. In terms of skill and potential, were Kevin Appier (A) and Andy Ashby (B) really all that different?

Assessing pitching skill and the potential to win, and turning that into a projected dollar value, is a challenge. One way to begin to get a handle on this is to use a tool I introduced at our Arizona symposium about five years ago.

The pitching matrix provides a means by which to group pitchers according to their skill and win potential, and then assign a dollar value estimate to each of those groups. We measure skill using our base performance value (BPV) gauge. We've determined in the past that the element possessing the strongest correlation to wins is offensive support, so we use Run Support to drive each pitcher's potential to post "W's."

The overall matrix looks like this...

RUN SUPPORT	S K I L L (B P V)			
	80+	60-79	40-59	Under 40
HIGH	$28+	$20	$13	$6
MOD HIGH	$23	$16	$10	$4
MOD LOW	$18	$12	$7	$2
LOW	$13	$8	$4	$0

How this reads... A pitcher with a projected BPV of 80 or over who plays on a high offensive club is valued at $28 or more. A pitcher with a projected BPV under 40, who plays on a poor offensive club, is valued at $0. All other variations fall within those outer boundaries on the grid.

The next task is to slot all the MLB teams into each level of projected run support. The final step is to slot each team's starting pitchers into the cells of the matrix based on their projected BPV.

A perfect model? Probably not, but it did provide some interesting insight and food-for-thought when we ran the analysis prior to the 2003 season...

• It seemed odd to find Curt Schilling and Randy Johnson in the $18 cell. However, based on our projections, Arizona's 2002 league-leading offense was on path to drop into the middle of the pack, which would significantly impact the duo's ability to continue their annual runs at 20 wins.

• Tom Glavine, $4? We've questioned his declining skill set for some time and he moved to a club projected to wallow in the depths of the NL in terms of run scoring.

• Brandon Duckworth and John Burkett in the $20 cell? Well, Duckworth had some skills potential on a PHI club projected to finish 4th in the NL in offense. Burkett was backed by a Red Sox' offensive lineup projected to pace the American League.

• Denny Neagle, $13? The design of the matrix gives all the Colorado pitchers a bit of a bump in value. There's no question about the level of offensive support, but will their pitchers keep them in enough ballgames? None of the COL starters were listed in any cell with a value higher than $13, however, so there was some small foundation of reality.

I don't believe that these anomalies invalidate the model. Rather, they point out potential areas of strength and weakness that we might be blind to given our preconceived notions about pitcher values. Was it conceivable back in March that Glavine might earn only $4? Improbable perhaps, but it pointed out that you should have considered some downside when the market set its value for him come Draft Day.

And, given that this is just another tool in our arsenal, and that it's all based on projections, nothing here is necessarily carved in stone.

There's one variable that the matrix does not seem to take into account. We'd all agree that the number of innings pitched a hurler compiles is a major driving force in the ability to win games. The correlation isn't perfect, but we'd probably all consider a 220 IP performance far more likely to rack up "W's" than a 140 IP season.

The matrix seemingly ignores this fact. However, if we believe that skill drives a pitcher's role, then the model still works. Recall that Esteban Loaiza, for instance, opened 2003 as the White Sox' #5 starter, a role that usually means no more than 140 IP at best. However, his terrific performance bought him more innings, and boosted his total over 200.

In short, the values in the pitching matrix should not be taken to the bank. However, the insightful tidbits this tool reveals should at least color your view of each hurler's potential Rotisserie value come Draft Day.

Got MILC?

In 2003, aliens landed in Kansas City and Anaheim, and switched the won-loss records of the Royals and the Angels. These same extra-terrestrials inhabited the body of Melvin Mora and transmuted his batting average with that of Pat Burrell.

For those who like to approach each season as a clean slate, these anomalies — if, in fact, that's what they were — lend support to keeping an open mind about every season. While we sat through six months, shaking our heads about Randy Johnson's ERA, or Billy Koch's saves total, or Brian Giles' HR output, these displays only served to remind us that anything is possible and risk-spreading is still a viable strategy.

But does this alien rumor have any merit? I think it does.

In the same way that aliens represent a great unknown in our culture, there is also a great unknown in baseball analysis. While we're bogged down in BPI's and DOM/DIS splits, there is still the qualitative aspect of baseball performance that we often forget.

In our fanalytic world, "qualitative" is akin to "unmeasurable," and that gives me the heebie-jeebies. But while this unmeasurable aspect is, well, unmeasurable, it is not beyond the limits of being fodder for some level of analysis.

Got MILC? (Oh no, here comes another Shandler acronym...)

Here are four unmeasurable elements that impact performance and can help define the anomalies and aberrations that our traditional fanalytics can't explain.

Maybe.

Momentum: Once a team or player gets going on a streak — or slump — the mere essence of the streak often feeds upon itself, perpetuating it beyond reason. Our base performance indicators can't explain or predict it, other than to slap a percentage play on the probability that it will eventually end. And, wouldn't you know it — it always does!

Intangibles: There are elements of performance that have little statistical basis and zero projectability, and are relegated to the netherworlds of "stuff that just happens because it can." These are not purely random events (we'll get to that in a minute), but low-probability occurrences that are built upon miniscule elements all fitting together at opportune times. These are things like a player's ability to step up his skills in key games (see Troy Glaus, 2002 post-season) or a 5.44 ERA pitcher pulling a no-hitter out of nowhere (see Scott Erickson, 1994). For teams, this can manifest itself as some unknown ability to fare well against certain opposing teams or pitchers (e.g. Curt Schilling has posted a 7.71 ERA vs the Cards over the past three years.).

Luck: This is the repository for all completely random events. The element of luck has no basis in skills whatsoever, other than providing a natural variability in numbers that we've come to expect (but still hate). A player can bat .275 one year and .245 the next, but still possess the same basic skill set. The 1987 Milwaukee Brewers opened their season 20-3 (see Momentum), then turned it around and immediately went 2-18 (also Momentum), but the combination of the two streaks in succession has to be considered luck.

Chemistry: Often, a diverse set of unremarkable skills on a team somehow meshes into something more than the sum of its parts. Add in a bit of Momentum, a few Intangibles and a dash of Luck... and you get the 2003 Kansas City Royals.

These variables are more psychological than statistical, more abstract than concrete, and more difficult to get our arms around. But they are all real parts of the game, and do shape the statistics that ultimately come out of them.

So, when we are faced with trying to validate an unusual performance, and we've exhausted all reasonable effort at statistical analysis, and logic, the next step is to cross the boundaries into the paranormal.

Some say that it's inconceivable that we represent the only intelligent life in the universe, and so the possibility of aliens has to exist. Similarly, just because we can't put a number on the MILC variables doesn't mean that they don't exist as well. Perhaps we have to accept that on faith.

Why We Still Fixate on Today

Every April, I talk about how the baseball season is a marathon, how you have to be excruciatingly patient and make decisions based on talent, not the fickle whims of major league managers. I write that baseball reality is fluid, which means that, whatever you accept as real today will change tomorrow.

Still, readers continue to question our in-season projections updates, especially those for players that had apparently "lost their jobs."

The loss of a job is not a terminal event, especially for players who have shown some level of skill in the past. But I recognize that it is human nature to consider current reality as fixed. And I wrote the following line in response to one of those e-mails:

The fluidity of baseball reality is a tough concept to grasp.

The comment was not intended to inflame, but to state a matter of fact. In our fervent desire to gain an edge in our leagues, we hang on every tidbit of information we can get our hands on. We then lock in on anything that looks remotely like reality. He pitched badly, he lost his job, cause, effect — and it's locked in. That opens up opportunities for us to find other players who can help our teams. And if those new players have even the slightest chance to claim the role, and keep it, we want to be the one to reap the benefits of that new reality.

But there are a variety of alternate realities that we lock out when we do this, from the possible failure of the new player, to the reclaiming of the role by the original player, to the emergence of yet another candidate. Our projections allow for the possibility of these other realities to occur.

It's a prudent approach, and a proven approach, but not a popular one.

The fact is, the fluidity of reality in general is a tough concept to grasp. No matter how much our logical brains understand and agree with the statement, we conduct our lives as if reality is fixed.

There is a certain structure we all need in our lives for comfort and security. We need to know that the same person will be waking up in our bed next to us each morning. We need to know that our car will start, there will be money in our wallet when we get to Starbucks (very important), and that there will be a job waiting for us when we arrive at our place of employment.

We hang on those realities and treat them as fixed. Subconsciously, we may know that there is a possibility, no matter how remote, that some of this might change tomorrow. But that is typically no more than as a passing thought. In fact, in most cases, even if the threat of losing our own job is a real possibility, we go into denial. We don't want to face the sequence of events that will likely upset the security of our fixed reality. We don't want to face the possibility of... losing control. And that's exactly what all this comes down to...

A fixed reality provides us with a greater sense of control.

So it is in fantasy baseball as well. We need the security of fixed realities in order to believe we have control over our teams. That's why we play these games in the first place. That's why fantasy baseball came into existence... to give us the chance to control a group of major league ballplayers like a general manager would.

When I tell you that baseball reality is fluid, that's an affront to your sense of control over your teams. I'm not trying to make trouble. I'm just trying to refocus your perception of reality.

One place where reality does *not* exist is with managerial statements about player roles. Roles are determined by skill and circumstance. Circumstance changes daily, as every ballgame provides new decision points for each manager.

But there is an overwhelming abundance of possibilities, which is beyond our comprehension, and beyond our control, and thus difficult to consider when managing our teams. It's easier to play this game with a firmer grasp of what we know to be true now. It's easier to react, as necessary, than to figure all the alternative realities into the mix. The fact that reality changes so often in baseball — which means we have to consider all possibilities — is what makes the concept of fluidity so tough to get a handle on.

It is especially apparent early in the year, when major league managers are already making carte blanche decisions based on a handful of at bats or innings pitched. This impatience at the upper levels makes things even more difficult for us.

But we can still take a perspective that allows us to best adjust for these changing realities. We can still exercise patience, consider a more objective stance to all the noise, and attempt to instill a bit more logic into the process. This won't nail every change, but at least we won't lock ourselves into roster management decisions based on events that are more fleeting than we want to accept.

Admittedly, this approach often flies in the face of common wisdom and requires you to challenge your own instincts. But, as a percentage play, it's the approach that provides the greatest return on your decisions.

In any given year, you can take a group of fast starters and slow starters and determine that those April performances did not shape their eventual finish. For instance, in 2002, C.C. Sabathia opened with a 6.82 ERA in April. Coming off of a superb rookie season, everyone was whispering the dreaded phrase, "sophomore slump." From May 1 on, Sabathia posted a sub-4.00 ERA and finished at 4.37 — virtually identical to his 2001 campaign. But because of the path he took to reach that 4.37 ERA, and the fact that his won-loss record dropped from 17-5 to 13-11 (no doubt due to a significantly weaker Indians offense), most people still consider 2002 as a drop-off from 2001. It wasn't.

Similarly, a certain 2003 Cy Young Award winner found himself on May 1 with an 0-2 record and a 4.89 ERA. For the rest of the season, Roy Halladay went 22-5 with an ERA of 2.97.

And the flipside is true as well. Oakland's Ramon Hernandez finished April with a .364 batting average. From May 1 on, he batted over 100 points lower, at .256. Matt Kinney's opening month boasted a 2.48 ERA. All his bandwagon jumpers weathered the subsequent five months with a 5.67 ERA (though many probably jumped off the wagon well before the crash was complete).

If you compiled a list of players who followed similar patterns each season, you would find that there are different players appearing on these lists each year. It is impossible to label anyone as a consistent slow starter or fast starter. Which means...

Virtually any player is vulnerable to a month of aberrant performance.

And if that month happens to be April, it's all the more noticeable because we don't have data from any other month to diffuse it. A 5.00 ERA in August can often go nearly unnoticed. But not in April.

Legitimizing the Other 20%

Percentage plays. That's what we're all about here. We use component skills analysis to identify performances that may improve or decline based on a series of rules, culled from years of research.

And then we'll say things like, "80% of those pitchers with a strand rate above or below a certain threshold will see their ERA regress to the mean." We're giving you an 80% probability that a certain roster management decision will yield a particular outcome.

And despite some dubious recommendations that often challenge your better judgment, these percentage plays continue to play out at an 80% rate, time after time.

But what about the other 20%?

Up until now, we've tossed off that other 20% as a residue by-product of playing the percentages. One of the foundation philosophies of this book is: "Long-term success dictates that you always chase the 80% and accept the fact that you will be wrong 20% of the time."

In the forecasting world, this is a harsh reality. There are too many variables for us to achieve a much better result. However, no matter how good an 80/20 play sounds in theory, it's all meaningless when we see other owners scarf up outliers like Albert Pujols and Alfonso Soriano.

In mid-April, HQ writer Jeff Howard sent me the following e-mail:

"I know that our primary focus at HQ is based on the analysis of hard data with very little subjective bias, however... every once in a while I see a hard-line stance on someone based on past BPI data that seems to fly in the face of the player's actual (not stat) performance to date.

"I am writing this in regards to the April 18 Market Watch column about Esteban Loaiza. Now, granted, he did pitch two games against the woeful Detroit offense but I watched both of them live on TV, as I did with his start last night against BAL and the previous one vs KC. This guy is throwing out of his mind right now. He has total control of four pitches and is just barely missing when he throws balls. Batters on the teams he has faced are very indecisive when they do swing. Many of them are getting off balance and lunging, making check swings. I may be wrong, but this looks to me like someone who has indeed learned something. I rode the HQ wagon on him a few years ago and he looked nothing like he does now mechanically.

"Doug Dennis and I had a conversation earlier this year about my drafting strategy and how it requires that someone be able to pick up free agent pitchers who can help during the season. He asked me how I was so "on" with my pitching pickups all the time. The truth is simply that I watch all of them pitch (with the benefit of the DTV MLB package) before I pick them up.

"I don't have to tell you that outings that look the same on paper can be very different in reality. Loaiza is not just getting bad hitters to get themselves out. He is shredding them, and the good hitters he faces are doing well just to put the ball in play. He struck out Sweeney twice, Ibanez and just about everyone else in KC's order last week. Almost every BAL hitter had a two-strike count when they punched one in play last night.

"I am not one for making predictions but I'll go out on a limb here and say he will make the All-Star team and end up with 15+ wins, a sub 3.80 ERA and more strikeouts than anyone imagined."

In the past, I've been accused of making statements that are pure heresy. I once commented (probably about 10 years ago now), that we would all fare better in our leagues if we did not watch our players perform. No ballpark. No TV. Certainly no DTV MLB package. The bias we acquire in watching those small performance samples clouds our ability to accurately analyze overall performance. Of course, it also takes away from the enjoyment of the game, so that's a hard-line stance I don't take any more.

However, there is a lot of merit to what Jeff writes. Our culture of objective analysis relies so heavily on historical precedent that sometimes we do not see the real changes until it's too late to do something about them.

My response to him:

"I think the problem is not so much a lack of first-hand observation but an inability to integrate what we see with the historical statistical analysis. However, the question I have to throw back at you is... how do we know this current level of performance is going to keep up? While he may look great now, there is no history of him being able to sustain this type of performance over 6 months. He's had good months before, he's had good Aprils before, and he's even been on my "A" list before. Perhaps he has turned the corner, but what evidence do we have that this is going to last? You can rely on your observation and say that this is a different pitcher, but is that enough? I don't know.

"I think we have to wait and see what happens. If he turns into Mark Prior, then perhaps we have to take a serious look at somehow integrating yet another discipline into our analytical process."

A look at the history of Esteban Loaiza bears this all out. The glimmers of hope in his numbers have had us on his bandwagon for several years. Here were the capsule commentaries from the last few *Baseball Forecasters...*

1999: Decent base skills, but allows far too many baserunners and has trouble stranding them. No signs of any great gains just yet, but he does have a good foundation to build on.

2000: Has shown hints of putting together solid numbers, and may be poised to take that next step up.

2001: Second straight season he's figured it out in the 2nd half. BPIs are nearly there for the next step up. UPSIDE: 15 wins, 3.75 ERA.

2002: With a decent skills set, he just can't seem to get over the hump, because:
- his velocity is a little slower
- hits are falling like crazy
- doesn't like facing LHers
- ballparks are smaller, right?
- that hump is plenty high

2003: H% and S% are supposed to be random and always regressing to the mean, but these trends are scary. Despite decent enough BPIs, external gauges have wreaked havoc with his ERA.

So, what represents reality? Will Loaiza revert to form and fall in with the 80% percentage play? Or was his incredible April — and Jeff's observations — two leading indicators of him falling into the other 20%?

The Performance Validation Model

We need a methodical process by which we can evaluate all the performance variables and draw some type of conclusion. Even if that conclusion is not definitive — which in most cases it won't be — we need a way to at least point us in some direction.

The task of creating this model faces several obstacles, most notably the challenge of integrating both objective and subjective variables. Recent baseball research, both here and elsewhere, has been focused on comprehensive quantitative analyses. That's not feasible here.

One place to start is with our laundry list of performance validation criteria. Using them as a base, I've come up with a condensed set of criteria for this analysis. Here they are, in more or less order of impact...

Historical performance: No matter what we see players do on the field, everything has to be benched in history to some extent. This reality can range from the subtle to the obvious. History tells us not to expect a 30-SB season out of Matt LeCroy, someone who has only 4 SBs in his entire pro career. That's the obvious. A more subtle tidbit might be that Adam Piatt once hit 39 HRs in Double-A ball, a fact that could explain a power spike at some point in the future.

Health: This variable can also be obvious or subtle, depending upon how much information we know and how much history we want to consider. A few different shades of the health variable:

• We know about Mike Sweeney's gimpy back and that it likely affected his performance this year. What we don't know is whether this injury was around longer than had been reported, which might explain the gimpy batting average he put up *before* he allegedly got hurt.

• We know that Ivan Rodriguez and Moises Alou somehow stayed in their respective lineups all season, and were allegedly healthy, but can we count on that lasting into 2004? Are Gil Meche owners at least a little bit nervous?

• And for all those Wade Miller and Derek Lowe owners who spent the season wondering, "Is there a hidden injury?"... all it takes is one little newsbite to validate what we are seeing. I call that the "Brian Tollberg Effect."

Role and usage: Any number of seemingly innocuous changes could mean wholesale shifts in a player's numbers. Some are as simple as a change in RBI opportunities being a result of moving further up or down in the batting order. But some are not as simple... Were this year's closer-to-starter experiments both failures since Danny Graves and Byung Hyun Kim either struggled or got hurt?

Leading indicators: The subtleties of base performance indicators can often reveal hidden explanations for outwardly extreme performance data. We're all learning to discount low ERAs that have been artificially deflated by high strand rates, or Mendoza-line batting averages unsupported by more favorable contact rates. Often, the leading indicator might just be a consistent trend in a player's history, such as the rising power skills displayed

218

over the past few years by Trot Nixon.

Mechanical changes: True adjustments to the manner in which a player approaches each element of his game can have far-reaching impact on performance. The problem is that the reporting of such changes in advance is more often noise than news. The biggest challenge in evaluating these adjustments is that we don't know whether the observed impact can be sustained over time, and by the time we can draw conclusions, it's often too late to do anything about it.

Ballpark effects: This effect is negligible for most parks. However, for the handful of stadiums that have marked offensive or pitching tendencies, this can provide nearly all of the support needed to explain aberrant performances.

Team environment: I've already talked about qualitative variables that can affect performance — momentum, intangibles, luck and chemistry. These can often manifest themselves in individual player surges and fades.

Age: Sometimes a player's performance can be attributed to the chronological arrival of his physical peak or decline. This is not something you'd usually rely on as your sole explaining criteria, but it can be a factor.

Caliber of competition: This factor is way down on the list because it only really works for very small data sets. Once we get much into May, most players have already faced a variety of strong and weak competition.

Personal and miscellaneous factors: We ask... "Has a player spent the winter frequenting workout rooms or banquet tables? Has the player undergone a family crisis? Experienced spiritual rebirth? Given up red meat?" Players all react differently to external circumstances. Given the way Marcus Giles played this season, it's not such a stretch to attribute his horrible 2002 at least in part to the family crises he went through.

One final piece of the puzzle, inside of which all these criteria need to be evaluated, is the issue of **WHEN?** When can you tell that a certain level of performance is for real? At what point does the number of accumulated AB or IP override any doubts? When do you have enough information to make a decision?

If Loaiza puts up his numbers over 40 IP, that is less likely to be a validation of performance than if he was able to maintain his levels over 100 IP. *At what point does maintaining performance provide its own validation?*

In many respects, this variable of "time" is even more important than any of the other variables. Eventually, if a player performs at a certain level long enough, the other variables are all irrelevant. It doesn't matter that Loaiza has an inconsistent history, or that Gil Meche has spent the last two years on the DL, or that Carlos Zambrano is only 22... if they manage to continue performing at their current levels long enough, their performances becomes self-validating. But when do we know that it is truly for real?

We're often asked how many AB or IP a player has to accumulate before his numbers are relevant. Obviously, 600 AB and 200 IP would provide a 100% percentage play for validating performance, but obviously, we don't have the luxury of waiting out an entire season. Most experts agree that 150 AB and 50 IP are the minimum playing time necessary, but I don't believe they provide enough evidence

for strong percentage plays. I'd estimate that about double these totals — 300 AB and 100 IP — are what is needed to provide us with the 80% play that we typically shoot for.

But fanalytic gamers don't have that much time. We have to make our decisions much earlier. That's why we need the evidence provided by the other variables — in tandem with playing time — to help us validate performance when we need to make our roster moves.

Every performance that we're trying to evaluate for validity is going to be held up against this series of variables. Our model needs to look at each one and ask questions like, "Does this player's health support his current performance?" and "Can we explain this player's performance by his new team environment, and if so, how much is that a factor?"

One way to "quantify" what is essentially unquantifiable, is to set up a scale to evaluate each variable. We can go one by one and assign points to how well that variable supports performance. We can ask, "Does this variable…"

- Fully validate the performance level (+5)
- Partially validate performance level (+1 to +4)
- Have little or no relevance to performance level (0)
- Partially contradict performance level (-1 to -4)
- Fully contradict performance level (-5)

Sure, it's subjective, but that's okay.

Each of the variables probably should also have its own scale, as the impact of health versus team environment is not equal, for example. The higher the score, the better we can validate a player's performance.

Or, we can just do a quick cut at the 80/20 percentage plays. For Loaiza:

80%: Expect a regression to his career level numbers
- It's been his history to be inconsistent
- He's posted excellent Aprils before
- His good April this year was against mostly weak opposition

20%: His current stats are a new level of performance
- He's shown the skills in the past; consistency has been the only issue
- According to the *Chicago Tribune* on April 4, manager Jerry Manuel said that he has added movement to his fastball and control to his breaking pitches since leaving Toronto
- Jeff Howard's first-hand observation confirms that fact
- New team environment might be the impetus to change

Typically, we'd consider that second point as noise, but the proof would be in the numbers. And he's put them up.

In a case like this, with such strong arguments on both sides, it no longer becomes an 80% percentage play. Subjectively, I'd probably make this a 60%-70% play, which in the grand scheme of things, may not be strong enough to follow with any conviction.

It can go either way. And that means you might have to trust your own gut. Evaluate each factor, assess each argument and decide which makes more sense. In most cases, you won't have a runaway winner, but this exercise can help show which might have a stronger tendency.

It's never black and white, but these wonderful shades of grey are what make player analysis so colorful.

The Rocky Path to Stardom

When it comes to well-hyped rookies who struggle in their first exposure to the majors, fantasy leaguers tend to be a little short in the patience department. The classic case of prospect anxiety occurred in the spring of 1996 when a certain mega-hyped future star was prepared to take yet another shot at a major league career.

You see, this supposed-slugger's rookie year was somewhat less than advertised. After pounding through the minors, he barely managed to stay above the Mendoza Line in his first 54 AB in the bigs in 1994. After only 11 hits — not a single one for extras bases — and 20 strikeouts, he was given a quick ticket back to Triple-A.

Back in the minors, he thrived again, batting over .300 and slugging over .600. In 1995, he got his second shot but struggled again, batting only .232 in 142 AB, with a barely .400 slugging average. By now, his eager fantasy owners were losing faith, and when 1996 arrived, they were likely chanting, "burn me once, shame on you. Burn me twice, shame on me."

Of course, those who kept the faith were rewarded with a 36 HR, .358 BA season from Alex Rodriguez. In the "Other Diamonds" section of this book, this is called the "A-Rod 10-Step Path to Stardom." While this is a "tongue-in-cheek" description of a typical path to stardom, there is a lot we can learn from it.

On a deep level, it may show how a player's ability to overcome adversity might lead to a more productive career. Those who are given the opportunity to make adjustments might be more apt to raise their ceilings. But "opportunity" is the key factor, and one that not all minor leaguers are afforded. How many chances will a Brandon Larson get? Perhaps he could become a productive major leaguer, but right now the Reds have him frozen at Step #5. As Deric McKamey once wrote, "Defense is what gets a prospect to the majors; offense is what keeps him there."

At face value, the 10-Step Path to Stardom tells us something very simple... if the game's top player today could struggle in his first few exposures to big league ball, we can certainly cut some slack to other struggling prospects. In fact, our recent history is overpopulated with productive major leaguers whose careers started off slowly. How many of you would have bailed on these disappointments after the following major league debuts?

	AB	H	HR	RBI	SB	BA
	===	===	==	===	==	===
Biggio,C	123	26	3	5	6	211
Bonds,B	413	92	16	48	36	223
Boone,B	129	25	4	15	1	194
Castilla,V	337	86	9	30	2	255
Chavez,E	356	88	13	50	1	247
Delgado,C	130	28	9	24	1	215
Edmonds,J	289	79	5	37	4	273
Finley,S	217	54	2	25	17	249
Floyd,C	334	94	4	41	10	281
Giambi,Jas	176	45	6	25	2	256
Glaus,T	165	36	1	23	1	218
Jones,A	106	23	5	13	3	217
Jordan,B	193	40	5	22	7	207
Kent,J	305	73	11	50	2	239
Nevin,P	156	28	2	13	1	179
Rodriguez,I	280	74	3	27	0	264

	AB	H	HR	RBI	SB	BA
Vaughn,M	219	57	4	32	2	260
Vidro,J	169	42	2	17	1	249
Vizquel,O	387	85	1	20	1	220
Williams,B	320	76	3	34	10	238
Williams,M	245	46	8	21	4	188

All of these players have had productive careers. For most, it was their batting average that took some time to adjust to major league pitching. For some — Edmonds, Finley, Floyd, Glaus, Nevin, I-Rod, Vaughn and Bernie Williams — their debuts displayed little indication that they would become major power sources.

Add to this list a whole slew of "cups of coffee" that were even more disappointing. How many of these players might have been "throw-ins" in some late-season dump deal?

	AB	H	HR	RBI	SB	BA
	===	===	==	===	==	===
Gonzalez,J	60	9	1	7	0	150
Green,S	33	3	0	1	1	091
Guerrero,V	27	5	1	1	0	185
Justice,D	51	12	1	3	2	235
Klesko,R	14	0	0	1	0	0
Koskie,C	29	4	1	2	0	138
Kotsay,M	52	10	0	4	3	192
Lofton,K	74	15	0	0	2	203
Palmeiro,R	73	18	3	12	1	247
Palmer,D	19	2	0	1	0	105
Perez,N	45	7	0	3	2	156
Piazza,M	69	16	1	7	0	232
Posada,J	14	1	0	0	0	071
Ramirez,M	53	9	2	5	0	170
Rodriguez,A	54	11	0	2	3	204
Salmon,T	79	14	2	6	1	177
Sanders,R	40	8	1	3	1	200
Sheffield,G	80	19	4	12	3	238
Soriano,A	50	9	2	3	2	180
Sosa,S	84	20	1	3	0	238
Stewart,S	38	8	0	1	2	211
Tejada,M	99	20	2	10	2	202
Thome,J	98	25	1	9	1	255
Ventura,R	45	8	0	7	0	178
Vina,F	45	10	0	2	6	222
Walker,L	47	8	0	4	1	170
Wilson,P	51	8	1	3	1	157
Womack,T	24	2	0	0	2	083

Nearly 30 players who would eventually become very productive, and less than half managed to bat even .200 in their first exposure to the majors. Only one managed to bat as high as .250.

The pitching side is equally intriguing. Lots of reasons to give up hope on these rookie bottom-feeders...

	W	L	SV	IP	ERA
	==	==	==	===	=====
Appier,K	1	4	0	22	9.14
Benitez,A	1	5	2	48	5.66
Dotel,O	8	3	0	85	5.38
Glavine,T	2	4	0	50	5.54
Guardado,E	3	8	0	95	6.18
Hampton,M	1	3	1	17	9.53
Hawkins,L	2	3	0	27	8.67
Leiter,A	2	2	0	23	6.35
Maddux,G	2	4	0	31	5.52
Miller,W	6	6	0	105	5.14
Mulder,M	9	10	0	154	5.44
Nen,R	1	1	0	23	6.35
Ortiz,Ra	2	3	0	48	6.52
Reynolds,S	1	3	0	25	7.11
Rhodes,A	0	3	0	36	8.00
Rivera,M	5	3	0	67	5.51
Schilling,C	0	3	0	15	9.82

Schmidt,J	2	2	0	25	5.76
Smoltz,J	2	7	0	64	5.48
Urbina,U	2	2	0	23	6.17
Vazquez,J	5	15	0	172	6.06
Weaver,J	9	12	0	164	5.55
Wolf,R	6	9	0	122	5.55

About two dozen productive arms and not a sub-5.00 ERA in the bunch. In fact, as bad as the debuts were for Glavine and Maddux, their futures got even bleaker in year #2. Glavine followed up with a 7-17, 4.56 ERA season; Maddux went 6-14 with a 5.61 ERA. In two years, the foundation of the Braves' decade-long run started out going 17-39 with an ERA over 5.00.

It makes Brett Myers' 4.43 ERA downright Gibsonesque by comparison. So those who've hung onto their patience skills with today's slow-starting rookies should rest easy.

The Realities of Cynicism

Albert Pujols, age 23.

Really now.

Ever since this phenom hit the bigs — big time — in 2001, there have been questions about his real age. After all, it's not very often that a 21-year-old with fewer than 100 at bats over Single-A ball hits 37 HRs and bats .329 in his rookie year... and then follows up with an equally impressive sophomore campaign... and then makes a triple-crown run in year #3.

And all of this by age 23.

Questions about his age arose almost immediately. Attention picked up after last year's Dominican Birth Certificate Carnage in which several hundred players were revealed to be years older than their stated ages. Pujols is Dominican, but he played high school ball in the U.S. The allegations were dismissed by the Cardinals on several occasions.

Still, the question keeps popping up in print from time to time. Sometimes it's just an idle speculation, other times a fleeting attempt to correlate his age with his performance. Never has anyone come right out and said, "Albert Pujols is older than 23," because nobody can prove it.

But then I came across an innocuous passage in Peter Golenbock's book, *Amazin'*, in which he interviews George Theodore, an equally innocuous player from the New York Mets of the late 1970's...

> *"I was really born in 1946. The Baseball Encyclopedia says I was born in 1947, and that's because when I signed my contract, I was told, 'You'll have a better chance if you're 21.' So I became a year younger, which I assume happens, whether [you're] in the Dominican Republic or not."*

After reading this, and then reading Michael Lewis' *Moneyball*, which describes the theater that Billy Beane produces for the media and the public, I realized that we're not exercising nearly enough cynicism these days. Statements emanating from inside MLB have limited credibility. We are told only what they want us to know.

So, just because we can't prove that Albert Pujols is older than his stated age doesn't mean it's not true. And while the evidence is largely circumstantial, we certainly do not have proof beyond a reasonable doubt that he is, in fact, 23.

If "proof beyond a reasonable doubt" is good enough for the courts, it's good enough for me. So I'll say it...

Albert Pujols is older than 23.

Go ahead, sue me.

This new revelation has far-reaching implications. For one, if Pujols is 27 — which is a number bandied about by some sources — we are actually witnessing a player experiencing his peak rather than one on the beginning rungs of the growth ladder. That means, if his numbers fall off a cliff during the 2008 season, we should not be analyzing why a 28-year-old would suddenly lose touch with his skills. We should be sitting back watching a 32-year-old naturally following his age-related bell curve.

Implication #2 is... if this scenario is true for Pujols, it could be equally true for others. Who's to say that those players throughout history who experienced precipitous drops in performance at relatively young ages weren't a few years older than reported? Maybe Jeff Cirillo's sudden collapse in 2002 from a perennial .300 hitter to a sub-.250 retread was because he's not 33, but maybe 37? Dale Murphy was a perennial .290-plus hitter in 1988 when his BA suddenly tanked to .226; he saw .250 only once over the final six years of his career. Maybe he wasn't 32 when that happened, but 36? And in 1991, Howard Johnson led the NL in HRs with 38 at age 31; in 1992 he hit only 7 and then struggled to achieve double-digit power output over the final three years of his career, the last one in Colorado.

There has to be a reason for these occurrences.

If age is not the issue, maybe there is other equally relevant information that's being kept from us. It's certainly not a stretch to assume that we don't know about every player's aches and pains, or marital situations, or sudden crises of faith. Yet, we're constantly bombarded by media assertions masquerading as absolute truth.

Things just don't happen for no reason, even if we can't figure it out from where we're sitting. Even after painstakingly analyzing all performance validation criteria, if you cannot come up with an answer, don't assume that one does not exist...

Maybe the player is hiding an injury, like Jason Kendall did in 2001 (and revealed long after the fact). Maybe the player is going through a messy divorce, like Frank Thomas did (and revealed long after the fact). Maybe a player needs some vision correction, or has changed his diet, or started a different workout regimen. Maybe a player is ticked off at his catcher for calling a wrong pitch and is too immature to get past it. Maybe a player just caught his roommate having an affair with his girlfriend. Maybe a player has found an ingenious new way to doctor the baseball before he goes into his windup. Maybe a player's elbow is hurting him but he has to play through it without telling a soul because he knows that there are three other players chomping at the bit to take his job away.

Or maybe the player is a few years older than what it says in the *Baseball Encyclopedia*.

We've become complacent about accepting the realities that we're being fed. Take this as a reminder... Reject blind faith and embrace cynicism. It will help create order in your fantasy baseball reality.

Realities of the "Process"

The core of *Moneyball* is the quest to find a more accurate way to measure future major league success. Author Michael Lewis tells us all about Billy Beane's apparently single-minded focus on the numbers, but there is another view we can take to explain what is going on.

There is a continuum in looking at developing successful sports performance...

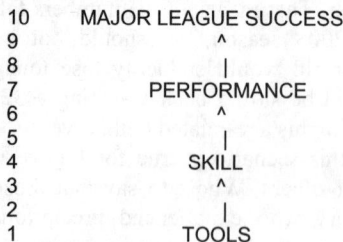

```
10      MAJOR LEAGUE SUCCESS
9               ^
8               |
7          PERFORMANCE
6               ^
5               |
4            SKILL
3               ^
2               |
1            TOOLS
```

Athletes work hard to develop along this scale, from 1 to 10, with the ultimate goal of succeeding in the majors. But each step in the process presents its own set of challenges, and success at any lower level does not guarantee success further up the scale.

Moving from TOOLS to SKILL requires that a player has the ability to harness his raw mechanical processes into something that has value for playing the game of baseball. It is good to be strong, for instance, but that does not necessarily convert to hitting a baseball with power. The best TOOLS do not guarantee success at any subsequent level.

Moving from SKILL to PERFORMANCE requires that a player assimilates his physical, mental and emotional assets into positive on-field results. It's good to have a 95 mph heater, for instance, but that won't help a pitcher who is unable to get his head back in the game after giving up a 3-run homerun. The best SKILL does not guarantee PERFORMANCE at any subsequent level.

Moving from PERFORMANCE to MAJOR LEAGUE SUCCESS is the final refinement of the process, requiring that the player has the ability to improve his game as conditions change, deal with the media, respond to fame, and all the high-level challenges — often, not specifically skill-related — that come along with playing on the grand stage.

Old School player development nearly always starts the process at point 1 on the scale, looking for players with tools, as early as high school. What Beane said was, let's skip points 1 and 2, and possibly even point 3, and focus only on players who've demonstrated signs of being capable of making that first jump into SKILL.

By starting the process at point 4, Beane already screens out many of those players who would not be able to convert their TOOLS to SKILL. Since the evaluation process at points 1-3 is mostly subjective in nature, he gains an edge by using statistical data to give him an early read in order to make that leap. In the end, the numbers are always the final judge of success, so it makes sense to use them, in some form, from the very beginning.

The Terrors of Aging

Players follow this process at their own pace, based on their physical, mental and emotional makeup. One of the most damaging mindsets is attaching an age level to expectations. Once a player reaches a certain age, if he hasn't achieved an expected level of success, he is dismissed from further consideration.

Admittedly, much of this mindset is driven by economics. A team would rather invest in a player who has 15-20 years of productivity ahead of him than one who has 7-10 years, even if the latter player would be twice as productive over that shorter span of time. While most players tend to reach their performance peak somewhere in the 27-31 age range, it is up to the front office to decide whether those peak-level stats will be compiled at the major league level or in the minors.

The underlying philosophy is one of impatience. Late-bloomers be damned.

Beane's innovative thinking (and the economics) might contribute to his open-mindedness on this issue as well. He's willing to try to catch lightning in a bottle with some older players, as evidenced by names like David McCarty and Billy McMillon on the OAK roster this year. Both players were prime commodities in their time, but aged too fast for their skills growth. The risk of taking a flyer on older prospects is low, and by targeting the key statistical indicators, Beane is still employing the same philosophy for uncovering hidden pockets of talent.

For the record, McMillon was posting a .401 on base percentage in the minors this year. Even McCarty's .351 BA was better than every OAK regular except Erubiel Durazo. In fact, Beane appeared to be stockpiling these types of bats on the roster of the Sacramento Rivercats, their Triple-A affiliate. During 2003, there were no fewer than nine batters on that team who were posting OB Avgs of .370 or better and were between the ages of 26 and 32.

Most fanalytic gamers ignore this end of the talent spectrum, perhaps prudently. But if you are ever going to catch that lightning, it's going to come from this caliber of forgotten talent.

That's where Esteban Loaiza came from.

The Lesson from Loaiza

From a forecasting perspective, the big stories of the year are always those that we follow closely with amazement and disbelief. They are players whose performances defy our expectations. They come out of nowhere, or refuse to fade, or can't manage to get on track no matter how positive the leading indicators are.

Albert Pujols was the big story of 2001, the player who came out of nowhere. In 2002, the big story was Alfonso Soriano, the player with horrible BPIs that refused to fade. This year, the big story has to be Esteban Loaiza.

In the earliest weeks of the season, HQ writer Jeff Howard went on record and called Loaiza's performance "for real." This defied all our analysis, chasing the 20% that I've always advised against. Yet, Loaiza never faded, not even when that 20th win seemed forever elusive. He had a great year, posting BPIs that ranked him among the Top 10 in all of baseball. Not bad for a guy who had 5-plus ERAs each of the past two years.

But what really happened here was not so much that we didn't see the talent, but that we lost patience. Loaiza had posted BPIs in the past that indicated solid potential. In fact, he was one of our prime sleepers in 1999, 2000 and 2001. His star faded a bit in our eyes last year and was snuffed out by the time this past March rolled around. After several years of failed expectations, we finally gave up on him. After all, he was 31. What more could we expect?

Age 31 is also that mystical "peak age" for pitchers. Skills continue to develop up until that point, more or less, so perhaps we can never really count out any pitcher in his 20s. A 28-year-old Triple-A journeyman may be seen as "over the hill" by most major league organizations, but he's really still on the rise of his growth curve. These are the arms that end up experiencing their peak while playing in places like Scranton.

Like Amaury Telemaco. Here is another pitcher who had a terrific pedigree when he was in the Cubs' system, but never succeeded in the bigs. For those who didn't notice, he pitched "lights-out" in Scranton/Wilkes-Barre this season, and despite a 1-4 record, posted solid BPIs while up with the Phillies. Nobody really takes him seriously because he is 29 (gasp!), but this is just the type of hurler who may have a few good years ahead of him.

Like, perhaps Doug Davis. Another one of our sleeper picks, as recently as 2002, and one we also eventually turned our backs on. His BPIs are not as strong as the previous two, but there he is with his 2.58 ERA in Milwaukee. At age 28.

Our friends at the *Baseball Prospectus* allege that "there is no such thing as a pitching prospect." Joe Sheehan has written several articles on this topic, and others have jumped on the bandwagon. Sheehan shows how the most highly prized pitching prospects have just as good a shot at making the bigs as anyone else, and how uncovering the Esteban Loaiza's is essentially a crapshoot.

I believe there *is* such a thing as a pitching prospect, but perhaps we have been **prospecting in the wrong places,** at least for our fanalytic purposes. Our love affair with young arms has blinded us to the fact that maybe we should be prospecting, not from the pool of green high school and college students, but from the vast wasteland of near-30 arms that are on the brink of maturity.

That is where the hidden pockets of skill may lie, both at the minor *and* major league levels. If our developmental philosophies were re-focused to grow arms over a longer-term developmental path, perhaps we might be able to find those hidden pockets more often.

Of course, instant gratification remains the unyielding force that runs the world, and economic realities preclude the viability of building a team on the backs of long-term investments. So we, as analysts, are left to keep our eyes open to the possibilities of the Esteban Loaizas.

Perhaps we have to maintain our patience, even when it hurts. Perhaps we have to jump on the pitching bandwagons sooner, and stay longer. This, of course, begs the questions, "How soon?" and "How long?"

And that is probably the next great frontier for forecasting analysis.

VII.
SABERMETRIC
TOOLS

Glossary

Avg: Batting Average (see also BA)

BA: Batting Average (see also Avg)

Base Performance Index (BPX): A comparison of a player's Base Performance Value to the overall level of talent in his league in a given year. This accounts for changes in overall talent level from one year to the next. A BPX value of 100 represents a skill set that is exactly at the league average. Values above 100 are above average performances; below 100 are below average performances.

Base Performance Indicator (BPI): A statistical formula that measures a single, isolated aspect of a player's raw skill and is almost always a situation independent evaluator. Although there are many such formulas, there are only a few that we are referring to when the term is used in this book. For batters, our BPIs are linear weighted power index (PX), speed score index (SX), walk rate (bb%), contact rate (ct%), batting eye (Eye) and expected batting average (xBA). For pitchers, our BPI's are control (bb/9), dominance (k/9), command (k/bb), opposition on base average (OOB), hit rate on balls in play (H%), strand rate (S%), and expected earned run average (xERA).

Base Performance Value (BPV): A single value that describes a player's overall raw skill level. This is more useful than any traditional statistical gauge to track player performance trends and project future statistical output. The actual BPV formula combines and weights several BPIs.

Batting BPV: *(Batting Eye x 20) + ((Batting Average - .300) / .003) + (Linear Weighted Power x 1.25)*

This formula combines the individual raw skills of batting eye, the ability to hit safely, and the ability to hit with power. **BENCHMARKS:** The best hitters will have a BPV of 50 or greater, and represent approximately the top 20% of all offensive players. (Note: Batting BPV does not appear in this edition of the *Forecaster* but does in the free projections update.)

Pitching BPV: *(Dominance Rate x 6) + (Command Ratio x 21) - (Opposition HR Rate x 30) - ((Opp. Batting Average - .275) x 200)*

This formula combines the individual raw skills of power, command, the ability to keep batters from reaching base, and the ability to prevent long hits, all characteristics that are unaffected by most external team factors. In tandem with a pitcher's strand rate, it provides a complete picture of the elements that contribute to a pitcher's ERA, and therefore serves as an accurate tool to project likely changes in ERA.

BENCHMARKS: We generally consider a BPV of 50 to be the minimum level required for long-term success. There are some veteran pitchers who rarely reach this level, but they are generally the types who are workhorse inning-eaters and post high ERA's. The elite of the bullpen aces will have BPV's in excess of 100 and it is rare for these stoppers to enjoy long term success with consistent levels under 75.

Baserunners per Innings Pitched: The ratio of hits and walks to innings pitched. Decreed as a base Rotisserie category, is also alternately called WHIP (walks, hits, innings pitched) and the highly-descriptive "Ratio." **BENCHMARKS:** Usually, a Br/IP of under 1.20 is considered top level and over 1.50 is indicative of poor performance. Levels under 1.00 — allowing fewer runners than IP — represent extraordinary performance and are rarely maintained over time.

Batters Faced per Game *(Craig Wright)*

((IP x 2.82) + H + BB) / G

A measure of pitcher usage and one of the leading indicators for potential pitcher burnout. (See Usage Warning Flags in the Forecaster's Toolbox.)

Batting Average (BA, or Avg): A grand old nugget that has long outgrown its usefulness, leaving its true value as nothing more than a link to baseball's past. But this remains deceptive. We revere .300 hitting superstars and scoff at .250 hitters, yet the difference between the two is 1 hit every 20 ABs. This 1 hit every five games is not nearly the wide variance that exists in our perceptions of what it means to be a .300 or .250 hitter. The bottom line is that BA is a poor evaluator of baseball performance. It neglects the offensive value of the base on balls and assumes that all hits are created equal.

Batting Eye (Eye)

(Walks / Strikeouts)

A measure of a player's strike zone judgment, the raw ability to distinguish between balls and strikes.

BENCHMARKS: The best hitters have eye ratios over 1.00 (indicating more walks than strikeouts) and are the most likely to be among a league's .300 hitters. At the other end of the scale are ratios less than 0.50, which represent batters who likely also have lower BA's. (See Forecaster's Toolbox for more research.)

bb%: Walk rate (hitters)

bb/9: Opposition Walks per 9 IP

BF/Gm: Batters Faced Per Game

BPI: Base Performance Indicator

BPV: Base Performance Value

BPX: Base Performance Index

Br/IP: Baserunners per Innings Pitched

Cmd: Command ratio

Command Ratio (Cmd)

(Strikeouts / Walks)

This is a measure of a pitcher's raw ability to get the ball over the plate. There is no more fundamental a skill than this, and so it is accurately used as a leading indicator to project future rises and falls in other gauges, such as ERA. Command is one of the best gauges to use to evaluate minor league performance. It is a prime component of a pitcher's base performance value.

BENCHMARKS: Baseball's upper echelon of command pitchers will have ratios in excess of 3.0. Pitchers with ratios under 1.0 — indicating that they walk more batters than they strike out — have virtually no potential for long term success. If you make no other changes in your approach to drafting a pitching staff, limiting your focus to only pitchers with a command ratio of 2.0 or better will substantially improve your odds of success. (See the Forecaster's Toolbox for more command ratio research.)

Contact Rate (ct%)

((AB - K) / AB)

Measures a batter's ability to get wood on the ball.

BENCHMARK: Those batters with the best contact skill will have levels of 90% or better. The hackers of society will have levels of 75% or less.

Control Rate (bb/9), or Opposition Walks per Game

BB Allowed x 9 / IP

Measures how many walks a pitcher allows per game equivalent. **BENCHMARK:** The best pitchers will have bb/9 levels of 3.0 or less.

Crickets: The sound heard when someone's opening draft bid on a player is also the only bid.

Ct%: Contact rate

Ctl: Control Rate

DIS%: PQS Disaster Rate

Dom: Dominance Rate

DOM%: PQS Domination Rate

Dominance Rate (k/9), or Opposition Strikeouts per Game

(K Allowed x 9 / IP)

Used in the BPV formula, it measures how many strikeouts a pitcher allows per game equivalent. **BENCHMARK:** The best pitchers will have k/9 levels of 6.0 or higher.

ERA Variance: The variance between a pitcher's ERA and his XERA, which is a measure of over or underachievement. A positive variance indicates the potential for a pitcher's ERA to rise. A negative variance indicates the potential for ERA improvement. (See Expected Earned Run Average.)

BENCHMARKS: Discount variances that are under 0.50. Any variance over 1.00 (one run per game) is regarded as a clear indicator of future change. Note that all variances over 0.50 are indicated by a "+" or "-" in the player boxes.

Expected Batting Average *(John Burnson)*

xH% x CT%, where

*xH% = GB% * (0.0022 PX + 0.0013 SX)*

*+ FB% * 0.1611*

*+ LD% * (-0.0023 SX + 0.8353)*

A hitter's batting average as calculated by multiplying the percentage of balls put in play (contact rate) by the chance that a ball in play falls for a hit. The likelihood that a ball in play falls for a hit is a product of the speed of the ball and distance it is hit (PX), the speed of the batter (SX), and distribution of ground balls, fly balls, and most importantly, line drives.

BENCHMARKS: In general, xBA's should approximate a hitter's batting average fairly closely. However, those hitters who have large variances between the two gauges are candidates for further analysis.

Expected Earned Run Average *(Gill and Reeve)*

(.575 x H [per 9 IP]) + (.94 x HR [per 9 IP]) + (.28 x BB [per 9 IP]) - (.01 x K [per 9 IP]) - Normalizing Factor

"xERA represents the expected ERA of the pitcher based on a normal distribution of his statistics. It is not influenced by situation-dependent factors." xERA erases the inequity between starters' and relievers' ERA's, eliminating the effect that a pitcher's success or failure has on another pitcher's ERA.

Similar to other gauges, the accuracy of this formula changes with the level of competition from one season to the next. The normalizing factor allows us to better approximate a pitcher's actual ERA. This value is usually somewhere around 2.77 and varies by league and year.

BENCHMARKS: In general, xERA's should approximate a pitcher's ERA fairly closely. However, those pitchers who have large variances between the two gauges are candidates for further analysis. (See ERA Variance.)

There is some confusion about how to interpret a pitcher's projected xERA as compared to his projected ERA.

The projected xERA is probably the more accurate gauge for looking ahead, as it is constructed solely from skills-related variables and situationally independent events.

The projected ERA is constructed from a trend analysis of historical ERAs, with some adjustments for leading indicators. The reason we include this at all is that pitching performance is also impacted by situationally *dependent* events — bullpen support, park factors, etc. — which are reflected better by ERA. The optimal approach, however, is to use *both* gauges as a range of the expectation for the coming year.

Eye: Batting Eye

G/F: Ground Ball to Fly Ball Ratio

Gopheritis (also, Acute Gopheritis and Chronic Gopheritis): The dreaded malady in which a pitcher is unable to keep the ball in the ballpark. Pitchers with gopheritis allow over 15% of their hits to leave the park, an approximate hr/9 level of 1.3 or higher.

Ground Ball / Fly Ball Ratio (G/F): A simple ratio of ground balls to fly balls. This has a variety of uses for both batters and pitchers. For batters, increased fly ball tendency may foretell a rise in power skills. For pitchers, the ability to keep the ball on the ground is usually necessary for long-term success.

BENCHMARKS: For batters, a G/F ratio over 1.80 may indicate a low ceiling for power potential. A G/F ratio under 1.00 may indicate a high ceiling. *(Mat Olkin)* Further study is needed to determine appropriate pitching benchmarks.

H%: Hits Allowed per Balls in Play

Hits Allowed per Balls in Play *(Voros McCracken)*

(H—HR) / ((IP x 2.82) + H - K - HR)

See Forecaster's Toolbox for a complete discussion on this gauge. **BENCHMARK:** The league average H% is 30%. Any +/- variance of 3% or more can affect a pitcher's ERA.

hr/9: Opposition Home Runs per 9 IP

IP/G: Innings Pitched per Game Appearance

k/9: Dominance rate (opposition strikeouts per 9 IP)

Leading Indicator: A statistical formula (usually a base performance indicator) that can be used to project likely future performance.

LIMA Plan: A strategy for Rotisserie leagues that allows you to target high skills pitchers at very low cost, thereby freeing up dollars for offense. LIMA is an acronym for Low Investment Mound Aces, and also pays tribute to Jose Lima, a $1 pitcher in 1998 who exemplified the power of the strategy. There are six steps to the strategy:

1. Budget a maximum of $60 (out of $260) for your pitching staff. This figure may vary slightly; keeper leagues can probably budget less, 5x5 leagues would need to budget more.

2. Allot no more than $30 of that budget for acquiring saves. That might mean one $30 stud, or several lower-priced closers.

3. Completely ignore the remaining pitching categories. When assembling the rest of your staff, only draft pitchers who:

- have a command ratio (K/BB) of 2.0 or better.
- have a strikeout rate of 6.0 or better.
- have a home run rate of 1.0 or less.

4. Draft as few innings as your league rules will allow. This enables you to better manage your staff during the season. And plan ahead; if your league has a 900 minimum innings rule, for instance, you only need two 180 IP starters to meet that requirement, surprisingly enough.

5. Maximize your batting acquisitions. With $200 or more to spend on hitters, you should be able to assemble an offense that ranks at or near the top of every batting category. But spend every penny and make sure all categories are covered.

6. Spread your risk. Risk minimization is an important element of value maximization, so spend no more than $29 for any player and try to keep the $1 picks to a minimum.

The overall goal is to ace the batting categories and carefully pick your pitching staff so that it will finish in the upper third in ERA/WHIP, in the upper third in saves, and somewhere around 9th-12th in wins. In a competitive league, that should usually generate enough points to win, and definitely enough to finish in the money. Worst case, you should have an excess of offense available that you can deal for arms.

The LIMA Plan works because it focuses on better allocation of resources. When fantasy leaguers pay big bucks for pitchers, they are not only paying for expected performance, they are also paying for better defined roles, which translates into more innings, more wins and more saves. But roles are highly variable, changing often during the course of a season. *The LIMA Plan says, let's invest in skill and let the roles fall where they may.* In the long run, better skills should translate into more innings, wins and saves anyway. And as it turns out, pitching skill costs much less than pitching roles do.

Linear Weights *(Pete Palmer)*

((Singles x .46) + (Doubles x .8) + (Triples x 1.02) + (Home runs x 1.4) + (Walks x .33) + (Stolen Bases x .3) - (Caught Stealing x .6) - ((At bats - Hits) x Normalizing Factor)

LW is also referred to as Batting Runs. Formula whose premise is that all events in baseball are linear, that is, the output (runs) is directly proportional to the input (offensive events). Each of these offensive events is then weighted according to its relative value in producing runs. Positive events — hits, walks, stolen bases — have positive values. Negative events — outs, caught stealing — have negative values.

The normalizing factor, representing the value of an out, is an offset to the particular level of offense in a given year. As such it changes every season, growing larger in high offense years and smaller in low offense years. The value is usually somewhere around .26 and varies by league.

LW is no longer included in the player forecast boxes, but the LW concept is used with the linear weighted power gauge.

Linear Weighted Power (LWPwr)

((((Doubles x .8) + (Triples x .8) + (Home runs x 1.4)) / At bats) x 365

An excerpt/variation of the LW formula that only considers events that are measures of a batter's raw power. A prime base performance indicator.

BENCHMARKS: Baseball's top sluggers usually top the 50 mark. Weak hitters will have a LWPwr level of under 20.

Linear Weighted Power Index (PX)

(Batter's LWPwr / League LWPwr) x 100

LWPwr is presented in this book in its normalized form to get a better read on a batter's accomplishment in each year. For instance, a 30-HR season today is not nearly as much of an accomplishment as 30 HRs hit in a lower offense year like 1995. A level of 100 equals league average power skills. Any player with a value over 100 has above average power skills, and those over 175 are the slugging elite.

LW: Linear Weights

LWPwr: Linear Weighted Power

Major League Equivalency *(Bill James):* A formula that converts a player's minor or foreign league statistics into a comparable performance in the major leagues. These are not projections, but rather conversions of current performance. Contains adjustments for the level of play in individual leagues and teams. Works best with Triple-A stats, not quite as well with Double-A stats, and hardly at all with the lower levels. Foreign conversions are still a work in process. James' formula only addressed batting. Our research has devised a similar methodology for pitchers, however, its best use comes when looking at MLE levels of BPI's, not traditional stats.

Mendoza Line: Named for Mario Mendoza, it represents the benchmark for batting futility. Usually refers to a .200 batting average, but can also be used for low levels of other statistical categories. Despite the "Mendoza Line" being used to describe a .200 hitter, Mendoza's lifetime batting average was actually a much loftier .215.

MLE: Major League Equivalency

Noise: Irrelevant or meaningless pieces of information that can distort the results of an analysis. In news, this is opinion or rumor that can invalidate valuable information. In forecasting, these are unimportant elements of statistical data that can artificially inflate or depress a set of numbers.

OB: On Base Average (batters)

OBA: Opposition On Base Average (pitchers)

On Base Average (OBA)

(H + BB) / (AB + BB)

Addressing one of the two deficiencies in BA, OB gives value to those events that get batters on base, but are not hits. By adding walks (and often, hit batsmen) into the basic batting average formula, we have a better gauge of a batter's ability to reach base safely. An OB of .350 can be read as "this batter gets on base 35% of the time."

Why this is a more important gauge than batting average... When a run is scored, there is no distinction made as to how that runner reached base. So, two thirds of the time — about how often a batter comes to the plate with the bases empty — a walk really is as good as a hit.

BENCHMARKS: We all know what a .300 hitter is, but what represents "good" for OB? That comparable level would likely be .400, with .275 representing the level of futility.

On Base Plus Slugging Average (OPS): A simple sum of the two gauges, it is considered as one of the better evaluators of overall performance. OPS combines the two basic elements of offensive production — the ability to get on base (OB) and the ability to advance baserunners (Slg).

BENCHMARKS: The game's top batters will have OPS levels over .900. The worst batters will have levels under .600.

Opposition Batting Average (OBA)

(Hits Allowed / ((IP x 2.82) + Hits Allowed))

A close approximation of the batting average achieved by opposing batters against a particular pitcher.

BENCHMARKS: The converse of the benchmark for batters, the best pitchers will have levels under .250; the worst pitchers levels over .300.

Opposition Home Runs per Game (hr/9)

(HR Allowed x 9 / IP)

Used in the BPV formula, it measures how many home runs a pitcher allows per game equivalent. **BENCHMARK**: The best pitchers will have hr/9 levels of under 1.0.

Opposition On Base Average (OOB)

(Hits Allowed + BB) / ((IP x 2.82) + H + BB)

A close approximation of the on base average achieved by opposing batters against a particular pitcher. **BENCHMARK**: The best pitchers will have levels under .300; the worst pitchers levels over .375.

Opposition Strikeouts per Game: See Dominance Rate.

Opposition Walks per Game: See Control Rate.

OPS: On Base Plus Slugging Average

Power/Finesse Rating

(BB + K) / IP

Measures the level by which a pitcher allows balls to be put into play and helps tie a pitcher's success to his team's level of defensive ability. In general, extreme power pitchers can be successful even with poor defensive teams. Extreme finesse pitchers usually cannot. Power pitchers tend to have greater longevity in the game. Finesse pitchers with poor defenses behind them are high risks to have poor won-loss records — even if they have acceptable ERAs.

BENCHMARKS: A level of 1.13 or greater describes the extreme power pitchers, or more aptly described as pure throwers. A level of .93 or lower describes an extreme finesse style, or a high contact pitcher. Tip... if you have to draft a pitcher from a poor defensive team, going with power over finesse will usually net you more wins in the long run.

PQS: Pure Quality Starts

PQS Disaster Rate *(Gene McCaffrey):* The percentage of a starting pitcher's outings that rate as a PQS-0 or PQS-1. See the Pitching Logs section for more information on DIS%.

PQS Domination Rate *(Gene McCaffrey):* The percentage of a starting pitcher's outings that rate as a PQS-4 or PQS-5. See the Pitching Logs section for more information on DOM%.

Pure Quality Starts: See page 132 for a complete description.

Pw: Linear Weighted Power

PX: Linear Weighted Power Index

R$: Rotisserie value

RAR: Runs Above Replacement

RC: Runs Created

RC/G: Runs Created Per Game

REff%: Relief Efficiency Per Cent

Reliever Efficiency Per Cent (REff%)

(Wins + Saves + Holds) / (Wins + Losses + SaveOpps + Holds)

This is a measure of the effectiveness of relief pitchers in pressure situations. How often does a reliever contribute positively to the outcome of the game? A record of consistent, positive impact on game outcomes breeds managerial confidence, and that confidence could pave the way to save opportunities. For those pitchers that are suddenly thrust into a closer's role, this formula helps gauge their potential to succeed based on past successes in similar roles.

BENCHMARK: Minimum of 80%.

Rotisserie Value (R$): The dollar value placed on a player's performance in a Rotisserie league, and designed to measure the impact that player has on the standings. These values are highly variable depending upon a variety of factors. In other words, a $30 player is only a $30 player if

- there is a 260-unit salary cap
- there are 12 teams in the league
- each team has a 23-man roster
- there are no freeze lists
- every other player is drafted at optimal value

Any variation in these factors will inflate or deflate a player's value. In addition, value will also be affected by the stage of the draft you are in, the position and category demands when the player comes up for bid, and the prevailing winds of the media.

In other words, **a $30 player is only a $30 player if someone in your draft pays $30 for him**.

There are a variety of methods to calculate value, most involving a delineation of a least valuable performance level (given league size and structure), and then assigning a certain dollar amount for incremental improvement from that base. The method we use is a variation of the Standings Gain Points method described in the book, *How to Value Players for Rotisserie Baseball,* by Art McGee.

Research has been showing a shift in how people play Rotisserie. The 5x5 game (adding runs scored and pitching strikeouts) has become the most prevalent variation. As many as 50% of you currently play in at least one mixed league, where the penetration into the player pool falls short of the standard 75%.

Does this invalidate the ratings in this book? No. Since values are driven by playing time, and our playing time projections are preliminary anyway, the best use for this data is to get a *general sense of value* no matter how you play the game.

In fact, since we currently have no idea whether Khalil Greene will really break camp as the Padres' shortstop, or who is going to be playing OF on the Mets next year, all the projected values are slightly inflated. They are roughly based on a 12-team AL and 13-team NL league. We've attempted to take into account as many contingencies as prudent, but the values will not total to anywhere near $3120, so don't waste your time adding them up, and save your irate e-mails.

A $25 player in this book might actually be worth $21. Or maybe $28. This level of precision is irrelevant in a process that is going to be driven by market forces anyway. So, don't obsess over it.

I always wonder how other writers manage to publish perfect Rotisserie values over the winter. Do they make their own arbitrary decisions as to which free agents are going to sign where, and who is going to land jobs in spring training? I'm not about to make those massive leaps of faith.

Bottom line... Some things you can predict, to other things you have to react. As roles become more defined closer to Opening Day, our online updates will provide better approximations of playing time, and projected Roto values that add up to $3120.

Runs Above Replacement (RAR): An estimate of the number of runs a player contributes above a "replacement level" player. "Replacement" is defined as the level of performance at which another player can easily be found at little or no cost to a team. What constitutes replacement level is a topic that is hotly debated. There are a variety of formulas and rules of thumb used to determine this level for each position (replacement level for a shortstop will be very different from replacement level for an outfielder). Our estimates appear below.

One of the major values of RAR for fantasy applications is that it can be used to assemble an integrated ranking of batters and pitchers for drafting purposes.

Batters create runs; pitchers save runs. But are batters and pitchers who have comparable RAR levels truly equal in value? In fact, pitchers might be considered to have higher value. Saving an additional run is more important than producing an additional run. A pitcher who throws a shutout is guaranteed to win that game, whereas no matter how many runs a batter produces, his team can still lose given a poor pitching outing.

To calculate RAR for batters:
- Start with a batter's runs created per game (RC/G).
- Subtract his position's replacement level RC/G.
- Multiply by number of games played, calculated as (AB - H + CS) / 25.5.

Replacement levels used in this book, for 2003:

POS	AL	NL
C	4.09	4.29
1B	5.38	5.51
2B	4.14	4.41
3B	4.51	4.25
SS	4.43	4.11
LF	5.33	5.59
CF	4.74	4.98
RF	5.15	5.61
DH	4.62	

To calculate RAR for pitchers:
- Start with the replacement level league ERA.
- Subtract the pitcher's ERA. (To calculate *projected* RAR, use the pitcher's XERA.)
- Multiply by number of games played, calculated as plate appearances (IP x 4.34) divided by 35.
- Multiply the resulting RAR level by 1.08 to account for the variance between earned runs and total runs.

RAR can also be used to calculate rough projected team won-loss records. *(Roger Miller)* Total the RAR levels for all the players on a team, divide by 10 and add to 53 wins.

Runs Created *(Bill James)*

(H + BB - CS) x (Total bases + (.55 x SB)) / (AB + BB)

A formula that converts all offensive events into a total of runs scored. As calculated for individual teams, the result approximates a club's actual run total with great accuracy.

Runs Created Per Game *(Bill James)*

Runs Created / ((AB - H + CS) / 25.5)

RC expressed on a per-game basis might be considered the hypothetical ERA compiled against a particular batter. Another way to look at it... a batter with a RC/G of 7.00 would be expected to score 7 runs per game if he were cloned nine times and faced an average pitcher in every at bat. Cloning batters is not a practice we recommend.

BENCHMARKS: Few players surpass the level of a 10.00 RC/G in any given season, but any level over 7.50 can still be considered very good. At the bottom of the scale are those who post RC/G levels below 3.00.

S%: Strand Rate

Save: There are six events that need to occur in order for a pitcher to post a single save...

1. The starting pitcher and middle relievers must pitch well.

2. The offense must score enough runs.

3. It must be a reasonably close game.

4. The manager must choose to put the pitcher in for a save opportunity.

5. The pitcher must pitch well and hold the lead.

6. The manager must let him finish the game.

Of these six events, only one is within the control of the relief pitcher. As such, projecting saves for a reliever has little to do with skill and a lot to do with opportunity. However, pitchers with excellent skills sets may create opportunity for themselves.

Situation Independent: Describing a statistical gauge that measures performance apart from the context of team, ballpark, or other outside variables. Home runs, inasmuch as they are unaffected by the performance of a batter's team, are often considered a situation independent stat (they are, however, affected by park dimensions). Strikeouts and Walks are better examples.

Conversely, RBI's are situation dependent because individual performance varies greatly by the performance of other batters on the team (you can't drive in runs if there is nobody on base). Similarly, pitching wins are as much a measure of the success of a pitcher as they are a measure of the success of the offense and defense performing behind that pitcher, and are therefore a poor measure of pitching performance alone.

Situation independent gauges are important for us to be able to separate a player's contribution to his team and isolate his performance so that we may judge it on its own merits.

Slg: Slugging Average

Slugging Average (Slg)

(Singles + (2 x Doubles) + (3 x Triples) + (4 x HR)) / AB

A measure of the total number of bases accumulated (or the minimum number of runners' bases advanced) per at bat. It is a misnomer; it is not a true measure of a batter's slugging ability because it includes singles. Slg also assumes that each type of hit has proportionately increasing value (i.e. a double is twice as valuable as a single, etc.) which is not true. For instance, with the bases loaded, a HR always scores four runs, a triple always scores three, but a double could score two or three and a single could score one, or two, or even three.

BENCHMARKS: The top 10%-15% of batters will have levels over .500. The bottom 5%-10% will have levels under .300.

Soft stats (also, Soft Skills): Batting eyes less than 0.50. Command ratios under 2.0. Strikeout rates below 5.0. Etc.

Soft-tosser: Pitcher with a strikeout rate of 5.0 or less.

Spd: Speed Score

Speed Score *(Bill James):* A measure of the various elements that comprise a runner's speed skills. Although this formula (a variation of James' original version) may be used as a leading indicator for stolen base output, SB attempts are controlled by managerial strategy which makes Spd somewhat less valuable.

The speed scores in this book are calculated as the mean value of the following four elements...

Stolen base efficiency = *(((SB + 3)/(SB + CS + 7)) - .4) x 20*

Stolen base frequency = *Square root of ((SB + CS)/(Singles + BB)) / .07*

Triples rating = *(3B / (AB - HR - K)) / .0016*

Runs scored as a percentage of times on base = *(((R - HR)/(H + BB - HR)) - .1) / .04*

Speed Score Index (SX)

(Batter's Spd / League Spd) x 100

Normalized speed scores are presented in this book to get a better read on a runner's accomplishment in context. A level of 100 equals league average speed skill. Values over 100 indicate above average skill, over 200 represent the Fleet of Feet Elite.

Strand Rate (S%)

(H + BB - ER) / (H + BB - HR)

This represents the percentage of allowed runners a pitcher strands, and measures both individual pitcher skill and bullpen effectiveness.

BENCHMARKS: The most adept at stranding runners will have S% levels over 75%. Once a pitcher's S% starts dropping down below 70%, he's going to have problems with his ERA. Those pitchers with strand rates over 80% will have artificially low ERAs, which will be prone to relapse. (See the Forecaster's Toolbox for more strand rate research.)

Strikeouts per Game: See Opposition Strikeouts per game.

SX: Speed Score Index

Vintage Eck Territory: A base performance value (BPV) level of 200 or over. Over the course of his career, Dennis Eckersely posted levels this high four times:

1989	345
1990	347
1991	226
1992	210

Vulture: A pitcher, typically a middle reliever, who accumulates an unusually high number of wins by preying on other pitchers' misfortunes. More accurately, this is a pitcher typically brought into a game after a starting pitcher has put his team behind, and then pitches well enough and long enough to allow his offense to take the lead, thereby "vulturing" a win from his starting pitcher.

Walk rate (bb%)

(BB / (AB + BB))

A measure of a batter's eye and plate patience.

BENCHMARKS: The best batters will have levels of over 10%. Those with the least plate patience will have levels of 5% or less.

Walks per Game: See Opposition Walks per Game.

Wasted talent: A player with a high level skill that is negated by a deficiency in another skill. For instance, basepath speed can be negated by poor on base ability. Pitchers with strong arms can be wasted because home plate is an elusive concept to them.

Wins: There are five events that need to occur in order for a pitcher to post a single win...

1. He must pitch well, allowing few runs.

2. The offense must score enough runs.

3. The defense must successfully field all batted balls.

4. The bullpen must hold the lead.

5. The manager must leave the pitcher in for 5 innings, and not remove him if the team is still behind.

Of these five events, only one is within the control of the pitcher. As such, projecting wins can be an exercise in futility.

xBA: Expected Batting Average

xERA: Expected ERA

CHEATER'S BOOKMARK

BATTING STATISTICS			BENCHMARKS			
			BAD	**'03 LG AVG**		**BEST**
Abbrv	**Term**	**Formula / Descr.**	**UNDER**	**AL**	**NL**	**OVER**
Avg	Batting Average	h/ab	250	268	269	300
xBA	Expected Batting Average	*See glossary*		271	270	
OB	On Base Average	(h+bb)/(ab+bb)	300	330	337	375
Slg	Slugging Average	total bases/ab	350	429	432	500
OPS	On Base plus Slugging	OB+Slg	650	759	769	875
bb%	Walk Rate	bb/(ab+bb)	5%	8%	9%	10%
ct%	Contact Rate	(ab-k) / ab	75%	82%	82%	85%
Eye	Batting Eye	bb/k	0.50	0.52	0.57	1.00
PX	Power Index	Normalized power skills	80	100	100	120
SX	Speed Index	Normalized speed skills	80	100	100	120
G/F	Groundball/Flyball Ratio	gb / fb		1.19	1.28	
RC/G	Runs Created per Game	*See glossary*	3.00	5.14	5.33	7.50
RAR	Runs Above Replacement	*See glossary*	-0			+25
BPV	Base Performance Value	*See glossary*	35	43	44	75
BPX	Base Performance Index	*See glossary*	80	100	100	120

PITCHING STATISTICS			BENCHMARKS			
			BAD	**'03 LG AVG**		**BEST**
Abbrv	**Term**	**Formula / Descr.**	**OVER**	**AL**	**NL**	**UNDER**
ERA	Earned Run Average	er*9/ip	5.00	4.51	4.31	4.00
Br/IP	Baserunners per Inning	(h+bb)/ip	1.50	1.39	1.39	1.25
BF/G	Batters Faced per Game	((ip*2.82)+h+bb)/g	28.0			
OBA	Opposition Batting Avg	Opp. h/ab	290	261	257	250
OOB	Opposition On Base Avg	Opp. (h+bb)/(ab+bb)	350	322	322	300
H%	Hits per balls in play	(h-hr)/((ip*2.82)+h-k-hr)		30%	30%	
xERA	Expected ERA	*See glossary*	5.00	4.53	4.40	4.00
Ctl	Control Rate	bb*9/ip		3.2	3.4	3.0
hr/9	Homerun Rate	hr*9/ip		1.1	1.1	1.0
S%	Strand Rate	(h+bb-er)/(h+bb-hr)		70%	72%	
DIS%	PQS Disaster Rate	% GS that are PQS 0/1		26%	23%	20%

			BAD	**'03 LG AVG**		**BEST**
			UNDER	**AL**	**NL**	**OVER**
RAR	Runs Above Replacement	*See glossary*	-0			+25
Dom	Dominance Rate	k*9/ip		6.2	6.7	6.5
Cmd	Command Ratio	k/bb		1.9	1.9	2.2
G/F	Groundball/Flyball Ratio	gb / fb		1.05	1.15	
BPV	Base Performance Value	*See glossary*	50	49	54	75
BPX	Base Performance Index	*See glossary*	80	100	100	120
DOM%	PQS Dominance Rate	% GS that are PQS 4/5		37%	42%	50%
Sv%	Saves Conversion Rate	(saves / save opps)		60%	70%	80%
REff%	Relief Effectiveness Rate	*See glossary*		64%	65%	80%

NOTES

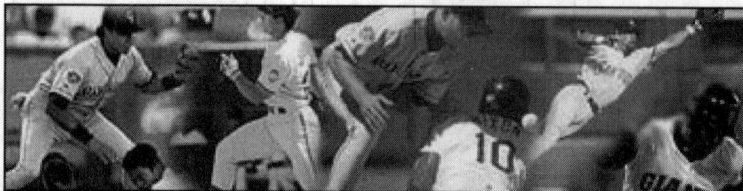